Using proven, field-tested technology, auto-graded **Excel Projects** allow instructors to seamlessly integrate Microsoft Excel® content into their course without having to manually grade spreadsheets. Students have the opportunity to practice important **finance skills** in Excel, helping them to master key concepts and gain proficiency with the program.

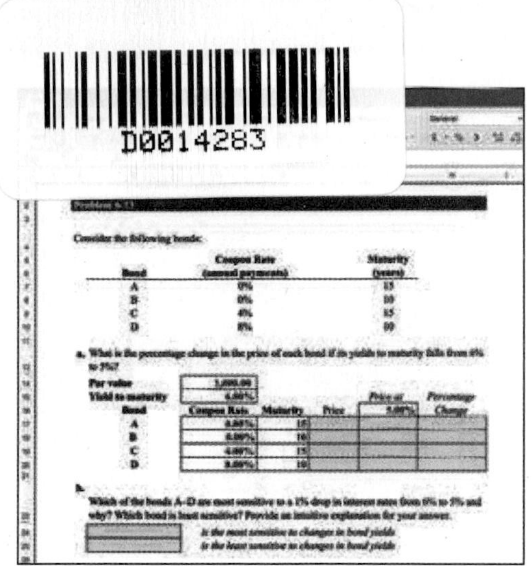

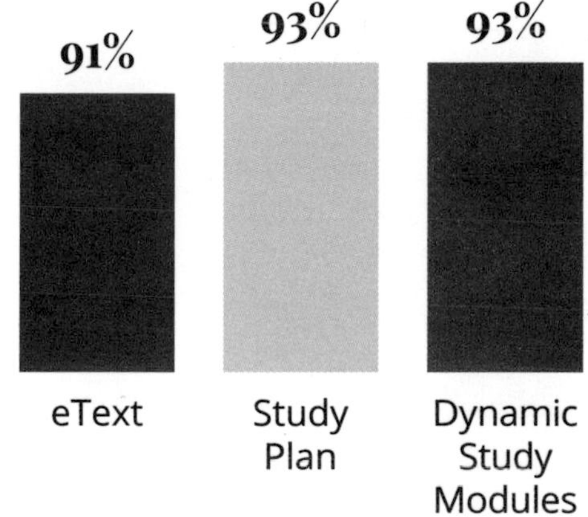

% of students who found learning tool helpful

Dynamic Study Modules help students study chapter topics effectively on their own by continuously assessing their **knowledge application** and performance in real time. These are available as graded assignments prior to class, and accessible on smartphones, tablets, and computers.

Pearson eText enhances student learning—both in and outside the classroom. Take notes, highlight, and bookmark important content, or engage with interactive lecture and example videos that bring learning to life (available with select titles). Accessible anytime, anywhere via MyLab or the app.

The **MyLab Gradebook** offers an easy way for students and instructors to view course performance. Item Analysis allows instructors to quickly see trends by analyzing details like the number of students who answered correctly/incorrectly, time on task, and median time spend on a question by question basis. And because it's correlated with the AACSB Standards, instructors can track students' progress toward outcomes that the organization has deemed important in preparing students to be **leaders.**

88%

of students would tell their instructor to keep using MyLab Finance

For additional details visit: www.pearson.com/mylab/finance

Principles of
Managerial Finance

The Pearson Series in Finance

Berk/DeMarzo
*Corporate Finance**
*Corporate Finance: The Core**

Berk/DeMarzo/Harford
*Fundamentals of Corporate Finance**

Brooks
*Financial Management: Core Concepts**

Copeland/Weston/Shastri
Financial Theory and Corporate Policy

Dorfman/Cather
Introduction to Risk Management and Insurance

Eakins/McNally
Corporate Finance Online

Eiteman/Stonehill/Moffett
*Multinational Business Finance**

Fabozzi
Bond Markets: Analysis and Strategies

Foerster
*Financial Management: Concepts and Applications**

Frasca
Personal Finance

Haugen
The Inefficient Stock Market: What Pays Off and Why
Modern Investment Theory

Holden
Excel Modeling in Corporate Finance
Excel Modeling in Investments

Hughes/MacDonald
International Banking: Text and Cases

Hull
Fundamentals of Futures and Options Markets
Options, Futures, and Other Derivatives

Keown
*Personal Finance: Turning Money into Wealth**

Keown/Martin/Petty
*Foundations of Finance: The Logic and Practice of Financial Management**

Madura
*Personal Finance**

McDonald
Derivatives Markets
Fundamentals of Derivatives Markets

Mishkin/Eakins
Financial Markets and Institutions

Moffett/Stonehill/Eiteman
*Fundamentals of Multinational Finance**

Pennacchi
Theory of Asset Pricing

Rejda/McNamara
Principles of Risk Management and Insurance

Smart/Gitman/Joehnk
*Fundamentals of Investing**

Solnik/McLeavey
Global Investments

Titman/Keown/Martin
*Financial Management: Principles and Applications**

Titman/Martin
Valuation: The Art and Science of Corporate Investment Decisions

Weston/Mitchell/Mulherin
Takeovers, Restructuring, and Corporate Governance

Zutter/Smart
*Principles of Managerial Finance**
*Principles of Managerial Finance—Brief Edition**

FIFTEENTH EDITION

Principles of Managerial Finance

Chad J. Zutter
University of Pittsburgh

Scott B. Smart
Indiana University

New York, NY

Vice President, Business, Economics, and UK Courseware: Donna Battista
Director of Portfolio Management: Adrienne D'Ambrosio
Senior Portfolio Manager: Kate Fernandes
Editorial Assistant: Caroline Fenn
Vice President, Product Marketing: Roxanne McCarley
Product Marketer: Kaylee Carlson
Product Marketing Assistant: Marianela Silvestri
Manager of Field Marketing, Business Publishing: Adam Goldstein
Executive Field Marketing Manager: Thomas Hayward
Vice President, Production and Digital Studio, Arts and Business: Etain O'Dea
Director of Production, Business: Jeff Holcomb
Managing Producer, Business: Alison Kalil
Content Producer: Meredith Gertz
Operations Specialist: Carol Melville
Design Lead: Kathryn Foot
Manager, Learning Tools: Brian Surette
Content Developer, Learning Tools: Sarah Peterson
Managing Producer, Digital Studio and GLP, Media Production and Development: Ashley Santora
Managing Producer, Digital Studio: Diane Lombardo
Digital Studio Producer: Melissa Honig
Digital Studio Producer: Alana Coles
Digital Content Team Lead: Noel Lotz
Digital Content Project Lead: Miguel Leonarte
Project Manager: Kathy Smith, Cenveo® Publisher Services
Interior Design: Cenveo® Publisher Services
Cover Design: Cenveo® Publisher Services
Cover Art: ChristopheHeylen/DigitalVision Vectors/Getty Images; Decha Anunthanapong/123RF; John Kuczala/DigitalVision/Getty Images; Sean Russell/Getty Images; MarsBars/E+/Getty Images; Panuwat Phimpha/Shutterstock
Printer/Binder: LSC Communications, Inc./Willard
Cover Printer: Phoenix Color/Hagerstown

Cataloging-in-Publication Data is available on file at the Library of Congress

ISBN 10: 0-13-447631-X
ISBN 13: 978-0-13-447631-5

2 18

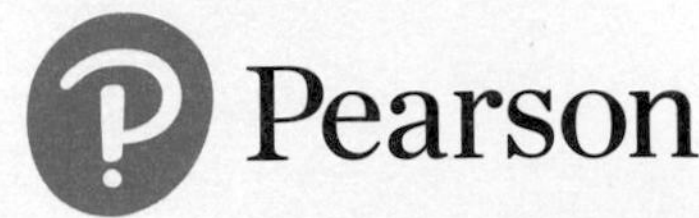

Dedicated to our good friend and mentor,

Dr. Lawrence J. Gitman,

who trusted us as coauthors and successors

of Principles of Managerial Finance.

CJZ

SBS

Brief Contents

Contents

PART 2 Financial Tools 75

5 Time Value of Money 189

▲ *Mega Millions Jackpot—Pay Me Now or Pay Me Later 190*

PART 4 Risk and the Required Rate of Return 345

9 The Cost of Capital 396

▲ J&J—Exceeding Expectations 397

PART 5 Long-Term Investment Decisions 429

11 Capital Budgeting Cash Flows 471

▲ *Moulson Coors Brewing Company—Brewing Up a Deal 472*

PART 6 Long-Term Financial Decisions 551

PART 7 Short-Term Financial Decisions 645

PART 8 Special Topics in Managerial Finance 725

About the Authors

Chad J. Zutter is a finance professor and the Dean's Excellence Faculty Fellow at the Katz Graduate School of Business at the University of Pittsburgh. Dr. Zutter received his B.B.A. from the University of Texas at Arlington and his Ph.D. from Indiana University. His research has a practical, applied focus and has been the subject of feature stories in, among other prominent outlets, *The Economist* and *CFO Magazine*. His papers have been cited in arguments before the U.S. Supreme Court and in consultation with companies such as Google and Intel. Dr. Zutter won the prestigious Jensen Prize for the best paper published in the *Journal of Financial Economics* and a best paper award from the *Journal of Corporate Finance*. He has won teaching awards at the Kelley School of Business at Indiana University and the Katz Graduate School of Business at the University of Pittsburgh. Prior to his career in academics, Dr. Zutter was a submariner in the U.S. Navy. Dr. Zutter and his wife have four children and live in Pittsburgh, Pennsylvania. In his free time he enjoys horseback riding and downhill skiing.

Scott B. Smart is a finance professor and the Whirlpool Finance Faculty Fellow at the Kelley School of Business at Indiana University. Dr. Smart received his B.B.A. from Baylor University and his M.A. and Ph.D. from Stanford University. His research focuses primarily on applied corporate finance topics and has been published in journals such as the *Journal of Finance*, the *Journal of Financial Economics*, the *Journal of Corporate Finance*, *Financial Management*, and others. His articles have been cited by business publications including *The Wall Street Journal*, *The Economist*, and *Business Week*. Winner of more than a dozen teaching awards, Dr. Smart has been listed multiple times as a top business school teacher by *Business Week*. He has held Visiting Professor positions at the University of Otago and Stanford University, and he worked as a Visiting Scholar for Intel Corporation, focusing on that company's mergers and acquisitions activity during the "Dot-com" boom in the late 1990s. As a volunteer, Dr. Smart currently serves on the boards of the Indiana University Credit Union and Habitat for Humanity. In his spare time he enjoys outdoor pursuits such as hiking and fly fishing.

About the Authors

Preface

NEW TO THIS EDITION

Finance is a dynamic discipline, as illustrated on this book's cover by the evolution of payment methods from coins and paper currency to bitcoin. As we made plans to publish the fifteenth edition, we were mindful of feedback from users of the fourteenth edition and of changes in managerial finance practices that have taken hold in recent years. For example, the Tax Cuts and Jobs Act of 2017 made sweeping changes to the corporate and personal tax codes. The new tax law changes the corporate tax from a progressive structure to one with a flat 21% tax rate. It also allows firms to immediately expense many types of capital assets while imposing limits on interest deductibility. This edition incorporates these changes and highlights how tax changes may alter firms' incentives in a variety of ways.

In every chapter, our changes were designed to make the material more up to date and more relevant for students. A number of new topics have been added at appropriate places, and new features appear in each chapter:

- We replaced nearly all of the chapter-opening vignettes with stories gathered from the business press in recent years that illustrate key ideas in each chapter. Many of the chapter openers feature companies such as Airbnb, Kroger, Netflix, Apple, Tesla, General Motors, Whirlpool, and Dell that are familiar to students. We designed these opening vignettes to impress upon students that the material they will see in each chapter is relevant for business in the "real world."
- At the end of each chapter we return to the opening vignette with an Opener-In-Review question that asks students to apply a concept that they have learned in the chapter to the business situation described in the chapter opener.
- We have rewritten all of the *Focus on Ethics* boxes, using new examples to highlight situations in which businesses or individuals have engaged in unethical behavior. The boxes explore the consequences of ethical lapses and the ways in which markets and governments play a role in enforcing ethical standards.
- New in this edition are Chapter Introduction Videos and animations. In the introduction videos the authors explain the importance of the chapter content within the context of managerial finance. The animations for select in-chapter figures and examples allow students to manipulate inputs to determine outputs in order to illustrate concepts and reinforce learning. MyLab Finance also offers new and updated Solution Videos that allow students to watch a video of the author discussing or solving in-chapter examples. We have also updated the financial calculator images that appear in the book to better match the financial calculator available on MyLab Finance.
- The chapter-ending Spreadsheet Exercises as well as select end-of-chapter problems in the text are now offered in MyLab Finance as auto-graded Excel Projects. Using proven, field-tested technology, auto-graded Excel Projects allow instructors to seamlessly integrate Microsoft Excel content into their course without having to manually grade spreadsheets. Students have the opportunity to practice important finance skills in Excel, helping them to master key concepts and gain proficiency with the program.

- We added new problems to each chapter, many of which require students to use real-world data and features of the new tax code to reach a solution.

The chapter sequence is essentially unchanged from the prior edition, but there are some noteworthy changes within each chapter. This edition contains nineteen chapters divided into eight parts. Each part is introduced by a brief overview, which is intended to give students an advance sense for the collective value of the chapters included in the part.

Part 1 contains two chapters. Chapter 1 provides an overview of the role of managerial finance in a business enterprise. It contains new, expanded content focusing on the goal of the firm and the broad principles that financial managers use in their pursuit of that goal. Chapter 2 describes the financial market context in which firms operate, with new coverage focusing on the transactions costs investors face when trading in secondary markets.

Part 2 contains three chapters focused on basic financial skills such as financial statement analysis, cash flow analysis, and time-value-of-money calculations. Chapter 3 provides an in-depth ratio analysis using real data from Whole Foods just prior to its acquisition by Amazon. The ratios provide opportunities for interesting discussion about some of the possible motives for that acquisition. We reorganized the flow of material in Chapter 4 to emphasize first the broad goals of strategic and operational financial planning and then the importance of cash flow within any financial plan. In Chapter 5, we rewrote much of the discussion to make time-value-of-money concepts simpler and more intuitive. We also added new coverage of growing perpetuities.

Part 3 focuses on bond and stock valuation. We placed these two chapters just ahead of the risk and return chapter to provide students with exposure to basic material on bonds and stocks that is easier to grasp than some of the more theoretical concepts in the next part. New in Chapter 6 is a discussion of the negative interest rates prevailing on government bonds in Japan and some European countries, as well as an expanded discussion of the tendency of the yield curve to invert prior to a recession. Chapter 7 offers new coverage of the use of price-to-earnings multiples to value stocks.

Part 4 contains the risk and return chapter as well as the chapter on the cost of capital. We believe that following the risk and return chapter with the cost of capital material helps students understand the important principle that the expectations of a firm's investors shape how the firm should approach major investment decisions (which are covered in Part 5). In other words, Part 4 is designed to help students understand where a project "hurdle rate" comes from before they start using hurdle rates in capital budgeting problems. Updates to Chapter 8 include new historical data on stocks, bonds, and Treasury bills, as well as examples and problems featuring real data on companies such as Apple, Google, Coca-Cola, and Wal-Mart. Chapter 9 contains new material on the use of market-value-based weights in the cost of capital calculation featuring actual data on the capital structure of Netflix. Throughout the chapter we have revised examples and problems to reflect today's low interest rate environment and the correspondingly low after-tax cost of debt faced by most public companies.

Part 5 contains three chapters on various capital budgeting topics. The first chapter focuses on capital budgeting methods such as payback and net present value analysis. A new feature of this chapter is an updated discussion of economic value added using data from Exxon Mobil Corp. The second chapter in this part explains how financial analysts construct cash flow projections, which are a required component of net present value analysis. The final chapter in this section describes how firms analyze the risks associated with capital investments.

Parts 6 deals with the topics of capital structure and payout policy. These two chapters contain updated material on trends in firms' use of leverage and their payout practices. Chapter 13 provides a new *Focus on Practice* box discussing how Qualcomm's highly skilled labor force turns what often is thought of as a variable cost into a fixed cost and thereby creates operating leverage. The chapter also contains new expanded coverage of the role that expected bankruptcy costs play in capital structure decisions. A new discussion in Chapter 14 highlights how and why companies have shifted their payout policies away from dividends and toward share repurchases over time.

Part 7 contains two chapters centered on working capital issues. A major development in business has been the extent to which firms have found new ways to economize on working capital investments. The first chapter in Part 7 explains why and how firms work hard to squeeze resources from their investments in current assets such as cash and inventory. The second chapter in this part focuses more on management of current liabilities.

Finally, Part 8 has three chapters covering a variety of topics, including hybrid securities, mergers and other forms of restructurings, and international finance. These subjects are some of the most dynamic areas in financial practice, and we have made a number of changes here to reflect current practices. Chapter 17 contains new examples of convertible securities issued by firms such as STMicroelectronics and Tesla. Chapter 18 covers important merger concepts with examples featuring recent transactions involving Anthem-Cigna, Fiat-Chrysler, Dow-DuPont, Berkshire Hathaway-Oncor, and Broadcom Ltd.-Maxlinear.

Although the text content is sequential, instructors can assign almost any chapter as a self-contained unit, enabling instructors to customize the text to various teaching strategies and course lengths.

Like the previous editions, the fifteenth edition incorporates a proven learning system, which integrates pedagogy with concepts and practical applications. It concentrates on the knowledge that is needed to make keen financial decisions in an increasingly competitive business environment. The strong pedagogy and generous use of examples—many of which use real data from markets or companies—make the text an easily accessible resource for in-class learning or out-of-class learning, such as online courses and self-study programs.

SOLVING TEACHING AND LEARNING CHALLENGES

The desire to write *Principles of Managerial Finance* came from the experience of teaching the introductory managerial finance course. Those who have taught the introductory course many times can appreciate the difficulties that some students have absorbing and applying financial concepts. Students want a book that speaks to them in plain English and explains how to apply financial concepts to solve real-world problems. These students want more than just description; they also want demonstration of concepts, tools, and techniques. This book is written with the needs of students in mind, and it effectively delivers the resources that students need to succeed in the introductory finance course.

Courses and students have changed since the first edition of this book, but the goals of the text have not changed. The conversational tone and wide use of examples set off in the text still characterize *Principles of Managerial Finance*.

Building on those strengths, fifteen editions, numerous translations, and well over half a million U.S. users, *Principles* has evolved based on feedback from both instructors and students, from adopters, nonadopters, and practitioners. In this edition, we have worked to ensure that the book reflects contemporary thinking and pedagogy to further strengthen the delivery of the classic topics that our users have come to expect. Below are descriptions of the most important resources in *Principles* that help meet teaching and learning challenges.

Users of *Principles of Managerial Finance* have praised the effectiveness of the book's **Teaching and Learning System**, which they hail as one of its hallmarks. The system, driven by a set of carefully developed learning goals, has been retained and polished in this fifteenth edition. The "walkthrough" on the pages that follow illustrates and describes the key elements of the Teaching and Learning System. We encourage both students and instructors to acquaint themselves at the start of the semester with the many useful features the book offers.

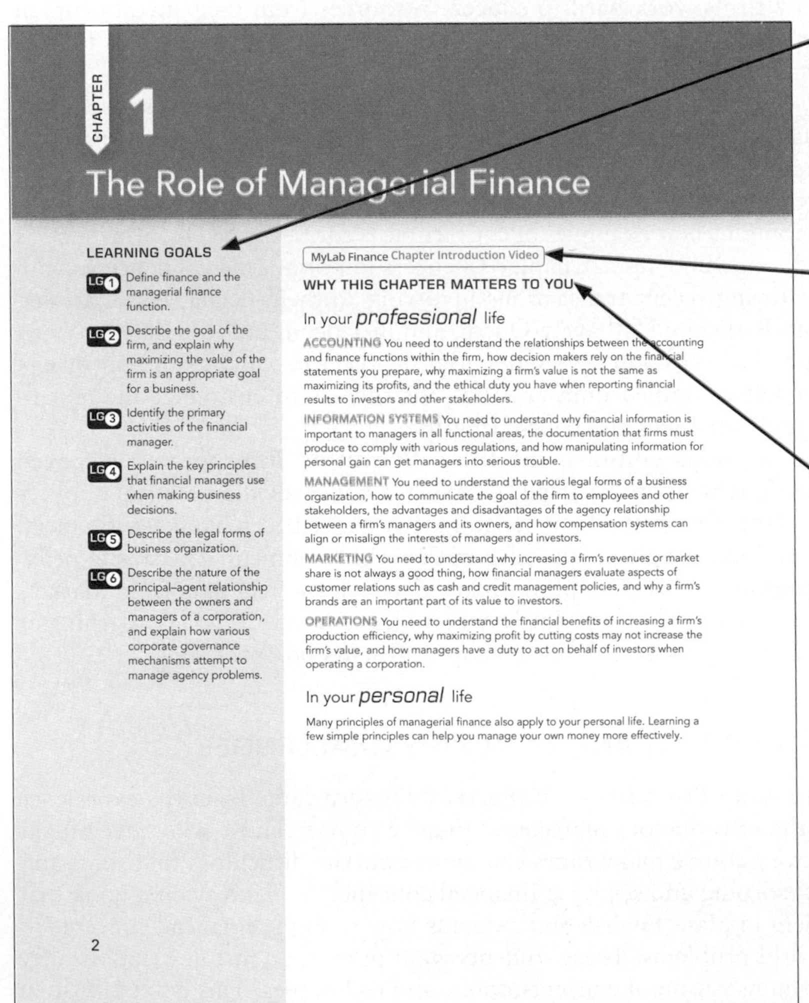

CHAPTER 1

The Role of Managerial Finance

LEARNING GOALS

LG1 Define finance and the managerial finance function.

LG2 Describe the goal of the firm, and explain why maximizing the value of the firm is an appropriate goal for a business.

LG3 Identify the primary activities of the financial manager.

LG4 Explain the key principles that financial managers use when making business decisions.

LG5 Describe the legal forms of business organization.

LG6 Describe the nature of the principal–agent relationship between the owners and managers of a corporation, and explain how various corporate governance mechanisms attempt to manage agency problems.

MyLab Finance Chapter Introduction Video

WHY THIS CHAPTER MATTERS TO YOU

In your *professional* life

ACCOUNTING You need to understand the relationships between the accounting and finance functions within the firm, how decision makers rely on the financial statements you prepare, why maximizing a firm's value is not the same as maximizing its profits, and the ethical duty you have when reporting financial results to investors and other stakeholders.

INFORMATION SYSTEMS You need to understand why financial information is important to managers in all functional areas, the documentation that firms must produce to comply with various regulations, and how manipulating information for personal gain can get managers into serious trouble.

MANAGEMENT You need to understand the various legal forms of a business organization, how to communicate the goal of the firm to employees and other stakeholders, the advantages and disadvantages of the agency relationship between a firm's managers and its owners, and how compensation systems can align or misalign the interests of managers and investors.

MARKETING You need to understand why increasing a firm's revenues or market share is not always a good thing, how financial managers evaluate aspects of customer relations such as cash and credit management policies, and why a firm's brands are an important part of its value to investors.

OPERATIONS You need to understand the financial benefits of increasing a firm's production efficiency, why maximizing profit by cutting costs may not increase the firm's value, and how managers have a duty to act on behalf of investors when operating a corporation.

In your *personal* life

Many principles of managerial finance also apply to your personal life. Learning a few simple principles can help you manage your own money more effectively.

2

Six **Learning Goals** at the start of the chapter highlight the most important concepts and techniques in the chapter. Students are reminded to think about the learning goals while working through the chapter by strategically placed **learning goal icons**.

To help students understand the relevance of a chapter within the overarching framework of managerial finance, every chapter has available in **MyLab Finance** a short chapter introduction video by an author.

Every chapter opens with a feature, titled **Why This Chapter Matters to You**, that helps motivate student interest by highlighting both professional and personal benefits from achieving the chapter learning goals.

Its first part, **In Your Professional Life**, discusses the intersection of the finance topics covered in the chapter with the concerns of other major business disciplines. It encourages students majoring in accounting, information systems, management, marketing, and operations to appreciate how financial acumen will help them achieve their professional goals.

The second part, **In Your Personal Life**, identifies topics in the chapter that will have particular application to personal finance. This feature also helps students appreciate the tasks performed in a business setting by pointing out that the tasks are not necessarily different from those that are relevant in their personal lives.

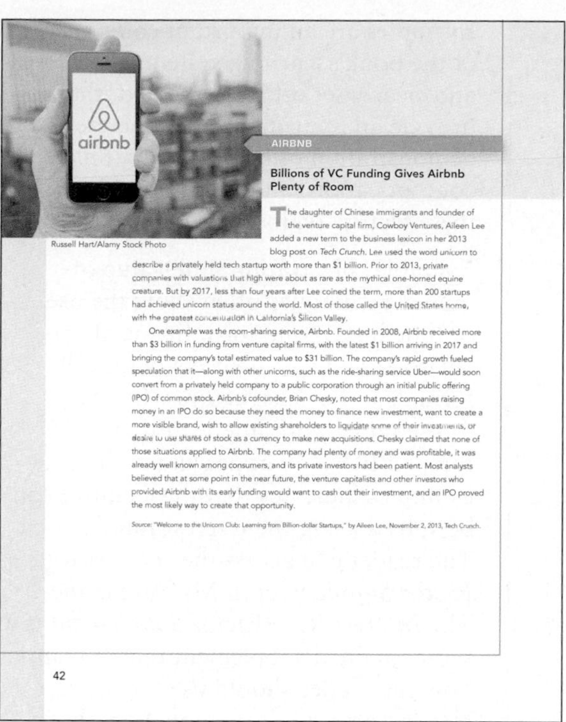

AIRBNB

Billions of VC Funding Gives Airbnb Plenty of Room

The daughter of Chinese immigrants and founder of the venture capital firm, Cowboy Ventures, Aileen Lee added a new term to the business lexicon in her 2013 blog post on *Tech Crunch*. Lee used the word *unicorn* to describe a privately held tech startup worth more than $1 billion. Prior to 2013, private companies with valuations that high were about as rare as the mythical one-horned equine creature. But by 2017, less than four years after Lee coined the term, more than 200 startups had achieved unicorn status around the world. Most of those called the United States home, with the greatest concentration in California's Silicon Valley.

One example was the room-sharing service, Airbnb. Founded in 2008, Airbnb received more than $3 billion in funding from venture capital firms, with the latest $1 billion arriving in 2017 and bringing the company's total estimated value to $31 billion. The company's rapid growth fueled speculation that it—along with other unicorns, such as the ride-sharing service Uber—would soon convert from a privately held company to a public corporation through an initial public offering (IPO) of common stock. Airbnb's cofounder, Brian Chesky, noted that most companies raising money in an IPO do so because they need the money to finance new investment, want to create a more visible brand, wish to allow existing shareholders to liquidate some of their investments, or desire to use shares of stock as a currency to make new acquisitions. Chesky claimed that none of those situations applied to Airbnb. The company had plenty of money and was profitable, it was already well known among consumers, and its private investors had been patient. Most analysts believed that at some point in the near future, the venture capitalists and other investors who provided Airbnb with its early funding would want to cash out their investment, and an IPO proved the most likely way to create that opportunity.

Source: "Welcome to the Unicorn Club: Learning from Billion-dollar Startups," by Aileen Lee, November 2, 2013, Tech Crunch.

Russell Hart/Alamy Stock Photo

42

Each chapter begins with a short **opening vignette** that describes a recent real-company event related to the chapter topic. These stories raise interest in the chapter by demonstrating its relevance in the business world. Most of these opening vignettes are entirely new to this edition. **New!** In MyLab Finance, users will find a brief video providing an overview of each chapter's content.

LG1 LG2

1.1 Finance and the Firm

The field of finance is broad and dynamic. Finance influences everything that firms do, from hiring personnel to building factories to launching new advertising campaigns. Because almost any aspect of business has important financial dimensions, many financially oriented career opportunities await those who understand the principles of finance described in this textbook. Even if you see yourself pursuing a career in another discipline such as marketing, operations, accounting, supply chain, or human resources, you'll find that understanding a few crucial ideas in finance will enhance your professional success. Knowing how financial managers think is important, especially if you're not one yourself, because they are often the gatekeepers of corporate resources. Fluency in the language of finance will improve your ability to communicate the value of your ideas to your employer. Financial knowledge will also make you a smarter consumer and a wiser investor with your own money.

Learning goal icons tie chapter content to the learning goals and appear next to related text sections and again in the chapter-end summary, end-of-chapter problems and exercises, and supplements such as the *Test Bank* and MyLab.

THE ROLE OF BUSINESS ETHICS

business ethics
Standards of conduct or moral judgment that apply to persons engaged in commerce.

Business ethics are the standards of conduct or moral judgment that apply to persons engaged in commerce. Violations of these standards involve a variety of actions: "creative accounting," earnings management, misleading financial forecasts, insider trading, fraud, excessive executive compensation, options backdating, bribery, and kickbacks. The financial press has reported many such violations in recent years, involving such well-known companies as Wells Fargo, where employees opened new accounts without authorization from customers, and Volkswagen, where engineers set up elaborate deceptions to get around pollution controls. In these and similar cases, the offending companies suffered various penalties, including fines levied by government agencies, damages paid to plaintiffs in lawsuits, or lost revenues from customers who abandoned the firms because of their errant behavior. Most companies have adopted formal

For help in study and review, boldfaced **key terms** and their definitions appear in the margin where they are first introduced. These terms are also boldfaced in the book's index and appear in the end-of-book glossary.

MATTER OF FACT

Finance Professors Aren't Like Everyone Else

Professionals who advise individual investors know that many people are more willing to invest in the stock market if it has been rising in the recent past and are less willing to do so if it has been falling. Such "trend-chasing" behavior often leaves investors worse off than if they had invested consistently over time. Classical finance theory suggests that past performance of the stock market is a very poor predictor of future performance, and therefore individuals should not base investment decisions on the market's recent history. A survey found that at least one group of investors did not fall prey to trend chasing in the stock market. When deciding whether to invest in stocks, finance professors were not influenced by the market's recent trend, presumably because they know that past performance does not predict the future. That's just one of the lessons in this book that can help you make better choices with your own money.

Source: Hibbert, Lawrence, and Prakash, 2012, "Do finance professors invest like everyone else?" *Financial Analysts Journal.*

Matter of Fact boxes provide interesting empirical facts, usually featuring recent data, that add background and depth to the material covered in the chapter.

IRF **EXAMPLE 5.10**

MyLab Finance Animation

In Example 5.8 involving Braden Company, we found the present value of Braden's $700, 5-year ordinary annuity discounted at 4% to be $3,116.28. We now assume that Braden's $700 annual cash in flow occurs at the *start* of each year and is thereby an annuity due. The following timeline illustrates the new situation.

Timeline for present value of an annuity due ($700 beginning-of-year cash flows, discounted at 4%, over 5 years)

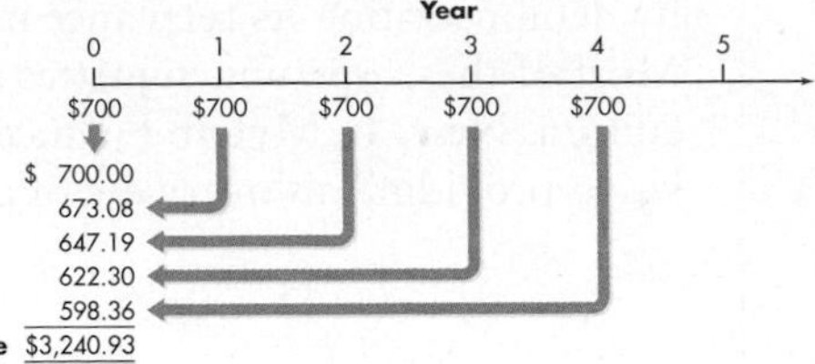

We can calculate its present value using a calculator or a spreadsheet.

MyLab Finance Financial Calculator

Note: Switch calculator to BEGIN mode.

Input	Function
700	PMT
4	I/Y
5	N
	CPT
	PV

Solution −3,240.93

Calculator use Before using your calculator to find the present value of an annuity due, you must either switch it to BEGIN mode or use the DUE key, depending on the specifics of your calculator. Then, using the inputs shown at the left, you will find the present value of the annuity due to be $3,240.93 (*Note:* Because we nearly always assume end-of-period cash flows, be sure to switch your calculator back to END mode when you have completed your annuity-due calculations.)

Spreadsheet use The following spreadsheet shows how to calculate the present value of the annuity due.

MyLab

	A	B
1	PRESENT VALUE OF AN ANNUITY DUE	
2	Annual annuity payment	$700
3	Annual rate of interest	4%
4	Number of years	5
5	Present value	−$3,240.93

Entry in Cell B5 is =PV(B3,B4,B2,0,1).
The minus sign appears before the $3,240.93 in B5 because the annuity's present value is a cost and therefore a cash outflow.

Examples are an important component of the book's learning system. Numbered and clearly set off from the text, they provide an immediate and concrete demonstration of how to apply financial concepts, tools, and techniques. Many of these feature real-world data.

Examples illustrating time-value-of-money techniques often show the use of time lines, equations, financial calculators, and spreadsheets (with cell formulas). For instructors who prefer to use tables with interest rate factors, an IRF icon appearing with some examples indicates that the example can be solved using the interest rate factors. The reader can access the *Interest Rate Factor Supplement* in MyLab Finance. The *Interest Rate Factor Supplement* is a self-contained supplement that explains how the reader should use the interest rate factors and documents how the in-chapter examples can be solved by using them.

MyLab Finance contains additional resources to demonstrate the examples. The MyLab Financial Calculator reference indicates that the reader can use the finance calculator tool in MyLab Finance to find the solution for an example by inputting the keystrokes shown in the calculator screenshot. The MyLab Finance Solution Video reference indicates that the reader can go to MyLab Finance to watch a video of the author discussing or solving the example. The MyLab Finance Video reference indicates that the reader can watch a video on related core topical areas.

IRF **PERSONAL FINANCE EXAMPLE 5.7**

MyLab Finance Animation

Fran Abrams wishes to determine how much money she will have after 5 years if she chooses annuity A, the ordinary annuity. She will deposit the $1,000 annual payments that the annuity provides at the end of each of the next 5 years into a savings account paying 7% annual interest. This situation is depicted on the following timeline.

Timeline for future value of an ordinary annuity ($1,000 end-of-year deposit, earning 7%, after 5 years)

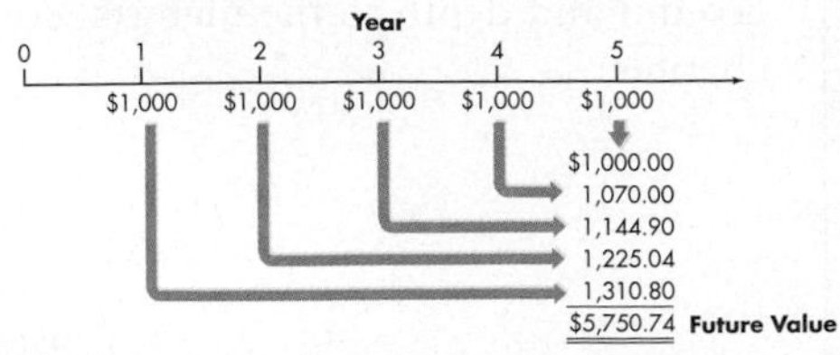

MyLab Finance Financial Calculator

As the figure shows, after 5 years, Fran will have $5,750.74 in her account. Note that because she makes deposits at the end of the year, the first deposit will earn

Personal Finance Examples demonstrate how students can apply managerial finance concepts, tools, and techniques to their personal financial decisions.

$$PV_0 = CF_1 \div r \tag{5.7}$$

Key Equations appear in green boxes throughout the text to help readers identify the most important mathematical relationships.

→ REVIEW QUESTIONS MyLab Finance Solutions

5–10 What is the difference between an ordinary annuity and an annuity due? Which is more valuable? Why?

5–11 What are the most efficient ways to calculate the present value of an ordinary annuity?

5–12 How can the formula for the future value of an annuity be modified to find the future value of an annuity due?

5–13 How can the formula for the present value of an ordinary annuity be modified to find the present value of an annuity due?

5–14 What is a perpetuity? Why is the present value of a perpetuity equal to the annual cash payment divided by the interest rate? Why doesn't this chapter provide an equation showing you how to calculate the future value of a perpetuity?

→ EXCEL REVIEW QUESTIONS MyLab Finance Solutions

5–15 Because tax time comes around every year, you smartly decide to make equal contributions to your IRA at the end of every year. Using the information provided at MyLab Finance, calculate the future value of your IRA contributions when you retire.

5–16 You have just graduated from college and begun your new career, and now it is time to buy your first home. Using the information provided at MyLab Finance, determine how much you can spend for your new dream home.

Review Questions appear at the end of each major text section. These questions challenge readers to stop and test their understanding of key concepts, tools, techniques, and practices before moving on to the next section.

NEW! Some sections have dedicated **Excel Review Questions** that ask students to demonstrate their ability to solve a financial problem using Excel.

FOCUS ON ETHICS *in practice*

Was the Deal for Manhattan a Swindle?

Most schoolchildren marvel when hearing Manhattan was purchased for a song in 1626. As the story goes, Peter Minuit of the Dutch West India Company gave the Lenape Native

about 787 Euros today after adjusting for inflation. Based on the recent exchange rate between the Euro and the U.S. dollar, that translates to about $871. Now, the deal looks a bit

to today, the sum would grow to roughly *4 trillion* guilders or $2 trillion. Based on New York City's Department of Finance property tax assessments, $2 trillion is roughly twice the

FOCUS ON PRACTICE *in practice*

New Century Brings Trouble for Subprime Mortgages

As the housing market began to boom at the end of the twentieth century and

adjustable rate mortgage (ARM), which featured a low introductory

Instead, borrowers in trouble could try to convince their lenders to allow

GLOBAL FOCUS *in practice*

Take an Overseas Assignment to Take a Step Up the Corporate Ladder

There is nothing like an extended stay in a foreign country to get a different perspective on world events, and there are sound career-enhancing reasons to work abroad. International experience can give you a competitive edge and may be vital to career advancement. Such experience goes far beyond mastering country-specific tax and accounting codes.

That's one message from the 2016 Global Mobility Trends Survey published by BGRS, a global human resources consulting company. The survey indicated that 61% of respondents said their company had communicated to employees that an international assignment was important to advance their careers. It's no wonder that companies place so much emphasis on international assignments, given that 80% of the survey respondents said the main purpose of having a globally mobile workforce was to facilitate important global business initiatives. The volume of international assignments reflected their importance to the success of a firm. The 2016 survey found that 63% of firms either increased or held steady the number of international assignments given to employees relative to the prior year, and 75% of firms said they expected the number of international assignments to remain the same or to increase through 2017.

On arrival in a foreign city, expatriates tend to live in a section of the city favored by other visitors from home. For security reasons, some executives also travel everywhere chauffeured by an English-speaking driver. It is possible for U.S. executives to live abroad for an extended period without soaking up much of the local culture. Doing so may increase one's comfort level, but at the loss of some of the valuable lessons to be learned from living abroad.

Overseas assignments do not come without some sacrifices. Long overseas postings can put stress on a family. The most common reason for turning down an international assignment (reported by 38% of survey respondents) involved family concerns, such as children's education, family adjustment, partner resistance, and language. The second most common reason (18%) for refusing an assignment was concern for a spouse's career, not unlike the same concern some employees have about a job that requires a cross-country transfer.

Yet as globalization has pushed companies across more borders, CFOs with international experience have found themselves in greater demand. Some chief executives value international experience in their CFOs more highly than either mergers and acquisitions or capital-raising experience.

► *If going abroad for a full-immersion assignment is not possible, what are some substitutes for a global assignment that may provide some—albeit limited—global experience?*

In Practice boxes offer insights into important topics in managerial finance through the experiences of real companies, both large and small. There are three categories of In Practice boxes:

Focus on Ethics boxes in every chapter help readers understand and appreciate important ethical issues and problems related to managerial finance. Nearly all of these boxes are brand new in this edition, and those that are not brand new have been substantially revised.

Focus on Practice boxes take a corporate focus that relates a business event or situation to a specific financial concept or technique.

Global Focus boxes look specifically at the managerial finance experiences of international companies.

All three types of In Practice boxes end with one or more *critical thinking questions* to help readers broaden the lesson from the content of the box.

SUMMARY

FOCUS ON VALUE

The time value of money is an important tool that financial managers and other market participants use to compare cash inflows and outflows occurring at different times. Because firms routinely make investments that produce cash inflows over long periods of time, the effective application of time-value-of-money techniques is extremely important. These techniques enable financial

REVIEW OF LEARNING GOALS

LG1 **Discuss the role of time value in finance, the use of computational tools, and the basic patterns of cash flow.** Financial managers and investors use time-value-of-money techniques when assessing the value of expected cash flow streams. Alternatives can be assessed by either compounding to find future value or discounting to find present value. Financial managers rely primarily on present-value techniques. Financial calculators and electronic spreadsheets

The end-of-chapter **Summary** consists of two sections. The first section, **Focus on Value**, explains how the chapter's content relates to the firm's goal of maximizing owner wealth. This feature helps reinforce understanding of the link between the financial manager's actions and share value.

The second part of the Summary, the **Review of Learning Goals**, restates each learning goal and summarizes the key material that was presented to support mastery of the goal. This review provides students with an opportunity to reconcile what they have learned with the learning goal and to confirm their understanding before moving forward.

OPENER-IN-REVIEW

The chapter opener described a lottery prize that could be taken as a $480 million lump sum payment or mixed stream of 30 payments, with the first payment of $11.42 million coming immediately, followed by 29 additional payments growing at 5% per year. If the lottery winner could earn 2% on cash invested today, should she take the lump sum or the mixed stream? What if the rate of return is 3%? What general principle do those calculations illustrate?

SELF-TEST PROBLEMS (Solutions in Appendix)

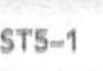

IRF

ST5–1 **Future values for various compounding frequencies** Delia Martin has $10,000 that she can deposit in any of three savings accounts for a 3-year period. Bank A compounds interest on an annual basis, bank B compounds interest twice each year, and bank C compounds interest each quarter. All three banks have a stated annual interest rate of 4%.

a. What amount would Ms. Martin have after 3 years, leaving all interest paid on deposit, in each bank?

b. What effective annual rate (EAR) would she earn in each of the banks?

c. On the basis of your findings in parts **a** and **b**, which bank should Ms. Martin deal with? Why?

d. If a fourth bank (bank D), also with a 4% stated interest rate, compounds interest continuously, how much would Ms. Martin have after 3 years? Does this alternative change your recommendation in part **c**? Explain why or why not.

Opener-In-Review questions at the end of each chapter revisit the opening vignette and ask students to apply lessons from the chapter to that business situation.

Self-Test Problems, keyed to the learning goals, give readers an opportunity to strengthen their understanding of topics by doing a sample problem. For reinforcement, solutions to the Self-Test Problems appear in the appendix at the back of the book. An IRF icon indicates that the Self-Test Problem can be solved using the interest rate factors. The reader can access the Interest Rate Factor Supplement in MyLab Finance.

WARM-UP EXERCISES All problems are available in MyLab Finance.

E5–1 Assume that a firm makes a $2,500 deposit into a short-term investment account. If this account is currently paying 0.7% (yes, that's right, less than 1%!), what will the account balance be after 1 year?

E5–2 If Bob and Judy combine their savings of $1,260 and $975, respectively, and deposit this amount into an account that pays 2% annual interest, compounded monthly, what will the account balance be after 4 years?

Warm-Up Exercises follow the Self-Test Problems. These short, numerical exercises give students practice in applying tools and techniques presented in the chapter.

PROBLEMS

All problems are available in MyLab Finance. The MyLab icon indicates problems in Excel format available in MyLab Finance.

LG2 P4–1 **Depreciation** On March 20, 2019, Norton Systems acquired two new assets. Asset A was research equipment costing $17,000 and having a 3-year recovery period. Asset B was duplicating equipment with an installed cost of $45,000 and a 5-year recovery period. Using the MACRS depreciation percentages in Table 4.2, prepare a depreciation schedule for each of these assets.

LG2 P4–2 **Depreciation** In early 2019, Sosa Enterprises purchased a new machine for $10,000 to make cork stoppers for wine bottles. The machine has a 3-year recovery period and is expected to have a salvage value of $2,000. Develop a depreciation schedule for this asset using the MACRS depreciation percentages in Table 4.2.

LG5 P4–20 **Integrative: Pro forma statements** Red Queen Restaurants wishes to prepare financial plans. Use the financial statements and the other information provided below to prepare the financial plans.

Comprehensive Problems, keyed to the learning goals, are longer and more complex than the Warm-Up Exercises. In this section, instructors will find multiple problems that address the important concepts, tools, and techniques in the chapter.

New! Excel templates for many end-of-chapter problems are available in MyLab Finance. These templates do not solve problems for students, but rather help students reach a solution faster by inputting data for them or by organizing facts presented in problems in a logical way.

A short descriptor identifies the essential concept or technique of the problem. Problems labeled as **Integrative** tie together related topics.

Personal Finance Problem

LG4 P4–11 **Preparation of cash budget** Sam and Suzy Sizeman need to prepare a cash budget for the last quarter of 2020 to make sure they can cover their expenditures during the period. Sam and Suzy have been preparing budgets for the past several years and have been able to identify the percentage of their income that they pay for most of

LG1 P4–22 **ETHICS PROBLEM** The SEC is trying to get companies to notify the investment community more quickly when a "material change" will affect their forthcoming financial results. In what sense might a financial manager be seen as "more ethical" if he or she follows this directive and issues a press release indicating that sales will not be as high as previously anticipated?

Personal Finance Problems specifically relate to personal finance situations and Personal Finance Examples in each chapter. These problems will help students see how they can apply the tools and techniques of managerial finance in managing their own finances.

All exercises and problems are available in MyLab Finance.

SPREADSHEET EXERCISE

You have been assigned the task of putting together a statement for the ACME Company that shows its expected inflows and outflows of cash over the months of July 2020 through December 2020.

Every chapter includes a **Spreadsheet Exercise**. This exercise gives students an opportunity to use Excel software to create one or more spreadsheets with which to analyze a financial problem. The spreadsheet to be created is often modeled on a table or Excel screenshot located in the chapter. Students can access working versions of the Excel screenshots in MyLab Finance.

Integrative Case 2

Track Software Inc.

Seven years ago, after 15 years in public accounting, Stanley Booker, CPA, resigned his position as manager of cost systems for Davis, Cohen, and O'Brien Public Accountants and started Track Software Inc. In the 2 years preceding his departure from Davis, Cohen, and O'Brien, Stanley had spent nights and weekends developing a sophisticated cost-accounting software program that became Track's initial product offering. As the firm grew, Stanley planned to develop and expand the software product offerings, all of which would be related to streamlining the accounting processes of medium- to large-sized manufacturers.

Although Track experienced losses during its first 2 years of operation—2013 and 2014—its profit has increased steadily from 2015 to the year just ended (2019). The firm's profit history, including dividend payments and contributions to retained earnings, is summarized in Table 1.

Stanley started the firm with a $100,000 investment: his savings of $50,000 as equity and a $50,000 long-term loan from the bank. He had hoped to maintain his initial 100% ownership in the corporation, but after experiencing a $50,000 loss during the first year of operation (2013), he sold 60% of the stock to a group of investors to obtain needed funds. Since then, no other stock transactions have taken place. Although he owns only 40% of the firm, Stanley actively manages all aspects of its activities; the other stockholders are not active in its management. The firm's stock was valued at $4.50 per share in 2018 and at $5.28 per share in 2019.

An **Integrative Case** at the end of each part of the book challenges students to use what they have learned over the course of several chapters. Additional chapter resources, such as Chapter Cases, Group Exercises, and numerous online resources, intended to provide further means for student learning and assessment are available in MyLab Finance at www.pearson.com/mylab/finance.

MyLab FINANCE

Reach Every Student by Pairing this Text with MyLab Finance

MyLab is the teaching and learning platform that empowers you to reach *every* student. By combining trusted author content with digital tools and a flexible platform, MyLab personalizes the learning experience and improves results for each student. Learn more about MyLab Finance at www.pearson.com/mylab/finance.

Deliver Trusted Content

You deserve teaching materials that meet your own high standards for your course. That's why Pearson partners with highly respected authors to develop interactive content and course-specific resources that you can trust—and that keep your students engaged.

Empower Each Learner

Each student learns at a different pace. Personalized learning pinpoints the precise areas where each student needs practice, giving all students the support they need—when and where they need it—to be successful.

Teach Your Course Your Way

Your course is unique. So whether you'd like to build your own assignments, teach multiple sections, or set prerequisites, MyLab gives you the flexibility to easily create *your* course to fit *your* needs.

Improve Student Results

When you teach with MyLab, student performance improves. That's why instructors have chosen MyLab for over 15 years, touching the lives of over 50 million students.

MyLab opens the door to a powerful Web-based tutorial, testing, and diagnostic learning system designed specifically for the Zutter/Smart, *Principles of Managerial Finance*. With MyLab, instructors can select an adaptable preconfigured course or create their own. Both options allow instructors to create, edit, and assign online homework, quizzes, and tests and track all student progress in the downloadable online gradebook. MyLab allows students to supplement and reinforce their in-class learning by taking advantage of a progress-driven Study Plan or self-selected practice problems, quizzes, and tests. For example, all end-of-chapter problems are assignable by instructors or selectable by students in MyLab, and because the problems have algorithmically generated values, no student will have the same homework as another or work the same problem twice; there is an unlimited opportunity for practice and testing. Students get the help they need, when they need it, from the robust tutorial options, including "View an Example" and "Help Me Solve This," which breaks the problem into steps and links to the relevant textbook page.

This fully integrated online system gives students the hands-on tutorial, practice, and diagnostic help they need to ensure they are effectively learning finance in the most efficient manner. Utilization of the resources available in MyLab Finance saves instructors time by enabling students to more effectively learn on their own and providing instructors with a full account of student progress, auto grading, and an online gradebook that can seamlessly link with a Learning Management System (e.g., Blackboard Learn, Brightspace by D2L, Canvas, or Moodle) or be downloaded to Excel.

The Multimedia Library in MyLab Finance provides students with access to a variety of chapter resources all intended to reinforce their learning and understanding of the textbook content. For example, students can access a Chapter Introduction Video for every chapter and dozens of Solution Videos for select in-chapter examples. Students can also access dynamic animations for select figures and examples throughout the book that provide them with the ability to control inputs and drive outputs to better understand the concepts.

The auto-graded Excel feature in MyLab Finance allows instructors to assign all Spreadsheet Exercises and select end-of-chapter problems without having to manually grade spreadsheets. Students have the opportunity to practice important finance skills in Excel and instructors have the ability to assess their learning without the hassle of time-consuming grading. Students simply download a spreadsheet, solve a finance problem in Excel, and then upload the file back to MyLab Finance. Students will receive personalized feedback on their work within minutes that allows them to pinpoint where they went wrong on any step of the problem.

Chapter Cases with automatically graded assessment are also provided in MyLab Finance. These cases have students apply the concepts they have learned to a more complex and realistic situation. These cases help strengthen practical application of financial tools and techniques.

MyLab also has Group Exercises that students can work together in the context of an ongoing company. Each group creates a company and follows it through the various managerial finance topics and business activities presented in the textbook.

MyLab Finance has an Interest Rate Factor Supplement that explains how to use the interest rate factors in time-value-of-money problems and works seamlessly with the textbook. The student can go directly to the IRF Supplement and see the in-chapter example solved using the interest rate factors. All examples that appear in the IRF Supplement are indicated in the text with an IRF icon.

Advanced reporting features in MyLab also allow you to easily report on AACSB accreditation and assessment in just a few clicks.

An online glossary, digital flashcards, financial calculator tutorials, videos, Spreadsheet Use examples from the text in Excel, and numerous other premium resources are available in MyLab.

DEVELOPING EMPLOYABILITY SKILLS

For students to succeed in a rapidly changing job market, they should be aware of their career options and how to go about developing a variety of skills. In this book and in MyLab Finance, we focus on developing these skills in a variety of ways.

Excel modeling skills—Each chapter contains a Spreadsheet Exercise that asks students to build an Excel model to help solve a business problem. Many

MyLab

	A	B
1	FUTURE VALUE OF AN ORDINARY ANNUITY	
2	Annual annuity payment	–$1,000
3	Annual rate of interest	7%
4	Number of years	5
5	Future value	$5,750.74

Entry in Cell B5 is =FV(B3,B4,B2,0,0).
The minus sign appears before the $1,000 in B2 because the annuity's payments are cash outflows.

chapters provide screenshots showing completed Excel models designed to solve in-chapter examples. Many chapters contain Excel Review Questions that prompt students to practice using Excel to solve specific types of problems. In addition, students can access the working Excel screenshots and solutions to the Excel Review Questions in MyLab Finance to further reenforce their learning and understanding. Also, in MyLab students will find dozens of Excel templates, marked in the text with a special icon, that help them model select end-of-chapter problems so they can reach a solution faster and with a deeper understanding of the underlying concepts. Finally, as mentioned above, every Excel Spreadsheet Exercise and select end-of-chapter problems can be assigned and auto graded.

Ethical reasoning skills—The *Focus on Ethics* boxes appearing in each chapter describe situations in which business professionals have violated ethical (and in some cases even legal) standards and have suffered consequences as a result. These boxes will help students recognize the ethical temptations they are likely to face while pursuing a finance career and the consequences that they may suffer if they behave unethically. Each chapter ends with an Ethics Problem that asks students to consider the ethical dimensions of some business decision.

Critical thinking skills—Nearly every significant financial decision requires critical thinking because making optimal decisions means weighing the marginal benefits and costs of alternative plans. To weigh those benefits and costs, one must first identify and quantify them. Nearly every chapter in this textbook discusses how financial analysts place a value on the net benefits associated with a particular decision. Students who master this material will be prepared to ask the tough questions necessary to assess whether a particular course of action creates value for shareholders.

Data analysis skills—Financial work is about data. Financial analysts have to identify the data that are relevant for a particular business problem, and they must know how to process that data in a way that leads to good decision making. In-chapter examples and end-of-chapter problems require students to sort out relevant from irrelevant data and to use the data that they have to make a clear recommendation about what course of action a firm should take.

TABLE OF CONTENTS OVERVIEW

The text's organization conceptually links the firm's actions and its value as determined in the financial market. We discuss every significant financial problem or decision in terms of both risk and return to assess the potential impact on owners' wealth. A Focus on Value element in each chapter's Summary helps reinforce the student's understanding of the link between the financial manager's actions and the firm's share value.

In organizing each chapter, we have adhered to a managerial decision-making perspective, relating decisions to the firm's overall goal of wealth maximization. Once a particular concept has been developed, its application is illustrated by an example, which is a hallmark feature of this book. These examples demonstrate, and solidify in the student's thought, financial decision-making considerations and their consequences.

INSTRUCTOR TEACHING RESOURCES

Supplements available to instructors at www.pearsonhighered.com/irc	Features of the Supplement
Instructor's Manual	• Overview of key topics • Detailed answers and solutions to all Opener-In-Review Questions, Warm-Up Exercises, end-of-chapter Problems, and Chapter Cases • Suggested answers to all critical thinking questions in chapter boxes, Ethics Problems, and Group Exercises • Spreadsheet Exercises • Group Exercises • Integrative Cases
Test Bank	More than 3,000 multiple-choice, true/false, short-answer, and graphing questions with these annotations: • Difficulty level (1 for straight recall, 2 for some analysis, 3 for complex analysis) • Type (Multiple-choice, true/false, short-answer, essay • Topic (The term or concept the question supports) • Learning outcome • AACSB learning standard (Ethical Understanding and Reasoning; Analytical Thinking Skills; Information Technology; Diverse and Multicultural Work; Reflective Thinking; Application of Knowledge)
Computerized TestGen	TestGen allows instructors to: • Customize, save, and generate classroom tests • Edit, add, or delete questions from the Test Item Files • Analyze test results • Organize a database of tests and student results
PowerPoints	Slides include all the figures and tables from the textbook. PowerPoints meet accessibility standards for students with disabilities. Features include, but are not limited to: • Keyboard and Screen Reader access • Alternative text for images • High color contrast between background and foreground colors

Acknowledgments

TO OUR COLLEAGUES, FRIENDS, AND FAMILY

Pearson sought the advice of a great many excellent reviewers, all of whom influenced the revisions of this book. The following individuals provided extremely thoughtful and useful comments for the preparation of the fifteenth edition:

Alan Blaylock, *Henderson State University*
Hsing Fang, *California State University, Los Angeles*
Carolyn Jarmon, *Empire State College*
Jerry Johnson, *Austin College*

Our special thanks go to the following individuals who contributed to the manuscript in the current and previous editions:

Saul W. Adelman
M. Fall Ainina
Gary A. Anderson
Ronald F. Anderson
James M. Andre
Gene L. Andrusco
Antonio Apap
David A. Arbeit
Allen Arkins
Saul H. Auslander
Peter W. Bacon
Richard E. Ball
Thomas Bankston
Alexander Barges
Charles Barngrover
Michael Becker
Omar Benkato
Robert Benson
Scott Besley
Douglas S. Bible
Charles W. Blackwell
Russell L. Block
Calvin M. Boardman
Paul Bolster
Robert J. Bondi
Jeffrey A. Born
Jerry D. Boswell
Denis O. Boudreaux
Kenneth J. Boudreaux
Thomas J. Boulton
Wayne Boyet
Ron Braswell
Christopher Brown
William Brunsen
Samuel B. Bulmash
Francis E. Canda
Omer Carey
Patrick A. Casabona
Johnny C. Chan
Robert Chatfield
K. C. Chen
Roger G. Clarke
Terrence M. Clauretie
Mark Cockalingam
Kent Cofoid
Boyd D. Collier
Thomas Cook
Maurice P. Corrigan
Mike Cudd
Donnie L. Daniel
Prabir Datta
Joel J. Dauten
Lee E. Davis
Irv DeGraw
Richard F. DeMong
Peter A. DeVito
R. Gordon Dippel
James P. D'Mello
Carleton Donchess
Thomas W. Donohue
Lorna Dotts
Vincent R. Driscoll
Betty A. Driver
David R. Durst
Dwayne O. Eberhardt
Ronald L. Ehresman
Ted Ellis
F. Barney English
Greg Filbeck
Ross A. Flaherty
Rich Fortin
Timothy J. Gallagher
George W. Gallinger
Sharon Garrison
Gerald D. Gay
Deborah Giarusso
R. H. Gilmer
Anthony J. Giovino
Lawrence J. Gitman
Michael Giuliano
Philip W. Glasgo
Jeffrey W. Glazer
Joel Gold
Ron B. Goldfarb
Dennis W. Goodwin
David A. Gordon
J. Charles Granicz
C. Ramon Griffin
Reynolds Griffith
Arthur Guarino
Lewell F. Gunter
Melvin W. Harju
John E. Harper
Phil Harrington
George F. Harris
George T. Harris
John D. Harris
Mary Hartman
R. Stevenson Hawkey

Roger G. Hehman
Harvey Heinowitz
Glenn Henderson
Russell H. Hereth
Kathleen T. Hevert
J. Lawrence Hexter
Douglas A. Hibbert
Roger P. Hill
Linda C. Hittle
James Hoban
Hugh A. Hobson
Keith Howe
Kenneth M. Huggins
Jerry G. Hunt
Mahmood Islam
James F. Jackson
Stanley Jacobs
Dale W. Janowsky
Jeannette R. Jesinger
Nalina Jeypalan
Timothy E. Johnson
Roger Juchau
Ashok K. Kapoor
Daniel J. Kaufman Jr.
Joseph K. Kiely
Terrance E. Kingston
Raj K. Kohli
Thomas M. Krueger
Lawrence Kryzanowski
Harry R. Kuniansky
William R. Lane
Richard E. La Near
James Larsen
Rick LeCompte
B. E. Lee
Scott Lee
Suk Hun Lee
Michael A. Lenarcic
A. Joseph Lerro
Thomas J. Liesz
Hao Lin
Alan Lines
Larry Lynch
Christopher K. Ma
James C. Ma
Dilip B. Madan
Judy Maese
James Mallet
Inayat Mangla
Bala Maniam
Timothy A. Manuel
Brian Maris
Daniel S. Marrone
William H. Marsh
John F. Marshall
Linda J. Martin
Stanley A. Martin
Charles E. Maxwell
Timothy Hoyt McCaughey
Lee McClain
Jay Meiselman
Vincent A. Mercurio
Joseph Messina
John B. Mitchell
Daniel F. Mohan
Charles Mohundro
Gene P. Morris
Edward A. Moses
Tarun K. Mukherjee
William T. Murphy
Randy Myers
Lance Nail
Donald A. Nast
Vivian F. Nazar
G. Newbould
Charles Ngassam
Alvin Nishimoto
Gary Noreiko
Dennis T. Officer
Kathleen J. Oldfather
Kathleen F. Oppenheimer
Richard M. Osborne
Jerome S. Osteryoung
Prasad Padmanabahn
Roger R. Palmer
Don B. Panton
John Park
Ronda S. Paul
Bruce C. Payne
Gerald W. Perritt
Gladys E. Perry
Stanley Piascik
Gregory Pierce
Mary L. Piotrowski
D. Anthony Plath
Jerry B. Poe
Gerald A. Pogue
Suzanne Polley
Ronald S. Pretekin
Fran Quinn
Rich Ravichandran
David Rayone
Walter J. Reinhart
Jack H. Reubens
Benedicte Reyes
William B. Riley Jr.
Ron Rizzuto
Gayle A. Russell
Patricia A. Ryan
Murray Sabrin
Kanwal S. Sachedeva
R. Daniel Sadlier
Hadi Salavitabar
Gary Sanger
Mukunthan Santhanakrishnan
William L. Sartoris
William Sawatski
Steven R. Scheff
Michael Schellenger
Michael Schinski
Tom Schmidt
Carl J. Schwendiman
Carl Schweser
Jim Scott
John W. Settle
Richard A. Shick
A. M. Sibley
Sandeep Singh
Surendra S. Singhvi
Stacy Sirmans
Barry D. Smith
Gerald Smolen
Ira Smolowitz
Jean Snavely
Joseph V. Stanford
John A. Stocker
Lester B. Strickler
Gordon M. Stringer
Elizabeth Strock
Donald H. Stuhlman
Sankar Sundarrajan
Philip R. Swensen
S. Tabriztchi
John C. Talbott
Gary Tallman
Harry Tamule
Richard W. Taylor
Rolf K. Tedefalk
Richard Teweles
Kenneth J. Thygerson
Robert D. Tollen
Emery A. Trahan
Barry Uze
Pieter A. Vandenberg
Nikhil P. Varaiya
Oscar Varela
Mark Vaughan
Kenneth J. Venuto
Sam Veraldi
James A. Verbrugge
Ronald P. Volpe

John M. Wachowicz Jr.
Faye (Hefei) Wang
William H. Weber III
Herbert Weinraub
Jonathan B. Welch
Grant J. Wells
Larry R. White
Peter Wichert
C. Don Wiggins
Howard A. Williams
Richard E. Williams
Glenn A. Wilt Jr.
Bernard J. Winger
Tony R. Wingler
Alan Wolk
I. R. Woods
John C. Woods
Robert J. Wright
Richard H. Yanow
Seung J. Yoon
Charles W. Young
Philip J. Young
Joe W. Zeman
John Zietlow
J. Kenton Zumwalt
Tom Zwirlein

Special thanks go to Alan Wolk of the University of Georgia for accuracy checking the quantitative content in the textbook. We are pleased by and proud of his efforts.

A hearty round of applause also goes to the publishing team assembled by Pearson—including Donna Battista, Kate Fernandes, Meredith Gertz, Melissa Honig, Miguel Leonarte, Kathy Smith, and others who worked on the book—for the inspiration and the perspiration that define teamwork. Also, special thanks to the formidable Pearson sales force in finance, whose ongoing efforts keep the business fun!

Finally, and most important, many thanks to our families for patiently providing support, understanding, and good humor throughout the revision process. To them we will be forever grateful.

Chad J. Zutter
Pittsburgh, Pennsylvania

Scott B. Smart
Bloomington, Indiana

PART ONE

Introduction to Managerial Finance

CHAPTERS IN THIS PART

Part 1 of *Principles of Managerial Finance* discusses the role of financial managers in businesses and the financial market environment in which firms operate. We argue that managers should aim to maximize the value of the firm and thereby maximize the wealth of its owners. Financial managers act on behalf of the firm's owners by making operating and investment decisions whose benefits exceed their costs. Such decisions create wealth for shareholders. Maximizing wealth is important because firms operate in a highly competitive financial market environment that offers shareholders many alternatives for investing. To raise the financial resources necessary to fund the firm's ongoing operations and future investment opportunities, managers must deliver value to the firm's investors. Without smart financial managers and access to financial markets, firms are unlikely to survive, let alone achieve the long-term goal of maximizing their value.

CHAPTER 1

The Role of Managerial Finance

LEARNING GOALS

LG1 Define finance and the managerial finance function.

LG2 Describe the goal of the firm, and explain why maximizing the value of the firm is an appropriate goal for a business.

LG3 Identify the primary activities of the financial manager.

LG4 Explain the key principles that financial managers use when making business decisions.

LG5 Describe the legal forms of business organization.

LG6 Describe the nature of the principal–agent relationship between the owners and managers of a corporation, and explain how various corporate governance mechanisms attempt to manage agency problems.

MyLab Finance Chapter Introduction Video

WHY THIS CHAPTER MATTERS TO YOU

In your *professional* life

ACCOUNTING You need to understand the relationships between the accounting and finance functions within the firm, how decision makers rely on the financial statements you prepare, why maximizing a firm's value is not the same as maximizing its profits, and the ethical duty you have when reporting financial results to investors and other stakeholders.

INFORMATION SYSTEMS You need to understand why financial information is important to managers in all functional areas, the documentation that firms must produce to comply with various regulations, and how manipulating information for personal gain can get managers into serious trouble.

MANAGEMENT You need to understand the various legal forms of a business organization, how to communicate the goal of the firm to employees and other stakeholders, the advantages and disadvantages of the agency relationship between a firm's managers and its owners, and how compensation systems can align or misalign the interests of managers and investors.

MARKETING You need to understand why increasing a firm's revenues or market share is not always a good thing, how financial managers evaluate aspects of customer relations such as cash and credit management policies, and why a firm's brands are an important part of its value to investors.

OPERATIONS You need to understand the financial benefits of increasing a firm's production efficiency, why maximizing profit by cutting costs may not increase the firm's value, and how managers have a duty to act on behalf of investors when operating a corporation.

In your *personal* life

Many principles of managerial finance also apply to your personal life. Learning a few simple principles can help you manage your own money more effectively.

BROOKDALE SENIOR LIVING

Is Brookdale's Management about to Be Retired?

Kristoffer Tripplaar/Alamy Stock Photo

For the owner and operator of Brookdale Senior Living Inc., which runs senior living facilities throughout the United States, 2016 proved difficult. The company's stock price started the year at $19.30 per share, but by year's end it had fallen 36% to $12.35. That drop took place in a year in which the broad stock market was up roughly 10%, so Brookdale's poor performance was especially irritating to its investors. Expressing frustration at Brookdale's lackluster performance, one of its largest shareholders, an investment management firm called Land and Buildings, issued a public letter to management and other shareholders demanding change. Specifically, the Land and Buildings letter called for Brookdale's management team to sell the physical real estate the company owned, distribute the proceeds from those sales directly to Brookdale shareholders, and sign contracts with the new property owners to manage the senior living facilities. Land and Buildings estimated that Brookdale could sell its real estate assets for as much as $21 per share, well above the company's then-current stock price. In other words, they were arguing that Brookdale's assets would be more valuable under someone else's control. Their letter concluded by saying, "It is time for Brookdale's Board of Directors to take affirmative action to ***maximize value***."

Less than 3 weeks later, investors learned that another firm was in talks to acquire part or all of Brookdale's assets, and the stock price moved up 20% in just 2 days. By mid-February, however, negotiations between Brookdale and its potential suitor had broken off, news that sent Brookdale's stock down more than 6% in a few hours.

The recent saga of Brookdale Senior Living illustrates several key ideas in finance. First, Brookdale's shareholders believe that management has a responsibility to operate the firm in a manner that maximizes the value of the company's stock. Second, the actions of Brookdale's management team seem to be at odds with what is desired by at least some of the firm's shareholders. Third, when a firm's financial performance remains subpar for an extended period, investors and other outside entities may try to reverse that trend by intervening, even if that calls for buying the company to wrest control from the existing management team.

Sources: "Land and Buildings issues letter to Brookdale Senior Living shareholders highlighting path to real estate monetization and maximizing shareholder value," Businesswire.com, December 20, 2016; "Activist shareholder pushes Brookdale to deliver on rumored deal," Seniorhousingnews.com, January 16, 2017; "Brookdale Senior Living shares fall after report Blackstone is no longer interested," cnbc.com, February 17, 2017.

LG1 LG2

1.1 Finance and the Firm

The field of finance is broad and dynamic. Finance influences everything that firms do, from hiring personnel to building factories to launching new advertising campaigns. Because almost any aspect of business has important financial dimensions, many financially oriented career opportunities await those who understand the principles of finance described in this textbook. Even if you see yourself pursuing a career in another discipline such as marketing, operations, accounting, supply chain, or human resources, you'll find that understanding a few crucial ideas in finance will enhance your professional success. Knowing how financial managers think is important, especially if you're not one yourself, because they are often the gatekeepers of corporate resources. Fluency in the language of finance will improve your ability to communicate the value of your ideas to your employer. Financial knowledge will also make you a smarter consumer and a wiser investor with your own money.

WHAT IS FINANCE?

finance
The science and art of how individuals and firms raise, allocate, and invest money.

managerial finance
Concerns the duties of the financial manager in a business.

Finance is the science and art of how individuals and firms raise, allocate, and invest money. The science of finance utilizes financial theories and concepts to establish general rules that can guide managers in their decisions. The art of finance involves adapting theory to particular business situations with their own unique circumstances. **Managerial finance** is concerned with the responsibilities of a financial manager working in a business. Though business finance is the primary focus of this book, the principles of finance apply to both personal and professional decision making. At the personal level, for instance, finance helps individuals decide how much of their earnings to spend, how much to save, and how to invest their savings. Financial thinking helps consumers decide when borrowing money is appropriate and enables them to critically evaluate loan offers with different terms. In a business context, finance involves the same types of decisions: how firms raise money from investors, how firms invest money in attempting to create value for their investors, and how firms decide whether to reinvest earnings in the business or distribute

MATTER OF FACT

Finance Professors Aren't Like Everyone Else

Professionals who advise individual investors know that many people are more willing to invest in the stock market if it has been rising in the recent past and are less willing to do so if it has been falling. Such "trend-chasing" behavior often leaves investors worse off than if they had invested consistently over time. Classical finance theory suggests that past performance of the stock market is a very poor predictor of future performance, and therefore individuals should not base investment decisions on the market's recent history. A survey found that at least one group of investors did not fall prey to trend chasing in the stock market. When deciding whether to invest in stocks, finance professors were not influenced by the market's recent trend, presumably because they know that past performance does not predict the future. That's just one of the lessons in this book that can help you make better choices with your own money.

Source: Hibbert, Lawrence, and Prakash, 2012, "Do finance professors invest like everyone else?" *Financial Analysts Journal.*

earnings back to investors. The keys to good financial decisions are much the same for businesses and individuals, which is why most students will benefit from an understanding of finance regardless of their profession. Learning the techniques of good financial analysis will not only help you make better financial decisions as a consumer but will also assist you in understanding the financial consequences of important business decisions, no matter what career path you follow.

WHAT IS A FIRM?

What is a firm? Put simply, a firm is a business organization that sells goods or services. However, a more complete answer attempts to explain why firms exist. They exist because investors want access to risky investment opportunities. In other words, firms are risky business organizations that, if not for investors' willingness to bear risk, would have difficulty generating the necessary investment capital to operate. For example, most investors do not have the expertise or wealth required to start a personal computer company, so instead they invest in a company like Apple. Even when a few individuals, such as Steve Jobs, Steve Wozniak, and Ronald Wayne, had the requisite expertise and wealth to start Apple Computer in a garage in 1976, vast amounts of additional money (i.e., investment capital) from investors were necessary for the firm to grow into what Apple is today. So, ultimately, firms are intermediaries that bring together investors and risky investment opportunities. Firms pool investment capital, make risky investment decisions, and manage risky investments all on behalf of investors who would otherwise not be able to do so effectively or efficiently on their own.

WHAT IS THE GOAL OF THE FIRM?

What goal should managers pursue? This question has no shortage of possible answers. Some might argue that managers should focus entirely on satisfying customers. Firms pursuing this goal could measure their products' market shares to gauge progress. Others suggest that managers must first inspire and motivate employees; in that case, employee turnover might be the key success metric to watch. Clearly, the goal or goals that managers select will affect many of the decisions they make, so choosing an objective is a critical determinant of how businesses operate.

Maximize Shareholder Wealth

Finance teaches that the primary goal of managers should be to maximize the wealth of the firm's owners—the stockholders or shareholders. Through the years, that recommendation has generated a lot of controversy. *The Economist* magazine once referred to shareholder value maximization as "the most powerful idea in business," but Jack Welch, the long-time Chief Executive Officer (CEO) of General Electric and a man *Fortune* magazine named "Manager of the Century," once called maximizing shareholder value "the dumbest idea in the world." Welch's assessment is particularly ironic because during his leadership, almost no company generated more wealth for its shareholders than General Electric. A $1,000 investment in GE stock made in 1981 when Welch took the reigns as CEO would have grown to roughly $67,000 by the time he retired in 2001. The simplest and best measure of stockholder wealth is the share price, so most finance textbooks (including ours) instruct managers to take actions that increase the firm's share price.

A common misconception is that when firms strive to make their shareholders happy, they do so at the expense of other constituencies such as customers, employees, or suppliers. This line of thinking ignores that in most cases, enriching shareholders requires managers to first satisfy the demands of these other interest groups, at least to some degree. Dividends ultimately received by stockholders come from the firm's profits. It is unlikely, then, that a firm whose customers are unhappy with its products, whose employees are looking for jobs at other firms, or whose suppliers are reluctant to ship raw materials will make shareholders rich because such a firm will likely be less profitable in the long run than one that better manages its relations with these stakeholder groups.

Therefore, we argue that the goal of the firm, as well as of managers, should be *to maximize the wealth of the owners for whom it is being operated*, which in most instances is equivalent to *maximizing the stock price*. This goal translates into a straightforward decision rule for managers: *Managers should take only*

FOCUS ON ETHICS *in practice*

Do Corporate Executives Have a Social Responsibility?

In a modern corporation, shareholders rely on management to oversee day-to-day operations. In this relationship, stockholders are principals and management their agents. Accordingly, the first duty of a corporation's management team is to maximize shareholder wealth. What role should social responsibility—that is, consideration of broader societal goals like slowing climate change—play in corporate decision making?

In a famous *New York Times* essay, Milton Friedman (winner of the 1976 Nobel Memorial Prize in Economic Sciences) argued corporate executives have no social responsibility. Their sole aim should be serving the pecuniary interests of their employers, the shareholders (subject, of course, to the constraints of the law). When executives use corporate resources to pursue other ends, they are spending someone else's money. Because it is practically impossible to guess exactly how individual shareholders would like to see their money spent to better the world—which specific social goals to pursue and how much to spend on each—management should focus exclusively on maximizing shareholder wealth and let shareholders use the proceeds to address social concerns on their own.

Friedman would acknowledge an exception to this doctrine. If use of corporate resources to pursue a social goal actually does more for stockholders financially than any alternative project (such as investment in a marketing campaign or new factories), then social responsibility is consistent with maximizing shareholder wealth. This may have been a consideration when Exxon Mobil—the world's largest publicly traded international oil and gas company—published its position on climate change:

> We have the same concerns as people everywhere—and that is how to provide the world with the energy it needs while reducing greenhouse gas emissions.
>
> The risk of climate change is clear and the risk warrants action. Increasing carbon emissions in the atmosphere are having a warming effect. There is a broad scientific and policy consensus that action must be taken to further quantify and assess the risks.
>
> ExxonMobil is taking action by reducing greenhouse gas emissions in its operations, helping consumers reduce their emissions, supporting research that leads to technology breakthroughs and participating in constructive dialogue on policy options.
>
> Addressing climate change, providing economic opportunity and lifting billions out of poverty are complex and interrelated issues requiring complex solutions. There is a consensus that comprehensive strategies are needed to respond to these risks.

► *How would Friedman view a sole proprietor's use of firm resources to pursue social goals?*

Friedman, Milton, "A Friedman Doctrine—The Social Responsibility Of Business Is to Increase Its Profits." *New York Times Magazine*, September 13, 1970, pp. 33, 122–26; Leube, Kurt R., *Essence of Friedman*. Stanford, CA: Hoover Institution Press, 1987; Exxon Mobil's Perspective on Climate Change: http://corporate.exxonmobil.com/en/current-issues/climate-policy/climate-perspectives/our-position *actions that they expect will increase the shareholders' wealth.* Although that objective sounds simple, its implementation is not always easy. To determine whether a particular course of action will increase or decrease shareholders' wealth, managers have to assess what return (i.e., cash inflows net of cash outflows) and risk (i.e., the uncertainty of the net cash flows) the action will bring. How managers do that is the focus of this book.

MATTER OF FACT

Firms Accelerate Dividends So That Shareholders Save on Taxes

One way that firms can maximize the wealth of shareholders is by thinking carefully about the taxes their shareholders must pay on dividends. Tax cuts enacted by Congress in 2003 lowered the tax rate on most dividends received by shareholders to a modest 15%. However, the legislation contained a provision by which the tax cuts would expire in 2013 unless Congress specifically acted to renew them. With a political compromise to renew the tax cuts looking unlikely in the 2012 election year, many firms announced plans to accelerate dividend payments they had planned to make in early 2013 to late 2012. The Washington Post Company, for example, announced that on December 27, 2012, it would pay out the entire $9.80 per share dividend that it had planned to distribute in 2013. What was the stock market's reaction to that announcement? Washington Post shares rose $5. By accelerating their dividend payments, companies such as Washington Post, Expedia, Inc., and luxury goods producer Coach, Inc., were increasing the wealth of their shareholders by helping them save taxes.

earnings per share (EPS)
The amount earned during the period on behalf of each outstanding share of stock, calculated by dividing the period's total earnings available for the firm's stockholders by the number of shares of stock outstanding.

Maximize Profit?

It might seem intuitive that maximizing a firm's share price is equivalent to maximizing its profits. That thought is not always correct, however.

Corporations commonly measure profits in terms of **earnings per share (EPS)**, which represent the amount earned during the period on behalf of each outstanding share of stock. Accountants calculate EPS by dividing the period's total earnings available for the firm's stockholders by the number of shares of stock outstanding.

EXAMPLE 1.1

MyLab Finance Solution Video

Nick Dukakis, the financial manager of Neptune Manufacturing, a producer of marine engine components, is choosing between two investments, Rotor and Valve. The following table shows the EPS Dukakis expects each investment to earn over its 3-year life.

	Earnings per share (EPS)			
Investment	Year 1	Year 2	Year 3	Total for years 1, 2, and 3
Rotor	$1.40	$1.00	$0.40	$2.80
Valve	0.60	1.00	1.40	3.00

If Dukakis thought he should make decisions to maximize profits, he would recommend that Neptune invest in Valve rather than Rotor because it results in higher total earnings per share over the 3-year period ($3.00 EPS compared with $2.80 EPS).

Does profit maximization lead to the highest possible share price? For at least three reasons, the answer is often no. First, timing is important. An investment that provides a small profit quickly may be preferable to one that produces a larger profit if that profit comes in the distant future. Second, profits and cash flows are not identical. The profit reported by a firm is simply an estimate of how it is doing, an estimate influenced by many different accounting choices made by firms when assembling their financial reports. Cash flow is a more straightforward measure of the money flowing into and out of the company than is profit. Companies must pay their bills with cash, not profits, so cash flow matters most to financial managers and investors. Third, risk is a major consideration. A firm that earns a low but reliable profit might be more valuable than another firm with profits that fluctuate a great deal (and therefore can be very high or very low at different times).

Timing Because a firm can earn a return on funds it receives, *the receipt of funds sooner rather than later is preferred.* In our example, even though the total earnings from Rotor are smaller than those from Valve, Rotor provides much greater earnings per share in the first year. It's possible that by investing in Rotor, Neptune Manufacturing can reinvest the earnings that it receives in year 1 to generate higher profits overall than if it had invested in project Valve. If the rate of return Neptune can earn on reinvested earnings is high enough, managers may do better to invest in project Rotor even though project Valve generates higher profits over the 3 years.

Cash Flows Profits do not necessarily result in cash flows available to stockholders. The accounting assumptions and techniques that a firm adopts can sometimes allow it to show a positive profit even when its cash outflows exceed cash inflows. For instance, suppose a retail electronics store buys a laptop from a supplier in December for $1,000 and sells it a few days later for $1,500. The profit on this transaction for the month of December is $500, but what is the cash flow? If the retailer pays its supplier $1,000 in December but allows its customer to pay for the laptop a month later in January, then the retailer actually has a net cash outflow in December.

For these and other reasons, higher earnings do not necessarily translate into a higher stock price. Earnings increases accompanied by increases in future cash flows are what produce higher stock prices. For example, a firm could increase its earnings by significantly reducing its equipment maintenance expenditures. If the reduced spending on maintenance results in lower product quality, however, the firm may impair its competitive position, and its stock price could drop as investors anticipate lower future cash flows and sell the stock. In this case, the earnings increase was accompanied by lower future cash flows and therefore a lower stock price.

risk
The chance that actual outcomes may differ from those expected.

risk averse
Requiring compensation to bear risk.

Risk Profit maximization also fails to account for **risk,** the chance that actual outcomes may differ from those expected. A basic premise in finance is that a tradeoff exists between return (cash flow) and risk. In general, stockholders are **risk averse,** which means they are willing to bear risk only if they expect compensation for doing so. In other words, investors demand higher returns on riskier investments, and they will accept lower returns on relatively safe investments. What this signifies in terms of the goal of the firm is that maximizing profits may not maximize the stock price. Suppose one firm is slightly more profitable than another, but investing in the firm with marginally higher profits also entails greater risk. Investors may well be willing to pay a higher price for the stock of the firm that produces lower but more predictable profits.

As another way to express this idea, we can say that cash flow and risk affect share price differently. Holding risk fixed, investors will pay more for the stock of a firm that generates higher cash flows and profits. In contrast, holding cash flow fixed, investors will pay more for shares that are less risky because they do not like risk. The key point, explored in more depth later, is that differences in risk can significantly affect the value of different investments. *Return and risk are, in fact, the key determinants of share price, which represents the wealth of the firm's owners.*

Maximize Stakeholders' Welfare?

stakeholders
Groups such as employees, customers, suppliers, creditors, and others who have a direct economic link to the firm but are not owners.

Critics of the view that managers should maximize the wealth of shareholders have advanced an alternative goal advocating a balanced consideration of the welfare of shareholders and other firm stakeholders. **Stakeholders** are individuals who are not owners of the firm but who nevertheless have some economic interest in it. Stakeholders include employees, suppliers, customers, and even members of the local community where a firm is located. Those who argue that firms should focus on stakeholders' interests maintain that shareholder value maximization as a business objective is far too narrow. This stakeholder view is widely held and indeed is reflected in the corporate law of countries such as Germany, France, and Japan, whereas the shareholder value maximization perspective is more common in the United States and the United Kingdom.

We see a number of flaws in recommending that firms neglect shareholder wealth maximization in favor of a broader stakeholder perspective. First, as we have already pointed out, maximizing shareholder wealth does not in any way imply that managers should ignore the interests of everyone connected to a firm who is not a shareholder. Managers cannot maximize the value of a firm if their employees, customers, and suppliers are constantly dissatisfied—all those stakeholders are free to do business with other firms. A recent study found that when firms were added to *Fortune* magazine's list of the best companies to work for (presumably a sign of labor-friendly practices), their stock prices jumped.[1] This evidence led the study's authors to conclude that the benefits of labor-friendly practices outweigh the costs. Apparently, what is good for employees is also good for shareholders.

Second, proponents of the stakeholder perspective often argue that in pursuit of maximizing shareholder value, managers take actions that push up the stock price in the short run to the detriment of the firm's long-run performance. In fact, to maximize shareholder value, managers must necessarily assess the long-term consequences of their actions because investors will certainly do so.

---

1. Olubunmi Faleye and Emery Trahan, "Labor-friendly corporate practices: Is what is good for employees good for shareholders?" *Journal of Investing*, June 2011.

To illustrate, consider that in March 2017, the online retailing giant Amazon reported that it earned a profit of $4.90 per share over the previous 12 months. Another company, Clorox, reported almost identical earnings per share of $4.92. Yet the stock prices of these two companies could not have been more different. Amazon was trading for $850 per share, whereas Clorox stock was selling for just $137. In other words, investors were willing to pay 6 times more for shares of Amazon even though it reported virtually the same EPS as Clorox. Why? Several factors may contribute, but the most plausible answer is that investors envision rosier long-term prospects for Amazon. If the only matter of concern to investors was short-term profits, then the prices of Amazon and Clorox should have been much closer because their profits, at least in the short term, were nearly identical.

Third, the stakeholder perspective is intrinsically difficult to implement, and advocates of the idea that managers should consider all stakeholders' interests along with those of shareholders do not typically indicate how managers should carry it out. For example, how much emphasis should managers place on the interests of different stakeholder groups? Are the interests of employees more or less important than the desires of customers? Should members of the local community who do no business with the firm have an equal say with the firm's suppliers? When different stakeholder groups disagree on the action a firm should take, how should managers make important decisions? In contrast, the goal of shareholder maximization clarifies what actions managers should take.

Fourth, many people misinterpret the statement that managers should maximize shareholder wealth as implying that managers should take any action, including illegal or unethical actions, that increases the stock price. Even the most ardent supporters of shareholder value maximization as the firm's primary goal acknowledge that managers must act within ethical and legal boundaries.

THE ROLE OF BUSINESS ETHICS

business ethics
Standards of conduct or moral judgment that apply to persons engaged in commerce.

Business ethics are the standards of conduct or moral judgment that apply to persons engaged in commerce. Violations of these standards involve a variety of actions: "creative accounting," earnings management, misleading financial forecasts, insider trading, fraud, excessive executive compensation, options backdating, bribery, and kickbacks. The financial press has reported many such violations in recent years, involving such well-known companies as Wells Fargo, where employees opened new accounts without authorization from customers, and Volkswagen, where engineers set up elaborate deceptions to get around pollution controls. In these and similar cases, the offending companies suffered various penalties, including fines levied by government agencies, damages paid to plaintiffs in lawsuits, or lost revenues from customers who abandoned the firms because of their errant behavior. Most companies have adopted formal ethical standards, although clearly adherence to and enforcement of those standards vary. The goal of such standards is to motivate business and market participants to adhere to both the letter and the spirit of laws and regulations concerned with business and professional practice. Most business leaders believe that businesses actually strengthen their competitive positions by maintaining high ethical standards.

Ethical Guidelines

Robert A. Cooke, a noted ethicist, suggests that the following questions be used to assess the ethical viability of a proposed action.[2]

1. Is the action arbitrary or capricious? Does it unfairly single out an individual or group?
2. Does the action violate the moral or legal rights of any individual or group?
3. Does the action conform to accepted moral standards?
4. Are there alternative courses of action that are less likely to cause actual or potential harm?

Clearly, considering such questions before taking an action can help ensure its ethical viability.

Today, many firms are addressing the issue of ethics by establishing corporate ethics policies that outline a set of fundamental principles guiding what their employees must or must not do. Some firms go further and make their ethical standards the centerpiece of their corporate image. For example, Google famously adopted the motto "Don't be evil." Even for Google, however, ethical dilemmas are unavoidable in business. The *Focus on Practice* box provides an example of ethical concerns confronting Google in the wake of the 2016 U.S. presidential election.

A major impetus toward the development of ethics policies has been the Sarbanes-Oxley Act of 2002. The act requires firms to disclose whether they have a code of ethics in place, and firms must report any waivers of those codes for senior management. Companies that do not have a code of ethics must explain why they have not adopted one. Many firms require their employees to sign a formal pledge to uphold the firm's ethics policies. Such policies typically apply to employee actions in dealing with all corporate stakeholders, including the public.

Ethics and Share Price

An effective ethics program can enhance corporate value by producing positive benefits. It can reduce potential litigation and judgment costs; maintain a positive corporate image; build shareholder confidence; and gain the loyalty, commitment, and respect of the firm's stakeholders. By maintaining and enhancing cash flow and reducing perceived risk, such actions can positively affect the firm's share price. Ethical behavior is therefore necessary for achieving the firm's goal of owner wealth maximization.

→ REVIEW QUESTIONS MyLab Finance Solutions

1–1 What is the goal of the firm and, therefore, of managers and employees? Discuss how one measures achievement of this goal.

1–2 For what three main reasons is profit maximization potentially inconsistent with wealth maximization?

2. Robert A. Cooke, "Business Ethics: A Perspective," in *Arthur Andersen Cases on Business Ethics* (Chicago: Arthur Andersen, September 1991), pp. 2 and 5.

FOCUS ON PRACTICE *in practice*

Must Search Engines Screen Out Fake News?

During his January 11, 2017, press conference, President-elect Donald Trump berated reporter Jim Acosta and his employer, CNN, saying, "You are fake news." For news organizations to question the validity of facts cited by politicians was nothing unusual, especially during an election year, but throughout the 2016 presidential election cycle, Trump turned that dynamic on its head through his confrontations with CNN and other news organizations. These exchanges sparked a debate about the responsibility of Google, Facebook, and other Internet-based companies to identify websites spreading fake news.

Google offers an interesting case study on value maximization and corporate ethics. In 2004, Google's founders provided "An Owner's Manual" for shareholders, which stated that "Google is not a conventional company" and that the company's ultimate goal "is to develop services that significantly improve the lives of as many people as possible." The founders stressed that running a successful business is not enough; they also want Google to make the world a better place. In light of that objective, what responsibility did Google have in helping voters distinguish real news from fake news? Just 1 month before the election, Google introduced a new "fact-check tag," to help readers assess the validity of news stories they were reading online. In subsequent months, Google introduced the fact-check tag to markets in other countries where elections were taking place, and it began new initiatives such as "CrossCheck," an effort to combine the work of human fact checkers with computer algorithms to identify fake news stories in France during its election cycle.

Google's famous corporate motto, "Don't Be Evil," is intended to convey a willingness to do the right thing even at the cost of sacrifice in the short run. Google's approach does not appear to be limiting its ability to maximize value, as the company's share price increased almost 1200% from 2004 to 2017!

▶ *Is the goal of maximizing shareholder wealth necessarily ethical or unethical?*

▶ *What responsibility, if any, does Google have in helping users assess the veracity of content they read online?*

Sources: "Labeling fact-check articles in Google News," by Richard Gingras, October 13, 2016, https://blog.google/topics/journalism-news/labeling-fact-check-articles-google-news/; "Google and Facebook combat fake news in France," BI Intelligence, February 7, 2017, businessinsider.com.

1–3 What is risk? Why must financial managers consider risk as well as return when they evaluate a decision alternative or action?

1–4 Is maximizing shareholder wealth inconsistent with having concern for the welfare of a firm's other stakeholders?

1.2 Managing the Firm

This book is about how managers running a firm can create value for the firm's investors through sound financial decision making. Responsibility for creating value does not rest solely or even primarily on the finance function. Marketers create value by identifying the unmet needs of customers, by making customers aware that their firm can meet those needs, and by establishing a solid brand. Employees working in the operations and supply chain functions contribute to a firm's value by streamlining manufacturing processes and securing reliable raw materials sources at reasonable cost. Human resources professionals help acquire and retain the talent firms need to achieve success. Accountants track the performance of the firm, help create financial plans and budgets, and ensure compliance with a host of regulatory requirements. And of course, financial managers advise all their peers in other functions on the financial consequences of their decisions.

The point is that nearly every employee, regardless of how his or her work helps enhance the firm's value, will interact with financial managers and will benefit from a basic working knowledge of financial principles. Every firm has limited resources, and employees in each part of a firm need some of those resources to function. Inside a firm, resource allocation is partly a matter of negotiation. Those who can make a better case that their work adds value will be more successful in acquiring the needed resources. Often the key to negotiating successfully in that environment is understanding the language of finance. To be a successful marketer or supply chain analyst or human resources professional, you must be able to explain how your work adds value in financial terms. This book will help you do just that.

Naturally our primary focus here is on what financial managers do. Therefore, we now turn to an overview of the managerial finance function.

THE MANAGERIAL FINANCE FUNCTION

Financial managers touch every part of a firm because everything that a firm does has some kind of financial impact. Employees in a firm's finance department help control costs on the factory floor. They analyze the market potential of new products and services. They quantify the costs and benefits of hiring additional workers. They assist in mitigating risks associated with unexpected movements in interest rates, commodity prices, and exchange rates. How do they accomplish all these things? The answer is that they rely on an essential set of principles and tools that are transferable to many different business applications. The managerial finance function is therefore not just about what financial managers do but also (and more importantly) about the methods they rely on daily.

Financial Managers' Key Decisions

Broadly speaking, most decisions that financial managers make, or help their colleagues in other functions make, fall into three broad categories: investment decisions, financing decisions, and working capital decisions. Some specialized areas of managerial finance do not fit neatly into any of these three categories, but the vast majority of decisions by financial managers relate to these broad areas.

investment decisions
Decisions that focus on how a company will spend its financial resources on long-term projects that ultimately determine whether the firm successfully creates value for its owners.

Investment decisions focus on how a company will spend its financial resources on long-term projects that ultimately determine whether the firm successfully creates value for its owners. For a semiconductor company like Intel, investment decisions revolve around how much money the firm should spend on new factories (each of which cost $5 billion to build), how much it should devote to research and development (Intel spends more than $12 billion annually), and how much the company should invest in its traditional microprocessors versus chips for newer wearable devices and products related to the Internet of Things. These are the most important decisions made by firms because they largely dictate whether a company succeeds or fails in the long run. Financial managers contribute to these decisions by performing a type of financial analysis known as capital budgeting, which we will discuss at length in subsequent chapters. Briefly, **capital budgeting** is a technique that helps managers decide which projects create the most value for shareholders. Essentially, capital budgeting identifies investment opportunities for which benefits exceed costs. Because value maximization requires managers to take actions only when benefits exceed costs, capital budgeting gives managers a tool for guiding investment decisions in a way that is directly linked to the goal of the firm.

capital budgeting
A technique that helps managers decide which projects create the most value for shareholders.

financing decisions
Decisions that determine how companies raise the money they need to pursue investment opportunities.

capital
The money that firms raise to finance their activities.

Once firms know how they want to invest resources, the next critical decision is where to obtain funding for those investments. **Financing decisions** determine how companies raise the money needed for investment opportunities. When firms are just getting started and as they continue to grow, they require capital from investors. **Capital** is the money raised by firms to finance their activities. For this reason, the financing decision may also be called the *capital structure decision*. Firms may raise capital by borrowing money from banks or other investors, or they may receive money from investors who want an ownership stake. Firms that are profitable can reinvest their earnings and thereby gain access to another form of capital. Although a firm's financing (or capital structure) decisions are almost certainly less important than its investment decisions, the mix of funding sources that a company uses has a number of important implications. For example, if a company chooses to borrow money, it is obligated to repay that money even if business conditions deteriorate. That's what happened to General Motors (GM) when it did not have enough cash to pay its debt and went bankrupt in June 2009. GM ultimately survived with the help of $51 billion in government assistance (of which about $39 billion was eventually repaid), but not every company that borrows money and later goes bankrupt is so fortunate. In contrast, borrowing money can benefit shareholders, in part because in the United States and many other countries, the tax code provides an incentive to borrow. Specifically, the U.S. corporate tax code allows firms to treat interest payments to lenders as a deductible business expense (which lowers the after-tax cost of borrowing for the firm), whereas tax laws do not give firms a deduction for cash dividend payments made to shareholders.

To visualize the difference between a firm's investment and financing decisions, refer to the balance sheet shown in Figure 1.1. Investment decisions generally refer to the items that appear on the left-hand side of the balance sheet, and financing decisions relate to the items on the right-hand side. Keep in mind, though, that financial managers make these decisions based on how they affect the firm's value, not on the accounting principles used to construct a balance sheet.

working capital decisions
Decisions that refer to the management of a firm's short-term resources.

Whereas the investment and financing decisions of firms often involve major strategic initiatives, on a day-to-day basis, financial managers spend more time making various types of short-term financial decisions. **Working capital decisions** refer to the management of a firm's short-term resources. These decisions involve tracking and forecasting the firm's cash position, making sure that the firm pays its bills on time and receives timely payments from customers, and calculating the optimal amount of inventory the firm should keep on hand. Collectively, the resources that a firm invests in items such as cash, inventory, accounts receivable, and accounts

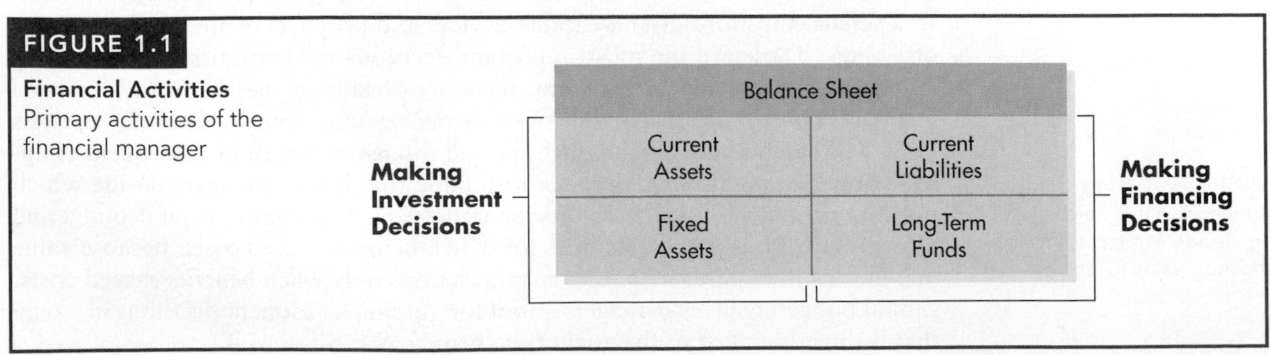

FIGURE 1.1
Financial Activities
Primary activities of the financial manager

payable are known as the firm's *working capital*. For many firms, the funds invested in working capital are considerable. For example, in July 2017, Apple reported that it held roughly $77 billion in cash in various short-term investments.

Principles That Guide Managers' Decisions

A financial manager performs many different roles in a large company, but no matter the job title, a common set of financial principles guide that manager's decisions and the advice he or she gives to colleagues working in different functions. Specifically, we highlight five key principles of great importance in managerial finance.

The Time Value of Money As we discussed earlier, timing matters in finance. Having money today is better than having it later because firms and individuals can invest the money on hand and earn a return on that money. Stating this idea another way, a dollar today is worth more than a dollar in the future. Investing a dollar today means that the dollar will grow to more than a dollar over time. The implication of this principle for managers is that, all else being equal, investments that provide faster payoffs are preferred over investments with distant payoffs. This does not suggest that firms must necessarily have an excessive focus on short-term results. Rather, the time value of money simply means that when an investment's payoffs come in the distant future, those payoffs must be larger to justify waiting for them.

The Tradeoff between Return and Risk "Nothing ventured, nothing gained" is a famous quote attributed to Benjamin Franklin. The equivalent financial principle is that a tradeoff exists between return and risk. Investors who want to earn higher returns must be willing to accept greater risk. Or, from the perspective of a business, a firm that puts investors' funds in riskier projects must offer those investors higher returns. For financial managers tasked with advising firms on investment decisions, this tradeoff means that any analysis of alternative investment projects quantify both the returns that investments may provide and the risks that they entail.

Cash Is King In discussing the differences between maximizing shareholder value and profits, we noted that cash flow and profit are not identical concepts. In finance, cash flow matters more than profit because firms can pay investors only with cash, not with profits. Ultimately, the cash flows that investors receive or expect to receive over time determine the value of the firm. If a firm is not generating positive cash flow, it cannot pay investors, even if its financial statements show that it is earning a profit. The same is true regarding a firm's dealings with its suppliers, employees, and anyone else to whom the firm owes money—those bills must be paid with cash.

Competitive Financial Markets When we think of the term *competition* in a business context, what usually comes to mind is the competition that occurs between firms in the markets for goods and services—Coke versus Pepsi, Samsung versus Apple, and so on. But firms also compete in another sense. They compete in the financial markets for access to capital controlled by investors. From time to time, most companies must raise money to fund new investments, and to succeed in raising money, firms have to convince participants in the financial markets that their ideas are as good or better than those of other firms seeking funding. Investors diligently search for the opportunities that provide the highest returns for a given risk level, so companies that cannot convince investors that their investment ideas will generate competitive rates of return may have difficulty raising capital.

Furthermore, at least for companies that have stock actively traded on stock exchanges, the financial markets constantly send signals to managers about how they are performing. Investors trade rapidly as they learn new information about companies, so stock prices also respond rapidly to news as it emerges. When investors hear positive news about a company (e.g., when a company announces better-than-expected financial results), the company's stock price moves up. On February 28, 2017, the stock price of the biotechnology firm Kite Pharma shot up almost 25% when the company released favorable results from clinical trials of one of the company's cancer-fighting drugs. On the other hand, stock prices fall when unfavorable news becomes known. In January 2017, shares of the toy manufacturer Mattel dropped 14% in a single day after the company announced disappointing financial results from the previous holiday shopping season.

How should managers respond to signals sent by the stock market? Although the opinions of investors as revealed by movements in a company's stock price are not always correct, managers should pay close attention to what the market is telling them. Investors have very strong incentives to evaluate the information they receive about companies in an unbiased way. If a company announces plans for a major new investment (e.g., the acquisition of another company) and its stock price falls, managers should recognize that the market is skeptical about the new investment, and they should carefully reconsider their plan to invest.

Incentives Are Important We have made a case for managers to operate firms with the aim of benefiting shareholders, but do managers behave this way? In many instances and for a variety of reasons, the answer is no. In part, this results from managers' incentives not being properly aligned with the interests of shareholders. For example, suppose one company makes an offer to purchase another company. The buyer's offer is quite attractive in the sense that the price offered is well above the current market price of the target company's stock. Accepting the offer seems like the best option for shareholders. However, the CEO of the target may decline the offer, knowing that if the acquisition takes place, he is likely to lose his job and the large salary that goes with it. Similarly, senior managers of the buyer in this example may not have their shareholders' best interests in mind. CEOs and other senior executives tend to earn higher pay when they run larger organizations, so perhaps the motivation to buy another company is about increasing management's compensation. In fact, CEO bonuses sometimes depend more on completing an acquisition deal than on whether that deal creates value for shareholders.

principal–agent problem
A problem that arises because the owners of a firm and its managers are not the same people and the agent does not act in the interest of the principal.

The example above illustrates a classic problem in finance known as the **principal–agent problem**. The principal–agent problem arises when the owners of a firm and its managers are not the same people. In this instance, what is best for shareholders and what managers believe to be in their own best interests may not be aligned. The principal–agent problem is particularly important in large corporations, in which a great degree of separation exists between the owners of a firm and its managers. We will explore the principal–agent problem, with potential solutions, as we study alternative ways of organizing businesses later in this chapter.

Organization of the Finance Function

The scope of the managerial finance function depends on the size of the firm. In very small firms, this function focuses largely on accounting and control issues. As a firm grows, the finance function typically separates from the accounting

treasurer
A key financial manager, who manages the firm's cash, oversees its pension plans, and manages key risks.

director of risk management
Works with the treasurer to manage risks that the firm faces related to movements in exchange rates, commodity prices, and interest rates.

department and becomes a unique organization linked directly to the company president or CEO through the chief financial officer (CFO). The lower portion of the organizational chart in Figure 1.2 shows the structure of the finance function in a typical medium to large firm.

Reporting to the CFO are the treasurer, the controller, the director of investor relations, and the director of internal audit. The **treasurer** manages the firm's cash, investing surplus funds when available and securing outside financing when needed. The treasurer also oversees a firm's pension plans and, together with the **director of risk management**, manages critical risks related to movements in foreign currency values, interest rates, and commodity prices.

FIGURE 1.2

Corporate Organization
The general organization of a corporation and the finance function (which is shown in yellow)

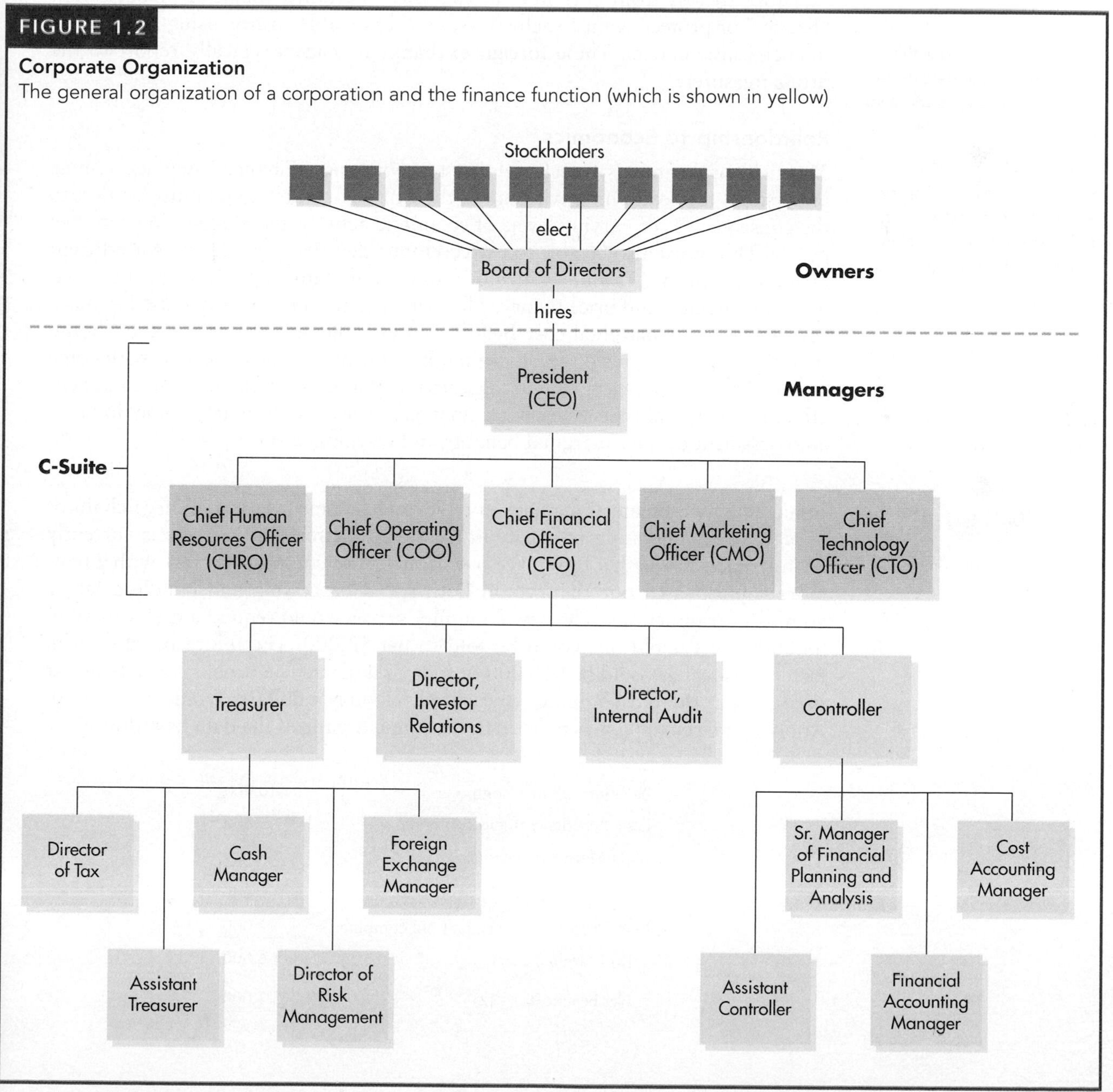

controller
The firm's chief accountant, who is responsible for the firm's accounting activities, such as corporate accounting, tax management, financial accounting, and cost accounting.

director of investor relations
The conduit of information between the firm and the investment community.

director of internal audit
Leads a team charged with making sure that all business units follow internal policies and comply with government regulations.

foreign exchange manager
The manager responsible for managing and monitoring the firm's exposure to loss from currency fluctuations.

marginal cost–benefit analysis
Economic principle that states that financial decisions should be made and actions taken only when the marginal benefits exceed the marginal costs.

The **controller** has a role more centered on accounting, budgeting, and tracking the performance of a business unit. The **director of investor relations** is the conduit of information between the firm and the investment community. The **director of internal audit** leads a team that is charged with making sure that all units within the firm are following internal policies and complying with government regulations. Some of these jobs have a very external focus, such as the treasurer, who must keep a close eye on a wide range of financial markets, and the director of investor relations, who communicates regularly with the outside investment community. Other jobs have a more internal focus, such as the controller position.

If international sales or purchases are important to a firm, it may well employ one or more finance professionals whose job is to monitor and manage the firm's exposure to loss from currency fluctuations. A trained financial manager can "hedge," or protect against such a loss, at a reasonable cost by using a variety of financial instruments. These **foreign exchange managers** typically report to the firm's treasurer.

Relationship to Economics

The field of finance is closely related to economics. Financial managers must understand the economic environment their firms operate in and must be alert to the consequences of varying levels of economic activity and changes in economic policy. They must also be able to use economic theories as guidelines for efficient business operation. Examples include supply-and-demand analysis, profit-maximizing strategies, and price theory. The primary economic principle used in managerial finance is **marginal cost–benefit analysis,** the tenet that managers should base financial decisions on the marginal benefits and costs associated with some action. That is, managers should take actions that generate higher marginal benefits than marginal costs. Nearly all financial decisions ultimately come down to an assessment of their marginal benefits and marginal costs.

EXAMPLE 1.2

Jamie Teng is a financial manager for Nord Department Stores, a large chain of upscale stores operating primarily in the western United States. She is currently trying to decide whether to replace one of the firm's computer servers with a new, more sophisticated one that would both speed processing and handle a larger volume of transactions. The new computer server would require a cash outlay of $8,000, and the old one could be sold to net $2,000. The future benefits from faster processing would be $10,000 in today's dollars. The benefits over a similar period from the old computer (measured in today's dollars) would be $3,000. Applying marginal cost–benefit analysis, Jamie organizes the data as follows:

Benefits with new computer	$10,000
Less: Benefits with old computer	3,000
(1) Marginal benefits	$ 7,000
Cost of new computer	$ 8,000
Less: Proceeds from sale of old computer	2,000
(2) Marginal costs	$ 6,000
Net benefit [(1) – (2)]	$ 1,000

Because the marginal benefits of $7,000 exceed the marginal costs of $6,000, Jamie recommends purchasing the new computer to replace the old one. The firm will experience a net benefit of $1,000 as a result of this action.

Relationship to Accounting

The firm's finance and accounting activities are closely related and generally overlap. In small firms, accountants often carry out the finance function; in large firms, financial analysts often help compile accounting information. We can, however, note two differences between finance and accounting; one is related to the emphasis on cash flows, and the other to decision making.

Emphasis on Cash Flows The accountant's primary function is to develop and report data for measuring the performance of the firm, assess its financial position, comply with and file reports required by securities regulators, and file and pay taxes. Using generally accepted accounting principles, the accountant prepares financial statements that recognize revenue at the time of sale (whether payment has been received or not) and recognize expenses when incurred. This approach is referred to as the **accrual basis.**

accrual basis
In preparation of financial statements, recognizes revenue at the time of sale and recognizes expenses when they are incurred.

The financial manager, in contrast, places primary emphasis on *cash flows,* the intake and outgo of cash. He or she maintains solvency of the firm by planning the cash flows necessary to satisfy its obligations and to acquire assets needed to achieve its goals. The financial manager uses this **cash basis** to recognize the revenues and expenses only with respect to actual inflows and outflows of cash. Whether a firm earns a profit or experiences a loss, it must have a sufficient flow of cash to meet its obligations as they come due.

cash basis
Recognizes revenues and expenses only with respect to actual inflows and outflows of cash.

EXAMPLE 1.3

MyLab Finance Solution Video

Nassau Corporation, a small yacht dealer, sold one yacht for $1,000,000 in the calendar year just ended. Nassau originally purchased the yacht for $800,000. Although the firm paid in full for the yacht during the year, at year's end it has yet to collect the $1,000,000 from the customer. The accounting view and the financial view of the firm's performance during the year are given by the following income and cash flow statements, respectively.

Accounting view (accrual basis)	
Nassau Corporation income statement for the year ended 12/31	
Sales revenue	$1,000,000
Less: Costs	800,000
Net profit	$ 200,000

Financial view (cash basis)	
Nassau Corporation cash flow statement for the year ended 12/31	
Cash inflow	$ 0
Less: Cash outflow	800,000
Net cash flow	−$800,000

In an accounting sense, Nassau Corporation is profitable, but in terms of actual cash flow, it has a problem. Its lack of cash flow resulted from the uncollected accounts receivable of $1,000,000. Without adequate cash inflows to meet its obligations, the firm will not survive, regardless of its level of profits.

As the example shows, accrual accounting data do not fully represent the circumstances of a firm. Thus, the financial manager must look beyond financial statements to gain insight into existing or developing problems. Of course, accountants are well aware of the importance of cash flows, and financial managers use and understand accrual-based financial statements. Nevertheless, the financial manager, by concentrating on cash flows, should be able to avoid insolvency and achieve the firm's financial goals.

PERSONAL FINANCE EXAMPLE 1.4 Individuals rarely use accrual concepts. Rather, they rely mainly on cash flows to measure their financial outcomes. Generally, individuals plan, monitor, and assess their financial activities using cash flows over a given period, typically a month or a year. Ann Bach projects her cash flows during October 2018 as follows:

	Amount	
Item	**Inflow**	**Outflow**
Net pay received	$4,400	
Rent		–$1,200
Car payment		–450
Utilities		–300
Groceries		–800
Clothes		–750
Dining out		–650
Gasoline		–260
Interest income	220	
Misc. expense		–425
Totals	$4,620	–$4,835

Ann subtracts her total outflows of $4,835 from her total inflows of $4,620 and finds that her net cash flow for October will be –$215. To cover the $215 shortfall, Ann will have to either borrow $215 (putting it on a credit card is a form of borrowing) or withdraw $215 from her savings. Alternatively, she may decide to reduce her outflows in areas of discretionary spending such as clothing purchases, dining out, or those items that make up the $425 of miscellaneous expense.

Decision Making The second major difference between finance and accounting involves decision making. Accountants devote most of their attention to the collection and presentation of financial data. Financial managers evaluate the accounting statements, develop additional data, and make decisions based on their assessment of the associated returns and risks. Of course, this does not mean that accountants never make decisions or that financial managers never gather data but rather that the primary emphases of accounting and finance are different.

→ **REVIEW QUESTIONS** MyLab Finance Solutions

1–5 What are the main types of decisions that financial managers make?

1–6 Why is it important that managers recognize that a tradeoff exists between risk and return? Why does that tradeoff exist?

1–7 What is the primary economic principle used in managerial finance?

1–8 What are the major differences between accounting and finance with respect to emphasis on cash flows and decision making?

1–9 If managers do not act in the best interests of shareholders, what role might incentives play in explaining that behavior?

1.3 Organizational Forms, Taxation, and the Principal–Agent Relationship

From a legal perspective, businesses can organize themselves in a variety of ways. Different organizational forms involve various tradeoffs related to ownership, control, taxation, liability, and other factors. In this section, we examine the pros and cons of alternative legal forms for businesses.

LEGAL FORMS OF BUSINESS ORGANIZATION

One of the most important decisions all businesses confront is how to choose a legal form of organization. This decision has very important financial implications. How a business is legally organized influences the risks borne by the firm's owners, how the firm can raise money, and how the firm's profits will be taxed. The three most common legal forms of business organization are the *sole proprietorship*, the *partnership*, and the *corporation*. Most businesses are organized as sole proprietorships, but the largest businesses are almost always organized as corporations. Even so, each type of organization has its advantages and disadvantages.

Sole Proprietorships

sole proprietorship
A business owned by one person and operated for his or her own profit.

A **sole proprietorship** is a for-profit business owned by one person. More than 70% of all U.S. businesses are sole proprietorships. The typical sole proprietorship is small, and the majority of sole proprietorships operate in the wholesale, retail, service, and construction industries.

Typically, the owner (proprietor) and a few employees operate the proprietorship. The proprietor raises capital from personal resources or by borrowing. The owner is responsible for all business decisions, so this form of organization appeals to entrepreneurs who enjoy working independently. Sole proprietorships do not pay taxes on their income as separate entities. Rather, income from sole proprietorships "passes through" to the owner and is taxed at the personal level.

unlimited liability
The condition of a sole proprietorship (or general partnership), giving creditors the right to make claims against the owner's personal assets to recover debts owed by the business.

A major drawback to the sole proprietorship is **unlimited liability**, which means that liabilities of the business are the entrepreneur's responsibility and that creditors can make claims against the entrepreneur's personal assets if the business fails to pay its debts.

TABLE 1.1 Strengths and Weaknesses of the Common Legal Forms of Business Organization

	Sole proprietorship	Partnership	Corporation
Strengths	• Owner receives all profits (and sustains all losses) • Low organizational costs • Income included and taxed on proprietor's personal tax return • Independence • Secrecy • Ease of dissolution	• Can raise more funds than sole proprietorships • Borrowing power enhanced by more owners • More available brain power and managerial skill • Income included and taxed on partner's personal tax return	• Owners have *limited liability*, which guarantees that they cannot lose more than they invested • Can achieve large size via sale of ownership (stock) • Ownership (stock) is readily transferable • Long life of firm • Can hire professional managers • Has better access to financing
Weaknesses	• Owner has *unlimited liability* in that total wealth can be taken to satisfy debts • Limited fund-raising power tends to inhibit growth • Proprietor must be jack-of-all-trades • Difficult to give employees long-run career opportunities • Lacks continuity when proprietor dies	• Owners have *unlimited liability* and may have to cover debts of other partners • Partnership is dissolved when a partner dies • Difficult to liquidate or transfer partnership	• Taxes are generally higher because corporate income is taxed, and dividends paid to owners are also taxed at a maximum 15% rate • More expensive to organize than other business forms • Subject to greater government regulation • Lacks secrecy because regulations require firms to disclose financial results

Partnerships

partnership
A business owned by two or more people and operated for profit.

articles of partnership
The written contract used to formally establish a business partnership.

A **partnership** consists of two or more owners doing business together for profit. Partnerships account for about 10% of all businesses, and they are typically larger than sole proprietorships. Partnerships are common in the accounting, law, finance, insurance, and real estate industries.

Most partnerships are established by a written contract known as **articles of partnership**. In a *general* (or *regular*) *partnership*, all partners have unlimited liability, and each partner is legally liable for all debts of the partnership. Like a sole proprietorship, a partnership is a pass-through business, meaning that partnerships do not pay income tax directly. Instead, income from the partnership flows through to the partners and is taxed at the individual level. Table 1.1 summarizes the strengths and weaknesses of proprietorships and partnerships.

Corporations

corporation
A legal business entity with rights and duties similar to those of individuals but with a legal identity distinct from its owners.

A **corporation** is a business entity owned by individuals, but the corporation itself is a legal entity distinct from its owners. A corporation has the legal powers of an individual. It can sue and be sued, make and be party to contracts, and acquire property in its own name. Although fewer than 20% of all U.S. businesses are incorporated, the largest businesses nearly always are; corporations account for roughly two-thirds of total business income.

MATTER OF FACT

Number of Businesses and Income Earned by Type of U.S. Firm

Although sole proprietorships greatly outnumber partnerships and corporations combined, they generate the lowest level of income. In total, sole proprietorships accounted for almost three-quarters of the number of business establishments in operation, but they earned just 10% of all business income. Corporations, on the other hand, accounted for just 17% of the number of businesses, but they earned almost two-thirds of all business income.

	Sole proprietorships	Partnerships	Corporations
Number of firms (millions)	25.3	3.4	5.8
Percentage of all firms	73%	10%	17%
Percentage of all business income	10%	26%	64%

Source: Overview of Approaches to Corporate Integration, Joint Committee on Taxation, United States Congress, May 17, 2016.

stockholders
The owners of a corporation, whose ownership, or *equity,* takes the form of common stock or, less frequently, preferred stock.

limited liability
A legal provision that limits stockholders' liability for a corporation's debt to the amount they initially invested in the firm by purchasing stock.

stock
A security that represents an ownership interest in a corporation.

dividends
Periodic distributions of cash to the stockholders of a firm.

board of directors
Group elected by the firm's stockholders and typically responsible for approving strategic goals and plans, setting general policy, guiding corporate affairs, and approving major expenditures.

One advantage of the corporate form is that corporations can raise money to expand by selling new stock to investors. Another advantage is that the owners of a corporation, its **stockholders** (whose ownership, or *equity,* takes the form of common or preferred stock), enjoy **limited liability,** meaning they are not personally liable for the firm's debts as are sole proprietors and partners. Their losses are limited to the amount they invested in the firm when they purchased shares of stock. In Chapter 7 you will learn more about stock, but for now we will simply say that **stock** is a security that represents an ownership interest in a corporation. Stockholders expect to earn a return by receiving **dividends**—periodic distributions of cash—or by realizing gains through increases in share price. Because the money to pay dividends generally comes from the profits that a firm earns, we refer to stockholders as *residual claimants.* They are paid last, after the corporation pays employees, suppliers, tax authorities, and lenders and anyone else to whom it owes money. Over time, if the firm does not generate enough cash to pay everyone else, there is no residual cash flow and nothing is available for stockholders. Table 1.1 lists the key strengths and weaknesses of corporations.

As noted in the upper portion of Figure 1.2, control of the corporation functions a little like a democracy. The stockholders vote periodically to elect members of the **board of directors,** which is typically responsible for approving strategic goals and plans, setting general policy, guiding corporate affairs, and approving major expenditures. Most importantly, the board decides when to hire or fire top managers and establishes compensation packages for the most senior executives. The board consists of "inside" directors, such as key corporate executives, and "outside" or "independent" directors, such as executives from other companies, major shareholders, and national or community leaders. Outside directors for major corporations receive compensation in the form of cash, stock, and stock options. This compensation often totals $250,000 per year or more.

TABLE 1.2 2018 Tax Rate Schedule for Single Taxpayer

Taxable income brackets			Tax calculation: Base tax	+	(Marginal rate × amount over bracket lower limit)	
$ 0	to	$ 9,525	$ 0	+	(10% × amount over	$ 0)
9,525	to	38,700	$ 953	+	(12% × amount over	$ 9,525)
38,700	to	82,500	$ 4,454	+	(22% × amount over	$ 38,700)
82,500	to	157,500	$ 14,090	+	(24% × amount over	$ 82,500)
157,500	to	200,000	$ 32,090	+	(32% × amount over	$157,500)
200,000	to	500,000	$ 45,690	+	(35% × amount over	$200,000)
Over 500,000			$150,690	+	(37% × amount over	$500,000)

president or chief executive officer (CEO)
Corporate official responsible for managing the firm's day-to-day operations and carrying out the policies established by the board of directors.

The **president or chief executive officer (CEO)** is responsible for managing day-to-day operations and carrying out the policies established by the board of directors. The CEO reports periodically to the firm's directors.

It is important to note the division between owners and managers in a large corporation, as shown by the dashed horizontal line in Figure 1.2. This separation is the source of the principal–agent problem mentioned earlier.

Business Organizational Forms and Taxation

Owners of pass-through businesses such as proprietorships and partnerships pay tax at the individual level, not at the business level. For individuals, income tax rates are progressive, meaning that the tax rate rises with income. Taxes also depend on the individual's filing status (e.g., whether they are single or married). Table 1.2 shows the tax rates applicable in 2018 for a single taxpayer.

EXAMPLE 1.5

MyLab Finance Solution Video

Dan Webster is the sole proprietor of Webster Manufacturing. This year Webster earned $80,000 before taxes from his business. Assuming that Dan has no other income, the taxes he will owe on his business income are as follows:

$$\begin{aligned} \text{Total taxes due} &= (0.10 \times \$9{,}525) + [0.12 \times (\$38{,}700 - \$9{,}525)] \\ &\quad + [0.22 \times (\$80{,}000 - \$38{,}700)] \\ &= \$953 + \$3{,}501 + \$9{,}086 \\ &= \$13{,}540 \end{aligned}$$

Notice that Webster's tax liability has two components. The first $4,454 in tax, denoted in Table 1.2 as the base tax, is calculated by multiplying 10% times Webster's first $9,525 in income and then multiplying 12% times Webster's next $29,175 in income. The sum of those two calculations is the $4,454 base tax from line 3 in Table 1.2. On top of that, Webster must pay an additional 22% in taxes on income above $38,700.

marginal tax rate
The tax rate that applies to the next dollar of income earned.

In a progressive tax rate structure like that shown in Table 1.2, there is a difference between the marginal tax rate and the average tax rate. The **marginal tax rate** represents the rate at which the next dollar of income is taxed. In Table 1.2, the marginal tax rate is 10% if the taxpayer earns less than $9,525. If income is more than $9,525 but less than $38,700, the marginal tax rate is 12%. As income rises, the marginal tax rate rises. In the example above, if Webster Manufacturing's earnings increase to $82,501, the last $1 in income would be taxed at the marginal rate of 24%.

average tax rate
Calculated by dividing taxes paid by taxable income.

The **average tax rate** equals taxes paid divided by taxable income. For many taxpayers, the average tax rate does not equal the marginal tax rate because tax rates change with income levels. In the example above, Webster Manufacturing's marginal tax rate is 22%, but its average tax rate is 16.9% ($13,540 ÷ $80,000). In most business decisions that managers make, it's the marginal tax rate that really matters. Remember that managers create value for shareholders by taking actions for which the marginal benefits exceed the marginal costs. Thus, managers should focus on the marginal tax rate because that determines the marginal taxes they will pay or avoid as a consequence of taking some action.

Figure 1.3 shows how marginal and average tax rates vary as an individual's taxable income rises. The blue line shows how the marginal tax rate increases in "steps" as income moves into each higher tax bracket (note: the graph omits the final 37% bracket for incomes above $500,000). The red line shows that the average tax increases with income too, but the average rate is generally less than the marginal rate. For example, a business owner with income of $300,000 faces a 35% marginal tax rate but pays an average tax rate of roughly 27% as illustrated in the following example.

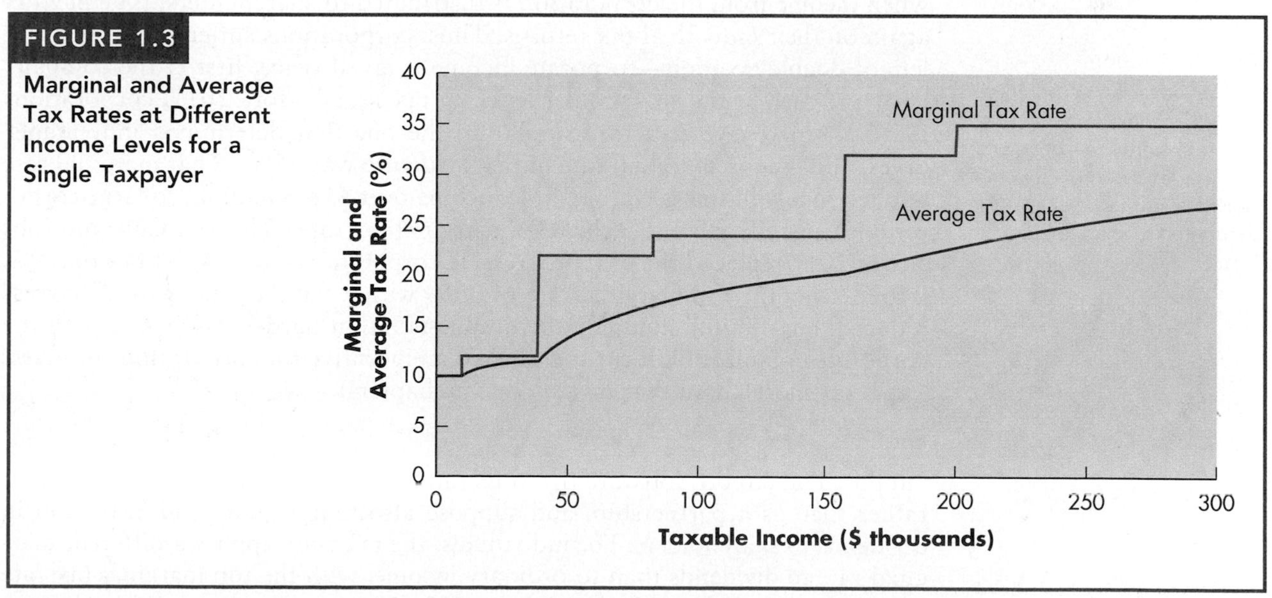

FIGURE 1.3
Marginal and Average Tax Rates at Different Income Levels for a Single Taxpayer

EXAMPLE 1.6

Peter Strong is a partner in Argaiv Software, and from that business he earned taxable income of \$300,000. Assuming that this is Peter's only source of income, from Table 1.2 we can see that based on Peter's tax bracket, he faces a marginal tax rate of 35%. How much in tax does Peter owe, and what is his average tax rate? Table 1.2 shows a base tax of \$45,690 for individuals with income above \$200,000 but below \$500,000. Here's where that base tax comes from:

$$\begin{aligned}\text{Base tax} &= (0.10 \times \$9{,}525) + (0.12 \times \$29{,}175) + (0.22 \times \$43{,}800)\\ &\quad + (0.24 \times \$75{,}000) + (0.32 \times \$42{,}500)\\ &= \$953 + \$3{,}501 + \$9{,}636 + \$18{,}000 + \$13{,}600\\ &= \$45{,}690\end{aligned}$$

In other words, based on his first \$200,000 in partnership earnings, Peter owes \$45,690 in taxes. In addition to that base tax, Peter must pay 35% tax on the last \$100,000 that he earns, so his total tax bill is

$$\text{Total taxes due} = \$45{,}690 + (0.35 \times \$100{,}000) = \$80{,}690$$

Given Peter's total tax bill, we can calculate the average tax rate by dividing taxes due by taxable income, as follows:

$$\text{Average tax rate} = \$80{,}690 \div \$300{,}000 = 0.269 = 26.9\%$$

Again we stress that in many cases the marginal tax rate and the average tax rate are not equal, and in such cases, managers should focus on the marginal tax rate when they make decisions about how to invest the firm's money.

Double taxation
A situation facing corporations in which income from the business is taxed twice—once at the business level and once at the individual level when cash is distributed to shareholders.

Taxation of corporations is quite different. A major disadvantage of the corporate form of organization is that a corporation itself pays taxes, and then when income from the corporation is distributed to shareholders, they pay tax again on their individual tax returns. Thus, corporations suffer from the problem of **double taxation**—corporate income is taxed twice, first at the company level and then at the shareholder level. In tax years before 2017, corporations faced a progressive structure similar to the one that determined individuals' taxes, and the top marginal rate in that structure was 35%. That marginal rate applied to any business with taxable income over \$18.3 million, so large corporations generally fell under the 35% marginal tax rate. The Tax Cuts and Jobs Act of 2017 replaced the old, progressive corporate tax with a flat tax of 21%. By replacing the top marginal rate of 35% with a flat 21% tax rate, Congress reduced, but did not eliminate the double-taxation burden associated with the corporate organization form and created an incentive for corporations to invest (we'll say more about that in subsequent chapters).

EXAMPLE 1.7

Suppose that Argaiv Software (from Example 1.6) is organized as a corporation rather than as a partnership, and suppose also that Argaiv paid \$300,000 in dividends to shareholders. For individuals, the tax code applies a different marginal rate to dividends than to ordinary income, with the top marginal tax rate on dividends equal to 23.8%. On the \$300,000 in corporate taxable income,

Argaiv will pay taxes of \$63,000 (0.21 × \$300,000), and its shareholders could pay as much as \$71,400 (0.238 × \$300,000) in taxes on the dividends that they receive. Therefore, the total tax burden faced by Argaiv and its shareholders is as high as \$134,400, compared to the total tax bill of \$80,690 that would be owed if Argaiv were organized as a partnership as in the previous example. The taxes paid on Argaiv dividends by its shareholders could be less than shown here if shareholders are not in the highest individual tax bracket.

ordinary income
Income earned by a business through the sale of goods or services.

capital gain
Income earned by selling an asset for more than it cost.

Regardless of their legal form, all businesses can earn ordinary income and capital gains. A corporation earns **ordinary income** through the sale of goods or services. A **capital gain** occurs if a firm sells an asset for more than its cost. Current law treats these two types of income differently in the taxation of individuals, but not for corporations. The law requires corporations to simply add capital gains to ordinary income when calculating taxes.

The law treats interest received by corporations as ordinary income (just like capital gains), but dividends received get a special tax break that moderates the effect of double taxation. Dividends the firm receives on common and preferred stock held in other corporations are usually subject to a 50% exclusion for tax purposes. The dividend exclusion in effect eliminates half of the potential tax liability from dividends received by the second and any subsequent corporations.

In calculating their taxes, corporations can deduct operating expenses, as well as interest expenses they pay to lenders. The tax deductibility of these expenses reduces their after-tax cost. The following example illustrates the benefit of tax deductibility.

EXAMPLE 1.8

MyLab Finance Solution Video

Two corporations, Debt Co. and No-Debt Co., earned \$200,000 before interest and taxes this year. During the year, Debt Co. paid \$30,000 in interest. No-Debt Co. had no debt and no interest expense. How do the after-tax earnings of these firms compare?

	Debt Co.	No-Debt Co.
Earnings before interest and taxes	\$200,000	\$200,000
Less: Interest expense	30,000	0
Earnings before taxes	\$170,000	\$200,000
Less: Taxes (21%)	35,700	42,000
Earnings after taxes	\$134,300	\$158,000
Difference in earnings after taxes	\$23,700	

Both firms face a 21% flat tax rate. Debt Co. had \$30,000 more interest expense than No-Debt Co., but Debt Co.'s earnings after taxes are only \$23,700 less than those of No-Debt Co. This difference is attributable to Debt Co.'s \$30,000 interest expense deduction, which provides a tax savings of \$6,300 (the tax bill is \$35,700 for Debt Co. versus \$42,000 for No-Debt Co.). The tax savings can be calculated directly by multiplying the 21% tax rate by the interest expense (0.21 × \$30,000 = \$6,300). Similarly, the \$23,700 after-tax interest expense can be calculated directly by multiplying 1 minus the tax rate by the interest expense [(1 − 0.21) × \$30,000 = \$23,700].

The tax deductibility of expenses reduces their actual (after-tax) cost to the firm as long as the firm is profitable. If a firm experiences a net loss in a given year, its tax liability is already zero. Even in this case, firms can deduct losses in one year from income earned in subsequent years (prior losses cannot offset more than 80% of taxable income in any subsequent year). Note that for both accounting and tax purposes interest is a tax-deductible expense, whereas dividends are not. Because dividends are not tax deductible, their after-tax cost is equal to the amount of the dividend.

Other Limited Liability Organizations

A number of other organizational forms provide owners with limited liability. The most popular are *limited partnership (LP), S corporation (S corp), limited liability company (LLC), and limited liability partnership (LLP)*. Each represents a specialized form or blending of the characteristics of the organizational forms described previously. What they have in common is that their owners enjoy limited liability, and they typically have fewer than 100 owners.

AGENCY PROBLEMS AND AGENCY COSTS

Large corporations have tens of thousands of different shareholders, and the vast majority of them have no direct managerial responsibility. The professional managers who run corporations are the *agents* of the shareholders, and they are entrusted to take actions or make decisions that are in the shareholders' best interests. As we have already noted, in many situations, managers may act in accordance with their own interests rather than on behalf of the shareholders. In most cases, if managers fail to do what shareholders want them to do, they will also fail to achieve the goal of maximizing shareholder wealth. The unavoidable conflict between a firm's principals (shareholders) and their agents (managers) gives rise to a variety of costs that owners must shoulder. **Agency costs** represent those costs that shareholders bear (or, equivalently, the loss in value that they endure) because managers pursue their own interests. Agency costs may include such things as an expensive private jet used by the CEO or the cost of hiring outside auditors to verify the accuracy of the financial reports produced by managers. Another type of agency cost arises when managers make suboptimal investment decisions, that is, making investments that decrease shareholder value or failing to make investments that would increase the firm's stock price. Of course, shareholders are generally sophisticated people, and they are aware of the consequences of delegating managerial responsibility to agents. So, to help ensure that managers act in ways consistent with the interests of shareholders, and therefore to mitigate agency costs, shareholders aim to establish a range of corporate governance practices. Society at large also influences corporate governance through the laws and regulations that governments establish and with which firms must comply.

agency costs
The costs that shareholders bear due to managers' pursuit of their own interests.

CORPORATE GOVERNANCE

corporate governance
The rules, processes, and laws by which companies are operated, controlled, and regulated.

Corporate governance refers to the rules, processes, and laws by which companies are operated, controlled, and regulated. It defines the rights and responsibilities of the corporate participants, such as the shareholders, board of directors, officers and managers, and other stakeholders, as well as the rules and procedures for making corporate decisions. A well-defined corporate governance structure is intended to benefit all corporate stakeholders by ensuring that the firm is run in a lawful and ethical fashion, in full compliance with all corporate regulations.

Both internal and external forces influence firms' corporate governance practices. In terms of internal influences, clearly shareholders, through the board of directors, exert influence on how a firm is governed. But when internal corporate governance mechanisms fail, external forces may step in. Many of the most important laws and regulations affecting U.S. corporations were passed in the wake of some kind of scandal, brought about in part because of corporate governance failures on a wide scale.

Internal Corporate Governance Mechanisms

Primary responsibility for establishing a firm's corporate governance policies rests with the board of directors. The board is responsible for hiring and firing the firm's CEO and for setting the terms of compensation for senior managers. One of the primary ways in which boards try to align the interests of managers and shareholders is through the structure of management compensation. Specifically, at most large companies, the pay of senior employees consists of a fixed base salary combined with a variable component that is tied to the firm's performance in some manner. For example, senior managers might receive an extra cash bonus if the firm meets particular revenue or earnings targets. A more direct way to create incentives for managers to act in shareholders' interests is through awards of stock options, restricted stock, and other forms of equity compensation. **Stock options** allow managers to buy shares of the company's stock at a fixed price. For example, suppose that a company's stock is worth $45 per share at the beginning of the year. The board might include 100,000 stock options in the CEO's compensation package. Suppose that each of those options allows the CEO to buy one share of stock for $45 at any time over the next few years. That gives the CEO a tremendous incentive to take actions that increase the stock price. If the stock price rises to $55, then the CEO can buy 100,000 shares for $45 each and then immediately resell them at the $55 market price, pocketing a profit of $1 million. The higher the stock price goes, the more the CEO benefits (and the more shareholders benefit, too). However, if the CEO takes actions that reduce the stock price below $45, then those stock options have little value.

stock options
Securities that allow managers to buy shares of stock at a fixed price.

Companies may link the pay of senior managers to the performance of the company's stock price in other ways. Firms often reward senior managers by giving them **restricted stock**, which are shares of stock that do not fully transfer from the company to the employee until certain conditions are met. These conditions might relate to the length of an employee's service or to meeting performance targets. When restricted stock is *fully vested*, ownership of the shares formally transfers to the employee. Obviously, the value of restricted shares is directly tied to the company's stock price. Often employees must wait several years (known as the *vesting period*) before their restricted stock is fully vested, and even then, companies may impose *minimum holding requirements*, meaning that an employee cannot immediately sell all their restricted shares, even if they are fully vested, as

restricted stock
Shares of stock paid out as part of a compensation package that do not fully transfer from the company to the employee until certain conditions are met.

MATTER OF FACT

CEO Pay Around the World

Both the amount that CEOs receive in compensation and the form their compensation takes vary greatly around the world. A 2016 report noted that median pay for CEOs in the United States was $14.9 million, nearly 3 times more than the median pay for CEOs from non-U.S. companies. British CEOs earned the second highest median pay at $10.5 million. On the European continent, German and French CEOs earned roughly half of what their British counterparts make, at $5.4 million and $4.0 million, respectively. Japanese CEOs received even less, with median pay at $1.5 million.

Given these large differences in total compensation, the base salaries of CEOs were surprisingly similar. For instance, the median base salary for a U.S. CEO was $5.1 million, compared with $4.1 million for a German CEO. What, then, caused the variations in total CEO pay? These were driven mostly by differences in the use of equity-based compensation. As an example, the portion of CEO pay coming in the form of stock or stock options was 60% for U.S. and U.K. firms, but in Germany and France, the fraction paid in equity totaled less than 24%. Japan was an even more dramatic outlier, with equity-based compensation accounting for just 10% of total CEO pay. Recall that the U.S. and U.K. legal systems emphasize the duty of managers to shareholders, whereas legal systems elsewhere place more emphasis on stakeholders. Those differences are reflected in equity-based CEO compensation around the world.

Source: "How CEO pay differs around the globe," Equilar.com press release, August 17, 2016.

long as the employee remains at the firm. Vesting requirements and minimum holding requirements ensure that the compensation of a firm's senior manager is always at least partially tied to the performance of the company's stock.

Corporate compensation plans have been closely scrutinized by stockholders, the Securities and Exchange Commission (SEC), and other government entities. The total compensation in 2016 for the chief executive officers of the 500 largest U.S. companies is considerable. For example, in 2016 Expedia's CEO, Dara Khosrowshahi, earned $94.6 million.

External Corporate Governance Mechanisms

If the board of directors does not effectively monitor senior management and establish sound governance practices, several external influences may emerge to fill the void. First, the firms' own investors may exert an effect on senior managers. Second, if investors cannot bring about change in an underperforming firm, an outside company may offer to take over the firm, in which case the senior management team would most likely be removed. Third, government regulations impose at least some minimal level of corporate governance standards with which firms must comply even if other internal and external governance mechanisms prove ineffective.

Individual versus Institutional Investors To better understand the role of shareholders in shaping a firm's corporate governance, it is helpful to differentiate between the two broad classes of owners: individuals and institutions. Generally, **individual investors** own relatively few shares and as a result do not typically have sufficient means to influence a firm's corporate governance. To pressure a firm, individual investors would have to vote collectively on

individual investors
Investors who own relatively small quantities of shares to meet personal investment goals.

matters such as electing directors. Coordinating the votes of thousands of individuals is difficult, so individual investors rarely exert much influence on corporations.

institutional investors
Investment professionals such as banks, insurance companies, mutual funds, and pension funds that are paid to manage and hold large quantities of securities on behalf of others.

Institutional investors have advantages over individual investors when it comes to influencing the corporate governance of a firm. **Institutional investors** are investment professionals paid to manage and hold large quantities of securities on behalf of individuals, businesses, and governments. Such investors include banks, insurance companies, mutual funds, and pension funds. Unlike individual investors, institutional investors often monitor and directly influence a firm's corporate governance by exerting pressure on management to perform, communicating their concerns to the firm's board, or even pressing for the election of their own slate of directors to the board. These large investors can also threaten to exercise their voting rights or liquidate their holdings if the board does not respond positively to their concerns. Because individual and institutional investors share the same goal, individual investors benefit from the monitoring activities of institutional investors.

activist investors
Investors who specialize in influencing management.

Activist investors, who may be wealthy individuals or institutional investors controlling a large pool of capital, specialize in influencing management. Activist shareholders may quickly assemble a significant ownership position in a firm to persuade senior managers to take specific actions, such as replacing existing board members with new ones favored by the activist. Activist investors typically emerge when a company has been underperforming, and their objective is to force managers to make changes to improve the firm's performance. To illustrate, in January 2017, the activist investing firm, Jana Partners, revealed that it had acquired a stake in the pharmaceutical giant Bristol-Myers Squibb. At the time, Bristol-Myers stock was trading for 20% less than it had just 1 year earlier, due in part to disappointing results from a clinical trial of a key drug. Just 1 month later, Bristol-Myers agreed to add three new directors to its board and to distribute $2 billion in cash to shareholders. No sooner had the company announced these changes than another activist, Carl Icahn, announced that he, too, had acquired a large block of Bristol-Myers stock. This fueled speculation that the company could become a takeover target because Icahn had previously pushed for the acquisition of underperforming companies by larger companies.

The Threat of Takeover When a firm's internal corporate governance structure is unable to keep agency problems in check, it is likely that rival managers will try to gain control of the firm. Because agency problems represent a misuse of the firm's resources and impose agency costs on the firm's shareholders, the firm's stock is generally depressed, making the firm an attractive takeover target. The threat of takeover by another firm that believes it can enhance the troubled firm's value by restructuring its management, operations, and financing can provide a strong source of external corporate governance. The constant threat of a takeover tends to motivate management to act in the best interests of the firm's owners.

Government Regulation

Government regulation shapes the corporate governance of all firms. During the past decade, corporate governance has received increased attention because of several high-profile corporate scandals involving abuse of corporate power and, in some cases, alleged criminal activity by corporate officers. The misdeeds derived from two main types of issues: (1) false disclosures in financial reporting and other material information releases and (2) undisclosed conflicts of interest between corporations and their analysts, auditors, and attorneys and between corporate directors, officers, and shareholders.

Asserting that an integral part of an effective corporate governance system is the provision for civil or criminal prosecution of individuals who conduct unethical or illegal acts in the name of the firm, in July 2002 the U.S. Congress passed the **Sarbanes-Oxley Act of 2002** (commonly called **SOX**). Sarbanes-Oxley was intended to eliminate many of the disclosure and conflict of interest problems that can arise when corporate managers are not held personally accountable for their firm's financial decisions and disclosures. SOX accomplished the following: established an oversight board to monitor the accounting industry, tightened audit regulations and controls, toughened penalties against executives who commit corporate fraud, strengthened accounting disclosure requirements and ethical guidelines for corporate officers, established corporate board structure and membership guidelines, established guidelines with regard to analyst conflicts of interest, mandated instant disclosure of stock sales by corporate executives, and increased securities regulation authority and budgets for auditors and investigators.

Sarbanes-Oxley Act of 2002 (SOX)
An act aimed at eliminating corporate disclosure and conflict of interest problems. Contains provisions concerning corporate financial disclosures and the relationships among corporations, analysts, auditors, attorneys, directors, officers, and shareholders.

→ REVIEW QUESTIONS MyLab Finance Solutions

1–10 Which legal form of business organization is most common? Which form do the largest businesses typically take and why?

1–11 Describe the roles of, and the relationships among, the major parties in a corporation: stockholders, board of directors, and managers. How are corporate owners rewarded for the risks they take?

1–12 Explain why corporations face a double taxation problem? For corporations, how are the marginal and average tax rates related?

1–13 Define agency problems, and describe how they give rise to agency costs. Explain how a firm's corporate governance structure can help avoid agency problems.

1–14 How can the firm structure management compensation to minimize agency problems?

1–15 How do market forces—both shareholder activism and the threat of takeover—prevent or minimize the agency problem? What role do institutional investors play in shareholder activism?

1.4 Developing Skills for Your Career

We began this chapter by arguing that regardless of your major, an understanding of finance would greatly enhance your career prospects. All business disciplines have a responsibility to contribute to the firm's goal of creating value, so understanding how to determine which actions create value and having the ability to explain the wisdom behind a particular course of action can help you succeed no matter what career path you've chosen. Below we highlight skills you can develop while working through this book.

CRITICAL THINKING

For many people working in a business, it is not obvious how the business creates value for its owners. In this text, we emphasize that value creation balances risk and return, so a critical evaluation of any proposed course of action requires an analysis of the risks of that action as well as its potential rewards. Virtually every chapter in this text provides guidance about how to make critical judgments regarding either the risks or the rewards (or both) tied to corporate decisions. By mastering those chapters will you learn how to apply criteria that lead to value-creating business decisions. You will learn the assumptions behind and the key relationships driving financial models, so even if your job does not involve building those models, you can help shape them by providing the data and analysis that the financial analysts at your firm use to provide financial justifications for key decisions. Your understanding of financial principles will also help you to identify weaknesses in financial analysis which, left uncorrected, might lead to suboptimal decisions.

COMMUNICATION AND COLLABORATION

In most large businesses today, employees work in cross-functional teams. If your aim is to work in marketing or supply chain or even general management, rest assured that working with a colleague from the finance department will be part of your regular routine. Thus, you need to understand how financial people think and the vocabulary they use to communicate with them effectively and persuasively. Developing a basic financial proficiency will help you gather and organize the information that the financial analyst on your team needs to demonstrate the value of your team's work to the larger organization.

FINANCIAL COMPUTING SKILLS

Though an in-depth discussion of using Excel or other computer programs to build complex financial models is beyond the scope of this text, we do provide an introduction to some of the Excel tools that see widespread practice in financial modeling. Even if your job does not involve building models in Excel, financial analysts in your firm will routinely present their analysis in that form, and your ability to respond and contribute to that analysis hinges upon your understanding of at least the basics of those models. Remember that finance is often the gatekeeper of corporate funds, so gaining support from the finance department may be an important step in marshaling the resources you need to do your job effectively. It's easier to gain that support if you are conversant in the basics of financial modeling in Excel.

SUMMARY

FOCUS ON VALUE

This chapter established the primary goal of the firm: **to maximize the wealth of the owners for whom the firm is being operated.** For public companies, this objective means that managers should act only on those opportunities that they expect will create value for owners by increasing the stock price. Doing so requires management to consider the returns and the risks of each proposed action and their combined effect on the value of the firm's stock.

REVIEW OF LEARNING GOALS

LG 1 **Define finance and the managerial finance function.** Finance is the science and art of how individuals and firms raise, allocate, and invest money. It affects virtually all aspects of business. Managerial finance is concerned with the duties of the financial manager working in a business. Financial managers administer the financial affairs of all types of businesses: private and public, large and small, profit seeking and not for profit. They perform such varied tasks as developing a financial plan or budget, extending credit to customers, evaluating proposed large expenditures, and raising money to fund the firm's operations.

LG 2 **Describe the goal of the firm, and explain why maximizing the value of the firm is an appropriate goal for a business.** The goal of the firm is to maximize its value and therefore the wealth of its shareholders. Maximizing the value of the firm means running the business in the interest of those who own it, the shareholders. Because shareholders are paid after other stakeholders, it is also generally necessary to satisfy the interests of other stakeholders to enrich shareholders.

LG 3 **Identify the primary activities of the financial manager.** Financial managers are primarily involved in three types of decisions. Investment decisions relate to how a company invests its capital to generate wealth for shareholders. Financing decisions relate to how a company raises the capital it needs to invest. Working capital decisions refer to the day-to-day management of a firm's short-term resources such as cash, receivables, inventory, and payables.

LG 4 **Explain the key principles that financial managers use when making business decisions.** The time value of money means that money is more valuable today than in the future because of the opportunity to earn a return on money that is on hand now. Because a tradeoff exists between risk and return, managers have to consider both factors for any investment they make. Managers should also focus more on cash flow than on accounting profit. Furthermore, managers need to recognize that market prices reflect information gathered by many different investors, so the price of a company's stock is an important signal of how the company is doing. Finally, although managers should act in shareholders' interest, they do not always do so, which requires various kinds of incentives to be in place so that the interests of managers and shareholders align to the greatest extent possible.

LG 5 **Describe the legal forms of business organization.** These are the sole proprietorship, the partnership, and the corporation. The corporation is dominant in the sense that most large companies are corporations, and a corporation's owners are its stockholders. Stockholders expect to earn a return by receiving dividends or by realizing gains through increases in share price.

LG 6 **Describe the nature of the principal–agent relationship between the owners and managers of a corporation, and explain how various corporate governance mechanisms attempt to manage agency problems.** The separation of owners and managers in a corporation gives rise to the classic principal–agent relationship, in which shareholders are the principals and managers are the agents. This arrangement works well when the agent makes decisions in the principal's best interest, but it can lead to agency problems when the interests of the principal and agent differ. A firm's corporate governance structure is intended to help ensure that managers act in the best interests of the firm's shareholders and other stakeholders, and it is usually influenced by both internal and external factors.

OPENER-IN-REVIEW

In the chapter opener, you learned that with Brookdale Senior Living's stock price trading around $12.35 per share, one of the firm's investors proposed an idea that might net the firm's shareholders $21 per share in cash. Suppose that Brookdale acted upon the suggestion of Land and Buildings and that as a result Brookdale was able to distribute $21 per share in cash to its investors. Suppose that after selling its real estate assets and paying out cash to shareholders, Brookdale's shares were worth $5 per share. Are Brookdale's investors better or worse off? Specifically, calculate the percentage change in the wealth of shareholders (including the cash they received and the change in the value of their stock) that would hypothetically occur if Brookdale acted according to this plan. Now suppose that Brookdale had 185.45 million shares outstanding. What is the total dollar value of wealth created (or destroyed) by the restructuring proposed by Land and Buildings?

SELF-TEST PROBLEM (Solution in Appendix)

ST1–1 **Emphasis on Cash Flows** Worldwide Rugs is a rug importer located in the United States that resells its import products to local retailers. Last year, Worldwide Rugs imported $2.5 million worth of rugs from around the world, all of which were paid for prior to shipping. On receipt of the rugs, the importer immediately resold them to local retailers for $3 million. To allow its retail clients time to resell the rugs, Worldwide Rugs sells to retailers on credit. Prior to the end of its business year, Worldwide Rugs collected 85% of its outstanding accounts receivable.

a. What is the accounting profit that Worldwide Rugs generated for the year?
b. Did Worldwide Rugs have a successful year from an accounting perspective?
c. What is the financial cash flow that Worldwide Rugs generated for the year?
d. Did Worldwide Rugs have a successful year from a financial perspective?
e. If the current pattern persists, what is your expectation for the future success of Worldwide Rugs?

WARM-UP EXERCISES All problems are available in MyLab Finance

LG5 E1–1 Ann and Jack have been partners for several years. Their firm, A & J Tax Preparation, has been very successful, as the pair agree on most business-related questions. One disagreement, however, concerns the legal form of their business. For the past 2 years, Ann has tried to convince Jack to incorporate. She believes there is no downside to incorporating and sees only benefits. Jack strongly disagrees; he thinks the business should remain a partnership forever.

First, take Ann's side, and explain the positive side to incorporating the business. Next, take Jack's side, and state the advantages to remaining a partnership. Last, what information would you want if you were asked to make the decision for Ann and Jack?

LG4 E1–2 As chief financial officer, you are responsible for weighing the financial pros and cons of the many investment opportunities developed by your company's research and development division. You are currently evaluating two competing 15-year projects that differ in several ways. Relative to your firm's current EPS, the first project is expected to generate above-average EPS during the first 5 years, average EPS during the second 5 years, and then below-average EPS during the last 5 years. The second project is expected to generate below-average EPS during the first 5 years, average EPS during the second 5 years, and then well-above-average EPS during the last 5 years.

Is the choice obvious if you expect the second investment to result in a larger overall earnings increase? Given the goal of the firm, what issues will you consider before making a final decision?

LG4 E1–3 The end-of-year parties at Yearling, Inc., are known for their extravagance. To thank the employees for their hard work, management provides the best food and entertainment. During the planning for this year's bash, a disagreement broke out between the treasurer's staff and the controller's staff. The treasurer's staff contended that the firm was running low on cash and might have trouble paying its bills over the coming months; they requested that cuts be made to the budget for the party. The controller's staff believed that any cuts were unwarranted, as the firm continued to be very profitable.

Can both sides be correct? Explain your answer.

LG5 E1–4 You have been made treasurer for a day at AIMCO, which develops technology for video conferencing. A manager of the satellite division has asked you to authorize a capital expenditure in the amount of $100,000. The manager states that this expenditure is necessary to continue a long-running project designed to use satellites to allow video conferencing anywhere on the planet. The manager admits that the satellite concept has been surpassed by recent technological advances in telephony, but he believes that AIMCO should continue the project because $2.5 million has already been spent over the past 15 years on this project. Although you believe the project will generate future cash outflows that exceed its inflows, the manager believes it would be a shame to waste the money and time already spent.

Use marginal cost–benefit analysis to make your decision regarding whether you should authorize the $100,000 expenditure to continue the project.

LG6

E1–5 Recently, some branches of Donut Shop, Inc., have dropped the practice of allowing employees to accept tips. Customers who once said, "Keep the change," now have to get used to waiting for their nickels. Management even instituted a policy of requiring that change be thrown out if a customer drives off without it. As a frequent customer who gets coffee and doughnuts for the office, you notice that the lines are longer and that more mistakes are being made in your order.

Explain why tips could be viewed as similar to stock options and why the delays and incorrect orders could represent a case of agency costs. If tips are gone forever, how could Donut Shop reduce these agency costs?

LG5

E1–6 In 2018 Ross Corporation had pretax ordinary income of $500,000 and sold for $150,000 an asset purchased in 2016 for $125,000. Calculate the 2018 tax liability for the company.

PROBLEMS

All problems are available in MyLab Finance. The MyLab icon indicates problems in Excel format available in MyLab Finance.

LG5

P1–1 **Liability comparisons** Merideth Harper has invested $25,000 in Southwest Development Company. The firm has recently declared bankruptcy and has $60,000 in unpaid debts. Explain the nature of payments, if any, by Merideth in each of the following situations.

a. Southwest Development Company is a sole proprietorship owned by Ms. Harper.

b. Southwest Development Company is a 50–50 partnership of Merideth Harper and Christopher Black.

c. Southwest Development Company is a corporation.

LG4

P1–2 **Accrual income versus cash flow for a period** Thomas Book Sales, Inc., supplies textbooks to college and university bookstores. The books are shipped with a proviso that they must be paid for within 30 days but can be returned for a full refund credit within 90 days. In 2018, Thomas shipped and billed book titles totaling $760,000. Collections, net of return credits, during the year totaled $690,000. The company spent $300,000 acquiring the books it shipped.

a. Using accrual accounting and the preceding values, show the firm's net profit for the past year.

b. Using cash accounting and the preceding values, show the firm's net cash flow for the past year.

c. Which of these statements is more useful to the financial manager? Why?

Personal Finance Problem

LG4

P1–3 **Cash flows** It is typical for Jane to plan, monitor, and assess her financial position using cash flows over a given period, typically a month. Jane has a savings account, and her bank loans money at 6% per year while it offers short-term investment rates of 5%. Jane's cash flows during August were as follows:

Item	Cash inflow	Cash outflow
Clothes		−$1,000
Interest received	$ 450	
Dining out		−500
Groceries		−800
Salary	4,500	
Auto payment		−355
Utilities		−280
Mortgage		−1,200
Gas		−222

a. Determine Jane's total cash inflows and cash outflows.
b. Determine the net cash flow for the month of August.
c. If there is a shortage, what are a few options open to Jane?
d. If there is a surplus, what would be a prudent strategy for her to follow?

P1–4 **Marginal cost–benefit analysis and the goal of the firm** Ken Allen, capital budgeting analyst for Bally Gears, Inc., has been asked to evaluate a proposal. The manager of the automotive division believes that replacing the robotics used on the heavy truck gear line will produce total benefits of $560,000 (in today's dollars) over the next 5 years. The existing robotics would produce benefits of $400,000 (also in today's dollars) over that same period. An initial cash investment of $220,000 would be required to install the new equipment. The manager estimates that the existing robotics can be sold for $70,000. Show how Ken will apply marginal cost–benefit analysis techniques to determine the following:
a. The marginal benefits of the proposed new robotics.
b. The marginal costs of the proposed new robotics.
c. The net benefit of the proposed new robotics.
d. What should Ken recommend that the company do? Why?
e. What factors besides the costs and benefits should be considered before the final decision is made?

P1–5 **Identifying agency problems, costs, and resolutions** Explain why each of the following situations is an agency problem and what costs to the firm might result from it. Suggest how the problem might be handled short of firing the individual(s) involved.
a. The front desk receptionist routinely takes an extra 20 minutes of lunch time to run personal errands.
b. Division managers are padding cost estimates to show short-term efficiency gains when the costs come in lower than the estimates.
c. The firm's chief executive officer has had secret talks with a competitor about the possibility of a merger in which she would become the CEO of the combined firms.
d. A branch manager lays off experienced full-time employees and staffs customer service positions with part-time or temporary workers to lower employment costs and raise this year's branch profit. The manager's bonus is based on profitability.

P1–6 **Corporate taxes** Tantor Supply, Inc., is a small corporation acting as the exclusive distributor of a major line of sporting goods. During 2018, the firm earned $92,500 before taxes.

a. Calculate the firm's tax liability.
b. How much are Tantor Supply's 2018 after-tax earnings?
c. What was the firm's average tax rate, based on your findings in part **a**?
d. What was the firm's marginal tax rate, based on your findings in part **a**?

P1–7 **Marginal and average tax rates** Using the tax rate schedule given in Table 1.2, perform the following:
a. Calculate the tax liability, after-tax earnings, and average tax rates for the following levels of partnership earnings before taxes: \$10,000; \$80,000; \$300,000; \$500,000; \$1 million; \$1.5 million; and \$2 million.
b. Plot the average tax rates (measured on the *y*-axis) against the pretax income levels (measured on the *x*-axis). What generalization can be made concerning the relationship between these variables?

P1–8 **Marginal tax rates** Using the tax rate schedule given in Table 1.2, perform the following:
a. Find the marginal tax rate for the following levels of sole proprietorship earnings before taxes: \$15,000; \$60,000; \$90,000; \$150,000; \$250,000; \$450,000; and \$1 million.
b. Plot the marginal tax rates (measured on the *y*-axis) against the pretax income levels (measured on the *x*-axis). Explain the relationship between these variables.

P1–9 **Interest versus dividend income** Last year, Shering Corporation had pretax earnings from operations of \$490,000. In addition, it received \$20,000 in income from interest on bonds it held in Zig Manufacturing and received \$20,000 in income from dividends on its 5% common stock holding in Tank Industries, Inc. Shering faces a flat 21% tax rate and is eligible for a 50% dividend exclusion on its Tank Industries stock.
a. Calculate the firm's tax on its operating earnings only.
b. Find the tax and the after-tax amount attributable to the interest income from Zig Manufacturing bonds.
c. Find the tax and the after-tax amount attributable to the dividend income from the Tank Industries, Inc., common stock.
d. Compare, contrast, and discuss the after-tax amounts resulting from the interest income and dividend income calculated in parts **b** and **c**.
e. What is the firm's total tax liability for the year?

P1–10 **Interest versus dividend expense** Michaels Corporation expects earnings before interest and taxes to be \$50,000 for the current period. Assuming a flat tax rate of 21%, compute the firm's earnings after taxes and earnings available for common stockholders (earnings after taxes and preferred stock dividends, if any) under the following conditions:
a. The firm pays \$12,000 in interest.
b. The firm pays \$12,000 in preferred stock dividends.

P1–11 Hemingway Corporation is considering expanding its operations to boost its income, but before making a final decision, it has asked you to calculate the corporate tax consequences of such a decision. Currently, Hemingway generates before-tax yearly income of \$200,000 and has no debt outstanding. Expanding operations would allow Hemingway to increase before-tax yearly income to $350,000. Hemingway can use either cash reserves or debt to finance its expansion. If Hemingway uses debt, it will have a yearly interest expense of $70,000.

Create a spreadsheet to conduct a tax analysis (assume a 21% flat tax rate) for Hemingway Corporation and determine the following:

a. What is Hemingway's current annual corporate tax liability?
b. What is Hemingway's current average tax rate?
c. If Hemingway finances its expansion using cash reserves, what will be its new corporate tax liability and average tax rate?
d. If Hemingway finances its expansion using debt, what will be its new corporate tax liability and average tax rate?
e. What would you recommend the firm do? Why?

P1–12 **ETHICS PROBLEM** What does it mean to say that managers should maximize shareholder wealth "subject to ethical constraints"? What ethical considerations might enter into decisions that result in cash flow and stock price effects that are less than they might otherwise have been?

SPREADSHEET EXERCISE

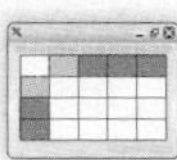

Assume that Monsanto Corporation is considering the replacement of some of its older and outdated carpet-manufacturing equipment. Its objective is to improve the efficiency of operations in terms of both speed and reduction in the number of defects. The company's finance department has compiled pertinent data to conduct a marginal cost–benefit analysis for the proposed equipment replacement.

The cash outlay for new equipment would be approximately $600,000. The net book value of the old equipment and its potential net selling price add up to $250,000. The total benefits over the life of the new equipment (measured in today's dollars) would be $900,000. The sum of benefits from the remaining life of the old equipment (measured in today's dollars) would be $300,000.

TO DO

Create a spreadsheet to conduct a marginal cost–benefit analysis for Monsanto Corporation, and determine the following:

a. The marginal benefits of the proposed new equipment.
b. The marginal costs of the proposed new equipment.
c. The net benefit of the proposed new equipment.
d. What would you recommend the firm do? Why?

MyLab Finance Visit www.pearson.com/mylab/finance **for Chapter Case:** ***Assessing the Goal of Sports Products, Inc.,*** Group Exercises, and numerous online resources.

CHAPTER 2

The Financial Market Environment

LEARNING GOALS

LG 1 Understand the role that financial institutions play in managerial finance.

LG 2 Understand the role that financial markets play in managerial finance.

LG 3 Describe the differences between the money market and the capital market.

LG 4 Understand the major regulations and regulatory bodies that affect financial institutions and markets.

LG 5 Describe the process of issuing common stock, including venture capital, going public, and the role of the investment bank.

LG 6 Understand what is meant by financial markets in crisis, and describe some of the root causes of the Great Recession.

MyLab Finance Chapter Introduction Video

WHY THIS CHAPTER MATTERS TO YOU

In your *professional* life

ACCOUNTING You need to understand how the firm raises external financing with the assistance of financial institutions in the financial markets.

INFORMATION SYSTEMS You need to understand how information flows between the firm and financial markets.

MANAGEMENT You need to understand why healthy financial institutions and markets are an integral part of a healthy economy and how a crisis in the financial sector can spread and affect almost any type of business.

MARKETING You need to understand why it is important for firms to communicate results to investors and how these communications lead to more favorable external financing terms for the firm in the financial markets.

OPERATIONS You need to understand why external financing is, for most firms, an essential aspect of ongoing operations.

In your *personal* life

Making financial transactions will be a regular occurrence throughout your life. These transactions may be as simple as depositing your paycheck in a bank or as complex as deciding how to allocate the money you save for retirement among different investment options. The content in this chapter will help you make better decisions when you conduct business in the financial markets.

Russell Hart/Alamy Stock Photo

AIRBNB

Billions of VC Funding Gives Airbnb Plenty of Room

The daughter of Chinese immigrants and founder of the venture capital firm, Cowboy Ventures, Aileen Lee added a new term to the business lexicon in her 2013 blog post on *Tech Crunch*. Lee used the word *unicorn* to describe a privately held tech startup worth more than $1 billion. Prior to 2013, private companies with valuations that high were about as rare as the mythical one-horned equine creature. But by 2017, less than four years after Lee coined the term, more than 200 startups had achieved unicorn status around the world. Most of those called the United States home, with the greatest concentration in California's Silicon Valley.

One example was the room-sharing service, Airbnb. Founded in 2008, Airbnb received more than $3 billion in funding from venture capital firms, with the latest $1 billion arriving in 2017 and bringing the company's total estimated value to $31 billion. The company's rapid growth fueled speculation that it—along with other unicorns, such as the ride-sharing service Uber—would soon convert from a privately held company to a public corporation through an initial public offering (IPO) of common stock. Airbnb's cofounder, Brian Chesky, noted that most companies raising money in an IPO do so because they need the money to finance new investment, want to create a more visible brand, wish to allow existing shareholders to liquidate some of their investments, or desire to use shares of stock as a currency to make new acquisitions. Chesky claimed that none of those situations applied to Airbnb. The company had plenty of money and was profitable, it was already well known among consumers, and its private investors had been patient. Most analysts believed that at some point in the near future, the venture capitalists and other investors who provided Airbnb with its early funding would want to cash out their investment, and an IPO proved the most likely way to create that opportunity.

Source: "Welcome to the Unicorn Club: Learning from Billion-dollar Startups," by Aileen Lee, November 2, 2013, Tech Crunch.

2.1 Financial Institutions

financial institution
An intermediary that channels the savings of individuals, businesses, and governments into loans or investments.

Most successful firms have ongoing needs for funds. **Financial institutions** serve as intermediaries by channeling the savings of individuals, businesses, and governments into loans or investments. Many financial institutions directly or indirectly pay savers interest on deposited funds; others provide services for a fee (e.g., checking accounts for which customers pay service charges). Some financial institutions accept customers' savings deposits and lend this money to other customers such as firms, others invest customers' savings in earning assets such as real estate or stocks and bonds, and still others do both. The government requires financial institutions to operate within established regulatory guidelines.

For financial institutions, the key suppliers of funds and the key demanders of funds are individuals, businesses, and governments. The savings that individual consumers place in financial institutions provide these institutions with a large portion of their funds. Individuals not only supply funds to financial institutions but also demand funds from them in the form of loans. However, individuals as a group are *net suppliers* for financial institutions: They save more money than they borrow.

Business firms also deposit some of their funds in financial institutions, primarily in checking accounts with various commercial banks. Like individuals, firms borrow funds from these institutions, but, unlike individuals, firms are *net demanders* of funds: They borrow more money than they save.

Governments maintain deposits of temporarily idle funds, certain tax payments, and Social Security payments in commercial banks. They do not borrow funds directly from financial institutions, although by selling their debt securities to various institutions, governments indirectly borrow from them. The government, like business firms, is typically a *net demander* of funds: It typically borrows more than it saves. We've all heard about the U.S. federal budget deficit.

Major types of financial institutions include commercial banks, investment banks, investment funds, insurance companies, and pension funds. Financial institutions offer a wide range of products and services for individual, business, and government clients.

COMMERCIAL BANKS, INVESTMENT BANKS, AND THE SHADOW BANKING SYSTEM

Commercial Banks

commercial banks
Institutions that provide savers with a secure place to invest their funds and that offer loans to individual and business borrowers.

Commercial banks are financial institutions that provide savers with a secure place to deposit or save funds for future use. Deposited funds generally earn a small rate of return, are available on demand, and are insured against loss. The largest commercial banks in the United States include JPMorgan Chase, Wells Fargo, Bank of America, Citibank, U.S. Bancorp, and PNC Bank. Commercial banks are among the most important financial institutions because they provide loans to both individuals and businesses to finance investments, such as the purchase of a new home or the expansion of a business.

The traditional business model of a commercial bank—taking in and paying interest on savings deposits and investing or lending those funds back out at higher interest rates—works to the extent that depositors trust their savings are safe. In the United States, most savings accounts at commercial banks are insured by the U.S. Federal Deposit Insurance Corporation (FDIC). The first $250,000 of deposits in an account at an FDIC-insured depository institution is covered dollar-for-dollar, principal plus any interest accrued or due the depositor. In the 1930s, FDIC insurance was put in place in response to the banking runs that occurred during the Great Depression. The same 1933 act of Congress that introduced deposit insurance, the **Glass-Steagall Act**, also created a separation between commercial banks and investment banks, meaning that an institution engaged in taking in deposits could not also engage in the somewhat riskier activities of securities underwriting and trading.

Glass-Steagall Act
An act of Congress in 1933 that created the Federal Deposit Insurance Corporation (FDIC) and separated the activities of commercial and investment banks.

Investment Banks

Investment banks are financial institutions that (1) assist companies in raising capital, (2) advise firms on major transactions such as mergers or financial restructurings, and (3) engage in trading and market-making activities. Some typical clients of investment banks include individuals with very high net worth, businesses, governments, pension funds, and other financial institutions. Size and reputation matter for investment banks. Large banks like Goldman Sachs, Morgan Stanley, Barclays, Credit Suisse, and Deutsche Bank have better connections, provide more services, and have greater capability of facilitating the unique transactions of their clients.

investment banks
Institutions that assist companies in raising capital, advise firms on major transactions such as mergers or financial restructurings, and engage in trading and market-making activities.

Commercial and investment banks remained essentially separate for more than 50 years, but Congress, with the approval of President Clinton, repealed Glass-Steagall in 1999. Companies that had formerly engaged only in the traditional activities of a commercial bank began competing with investment banks for underwriting and other services. Some of the largest commingled banks are JPMorgan Chase, Bank of America Merrill Lynch, and Citigroup.

Shadow Banking System

The past 25 years have witnessed tremendous growth in what has come to be known as the shadow banking system. The **shadow banking system** describes a group of financial institutions that engage in lending activities, much like traditional banks, but that do not accept deposits and are therefore not subject to the same regulations with which traditional depository institutions must comply. For example, financial institutions such as mutual funds, insurance companies, or pension funds might have excess cash to invest, and a large corporation might need short-term financing to cover seasonal cash flow needs. Investment banks can act as an intermediary between these two parties and help facilitate a loan and thereby become part of the shadow banking system. The Financial Stability

shadow banking system
A group of institutions that engage in lending activities, much like traditional banks, but that do not accept deposits and therefore are not subject to the same regulations as traditional banks.

MATTER OF FACT

Consolidation in the U.S. Banking Industry

The U.S. banking industry has been going through a long period of consolidation. According to the Federal Deposit Insurance Corporation (FDIC), the number of commercial banks in the United States declined from 14,400 in early 1984 to 4,964 by October 2017, a decline of more than 65%. The decline is concentrated among small community banks, which larger institutions have been acquiring at a rapid pace.

Board's *Global Shadow Banking Monitoring Report 2016* indicates that the shadow banking system financed $34 trillion in assets in 27 countries, and in the United States alone it financed $13.8 trillion in assets.

→ **REVIEW QUESTIONS** MyLab Finance Solutions

2–1 What are financial institutions? Describe the role they play within the financial market environment.
2–2 Who are the key customers of financial institutions? Who are net suppliers, and who are net demanders of funds?
2–3 Describe the role of commercial banks, investment banks, and the shadow banking system within the financial market environment.

LG2 LG3

2.2 Financial Markets

financial markets
Forums in which suppliers of funds and demanders of funds can transact business directly.

Whereas savers who deposit funds into financial institutions have no direct knowledge of how those funds are lent, suppliers of funds in the financial markets know where their money goes. **Financial markets** are forums in which suppliers and demanders of funds can transact business directly. The two key financial markets are the money market and the capital market. Short-term debt instruments, or marketable securities, trade in the *money market.* Long-term securities—bonds and stocks—trade in the *capital market.*

private placement
The sale of a new security directly to an investor or group of investors.

public offering
The sale of either bonds or stocks to the general public.

To raise money, firms can use either private placements or public offerings. A **private placement** involves the sale of a new security directly to an investor or group of investors, such as an insurance company or a pension fund. When firms need to raise large sums of money by selling securities, they usually do so through a **public offering**, which is the sale of either bonds or stocks to the general public.

primary market
Financial market in which securities are initially issued; the only market in which the issuer is directly involved in the transaction.

secondary market
Financial market in which pre-owned securities (those that are not new issues) are traded.

When a company or government entity sells stocks or bonds to investors and receives cash in return, it issues securities in the **primary market**. After the primary market transaction occurs, any further trading in the security does not involve the issuer directly, and the issuer receives no additional money from subsequent transactions. Once the securities begin to trade between investors, they become part of the **secondary market**. On large stock exchanges, billions of shares may trade between buyers and sellers on a single day, and these trades are all secondary market transactions. Money flows from the investors buying stocks to the investors selling them, and the company whose stock investors are trading remains largely unaffected by the transactions. Thus, we can say that the secondary market is where investors trade securities that were originally issued in the primary market.

THE RELATIONSHIP BETWEEN INSTITUTIONS AND MARKETS

Financial institutions actively participate in the financial markets as both suppliers and demanders of funds. Figure 2.1 depicts the general flow of funds through and between financial institutions and financial markets as well as the mechanics of private placement transactions. Domestic or foreign individuals, businesses, and governments may supply and demand funds. We next briefly discuss the

FIGURE 2.1

Flow of Funds

Flow of funds for financial institutions and markets

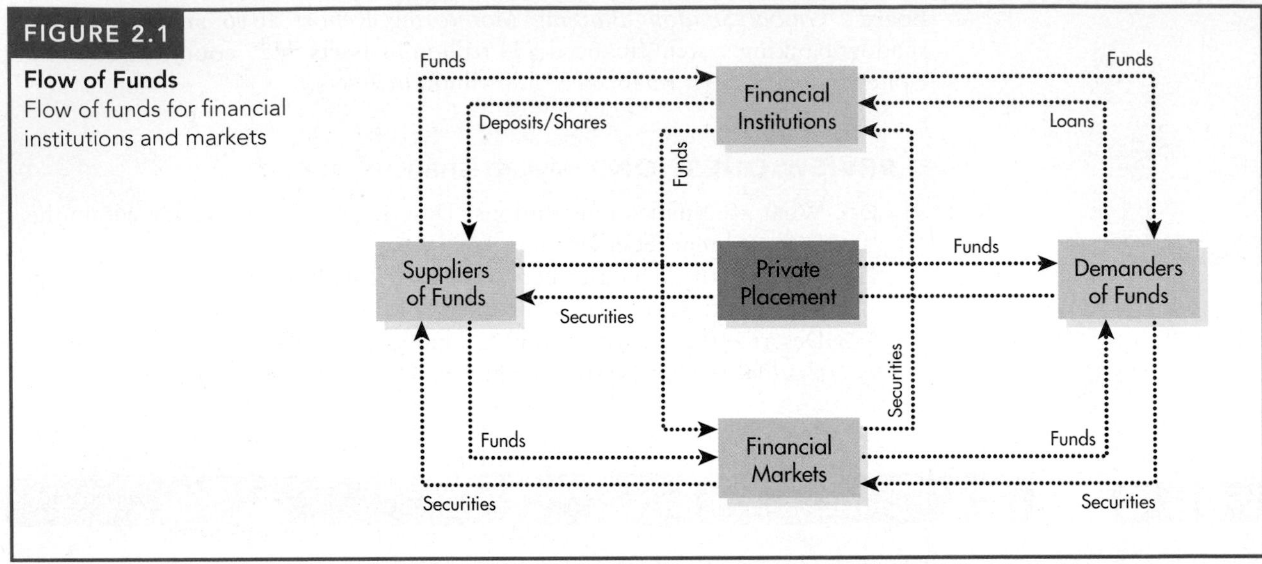

money market, including its international equivalent, the *Eurocurrency market.* We then end this section with a look at the capital market, which is the market where firms issue long-term securities such as stocks and bonds.

THE MONEY MARKET

money market
A market where investors trade highly liquid securities with maturities of 1 year or less.

The **money market** is a market where investors trade highly liquid securities with maturities of 1 year or less. The money market exists because some individuals, businesses, governments, and financial institutions have temporarily idle funds they wish to invest in a relatively safe, interest-bearing asset. At the same time, other individuals, businesses, governments, and financial institutions find themselves in need of seasonal or temporary financing. The money market brings together these suppliers and demanders of short-term funds.

marketable securities
Short-term debt instruments, such as U.S. Treasury bills, commercial paper, and negotiable certificates of deposit issued by government, business, and financial institutions, respectively.

In the money market, buyers and sellers trade **marketable securities**, which are short-term debt instruments such as U.S. Treasury bills, commercial paper, and negotiable certificates of deposit issued by government, business, and financial institutions, respectively. Investors generally consider marketable securities to be among the least risky investments available.

Eurocurrency market
International equivalent of the domestic money market.

The international equivalent of the domestic money market is the **Eurocurrency market.** This market for short-term bank deposits is denominated in U.S. dollars or other major currencies. Eurocurrency deposits arise when a corporation or individual makes a bank deposit in a currency other than the local currency of the country where the bank is located. For example, if a multinational corporation were to deposit U.S. dollars in a London bank, this action would create a Eurodollar deposit (a dollar deposit at a bank in Europe). Nearly all Eurodollar deposits are *time deposits,* which means the bank would promise to repay the deposit, with interest, at a fixed date in the future—in 6 months, for example. During the interim, the bank is free to lend this dollar deposit to creditworthy corporate or government borrowers. If the bank cannot find a borrower on its own, it may lend the deposit to another international bank.

THE CAPITAL MARKET

capital market
A market that enables suppliers and demanders of long-term funds to make transactions.

The **capital market** enables suppliers and demanders of long-term funds to make transactions. Businesses and governmental entities are the major issuers of securities in the capital market. The broker and dealer markets that provide a forum for bond and stock transactions form the backbone of the capital market. Although the United States has the world's largest and most active capital markets, in recent decades capital markets have experienced tremendous growth in countries all over the world.

Key Securities Traded: Bonds and Stocks

Securities traded in the capital market fall into two broad categories: *debt* and *equity*. The term debt refers to a loan that a borrower must repay. Equity, in contrast, refers to a security issued by a business that provides the security holder with an ownership stake in the firm. The main type of debt security is a *bond,* whereas the main equity security is *common stock. Preferred stock* has features of both debt and equity, and for that reason we refer to preferred stock as a hybrid security.

bond
Long-term debt instrument used by business and government to raise large sums of money, generally from a diverse group of lenders.

Bonds are long-term debt instruments used by business and government to raise large sums of money, generally from a diverse group of lenders. Bonds typically pay periodic interest at a *stated interest rate.* The borrower pays interest on the bond's *principal* until the bond's *maturity date*, at which point the borrower repays the principal to the bondholders. Bond issuers have a legal commitment to make interest and principal payments to investors, and failure to do so may result in the borrower going bankrupt.

common stock
A unit of ownership, or equity, in a corporation.

Shares of **common stock** are units of ownership, or equity, in a corporation. Common stockholders earn a return by receiving dividends—periodic distributions of cash—or by realizing increases in share price. Firms have no obligation to pay dividends on common stock, and in fact most young firms tend to reinvest their earnings rather than pay them out as dividends. Eventually, as they grow and mature, most firms do pay dividends and raise them over time.

preferred stock
A special form of ownership having a fixed periodic dividend that must be paid prior to payment of any dividends to common stockholders.

Preferred stock is a hybrid form of ownership that has features of both a bond and a common stock. Firms promise to pay preferred stockholders a fixed periodic dividend, much like the fixed interest payments that bonds offer. Firms must also pay dividends to preferred stockholders before they pay dividends to common stockholders. In other words, like bonds, preferred stock has "preference" over common stock. However, if a firm cannot pay dividends, preferred stockholders cannot force it into bankruptcy as bondholders can when a firm does not make interest and principal payments.

The market prices of both common and preferred stocks can fluctuate, but because preferred dividends are fixed, whereas firms may increase or decrease dividends on common shares without limit, common stock prices tend to fluctuate more. See the *Focus on Practice* box for the story of one legendary stock price and the equally legendary man who brought it about.

Broker Markets and Dealer Markets

liquidity
The ability to quickly buy or sell a security without having an impact on the security's price.

The vast majority of trades made by investors take place in the secondary market. Print media sources like the *Wall Street Journal* and online resources like Yahoo! Finance (finance.yahoo.com) report information on secondary market transactions. A desirable feature of secondary markets for traders is **liquidity**,

FOCUS ON PRACTICE *in practice*

Berkshire Hathaway: Can Buffett Be Replaced?

In early 1980, investors could buy one share of Berkshire Hathaway Class A common stock (stock symbol: BRKA) for $285. That may have seemed expensive at the time, but by August 2017 the price of just one share had climbed to $270,235. The wizard behind such phenomenal growth in shareholder value is the chairman of Berkshire Hathaway, Warren Buffett, nicknamed the Oracle of Omaha.

With his partner, Vice-Chairman Charlie Munger, Buffett runs a large conglomerate of dozens of subsidiaries with 367,000 employees and more than $223 billion in annual revenues. He makes it look easy. In his words, "I've taken the easy route, just sitting back and working through great managers who run their own shows. My only tasks are to cheer them on, sculpt and harden our corporate culture, and make major capital-allocation decisions. Our managers have returned this trust by working hard and effectively."*

Buffett's style of corporate leadership seems rather laid back, but behind that "aw-shucks" manner is one of the best analytical minds in business. He believes in aligning managerial incentives with performance. Berkshire employs many different incentive arrangements, their terms depending on such elements as the economic potential or capital intensity of a CEO's business. Whatever the compensation arrangement, Buffett tries to keep it both simple and fair. Buffett himself receives an annual salary of $100,000, which isn't much in this age of supersized CEO compensation packages. Listed for many years among the world's wealthiest people, Buffett has donated most of his Berkshire stock to the Bill and Melinda Gates Foundation.

Berkshire's annual report is a must-read for many investors due to the popularity of Buffett's annual letter to shareholders with his homespun take on such topics as investing, corporate governance, and corporate leadership. Shareholder meetings in Omaha, Nebraska, have turned into cult-like gatherings, with thousands traveling to listen to Buffett answer questions from shareholders. One question that has been firmly answered is that of Buffett's ability to create shareholder value.

The next question, not yet answered, is whether Berkshire Hathaway can successfully replace Buffett (age 87) and Munger (age 93). Several times in recent years Buffett has said publicly that his successor already works at Berkshire and has the full support of the company's board, but as yet no one has been specifically named as successor. Berkshire shareholders hope that Buffett's special wisdom applies as well to identifying new managerial talent as it does to making strategic investment decisions.

► *Thinking about the principal-agent problem from Chapter 1, why might Buffett use different incentive systems in firms with different growth prospects?*

Source: *Berkshire Hathaway, Inc., "Letter to Shareholders of Berkshire Hathaway, Inc.," *2006 Annual Report,* p. 4.

market order
An order to either buy or sell a security at the prevailing market prices.

bid price
The highest price a buyer in the market is willing to pay for a security.

ask price
The lowest price a seller in the market is willing to accept for a security.

which refers to the ability to quickly buy or sell a security without having an impact on the security's price. If a security trades in an illiquid market, selling or buying that security quickly may prove difficult and may require a price concession by the investor to facilitate the trade.

The typical secondary market trade requires an investor to submit an order to a brokerage service, for which the brokerage charges the investor a fee called a commission. The simplest type of trade involves a **market order**, which is an order to either sell or buy a security at the prevailing *bid* or *ask* price, respectively. The **bid price** is the highest price a buyer in the market is willing to pay for a security, and the **ask price** is the lowest price a seller in the market is willing to accept for a security. In effect, an investor pays the ask price when buying securities and receives the bid price when selling them. An example will help illustrate this concept.

EXAMPLE 2.1

MyLab Finance Solution Video

Mark instructs his broker to submit a market order to buy 100 shares of Facebook common stock. At the time, the ask price for Facebook is $138.79, and the bid price is $138.71. Remember, the ask price is the lowest price offered in the market to sell Facebook to a potential buyer. Since Mark is trying to buy

Facebook stock, and he wants to buy at the lowest possible price, he will pay \$138.79, plus whatever commissions his broker charges. If, however, Mark already owned Facebook stock and wanted to sell it, he would be looking for the market's best offer to buy, the bid price. In that case, Mark would sell his shares for \$138.71, less commissions charged by the broker.

bid/ask spread
The difference between the bid and ask prices.

The difference between the bid and ask prices is the **bid/ask spread.**

$$\text{Bid/Ask Spread} = \text{Ask Price} - \text{Bid Price} \tag{2.1}$$

market makers
Securities dealers who "make markets" by offering to buy or sell certain securities at stated prices.

The bid/ask spread is a kind of trading cost that investors may pay when they trade through a market maker. A **market maker** is a securities dealer who makes a market in one or more securities by offering to buy or sell them at stated bid/ask prices. The bid/ask spread represents income to the market maker in much the same way that commission is income for the broker who submits the order. When an investor submits an order through a broker, the brokerage service sends the order, usually electronically, to a market maker to execute the trade. How the market maker executes the order depends on whether the secondary market where the trade takes place is a broker market or a dealer market.

broker market
The securities exchanges on which the two sides of a transaction, the buyer and seller, are brought together to trade securities.

The essential difference between broker and dealer markets is a technical point that deals with the way trades are executed. When a trade occurs in a **broker market**, the market maker brings the buyer's order and the seller's order together to execute the trade at the midpoint of the bid/ask spread. In other words, Party A sells his or her securities directly to the buyer, Party B. Note that this kind of market will have a high degree of liquidity if many investors want to buy and many want to sell. In this case the market maker acts as a broker and by doing so forgoes collecting the bid/ask spread. This means that the only transaction cost for each trader is their brokerage commission.

dealer market
The market in which the buyer and seller are not brought together directly but instead have their orders executed by securities dealers who "make markets" in the given security.

In contrast, when trades occur in a **dealer market** the buyer's and the seller's orders are not brought directly together. Instead, market makers execute the buy/sell market orders they receive using their own inventory of securities. Essentially, two separate trades take place: Party A sells her securities (say, IBM stock) to a dealer at the bid price, and Party B buys his securities (IBM stock) from another, or possibly even the same, dealer at the ask price. This type of market will have good liquidity if dealers are willing to buy and sell quickly in response to the orders they receive. In this case, the market maker acts as a dealer and by doing so collects one-half of the bid/ask spread for each side of the trade. If the same dealer executes both sides of the trade, she collects the full bid/ask spread. In a dealer market, the total transaction cost for each of the traders is one-half the bid/ask spread plus the brokerage commission. You can see that the key difference between broker and dealer markets is whether other traders provide liquidity or whether dealers perform that function. In broker markets the orders from investors provide liquidity, and in dealer markets the dealers provide liquidity.

PERSONAL FINANCE EXAMPLE 2.2

MyLab Finance Solution Video

Assume that the current bid price for Merck & Co. stock is \$63.25 and the ask price is \$63.45. Suppose you have an E*TRADE brokerage account that charges a \$6.95 commission for online equity trades. What is the current bid/ask spread for Merck?

$$\text{Bid/Ask Spread} = \$63.45 - \$63.25 = \$0.20$$

Inserting the current bid and ask prices into Equation 2.1, you find that the bid/ask spread for Merck is \$0.20. What would your total transaction costs be if you purchased 100 shares of Merck by submitting a market order via your E*TRADE account? Assume the trade is sent to a broker market for execution, and the market maker matches your order with a 100-share sell order for Merck from another investor. In this case your order will be executed at the midpoint of the bid/ask spread (\$63.35), so you will pay only the brokerage commission.

$$\text{Total Transaction Costs} = \text{Brokerage Commission} = \$6.95$$

Now what would your total transaction costs be if you purchased 100 shares of Merck by submitting a market order via your E*TRADE account, and it is routed to a dealer market for execution?

$$\begin{aligned}\text{Total Transaction Costs} &= (\text{Number of Shares} \times 1/2 \text{ the Bid/Ask Spread}) \\ &\quad + \text{Brokerage Commission} \\ &= (100 \times 1/2 \times \$0.20) + \$6.95 \\ &= \$10 + \$6.95 = \$16.95\end{aligned}$$

Depending on where your brokerage routes your order, you find that your total transaction costs are either \$6.95 in a broker market or \$16.95 in a dealer market.

Because any stock that trades in the secondary market has a bid price and an ask price, it may seem difficult to answer the question, what is the market value of the stock? In the previous example, is the market value of Merck \$63.45 or \$63.25? A fairly common convention is to refer to the midpoint of the bid/ask spread as the stock's market value. In this case, we could say that Merck's market value is \$63.35, which is halfway between the bid and ask prices.

$$\text{Midpoint of the Bid/Ask Spread} = (\$63.45 + \$63.25) \div 2 = \$63.35$$

securities exchanges
Organizations that provide the marketplace in which firms can raise funds through the sale of new securities and purchasers can resell securities.

Broker Markets Most broker markets consist of national or regional **securities exchanges**, which are organizations that provide a physical marketplace where traders can buy and sell securities. Note that most broker markets are actually broker/dealer markets in the sense that when executing trades the market maker must act as a broker first, when public orders are available to provide the necessary liquidity, and as a dealer second, when there are no public orders to provide the requisite liquidity.

If you are like most people, the first name that comes to mind in association with the "stock market" is the New York Stock Exchange, known as the NYSE. In fact, the NYSE is the dominant broker market, accounting for a little more than 25% of the total dollar volume of all trades in the U.S. stock market in 2016. Internet-based brokerage systems enable investors to place their buy and sell orders electronically, and those orders execute on the NYSE in seconds, thanks to sophisticated telecommunication devices.

For a firm to list its securities for trading on a stock exchange, it must file an application for listing and meet a number of requirements. For example, to be eligible for listing on the NYSE, a firm must have aggregate pretax earnings of at least \$10 million over the previous 3 years, with at least \$2 million in each of the previous 2 years, and greater than zero in each of the previous 3 years; at least 400 stockholders owning 100 or more shares; at least 1.1 million shares of publicly held stock outstanding; a market value of publicly held shares of at least $40 million; and a public share price of at least $4. Firms that earn listing status on the NYSE are among the largest public companies, and their shares often trade in multiple venues in addition to the NYSE. Accordingly, trading in NYSE-listed stocks accounted for more than 47% of all U.S. stock trades in 2016.

Dealer Markets A key feature of the dealer market is that it has no centralized trading floors. Instead, it is composed of a large number of market makers linked together via a mass-telecommunications network.

Of note, most dealer markets are technically dealer/broker markets in the sense that when executing trades the market maker can act as dealer first, whenever it suits her to provide liquidity, and as broker second, whenever it doesn't suit her to provide liquidity. If a market maker in a dealer market receives an order she does not want to execute, she can simply route the order along to another market maker for execution. For example, she might route the order to a broker market. The two most recognizable dealer markets are the **Nasdaq market**, an all-electronic trading platform used to execute securities trades, and the **over-the-counter (OTC) market**, where investors trade smaller, unlisted securities. Together these two dealer markets account for about 25% of all shares traded in the United States, with the Nasdaq accounting for the overwhelming majority of those trades. (As an aside, the primary market is also a dealer market because all new issues are sold to the investing public by securities dealers, acting on behalf of the investment bank.)

Nasdaq market
An all-electronic trading platform used to execute securities trades.

over-the-counter (OTC) market
Market where smaller, unlisted securities are traded.

Founded in 1971, the *National Association of Securities Dealers Automated Quotation System,* or simply *Nasdaq,* had its origins in the OTC market but today is a totally separate entity that's no longer part of the OTC market. In fact, in 2006 the Securities and Exchange Commission (SEC) formally recognized the Nasdaq as a "listed exchange," essentially giving it the same stature and prestige as the NYSE.

In recent years, the distinctions between broker and dealer markets have blurred. Electronic trading platforms, using sophisticated algorithms, place buy and sell orders very rapidly (so-called high-frequency trading), often without any human intervention. These algorithms may allow trading firms to speculate on a stock's price movements, or they may be used to take a single, large buy or sell order and break it into many smaller orders in an effort to minimize the price impact of buying or selling a large quantity of shares. An increasing amount of trading takes place today "off exchange," often in private trading venues known as "dark pools." Roughly one-third of secondary market trading occurs in these off-exchange environments.

International Capital Markets

Eurobond market
The market in which corporations and governments typically issue bonds denominated in dollars and sell them to investors located outside the United States.

Although U.S. capital markets are by far the world's largest, important debt and equity markets exist outside the United States. In the **Eurobond market**, corporations and governments typically issue bonds denominated in dollars and sell them to investors located outside the United States. A U.S. corporation might, for example, issue dollar-denominated bonds that investors in Belgium, Germany, or Switzerland would purchase. Through the Eurobond market,

MATTER OF FACT

NYSE Is the World's Largest Stock Exchange

According to The Money Project, in 2016 the world boasted 60 major stock exchanges with a combined total market value of $69 trillion. The largest stock market in the world, as measured by the total market value of securities listed on that market, is the NYSE, with listed securities worth more than $18.5 trillion, or about 27% of the total market value for all major exchanges globally. The NYSE's total market capitalization is larger than the total market capitalizations of the world's 50 smallest major exchanges combined. The next largest is the Nasdaq at $7.5 trillion, with exchanges in Tokyo and Shanghai not far behind at $4.9 trillion and $4.5 trillion, respectively.

issuing firms and governments can tap a much larger pool of investors than would be generally available in the local market.

The *foreign bond market* is an international market for long-term debt securities. A **foreign bond** is a bond issued by a foreign corporation or government that is denominated in the investor's home currency and sold in the investor's home market. A bond issued by a U.S. company that is denominated in Swiss francs and sold in Switzerland is a foreign bond. Although the foreign bond market is smaller than the Eurobond market, many issuers have found it useful in tapping debt markets around the world.

foreign bond
A bond that is issued by a foreign corporation or government and is denominated in the investor's home currency and sold in the investor's home market.

Finally, the **international equity market** allows corporations to sell blocks of shares to investors in a number of different countries simultaneously. This market enables corporations to raise far larger amounts of capital than they could in any single market. International equity sales have been indispensable to governments that have sold state-owned companies to private investors.

international equity market
A market that allows corporations to sell blocks of shares to investors in a number of different countries simultaneously.

THE ROLE OF CAPITAL MARKETS

From a firm's perspective, a capital market should be a liquid market where firms can interact with investors to obtain valuable external financing resources. From investors' perspectives, a capital market should be an **efficient market** that establishes correct prices for the securities that firms sell and allocates funds to their most productive uses. This role is especially true for securities actively traded in broker or dealer markets, where intense competition among investors determines the prices of securities.

efficient market
A market that establishes correct prices for the securities that firms sell and allocates funds to their most productive uses.

The Efficient-Market Hypothesis

Active stock markets, such as the NYSE and the Nasdaq market, may be *efficient* if they are made up of many rational competitive investors who react quickly and objectively to new information. The **efficient market hypothesis (EMH)**, which is the basic theory describing the behavior of such a market, specifically states the following:

1. Securities are typically in equilibrium, which means they are fairly priced and their expected returns equal their required returns.
2. At any point in time, security prices fully reflect all information available about the firm and its securities, and these prices react swiftly to new information.
3. Because stocks are fully and fairly priced, investors need not waste their time trying to find mispriced (undervalued or overvalued) securities.

efficient market hypothesis (EMH)
Theory describing the behavior of a market in which (1) securities are in equilibrium, (2) security prices fully reflect all available information and react swiftly to new information, and (3) because stocks are fully and fairly priced, investors need not waste time looking for mispriced securities.

The price of an individual security is determined by the interaction between buyers and sellers in the market. If the market is efficient, the price of a stock is an unbiased estimate of its true value. In this context, the term *unbiased* means that stock prices are neither systematically overpriced nor underpriced. Investors compete with one another for information about a stock's true value, so at any given time, a stock's price reflects all the information known about the stock. Changes in the price reflect new information that investors learn about and act on. For example, suppose that a certain company's stock currently trades at $40 per share. If this company announces that sales of a new product have been higher than expected, and if investors have not already anticipated that announcement, investors will raise their estimate of what the stock is truly worth. At $40, the stock is a relative bargain, so temporarily more buyers than sellers will want to trade the stock, and its price will have to rise to restore equilibrium in the market. The more efficient the market is, the more rapidly this whole process works. In theory, even information known only to insiders may become incorporated in stock prices, as the *Focus on Ethics* box on page 53 explains.

New information is, almost by definition, unpredictable. For example, it is well known that retail companies in the United States have a spike in sales near the end of the calendar year as the holiday season approaches. When a firm reports higher sales near the end of the year, it is not new information because investors in the market are aware of the seasonal pattern and anticipate that sales will be higher in the fourth quarter than at any other time of year. To the market, new information would be a report from a retailer that its sales were higher (or lower) in the fourth quarter than investors had already expected. Because it is unanticipated, new information has a random quality (i.e., sometimes firms announce better-than-expected results, and sometimes they announce worse-than-expected results). As new information arrives, stock prices quickly respond, and those price movements will appear to occur at random. Therefore, one sign of stock market efficiency is that changes in stock prices are nearly impossible to predict, even by professional investors.

Not everyone agrees that prices in financial markets are as efficient as described in the preceding paragraph. Advocates of *behavioral finance,* an emerging field that blends ideas from finance and psychology, argue that stock prices and prices of other securities can deviate from their true values for extended periods and that these deviations may lead to predictable patterns in stock prices. One of the most widely recognized proponents of behavioral finance, Richard Thaler, won the 2017 Nobel Prize in Economics for his work challenging the efficient markets hypothesis. Thaler's early research provided evidence that stocks that had performed poorly in the past displayed a predictable tendency to rebound, giving investors aware of that pattern a profit opportunity.

Just how efficient are prices in financial markets? One sign that markets are quite efficient is that very few professional investors, such as mutual fund and pension fund managers, earn returns that beat the average return in the market. In 2016, fewer than 40% of mutual funds earned a return that beat the return on the S&P500 stock index. Fewer than 18% beat the S&P500 over the 15-year period from 2002 to 2016. Moreover, the funds that do beat the S&P500 return change over time, meaning that funds that perform well in the past are not particularly likely to repeat that performance. A 2017 study identified mutual funds that had outperformed the S&P500 for a 3-year period and then studied the performance of those funds over the subsequent 3 years. Only 5% of fund managers

FOCUS ON ETHICS *in practice*

Should Insider Trading Be Legal?

In May 2017, a federal jury convicted Doug DeCinces of insider trading for scoring nearly $1.3 million from a stock tip about a pending corporate acquisition. The tip came from a close friend who happened to be CEO of the target firm. DeCinces has already agreed to pay $2.5 million to settle the civil complaint with the Securities and Exchange Commission (SEC) and now faces up to 280 years in prison. This story is common; between 2002 and 2016, the SEC pursued 740 insider-trading cases against 1,572 defendants/respondents. What is unusual is this defendant's prior career—DeCinces spent 15 years playing third base for the Baltimore Orioles and California Angels.

Congress created the modern legal framework for regulating securities markets in 1933 and 1934. The SEC defines insider trading as trading a security, in breach of a fiduciary duty or other relationship of trust and confidence, while in possession of material, nonpublic information about the security. The integrity of securities markets is important to the overall economy because growth in income and jobs depends on scarce investor funds flowing to those firms with the best prospects. When securities markets are efficient, prices send clear signals about the best place to invest. The SEC prosecutes insider trading to ensure a fair, level playing field for all investors. Were the public to see securities markets as profitable only to insiders, they might shy away. And without large numbers of active buyers and sellers, markets would send distorted price signals, and economic growth would suffer.

Interestingly, many finance and law professors believe insider trading should be legal. Perhaps the most famous proponent is Henry Manne, who has argued that SEC efforts to stop insider trading have proved as ineffective as Prohibition in deterring bootlegging. Manne and others have also emphasized efficient allocation of investor funds depends on securities prices reflecting all relevant information, not just what happens to be public. Finally, they express skepticism at the idea that insider trading will drive the public away from securities—noting many markets (such as the ones for professional athletes, real estate, and used cars) function well despite unequal distributions of information. However, the scholar most closely associated with the idea of efficient markets, Nobel Prize winner Eugene Fama, does not believe that insider trading should be allowed, based on concerns that doing so would create an incentive for managers to hold back information about the firms they manage for reasons of personal gain.

In the end, the question of whether to decriminalize insider trading comes down to a tradeoff—the social cost of security price signals potentially distorted by fewer buyers/sellers against the social benefit of signals reflecting all relevant information. SEC enforcement policies may unintentionally acknowledge this tradeoff—prosecutions are comparatively rare, but convictions lead to severe punishment. The 740 insider-trading cases since 2002 translate into an average of just 49 per year, compared with billions of U.S. securities transactions. But, as Doug DeCinces found out, when caught, the SEC can be a stern umpire.

► *Suppose insider trading were legal. Would it still present an ethical issue for insiders wishing to trade on non-public information?*

Sources: "Former Angels star Doug DeCinces found guilty in insider trading deal that netted him $1 million-plus," *The Orange County Register*, May 12, 2017 (accessed online: http://www.ocregister.com/2017/05/12/forrmer-angels-star-doug-decinces-found-guilty-in-insider-trading-deal-that-netted-him-1-million-plus/). "Busting Insider Trading: As Pointless as Prohibition." *Wall Street Journal*, April 28, 2014 (accessed online: https://www.wsj.com/articles/henry-g-mannebusting-insider-trading-as-pointless-as-prohibition-1398720501).

who beat the S&P500 for 3 years managed to repeat that feat.[1] That relatively few professional managers outperform the overall market consistently is exactly what the efficient markets hypothesis predicts.

The extent to which stock markets are efficient will be debated for a long time. Clearly, prices do move in response to new information, and for most investors and corporate managers, the best advice is probably to use caution

1 "Fleeting Alpha: Evidence From the SPIVA Persistence Scorecards," by Ryan Poirier and Aye M. Soe, S&P Dow Jones Indices, February 2017.

when betting against the market. Identifying securities over- or undervalued by the market is extremely difficult, and very few people have demonstrated an ability to bet against the market correctly for an extended period.

→ **REVIEW QUESTIONS** MyLab Finance Solutions

2–4 What role do financial markets play in our economy? What are primary and secondary markets? What relationship exists between financial institutions and financial markets?

2–5 What is a private placement versus a public offering?

2–6 What is the money market? What is the Eurocurrency market?

2–7 What is the capital market? What are broker markets? What are dealer markets? How do they differ?

2–8 Describe the role of capital markets from the firm's and investors' perspectives. What is the efficient market hypothesis?

2.3 Regulation of Financial Markets and Institutions

With the hope of fostering fair, efficient, and stable financial markets, governments regulate financial institutions and markets, usually as much or more than almost any other sector in the economy. This section provides an overview of the financial regulatory landscape in the United States.

REGULATIONS GOVERNING FINANCIAL INSTITUTIONS

Federal Deposit Insurance Corporation (FDIC)
An agency created by the Glass-Steagall Act that provides insurance for deposits at banks and monitors banks to ensure their safety and soundness.

Gramm-Leach-Bliley Act
An act that allows business combinations (i.e., mergers) between commercial banks, investment banks, and insurance companies and thus permits these institutions to compete in markets that prior regulations prohibited them from entering.

As mentioned in Section 2.1, Congress passed the Glass-Steagall Act in 1933 during the depths of the Great Depression. The early 1930s witnessed a series of banking panics that caused almost one-third of the nation's banks to fail. Troubles within the banking sector and other factors contributed to the worst economic contraction in U.S. history, in which industrial production fell by more than 50%, the unemployment rate peaked at almost 25%, and stock prices dropped roughly 86%. The Glass-Steagall Act attempted to calm the public's fears about the banking industry by establishing the **Federal Deposit Insurance Corporation** (FDIC), which provided deposit insurance, effectively guaranteeing that individuals would not lose their money if they held it in a bank that failed. The FDIC was also charged with examining banks on a regular basis to ensure they were "safe and sound." The Glass-Steagall Act also prohibited institutions that took deposits from engaging in activities such as securities underwriting and trading, thereby effectively separating commercial banks from investment banks.

Over time, U.S. financial institutions faced competitive pressures from both domestic and foreign businesses that engaged in facilitating loans or making loans directly. Because these competitors either did not accept deposits or were located outside the United States, they were not subject to the same regulations as domestic banks. As a result, domestic banks began to lose market share in their core businesses. Pressure mounted to repeal the Glass-Steagall Act so that U.S. banks could compete more effectively, and in 1999 Congress enacted and President Clinton signed the **Gramm-Leach-Bliley Act**, which allows commercial banks, investment banks, and insurance companies to consolidate and compete for business in a wider range of activities.

In the aftermath of the recent financial crisis and recession, Congress passed the Dodd-Frank Wall Street Reform and Consumer Protection Act in July 2010. In print, the new law runs for hundreds of pages and calls for the creation of several new agencies, including the Financial Stability Oversight Council, the Office of Financial Research, and the Bureau of Consumer Financial Protection. The act also realigns the duties of several existing agencies and requires existing and new agencies to report to Congress regularly. Nearly a decade after Dodd-Frank became law, the various agencies affected or created by the new law were still writing rules specifying how the new law's provisions would be implemented. Exactly how the new legislation will affect financial institutions and markets, or whether it will even survive with the new administration of President Trump in the White House, remains unclear.

REGULATIONS GOVERNING FINANCIAL MARKETS

Securities Act of 1933
An act that regulates the sale of securities to the public via the primary market.

During the Great Depression, Congress passed two other pieces of legislation that had an enormous effect on the regulation of financial markets. The **Securities Act of 1933** imposed new regulations governing the sale of new securities. The 1933 act was intended to regulate activity in the primary market in which securities are initially issued to the public. The act was designed to ensure that the sellers of new securities provided extensive disclosures to the potential buyers of those securities.

Securities Exchange Act of 1934
An act that regulates the trading of securities such as stocks and bonds in the secondary market.

Securities and Exchange Commission (SEC)
The primary government agency responsible for enforcing federal securities laws.

The **Securities Exchange Act of 1934** regulates the secondary trading of securities such as stocks and bonds. The Securities Exchange Act of 1934 also created the **Securities and Exchange Commission** (SEC), which is the primary agency responsible for enforcing federal securities laws. In addition to the one-time disclosures required of security issuers by the Securities Act of 1933, the Securities Exchange Act of 1934 requires ongoing disclosure by companies whose securities trade in secondary markets. Companies must make a 10-Q filing every quarter and a 10-K filing annually. The 10-Q and 10-K forms contain detailed information about the financial performance of the firm during the relevant period. Today, these forms are available online through EDGAR (Electronic Data Gathering, Analysis, and Retrieval) on the SEC's website. The 1934 act also imposes limits on the extent to which corporate "insiders," such as senior managers, can trade in their firm's securities.

How much regulation of financial institutions and markets is appropriate? The debate surrounding that question may never end, but most countries do regulate the financial sectors of their economies to some degree. Trust is essential to the development of financial markets—without it, savers would be reluctant to supply funds to firms that need money to finance investment. To the extent that regulations enhance trust, they may encourage broader participation in financial markets, which in turn contributes to a growing economy.

→ REVIEW QUESTIONS MyLab Finance Solutions

2–9 Why do you think that so many pieces of important legislation related to financial markets and institutions were passed during the Great Depression?

2–10 What different aspects of financial markets do the Securities Act of 1933 and the Securities Exchange Act of 1934 regulate?

LG5

2.4 The Securities Issuing Process

As net demanders of funds, businesses sometimes find it necessary to access the capital market to raise external financing by selling new securities to investors. Companies use the new financing to fund operations or strategic investments that maximize the value of the firm. Most businesses will issue a mix of debt and equity securities over time, and they can issue both security types through a private placement or a public offering. The process for issuing debt and that for issuing equity are more similar than not, so for brevity the remainder of this section discusses the procedure for issuing common stock.

Because of the high risk associated with a business startup, a firm's initial financing typically comes from its founders in the form of a common stock investment. Until the founders have made an equity investment, it is highly unlikely that others will contribute either equity or debt capital. Early-stage outside investors in the firm's equity, as well as lenders who provide debt capital, want assurance they are taking no more risk than the founders. In addition, they want confirmation that the founders are confident enough in their vision for the firm that they are willing to risk their own money.

private equity
External equity financing that is raised via a private placement, typically by private early-stage firms with attractive growth prospects.

angel financing
Private equity financing provided to a young firm by a wealthy individual investing his or her own money.

venture capital
Equity financing provided by a firm that specializes in financing young, rapidly growing firms. Venture capital firms raise pools of money from outside investors which they then use to purchase equity stakes in small private companies.

angel investors (angels)
Wealthy individual investors who make their own investment decisions and are willing to invest in promising startups in exchange for a portion of the firm's equity.

venture capitalists (VCs)
Formal business entities that take in private equity capital from many individual investors, often institutional investors such as endowments and pension funds or individuals of high net worth, and make private equity investment decisions on their behalf.

ISSUING COMMON STOCK

Typically, the initial rounds of external financing for business startups with attractive growth prospects come from private investors via a private equity placement. Then, as the firm establishes the market potential of its product or service and begins to generate revenues, cash flow, and profits, it will often "go public" by issuing shares of common stock to a much broader group of investors.

Before we consider the initial public sale of equity, let's discuss some key aspects of early-stage equity financing.

Private Equity

Private equity is equity financing that is raised via a private placement, typically by early-stage firms with attractive growth prospects. Rapidly growing firms will usually require multiple rounds of private equity financing as they make early investments and develop operational capabilities. When the private equity financing comes from angel investors or venture capitalists, we refer to it as **angel financing** or **venture capital**, respectively. **Angel investors** (or **angels**) tend to be wealthy individual investors who make their own investment decisions and are willing to invest in promising startups in exchange for a portion of the firm's equity. In contrast, **venture capitalist** (VC) firms are businesses that take in money from many individual investors, often institutional investors such as endowments and pension funds or individuals of high net worth, and make investment decisions on their behalf. VCs typically maintain strong oversight in the firms they finance. They ordinarily take a seat on the firm's board of directors and have clearly defined exit strategies, often divesting their investment in the firm when it goes public or shortly thereafter. In 2016, VCs provided almost $50 billion in financing to U.S. businesses.

Organization and Investment Stages Venture capital investors tend to be organized in one of four basic ways, as described in Table 2.1. The *VC limited*

TABLE 2.1 Organization of Venture Capital Investors

Organization	Description
Small business investment companies (SBICs)	Corporations chartered by the federal government that can borrow at attractive rates from the U.S. Treasury and use the funds to make venture capital investments in private companies.
Financial VC funds	Subsidiaries of financial institutions, particularly banks, set up to help young firms grow and, it is hoped, become major customers of the institution.
Corporate VC funds	Firms, sometimes subsidiaries, established by nonfinancial firms, typically to gain access to new technologies that the corporation can access to further its own growth.
VC limited partnerships	Limited partnerships organized by professional VC firms, which serve as the general partner and organize, invest, and manage the partnership using the limited partners' funds; the professional VCs ultimately liquidate the partnership and distribute the proceeds to all partners.

partnership is the most common structure. The primary objective of these funds is to earn high returns.

VCs can invest in early-stage companies, later-stage companies, or buyouts and acquisitions. Generally, VCs invest about 40% to 50% of their resources in early-stage companies (for startup funding and expansion), and they invest a similar percentage in later-stage companies (for marketing, production expansion, and preparation for public offering). VCs invest just 5% to 10% of their funds in transactions involving the buyout or acquisition of other companies. Generally, VCs look for annual rates of return ranging from 20% to 50% or more, depending on both the development stage and the attributes of each company. VCs require higher returns on their riskier, early-stage investments than on later-stage investments.

Deal Structure and Pricing Regardless of the development stage, when VCs invest they do so under a legal agreement that clearly defines the deal structure and pricing. The deal structure allocates responsibilities and ownership interests between the existing owners (typically the founders) and the venture capitalist, and its terms depend on numerous factors related to the founders; the business structure, stage of development, and outlook; and other market and timing issues. The deal pricing is a function of the value of the business, the amount of funding provided, and the perceived risk of business operations. To control the VC's risk exposure and to help ensure the firm's success, the agreement will typically contain covenants or provisions that subject the firm to constraints or stipulations, such as tying the actual funding amount to the achievement of measurable milestones. The agreement will also have an explicit exit strategy for the VC that defines when and how the venture capital must be repaid. For example, VCs often tie their exit strategy to the firm's initial public offering of equity.

Venture capitalists will require more equity ownership and pay less for it the riskier and less developed the business. For this reason, financial managers strive to maximize the firm's earnings and minimize the risk of the firm's cash flows. Doing so will maximize the firm's value and minimize the cost of venture capital financing.

Going Public

When a firm wishes to sell its stock in the primary market, it has three alternatives. It can make (1) a *private placement,* in which the firm sells new securities directly to an investor or group of investors; (2) a *rights offering,* in which the firm sells new shares to existing stockholders; or (3) a *public offering,* in which it offers its shares for sale to the general public. Here we focus on public offerings, particularly the **initial public offering (IPO)**, which is the first public sale of a firm's stock. IPOs are typically made by small, rapidly growing companies that either require additional capital to continue growing or have met a milestone for going public that was established in an earlier agreement to obtain VC funding.

initial public offering (IPO)
The first public sale of a firm's stock.

To go public, the firm must first obtain approval from its current shareholders, the investors who own its privately issued stock. Next, the company's auditors and lawyers must certify that all the company's financial documents are as accurate as possible. The company then hires an investment bank willing to facilitate the offering. This investment bank provides the issuer with advice about important aspects of the issuing process. We'll discuss the role of the investment bank in more detail in the next section.

Next, with the help of the investment bank, the company files a registration statement with the SEC. One portion of this statement is called the **prospectus.** It describes the crucial aspects of the company issuing stock and the terms of the stock offering. During the waiting period between the statement's filing and its approval, prospective investors can receive a preliminary prospectus. This preliminary version is called a **red herring** because a notice printed in red on the front cover indicates the tentative nature of the document. The cover page of the preliminary prospectus describing the 2017 stock issue of Snap Inc., the parent company of Snapchat, appears in Figure 2.2. Although the preliminary document is incomplete, it still conveys considerable information to prospective investors. For example, Snap's IPO is selling 200,000,000 shares of non-voting Class A Common Stock in its IPO. Notice that Snap has three classes of common stock. The Class B shares have one vote per share and are convertible into one share of Class A. The Class C shares have 10 votes per share and are convertible into one share of Class B, and the founders are the exclusive owners of the super-voting Class C common stock. Thus, they have total voting control even after going public.

prospectus
A portion of a security registration statement that describes the key aspects of the issue, the issuer, and its management and financial position.

red herring
A preliminary prospectus made available to prospective investors during the waiting period between the registration statement's filing with the SEC and its approval.

After the SEC approves the registration statement, the investment community can begin analyzing the company's prospects. However, from the time it files until at least 1 month after the IPO is complete, the company must observe a *quiet period* during which the law places restrictions on what company officials may say about the company. The purpose of the quiet period is to make sure that all potential investors have access to the same information about the company—the information presented in the preliminary prospectus—and that no one is privy to any unpublished data that might confer an unfair advantage.

The investment banks and company executives promote the company's stock offering through a *roadshow,* a series of presentations to potential investors around the country and sometimes overseas. In addition to providing investors with information about the new issue, roadshow sessions help investment banks gauge demand for the offering and set a preliminary offer price range. Figure 2.2 shows that the preliminary offer price range for Snap is between $14 and $16. After the investment bank sets terms and prices the issue, the SEC must approve the offering.

FIGURE 2.2

Cover of a Preliminary Prospectus for a Stock Issue

Some of the key factors related to the 2017 Class A common stock issue by Snap Inc. are summarized on the cover of the preliminary prospectus. The disclaimer printed in red across the top of the page is what gives the preliminary prospectus its "red herring" name.

Source: From SEC filing Form S-1/A, Copyright © U.S. Securities and Exchange Commission.

The information in this preliminary prospectus is not complete and may be changed. These securities may not be sold until the registration statement filed with the Securities and Exchange Commission is effective. This preliminary prospectus is not an offer to sell nor does it seek an offer to buy these securities in any jurisdiction where the offer or sale is not permitted.

PROSPECTUS (Subject to Completion)
Dated February 24, 2017

200,000,000 Shares

Snap Inc.

Class A Common Stock

This is an initial public offering of shares of non-voting Class A common stock of Snap Inc.

Snap Inc. is offering to sell 145,000,000 shares of Class A common stock in this offering. The selling stockholders identified in this prospectus are offering an additional 55,000,000 shares of Class A common stock. We will not receive any of the proceeds from the sale of the shares being sold by the selling stockholders.

We have three classes of common stock: Class A common stock, Class B common stock, and Class C common stock. The rights of the holders of Class A common stock, Class B common stock, and Class C common stock are identical, except with respect to voting, conversion, and transfer rights. Class A common stock is non-voting. Anyone purchasing Class A common stock in this offering will therefore not be entitled to any votes. Each share of Class B common stock is entitled to one vote and is convertible into one share of Class A common stock. Each share of Class C common stock is entitled to ten votes and is convertible into one share of Class B common stock. The Class C common stock, which is held by our founders, each of whom is an executive officer and a director of the company, will represent approximately 88.5% of the voting power of our outstanding capital stock following this offering.

Before this offering, there has been no public market for our Class A common stock. It is currently estimated that the initial public offering price will be between $14.00 and $16.00 per share. Our Class A common stock has been approved for listing on the New York Stock Exchange under the symbol "SNAP."

We are an "emerging growth company" under the Jumpstart Our Business Startups Act of 2012, have elected to comply with reduced public company reporting requirements, and may elect to comply with reduced public company reporting requirements in future filings.

See "Risk Factors" beginning on page 15 to read about factors you should consider before buying our Class A common stock.

	Price to Public	Underwriting Discounts and Commissions (1)	Proceeds to Snap Inc.	Proceeds to Selling Stockholders
Per share	$	$	$	$
Total	$	$	$	$

(1) See "Underwriting" for a description of the compensation payable to the underwriters.

At our request, the underwriters have reserved up to 7.0% of the shares of Class A common stock offered by this prospectus for sale, at the initial public offering price, to certain institutions as well as individuals associated with us. See "Underwriting—Directed Share Program."

To the extent that the underwriters sell more than 200,000,000 shares of Class A common stock, the underwriters have the option to purchase up to an additional 30,000,000 shares of Class A common stock from us and certain of the selling stockholders at the initial public offering price less the underwriting discount.

The Securities and Exchange Commission and state securities regulators have not approved or disapproved of these securities or determined if this prospectus is truthful or complete. Any representation to the contrary is a criminal offense.

The underwriters expect to deliver the shares against payment in New York, New York on , 2017.

Morgan Stanley *Goldman, Sachs & Co.* *J. P. Morgan* *Deutsche Bank Securities*

Barclays *Credit Suisse* *Allen & Company LLC*

Prospectus dated , 2017

The Investment Bank's Role

investment bank
Financial intermediary that specializes in selling new security issues and advising firms with regard to major financial transactions.

underwriting
The role of the investment bank in bearing the risk of reselling, at a profit, the securities purchased from an issuing corporation at an agreed-on price.

IPO offer price
The price at which the issuing firm sells its securities.

originating investment bank
The investment bank initially hired by the issuing firm, it brings other investment banks in as partners to form an underwriting syndicate.

underwriting syndicate
A group of other banks formed by the originating investment bank to share the financial risk associated with underwriting new securities.

tombstone
The list of underwriting syndicate banks, presented in such a way to indicate a syndicate member's level of involvement, located at the bottom of the IPO prospectus cover page.

selling group
A large number of brokerage firms that join the originating investment bank(s); each accepts responsibility for selling a certain portion of a new security issue on a commission basis.

An **investment bank** (such as Morgan Stanley or Goldman Sachs) is a financial intermediary that specializes in selling new security issues and advising firms with regard to major financial transactions. The investment bank is responsible for promoting the stock and facilitating the sale of the company's IPO shares. The main activity of the investment bank is **underwriting**, and this is why investment banks that assist with a security offering are called *underwriters*. The underwriting process requires the investment bank to guarantee the issuer a price for its securities, called the *IPO offer price*. In so doing, the bank effectively purchases the securities from the issuing firm and bears the risk of reselling them to the public. The **IPO offer price** is the price at which the issuing firm sells the securities to the primary market investors, and it represents the actual proceeds received by the company for each security that it issues, before subtracting fees charged by the investment banker.

In most security offerings, the investment bank hired by the issuing firm, often called the **originating investment bank**, brings in other investment banks as partners to form an **underwriting syndicate**. The syndicate banks share the financial risk associated with buying the entire issue from the issuer and reselling the new securities to the public. The cover page of the IPO prospectus, known as the **tombstone,** lists the syndicate banks; the names of the originating bank and other banks responsible for selling a large percentage of the offering appear in a larger font than the names of other banks in the syndicate. The preliminary prospectus for Snap's IPO in Figure 2.2 shows that the underwriting syndicate comprised seven investment banks (Morgan Stanley, Goldman Sachs, JPMorgan, Deutsche Bank, Barclays, Credit Suisse, and Allen & Company). Of these seven banks, Morgan Stanley was the originating bank and had the largest involvement in the offer, with responsibility for selling 30% of the shares. In many cases, the underwriting syndicate may form a **selling group**, which is composed of other financial institutions that help sell IPO shares but have no underwriting responsibility and therefore bear no risk if they are unable to sell the shares they are allocated. Members of the selling group earn a fee known as the *selling concession*.

To facilitate selling the shares, the underwriting syndicate and members of the selling group solicit buying interest from potential primary market investors. The primary market investors are the initial purchasers of the securities and generally consist of various institutional investors such as pension funds, mutual funds, and hedge funds. Once a sufficient number of primary market investors are identified, the originating investment bank and the issuing firm agree on a final IPO offer price and the shares are sold to primary market investors. Figure 2.3 depicts the selling process for a security issue.

Compensation for underwriting and selling services comes via underwriting fees that the investment banks collect in the form of a discounted price when they purchase the shares from the issuing firm. For example, the final prospectus for Snap's IPO, shown in Figure 2.4, provides all final information pertaining to the offering. You can see that the final IPO offer price, indicated as *Price to Public*, is \$17 and the *Proceeds to Snap Inc.* and *Proceeds to Selling Stockholders* is only \$16.575; therefore, the underwriting discount or commission is \$0.425 per share. This underwriting discount or commission represents a 2.5% underwriting fee paid to the underwriters by the issuing firm. The \$0.425 per share fee may not seem very large, but when you consider that the underwriting syndicate

FIGURE 2.3

The Selling Process for a Large Security Issue
The investment banker hired by the issuing corporation may form an underwriting syndicate. The underwriting syndicate buys the entire security issue from the issuing corporation at an agreed-on price. The underwriters then have the opportunity (and bear the risk) of reselling the issue to the public at a profit. Both the originating investment banker and the other syndicate members put together a selling group to sell the issue on a commission basis to investors.

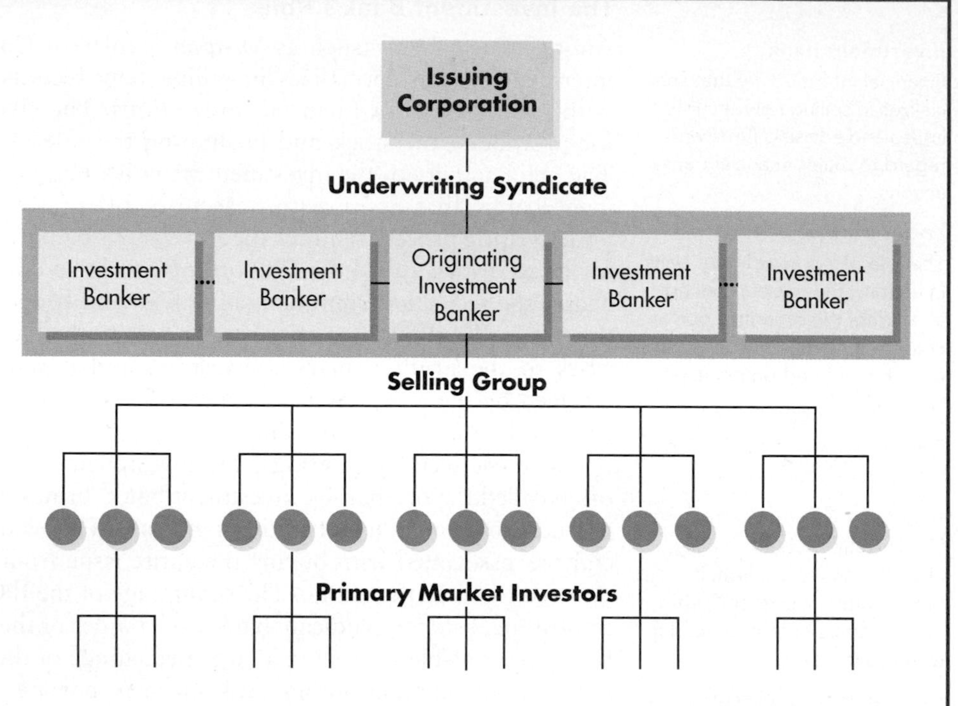

total proceeds
The total amount of proceeds for all shares sold in the IPO. Calculated as the IPO offer price times the number of IPO shares issued.

underwrote 200 million shares for Snap, it translates to a total underwriting fee of \$85,000,000 on **total proceeds** of $\$17 \times 200{,}000{,}000 = \$3.4$ billion, where total proceeds equal the offer price times the number of shares sold in the IPO.

$$\text{Total Proceeds} = (\text{IPO Offer Price} \times \text{\# of IPO Shares Issued}) \quad (2.2)$$

Recall that Morgan Stanley, the originating bank, was responsible for 30% of the shares offered, so that means Morgan Stanley alone collected \$25,500,000. The 2.5% underwriting fee that Snap negotiated was actually low by industry standards, because most firms going public pay a 7% fee. After subtracting the underwriting fee, Snap and its selling shareholders realized net proceeds of \$2,403,375,000 and \$911,625,000, respectively.

market price
The price of the firm's shares as determined by the interaction of buyers and sellers in the secondary market.

market capitalization
The total market value of a publicly traded firm's outstanding stock. Calculated as the market price times the number of shares of stock outstanding.

Though the investment banker together with the company going public set the IPO offer price, once trading begins in the secondary market, the interaction of buyers and sellers determines the **market price** of the firm's shares. The market price fluctuates as the balance of buyers and sellers shifts. Trading in the secondary market also establishes the newly public firm's **market capitalization**, which is the total market value of the firm's outstanding stock. A firm's market capitalization equals the market price of the firm's shares times the number of shares outstanding.

$$\text{Market Capitalization} = (\text{Market Price of Stock} \times \text{\# of Shares of Stock Outstanding}) \quad (2.3)$$

FIGURE 2.4

Cover of a Final Prospectus for a Stock Issue

The final key factors related to the 2017 Class A common stock issue by Snap Inc. are summarized on the cover of the final prospectus.

Source: From SEC filing Form 424B4. Copyright © U.S. Securities and Exchange Commission.

Filed Pursuant to Rule 424(b)(4)
Registration No. 333-215866

PROSPECTUS

200,000,000 Shares

Snap Inc.

Class A Common Stock

This is an initial public offering of shares of non-voting Class A common stock of Snap Inc.

Snap Inc. is offering to sell 145,000,000 shares of Class A common stock in this offering. The selling stockholders identified in this prospectus are offering an additional 55,000,000 shares of Class A common stock. We will not receive any of the proceeds from the sale of the shares being sold by the selling stockholders.

We have three classes of common stock: Class A common stock, Class B common stock, and Class C common stock. The rights of the holders of Class A common stock, Class B common stock, and Class C common stock are identical, except with respect to voting, conversion, and transfer rights. Class A common stock is non-voting. Anyone purchasing Class A common stock in this offering will therefore not be entitled to any votes. Each share of Class B common stock is entitled to one vote and is convertible into one share of Class A common stock. Each share of Class C common stock is entitled to ten votes and is convertible into one share of Class B common stock. The Class C common stock, which is held by our founders, each of whom is an executive officer and a director of the company, will represent approximately 88.5% of the voting power of our outstanding capital stock following this offering.

Before this offering, there has been no public market for our Class A common stock. The initial public offering price is $17.00 per share. Our Class A common stock has been approved for listing on the New York Stock Exchange under the symbol "SNAP."

We are an "emerging growth company" under the Jumpstart Our Business Startups Act of 2012, have elected to comply with reduced public company reporting requirements, and may elect to comply with reduced public company reporting requirements in future filings.

See "Risk Factors" beginning on page 15 to read about factors you should consider before buying our Class A common stock.

	Price to Public	Underwriting Discounts and Commissions (1)	Proceeds to Snap Inc.	Proceeds to Selling Stockholders
Per share	*$17.00*	*$0.425*	*$16.575*	*$16.575*
Total	*$3,400,000,000.00*	*$85,000,000.00*	*$2,403,375,000.00*	*$911,625,000.00*

(1) See "Underwriting" for a description of the compensation payable to the underwriters.

At our request, the underwriters have reserved up to 7.0% of the shares of Class A common stock offered by this prospectus for sale, at the initial public offering price, to certain institutions as well as individuals associated with us. See "Underwriting—Directed Share Program."

To the extent that the underwriters sell more than 200,000,000 shares of Class A common stock, the underwriters have the option to purchase up to an additional 30,000,000 shares of Class A common stock from us and certain of the selling stockholders at the initial public offering price less the underwriting discount.

The Securities and Exchange Commission and state securities regulators have not approved or disapproved of these securities or determined if this prospectus is truthful or complete. Any representation to the contrary is a criminal offense.

The underwriters expect to deliver the shares against payment in New York, New York on March 7, 2017.

Morgan Stanley *Goldman, Sachs & Co.* *J. P. Morgan* *Deutsche Bank Securities*

Barclays *Credit Suisse* *Allen & Company LLC*

The market price of Snap's stock was \$24.48 per share after its first day of secondary market trading, and Snap had 661,834,416 shares of stock outstanding following its IPO. Inserting these values into equation 2.3, we find that Snap's market capitalization is about \$16 billion.

The primary market investors who purchase shares in an IPO often earn a substantial profit once the shares start trading in the secondary market. For most IPOs, the offer price at which primary market investors purchase shares is well below what investors in the secondary market are willing to pay for the shares. For Snap's IPO the offer price was \$17 per share, as shown in Figure 2.4, and its stock finished trading on its first day in the secondary market at \$24.48 a share. For investors who purchased Snap shares from the underwriting syndicate (or the selling group), that's a one-day gain of \$7.48 (\$24.48 − \$17). To put that number in focus, investors who purchased Snap stock at the \$17 offer price earned a return on their investment of 44% in just one day. This represents a profit of almost \$1.5 billion for those investors who had the opportunity to buy Snap shares at the offer price. However, it represents a substantial cost to Snap. To put this differently, had Snap and its selling stockholders sold their stock for what the market was willing to pay, they could have generated an additional \$1.5 billion in total proceeds, but instead they "left the money on the table" for investors.

IPO market price
The final trading price on the first day in the secondary market.

IPO underpricing
The percentage change from the final IPO offer price to the IPO market price, which is the final trading price on the first day in the secondary market; this is also called the IPO initial return.

The percentage change from the final IPO offer price to the **IPO market price**, which is the final trading price on the first day in the secondary market, is called the **IPO underpricing.**

$$\text{IPO Underpricing} = (\text{Market Price} - \text{Offer Price}) \div \text{Offer Price} \quad (2.4)$$

The term *underpricing* applies because the offer price is usually set below what secondary market investors are willing to pay. Selling shares at what appears to be a below-market price might seem unusual, but surprisingly IPOs are underpriced more often than not in virtually every country around the world. In the United States the average IPO that took place between 1980 and 2016 was underpriced by 17.9%. You might wonder, and you would not be alone, why issuers don't insist that investment banks sell their shares at the price the secondary market is willing to pay to generate the maximum IPO proceeds. Many theories and empirical studies aim to answer this question, and the best answers recognize that the IPO process is full of uncertainty for all parties involved. Neither the firm issuing shares in the deal, nor its investment bankers, nor even the primary market investors who bid for shares during the IPO roadshow know what the eventual market price of the stock will be. By underpricing their shares and leaving some money on the table for the primary market investors, IPO firms create incentives for all necessary parties to participate in the IPO process.

EXAMPLE 2.3

MyLab Finance Solution Video

With baby boomers retiring and hitting the open roads of America in droves, the largest U.S. recreational vehicle dealer, Camping World, decided it was time to go public. Its IPO took place on October 7, 2016, at which time the company sold 11.4 million shares at an IPO offer price of \$22 per share. Checking prices for Camping World on Yahoo! Finance, you can find that the IPO market price at the close of secondary market trading on October 7 was \$22.50. With this information you can calculate the IPO underpricing using Equation 2.4.

$$\begin{aligned}\text{IPO Underpricing} &= (\text{Market Price} - \text{Offer Price}) \div \text{Offer Price}\\ &= (\$22.50 - \$22) \div \$22 = 0.0227 \text{ or } 2.27\%\end{aligned}$$

Camping World's IPO underpricing of 2.27% is considerably less than the 44% underpricing for Snap Inc. This demonstrates another interesting fact about IPOs, specifically, that the degree to which IPOs are underpriced varies tremendously from one deal to another and one time to another. Usually, smaller IPOs are underpriced more than larger ones, but that was not the case here. Camping World raised $250.8 million in its offering, which is a small fraction of the $3.4 billion raised in Snap's IPO.

→ **REVIEW QUESTIONS** MyLab Finance Solutions

2–11 What is the difference between an angel investor (angel) and a venture capitalist (VC)?

2–12 What four ways do VCs use to organize their businesses? How do they structure and price their deals?

2–13 What general procedures must a private firm follow to go public via an initial public offering (IPO)?

2–14 What role does an investment bank play in a public offering? Describe an underwriting syndicate.

2.5 Financial Markets in Crisis

Modern economies are vulnerable when financial markets are in a state of crisis. For example, in 2008, the U.S. financial system, as well as financial systems around the world, appeared to be on the verge of collapse. Troubles in the financial sector spread to other industries, and a severe global recession ensued. In this section, we outline some of the main causes and consequences of the financial market crises that led to the Great Recession.

FINANCIAL INSTITUTIONS AND REAL ESTATE FINANCE

In the classic film, *It's a Wonderful Life,* the central character is George Bailey, who runs a financial institution called the Bailey Building and Loan Association. In a key scene in that movie, a bank run is about to occur, and depositors demand that George return the money they had invested in the Building and Loan. George pleads with one man to keep his funds at the bank, saying:

> You're thinking of this place all wrong, as if I have the money back in a safe. The money's not here. Your money is in Joe's house. That's right next to yours—and then the Kennedy house, and Mrs. Maklin's house, and a hundred others. You're lending them the money to build, and then they're going to pay it back to you as best they can. What are you going to do, foreclose on them?*

securitization The process of pooling mortgages or other types of loans and then selling claims or securities against that pool in the secondary market.

mortgage-backed securities Securities that represent claims on the cash flows generated by a pool of mortgages.

This scene offers a realistic portrayal of the role that financial institutions played in allocating credit for investments in residential real estate for many years. Local banks took deposits and made loans to local borrowers. However, since the 1970s, neighbors no longer hold each others' mortgages—securitization has changed the way that mortgage finance works. **Securitization** refers to the process of pooling mortgages or other types of loans and then selling claims or securities against that pool in a secondary market. These securities, called **mortgage-backed securities**, can be purchased by individual investors, mutual funds, or virtually any

*"It's a Wonderful Life." Dir. Frank Capra. Perf. James Stewart, Donna Reed, Lionel Barrymore, and Thomas Mitchell. RKO Radio Pictures, 1946.

other investor. As homeowners repay their loans, those payments eventually make their way into the hands of investors who hold the mortgage-backed securities. Therefore, a primary risk associated with mortgage-backed securities is that homeowners may not be able to, or may choose not to, repay their loans. Banks today still lend money to individuals who want to build or purchase new homes, but they typically bundle those loans together and sell them to organizations that securitize them and pass them on to investors all over the world.

Falling Home Prices and Delinquent Mortgages

Prior to the 2008 financial crisis, most investors viewed mortgage-backed securities as relatively safe investments. Figure 2.5 illustrates one of the main reasons for this view. The figure shows the behavior of the Standard & Poor's Case-Shiller Index, a barometer of home prices in 10 major U.S. cities, in each month from January 1987 to January 2017. Historically, declines in the index were relatively infrequent, and between July 1995 and April 2006 the index rose continuously without posting even a single monthly decline. When house prices are rising, the gap between what homes are worth and what borrowers owe on their mortgages widens. Lenders will allow borrowers who have difficulty making payments on their mortgages to tap this built-up home equity to refinance their loans and lower their payments. Therefore, rising home prices helped keep mortgage default rates low from the mid-1990s through early 2006. Investing in real estate and mortgage-backed securities seemed to involve very little risk during this period.

In part because real estate investments seemed relatively safe, lenders began relaxing their standards for borrowers. This change led to tremendous growth in a category of loans called subprime mortgages. **Subprime mortgages** are mortgage loans made to borrowers with lower incomes and poorer credit histories as compared to "prime" borrowers. Loans granted to subprime borrowers often have adjustable, rather than fixed, interest rates, which makes subprime borrowers particularly vulnerable if interest rates rise. Many of these borrowers (and

subprime mortgages
Mortgage loans made to borrowers with lower incomes and poorer credit histories as compared to "prime" borrowers.

FIGURE 2.5

House Prices Soar and Then Crash

The figure shows the Standard & Poor's Case-Shiller Home Price Index from January 1987 through January 2017 and illustrates that home prices rose almost without interruption for nearly a decade before experiencing a sharp collapse starting in May 2006.

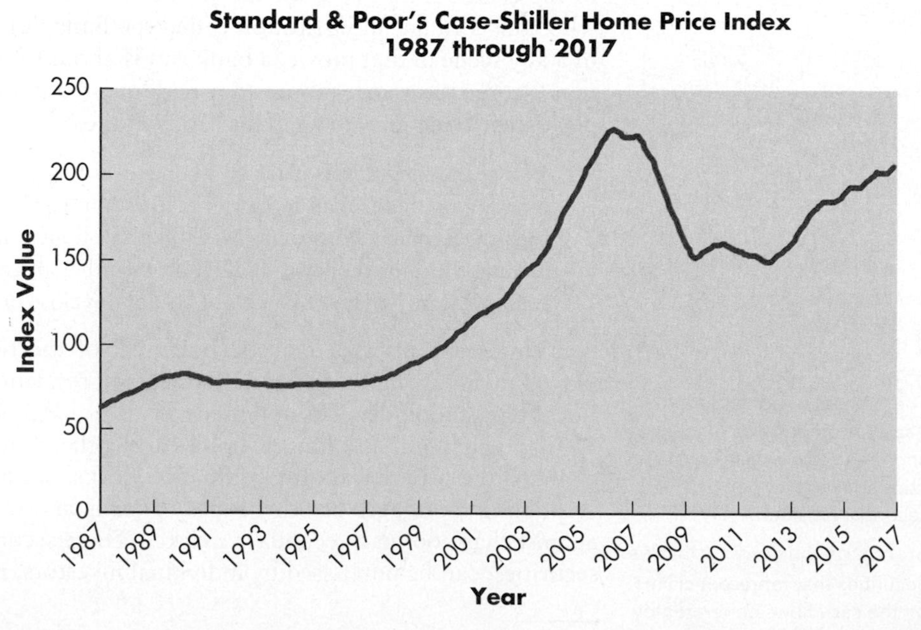

lenders) assumed that rising home prices would allow refinancing of their loans if they had difficulties making payments. Partly through the growth of subprime mortgages, banks and other financial institutions gradually increased their investments in real estate loans. In 2000, real estate loans accounted for less than 40% of the total loan portfolios of large banks. By 2007, real estate loans grew to more than half of all loans made by large banks, and the fraction of these loans in the subprime category increased as well.

Unfortunately, as Figure 2.5 shows, home prices fell almost without interruption from May 2006 through May 2009. Over that 3-year period, home prices fell on average by more than 30%. Not surprisingly, when homeowners struggled to make mortgage payments, refinancing was no longer an option, and delinquency rates and foreclosures began to climb. By 2009, nearly 25% of subprime borrowers were behind schedule on their mortgage payments. Some borrowers, recognizing that the value of their homes was far less than the amount they owed on their mortgages, simply walked away and let lenders repossess their homes.

Crisis of Confidence in Banks

With delinquency rates rising, the value of mortgage-backed securities began to fall and so did the fortunes of financial institutions that had invested heavily in real estate assets. In March 2008, the Federal Reserve provided financing for the acquisition (i.e., the rescue) of Bear Stearns by JPMorgan Chase. Later that year, Lehman Brothers filed for bankruptcy. Throughout 2008 and 2009, the Federal Reserve, President Bush, and finally President Obama took unprecedented steps to try to shore up the banking sector and stimulate the economy, but these measures could not completely avert the crisis.

Figure 2.6 shows the behavior of the Standard & Poor's Banks Select Industry Index, which tracks bank stocks. According to the index, bank stocks fell 77% between May 2007 and March 2009, and the number of bank failures skyrocketed. According to the FDIC, only three banks failed in 2007. In 2008, that

FIGURE 2.6

Bank Stocks Plummet During Financial Crisis

The graph shows the Standard and Poor's Banks Select Industry Index from March 2007 to March 2017. Concerns about the health of U.S. financial institutions drove bank stocks down by 77% between May 2007 and March 2009.

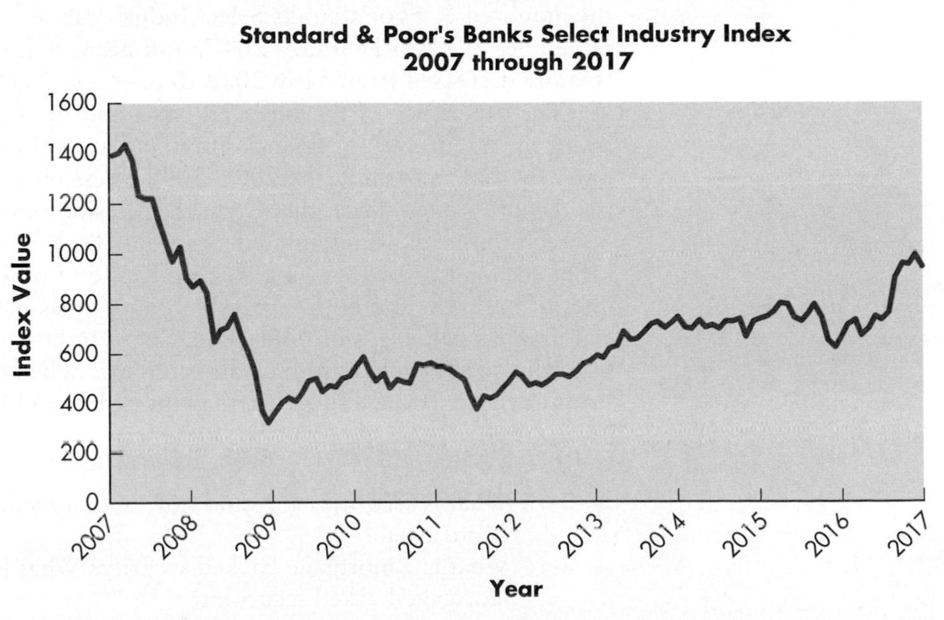

number rose by a factor of 8 to 25 failed banks, and the number increased nearly 6 times to 140 failures in 2009. Although the economy began to recover in 2010, bank failures continued at a rapid pace, with 157 institutions failing that year, followed by 92 more failures in 2011. It was not until 2015 that bank failures fell back into the single digits.

SPILLOVER EFFECTS AND RECOVERY FROM THE GREAT RECESSION

As banks came under intense financial pressure in 2008, they began to tighten their lending standards and dramatically reduce the quantity of loans they made. In the aftermath of the Lehman Brothers bankruptcy, lending in the money market contracted very sharply. Corporations that had relied on the money market as a source of short-term funding found they could no longer raise money in this market or could do so only at extraordinarily high rates.

As a consequence, businesses began to hoard cash and cut back on expenditures, and economic activity contracted. Gross domestic product (GDP) declined in five out of six quarters starting in the first quarter of 2008, and the economy shed more than 8 million jobs in 2008–2009 as the unemployment rate reached 10%. In response to the Great Recession, Congress passed an $862 billion stimulus package in an attempt to revive the economy, and the Federal Reserve pushed short-term interest rates close to 0%. Although the economy began to recover in 2009, the recovery was very slow. Not until May 2014 did total employment equal what it had been prior to the start of the recession, and not until September 2015 did the unemployment rate once again achieve pre-recession levels of 5% or less.

As the recession subsided and financial institutions eased credit constraints, positive economic indicators started to emerge. Figure 2.5 shows that housing prices began to recover in earnest, and mortgage default rates subsided to pre-crisis levels in March 2012. The average home price increased 42% from March 2012 to May 2017, and as of May 2017 the Case-Shiller Home Price Index was within 7% of its all-time high in April 2006. Figure 2.6 shows that the Standard & Poor's Banks Select Industry Index rose 136% from the end of December 2011 to February 2017, and according to the FDIC, bank failures steadily decreased from 51 in 2012 to only 5 in 2016.

The experience of the financial crisis and the recession that followed illustrates the importance of financial markets to the functioning of a market economy. By some measures, the 2008–2009 recession was the worst experienced in the United States since the Great Depression. Indeed, many parallels exist between those two economic contractions. Both were preceded by a period of rapid economic growth, rising stock prices, and movements by banks into new lines of business, and both involved a major crisis in the financial sector. Financial markets help transfer funds from savers to borrowers, and the smooth flow of credit is vital to the health of the economy. When that flow is interrupted and firms are denied access to credit, they invest less and hire fewer people.

→ REVIEW QUESTIONS MyLab Finance Solutions

2–15 What is securitization, and how does it facilitate investment in real estate assets?

2–16 What is a mortgage-backed security? What basic risk is associated with mortgage-backed securities?

2–17 How do rising home prices contribute to low mortgage delinquencies?
2–18 Why do falling home prices create an incentive for homeowners to default on their mortgages even if they can afford to make the monthly payments?
2–19 Why does a crisis in the financial sector spill over into other industries?

SUMMARY

THE ROLE OF FINANCIAL INSTITUTIONS AND MARKETS

This chapter described why financial institutions and markets are an integral part of managerial finance. Companies cannot get started or survive without raising capital, and financial institutions and markets give firms access to the financing necessary for growth. As we have seen in recent years, however, financial markets can be quite turbulent, and when large financial institutions get into trouble, access to capital is reduced and firms throughout the economy suffer as a result.

REVIEW OF LEARNING GOALS

LG 1 Understand the role that financial institutions play in managerial finance. Financial institutions bring net suppliers of funds and net demanders together to help translate the savings of individuals, businesses, and governments into loans and other types of investments. The net suppliers of funds are generally individuals or households who save more money than they borrow. Businesses and governments are generally net demanders of funds, meaning they borrow more money than they save.

LG 2 Understand the role that financial markets play in managerial finance. Like financial institutions, financial markets help businesses raise the external financing they need to fund new investments for growth. Financial markets provide a forum in which savers and borrowers can transact business directly. Businesses and governments issue debt and equity securities directly to the public in the primary market. Subsequent trading of these securities between investors occurs in the secondary market.

LG 3 Describe the differences between the money market and the capital market. In the money market, savers who want a temporary place to deposit funds where they can earn interest interact with borrowers who have a short-term need for funds. Marketable securities, including Treasury bills, commercial paper, and other instruments, are the main securities traded in the money market. The Eurocurrency market is the international equivalent of the domestic money market.

In contrast, the capital market is the forum in which savers and borrowers interact on a long-term basis. Firms issue either debt (bonds) or equity (stock) securities in the capital market. Once issued, these securities trade on secondary markets that are either broker markets or dealer markets. An important function of the capital market is to determine the underlying value of the securities issued by businesses. In an efficient market, the price of a security is an unbiased estimate of its true value.

LG 4 **Understand the major regulations and regulatory bodies that affect financial institutions and markets.** The Glass-Steagall Act created the FDIC and imposed a separation between commercial and investment banks. The act was designed to limit the risks that banks could take and to protect depositors. More recently, the Gramm-Leach-Bliley Act essentially repealed the elements of Glass-Steagall pertaining to the separation of commercial and investment banks. After the recent financial crisis, much debate has occurred regarding the proper regulation of large financial institutions. The Dodd-Frank Act was passed in 2010 and contained a host of new regulatory requirements, the effects of which are yet to be determined.

The Securities Act of 1933 and the Securities Exchange Act of 1934 are the major pieces of legislation shaping the regulation of financial markets. The 1933 act focuses on regulating the sale of securities in the primary market, whereas the 1934 act deals with regulations governing transactions in the secondary market. The 1934 act also created the Securities and Exchange Commission, the primary body responsible for enforcing federal securities laws.

LG 5 **Describe the process of issuing common stock, including venture capital, going public, and the investment bank.** The initial external financing for business startups with attractive growth prospects typically comes in the form of private equity raised via a private equity placement. These investors can be either angel investors or venture capitalists (VCs). VCs usually invest in both early-stage and later-stage companies that they hope to take public to cash out their investments.

The first public issue of a firm's stock is called an initial public offering (IPO). The company selects an investment bank to advise it and to sell the securities. The lead investment bank may form a selling syndicate with other investment banks. The IPO process includes getting SEC approval, promoting the offering to investors, and pricing the issue.

LG 6 **Understand what is meant by financial markets in crisis, and describe some of the root causes of the Great Recession.** The financial crisis was caused by several factors related to investments in real estate. Financial institutions lowered their standards for lending to prospective homeowners, and institutions also invested heavily in mortgage-backed securities. When home prices fell and mortgage delinquencies rose, the value of the mortgage-backed securities held by banks plummeted, causing some banks to fail and many others to restrict the flow of credit to business. That, in turn, contributed to a severe recession in the United States that became known as the Great Recession.

OPENER-IN-REVIEW

In the chapter opener, you read about the spectacular rise of Airbnb. One of the early investors in Airbnb was the venture capital firm Sequoia Capital, which contributed $600,000 in 2009. Assume that by making that early-stage investment, Sequoia Capital purchased a 10% ownership stake in Airbnb. If the company was worth $31 billion in 2017, how much had the value of Airbnb grown in those 8 years?

SELF-TEST PROBLEM (Solution in Appendix)

ST2–1 **Transaction costs** Assume that you use a TD Ameritrade brokerage account and place your stock trades through the Interactive Voice Response (IVR) Phone System, which charges a $34.99 commission per stock trade. You would like to sell 1,500 shares of Microsoft Corporation, which is listed on the Nasdaq stock exchange, so you check the real-time quotes through TD Ameritrade and see a bid price of $57.31 and an ask price of $57.33.

a. What is the current bid/ask spread for Microsoft?

b. If you place the sell order and TD Ameritrade routes the order to Microsoft's listing exchange, what are your likely total transaction costs? (*Hint:* Nasdaq is a dealer market.)

c. What are your total transaction costs if the Nasdaq dealer who receives your order decides to act as broker and allows a public order to buy 1,500 shares of Microsoft to satisfy your order?

d. Regardless of how your trade is executed, based on the bid/ask spread what is the market value of your trade?

WARM-UP EXERCISES All problems are available in MyLab Finance

E2–1 What does it mean when we say that individuals as a group are net suppliers of funds for financial institutions? What do you think the consequences might be for financial markets if individuals consumed more of their incomes and thereby reduced the supply of funds available to financial institutions?

E2–2 You are the chief financial officer (CFO) of Gaga Enterprises, an edgy fashion design firm. Your firm needs $10 million to expand production. How do you think the process of raising this money will vary if you raise it with the help of a financial institution versus raising it directly in the financial markets?

LG3

E2–3 For what kinds of needs do you think a firm would issue securities in the money market versus the capital market?

LG4

E2–4 Over the past 100 years, the level of government regulation of financial institutions and markets has ebbed and flowed or, as some economists might argue, has ebbed and flooded. Although the laws and regulatory agencies created by the government have various defined and not-so-well-defined goals, what, might you argue, is the single biggest benefit of government regulation?

LG5

E2–5 Angina Inc. has 5 million shares outstanding. The firm is considering issuing an additional 1 million shares. After selling these shares at their $20 per share offering price and netting 95% of the sale proceeds, the firm is obligated by an earlier agreement to sell an additional 250,000 shares at 90% of the offering price. In total, how much cash will the firm net from these stock sales?

E2–6 Your broker calls to offer you the investment opportunity of a lifetime, the chance to invest in mortgage-backed securities. The broker explains that these securities are entitled to the principal and interest payments received from a pool of residential mortgages. List some of the questions you would ask your broker that would help in assessing the risk of this investment opportunity.

PROBLEMS

All problems are available in MyLab Finance. The MyLab icon indicates problems in Excel format available in MyLab Finance.

P2–1 **Transaction costs** You would like to purchase one Class A share of Berkshire Hathaway through your Scottrade brokerage account. Scottrade charges a $7 commission for online trades. You log into your account, check the real-time quotes for Berkshire Hathaway (you see a bid price of $262,850 and an ask price of $263,770) and submit your order.

a. What is the current bid/ask spread for Berkshire Hathaway Class A shares?

b. If Scottrade routes your buy order to the NYSE, where Berkshire Hathaway is listed, what's the potential minimum your total transaction costs will be?

c. If, instead, Scottrade routes your buy order to the Nasdaq, where Berkshire Hathaway is not listed, what's the potential maximum your total transaction costs will be?

d. Regardless of how your trade is executed, based on the bid/ask spread what is the market value of your trade?

P2–2 **Transaction costs** In late December you decide, for tax purposes, to sell a losing position that you hold in Twitter, which is listed on the NYSE, so that you can capture the loss and use it to offset some capital gains, thus reducing your taxes for the current year. However, since you still believe that Twitter is a good long-term investment, you wish to buy back your position in February the following year. To get this done you call your Charles Schwab brokerage account manager and request that he immediately sell your 1,200 shares of Twitter and then in early February buy them back. Charles Schwab charges a commission of $4.95 for online stock trades and for broker-assisted trades there is an additional $25.00 service charge, so the total commission is $29.95.

a. Suppose that your total transaction costs for selling the 1,200 shares of Twitter in December were $59.95. What was the bid/ask spread for Twitter at the time your trade was executed?

b. Given that Twitter is listed on the NYSE, do your total transaction costs for December seem reasonable? Explain why or why not.

c. When your February statement arrives in the mail, you see that your total transaction costs for buying the 1,200 shares of Twitter were $47.95. What was the bid/ask spread for Twitter at the time your trade was executed?

d. What are your total round-trip transaction costs for both selling and buying the shares, and what could you have done differently to reduce the total costs?

P2–3 **Initial public offering** On April 13, 2017, Yext Inc. completed its IPO on the NYSE. Yext sold 10,500,000 shares of stock at an offer price of $11 with an underwriting discount of $0.77 per share. Yext's closing stock price on the first day of trading on the secondary market was $13.41, and 85,489,470 shares were outstanding.

a. Calculate the total proceeds for Yext's IPO.
b. Calculate the percentage underwriter discount.
c. Calculate the dollar amount of the underwriting fee for Yext's IPO.
d. Calculate the net proceeds for Yext's IPO.
e. Calculate Yext's IPO underpricing.
f. Calculate Yext's market capitalization.

P2–4 **Initial public offering** A Brazilian company called Netshoes completed its IPO on April 12, 2017, and listed on the NYSE. Netshoes sold 8,250,000 shares of stock to primary market investors at an IPO offer price of $18, with an underwriting discount of 6.5%. Secondary market investors, however, were paying only $16.10 per share for Netshoes' 31,025,936 shares of stock outstanding.

a. Calculate the total proceeds for Netshoes' IPO.
b. Calculate the dollar amount of the underwriting fee for Netshoes' IPO.
c. Calculate the net proceeds for Netshoes' IPO.
d. Calculate market capitalization for Netshoes' outstanding stock.
e. Calculate IPO underpricing for Netshoes' IPO.
f. Explain the IPO underpricing for Netshoes.

P2–5 **ETHICS PROBLEM** The Securities Exchange Act of 1934 limits, but does not prohibit, corporate insiders from trading in their own firm's shares. What ethical issues might arise when a corporate insider wants to buy or sell shares in the firm where he or she works?

SPREADSHEET EXERCISE

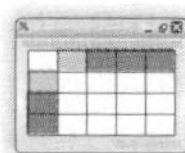

MuleSoft, Inc. conducted its IPO on March 17, 2017 for the principal purposes of increasing its capitalization and financial flexibility, creating a public market for its Class A common stock, and enabling access to the public equity markets for it and its stockholders. MuleSoft sold 13 million shares for an IPO offer price of $17 per share. The underwriting discount was $1.19 per share. MuleSoft intends to use the net proceeds from the offering to the firm for general corporate purposes, such as working capital, operating expenses, and capital expenditures, and to possibly acquire complementary businesses, products, services or technologies. MuleSoft's closing stock price was $24.75 after the first day of trading on the NYSE and there were 125,991,577 shares of stock outstanding.

TO DO

Create a spreadsheet to conduct an analysis of MuleSoft's IPO, and determine the following:

a. Calculate the total proceeds for MuleSoft's IPO.
b. Calculate the percentage underwriter discount for MuleSoft's IPO.
c. Calculate the dollar amount of the underwriting fee for MuleSoft's IPO.
d. Calculate the net proceeds for MuleSoft's IPO.
e. Calculate the percentage IPO underpricing for MuleSoft's IPO.
f. Calculate the market capitalization for MuleSoft's IPO after the first day of trading in the secondary market.

MyLab Finance Visit www.pearson.com/mylab/finance for **Chapter Case: *The Pros and Cons of Being Publicly Listed,*** Group Exercises, and numerous online resources.

Integrative Case 1

Merit Enterprise Corp.

Sara Lehn, chief financial officer of Merit Enterprise Corp., was reviewing her presentation one last time before her upcoming meeting with the board of directors. Merit's business had been brisk for the past 2 years, and the company's CEO was pushing for a dramatic expansion of Merit's production capacity. Executing the CEO's plans would require $4 billion in new capital in addition to $2 billion in excess cash built up by the firm. Sara's immediate task was to brief the board on options for raising the needed $4 billion.

Unlike most companies its size, Merit had maintained its status as a private company, financing its growth by reinvesting profits and, when necessary, borrowing from banks. Whether Merit could follow that same strategy to raise the $4 billion necessary to expand at the pace envisioned by the firm's CEO was uncertain, although it seemed unlikely to Sara. She had identified the following two options for the board to consider.

Option 1: Merit could approach JPMorgan Chase, a bank that had served Merit well for many years with seasonal credit lines as well as medium-term loans. Lehn believed that JPMorgan was unlikely to make a $4 billion loan to Merit on its own, but it could probably gather a group of banks together to make a loan of this magnitude. However, the banks would undoubtedly demand that Merit limit further borrowing and provide JPMorgan with periodic financial disclosures so that it could monitor Merit's financial condition as Merit expanded its operations.

Option 2: Merit could convert to public ownership, issuing stock to the public in the primary market. With Merit's excellent financial performance in recent years, Sara thought that its stock could command a high price in the market and that many investors would want to participate in any stock offering that Merit conducted.

Becoming a public company would also allow Merit, for the first time, to offer employees compensation in the form of stock or stock options, thereby creating stronger incentives for employees to help the firm succeed. Sara also knew, however, that public companies faced extensive disclosure requirements and other regulations that Merit had never had to confront as a private firm. Furthermore, with stock trading in the secondary market, who knew what kind of individuals or institutions might wind up holding a large chunk of Merit stock?

TO DO

a. Discuss the pros and cons of option 1, and prioritize your thoughts. What are the most positive aspects of this option, and what are the biggest drawbacks?
b. Do the same for option 2.
c. Which option do you think Sara should recommend to the board, and why?

PART TWO Financial Tools

CHAPTERS IN THIS PART

In Part Two, you will learn about some of the basic analytical tools that financial managers use almost every day. Chapter 3 reviews the main financial statements used as a firm's primary means of communication with investors, analysts, and the rest of the business community. The chapter also demonstrates some simple tools for analyzing the information contained in financial statements; these tools will help managers to identify and diagnose financial problems.

Firms create financial statements using the accrual principles of accounting; in finance, though, cash flow is what really matters. Chapter 4 shows how to use financial statements in determining the amount of cash flow a firm is generating and the ways in which it is spending that cash flow. It also explains how firms develop short-term and long-term financial plans.

Managers must decide whether the cash flows that investments produce over time justify their up-front costs. Chapter 5 illustrates techniques for making these sorts of judgments.

CHAPTER 3

Financial Statements and Ratio Analysis

LEARNING GOALS

LG 1 Review the contents of the stockholders' report and the procedures for consolidating international financial statements.

LG 2 Understand who uses financial ratios and how.

LG 3 Use ratios to analyze a firm's liquidity and activity.

LG 4 Discuss the relationship between debt and financial leverage, as well as the ratios used to analyze a firm's debt.

LG 5 Use ratios to analyze a firm's profitability and its market value.

LG 6 Use a summary of financial ratios and the DuPont system of analysis to perform a complete ratio analysis.

MyLab Finance Chapter Introduction Video

WHY THIS CHAPTER MATTERS TO YOU

In your *professional* life

ACCOUNTING You need to understand how your colleagues in the finance field function as well as how outside investors analyze the four essential financial statements that the accounting department compiles. You especially need to understand how analysts use key financial ratios to assess a firm's health.

INFORMATION SYSTEMS You need to understand what data are included in the firm's financial statements so you can design systems that will supply such data to those who prepare the statements and to those who use the data for ratio calculations.

MANAGEMENT You need to understand why different firm stakeholders will have an interest in the firm's financial statements and how those stakeholders will analyze the statements to assess the firm's performance—and yours.

MARKETING You need to understand the effects your decisions will have on the financial statements, particularly the income statement and the statement of cash flows, and how analysis of ratios, especially those involving sales figures, will affect the firm's decisions about inventory, credit policies, and pricing decisions.

OPERATIONS You need to understand how the costs of operations are reflected in the firm's financial statements and how analysis of ratios—particularly those involving assets, cost of goods sold, or inventory—may affect requests for new equipment or facilities.

In your *personal* life

A routine step in personal financial planning is to prepare and analyze personal financial statements so that you can monitor progress toward your financial goals. Also, to build and monitor your investment portfolio, you need to understand and analyze corporate financial statements.

KROGER

Ratios Point to Trouble at Kroger

Sean Pavone/Alamy Stock Photo

On Thursday, March 2, 2017, Kroger issued its fiscal year financial results. The company reported a 12th consecutive year of market-share gains and profits of $0.53 per share; results that were slightly higher than the consensus forecast among Wall Street stock analysts. If Kroger's financial results were better than expected, why did the stock price fall 9% on the day of Kroger's earnings announcement? A report by the investment research website Marketrealist.com pointed to two main reasons. First, although Kroger's earnings beat expectations, sales and earnings were actually lower than they had been in the same quarter in the prior year. Still, analysts had anticipated that decline and had incorporated it into their forecasts, so a decrease in revenues and earnings alone should not have caused such a dramatic decline in the stock.

In addition to the profit decline, Kroger reported a reduction in their *gross profit margin*. The gross profit margin indicates how much gross profit (i.e., sales minus cost of goods sold) a company earns per dollar of revenue that it generates. It's an important metric because a higher gross margin suggests that a firm has greater pricing power in the market, which may reflect the strength of a company's brand or other positive aspects of its competitive position in its market. In Kroger's March 2017 financial results, two bad things were happening at once. Sales were down, which one would expect to lead to a decline in earnings. But perhaps more important than that, Kroger's competitive position seemed to be eroding as its profits per dollar of sales fell by close to 10%.

Financial statements contain a wealth of information, but digesting that information is not easy. One way analysts put financial data into perspective is by calculating a variety of financial ratios. These ratios help give them an idea of how a firm is performing, not only in an absolute sense, but also relative to its competitors. In this chapter, you'll learn how to use financial ratios to assess a company's performance.

Source: Sonya Bells, "Kroger's fiscal 4Q17 EPS falls 7% as deflation hits margins and comps," March 4, 2017, marketrealist.com.

LG1

3.1 The Stockholders' Report

generally accepted accounting principles (GAAP) The practice and procedure guidelines used to prepare and maintain financial records and reports; authorized by the Financial Accounting Standards Board (FASB).

Financial Accounting Standards Board (FASB) The accounting profession's rule-setting body, which authorizes generally accepted accounting principles (GAAP).

Public Company Accounting Oversight Board (PCAOB) A not-for-profit corporation established by the Sarbanes-Oxley Act of 2002 to protect the interests of investors and further the public interest in the preparation of informative, fair, and independent audit reports.

stockholders' report Annual report that publicly owned corporations must provide to stockholders; it summarizes and documents the firm's financial activities during the past year.

letter to stockholders Typically, the first element of the annual stockholders' report and the primary communication from management.

Every corporation has many uses for the standardized reports of its financial activities. Periodically, companies prepare reports for regulators, creditors (lenders), owners, and management. The guidelines they use to prepare and maintain financial records are known as **generally accepted accounting principles (GAAP).** The accounting profession's rule-setting body, the **Financial Accounting Standards Board (FASB)**, authorizes these accounting principles.

In addition, the *Sarbanes-Oxley Act of 2002*, enacted in an effort to eliminate many disclosure and conflict of interest problems of corporations, established the **Public Company Accounting Oversight Board (PCAOB)**, a not-for-profit corporation that oversees auditors of public corporations. Congress charged the PCAOB with protecting the interests of investors and furthering the public interest in the preparation of informative, fair, and independent audit reports. Legislators hoped that the PCAOB would instill confidence in investors with regard to the accuracy of public corporations' audited financial statements.

The U.S. Securities and Exchange Commission (SEC)—the federal regulatory body that governs the sale and listing of securities—requires publicly owned corporations with more than $5 million in assets and 500 or more stockholders to provide their stockholders with an annual **stockholders' report.** The stockholders' report summarizes and documents the firm's financial activities during the past year. It begins with a letter to the stockholders from the firm's chief executive officer or chairman of the board.

THE LETTER TO STOCKHOLDERS

The **letter to stockholders** is the primary communication from management in the annual report. It describes the events that managers believe had the greatest effect on the firm during the year. It also typically discusses management philosophy, corporate governance issues, strategies, and plans for the coming year.

GLOBAL FOCUS *in practice*

More Countries Adopt International Financial Reporting Standards

In the United States, public companies must report financial results using GAAP. However, accounting standards vary around the world, and that makes comparing the financial results of firms located in different countries quite challenging. In recent years, many countries have adopted a system of accounting principles known as International Financial Reporting Standards (IFRS). Those principles are established by an independent standards-setting body known as the International Accounting Standards Board (IASB). The IASB designs these standards with the goal of making financial statements everywhere understandable, reliable, comparable, and accurate. More than 80 countries now require listed firms to comply with IFRS, and dozens more permit or require firms to follow IFRS to some degree.

Why hasn't the United States followed the global trend of IFRS adoption? Some argue that GAAP is still the "gold standard" and that a movement to IFRS would lower the overall quality of financial reporting made by U.S. firms. It is true that IFRS generally requires less detail than GAAP. Even so, the Securities and Exchange Commission has expressed its view that U.S. investors will benefit as GAAP and IFRS converge, although there is no requirement that firms in the United States will switch to IFRS in the near future.

► *What costs and benefits might be associated with a switch to IFRS in the United States?*

THE FOUR KEY FINANCIAL STATEMENTS

The four key financial statements required by the SEC for reporting to shareholders are (1) the income statement, (2) the balance sheet, (3) the statement of stockholders' equity, and (4) the statement of cash flows. The financial statements from the 2019 stockholders' report of Bartlett Company, a manufacturer of metal fasteners, are presented and briefly discussed in this section. Most likely, you have studied these four financial statements in an accounting course, so the purpose here is to refresh your memory of the basics rather than provide an exhaustive review.

Income Statement

income statement
Provides a financial summary of the firm's operating results during a specified period.

The **income statement** provides a financial summary of the firm's operating results during a specified period, usually one quarter or one year. Companies produce and release to the public quarterly and annual income statements based on their fiscal year, which may or may not align with a calendar year. Kroger's fiscal year, for example, ends on or near January 31, so the company would report earnings for the fiscal year 2017 in January 2018. About 70% of U.S. public companies align their fiscal year with the calendar year. Most large companies produce income statements at least monthly, but they use these statements internally and do not publicly release them.

FOCUS ON ETHICS *in practice*

Earnings Shenanigans

Near the end of each quarter, many publicly traded companies unveil performance numbers in a Wall Street ritual known as "earnings season." Interest is high as media outlets race to report the announcements, analysts pore over the figures, and investors trade on the implications. The most anticipated metric is normally earnings per share (EPS), which for each firm is compared to the consensus forecast of market analysts. Firms beating the forecast tend to enjoy jumps in share prices while those falling short, by even a small amount, tend to suffer price declines.

Pressure to meet or beat market expectations can push executives to unethical, and sometimes illegal, acts of financial misrepresentation. In April 2016, Logitech International S.A., a leading producer of peripherals for computers (like its famous mouse) and other electronics, agreed to a $7.5 million penalty to settle with the U.S. Securities and Exchange Commission (SEC) for fraudulently underreporting losses on a new product in 2011 and, more generally, understating likely expenses on product warranties in 2012/2013—all just to meet earnings expectations.

In October 2010, Logitech launched "Revue"—a device for streaming online media on a television. Demand fell far short of expectations, resulting in well over 100,000 unsold units by fourth quarter 2011. Generally Accepted Accounting Principles (GAAP) require valuing such inventory at market value if the firm foresees slashing the sales price below cost. Yet Logitech failed to fully mark down unsold Revues, thereby seriously overstating 2011 operating income. On a broader scale, Logitech also artificially boosted income in 2012 and 2013 by understating the number of its products covered by warranties as well as the size of likely claims on defective devices.

In his 2002 letter to shareholders, Berkshire Hathaway President, CEO, and Board Chairman Warren Buffett shared three enduring nuggets of wisdom to keep in mind when looking at financials: (i) weak accounting practices typically signify bigger problems, (ii) unintelligible information usually indicates shifty management, and (iii) earnings often fall short of rosy forecasts because firms seldom operate in predictable environments. The Sage of Omaha closed the newsletter on a prophetic note: "Managers that always promise to 'make the numbers' will at some point be tempted to make up the numbers."

► *Logitech understated potential warranty expenses by assuming customers would submit defective-product claims within one quarter—even though warranties extended for many years. Suppose instinct tells you the assumption is reasonable and ethical because problems with electronic devices occur soon after purchase or not at all. What evidence might you compile to challenge your instincts and satisfy auditors?*

"SEC Announced Financial Fraud Cases," U.S. Securities and Exchange Press Release 2016-74 (April 19, 2016). Two executives also lost their jobs and agreed to pay five-figure fines. Link: https://www.sec.gov/news/pressrelease/2016-74.html.

Table 3.1 presents Bartlett Company's income statements for the years ended December 31, 2019 and 2018. The 2019 statement begins with sales revenue, which is the total dollar amount of sales during the period. Next we subtract the cost of goods sold to obtain Bartlett's gross profit of $986,000, which represents the amount remaining to pay operating, financial, and tax costs. Then we deduct operating expenses—which include selling expense, general and administrative expense, lease expense, and depreciation expense—to arrive at *operating profits* of $418,000. Operating profits represent what the company earned from producing and selling products before deducting any costs related to debt financing (i.e., interest expense) and taxes. For this reason, operating profit is often called *earnings before interest and taxes,* or *EBIT.* Finally we deduct the cost of any debt financing—interest expense—to find *net profits* (or *earnings*) *before taxes*. After subtracting $93,000 in 2019 interest, Bartlett Company had $325,000 of net profits before taxes.

Once we have the before-tax profit, we can calculate taxes due based on the appropriate tax rates. Deducting taxes leaves us with *net profits* (or *earnings*) *after taxes,* also referred to as *net income*. Bartlett Company's net profits after taxes for 2019 were $231,000. We must subtract preferred stock dividends (if the firm has preferred stock) from net profits after taxes to arrive at *earnings available for common stockholders,* which is the amount earned by the firm on behalf of its common stockholders.

TABLE 3.1 Bartlett Company Income Statements ($000)

	For the years ended December 31	
	2019	2018
Sales revenue	$3,074	$2,567
Less: Cost of goods sold	2,088	1,711
Gross profits	$ 986	$ 856
Less: Operating expenses		
Selling expense	$ 100	$ 108
General and administrative expenses	194	187
Other operating expenses	35	35
Depreciation expense	239	223
Total operating expense	$ 568	$ 553
Operating profits	$ 418	$ 303
Less: Interest expense	93	91
Net profits before taxes	$ 325	$ 212
Less: Taxes	94	64
Net profits after taxes	$ 231	$ 148
Less: Preferred stock dividends	10	10
Earnings available for common stockholders	$ 221	$ 138
Earnings per share (EPS)[a]	$2.90	$1.81
Dividend per share (DPS)[b]	$1.29	$0.75

[a]Calculated by dividing the earnings available for common stockholders by the number of shares of common stock outstanding: 76,262 in 2019 and 76,244 in 2018. Earnings per share in 2019: $221,000 ÷ 76,262 = $2.90; in 2018: $138,000 ÷ 76,244 = $1.81.

[b]Calculated by dividing the dollar amount of dividends paid to common stockholders by the number of shares of common stock outstanding. Dividends per share in 2019: $98,000 ÷ 76,262 = $1.29; in 2018: $57,183 ÷ 76,244 = $0.75.

Dividing earnings available for common stockholders by the number of shares of common stock outstanding results in *earnings per share (EPS)*. EPS represent the number of dollars earned during the period on behalf of each outstanding share of common stock. In 2019, Bartlett Company earned $221,000, and it had 76,262 common shares outstanding. Dividing earnings available for common stockholders by shares outstanding results in earnings per share of $2.90.

dividend per share (DPS)
The dollar amount of cash distributed during the period on behalf of each outstanding share of common stock.

Companies are not legally required to pay dividends to shareholders, and in fact many firms do not pay dividends, preferring to reinvest their earnings in new assets to finance growth. However, many companies do pay dividends, and management (along with the board of directors) determines the size of the payments. In 2019, Bartlett decided to pay $98,000 in dividends to shareholders, which translates into a **dividend per share** of $1.29. Because Bartlett pays cash dividends to its shareholders, the income statement shows how much cash the company paid to each share in 2019.

PERSONAL FINANCE EXAMPLE 3.1 Jan and Jon Smith, a mid-30s married couple with no children, prepared a personal income and expense statement, which is similar to a corporate income statement. A condensed version of their income and expense statement follows.

Jan and Jon Smith's Income and Expense Statement for the Year Ended December 31, 2019

Income	
Salaries	$91,500
Interest received	195
Dividends received	120
(1) Total income	$91,815
Expenses	
Mortgage payments	$11,500
Auto loan payments	4,280
Utilities	3,180
Home repairs and maintenance	1,050
Food	8,235
Car expense	5,450
Health care and insurance	3,150
Clothes, shoes, accessories	2,745
Insurance	1,380
Taxes	36,600
Appliance and furniture payments	1,250
Recreation and entertainment	4,575
Tuition and books for Jan	3,830
Personal care and other items	915
(2) Total expenses	$88,140
(3) Cash surplus (or deficit) [(1) – (2)]	$ 3,675

During the year, the Smiths had total income of $91,815 and total expenses of $88,140, which left them with a cash surplus of $3,675. They can save and invest the surplus. Notice that the $3,675 represents just about 4% of the Smiths' total income. Most financial advisors would suggest a much higher savings rate, so Jan and Jon may want to take a hard look at their budget to see where they can cut expenses.

Balance Sheet

balance sheet
Summary statement of the firm's financial position at a given point in time.

The **balance sheet** presents a summary statement of the firm's financial position at a given time. The statement balances the firm's assets (what it owns) against its financing, which can be either debt (what it owes) or equity (what owners provided). Bartlett Company's balance sheets as of December 31 of 2019 and 2018 appear in Table 3.2. They show a variety of asset, liability (debt), and equity accounts.

TABLE 3.2 Bartlett Company Balance Sheets ($000)

	December 31	
Assets	**2019**	**2018**
Cash	$ 363	$ 288
Marketable securities	68	51
Accounts receivable	503	365
Inventories	289	300
Total current assets	$1,223	$1,004
Land and buildings	$2,072	$1,903
Machinery and equipment	1,866	1,693
Furniture and fixtures	358	316
Vehicles	275	314
Other (includes financial leases)	98	96
Total gross fixed assets (at cost)	$4,669	$4,322
Less: Accumulated depreciation	2,295	2,056
Net fixed assets	$2,374	$2,266
Total assets	$3,597	$3,270
Liabilities and Stockholders' Equity		
Accounts payable	$ 382	$ 270
Notes payable	79	99
Accruals	159	114
Total current liabilities	$ 620	$ 483
Long-term debt (includes financial leases)	1,023	967
Total liabilities	$1,643	$1,450
Preferred stock: cumulative 5%, $100 par, 2,000 shares authorized and issued	$ 200	$ 200
Common stock: $2.50 par, 100,000 shares authorized, shares issued and outstanding in 2019: 76,262; in 2018: 76,244	191	191
Paid-in capital in excess of par on common stock	428	417
Retained earnings	1,135	1,012
Total stockholders' equity	$1,954	$1,820
Total liabilities and stockholders' equity	$3,597	$3,270

current assets
Short-term assets, expected to be converted into cash within 1 year.

current liabilities
Short-term liabilities, expected to be paid within 1 year.

The balance sheet makes a clear distinction between short-term and long-term assets and liabilities. The **current assets** and **current liabilities** are short-term assets and liabilities, which means that the firm will convert them into cash (current assets) or pay them (current liabilities) within 1 year. The balance sheet classifies all other assets and liabilities, along with stockholders' equity, as long-term, or fixed, because they will likely remain on the firm's books for more than 1 year.

Accountants refer to an item on the balance sheet as being *liquid* if the item is easy to convert into cash quickly without much loss in value. The balance sheet lists assets from the most liquid—cash—down to the least liquid. Marketable securities are very liquid short-term investments, such as U.S. Treasury bills or certificates of deposit, held by the firm. Most financial analysts view marketable securities as almost perfect substitutes for cash because they are so easy to sell quickly. Accounts receivable represent the total monies owed the firm by its customers on credit sales. They are not as liquid as cash and marketable securities because some uncertainty always exists regarding whether a firm's customers will pay their bills. Inventories include raw materials, work in process (partially finished goods), and finished goods held by the firm. Inventories are even less liquid because the firm must first sell the finished product and then collect on the sale. The entry for gross fixed assets is the original cost of all fixed (long-term) assets owned by the firm. Net fixed assets represent the difference between gross fixed assets and accumulated depreciation, the total expense recorded for the depreciation of fixed assets. The value of any item listed on the balance sheet is called its *book value*.

long-term debt
Debt for which payment is not due in the current year.

Similarly, the balance sheet lists the liabilities and equity accounts from short-term to long-term. Current liabilities include accounts payable, amounts owed for credit purchases by the firm; notes payable, outstanding short-term loans, typically from commercial banks; and accruals, amounts owed for services for which a bill may not or will not be received. Examples of accruals include taxes due the government and wages due employees. **Long-term debt** represents debt for which payment is not due in the current year. Stockholders' equity refers to the owners' claims on the firm. The preferred stock entry shows the historical proceeds from the sale of preferred stock ($200,000 for Bartlett Company).

paid-in capital in excess of par
The amount of proceeds in excess of the par value received from the original sale of common stock.

retained earnings
The cumulative total of all earnings, net of dividends, that have been retained and reinvested in the firm since its inception.

Next, the amount paid by the original purchasers of common stock appears in two separate entries—common stock and paid-in capital in excess of par on common stock. The common stock entry is the *par value* of common stock. Par value is an arbitrary number assigned to shares of stock when they are first created. The par value is not related to the price investors pay for the stock that a company issues. **Paid-in capital in excess of par** represents the amount of proceeds in excess of the par value received from the original sale of common stock. The sum of the common stock and paid-in capital accounts divided by the number of shares outstanding represents the original price per share received by the firm on a single issue of common stock. Bartlett Company therefore received about $8.12 per share [($191,000 par + $428,000 paid-in capital in excess of par) ÷ 76,262 shares] from the sale of its common stock.

Finally, **retained earnings** represent the cumulative total of all earnings, net of dividends, that the company has retained and reinvested in the firm since its inception. It is important to recognize that retained earnings do not represent a pool of cash that the firm can draw upon. Rather, they are funds already reinvested in the business.

Bartlett Company's balance sheets in Table 3.2 show that the firm's total assets increased from $3,270,000 in 2018 to $3,597,000 in 2019. The $327,000 increase was due to increases of $219,000 in current assets and $108,000 in net fixed assets. The asset increase, in turn, appears to have been financed mainly by increases of $123,000 in retained earnings and $193,000 in total liabilities. Better insight into these changes can be derived from the statement of cash flows, which we will discuss shortly.

PERSONAL FINANCE EXAMPLE 3.2 The following personal balance sheet for Jan and Jon Smith—the couple introduced earlier, who are married, in their mid-30s, and have no children—is similar to a corporate balance sheet.

Jan and Jon Smith's Balance Sheet: December 31, 2019

Assets		Liabilities and Net Worth	
Cash on hand	$ 90	Credit card balances	$ 665
Checking accounts	575	Utility bills	265
Savings accounts	760	Medical bills	75
Money market funds	800	Other current liabilities	45
Total liquid assets	$ 2,225	Total current liabilities	$ 1,050
Stocks and bonds	$ 2,250	Real estate mortgage	$120,000
Mutual funds	1,500	Auto loans	14,250
Retirement funds, IRA	2,000	Education loan	13,800
Total investments	$ 5,750	Personal loan	4,000
Real estate	$180,000	Furniture loan	800
Cars	34,000	Total long-term liabilities	$152,850
Household furnishings	3,700	Total liabilities	$153,900
Jewelry and artwork	1,500	Net worth (N/W)	73,275
Total personal property	$219,200		
Total assets	$227,175	Total liabilities and net worth	$227,175

The Smiths have total assets of $227,175 and total liabilities of $153,900. Personal net worth (N/W) is a "plug figure"—the difference between total assets and total liabilities—which in the case of Jan and Jon Smith is $73,275.

statement of stockholders' equity
Shows all equity account transactions that occurred during a given year.

statement of retained earnings
Reconciles the net income earned during a given year, and any cash dividends paid, with the change in retained earnings between the start and the end of that year. An abbreviated form of the *statement of stockholders' equity*.

Statement of Retained Earnings

The statement of retained earnings is an abbreviated form of the statement of stockholders' equity. Unlike the **statement of stockholders' equity,** which shows all equity account transactions that occurred during a given year, the **statement of retained earnings** reconciles the net income earned during a given year, and any cash dividends paid, with the change in retained earnings between the start and the end of that year. Table 3.3 presents this statement for Bartlett Company for the year ended December 31, 2019. The statement shows that the

TABLE 3.3 Bartlett Company Statement of Retained Earnings ($000) for the Year Ended December 31, 2019

Retained earnings balance (January 1, 2019)	$1,012
Plus: Net profits after taxes (for 2019)	231
Less: Cash dividends (paid during 2019)	
Preferred stock	10
Common stock	98
Total dividends paid	$ 108
Retained earnings balance (December 31, 2019)	$1,135

company began the year with $1,012,000 in retained earnings and had net profits after taxes of $231,000, from which it paid a total of $108,000 in dividends, resulting in year-end retained earnings of $1,135,000. Thus, the net increase for Bartlett Company was $123,000 ($231,000 net profits after taxes minus $108,000 in dividends) during 2019.

Statement of Cash Flows

statement of cash flows
Provides a summary of the firm's operating, investment, and financing cash flows and reconciles them with changes in its cash and marketable securities during the period.

The **statement of cash flows** is a summary of the cash flows over the period. The statement provides insight into the firm's operating, investment, and financing cash flows and reconciles them with changes in its cash and marketable securities during the period. Bartlett Company's statement of cash flows for the year ended December 31, 2019, appears in Table 3.4. We provide further insight into this statement in our discussion of cash flow later in this text.

NOTES TO THE FINANCIAL STATEMENTS

notes to the financial statements
Explanatory notes keyed to relevant accounts in the statements; they provide detailed information on the accounting policies, procedures, calculations, and transactions underlying entries in the financial statements.

Included with published financial statements are explanatory notes keyed to the relevant accounts in the statements. These **notes to the financial statements** provide detailed information on the accounting policies, procedures, calculations, and transactions underlying entries in the financial statements. Common issues addressed by these notes include revenue recognition, income taxes, breakdowns of fixed asset accounts, debt and lease terms, and contingencies. Since passage of Sarbanes-Oxley, notes to the financial statements have also included some details about compliance with that law. Professional securities analysts use the data in the statements and notes to develop estimates of the value of securities that the firm issues, and these estimates influence the actions of investors and therefore the firm's share value.

CONSOLIDATING INTERNATIONAL FINANCIAL STATEMENTS

Financial Accounting Standards Board (FASB) Standard No. 52
Mandates that U.S.–based companies translate their foreign-currency-denominated assets and liabilities into U.S. dollars, for consolidation with the parent company's financial statements. This process is done by using the *current rate (translation) method.*

So far, we've discussed financial statements involving only one currency, the U.S. dollar. The issue of how to consolidate a company's foreign and domestic financial statements has bedeviled the accounting profession for many years. The current policy is described in **Financial Accounting Standards Board (FASB) Standard No. 52,**

TABLE 3.4 **Bartlett Company Statement of Cash Flows ($000) for the Year Ended December 31, 2019**

Cash Flow from Operating Activities	
Net profits after taxes	$ 231
Depreciation	239
Increase in accounts receivable	−138[a]
Decrease in inventories	11
Increase in accounts payable	112
Increase in accruals	45
Cash provided by operating activities	$ 500
Cash Flow from Investment Activities	
Increase in gross fixed assets	−347
Change in equity investments in other firms	0
Cash provided by investment activities	−$ 347
Cash Flow from Financing Activities	
Decrease in notes payable	−20
Increase in long-term debts	56
Changes in stockholders' equity[b]	11
Dividends paid	−108
Cash provided by financing activities	−$ 61
Net increase in cash and marketable securities	$ 92

[a]As is customary, parentheses are used to denote a negative number, which in this case is a cash outflow.

[b]Retained earnings are excluded here because their change is actually reflected in the combination of the "net profits after taxes" and "dividends paid" entries.

which mandates that U.S. companies translate their foreign-currency-denominated assets and liabilities into U.S. dollars for consolidation with the parent company's financial statements. This process is done with a technique called the **current rate (translation) method**, under which all of a U.S. parent company's foreign-currency-denominated assets and liabilities are converted into dollar values using the exchange rate prevailing at the fiscal year ending date (the current rate). Income statement items are treated similarly. Equity accounts, in contrast, are translated into dollars by using the exchange rate that prevailed when the parent's equity investment was made (the historical rate). Retained earnings are adjusted to reflect each year's operating profits or losses.

current rate (translation) method
Technique used by U.S.–based companies to translate their foreign-currency-denominated assets and liabilities into U.S. dollars, for consolidation with the parent company's financial statements, using the year-end (current) exchange rate.

→ REVIEW QUESTIONS MyLab Finance Solutions

3–1 What roles do GAAP, the FASB, and the PCAOB play in the financial reporting activities of public companies?

3–2 Describe the purpose of each of the four major financial statements.

3–3 Why are the notes to the financial statements important to professional securities analysts?

3–4 How is the current rate (translation) method used to consolidate a firm's foreign and domestic financial statements?

3.2 Using Financial Ratios

ratio analysis
Involves methods of calculating and interpreting financial ratios to analyze and monitor the firm's performance.

The information contained in the four basic financial statements has major significance to a variety of interested parties who regularly need to have relative measures of the company's performance. *Relative* is the key word here, because the analysis of financial statements is based on the use of *ratios* or *relative values*. **Ratio analysis** involves methods of calculating and interpreting financial ratios to analyze and monitor the firm's performance. The basic inputs required to conduct ratio analysis are the firm's income statement and balance sheet.

INTERESTED PARTIES

Ratio analysis of a firm's financial statements is of interest to shareholders, creditors, and the firm's own management. Both present and prospective shareholders are interested in the firm's current and future level of risk and return, which directly affect share price. The firm's creditors concern themselves primarily with the short-term liquidity of the company and its ability to make interest and principal payments. A secondary concern of creditors is the firm's profitability; they want assurance that the business is healthy. Management, like stockholders, focuses on all aspects of the firm's financial situation, and it uses ratios to monitor the firm's performance from period to period.

TYPES OF RATIO COMPARISONS

Ratio analysis is not merely the calculation of a given ratio. More important is the *interpretation* of the ratio value. Usually, the value of a particular ratio is less important than how it changes over time or how it compares to the same ratios for competing firms. Looking at ratios over time or in comparison to other firms in the same industry allows users of financial ratios to make more refined judgments about a company's performance.

Cross-Sectional Analysis

cross-sectional analysis
Comparison of different firms' financial ratios at the same point in time; involves comparing the firm's ratios with those of other firms in its industry or with industry averages.

benchmarking
A type of *cross-sectional analysis* in which the firm's ratio values are compared with those of a key competitor or with a group of competitors that it wishes to emulate.

Cross-sectional analysis involves the comparison of different firms' financial ratios at the same point in time. Analysts are often interested in how well a firm has performed in relation to other firms in its industry. Frequently, a firm will compare its ratio values with those of a key competitor, a group of competitors, or even top-performing firms from other industries that it wishes to emulate. Nearly all users of financial ratios employ this type of cross-sectional analysis, called **benchmarking**.

One simple type of benchmarking compares a particular company's financial ratios to the industry averages. Several sources publish industry average ratios, including the *Almanac of Business and Industrial Financial Ratios, Dun & Bradstreet's Industry Norms and Key Business Ratios, RMA Annual Statement Studies, Value Line*, and various online sources. Table 3.5 illustrates a brief cross-sectional ratio analysis by comparing several ratios for pairs of firms that compete with each other as well as for the industry average value.

Analysts have to exercise great care when drawing conclusions from ratio comparisons. It's tempting to assume that if one ratio for a particular firm is

TABLE 3.5 Financial Ratios for Select Firms and Their Industry Average Values

	Current ratio	Quick ratio	Inventory turnover	Average collection period (days)	Total asset turnover	Debt ratio	Net profit margin	Return on total assets	Return on common equity	Price to earnings ratio
Apple	1.4	1.3	61.6	49.6	0.7	0.6	21.2%	14.2%	35.6%	16.9
Hewlett-Packard	1.0	0.7	8.8	31.1	1.7	0.7	5.2	8.6	16.4	10.7
Computers	1.5	0.6	21.0	57.0	0.8	0.4	15.6	11.9	32.3	16.0
Home Depot	1.3	0.4	4.3	5.3	1.6	0.5	4.0	6.5	13.7	22.7
Lowe's	1.3	0.2	3.7	0.0	1.4	0.4	3.7	5.4	9.3	20.6
Building materials	2.8	0.8	3.7	5.3	1.6	0.3	4.0	6.5	13.7	26.2
Kroger	0.8	0.2	11.5	5.8	3.2	0.8	1.9	6.0	30.0	13.6
Whole Foods Market	1.5	1.1	19.9	5.6	2.5	0.5	3.2	8.0	15.7	18.0
Grocery stores	1.3	0.7	11.1	7.5	2.4	0.6	2.1	3.1	9.8	20.8
Target	0.9	0.3	5.9	3.9	1.8	0.7	3.8	7.1	24.4	10.7
Walmart	0.9	0.3	9.0	3.7	2.4	0.6	3.5	8.4	20.3	16.3
Merchandise stores	1.7	0.6	4.1	3.7	2.3	0.5	1.5	4.9	10.8	37.1

The data used to calculate these ratios are drawn from the Compustat North American database.

above the industry norm, it signifies that the firm is performing well, at least along the dimension measured by that ratio. However, ratios may be above or below the industry norm for both positive and negative reasons, and it is necessary to determine why a firm's performance differs from that of its industry peers. *Thus, ratio analysis on its own is probably most useful in highlighting areas for further investigation.*

EXAMPLE 3.3

MyLab Finance Solution Video

In early 2019, Mary Boyle, the chief financial analyst at Caldwell Manufacturing, a producer of heat exchangers, gathered data on the firm's financial performance during 2018, the year just ended. She calculated a variety of ratios and obtained industry averages. She was especially interested in inventory turnover, which reflects the speed with which the firm moves its inventory from raw materials through production into finished goods and to the customer as a completed sale. Generally, analysts like to see higher values of this ratio because they indicate a quicker turnover of inventory and more efficient inventory management. Caldwell Manufacturing's inventory turnover for 2018 and the industry average inventory turnover were as follows:

	Inventory Turnover, 2018
Caldwell Manufacturing	14.8
Industry average	9.7

Initially, Mary believed these data showed that the firm had managed its inventory much better than the average firm in the industry. The turnover was nearly 53% faster than the industry average. On reflection, however, she realized that a very high inventory turnover could be a sign that the firm is not holding enough inventories. The consequence of low inventory could be excessive stockouts (insufficient inventory to meet customer needs). Discussions with people in the manufacturing and marketing departments did, in fact, uncover such a problem. Inventories of raw materials during the year were extremely low, resulting in numerous production delays that hindered the firm's ability to meet demand and resulted in disgruntled customers and lost sales. A ratio that initially appeared to reflect extremely efficient inventory management was actually the symptom of a major problem.

Time-Series Analysis

time-series analysis
Evaluation of the firm's financial performance over time using financial ratio analysis.

Time-series analysis evaluates performance over time. Comparison of current to past performance, using ratios, enables analysts to assess the firm's progress and to spot trends. Any significant year-to-year changes may indicate a problem, especially if the same trend is not an industry-wide phenomenon.

Combined Analysis

The most informative approach to ratio analysis combines cross-sectional and time-series analyses. A combined view makes it possible to assess the trend in the behavior of the ratio in relation to the trend for the industry. Figure 3.1 depicts this type of approach. The figure shows the net profit margin for American Airlines as well as the U.S. airline industry from 2013 to 2016. A glance at the figure reveals several interesting patterns. First, American Airlines was more profitable than the industry in 2014 and 2015, but it lagged the industry in 2013 and 2016. In other words, relative to industry profitability, American's net profit margin shows no discernible trend. Second, the airline industry seems quite volatile, with industry net profit margins fluctuating from a low of 4.4% in 2014 to a high of

FIGURE 3.1

Combined Analysis
Combined cross-sectional and time-series view of American Airline's net profit margin, 2013–2016

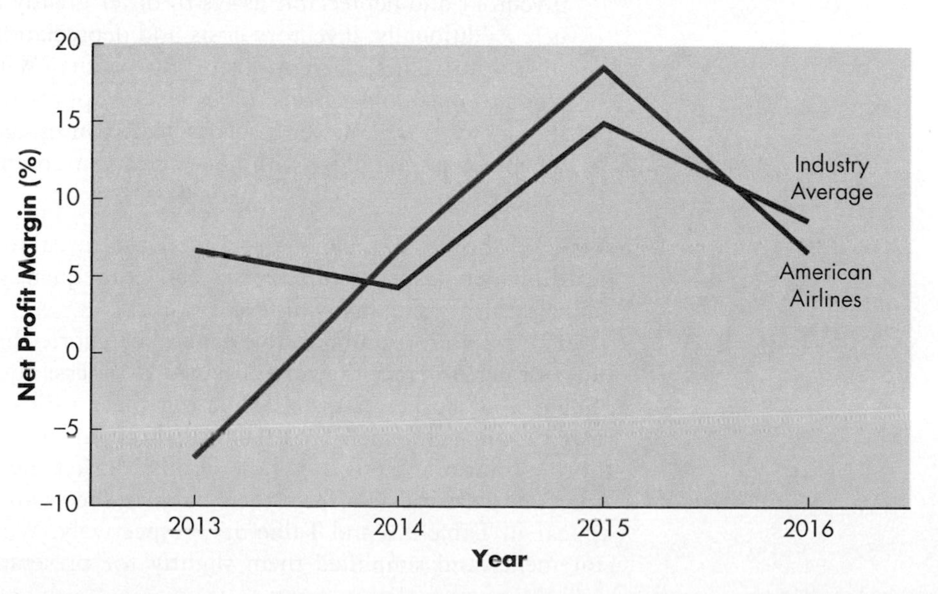

15.0% in 2015. Like American, the airline industry's profitability does not exhibit any particular trend over this period. Third, American Airlines' profits are even more volatile than the industry's, ranging from –6.9% to 18.6% during this 4-year period. Of course, it makes sense that the financial results of one company would fluctuate more than the industry average, because grouping firms together and taking an average smooths out some of the ups and downs that individual firms experience.

CAUTIONS ABOUT USING RATIO ANALYSIS

Before discussing specific ratios, we should consider the following cautions about their use:

1. Ratios that reveal large deviations from the norm merely indicate the possibility of a problem. Analysts must do additional work to determine whether a problem exists and to isolate the causes of the problem.
2. A single ratio does not generally provide sufficient information on which to judge the overall performance of the firm. However, if an analysis focuses only on certain specific aspects of a firm's financial position, one or two ratios may suffice.
3. Analysts should take care to use financial statements dated at the same point in the year before calculating ratios for different companies. Otherwise, the effects of seasonality may produce erroneous conclusions and decisions.
4. It is preferable to use audited financial statements for ratio analysis. If statements have not been audited, the data in them may not reflect the firm's true financial condition.
5. The financial data being compared should have been constructed using the same set of accounting principles, such as GAAP. The use of differing accounting treatments can distort the results of ratio comparisons.
6. Results can be distorted by high inflation, which can cause the book values of inventory and depreciable assets to differ greatly from their replacement values. Additionally, inventory costs and depreciation write-offs can differ from their true values, thereby distorting profits. Without adjustment, inflation tends to make older firms (older assets) appear more efficient and profitable than newer firms (newer assets). Clearly, in using ratios, you must be careful when comparing older with newer firms or comparing a firm to itself over a long period.

As noted above, no single financial ratio can reveal much about a firm's financial health, which has many different facets. Consequently, financial experts typically analyze a firm using many different ratios.

Financial ratios fall into five general categories based upon the specific attributes of performance they are designed to assess: liquidity, activity, debt, profitability, and market ratios. Calculating these ratios requires, at a minimum, a firm's income statement and balance sheet. In the next section we will begin a thorough ratio analysis of Whole Foods Market Inc. (prior to its acquisition by Amazon) by using data from their balance sheets and income statements, which appear in Table 3.6 and Table 3.7, respectively. We have condensed the actual statements and simplified them slightly for presentation here. Note, however,

TABLE 3.6 Whole Foods Market Inc. Balance Sheets for 2016 and 2015 ($ millions)

Assets	2016	2015	Liabilities and Equity	2016	2015
Cash	$ 852	$ 519	Accounts payable	$ 307	$ 295
Accounts receivable	242	218	Other current liabilities	1,034	957
Inventory	517	500	Total current liabilities	$1,341	$1,252
Other current assets	364	307	Long-term debt	1,776	720
Total current assets	$1,975	$1,544	Total liabilities	$3,117	$1,972
Property, plant, and equipment (net)	3,442	3,163	Common stock	907	1,780
Other long-term assets	924	1,034	Retained earnings	2,317	1,989
Total fixed assets	$4,366	$4,197	Total equity	$3,224	$3,769
Total assets	$6,341	$5,741	Total liabilities plus equity	$6,341	$5,741

Note: The company had 318.3 million and 348.9 million shares outstanding in 2016 and 2015, respectively.

TABLE 3.7 Whole Foods Market Inc. Income Statements for 2016 and 2015 ($ millions)

	2016	2015
Sales	$15,724	$15,389
Less: Cost of goods sold	10,313	9,973
Gross profit	$ 5,411	$ 5,416
Less: Selling, general, and administrative expenses	4,477	4,472
Other operating expenses	77	83
Operating profit (EBIT)	$ 857	$ 861
Less: Interest expense	41	0
Plus: Other income	11	17
Pre-tax income	$ 827	$ 878
Less: Taxes	320	342
Net income	$ 507	$ 536
Dividends paid	$ 177	$ 186

that you could analyze almost any company using the ratios presented in the remainder of this chapter. Of course, many companies in different industries use ratios that focus on aspects particular to their industry.

→ REVIEW QUESTIONS MyLab Finance Solutions

3–5 With regard to financial ratio analysis, how do the viewpoints held by the firm's present and prospective shareholders, creditors, and management differ?

3–6 What is the difference between cross-sectional and time-series ratio analysis? What is benchmarking?

3–7 When performing cross-sectional ratio analysis, the analyst should pay primary attention to what types of deviations from the norm? Why?

3–8 Why is it preferable to compare ratios calculated using financial statements that are dated at the same point in time during the year?

LG3

3.3 Liquidity Ratios

liquidity
A firm's ability to satisfy its short-term obligations as they come due.

The **liquidity** of a firm reflects its ability to satisfy its short-term obligations as they come due. Generally speaking, a firm with greater liquidity will have an easier time paying its bills and is less likely to become insolvent. Because a common precursor to financial distress and bankruptcy is low or declining liquidity, these ratios can provide early warning signs that a company has cash flow problems that could cause the business to fail. Clearly, the ability of a firm to pay its bills is desirable, so having enough liquidity for day-to-day operations is important. However, liquid assets, like cash held at banks and marketable securities, do not earn a particularly high rate of return, so shareholders will not want a firm to overinvest in liquidity.

How much liquidity is enough? The liquidity needed depends on a variety of factors, including the firm's size, its access to short-term financing sources like bank credit lines, and the volatility of its business. Larger firms with access to bank credit need less liquidity than smaller firms that may not be able to borrow in a crisis. All firms have to balance the need for safety that liquidity provides against the low returns that liquid assets generate for investors. Beyond safety, liquidity provides other benefits. For example, a firm with large cash reserves will be able to make strategic investments quickly rather than going through the process of raising additional funds to invest.

We can make some general statements about the optimal liquidity position for a firm, though quantifying that precisely is probably impossible. To the extent that a firm needs liquidity for safety, then a firm in an industry that is volatile (like airlines, as we saw in Figure 3.1) needs more liquidity than one in a more stable industry. Within a single industry, a firm that is itself riskier than others in the industry (e.g., a firm that has more long-term debt) probably requires more liquidity. From the strategic investment perspective, a firm in an industry where the competitive dynamics are changing rapidly or consolidation is taking place may need the ability to make sudden strategic investments, and that need could justify a higher investment in liquid assets.

Though determining exactly how much liquidity a firm needs represents a challenge, measuring a firm's liquidity is relatively straightforward. The two most common measures of liquidity are the current ratio and the quick (acid-test) ratio.

CURRENT RATIO

current ratio
A measure of liquidity calculated by dividing the firm's current assets by its current liabilities.

The **current ratio** measures liquidity by comparing a firm's current assets to its current liabilities. The mathematical expression for the current ratio is

$$\text{Current ratio} = \text{Current assets} \div \text{Current liabilities} \quad (3.1)$$

The data required to calculate the current ratios for Whole Foods in 2016 and 2015 appear in Table 3.6. The current ratios for Whole Foods in those 2 years are

$$2016\text{: } \$1{,}975 \div \$1{,}341 = 1.47$$

$$2015\text{: } \$1{,}544 \div \$1{,}252 = 1.23$$

MATTER OF FACT

Determinants of Liquidity Needs

Glance back at the first column of data in Table 3.5, which shows the current ratio for a variety of companies and industries. Notice that the industry with the highest current ratio (i.e., most liquidity) is building materials, an industry notoriously sensitive to business cycle swings. The current ratio for that industry is 2.8, indicating that the typical firm in that business has almost 3 times as much in current assets as in current liabilities. Two of the largest competitors in that industry, The Home Depot and Lowe's, operate with a current ratio of 1.3, less than half the industry average. Does this ratio mean that these firms have a liquidity problem? Not necessarily. Large enterprises generally have well-established relationships with banks that can provide lines of credit and other short-term loan products in the event that the firm needs liquidity. Smaller firms may not have the same access to credit and therefore tend to operate with more liquidity.

Whole Foods increased its liquidity position in 2016 to a level slightly above the industry average, as shown in Table 3.5. The grocery industry is one in which cash flows are relatively stable and predictable—people have to eat whether the economy is booming or in recession. Ordinarily, we would therefore expect grocers to maintain less liquidity than firms in most other industries. Indeed, Table 3.5 shows that the average current ratio in the grocery industry (1.3) is less than that in industries such as computers (1.5), building materials (2.8), and retail merchandise stores (1.7). However, prior to its acquisition by Amazon, Whole Foods occupied a unique position in the grocery industry, one that catered to upscale consumers by offering gourmet, organic food products at higher prices compared to traditional grocers such as Kroger. Imagine what might happen to Whole Foods in a recession. Customers cut back spending on luxury items first, which might mean a switch from Whole Foods to a grocery provider with lower prices. Thus, we expect Whole Foods to be riskier than the average grocery company, and that in turn may justify their relatively high current ratio.

PERSONAL FINANCE EXAMPLE 3.4

MyLab Finance Solution Video

Individuals, like corporations, can use financial ratios to analyze and monitor their performance. Typically, personal finance ratios are calculated using the personal income and expense statement and personal balance sheet for the period of concern. Here we use these statements, presented in the preceding personal finance examples, to demonstrate calculation of Jan and Jon Smith's liquidity ratio for calendar year 2019.

The personal *liquidity ratio* is calculated by dividing total liquid assets by total current debt. It indicates the percentage of annual debt obligations that an individual can meet using current liquid assets. The Smiths' total liquid assets were \$2,225. Their total current debts are \$18,080 (total current liabilities of \$1,050 + mortgage payments of \$11,500 + auto loan payments of \$4,280 + appliance and furniture payments of \$1,250). Substituting these values into the ratio formula, we get

$$\text{Liquidity ratio} = \frac{\text{Total liquid assets}}{\text{Total current debts}} = \frac{\$2{,}225}{\$18{,}880} = 0.123, \text{ or } 12.3\%$$

The ratio indicates that the Smiths can cover only about 12% of their existing 1-year debt obligations with their current liquid assets. Clearly, the Smiths plan to meet these debt obligations from their income, but this ratio suggests that their liquid funds do not provide a large cushion. As one of their goals, they should probably build up a larger fund of liquid assets to meet unexpected expenses.

QUICK (ACID-TEST) RATIO

quick (acid-test) ratio
A measure of liquidity calculated by dividing the firm's current assets less inventory by its current liabilities.

The **quick (acid-test) ratio** is similar to the current ratio except that it excludes inventory, which is generally the least liquid current asset. The generally low liquidity of inventory results from two primary factors: (1) Many types of inventory cannot be easily sold because they are partially completed items, special-purpose items, and the like; and (2) inventory is typically sold on credit, which means that it becomes an account receivable before being converted into cash. An additional problem with inventory as a liquid asset is that the times when companies face a dire need for liquidity, when business is bad, are precisely the times when it is most difficult to convert inventory into cash by selling it. The quick ratio is calculated as

$$\text{Quick ratio} = \frac{\text{Current assets} - \text{Inventory}}{\text{Current liabilities}} \tag{3.2}$$

The quick ratio calculations for Whole Foods show that the company increased its most liquid assets significantly in 2016. A glance back at the balance sheet makes it clear that Whole Foods dramatically increased its cash holdings in 2016, whereas most other current asset and liability accounts did not change as much. The consequence was a jump in the quick ratio, as shown below:

$$2016\text{:}\ \frac{\$1{,}975 - \$517}{\$1{,}341} = \frac{\$1{,}458}{\$1{,}341} = 1.09$$

$$2015\text{:}\ \frac{\$1{,}544 - \$500}{\$1{,}252} = \frac{\$1{,}044}{\$1{,}252} = 0.83$$

The important question arising from these calculations is whether Whole Foods was building up cash because it perceived a need for greater financial safety, because it was planning to use the cash for a major investment, or for some other reason.

MATTER OF FACT

The Importance of Inventories

Turn again to Table 3.5 and examine the columns listing current and quick ratios for different firms and industries. Notice that Apple has a current ratio of 1.4, almost identical to current ratios for Home Depot and Lowe's, which are both 1.3. The quick ratios for Home Depot and Lowe's are much lower than their current ratios, but for Apple that is not true—that firm's current and quick ratios are nearly equal. Why? First, Apple relies primarily on contract manufacturers to make its products, so it holds little or no inventory while its devices are being made. Second, the popularity of Apple's products means that inventory does not sit on retail store shelves very long. In contrast, all it takes is a trip to your local Home Depot or Lowe's store to see that the business model in this industry requires a massive investment in inventory, which implies that the quick ratio will be much less than the current ratio for building materials firms.

As with the current ratio, the quick ratio level that a firm should strive to achieve depends largely on the nature of the business in which it operates. The quick ratio provides a better measure of overall liquidity only when a firm's inventory cannot be easily converted into cash. If inventory is liquid, the current ratio is a preferred measure of overall liquidity.

→ **REVIEW QUESTIONS** MyLab Finance Solutions

3–9 Under what circumstances would the current ratio be the preferred measure of overall firm liquidity? Under what circumstances would the quick ratio be preferred?

3–10 In Table 3.5, most of the specific firms listed have current ratios that fall below the industry average. Why? One exception to this general pattern is Whole Foods Market, which competes at the very high end of the retail grocery market. Why might Whole Foods Market operate with greater-than-average liquidity?

3.4 Activity Ratios

activity ratios
Measure the speed with which various accounts are converted into sales or cash, or inflows or outflows.

Activity ratios measure the speed with which various asset and liability accounts are converted into sales or cash. Activity ratios measure how efficiently a firm operates along a variety of dimensions, such as inventory management, disbursements, and collections. A number of ratios measure the activity of the most important current accounts, which include inventory, accounts receivable, and accounts payable. We can use ratios to assess the efficiency with which a firm manages its total assets as well.

INVENTORY TURNOVER

inventory turnover ratio
Measures the activity, or liquidity, of a firm's inventory.

For firms whose business involves holding significant inventory balances, the **inventory turnover ratio** is a metric used by analysts to judge the effectiveness of inventory management practices. Here again, the value of the inventory ratio that represents good management depends on the nature of the business. As you would expect (and as you will soon see), grocery stores turn their inventory over quite rapidly. After all, many items in a grocer's inventory spoil quickly. In contrast, a firm that manufactures heavy equipment will turn its inventory over much more slowly, partly because the manufacturing process itself takes a long time, requiring a large investment in raw materials and work-in-process inventory. The formula for calculating inventory is

$$\text{Inventory turnover} = \text{Cost of goods sold} \div \text{Inventory} \quad (3.3)$$

Remember that cost of goods sold represents the cost of all items sold by the firm in a year, whereas inventory refers to the goods on hand at any moment. Thus, when calculating this ratio, we arrive at a figure that represents the number of times per year the company "turns over," or sells, its inventory balance. To calculate inventory turnover for Whole Foods, we need information from their income statement and balance sheet. Calculations show that Whole Foods turned its inventory 19.9 times in both 2015 and 2016.

$$2016: \$10{,}313 \div \$517 = 19.9$$
$$2015: \$9{,}973 \div \$500 = 19.9$$

average age of inventory
Average number of days' sales in inventory.

Another inventory activity ratio measures how many days of inventory the firm has on hand. You can easily convert inventory turnover into an **average age of inventory** by dividing the turnover ratio into 365. For example, if Whole Foods sells its inventory 19.9 times within a single year, then that means its inventory balance lasts, on average, about 18.3 days (365 ÷ 19.9 = 18.3). Obviously, some items in inventory turn every day or two, such as freshly baked bread or ready-to-eat food cooked in the store. If these items do not sell rapidly, they spoil and go to waste. Other items, like canned goods or cleaning supplies, do not sell as rapidly. On average, though, the typical item in a Whole Foods store sells in about 18 days, and that figure didn't change in 2016.

To illustrate how much financial ratios can vary across industries, consider the Oregon-based company Willamette Valley Vineyards. Wine producers age most varieties of wine they make before selling them to customers. In its recent financial statements, Willamette reported that it held $10.63 million in inventory and its cost of goods sold for the year was $7.1 million. Plugging those numbers into Equation 3.3 reveals that Willamette's inventory turnover ratio was just 0.67 times per year. Dividing that number into 365 tells us that the average product made by Willamette stays in inventory for 544 days!

AVERAGE COLLECTION PERIOD

average collection period
The average amount of time needed to collect accounts receivable.

The **average collection period,** or average age of accounts receivable, is useful in evaluating credit and collection policies. It equals the accounts receivable balance divided by average daily sales:[1]

$$\text{Average collection period} = \frac{\text{Accounts receivable}}{\text{Average sales per day}} = \frac{\text{Accounts receivable}}{\frac{\text{Annual sales}}{365}} \qquad (3.4)$$

Applying data from Whole Foods' income statement and balance sheet to Equation 3.4, we find that the company's collection period is exceedingly short at just over 5 days.

$$2016: \frac{\$242}{\frac{\$15{,}724}{365}} = 5.6 \text{ days}$$

$$2015: \frac{\$218}{\frac{\$15{,}389}{365}} = 5.2 \text{ days}$$

1. The formula as presented assumes, for simplicity, that all sales are made on a credit basis. If that is not the case, *average credit sales per day* should be substituted for average sales per day.

A result like this for a grocery store company isn't particularly surprising. Most customers pay with cash, a check, or a credit card. Accounting practices treat all those payment forms as cash sales. That is, when a customer pays Whole Foods with a credit card (as long as the card is a Visa, MasterCard, or any card not issued by Whole Foods), the transaction goes to cash on the firm's balance sheet, not to accounts receivable. The low collection period for Whole Foods really reflects that they make very few sales on credit—not that they collect quickly when they do sell on credit.

To get a different perspective on the average collection period, let's examine financial data from Whirlpool Corp. Whirlpool manufactures consumer durable goods like ovens, refrigerators, washers, and dryers. It sells very little directly to consumers. Instead, Whirlpool sells to appliance retailers like Best Buy, Lowe's, Home Depot and others. Nearly all these sales occur on credit, with Whirlpool giving its retail partners some time to sell the appliances before they have to submit payment back to Whirlpool.

In 2016 Whirlpool's receivables balance was $2.7 billion, with sales of $20.7 billion. Plugging those numbers into Equation 3.4 shows that Whirlpool's average collection period was just less than 48 days. The year before, the company's collection period numbered about 44 days, so collections appear to have slowed a little in 2016. A slowdown in collections would not be unusual in an economy that was losing steam as customers struggled to pay their bills on time. However, the U.S. economy performed relatively well in 2016, so does the slowing collection period indicate an internal problem with Whirlpool's collection efforts?

Although the overall economy performed well in 2016, many parts of the brick-and-mortar retail segment struggled, largely (though not entirely) due to competition from Amazon. Two of Whirlpool's biggest U.S. customers, Sears and Best Buy, reported declining or flat sales that year, and managers at Sears took the unusual step of publicly announcing that they were not sure the company could survive in the long term. The situation was better at Home Depot, where sales increased, but their payables rose even faster, suggesting that Home Depot was taking more time to pay its suppliers. The increase in Whirlpool's collection period from 44 to 48 days may not seem like a major change, but it represents hundreds of millions of additional dollars tied up in the company's accounts receivable.

The average collection period is meaningful only in relation to the firm's credit terms. If Whirlpool had extended its credit terms slightly in 2016, then that alone could explain the increase in its collection period. If Whirlpool implemented no change in credit terms in 2016, then the rising collection period could easily

MATTER OF FACT

Who Gets Credit?

Notice in Table 3.5 the vast differences across industries in the average collection periods. Companies in the building materials, grocery, and merchandise store industries collect in just a few days, whereas firms in the computer industry take a month or two to collect on their sales. This difference exists primarily because these industries serve very different customers. Grocery and retail stores serve individuals who pay cash or use credit cards (which, to the store, are essentially the same as cash). Computer manufacturers sell to retail chains, businesses, and other large organizations that negotiate agreements allowing them to pay well after the sale is made.

indicate either deteriorating financial conditions among Whirlpool's customers or perhaps even problems with its collections department. Either situation would require further attention from the company's financial management team.

AVERAGE PAYMENT PERIOD

average payment period
The average amount of time needed to pay accounts payable.

The **average payment period,** or average age of accounts payable, is calculated in the same manner as the average collection period:

$$\text{Average payment period} = \frac{\text{Accounts payable}}{\text{Average purchases per day}} = \frac{\text{Accounts payable}}{\frac{\text{Annual purchases}}{365}} \quad (3.5)$$

The difficulty in calculating this ratio stems from the need to find annual purchases,[2] a value not available in published financial statements. Ordinarily, purchases are estimated as a given percentage of cost of goods sold. If we assume that Whole Foods' purchases equaled 70% of its cost of goods sold, its average payment period is

$$2016\text{: } \frac{\$307}{\frac{0.70 \times \$10{,}313}{365}} = 15.5 \text{ days}$$

$$2015\text{: } \frac{\$295}{\frac{0.70 \times \$9{,}973}{365}} = 15.4 \text{ days}$$

Whole Foods pays for purchases in about 15 days, a figure that barely moved in 2016. As was true with the average collection period, we can make judgments about Whole Foods' 15-day average payment period only if we know the credit terms offered by their suppliers. If Whole Foods' suppliers have extended, on average, 15-day credit terms, an analyst would conclude that the company is doing a good job of paying its bills on time. Although we have no information about the credit terms granted to Whole Foods, there are likely no issues of concern here because the payment period remained virtually fixed for 2 years.

TOTAL ASSET TURNOVER

total asset turnover
Indicates the efficiency with which the firm uses its assets to generate sales.

The **total asset turnover** is a measure of the efficiency with which the firm uses its assets to generate sales. This ratio simply indicates how many dollars of sales a firm produces for each dollar of assets that it has invested in the business. The formula for total asset turnover is

$$\text{Total asset turnover} = \text{Sales} \div \text{Total assets} \quad (3.6)$$

2. Technically, we should use annual *credit* purchases—rather than annual purchases—in calculating this ratio. For simplicity, we ignore this refinement here.

MATTER OF FACT

Sell It Fast

Observe in Table 3.5 that the grocery business has more rapid total asset turnover than any other industry. That makes sense because inventory is among the most valuable assets held by these firms, and grocery stores must sell baked goods, dairy products, and produce quickly or throw such items away when they spoil. It's true that some items in a grocery store have a shelf life longer than anyone really wants to know (think Twinkies), but on average a grocery store has to replace its entire inventory in just a few days or weeks, and that practice contributes to the rapid turnover of the firm's total assets.

For Whole Foods, the total asset turnover figures for 2015 and 2016 are

$$2016: \$15{,}724 \div \$6{,}341 = 2.48$$
$$2015: \$15{,}389 \div \$5{,}741 = 2.68$$

Whole Foods' asset turnover slowed a bit in 2016, and that would concern managers if it was part of a long-term trend for the company. Looking back at Table 3.5, we see that the average asset turnover ratio for the grocery industry is 2.4, so Whole Foods' performance is in line with the industry norm.

Generally, the higher a firm's total asset turnover, the more efficiently its assets have been used. This measure is probably of greatest interest to management because it indicates whether the firm's operations have been financially efficient.

→ **REVIEW QUESTION** MyLab Finance Solutions

3–11 To assess the firm's average collection period and average payment period ratios, what additional information is needed, and why?

LG4

3.5 Debt Ratios

The debt position of a firm indicates the amount of money the firm uses that does not come from shareholders, but rather from lenders. In general, analysts center most on long-term debts that commit the firm to a stream of contractual payments over many years. The greater the debt, the greater is the firm's risk of being unable to meet its contractual debt payments. Because firms must satisfy creditors' claims before they can pay shareholders, current and prospective shareholders pay close attention to the firm's ability to repay debts. Lenders are also concerned about the firm's indebtedness, because holding everything else constant, a firm with more debt has a greater risk of failing to repay its lenders.

In general, the more debt a firm uses in relation to its total assets, the greater is its financial leverage. The term **financial leverage** refers to the degree to which a firm uses debt financing (or other types of fixed-cost financing, such as preferred stock) and to the effects of debt financing. When a firm finances more of its investment by borrowing money, the expected return on the investment increases, but so does the risk.

financial leverage
The magnification of risk and return through the use of fixed-cost financing, such as debt and preferred stock.

EXAMPLE 3.5

Patty Akers is incorporating her new business. After much analysis, she determined that an initial investment of $50,000—$20,000 in current assets and $30,000 in fixed assets—is necessary. These funds can be obtained in one of two ways. The first is the *no-debt plan,* under which she would invest the full $50,000 without borrowing. The other alternative, the *debt plan,* involves investing $25,000 and borrowing the balance of $25,000 at 6% annual interest.

Patty expects $30,000 in sales, $18,000 in operating expenses, and a 21% tax rate. Projected balance sheets and income statements associated with the two plans appear below in Table 3.8. The no-debt plan results in after-tax profits of $9,480, which represent a 19% rate of return on Patty's $50,000 investment. The debt plan results in $8,295 of after-tax profits, which represent a 33.2% rate of return on Patty's investment of $25,000. The debt plan provides Patty with a higher rate of return, but also has a greater risk because the annual $1,500 of interest must be paid whether Patty's business is profitable or not.

The previous example demonstrates that *with increased debt comes greater risk as well as higher potential return.* Therefore, the greater the financial leverage, the greater the potential risk and return. A detailed discussion of the effect of debt on the firm's risk, return, and value appears later in this text. For now we will focus on how analysts use financial leverage ratios to assess a firm's debt position.

degree of indebtedness
Ratios that measure the amount of debt relative to other significant balance sheet amounts.

Leverage measures are of two general types: measures of the degree of indebtedness and measures of the ability to repay debts. The **degree of indebtedness** ratios measure the amount of debt relative to other significant balance sheet amounts. Two common measures of the degree of indebtedness are the debt ratio and the debt-to-equity ratio.

TABLE 3.8 **Financial Statements Associated with Patty's Alternatives**

Balance sheets	**No-debt plan**	**Debt plan**
Current assets	$20,000	$20,000
Fixed assets	30,000	30,000
Total assets	$50,000	$50,000
Debt (6% interest)	$ 0	$25,000
(1) Equity	50,000	25,000
Total liabilities and equity	$50,000	$50,000
Income Statements		
Sales	$30,000	$30,000
Less: Operating expenses	18,000	18,000
Operating profits	$12,000	$12,000
Less: Interest expense	0	0.06 × $25,000 = $ 1,500
Net profits before taxes	$12,000	$10,500
Less: Taxes (rate = 21%)	2,520	2,205
(2) Net profits after taxes	$ 9,480	$ 8,295
Return on equity [(2) ÷ (1)]	$\frac{\$9,480}{\$50,000} = 19\%$	$\frac{\$8,295}{\$25,000} = 33.2\%$

ability to repay debt

coverage ratios
Ratios that measure a firm's ability to make required debt payments and to pay other fixed charges such as lease payments.

The second type of leverage measures focuses on a firm's **ability to repay debt.** These ratios compare the income that a firm earns to the fixed payments (for debts and obligations such as leases) that it is obliged to make. These ratios are also called **coverage ratios,** and they help analysts assess whether a company can *service their debts* (i.e., make payments on time). Typically, lenders prefer higher coverage ratios, but a very high ratio might indicate that the firm's management is too conservative and could earn higher returns by borrowing more. In general, lower coverage ratios mean that a firm is less likely to repay its debt in full and on time. If a firm is unable to pay these obligations, its creditors may seek immediate repayment, which in most instances would force a firm into bankruptcy. Two popular coverage ratios are the times interest earned ratio and the fixed-payment coverage ratio.

DEBT RATIO

debt ratio
Measures the proportion of total assets financed by the firm's creditors.

The **debt ratio** measures the proportion of total assets financed by the firm's creditors. A higher debt ratio means that a firm is using a larger amount of other people's money to finance its operations, or equivalently, the firm is using greater financial leverage. The formula for debt ratio is

$$\text{Debt ratio} = \text{Total liabilities} \div \text{Total assets} \quad (3.7)$$

Plugging values from Whole Foods' balance sheet into Equation 3.7, we find that the company's debt ratios are

$$\text{2016: } \$3{,}117 \div \$6{,}341 = 0.49 = 49\%$$
$$\text{2015: } \$1{,}972 \div \$5{,}741 = 0.34 = 34\%$$

This value indicates that the company has financed close to half its assets with debt as of 2016 and that the company dramatically increased its debt ratio that year. An increase in the debt ratio could reflect a strategic financial decision by Whole Foods' management to position the company in a way that would allow it to earn higher returns while taking greater risk. In fact, a reading of management's commentary that accompanies the financial statements in the annual report indicates that in the past year the firm issued new long-term notes (i.e., it borrowed money) and used some of the proceeds from that borrowing to repurchase shares, thus shifting its financing mix away from equity toward debt.

DEBT-TO-EQUITY RATIO

debt-to-equity ratio
Measures the relative proportion of total liabilities and common stock equity used to finance the firm's total assets.

The **debt-to-equity ratio** measures the relative proportion of total liabilities to common stock equity used to finance the firm's assets. As with debt ratio, a higher debt-to-equity ratio means that the firm uses more financial leverage. The debt-to-equity ratio is calculated as

$$\text{Debt-to-equity ratio} = \text{Total liabilities} \div \text{Common stock equity} \quad (3.8)$$

The debt-to-equity ratios for Whole Foods look like this

$$\text{2016: } \$3{,}117 \div \$3{,}224 = 0.97$$
$$\text{2015: } \$1{,}972 \div \$3{,}769 = 0.52$$

This result tells us that in 2016, for every $1.00 common stockholders have invested in Whole Foods, the company owes about 97¢ to creditors. These ratios show even more dramatically the shift in the company's financing mix away from equity toward debt. Of note, several methods exist for calculating the debt-to-equity ratio. A common alternative uses only long-term debt in the numerator. In that case, the ratios for Whole Foods are

$$2016\text{: } \$1{,}776 \div \$3{,}224 = 0.55$$
$$2015\text{: } \$720 \div \$3{,}769 = 0.19$$

When conducting ratio analyses, some financial analysts choose to consider all stockholders, including both preferred and common stockholders, rather than only common stockholders, in which case they use values relevant to all stockholders, such as net profits after taxes (instead of earnings available for common stockholders) and total stockholders' equity (instead of common stock equity). Clearly, different methods can lead to very different results, although in this case the two methods produce the same results because Whole Foods has only common stock outstanding. Here again we note that high versus low debt ratios reflect a tradeoff, specifically that higher debt leads to both higher return and risk. Making blanket statements that a firm clearly has too much or too little debt is difficult, except perhaps when the firm's debts are so high that it can't repay them. Assessing a firm's ability to repay debts is the focus of the coverage ratios that we turn to next.

TIMES INTEREST EARNED RATIO

times interest earned ratio
Measures the firm's ability to make contractual interest payments; sometimes called the *interest coverage ratio.*

The **times interest earned ratio,** sometimes called the *interest coverage ratio,* measures the firm's ability to make contractual interest payments. The higher its value, the better able the firm is to fulfill its interest obligations. The times interest earned ratio is calculated as

$$\text{Times interest earned ratio} = \text{Earnings before interest and taxes} \div \text{Interest} \quad (3.9)$$

The figure for earnings before interest and taxes (EBIT) is the same as that for operating profits shown in the income statement. The income statement for Whole Foods in 2015 shows interest expense of $0, so we cannot use Equation 3.9 in that year. The times interest earned ratio in 2016 is

$$\text{Time interest earned ratio} = \$857 \div \$41 = 20.9$$

At first glance, this ratio seems to indicate that Whole Foods has EBIT more than 20 times what it needs to cover the interest charges on its debt. If that were true, it would indicate that the company should have no problem meeting its long-term obligations. However, the figure may be somewhat misleading because Whole Foods leases many of its properties. Lease payments are very similar to interest payments in the sense that the payments are fixed and the firm must make those payments whether business is good or bad. In other words, lease expenses influence a firm's risk and return profile in much the same way that borrowing money does.

FIXED-PAYMENT COVERAGE RATIO

fixed-payment coverage ratio
Measures the firm's ability to meet all fixed-payment obligations.

The **fixed-payment coverage ratio** measures the firm's ability to meet all fixed-payment obligations such as loan interest and principal, lease payments, and preferred stock dividends. As is true of the times interest earned ratio, the higher this value, the better. The formula for the fixed-payment coverage ratio is

$$\text{Fixed-payment coverage ratio} = \frac{\text{Earnings before interest and taxes} + \text{Lease payments}}{\text{Interest} + \text{Lease payments} + \{(\text{Principal payments} + \text{Preferred stock dividends}) \times [1/(1-T)]\}} \quad (3.10)$$

where T is the corporate tax rate applicable to the firm's income. The term $1/(1 - T)$ is included to adjust the after-tax principal and preferred stock dividend payments back to a before-tax equivalent that is consistent with the before-tax values of all other terms. Unfortunately, from the abbreviated financial statements in Tables 3.6 and 3.7, we cannot calculate this ratio for Whole Foods.

Like the times interest earned ratio, the fixed-payment coverage ratio measures risk. The lower this ratio, the greater is the risk to both lenders and owners; the greater this ratio, the lower is the risk. This ratio allows interested parties to assess the firm's ability to meet additional fixed-payment obligations without being driven into bankruptcy.

→ **REVIEW QUESTIONS** MyLab Finance Solutions

3–12 What is financial leverage?

3–13 What ratio measures the firm's degree of indebtedness? What ratios assess the firm's ability to service debts?

3.6 Profitability Ratios

There are many measures of profitability. As a group, these measures enable analysts to evaluate the firm's profits with respect to its sales, assets, or the owners' investment. Owners, creditors, and managers pay close attention to boosting profits because of the great importance the market places on them.

COMMON-SIZE INCOME STATEMENTS

common-size income statement
An income statement in which each item is expressed as a percentage of sales.

A useful tool for evaluating profitability in relation to sales is the **common-size income statement.** Each item on this statement is expressed as a percentage of sales. Common-size income statements prove especially useful when comparing performance across years because it is easy to see if certain categories of expenses are trending up or down as a percentage of the total volume of business that the company transacts. Three frequently cited ratios of profitability that come directly from the common-size income statement are (1) the gross profit margin, (2) the operating profit margin, and (3) the net profit margin.

TABLE 3.9 Whole Foods Common-Size Income Statements

	2016	2015	Evaluation[a] 2015–2016
Sales revenue	100.0%	100.0%	
Less: Cost of goods sold	65.6	64.8	Worse
(1) Gross profit margin	34.4%	35.2%	Worse
Less: Operating expenses			
Less: Selling, general, and administrative expenses	28.5%	29.1%	Better
Other operating expenses	0.5	0.5	Same
(2) Operating profit margin	5.4%	5.6%	Worse
Less: Interest expense	0.3	0.0	
Plus: Other income	0.1%	0.1%	
Pre-tax income	5.2%	5.7%	Worse
Less: Taxes	2.0	2.2	Better
(3) Net profit margin	3.2%	3.5%	Worse

[a]Subjective assessments based on data provided.

Table 3.9 shows common-size income statements for 2016 and 2015 for Whole Foods. These statements reveal that the firm's cost of goods sold increased from 64.8% of sales in 2015 to 65.6% in 2016, resulting in a worsening gross profit margin. Operating income and net income fell as well, but a decline in operating expenses helped to moderate the company's decline in income.

GROSS PROFIT MARGIN

gross profit margin
Measures the percentage of each sales dollar remaining after the firm has paid for its goods.

The **gross profit margin** measures the percentage of each sales dollar remaining after the firm has paid for its cost of goods sold. The higher the gross profit margin, the better. Analysts pay close attention to changes in a company's gross profit margin, particularly when a company's profits depend on its intellectual property (like high technology) or its brand value. The reason why the gross profit margin is so important is simple. You can loosely think of the gross profit margin as a measure of the "markup" on a firm's products. A company with a high gross profit margin is able to charge a high price relative to what it spends to make a product, and that is an indicator of a strong competitive position in the market. Conversely, a thin gross profit margin suggests that the company cannot charge a great deal more than the production costs of the product, which is a sign that the company operates in a highly competitive environment or has noncompetitive manufacturing costs. When analysts see a dip in a company's gross profit margin, they may interpret it as a sign of a weakening competitive position.

To understand this point, look at Figure 3.2, which shows how Apple's introduction of the iPhone changed that company's gross margin. Apple sold its first iPhone in the fourth quarter of its 2007 fiscal year, and the company quickly increased its share of the smartphone market from nothing to 17% by the third quarter of 2009. Over that same period, Apple's gross margin improved from

FIGURE 3.2

Apple Gross Margin and Share of Smartphone Market 2004–2016

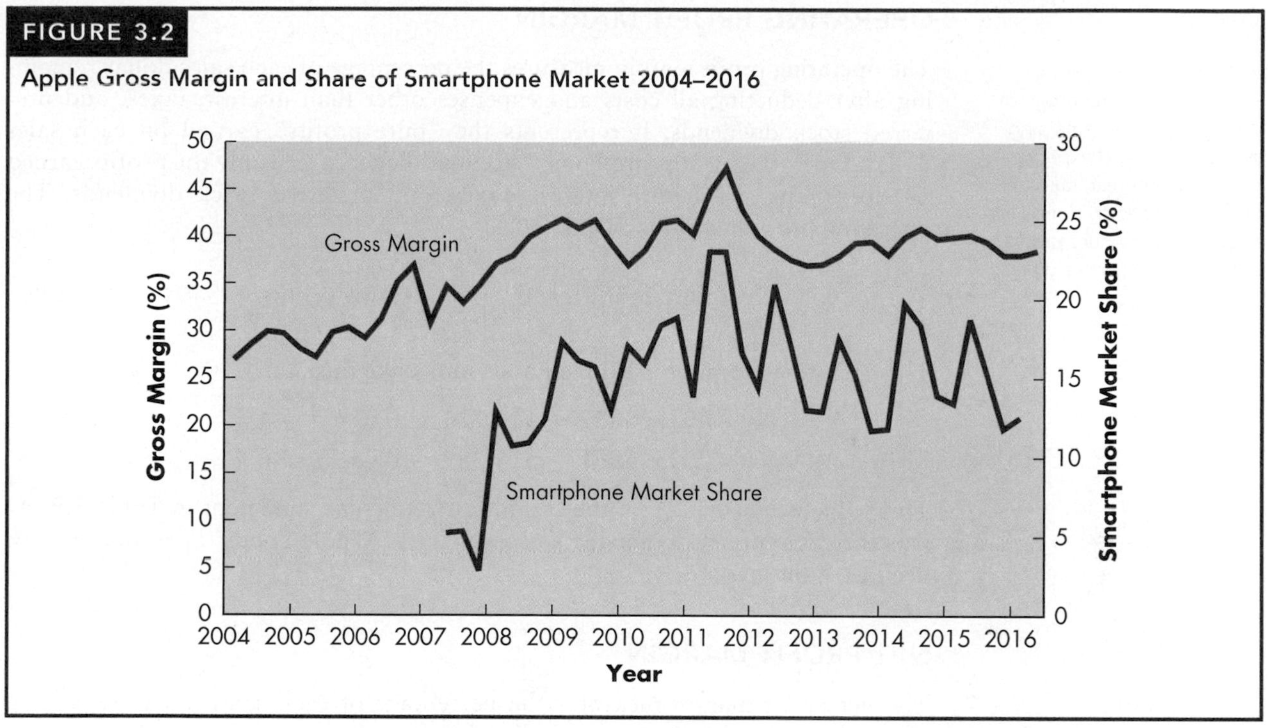

34.7% to 41.8%. That increased gross profit margin meant that for every dollar of revenue Apple generated, it earned roughly an additional 7¢ in gross profit. For several years, Apple's competitive position strengthened as the share of the firm's total revenues coming from smartphones increased. By the middle of 2012, Apple's gross margin and its share of the smartphone market peaked at 47% and 23%, respectively. Since then, competition has reduced Apple's share of smartphone sales and its gross margin, although Apple is still much more profitable than it was before it launched the iPhone.

The formula for the gross profit margin is

$$\text{Gross profit margin} = \frac{\text{Sales} - \text{Cost of goods sold}}{\text{Sales}} = \frac{\text{Gross profits}}{\text{Sales}} \tag{3.11}$$

Returning to our running ratio analysis of Whole Foods' financial performance, we see that their gross profit margin for 2016 and 2015 is

$$2016\text{:} \ \frac{\$15{,}724 - \$10{,}313}{\$15{,}724} = 0.344 = 34.4\%$$

$$2015\text{:} \ \frac{\$15{,}389 - \$9{,}973}{\$15{,}389} = 0.352 = 35.2\%$$

We can also see that the gross profit margin is labeled (1) on the common-size income statement in Table 3.9. Whole Foods' gross profit margin slipped a bit in 2016, which is a worrisome sign that managers would want to watch carefully.

OPERATING PROFIT MARGIN

operating profit margin
Measures the percentage of each sales dollar remaining after all costs and expenses *other than* interest, taxes, and preferred stock dividends are deducted; the "pure profits" earned on each sales dollar.

The **operating profit margin** measures the percentage of each sales dollar remaining after deducting all costs and expenses other than interest, taxes, and preferred stock dividends. It represents the "pure profits" earned on each sales dollar. Operating profits are "pure" because they measure only the profits earned on operations and ignore interest, taxes, and preferred stock dividends. The operating profit margin is calculated as

$$\text{Operating profit margin} = \text{Operating profits} \div \text{Sales} \quad (3.12)$$

The operating margin for Whole Foods looks like this:

$$2016\text{: } \$857 \div \$15{,}724 = 0.054 = 5.4\%$$
$$2015\text{: } \$861 \div \$15{,}389 = 0.056 = 5.6\%$$

This value is labeled (2) on the common-size income statement in Table 3.9. As was the case with the company's gross margin, Whole Foods' operating margin declined a bit in 2016.

NET PROFIT MARGIN

net profit margin
Measures the percentage of each sales dollar remaining after all costs and expenses, *including* interest, taxes, and preferred stock dividends, have been deducted.

The **net profit margin** measures the percentage of each sales dollar remaining after all costs and expenses, including interest, taxes, and preferred stock dividends, have been deducted. Naturally, managers and analysts view a high net profit margin in a positive light. The higher the firm's net profit margin, the better. The net profit margin is calculated as

$$\text{Net profit margin} = \text{Earnings available for common stockholders} \div \text{Sales} \quad (3.13)$$

Applying Equation 3.13 to the numbers in Whole Foods' income statements, we find that their net profit margin is

$$2016\text{: } \$507 \div \$15{,}724 = 0.032 = 3.2\%$$
$$2015\text{: } \$536 \div \$15{,}389 = 0.034 = 3.4\%$$

This value is labeled (3) on the common-size income statement in Table 3.9. Does it surprise you that Whole Foods makes just a little more than 3¢ of net profit for each dollar of groceries that it sells? The grocery industry earns notoriously thin net profit margins, largely because food products are undifferentiated. An apple you buy at one grocery store looks and tastes pretty much like an apple you buy anywhere else, so grocery pricing tends to be very competitive. Notice in Table 3.5, however, that Whole Foods' net profit margin is a little higher than Kroger's, which is consistent with Whole Foods' strategy to sell more unique food items to upscale customers.

The net profit margin is a commonly cited measure of the firm's success with respect to earnings on sales. "Good" net profit margins differ considerably across industries. A net profit margin of 2% or less would not be unusual for a grocery store, whereas a net profit margin of 10% would be low for a retail jewelry store.

EARNINGS PER SHARE (EPS)

The firm's earnings per share (EPS) is generally of interest to present or prospective stockholders and management. As we noted earlier, EPS represents the number of dollars earned during the period on behalf of each outstanding share of common stock. Unlike most of the ratios we've studied so far, EPS is not a figure that analysts can compare across companies in a meaningful way. That's because every company has a different number of common shares outstanding. If we observe that Whole Foods has EPS that are roughly 3 times greater than Kroger's EPS, we cannot conclude that managers at Whole Food are doing a better job. The difference in EPS is a function of both the profits earned by each company and the number of outstanding shares. Therefore, analysts look closely at how EPS change over time for a particular company and at how a firm's EPS compare to its stock price (as we will see shortly). Earnings per share is calculated as

$$\text{Earnings per share} = \frac{\text{Earnings available for common stockholders}}{\text{Number of shares of common stock outstanding}} \quad (3.14)$$

The note to Whole Foods' balance sheet in Table 3.6 tells us how many shares of stock the company had outstanding in 2015 and 2016, so combining that information with the net income figures from Table 3.7 we have

$$2016\text{: } \$507 \div 318.3 = \$1.59$$

$$2015\text{: } \$536 \div 348.9 = \$1.54$$

Notice an interesting pattern here. Whole Foods earned a smaller net profit in 2016 ($507 versus $536 in 2015) and a smaller net profit margin (3.2% versus 3.4% in 2015), but it reported higher earnings per share in 2016 ($1.59 versus $1.54). How did the company earn less money overall and at the same time earn more per share? The answer is that Whole Foods repurchased shares in 2016, so the total number of outstanding shares declined. Firms repurchase shares for many reasons. One reason is to put excess cash held by a company into the hands of shareholders, but another may be to increase the EPS figure. We will return to the motivations for and consequences of share repurchases later in this book.

Besides repurchasing shares, firms can return cash to shareholders by paying dividends. The dollar amount of cash actually distributed to each share is the *dividend per share (DPS)*. Table 3.7 shows that Whole Foods paid $177 million and $186 million in dividends in 2016 and 2015, respectively. Dividing those figures by the number of outstanding shares in each year, we see that the company paid DPS of about $0.56 in 2016 and $0.53 in 2015. Thus, although Whole Foods decreased its total dividend payments in 2016, the DPS increased because the company decreased the number of outstanding shares that year. Notice that Whole Foods' DPS are quite a bit less than its EPS. Most firms that pay dividends do not pay out all earnings as dividends. Instead, they reinvest some of their earnings to help finance future investment and growth.

RETURN ON TOTAL ASSETS (ROA)

return on total assets (ROA)
Measures the overall effectiveness of management in generating profits with its available assets; also called the *return on investment (ROI)*.

The **return on total assets (ROA)**, one of several ratios that are sometimes called the *return on investment (ROI)*, measures the overall effectiveness of management in generating profits with its available assets. The return on total assets is calculated as

$$\text{ROA} = \text{Earnings available for common stockholders} \div \text{Total assets} \quad (3.15)$$

For Whole Foods, the ROA results for 2016 and 2015 are

$$2016\text{: } \$507 \div \$6{,}341 = 0.080 = 8.0\%$$
$$2015\text{: } \$536 \div \$5{,}741 = 0.093 = 9.3\%$$

The numbers here tell us that Whole Foods earned about 9.3¢ for each dollar of assets in 2015, but it earned just 8¢ in 2016.

The decline in Whole Foods' ROA in 2016 is one of the more alarming changes we've identified in this ratio analysis of the firm's performance. This drop occurred because net income fell about 5.4% in 2016, while total assets increased by 10.4%. Whole Foods invested more assets in its business and simultaneously earned less income—clearly not an outcome desired by the company or its investors. Financial analysts working at Whole Foods or at outside firms that might invest in Whole Foods' stock would surely investigate this result in more depth, and in so doing they would explore several questions. First, the analysis here examines just 2 years of data. Analysts could easily calculate the company's ROA going back several more years to see if Whole Foods' ROA in 2015 was unusually good. In that case, the 2016 ROA of 8.0% might be more in line with the company's long-term performance and would therefore not be a cause for alarm. Second, if analysts look at a longer time series of Whole Foods' financial numbers and find that 8% is, in fact, a poor outcome by historical standards, they would want to know if 2016 was also a bad year for the industry as a whole. If the industry performed well in 2016, that would make Whole Foods' dip more worrisome. Third, one reason the ROA might decline in a particular year is that the firm made a large investment that takes time to pay off. That hypothesis seems consistent with the 10.4% increase in Whole Foods' assets in 2016, but analysts would comb Whole Foods' public disclosures carefully to learn how the company invested its additional assets in 2016 and whether it is reasonable to expect those investments to generate positive earnings and cash flows in 2017 and beyond.

RETURN ON EQUITY (ROE)

return on equity (ROE)
Measures the return earned on the common stockholders' investment in the firm.

The **return on equity** (ROE) ratio is similar to ROA, except that it focuses on the earnings that a company generates relative to the equity invested in the firm rather than the assets invested. The equation for ROE is

$$\text{ROE} = \text{Earnings available for common stockholders} \div \text{Common stock equity} \quad (3.16)$$

Before checking the ROE numbers for Whole Foods, take a moment to compare the equations for ROA (Equation 3.15) and ROE (Equation 3.16). The two equations share the same numerator, earnings available for common stockholders.

They differ only because the denominator for ROE is common stock equity, whereas the denominator for ROA is total assets. From the basic equation in accounting, we know that on a balance sheet, the firm's total assets equal the sum of liabilities and equity (A = L + E). This means that as long as a firm has at least some liabilities on its balance sheet, its common stock equity will always be less than its assets. If equity is less than assets, then the denominator of the ROE calculation will always be less than the denominator for ROA. Given that the two ratios share the same numerator, we can make the following general statements about the relation between ROA and ROE.

- When a firm has positive earnings available for common stockholders, its ROE will be greater than its ROA (ROE > ROA if earnings are positive).
- When a firm does not have positive earnings available for common stockholders (e.g., when the firm experiences a loss), its ROE will be more negative than its ROA (ROE < ROA if earnings are negative).

A simplified way of stating this relationship is that in good times, the return on a firm's equity is even better than the return on its assets, but in bad times, the return on a firm's equity is worse than the return on its assets. Now let's look at the ROE results for Whole Foods, which are

$$2016: \$507 \div \$3{,}224 = 0.157 = 15.7\%$$
$$2015: \$536 \div \$3{,}769 = 0.142 = 14.2\%$$

Two observations are important here. First, in both years Whole Foods' ROE exceeds its ROA. Second, although the firm's ROA fell in 2016 (from 9.3% to 8.0%), its ROE actually went up that year (from 14.2% to 15.7%). At first glance this seems quite odd. These two ratios are both designed to measure a company's profitability, but for the same company in the same year, one ratio fell while the other rose. Why did this happen, and what are we to make of this apparent contradiction?

As we noted above, the difference between ROE and ROA arises because a firm's assets typically exceed its common stock equity, with the difference being the firm's liabilities. The more a firm borrows, the larger is the gap between its assets and its equity. Likewise, if a firm uses debt financing to a great extent, then the ROA and ROE ratios can tell very different stories. In 2016, Whole Foods increased its total assets by 10.4%, but the firm's common stock equity actually fell by 14.5%. The only way to make both of those things happen at the same time is to borrow more, and Whole Foods' balance sheet shows that the company did just that. Total liabilities increased in 2016 from $1,972 to $3,117, a 58% jump! In 2016, Whole Foods made some major changes to the right-hand side of its balance sheet. It accomplished this primarily by borrowing money and using that money to retire some of its outstanding common stock. The bottom of Table 3.6 indicates that Whole Foods reduced common stock shares outstanding by 30.6 million in 2016.

The ROA and ROE ratios reflect this dramatic shift in Whole Foods' mix of debt and equity financing in two ways. First, it is the change in financing mix that creates a situation in which the ROA falls and the ROE rises in the same year. The ROA fell in 2016 because the company's earnings fell at the same time its assets increased. However, the ROE actually rose because Whole Foods' equity fell even faster than its earnings. In other words, the company earned a lower profit in 2016, but many fewer shareholders had a claim on those profits. The second way the change in financing mix influences the ROA and ROE ratios is that the gap between those two ratios widens with more debt and less equity financing. Below we repeat the ROA and ROE values for 2015 and 2016 and highlight the differences between them.

	2016	2015
ROE	15.7%	14.2%
ROA	8.0	9.3
Difference (ROE − ROA)	7.7	4.9

As we stated earlier, when a company finances its activities, at least in part, by borrowing money, we say that the firm employs *financial leverage*. You can understand why we use that term if you look at the differences in ROA and ROE above. In 2016, Whole Foods used much more debt (i.e., more leverage), and that resulted in an ROE almost twice as large as the ROA. In other words, by borrowing money Whole Foods magnified or levered up the return that shareholders earned relative to the underlying return on the firm's overall asset base. In 2015 the ROE was also higher than the ROA, but not to the same degree because Whole Foods did not rely as heavily on borrowed funds that year. Of course, the favorable ROE outcome in 2016 might have been quite different if Whole Foods had earned a loss that year. In that case, the ROE would have been substantially worse than the ROA.

The general lesson here is one that we will return to repeatedly in this text. When firms borrow money, they magnify the returns that shareholders earn in good times, but they also magnify the losses that shareholders endure in bad times. The earnings of a company with more debt will experience higher highs and lower lows compared to a company with less debt. The more a firm borrows, the greater will be the volatility of its earnings.

→ **REVIEW QUESTIONS** MyLab Finance Solutions

3–14 What three ratios of profitability appear on a common-size income statement?

3–15 What would explain a firm having a high gross profit margin and a low net profit margin?

3–16 A firm's ROE is typically not equal to its ROA. Why? When would a firm's ROA equal its ROE?

LG5

3.7 Market Ratios

market ratios
Relate a firm's market value, as measured by its current share price, to certain accounting values.

Market ratios relate the firm's market value, as measured by its current share price, to certain accounting values. These ratios give insight into how investors in the marketplace believe the firm is doing in terms of risk and return. An interesting aspect of these ratios is that they combine backward-looking and forward-looking perspectives. A firm's stock price is intrinsically forward looking because what investors are willing to pay for a stock is based much more on how they think a company will perform in the future than on how it has performed in the past. Accounting values, in contrast, have an inherently historical perspective. Here we consider two widely quoted market ratios, one that focuses on earnings and another that emphasizes book value.

PRICE/EARNINGS (P/E) RATIO

price/earnings (P/E) ratio
Measures the amount that investors are willing to pay for each dollar of a firm's earnings; the higher the P/E ratio, the greater the investor confidence.

The **price/earnings (P/E) ratio** is one of the most widely quoted financial ratios in the investments community. The P/E ratio measures the amount that investors are willing to pay for each dollar of a firm's earnings. A variety of factors can influence whether a firm's P/E ratio is high or low, but one of the primary determinants of the P/E ratio is the rate of growth that investors believe a firm will achieve. Other things being equal, investors will pay a higher price for the shares of a firm they expect to grow rapidly, so fast-growing firms tend to have higher P/E ratios than more stable companies. Another factor that influences this ratio is risk. Holding everything else constant, investors will pay a higher price for a firm they believe is less risky. Therefore, the P/E ratio may be high if a firm's growth prospects are good, if its risk is low, or (as we will soon see) for other reasons. The P/E ratio is calculated as

$$\text{P/E ratio} = \text{Market price per share of common stock} \div \text{Earnings per share} \quad (3.17)$$

Before examining the P/E ratio for Whole Foods, let's take a look at the long-term behavior of P/E ratios in the broad stock market. The blue line in Figure 3.3 shows the average P/E ratio for all U.S. stocks on a monthly basis from January 1976 to September 2016, and the vertical grey bars show periods in which the U.S. economy was in recession. The horizontal line in the figure indicates that from 1976 to 2016, the average stock had a P/E ratio of about 19.9. However,

FIGURE 3.3

Average P/E Ratio for U.S. Stocks
Average P/E ratio for all U.S. stocks on a monthly basis from January 1976 to September 2016

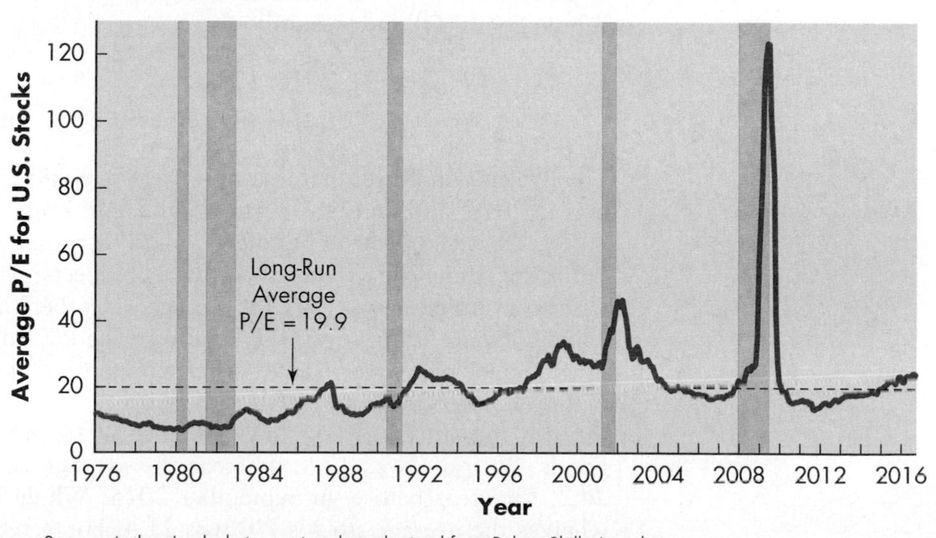

Source: Authors' calculations using data obtained from Robert Shiller's website

P/E ratios fluctuated dramatically, ranging from a low of 6.8 in April 1980 to a high of 123.7 in May 2009.

We can plausibly link some of the fluctuations in P/E ratios to changes in investors' expectations about growth. The average P/E ratio fell in the late 1970s and into the early 1980s, which is consistent with the view that investors had low growth expectations. Indeed, two recessions occurred in the early 1980s, and economic growth was slow by historical standards until the second recession ended. Generally speaking, the mid-1980s through the decade of the 1990s was a period of above-average economic growth, and the average P/E ratio in the U.S. stock market trended up throughout that period. In contrast, economic growth was tepid by historical standards in the 2000s, and the average P/E ratio fell again during that time, with one very obvious and very large exception.

Notice in Figure 3.3 the extremely high P/E ratios that prevailed in the stock market during much of 2008 and 2009. Those unusually high numbers reveal an important lesson about the difficulties of interpreting P/E ratios. We know that the U.S. economy experienced a deep recession in 2008 and 2009. If a high P/E ratio is a sign that investors expect rapid earnings growth, then a recession seems like a strange time to observe high P/E ratios in the stock market. In fact, the market's average P/E ratio was high at this time not because investors expected very rapid earnings growth in the future, but because total corporate earnings during the recession were extremely low. In inflation-adjusted terms, corporate earnings were lower in 2009 than they had been since 1922! In other words, the "E" in the denominator of the P/E ratio fell dramatically in the recession, and that caused an unusual spike in the P/E ratio. To put it differently, although the recession probably caused investors to revise downward their expectations about future earnings growth, the actual earnings that companies generated during the recession fell even faster, so the net result was a huge jump in the market's average P/E ratio.

With the stock market's historical P/E ratios providing some perspective, let's examine Whole Foods' P/E ratio. At the end of the 2016 fiscal year, the price of Whole Foods' common stock was \$28.35, and a year earlier the price was \$31.65. Using these values and the EPS figures provided earlier, we can calculate Whole Foods' P/E ratios as follows:

$$2016\text{: } \$28.35 \div \$1.59 = 17.83$$

$$2015\text{: } \$31.65 \div \$1.53 = 20.69$$

The P/E ratio indicates that investors were paying \$17.83 for each \$1.00 of earnings in 2016, and that figure was down significantly from the 2015 P/E ratio of 20.69. Does the drop in Whole Foods' P/E ratio signal that investors are less optimistic about the company's growth prospects? To answer that question, it is wise to examine how P/E ratios changed at other firms during this period. We could compare Whole Foods' P/E ratio to the P/E ratios of other grocery chains, other retail stores, or some other comparison group. For example, using Figure 3.3 we can compare the P/E ratio for Whole Foods to the average P/E ratio in the stock market. In September 2016, when Figure 3.3 ends, Whole Foods' P/E ratio was 17.8, whereas the average U.S. stock had a P/E ratio of 24.2. The year before, in September 2015, Whole Foods' P/E ratio was 20.7, whereas the average stock's P/E was 21.4. For 2 years in a row, Whole Foods' P/E was below the average value for all U.S. stocks, but perhaps more worrisome for Whole Foods' managers and investors, the company's P/E ratio fell in 2016 while the P/E ratio of the average U.S. stock actually rose.

MARKET/BOOK (M/B) RATIO

market/book (M/B) ratio
Provides an assessment of how investors view the firm's performance. Firms expected to earn high returns relative to their risk typically sell at higher M/B multiples.

The **market/book (M/B) ratio** provides an assessment of how investors view the firm's performance by comparing the market price of the firm's common stock (i.e., what investors are willing to pay for the stock) to the book value of common stock (i.e., the value shown on the balance sheet). For most companies, the M/B ratio will be greater than 1, and often it is much greater than that. Remember that the values shown on a company's balance sheet are based largely on historical costs, whereas the market value of a company's stock is inherently based on how investors believe the company will perform in the future. Furthermore, recall that the objective of managers is to create value for shareholders. One way to demonstrate that managers are creating value is to show that the value investors are willing to pay for the stock is greater than the historical-cost-based book value of the firm's shares. In other words, when the firm's market value exceeds its book value, then managers have created value that exceeds the costs of the assets they have invested in.

To calculate the firm's M/B ratio, we first need to find the *book value per share of common stock:*

$$\frac{\text{Book value per share}}{\text{of common stock}} = \frac{\text{Total common stock equity}}{\text{Number of shares of common stock outstanding}} \quad (3.18)$$

For Whole Foods, we see in Table 3.6 that the company reported a total equity balance of \$3,224 million in 2016, and it had 318.3 million shares of common stock outstanding.[3] This results in a book value per share of

$$\begin{array}{c}\text{Book value per share}\\ \text{of common stock}\end{array} = \frac{\$3{,}224}{318.3} = \$10.13$$

In 2015, the company reported equity of \$3,769 and 348.9 million outstanding shares, so book value per share that year was \$10.80. With this information in hand, we can calculate the market/book ratio. The formula for the market/book ratio is

$$\text{Market/book (M/B) ratio} = \frac{\text{Market price per share of common stock}}{\text{Book value per share of common stock}} \quad (3.19)$$

Previously, we noted that Whole Foods' stock price was trading at \$28.35 at the end of its 2016 fiscal year and at \$31.65 at the end of 2015. Using those numbers and the book value per share figures above, we find that Whole Foods' M/B ratios look like this:

$$2016\text{: } \$28.35 \div \$10.13 = 2.80$$
$$2015\text{: } \$31.65 \div \$10.80 = 2.93$$

3. Whole Foods has no preferred stock, so total equity equals common stock equity. For firms with outstanding preferred shares, we would subtract the book value of preferred shares from total equity to obtain common stock equity.

Just as Whole Foods' P/E ratio fell in 2016, so did its M/B ratio. In 2015, investors were willing to pay $2.93 for each $1 of book value, but in 2016 they paid only $2.80 per $1 of book value.

The stocks of firms that investors expect to perform well—firms that improve profits, increase their market share, or launch successful products—typically sell at higher M/B ratios than the stocks of firms with less attractive outlooks. For Whole Foods, the M/B ratio provides a mixed signal. On the one hand, the market value of the firm's shares is close to 3 times greater than the book value. On the other hand, investors seem to have cooled a bit on the company in 2016.

→ **REVIEW QUESTION** MyLab Finance Solutions

3–17 What do the price/earnings (P/E) ratio and the market/book (M/B) ratio reveal about how investors assess a firm's performance? What caveats must investors keep in mind when evaluating these ratios?

3.8 A Complete Ratio Analysis

In this section we summarize the ratio analysis that we've performed for Whole Foods, and we introduce another approach for using ratios to diagnose problems with a firm's profitability—the DuPont method.

SUMMARY OF WHOLE FOODS' FINANCIAL CONDITION

Table 3.10 summarizes many of the ratios we've calculated for Whole Foods. The table shows ratio values for 2015 and 2016, the industry average ratio (where available), and the formula for each ratio. Using these data, we can discuss the five key aspects of the firm's performance: liquidity, activity, debt, profitability, and market.

Liquidity

The overall liquidity of the firm increased significantly in 2016, rising above the industry norm. The company should therefore encounter no difficulties in paying short-term liabilities, but investors may develop concerns that the company is overinvesting in liquidity if this trend continues.

Activity

Whole Foods' inventory turnover has been steady for 2 consecutive years and is well above the industry average. Although the grocery chain's receivables collection period increased slightly in 2016, the company does not sell a great deal on credit, and its collections still seem to be better than average for the industry. The speed with which the company pays its bills has not changed materially in the past 2 years. Overall, then, we conclude that Whole Foods is managing its current assets and liabilities reasonably well.

Whole Foods' total asset turnover slowed to a significant degree in 2016, and the company is just about at the industry average on this metric. Recall that Whole Foods made a significant investment in new assets in 2016, and no asset category increased faster than cash, which jumped 64%. Holding more cash is not likely to help the company generate more revenue, so until Whole Foods puts its cash to use by investing in revenue-generating assets, its total asset turnover is not likely to return to the 2015 level the company achieved. Firms that hold too much cash sometimes become the target of a takeover attempt as the acquiring firm views the target's excess cash as an under-performing asset.

Debt

Whole Foods' indebtedness increased sharply in 2016, though the company still uses less debt than does the average grocery company. Given that the company is generating more than enough cash flow to cover its interest payments, the increase in debt is not likely to be a major source of concern, even though it will increase the company's risk profile.

Profitability

Whole Foods was more profitable than the average grocery firm in 2016 by all measures. The company's net profit margin, ROA, and ROE all exceeded the industry average. Even so, managers and investors will not want to see a continuation of the decline in net margin and ROA that occurred in 2016. As we have discussed above, although the company increased its ROE, it did so primarily by replacing equity with debt on its balance sheet, not by making the business intrinsically more profitable. A look at the market ratios also suggests that investors do not view everything about the company's performance in a positive light.

Market

Both the P/E and M/B ratios fell in 2016, suggesting that investors have a little less confidence in the firm in 2016. However, both of these ratios are above the industry average. The declines in these ratios may reflect investors' concerns about deteriorating fundamental profitability in the business, reduced growth prospects, or other factors such as increased risk arising from greater financial leverage.

Overall, the ratio analysis for Whole Foods told a mixed story at the end of 2016. The company was profitable and growing. It showed no signs of difficulty in paying its debts. However, there were some indications that the firm's profits were coming under pressure. Furthermore, the market value ratios indicate that investors were not quite as optimistic about Whole Foods as they were in 2015.

Another sign of investor discontent emerged in April 2017, when the activist hedge fund, Jana Partners, announced that it had accumulated a block of 9% of the company's common stock, making it the company's largest shareholder. Jana publicly challenged the board and senior management of Whole Foods and proposed its own slate of 4 candidates for the board of directors. Whole Foods responded by offering to appoint 2 of Jana's 4 candidates to the board if the hedge fund agreed to refrain from publicly criticizing the company for 2 years. Jana refused, but as this book was going to press, Amazon announced that it was buying Whole Foods for $13.7 billion in cash. That price tag represented a 27% premium over the then-current market price of Whole Foods stock and a major win for Jana Partners.

TABLE 3.10 Summary of Whole Foods' Ratios (2015–2016, Including 2016 Industry Averages)

		Year		Industry average	Evaluation		
Ratio	Formula	2015	2016	2016	Cross-sectional 2016	Time-series 2015–2016	Overall
Liquidity							
Current ratio	$\frac{\text{Current assets}}{\text{Current liabilities}}$	1.23	1.47	1.32	OK	OK	OK
Quick (acid-test) ratio	$\frac{\text{Current assets} - \text{Inventory}}{\text{Current liabilities}}$	0.83	1.09	0.76	OK	OK	OK
Activity							
Inventory turnover	$\frac{\text{Cost of goods sold}}{\text{Inventory}}$	19.9	19.9	11.1	OK	OK	OK
Average collection period	$\frac{\text{Accounts receivable}}{\text{Average sales per day}}$	5.2 days	5.6 days	7.5 days	OK	OK	OK
Average payment period	$\frac{\text{Accounts payable}}{\text{Average purchases per day}}$	15.4 days	15.5 days	17.1 days	OK	OK	OK
Total assets turnover	$\frac{\text{Sales}}{\text{Total assets}}$	2.68	2.48	2.4	OK	Watch	OK
Debt							
Debt ratio	$\frac{\text{Total liabilities}}{\text{Total assets}}$	34%	49%	60.0%	OK	Watch	OK
Debt/equity ratio	$\frac{\text{Total liabilities}}{\text{Common stock equity}}$	0.52	0.97	1.50	OK	Watch	OK
Times interest earned ratio	$\frac{\text{Earnings before interest and taxes}}{\text{Interest}}$	NA	20.9	4.3	OK	OK	OK

Ratio	Formula	Year 2015	Year 2016	Industry average 2016	Evaluation: Cross-sectional 2016	Evaluation: Time-series 2015–2016	Evaluation: Overall
Profitability							
Gross profit margin	$\frac{\text{Gross profits}}{\text{Sales}}$	35.2%	34.4%	30.0%	OK	OK	OK
Operating profit margin	$\frac{\text{Operating profits}}{\text{Sales}}$	5.6%	5.4%	6.1%	Watch	Watch	Watch
Net profit margin	$\frac{\text{Earnings available for common stockholders}}{\text{Sales}}$	3.4%	3.2%	2.1%	OK	Watch	OK
Earnings per share (EPS)	$\frac{\text{Earnings available for common stockholders}}{\text{Number of shares of common stock outstanding}}$	\$1.54	\$1.59	NA	NA	OK	OK
Return on total assets (ROA)	$\frac{\text{Earnings available for common stockholders}}{\text{Total assets}}$	9.3%	8.0%	3.1%	OK	Watch	Watch
Return on equity (ROE)	$\frac{\text{Earnings available for common stockholders}}{\text{Common stock equity}}$	14.2%	15.7%	13.8%	Good	OK	Good
Market							
Price/earnings (P/E) ratio	$\frac{\text{Market price per share of common stock}}{\text{Earnings per share}}$	20.69	17.83	15.2	OK	Watch	OK
Market/book (M/B) ratio	$\frac{\text{Market price per share of common stock}}{\text{Book value per share of common stock}}$	2.93	2.80	2.60	OK	Watch	OK

DUPONT SYSTEM OF ANALYSIS

DuPont system of analysis
System used to dissect the firm's financial statements and to assess its financial condition.

Analysts use the **DuPont system of analysis** to dissect the firm's financial statements and to assess its financial condition. It merges information from the income statement and the balance sheet into two summary measures of profitability, return on total assets (ROA) and return on common equity (ROE), and then decomposes those measures to identify underlying drivers of the firm's performance. Figure 3.4 depicts the basic DuPont system with 2016 financial information from Whole Foods. The upper portion of the chart summarizes the income statement activities, and the lower portion summarizes the balance sheet activities.

DuPont Formula

DuPont formula
Multiplies the firm's *net profit margin* by its *total asset turnover* to calculate the firm's *return on total assets (ROA)*.

The DuPont system first brings together the net profit margin, which measures the firm's profitability on sales, with its total asset turnover, which indicates how efficiently the firm has used its assets to generate sales. In the **DuPont formula,** the product of these two ratios results in the return on total assets (ROA):

$$\text{ROA} = \text{Net profit margin} \times \text{Total asset turnover}$$

Substituting the appropriate formulas for net profit margin and total asset turnover into the equation and simplifying results in the formula for ROA given earlier,

$$\text{ROA} = \frac{\text{Earnings available for common stockholders}}{\text{Sales}} \times \frac{\text{Sales}}{\text{Total assets}} = \frac{\text{Earnings available for common stockholders}}{\text{Total assets}}$$

When we substitute the 2016 values of the net profit margin and total asset turnover for Whole Foods, calculated earlier, into the DuPont formula, the result is

$$\text{ROA} = 3.2\% \times 2.48 = 7.9\%$$

Except for a small difference in rounding, this value is the same as that calculated directly in Section 3.6 (page 108). The DuPont formula enables the firm to break down its return into profit-on-sales and efficiency-of-asset-use components. One way to think about this type of analysis is that it demonstrates two "channels" through which a firm may achieve a given level of ROA. A firm may achieve its target ROA either by having a strong net profit margin or by turning over its assets rapidly. Firms can adopt strategies that emphasize either of these channels to achieve an acceptable ROA.

To illustrate this idea, return to Table 3.5 and focus your attention on the ratios for Target and Walmart. Clearly, these two companies compete against each other, yet they have adopted different strategies. Target stores typically have a more open layout with better lighting compared to Walmart stores, and Target's prices are a bit higher. Walmart typically charges lower prices, but it crams its stores with items that turn over rapidly. In Table 3.5, observe that these two companies earned fairly similar ROAs—7.1% for Target and 8.4% for Walmart. They achieved these results in different ways. Target had a higher net profit margin (3.8% versus 3.5% at Walmart) mostly because it charged higher prices. But Walmart turned its assets much faster (2.4 times per year versus 1.8 times for Target). Strategically, Target has decided to compete by attracting a more upscale consumer who wants a more relaxed shopping experience and is willing to pay more than the typical Walmart customer. If Target decided to cut its prices to compete on that dimension with Walmart, it would need to increase its asset turnover; otherwise, its ROA would fall.

FIGURE 3.4

DuPont System of Analysis

The DuPont system of analysis with application to Whole Foods (2016)

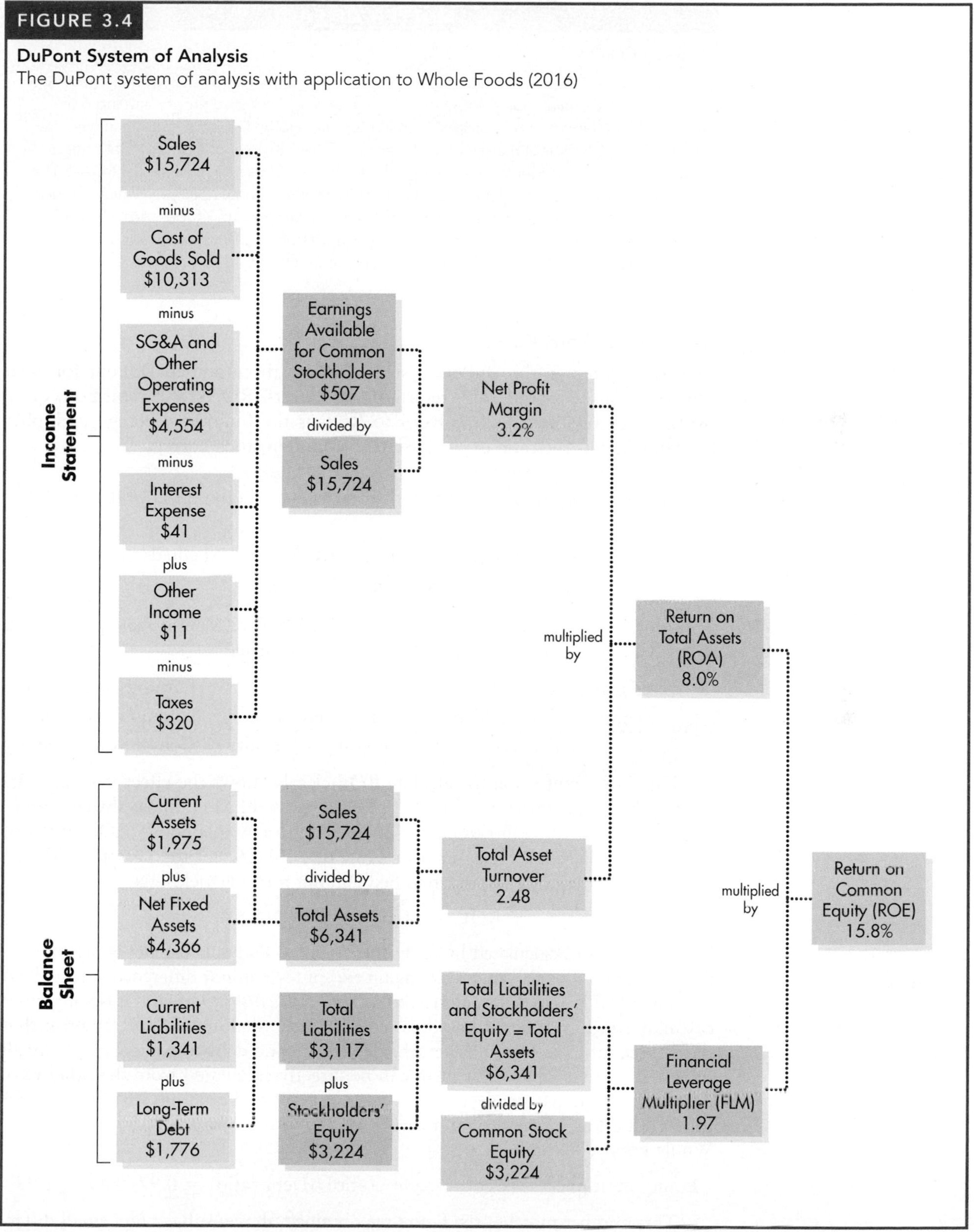

MATTER OF FACT

Dissecting ROA

Return to Table 3.5, and examine the ROA figures for Home Depot and Kroger. Those two firms have very similar ROAs, with Home Depot earning 6.5% and Kroger earning 6.0%. Now look at their net profit margins. By that measure, Home Depot is more than twice as profitable as Kroger (net margin of 4.0% versus 1.9% for Kroger). If Home Depot's net profit margin is so much bigger than Kroger's, why do the two firms earn very similar ROAs? The answer lies in total asset turnover. Kroger turns its assets 3.2 times per year, which is much faster than Home Depot's asset turnover of 1.6 times. Simply put, Kroger uses its assets twice as efficiently as Home Depot, but Home Depot's net profit margin is about twice as large as Kroger's; the end result is that both firms earn close to a 6% ROA.

Modified DuPont Formula

modified DuPont formula
Relates the firm's *return on total assets (ROA)* to its *return on equity (ROE)* using the *financial leverage multiplier (FLM)*.

financial leverage multiplier (FLM)
The ratio of the firm's total assets to its common stock equity.

The second step in the DuPont system employs the **modified DuPont formula.** This formula relates the firm's return on total assets (ROA) to its return on equity (ROE). The key ratio linking ROA to ROE is the **financial leverage multiplier (FLM)**, which is the ratio of total assets to common stock equity:

$$\text{Financial leverage multiplier (FLM)} = \text{Total assets} \div \text{Common stock equity} \quad (3.20)$$

Next, it's easy to see that the product of ROA and FLM equals the firm's ROE.

$$\text{ROE} = \text{ROA} \times \text{FLM}$$

Substituting the appropriate formulas for ROA and FLM into the equation and simplifying results in the formula for ROE given earlier:

$$\text{ROE} = \frac{\text{Earnings available for common stockholders}}{\text{Total assets}} \times \frac{\text{Total assets}}{\text{Common stock equity}} = \frac{\text{Earnings available for common stockholders}}{\text{Common stock equity}}$$

Using this expression to calculate ROE clearly shows the effect that financial leverage has in magnifying a firm's ROA because the FLM is almost always a number greater than 1.0. Substituting the 2016 values for Whole Foods' ROA of 8.0%, calculated earlier, and the company's FLM of 1.97 ($6,341 total assets ÷ $3,224 common stock equity) into the modified DuPont formula yields

$$\text{ROE} = 8.0\% \times 1.97 = 15.8\%$$

The 15.8% ROE calculated by using the modified DuPont formula is the same as that calculated directly (page 109), again except for a minor difference in rounding.

The FLM is also often referred to as the *equity multiplier,* and it is sometimes calculated using total stockholders' equity in the denominator. Recognize that these three ratios—the multiplier, the debt ratio, and debt-to-equity ratio—are all related such that any one of them can be directly calculated from the other two. For example, if we divide the debt-to-equity ratio (Equation 3.8) by the debt ratio (Equation 3.7), we obtain the FLM. Using the relevant 2016 numbers for Whole Foods, we have

$$\text{Equity multiplier} = (\text{Debt-to-equity ratio})/(\text{Debt ratio}) = 0.97/0.49 = 1.98$$

This number matches the figure we obtained above, subject to a small difference in rounding.

Applying the DuPont System

The advantage of the DuPont system is that it allows the firm to break its return on equity into a profit-on-sales component (net profit margin), an efficiency-of-asset-use component (total asset turnover), and a use-of-financial-leverage component (financial leverage multiplier). Analysts can decompose the total return to owners into these important components.

The use of the DuPont system of analysis as a diagnostic tool is best explained using Figure 3.4. Beginning with the rightmost value—the ROE—the financial analyst moves to the left, dissecting and analyzing the inputs to the formula to isolate the probable cause of the resulting above-average (or below-average) value.

EXAMPLE 3.6

MyLab Finance Solution Video

In Table 3.8 we saw that Whole Foods' 2016 ROE was 15.7%, above the 13.8% industry average. What are the drivers of this difference? Start at the far right of Figure 3.4 and move left. Whole Foods' ROA was 8.0%, well above the industry average of 3.1%. Whole Foods' FLM was just under 2.0, whereas the industry average was 2.5.[4] Therefore, Whole Foods' shareholders enjoyed a higher-than-average ROE because the firm's underlying profitability, its ROA, was much higher than that of the typical grocery chain. Continuing to move left in Figure 3.4, we see that the ROA figure resulted from Whole Foods' above-average net profit margin of 3.2% and its asset turnover of 2.48, which just barely rose above the industry average.

→ REVIEW QUESTIONS MyLab Finance Solutions

3–18 Financial ratio analysis is often divided into five areas: liquidity, activity, debt, profitability, and market ratios. Differentiate each of these areas of analysis from the others. Which is of greatest concern to creditors?

3–19 Describe how you would use a large number of ratios to perform a complete ratio analysis of the firm.

3–20 What three areas of analysis are combined in the modified DuPont formula? Explain how the manager uses the DuPont system of analysis to dissect the firm's results and isolate their causes.

SUMMARY

FOCUS ON VALUE

Financial managers review and analyze the firm's financial statements periodically, both to uncover developing problems and to assess the firm's progress toward achieving its goals. These actions are aimed at **preserving and creating value for the firm's owners.** Financial ratios enable financial managers to monitor the pulse of the firm and its progress toward its strategic goals. Although financial statements and financial ratios rely on accrual concepts, they can provide useful insights into important aspects of risk and return (cash flow) that affect share price.

4. We estimate the industry average FLM by dividing the industry average debt-to-equity ratio of 1.5 in Table 3.8 by the industry average debt ratio of 0.6.

REVIEW OF LEARNING GOALS

LG 1 **Review the contents of the stockholders' report and the procedures for consolidating international financial statements.** The annual stockholders' report, which publicly owned corporations must provide to stockholders, documents the firm's financial activities of the past year. It includes the letter to stockholders and other information about the firm's activities and strategies. It also contains four key financial statements: the income statement, the balance sheet, the statement of stockholders' equity (or its abbreviated form, the statement of retained earnings), and the statement of cash flows. Notes describing the technical aspects of the financial statements follow. Financial statements of companies that have operations whose cash flows are denominated in one or more foreign currencies must be translated into U.S. dollars in accordance with *FASB Standard No. 52.*

LG 2 **Understand who uses financial ratios and how.** Ratio analysis enables stockholders, lenders, and the firm's managers to evaluate the firm's financial performance. It can be performed on a cross-sectional or a time-series basis. Benchmarking is a popular type of cross-sectional analysis. Users of ratios should understand the cautions that apply to their use.

LG 3 **Use ratios to analyze a firm's liquidity and activity.** Analysts can assess a firm's liquidity, or the ability of the firm to pay its bills as they come due, by calculating the current ratio and the quick (acid-test) ratio. Activity ratios measure the speed with which accounts are converted into sales or cash. Analysts use the inventory turnover ratio, the accounts receivable collection period, and the average payment period (for accounts payable) to assess the activity of those current assets and liabilities. Total asset turnover measures the efficiency with which the firm uses its assets to generate sales.

LG 4 **Discuss the relationship between debt and financial leverage, as well as the ratios used to analyze a firm's debt.** The more debt a firm uses, the greater its financial leverage, which magnifies both risk and return. Financial debt ratios measure both the degree of indebtedness and the ability to service debts. A common measure of indebtedness is the debt ratio. The ability to pay fixed charges can be measured by times interest earned and fixed-payment coverage ratios.

LG 5 **Use ratios to analyze a firm's profitability and its market value.** The common-size income statement, which shows each item as a percentage of sales, can be used to determine gross profit margin, operating profit margin, and net profit margin. Other measures of profitability include earnings per share, return on total assets, and return on common equity. Market ratios include the price/earnings ratio and the market/book ratio.

LG 6 **Use a summary of financial ratios and the DuPont system of analysis to perform a complete ratio analysis.** A summary of all ratios can be used to perform a complete ratio analysis using cross-sectional and time-series analysis. The DuPont system of analysis is a diagnostic tool used to find the key areas responsible for the firm's financial performance. It enables the firm to break the return on common equity into three components: profit on sales, efficiency of asset use, and use of financial leverage.

OPENER-IN-REVIEW

For the quarter ended January 28, 2017, Kroger reported sales of $27.61 billion and cost of goods sold of $21.47 billion. What was the company's gross profit margin that quarter?

SELF-TEST PROBLEMS (Solutions in Appendix)

ST3–1 **Ratio formulas and interpretations** Without referring to the text, indicate for each of the following ratios the formula for calculating it and the kinds of problems, if any, the firm may have if that ratio is too high relative to the industry average. What if the ratio is too low relative to the industry average? Create a table similar to the one that follows and fill in the empty blocks.

Ratio	Too high	Too low
Current ratio =		
Inventory turnover =		
Times interest earned =		
Gross profit margin =		
Return on total assets =		
Price/earnings (P/E) ratio =		

ST3–2 **Balance sheet completion using ratios** Complete the 2019 balance sheet for O'Keefe Industries, using the information that follows it.

O'Keefe Industries Balance Sheet December 31, 2019

Assets		Liabilities and Stockholders' Equity	
Cash	$32,720	Accounts payable	$120,000
Marketable securities	25,000	Notes payable	
Accounts receivable		Accruals	$ 20,000
Inventories		Total current liabilities	
Total current assets		Long-term debt	
Net fixed assets		Stockholders' equity	$600,000
Total assets	$	Total liabilities and stockholders' equity	$

The following financial data for 2019 are also available:

1. Sales totaled $1,800,000.
2. The gross profit margin was 25%.
3. Inventory turnover was 6.0.
4. There are 365 days in the year.
5. The average collection period was 40 days.
6. The current ratio was 1.60.
7. The total asset turnover ratio was 1.20.
8. The debt ratio was 60%.

WARM-UP EXERCISES All problems are available in MyLab Finance

E3–1 You are a summer intern at the office of a local tax preparer. To test your basic knowledge of financial statements, your manager gives you the following list of accounts and asks you to prepare a simple income statement using those accounts.

Accounts	($000,000)
Depreciation	$ 25
General and administrative expenses	22
Sales	345
Sales expenses	18
Cost of goods sold	255
Lease expense	4
Interest expense	3

a. Arrange the accounts into a well-labeled income statement. Make sure you label and solve for gross profit, operating profit, and net profit before taxes.

b. Using a 21% tax rate, calculate taxes paid and net profit after taxes.

c. Assuming a dividend of $1.10 per share with 4.25 million shares outstanding, calculate EPS and additions to retained earnings.

LG 1

E3–2 Explain why the income statement can also be called a "profit-and-loss statement." What exactly does the word *balance* mean in the title of the balance sheet? Why do we balance the two halves?

LG 1

E3–3 Cooper Industries Inc. began 2019 with retained earnings of $25.32 million. During the year, it paid four quarterly dividends of $0.35 per share to 2.75 million common stockholders. Preferred stockholders, holding 500,000 shares, were paid two semiannual dividends of $0.75 per share. The firm had a net profit after taxes of $5.15 million. Prepare the statement of retained earnings for the year ended December 31, 2019.

LG 3

E3–4 Bluestone Metals Inc. is a metal fabrication firm that manufactures prefabricated metal parts for customers in a variety of industries. The firm's motto is "If you need it, we can make it." The CEO of Bluestone recently held a board meeting during which he said that the company had the capability to build any of its products using a lean manufacturing model that allowed the company to keep inventory levels low. As an investor, you have calculated some ratios to analyze the firm's performance. Bluestone's current ratios and quick ratios for the past 6 years are as follows:

	2014	2015	2016	2017	2018	2019
Current ratio	1.2	1.4	1.3	1.6	1.8	2.2
Quick ratio	1.1	1.3	1.2	0.8	0.6	0.4

What do you think of the CEO's claim that the firm's manufacturing process allows it to keep inventories low?

LG 6

E3–5 If we know that a firm has a net profit margin of 4.5%, total asset turnover of 0.72, and a financial leverage multiplier of 1.43, what is its ROE? What is the advantage to using the DuPont system to calculate ROE over the direct calculation of earnings available for common stockholders divided by common stock equity?

PROBLEMS

All problems are available in MyLab Finance. The MyLab icon indicates problems in Excel format available in MyLab Finance.

P3–1 **Financial statement account identification** Mark each of the accounts listed in the following table as follows:

a. In column (1), indicate in which statement—income statement (IS) or balance sheet (BS)—the account belongs.

b. In column (2), indicate whether the account is a current asset (CA), current liability (CL), expense (E), fixed asset (FA), long-term debt (LTD), revenue (R), or stockholders' equity (SE).

Account name	(1) Statement	(2) Type of account
Accounts payable	____	____
Accounts receivable	____	____
Accruals	____	____
Accumulated depreciation	____	____
Administrative expense	____	____
Buildings	____	____
Cash	____	____
Common stock (at par)	____	____
Cost of goods sold	____	____
Depreciation	____	____
Equipment	____	____
General expense	____	____
Interest expense	____	____
Inventories	____	____
Land	____	____
Long-term debts	____	____
Machinery	____	____
Marketable securities	____	____
Notes payable	____	____
Operating expense	____	____
Paid-in capital in excess of par	____	____
Preferred stock	____	____
Preferred stock dividends	____	____
Retained earnings	____	____
Sales revenue	____	____
Selling expense	____	____
Taxes	____	____
Vehicles	____	____

P3–2 Income statement preparation On December 31, 2019, Cathy Chen, a self-employed certified public accountant (CPA), completed her first full year in business. During the year, she charged her clients $360,000 for accounting services. She had two employees, a bookkeeper and a clerical assistant. In addition to her *monthly* salary of $8,000, Ms. Chen paid *annual* salaries of $48,000 and $36,000 to the bookkeeper and the clerical assistant, respectively. Employment taxes and benefit costs for Ms. Chen and her employees totaled $34,600 for the year. Expenses for office supplies, including postage, totaled $10,400 for the year. In addition, Ms. Chen spent $17,000 during the year on tax-deductible travel and entertainment associated with client visits and new business development. Lease payments for the office space rented (a tax-deductible expense) were $2,700 *per month*. Depreciation expense on the office furniture and fixtures was $15,600 for the year. During the year, Ms. Chen paid interest of $15,000 on the $120,000 borrowed to start the business. She paid an average tax rate of 30% during 2019.

a. Prepare an income statement for Cathy Chen, CPA, for the year ended December 31, 2019.
b. Evaluate her 2019 financial performance.

Personal Finance Problem

P3–3 Income statement preparation Adam and Arin Adams have collected their personal income and expense information and have asked you to put together an income and expense statement for the year ended December 31, 2019. You have received the following information from the Adams family.

Adam's salary	$45,000	Utilities	$ 3,200
Arin's salary	30,000	Groceries	2,200
Interest received	500	Medical	1,500
Dividends received	150	Property taxes	1,659
Auto insurance	600	Income tax, Social Security	13,000
Home insurance	750	Clothes and accessories	2,000
Auto loan payment	3,300	Gas and auto repair	2,100
Mortgage payment	14,000	Entertainment	2,000

a. Create a personal *income and expense statement* for the period ended December 31, 2019. It should be similar to a corporate income statement.
b. Did the Adams family have a cash surplus or cash deficit?
c. If the result is a surplus, how can the Adams family use that surplus?

LG1

P3–4 Calculation of EPS and retained earnings Everdeen Mining Inc. ended 2019 with a net profit *before* taxes of $436,000. The company is subject to a 21% tax rate and must pay $64,000 in preferred stock dividends before distributing any earnings on the 170,000 shares of common stock currently outstanding.

a. Calculate Everdeen's 2019 earnings per share (EPS).
b. If the firm paid common stock dividends of $0.80 per share, how many dollars would go to retained earnings?

P3–5 **Balance sheet preparation** Use the appropriate items from the following list to prepare Mellark's Baked Goods balance sheet at December 31, 2019.

Item	Value ($000) at December 31, 2019	Item	Value ($000) at December 31, 2019
Accounts payable	$ 220	Inventories	$ 375
Accounts receivable	450	Land	100
Accruals	55	Long-term debts	420
Accumulated depreciation	265	Machinery	420
Buildings	225	Marketable securities	75
Cash	215	Notes payable	475
Common stock (at par)	90	Paid-in capital in excess of par	360
Cost of goods sold	2,500		
Depreciation expense	45	Preferred stock	100
Equipment	140	Retained earnings	210
Furniture and fixtures	170	Sales revenue	3,600
General expense	320	Vehicles	25

P3–6 **Effect of net income on a firm's balance sheet** Conrad Air Inc. reported net income of $1,365,000 for the year ended December 31, 2020. Show how Conrad's balance sheet would change from 2019 to 2020 depending on how Conrad "spent" those earnings as described in the scenarios that appear below.

Conrad Air Inc. Balance Sheet as of December 31, 2019

Assets		Liabilities and Stockholders' Equity	
Cash	$ 120,000	Accounts payable	$ 70,000
Marketable securities	35,000	Short-term notes	55,000
Accounts receivable	45,000	Current liabilities	$ 125,000
Inventories	$ 130,000	Long-term debt	2,700,000
Current assets	$ 330,000	Total liabilities	$2,825,000
Equipment	$2,970,000	Common stock	$ 500,000
Buildings	1,600,000	Retained earnings	1,575,000
Fixed assets	$4,570,000	Stockholders' equity	$2,075,000
Total assets	$4,900,000	Total liabilities and equity	$4,900,000

a. Conrad paid no dividends during the year and invested the funds in marketable securities.
b. Conrad paid dividends totaling $500,000 and used the balance of the net income to retire (pay off) long-term debt.
c. Conrad paid dividends totaling $500,000 and invested the balance of the net income in building a new hangar.
d. Conrad paid out all $1,365,000 as dividends to its stockholders.

P3–7 Initial sale price of common stock Hudson-Perry Recordings Inc. has one issue of preferred stock and one issue of common stock outstanding. Given their stockholders' equity account that follows, determine the original price per share at which the firm sold its single issue of common stock.

Stockholders' Equity ($000)	
Preferred stock	$ 225
Common stock ($0.10 par, 1,400,000 shares outstanding)	140
Paid-in capital in excess of par on common stock	19,460
Retained earnings	1,800
Total stockholders' equity	$21,625

P3–8 Statement of retained earnings Hayes Enterprises began 2019 with a retained earnings balance of $928,000. During 2019, the firm earned $377,000 after taxes. From this amount, preferred stockholders were paid $47,000 in dividends. At year-end 2019, the firm's retained earnings totaled $1,048,000. The firm had 140,000 shares of common stock outstanding during 2019.

a. Prepare a statement of retained earnings for the year ended December 31, 2019, for Hayes Enterprises. (*Note:* Be sure to calculate and include the amount of cash dividends paid in 2019.)
b. Calculate the firm's 2019 earnings per share (EPS).
c. How large a per-share cash dividend did the firm pay on common stock during 2019?

P3–9 Changes in stockholders' equity Listed are the equity sections of balance sheets for years 2018 and 2019 as reported by Mountain Air Ski Resorts Inc. The overall value of stockholders' equity has risen from $2,000,000 to $7,500,000. Use the statements to discover how and why that happened.

Mountain Air Ski Resorts Inc.
Balance Sheets (partial)

Stockholders' equity	2018	2019
Common stock ($1.00 par)		
Authorized: 5,000,000 shares		
Outstanding: 1,500,000 shares 2019		$1,500,000
500,000 shares 2018	$ 500,000	
Paid-in capital in excess of par	500,000	4,500,000
Retained earnings	1,000,000	1,500,000
Total stockholders' equity	$2,000,000	$7,500,000

The company paid total dividends of $200,000 during fiscal 2019.

a. What was Mountain Air's net income for fiscal 2019?
b. How many new shares did the corporation issue and sell during the year?
c. At what average price per share did the new stock sold during 2019 sell?
d. At what price per share did Mountain Air's original 500,000 shares sell?

P3–10 **Ratio comparisons** Robert Arias recently inherited a stock portfolio from his uncle. Wishing to learn more about the companies in which he is now invested, Robert performs a ratio analysis on each one and decides to compare them to one another. Some of his ratios are listed below.

Ratio	Island Electric Utility	Burger Heaven	Fink Software	Roland Motors
Current ratio	1.10	1.3	6.8	4.5
Quick ratio	0.90	0.82	5.2	3.7
Debt ratio	0.68	0.46	0.0	0.35
Net profit margin	6.2%	14.3%	28.5%	8.4%

Assuming that his uncle was a wise investor who assembled the portfolio with care, Robert finds the wide differences in these ratios confusing. Help him out.

a. What problems might Robert encounter in comparing these companies to one another on the basis of their ratios?

b. Why might the current and quick ratios for the electric utility and the fast-food stock be so much lower than the same ratios for the other companies?

c. Why might it be all right for the electric utility to carry a large amount of debt, but not the software company?

d. Why wouldn't investors invest all their money in software companies instead of in less profitable companies? (Focus on risk and return.)

P3–11 **Liquidity management** Bauman Company's total current assets, total current liabilities, and inventory for each of the past 4 years follow:

Item	2016	2017	2018	2019
Total current assets	$16,950	$21,900	$22,500	$27,000
Total current liabilities	9,000	12,600	12,600	17,400
Inventory	6,000	6,900	6,900	7,200

a. Calculate the firm's current and quick ratios for each year. Compare the resulting time series for these measures of liquidity.

b. Comment on the firm's liquidity over the 2016–2019 period.

c. If you were told that Bauman Company's inventory turnover for each year in the 2016–2019 period and the industry averages were as follows, would this information support or conflict with your evaluation in part **b**? Why?

Inventory turnover	2016	2017	2018	2019
Bauman Company	6.3	6.8	7.0	6.4
Industry average	10.6	11.2	10.8	11.0

Personal Finance Problem

LG 3

P3–12 Liquidity ratio Josh Smith has compiled some of his personal financial data to determine his liquidity position. The data are as follows.

Account	Amount
Cash	$3,200
Marketable securities	1,000
Checking account	800
Credit card payables	1,200
Short-term notes payable	900

a. Calculate Josh's liquidity ratio.

b. Several of Josh's friends have told him that they have liquidity ratios of about 1.8. How would you analyze Josh's liquidity relative to his friends?

MyLab

P3–13 Inventory management Three companies that compete in the footwear market are Foot Locker, Finish Line, and DSW. The table below shows inventory levels and cost of goods sold for each company for the 2016, 2015, and 2014 fiscal years. Calculate the inventory turnover ratio for each company in each year and summarize your findings. All values are in $ millions.

Foot Locker	**2016**	**2015**	**2014**
Cost of goods sold	$4,907	$4,777	$4,372
Inventory	1,285	1,250	1,220
Finish Line			
Cost of goods sold	$1,306	$1,237	$1,123
Inventory	377	343	304
DSW			
Cost of goods sold	$1,852	$1,741	$1,629
Inventory	484	451	398

P3–14 Accounts receivable management The table below shows that Blair Supply had an end-of-year accounts receivable balance of $300,000. The table also shows how much of the receivables balance originated in each of the previous 6 months. The company had annual sales of $2.4 million, and it normally extends 30-day credit terms to its customers.

Month of origin	Accounts receivable
July	$ 3,875
August	2,000
September	34,025
October	15,100
November	52,000
December	193,000
Year-end accounts receivable	$300,000

a. Use the year-end total to evaluate the firm's collection system.

b. If 70% of the firm's sales occur between July and December, would this information affect the validity of your conclusion in part **a**? Explain.

P3–15 Interpreting liquidity and activity ratios The table below shows key financial data for three firms that compete in the consumer products market: Procter & Gamble, Colgate-Palmolive, and Clorox. All dollar values are in thousands.

	Procter & Gamble	Colgate-Palmolive	Clorox
Sales	$65,231	$15,195	$5,875
Cost of goods sold	32,967	6,072	3,233
Receivables	4,729	1,411	514
Inventory	4,787	1,171	501
Total current assets	25,572	4,338	1,549
Total current liabilities	28,891	3,305	2,037
Total assets	117,033	12,123	4,568

a. Calculate each of the following ratios for all three companies: current ratio, quick ratio, inventory turnover, average collection period, total asset turnover.

b. Which company is in the position of having greatest liquidity?

c. Would you say that the three companies exhibit similar performance or quite different performance in terms of collecting receivables? Why do you think that might be?

d. Which company has the most rapid inventory turnover? Which company appears to be least efficient in terms of total asset turnover? Are your answers to those questions a little surprising? If a company is best at inventory turnover and worst at total asset turnover, what do you think that means?

P3–16 Debt analysis Springfield Bank is evaluating Creek Enterprises, which has requested a $4,000,000 loan, to assess the firm's financial leverage and financial risk. On the basis of the debt ratios for Creek, along with the industry average and Creek's recent financial statements (following), evaluate and recommend appropriate action on the loan request.

Creek Enterprises Income Statement for the Year Ended December 31, 2019	
Sales revenue	$30,000,000
Less: Cost of goods sold	21,000,000
Gross profits	$ 9,000,000
Less: Operating expenses	
Selling expense	$ 3,000,000
General and administrative expenses	1,800,000
Lease expense	200,000
Depreciation expense	1,000,000
Total operating expense	$ 6,000,000
Operating profits	$ 3,000,000
Less: Interest expense	1,000,000
Net profits before taxes	$ 2,000,000
Less: Taxes (rate = 21%)	420,000
Net profits after taxes	$ 1,580,000
Less: Preferred stock dividends	100,000
Earnings available for common stockholders	$ 1,480,000

Creek Enterprises Balance Sheet December 31, 2019			
Assets		**Liabilities and Stockholders' Equity**	
Cash	$ 1,000,000	Accounts payable	$ 8,000,000
Marketable securities	3,000,000	Notes payable	8,000,000
Accounts receivable	12,000,000	Accruals	500,000
Inventories	7,500,000	Total current liabilities	$16,500,000
Total current assets	$23,500,000	Long-term debt (includes financial leases)[b]	$20,000,000
Land and buildings	$11,000,000		
Machinery and equipment	20,500,000	Preferred stock (25,000 shares, $4 dividend)	$ 2,500,000
Furniture and fixtures	8,000,000		
Gross fixed assets (at cost)[a]	$39,500,000	Common stock (1 million shares at $5 par)	5,000,000
Less: Accumulated depreciation	13,000,000		
Net fixed assets	$26,500,000	Paid-in capital in excess of par value	4,000,000
Total assets	$50,000,000		
		Retained earnings	2,000,000
		Total stockholders' equity	$13,500,000
		Total liabilities and stockholders' equity	$50,000,000

[a]The firm has a 4-year financial lease requiring annual beginning-of-year payments of $200,000. Three years of the lease have yet to run.

[b]Required annual principal payments are $800,000.

Industry averages	
Debt ratio	0.51
Times interest earned ratio	7.30
Fixed-payment coverage ratio	1.85

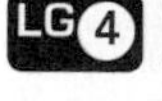

MyLab

P3–17 Profitability analysis The table below shows 2016 total revenues, cost of goods sold, earnings available for common stockholders, total assets, and stockholders' equity for three companies competing in the bottled drinks market: The Coca-Cola Company, Pepsico Inc., and Dr Pepper Snapple Group. All dollar values are in thousands.

	Coca-Cola	Pepsico	Dr Pepper
Revenues	$41,863	$62,799	$6,440
Cost of goods sold	16,465	28,209	2,582
Earnings	6,527	6,329	847
Total assets	87,270	74,129	9,791
Shareholders equity	23,062	11,246	2,134

a. Use the information given to analyze each firm's profitability in as many different ways as you can. Which company is most profitable? Why is this question difficult to answer?

b. For each company, ROE > ROA. Why is that so? Look at the difference between ROE and ROA for each company. Does that difference help you determine which firm uses the highest percentage of debt to finance its activities?

P3-18 Using Tables 3.1, 3.2, and 3.3, conduct a complete ratio analysis of the Bartlett Company for the years 2018 and 2019. You should assess the firm's liquidity, activity, debt, and profitability ratios. Highlight any particularly positive or negative developments that you uncover when comparing ratios from 2018 and 2019.

P3–19 **Common-size statement analysis** A common-size income statement for Creek Enterprises' 2018 operations follows. Using the firm's 2019 income statement presented in Problem 3–16, develop the 2019 common-size income statement and compare it with the 2018 statement. Which areas require further analysis and investigation?

Creek Enterprises Common-Size Income Statement for the Year Ended December 31, 2018	
Sales revenue ($35,000,000)	100.0%
Less: Cost of goods sold	65.9
Gross profits	34.1%
Less: Operating expenses	
Selling expense	12.7%
General and administrative expenses	6.3
Lease expense	0.6
Depreciation expense	3.6
Total operating expense	23.2%
Operating profits	10.9%
Less: Interest expense	1.5
Net profits before taxes	9.4%
Less: Taxes (rate = 21%)	2.0
Net profits after taxes	7.4%
Less: Preferred stock dividends	0.1
Earnings available for common stockholders	7.3%

P3–20 **The relationship between financial leverage and profitability** Pelican Paper Inc. and Timberland Forest Inc. are rivals in the manufacture of craft papers. Some financial statement values for each company follow. Use them in a ratio analysis that compares the firms' financial leverage and profitability.

Item	Pelican Paper	Timberland Forest
Total assets	$10,000,000	$10,000,000
Total equity (all common)	9,000,000	5,000,000
Total debt	1,000,000	5,000,000
Annual interest	100,000	500,000
Total sales	25,000,000	25,000,000
EBIT	6,250,000	6,250,000
Earnings available for common stockholders	3,690,000	3,450,000

a. Calculate the following debt and coverage ratios for the two companies. Discuss their financial risk and ability to cover the costs in relation to each other.
   1. Debt ratio
   2. Times interest earned ratio

b. Calculate the following profitability ratios for the two companies. Discuss their profitability relative to one another.
   1. Operating profit margin
   2. Net profit margin
   3. Return on total assets
   4. Return on common equity

c. In what way has the larger debt of Timberland Forest made it more profitable than Pelican Paper? What are the risks that Timberland's investors undertake when they choose to purchase its stock instead of Pelican's?

P3-21 Analysis of debt ratios Financial information from fiscal year 2016 for two companies competing in the cosmetics industry—The Estée Lauder Companies and e.l.f. Beauty Inc.—appears in the table below. All dollar values are in thousands.

	Estée Lauder	e.l.f. Beauty
Total assets	$9,223,300	$414,729
Total liabilities	5,636,000	273,867
EBIT	1,625,900	26,095
Interest expense	70,700	16,283

a. Calculate the debt ratio and the times interest earned ratio for each company. In what way are these companies similar in terms of their debt usage, and in what way are they very different?

b. Calculate the ratio of interest expense to total liabilities for each company. Conceptually, what do you think this ratio is trying to measure? Why are the values of this ratio dramatically different for these two firms? Suggest some reasons.

P3–22 Ratio proficiency McDougal Printing Inc. had sales totaling $40,000,000 in fiscal year 2019. Some ratios for the company are listed below. Use this information to determine the dollar values of various income statement and balance sheet accounts as requested.

McDougal Printing Inc. Year Ended December 31, 2019	
Sales	$40,000,000
Gross profit margin	80%
Operating profit margin	35%
Net profit margin	8%
Return on total assets	16%
Return on common equity	20%
Total asset turnover	2
Average collection period	62.2 days

Calculate values for the following:

a. Gross profits

b. Cost of goods sold

c. Operating profits
d. Operating expenses
e. Earnings available for common stockholders
f. Total assets
g. Total common stock equity
h. Accounts receivable

P3–23 **Cross-sectional ratio analysis** Use the accompanying financial statements for Fox Manufacturing Company for the year ended December 31, 2019, along with the industry average ratios below, to do the following:

a. Prepare and interpret a complete ratio analysis of the firm's 2019 operations.
b. Summarize your findings and make recommendations.

Fox Manufacturing Company Income Statement for the Year Ended December 31, 2019	
Sales revenue	$600,000
Less: Cost of goods sold	460,000
Gross profits	$140,000
Less: Operating expenses	
General and administrative expenses	$ 30,000
Depreciation expense	30,000
Total operating expense	$ 60,000
Operating profits	$ 80,000
Less: Interest expense	10,000
Net profits before taxes	$ 70,000
Less: Taxes	27,100
Net profits after taxes (*Hint:* Earnings available for common stockholders as there are no preferred stockholders)	$ 42,900
Earnings per share (EPS)	$2.15

Ratio	Industry average, 2019
Current ratio	2.35
Quick ratio	0.87
Inventory turnover[a]	4.55
Average collection period[a]	35.8 days
Total asset turnover	1.09
Debt ratio	0.300
Times interest earned ratio	12.3
Gross profit margin	0.202
Operating profit margin	0.135
Net profit margin	0.091
Return on total assets (ROA)	0.099
Return on common equity (ROE)	0.167
Earnings per share (EPS)	$3.10

[a]Based on a 365-day year and on end-of-year figures.

Fox Manufacturing Company Balance Sheet December 31, 2019	
Assets	
Cash	$ 15,000
Marketable securities	7,200
Accounts receivable	34,100
Inventories	82,000
Total current assets	$138,300
Net fixed assets	270,000
Total assets	$408,300
Liabilities and Stockholders' Equity	
Accounts payable	$ 57,000
Notes payable	13,000
Accruals	5,000
Total current liabilities	$ 75,000
Long-term debt	$150,000
Common stock equity (20,000 shares outstanding)	$110,200
Retained earnings	73,100
Total stockholders' equity	$183,300
Total liabilities and stockholders' equity	$408,300

P3–24 Financial statement analysis The financial statements of Zach Industries for the year ended December 31, 2019, follow.

Zach Industries Income Statement for the Year Ended December 31, 2019	
Sales revenue	$160,000
Less: Cost of goods sold	106,000
Gross profits	$ 54,000
Less: Operating expenses	
Selling expense	$ 16,000
General and administrative expenses	10,000
Lease expense	1,000
Depreciation expense	10,000
Total operating expense	$ 37,000
Operating profits	$ 17,000
Less: Interest expense	6,100
Net profits before taxes	$ 10,900
Less: Taxes	4,360
Net profits after taxes	$ 6,540

Zach Industries Balance Sheet December 31, 2019	
Assets	
Cash	$ 500
Marketable securities	1,000
Accounts receivable	25,000
Inventories	45,500
Total current assets	$ 72,000
Land	$ 26,000
Buildings and equipment	90,000
Less: Accumulated depreciation	38,000
Net fixed assets	$ 78,000
Total assets	$150,000
Liabilities and Stockholders' Equity	
Accounts payable	$ 22,000
Notes payable	47,000
Total current liabilities	$ 69,000
Long-term debt	22,950
Common stock[a]	31,500
Retained earnings	26,550
Total liabilities and stockholders' equity	$150,000

[a]The firm's 3,000 outstanding shares of common stock closed 2019 at a price of $25 per share.

a. Use the preceding financial statements to complete the following table. Assume that the industry averages given in the table are applicable for both 2018 and 2019.

Ratio	Industry average	Actual 2018	Actual 2019
Current ratio	1.80	1.84	______
Quick ratio	0.70	0.78	______
Inventory turnover[a]	2.50	2.59	______
Average collection period[a]	37.5 days	36.5 days	______
Debt ratio	65%	67%	______
Times interest earned ratio	3.8	4.0	______
Gross profit margin	38%	40%	______
Net profit margin	3.5%	3.6%	______
Return on total assets	4.0%	4.0%	______
Return on common equity	9.5%	8.0%	______
Market/book ratio	1.1	1.2	______

[a]Based on a 365-day year and on end-of-year figures.

b. Analyze Zach Industries' financial condition as it is related to (1) liquidity, (2) activity, (3) debt, (4) profitability, and (5) market. Summarize the company's overall financial condition.

P3–25 **Integrative: Complete ratio analysis** Given the following financial statements, historical ratios, and industry averages, calculate Sterling Company's financial ratios for the most recent year. (Assume a 365-day year.)

Sterling Company Income Statement for the Year Ended December 31, 2019	
Sales revenue	$10,000,000
Less: Cost of goods sold	7,500,000
Gross profits	$ 2,500,000
Less: Operating expenses	
Selling expense	$ 300,000
General and administrative expenses	650,000
Lease expense	50,000
Depreciation expense	200,000
Total operating expense	$ 1,200,000
Operating profits	$ 1,300,000
Less: Interest expense	200,000
Net profits before taxes	$ 1,100,000
Less: Taxes (rate = 21%)	231,000
Net profits after taxes	$ 869,000
Less: Preferred stock dividends	50,000
Earnings available for common stockholders	$ 819,000
Earnings per share (EPS)	$4.10

Sterling Company Balance Sheet December 31, 2019

Assets		Liabilities and Stockholders' Equity	
Cash	$ 200,000	Accounts payable[a]	$ 900,000
Marketable securities	50,000	Notes payable	200,000
Accounts receivable	800,000	Accruals	100,000
Inventories	950,000	Total current liabilities	$ 1,200,000
Total current assets	$ 2,000,000	Long-term debt (includes financial leases)	$ 3,000,000
Gross fixed assets (at cost)	$12,000,000		
Less: Accumulated depreciation	3,000,000	Preferred stock (25,000 shares, $2 dividend)	$ 1,000,000
Net fixed assets	$ 9,000,000		
Other assets	1,000,000	Common stock (200,000 shares at $3 par)[b]	600,000
Total assets	$12,000,000	Paid-in capital in excess of par value	5,200,000
		Retained earnings	1,000,000
		Total stockholders' equity	$ 7,800,000
		Total liabilities and stockholders' equity	$12,000,000

[a]Annual credit purchases of $6,200,000 were made during the year.

[b]On December 31, 2019, the firm's common stock closed at $39.50 per share.

Analyze its overall financial situation from both a cross-sectional and a time-series viewpoint. Break your analysis into evaluations of the firm's liquidity, activity, debt, profitability, and market.

Historical and Industry Average Ratios for Sterling Company			
Ratio	**Actual 2017**	**Actual 2018**	**Industry average, 2019**
Current ratio	1.40	1.55	1.85
Quick ratio	1.00	0.92	1.05
Inventory turnover	9.52	9.21	8.60
Average collection period	45.6 days	36.9 days	35.5 days
Average payment period	59.3 days	61.6 days	46.4 days
Total asset turnover	0.74	0.80	0.74
Debt ratio	0.20	0.20	0.30
Times interest earned ratio	8.2	7.3	8.0
Fixed-payment coverage ratio	4.5	4.2	4.2
Gross profit margin	0.30	0.27	0.25
Operating profit margin	0.12	0.12	0.10
Net profit margin	0.062	0.062	0.053
Return on total assets (ROA)	0.045	0.050	0.040
Return on common equity (ROE)	0.061	0.067	0.066
Earnings per share (EPS)	$1.75	$2.20	$1.50
Price/earnings (P/E) ratio	12.0	10.5	11.2
Market/book (M/B) ratio	1.20	1.05	1.10

LG 6

P3–26 DuPont system of analysis Use the following 2016 financial information for ATT and Verizon to conduct a DuPont system of analysis for each company.

	ATT	Verizon
Sales	$163,786	$125,980
Earnings available for common stockholders	13,333	13,608
Total assets	403,821	244,180
Stockholders' equity	124,110	24,032

a. Which company has the higher net profit margin? Higher asset turnover?
b. Which company has the higher ROA? The higher ROE?

LG 6

P3–27 Complete ratio analysis, recognizing significant differences Home Health Inc. has come to Jane Ross for a yearly financial checkup. As a first step, Jane has prepared a complete set of ratios for fiscal years 2018 and 2019. She will use them to look for significant changes in the company's situation from one year to the next.

Home Health Inc. Financial Ratios		
Ratio	**2018**	**2019**
Current ratio	3.25	3.00
Quick ratio	2.50	2.20
Inventory turnover	12.80	10.30
Average collection period	42.6 days	31.4 days
Total asset turnover	1.40	2.00
Debt ratio	0.45	0.62
Times interest earned ratio	4.00	3.85
Gross profit margin	68%	65%
Operating profit margin	14%	16%

Home Health Inc. Financial Ratios (Continued)		
Ratio	2018	2019
Net profit margin	8.3%	8.1%
Return on total assets	11.6%	16.2%
Return on common equity	21.1%	42.6%
Price/earnings ratio	10.7	9.8
Market/book ratio	1.40	1.25

a. To focus on the degree of change, calculate the year-to-year proportional change by subtracting the year 2018 ratio from the year 2019 ratio and then dividing the difference by the year 2018 ratio. Multiply the result by 100. Preserve the positive or negative sign. The result is the percentage change in the ratio from 2018 to 2019. Calculate the proportional change for the ratios shown here.

b. For any ratio that shows a year-to-year difference of 10% or more, state whether the difference is in the company's favor or not.

c. For the most significant changes (25% or more), look at the other ratios and cite at least one other change that may have contributed to the change in the ratio you are discussing.

P3–28 **ETHICS PROBLEM** Do some reading in periodicals or on the Internet to find out more about the Sarbanes-Oxley Act's provisions for companies. Select one of those provisions, and indicate why you think financial statements will be more trustworthy if company financial executives implement this provision of SOX.

SPREADSHEET EXERCISE

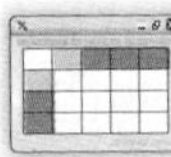

The income statement and balance sheet are the primary reports that a firm constructs for use by management and for distribution to stockholders, regulatory bodies, and the general public. They are the primary sources of historical financial information about the firm. Dayton Products Inc. is a moderate-sized manufacturer. The company's management has asked you to perform a detailed financial statement analysis of the firm.

The income statements for the years ending December 31, 2019 and 2018, respectively, are presented in the following table.

Annual Income Statements (Values in Millions)		
	For the year ended	
	December 31, 2019	December 31, 2018
Sales	$178,909	$187,510
Cost of goods sold	109,701	111,631
Selling, general, and administrative expenses	12,356	12,900
Other tax expense	33,572	33,377
Depreciation and amortization	12,103	7,944
Other income (add to EBIT to arrive at EBT)	3,147	3,323
Interest expense	398	293
Income tax rate	21%	21%
Dividends paid per share	$1.15	$0.91
Basic EPS from total operations	$1.64	$2.87

You also have the following balance sheet information as of December 31, 2019 and 2018, respectively.

Annual Balance Sheets (Values in Millions)		
	December 31, 2019	December 31, 2018
Cash	$ 9,090	$ 6,547
Receivables	21,163	19,549
Inventories	8,068	7,904
Other current assets	1,831	1,681
Property, plant, and equipment, gross	204,960	187,519
Accumulated depreciation and depletion	110,020	97,917
Other noncurrent assets	19,413	17,891
Accounts payable	13,792	22,862
Short-term debt payable	4,093	3,703
Other current liabilities	15,290	3,549
Long-term debt payable	6,655	7,099
Deferred income taxes	16,484	16,359
Other noncurrent liabilities	21,733	16,441
Retained earnings	76,458	73,161
Total common shares outstanding	6.7 billion	6.8 billion

TO DO

a. Create a spreadsheet similar to Table 3.1 to model the following:
   (1) A multiple-step comparative income statement for Dayton Inc. for the periods ending December 31, 2019 and 2018. You must calculate the cost of goods sold for the year 2019.
   (2) A common-size income statement for Dayton Inc. covering the years 2019 and 2018.

b. Create a spreadsheet similar to Table 3.2 to model the following:
   (1) A detailed, comparative balance sheet for Dayton Inc. for the years ended December 31, 2019 and 2018.
   (2) A common-size balance sheet for Dayton Inc. covering the years 2019 and 2018.

c. Create a spreadsheet similar to Table 3.10 to perform the following analysis:
   (1) Create a table that reflects both 2019 and 2018 operating ratios for Dayton Inc., segmented into (a) liquidity, (b) activity, (c) debt, (d) profitability, and (e) market. Assume that the current market price for the stock is $90.
   (2) Compare the 2019 ratios to the 2018 ratios. Indicate whether the results "outperformed the prior year" or "underperformed relative to the prior year."

MyLab Finance Visit www.pearson.com/mylab/finance for **Chapter Case: *Assessing Martin Manufacturing's Current Financial Position,*** Group Exercises, and numerous online resources.

CHAPTER 4

Long- and Short-Term Financial Planning

LEARNING GOALS

LG 1 Understand the financial planning process, including long-term (strategic) financial plans and short-term (operating) financial plans.

LG 2 Understand tax depreciation procedures and the effect of depreciation on the firm's cash flows.

LG 3 Discuss the firm's statement of cash flows, operating cash flow, and free cash flow.

LG 4 Discuss the cash-planning process and the preparation, evaluation, and use of the cash budget.

LG 5 Explain the procedures used to prepare and evaluate the pro forma income statement and the pro forma balance sheet.

LG 6 Evaluate the approaches to pro forma financial statement preparation and the common uses of pro forma statements.

MyLab Finance Chapter Introduction Video

WHY THIS CHAPTER MATTERS TO YOU

In your *professional* life

ACCOUNTING You need to understand how depreciation is used for both tax and financial reporting purposes; how to develop the statement of cash flows; the primary focus on cash flows, rather than accruals, in financial decision making; and how pro forma financial statements are used within the firm.

INFORMATION SYSTEMS You need to understand the data that must be kept to record depreciation for tax and financial reporting, the information required for strategic and operating plans, and what data are necessary as inputs for preparing cash plans and profit plans.

MANAGEMENT You need to understand the difference between strategic and operating plans, and the role of each; the importance of focusing on the firm's cash flows; and how use of pro forma statements can head off trouble for the firm.

MARKETING You need to understand the central role that marketing plays in formulating the firm's long-term strategic plans and the importance of the sales forecast as the key input for both cash planning and profit planning.

OPERATIONS You need to understand how depreciation affects the value of the firm's plant assets, how the results of operations are captured in the statement of cash flows, that operations provide key inputs into the firm's short-term financial plans, and the distinction between fixed and variable operating costs.

In your *personal* life

Individuals, like corporations, should focus on cash flow when planning and monitoring finances. You should establish short- and long-term financial goals (destinations) and develop personal financial plans (road maps) that will guide their achievement. Cash flows and financial plans are as important for individuals as for corporations.

NETFLIX INC.

Not Streaming at Netflix—Cash Flow

360b/Alamy Stock Photo

On January 18, 2017, Netflix announced that it had made a profit of almost $187 million the previous year and added nearly 2 million new subscribers. Those numbers exceeded Wall Street analysts' expectations, and Netflix stock jumped more than 8% on the news. On the basis of that information, you might think that Netflix was bringing in cash faster than it streamed movies. In reality, the company reported that it spent almost $1.5 billion more cash on its operations than it brought in during 2016. How is it possible for a company to report a large profit when it is generating negative cash flow from operations? In the case of Netflix, the company was investing heavily in new licenses and other agreements with movie studios and television broadcasters that would allow it to stream content that its subscribers would want to see for years to come. The costs of those agreements do not immediately show up as an expense on the Netflix income statement, which means that the company's earnings appear much greater than its true cash flows.

A company can't survive for long if it is generating massive cash outflows. If that's true, how did Netflix stay afloat in 2016, and why were investors in the stock market so thrilled by the company's financial disclosures? Netflix survived, and even thrived, in 2016 largely due to two actions. First, it drew down its reserves of cash and marketable securities by about $0.5 billion. Second, it managed to persuade lenders to provide roughly $1 billion in new loans that year. Those two sources provided Netflix with enough cash to continue investing heavily in new content agreements with companies like Disney, and investors believed that those agreements, along with the rapidly expanding user base, would eventually allow Netflix to do something even more important than earn profit—generate positive cash flow.

The situation at Netflix is not particularly uncommon. Even when a firm is reporting positive earnings, its cash flow picture may be quite different. When a firm is expanding, as Netflix has been for several years, it may have to make additional investments in inventory, receivables, and other assets. Cash outlays for those investments do not necessarily show up immediately in the profit calculation, but they do reduce *free cash flow,* a performance measure that financial analysts watch closely. Cash flow is the primary driver of a firm's value, and firms must have cash, not earnings, to pay their bills. After reading this chapter, you'll understand the differences between cash flow and profit, and you'll see why companies must plan carefully to have the cash needed for survival in the short run so they can generate value for their stockholders in the long run.

LG 1 4.1 The Financial Planning Process

Financial planning is an important aspect of the firm's operations because it provides road maps for guiding, coordinating, and controlling actions to achieve the firm's objective of creating value for shareholders. The financial planning process is highly collaborative across functions because the inputs required to build a financial plan come from every part of the firm. Two key aspects of the financial planning process are *cash planning* and *profit planning.* Cash planning involves preparation of the firm's cash budget, a tool that managers use to ensure they put excess cash to work or have outside financing lined up when the firm is not generating enough internal cash to cover expenses. Profit planning involves preparation of pro forma statements, which project what a firm's balance sheet and income statement will look like in future years. Both the cash budget and the pro forma statements are useful for internal financial planning, and sometimes lenders want to see a firm's financial projections before they approve loans.

financial planning process
Planning that begins with long-term, or strategic, financial plans that in turn guide the formulation of short-term, or operating, plans and budgets.

The **financial planning process** begins with long-term, or *strategic,* financial plans. These plans, in turn, guide the formulation of short-term, or *operating,* plans and budgets. Generally, the short-term plans and budgets implement the firm's long-term strategic objectives. Although the remainder of this chapter places primary emphasis on short-term financial plans and budgets, a few preliminary comments on long-term financial plans are in order.

LONG-TERM (STRATEGIC) FINANCIAL PLANS

long-term (strategic) financial plans
Plans that lay out a company's financial actions and the anticipated impact of those actions over periods ranging from 2 to 10 years.

Long-term (strategic) financial plans lay out a company's financial actions and the anticipated effect of those actions over periods ranging from 2 to 10 years. These plans reflect the company's strategies for how it will compete in its markets to create value for shareholders. Integrated across functional areas, the plans require input from all areas of the firm, including research and development, marketing, operations, human resources, accounting, and, of course, finance. The plans specify the magnitude and timing of major investments the firm must make (as well as former investments the firm will abandon), and they forecast when and how those investments will pay off. Long-term financial plans describe how a firm will develop and execute marketing plans to promote its products and services, and these plans make projections for how many employees the firm will need to achieve its goals. Many firms adopt a 5-year strategic planning process in which managers revise the 5-year plan at least annually as significant new information becomes available. Firms subject to high degrees of operating uncertainty, relatively short production cycles, or both, tend to use shorter planning horizons.

From a financial perspective, long-term plans have two main objectives. First, long-term plans describe how a firm will build value for shareholders by creating new products and services that customers want. Second, long-term plans help managers determine whether they will need to raise additional external capital by selling stock or borrowing money, or whether the firm will generate sufficient cash flow to retire debt, pay dividends, or repurchase shares. In other words, long-term plans influence both of the main types of decisions that financial managers face: investment decisions and financing decisions. A series of annual budgets support the long-term plans by providing intermediate goals for managers.

SHORT-TERM (OPERATING) FINANCIAL PLANS

short-term (operating) financial plans
Plans that specify short-term financial actions and the anticipated impact of those actions.

Short-term (operating) financial plans specify short-term financial actions and the anticipated effect of those actions. These plans most often cover a 1- to 2-year period. Key inputs include the sales forecast and various forms of operating and financial data. Key outputs include a number of operating budgets, the cash budget, and pro forma financial statements. The entire short-term financial planning process is outlined in Figure 4.1. Here we focus solely on cash and profit planning from the financial manager's perspective.

Short-term financial planning begins with the sales forecast. From that forecast, companies develop production plans that take into account lead (preparation) times and include estimates of the resources required to achieve the sales forecast, such as raw materials for manufacturing firms or new personnel for services firms. Once managers estimate the costs of acquiring and deploying those resources, the firm can prepare a pro forma income statement and cash budget. With these basic inputs, the firm can finally develop a pro forma balance sheet.

PERSONAL FINANCE EXAMPLE 4.1 The first step in personal financial planning requires you to define your goals. Whereas in a corporation the goal is to maximize shareholder wealth, individuals typically have several different financial goals. These might have short-, medium-, or long-term horizons, and they depend on your age, income, family status, and other factors.

Set your personal financial goals carefully and realistically. Each goal should be clearly defined and have a priority, time frame, and cost estimate. For example, a college senior's intermediate-term goal in 2019 might include earning a master's degree at a cost of $60,000 by 2021, and his or her long-term goal might be to buy a condominium at a cost of $250,000 by 2025.

Throughout the remainder of this chapter, we will concentrate on the key outputs of the short-term financial planning process: the cash budget, the pro

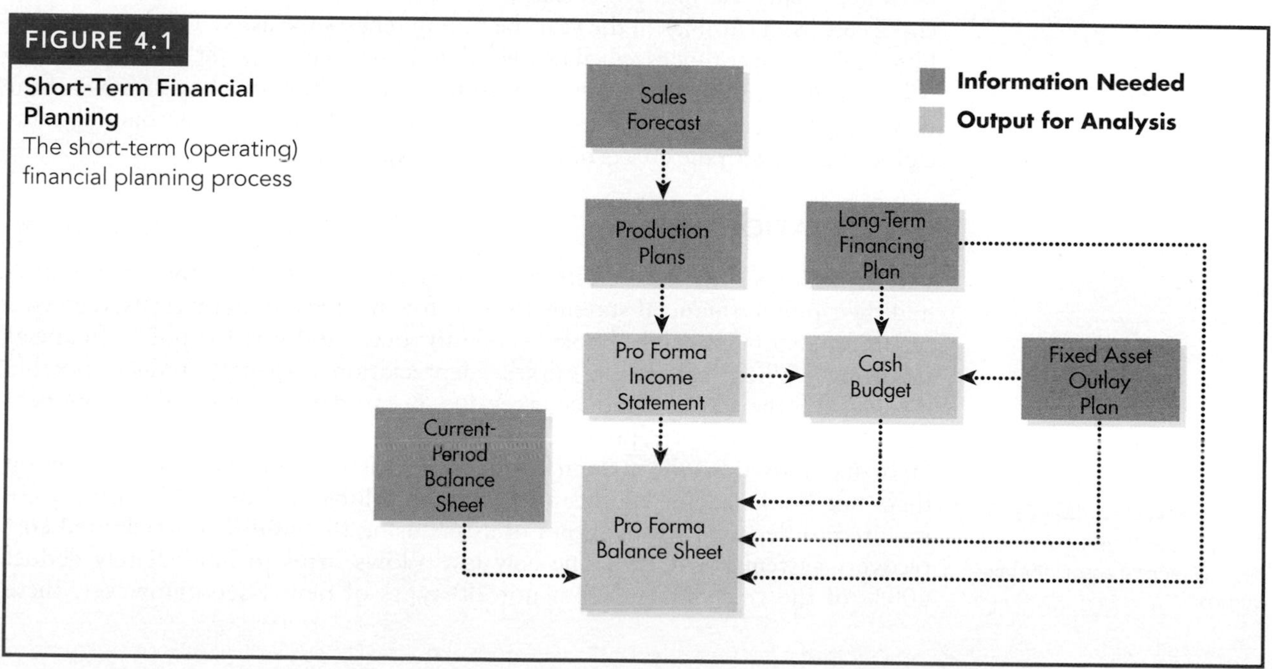

FIGURE 4.1
Short-Term Financial Planning
The short-term (operating) financial planning process

forma income statement, and the pro forma balance sheet. First, however, we turn our attention to the subject of cash flow, focusing on why cash flow differs from profit and on different cash flow measures that may be important to managers and investors.

→ **REVIEW QUESTIONS** MyLab Finance Solutions

4–1 What is the financial planning process? Contrast long-term (strategic) financial plans with short-term (operating) financial plans.

4–2 Which three statements result as part of the short-term (operating) financial planning process?

LG2 LG3

4.2 Measuring the Firm's Cash Flow

"Cash is king" is an old saying in finance. Cash flow is the primary ingredient in any financial valuation model. If an analyst wants to put a value on an investment that a firm is considering, estimating cash flow is central to the valuation process. This chapter explains where the cash flow numbers used in valuations come from.

Though a company's earnings deservedly receive much attention from outside investors, earnings and cash flows are not equal. When companies calculate their earnings, they do so using accrual-based generally accepted accounting principles (GAAP), and those principles are designed to achieve objectives other than simply reporting cash inflows and outflows. For example, if a company pays cash today for an asset that it will use for many years, like a piece of equipment, GAAP does not permit firms to deduct the entire cost of that asset as an expense against earnings in the current year. Rather, firms must spread out the cost of the asset over several years, recognizing that the asset's useful life is more than 1 year. Accounting principles reflect the view that charging smaller expenses over an asset's useful life more fairly represents the firm's financial performance than does deducting an asset's entire cost from earnings in the year the firm purchases the asset. This allocation of historical cost over time is called **depreciation.** In finance, we want to know exactly when a firm spends and receives cash, so to calculate how much cash flow a firm generates, financial analysts must "unwind" some of the effects of accounting principles, starting with the effects of depreciation expenses.

depreciation
A portion of the costs of fixed assets charged against annual revenues over time.

DEPRECIATION

U.S. law allows firms to use different depreciation methods in their tax returns and their public financial statements, and for this reason many firms keep two separate sets of financial "books"—one for taxes and one for public financial reporting. When calculating taxes, depreciation expenses reduce taxable income, and thereby also reduce taxes due. Because of the time value of money, firms would rather save taxes today than save taxes tomorrow, so businesses favor methods that allow them to depreciate assets as rapidly as possible on their tax books. Prior to the Tax Cuts and Jobs Act of 2017, firms were required to depreciate most types of assets using the **modified accelerated cost recovery system (MACRS)**. The new law allows firms to immediately deduct 100% of the cost of many (but not all) types of new assets. However, these

modified accelerated cost recovery system (MACRS)
System used to determine the depreciation of assets for tax purposes.

"bonus depreciation" deductions will be phased out gradually over several years without further Congressional action. For financial reporting purposes, firms can choose from several different methods for calculating depreciation expenses. All of those methods use a formula that relies on an asset's depreciable value and its depreciable life.

Depreciable Value of an Asset

Under the MACRS procedures and the new law, the depreciable value of an asset (the amount to be depreciated) is its full cost, including outlays for installation. Even if the asset will have some salvage value at the end of its useful life, the firm can still take depreciation deductions equal to the asset's full initial cost.

EXAMPLE 4.2

MyLab Finance Solution Video

Baker Corporation acquired a new machine at a cost of $38,000, with installation costs of $2,000. When the machine is retired from service, Baker expects to sell it for scrap metal and receive $1,000. Regardless of its expected salvage value, the depreciable value of the machine is $40,000: $38,000 cost + $2,000 installation cost.

Depreciable Life of an Asset

depreciable life
Time period over which an asset is depreciated.

The period over which an asset is depreciated is called its **depreciable life.** For any particular asset, the shorter the depreciable life, the larger the annual depreciation deductions will be, and the larger will be the tax savings associated with those deductions, all other things being equal. Accordingly, the Tax Cuts and Jobs Act of 2017 makes investments in many types of new assets more attractive by accelerating the depreciation deductions (and hence the tax savings) associated with those investments. The new law allows firms to depreciate 100% of an asset's cost in the year it is purchased, though some types of assets are not eligible for this bonus depreciation.

MACRS recovery period
The appropriate depreciable life of a particular asset as determined by MACRS.

Because firms must still gradually depreciate the cost of some assets, and because the MACRS provisions will once again be the norm for most assets in a few years, we describe the basic MACRS system here. There are six **MACRS recovery periods**—3, 5, 7, 10, 15, and 20 years—with longer recovery periods for some types of property investments. Corresponding to each of these recovery periods is a property class that includes specific assets defined by the tax law. For instance, under MACRS, office furniture, such as desks and filing cabinets, falls into the 7-year recovery period class. Table 4.1 lists some of the assets in each of the first four property classes.

DEPRECIATION METHODS

For financial reporting purposes, companies can use a variety of depreciation methods (straight-line, double declining balance, and sum-of-the-years'-digits). For tax purposes, when using MACRS, firms usually depreciate assets in the first four MACRS property classes by the double-declining balance method, using a half-year convention (meaning that a half-year's depreciation is taken in the year the asset is purchased) and switching to straight-line when advantageous. Table 4.2

TABLE 4.1 First Four Property Classes under MACRS

Property class (recovery period)	Definition
3 years	Research equipment and certain special tools
5 years	Computers, printers, copiers, duplicating equipment, cars, light-duty trucks, qualified technological equipment, and similar assets
7 years	Office furniture, fixtures, most manufacturing equipment, railroad track, and single-purpose agricultural and horticultural structures
10 years	Equipment used in petroleum refining or in the manufacture of tobacco products and certain food products

TABLE 4.2 Rounded Depreciation Percentages by Recovery Year Using MACRS for First Four Property Classes

	Percentage by recovery year[a]			
Recovery year	3 years	5 years	7 years	10 years
1	33%	20%	14%	10%
2	45	32	25	18
3	15	19	18	14
4	7	12	12	12
5		12	9	9
6		5	9	8
7			9	7
8			4	6
9				6
10				6
11				4
Totals	100%	100%	100%	100%

[a]These percentages have been rounded to the nearest whole percent.

shows the approximate percentages (rounded to the nearest whole percent) written off each year for the first four property classes.

For assets depreciated under MACRS, the half-year convention assumes that, on average, firms acquire assets in the middle of the year, so the allowable depreciation deduction in the first year is smaller than it would be if firms could take a full year's worth of depreciation in the year they purchase an asset. Because firms can take only a half-year's worth of depreciation in the first year, they can take an extra half-year in the year after the asset's useful life officially ends. To illustrate, observe that in Table 4.2 an asset falling in the 3-year recovery class is depreciated over 4 years, an asset in the 5-year recovery class is depreciated over 6 years, and so on. The first and last year's depreciation charges represent a half-year's worth of depreciation.

EXAMPLE 4.3

Baker Corporation acquired, for an installed cost of $40,000, a machine having a recovery period of 5 years. Using the applicable percentages from Table 4.2, Baker calculates the depreciation in each year as follows:

Year	Cost	Percentages (from Table 4.2)	Depreciation
1	$40,000	20%	$40,000 × 20% = $ 8,000
2	40,000	32	$40,000 × 32% = $12,800
3	40,000	19	$40,000 × 19% = $ 7,600
4	40,000	12	$40,000 × 12% = $ 4,800
5	40,000	12	$40,000 × 12% = $ 4,800
6	40,000	5	$40,000 × 5% = $ 2,000
Totals		100%	$40,000

Column 3 shows that the full cost of the asset is written off over 6 recovery years.

DEVELOPING THE STATEMENT OF CASH FLOWS

The statement of cash flows, introduced in Chapter 3, summarizes the firm's cash flow over a given period. Keep in mind that analysts typically lump cash and marketable securities together when assessing the firm's liquidity because both cash and marketable securities represent a reservoir of liquidity. That reservoir is increased by cash inflows and decreased by cash outflows.

Notice how the three sections of the statement of cash flows reflect the three fundamental functions of firms. Firms take in money from investors, they invest that money in risky assets, and they operate those assets to generate cash flows for a return to investors. Accordingly, the statement of cash flows shows that a firm's cash flows fall into three categories: (1) cash flow from operating activities, (2) cash flow from investment activities, and (3) cash flow from financing activities. **Cash flow from operating activities** includes the cash inflows and outflows directly related to the sale and production of the firm's products and services. **Cash flow from investment activities** includes the cash flows associated with the purchase and sale of both fixed assets and equity investments in other firms. Clearly, purchase transactions would result in cash outflows, whereas sales transactions would generate cash inflows. **Cash flow from financing activities** results from debt and equity financing transactions. Borrowing on either a short-term or long-term basis would result in a corresponding cash inflow; repaying debt would result in an outflow. Similarly, the sale of the company's stock would result in a cash inflow; the repurchase of stock or payment of cash dividends would result in an outflow.

cash flow from operating activities
Cash flows directly related to sale and production of the firm's products and services.

cash flow from investment activities
Cash flows associated with purchase and sale of both fixed assets and equity investments in other firms.

cash flow from financing activities
Cash flows that result from debt and equity financing transactions; includes incurrence and repayment of debt, cash inflows from the sale of stock, and cash outflows to repurchase stock or pay cash dividends.

Classifying Inflows and Outflows of Cash

The statement of cash flows groups the inflows and outflows of cash into these three categories and summarizes the firm's overall cash position. The information required to construct the statement of cash flows comes from the income statement and the balance sheet. But which items on those statements represent cash inflows and which represent outflows? In some cases, the answers are quite intuitive. When a firm earns positive net income, for example, that counts as a cash inflow. Perhaps less intuitively, when a firm's income statement shows a deduction for depreciation expense, that too is a cash inflow. Remember that depreciation expense is just an accounting entry designed to smooth out the reported cost of an asset over time. When a firm deducts depreciation on its income statement, there is no cash outlay directly tied to that deduction. That fact alone would mean that the firm's net income is less than its cash flow, so we add depreciation expense back to net income to get a clearer picture of the cash flow a company earns.

Similarly, changes in accounts on a firm's balance sheet reflect inflows and outflows of cash. In general, increases in asset accounts on the balance sheet are associated with cash outflows tied to investments that a firm has made in new assets. If we see that a firm reports higher fixed assets from one year to the next, that means cash outflow is tied to the acquisition of those new assets. The same is true if current assets such as inventory and receivables increase on the balance sheet. In contrast, decreases in asset balances point toward cash inflows. If this year's balance sheet shows lower gross fixed asset balances, then the firm generated cash by selling fixed assets. If inventory or receivables balances are lower this year, the firm generated cash by selling inventories or collecting accounts receivable.

Conversely, increases in items on the right-hand side of the balance sheet (i.e., liabilities and equity) reflect cash inflows. If a firm borrows more, it receives a cash inflow and the value of debt on the balance sheet increases. If a firm sells more stock, it receives a cash inflow and the value of common stock equity on the balance sheet increases. The opposite is true when liabilities and equity accounts fall. A reduction in debts signals that a firm spent cash paying back money that it previously borrowed. A reduction in common stock equity suggests that the firm repurchased outstanding shares of stock. Table 4.3 classifies the basic inflows (sources) and outflows (uses) of cash.

We can make a few additional points about the classification scheme in Table 4.3:

1. A *decrease* in an asset, such as the firm's cash balance, is an *inflow of cash.* Why? It is because cash that has been tied up in the asset is released and can be used for some other purpose, such as repaying a loan. In contrast, an *increase* in the firm's cash balance is an *outflow of cash* because additional cash is being tied up in the firm's cash balance.

   The classification of decreases and increases in a firm's cash balance is difficult for many to grasp. To clarify, imagine that you store all your cash in a bucket. Your cash balance is represented by the amount of cash in the bucket. When you need cash, you withdraw it from the bucket, which decreases your cash balance and provides an inflow of cash to you. Conversely, when you have excess cash, you deposit it in the bucket, which

MATTER OF FACT

Apple's Cash Flows

In its 2016 annual report, Apple reported more than $65 billion in cash from its operating activities. It used much of that cash flow on investment activities, spending roughly $31 billion to increase its holdings of marketable securities (i.e., to build up cash reserves). With plans to open a new headquarters building the next year, Apple spent almost $13 billion to acquire new property, plant, and equipment. By contrast, the cash flow from financing activities was relatively minor. The company spent almost $30 billion on share repurchases in 2016, but that was largely offset by the $22 billion Apple raised by issuing new debt.

TABLE 4.3 Inflows and Outflows of Cash

Inflows (sources)	Outflows (uses)
Decrease in any asset	Increase in any asset
Increase in any liability	Decrease in any liability
Net profits after taxes	Net loss after taxes
Depreciation and other noncash charges	Dividends paid
Sale of stock	Repurchase or retirement of stock

increases your cash balance and represents an outflow of cash from you. Focus on the movement of funds in and out of your pocket. A decrease in cash (from the bucket) is an inflow (to your pocket); an increase in cash (in the bucket) is an outflow (from your pocket).

noncash charge
An expense that is deducted on the income statement but does not involve the actual outlay of cash during the period; includes depreciation, amortization, and depletion.

2. Depreciation (like amortization and depletion) is an example of a **noncash charge**, an expense that is deducted on the income statement but does not involve an actual outlay of cash. Therefore, when measuring the amount of cash flow generated by a firm, we have to add depreciation and any other noncash expenses back to net income; if we don't, we will understate the cash truly generated by the firm. For this reason, depreciation appears as a source of cash in Table 4.3.
3. Because depreciation is treated as a separate cash inflow, only changes in gross rather than net fixed assets appear on the statement of cash flows. The change in net fixed assets is equal to the change in gross fixed assets minus the depreciation charge. Therefore, if we treated depreciation as a cash inflow as well as the reduction in net (rather than gross) fixed assets, we would be double counting depreciation.
4. Direct entries of changes in retained earnings are not included on the statement of cash flows. Instead, entries for items that affect retained earnings appear as net profits or losses after taxes and dividends are paid.

Preparing the Statement of Cash Flows

The statement of cash flows uses data from the income statement, along with the beginning- and end-of-period balance sheets. Tables 4.4 and 4.5 show the income statement for the year ended December 31, 2019 and the December 31 balance

TABLE 4.4 Baker Corporation 2019 Income Statement ($000)

Sales revenue	$1,700
Less: Cost of goods sold	1,000
Gross profits	$ 700
Less: Operating expenses	
Selling, general, and administrative expense	$ 230
Depreciation expense	100
Total operating expense	$ 330
Earnings before interest and taxes (EBIT)	$ 370
Less: Interest expense	70
Net profits before taxes	$ 300
Less: Taxes (rate = 21%)	63
Net profits after taxes	$ 237
Less: Preferred stock dividends	10
Earnings available for common stockholders	$ 227
Earnings per share (EPS)[a]	$ 2.27
Common stock dividends per share (DPS)[b]	$ 0.70

[a]Calculated by dividing the earnings available for common stockholders by the number of shares of common stock outstanding ($170,000 ÷ 100,000 shares = $1.70 per share).

[b]The firm's board decided to pay $70,000 in dividends to common shareholders, so dividends per share are $0.70 ($70,000 ÷ 100,000 shares = $0.70 per share).

TABLE 4.5 Baker Corporation Balance Sheets ($000)

	December 31	
Assets	**2019**	**2018**
Cash and marketable securities	$1,057	$ 500
Accounts receivable	400	500
Inventories	600	900
Total current assets	$2,000	$1,900
Land and buildings	$1,200	$1,050
Machinery and equipment, furniture and fixtures, vehicles, and other	1,300	1,150
Total gross fixed assets (at cost)	$2,500	$2,200
Less: Accumulated depreciation	1,300	1,200
Net fixed assets	$1,200	$1,000
Total assets	$3,257	$2,900
Liabilities and stockholders' equity		
Accounts payable	$ 700	$ 500
Notes payable	600	700
Accruals	100	200
Total current liabilities	$1,400	$1,400
Long-term debt	600	400
Total liabilities	$2,000	$1,800
Preferred stock	$ 100	$ 100
Common stock: $1.20 par, 100,000 shares outstanding in 2019 and 2018	120	120
Paid-in capital in excess of par on common stock	380	380
Retained earnings	657	500
Total stockholders' equity	$1,257	$1,100
Total liabilities and stockholders' equity	$3,257	$2,900

sheets for 2018 and 2019 for Baker Corporation. Table 4.6 presents the statement of cash flows for the year ended December 31, 2019, for Baker Corporation. Note that all cash inflows as well as net profits after taxes and depreciation are treated as positive values. All cash outflows, any losses, and dividends paid are treated as negative values. The items in each category—operating, investment, and financing—are totaled, and the three totals are added to get the "Net increase (decrease) in cash and marketable securities" for the period. As a check, this value should reconcile with the actual change in cash and marketable securities for the year, which is obtained from the beginning- and end-of-period balance sheets.

Interpreting the Statement

The statement of cash flows allows the financial manager and other interested parties to analyze the firm's cash flow. The manager should pay special attention both to the major categories of cash flow and to the individual items of cash inflow and outflow, to look for any developments that are contrary to the company's financial policies. In addition, analysts can use the statement to evaluate progress toward projected goals or to isolate inefficiencies. The financial manager

TABLE 4.6 **Baker Corporation Statement of Cash Flows ($000) for the Year Ended December 31, 2019**

Cash flow from operating activities	
Net profits after taxes	$237
Depreciation	100
Decrease in accounts receivable	100
Decrease in inventories	300
Increase in accounts payable	200
Decrease in accruals	−100
Cash provided by operating activities	$837
Cash flow from investment activities	
Increase in gross fixed assets	−$300
Changes in equity investments in other firms	0
Cash provided by investment activities	−$300
Cash flow from financing activities	
Decrease in notes payable	−$100
Increase in long-term debt	200
Changes in stockholders' equity[a]	0
Dividends paid (common and preferred)	−80
Cash provided by financing activities	$ 20
Net increase in cash and marketable securities	$557

[a]Retained earnings are excluded here because their change is actually reflected in the combination of the "Net profits after taxes" and "Dividends paid" entries.

also can prepare a statement of cash flows developed from projected financial statements to determine whether planned actions are desirable in view of the resulting cash flows.

operating cash flow (OCF)
The cash flow a firm generates from its normal operations; calculated as net operating profits after taxes (NOPAT) plus depreciation.

net operating profits after taxes (NOPAT)
A firm's earnings before interest and after taxes, EBIT × (1 − *T*).

Operating Cash Flow A firm generates its **operating cash flow (OCF)** from its normal operations: producing and selling its output of goods or services. Various definitions of OCF appear in the financial literature. The definition introduced here excludes interest expense. We exclude interest expense because we want a measure that captures the cash flow generated by the firm's operations, not by how those operations are financed. The first step is to calculate **net operating profits after taxes (NOPAT)**, which represent the firm's earnings before interest and after taxes. Letting T equal the applicable corporate tax rate, we calculate NOPAT as

$$\text{NOPAT} = \text{EBIT} \times (1 - T) \tag{4.1}$$

To convert NOPAT to operating cash flow (OCF), we merely add back depreciation:

$$\text{OCF} = \text{NOPAT} + \text{Depreciation} \tag{4.2}$$

We can substitute the expression for NOPAT from Equation 4.1 into Equation 4.2 to get a single equation for OCF:

$$OCF = [EBIT \times (1 - T)] + \text{Depreciation} \quad (4.3)$$

EXAMPLE 4.4

MyLab Finance Solution Video

Substituting the values for Baker Corporation from its income statement (Table 4.4) into Equation 4.3, we get

$$OCF = [\$370 \times (1.00 - 0.21)] + \$100 = \$292.3 + \$100 = \$392.3$$

During 2019, Baker Corporation generated \$392,300 of cash flow from producing and selling its output. Therefore, we can conclude that Baker's operations are generating positive cash flows.

FREE CASH FLOW

free cash flow (FCF)
The amount of cash flow available to investors (creditors and owners) after the firm has met all operating needs and paid for investments in net fixed assets and net current assets.

The firm's **free cash flow (FCF)** represents the cash available to investors—the providers of debt (creditors) and equity (owners)—after the firm has met all operating needs and paid for net investments in fixed assets and current assets. Conceptually, free cash flow is the cash flow that firms can distribute to investors, but as the *Focus on Ethics* box explains, sometimes an unexpected flood of free cash flows tempts managers to waste those funds rather than putting them in investors' hands.

Free cash flow can be defined as

$$\begin{aligned} FCF = OCF &- \text{Net fixed asset investment (NFAI)} \\ &- \text{Net current asset investment (NCAI)} \end{aligned} \quad (4.4)$$

The *net fixed asset investment (NFAI)* is the net investment the firm makes in fixed assets and refers to purchases minus sales of fixed assets. You can calculate the NFAI using

$$NFAI = \text{Change in net fixed assets} + \text{Depreciation} \quad (4.5)$$

The NFAI is also equal to the change in gross fixed assets from one year to the next.

EXAMPLE 4.5

Using the Baker Corporation's balance sheets in Table 4.5, we see that its change in net fixed assets between 2018 and 2019 was \$200 (\$1,200 in 2019 – \$1,000 in 2018). Substituting this value and the \$100 of depreciation for 2019 into Equation 4.5, we get Baker's net fixed asset investment (NFAI) for 2019:

$$NFAI = \$200 + \$100 = \$300$$

Baker Corporation therefore invested a net \$300,000 in fixed assets during 2019. This amount would, of course, represent a cash outflow to acquire fixed assets during 2019.

FOCUS ON ETHICS *in practice*

Is Excess Cash Always a Good Thing?

In Shakespeare's *As You Like It*, Rosalind—the lovesick heroine—wonders, "Can one desire too much of a good thing?" By "thing," she specifically meant love, but the implied answer has transformed the question into a common expression—you can't get enough of a good thing. As the chapter notes, free cash flow is a good thing because a firm blessed with it has already met all operating needs and paid for all investments in net current and net fixed assets. But once a firm has covered these, is more cash always better?

Paradoxically, Harvard finance professor Michael Jensen replied, "not always," in a classic 1986 paper. To argue the point, Jensen returned to the potential conflict between shareholders (principals) and management (their agents). Shareholders want management to focus on share price. But sometimes the CEO has a different agenda—such as boosting company size, perhaps to raise his profile and trigger lucrative employment offers from other firms. The weaker the shareholders' control, the more likely management will pursue its own interests. And free cash flow, according to Jensen, gives management resources to play with.

Imagine a mature firm with healthy cash flows but an uncertain future. In the original article, Jensen pointed to the oil industry, which remains a good example. Between 1973 and 1980, supply disruptions from Middle Eastern conflict and the Iranian Revolution produced an 11-fold increase in crude-oil prices. Because it is tough to reduce commutes or trade in gas-guzzlers overnight, oil companies reaped a short-term bonanza, pumping out billions in free cash flow. In the long run, however, consumers can move and buy new cars; firms can also build more energy-efficient factories. They did and by 1986 oil prices were 71% below the 1980 peak. In the meantime, however, oil companies spent that mountain of cash on exploration and acquisitions of firms outside the oil business—neither of which did more for shareholders than they could have done for themselves had oil-company management simply paid out the surplus cash as dividends.

This is not to imply more free cash flow is always bad. Often, small, younger firms find themselves in the exact opposite position of early 1980s oil companies—they are flush with great projects but cash poor. Because of their short track record and thin collateral, such firms often must fund investment projects with internal funds because borrowing is too expensive or impossible. In this case, excess cash is great because it allows management to exploit opportunities that might otherwise go by the wayside.

The bottom line for management is—the best way to keep shareholders happy is to focus on what is best for them. Or, as the Bard more poetically put it in *King Lear*, "How, in one house, should many people under two commands hold amity? 'Tis hard; almost impossible."

► *Suppose unexpected events in the market for your product leave you with significant free cash flow. What benchmark should you use in determining the best (and most ethical) use of those funds?*

Source: Michael C. Jensen, "Agency Costs of Free Cash Flow, Corporate Finance, and Takeovers," *American Economic Review* 76 (1986): 323–329.

Looking at Equation 4.5, we see that if net fixed assets decline by an amount exceeding the depreciation for the period, the NFAI would be negative. A negative NFAI represents a net cash inflow attributable to the firm selling more assets than it acquired during the year.

The *net current asset investment (NCAI)* represents the net investment made by the firm in its current (operating) assets. "Net" refers to the difference between current assets and the sum of accounts payable and accruals. Notes payable are not included in the NCAI calculation because they represent a negotiated creditor claim on the firm's free cash flow. The NCAI calculation is

$$\text{NCAI} = \text{Change in current assets} - \text{Change in (accounts payable + accruals)} \quad (4.6)$$

EXAMPLE 4.6

Looking at the Baker Corporation's balance sheets for 2018 and 2019 in Table 4.5, we see that the change in current assets between 2018 and 2019 is \$157 (\$2,057 in 2019 − \$1,900 in 2018). The difference between Baker's accounts payable plus accruals of \$800 in 2019 (\$700 in accounts payable + \$100 in accruals) and of \$700 in 2018 (\$500 in accounts payable + \$200 in accruals) is \$100 (\$800 in 2019 − \$700 in 2018). Substituting into Equation 4.6 the change in current assets and the change in the sum of accounts payable plus accruals for Baker Corporation, we get its 2019 NCAI:

$$\text{NCAI} = \$157 - \$100 = \$57$$

So, during 2019 Baker Corporation made a \$57 investment in its current assets net of accounts payable and accruals.

Now we can substitute Baker Corporation's 2019 operating cash flow (OCF) of \$392.3, its net fixed asset investment (NFAI) of \$300, and its net current asset investment (NCAI) of \$57 into Equation 4.4 to find its free cash flow (FCF):

$$\text{FCF} = \$392.3 - \$300 - \$57 = \$35.3$$

We can see that during 2019 Baker generated \$35,300 of free cash flow, which it can use to pay its investors: creditors (payment of interest) and owners (payment of dividends). Thus, the firm generated adequate cash flow to cover all its operating costs and investments and had free cash flow available to pay investors. However, Baker's interest expense in 2019 was \$70,000, so the firm is not generating enough FCF to provide a sufficient return to its investors.

By generating more cash flow than it needs to pay bills and invest in new current and fixed assets, a firm creates value for shareholders. The *Focus on Practice* box discusses LinkedIn's free cash flow. In the next section, we consider various aspects of financial planning for cash flow and profit.

FOCUS ON PRACTICE *in practice*

Free Cash Flow at LinkedIn

A February 2016 analyst report questioned whether the professional networking company LinkedIn was being run for the benefit of shareholders or management. The report noted that in the previous year LinkedIn showed an operating cash flow of \$807 million. From that sum, the company invested \$507 million in new assets, leaving free cash flow of \$300 million. On the face of it, that seems like good news. However, the analyst's report noted that LinkedIn's cash flow was heavily influenced by its employee stock option plan. Under this plan, employees have the right to buy stock at a fixed price. That right is especially valuable if the market price of the company's stock rises. When employees exercise their right to buy, they write a check to LinkedIn and the company issues new shares. LinkedIn's financial records showed that it received \$510 million from employees purchasing stock at below-market prices. Excluding that, the company's free cash flow was negative.

► *Free cash flow is often considered a more reliable measure of a company's income than reported earnings. In what possible ways might corporate accountants change earnings to present a more favorable earnings statement?*

Source: Paulo Santos, "Is LinkedIN Run Solely for Its Employees' Benefit?" February 11, 2016, https://seekingalpha.com/article/3886576-linkedin-run-solely-employees-benefit

→ **REVIEW QUESTIONS** MyLab Finance Solutions

4–3 Briefly describe the first four modified accelerated cost recovery system (MACRS) property classes and recovery periods. Explain how the depreciation percentages are determined by using the MACRS recovery periods.

4–4 Describe the overall cash flow through the firm in terms of cash flow from operating activities, cash flow from investment activities, and cash flow from financing activities.

4–5 Explain why a decrease in cash is classified as a cash inflow (source) and why an increase in cash is classified as a cash outflow (use) in preparing the statement of cash flows.

4–6 Why is depreciation (as well as amortization and depletion) considered a noncash charge?

4–7 Describe the general format of the statement of cash flows. How are cash inflows differentiated from cash outflows on this statement?

4–8 Why do we exclude interest expense from operating cash flow?

4–9 Define and differentiate between a firm's operating cash flow (OCF) and its free cash flow (FCF).

4.3 Cash Planning: Cash Budgets

cash budget (cash forecast)
A statement of the firm's planned inflows and outflows of cash that managers use to estimate its short-term cash requirements.

The **cash budget**, or **cash forecast**, is a statement of the firm's planned inflows and outflows of cash. Managers use the cash budget to estimate the firm's short-term cash requirements, with particular attention to planning for surplus cash and for cash shortages.

Typically, the cash budget covers 1 year, divided into smaller time intervals. The number of intervals depends on the nature of the business. The more seasonal and uncertain a firm's cash flows, the greater the number of intervals. Because many firms are confronted with a seasonal cash flow pattern, the cash budget is quite often presented on a monthly basis. Firms with stable patterns of cash flow may use quarterly or annual time intervals.

THE SALES FORECAST

sales forecast
The prediction of the firm's sales over a given period, based on external and/or internal data; used as the key input to the short-term financial planning process.

The key input to the short-term financial planning process is the firm's **sales forecast**. The marketing department often plays the major role in putting together this projection of sales over the coming year. On the basis of the sales forecast, the financial manager estimates the monthly cash flows that will result from projected sales and from outlays related to production, inventory, and sales. The manager also determines the level of fixed assets required and the amount of financing, if any, needed to support the firm's activities during the year. In practice, obtaining good data proves the most difficult aspect of forecasting. The sales forecast may be based on an analysis of external data, internal data, or a combination of the two.

external forecast
A sales forecast based on the relationships observed between the firm's sales and certain key external economic indicators.

An **external forecast** is based on the relationships observed between the firm's sales and certain key external economic indicators such as the gross domestic product (GDP), new housing starts, consumer confidence, and disposable personal income. Constructing an external forecast calls for a *top-down approach*, which means that the company first looks at the big picture, such as how fast GDP will be growing. From there, the company identifies the markets it will compete in and makes projections for the share of each market it can capture. These high-level factors eventually lead to an overall sales forecast for the firm.

internal forecast
A sales forecast based on a buildup, or consensus, of sales forecasts through the firm's own sales channels.

Internal forecasts are based on a consensus of sales forecasts through the firm's own sales channels, using a *bottom-up approach*. Managers charged with creating an internal forecast ask the firm's salespeople to estimate how many units of each type of product they expect to sell in the coming year. The sales manager collects and aggregates these forecasts and then makes adjustments to them based on a range of factors to arrive at the firm's overall sales forecast.

Firms generally use a combination of external and internal forecast data to make the final sales forecast. The internal data provide insight into sales expectations, and the external data provide a means of adjusting these expectations to take into account general economic factors. The nature of the firm's product also often affects the mix and types of forecasting methods used.

PREPARING THE CASH BUDGET

Table 4.7 illustrates the general format of a cash budget. The budget begins by calculating total cash receipts and disbursements to arrive at the net cash inflow or outflow, which is then added to the beginning cash balance. The resulting ending cash balance shows how much cash the firm would have on hand without seeking additional financing. Most firms have a minimum cash balance they want to keep on hand at all times, so the cash budget compares the ending cash balance to the minimum desired balance. If the ending cash balance exceeds the minimum, the firm has excess cash it can invest in marketable securities or other assets. If the ending cash balance falls short of the minimum balance requirement, then the firm will seek additional financing, most likely in the form of short-term borrowing.

The following discussion, along with Tables 4.8 and 4.9, illustrates each of the cash budget's components individually. Table 4.10 presents the completed cash budget for Coulson Industries.

Total Cash Receipts

total cash receipts
All of a firm's inflows of cash during a given financial period.

Total cash receipts include all inflows of cash during a given period. The most common components of cash receipts are cash sales, collections of accounts receivable, and other cash receipts. Note that to estimate cash receipts, analysts have to gather information from a variety of sources within the firm, including people from marketing and sales as well as those employees who oversee collections.

TABLE 4.7 The General Format of the Cash Budget

	Jan.	Feb.	...	Nov.	Dec.
Total cash receipts	$XXA	$XXH		$XXN	$XXU
Less: Total cash disbursements	XXB	XXI	...	XXO	XXV
Net cash flow	$XXC	$XXJ		$XXP	$XXW
Add: Beginning cash	XXD	XXE	XXK	XXQ	XXR
Ending cash	$XXE ↗	$XXK ↗	↗	$XXR ↗	$XXX
Less: Minimum cash balance	XXF	XXL	...	XXS	XXY
Required total financing		$XXM		$XXT	
Excess cash balance	$XXG				$XXZ

EXAMPLE 4.7

Coulson Industries, a defense contractor, is developing a cash budget for October, November, and December. Coulson's sales in August and September were $100,000 and $200,000, respectively. Sales of $400,000, $300,000, and $200,000 have been forecast for October, November, and December, respectively. Historically, 20% of the firm's sales have been for cash, 50% have generated accounts receivable collected after 1 month, and the remaining 30% have generated accounts receivable collected after 2 months. Bad-debt expenses (uncollectible accounts) have been negligible. In December, the firm will receive a $30,000 dividend from stock in a subsidiary. The schedule of expected cash receipts for the company appears in Table 4.8. It contains the following:

Forecast sales Coulson expects sales to rise from August to October before falling slightly in November and December.

Cash sales The cash sales shown for each month represent 20% of the total sales forecast for that month.

Collections of A/R These entries represent the collection of accounts receivable (A/R) resulting from sales in earlier months.

Lagged 1 month These figures represent sales made in the preceding month that generated accounts receivable collected in the current month. Because 50% of the current month's sales are collected 1 month later, the collections of A/R with a 1-month lag shown for September represent 50% of the sales in August, collections for October represent 50% of September sales, and so on.

Lagged 2 months These figures represent sales made 2 months earlier that generated accounts receivable collected in the current month. Because 30% of sales are collected 2 months later, the collections with a 2-month lag shown for October represent 30% of the sales in August, and so on.

Other cash receipts These are cash receipts expected from sources other than sales. Interest received, dividends received, proceeds from the sale of equipment, stock and bond sale proceeds, and lease receipts may show up here. For Coulson Industries, the only other cash receipt is the $30,000 dividend due in December.

Total cash receipts This figure represents the total of all the cash receipts listed for each month. For Coulson Industries, the figures for August and September represent actual cash inflows, whereas the figures for October, November, and December are forecasts based on expected sales and collections patterns.

Total Cash Disbursements

total cash disbursements All outlays of cash by the firm during a given financial period.

Total cash disbursements include all outlays of cash by the firm during a given period. The most common cash disbursements are

Cash purchases	Fixed-asset outlays
Payments of accounts payable	Interest payments
Rent (and lease) payments	Cash dividend payments
Wages and salaries	Principal payments (loans)
Tax payments	Repurchases or retirements of stock

TABLE 4.8 A Schedule of Projected Cash Receipts for Coulson Industries ($000)

Sales forecast	Aug. $100	Sept. $200	Oct. $400	Nov. $300	Dec. $200
Cash sales (0.20)	$20	$40	$ 80	$ 60	$ 40
Collections of A/R:					
Lagged 1 month (0.50)		50	100	200	150
Lagged 2 months (0.30)			30	60	120
Other cash receipts					30
Total cash receipts	$20	$90	$210	$320	$340

Here, too, note that the information required to estimate total cash disbursements comes from a wide range of sources. The human resources department would have the best access to information about disbursements for employee salaries, wages, and benefits. The operations department would be in the best position to provide data on purchases of raw materials and purchases of new fixed assets. The accounting department would have responsibility for the firm's tax payments. In short, for financial managers to put together a cash budget, they must be engaged with practically every part of a firm.

It is important to recognize that *depreciation and other noncash charges are NOT included in the cash budget* because they merely represent a scheduled write-off of an earlier cash outflow. The impact of depreciation, as we noted earlier, is reflected in the reduced cash outflow for tax payments.

EXAMPLE 4.8

Coulson Industries has gathered the following data needed for preparing a cash disbursements schedule for October, November, and December.

Purchases The firm's purchases represent 70% of sales. Of this amount, Coulson pays 10% in cash up front. It pays 70% in the month immediately following the month of purchase, as highlighted in Table 4.9 by the row labeled *lagged 1 month*. The company pays the remaining 20% 2 months following the month of purchase, as Table 4.9 shows in the row labeled *lagged 2 months*.

Rent payments Coulson will pay rent of $5,000 each month.

Wages and salaries Fixed salaries for the year are $96,000, or $8,000 per month. In addition, Coulson's financial managers estimate that wages equal 10% of monthly sales.

Tax payments Coulson must pay taxes of $25,000 in December.

Fixed-asset outlays The company will pay cash for new machinery costing $130,000 in November.

Interest payments An interest payment of $10,000 is due in December.

Cash dividend payments Coulson will pay cash dividends of $20,000 in October.

Principal payments (loans) A $20,000 principal payment is due in December.

TABLE 4.9 A Schedule of Projected Cash Disbursements for Coulson Industries ($000)

Purchases (0.70 × sales)	Aug. $70	Sept. $140	Oct. $280	Nov. $210	Dec. $140
Cash purchases (0.10)	$7	$14	$ 28	$ 21	$ 14
Payments of A/P:					
Lagged 1 month (0.70)		49	98	196	147
Lagged 2 months (0.20)			14	28	56
Rent payments			5	5	5
Wages and salaries			48	38	28
Tax payments					25
Fixed-asset outlays				130	
Interest payments					10
Cash dividend payments			20		
Principal payments					20
Total cash disbursements	$7	$63	$213	$418	$305

net cash flow
The mathematical difference between the firm's cash receipts and its cash disbursements in each period.

ending cash
The sum of the firm's beginning cash and its net cash flow for the period.

required total financing
Amount of funds needed by the firm if the ending cash for the period is less than the desired minimum cash balance; typically represented by notes payable.

excess cash balance
The (excess) amount available for investment by the firm if the period's ending cash is greater than the desired minimum cash balance; assumed to be invested in marketable securities.

Repurchases or retirements of stock No repurchase or retirement of stock is expected between October and December.

Table 4.9 presents the firm's cash disbursements schedule, using the preceding data.

Net Cash Flow, Ending Cash, Financing, and Excess Cash

Look back at the general-format cash budget in Table 4.7. We have inputs for the first two entries, and we now continue calculating the firm's cash needs. We find the firm's **net cash flow** by subtracting the cash disbursements from cash receipts in each period. Then we add beginning cash to the firm's net cash flow to determine the **ending cash** for each period.

Finally, we subtract the desired minimum cash balance from ending cash to find the **required total financing** or the **excess cash balance**. If the ending cash is less than the minimum cash balance, financing is required. Most managers view such financing as short term, so we will assume that any short-term borrowing the firm does will appear on the balance sheet as notes payable. If the ending cash is greater than the minimum cash balance, *excess cash* exists. Managers usually invest any excess cash in liquid, short-term, interest-paying marketable securities.

EXAMPLE 4.9

Table 4.10 presents Coulson Industries' cash budget. The company wishes to maintain, as a reserve for unexpected needs, a minimum cash balance of $25,000. For Coulson Industries to keep this ending cash balance, it will need total borrowing of $76,000 in November and $41,000 in December. In October, the firm will have an excess cash balance of $22,000, which it can invest in an interest-earning marketable security. The required total financing figures in the cash budget refer to how much Coulson will owe at the end of the month; they do not represent the monthly changes in borrowing.

We can easily find the monthly changes in borrowing and in excess cash by further analyzing the cash budget. In October, the $50,000 beginning

TABLE 4.10 A Cash Budget for Coulson Industries ($000)

	Oct.	Nov.	Dec.
Total cash receipts[a]	$210	$320	$340
Less: Total cash disbursements[b]	213	418	305
Net cash flow	−$ 3	−$ 98	$ 35
Add: Beginning cash	50	47	−51
Ending cash	$ 47	−$ 51	−$ 16
Less: Minimum cash balance	25	25	25
Required total financing (notes payable)[c]		$ 76	$ 41
Excess cash balance (marketable securities)[d]	$ 22		

[a]From Table 4.8.

[b]From Table 4.9.

[c]Values are placed in this line when the ending cash is less than the desired minimum cash balance. These amounts are typically financed short term and therefore are represented by notes payable.

[d]Values are placed in this line when the ending cash is greater than the desired minimum cash balance. These amounts are typically assumed to be invested short term and therefore are represented by marketable securities.

cash, which becomes $47,000 after the $3,000 net cash outflow, results in a $22,000 excess cash balance (i.e., Coulson has $22,000 in cash above the $25,000 minimum). In November, Coulson has a net cash outflow of $98,000. From that we subtract the existing cash and marketable securities balance of $47,000 and find that the firm has a cash deficit of $51,000. Because Coulson wants a minimum of $25,000 of cash on hand at all times, in November the firm must borrow $76,000, enough to cover the cash deficit and replenish the cash balance to the desired minimum. In December, Coulson earns net cash inflows of $35,000, which it uses to repay some of its short-term borrowings, reducing the outstanding short-term debt from $76,000 to $41,000. In summary, the financial activities for each month would be as follows:

October: **Invest the $22,000** excess cash balance in marketable securities.

November: Liquidate the $22,000 of marketable securities and **borrow $76,000** (notes payable).

December: **Repay $35,000** of notes payable to leave $41,000 of outstanding required total financing.

At the end of each of the 3 months, Coulson expects the following balances in cash, marketable securities, and notes payable:

	End-of-month balance ($000)		
Account	Oct.	Nov.	Dec.
Cash	$25	$25	$25
Marketable securities	22	0	0
Notes payable	0	76	41

EVALUATING THE CASH BUDGET

The cash budget indicates whether managers should expect a cash shortage or surplus in each of the months covered by the forecast. It is a critical planning tool because it helps managers secure borrowing arrangements, such as bank lines of credit, before the firm actually needs the money. As time passes, managers refer back to the cash budget to compare projections to the firm's actual performance. Such a comparison allows managers to identify problems in which actual cash inflows and outflows vary from the budget's forecast.

Cash budgets are just as important to individuals. Nearly all financial advisors tell their clients that they should have money saved in liquid assets sufficient to cover a few months of expenses in the event of an emergency. Individuals following this advice know how much money they need in their emergency fund only if they have a good idea of what their monthly cash expenses (i.e., disbursements) will be. Similarly, individuals can use cash budgets to identify periods when they will have excess funds to invest or when they will need to borrow money.

PERSONAL FINANCE EXAMPLE 4.10 Individuals need to prepare budgets to make sure they can cover their current expenses (cash outflows) and save for the future. The personal budget is a short-term financial planning report that helps individuals or families achieve short-term financial goals. Personal budgets typically cover a 1-year period, broken into months.

A condensed version of a personal budget for the first quarter (3 months) is shown below.

	Jan.	Feb.	Mar.
Income			
Take-home pay	$4,775	$4,775	$4,775
Investment income			90
(1) Total income	$4,775	$4,775	$4,865
Expenses			
(2) Total expenses	$4,026	$5,291	$7,396
Cash surplus or deficit [(1) − (2)]	$ 749	−$ 516	−$2,531
Cumulative cash surplus or deficit	$ 749	$ 233	−$2,298

The personal budget shows a cash surplus of $749 in January, followed by monthly deficits in February and March of $516 and $2,531, resulting in a cumulative deficit of $2,298 through March. Clearly, to cover the deficit, some action—such as increasing income, reducing expenses, drawing down savings, or borrowing—will be necessary to bring the budget into balance. Borrowing by using credit can offset a deficit in the short term but can lead to financial trouble if done repeatedly.

COPING WITH UNCERTAINTY IN THE CASH BUDGET

Forecasts are almost inevitably wrong, at least to some degree. That doesn't mean that putting together a cash budget is pointless. Instead, it indicates that managers need to understand that a firm's actual experience will not match the projections included in the cash budget exactly and that plans to invest surplus cash or to borrow money have to be flexible enough to adjust to actual outcomes. Of course, the best way to deal with uncertainty in the cash budget is to incorporate the most careful and accurate forecasts possible. Aside from careful estimation of cash budget inputs, there are two ways of coping with uncertainty in the cash budget. One is to conduct a *scenario analysis,* in which analysts prepare several cash budgets, based on pessimistic, most likely, and optimistic forecasts. From this range of cash flows, the financial manager can determine the amount of financing necessary to cover the most adverse situation. The use of several cash budgets, based on differing scenarios, also should give the financial manager a sense of the riskiness of various alternatives.

EXAMPLE 4.11

Table 4.11 presents the summary of Coulson Industries' cash budget prepared for each month, using pessimistic, most likely, and optimistic estimates of total cash receipts and disbursements. The most likely estimate is based on the expected outcomes presented earlier.

During October, Coulson will, at worst, need $15,000 of financing and, at best, will have a $62,000 excess cash balance. During November, its financing requirement could be as high as $185,000, or it could experience an excess cash balance of $5,000. The December projections show maximum borrowing of $190,000, with a possible excess cash balance of $107,000. By considering extreme values in the pessimistic and optimistic outcomes, Coulson Industries

TABLE 4.11 A Scenario Analysis of Coulson Industries' Cash Budget ($000)

	October			November			December		
	Pessimistic	Most likely	Optimistic	Pessimistic	Most likely	Optimistic	Pessimistic	Most likely	Optimistic
Total cash receipts	$ 160	$210	$285	$ 210	$320	$410	$275	$340	$422
Less: Total cash disbursements	200	213	248	380	418	467	280	305	320
Net cash flow	−$ 40	−$ 3	$ 37	−$170	−$ 98	−$ 57	−$ 5	$ 35	$102
Add: Beginning cash	50	50	50	10	47	87	− 160	−51	30
Ending cash	$ 10	$ 47	$ 87	−$160	−$ 51	$ 30	−$165	−$ 16	$132
Less: Minimum cash balance	25	25	25	25	25	25	25	25	25
Required total financing	$ 15			$ 185	$ 76		$190	$ 41	
Excess cash balance		$ 22	$ 62			$ 5			$107

should be better able to plan its cash requirements. For the 3-month period, the peak borrowing requirement under the worst circumstances would be $190,000, which happens to be considerably greater than the most likely estimate of $76,000.

A second and much more sophisticated way of coping with uncertainty in the cash budget is *simulation*. By simulating the occurrence of sales and other uncertain events, the firm can develop a probability distribution of its ending cash flows for each month. The financial decision maker can then use the probability distribution to determine the amount of financing needed to protect the firm adequately against a cash shortage.

CASH FLOW WITHIN THE MONTH

Because the cash budget shows cash flows only on a monthly basis, the information provided by the cash budget is not necessarily adequate for ensuring solvency. A firm must look more closely at its pattern of daily cash receipts and cash disbursements to ensure that adequate cash is available for paying bills as they come due.

The synchronization of cash flows in the cash budget at month's end does not ensure that the firm will be able to meet its daily cash requirements. Because a firm's cash flows are generally quite variable when viewed daily, effective cash planning requires a look beyond the cash budget. The financial manager must therefore plan and monitor cash flow more frequently than on a monthly basis. The greater the variability of cash flows from day to day, the greater the amount of attention required.

→ REVIEW QUESTIONS MyLab Finance Solutions

4–10 What is the purpose of the cash budget? What role does the sales forecast play in its preparation?

4–11 Briefly describe the basic format of the cash budget.

4–12 How can the two "bottom lines" of the cash budget be used to determine the firm's short-term borrowing and investment requirements?

4–13 What is the cause of uncertainty in the cash budget, and what two techniques can be used to cope with this uncertainty?

LG5

4.4 Profit Planning: Pro Forma Statements

pro forma statements
Projected, or forecast, income statements and balance sheets.

Whereas cash planning focuses on forecasting cash flows, *profit planning* has a broader emphasis that encapsulates the firm's overall financial position. Shareholders, creditors, and the firm's management pay close attention to **pro forma statements**, which are projected income statements and balance sheets. Firms construct pro forma financial statements by studying past relationships between key accounts on the income statement and balance sheet and making judgments about whether those relationships will continue in the near future. Many of the financial ratios introduced earlier in this text play an important role in the creation of pro forma financial statements.

Managers require two main inputs to prepare pro forma statements: (1) financial statements for at least the preceding year and (2) the sales forecast for the coming year. Given those inputs, managers make a variety of assumptions based on historical financial relationships to construct projected income statements and balance sheets. To illustrate this process, we will focus on the company Fair Traders Inc., which works with artists in developing countries to produce and sell handmade dinner plates and mugs.

PRECEDING YEAR'S FINANCIAL STATEMENTS

The income statement for the firm's 2019 operations is given in Table 4.12. It indicates that Fair Traders had sales of $100,000, total cost of goods sold of $80,000, net profits before taxes of $9,000, and net profits after taxes of $7,650. The firm paid $4,000 in cash dividends, leaving $3,650 to be transferred to retained earnings. The firm's balance sheet for 2019 is given in Table 4.13.

SALES FORECAST

As with the cash budget, the key input for pro forma statements is the sales forecast. Fair Traders' sales forecast for the coming year (2020), based on both external and internal data, appears in Table 4.14. The unit sale prices of the products reflect an increase from $20 to $25 for mugs and from $40 to $50 for plates. These increases are necessary to cover anticipated rises in costs.

TABLE 4.12 Fair Traders Income Statement for the Year Ended December 31, 2019

Sales revenue	
Mugs (1,000 units at $20/unit)	$ 20,000
Plates (2,000 units at $40/unit)	80,000
Total sales	$100,000
Less: Cost of goods sold	
Labor	$ 28,500
Materials	13,500
Overhead	38,000
Total cost of goods sold	$ 80,000
Gross profits	$ 20,000
Less: Operating expenses	10,000
Operating profits	$ 10,000
Less: Interest expense	1,000
Net profits before taxes	$ 9,000
Less: Taxes (assumed rate = 15%)	1,350
Net profits after taxes	$ 7,650
Less: Common stock dividends	4,000
To retained earnings	$ 3,650

TABLE 4.13 Fair Traders Balance Sheet, December 31, 2019

Assets		Liabilities and stockholders' equity	
Cash	$ 6,000	Accounts payable	$ 7,000
Marketable securities	4,000	Taxes payable	300
Accounts receivable	13,000	Notes payable	8,300
Inventories	16,000	Other current liabilities	3,400
Total current assets	$39,000	Total current liabilities	$19,000
Net fixed assets	51,000	Long-term debt	18,000
Total assets	$90,000	Total liabilities	$37,000
		Common stock	30,000
		Retained earnings	23,000
		Total liabilities and stockholders' equity	$90,000

TABLE 4.14 2020 Sales Forecast for Fair Traders

Unit sales		Dollar sales	
Mugs	1,500	Mugs ($25/unit)	$ 37,500
Plates	1,950	Plates ($50/unit)	97,500
		Total	$135,000

→ **REVIEW QUESTION** MyLab Finance Solutions

4–14 What is the purpose of pro forma statements? What inputs are required for preparing them using the simplified approaches?

4.5 Preparing the Pro Forma Income Statement

percent-of-sales method
A simple method for developing the pro forma income statement; it forecasts sales and then expresses the various income statement items as percentages of projected sales.

A simple method for developing a pro forma income statement is the **percent-of-sales method.** It forecasts sales and then expresses the various income statement items as percentages of projected sales. The percentages used are likely to be the percentages of sales for those items in the previous year. By using dollar values taken from Fair Traders' 2019 income statement (Table 4.12), we find that these percentages are

$$\frac{\text{Cost of goods sold}}{\text{Sales}} = \frac{\$80,000}{\$100,000} = 0.800 = 80.0\%$$

$$\frac{\text{Operating expenses}}{\text{Sales}} = \frac{\$10,000}{\$100,000} = 0.100 = 10.0\%$$

$$\frac{\text{Interest expense}}{\text{Sales}} = \frac{\$1,000}{\$100,000} = 0.010 = 1.0\%$$

TABLE 4.15 A Pro Forma Income Statement, Using the Percent-of-Sales Method, for Fair Traders for the Year Ended December 31, 2020

Sales revenue	$135,000
Less: Cost of goods sold (0.80)	108,000
Gross profits	$ 27,000
Less: Operating expenses (0.10)	13,500
Operating profits	$ 13,500
Less: Interest expense (0.01)	1,350
Net profits before taxes	$ 12,150
Less: Taxes (assumed rate = 15%)	1,823
Net profits after taxes	$ 10,327
Less: Common stock dividends	4,000
To retained earnings	$ 6,327

Applying these percentages to the firm's forecast sales of $135,000 (developed in Table 4.14), we get the 2020 pro forma income statement shown in Table 4.15. We have assumed that Fair Traders will pay $4,000 in common stock dividends, so the expected contribution to retained earnings is $6,327. This represents a considerable increase over $3,650 in the preceding year (see Table 4.12).

CONSIDERING TYPES OF COSTS AND EXPENSES

The technique used to prepare the pro forma income statement in Table 4.15 assumes that all the firm's costs and expenses are variable. That is, for a given percentage increase in sales, the same percentage increase in cost of goods sold, operating expenses, and interest expense would result. For example, as Fair Traders' sales increased by 35%, we assumed that its costs of goods sold also increased by 35%. On the basis of this assumption, the firm's net profits before taxes also increased by 35%.

Because this approach assumes that all costs are variable, it may understate the increase in profits that will occur when sales increase if some of the firm's costs are fixed. Similarly, if sales decline, the percentage-of-sales method may overstate profits if some costs are fixed and do not fall when revenues decline. Therefore, a pro forma income statement constructed using the percentage-of-sales method generally tends to understate profits when sales are increasing and overstate profits when sales are decreasing. The best way to adjust for the presence of fixed costs when preparing a pro forma income statement is to break the firm's historical costs and expenses into fixed and variable components. We discuss the potential returns as well as risks resulting from use of fixed (operating and financial) costs to create "leverage" elsewhere in this text. The main point is to recognize that fixed costs make a firm's profits more volatile than its revenues. That is, when both profits and sales are rising, profits tend to increase at a faster rate, but when profits and sales are in decline, the percentage drop in profits is often greater than the rate of decline in sales.

EXAMPLE 4.12

MyLab Finance Solution Video

Fair Traders' 2019 actual and 2020 pro forma income statements, broken into fixed and variable cost and expense components, follow:

Fair Traders Income Statements

	2019 Actual	2020 pro forma
Sales revenue	$100,000	$135,000
Less: Cost of goods sold		
Fixed cost	40,000	40,000
Variable cost (0.40 × sales)	40,000	54,000
Gross profits	$ 20,000	$ 41,000
Less: Operating expenses		
Fixed expense	$ 5,000	$ 5,000
Variable expense (0.05 × sales)	5,000	6,750
Operating profits	$ 10,000	$ 29,250
Less: Interest expense (all fixed)	1,000	1,000
Net profits before taxes	$ 9,000	$ 28,250
Less: Taxes (assumed rate = 15%)	1,350	4,238
Net profits after taxes	$ 7,650	$ 24,012

Breaking Fair Traders' costs and expenses into fixed and variable components provides a more accurate projection of its pro forma profit. By assuming that *all* costs are variable (as shown in Table 4.15), we find that projected net profits before taxes would continue to equal 9% of sales (in 2019, $9,000 net profits before taxes ÷ $100,000 sales). Therefore, the 2020 net profits before taxes would have been $12,150 (0.09 × $135,000 projected sales) instead of the $28,250 obtained by using the firm's fixed-cost–variable-cost breakdown.

When using a simplified approach to prepare a pro forma income statement, analysts should break down costs and expenses into fixed and variable components.

→ REVIEW QUESTIONS MyLab Finance Solutions

4–15 How is the percent-of-sales method used to prepare pro forma income statements?

4–16 Why does the presence of fixed costs lead to errors in a pro forma income statement constructed using the percent-of-sales method? What is a better method?

LG5

4.6 Preparing the Pro Forma Balance Sheet

A number of simplified approaches are available for preparing the pro forma balance sheet. One involves estimating each balance sheet account as a fixed percentage of sales. A better and more common approach is the **judgmental approach**, under which the firm estimates the values of certain balance sheet accounts and

judgmental approach
A simplified approach for preparing the pro forma balance sheet under which the firm estimates the values of certain balance sheet accounts and uses its external financing as a balancing, or "plug," figure.

uses its external financing as a balancing, or "plug," figure. The judgmental approach represents an improved version of the percent-of-sales approach to pro forma balance sheet preparation. The judgmental approach requires only slightly more information and should yield better estimates than the somewhat naive percent-of-sales approach.

To apply the judgmental approach in preparing Fair Traders' 2020 pro forma balance sheet, we make a number of assumptions about levels of various balance sheet accounts:

1. A minimum cash balance of $6,000 is desired.
2. Marketable securities will remain unchanged from their current level of $4,000.
3. Accounts receivable on average represent about 45 days of sales (about 1/8 of a year). Because Fair Traders' annual sales are projected to be $135,000, accounts receivable should average $16,875 (1/8 × $135,000).
4. The ending inventory should remain at a level of about $16,000, of which 25% (approximately $4,000) should be raw materials and the remaining 75% (approximately $12,000) should consist of finished goods.
5. A new machine costing $20,000 will be purchased. Total depreciation for the year is $8,000. Adding the $20,000 acquisition to the existing net fixed assets of $51,000 and subtracting the depreciation of $8,000 yields net fixed assets of $63,000.
6. Purchases will represent approximately 30% of annual sales, which in this case is approximately $40,500 (0.30 × $135,000). The firm estimates that it can take 73 days on average to satisfy its accounts payable. Thus accounts payable should equal one-fifth (73 days ÷ 365 days) of the firm's purchases, or $8,100 (1/5 × $40,500).
7. Taxes payable will equal one-fourth of the current year's tax liability, which equals $455 (one-fourth of the tax liability of $1,823 shown in the pro forma income statement in Table 4.15).
8. Notes payable will remain unchanged from their current level of $8,300.
9. No change in other current liabilities is expected. They remain at the level of the previous year: $3,400.
10. The firm's long-term debt and its common stock will remain unchanged at $18,000 and $30,000, respectively; no issues, retirements, or repurchases of bonds or stocks are planned.
11. Retained earnings will increase from the beginning level of $23,000 (from the balance sheet dated December 31, 2019, in Table 4.13) to $29,327. The increase of $6,327 represents the amount of retained earnings calculated in the year-end 2020 pro forma income statement in Table 4.15.

external financing required ("plug" figure)
Under the judgmental approach for developing a pro forma balance sheet, the amount of external financing needed to bring the statement into balance. It can be either a positive or a negative value.

A 2020 pro forma balance sheet for Fair Traders based on these assumptions is presented in Table 4.16. A **"plug" figure**—called the **external financing required**—of $8,293 is needed to bring the statement into balance. This means that the firm will have to obtain about $8,300 of additional external financing to support the increased sales level of $135,000 for 2020.

A positive value for "external financing required," like that shown in Table 4.16, means that, based on its plans, the firm will not generate enough internal financing to support its forecast growth in assets. To support the forecast level of operation, the firm must raise funds externally by using debt and/or equity financing or by reducing dividends. Once managers decide what form of

TABLE 4.16 **A Pro Forma Balance Sheet, Using the Judgmental Approach, for Fair Traders (December 31, 2020)**

Assets			Liabilities and stockholders' equity	
Cash		$ 6,000	Accounts payable	$ 8,100
Marketable securities		4,000	Taxes payable	455
Accounts receivable		16,875	Notes payable	8,300
Inventories			Other current liabilities	3,400
Raw materials	$ 4,000		Total current liabilities	$ 20,255
Finished goods	12,000		Long-term debt	18,000
Total inventory		16,000	Total liabilities	$ 38,255
Total current assets		$ 42,875	Common stock	30,000
Net fixed assets		63,000	Retained earnings	29,327
Total assets		$105,875	Total	$ 97,582
			External financing required[a]	8,293
			Total liabilities and stockholders' equity	$105,875

[a]The amount of external financing needed to force the firm's balance sheet to balance. Because of the nature of the judgmental approach, the balance sheet is not expected to balance without some type of adjustment.

financing the firm will employ, they modify the pro forma balance sheet to replace "external financing required" with the planned increases in the debt and/or equity accounts.

A negative value for "external financing required" indicates that, based on its plans, the firm will generate more financing internally than it needs to support its forecast growth in assets. In this case, funds are available for use in repaying debt, repurchasing stock, increasing dividends, or investing in new assets. Once managers decide what they will do with the additional cash flow that the firm will generate, they replace the "external financing required" line item in the pro forma balance sheet with the planned changes to other accounts.

→ **REVIEW QUESTIONS** MyLab Finance Solutions

4–17 Describe the judgmental approach for simplified preparation of the pro forma balance sheet.

4–18 What is the significance of the "plug" figure, external financing required? Differentiate between strategies associated with positive values and with negative values for external financing required.

LG6

4.7 Evaluation of Pro Forma Statements

It is difficult to forecast the many variables involved in preparing pro forma statements. As a result, investors, lenders, and managers frequently use the techniques presented in this chapter to make rough estimates of pro forma financial statements. It is nonetheless important to recognize the weaknesses of these simplified approaches. The weaknesses lie in two assumptions: (1) that the firm's past financial condition is an accurate indicator of its future and (2) that managers can force certain accounts to take on "desired" values. Despite their weaknesses, pro forma financial statements remain useful to managers.

However pro forma statements are prepared, analysts must understand how to use them in making financial decisions. Both financial managers and lenders can use pro forma statements to analyze the firm's inflows and outflows of cash, as well as its liquidity, activity, debt, profitability, and market value. They can calculate various ratios from the pro forma income statement and balance sheet to evaluate performance. They can even construct a pro forma statement of cash flows from the pro forma balance sheet and income statement. After analyzing the pro forma statements, the financial manager can take steps to adjust planned operations to achieve short-term financial goals. For example, if projected profits on the pro forma income statement are too low, a variety of pricing and/or cost-cutting actions might be initiated. If the projected level of accounts receivable on the pro forma balance sheet is too high, changes in credit or collection policy may be called for. Pro forma statements are therefore of great importance in solidifying the firm's financial plans for the coming year. Pro forma forecast statements also provide a "baseline" for managers to evaluate ongoing performance as the year begins. They enable questions such as "Why are our actuals above (or below) our prior expectations?" and "What has changed in our operations?"

→ REVIEW QUESTIONS MyLab Finance Solutions

4–19 What are the two basic weaknesses of the simplified approaches to preparing pro forma statements?

4–20 What is the financial manager's objective in evaluating pro forma statements?

SUMMARY

FOCUS ON VALUE

Cash flow, the lifeblood of the firm, is a key determinant of the value of the firm. The financial manager must plan and manage the firm's cash flow. The goal is to ensure the firm's solvency and to generate positive cash flow for the firm's owners. Both the magnitude and the risk of the cash flows generated on behalf of the owners determine the firm's value.

To carry out the responsibility **to create value for owners,** the financial manager uses tools such as cash budgets and pro forma financial statements as part of the process of generating positive cash flow. Good financial plans should result in positive free cash flows. Clearly, the financial manager must deliberately and carefully plan and manage the firm's cash flows to achieve the firm's goal of maximizing share price.

REVIEW OF LEARNING GOALS

LG1 **Understand the financial planning process, including long-term (strategic) financial plans and short-term (operating) financial plans.** The two key aspects of the financial planning process are cash planning and profit planning. Cash planning involves the cash budget or cash forecast. Profit planning relies on the pro forma income statement and balance sheet. Long-term (strategic) financial plans act as a guide for preparing short-term (operating) financial plans. Long-term plans tend to cover periods ranging from 2 to 10 years; short-term plans most often cover a 1- to 2-year period.

LG2 **Understand tax depreciation procedures and the effect of depreciation on the firm's cash flows.** Depreciation is an important factor affecting a firm's cash flow. An asset's depreciable value and depreciable life are determined by using the MACRS standards in the federal tax code. MACRS groups assets (excluding real estate) into six property classes based on length of recovery period.

LG3 **Discuss the firm's statement of cash flows, operating cash flow, and free cash flow.** The statement of cash flows is divided into cash flow from operating, investment, and financing activities. It reconciles changes in the firm's cash flows with changes in cash and marketable securities for the period. Interpreting the statement of cash flows involves both the major categories of cash flow and the individual items of cash inflow and outflow. Free cash flow, which analysts use to value companies, is the amount of cash flow available to creditors and owners.

LG4 **Discuss the cash-planning process and the preparation, evaluation, and use of the cash budget.** The cash-planning process uses the cash budget, based on a sales forecast, to estimate short-term cash surpluses and shortages. The cash budget is typically prepared for a 1-year period divided into months. It nets cash receipts and disbursements for each period to calculate net cash flow. Ending cash is estimated by adding beginning cash to the net cash flow. By subtracting the desired minimum cash balance from the ending cash, the firm can determine required total financing or the excess cash balance. To cope with uncertainty in the cash budget, scenario analysis or simulation can be used. A firm must also consider its pattern of daily cash receipts and cash disbursements.

LG5 **Explain the procedures used to prepare and evaluate the pro forma income statement and the pro forma balance sheet.** A pro forma income statement can be developed by calculating past percentage relationships between certain cost and expense items and the firm's sales and then applying these percentages to forecasts. Because this approach implies that all costs and expenses are variable, it tends to understate profits when sales are increasing and to overstate profits when sales are decreasing. This problem can be avoided by breaking down costs and expenses into fixed and variable components. In this case, the fixed components remain unchanged from the most recent year, and the variable costs and expenses are forecast on a percent-of-sales basis.

Under the judgmental approach, the values of certain balance sheet accounts are estimated and the firm's external financing is used as a balancing, or "plug," figure. A positive value for "external financing required" means that the firm will not generate enough internal financing to support its forecast growth in assets and will have to raise funds externally or reduce dividends. A negative value for "external financing required" indicates that the firm will generate more financing internally than it needs to support its forecast growth in assets and funds will be available for use in repaying debt, repurchasing stock, or increasing dividends.

LG6 **Evaluate the approaches to pro forma financial statement preparation and the common uses of pro forma statements.** Simple approaches for preparing pro forma statements assume that the firm's past financial condition is an accurate indicator of the future. Pro forma statements are commonly used to forecast and analyze the firm's profitability and overall financial performance so that managers can make adjustments to operations to achieve short-term financial goals.

OPENER-IN-REVIEW

The chapter opener described a company that reported increases in revenues and profits, but even so, the company's free cash flow was negative. Explain why a profitable, expanding business may have negative free cash flow.

SELF-TEST PROBLEMS (Solutions in Appendix)

ST4–1 **Depreciation and cash flow** A firm expects to have earnings before interest and taxes (EBIT) of $160,000 in each of the next 6 years. It pays annual interest of $15,000. The firm is considering the purchase of an asset that costs $140,000, requires $10,000 in installation cost, and has a recovery period of 5 years. It will be the firm's only asset, and the asset's depreciation is already reflected in its EBIT estimates.

a. Calculate the annual depreciation for the asset purchase using the MACRS depreciation percentages in Table 4.2.

b. Calculate the firm's operating cash flows for each of the 6 years, using Equation 4.3. Assume that the firm is subject to a 21% tax rate on all the profit that it earns.

c. Suppose that the firm's net fixed assets, current assets, accounts payable, and accruals had the following values at the start and end of the final year (year 6). Calculate the firm's free cash flow (FCF) for that year.

Account	Year 6 start	Year 6 end
Net fixed assets	$ 7,500	$ 0
Current assets	90,000	110,000
Accounts payable	40,000	45,000
Accruals	8,000	7,000

d. Compare and discuss the significance of each value calculated in parts **b** and **c**.

ST4–2 **Cash budget and pro forma balance sheet inputs** Jane McDonald, a financial analyst for Carroll Company, has prepared the following sales and cash disbursement estimates for the period February–June of the current year.

Month	Sales	Cash disbursements
February	$500	$400
March	600	300
April	400	600
May	200	500
June	200	200

McDonald notes that, historically, 30% of sales have been for cash. Of *credit sales,* the firm collects 70% 1 month after the sale, and it collects the remaining 30% 2 months after the sale. The firm wishes to maintain a minimum ending balance in its cash account of $25. The firm will invest balances above this amount in short-term government securities (marketable securities), whereas any deficits would be financed through short-term bank borrowing (notes payable). The beginning cash balance at April 1 is $115.

a. Prepare cash budgets for April, May, and June.

b. How much financing, if any, at a maximum would Carroll Company require to meet its obligations during this 3-month period?

c. A pro forma balance sheet dated at the end of June is to be prepared from the information presented. Give the size of each of the following: cash, notes payable, marketable securities, and accounts receivable.

ST4–3 **Pro forma income statement** Euro Designs Inc. expects sales during 2020 to rise from the 2019 level of $3.5 million to $3.9 million. Because of a scheduled large loan payment, the interest expense in 2020 is expected to drop to $325,000. The firm plans to increase its cash dividend payments during 2020 to $320,000. The company's year-end 2019 income statement follows.

Euro Designs Inc. Income Statement for the Year Ended December 31, 2019	
Sales revenue	$3,500,000
Less: Cost of goods sold	1,925,000
Gross profits	$1,575,000
Less: Operating expenses	420,000
Operating profits	$1,155,000
Less: Interest expense	400,000
Net profits before taxes	$ 755,000
Less: Taxes (rate = 21%)	158,550
Net profits after taxes	$ 596,450
Less: Cash dividends	250,000
To retained earnings	$ 346,450

a. Use the percent-of-sales method to prepare a 2020 pro forma income statement for Euro Designs Inc.

b. Explain why the statement may underestimate the company's actual 2020 pro forma income.

WARM-UP EXERCISES

All problems are available in MyLab Finance

LG2 **E4–1** The installed cost of a new computerized controller was $65,000. Calculate the depreciation schedule by year assuming a recovery period of 5 years and using the appropriate MACRS depreciation percentages given in Table 4.2.

LG3 **E4–2** Classify the following changes in each of the accounts as either an inflow or an outflow of cash. During the year (a) marketable securities increased, (b) land and buildings decreased, (c) accounts payable increased, (d) vehicles decreased, (e) accounts receivable increased, and (f) dividends were paid.

LG3 **E4–3** Determine the operating cash flow (OCF) for Kleczka LLC, based on the following data. (All values are in thousands of dollars.) During the year the firm had sales of $2,500, cost of goods sold totaled $1,800, operating expenses totaled $300, and depreciation expenses were $200. The firm is in the 35% tax bracket.

LG3 **E4–4** During the year, Xero Inc. experienced an increase in net fixed assets of $300,000 and had depreciation of $200,000. It also experienced an increase in current assets of $150,000 and an increase in accounts payable and accruals of $75,000. If operating cash flow (OCF) for the year was $700,000, calculate the firm's free cash flow (FCF) for the year.

LG5 **E4–5** Rimier Corp. forecasts sales of $650,000 for 2020. Assume that the firm has fixed costs of $250,000 and variable costs amounting to 35% of sales. Operating expenses are estimated to include fixed costs of $28,000 and a variable portion equal to 7.5% of sales. Interest expenses for the coming year are estimated to be $20,000. Estimate Rimier's net profits before taxes for 2020.

PROBLEMS

All problems are available in MyLab Finance. The MyLab icon indicates problems in Excel format available in MyLab Finance.

LG2 **P4–1** **Depreciation** On March 20, 2019, Norton Systems acquired two new assets. Asset A was research equipment costing $17,000 and having a 3-year recovery period. Asset B was duplicating equipment with an installed cost of $45,000 and a 5-year recovery period. Using the MACRS depreciation percentages in Table 4.2, prepare a depreciation schedule for each of these assets.

LG2 **P4–2** **Depreciation** In early 2019, Sosa Enterprises purchased a new machine for $10,000 to make cork stoppers for wine bottles. The machine has a 3-year recovery period and is expected to have a salvage value of $2,000. Develop a depreciation schedule for this asset using the MACRS depreciation percentages in Table 4.2.

LG2 LG3 **P4–3** **MACRS depreciation expense and accounting cash flow** Pavlovich Instruments Inc., a maker of precision telescopes, expects to report pretax income of $430,000 this year. The company's financial manager is considering the timing of a purchase of new computerized lens grinders. The grinders will have an installed cost of $80,000 and a cost recovery period of 5 years. They will be depreciated using the MACRS schedule.

a. If the firm purchases the grinders before year's end, what depreciation expense will it be able to claim this year? (Use Table 4.2.)
b. If the firm reduces its reported income by the amount of the depreciation expense calculated in part a, what tax savings will result?

P4–4 **Depreciation and accounting cash flow** A firm in the third year of depreciating its only asset, which originally cost $180,000 and has a 5-year MACRS recovery period, has gathered the following data relative to the current year's operations.

Accruals	$ 15,000
Current assets	120,000
Interest expense	15,000
Sales revenue	400,000
Inventory	70,000
Total costs before depreciation, interest, and taxes	290,000
Tax rate on ordinary income	21%

a. Use the relevant data to determine the operating cash flow (see Equations 4.2 and 4.3) for the current year.
b. Explain the impact that depreciation, as well as any other noncash charges, has on a firm's cash flows.

P4–5 **Classifying inflows and outflows of cash** Classify each of the following items as an inflow (I) or an outflow (O) of cash.

Item	Change ($)	Item	Change ($)
Cash	−300	Accounts receivable	+1,700
Accounts payable	−1,200	Net profits	+900
Notes payable	+1,500	Depreciation	+1,100
Long-term debt	+1,000	Repurchase of stock	+900
Inventory	+200	Cash dividends	+800
Fixed assets	+400	Sale of stock	+1,000

P4–6 **Finding operating and free cash flows** Consider the following balance sheets and selected data from the income statement of Keith Corporation.

Keith Corporation Balance Sheets

	December 31	
Assets	**2019**	**2018**
Cash	$ 1,500	$ 1,000
Marketable securities	1,800	1,200
Accounts receivable	2,000	1,800
Inventories	2,900	2,800
Total current assets	$ 8,200	$ 6,800
Gross fixed assets	$29,500	$28,100
Less: Accumulated depreciation	14,700	13,100
Net fixed assets	$14,800	$15,000
Total assets	$23,000	$21,800

(continued)

Keith Corporation Balance Sheets *(continued)*		
	December 31	
Liabilities and stockholders' equity	**2019**	**2018**
Accounts payable	$ 1,600	$ 1,500
Notes payable	2,800	2,200
Accruals	200	300
Total current liabilities	$ 4,600	$ 4,000
Long-term debt	5,000	5,000
Total liabilities	$ 9,600	$ 9,000
Common stock	$10,000	$10,000
Retained earnings	3,400	2,800
Total stockholders' equity	$13,400	$12,800
Total liabilities and stockholders' equity	$23,000	$21,800

Keith Corporation Income Statement Data (2019)	
Depreciation expense	$1,600
Earnings before interest and taxes (EBIT)	2,700
Interest expense	367
Net profits after taxes	1,400
Tax rate	21%

a. Calculate the firm's net operating profit after taxes (NOPAT) for the year ended December 31, 2019, using Equation 4.1.
b. Calculate the firm's operating cash flow (OCF) for the year ended December 31, 2019, using Equation 4.3.
c. Calculate the firm's free cash flow (FCF) for the year ended December 31, 2019, using Equation 4.4.
d. Interpret, compare, and contrast your cash flow estimates in parts **b** and **c**.

P4-7 **Statement of cash flows** Below we reproduce the stockholders' equity section of the 2019 and 2018 balance sheets for Baker Corporation, which also appear as part of Table 4.5.

Account	2019	2018
Preferred stock	$ 100	$ 100
Common stock (par)	120	120
Paid-in capital	380	380
Retained earnings	657	500
Total stockholders' equity	1,257	1,100

a. The Baker Corporation statement of cash flows in Table 4.6 shows a $0 cash inflow resulting from changes in stockholders' equity, yet the balance sheet shows that stockholders' equity increased by $157 in 2019. Can you explain this apparent contradiction?
b. Will the statement of cash flows for Baker Corporation show a $0 cash inflow resulting from the change in stockholders' equity every year, or are other values possible? Explain how Baker's statement of cash flows could show a positive cash inflow resulting from a change in stockholders' equity in some future year?

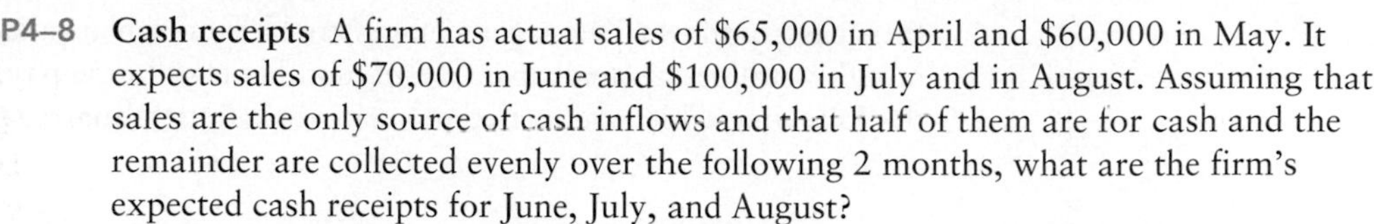

P4–8 Cash receipts A firm has actual sales of $65,000 in April and $60,000 in May. It expects sales of $70,000 in June and $100,000 in July and in August. Assuming that sales are the only source of cash inflows and that half of them are for cash and the remainder are collected evenly over the following 2 months, what are the firm's expected cash receipts for June, July, and August?

P4–9 Cash disbursements schedule Maris Brothers Inc. needs a cash disbursement schedule for the months of April, May, and June. Use the format of Table 4.9 and the following information in its preparation.

Sales: February = $500,000; March = $500,000; April = $560,000; May = $610,000; June = $650,000; July = $650,000

Purchases: Purchases are calculated as 60% of the next month's sales, 10% of purchases are made in cash, 50% of purchases are paid for 1 month after purchase, and the remaining 40% of purchases are paid for 2 months after purchase.

Rent: The firm pays rent of $8,000 per month.

Wages and salaries: Base wage and salary costs are fixed at $6,000 per month plus a variable cost of 7% of the current month's sales.

Taxes: A tax payment of $54,500 is due in June.

Fixed asset outlays: New equipment costing $75,000 will be bought and paid for in April.

Interest payments: An interest payment of $30,000 is due in June.

Cash dividends: Dividends of $12,500 will be paid in April.

Principal repayments and retirements: No principal repayments or retirements are due during these months.

LG4

P4–10 Cash budget: Basic Grenoble Enterprises had sales of $50,000 in March and $60,000 in April. Forecast sales for May, June, and July are $70,000, $80,000, and $100,000, respectively. The firm has a cash balance of $5,000 on May 1 and wishes to maintain a minimum cash balance of $5,000. Given the following data, prepare and interpret a cash budget for the months of May, June, and July.

(1) The firm makes 20% of sales for cash, 60% are collected in the next month, and the remaining 20% are collected in the second month following sale.
(2) The firm receives other income of $2,000 per month.
(3) The firm's actual or expected purchases, all made for cash, are $50,000, $70,000, and $80,000 for the months of May through July, respectively.
(4) Rent is $3,000 per month.
(5) Wages and salaries are 10% of the previous month's sales.
(6) Cash dividends of $3,000 will be paid in June.
(7) Payment of principal and interest of $4,000 is due in June.
(8) A cash purchase of equipment costing $6,000 is scheduled in July.
(9) Taxes of $6,000 are due in June.

Personal Finance Problem

LG4

P4–11 Preparation of cash budget Sam and Suzy Sizeman need to prepare a cash budget for the last quarter of 2020 to make sure they can cover their expenditures during the period. Sam and Suzy have been preparing budgets for the past several years and have been able to identify the percentage of their income that they pay for most of their cash outflows. These percentages are based on their take-home pay (e.g., monthly utilities normally run 5% of monthly take-home pay). The information in the following table can be used to create their fourth-quarter budget for 2020.

Income	
Monthly take-home pay	$4,900
Expenses	
Housing	30.0%
Utilities	5.0%
Food	10.0%
Transportation	7.0%
Medical/dental	0.5%
Clothing for October and November	3.0%
Clothing for December	$ 440
Property taxes (November only)	11.5%
Appliances	1.0%
Personal care	2.0%
Entertainment for October and November	6.0%
Entertainment for December	$1,500
Savings	7.5%
Other	5.0%
Excess cash	4.5%

a. Prepare a quarterly cash budget for Sam and Suzy covering the months October through December 2020.
b. Are there individual months that incur a deficit?
c. What is the cumulative cash surplus or deficit by the end of December 2020?

P4–12 **Cash budget: Advanced** The actual sales and purchases for Xenocore Inc. for September and October 2019, along with its forecast sales and purchases for the period November 2019 through April 2020, follow.

The firm makes 20% of all sales for cash and collects on 40% of its sales in each of the 2 months following the sale. Other cash inflows are expected to be $12,000 in September and April, $15,000 in January and March, and $27,000 in February. The firm pays cash for 10% of its purchases. It pays for 50% of its purchases in the following month and for 40% of its purchases 2 months later.

Year	Month	Sales	Purchases
2019	September	$210,000	$120,000
2019	October	250,000	150,000
2019	November	170,000	140,000
2019	December	160,000	100,000
2020	January	140,000	80,000
2020	February	180,000	110,000
2020	March	200,000	100,000
2020	April	250,000	90,000

Wages and salaries amount to 20% of the preceding month's sales. Rent of $20,000 per month must be paid. Interest payments of $10,000 are due in January and April. A principal payment of $30,000 is also due in April. The firm expects to pay cash dividends of $20,000 in January and April. Taxes of $80,000 are due in April. The firm also intends to make a $25,000 cash purchase of fixed assets in December.

a. Assuming that the firm has a cash balance of $22,000 at the beginning of November, determine the end-of-month cash balances for each month, November through April.
b. Assuming that the firm wishes to maintain a $15,000 minimum cash balance, determine the required total financing or excess cash balance for each month, November through April.
c. If the firm were requesting a line of credit to cover needed financing for the period November to April, how large would this line have to be? Explain your answer.

P4–13 Cash flow concepts The following represent financial transactions that Johnsfield & Co. will be undertaking in the next planning period. For each transaction, check the statement or statements that will be affected immediately.

	Statement		
Transaction	**Cash budget**	**Pro forma income statement**	**Pro forma balance sheet**
Cash sale			
Credit sale			
Accounts receivable are collected			
Asset with 5-year life is purchased			
Depreciation is taken			
Amortization of goodwill is taken			
Sale of common stock			
Retirement of outstanding bonds			
Fire insurance premium is paid for the next 3 years			

P4–14 Cash budget: Scenario analysis Trotter Enterprises Inc. has gathered the following data to plan for its cash requirements and short-term investment opportunities for October, November, and December. All amounts are shown in thousands of dollars.

	October			November			December		
	Pessi-mistic	Most likely	Opti-Mistic	Pessi-mistic	Most likely	Opti-mistic	Pessi-mistic	Most likely	Opti-mistic
Total cash receipts	$260	$342	$462	$200	$287	$366	$191	$294	$353
Total cash disbursements	285	326	421	203	261	313	287	332	315

a. Prepare a scenario analysis of Trotter's cash budget using −\$20,000 as the beginning cash balance for October and a minimum required cash balance of \$18,000.
b. Use the analysis prepared in part **a** to predict Trotter's financing needs and investment opportunities over the months of October, November, and December. Discuss how knowledge of the timing and amounts involved can aid the planning process.

LG4

P4–15 **Multiple cash budgets: Scenario analysis** Brownstein Inc. expects sales of \$100,000 during each of the next 3 months. It will make monthly purchases of \$60,000 during this time. Wages and salaries are \$10,000 per month plus 5% of sales. Brownstein expects to make a tax payment of \$20,000 in the next month and a \$15,000 purchase of fixed assets in the second month and to receive \$8,000 in cash from the sale of an asset in the third month. All sales and purchases are for cash. Beginning cash and the minimum cash balance are assumed to be zero.
a. Construct a cash budget for the next 3 months.
b. Brownstein is unsure of the sales levels, but all other figures are certain. If the most pessimistic sales figure is \$80,000 per month and the most optimistic is \$120,000 per month, what are the monthly minimum and maximum ending cash balances that the firm can expect for each of the 1-month periods?
c. Briefly discuss how the financial manager can use the data in parts **a** and **b** to plan for financing needs.

LG5

P4–16 **Pro forma income statement** The marketing department of Metroline Manufacturing estimates that its sales in 2020 will be \$1.5 million. Interest expense is expected to remain unchanged at \$35,000, and the firm plans to pay \$70,000 in cash dividends during 2020. Metroline Manufacturing's income statement for the year ended December 31, 2019, and a breakdown of the firm's cost of goods sold and operating expenses into their fixed and variable components are given below.
a. Use the percent-of-sales method to prepare a pro forma income statement for the year ended December 31, 2020.
b. Use fixed and variable cost data to develop a pro forma income statement for the year ended December 31, 2020.
c. Compare and contrast the statements developed in parts **a** and **b**. Which statement probably provides the better estimate of 2020 income? Explain why.

Metroline Manufacturing Income Statement for the Year Ended December 31, 2019	
Sales revenue	\$1,400,000
Less: Cost of goods sold	910,000
Gross profits	\$ 490,000
Less: Operating expenses	120,000
Operating profits	\$ 370,000
Less: Interest expense	35,000
Net profits before taxes	\$ 335,000
Less: Taxes (rate = 40%)	134,000
Net profits after taxes	\$ 201,000
Less: Cash dividends	66,000
To retained earnings	\$ 135,000

Metroline Manufacturing Breakdown of Costs and Expenses into Fixed and Variable Components for the Year Ended December 31, 2019	
Cost of goods sold	
Fixed cost	\$210,000
Variable cost	700,000
Total costs	\$910,000
Operating expenses	
Fixed expenses	\$ 36,000
Variable expenses	84,000
Total expenses	\$120,000

LG5

P4–17 Pro forma income statement: Scenario analysis Allen Products LP. wants to do a scenario analysis for the coming year. The pessimistic prediction for sales is \$900,000; the most likely amount of sales is \$1,125,000; and the optimistic prediction is \$1,280,000. Allen's income statement for the most recent year follows.

Allen Products LP. Income Statement for the Year Ended December 31, 2019	
Sales revenue	\$937,500
Less: Cost of goods sold	421,875
Gross profits	\$515,625
Less: Operating expenses	234,375
Operating profits	\$281,250
Less: Interest expense	30,000
Net profits before taxes	\$251,250
Less: Taxes (rate = 25%)	62,813
Net profits after taxes	\$188,437

a. Use the percent-of-sales method, the income statement for December 31, 2019, and the sales revenue estimates to develop pessimistic, most likely, and optimistic pro forma income statements for the coming year.

b. Explain how the percent-of-sales method could result in an overstatement of profits for the pessimistic case and an understatement of profits for the most likely and optimistic cases.

c. Restate the pro forma income statements prepared in part **a** to incorporate the following assumptions about the 2019 costs:

\$250,000 of the cost of goods sold is fixed; the rest is variable.
\$180,000 of the operating expenses is fixed; the rest is variable.
All the interest expense is fixed.

d. Compare your findings in part **c** to your findings in part **a**. Do your observations confirm your explanation in part **b**?

LG5

P4–18 Pro forma balance sheet: Basic Leonard Industries wishes to prepare a pro forma balance sheet for December 31, 2020. The firm expects 2020 sales to total \$3,000,000. The following information has been gathered:

(1) A minimum cash balance of \$50,000 is desired.
(2) Marketable securities are expected to remain unchanged.
(3) Accounts receivable represent 10% of sales.
(4) Inventories represent 12% of sales.
(5) A new machine costing \$90,000 will be acquired during 2020. Total depreciation for the year will be \$32,000.
(6) Accounts payable represent 14% of sales.
(7) Accruals, other current liabilities, long-term debt, and common stock are expected to remain unchanged.
(8) The firm's net profit margin is 4%, and it expects to pay out \$70,000 in cash dividends during 2020.
(9) The December 31, 2019, balance sheet follows.

Leonard Industries Balance Sheet December 31, 2019			
Assets		**Liabilities and stockholders' equity**	
Cash	$ 45,000	Accounts payable	$ 395,000
Marketable securities	15,000	Accruals	60,000
Accounts receivable	255,000	Other current liabilities	30,000
Inventories	340,000	Total current liabilities	$ 485,000
Total current assets	$ 655,000	Long-term debt	350,000
Net fixed assets	600,000	Total liabilities	$ 835,000
Total assets	$1,255,000	Common stock	200,000
		Retained earnings	220,000
		Total liabilities and stockholders' equity	$1,255,000

a. Use the judgmental approach to prepare a pro forma balance sheet dated December 31, 2020, for Leonard Industries.

b. How much, if any, additional financing will Leonard Industries require in 2020? Discuss.

c. Could Leonard Industries adjust its planned 2020 dividend to avoid the situation described in part **b**? Explain how.

P4–19 **Pro forma balance sheet** Peabody & Peabody has 2019 sales of $10 million. It wishes to analyze expected performance and financing needs for 2021, which is 2 years ahead. Given the following information, respond to parts **a** and **b**.

(1) The percent of sales for items that vary directly with sales are as follows:

Accounts receivable, 12%
Inventory, 18%
Accounts payable, 14%
Net profit margin, 3%

(2) Marketable securities and other current liabilities are expected to remain unchanged.
(3) A minimum cash balance of $480,000 is desired.
(4) A new machine costing $650,000 will be acquired in 2020, and equipment costing $850,000 will be purchased in 2021. Total depreciation in 2020 is forecast as $290,000, and in 2021 $390,000 of depreciation will be taken.
(5) Accruals are expected to rise to $500,000 by the end of 2021.
(6) No sale or retirement of long-term debt is expected.
(7) No sale or repurchase of common stock is expected.
(8) The dividend payout of 50% of net profits is expected to continue.
(9) Sales are expected to be $11 million in 2020 and $12 million in 2021.
(10) The December 31, 2019, balance sheet follows.

Peabody & Peabody Balance Sheet December 31, 2019 ($000)			
Assets		**Liabilities and stockholders' equity**	
Cash	$ 400	Accounts payable	$1,400
Marketable securities	200	Accruals	400
Accounts receivable	1,200	Other current liabilities	80
Inventories	1,800	Total current liabilities	$1,880
Total current assets	$3,600	Long-term debt	2,000
Net fixed assets	4,000	Total liabilities	$3,880
Total assets	$7,600	Common equity	3,720
		Total liabilities and stockholders' equity	$7,600

a. Prepare a pro forma balance sheet dated December 31, 2021.
b. Discuss the financing changes suggested by the statement prepared in part **a.**

P4–20 **Integrative: Pro forma statements** Red Queen Restaurants wishes to prepare financial plans. Use the financial statements and the other information provided below to prepare the financial plans.

The following financial data are also available:
(1) The firm has estimated that its sales for 2020 will be $900,000.
(2) The firm expects to pay $35,000 in cash dividends in 2020.
(3) The firm wishes to maintain a minimum cash balance of $30,000.
(4) Accounts receivable represent approximately 18% of annual sales.
(5) The firm's ending inventory will change directly with changes in sales in 2020.
(6) A new machine costing $42,000 will be purchased in 2020. Total depreciation for 2020 will be $17,000.
(7) Accounts payable will change directly in response to changes in sales in 2020.
(8) Taxes payable will equal one-fourth of the tax liability on the pro forma income statement.
(9) Marketable securities, other current liabilities, long-term debt, and common stock will remain unchanged.

a. Prepare a pro forma income statement for the year ended December 31, 2020, using the percent-of-sales method.
b. Prepare a pro forma balance sheet dated December 31, 2020, using the judgmental approach.
c. Analyze these statements, and discuss the resulting external financing required.

Red Queen Restaurants Income Statement for the Year Ended December 31, 2019	
Sales revenue	$800,000
Less: Cost of goods sold	600,000
Gross profits	$200,000
Less: Operating expenses	100,000
Net profits before taxes	$100,000
Less: Taxes (rate = 21%)	21,000
Net profits after taxes	$ 79,000
Less: Cash dividends	20,000
To retained earnings	$ 59,000

Red Queen Restaurants Balance Sheet December 31, 2019			
Assets		**Liabilities and stockholders' equity**	
Cash	$ 32,000	Accounts payable	$100,000
Marketable securities	18,000	Taxes payable	20,000
Accounts receivable	150,000	Other current liabilities	5,000
Inventories	100,000	Total current liabilities	$125,000
Total current assets	$300,000	Long-term debt	200,000
Net fixed assets	350,000	Total liabilities	$325,000
Total assets	$650,000	Common stock	150,000
		Retained earnings	175,000
		Total liabilities and stockholders' equity	$650,000

P4–21 **Integrative: Pro forma statements** Provincial Imports Inc. has assembled past (2019) financial statements (income statement and balance sheet below) and financial projections for use in preparing financial plans for the coming year (2020).

Provincial Imports Inc. Income Statement for the Year Ended December 31, 2019	
Sales revenue	$5,000,000
Less: Cost of goods sold	2,750,000
Gross profits	$2,250,000
Less: Operating expenses	850,000
Operating profits	$1,400,000
Less: Interest expense	200,000
Net profits before taxes	$1,200,000
Less: Taxes (rate = 21%)	252,000
Net profits after taxes	$ 948,000
Less: Cash dividends	288,000
To retained earnings	$ 660,000

Provincial Imports Inc.
Balance Sheet December 31, 2019

Assets		Liabilities and stockholders' equity	
Cash	$ 200,000	Accounts payable	$ 700,000
Marketable securities	225,000	Taxes payable	95,000
Accounts receivable	625,000	Notes payable	200,000
Inventories	500,000	Other current liabilities	5,000
Total current assets	$1,550,000	Total current liabilities	$1,000,000
Net fixed assets	1,400,000	Long-term debt	500,000
Total assets	$2,950,000	Total liabilities	$1,500,000
		Common stock	75,000
		Retained earnings	1,375,000
		Total liabilities and equity	$2,950,000

Information related to financial projections for the year 2020 is as follows:

(1) Projected sales are $6,000,000.
(2) Cost of goods sold in 2019 includes $1,000,000 in fixed costs.
(3) Operating expense in 2019 includes $250,000 in fixed costs.
(4) Interest expense will remain unchanged.
(5) The firm will pay cash dividends amounting to 40% of net profits after taxes.
(6) Cash and inventories will double.
(7) Marketable securities, notes payable, long-term debt, and common stock will remain unchanged.
(8) Accounts receivable, accounts payable, and other current liabilities will change in direct response to the change in sales.
(9) A new computer system costing $356,000 will be purchased during the year. Total depreciation expense for the year will be $110,000.
(10) The tax rate will remain at 21% and taxes payable are 38% of the tax liability on the income statement.

a. Prepare a pro forma income statement for the year ended December 31, 2020, using the fixed cost data given to improve the accuracy of the percent-of-sales method.

b. Prepare a pro forma balance sheet as of December 31, 2020, using the information given and the judgmental approach. Include a reconciliation of the retained earnings account.

c. Analyze these statements, and discuss the resulting external financing required.

LG 1

P4–22 **ETHICS PROBLEM** The SEC is trying to get companies to notify the investment community more quickly when a "material change" will affect their forthcoming financial results. In what sense might a financial manager be seen as "more ethical" if he or she follows this directive and issues a press release indicating that sales will not be as high as previously anticipated?

SPREADSHEET EXERCISE

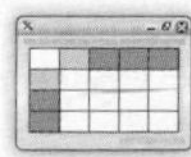

You have been assigned the task of putting together a statement for the ACME Company that shows its expected inflows and outflows of cash over the months of July 2020 through December 2020.

You have been given the following data for ACME Company:

(1) Expected gross sales for May through December, respectively, are $300,000, $290,000, $425,000, $500,000, $600,000, $625,000, $650,000, and $700,000.
(2) 12% of the sales in any given month are collected during that month. However, the firm has a credit policy of 3/10 net 30, so factor a 3% discount into the current month's sales collection.
(3) 75% of the sales in any given month are collected during the following month after the sale.
(4) 13% of the sales in any given month are collected during the second month following the sale.
(5) The expected purchases of raw materials in any given month are based on 60% of the expected sales during the following month.
(6) The firm pays 100% of its current month's raw materials purchases in the following month.
(7) Wages and salaries are paid on a monthly basis and are based on 6% of the current month's expected sales.
(8) Monthly lease payments are 2% of the current month's expected sales.
(9) The monthly advertising expense amounts to 3% of sales.
(10) R&D expenditures are expected to be allocated to August, September, and October at the rate of 12% of sales in those months.
(11) During December a prepayment of insurance for the following year will be made in the amount of $24,000.
(12) During the months of July through December, the firm expects to have miscellaneous expenditures of $15,000, $20,000, $25,000, $30,000, $35,000, and $40,000, respectively.
(13) Taxes will be paid in September in the amount of $40,000 and in December in the amount of $45,000.
(14) The beginning cash balance in July is $15,000.
(15) The target cash balance is $15,000.

TO DO

a. Prepare a cash budget for July 2020 through December 2020 by creating a combined spreadsheet that incorporates spreadsheets similar to those in Tables 4.8, 4.9, and 4.10. Divide your spreadsheet into three sections:
   (1) Total cash receipts
   (2) Total cash disbursements
   (3) Cash budget covering the period of July through December

   The cash budget should reflect the following:
   (1) Beginning and ending monthly cash balances
   (2) The required total financing in each month required
   (3) The excess cash balance in each month with excess

b. Based on your analysis, briefly describe the outlook for this company over the next 6 months. Discuss its specific obligations and the funds available to meet them. What could the firm do in the case of a cash deficit? (Where could it get the money?) What should the firm do if it has a cash surplus?

MyLab Finance Visit www.pearson.com/mylab/finance for **Chapter Case: *Preparing Martin Manufacturing's 2020 Pro Forma Financial Statements,*** Group Exercises, and numerous online resources.

CHAPTER 5

Time Value of Money

LEARNING GOALS

LG 1 Discuss the role of time value in finance, the use of computational tools, and the basic patterns of cash flow.

LG 2 Understand the concepts of future value and present value, their calculation for single cash flow amounts, and the relationship between them.

LG 3 Find the future value and the present value of both an ordinary annuity and an annuity due, and find the present value of a perpetuity.

LG 4 Calculate both the future value and the present value of a mixed stream of cash flows.

LG 5 Understand the effect that compounding interest more frequently than annually has on future value and on the effective annual rate of interest.

LG 6 Describe the procedures involved in (1) determining deposits needed to accumulate a future sum, (2) loan amortization, (3) finding interest or growth rates, and (4) finding an unknown number of periods.

MyLab Finance Chapter Introduction Video

WHY THIS CHAPTER MATTERS TO YOU

In your *professional* life

ACCOUNTING You need to understand time-value-of-money calculations to account for certain transactions such as loan amortization, lease payments, and bond interest rates.

INFORMATION SYSTEMS You need to understand time-value-of-money calculations to design systems that accurately measure and value the firm's cash flows.

MANAGEMENT You need to understand time-value-of-money calculations so that your management of cash receipts and disbursements enables the firm to receive the greatest value from its cash flows.

MARKETING You need to understand time value of money because funding for new programs and products must be justified financially using time-value-of-money techniques.

OPERATIONS You need to understand time value of money because it affects the value of investments in new equipment, in new processes, and in inventory.

In your *personal* life

Time-value-of-money techniques are widely used in personal financial planning. With them, you can calculate how much wealth you can accumulate by saving and investing money over time. You can determine how much money you need to set aside now to reach a particular savings target in the future. You can compare the values of lump-sum payments to streams of cash flows such as annuities. You can calculate payments for consumer loans such as auto loans and home mortgages, or given those payments, you can determine the interest rate that a lender is charging you. Time-value-of-money techniques can help you with almost any major financial decision that you face over your lifetime.

David L. Ryan/Boston Globe/Getty images

MEGA MILLIONS JACKPOT

Pay Me Now or Pay Me Later

Each week millions of people buy lottery tickets in the hope of getting rich quick. In August 2017, someone in Massachusettes got the surprise of a lifetime upon learning she held the winning ticket to the $758.7 million Powerball jackpot, the second-largest lottery prize in U.S. history. The winner, 52-year-old hospital worker Mavis Wanczyk, could choose to take the prize in the form of an immediate $480 million payment, or she could collect her winnings gradually over time. Specifically, Ms. Wanczyk could elect to receive 30 annual payments, starting with an immediate payment of $11.42 million with subsequent payments growing at 5% per year. The sum of those 30 payments equals the advertised lottery jackpot of $758.7 million.

Why would anyone take $480 million rather than $758.7 million? One answer is that the $480 million comes right away, and with that money in hand, the winner can invest the money and earn a return. Because of that opportunity, having $480 million today is much more valuable than having it at some point in the distant future. How much more valuable depends on several factors, especially the rate of return the winner can earn on investments. Winners of huge lottery jackpots have to make an early decision about whether it is better to take a lump sum and invest it or better to take the larger annuity payments spread out over many years. In this chapter, you'll learn how to make such a comparison . . . just in case.

5.1 The Role of Time Value in Finance

The *time value of money* refers to the observation that it is better to receive money sooner than later. You can invest money you have in hand today to earn a positive rate of return, producing more money tomorrow. For that reason, a dollar today is worth more than a dollar in the future. In business situations, managers constantly face tradeoffs when actions that require cash outflows today may produce cash inflows later. Because cash that comes in the future is worth less than cash that firms spend up front, managers need a set of tools for comparing cash inflows and outflows that occur at different times. Individuals can use those tools also when making decisions about investing or borrowing money. This chapter introduces you to those tools.

FUTURE VALUE VERSUS PRESENT VALUE

Suppose that a firm has an opportunity to spend $15,000 today on some investment that will produce $17,000 spread out over the next 5 years as follows:

Year 1	$3,000
Year 2	5,000
Year 3	4,000
Year 4	3,000
Year 5	2,000

Is this investment a wise one? It might seem that the obvious answer is yes because the firm spends $15,000 and receives $17,000. Remember, though, that the value of the dollars the firm receives in the future is less than the value of the dollars they spend today. Therefore, it is not clear whether the $17,000 inflows are enough to justify the initial investment.

Time-value-of-money analysis helps managers answer questions like this one. The idea is that managers need a way to compare cash today versus cash in the future. There are two equivalent ways of doing so. One way is to ask the question, what amount of money in the future is equivalent to $15,000 today? In other words, what is the *future value* of $15,000? The other approach asks, what amount today is equivalent to $17,000 paid out over the next 5 years as outlined above? In other words, what is the *present value* of the stream of cash flows coming in the next 5 years?

timeline
A horizontal line on which time zero appears at the leftmost end and future periods are marked from left to right; can be used to depict investment cash flows.

A **timeline** depicts the cash flows associated with a given investment. It is a horizontal line on which time zero appears at the leftmost end and future periods are marked from left to right. A timeline illustrating our hypothetical investment problem appears in Figure 5.1. The cash flows occurring at time zero

FIGURE 5.1

Timeline
Timeline depicting an investment's cash flows

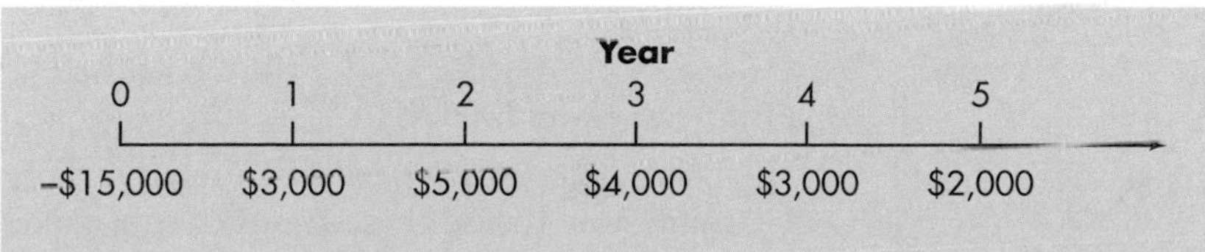

FIGURE 5.2

Compounding and Discounting
Timeline showing compounding to find future value and discounting to find present value

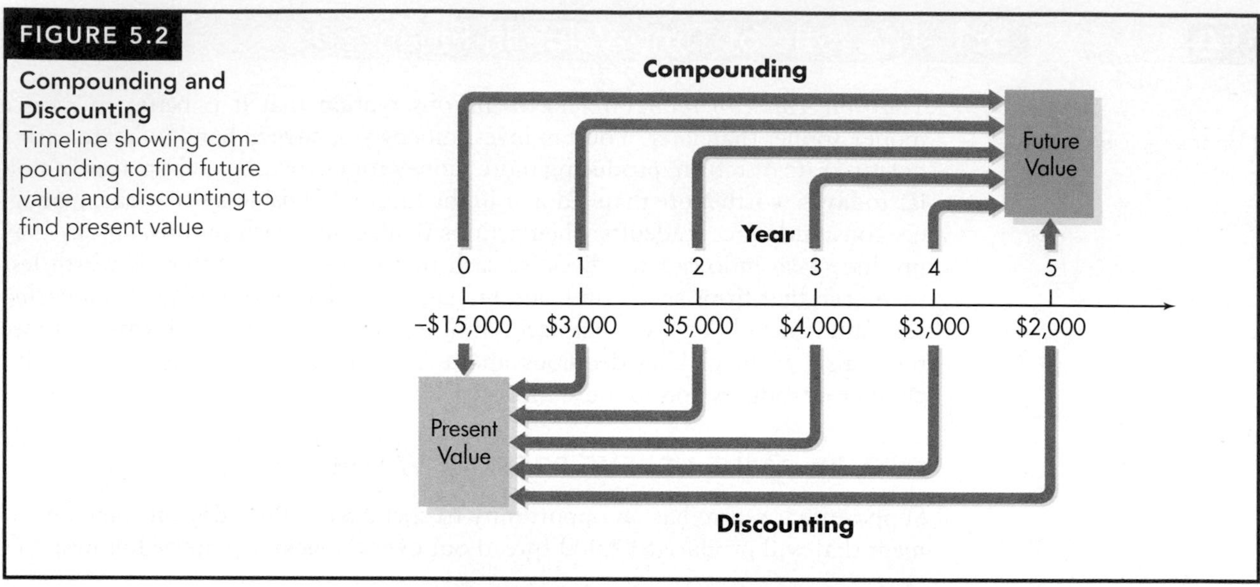

(today) and at subsequent 1-year intervals are below the line; the negative values represent *cash outflows* ($15,000 invested today at time zero), and the positive values represent *cash inflows* ($3,000 inflow in 1 year, $5,000 inflow in 2 years, and so on).

To make the correct investment decision, managers must compare the cash flows depicted in Figure 5.1 at a single point in time. Typically, that point is either the end or the beginning of the investment's life. The future value technique uses *compounding* to find the *future value* of each cash flow at the end of the investment's life and then sums these values to find the investment's future value. This approach is depicted above the timeline in Figure 5.2. The figure shows that the future value of each cash flow is measured at the end of the investment's 5-year life. Alternatively, the present value technique uses *discounting* to find the *present value* of each cash flow at time zero and then sums these values to find the investment's value today. Application of this approach is depicted below the timeline in Figure 5.2. In practice, when making investment decisions, managers usually adopt the present value approach.

COMPUTATIONAL TOOLS

Finding present and future values can involve time-consuming calculations. Although you should understand the concepts and mathematics underlying these calculations, financial calculators and spreadsheets streamline the application of time value techniques.

Financial Calculators

Financial calculators include numerous preprogrammed financial routines. Learning how to use these routines can make present and future value calculations a breeze.

FIGURE 5.3

Calculator Keys
Important financial keys on the typical calculator

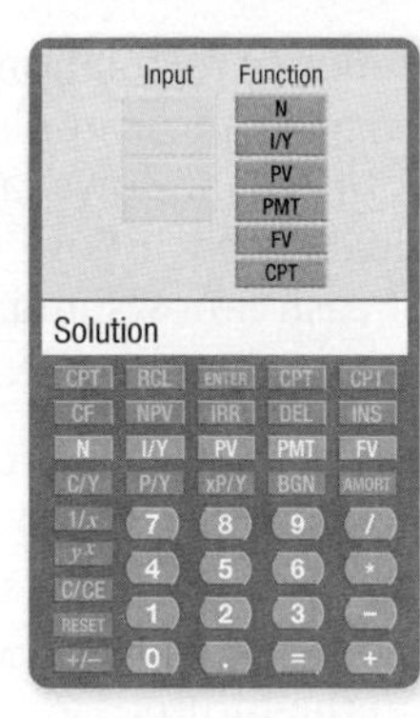

N — Number of periods
I/Y — Interest rate per period
PV — Present value
PMT — Payment amount per period
FV — Future value
CPT — Compute key used to initiate financial calculation once all input values have been entered

We focus primarily on the keys highlighted in Figure 5.3. We typically use four of the five keys shown in third row on the calculator, along with the compute (**CPT**) key to calculate the value of a fifth key. That is, one of the five keys in the third row represents the unknown value we want to calculate. There are also more sophisticated menu-driven functions such as the CF, NPV, and IRR keystrokes: After you select the appropriate routine, the calculator prompts you to enter the appropriate input value. Throughout this book our examples provide the typical keystrokes for the time-value-of-money calculations. It may be necessary for you to refer to your specific calculator's reference guide for complete instructions about how to use your financial calculator.

Once you understand the underlying concepts, you probably will want to use a calculator to streamline calculations. With a little practice, you can increase both the speed and the accuracy of your financial computations. Remember that conceptual understanding of the material is the objective. An ability to solve problems with the aid of a calculator does not necessarily reflect such an understanding, so don't just settle for answers. Work with the material until you are sure that you also understand the concepts.

Electronic Spreadsheets

Like financial calculators, electronic spreadsheets have built-in routines that simplify time-value calculations. We provide in the text a number of spreadsheet solutions that identify the cell entries for calculating time values. The value for each variable is entered in a cell in the spreadsheet, and the calculation is programmed using an equation that links the individual cells. Changing any input variable automatically changes the solution as a result of the equation linking the cells.

Cash Flow Signs

To provide a correct answer, financial calculators and electronic spreadsheets require that users designate whether a cash flow represents an inflow or an outflow. Entering positive numbers designates cash inflows, while entering negative numbers designates cash outflows. By entering the cash flows correctly, you are providing the financial calculator or electronic spreadsheet the calculation's timeline. With accurate cash flows entered, answers provided by financial calculators or electronic spreadsheets will indicate the proper result.

BASIC PATTERNS OF CASH FLOW

Applications of time-value-of-money calculations to financial problems are almost infinite in variety. One way to place those applications into different categories is based on the general patterns of cash inflows and outflows. Some financial problems involve comparing a single cash inflow to a single cash outflow. Others involve comparing streams of cash inflows and outflows. Here are the basic cash flow patterns that we will study in this chapter.

Single amount: A lump sum amount either currently held or expected at some future date. For example, we might want to know how much a $1,000 investment made today might be worth in 5 years. Or we might wish to know how much money we have to set aside today to cover some specific one-time payment we'll have to make in the future.

Annuity: A level periodic stream of cash flow. Many financial arrangements involve making or receiving a fixed payment each month or each year for several years. The classic example from consumer finance is the home mortgage. Time-value-of-money techniques help us determine what the monthly mortgage payment will be given the size of the loan required to buy a home.

Mixed stream: A stream of cash flow that is not an annuity; a stream of unequal periodic cash flows that reflect no particular pattern. Most business investment decisions fall into this category. Two examples appear below. Mixed stream A involves an immediate cash outflow of $4,400, followed by cash inflows of varying amounts for the next 6 years. Mixed stream B has a cash outflow of $50 up front, followed by alternating cash inflows and outflows.

	Mixed cash flow stream	
Year	A	B
0	−$4,400	−$ 50
1	100	50
2	800	−100
3	1,200	280
4	1,200	−60
5	1,400	
6	300	

Regardless of whether a specific financial problem involves a lump sum, an annuity, or a mixed stream, the tools and concepts required to make valid comparisons of cash flows across time are similar, as we will see in the rest of this chapter.

→ REVIEW QUESTIONS MyLab Finance Solutions

5–1 What is the difference between future value and present value? Which approach is generally preferred by financial managers?

5–2 Define and differentiate among the three basic patterns of cash flow: (1) a single amount, (2) an annuity, and (3) a mixed stream.

5.2 Single Amounts

Although most real-world financial problems require managers to make comparisons between streams of cash flow over time, some problems are simpler and involve lump sums or single cash flows at a particular point in time. Furthermore, understanding how to apply time-value-of-money methods to lump sum problems is key to knowing how to handle more complex decisions, so we will begin by studying the comparison of lump sums at different times.

FUTURE VALUE OF A SINGLE AMOUNT

The most basic time-value-of-money concepts and computations concern single payments or receipts that occur in the present or in the future. We begin by considering problems that involve finding the future value of cash that is on hand immediately. Then we will use the underlying concepts to solve problems that determine the value today of cash that will be received or paid in the future.

We often need to know to what extent the money we invest now will grow in the future. For example, if you deposit \$500 today into an account that pays 2% annual interest, how much would you have in the account in 10 years? **Future value** is the value on some future date of money that you invest today. The future value depends on how much money you invest now, how long it remains invested, and the interest rate earned by the investment.

future value
The value on some future date of money that you invest today.

The Concept of Future Value

Perhaps the most powerful of all time-value-of-money concepts is that of compound interest. **Compound interest** is interest paid on an investment's original principal and on interest that has accumulated over previous periods. The term **principal** may refer to the original amount of money placed into an investment or to the balance on which an investment pays interest. Compound interest works by adding the interest earned from one period to the original principal, to create a new principal value for the next period. Thus, an investor receives (or a borrower pays) interest not only on the original principal but also on interest that has been earned in previous periods and added to the original principal balance. The process of adding interest to an investment's principal and paying interest on the new, higher balance is called *compounding*. Compounding may occur daily, monthly, annually, or at almost any time interval. Annual compounding is the simplest type, so we will begin with examples of annual compounding.

compound interest
Interest that is earned on a given deposit and has become part of the principal at the end of a specified period.

principal
The amount of money on which interest is paid.

To calculate the future value of a sum of money that we have on hand today, we will apply compound interest over time. To compute the future value, we must know the present value, or the amount of money we have today; the interest rate; the number of periods that the investment will earn interest; and the compounding interval, that is, the number of times per year that interest compounds. A simple example illustrates the concept of future value with annual compounding.

PERSONAL FINANCE EXAMPLE 5.1

MyLab Finance Solution Video

If Fred Moreno places $100 in an account paying 8% interest compounded annually (i.e., interest is added to the $100 principal 1 time per year), after 1 year he will have $108 in the account. That's just the initial principal of $100 plus 8% ($8) in interest. The future value at the end of the first year is

$$\text{Future value at end of year 1} = \$100 \times (1 + 0.08) = \$108$$

If Fred were to leave this money in the account for another year, he would be paid interest at the rate of 8% on the new principal of $108. After 2 years there would be $116.64 in the account. This amount would represent the principal after the first year ($108) plus 8% of the $108 ($8.64) in interest. The future value after 2 years is

$$\begin{aligned}\text{Future value after 2 years} &= \$108 \times (1 + 0.08) \\ &= \$116.64\end{aligned}$$

Substituting the expression $100 × (1 + 0.08) from the first-year calculation for the $108 value in the second-year calculation gives us

$$\begin{aligned}\text{Future value after 2 years} &= \$100 \times (1 + 0.08) \times (1 + 0.08) \\ &= \$100 \times (1 + 0.08)^2 \\ &= \$116.64\end{aligned}$$

The equations in the preceding example lead to a general formula for calculating future value.

The Equation for Future Value

We can generalize the basic relationship illustrated in Example 5.1 to find the future value of a lump sum in any situation. We use the following notation for the various inputs:

FV_n = future value after n periods

PV_0 = initial principal, or present value when time = 0

r = annual rate of interest (*Note:* Financial calculators often use **I/Y** to represent the interest rate.)

n = number of periods (typically years) that the money remains invested

The general equation for the future value after n periods is

$$FV_n = PV_0 \times (1 + r)^n \quad (5.1)$$

The following example shows how to apply Equation 5.1.

IRF PERSONAL FINANCE EXAMPLE 5.2

Jane Farber places $800 in a savings account paying 3% interest compounded annually. She wants to know how much money will be in the account after 5 years. Substituting $PV_0 = \$800$, $r = 0.03$, and $n = 5$ into Equation 5.1 gives the future value after 5 years:

$$FV_5 = \$800 \times (1 + 0.03)^5 = \$800 \times (1.15927) = \$927.42$$

We can depict this situation on a timeline as follows:

Timeline for future value of a single amount ($800 initial principal, earning 3%, after 5 years)

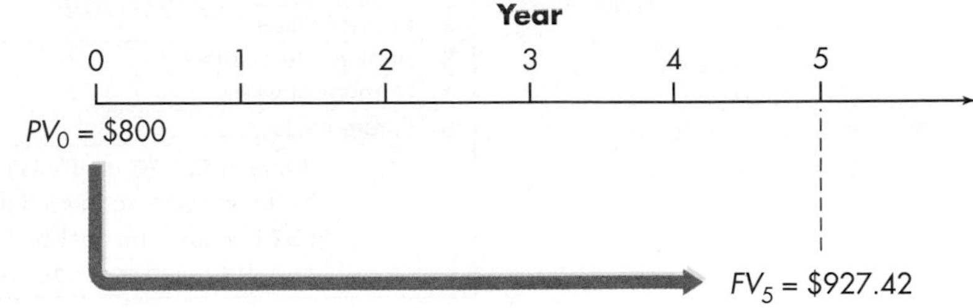

Although solving the equation in the preceding example is not particularly difficult, using a financial calculator or electronic spreadsheet simplifies the calculation.

PERSONAL FINANCE EXAMPLE 5.3 In Personal Finance Example 5.2, Jane Farber places $800 in her savings account at 3% interest compounded annually and wishes to find out how much will be in the account after 5 years.

MyLab Finance Financial Calculator

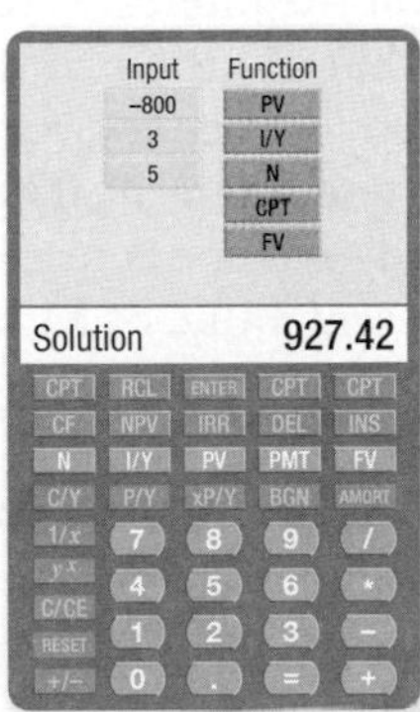

Calculator use[1] We can use a financial calculator to find the future value directly. First enter –800 and depress **PV**; next enter 5 and depress **N**; then enter 3 and depress **I/Y** (which is equivalent to "*r*" in our notation); finally, to calculate the future value, depress **CPT** and then **FV**. The future value of $927.42 should appear on the calculator display as shown at the left. Remember that the calculator differentiates inflows from outflows by preceding the outflows with a negative sign. For example, in the problem just demonstrated, the $800 present value (PV), because we entered it as a negative number, is considered an outflow. Therefore, the calculator shows the future value (FV) of $927.42 as a positive number to indicate that it is the resulting inflow. Had we entered $800 present value as a positive number, the calculator would show the future value of $927.42 as a negative number. Simply stated, *the cash flows—present value (PV) and future value (FV)—will have opposite signs.* (*Note:* In future examples of calculator use, we will use only a display similar to that shown here. If you need a reminder of the procedures involved, review this paragraph.)

Spreadsheet use Excel offers a mathematical function that makes the calculation of future values easy. The format of that function is FV(rate,nper,pmt,pv,type). The terms inside the parentheses are inputs that Excel requires to calculate the future value. The terms *rate* and *nper* refer to the interest rate and the number of time periods, respectively. The term *pv* represents the lump sum (or present value) that you are investing today. For now, we will ignore the other two inputs, *pmt* and *type,* and enter a value of zero for each. The following Excel spreadsheet shows how to use this function to calculate the future value.

1. Many calculators allow the user to set the number of payments per year. Most of these calculators are preset for monthly payments, or 12 payments per year. Because we work primarily with annual payments—one payment per year—it is important to be sure that your calculator is set for one payment per year. Although most calculators are preset to recognize that all payments occur at the end of the period, it is also important to make sure that your calculator is correctly set on the END mode. To avoid including previous data in current calculations, always clear all registers of your calculator before inputting values and making each computation. You can punch the known values into the calculator in any order; the order specified in this as well as other demonstrations of calculator use included in this text merely reflects convenience and personal preference.

	A	B
1	FUTURE VALUE OF A SINGLE AMOUNT	
2	Present value	–$800
3	Annual rate of interest	3%
4	Number of years	5
5	Future value	$927.42

Entry in Cell B5 is =FV(B3,B4,0,B2,0).
The minus sign appears before the $800 in B2 because the cost of the investment is treated as a cash outflow.

Changing any of the values in cells B2, B3, or B4 automatically changes the result shown in cell B5 because the formula in that cell links back to the others. As with the calculator, Excel reports cash inflows as positive numbers and cash outflows as negative numbers. In the example here, we have entered the $800 present value as a negative number, which causes Excel to report the future value as a positive number. Logically, Excel treats the $800 present value as a cash outflow, as if you are paying for the investment you are making, and it treats the future value as a cash inflow when you reap the benefits of your investment 5 years later.

A Graphical View of Future Value

Figure 5.4 illustrates how the future value of $1 depends on the interest rate and the number of periods that money is invested. It shows that (1) the higher the interest rate, the higher the future value, and (2) the longer the money remains invested, the higher the future value. Note that for an interest rate of 0%, the future value always equals the present value ($1.00). For any interest rate greater than zero, however, the future value is greater than the present value of $1.00.

Compound Interest versus Simple Interest

simple interest
Interest that is earned only on an investment's original principal and not on interest that accumulates over time.

Before turning our attention to the concept of present value, we should make a distinction between compound interest, a concept that we have applied in all of our examples so far, and simple interest. **Simple interest** is interest earned only

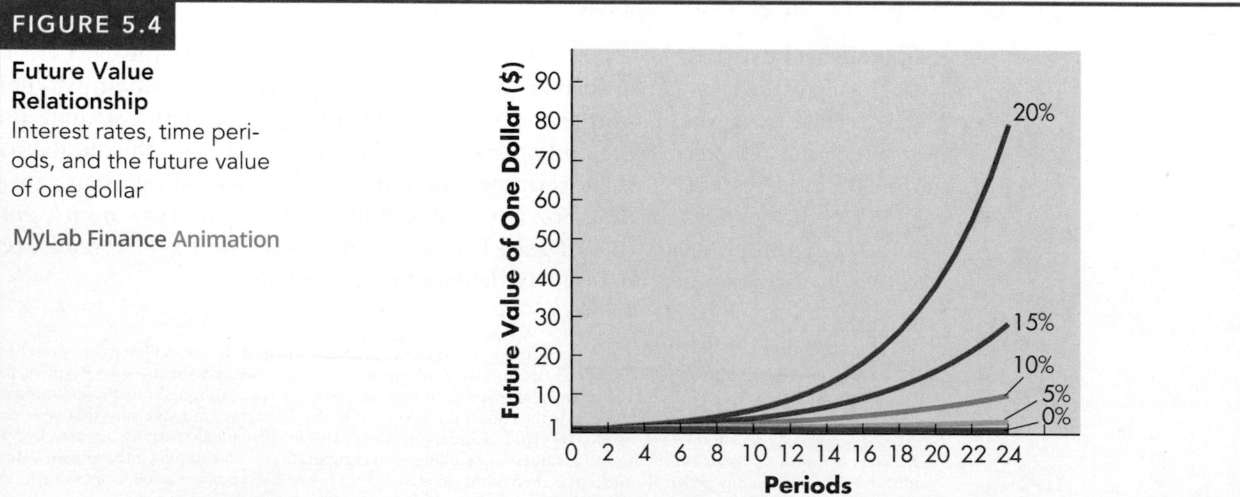

FIGURE 5.4

Future Value Relationship
Interest rates, time periods, and the future value of one dollar

MyLab Finance Animation

TABLE 5.1 Simple Interest versus Compound Interest

	Account Balance	
Time (year)	Simple Interest	Compound Interest
0 (initial deposit)	$1,000	$1,000.00
1	1,050	1,050.00
2	1,100	1,102.50
3	1,150	1,157.62
4	1,200	1,215.51
5	1,250	1,276.28
10	1,500	1,628.89

on an investment's original principal and not on accumulated interest. Naturally money accumulates faster when an investment earns compound interest rather than simple interest. When the interest rate is very low and the time that money remains invested is very short, the difference between earning compound interest and simple interest is small. But at higher interest rates and for longer investment horizons, the differences can be quite substantial. Table 5.1 illustrates this concept by showing how much money accumulates over time if an investor places $1,000 into an account earning 5% interest. If the account pays simple interest, then the investor receives exactly $50 in interest every period, so after 1 year the account balance is $1,050, after 2 years the balance is $1,100, and so on. If the account pays compound interest, the balance grows much faster because the investor earns more than $50 in interest every period after the first one. After 10 years, the account paying 5% simple interest is worth $1,500, but the account paying compound interest is worth $1,628.89.

Our focus thus far has been on determining how fast money will grow over time. In many business and personal finance problems, the relevant question is not what the future value of an investment will be, but rather how much a future cash flow (or stream of cash flows) is worth today.

PRESENT VALUE OF A SINGLE AMOUNT

Most investments made by businesses and individuals involve an exchange of money today for money in the future. For example, a company must spend money today to build a plant, but over time the products made in that plant will generate cash inflows for the firm. Therefore, the firm must decide whether those future cash inflows are worth the cost of building the plant. In much the same way, an individual investor buys a stock because it will pay dividends and may sell in the future at a higher price than it sells for today. The investor must decide if the price required to buy the stock today is worth the future dividends and capital gains the stock may provide in the future. Thus, both businesses and individuals need a way to determine the *present value* of cash flows that come in the future.

present value
The value in today's dollars of some future cash flow.

The **present value** is the value in today's dollars of some future cash flow. An equivalent definition is that the present value is the amount that one would have to invest today such that the investment would grow to a particular value in the future. For example, suppose an individual is presented with an investment opportunity that will pay $5,000 three years from now. The present value represents the amount of money the investor would pay today for the right to receive that $5,000 cash inflow in 3 years. Like future value, present value depends on the interest rate and the timing of cash flows.

The Concept of Present Value

discounting cash flows
The process of finding present values; the inverse of compounding interest.

The process of finding present values is often referred to as **discounting cash flows.** Present value calculations answer the following question: If you can earn r percent on your money, what is the most you would be willing to pay now for an opportunity to receive FV_n dollars n periods from today?

This process is actually the inverse of compounding interest. Instead of finding the future value of present dollars invested at a given rate, discounting determines the present value of a future amount, assuming an opportunity to earn a certain return on the money. This annual rate of return is variously referred to as the *discount rate, required return, cost of capital,* and *opportunity cost.* We use these terms interchangeably in this text.

PERSONAL FINANCE EXAMPLE 5.4 Paul Shorter has an opportunity to receive $300 one year from now. What is the most that Paul should pay now for this opportunity? The answer depends in part on what Paul's current investment opportunities are (i.e., what his opportunity cost is). Suppose Paul can earn a return of 2% on money that he has on hand today. To determine how much he'd be willing to pay for the right to receive $300 one year from now, Paul can think about how much of his own money he'd have to set aside right now to earn $300 by next year. Letting PV_0 equal this unknown amount and using the same notation as in the future value discussion, we have

$$PV_0 \times (1 + 0.02) = \$300$$

Solving for PV_0 gives us

$$PV_0 = \frac{\$300}{(1 + 0.02)}$$
$$= \$294.12$$

The value today ("present value") of $300 received 1 year from today, given an interest rate of 2%, is $294.12. That is, investing $294.12 today at 2% would result in $300 in 1 year. Given his opportunity cost (or his required return) of 2%, Paul should not pay more than $294.12 for this investment. Doing so would mean that he would earn a return of less than 2% on this investment. That's unwise if he has other similar investment opportunities that pay 2%. However, if Paul could buy this investment for less than $294.12, he would earn a return greater than his 2% opportunity cost.

The Equation for Present Value

We can find the present value of a future amount mathematically by solving Equation 5.1 for PV_0. In other words, the present value, PV_0, of some future amount, FV_n, to be received n periods from now, assuming an interest rate (or opportunity cost) of r, equals

$$PV_0 = \frac{FV_n}{(1 + r)^n} \tag{5.2}$$

IRF PERSONAL FINANCE EXAMPLE 5.5 Pam Valenti has been offered an investment opportunity that will pay her \$1,700 eight years from now. Pam has other investment opportunities available to her that pay 4%, so she will require a 4% return on this opportunity. How much should Pam pay for this opportunity? In other words, what is the present value of \$1,700 that comes in 8 years if the opportunity cost is 4%? Substituting $FV_8 = \$1{,}700$, $n = 8$, and $r = 0.04$ into Equation 5.2 yields

$$PV_0 = \frac{\$1{,}700}{(1 + 0.04)^8} = \frac{\$1{,}700}{1.36857} = \$1{,}242.17$$

The following timeline shows this analysis.

Timeline for present value of a single amount (\$1,700 future amount, discounted at 4%, for 8 years)

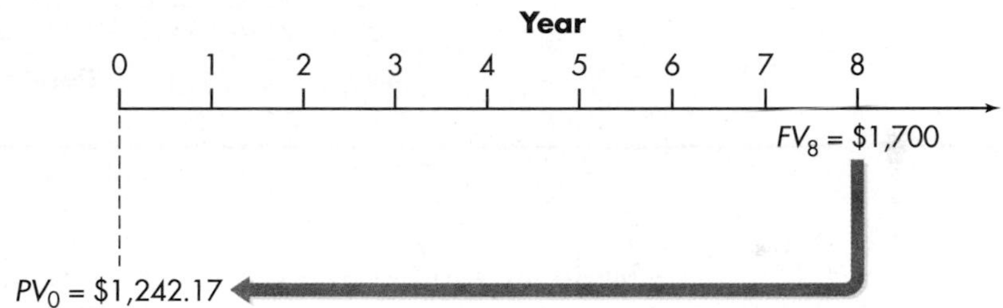

MyLab Finance Financial Calculator

Calculator use Using the calculator's financial functions and the inputs shown at the left, you should find the present value to be \$1,242.17. Notice that the calculator result is represented as a negative value to indicate that the present value is a cash outflow (i.e., the investment's cost).

Spreadsheet use The format of Excel's present value function is very similar to the future value function covered earlier. The appropriate syntax is PV(rate,nper,pmt,fv,type). The input list inside the parentheses is the same as in Excel's future value function with one exception. The present value function contains the term *fv,* which represents the future lump sum payment (or receipt) whose present value you are trying to calculate. The following Excel spreadsheet illustrates how to use this function to calculate the present value.

	A	B
1	PRESENT VALUE OF A SINGLE AMOUNT	
2	Future value	\$1,700
3	Annual rate of interest	4%
4	Number of years	8
5	Present value	–\$1,242.17

Entry in Cell B5 is =PV(B3,B4,0,B2,0).
The minus sign appears before the \$1,242.17 in B5 because the cost of the investment is treated as a cash outflow.

A Graphical View of Present Value

Figure 5.5 illustrates how the present value of \$1 depends on the interest rate (or discount rate) and the number of periods an investor must wait to receive \$1. The figure shows that, everything else being equal, (1) the higher the discount

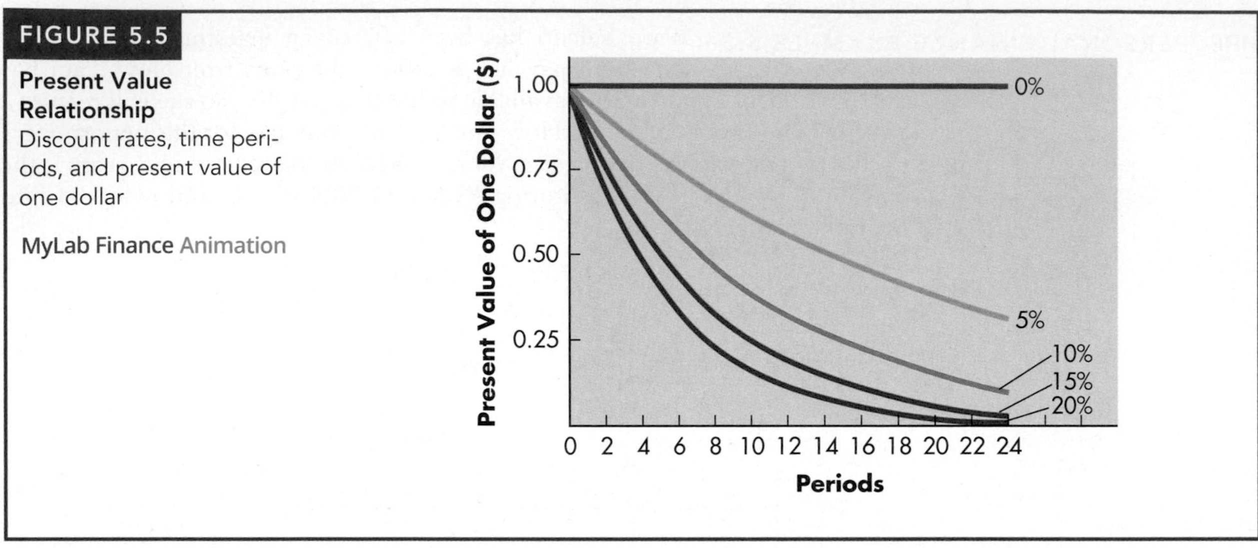

FIGURE 5.5

Present Value Relationship
Discount rates, time periods, and present value of one dollar

MyLab Finance Animation

rate, the lower the present value; and (2) the longer the waiting period, the lower the present value. Also note that if the discount rate is 0%, the present value of $1 always equals $1 no matter when that dollar arrives. But for any discount rate greater than zero, the present value is less than $1.

→ REVIEW QUESTIONS MyLab Finance Solutions

5–3 How is the compounding process related to the payment of interest on savings? What is the general equation for future value?

5–4 What effect would a decrease in the interest rate have on the future value of a deposit? What effect would an increase in the holding period have on future value?

5–5 What is meant by "the present value of a future amount"? What is the general equation for present value?

5–6 What effect does increasing the required return have on the present value of a future amount? Why?

5–7 How are present value and future value calculations related?

→ EXCEL REVIEW QUESTIONS MyLab Finance Solutions

5–8 It is tax time and you would like to make a tax-deductible contribution to an individual retirement account (IRA). Using the information provided at MyLab Finance, find the future value of an IRA contribution that grows until you retire.

5–9 It is never too soon to begin investing for a child's college education. Using the information provided at MyLab Finance, determine the present value you would need to invest today to ensure that your child receives the college education she deserves.

5.3 Annuities

How much would you pay today for an investment that pays $3,000 at the end of each of the next 20 years, given that you can earn 7% on other investments? How much will you have after 5 years if your employer withholds and invests $1,000 of your bonus at the end of each of the next 5 years, guaranteeing you a 9% annual rate of return? To answer these questions, you need to understand the application of time value of money to *annuities.*

annuity
A stream of equal periodic cash flows over a specified time period. These cash flows can be inflows or outflows of funds.

An **annuity** is a stream of equal periodic cash flows over a specified time. These cash flows may arrive at annual intervals, but they can also occur at other intervals, such as monthly rent or car payments. The cash flows in an annuity can be inflows (the $3,000 received at the end of each of the next 20 years) or outflows (the $1,000 invested at the end of each of the next 5 years).

ordinary annuity
An annuity for which the cash flow occurs at the end of each period.

annuity due
An annuity for which the cash flow occurs at the beginning of each period.

TYPES OF ANNUITIES

Annuities are of two general types. For an **ordinary annuity**, the cash flow occurs at the *end* of each period. For an **annuity due**, the cash flow occurs at the *beginning* of each period.

PERSONAL FINANCE EXAMPLE 5.6 Fran Abrams is evaluating two annuities. Both annuities pay $1,000 per year, but annuity A is an ordinary annuity, while annuity B is an annuity due. To better understand the difference between these annuities, she has listed their cash flows in Table 5.2. The two annuities differ only in the timing of their cash flows: The cash flows occur sooner with the annuity due than with the ordinary annuity.

Although the cash flows of both annuities in Table 5.2 total $5,000, the annuity due would have a higher future value than the ordinary annuity because each of its five annual cash flows can earn interest for 1 year more than each of the ordinary annuity's cash flows. In general, as we will demonstrate later in this chapter, *the value (present or future) of an annuity due is always greater than the value of an otherwise identical ordinary annuity.*

TABLE 5.2 **Comparison of Ordinary Annuity and Annuity Due Cash Flows ($1,000, 5 Years)**

	Annual cash flows	
Year	Annuity A (*ordinary*)	Annuity B (*annuity due*)
0	$ 0	$1,000
1	1,000	1,000
2	1,000	1,000
3	1,000	1,000
4	1,000	1,000
5	1,000	0
Totals	$5,000	$5,000

FINDING THE FUTURE VALUE OF AN ORDINARY ANNUITY

One way to find the future value of an ordinary annuity is to calculate the future value of each cash flow and then add up those figures. Fortunately, several shortcuts lead to the answer. You can calculate the future value after n years of an ordinary annuity that makes n annual cash payments equal to CF_1 by using Equation 5.3:

$$FV_n = CF_1 \times \left\{ \frac{[(1 + r)^n - 1]}{r} \right\} \tag{5.3}$$

As before, in this equation r represents the interest rate, and n represents the number of payments in the annuity (or, equivalently, the number of years over which the annuity is spread). The subscript 1 on the term CF_1 highlights that with an ordinary annuity, the first payment comes after 1 year (or, more generally, after 1 *period*). The calculations required to find the future value of an ordinary annuity are illustrated in the following example.

IRF PERSONAL FINANCE EXAMPLE 5.7

MyLab Finance Animation

Fran Abrams wishes to determine how much money she will have after 5 years if she chooses annuity A, the ordinary annuity. She will deposit the $1,000 annual payments that the annuity provides at the end of each of the next 5 years into a savings account paying 7% annual interest. This situation is depicted on the following timeline.

Timeline for future value of an ordinary annuity ($1,000 end-of-year deposit, earning 7%, after 5 years)

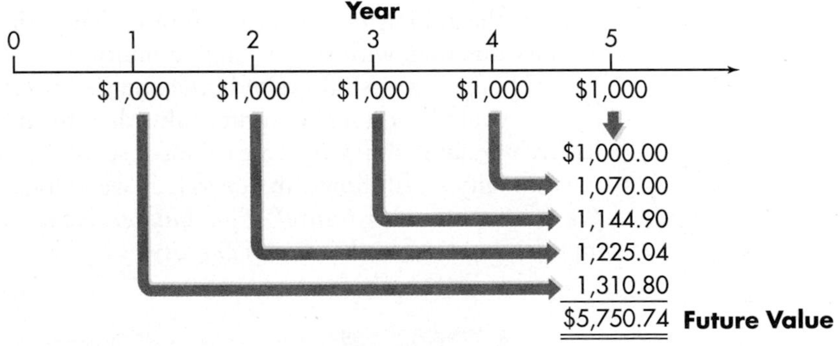

MyLab Finance Financial Calculator

Input	Function
−1000	PMT
7	I/Y
5	N
	CPT
	FV

Solution 5,750.74

As the figure shows, after 5 years, Fran will have $5,750.74 in her account. Note that because she makes deposits at the end of the year, the first deposit will earn interest for 4 years, the second for 3 years, and so on. Plugging the relevant values into Equation 5.3, we have

$$FV_5 = \$1{,}000 \times \left\{ \frac{[(1 + 0.07)^5 - 1]}{0.07} \right\} = \$5{,}750.74$$

Calculator use Using the calculator inputs shown at the left, you can confirm that the future value of the ordinary annuity equals $5,750.74. In this example, we enter the $1,000 annuity payment as a negative value, which in turn causes the calculator to report the resulting future value as a positive value. You can think of each $1,000 deposit that Fran makes into her investment account as a payment into the account or a cash outflow, and after 5 years the future value is the balance in the account, or the cash inflow that Fran receives as a reward for investing.

Spreadsheet use To calculate the future value of an annuity in Excel, we will use the same future value function that we used to calculate the future value of a lump sum, but we will add two new input values. Recall that the future value function's syntax is FV(rate,nper,pmt,pv,type). We have already explained the terms *rate, nper,* and *pv* in this function. The term *pmt* refers to the annual payment the annuity offers. The term *type* is an input that lets Excel know whether the annuity being valued is an ordinary annuity (in which case the input value for *type* is 0 or omitted) or an annuity due (in which case the correct input value for *type* is 1). In this particular problem, the input value for *pv* is 0 because there is no up-front money received that is separate from the annuity. The only cash flows are those that are part of the annuity stream. The following Excel spreadsheet demonstrates how to calculate the future value of the ordinary annuity.

	A	B
1	FUTURE VALUE OF AN ORDINARY ANNUITY	
2	Annual annuity payment	–$1,000
3	Annual rate of interest	7%
4	Number of years	5
5	Future value	$5,750.74

Entry in Cell B5 is =FV(B3,B4,B2,0,0).
The minus sign appears before the $1,000 in B2 because the annuity's payments are cash outflows.

FINDING THE PRESENT VALUE OF AN ORDINARY ANNUITY

Quite often in finance, we need to find the present value of a stream of cash flows spread over several future periods. An annuity is, of course, a stream of equal periodic cash flows. The method for finding the present value of an ordinary annuity is similar to the method just discussed. One approach is to calculate the present value of each cash flow in the annuity and then add up those present values. Alternatively, the algebraic shortcut for finding the present value of an ordinary annuity that makes an annual payment of CF_1 for n years looks like

$$PV_0 = \left(\frac{CF_1}{r}\right) \times \left[1 - \frac{1}{(1 + r)^n}\right] \tag{5.4}$$

Of course, the simplest approach is to solve problems like this one with a financial calculator or spreadsheet program.

IRF EXAMPLE 5.8

MyLab Finance Solution Video
MyLab Finance Animation

Braden Company, a small producer of plastic toys, wants to determine the most it should pay for a particular ordinary annuity. The annuity consists of cash inflows of $700 at the end of each year for 5 years. The firm requires the annuity to provide a minimum return of 4%. The following timeline depicts this situation.

Timeline for present value of an ordinary annuity ($700 end-of-year cash flows, discounted at 4%, over 5 years)

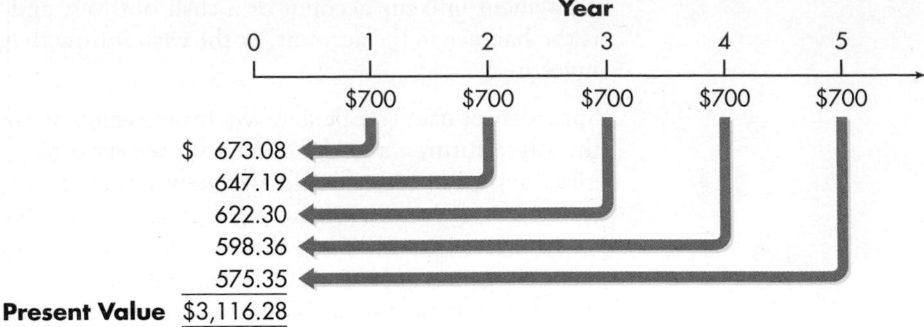

Table 5.3 shows that one way to find the present value of the annuity is to simply calculate the present values of all the cash payments using the present value equation (Equation 5.2) and sum them. This procedure yields a present value of $3,116.28. Calculators and spreadsheets offer streamlined methods for arriving at this figure.

TABLE 5.3 Long Method for Finding the Present Value of an Ordinary Annuity

Year (n)	Cash flow	Present value calculation	Present value
1	$700	$\frac{\$700}{(1 + 0.04)^1} =$	$ 673.08
2	700	$\frac{\$700}{(1 + 0.04)^2} =$	$ 647.19
3	700	$\frac{\$700}{(1 + 0.04)^3} =$	$ 622.30
4	700	$\frac{\$700}{(1 + 0.04)^4} =$	$ 598.36
5	700	$\frac{\$700}{(1 + 0.04)^5} =$	$ 575.35
		Present value of annuity	$3,116.28

MyLab Finance Financial Calculator

Input	Function
700	PMT
4	I/Y
5	N
	CPT
	PV
Solution	–3,116.28

Calculator use Using the calculator's inputs shown at the left, you will find the present value of the ordinary annuity to be $3,116.28. Because the present value in this example is a cash outflow representing what Braden Company is willing to pay for the annuity, we show it as a negative value in the calculator display.

Spreadsheet use The following spreadsheet shows how to calculate present value of the ordinary annuity.

	A	B
1	PRESENT VALUE OF AN ORDINARY ANNUITY	
2	Annual annuity payment	$700
3	Annual rate of interest	4%
4	Number of years	5
5	Present value	–$3,116.28

Entry in Cell B5 is =PV(B3,B4,B2,0,0).
The minus sign appears before the $3,116.28 in B5 because the annuity's present value is a cost and therefore a cash outflow.

FINDING THE FUTURE VALUE OF AN ANNUITY DUE

We now turn our attention to annuities due. Remember that the cash flows of an annuity due occur at the *start of the period*. In other words, if we are dealing with annual payments, each payment in an annuity due comes 1 year earlier than it would in an ordinary annuity, which in turn means that each payment can earn an extra year of interest. That is why the future value of an annuity due exceeds the future value of an otherwise identical ordinary annuity.

The algebraic shortcut for the future value after n years of an annuity due that makes n annual payments of CF_0 is

$$FV_n = CF_0 \times \left\{\frac{[(1+r)^n - 1]}{r}\right\} \times (1+r) \qquad (5.5)$$

Compare this equation with Equation 5.3, which shows how to calculate the future value of an ordinary annuity. The two equations are nearly identical but do show two differences. In Equation 5.5 we use the term CF_0 rather than CF_1 to highlight that for an annuity due, the first payment comes right away (at the beginning of the first year when time = 0). In addition, Equation 5.5 has an added term, $(1 + r)$, at the end. In other words, the value obtained from Equation 5.5 will be $(1 + r)$ times greater than the value in Equation 5.3 if the other inputs (the annual cash flow and the number of payments) are the same. That makes sense because all the payments in the annuity due earn 1 more year of interest than do payments in the ordinary annuity.

IRF PERSONAL FINANCE EXAMPLE 5.9 Recall from an earlier example, illustrated in Table 5.2, that Fran Abrams wanted to choose between an ordinary annuity and an annuity due, both offering similar terms except for the timing of cash flows. We calculated the future value of the ordinary annuity in Example 5.7, but we now want to calculate the future value of the annuity due. The timeline on the next page depicts this situation. Take care to notice on the timeline that when we use Equation 5.5 (or any of the shortcuts that follow) we are calculating the future value of Fran's annuity due after 5 years even though the fifth and final payment in the annuity due comes after 4 years (which is equivalent to the beginning of year 5). We can calculate the future value of an annuity due using a calculator or a spreadsheet.

MyLab Finance Animation

MyLab Finance Financial Calculator

Note: Switch calculator to BEGIN mode.

Input	Function
−1000	PMT
7	I/Y
5	N
	CPT
	FV

Solution 6,153.29

Calculator use Before using your calculator to find the future value of an annuity due, you must either switch it to BEGIN mode or use the DUE key, depending on the specific calculator. Then, using the inputs shown at the left, you will find the future value of the annuity due to be $6,153.29. (*Note:* Because we nearly always assume end-of-period cash flows, be sure to switch your calculator back to END mode when you have completed your annuity-due calculations.)

Timeline for future value of an annuity due ($1,000 beginning-of-year deposit, earning 7%, after 5 years)

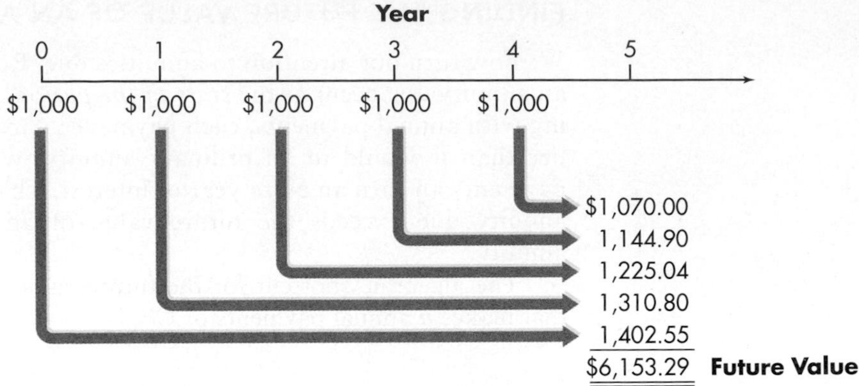

Spreadsheet use The following Excel spreadsheet illustrates how to calculate the future value of the annuity due. Remember that for an annuity due the *type* input value must be set to 1, and we must also specify the *pv* input value as 0 because there is no upfront cash other than what is part of the annuity stream.

	A	B
1	FUTURE VALUE OF AN ANNUITY DUE	
2	Annual annuity payment	–$1,000
3	Annual rate of interest	7%
4	Number of years	5
5	Future value	$6,153.29

Entry in Cell B5 is =FV(B3,B4,B2,0,1). The minus sign appears before the $1,000 in B2 because the annuity's payments are cash outflows.

Comparison of an Annuity Due with an Ordinary Annuity Future Value

The future value of an annuity due is always greater than the future value of an otherwise identical ordinary annuity. We can see that by comparing the future values after 5 years of Fran Abrams's two annuities:

$$\text{Ordinary annuity} = \$5{,}750.74 \quad \text{versus} \quad \text{Annuity due} = \$6{,}153.29$$

Because the cash flow of the annuity due occurs at the beginning of the period rather than at the end (i.e., each payment comes 1 year sooner in the annuity due), its future value is greater. How much greater? It is interesting to calculate the percentage difference between the value of the annuity and the value of the annuity due:

$$(\$6{,}153.29 - \$5{,}750.74) \div \$5{,}750.74 = 0.07 = 7\%$$

Recall that the interest rate in this example is 7%. It is no coincidence that the annuity due is 7% more valuable than the annuity. An extra year of interest on each of the annuity due's payments makes the annuity due 7% more valuable than the annuity.

FINDING THE PRESENT VALUE OF AN ANNUITY DUE

We can also find the present value of an annuity due. By adjusting the ordinary annuity present value calculation, we can easily perform this calculation. Because the cash flows of an annuity due occur at the beginning rather than end of the period, we discount each annuity due cash flow 1 fewer period than an ordinary annuity. The algebraic formula for the present value of an annuity due is

$$PV_0 = \left(\frac{CF_0}{r}\right) \times \left[1 - \frac{1}{(1 + r)^n}\right] \times (1 + r) \tag{5.6}$$

Notice the similarity between this equation and Equation 5.4. The two equations are identical except that Equation 5.6 uses CF_0 to indicate that the first cash flow arrives immediately in an annuity due, and Equation 5.6 has an extra term at the end, $(1 + r)$. The reason for this extra term is the same as when we calculated the future value of the annuity due. In the annuity due, each payment arrives 1 year earlier (compared to the ordinary annuity), so each payment has a higher present value. To be specific, each payment of the annuity due is discounted one less period so it's worth r% more than each ordinary annuity payment.

IRF EXAMPLE 5.10

MyLab Finance Animation

In Example 5.8 involving Braden Company, we found the present value of Braden's $700, 5-year ordinary annuity discounted at 4% to be $3,116.28. We now assume that Braden's $700 annual cash in flow occurs at the *start* of each year and is thereby an annuity due. The following timeline illustrates the new situation.

Timeline for present value of an annuity due ($700 beginning-of-year cash flows, discounted at 4%, over 5 years)

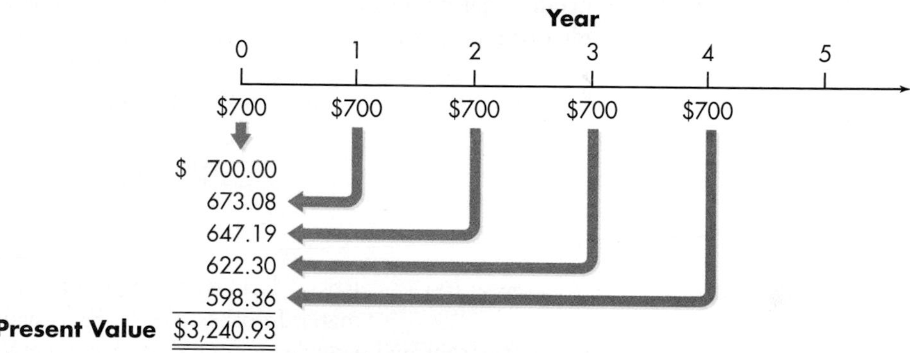

We can calculate its present value using a calculator or a spreadsheet.

MyLab Finance Financial Calculator

Note: Switch calculator to BEGIN mode.

Input	Function
700	PMT
4	I/Y
5	N
	CPT
	PV

Solution −3,240.93

Calculator use Before using your calculator to find the present value of an annuity due, you must either switch it to BEGIN mode or use the DUE key, depending on the specifics of your calculator. Then, using the inputs shown at the left, you will find the present value of the annuity due to be $3,240.93 (*Note:* Because we nearly always assume end-of-period cash flows, be sure to switch your calculator back to END mode when you have completed your annuity-due calculations.)

Spreadsheet use The following spreadsheet shows how to calculate the present value of the annuity due.

MyLab

	A	B
1	PRESENT VALUE OF AN ANNUITY DUE	
2	Annual annuity payment	$700
3	Annual rate of interest	4%
4	Number of years	5
5	Present value	$3,240.93

Entry in Cell B5 is =PV(B3,B4,B2,0,1).
The minus sign appears before the $3,240.93 in B5 because the annuity's present value is a cost and therefore a cash outflow.

Comparison of an Annuity Due with an Ordinary Annuity Present Value

The present value of an annuity due is always greater than the present value of an otherwise identical ordinary annuity. We can verify this statement by comparing the present values of the Braden Company's two annuities:

$$\text{Ordinary annuity} = \$3{,}116.28 \quad \text{versus} \quad \text{Annuity due} = \$3{,}240.93$$

Because the cash flows of the annuity due occur at the beginning of each period rather than at the end, their present values are greater. If we calculate the percentage difference in the values of these two annuities, we will find that the annuity due is 4% more valuable than the annuity (remember that 4% is the discount rate that Braden uses):

$$(\$3{,}240.93 - \$3{,}116.28) \div \$3{,}116.28 = 0.04 = 4\%$$

FINDING THE PRESENT VALUE OF A PERPETUITY

perpetuity
An annuity with an infinite life, providing continual annual cash flow.

A **perpetuity** is an annuity with an infinite life. In other words, it is an annuity that never stops providing a cash flow at the end of each year.

A number of business and personal investment decisions involve payouts that occur indefinitely into the future and are therefore excellent applications of the idea of a perpetuity. Fortunately, the calculation for the present value of a perpetuity is one of the easiest in finance. If a perpetuity pays an annual cash flow of CF_1, starting 1 year from now, the present value of the cash flow stream is

$$PV_0 = CF_1 \div r \tag{5.7}$$

PERSONAL FINANCE EXAMPLE 5.11 Ross Clark wishes to endow a chair in finance at his alma mater. In other words, Ross wants to make a lump sum donation today that will provide an annual stream of cash flows to the university forever. The university indicated that the annual cash flow required to support an endowed chair is $400,000 and that it will invest money Ross donates today in assets earning a 5% return. If Ross wants to give money today so that the university will begin receiving annual cash flows next year, how large must his contribution be? To determine the amount Ross must give the university to fund the chair, we must calculate the present value of a $400,000 perpetuity discounted at 5%. Using Equation 5.7, we can determine that this present value is $8 million when the interest rate is 5%:

$$PV_0 = \$400{,}000 \div 0.05 = \$8{,}000{,}000$$

In other words, to generate $400,000 every year for an indefinite period requires $8,000,000 today if Ross Clark's alma mater can earn 5% on its investments. If the university earns 5% interest annually on the $8,000,000, it can withdraw $400,000 per year indefinitely without ever touching the original $800,000 donation.

Many financial applications require analysts to calculate the present value of a cash flow stream that continues forever (i.e., a perpetuity) and grows at a steady rate. Calculating the present value of a growing perpetuity is not much more complicated than finding the present value of a level perpetuity. For a cash flow stream that begins next year, pays an initial cash flow of CF_1, and grows after next year at a constant rate g forever, the present value of the growing perpetuity is

$$PV_0 = \left(\frac{CF_1}{r - g}\right) \tag{5.8}$$

Equation 5.8 applies only when the discount rate is greater than the growth rate in cash flows (i.e., $r > g$). If the interest rate is less than or equal to the growth rate, cash flows grow so fast that the present value of the stream is infinite.

PERSONAL FINANCE EXAMPLE 5.12 Suppose, after consulting with his alma mater, Ross Clark learns that the university requires the endowment to provide a $400,000 cash flow next year, but subsequent annual cash flows must grow by 2% per year to keep up with inflation. How much does Ross need to donate today to cover this requirement? Plugging the relevant values into Equation 5.8, we have:

$$PV_0 = \frac{\$400{,}000}{0.05 - 0.02} = \$13{,}333{,}333$$

Compared to the level perpetuity providing $400,000 per year, the growing perpetuity requires Ross to make a much larger initial donation, $13.3 million versus $8 million.

→ REVIEW QUESTIONS MyLab Finance Solutions

5–10 What is the difference between an ordinary annuity and an annuity due? Which is more valuable? Why?

5–11 What are the most efficient ways to calculate the present value of an ordinary annuity?

5–12 How can the formula for the future value of an annuity be modified to find the future value of an annuity due?

5–13 How can the formula for the present value of an ordinary annuity be modified to find the present value of an annuity due?

5–14 What is a perpetuity? Why is the present value of a perpetuity equal to the annual cash payment divided by the interest rate? Why doesn't this chapter provide an equation showing you how to calculate the future value of a perpetuity?

→ EXCEL REVIEW QUESTIONS MyLab Finance Solutions

5–15 Because tax time comes around every year, you smartly decide to make equal contributions to your IRA at the end of every year. Using the information provided at MyLab Finance, calculate the future value of your IRA contributions when you retire.

5–16 You have just graduated from college and begun your new career, and now it is time to buy your first home. Using the information provided at MyLab Finance, determine how much you can spend for your new dream home.

5–17 Rather than making contributions to an IRA at the end of each year, you decide to make equal contributions at the beginning of each year. Using the information provided at MyLab Finance, solve for the future value of your IRA contributions when you retire.

LG4

5.4 Mixed Streams

mixed stream
A stream of unequal periodic cash flows that reflect no particular pattern.

Two types of cash flow streams are possible, the annuity and the mixed stream. Whereas an annuity is a pattern of equal periodic cash flows, a **mixed stream** consists of unequal periodic cash flows that reflect no particular pattern. Financial managers frequently need to evaluate opportunities that they expect to provide mixed streams of future cash flows. Here we consider both the future value and the present value of mixed streams.

FUTURE VALUE OF A MIXED STREAM

Determining the future value of a mixed stream of cash flows is straightforward. We compute the future value of each cash flow at the specified future date and then add all the individual future values to find the total future value.

IRF EXAMPLE 5.13

Shrell Industries, a cabinet manufacturer, expects to receive the following mixed stream of cash flows over the next 5 years from one of its small customers.

Time	Cash flow
0	\$ 0
1	11,500
2	14,000
3	12,900
4	16,000
5	18,000

If Shrell expects to earn 8% on its investments, how much will it accumulate after 5 years if it immediately invests these cash flows when they are received? This situation is depicted on the following timeline.

Timeline for future value of a mixed stream (end-of-year cash flows, compounded at 8% to the end of year 5)

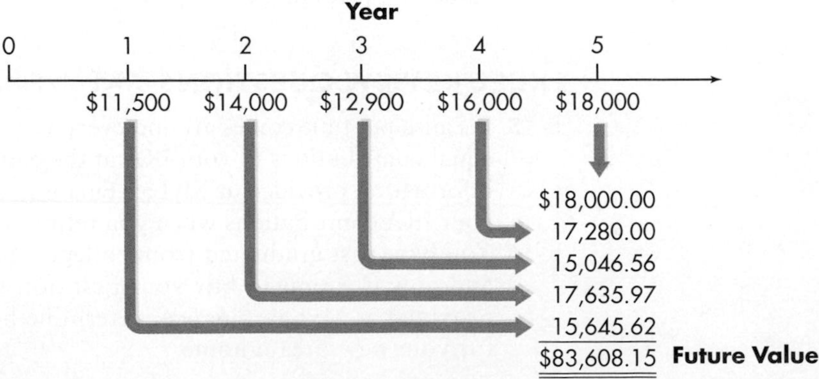

MyLab Finance Financial Calculator

Input	Function
0	CF_0
11500	CF_1
14000	CF_2
12900	CF_3
16000	CF_4
18000	CF_5
8	I/Y
	CPT
	NPV

Solution 56,902.30

Calculator use Most financial calculators do not have a built-in function for finding the future value of a mixed stream of cash flows, but most of them have a function for finding the present value. Once you have the present value of the mixed stream, you can move it forward in time to find the future value. To accomplish this task you must first enter the mixed stream of cash flows into your financial calculator's cash flow register, usually denoted by the CF key, starting with the cash flow at time zero. Be sure to enter cash flows correctly as either cash inflows or outflows. Once you enter the cash flows, you will need to use the calculator's net present value (NPV) function to find the present value of the cash flows. For Shrell, enter the following into your calculator's cash flow register: $CF_0 = 0$, $CF_1 = 11{,}500$, $CF_2 = 14{,}000$, $CF_3 = 12{,}900$, $CF_4 = 16{,}000$, $CF_5 = 18{,}000$. Next enter the interest rate of 8% and then solve for the NPV, which is the present value of the mixed stream of cash flows at time zero. The present value of the mixed stream of cash flows is $56,902.30, so you need to move this amount forward to the end of year 5 to find the future of the mixed stream. Enter −56,902.30 as the PV, 5 for N, 8 for I/Y, and then compute FV.

MyLab Finance Financial Calculator

Input	Function
−56902.30	PV
8	I/Y
5	N
	CPT
	FV

Solution 83,608.15

You will find that the future value at the end of year 5 of Shrell's mixed cash flows is $83,608.15. An alternative approach to using the calculator's cash flow register and NPV function is to find the future value at time 5 of each cash flow and then sum the individual future values to find the future value of Shrell's mixed stream. Finding the future value of a single cash flow was demonstrated earlier (in Personal Finance Example 5.3). As you have already discovered, summing the individual future values of Shrell Industries' mixed cash flow stream results in a future value of $83,608.15 after 5 years.

Spreadsheet use A relatively simple way to use Excel to calculate the future value of a mixed stream is to use the Excel net present value (NPV) function combined with the future value (FV) function discussed on page 197. The syntax of the NPV function is NPV(rate, value1, value2, value 3, . . .). The rate argument is the interest rate, and value1, value2, value3, . . . represent a stream of cash flows. The NPV function assumes that the first payment in the stream arrives 1 year in the future and that all subsequent payments arrive at 1-year intervals.

To find the future value of a mixed stream, the trick is to use the NPV function to first find the present value of the mixed stream and then find the future of this present value lump sum amount. The Excel spreadsheet below illustrates this approach (notice that the NPV appears as an outflow because it represents the net present value of the stream of investment costs).

	A	B
1	FUTURE VALUE OF A MIXED STREAM	
2	Year	Cash Flow
3	1	$11,500
4	2	$14,000
5	3	$12,900
6	4	$16,000
7	5	$18,000
8	Annual rate of interest	8%
9	NPV	$56,902.30
10	Number of years	5
11	Future value	$83,608.15

Entry in Cell B9 is =NPV(B8,B3:B7).
Entry in Cell B11 is =-FV(B8,B10,0,B9,0).

PRESENT VALUE OF A MIXED STREAM

Finding the present value of a mixed stream of cash flows is similar to finding the future value of a mixed stream. We determine the present value of each future cash flow and then add all the individual present values together to find the total present value.

IRF EXAMPLE 5.14

MyLab Finance Solution Video

Frey Company, a shoe manufacturer, has the opportunity to receive the following mixed stream of cash flows over the next 5 years.

Time	Cash flow
0	$ 0
1	400
2	800
3	500
4	400
5	300

If the firm must earn at least 9% on its investments, what is the most it should pay for this opportunity? This situation is depicted on the following timeline.

Timeline for present value of a mixed stream (end-of-year cash flows, discounted at 9% over the corresponding number of years)

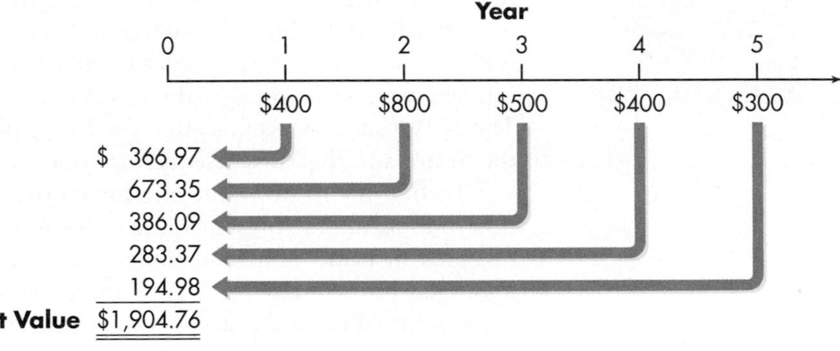

MyLab Finance Financial Calculator

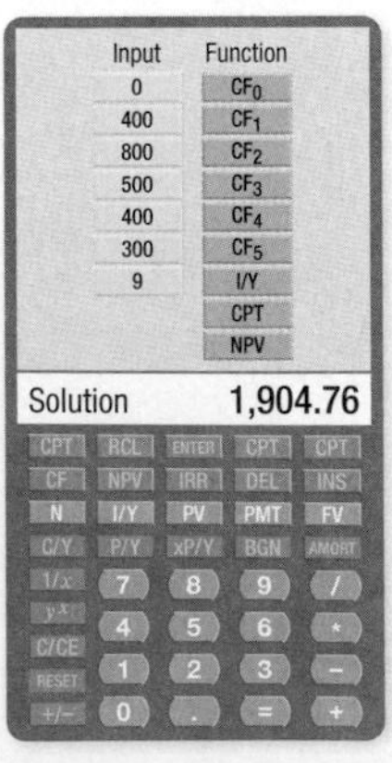

Calculator use You can use the NPV function on your financial calculator to find the present value of the mixed cash flow stream. Recall that to accomplish this task you must first enter the mixed stream of cash flows into your financial calculator's cash flow register by using the CF key. For Frey enter the following into your calculator's cash flow register: $CF_0 = 0$, $CF_1 = 400$, $CF_2 = 800$, $CF_3 = 500$, $CF_4 = 400$, $CF_5 = 300$. Next enter the interest rate of 9% and then solve for the NPV. The present value of Frey Company's mixed cash flow stream found using a calculator is $1,904.76.

Spreadsheet use To calculate the present value of a mixed stream in Excel, we will use the NPV function. The present value of the mixed stream of future cash flows can be calculated as shown on the following Excel spreadsheet.

	A	B
1	PRESENT VALUE OF A MIXED STREAM	
2	Year	Cash Flow
3	1	$400
4	2	$800
5	3	$500
6	4	$400
7	5	$300
8	Annual rate of interest	9%
9	Present value	$1,904.76
	Entry in Cell B9 is =NPV(B8,B3:B7).	

→ **REVIEW QUESTION** MyLab Finance Solutions

5–18 How do you calculate the future value of a mixed stream of cash flows? How do you calculate the present value of a mixed stream?

→ **EXCEL REVIEW QUESTION** MyLab Finance Solutions

5–19 To give yourself a financial head start after college, you have decided to work summer jobs and invest the money you earn until after graduation. You expect that your earnings each summer will vary depending on the job you get. Using the information provided at MyLab Finance, find the value of your financial head start after graduation.

5.5 Compounding Interest More Frequently Than Annually

Interest often compounds more frequently than once a year. Savings institutions compound interest semiannually, quarterly, monthly, weekly, daily, or even continuously. This section discusses various issues and techniques related to these more frequent compounding intervals.

SEMIANNUAL COMPOUNDING

semiannual compounding
Compounding of interest over two periods within the year.

Semiannual compounding of interest involves an investment with two compounding periods within the year. Rather than paying the stated interest rate once a year, the investment pays one-half of the stated interest rate twice a year.

IRF **PERSONAL FINANCE EXAMPLE 5.15** Fred Moreno has decided to invest $100 in a savings account paying 8% interest compounded semiannually. If he leaves his money in the account for 24 months (2 years), he will receive 4% interest compounded over four periods, each of which is 6 months long. Table 5.4 shows that after 12 months (1 year) with 8% semiannual compounding, Fred will have $108.16; after 24 months (2 years), he will have $116.99.

TABLE 5.4 Future Value from Investing $100 at 8% Interest Compounded Semiannually over 24 Months (2 Years)

Period	Beginning principal	Future value calculation	Future value at end of period
6 months	$100.00	$100.00 × (1 + 0.04) =	$104.00
12 months	104.00	$104.00 × (1 + 0.04) =	$108.16
18 months	108.16	$108.16 × (1 + 0.04) =	$112.49
24 months	112.49	$112.49 × (1 + 0.04) =	$116.99

QUARTERLY COMPOUNDING

quarterly compounding
Compounding of interest over four periods within the year.

Quarterly compounding of interest involves four compounding periods within the year. One-fourth of the stated interest rate is paid four times a year.

IRF PERSONAL FINANCE EXAMPLE 5.16 Fred Moreno has found an institution that will pay him 8% interest compounded quarterly. If he leaves his money in this account for 24 months (2 years), he will receive 2% interest compounded over eight periods, each of which is 3 months long. Table 5.5 shows the amount Fred will have at the end of each period. After 12 months (1 year), with 8% quarterly compounding, Fred will have $108.24; after 24 months (2 years), he will have $117.17.

TABLE 5.5 Future Value from Investing $100 at 8% Interest Compounded Quarterly over 24 Months (2 Years)

Period	Beginning principal	Future value calculation	Future value at end of period
3 months	$100.00	$100.00 × (1 + 0.02) =	$102.00
6 months	102.00	$102.00 × (1 + 0.02) =	$104.04
9 months	104.04	$104.04 × (1 + 0.02) =	$106.12
12 months	106.12	$106.12 × (1 + 0.02) =	$108.24
15 months	108.24	$108.24 × (1 + 0.02) =	$110.41
18 months	110.41	$110.41 × (1 + 0.02) =	$112.62
21 months	112.62	$112.62 × (1 + 0.02) =	$114.87
24 months	114.87	$114.87 × (1 + 0.02) =	$117.17

Table 5.6 compares values for Fred Moreno's $100 at the end of years 1 and 2, given annual, semiannual, and quarterly compounding periods at the 8% rate. The table shows that *the more frequently interest compounds, the greater the amount of money that accumulates.* This statement is true for any interest rate above zero for any period of time.

TABLE 5.6 Future Value at the End of Years 1 and 2 from Investing $100 at 8% Interest, Given Various Compounding Periods

	Compounding period		
End of year	Annual	Semiannual	Quarterly
1	$108.00	$108.16	$108.24
2	116.64	116.99	117.17

A GENERAL EQUATION FOR COMPOUNDING

We can rewrite the future value formula (Equation 5.1) for situations when compounding takes place more than once per year. If m equals the number of times per year interest is compounded, the formula for the future value of a lump sum becomes

$$FV_n = PV_0 \times \left(1 + \frac{r}{m}\right)^{m \times n} \qquad (5.9)$$

If $m = 1$, Equation 5.9 reduces to Equation 5.1. Thus, if interest compounds annually, Equation 5.9 will provide the same result as Equation 5.1. We illustrate the application of Equation 5.9 with a simple example.

PERSONAL FINANCE EXAMPLE 5.17 The preceding examples calculated the amount that Fred Moreno would have after 2 years if he deposited \$100 at 8% interest compounded semiannually or quarterly. For semiannual compounding, m would equal 2 in Equation 5.9; for quarterly compounding, m would equal 4. Substituting the appropriate values for semiannual and quarterly compounding into Equation 5.9, we find that

1. *For semiannual compounding:*

$$FV_2 = \$100 \times \left(1 + \frac{0.08}{2}\right)^{2\times 2} = \$100 \times (1 + 0.04)^4 = \$116.99$$

2. *For quarterly compounding:*

$$FV_2 = \$100 \times \left(1 + \frac{0.08}{4}\right)^{4\times 2} = \$100 \times (1 + 0.02)^8 = \$117.17$$

These results agree with the values for FV_2 in Tables 5.4 and 5.5.

If the interest were compounded monthly, weekly, or daily, m would equal 12, 52, or 365, respectively.

USING COMPUTATIONAL TOOLS FOR COMPOUNDING

As before, we can simplify the computation process by using a calculator or spreadsheet program.

PERSONAL FINANCE EXAMPLE 5.18 Fred Moreno wished to find the future value of \$100 invested at 8% interest compounded both semiannually and quarterly for 2 years.

MyLab Finance Financial Calculator

Input	Function
−100	PV
4	I/Y
4	N
	CPT
	FV
Solution	116.99

Calculator use If the calculator were used for the semiannual compounding calculation, the number of periods would be 4, and the interest rate would be 4%. The future value of \$116.99 will appear on the calculator display as shown to the left.

For the quarterly compounding case, the number of periods would be 8 and the interest rate would be 2%. The future value of \$117.17 will appear on the calculator display as shown on the next page.

Spreadsheet use The future value of the single amount with semiannual and quarterly compounding also can be calculated as shown on the following Excel spreadsheet.

MyLab Finance Financial Calculator

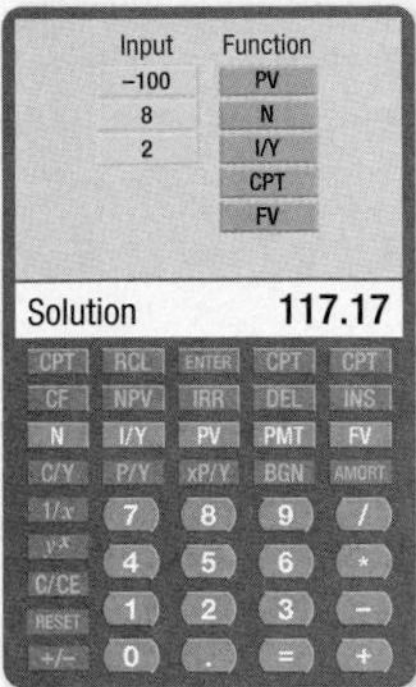

	A	B
1	FUTURE VALUE OF A SINGLE AMOUNT WITH SEMIANNUAL AND QUARTERLY COMPOUNDING	
2	Present value	–$100
3	Annual rate of interest	8%
4	Compounding frequency - semiannual	2
5	Number of years	2
6	Future value with semiannual compounding	$116.99
7	Present value	–$100
8	Annual rate of interest	8%
9	Compounding frequency - quarterly	4
10	Number of years	2
11	Future value with quarterly compounding	$117.17

Entry in Cell B6 is =FV(B3/B4,B5*B4,0,B2,0).
Entry in Cell B11 is =FV(B8/B9,B10*B9,0,B7,0).
The minus sign appears before the $100 in B2 and B7 because the cost of the investment is treated as a cash outflow.

CONTINUOUS COMPOUNDING

continuous compounding Compounding of interest, literally, all the time. Equivalent to compounding interest an infinite number of times per year.

As the number of compounding periods per year gets very large, we approach a situation in which we compound interest continuously. In this case interest compounds every second (or even every nanosecond)—literally, interest compounds all the time. In this case, m in Equation 5.9 would approach infinity, and as m approaches infinity, Equation 5.9 converges to

$$FV_n = PV_0 \times e^{r \times n} \tag{5.10}$$

where e is the exponential function,[2] which has a value of approximately 2.7183.

IRF PERSONAL FINANCE EXAMPLE 5.19

To find the value after 2 years ($n = 2$) of Fred Moreno's $100 deposit ($PV_0 = \$100$) in an account paying 8% annual interest ($r = 0.08$) compounded continuously, we can substitute into Equation 5.10:

MyLab Finance Financial Calculator

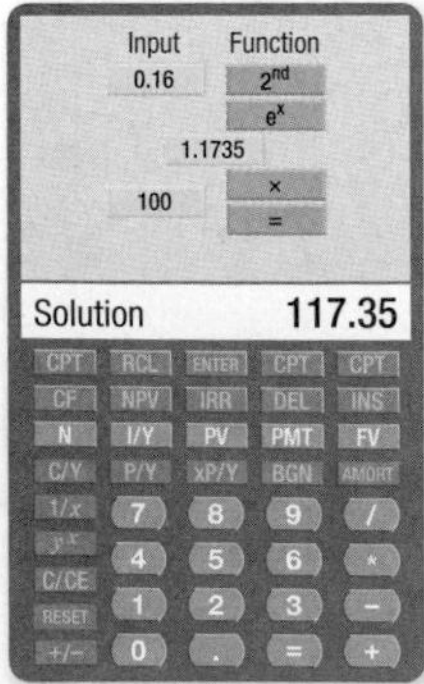

$$\begin{aligned} FV_2 \text{ (continuous compounding)} &= \$100 \times e^{0.08 \times 2} \\ &= \$100 \times 2.7183^{0.16} \\ &= \$100 \times 1.1735 = \$117.35 \end{aligned}$$

Calculator use To find this value using the calculator, you must first find the value of $e^{0.16}$ by punching in 0.16 and then pressing 2nd and then e^x to get 1.1735. Next multiply this value by $100 to obtain the future value of $117.35, as shown at the left. (*Note:* On some calculators, you may not have to press 2nd before pressing e^x.)

Spreadsheet use The following Excel spreadsheet shows how to calculate the future value of Fred's deposit with continuous compounding.

2. Most calculators have the exponential function, typically noted by e^x. The use of this key is especially helpful in calculating future value when interest is compounded continuously.

MyLab

	A	B
1	FUTURE VALUE OF A SINGLE AMOUNT WITH CONTINUOUS COMPOUNDING	
2	Present value	$100
3	Annual rate of interest, compounded continuously	8%
4	Number of years	2
5	Future value with continuous compounding	$117.35
	Entry in Cell B5 is =B3*EXP(B3*B4).	

As expected, Fred's deposit grows more with continuous compounding than it does with semiannual ($116.99) or quarterly ($117.17) compounding. In fact, continuous compounding produces a greater future value than any other compounding frequency.

NOMINAL AND EFFECTIVE ANNUAL RATES OF INTEREST

nominal (stated) annual rate
Contractual annual rate of interest charged by a lender or promised by a borrower.

effective (true) annual rate (EAR)
The annual rate of interest actually paid or earned.

Both businesses and investors need to make objective comparisons of loan costs or investment returns over different compounding periods. To put interest rates on a common basis for comparison, we distinguish between nominal and effective annual rates. The **nominal, or stated, annual rate** is the contractual annual rate of interest charged by a lender or promised by a borrower. The **effective, or true, annual rate (EAR)** is the annual rate of interest actually paid or earned. The effective annual rate reflects the effects of compounding frequency, whereas the nominal annual rate does not.

Using the notation introduced earlier, we can calculate the effective annual rate, EAR, by substituting values for the nominal annual rate, r, and the compounding frequency, m, into the equation

$$EAR = \left(1 + \frac{r}{m}\right)^m - 1 \tag{5.11}$$

We can apply Equation 5.11 using data from preceding examples.

PERSONAL FINANCE EXAMPLE 5.20 Fred Moreno wishes to find the effective annual rate associated with an 8% nominal annual rate ($r = 0.08$) when interest is compounded (1) annually ($m = 1$), (2) semiannually ($m = 2$), and (3) quarterly ($m = 4$). Substituting these values into Equation 5.11, we get

1. *For annual compounding:*

$$EAR = \left(1 + \frac{0.08}{1}\right)^1 - 1 = (1 + 0.08)^1 - 1 = 1 + 0.08 - 1 = 0.08 = 8\%$$

2. *For semiannual compounding:*

$$EAR = \left(1 + \frac{0.08}{2}\right)^2 - 1 = (1 + 0.04)^2 - 1 = 1.0816 - 1 = 0.0816 = 8.16\%$$

3. *For quarterly compounding:*

$$EAR = \left(1 + \frac{0.08}{4}\right)^4 - 1 = (1 + 0.02)^4 - 1 = 1.0824 - 1 = 0.0824 = 8.24\%$$

Calculator use To find the *EAR* using the calculator, you first need to enter the nominal annual rate and the compounding frequency per year. Most financial calculators have a NOM key for entering the nominal rate and either a P/Y or C/Y key for entering the compounding frequency per year. Once you enter these inputs, depress the EFF or CPT key to display the corresponding effective annual rate.

Spreadsheet use You can convert nominal interest rates to effective rates (or vice versa) using Excel's EFFECT and NOMINAL functions. To find the *EAR*, the EFFECT function asks you to input the nominal annual rate and the compounding frequency. If you input an *EAR* and the compounding frequency, the NOMINAL function provides the nominal annual rate or the annual percentage rate (APR). Interest rate conversions from the 8% *APR* to the semiannual *EAR* and from the quarterly *EAR* back to the 8% *APR* are shown on the following Excel spreadsheet.

	A	B
1	INTEREST RATE CONVERSION NOMINAL VS. EFFECTIVE ANNUAL RATE	
2	Nominal annual rate of interest	8%
3	Compounding frequency - semiannual	2
4	Effective annual rate of interest	8.16%
5	Nominal annual rate of interest	8%
6	Compounding frequency - quarterly	4
7	Effective annual rate of interest	8.24%
	Entry in Cell B4 is =EFFECT(B2,B3). Entry in Cell B5 is =NOMINAL(B7,B6).	

These examples demonstrate two important points. First, the nominal rate equals the effective rate if compounding occurs annually. Second, the effective annual rate increases with increasing compounding frequency, up to a limit that occurs with continuous compounding.[3]

annual percentage rate (APR)
The nominal annual rate of interest, found by multiplying the periodic rate by the number of periods in one year, that must be disclosed to consumers on credit cards and loans as a result of "truth-in-lending laws."

annual percentage yield (APY)
The effective annual rate of interest that must be disclosed to consumers by banks on their savings products as a result of "truth-in-savings laws."

At the consumer level, "truth-in-lending laws" require disclosure on credit card and loan agreements of the **annual percentage rate (APR)**. The APR is the nominal annual rate, which is found by multiplying the periodic rate by the number of periods in 1 year. For example, a bank credit card that charges 1.5% per month (the periodic rate) would have an APR of 18% (1.5% per month × 12 months per year).

"Truth-in-savings laws," in contrast, require banks to quote the **annual percentage yield (APY)** on their savings products. The APY is the effective annual rate a savings product pays. For example, a savings account that pays 0.75% per month would have an APY of 9.38% $[(1.0075)^{12} - 1]$.

Quoting loan interest rates at their lower nominal annual rate (the APR) and savings interest rates at the higher effective annual rate (the APY) offers two advantages. First, it tends to standardize disclosure to consumers. Second, it enables financial institutions to quote the most attractive interest rates: low loan rates and high savings rates.

3. The effective annual rate for this extreme case can be found by using the equation

$$EAR \text{ (continuous compounding)} = e^r - 1 \quad (5.11a)$$

For the 8% nominal annual rate ($r = 0.08$), substitution into Equation 5.10a results in an effective annual rate of

$$e^{0.08} - 1 = 1.0833 - 1 = 0.0833 = 8.33\%$$

in the case of continuous compounding. This result is the highest effective annual rate attainable with an 8% nominal rate.

→ **REVIEW QUESTIONS** MyLab Finance Solutions

5–20 What effect does compounding interest more frequently than annually have on (**a**) future value and (**b**) the effective annual rate (EAR)? Why?

5–21 How does the future value of a deposit subject to continuous compounding compare to the value obtained by annual compounding?

5–22 Differentiate between a nominal annual rate and an effective annual rate (EAR). Define annual percentage rate (APR) and annual percentage yield (APY).

FOCUS ON ETHICS *in practice*

Was the Deal for Manhattan a Swindle?

Most schoolchildren marvel when hearing Manhattan was purchased for a song in 1626. As the story goes, Peter Minuit of the Dutch West India Company gave the Lenape Native Americans beads and trinkets worth a mere $24 for the island.

But wait. A letter written by Dutch merchant, Pieter Schage, on November 5, 1626 to the directors of the Dutch West India Company confirmed the transaction but valued the goods (which more likely were kettles, muskets, powder, and axes) at 60 Dutch guilders. According to the *International Institute of Social History,* 60 Dutch guilders in 1626 are worth about 787 Euros today after adjusting for inflation. Based on the recent exchange rate between the Euro and the U.S. dollar, that translates to about $871. Now, the deal looks a bit better for the Lenape. But the surface area of Manhattan comprises 636,000 square feet, and condos there sell for an average of $1,700 *per square foot.* So even after adjusting for price changes since 1626, Minuit still looks pretty sly.

Before closing the case, consider one more factor. The average annualized return on U.S. stocks over the last 200 years was 6.6%. If 60 Dutch guilders were invested at 6.6% from 1626 to today, the sum would grow to roughly *4 trillion* guilders or $2 trillion. Based on New York City's Department of Finance property tax assessments, $2 trillion is roughly twice the value of all New York City real estate today!

Of course, when the deal for Manhattan was struck, the first asset trading of any kind on a street called Wall lay over 80 years in the future, so the Lenape could not salt the receipts away in stocks. Still, the illustration makes the larger point—compounding is a magical thing! And given this magic, it is less clear who fleeced whom.

▶ *People without finance training often fail to appreciate the power of compound interest. Consider the following data for a typical credit card:*

Outstanding Balance: $5,000
Annual Percentage Rate (APR): 12%
Minimum Payment: Larger of [(1% + APR/12) × balance] or $25

	Minimum Payment Only	$100 Payment Each Month
Monthly Payments to Zero Balance	208	71
Total Interest Paid	$4,242	$1,993

The first minimum payment is $100, but that minimum will decline each month as the outstanding balance shrinks. Making the minimum payment every month means that the borrower takes 17 years to pay off the card, paying more than $4,000 in interest along the way. By paying $100 each month, however, the borrower repays the debt in one-third the time and at less than half the interest cost.

How much responsibility do lenders have to educate borrowers? Does the fact that the government requires disclosure statements with a few standardized examples illustrating the time value of money change your answer?

→ **EXCEL REVIEW QUESTIONS** MyLab Finance Solutions

5–23 You are responsible for managing your company's short-term investments and you know that the compounding frequency of investment opportunities is quite important. Using the information provided at MyLab Finance, calculate the future value of an investment opportunity based on various compounding frequencies.

5–24 What if your short-term investments provide continuous compounding? Using the information provided at MyLab Finance, determine the future value of an investment opportunity based on continuous compounding.

5–25 Rather than comparing future values, you often compare the effective annual rates of various investment opportunities with differing compounding frequencies. Using the information provided at MyLab Finance, solve for the effective annual rates of several investment opportunities with different compounding frequencies.

LG6

5.6 Special Applications of Time Value

Future-value and present-value techniques have a number of important applications in finance. We'll study four of them in this section: (1) determining deposits needed to accumulate a future sum, (2) loan amortization, (3) finding interest or growth rates, and (4) finding an unknown number of periods.

DETERMINING DEPOSITS NEEDED TO ACCUMULATE A FUTURE SUM

Suppose that you want to buy a house 5 years from now, and you estimate that an initial down payment of \$30,000 will be required at that time. To accumulate the \$30,000, you will wish to make equal annual end-of-year deposits into an account paying annual interest of 6%. The solution to this problem is closely related to the process of finding the future value of an annuity. You must determine what size annuity will have a future value of \$30,000 after 5 years.

Earlier in the chapter we used Equation 5.3 to find the future value of an ordinary annuity that made a payment, CF_1, each year. In the current problem, we know the future value we want to achieve, \$30,000, but we want to solve for the annual cash payment that we'd have to save to achieve that goal. Solving Equation 5.3 for CF_1 gives

$$CF_1 = FV_n \div \left\{\frac{[(1+r)^n - 1]}{r}\right\} \tag{5.12}$$

Plugging the relevant values into Equation 5.12, we find that the annual deposit required is \$5,321.89.

$$CF_1 = \$30{,}000 \div \left\{\frac{[(1+0.06)^5 - 1]}{0.06}\right\} = \$30{,}000 \div \left\{\frac{0.3382256}{0.06}\right\} = \$5{,}321.89$$

As a practical matter, to solve problems like this one, analysts nearly always use a calculator or Excel as demonstrated in the following example.

PERSONAL FINANCE EXAMPLE 5.21 As just stated, you want to determine the equal annual end-of-year deposits required to accumulate $30,000 after 5 years, given an interest rate of 6%.

MyLab Finance Financial Calculator

Calculator use Using the calculator inputs shown at the left, you will find the annual deposit amount to be $5,321.89. Thus, if $5,321.89 is deposited at the end of each year for 5 years at 6% interest, there will be $30,000 in the account after 5 years.

Spreadsheet use In Excel, solving for the annual cash flow that helps you reach the $30,000 means using the payment function. Its syntax is PMT (rate,nper,pv, fv,type). We have previously discussed all the inputs in this function. The following Excel spreadsheet illustrates how to use this function to find the annual payment required to save $30,000.

	A	B
1	ANNUAL DEPOSITS AMOUNT TO ACCUMULATE A FUTURE SUM	
2	Future value	$30,000
3	Annual rate of interest	6%
4	Number of years	5
5	Annual annuity payment	–$5,321.89

Entry in Cell B5 is =PMT(B3,B4,0,B2,0).
The minus sign appears before the annuity payment in B5 because deposit amounts are cash outflows for the investor.

LOAN AMORTIZATION

loan amortization
The determination of the equal periodic loan payments necessary to provide a lender with a specified interest return and to repay the loan principal over a specified period.

loan amortization schedule
A schedule of equal payments to repay a loan. It shows the allocation of each loan payment to interest and principal.

The term **loan amortization** refers to a situation in which the borrower makes fixed periodic payments and gradually pays down the loan principal over time. A **loan amortization schedule** is a record of the payments that a borrower makes, including the interest and principal components of each payment, and the schedule shows the remaining loan balance after each payment. Many consumer loans such as home mortgages and car loans are typically structured as amortizing loans. In terms of time-value-of-money-concepts, the stream of fixed payments in an amortizing loan has the same present value as the original principal. In other words, given the principal, the interest rate, and the term (i.e., the length of time that the borrower makes payments) of the loan, we can calculate the periodic loan payment by finding an annuity that has the same present value as the loan principal.

Earlier in the chapter, Equation 5.4 demonstrated how to find the present value of an ordinary annuity given information about the number of time periods, the interest rate, and the annuity's periodic payment. We can rearrange that equation to solve for the payment, our objective in this problem:

$$CF_1 = (PV_0 \times r) \div \left[1 - \frac{1}{(1 + r)^n}\right] \tag{5.13}$$

PERSONAL FINANCE EXAMPLE 5.22 Alex May borrows \$6,000 from a bank. The bank requires Alex to repay the loan fully in 4 years by making four end-of-year payments. The interest rate on the loan is 10%. What is the loan payment that Alex will have to make each year? Plugging the appropriate values into Equation 5.13, we have

$$CF_1 = (\$6{,}000 \times 0.10) \div \left[1 - \frac{1}{(1 + 0.10)^4}\right] = \$600 \div 0.316987 = \$1{,}892.82$$

MyLab Finance Financial Calculator

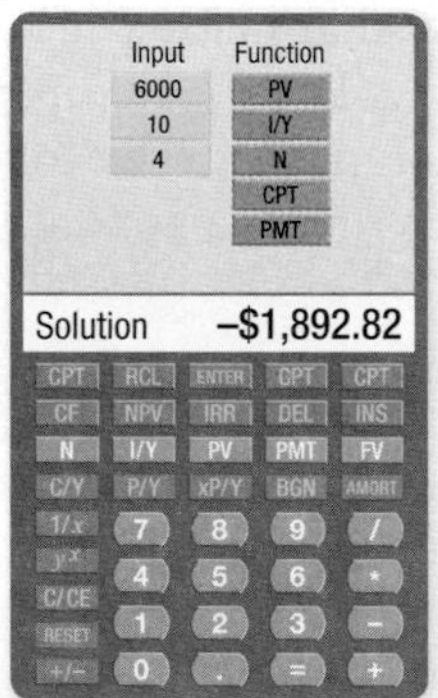

Calculator use Using the calculator inputs shown at the left, you verify that Alex's annual payment will be \$1,892.82. Thus, to repay the interest and principal on a \$6,000, 10%, 4-year loan, equal annual end-of-year payments of \$1,892.82 are necessary.

Table 5.7 provides a loan amortization schedule that shows the principal and interest components of each payment. The portion of each payment that represents interest (column 3) declines over time, and the portion going to principal repayment (column 4) increases. Every amortizing loan displays this pattern; as each payment reduces the principal, the interest component declines, leaving a larger portion of each subsequent loan payment to repay principal. Notice that after Alex makes the fourth payment, the remaining loan balance is zero.

Spreadsheet use The first spreadsheet below shows how to calculate the annual loan payment, and the second spreadsheet illustrates the construction of an amortization schedule.

	A	B
1	ANNUAL PAYMENT AMOUNT TO REPAY A LOAN	
2	Present value	\$6,000
3	Annual rate of interest	10%
4	Number of years	4
5	Annual loan payment	–\$1,892.82

Entry in Cell B5 is =PMT(B3,B4,B2,0,0). The minus sign appears before the loan payment in B5 because loan payments are cash outflows for the borrower.

TABLE 5.7 Loan Amortization Schedule (\$6,000 Principal, 10% Interest, 4-Year Repayment Period)

			Payments		
End-of-year	Beginning-of-year principal (1)	Loan payment (2)	Interest [0.10 × (1)] (3)	Principal [(2) − (3)] (4)	End-of-year principal [(1) − (4)] (5)
1	\$6,000.00	\$1,892.82	\$600.00	\$1,292.82	\$4,707.18
2	4,707.18	1,892.82	470.72	1,422.10	3,285.08
3	3,285.08	1,892.82	328.51	1,564.31	1,720.77
4	1,720.77	1,892.82	172.08	1,720.74	—[a]

[a]Because of rounding, a slight difference (\$0.03) exists between the beginning-of-year-4 principal (in column 1) and the year-4 principal payment (in column 4).

	A	B	C	D	E
1	LOAN AMORTIZATION SCHEDULE				
2			Loan principal	$6,000	
3			Annual rate of interest	10%	
4			Number of years	4	
5		Annual annuity payments			
6	Year	Total	To Interest	To Principal	Year-End Principal
7	0				$6,000.00
8	1	–$1,892.82	–$600.00	–$1,292.82	$4,707.18
9	2	–$1,892.82	–$470.72	–$1,422.11	$3,285.07
10	3	–$1,892.82	–$328.51	–$1,564.32	$1,720.75
11	4	–$1,892.82	–$172.07	–$1,720.75	$0.00

Key Cell Entries
Cell B8 is =PMT(D3,D4,D2,0,0), copy to B9:B11
Cell C8 is =-D3*E7, copy to C9:C11
Cell D8 is =B8-C8, copy to D9:D11
Cell E8 is =E7+D8, copy to E9:E11
The minus sign appears before the loan payments because these are cash outflows for the borrower.

To attract home buyers who could not afford fixed-rate 30-year mortgages requiring equal monthly payments, lenders offered mortgages low "teaser" interest rates that adjusted over time. Recall from Chapter 2 that *subprime mortgages* are mortgage loans made to borrowers with lower incomes and poorer credit histories as compared to "prime" borrowers. The *Focus on Practice* box discusses how such mortgages have worked out for some "subprime" borrowers.

FINDING INTEREST OR GROWTH RATES

One of the performance measures that investors and corporate managers focus on most is growth. How fast a firm can grow its sales, earnings, or cash flows is an important signal about its competitive position in the market. Similarly,

FOCUS ON PRACTICE *in practice*

New Century Brings Trouble for Subprime Mortgages

As the housing market began to boom at the end of the twentieth century and into the early twenty-first, the market share of subprime mortgages climbed from near 0% in 1997 to about 20% of mortgage originations in 2006. Several factors combined to fuel the rapid growth of lending to borrowers with tarnished credit, including a low interest rate environment, loose underwriting standards, and innovations in mortgage financing such as "affordability programs" to increase rates of homeownership among lower-income borrowers.

Particularly attractive to new home buyers was the hybrid adjustable rate mortgage (ARM), which featured a low introductory interest rate that reset upward after a preset period of time. Interest rates began a steady upward trend beginning in late 2004. In 2006, some $300 billion worth of adjustable ARMs were reset to higher rates. In a market with rising home values, a borrower has the option to refinance the mortgage, using some of the equity created by the home's increasing value to reduce the mortgage payment. After 2006, however, home prices started a 3-year slide, so refinancing was not an option for many subprime borrowers. Instead, borrowers in trouble could try to convince their lenders to allow a "short sale," in which the borrower sells the home for whatever the market will bear and the lender agrees to accept the proceeds from that sale as settlement for the mortgage debt. For lenders and borrowers alike, foreclosure is the last, worst option.

► *As a reaction to problems in the subprime area, lenders tightened lending standards. What effect do you think this change had on the housing market?*

people who want to judge their own performance as investors look at the growth rate in the value of their investment portfolio or in the prices of particular stocks they own. Finding a growth rate involves the same mathematics as finding an interest rate, because the interest rate determines how fast money grows over time. To calculate a growth rate, we again make use of Equation 5.1, but in this case we want to solve for the interest rate (or growth rate) representing the increase in value of some investment between two time periods. Solving Equation 5.1 for r, we have

$$r = \left(\frac{FV_n}{PV_0}\right)^{1/n} - 1 \tag{5.14}$$

The simplest situation is one in which an investment's value has changed over time, and you want to know what compound annual rate of growth (or interest) is consistent with the change in value that occurred over time.

PERSONAL FINANCE EXAMPLE 5.23 Consumers across the United States are familiar with Dollar Tree stores, which offer a vast array of items that cost just \$1. Most shoppers at Dollar Tree probably do not know that the company's stock was one of the best-performing stocks during the decade that ended in 2016. An investor who purchased a \$10 share of Dollar Tree stock at the end of 2006 saw the firm's stock price grow to \$70 by 2016's close. What compound annual growth rate does that increase represent? Or, equivalently, what average annual rate of interest did shareholders earn over that period? Let the initial \$10 price represent the stock's present value in 2006, and let \$70 represent the stock's future value 10 years later. Plugging the appropriate values into Equation 5.13, we find that Dollar Tree stock increased almost 21.5% per year over this decade.

$$r = (\$70 \div \$10)^{(1/10)} - 1 = 0.2148 = 21.48\%$$

MyLab Finance Financial Calculator

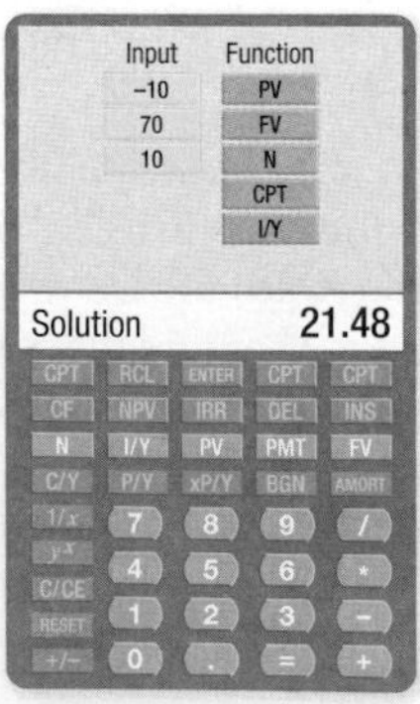

Calculator use Using the calculator to find the interest or growth rate, we treat the earliest value as a present value, *PV*, and the latest value as a future value, *FV*. (*Note:* Most calculators require either the *PV* or the *FV* value to be input as a negative value to calculate an unknown interest or growth rate.) If we think of an investor buying Dollar Tree stock for \$10 at the end of 2016, we treat that \$10 payment as a cash outflow. Then the \$70 future value represents a cash inflow, as if the investor sold the stock in 2016 and received cash. The calculator screenshot confirms that the growth rate in Dollar Tree stock over this period was 21.48%.

Spreadsheet use The following spreadsheet shows how to find Dollar Tree's growth rate using Excel's RATE function. The syntax of that function is RATE(nper,pmt,pv,fv,type,guess). We have encountered the function's arguments *nper*, *pmt*, *pv*, *fv*, and *type* previously. In this problem, \$10 is the present value, and \$70 is the future value. We set the arguments *pmt* and *type* to zero because those arguments are needed to work with annuities, but we are calculating the growth rate by comparing two lump sums. The new argument in this function is *guess*, which in nearly all applications you can set to zero.

	A	B
1	SOLVING FOR INTEREST OR GROWTH RATE OF A SINGLE AMOUNT INVESTMENT	
2	Present value	–$10
3	Future value	$70
4	Number of years	10
5	Annual rate of interest	21.48%
	Entry in Cell B5 is =RATE(B4,0,B2,B3,0,0). The minus sign appears before the $10 in B2 because we treat the investment's cost as a cash outflow.	

Sometimes individuals want to know the interest rate that is associated with a stream of cash flows rather than two lump sums. For example, if you pay a lump sum today in exchange for a stream of cash flows over several years, what rate of return is implicit in this arrangement? The most straightforward problem of this type involves solving for the interest rate embedded in an annuity.

PERSONAL FINANCE EXAMPLE 5.24 Jan Jacobs can borrow $2,000 today, and she must repay the loan in equal end-of-year payments of $482.57 over 5 years. Notice that Jan's payments will total $2,412.85 (i.e., $482.57 per year × 5 years). That's more than she borrowed, so she is clearly paying interest on this loan, as we'd expect. The question is, what annual interest rate is Jan paying? You could calculate the percentage difference between what Jan borrowed and what she repaid as follows:

$$\frac{\$2{,}412.85 - \$2{,}000}{\$2{,}000} = 0.206 = 20.6\%$$

Unfortunately, for two reasons this calculation does not tell us what interest rate Jan is paying. First, this calculation sums Jan's payments over 5 years, so it does not reveal the interest rate on her loan *per year*. Second, because each of Jan's payments comes at a different time, it is not valid to simply add them up. Time-value-of-money principles tell us that even though each payment is for $482.57, the payments have different values because they occur at different times. The key idea in this problem is that there is some interest rate at which the present value of the loan payments is equal to the loan principal. It's this interest rate that equates the loan principal to the present value of payments that we want to find. Solving for that algebraically is very difficult, so we rely on a calculator or spreadsheet to find the solution.

MyLab Finance Financial Calculator

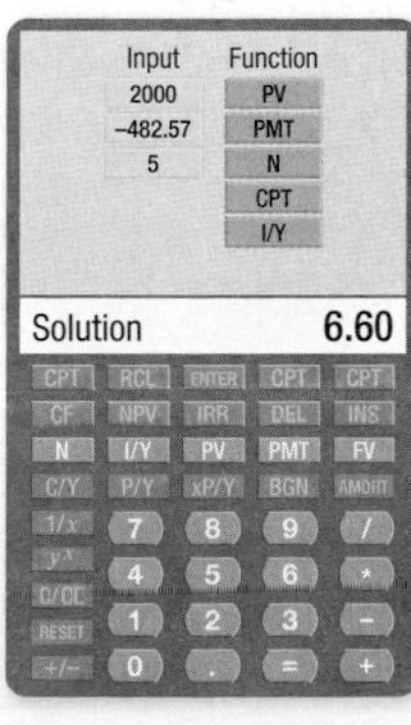

Calculator use (*Note:* Most calculators require you to input either the *PMT* or the *PV* value as a negative number to calculate an unknown interest rate on an equal-payment loan. We take the approach of treating PMT as a cash outflow with a negative number.) Using the inputs shown at the left, you will find that the interest rate on this loan is 6.6%.

Spreadsheet use You can also calculate the interest on this loan as shown on the following Excel spreadsheet.

	A	B
1	SOLVING FOR INTEREST OR GROWTH RATE OF AN ORDINARY ANNUITY	
2	Present value	$2,000
3	Annual annuity amount	–$482.57
4	Number of years	5
5	Annual rate of interest	6.60%

Entry in Cell B5 is =RATE(B4,B3,B2,0,0). The minus sign appears before the $482.57 in B3 because we treat the loan payment as a cash outflow.

FINDING AN UNKNOWN NUMBER OF PERIODS

Sometimes individuals want to know how long it will take them to reach a particular savings goal if they set aside a lump sum today or if they make fixed deposits into an investment account each year. The simplest situation is when a person wishes to determine the number of periods, n, it will take for an initial deposit, PV_0, to grow to a specified future amount, FV_n, given a stated interest rate, r. To solve this problem, we will once again rely on the basic future value relationship described in Equation 5.1, except that here we want to solve for n rather than FV_n.

If we solve Equation 5.1 for n, we obtain the following equation

$$n = \frac{\log\left(\frac{FV_n}{PV_0}\right)}{\log(1 + r)} \tag{5.15}$$

In other words, to find the number of periods it takes to accumulate FV_n dollars starting with PV_0 dollars and earning rate r, we first take the logarithm of the ratio of the future value to the present value. Then we divide that by the logarithm of 1 plus the interest rate.

PERSONAL FINANCE EXAMPLE 5.25 Ann Bates wishes to determine how long it will take for her initial $1,000 deposit, earning 8% annual interest, to grow to $2,500. Applying Equation 5.15, at an 8% annual rate of interest, how many years, n, will it take for Ann's $1,000, PV_0, to grow to $2,500, FV_n?

MyLab Finance Financial Calculator

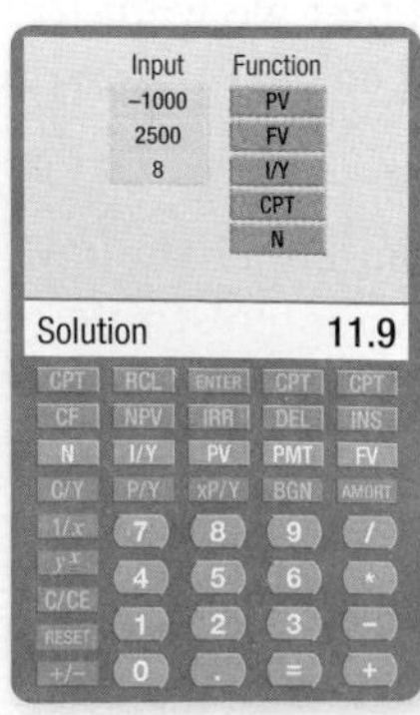

$$n = \frac{\log\left(\frac{\$2{,}500}{\$1{,}000}\right)}{\log(1.08)} = \frac{0.39794}{0.03342} = 11.9$$

Ann will have to wait almost 12 years to reach her savings goal of $2,500.

Calculator use Using the calculator, we treat the initial value as the present value, PV, and the latest value as the future value, FV. (*Note:* Most calculators require either the PV or the FV value to be input as a negative number to calculate an unknown number of periods. We treat Ann's $1,000 initial deposit as a cash flow and give it a negative number.) Using the inputs shown at the left, we verify that it will take Ann 11.9 years to reach her $2,500 goal.

Spreadsheet use You can calculate the number of years for the present value to grow to a specified future value using Excel's NPER function, as shown below.

	A	B
1	SOLVING FOR THE YEARS OF A SINGLE AMOUNT INVESTMENT	
2	Present value	–$1,000
3	Future value	$2,500
4	Annual rate of interest	8%
5	Number of years	11.9

Entry in Cell B5 is =NPER(B4,0,B2,B3,0).
The minus sign appears before the $1,000 in B2 because we treat the initial deposit as a cash outflow.

A similar type of problem involves finding the number of level payments required to pay off a loan. That is, suppose we know the loan principal, the loan payment, and the interest rate. With that information we can determine how many payments will be required to completely repay the loan. Here again the loan principal is the present value, and we want a stream of annuity payments that have the same present value. We know the interest rate, but we do not know how many loan payments are required.

PERSONAL FINANCE EXAMPLE 5.26 Bill Smart can borrow $25,000 at a 7.25% annual interest rate. The lender requires Bill to make equal, end-of-year payments of $3,878.07. Bill wishes to determine how long it will take to fully repay the loan. The algebraic solution to this problem is a bit tedious, so we will find the answer with a calculator or spreadsheet.

MyLab Finance Financial Calculator

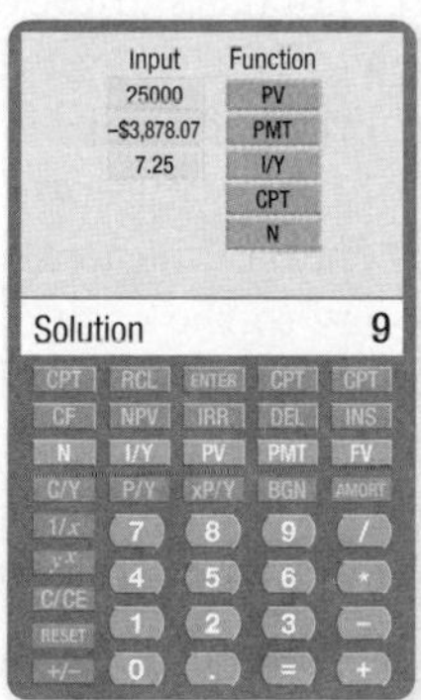

Calculator use (*Note:* Most calculators require either the *PV* or the *PMT* value to be input as a negative number to calculate an unknown number of periods. We treat the loan payments as cash outflows here and show them with a negative number.) Using the inputs at the left, you will find the number of periods to be 9 years. So, after making 9 payments of $3,878.07, Bill will have a zero outstanding balance.

Spreadsheet use The number of years to pay off the loan also can be calculated as shown on the following Excel spreadsheet.

	A	B
1	SOLVING FOR THE YEARS TO REPAY A SINGLE LOAN AMOUNT	
2	Present value	$25,000
3	Annual payment amount	–$3,878.07
4	Annual rate of interest	7.25%
5	Number of years	9.0

Entry in Cell B5 is =NPER(B4,B3,B2,0,0).
The minus sign appears before the $3,878.07 in B3 because we treat the loan payments as cash outflows.

→ REVIEW QUESTIONS MyLab Finance Solutions

5–26 How can you determine the size of the equal, end-of-year deposits necessary to accumulate a certain future sum at the end of a specified future period at a given annual interest rate?

5–27 Describe the procedure used to amortize a loan into a series of equal periodic payments.

5–28 How can you determine the unknown number of periods when you know the present and future values—single amount or annuity—and the applicable rate of interest?

→ EXCEL REVIEW QUESTIONS MyLab Finance Solutions

5–29 You want to buy a new car as a graduation present for yourself, but before finalizing a purchase you need to consider the monthly payment amount. Using the information provided at MyLab Finance, find the monthly payment amount for the car you are considering.

5–30 As a finance major, you realize that you can quickly estimate your retirement age by knowing how much you need to retire, how much you can contribute each month to your retirement account, and what rate of return you can earn on your retirement investments. With that information, you can solve for the number of years it will take to save the money you need to retire. Using the information provided at MyLab Finance, estimate the age at which you will be able to retire.

SUMMARY

FOCUS ON VALUE

The time value of money is an important tool that financial managers and other market participants use to compare cash inflows and outflows occurring at different times. Because firms routinely make investments that produce cash inflows over long periods of time, the effective application of time-value-of-money techniques is extremely important. These techniques enable financial managers to compare the costs of investments they make today to the cash inflows those investments will generate in future years. Such comparisons help managers achieve the firm's overall goal of share price maximization. It will become clear later in this text that the application of time-value techniques is a key part of the valuation process needed to make wealth-maximizing decisions.

REVIEW OF LEARNING GOALS

LG 1 **Discuss the role of time value in finance, the use of computational tools, and the basic patterns of cash flow.** Financial managers and investors use time-value-of-money techniques when assessing the value of expected cash flow streams. Alternatives can be assessed by either compounding to find future value or discounting to find present value. Financial managers rely primarily on present-value techniques. Financial calculators and electronic spreadsheets streamline the application of time-value techniques. Cash flow patterns are of three types: a single amount or lump sum, an annuity, or a mixed stream.

LG 2 **Understand the concepts of future value and present value, their calculation for single amounts, and the relationship between them.** Future value (FV) relies on compound interest to translate current dollars into future dollars. The initial principal or deposit in one period, along with the interest earned on it, becomes the beginning principal of the following period.

The present value (PV) of a future amount is the amount of money today that is equivalent to the given future amount, considering the return that can be earned. Present value is the inverse of future value.

LG 3 **Find the future value and the present value of both an ordinary annuity and an annuity due, and find the present value of a perpetuity.** An annuity is a pattern of equal periodic cash flows. For an ordinary annuity, the cash flows occur at the end of the period. For an annuity due, cash flows occur at the beginning of the period.

The future or present value of an ordinary annuity can be found by using algebraic equations, a financial calculator, or a spreadsheet program. The value of an annuity due is always $r\%$ greater than the value of an identical annuity. The present value of a perpetuity—an infinite-lived annuity—equals the annual cash payment divided by the discount rate. The present value of a growing perpetuity equals the initial cash payment divided by the difference between the discount rate and the growth rate.

LG 4 **Calculate both the future value and the present value of a mixed stream of cash flows.** A mixed stream of cash flows consists of unequal periodic cash flows that reflect no particular pattern. The future value of a mixed stream of cash flows is the sum of the future values of each cash flow. Similarly, the present value of a mixed stream of cash flows is the sum of the present values of the individual cash flows.

LG 5 **Understand the effect that compounding interest more frequently than annually has on future value and on the effective annual rate of interest.** Interest can compound at intervals ranging from annually to daily and even continuously. The more often interest compounds, the larger the future amount that will be accumulated, and the higher the effective, or true, annual rate (EAR).

The annual percentage rate (APR)—a nominal annual rate—is quoted on credit cards and loans. The annual percentage yield (APY)—an effective annual rate—is quoted on savings products.

LG 6 **Describe the procedures involved in (1) determining deposits needed to accumulate a future sum, (2) loan amortization, (3) finding interest or growth rates, and (4) finding an unknown number of periods.** (1) The periodic deposit to accumulate a given future sum can be found by solving the equation for the future value of an annuity for the annual payment. (2) A loan can be amortized into equal periodic payments by solving the equation for the present value of an annuity for the periodic payment. (3) Interest or growth rates can be estimated by finding the unknown interest rate in the equation for the present value of a single amount or an annuity. (4) The number of periods can be estimated by finding the unknown number of periods in the equation for the present value of a single amount or an annuity.

OPENER-IN-REVIEW

The chapter opener described a lottery prize that could be taken as a $480 million lump sum payment or mixed stream of 30 payments, with the first payment of $11.42 million coming immediately, followed by 29 additional payments growing at 5% per year. If the lottery winner could earn 2% on cash invested today, should she take the lump sum or the mixed stream? What if the rate of return is 3%? What general principle do those calculations illustrate?

SELF-TEST PROBLEMS (Solutions in Appendix)

IRF

ST5–1 **Future values for various compounding frequencies** Delia Martin has $10,000 that she can deposit in any of three savings accounts for a 3-year period. Bank A compounds interest on an annual basis, bank B compounds interest twice each year, and bank C compounds interest each quarter. All three banks have a stated annual interest rate of 4%.

a. What amount would Ms. Martin have after 3 years, leaving all interest paid on deposit, in each bank?

b. What effective annual rate (EAR) would she earn in each of the banks?

c. On the basis of your findings in parts **a** and **b**, which bank should Ms. Martin deal with? Why?

d. If a fourth bank (bank D), also with a 4% stated interest rate, compounds interest continuously, how much would Ms. Martin have after 3 years? Does this alternative change your recommendation in part **c**? Explain why or why not.

LG3
IRF

ST5–2 **Future values of annuities** Ramesh Abdul has the opportunity to invest in either of two annuities, each of which will cost $38,000 today. Annuity X is an annuity due that makes 6 cash payments of $9,000. Annuity Y is an ordinary annuity that makes 6 cash payments of $10,000. Assume that Ramesh can earn 15% on his investments.

a. On a purely intuitive basis (i.e., without doing any math), which annuity do you think is more attractive? Why?

b. Find the future value after 6 years for both annuities.

c. Use your finding in part **b** to indicate which annuity is more attractive. Why? Compare your finding to your intuitive response in part **a**.

LG2 LG3 LG4
IRF

ST5–3 **Present values of single amounts and streams** You have a choice of accepting either of two 5-year cash flow streams or single amounts. One cash flow stream is an ordinary annuity, and the other is a mixed stream. You may accept alternative A or B, either as a cash flow stream or as a single amount. Given the cash flow stream and single amounts associated with each (see the following table), and assuming a 9% opportunity cost, which alternative (A or B) and in which form (cash flow stream or single amount) would you prefer?

Year	Cash flow stream	
	Alternative A	Alternative B
1	$700	$1,100
2	700	900
3	700	700
4	700	500
5	700	300
	Single amount	
At time zero	$2,825	$2,800

LG6 IRF

ST5–4 **Deposits needed to accumulate a future sum** Judi Janson wishes to accumulate $8,000 by making equal, end-of-year deposits over the next 5 years. If Judi can earn 7% on her investments, how much must she deposit at the end of each year to meet this goal?

WARM-UP EXERCISES All problems are available in MyLab Finance.

LG2

E5–1 Assume that a firm makes a $2,500 deposit into a short-term investment account. If this account is currently paying 0.7% (yes, that's right, less than 1%!), what will the account balance be after 1 year?

LG2 LG5

E5–2 If Bob and Judy combine their savings of $1,260 and $975, respectively, and deposit this amount into an account that pays 2% annual interest, compounded monthly, what will the account balance be after 4 years?

LG3

E5–3 Gabrielle just won $2.5 million in the state lottery. She is given the option of receiving a lump sum of $1.3 million now, or she can elect to receive $100,000 at the end of each of the next 25 years. If Gabrielle can earn 5% annually on her investments, which option should she take?

LG4

E5–4 Your firm has the option of making an investment in new software that will cost $130,000 today but will save the company money over several years. You estimate that the software will provide the savings shown in the following table over its 5-year life.

Year	Savings estimate
1	$35,000
2	50,000
3	45,000
4	25,000
5	15,000

Should the firm make this investment if it requires a minimum annual return of 9% on all investments?

E5–5 Joseph is a friend of yours. He has plenty of money but little financial sense. He received a gift of $12,000 for his recent graduation and is looking for a bank in which to deposit the funds. Partners' Savings Bank offers an account with an annual interest rate of 3% compounded semiannually, whereas Selwyn's offers an account with a 2.75% annual interest rate compounded continuously. Calculate the value of the two accounts after 1 year, and recommend to Joseph which account he should choose.

E5–6 Jack and Jill have just had their first child. If they expect that college will cost $150,000 per year in 18 years, how much should the couple begin depositing annually at the end of each of the next 18 years to accumulate enough funds to pay 1 year of tuition 18 years from now? Assume they can earn a 6% annual rate of return on their investment.

PROBLEMS

All problems are available in MyLab Finance. The MyLab icon indicates problems in Excel format available in MyLab Finance.

P5–1 **Using a timeline** The financial manager at Starbuck Industries is considering an investment that requires an initial outlay of $25,000 and is expected to produce cash inflows of $3,000 at the end of year 1, $6,000 at the end of years 2 and 3, $10,000 at the end of year 4, $8,000 at the end of year 5, and $7,000 at the end of year 6.

a. Draw and label a timeline depicting the cash flows associated with Starbuck Industries' proposed investment.

b. Use arrows to demonstrate, on the timeline in part **a**, how compounding to find future value can be used to measure all cash flows at the end of year 6.

c. Use arrows to demonstrate, on the timeline in part **b**, how discounting to find present value can be used to measure all cash flows at time zero.

d. Which of the approaches—future value or present value—do financial managers rely on most often for decision making?

P5–2 **Future value calculation** Without referring to the preprogrammed function on your financial calculator, use the basic formula for future value along with the given interest rate, r, and the number of periods, n, to calculate the future value of $1 in each of the cases shown in the following table.

Case	Interest rate, r	Number of periods, n
A	12%	2
B	6	3
C	9	2
D	3	4

P5–3 **Future value** You have $100 to invest. If you put the money into an account earning 5% interest compounded annually, how much money will you have in 10 years? How much money will you have in 10 years if the account pays 5% simple interest?

MyLab

P5–4 **Future values** For each of the cases shown in the following table, calculate the future value of the single cash flow deposited today and held until the end of the deposit period if the interest is compounded annually at the rate specified.

Case	Single cash flow	Interest rate	Deposit period (years)
A	$ 200	5%	20
B	4,500	8	7
C	10,000	9	10
D	25,000	10	12
E	37,000	11	5
F	40,000	12	9

Personal Finance Problem

P5–5 **Time value** You have $1,500 to invest today at 7% interest compounded annually.
a. Find how much you will have accumulated in the account after (1) 3 years, (2) 6 years, and (3) 9 years.
b. Use your findings in part **a** to calculate the amount of interest earned in (1) the first 3 years (years 1 to 3), (2) the second 3 years (years 4 to 6), and (3) the third 3 years (years 7 to 9).
c. Compare and contrast your findings in part **b**. Explain why the amount of interest earned increases in each succeeding 3-year period.

Personal Finance Problem

P5–6 **Time value** As part of your financial planning, you wish to purchase a new car 5 years from today. The car you wish to purchase costs $14,000 today, and your research indicates that its price will increase by 2% to 4% per year over the next 5 years.
a. Estimate the price of the car in 5 years if inflation is (1) 2% per year and (2) 4% per year.
b. How much more expensive will the car be if the rate of inflation is 4% rather than 2%?
c. Estimate the price of the car if inflation is 2% for the next 2 years and 4% for 3 years after that.

Personal Finance Problem

MyLab

P5–7 **Time value** You can deposit $10,000 into an account paying 9% annual interest either today or exactly 10 years from today. How much better off will you be 40 years from now if you decide to make the initial deposit today rather than 10 years from today?

Personal Finance Problem

P5–8 **Time value** Misty needs to have $15,000 in 5 years to fulfill her goal of purchasing a small sailboat. She is willing to invest a lump sum today and leave the money untouched for 5 years until it grows to $15,000, but she wonders what sort of investment return she will need to earn to reach her goal. Use your calculator or spreadsheet to figure out the approximate annually compounded rate of return that Misty needs in each of these cases:
a. Misty can invest $10,200 today.
b. Misty can invest $8,150 today.
c. Misty can invest $7,150 today.

Personal Finance Problem

LG 2

P5–9 Single-payment loan repayment A person borrows $200 that he must repay in a lump sum no more than 8 years from now. The interest rate is 8.5% annually compounded. The borrower can repay the loan at the end of any earlier year with no prepayment penalty.

a. What amount will be due if the borrower repays the loan after 1 year?

b. How much would the borrower have to repay after 4 years?

c. What amount is due at the end of the eighth year?

LG 2

P5–10 Present value calculation Without referring to the preprogrammed function on your financial calculator, use the basic formula for present value, along with the given discount rate, *r*, and the number of periods, *n*, to calculate the present value of $1 in each of the cases shown in the following table.

Case	Discount rate, *r*	Number of periods, *n*
A	2%	4
B	10	2
C	5	3
D	13	2

LG 2 

P5–11 Present values For each of the cases shown in the following table, calculate the present value of the cash flow, discounting at the rate given and assuming that the cash flow is received at the end of the period noted.

Cash	Single cash flow	Discount rate	End of period (years)
A	$ 7,000	12%	4
B	28,000	8	20
C	10,000	14	12
D	150,000	11	6
E	45,000	20	8

LG 2

P5–12 Present value concept Answer each of the following questions.

a. How much money would you have to invest today to accumulate $6,000 after 6 years if the rate of return on your investment is 12%?

b. What is the present value of $6,000 that you will receive after 6 years if the discount rate is 12%?

c. What is the most you would spend today for an investment that will pay $6,000 in 6 years if your opportunity cost is 12%?

d. Compare, contrast, and discuss your findings in parts **a** through **c**.

Personal Finance Problem

LG 2

P5–13 Time value Jim Nance has been offered an investment that will pay him $500 three years from today.

a. If his opportunity cost is 7% compounded annually, what value should he place on this opportunity today?

b. What is the most he should pay to purchase this investment today?

c. If Jim can purchase this investment for less than the amount calculated in part **a**, what does that imply about the rate of return he will earn on the investment?

LG2

P5–14 **Time value** An Iowa state savings bond can be converted to $100 at maturity 6 years from purchase. If the state bonds are to be competitive with U.S. savings bonds, which pay 3% annual interest (compounded annually), at what price must the state sell its bonds? Assume no cash payments on savings bonds prior to redemption.

Personal Finance Problem

LG2

P5–15 **Time value and discount rates** You just won a lottery that promises to pay you $1,000,000 exactly 10 years from today. A company approaches you today, offering cash in exchange for your winning lottery ticket.

a. What is the least you will sell your claim for if you can earn the following rates of return on similar-risk investments during the 10-year period?
(1) 6%
(2) 9%
(3) 12%

b. Rework part **a** under the assumption that the $1,000,000 payment will be received in 15 rather than 10 years.

c. On the basis of your findings in parts **a** and **b**, discuss the effect of both the size of the rate of return and the time until receipt of payment on the present value of a future sum.

Personal Finance Problem

P5–16 **Time value comparisons of single amounts** In exchange for a $23,000 payment today, a well-known company will allow you to choose one of the alternatives shown in the following table. Your opportunity cost is 9%.

Alternative	Single amount
A	$28,500 at end of 3 years
B	$54,000 at end of 9 years
C	$160,000 at end of 20 years

a. Find the value today of each alternative.
b. Are all the alternatives acceptable? That is, are they worth $23,000 today?
c. Which alternative, if any, will you take?

Personal Finance Problem

MyLab

P5–17 **Cash flow investment decision** Tom Alexander has an opportunity to purchase any of the investments shown in the following table. The purchase price, the amount of the single cash inflow, and its year of receipt are given for each investment. Which purchase recommendations would you make, assuming that Tom can earn 10% on his investments?

Investment	Price	Single cash inflow	Year of receipt
A	$18,000	$30,000	5
B	600	3,000	20
C	3,500	10,000	10
D	1,000	15,000	40

P5–18 Calculating deposit needed You put $10,000 in an account earning 5%. After 3 years, you make another deposit into the same account. Four years later (that is, 7 years after your original $10,000 deposit), the account balance is $20,000. What was the amount of the deposit at the end of year 3?

P5–19 Future value of an annuity For each case in the accompanying table, answer the questions that follow.

Case	Annuity payment	Interest rate	Annuity length (years)
A	$ 2,500	8%	10
B	500	12	6
C	30,000	20	5
D	11,500	9	8
E	6,000	14	30

a. Calculate the future value of the annuity, assuming that it is
   (1) An ordinary annuity.
   (2) An annuity due.

b. Compare your findings in parts **a**(1) and **a**(2). All else being identical, which type of annuity—ordinary or annuity due—is preferable? Explain why.

P5–20 Present value of an annuity Consider the following cases.

Case	Annuity payment	Interest rate	Annuity length (years)
A	$ 12,000	7%	3
B	55,000	12	15
C	700	20	9
D	140,000	5	7
E	22,500	10	5

a. Calculate the present value of the annuity, assuming that it is
   (1) An ordinary annuity.
   (2) An annuity due.

b. Compare your findings in parts **a**(1) and **a**(2). All else being identical, which type of annuity—ordinary or annuity due—is preferable? Explain why.

Personal Finance Problem

P5–21 Time value: Annuities Marian Kirk wishes to select the better of two 10-year annuities. Annuity 1 is an ordinary annuity of $2,500 per year for 10 years. Annuity 2 is an annuity due of $2,300 per year for 10 years.

a. Find the future value of both annuities 10 years from now, assuming that Marian can earn (1) 6% annual interest and (2) 10% annual interest.

b. Use your findings in part **a** to indicate which annuity has the greater future value after 10 years for both the (1) 6% and (2) 10% interest rates.

c. Find the present value of both annuities, assuming that Marian can earn (1) 6% annual interest and (2) 10% annual interest.

d. Use your findings in part **c** to indicate which annuity has the greater present value for both (1) 6% and (2) 10% interest rates.
e. Briefly compare, contrast, and explain any differences between your findings using the 6% and 10% interest rates in parts **b** and **d.**

Personal Finance Problem

P5–22 **Retirement planning** Hal Thomas, a 25-year-old college graduate, wishes to retire at age 65. To supplement other sources of retirement income, he can deposit $2,000 each year into a tax-deferred individual retirement arrangement (IRA). The IRA will earn a 10% return over the next 40 years.

a. If Hal makes end-of-year $2,000 deposits into the IRA, how much will he have accumulated in 40 years when he turns 65?
b. If Hal decides to wait until age 35 to begin making end-of-year $2,000 deposits into the IRA, how much will he have accumulated when he retires 30 years later?
c. Using your findings in parts **a** and **b,** discuss the impact of delaying deposits into the IRA for 10 years (age 25 to age 35) on the amount accumulated by the end of Hal's sixty-fifth year.
d. Rework parts **a, b,** and **c,** assuming that Hal makes all deposits at the beginning, rather than end, of each year. Discuss the effect of beginning-of-year deposits on the future value accumulated by the end of Hal's sixty-fifth year.

Personal Finance Problem

P5–23 **Value of a retirement annuity** An insurance agent is trying to sell you an annuity that will provide you with $12,000 at the end of each of the next 25 years. If you don't purchase this annuity, you can invest your money and earn a return of 9%. What is the most you would pay for this annuity right now?

Personal Finance Problem

P5–24 **Funding your retirement** Emily Jacob is 45 years old and has saved nothing for retirement. Fortunately, she just inherited $75,000. Emily plans to put a large portion of that money into an investment account earning an 11% return. She will let the money accumulate for 20 years, when she will be ready to retire. She would like to deposit enough money today so she could begin making withdrawals of $50,000 per year starting at age 66 (21 years from now) and continuing for 24 additional years, when she will make her last withdrawal at age 90. Whatever remains from her inheritance, Emily will spend on a shopping spree. Emily will continue to earn 11% on money in her investment account during her retirement years, and she wants the balance in her retirement account to be $0 after her withdrawal on her ninetieth birthday.

a. How much money must Emily set aside now to achieve that goal? It may be helpful to construct a timeline to visualize the details of this problem.
b. Emily realizes that once she retires she will want to have less risky investments that will earn a slightly lower rate of return, 8% rather than 11%. If Emily can earn 11% on her investments from now until age 65, but she earns just 8% on her investments from age 65 to 90, how much money does she need to set aside today to achieve her goal?
c. Suppose Emily puts all of the $75,000 that she inherited into the account earning 11%. As in part **b,** she will earn only an 8% return on her investments after age 65. If Emily withdraws $50,000 as planned on each birthday from age 66 to age 90, how much will be left in her account for her heirs after her last withdrawal?

Personal Finance Problem

P5–25 **Value of an annuity versus a single amount** Assume that you just won the state lottery. Your prize can be taken either in the form of $40,000 at the end of each of the next 25 years (i.e., $1,000,000 over 25 years) or as a single amount of $500,000 paid immediately.

a. If you expect to earn 5% annually on your investments over the next 25 years, ignoring taxes and other considerations, which alternative should you take? Why?

b. Would your decision in part **a** change if you could earn 7% rather than 5% on your investments over the next 25 years? Why?

c. At approximately what interest rate would you be indifferent between the two options?

P5–26 **Perpetuities** Consider the data in the following table.

Perpetuity	Annual payment	Discount rate
A	$ 20,000	8%
B	100,000	10
C	3,000	6
D	60,000	5

Determine the present value of each perpetuity.

P5–27 **Perpetuities** Suppose that today's date is January 1, 2019. You have the opportunity to make an investment that will pay you $100 on January 1 of every year, starting in 2020 and continuing forever. Assume the relevant discount rate is 7%.

a. What would you pay now for this investment?

b. Suppose the investment's first cash flow comes immediately, on January 1, 2019, with subsequent cash payments every January 1 thereafter. Now how much would you pay? It might be helpful to draw the first few years of a timeline here and compare it to the situation in part **a**.

c. Suppose the investment's first cash flow is 3 years from now, on January 1, 2022. On every January 1 thereafter you will receive $100. How much is this worth to you today, January 1, 2019?

P5–28 **Perpetuities** You are evaluating an investment that will pay $75 in 1 year, and it will continue to make payments at annual intervals thereafter, but the payments will grow by 4% forever.

a. What is the present value of the first $75 payment if the discount rate is 10%?

b. How much cash will this investment pay 100 years from now? What is the present value of the 100th payment? Again, use a 10% discount rate.

c. What is the present value of the entire growing stream of perpetual cash flows?

d. Explain why the answers to parts **a** and **b** help to explain why an infinite stream of growing cash flows has a finite present value?

Personal Finance Problem

P5–29 **Creating an endowment** On completion of her introductory finance course, Marla Lee was so pleased with the amount of useful and interesting knowledge she gained that she convinced her parents, who were wealthy alumni of the university she was attending, to create an endowment. The endowment will provide for three students from low-income families to take the introductory finance course each year in perpetuity. The cost of taking the finance course this year is $200 per student (or $600 for 3 students), but that cost will grow by 2% per year forever. Marla's parents will create the endowment by making a single payment to the university today. The university expects to earn 6% per year on these funds.

a. What will it cost 3 students to take the finance class next year?
b. How much will Marla's parents have to give the university today to fund the endowment if it starts paying out cash flow next year?
c. What amount would be needed to fund the endowment if the university could earn 9% rather than 6% per year on the funds?

P5–30 Value of a mixed stream For each of the mixed streams of cash flows shown in the following table, determine the future value at the end of the final year if deposits are made into an account paying annual interest of 12%, assuming that no withdrawals are made during the period and that the deposits are made

a. At the *end* of each year (i.e., the first deposit occurs 1 year from now)
b. At the *beginning* of each year (i.e., the first deposit occurs immediately)

	Cash flow stream		
Year	A	B	C
1	$ 900	$30,000	$1,200
2	1,000	25,000	1,200
3	1,200	20,000	1,000
4		10,000	1,900
5		5,000	

Personal Finance Problem

P5–31 Value of a single amount versus a mixed stream Gina Vitale has just contracted to sell a small parcel of land that she inherited a few years ago. The buyer is willing to pay $24,000 now, or the buyer will make a series of 5 payments starting now and continuing at annual intervals as shown in the table below. Because Gina doesn't really need the money today, she plans to let it accumulate in an account that earns 7% annual interest. Given her desire to buy a house 5 years after selling the lot, she decides to choose the payment alternative—either the lump sum or the mixed stream—that provides the higher future value after 5 years. Which alternative will she choose?

Mixed stream	
Time	Cash flow
0	$ 2,000
1	4,000
2	6,000
3	8,000
4	10,000

LG4 

P5–32 Value of mixed streams Find the present value of the streams of cash flows shown in the following table. Assume that the opportunity cost is 12%.

A		B		C	
Year	Cash flow	Year	Cash flow	Year	Cash flow
1	−$2,000	1	$10,000	1–5	$10,000/yr
2	3,000	2–5	5,000/yr	6–10	8,000/yr
3	4,000	6	7,000		
4	6,000				
5	8,000				

LG4

P5–33 Present value: Mixed streams Consider the mixed streams of cash flows shown in the following table.

	Cash flow stream	
Year	A	B
0	−$50,000	$10,000
1	40,000	20,000
2	30,000	30,000
3	20,000	40,000
4	10,000	−50,000
Totals	$50,000	$50,000

a. Find the present value of each stream using a 5% discount rate.
b. Compare the calculated present values and discuss them in light of the undiscounted cash flows totaling $50,000 in each case. Is there some discount rate at which the present values of the two streams would be equal?

LG1 LG4

P5–34 Value of a mixed stream Harte Systems Inc., a maker of electronic surveillance equipment, is considering selling the rights to market its home security system to a well-known hardware chain. The proposed deal calls for the hardware chain to pay Harte $30,000 and $25,000 at the end of years 1 and 2 and to make annual year-end payments of $15,000 in years 3 through 9. A final payment to Harte of $10,000 would be due at the end of year 10.
a. Lay out the cash flows involved in the offer on a timeline.
b. If Harte applies a required rate of return of 12% to them, what is the present value of this series of payments?
c. A second company has offered Harte an immediate one-time payment of $100,000 for the rights to market the home security system. Which offer should Harte accept?

LG4

P5-35 Value of a mixed stream Herr Mining Company plans to open a new coal mine. Developing the mine will cost $1 million right away, but cash flows of $4 million will arrive starting in 1 year and then continuing for the next 4 years (i.e., years 2 through 5). After that, no coal will remain, and Herr must spend $22 million to restore the land surrounding the mine to its original condition.
a. Construct a timeline showing the cash flows starting at time zero and extending until time 6.

b. What is the total undiscounted cash flow associated with this project over its 6-year life? Given this answer, do you think there is any way that the project can be financially attractive to Herr Mining? Why or why not?
c. Calculate the present value of the project's cash flows, assuming the company's opportunity cost is 5%. What if the opportunity cost is 10%? Comment on what you find.

P5–36 Relationship between future value and present value: Mixed stream Using the information in the accompanying table, answer the questions that follow.

Year	Cash flow
0	$ 0
1	800
2	900
3	1,000
4	1,500
5	2,000

a. Determine the present value of the mixed stream of cash flows, using a 5% discount rate.
b. Suppose you had a lump sum equal to your answer in part **a** on hand today. If you invested this sum for 5 years and earned a 5% return each year, how much would you have after 5 years?
c. Determine the future value 5 years from now of the mixed stream, using a 5% interest rate. Compare your answer here to your answers in part **b**.
d. How much would you be willing to pay for this stream, assuming that you can at best earn 5% on your investments?

LG4

P5–37 Relationship between future value and present value: Mixed stream The table below shows a mixed cash flow stream starting in 1 year, except that the cash flow for year 3 is missing.

Year 1	$10,000
Year 2	5,000
Year 3	
Year 4	20,000
Year 5	3,000

Suppose you somehow know that the present value of the entire stream is $32,911.03 and that the discount rate is 4%. What is the amount of the missing cash flow in year 3?

LG5

P5–38 Changing compounding frequency Using annual, semiannual, and quarterly compounding periods for each of the following, (1) calculate the future value if $5,000 is deposited initially, and (2) determine the effective annual rate (EAR).
a. At 12% annual interest for 5 years.
b. At 16% annual interest for 6 years.
c. At 20% annual interest for 10 years.

P5–39 Compounding frequency, time value, and effective annual rates For each of the cases in the table below:

a. Calculate the future value at the end of the specified deposit period.
b. Determine the effective annual rate, EAR.
c. Compare the nominal annual rate, *r*, to the effective annual rate, EAR. What relationship exists between compounding frequency and the nominal and effective annual rates?

Case	Amount of initial deposit	Nominal annual rate, *r*	Compounding frequency, *m* (times/year)	Deposit period (years)
A	$ 2,500	6%	2	5
B	50,000	12	6	3
C	1,000	5	1	10
D	20,000	16	4	6

LG5

P5–40 Continuous compounding For each of the cases in the following table, find the future value at the end of the deposit period, assuming that interest is compounded continuously at the given nominal annual rate.

Case	Amount of initial deposit	Nominal annual rate, *r*	Deposit period (years), *n*
A	$1,000	9%	2
B	600	10	10
C	4,000	8	7
D	2,500	12	4

Personal Finance Problem

LG5

P5–41 Compounding frequency and time value You plan to invest $2,000 in an individual retirement account (IRA) today at a nominal annual rate of 8%, which is expected to apply to all future years.

a. How much will you have in the account after 10 years if interest is compounded (1) annually, (2) semiannually, (3) daily (assume a 365-day year), and (4) continuously?
b. What is the effective annual rate (EAR) for each compounding period in part **a**?
c. How much greater will your IRA balance be in 10 years if interest compounds continuously rather than annually?
d. How does the compounding frequency affect the future value and effective annual rate for a given deposit? Explain in terms of your findings in parts **a** through **c**.

Personal Finance Problem

 LG5

P5–42 Annuities and compounding Janet Boyle intends to deposit $300 per year in a credit union for the next 10 years, and the credit union pays an annual interest rate of 8%.

a. Determine the future value that Janet will have in 10 years, given that end-of-period deposits are made and no interest is withdrawn, if
   (1) $300 is deposited annually and the credit union pays interest annually.
   (2) $150 is deposited semiannually and the credit union pays interest semiannually.
   (3) $75 is deposited quarterly and the credit union pays interest quarterly.

b. Use your findings in part a to discuss the effect of more frequent deposits and compounding of interest on the future value of an annuity.

P5–43 **Deposits to accumulate future sums** For each case shown in the following table, determine the amount of the equal, end-of-year deposits necessary to accumulate the given sum at the end of the specified period, assuming the stated annual interest rate.

Case	Sum to be accumulated	Accumulation period (years)	Interest rate
A	$ 5,000	3	12%
B	100,000	20	7
C	30,000	8	10
D	15,000	12	8

Personal Finance Problem

P5–44 **Creating a retirement fund** To supplement your retirement, you estimate that you need to accumulate $220,000 exactly 42 years from today. You plan to make equal, end-of-year deposits into an account paying 8% annual interest.

a. How large must the annual deposits be to create the $220,000 fund in 42 years?

b. If you can afford to deposit only $600 per year into the account, how much will you have accumulated in 42 years?

Personal Finance Problem

LG6

P5–45 **Accumulating a growing future sum** A retirement home at Deer Trail Estates now costs $185,000. Inflation is expected to increase this price by 6% per year over the 20 years before C. L. Donovan retires. If Donovan earns 10% on his investments, how large must an equal, end-of-year deposit be to provide the cash needed to buy the home 20 years from now?

Personal Finance Problem

P5–46 **Inflation, time value, and annual deposits** While vacationing in Florida, John Kelley saw the vacation home of his dreams. It was listed with a sale price of $200,000. The only catch is that John is 40 years old and plans to continue working until he is 65. John believes that prices generally increase at the overall rate of inflation and that he can earn 9% on his investments. He is willing to invest a fixed amount at the end of each of the next 25 years to fund the cash purchase of such a house (one that can be purchased today for $200,000) when he retires.

a. Inflation is expected to average 5% per year for the next 25 years. What will John's dream house cost when he retires?

b. How much must John invest at the end of each of the next 25 years to have the cash purchase price of the house when he retires?
c. If John invests at the beginning instead of at the end of each of the next 25 years, how much must he invest each year?

P5–47 **Loan payment** Determine the equal, end-of-year payment required each year over the life of the loans shown in the following table to repay them fully during the stated term of the loan.

Loan	Principal	Interest rate	Term of loan (years)
A	$12,000	8%	3
B	60,000	12	10
C	75,000	10	30
D	4,000	15	5

Personal Finance Problem

P5–48 **Loan amortization schedule** Joan Messineo borrowed $45,000 at a 4% annual rate of interest that she must repay over 3 years. The loan is amortized into three equal, end-of-year payments.
a. Calculate the end-of-year loan payment.
b. Prepare a loan amortization schedule showing the interest and principal breakdown of each of the three loan payments.
c. Explain why the interest portion of each payment declines with the passage of time.

P5–49 **Loan interest deductions** Liz Rogers just closed a $10,000 business loan that she must repay in three equal, end-of-year payments. The interest rate on the loan is 13%. As part of her firm's detailed financial planning, Liz wishes to determine the annual interest deduction attributable to the loan. (Because it is a business loan, the interest portion of each loan payment is tax-deductible to the business.)
a. Determine the firm's annual loan payment.
b. Prepare an amortization schedule for the loan.
c. How much interest expense will Liz's firm have in *each* of the next 3 years as a result of this loan?

Personal Finance Problem

P5–50 **Monthly loan payments** Tim Smith is shopping for a used luxury car. He has found one priced at $30,000. The dealer has told Tim that if he can come up with a down payment of $5,000, the dealer will finance the balance of the price at a 6% annual rate over 3 years (36 months).
a. Assuming that Tim accepts the dealer's offer, what will his *monthly* (end-of-month) payment amount be?
b. Use a financial calculator or spreadsheet to help you figure out what Tim's *monthly* payment would be if the dealer were willing to finance the balance of the car price at a 4% annual rate.

P5–51 **Growth rates** Jamie El-Erian is a savvy investor. On January 1, 2010, she bought shares of stock in Amazon, Chipotle Mexican Grill, and Netflix. The table below shows the price she paid for each stock, the price she received when she eventually sold her shares, and the date on which she sold each stock. Calculate the average annual growth in each company's share price over the time that Jamie held its stock.

Stock	Purchase price	Selling price	Sale date
Amazon	$134	$754	January 1, 2017
Chipotle	88	301	January 1, 2013
Netflix	8	110	January 1, 2016

Personal Finance Problem

LG6

P5–52 **Rate of return** Rishi Singh has $1,500 to invest. His investment counselor suggests that Rishi should buy an investment that pays no interest but will be worth $2,000 after 3 years.

a. What average annual rate of return will Rishi earn with this investment?

b. Rishi is considering another investment, of equal risk, that earns an annual return of 8%. Which investment should he make, and why?

Personal Finance Problem

LG6

P5–53 **Rate of return and investment choice** Clare Jaccard has $5,000 to invest. Because she is only 25 years old, she is not concerned about the length of the investment's life. What she is sensitive to is the rate of return she will earn on the investment. With the help of her financial advisor, Clare has isolated four equally risky investments, each providing a single cash flow at the end of its life, as shown in the following table. All the investments require an initial $5,000 payment.

Investment	Future cash inflow	Investment life (years)
A	$ 8,400	6
B	15,900	15
C	7,600	4
D	13,000	10

a. Calculate, to the nearest 1%, the average annual rate of return on each of the four investments available to Clare.

b. Which investment would you recommend to Clare, given her goal of maximizing the rate of return?

LG6

P5–54 **Rate of return: Annuity** What is the rate of return on an investment of $10,606 if the investor will receive $2,000 each year for the next 10 years?

Personal Finance Problem

LG6

P5–55 **Choosing the best annuity** Raina Herzig wishes to choose the best of four annuities available to her. In each case, in exchange for paying a lump sum today, she will receive equal, end-of-year cash payments for a specified number of years. She considers the annuities equally risky and is not concerned about their differing lives.

Her decision will be based solely on the rate of return she will earn on each annuity. The following table shows the key terms of the four annuities.

Annuity	Cost of annuity today	Annual cash flow	Life (years)
A	$30,000	$3,100	20
B	25,000	3,900	10
C	40,000	4,200	15
D	35,000	4,000	12

a. Calculate, to the nearest 1%, the rate of return on each of the four annuities Raina is considering.
b. Given Raina's stated decision criterion, which annuity would you recommend?

Personal Finance Problem

P5–56 **Interest rate for an annuity** Anna Waldheim was seriously injured in an industrial accident. She sued the responsible parties and was awarded a judgment of $2,000,000. Today, she and her attorney are attending a settlement conference with the defendants. The defendants have made an initial offer of $156,000 per year for 25 years. Anna plans to counteroffer at $255,000 per year for 25 years. Both the offer and the counteroffer have a present value of $2,000,000, the amount of the judgment. Both assume payments at the end of each year.
a. What interest rate assumption have the defendants used in their offer (rounded to the nearest whole percent)?
b. What interest rate assumption have Anna and her lawyer used in their counteroffer (rounded to the nearest whole percent)?
c. Anna is willing to settle for an annuity that carries an interest rate assumption of 9%. What annual payment would be acceptable to her?

Personal Finance Problem

P5–57 **Loan rates of interest** John Flemming has been shopping for a loan to finance the purchase of a used car. He has found three possibilities that seem attractive and wishes to select the one with the lowest interest rate. The information available with respect to each of the three $5,000 loans is shown in the following table. Each loan requires John to make one payment at the end of each year.

Loan	Principal	Annual payment	Term (years)
A	$5,000	$1,352.81	5
B	5,000	1,543.21	4
C	5,000	2,010.45	3

a. Determine the interest rate associated with each of the loans.
b. Which loan should John take?

P5–58 **Number of years needed to acccumulate a future amount** For each of the following cases, determine the number of years it will take for the initial deposit to grow to equal the future amount at the given interest rate.

Case	Initial deposit	Future amount	Interest rate
A	$ 300	$ 1,000	7%
B	12,000	15,000	5
C	9,000	20,000	10
D	100	500	9
E	7,500	30,000	15

Personal Finance Problem

LG6

P5–59 Time to accumulate a given sum Manuel Rios wishes to determine how long it will take an initial deposit of $10,000 to double.

a. If Manuel earns 10% annual interest on the deposit, how long will it take for him to double his money?

b. How long will it take if he earns only 7% annual interest?

c. How long will it take if he can earn 12% annual interest?

d. Reviewing your findings in parts **a**, **b**, and **c**, indicate what relationship exists between the interest rate and the amount of time it will take Manuel to double his money.

P5–60 Number of years to provide a given return In each of the following cases, determine the number of years that the given ordinary annuity cash flows must continue to provide the desired rate of return given the cost of the annuity.

Case	Cost of annuity	Annuity payment	Desired rate of return
A	$ 1,000	$ 250	11%
B	150,000	30,000	15
C	80,000	10,000	10
D	600	275	9
E	17,000	3,500	6

Personal Finance Problem

LG6

P5–61 Time to repay installment loan Mia Salto wishes to determine how long it will take to repay a $14,000 loan given that the lender requires her to make annual end-of-year installment payments of $2,450.

a. If the interest rate on the loan is 12%, how long will it take her to repay the loan fully?

b. How long will it take if the interest rate is 9%?

c. How long will it take if she has to pay 15% annual interest?

d. Reviewing your answers in parts **a**, **b**, and **c**, describe the general relationship between the interest rate and the amount of time it will take Mia to repay the loan fully.

LG6

P5–62 ETHICS PROBLEM Samantha Fong sold her home in San Francisco in 2017 for $1.5 million, which was the median home price for that city. Samantha had lived in that house for 17 years, having purchased it from Michael Shoven in 2000 for $545,000. What average annual rate of return did Samantha earn on her home, ignoring things such as property taxes and the costs of maintaining the home?

Would you say that Samantha somehow "swindled" Michael? Would your answer to that question be influenced by the knowledge that from 2000 to 2017, the average annual return on U.S. stocks was a little less than 6%?

SPREADSHEET EXERCISE

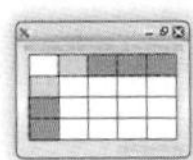

At the end of 2019, Uma Corporation is considering a major long-term project in an effort to remain competitive in its industry. The production and sales departments have determined the potential annual cash flow savings that could accrue to the firm if it acts soon. Specifically, they estimate that a mixed stream of future cash flow savings will occur at the end of the years 2020 through 2025. The years 2026 through 2030 will see consecutive $90,0000 cash flow savings at the end of each year. The firm estimates that its discount rate over the first 6 years will be 7%. The expected discount rate over the years 2026 through 2030 will be 11%.

The project managers will find the project acceptable if it results in present cash flow savings of at least $860,000. The following cash flow savings data are supplied to the finance department for analysis.

Year	Cash flow savings
2020	$110,000
2021	120,000
2022	130,000
2023	150,000
2024	160,000
2025	150,000
2026	90,000
2027	90,000
2028	90,000
2029	90,000
2030	90,000

TO DO

Create spreadsheets similar to Table 5.3, and then answer the following questions.

a. Determine the value (at the end of 2019) of the future cash flow savings expected to be generated by this project.

b. Based solely on the one criterion set by management, should the firm undertake this specific project? Explain.

c. What is the "interest rate risk," and how might it influence the recommendation made in part **b**? Explain.

MyLab Finance Visit www.pearson.com/mylab/finance for **Chapter Case: *Funding Jill Moran's Retirement Annuity,*** Group Exercises, and numerous online resources.

Integrative Case 2

Track Software Inc.

Seven years ago, after 15 years in public accounting, Stanley Booker, CPA, resigned his position as manager of cost systems for Davis, Cohen, and O'Brien Public Accountants and started Track Software Inc. In the 2 years preceding his departure from Davis, Cohen, and O'Brien, Stanley had spent nights and weekends developing a sophisticated cost-accounting software program that became Track's initial product offering. As the firm grew, Stanley planned to develop and expand the software product offerings, all of which would be related to streamlining the accounting processes of medium- to large-sized manufacturers.

Although Track experienced losses during its first 2 years of operation—2013 and 2014—its profit has increased steadily from 2015 to the year just ended (2019). The firm's profit history, including dividend payments and contributions to retained earnings, is summarized in Table 1.

Stanley started the firm with a $100,000 investment: his savings of $50,000 as equity and a $50,000 long-term loan from the bank. He had hoped to maintain his initial 100% ownership in the corporation, but after experiencing a $50,000 loss during the first year of operation (2013), he sold 60% of the stock to a group of investors to obtain needed funds. Since then, no other stock transactions have taken place. Although he owns only 40% of the firm, Stanley actively manages all aspects of its activities; the other stockholders are not active in its management. The firm's stock was valued at $4.50 per share in 2018 and at $5.28 per share in 2019.

TABLE 1

Track Software Inc.,
Profit, Dividends, and Retained Earnings, 2013–2019

Year	Net profits after taxes	Dividends paid	Contribution to retained earnings
2013	–$50,000	$ 0	–$50,000 – 0 = –$50,000
2014	–20,000	0	–20,000 – 0 = –20,000
2015	15,000	0	15,000 – 0 = 15,000
2016	35,000	0	35,000 – 0 = 35,000
2017	40,000	1,000	40,000 – 1,000 = 39,000
2018	43,000	3,000	43,000 – 3,000 = 40,000
2019	48,000	5,000	48,000 – 5,000 = 43,000

Stanley has just prepared the firm's 2019 income statement, balance sheet, and statement of retained earnings, shown in Tables 2, 3, and 4, respectively, along with the 2018 balance sheet. In addition, he has compiled the 2018 ratio values and industry average ratio values for 2019, which are applicable to both 2018 and 2019 and are summarized in Table 5. He is quite pleased to have achieved record earnings of $48,000 in 2019, but he is concerned about the firm's cash flows. Specifically, he is finding it more and more difficult to pay the firm's bills in a timely manner and generate cash flows to investors, both creditors and owners. To gain insight into these cash flow problems, Stanley is planning to determine the firm's 2019 operating cash flow (OCF) and free cash flow (FCF).

Stanley is further frustrated that the firm cannot afford to hire a software developer to complete development of a cost estimation package that he believes has "blockbuster" sales potential. Stanley began development of this package 2 years ago, but the firm's growing complexity has forced him to devote more of his time to administrative duties, thereby halting development. Stanley's reluctance to fill this position stems from his concern that the added $80,000 per year in salary and benefits for the position would certainly lower the firm's earnings per share (EPS) over the next couple of years. Although the project's success is in no way guaranteed, Stanley believes that if the money were spent to hire the software developer, the firm's sales and earnings would significantly rise once the 2- to 3-year development, production, and marketing process was completed.

With all these concerns in mind, Stanley set out to review the various data to develop strategies that would help ensure a bright future for Track Software. Stanley believed that as part of this process, a thorough ratio analysis of the firm's 2019 results would provide important additional insights.

TABLE 2

Track Software Inc., Income Statement ($000) for the Year Ended December 31, 2019

Sales revenue	$1,550
Less: Cost of goods sold	1,030
Gross profits	$ 520
Less: Operating expenses	
Selling expense	$ 150
General and administrative expenses	270
Depreciation expense	11
Total operating expense	$ 431
Operating profits (EBIT)	$ 89
Less: Interest expense	29
Net profits before taxes	$ 60
Less: Taxes (20%)	12
Net profits after taxes	$ 48

TABLE 3

Track Software Inc., Balance Sheet ($000)		
	December 31	
Assets	2019	2018
Cash	$ 12	$ 31
Marketable securities	66	82
Accounts receivable	152	104
Inventories	191	145
Total current assets	$421	$362
Gross fixed assets	$195	$180
Less: Accumulated depreciation	63	52
Net fixed assets	$132	$128
Total assets	$553	$490
Liabilities and stockholders' equity		
Accounts payable	$136	$126
Notes payable	200	190
Accruals	27	25
Total current liabilities	$363	$341
Long-term debt	38	40
Total liabilities	$401	$381
Common stock (50,000 shares outstanding at $0.40 par value)	$ 20	$ 20
Paid-in capital in excess of par	30	30
Retained earnings	102	59
Total stockholders' equity	$152	$109
Total liabilities and stockholders' equity	$553	$490

TABLE 4

Track Software Inc., Statement of Retained Earnings ($000) for the Year Ended December 31, 2019	
Retained earnings balance (January 1, 2019)	$ 59
Plus: Net profits after taxes (for 2019)	48
Less: Cash dividends on common stock (paid during 2019)	5
Retained earnings balance (December 31, 2019)	$102

TABLE 5

Ratio	Actual 2018	Industry average 2019
Current ratio	1.06	1.82
Quick ratio	0.63	1.10
Inventory turnover	10.40	12.45
Average collection period	29.6 days	20.2 days
Total asset turnover	2.66	3.92
Debt ratio	0.78	0.55
Times interest earned ratio	3.0	5.6
Gross profit margin	32.1%	42.3%
Operating profit margin	5.5%	12.4%
Net profit margin	3.0%	4.0%
Return on total assets (ROA)	8.0%	15.6%
Return on common equity (ROE)	36.4%	34.7%
Price/earnings (P/E) ratio	5.2	7.1
Market/book (M/B) ratio	2.1	2.2

TO DO

a. (1) On what financial goal does Stanley seem to be focusing? Is it the correct goal? Why or why not?
(2) Could a potential agency problem exist in this firm? Explain.

b. Calculate the firm's earnings per share (EPS) for each year, recognizing that the number of shares of common stock outstanding has remained unchanged since the firm's inception. Comment on the EPS performance in view of your response in part **a.**

c. Use the financial data presented to determine Track's operating cash flow (OCF) and free cash flow (FCF) in 2019. Evaluate your findings in light of Track's current cash flow difficulties.

d. Analyze the firm's financial condition in 2019 as it relates to (1) liquidity, (2) activity, (3) debt, (4) profitability, and (5) market, using the financial statements provided in Tables 2 and 3 and the ratio data included in Table 5. Be sure to evaluate the firm on both a cross-sectional and a time-series basis.

e. What recommendation would you make to Stanley regarding hiring a new software developer? Relate your recommendation here to your responses in part **a.**

f. Track Software paid $5,000 in dividends in 2019. Suppose that an investor approached Stanley about buying 100% of his firm. If this investor believed that by owning the company he could extract $5,000 per year in cash from the company in perpetuity, what do you think the investor would be willing to pay for the firm if the required return on this investment is 10%?

g. Suppose you believed that the FCF generated by Track Software in 2019 could continue forever. You are willing to buy the company in order to receive this perpetual stream of free cash flow. What are you willing to pay if you require a 10% return on your investment?

PART THREE

Valuation of Securities

CHAPTERS IN THIS PART

In Part Two, you learned how to use time-value-of-money tools to compare cash flows at different times. In Part Three, you will put those tools to use by valuing the two most common types of securities: bonds and stocks.

Chapter 6 introduces you to the world of interest rates and bonds. Although bonds are among the safest investments available, they are not without risk. The primary risk is that market interest rates will fluctuate. Those fluctuations cause bond prices to move, and those movements affect the returns that bond investors earn. Chapter 6 explains why interest rates vary from one bond to another and the factors that cause interest rates to move over time.

Chapter 7 focuses on stock valuation. It explains the characteristics of stock that distinguish it from debt and describes the differences between common and preferred stock. You'll have another chance to practice time-value-of-money techniques as Chapter 7 illustrates how to value stocks by discounting either (1) the dividends that stockholders receive or (2) the free cash flows that the firm generates over time.

CHAPTER 6

Interest Rates and Bond Valuation

LEARNING GOALS

LG 1 Describe interest rate fundamentals, the term structure of interest rates, and risk premiums.

LG 2 Review the legal aspects of bond financing and bond cost.

LG 3 Discuss the general features, yields, prices, ratings, popular types, and international issues of corporate bonds.

LG 4 Understand the key inputs and basic model used in the bond valuation process.

LG 5 Apply the basic valuation model to bonds, and describe the impact of required return and time to maturity on bond prices.

LG 6 Explain yield to maturity (YTM), its calculation, and the procedure used to value bonds that pay interest semiannually.

MyLab Finance Chapter Introduction Video

WHY THIS CHAPTER MATTERS TO YOU

In your *professional* life

ACCOUNTING You need to understand interest rates and the various types of bonds to be able to account properly for amortization of bond premiums and discounts and for bond issues and retirements.

INFORMATION SYSTEMS You need to understand the data that are necessary to track bond valuations and bond amortization schedules.

MANAGEMENT You need to understand the behavior of interest rates and how they affect the types of funds the firm can raise and the timing and cost of bond issues and retirements.

MARKETING You need to understand how the interest rate level and the firm's ability to issue bonds may affect the availability of financing for marketing research projects and new-product development.

OPERATIONS You need to understand how the interest rate level may affect the firm's ability to raise funds to maintain and grow the firm's production capacity.

In your *personal* life

Interest rates have a direct impact on personal financial planning. Movements in interest rates occur frequently and affect the returns from and values of savings and investments. The rate of interest you are charged on credit cards and loans can have a profound effect on your personal finances. Understanding the basics of interest rates is important to your personal financial success.

ASTON MARTIN BOND ISSUE

The Name Is Bond—Junk Bond

BFA/United Artists/Alamy Stock Photo

Featured in films ranging from the 1963 spy classic *Goldfinger* to 2015's *Spectre*, Aston Martin luxury sports cars have claimed an enviable position in pop culture as the vehicle of choice for James Bond. In April 2017, Aston Martin executives were hoping that a different kind of bond would help to revive the struggling company. Aston Martin borrowed heavily in 2011, and the company's subsequent poor financial performance caused the price of its outstanding bonds to fall by 39%. Because investors viewed the company's bonds as quite risky, the interest rates on Aston Martin's bonds were steep, paying as much as 10.25%. Fortunately for Aston Martin, an Italian investor bought a large stake in the company in 2012, and that new investment enabled the automaker to introduce its first new car model in years in 2016 and a luxury, three-person submarine with a $4 million sticker price in 2017. New products revved up profits, so in 2017 Aston Martin executives went to the bond market once again to raise money.

The company brought in the equivalent of $660 million in new financing by issuing bonds, some denominated in U.S. dollars and some denominated in British pounds, to investors around the world. The company planned to use the proceeds from the bond sale to refinance existing debt, which was set to mature in 2018. With an improved financial outlook, Aston Martin didn't look as risky to investors in 2017 as it had several years earlier, so the interest rates on its new bonds were much lower at 5.75%. That rate, however, was still much higher than the rate some other companies were paying at the time. Microsoft, for example, raised $17 billion in a January 2017 bond issue with interest rates as low as 3.34%.

Investors naturally want to assess the risks associated with a company's bonds, and independent bond-rating agencies help them do that. Those agencies assign letter grades to new bond issues, and the grades indicate the likelihood that the borrower will be able to repay the principal and interest as promised. Broadly speaking, bonds fall into one of two categories based on the ratings they receive. Bonds given a relatively high rating are known as *investment grade bonds*, whereas bonds assigned lower ratings are called *junk bonds* or, more kindly, *high-yield bonds*. Microsoft's 2017 bond issue received the highest possible rating of AAA, which is why that company could borrow at such a low interest rate. Aston Martin's bonds, in contrast, earned a rating of B, placing the company's debt, unlike its automobiles, firmly in the junk category.

6.1 Interest Rates and Required Returns

As noted earlier in this text, financial institutions and markets create the mechanism through which funds flow between savers (suppliers of funds) and borrowers (demanders of funds). All else being equal, savers would like to earn as much interest as possible, and borrowers would like to pay as little as possible. The interest rate prevailing in the market at any given time reflects the equilibrium between savers and borrowers.

INTEREST RATE FUNDAMENTALS

The *interest rate* or *required return* represents the cost of money. It is the compensation that a supplier of funds expects and a demander of funds must pay. Usually the term **interest rate** applies to debt instruments such as bank loans or bonds, whereas the term **required return** applies to almost any kind of investment. In fact, the meanings of these two terms are quite similar because in both cases the supplier is compensated for providing funds to the demander.

interest rate
Usually applied to debt instruments such as bank loans or bonds; the compensation paid by the borrower of funds to the lender; from the borrower's point of view, the cost of borrowing funds.

required return
Usually applied to equity instruments such as common stock; the cost of funds obtained by selling an ownership interest.

When we speak about the interest rate or the required return on an investment, we may take either a historical perspective (i.e., what return did an investment actually provide?) or a forward-looking perspective (i.e., what return should we expect the investment to provide in the future given its risk?). Both perspectives are important. Looking at historical data to measure the *actual returns* that different types of investments have provided helps managers and investors form better judgments about the *expected returns* that are the focus of the forward-looking approach. In a decision-making context, expected returns weigh more heavily than do actual returns.

Broadly speaking, interest rates are determined by the interaction of supply and demand, just as prices of other goods and services are determined. When the demand for funds is low and the supply of savings is high, interest rates are low. Figure 6.1 illustrates this supply–demand relationship. The equilibrium interest rate, r_0, occurs at the intersection of the supply function (labeled S_0) and the demand function (labeled D).

FIGURE 6.1

Supply–Demand Relationship
Supply of savings and demand for investment funds

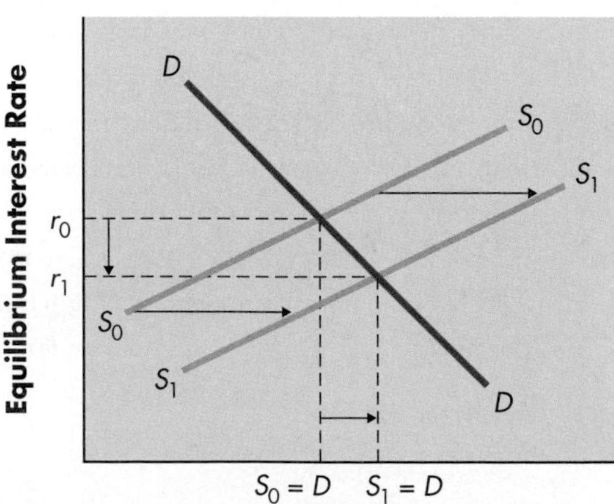

The equilibrium interest rate changes as economic forces alter either the supply of or the demand for funds. To combat a recession, the Board of Governors of the Federal Reserve System might initiate actions to increase the supply of credit in the economy, causing the supply function in Figure 6.1 to shift down and to the right to S_1. The result would be a lower equilibrium interest rate, r_1. With a lower cost of money, firms might find that investments previously viewed as unattractive are now worth undertaking, and as firms hire more workers and spend more on plant and equipment, the economy begins to expand again.

inflation
A rising trend in the prices of most goods and services.

liquidity preference
A general tendency for investors to prefer short-term (i.e., more liquid) securities.

A variety of factors can influence the equilibrium interest rate. One factor is **inflation**, an increase in the prices of most goods and services. Typically, savers demand higher returns (i.e., higher interest rates) when inflation is high because they want their investments to outpace rising prices—they want their purchasing power to increase so they can increase their consumption in the future as a result of having saved and invested money. A second factor influencing interest rates is risk. When people perceive a particular investment as riskier, they will expect a higher return on that investment as compensation for bearing the risk. A third factor that can affect the interest rate is a **liquidity preference** among investors. The term *liquidity preference* refers to the general tendency of investors to prefer short-term securities (i.e., securities that are more liquid). If, all other things being equal, investors would prefer to buy short-term rather than long-term securities, interest rates on short-term instruments such as Treasury bills will be lower than rates on longer-term securities. Investors will hold these securities, despite the relatively low return they offer, because they meet investors' preferences for liquidity.

Negative Interest Rates

Almost as long as there have been borrowers and lenders, both parties assumed that interest rates could only be positive. That is, borrowers would have to repay lenders more money than they originally borrowed. In many parts of the world, that assumption has been turned upside down. Starting in 2014, central banks in several European economies and in Japan instituted policies that resulted in negative interest rates. When a loan carries an interest rate below zero, the lender essentially pays interest to the borrower rather than the other way around.

Central banks in Europe and Japan instituted negative interest rate policies (NIRPs) to combat weak economic growth. These policies work through linkages in the banking system and the broader financial system. Each nation's central bank requires commercial banks in that country to have accounts at the central bank, where they deposit reserves. When a central bank decides to push interest rates below zero, it starts by charging commercial banks interest on their reserves rather than paying interest to those banks. In other words, the first step in creating negative interest rates is for the central bank to essentially impose a tax on the commercial banks. That action has ripple effects throughout the financial system, and other interest rates, such as those on government bonds, may turn negative too. By the fall of 2016, outstanding government bonds paying negative interest rates accounted for more than $12 trillion globally.

A natural question is, why would anyone buy an investment if it paid an interest rate below zero? The answer is that there is no good, safe alternative offering a better return. Consumers and other investors who do not have large amounts of money to invest could hold cash at home and earn a 0% return, and indeed signs of more cash hoarding (such as an increase in demand for home

MATTER OF FACT

Fear Turns T-Bill Rates Negative

Near the height of the financial crisis in December 2008, interest rates on Treasury bills briefly turned negative, meaning that investors paid more to the Treasury than the Treasury promised to pay back. Why would people put their money into an investment they *know* will lose money? Remember that 2008 saw the demise of Lehman Brothers, and fears that other commercial banks and investments banks might fail were rampant. Evidently, some investors were willing to pay the U.S. Treasury to keep their money safe for a short time.

safes and large-denomination bills) materialized after the NIRPs were put in place. Even so, holding cash is risky because cash can be stolen or lost in a fire. For institutional investors who have millions or billions to invest, holding cash is very costly. Buying a government bond with a (slightly) negative interest rate may be the only way to keep money secure. So far, widespread negative interest rates have been confined to Europe and Japan, but interest rates on some U.S. government securities have been negative for brief periods.

Nominal and Real Interest Rates

nominal rate of interest
The actual rate of interest charged by the supplier of funds and paid by the demander.

The **nominal rate of interest** is the actual rate of interest charged by the supplier of funds and paid by the demander. Interest rates quoted online or at financial institutions are nominal interest rates. The nominal interest rate is also the rate at which an investor's money will grow over time. However, because of inflation's effect on the value of money, the nominal interest rate does not adequately capture the increase in an investor's purchasing power over time.

For example, if you put \$50 into an investment that promises to pay 3% interest, at the end of the year you will have \$51.50 (the initial \$50 plus a \$1.50 return). Your nominal return is 3%, but this does not necessarily mean that you are better off at the end of the year because the nominal return does not take into account the effects of inflation. Assume that at the beginning of the year, one bag of groceries costs \$50. You can either make the \$50 investment that offers a 3% nominal return or use that money to buy one bag of groceries. During the year, suppose grocery prices rise by 3%. This means that by the end of the year one bag of groceries costs \$51.50. If you invest your money rather than spend it on groceries, by year's end you will have \$51.50, still just enough to buy one bag of groceries. In other words, your purchasing power did not increase at all during the year. The **real interest rate** on an investment measures the increase in purchasing power that the investment provides. In the current example, the real rate of return is 0% even though the nominal rate of return is 3%. In dollar terms, by investing \$50 you increased your wealth by 3% to \$51.50, but in terms of purchasing power you are no better off because you can only buy the same amount of goods that you could have bought before you made the investment.

real rate of interest
The rate of return on an investment measured not in dollars but in the increase in purchasing power that the investment provides. The real rate of interest measures the rate of increase in purchasing power.

We can express the relationship between the nominal interest rate, the real interest rate, and the expected inflation rate as follows:

$$(1 + r) = (1 + r^*)(1 + i) \tag{6.1}$$

$$r^* \approx r - i \tag{6.1a}$$

where

r = nominal interest rate

r^* = real interest rate

i = expected inflation rate

Equation 6.1 shows that 1 plus the nominal interest rate equals the product of 1 plus the real interest rate and 1 plus the expected inflation rate. Equation 6.1a reveals that the real rate is *approximately* equal to the difference between the nominal rate and the expected inflation rate. This approximation is quite good when interest rates and expected inflation are low. In market environments with high interest and inflation rates, however, the approximation in Equation 6.1a becomes less accurate.

PERSONAL FINANCE EXAMPLE 6.1

MyLab Finance Solution Video

Burt Gummer is a survivalist who constantly worries that the apocalypse may happen any day now. To be prepared, Burt stores food with a long shelf life in his basement. Burt has $100 to add to his food stores, and he is considering the purchase of 100 cans of Spam for $1 each. Burt expects the inflation rate over the coming year to be 9%, so a can of Spam will cost $1.09 each in a year. Burt's wife, Heather, has heard of an investment that will pay a 21% nominal return over the next year, so she thinks Burt should invest the money rather than use it to buy Spam.

Equation 6.1a says that the approximate real return on Burt's potential investment is 12%:

$$12\% \approx 21\% - 9\%$$

On the basis of this calculation, Burt might expect that if he invests $100, he could buy 112 cans of Spam next year rather than 100 cans this year (a 12% increase in purchasing power). Suppose that Burt invests the money, earns a 21% rate of return, and 1 year later has $121. By that time, one can of Spam costs $1.09, so Burt is just barely able to purchase 111 cans (111 cans × $1.09 = $120.99). Burt's purchasing power has increased by 11%, not by the 12% that he expected. Equation 6.1 reveals that the exact real return on Burt's investment is 11%:

$$(1 + 0.21) = (1 + r^*)(1 + 0.09)$$

$$\frac{1.21}{1.09} = 1 + r^*$$

$$1.110 - 1 = 0.11 = 11\% = r^*$$

Nominal Interest Rates, Inflation, and Risk

Nominal interest rates are affected not only by inflation but also by risk. Just as investors demand higher rates of return when expected inflation is high, they also demand higher returns on risky investments than on safe ones. Otherwise, investors have little incentive to bear the additional risk. Therefore, *investors will demand a higher nominal rate of return on risky investments*. The additional return that investors require as compensation for bearing risk is called the risk premium (RP).

Before discussing the impact of risk on interest rates, we find it useful to establish a benchmark rate of return in the absence of risk. Suppose some investment offers a return that is completely free of risk. Denote this rate of return as the risk-free rate, R_F. By definition, the return on this investment is not affected by risk, but it is affected by investors' inflation expectations. The higher the inflation rate that investors expect over the investment's life, the higher the nominal return they will demand, even in the absence of risk. Therefore, the nominal rate of interest on a risk-free investment is the sum of the real return that investors require and the inflation rate that they expect.[1] We could say that the risk-free rate reflects a premium, over and above the real interest rate, based on expected inflation. Mathematically, this relationship is given by Equation 6.2:

$$R_F = r^* + i \tag{6.2}$$

The premium for expected inflation in Equation 6.2 represents the rate of inflation that investors expect over the life of an investment. The expected inflation premium changes over time in response to many factors, such as shifts in monetary and fiscal policies, currency movements, and international political events.

Although in practice no investment is completely free of risk, securities issued by the U.S. government are widely regarded as the safest investments in the world. *Treasury bills* (*T-bills*) are short-term IOUs issued by the U.S. Treasury that mature in 1 year or less. The Treasury also issues longer-term securities such as *Treasury notes*, which have maturities ranging from 2 to 10 years, and *Treasury bonds*, which mature in 30 years. These securities are as close as we can get in the real world to a risk-free investment, so the rate of return offered by Treasury bills is a common proxy for the risk-free rate in Equation 6.2. You can find nominal rates of return on T-bills on the web and from many other sources. Figure 6.2 illustrates how the rate of inflation and the risk-free interest rate moved from 1961 through 2016. The blue line in the figure plots the interest rate on a 1-year T-bill each year, and the red line plots the inflation that occurred during that calendar year. The difference between the two lines is therefore the real rate of return that investors actually earned during the year (as opposed to the real rate that they expected to earn at the start of each calendar year).

During this period, the two rates tended to move in a similar fashion. Note that T-bill rates were slightly above the inflation rate most of the time, meaning that T-bills generally offered a small positive real return (about 1.3% on average). Between 1978 and the early 1980s, inflation and interest rates were quite high, peaking at around 14% in 1980–1981. Since then, T-bill rates have gradually declined. To combat a severe recession, the Federal Reserve pushed interest rates down to almost 0% in 2009 and kept them there for several years. Even though the economy experienced a positive inflation rate in every year since 2009, the Fed kept interest rates near zero, so the real interest rate in those years was actually negative.

Now consider some alternative investment, j, that is not risk free. Because this investment is risky, investors will demand a risk premium, RP_j, over and above the risk-free rate. Thus, the nominal return on security j equals

$$r_j = R_F + RP_j \tag{6.3}$$

The size of the risk premium, RP_j, depends on many factors. One factor that matters a great deal is the type of security under consideration. As the chapter opener about Aston Martin explained, investment grade bonds have lower risk premiums than junk

1. Here again we are making use of the approximate relationship between the nominal rate, the real rate, and inflation. By rearranging Equation 6.1a, we see that the nominal rate approximately equals the real rate plus the inflation rate.

FIGURE 6.2

Inflation and the Risk-free Interest Rates
Relationship between annual rate of inflation and 1-year U.S. Treasury bill rate, 1961–2016

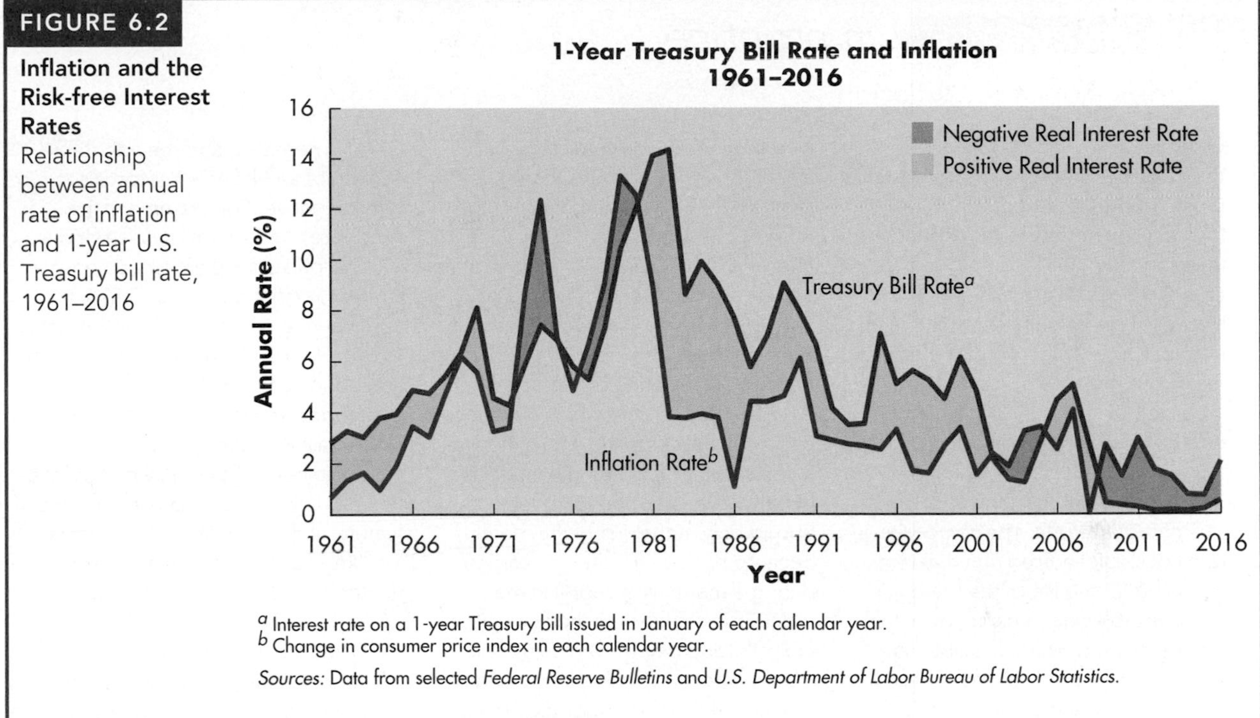

[a] Interest rate on a 1-year Treasury bill issued in January of each calendar year.
[b] Change in consumer price index in each calendar year.
Sources: Data from selected *Federal Reserve Bulletins* and *U.S. Department of Labor Bureau of Labor Statistics.*

bonds, and likewise preferred stocks usually have lower risk premiums than common stocks. In addition, attributes of the entity issuing the security affect the risk premium. Common stocks issued by large companies usually have lower risk premiums than stocks issued by small companies, for example. We will have a great deal more to say about risk premiums later in this text.

term structure of interest rates
The relationship between the maturity and rate of return for bonds with similar levels of risk.

yield curve
A graphic depiction of the term structure of interest rates.

yield to maturity (YTM)
Compound annual rate of return earned on a debt security purchased on a given day and held to maturity. An estimate of the market's required return on a particular bond.

normal yield curve
An upward-sloping yield curve indicates that long-term interest rates are generally higher than short-term interest rates.

inverted yield curve
A downward-sloping yield curve indicates that short-term interest rates are generally higher than long-term interest rates.

TERM STRUCTURE OF INTEREST RATES

The **term structure of interest rates** is the relationship between the maturity and rate of return for bonds with similar levels of risk. A graph of this relationship is called the **yield curve**. A quick glance at the yield curve tells analysts how rates vary between short-, medium-, and long-term bonds, but it may also provide information on where interest rates and the economy in general are headed in the future. Usually, when analysts examine the term structure of interest rates, they focus on Treasury securities because they are free of default risk.

Yield Curves

A bond's **yield to maturity (YTM)** (discussed in greater detail later in this chapter) represents the compound annual rate of return that an investor earns on the bond, assuming the bond makes all promised payments and the investor holds the bond to maturity. In most cases the YTM is a reasonably good measure of the market's required return on a bond. In a yield curve, the YTM is plotted on the vertical axis and time to maturity is plotted on the horizontal axis. Most of the time, long-term interest rates are higher than short-term rates, and we have a **normal yield curve** that slopes upward. Occasionally, short-term rates are higher than long-term rates, and we have an **inverted yield curve**. Finally, at times little

FOCUS ON PRACTICE *in practice*

I-Bonds Adjust for Inflation

One disadvantage of bonds is that they usually offer a fixed interest rate. Once a bond is issued, its interest rate typically cannot adjust as expected inflation changes. This rigidity presents a serious risk to bond investors because if inflation rises while the nominal rate on the bond remains fixed, the real rate of return falls.

The U.S. Treasury Department now offers the I-bond, which is an inflation-adjusted savings bond. A Series-I bond earns interest through the application of a *composite rate*. The composite rate consists of a *fixed rate* that remains the same for the life of the bond and an *adjustable rate* equal to the actual rate of inflation. The adjustable rate changes twice per year and is based on movements in the Consumer Price Index for All Urban Consumers (CPI-U). This index tracks the prices of thousands of goods and services, so an increase in this index indicates that inflation has occurred. As the rate of inflation moves up and down, I-bond interest rates adjust (with a short lag). Interest earnings are exempt from state and local income taxes, and are payable only when an investor redeems an I-bond. I-bonds are issued at face value in any denomination of $25 or more.

The I-bond is not without its drawbacks. Any redemption within the first 5 years results in a 3-month interest penalty. Also, you should redeem an I-bond only at the first of the month because none of the interest earned during a month is included in the redemption value until the first day of the following month. The adjustable rate feature of I-bonds can work against investors (i.e., it can lower their returns) if deflation occurs. **Deflation** refers to a general trend of falling prices, so when deflation occurs, the change in the CPI-U is negative, and the adjustable portion of an I-bond's interest also turns negative. For example, if the fixed-rate component on an I-bond is 2% and prices fall 0.5% (stated equivalently, the inflation rate is –0.5%), the nominal rate on an I-bond will be just 1.5% (2% – 0.5%). The nominal rate on an I-bond cannot fall below zero, no matter how much deflation takes place. In the past 80 years, periods of deflation have been very rare, whereas inflation has been an almost ever-present feature of the economy, so investors are likely to enjoy the inflation protection that I-bonds offer in the future.

► *What effect do you think the inflation-adjusted interest rate has on the price of an I-bond in comparison with similar bonds having no allowance for inflation?*

flat yield curve
A yield curve that indicates that interest rates do not vary much at different maturities.

or no difference exists between short-term and long-term rates, and we have a **flat yield curve**. Figure 6.3 shows four historical yield curves for U.S. Treasury securities: one from February 2002, a second from July 2006, a third from February 2007, and a fourth from May 2017.

FIGURE 6.3

Treasury Yield Curves
Yield curves for U.S. Treasury securities: February 2002; July 2006; February 2007; and May 2017

MyLab Finance Animation

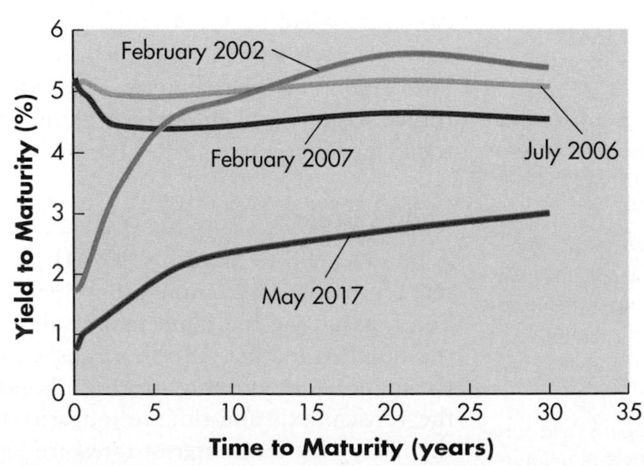

Source: https://www.treasury.gov/resource-center/data-chart-center/interest-rates/Pages/TextView.aspx?data=yield

deflation
A general trend of falling prices.

Observe that both the position and the shape of the yield curves change over time. The yield curve of February 2002 was upward sloping and relatively steep, with long-term rates well above short-term rates. The yield curve from May 2017 was also upward sloping, but it was not as steep as the yield curve in 2002, and at every maturity, rates were lower in 2017 than in 2002. The lower rates in 2017 were a function of both intervention by the Federal Reserve to keep rates low and the lower rate of inflation prevailing in the economy then compared to 2002. The yield curve from July 2006 was almost flat, with very little difference between yields on short-term and long-term Treasury securities. Finally, the yield curve from February 2007 was inverted, or downward sloping. Historically, a downward-sloping yield curve occurs infrequently and is often a sign that the economy is weakening. Most recessions in the United States have been preceded by an inverted yield curve.

Figure 6.4 demonstrates that last point. The grey bars in the figure indicate periods during which the U.S. economy was in recession. The line in the figure plots the difference between the yield to maturity on a 5-year Treasury note and the yield to maturity on a 1-year Treasury bill. Figure 6.4 shows that most of the time the 5-year note has a higher yield than the 1-year bill, but notice that when the line dips below 0% (i.e., when the yield curve is downward sloping), a recession almost always follows within a few months. In addition, notice how the difference in yields tends to be highest soon after a recession ends. This means that the slope of the yield curve is very steep as the economy pulls out of a recession and begins growing rapidly. Thus, the slope of the yield curve is a good predictor of overall economic activity: A negative slope foreshadows a recession, whereas a steep positive slope predicts an economic boom.

The shape of the yield curve may affect the firm's financing decisions. A financial manager who faces a downward-sloping yield curve may be tempted to rely more heavily on cheaper, long-term financing. However, a risk in following this strategy is that interest rates may fall in the future, so long-term rates that seem cheap today may be relatively expensive tomorrow. Likewise, when the yield curve is upward sloping, the manager may believe it wise to use cheaper,

FIGURE 6.4

The Slope of the Yield Curve and the Business Cycle
The difference in rates between 5-year and 1-year Treasury securities and its relationship to the business cycle

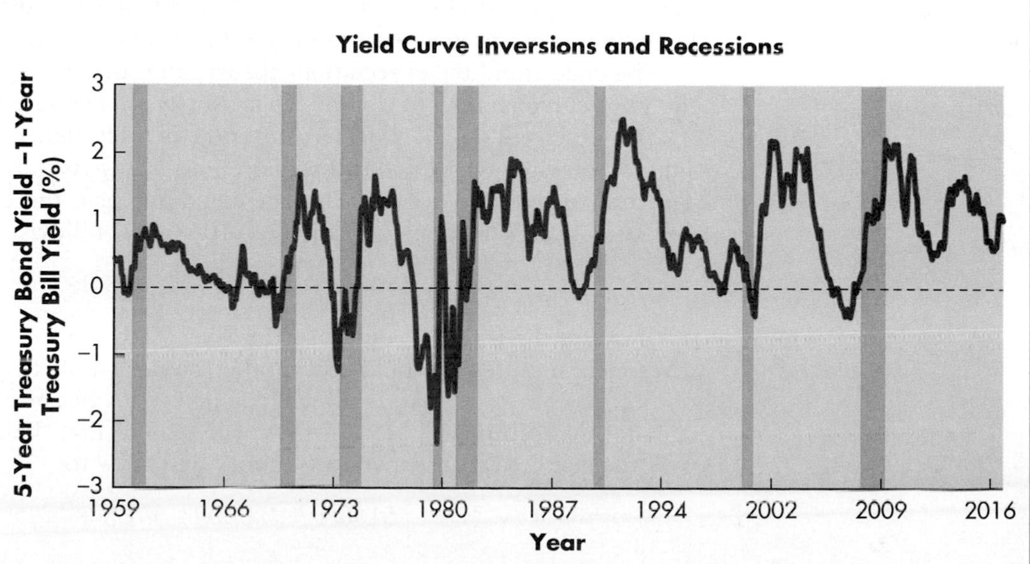

MATTER OF FACT

Bond Yields Hit Record Lows

On July 8, 2016, the 10-year Treasury note yield reached an all-time low of 1.366%. That was good news for the housing market. Many mortgage rates are linked to rates on Treasury securities. For example, the traditional 30-year mortgage rate is typically linked to the yield on 10-year Treasury notes. With mortgage rates reaching new lows, potential buyers found they could afford more expensive homes, and existing homeowners were able to refinance their existing loans, lowering their monthly mortgage payments and leaving them with more money to spend on other things. This kind of activity is precisely what the Federal Reserve hoped to stimulate by keeping interest rates low during the economic recovery.

short-term financing. Relying on short-term financing has its own risks. Firms that borrow on a short-term basis may see their costs rise if interest rates go up. Even more serious is the risk that a firm may not be able to refinance a short-term loan when it comes due. A variety of factors influence the choice of loan maturity, but the shape of the yield curve is something that managers must consider when making decisions about short-term versus long-term borrowing.

Theories of the Term Structure

Three theories are frequently cited to explain the general shape of the yield curve: the expectations theory, the liquidity preference theory, and the market segmentation theory.

expectations theory
The theory that the yield curve reflects investor expectations about future interest rates; an expectation of rising interest rates results in an upward-sloping yield curve, and an expectation of declining rates results in a downward-sloping yield curve.

Expectations Theory One theory of the term structure of interest rates, the **expectations theory**, suggests that the yield curve reflects investor expectations about future interest rates. The expectations theory asserts that when deciding whether to buy long-term or short-term bonds, investors seek only to maximize their expected return. As a consequence, when investors expect short-term interest rates to rise in the future (perhaps because investors believe that inflation will rise in the future), today's long-term rates will be higher than current short-term rates, and the yield curve will be upward sloping. The opposite is true when investors expect declining short-term rates: Today's short-term rates will be higher than current long-term rates, and the yield curve will be inverted.

To understand the expectations theory, consider this example. Suppose that the yield curve is upward sloping, as it usually is. The rate on a 1-year T-bill is 2%, and the rate on a 2-year Treasury note is a bit higher at 2.5%. Now, consider an investor who has \$100 to place into a low-risk investment for 2 years. The investor has two options. First, he could purchase the 2-year Treasury note, and after 2 years he would accumulate \$105.06, as follows:

$$\$100(1 + 0.025)^2 = \$105.06$$

Instead, the investor could buy the 1-year T-bill paying 2%, and when that investment matures, he could buy another 1-year T-bill. Today the investor does not know what return the T-bill will pay next year, but he has some expectation of what that return will be, which we will denote $E(r)$. Following this strategy, over the next 2 years the investor's money will grow to

$$\$100(1 + 0.020)(1 + E(r))$$

The expectations theory says that equilibrium occurs when investors are indifferent between these two options because both offer the same expected return. In other words, equilibrium occurs when the investor expects to accumulate the same amount of money no matter which option she chooses. If we set the return on these two strategies to be equal to each other, we see that the only way such an equilibrium can exist in this example is if the investor believes that the rate next year on a 1-year T-bill will be 3%:

$$\$100(1 + 0.025)^2 = \$100(1 + 0.020)(1 + E(r))$$
$$(1 + 0.025)^2 = (1 + 0.020)(1 + E(r))$$
$$E(r) = 0.030 = 3.0\%$$

To recap, we began the example with a yield curve that was upward sloping. According to the expectations theory, an upward-sloping yield curve must mean that investors expect interest rates to rise in the future. Only because they expect short-term rates to rise are they willing to purchase a short-term bond today that offers a lower return than today's long-term bond offers. In this example, the investor is indifferent between the two options—buying the Treasury note and earning 2.5% for 2 consecutive years or buying a T-bill today that pays 2% and another T-bill that the investor expects will pay 3.0% next year. The table below summarizes the fact situation in this example.

Investment strategy	Rate earned this year (%)	Rate earned (or expected) next year (%)	Compound return over 2 years (%)
Buy 2-year note today	2.5	2.5	5.06
Buy 1-year T-bill, then reinvest in another T-bill next year	2.0	3.0	5.06

According to the expectations theory, an upward-sloping yield curve means that investors expect interest rates to rise, and by the same logic, a downward-sloping yield curve means that investors expect interest rates to fall.

EXAMPLE 6.2

Suppose that a 1-year T-bill currently offers a 3.5% return and a 2-year Treasury note offers a 3.0% annual return. Thus, the short-term rate is higher than the long-term rate and the yield curve slopes down. According to the expectations theory, what belief must investors hold about the rate of return that a 1-year T-bill will offer next year? First, recognize that by purchasing the 2-year note, investors can earn a return of 6.09% over 2 years:

$$(1 + 0.030)^2 = 1.0609$$

If the market is in equilibrium, then the expected return on a strategy of purchasing a sequence of two 1-year T-bills must offer the same return, so we have

$$(1 + 0.035)(1 + \mathrm{E(r)}) = 1.0609$$
$$1 + \mathrm{E(r)} = 1.0609 \div 1.035$$
$$\mathrm{E(r)} = 0.025 = 2.5\%$$

Investors believe the T-bill will offer a 2.5% return next year, which is lower than the 3.0% return currently offered by 1-year T-bills. In other words, investors are indifferent between earning 3.0% for 2 consecutive years on the Treasury note or earning 3.5% this year and 2.5% next year on a sequence of two 1-year T-bills. Thus, today's downward-sloping yield curve implies that investors expect falling rates.

Liquidity Preference Theory Most of the time, yield curves are upward sloping, which, according to the expectations theory, means that investors expect interest rates to rise. An alternative explanation for the typical upward slope of the yield curve is the **liquidity preference theory**. This theory holds that, all else being equal, investors generally prefer to buy short-term securities, while issuers prefer to sell long-term securities. For investors, short-term securities are attractive because they are highly liquid and their prices are not particularly volatile.[2] Hence, investors will accept somewhat lower rates on short-term bonds because they are less risky than long-term bonds. Conversely, when firms or governments want to lock in their borrowing costs for a long period by selling long-term bonds, those bonds have to offer higher rates to entice investors away from the short-term securities they prefer. Borrowers are willing to pay somewhat higher rates because long-term debt allows them to eliminate or reduce the risk of not being able to refinance short-term debts when they come due. Borrowing on a long-term basis also reduces uncertainty about future borrowing costs.

liquidity preference theory
Theory suggesting that long-term rates are generally higher than short-term rates (hence, the yield curve is upward sloping) because investors perceive short-term investments as more liquid and less risky than long-term investments. Borrowers must offer higher rates on long-term bonds to entice investors away from their preferred short-term securities.

Market Segmentation Theory The **market segmentation theory** suggests that the market for loans is totally segmented on the basis of maturity and that the supply of and demand for loans within each segment determine its prevailing interest rate. In other words, the equilibrium between suppliers and demanders of short-term funds, such as seasonal business loans, would determine prevailing short-term interest rates, and the equilibrium between suppliers and demanders of long-term funds, such as real estate loans, would determine prevailing long-term interest rates. The slope of the yield curve would be determined by the general relationship between the prevailing rates in each market segment. For example, an upward-sloping yield curve indicates greater borrowing demand relative to the supply of funds in the long-term segment of the debt market relative to the short-term segment.

market segmentation theory
Theory suggesting that the market for loans is segmented on the basis of maturity and that the supply of and demand for loans within each segment determine its prevailing interest rate; the slope of the yield curve is determined by the general relationship between the prevailing rates in each market segment.

All three term structure theories have merit, so the slope of the yield curve is affected by (1) interest rate expectations, (2) liquidity preferences, and (3) the comparative equilibrium of supply and demand in the short- and long-term market segments. Upward-sloping yield curves result from expectations of rising interest rates, lender preferences for shorter-maturity loans, and greater supply of short-term loans than of long-term loans relative to demand. The opposite conditions would result in a downward-sloping yield curve. At any time, the interaction of these three forces determines the prevailing slope of the yield curve.

---

2. Later in this chapter, we demonstrate that debt instruments with longer maturities are more sensitive to changing market interest rates. For a given change in market rates, the prices (i.e., values) of longer-term bonds will fluctuate more (up or down) than the prices of bonds with shorter maturities.

RISK PREMIUMS: ISSUER AND ISSUE CHARACTERISTICS

So far, we have considered only risk-free U.S. Treasury securities. We now reintroduce the risk premium and assess it in view of risky non-Treasury issues. Recall Equations 6.2 and 6.3:

$$R_F = r^* + i$$

$$r_j = R_F + RP_j$$

In words, the nominal rate of interest for security j (r_j) is equal to the risk-free rate, consisting of the real rate of interest (r^*) plus the expected inflation rate (i), plus the risk premium (RP_j). The *risk premium* varies with specific issuer and issue characteristics.

EXAMPLE 6.3

MyLab Finance Solution Video

The nominal interest rates on a number of classes of long-term securities in May 2017 were as follows:

Security	Nominal interest rate
5-Year U.S. Treasury notes	1.81%
Corporate bonds:	
Investment grade	3.37
High-yield	7.67

Because the U.S. Treasury bond would represent the risk-free rate for a 5-year investment, we can calculate the risk premium of the other securities by subtracting the risk-free rate, 1.81%, from rates offered by each of the other corporate securities:

Security	Risk premium
Corporate bonds:	
Investment grade	3.37% − 1.81% = 1.56%
High-yield	7.67% − 1.81% = 5.86%

These risk premiums reflect differing issuer and issue risks. Junk bonds have a higher risk premium than investment grade bonds, and that higher risk premium is the compensation that investors demand for bearing the higher default risk of lower-quality bonds.

The risk premium consists of a number of issuer- and issue-related components, including business risk, financial risk, interest rate risk, liquidity risk, and tax risk, as well as the purely debt-specific risks—default risk and contractual provision risk—briefly defined in Table 6.1. In general, the highest risk premiums and therefore the highest nominal interest rates are associated with securities issued by firms with a high risk of default and from long-term maturities that have unfavorable contractual provisions.

TABLE 6.1 Debt-Specific Risk Premium Components

Component	Description
Default risk	The possibility that the issuer of debt will not pay the contractual interest or principal as scheduled. The greater the uncertainty as to the borrower's ability to meet these payments, the greater the risk premium. High bond ratings reflect low default risk, and low bond ratings reflect high default risk.
Contractual provision risk	Conditions that are often included in a debt agreement or a stock issue. Some of these reduce risk, whereas others may increase risk. For example, a provision allowing a bond issuer to retire its bonds prior to their maturity under favorable terms increases the bond's risk.

→ **REVIEW QUESTIONS** MyLab Finance Solutions

6–1 What is the real rate of interest? Differentiate it from the nominal rate of interest.

6–2 What is the term structure of interest rates, and how is it related to the yield curve?

6–3 For a given class of similar-risk securities, what does each of the following yield curves reflect about interest rates: (**a**) downward sloping, (**b**) upward sloping, and (**c**) flat? What is the "normal" shape of the yield curve?

6–4 Briefly describe the following theories of the general shape of the yield curve: (**a**) expectations theory, (**b**) liquidity preference theory, and (**c**) market segmentation theory.

6–5 List and briefly describe the potential issuer- and issue-related risk components that are embodied in the risk premium. Which are the purely debt-specific risks?

LG2 LG3

6.2 Government and Corporate Bonds

municipal bond
A bond issued by a state or local government body.

corporate bond
A long-term debt instrument indicating that a corporation has borrowed a certain amount of money and promises to repay it in the future under clearly defined terms.

When governments and corporations need to borrow money, they often do so by issuing bonds. In addition to the Treasury bills, notes, and bonds issued by the federal government, state and local governments issue bonds known as **municipal bonds**. A **corporate bond** is a long-term debt instrument indicating that a corporation has borrowed a certain amount of money and promises to repay it in the future under clearly defined terms.

The features of government and corporate bonds are similar. Most bonds are issued with maturities of 10 to 30 years and with a **par value, principal**, or **face value**, of $1,000. A bond's **coupon rate** represents the percentage of the bond's par value that will be paid to bondholders annually as interest. Most bonds make two interest payments per year (i.e., semiannual payments), and in that case the bond pays one-half of the coupon rate every 6 months. Bond's are sometimes called *fixed-income securities* because the coupon payments they make either do not change or change only according to a specified formula that is not linked to the issuer's financial performance.

par value, face value, principal
The amount of money the borrower must repay at maturity, and the value on which periodic interest payments are based.

coupon rate
The percentage of a bond's par value that will be paid annually, typically in two equal semiannual payments, as interest.

bond indenture
A legal document that specifies both the rights of the bondholders and the duties of the issuing corporation.

standard debt provisions
Provisions in a bond indenture specifying certain record-keeping and general business practices that the bond issuer must follow; normally, they do not place a burden on a financially sound business.

restrictive covenants
Provisions in a bond indenture that place operating and financial constraints on the borrower.

subordination
In a bond indenture, the stipulation that subsequent creditors agree to wait until all claims of the senior debt are satisfied.

LEGAL ASPECTS OF CORPORATE BONDS

Certain legal arrangements are required to protect purchasers of bonds. Bondholders are protected primarily through the indenture and the trustee.

Bond Indenture

A **bond indenture** is a legal document that specifies both the rights of the bondholders and the duties of the bond issuer. Included in the indenture are descriptions of the amount and timing of all interest and principal payments, as well as descriptions of specific actions that the borrower must take or must not take. Corporate borrowers commonly must (1) maintain satisfactory accounting records in accordance with generally accepted accounting principles (GAAP), (2) periodically supply audited financial statements, (3) pay taxes and other liabilities when due, and (4) maintain all facilities in good working order.

Standard Provisions The **standard debt provisions** in the bond indenture specify certain record-keeping and general business practices that the bond issuer must follow.

Restrictive Provisions Bond indentures also normally include certain **restrictive covenants**, which place operating and financial constraints on the borrower. These provisions help protect the bondholder against increases in borrower risk. Without them, the borrower could increase the firm's risk but not have to pay increased interest to compensate for the increased risk.

The most common restrictive covenants do the following:

1. Place limits on the values of certain accounting ratios that must be maintained while the debt is outstanding. Examples of some ratios with levels constrained by debt covenants are the interest coverage ratio, the current ratio, and the debt-to-equity ratio. Many of these ratios require a minimum level of liquidity, to ensure against loan default.
2. Prohibit or limit the sale of accounts receivable or other assets to generate cash. Selling receivables could cause a long-run cash shortage if proceeds were used to meet current obligations. Violations of this type of covenant could force the borrower to repay outstanding bonds immediately.
3. Impose fixed-asset restrictions. The borrower must maintain a specified level of fixed assets to guarantee its ability to repay the bonds.
4. Constrain subsequent borrowing. Additional long-term debt may be prohibited, or additional borrowing may be subordinated to the original loan. **Subordination** means that subsequent creditors agree to wait until all claims of the *senior debt* are satisfied.
5. Limit the firm's annual cash dividend payments to a specified percentage or amount.

Other restrictive covenants are sometimes included in bond indentures.

The violation of any standard or restrictive provision by the borrower may give bondholders the right to demand immediate repayment of the debt, or it may trigger some other change, such as a rating downgrade or a renegotiation of the terms of the indenture. Generally, bondholders evaluate any violation to determine whether it jeopardizes the loan. They may then decide to demand immediate repayment, continue the loan, or alter the terms of the bond indenture.

sinking-fund requirement
A restrictive provision often included in a bond indenture, providing for the systematic retirement of bonds prior to their maturity.

collateral
A specific asset against which bondholders have a claim in the event that a borrower defaults on a bond.

secured bond
A bond backed by some form of collateral.

unsecured bond
A bond backed only by the borrower's ability to repay the debt.

trustee
A paid individual, corporation, or commercial bank trust department that acts as the third party to a bond indenture and can take specified actions on behalf of the bondholders if the terms of the indenture are violated.

Sinking-Fund Requirements Another common restrictive provision is a **sinking-fund requirement**. Its objective is to provide for the systematic retirement of bonds prior to their maturity. To carry out this requirement, the corporation makes semiannual or annual payments that are used to retire bonds by purchasing them in the marketplace.

Security or Collateral The bond indenture identifies any collateral pledged against the bond and specifies how it must be maintained. **Collateral** refers to a specific asset against which bondholders have a claim in the event that the borrower defaults on the bond. The protection of bond collateral is crucial to guarantee the safety of a bond issue. A bond backed by some form of collateral is called a **secured bond**, whereas a bond backed only by the ability of the borrower to repay is called an **unsecured bond**.

Trustee

A **trustee** is a third party to a bond indenture. The trustee can be an individual, a corporation, or (most often) a commercial bank trust department. The trustee is paid to act as a "watchdog" on behalf of the bondholders and can take specified actions on behalf of the bondholders if the terms of the indenture are violated.

COST OF BONDS TO THE ISSUER

The cost of bond financing is generally greater than the issuer would have to pay for short-term borrowing. The major factors that affect the cost, which is the rate of interest paid by the bond issuer, are the bond's maturity, the size of the offering, the issuer's risk, and the basic cost of money.

Impact of Bond Maturity

Generally, as we noted earlier in Section 6.1, long-term debt pays higher interest rates than short-term debt. In a practical sense, the longer the maturity of a bond, the more sensitive the price of the bond will be to future changes in interest rates, which increases the risks of long-term bonds to investors. In addition, the longer the term, the greater the chance that the issuer might default.

Impact of Offering Size

The size of the bond offering also affects the interest cost of borrowing, but in an inverse manner: Bond flotation and administration costs per dollar borrowed are likely to decrease as offering size increases. However, the risk to the bondholders may increase, because larger offerings result in greater risk of default, all other factors held constant.

Impact of Issuer's Risk

The greater the issuer's *default risk*, the higher the interest rate. Some risk can be reduced through inclusion of appropriate restrictive provisions in the bond indenture. Clearly, bondholders must be compensated with higher returns for taking greater risk. Frequently, bond buyers rely on bond ratings (discussed later) to determine the issuer's overall risk.

Impact of the Cost of Money

The cost of money in the capital market is the basis for determining a bond's coupon rate. Generally, the rate on U.S. Treasury securities of equal maturity is used as the lowest-risk cost of money. To that basic rate is added a *risk premium* (as described earlier in this chapter) that reflects the factors mentioned above (maturity, offering size, and issuer's risk).

GENERAL FEATURES OF A BOND ISSUE

Three features sometimes included in a corporate bond issue are a conversion feature, a call feature, and stock purchase warrants. These features provide the issuer or the purchaser with certain opportunities for replacing or retiring the bond or supplementing it with some type of equity issue.

conversion feature
A feature of convertible bonds that allows bondholders to change each bond into a stated number of shares of common stock.

Convertible bonds offer a **conversion feature** that allows bondholders to convert each bond into shares of the bond issuer's common stock. Bondholders convert their bonds into stock only when the market price of the stock is such that conversion will provide a profit for the bondholder. In other words, if the market price of the bond issuer's stock rises enough, it makes sense for bondholders to convert their bonds into shares rather than to accept cash repayment of the bond principal. Because the bond conversion feature gives investors the opportunity to participate in the appreciation of the issuer's common stock, a conversion feature is desirable from the perspective of bondholders. As a result, they will accept a lower interest rate on convertible bonds compared to bonds without the conversion feature, all other factors being equal.

call feature
A feature included in nearly all corporate bond issues that gives the issuer the opportunity to repurchase bonds at a stated call price prior to maturity.

call price
The stated price at which a bond may be repurchased, by use of a call feature, prior to maturity.

call premium
The amount by which a bond's call price exceeds its par value.

Nearly all corporate bond issues include a **call feature**. That feature gives the issuer the opportunity to repurchase bonds prior to maturity. The **call price** is the stated price at which the issuer may repurchase bonds prior to maturity. Sometimes the call feature can be exercised only during a certain period. As a rule, the call price exceeds the par value of a bond by an amount equal to 1 year's interest. For example, a \$1,000 bond with a 5% coupon rate would be callable for around $\$1{,}050\,[\$1{,}000 + (0.05 \times \$1{,}000)]$. The amount by which the call price exceeds the bond's par value is commonly referred to as the **call premium**. This premium compensates bondholders for having the bond called away from them; to the issuer, it represents the cost of calling the bonds.

The call feature enables an issuer to call an outstanding bond when interest rates fall and issue a new bond at a lower interest rate. When interest rates rise, the call privilege will not be exercised, except possibly to meet sinking-fund requirements. Of course, to sell a callable bond in the first place, the issuer must pay a higher interest rate than that on noncallable bonds of equal risk, to compensate bondholders for the risk of having the bonds called away from them.

stock purchase warrants
Instruments that give their holders the right to purchase a certain number of shares of the issuer's common stock at a specified price over a certain period of time.

Bonds occasionally have stock purchase warrants attached as "sweeteners" to make them more attractive to prospective buyers. **Stock purchase warrants** are instruments that give their holders the right to purchase a certain number of shares of the issuer's common stock at a specified price over a certain period of time. Their inclusion typically enables the issuer to pay a slightly lower coupon rate than would otherwise be required.

BOND YIELDS

In the bond market, we use several conventions for measuring a bond's rate of return. Unfortunately for students who are new to the field, the names of different return measures are rather similar, as all of them incorporate the word *yield*. That term has slightly different meanings in different contexts. The three most widely reported measures of a bond's return are its *current yield*, its *yield to maturity (YTM)*, and its *yield to call (YTC)*. Each of these terms defines a bond's return in a slightly different way.

current yield
A measure of a bond's cash return for the year; calculated by dividing the bond's annual interest payment by its current price.

The simplest yield measure is the **current yield**, the annual interest payment divided by the current price. For example, a $1,000 par-value bond with an 8% coupon rate that currently sells for $970 would have a current yield of 8.25% $[(0.08 \times \$1{,}000) \div \$970]$. This measures how much interest a bondholder receives as a percentage of the bond's market price. However, a bond's total return depends not just on the interest payments it makes but also on the change in the bond's price that occurs. Because it focuses only on the interest that a bond pays, the current yield is not an especially accurate measure of a bond's rate of return. Both the yield to maturity and the yield to call measures provide a more complete picture of a bond's return, and we'll return to those concepts later in this chapter.

BOND PRICES

Because most corporate bonds are purchased and held by institutional investors, such as banks, insurance companies, and mutual funds, rather than individual investors, bond trading and price data are not readily available to individuals. Even so, it is important to understand market conventions for quoting bond prices and yields. Table 6.2 includes some data on the bonds of five companies. A quote for a bond issued by Verizon appears in the table's first row. The second column shows that Verizon's bond has a coupon rate of 4.522%, and the third column indicates that the bond matures on September 15, 2048. The fourth column lists the bond's closing price *expressed as a percentage of the bond's par value.* Most corporate bonds are issued with a *par,* or *face, value* of $1,000. The Verizon bond has a $1,000 par value and is quoted at 91.98, or $919.80 (0.9198 × $1,000). The final column of Table 6.2 shows the bond's *yield to maturity (YTM),* which, as we will see, is the compound

TABLE 6.2 Data on Selected Bonds

Company	Coupon	Maturity	Price	Yield (YTM)
Verizon	4.522%	Sep. 15, 2048	91.98	5.033%
Ford	5.291	Dec. 8, 2046	101.98	5.158
Marathon	5.000	Sep. 15, 2054	91.75	5.524
Humana	3.150	Dec. 1, 2022	101.73	2.799
Kohls	4.750	Dec. 15, 2023	104.48	3.947

Bond data from http://finra-markets.morningstar.com/BondCenter/ActiveUSCorpBond.jsp, accessed on April 28, 2017.

annual rate of return that would be earned on the bond if it were purchased and held to maturity. Given its 4.522% coupon rate and its price of $919.80, the Verizon bond offers a yield to maturity of 5.033%. Note that the YTM is above the coupon rate. The reason is that the Verizon bond currently sells below its $1,000 par value, so an investor who buys the bond today and holds it until it matures will receive interest payments of $45.22 each year *and* a capital gain of $81.20 ($1,000 − $919.80) when the bond matures. The capital gain component adds to the bond's total return, which boosts its YTM above its coupon rate.

BOND RATINGS

Independent agencies such as Moody's, Fitch, and Standard & Poor's assess the riskiness of publicly traded bond issues. These agencies derive their ratings by using financial ratio and cash flow analyses to assess the likely payment of bond interest and principal. Table 6.3 summarizes these ratings. For discussion of ethical issues related to the bond-rating agencies, see the *Focus on Ethics* box.

Normally, an inverse relationship exists between the quality of a bond and the rate of return that it must provide bondholders: High-quality (high-rated) bonds provide lower returns than lower-quality (low-rated) bonds, reflecting the lender's risk–return tradeoff. When considering bond financing, the financial manager must focus on the expected ratings of the bond issue because these ratings directly affect the interest rate that the issuer must pay investors.

COMMON TYPES OF BONDS

We can classify bonds in a variety of ways. Here we break them into traditional bonds (the basic types that have been around for years) and contemporary bonds (newer, more innovative types). The traditional types of bonds are summarized

TABLE 6.3 Moody's and Standard & Poor's Bond Ratings

Moody's	Interpretation	Standard & Poor's	Interpretation
Aaa	Prime quality	AAA	Investment grade
Aa	High grade	AA	
A	Upper medium grade	A	
Baa	Medium grade	BBB	
Ba	Lower medium grade or speculative	BB	Speculative
B	Speculative	B	
Caa	From very speculative	CCC	
Ca	to near or in default	CC	
C	Lowest grade	C	Income bond
		D	In default

Note: Some ratings may be modified to show relative standing within a major rating category; for example, Moody's uses numerical modifiers (1, 2, 3), whereas Standard & Poor's uses plus (+) and minus (−) signs.

Sources: Moody's Investors Service, Inc., and Standard & Poor's Corporation.

TABLE 6.4 Characteristics and Priority of Lender's Claim of Traditional Types of Bonds

Bond type	Characteristics	Priority of lender's claim
Unsecured bonds		
Debentures	Unsecured bonds that only creditworthy firms can issue. Convertible bonds are normally debentures.	Claims are the same as those of any general creditor. May have other unsecured bonds subordinated to them.
Subordinated debentures	Claims are not satisfied until those of the creditors holding certain (senior) debts have been fully satisfied.	Claim is that of a general creditor but not as good as a senior debt claim.
Income bonds	Payment of interest is required only when earnings are available. Commonly issued in reorganization of a failing firm.	Claim is that of a general creditor. Are not in default when interest payments are missed because they are contingent only on earnings being available.
Secured Bonds		
Mortgage bonds	Secured by real estate or buildings.	Claim is on proceeds from sale of mortgaged assets; if not fully satisfied, the lender becomes a general creditor. The first-mortgage claim must be fully satisfied before distribution of proceeds to second-mortgage holders and so on. A number of mortgages can be issued against the same collateral.
Collateral trust bonds	Secured by stock and (or) bonds that are owned by the issuer. Collateral value is generally 25% to 35% greater than bond value.	Claim is on proceeds from stock and/or bond collateral; if not fully satisfied, the lender becomes a general creditor.
Equipment trust certificates	Used to finance "rolling stock," such as airplanes, trucks, boats, railroad cars. A trustee buys the asset with funds raised through the sale of trust certificates and then leases it to the firm; after making the final scheduled lease payment, the firm receives title to the asset. A type of leasing.	Claim is on proceeds from the sale of the asset; if proceeds do not satisfy outstanding debt, trust certificate lenders become general creditors.

debentures
subordinated debentures
income bonds
mortgage bonds
collateral trust bonds
equipment trust certificates
See Table 6.4.

in terms of their key characteristics and priority of lender's claim in Table 6.4. Note that the first three types—**debentures, subordinated debentures,** and **income bonds**—are unsecured, whereas the last three—**mortgage bonds, collateral trust bonds,** and **equipment trust certificates**—are secured.

zero- (or low-) coupon bonds
junk (high-yield) bonds
floating-rate bonds
extendible notes
putable bonds
See Table 6.5.

Table 6.5 describes the key characteristics of five contemporary types of bonds: **zero- (or low-) coupon bonds, junk (high-yield) bonds, floating-rate bonds, extendible notes,** and **putable bonds.** These bonds can be either unsecured or secured. Changing capital market conditions and investor preferences have spurred further innovations in bond financing in recent years and will probably continue to do so.

INTERNATIONAL BOND ISSUES

Companies and governments borrow internationally by issuing bonds in two principal financial markets: the Eurobond market and the foreign bond market. Both give borrowers the opportunity to obtain large amounts of long-term

FOCUS ON ETHICS *in practice*

"Can Bond Ratings Be Trusted?"

Nationally Recognized Statistical Rating Organizations (NRSROs), or credit-rating agencies, provide investors with independent assessments of a debt issuer's ability to make scheduled interest and principal payments. NRSROs assess corporate bonds, government bonds, municipal bonds, and debt obligations backed by collateral, such as mortgage-backed securities (MBSs). Broadly speaking, all NRSROs use the same approach for evaluating a debt instrument—feed quantitative data and qualitative judgments into a statistical model, then use the resulting default probability to award a letter grade on a continuum from "extremely unlikely" to "almost certain." Moody's, Standard & Poor's, and Fitch dominate the credit-ratings business, accounting for nearly 95% of the market. The reputations of the Big Three—each has been in business over 100 years—make their ratings highly coveted. But the Great Recession of 2007-09 tarnished those reputations.

The pre-recession housing boom and strong demand for highly rated debt boosted the value of outstanding mortgage-backed securities to over $11 trillion by 2008, or 35% of U.S. bond market debt. This trend made the business of rating MBSs very lucrative, perhaps leading NRSROs to overlook potential flaws in their default-risk models. From 2000 to 2007, MBSs accounted for nearly half of Moody's rating revenues; in 2006 alone, Moody's awarded a "AAA" rating to an average of 30 MBSs *every day*. But when home prices across the U.S. started to tumble in 2007, the flaws in the models of default risk became apparent as home mortgage defaults soared. Ultimately, Moody's had to downgrade 83% of the $869 billion in MBSs rated AAA in 2006. The fallout from widespread MBS "ratings inflation" brought down two of the nation's largest investment banks—Bear Stearns and Lehman Brothers—and contributed to the worst recession since the Great Depression.

In the post-game analysis, many blamed fraud for the ratings inflation, as suggested by an internal December 2006 Standard & Poor's email that proclaimed "Let's hope we are all wealthy and retired by the time this house of cards falters."* Others pointed to a flawed system whereby the issuer of the debt instrument, not the investor, pays the NRSRO. But these explanations cannot tell the whole story—several large financial institutions that paid for ratings of complex MBSs were undone by their own holdings when those ratings turned out to be inflated. Moreover, ratings inflation did not extend to the traditional bread-and-butter of the business—corporate bonds—despite the fact issuers also pay for those ratings.

▶ *What ethical issues could arise because companies or governments issuing debt—not investors—pay NRSROs to rate those instruments?*

▶ *Why do you think NRSROs inflated ratings for new complex MBSs but not traditional corporate bonds in the run-up to the Great Recession?*

*From House Committee on Oversight and Government Reform

debt financing quickly, in the currency of their choice and with flexible repayment terms.

Eurobond
A bond issued by an international borrower and sold to investors in countries with currencies other than the currency in which the bond is denominated.

foreign bond
A bond that is issued by a foreign corporation or government and is denominated in the investor's home currency and sold in the investor's home market.

A **Eurobond** is issued by an international borrower and sold to investors in countries with currencies other than the currency in which the bond is denominated. An example is a dollar-denominated bond issued by a U.S. corporation and sold to Belgian investors. From the founding of the Eurobond market in the 1960s until the mid-1980s, "blue chip" U.S. corporations were the largest single class of Eurobond issuers. Some of these companies were able to borrow in this market at interest rates below those the U.S. government paid on Treasury bonds. As the market matured, issuers became able to choose the currency in which they borrowed, and European and Japanese borrowers rose to prominence. In more recent years, the Eurobond market has become much more balanced in terms of the mix of borrowers, total issue volume, and currency of denomination.

In contrast, a **foreign bond** is issued by a foreign corporation or government and is denominated in the investor's home currency and sold in the investor's

TABLE 6.5 Characteristics of Contemporary Types of Bonds

Bond type	Characteristics[a]
Zero- (or low-) coupon bonds	Issued with no (zero) or a very low coupon (stated interest) rate and sold at a large discount from par. A significant portion (or all) of the investor's return comes from gain in value (i.e., par value minus purchase price). Generally callable at par value.
Junk (high-yield) bonds	Debt rated Ba or lower by Moody's or BB or lower by Standard & Poor's. Commonly used by rapidly growing firms to obtain growth capital, most often as a way to finance mergers and takeovers. High-risk bonds with high yields, often yielding 2% to 3% more than the best-quality corporate debt.
Floating-rate bonds	Stated interest rate is adjusted periodically within stated limits in response to changes in specified money market or capital market rates. Popular when future inflation and interest rates are uncertain. Tend to sell at close to par because of the automatic adjustment to changing market conditions. Some issues provide for annual redemption at par at the option of the bondholder.
Extendible notes	Short maturities, typically 1 to 5 years, that can be renewed for a similar period at the option of holders. Similar to a floating-rate bond. An issue might be a series of 3-year renewable notes over a period of 15 years; every 3 years, the notes could be extended for another 3 years, at a new rate competitive with market interest rates at the time of renewal.
Putable bonds	Bonds that can be redeemed at par (typically, $1,000) at the option of their holder either at specific dates after the date of issue and every 1 to 5 years thereafter or when and if the firm takes specified actions, such as being acquired, acquiring another company, or issuing a large amount of additional debt. In return for its conferring the right to "put the bond" at specified times or when the firm takes certain actions, the bond's yield is lower than that of a nonputable bond.

[a] The claims of lenders (i.e., bondholders) against issuers of each of these types of bonds vary, depending on the bonds' other features. Each of these bonds can be unsecured or secured.

home market. A Swiss-franc–denominated bond issued in Switzerland by a U.S. company is an example of a foreign bond. The largest foreign bond markets include the United Kingdom, Japan, Switzerland, and the United States. Some types of foreign bonds have particularly unusual names. For example, a *bulldog bond* is a foreign bond issued in Britain and a *samurai bond* is one issued in Japan.

→ REVIEW QUESTIONS MyLab Finance Solutions

6–6 What are typical maturities, denominations, and interest payments of a corporate bond? What mechanisms protect bondholders?

6–7 Differentiate between standard debt provisions and restrictive covenants included in a bond indenture. What are the consequences if a bond issuer violates any of these covenants?

6–8 How is the cost of bond financing typically related to the cost of short-term borrowing? In addition to the maturity of a bond, what other major factors affect its cost to the issuer?

6–9 What is a conversion feature? A call feature? What are stock purchase warrants?

6–10 What is the current yield for a bond? How are bond prices quoted? How are bonds rated, and why?

6–11 Compare the basic characteristics of Eurobonds and foreign bonds.

6.3 Valuation Fundamentals

valuation
The process that links risk and return to determine the worth of an asset.

Valuation is the process that links risk and return to determine the worth of an asset. It is a relatively simple process that investors and managers apply to *expected* streams of cash flows from bonds, stocks, income properties, oil wells, and so on. To determine an asset's value, a financial manager uses the time-value-of-money techniques presented in Chapter 5 and the concepts of risk and return that we will develop in Chapter 8.

For two major reasons, understanding the valuation process is crucial for financial managers. First, firms often issue securities such as bonds and stocks to investors, so managers must grasp how investors will value those securities. Second, financial managers must often decide whether some investment opportunity available to a firm will generate sufficient cash flows to justify its cost. To make that judgment, managers work to place a value on an investment project's cash flows and then compare that estimate of the investment's value to its cost. Making investments that are worth more than they cost is central to creating value for shareholders, which is the primary goal of financial management.

KEY INPUTS

The valuation process has three key inputs: (1) cash flows; (2) timing; and (3) a measure of risk, which determines the required return. Each input is described below.

Cash Flows

The value of any asset depends on the cash flow(s) it is *expected* to provide over time. To have value, an asset does not have to provide an annual cash flow; it can provide an intermittent cash flow or even a single cash flow over the period.

PERSONAL FINANCE EXAMPLE 6.4 Celia Sargent wishes to estimate the value of three assets she is considering investing in: common stock in Michaels Enterprises, an interest in an oil well, and an original painting by a well-known artist. Her cash flow estimates for each are as follows:

Stock in Michaels Enterprises: Expect to receive cash dividends of $300 per year indefinitely.

Oil well: Expect to receive cash flows of $2,000 after 1 year, $4,000 after 2 years, and $10,000 after 4 years, when the well will run dry.

Original painting: Expect to sell the painting in 5 years for $85,000.

With these cash flow estimates, Celia has taken the first step toward placing a value on each of the assets.

Timing

In addition to making cash flow estimates, we must know the timing of the cash flows. For example, Celia expects the cash flows of \$2,000, \$4,000, and \$10,000 for the oil well to occur after 1, 2, and 4 years, respectively. The combination of the cash flow and its timing defines the return expected from the asset.

Risk and Required Return

The risk associated with a cash flow stream also affects its value. Holding the size of the cash flow stream constant, the more risky a cash flow stream is (i.e., the more uncertainty about the amount and timing of the cash flow stream), the less valuable the stream will be. In the valuation process, we account for greater risk by discounting cash flows at a higher rate (i.e., by requiring a higher rate of return). The higher the risk, the greater the required return, and the lower the risk, the less the required return.

PERSONAL FINANCE EXAMPLE 6.5 Let's return to Celia Sargent's task of placing a value on the original painting and consider two scenarios.

Scenario 1: Certainty A major art gallery has contracted to buy the painting for \$85,000 after 5 years. Because this contract is already signed and the art gallery is well established and reliable, Celia views this asset as "money in the bank." She thus would use something close to the prevailing risk-free rate of 3% as the required return when calculating the value of the painting.

Scenario 2: High risk The values of original paintings by this artist have fluctuated widely over the past 10 years. Although Celia expects to sell the painting for \$85,000, she realizes that its sale price in 5 years could range between \$30,000 and \$140,000. Because of the high uncertainty surrounding the painting's value, Celia believes that a 15% required return is appropriate.

These two estimates of the appropriate required return illustrate how the discount rate accounts for risk in the valuation process. Although adjusting the discount rate for risk has a subjective element, analysts use historical data and a variety of analytical methods to estimate the required return with as much precision as possible.

BASIC VALUATION MODEL

The value of an asset is *the present value of all the future cash flows it is expected to provide*. Therefore, calculating an asset's value means discounting the expected cash flows back to the present using a discount rate or required return commensurate with the asset's risk. Using the present value techniques explained in Chapter 5, we can express the value of any asset at time zero, V_0, as

$$V_0 = \frac{CF_1}{(1 + r)^1} + \frac{CF_2}{(1 + r)^2} + \ldots + \frac{CF_n}{(1 + r)^n} \tag{6.4}$$

where

V_0 = value of the asset at time zero
CF_t = cash flow *expected* in year t
r = required return (discount rate)
n = time period (investment's life or investor's holding period)

We can use the basic idea behind Equation 6.4 to determine the value of many different kinds of assets.

IRF PERSONAL FINANCE EXAMPLE 6.6 Celia Sargent values each asset by discounting its cash flows as indicated by Equation 6.4. Because Michael's stock pays a perpetual stream of $300 dividends, Equation 6.4 reduces to Equation 5.7, which says that the present value of a perpetuity equals the dividend payment divided by the required return. Celia decides that a 12% discount rate is appropriate for this investment, so her estimate of the value of Michael's Enterprises stock is

$$\$300 \div 0.12 = \$2{,}500$$

Next, Celia values the oil well investment, which she believes is the most risky of the three investments. Discounting the oil well's cash flows using a 20% required return, Celia estimates the well's value to be

$$\frac{\$2{,}000}{(1 + 0.20)^1} + \frac{\$4{,}000}{(1 + 0.20)^2} + \frac{\$10{,}000}{(1 + 0.20)^4} = \$9{,}266.98$$

Finally, Celia estimates the value of the painting by discounting the expected $85,000 cash payment in 5 years at 15%:

$$\$85{,}000 \div (1 + 0.15)^5 = \$42{,}260.02$$

Note that, regardless of the pattern of the asset's expected cash flows, Celia can use the basic valuation equation to determine the asset's value.

→ REVIEW QUESTIONS MyLab Finance Solutions

6–12 Why is it important for financial managers to understand the valuation process?
6–13 What are the three key inputs to the valuation process?
6–14 Does the valuation process apply only to assets that provide an annual cash flow? Explain.
6–15 Define and specify the general equation for the value of any asset, V_0.

LG5 LG6

6.4 Bond Valuation

Customizing the basic valuation equation to value specific securities such as bonds, preferred stock, and common stock is relatively straightforward. We describe bond valuation in this chapter, and we cover the valuation of common stock and preferred stock elsewhere in this text in Chapter 7.

BOND FUNDAMENTALS

Bonds are long-term debt instruments used by business and government to raise large sums of money, typically from a diverse group of lenders. Most corporate bonds pay interest semiannually (every 6 months) at a stated coupon rate; have an initial maturity of 10 to 30 years; and have a par value, principal, or face value, of $1,000 that the borrower must repay at maturity.

EXAMPLE 6.7

On January 1, 2018, Mills Company issued a 6% coupon rate, 10-year bond with a $1,000 par value that pays interest annually. Investors who buy this bond receive the contractual right to two types of cash flows: (1) $60 annual interest (6% coupon rate × $1,000 par value) distributed at the end of each year and (2) the $1,000 par value at the end of the tenth year.

We will use the Mills Company bond to see how the market prices bonds. We use the terms price and value (or pricing and valuation) interchangeably, reflecting a view that the participants in the bond market determine the price of a bond using the valuation principles outlined here.

BOND VALUATION

Valuing a bond is a simple application of Equation 6.4. The market price of a bond should equal the present value of the payments its issuer is contractually obligated to make. Those payments include a series of coupon (i.e., interest) payments and a final payment to return the bond's par value to the investor when the bond matures. The basic model for the value, B_0, of a bond is given by

$$B_0 = \frac{C}{(1+r)^1} + \frac{C}{(1+r)^2} + \frac{C}{(1+r)^3} + \ldots + \frac{C}{(1+r)^n} + \frac{M}{(1+r)^n}$$

$$B_0 = \left[\sum_{t=1}^{n} \frac{C}{(1+r)^t}\right] + \left[\frac{M}{(1+r)^n}\right] \tag{6.5}$$

where

B_0 = value (or price) of the bond at time zero
C = annual coupon interest payment in dollars
n = number of years to maturity
M = par value in dollars
r = required return on the bond

Notice that the stream of cash flows provided by a bond is composed of an annuity paying $\$C$ for n years plus a lump sum payment of $\$M$ when the bond matures. Determining the value of a bond today means calculating the present value of the annuity of coupon payments and adding to that the present value of the bond's par value paid at maturity. Therefore, an alternative mathematical approach to calculating a bond's price makes use of the formulas for the present value of an annuity and the present value of a lump sum, discussed previously in this text.

$$B_0 = \left(\frac{C}{r}\right)\left[1 - \frac{1}{(1+r)^n}\right] + \frac{M}{(1+r)^n} \quad (6.5a)$$

The first term in Equation 6.5a is the formula for the present value of an annuity, and the second term is the present value of a lump sum. We can calculate a bond's value by using Equations 6.5 or 6.5a, or by using a financial calculator or spreadsheet.

IRF EXAMPLE 6.8

Tim Sanchez wishes to determine the current value of the Mills Company bond. If the bond pays interest annually and the required return on the bond is 6% (equal to its coupon rate), then we can calculate the bond's value using Equation 6.5a:

$$B_0 = \left(\frac{\$60}{0.06}\right)\left[1 - \frac{1}{(1+0.06)^{10}}\right] + \frac{\$1{,}000}{(1+0.06)^{10}}$$

$$B_0 = \$1{,}000[0.44161] + \$558.39 = \$441.61 + \$558.39 = \$1{,}000.00$$

The timeline below depicts the computations involved in finding the bond value.

Timeline for bond valuation (Mills Company's 6% coupon rate, 10-year maturity, $1,000 par, January 1, 2018, issue date, paying annual interest, and required rate of return of 6%)

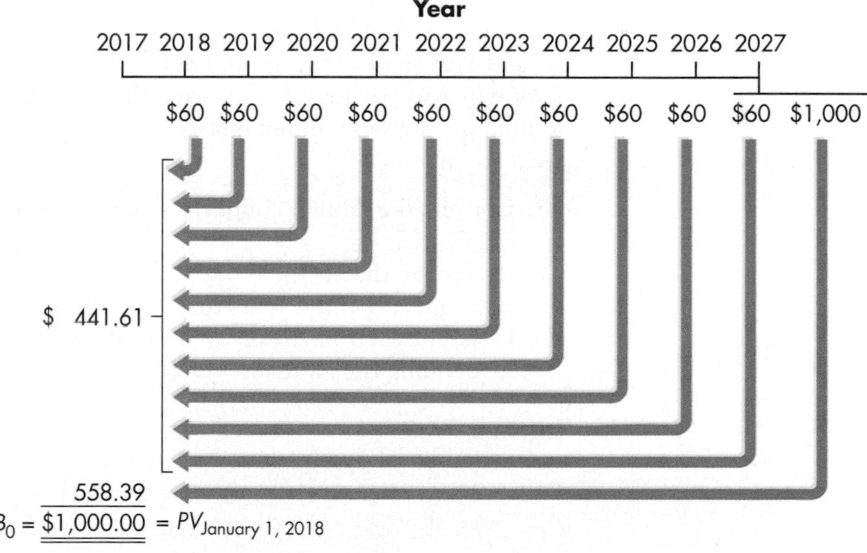

MyLab Finance Financial Calculator

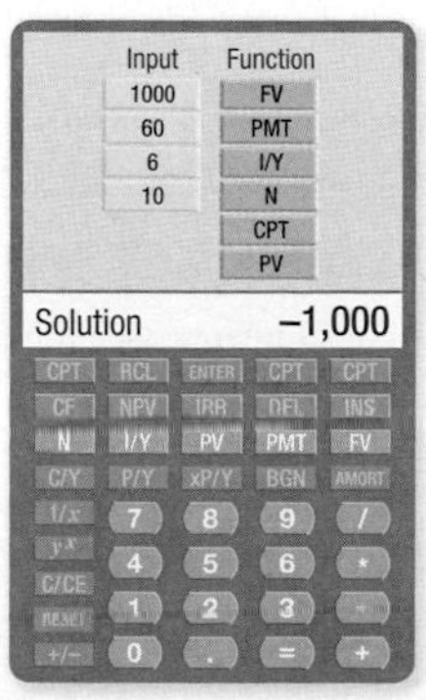

Calculator use Using the Mills Company's inputs shown at the left, you should find the bond value to be exactly $1,000. If you compare the calculator keystrokes to the ones we displayed when we used a calculator to find the present value of an ordinary annuity earlier in this text, you will see that there is an additional term here, namely, the $1,000 future value (FV). We must add that to our sequence of keystrokes because the bond pays out an annuity plus a lump sum at the end. When we add the FV keystroke, we are capturing the value of that final lump sum payment when the bond matures. Note that *the calculated bond value is equal to its par value, which will always be the case when the required return is equal to the coupon rate.*

Spreadsheet use We can also calculate the value of the Mills Company bond as shown in the following Excel spreadsheet.

	A	B
1	VALUATION FOR ANNUAL BOND	
2	Par value	$1,000
3	Coupon interest rate	6%
4	Annual Interest payment	$60
5	Required rate of return	6%
6	Number of years to maturity	10
7	Bond value	–$1,000.00

Entry in Cell B4 is =B2*B3.
Entry in Cell B7 is =PV(B5,B6,B4,B2,0).
The minus sign appears before the $1,000.00 in B7 because the bond's price is a cost for the investor.

SEMIANNUAL INTEREST RATES AND BOND VALUES

As a practical matter, most bonds make semiannual rather than annual interest payments. Continuing with the example of the Mills Company bond, we note that if it paid interest semiannually rather than annually, then investors would receive an annuity of 20 coupon payments (2 payments per year for 10 years) of $30 each (half of the annual $60 coupon paid every 6 months), and of course they will also receive $1,000 when the bond matures. Calculating the value for a bond paying semiannual interest requires three changes to the approach we've used so far:

1. Convert the annual coupon payment, C, to a semiannual payment by dividing C by 2.
2. Recognize that if the bond has n years to maturity it will make $2n$ coupon payments (i.e., in n years there are $2n$ semiannual periods).
3. Discount each payment by using the semiannual required return calculated by dividing the annual required return, r, by 2.[3]

3. As we noted in Chapter 5, the effective annual rate of interest, *EAR*, for stated interest rate r, when interest is paid semiannually ($m = 2$) can be found by using Equation 5.10:

$$EAR = \left(1 + \frac{r}{2}\right)^2 - 1$$

For example, a bond with a 12% required stated annual return, r_d, that pays semiannual interest would have an effective annual rate of

$$EAR = \left(1 + \frac{0.12}{2}\right)^2 - 1 = (1.06)^2 - 1 = 1.1236 - 1 = 0.1236 = 12.36$$

Because most bonds pay semiannual interest at semiannual rates equal to 50% of the stated annual rate, their effective annual rates are generally higher than their stated annual rates.

Substituting these three changes into Equations 6.5 and 6.5a yields

$$B_0 = \frac{\frac{C}{2}}{\left(1+\frac{r}{2}\right)^1} + \frac{\frac{C}{2}}{\left(1+\frac{r}{2}\right)^2} + \frac{\frac{C}{2}}{\left(1+\frac{r}{2}\right)^3} + \ldots + \frac{\frac{C}{2}}{\left(1+\frac{r}{2}\right)^{2n}} + \frac{M}{\left(1+\frac{r}{2}\right)^{2n}}$$

$$B_0 = \left[\sum_{t=1}^{2n} \frac{\frac{C}{2}}{\left(1+\frac{r}{2}\right)^t}\right] + \left[\frac{M}{\left(1+\frac{r}{2}\right)^{2n}}\right] \quad (6.6)$$

and

$$B_0 = \left(\frac{C/2}{r/2}\right)\left[1 - \frac{1}{\left(1+\frac{r}{2}\right)^{2n}}\right] + \frac{M}{\left(1+\frac{r}{2}\right)^{2n}} \quad (6.6a)$$

IRF EXAMPLE 6.9

Assuming that the Mills Company bond pays interest semiannually and that the required annual return, r, is 6%, we can use Equation 6.6a to find the value of the bond:

$$B_0 = \left(\frac{\$60/2}{0.06/2}\right)\left[1 - \frac{1}{\left(1+\frac{0.06}{2}\right)^{2(10)}}\right] + \frac{\$1{,}000}{\left(1+\frac{0.06}{2}\right)^{2(10)}}$$

$$B_0 = \$1{,}000[0.44632] + \$553.68 = \$446.32 + \$553.68 = \$1{,}000$$

As before, because the required rate on this bond equals the coupon rate, the bond sells at par value. We will soon see that when the required return does not equal the coupon rate, the bond may sell above or below par value.

MyLab Finance Financial Calculator

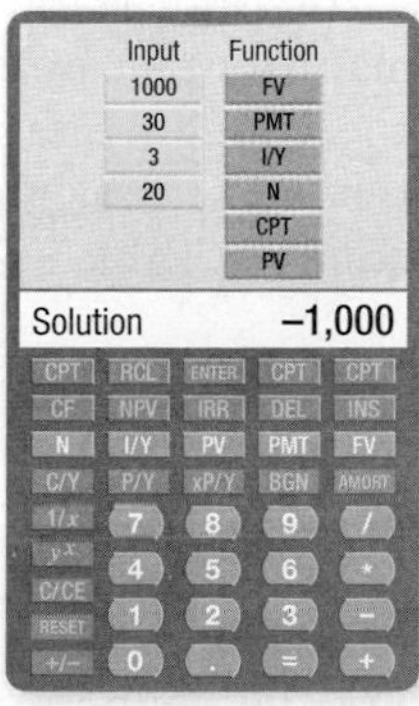

Calculator use When using a calculator to find the price of a bond that pays interest semiannually, we must double the number of periods and divide both the required annual return and the annual coupon payment by 2. For the Mills Company bond, we would use 20 periods (2 × 10 years), a semiannual required return of 3% (6% ÷ 2), and an interest payment of $30 ($60 ÷ 2). Using these inputs, you should find the bond value with semiannual interest to be $1,000, as shown at the left.

Spreadsheet use The value of the Mills Company bond paying semiannual interest at an annual required return of 6% also can be calculated as shown in the following Excel spreadsheet.

	A	B
1	VALUATION FOR SEMIANNUAL BOND	
2	Par value	$1,000
3	Coupon interest rate	6%
4	Interest payments per year	2
5	Interest payment	$30
6	Required rate of return	6%
7	Number of years to maturity	10
8	Bond value	–$1,000

Entry in Cell B5 is =B2*B3/B4.
Entry in Cell B8 is =PV(B6/B4,B7*B4,B5,B2,0).
The minus sign appears before the $1,000
in B8 because the bond's price is a cost for the investor.

CHANGES IN BOND VALUES

The price of a bond in the marketplace does not remain fixed at its par value. In Table 6.2 you saw that the prices of bonds often differ from their par values. Some bonds are valued below par (current price below 100), and others are valued above par (current price above 100). A variety of forces in the economy, as well as the passage of time, affect bond values. The most important thing to know about bond prices is that they move in the opposite direction of required returns. When the required return rises, the bond price falls, and when the required return falls, the bond price rises.

Required Returns and Bond Values

Whenever the required return on a bond differs from the bond's coupon rate, the bond's price will differ from its par value. The required return is likely to differ from the coupon rate because either (1) economic conditions have changed since the bond was issued, causing a shift in the cost of funds; or (2) the bond issuer's risk has changed. Increases in the cost of funds or in risk will raise the required return; decreases in the cost of funds or in risk will lower the required return.

discount
The amount by which a bond sells below its par value.

premium
The amount by which a bond sells above its par value.

When the required return is greater than the coupon rate, the bond's value will be less than its par value. In this case, the bond sells at a **discount**. Looking back at Table 6.2 on page 274, you can see that the Verizon and Marathon bonds sell at a discount, and these bonds have a yield to maturity that exceeds the coupon rate. When the required return falls below the coupon rate, the bond's value will be greater than par. In this situation, the bond sells at a **premium**, which is the case for the Ford, Humana, and Kohls bonds in Table 6.2.

IRF EXAMPLE 6.10

MyLab Finance Solution Video

Let's reconsider the Mills Company bond paying a 6% coupon rate and maturing in 10 years (assume annual interest payments for simplicity). Initially, we assumed that the required return on this bond was 6%, and in that case the bond's value was $1,000, equal to par value. Let's see what happens to the bond's value if the required return is higher or lower than the coupon rate. Table 6.6 shows that at an 8% required return, the bond sells at a discount

MyLab Finance Financial Calculator

Input	Function
1000	FV
60	PMT
8	I/Y
10	N
	CPT
	PV
Solution	−865.80

Input	Function
1000	FV
60	PMT
4	I/Y
10	N
	CPT
	PV
Solution	−1,162.22

TABLE 6.6 Bond Values for Various Required Returns (Mills Company's 6% Coupon Interest Rate, 10-Year Maturity, $1,000 Par, January 1, 2018, Issue Date, Paying Annual Interest)

Required return, r	Bond value, B_0	Status
8%	$ 865.80	Discount
6	1,000.00	Par value
4	1,162.22	Premium

with a value of $865.80, but if the required return is 4%, the bond sells at a premium with a value of $1,162.22.

Calculator use Using the inputs shown at the left for the two different required returns, you will find the value of the bond to be below or above par. At an 8% required return, the bond would sell for $865.80, which is a discount of $134.20 below par value. At a 4% required return, the bond would sell for $1,162.22, which is a premium of $162.22 above par value. Figure 6.5 illustrates the inverse relationship between the required return and the price of the Mills Company bond.

Spreadsheet use The values for the Mills Company bond at required returns of 8% and 6% also can be calculated as shown in the following Excel spreadsheet. Once this spreadsheet has been configured, you can calculate the bond price for any required return by simply changing the input values.

FIGURE 6.5

Bond Values and Required Returns

Bond values and required returns (Mills Company's 6% coupon interest rate, 10-year maturity, $1,000 par, January 1, 2018, issue date, paying annual interest)

MyLab Finance Animation

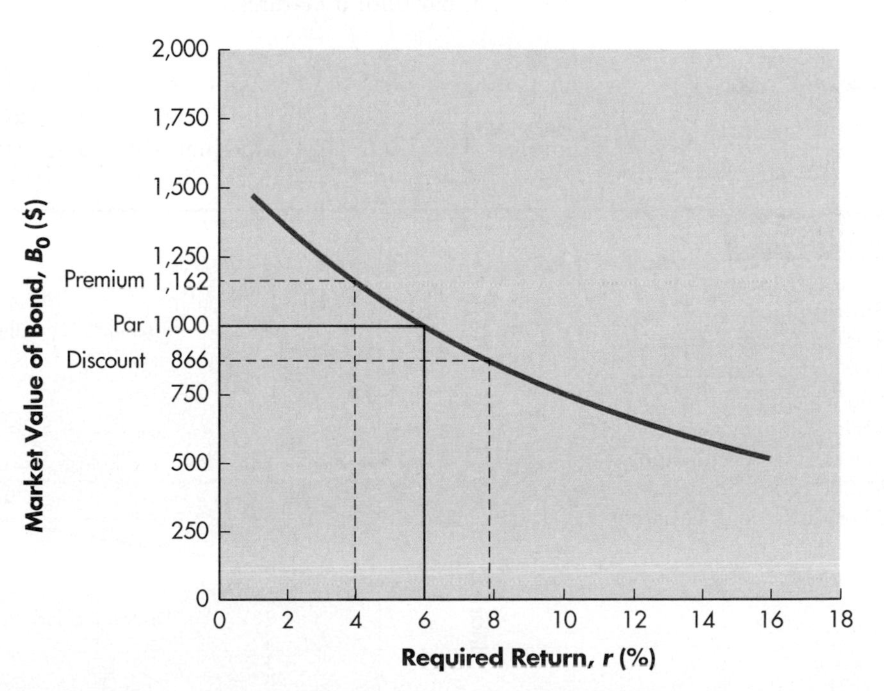

	A	B	C
1	VALUATION FOR ANNUAL BOND		
2	Par value	$1,000	$1,000
3	Coupon interest rate	6%	6%
4	Annual interest payment	$60	$60
5	Required rate of return	8%	4%
6	Number of years to maturity	10	10
7	Bond value	–$865.80	–$1,162.22

Entry in Cell B7 is =PV(B5,B6,B4,B2,0).
Note that the bond trades at a discount (i.e., below par) because the bond's coupon rate is below investors' required rate of return.

Entry in Cell C7 is =PV(C5,C6,C4,C2,0).
Note that the bond trades at a premium (i.e., above par) because the bond's coupon rate is above investors' required rate of return.

Time to Maturity and Bond Values

Whenever the required return is different from the coupon rate, the amount of time to maturity affects a bond's price. An additional factor is whether required returns are constant or change over the life of the bond.

Constant Required Returns When the required return is different from the coupon rate and is constant until maturity, the value of the bond will approach its par value as the passage of time brings the bond's maturity date closer. (Of course, when the required return equals the coupon rate, the bond's value will remain at par until it matures.)

EXAMPLE 6.11

Figure 6.6 depicts the behavior of the bond values calculated earlier and presented in Table 6.6 for Mills Company's 6% coupon rate bond paying annual interest and having 10 years to maturity. Each of the three required returns—8%,

FIGURE 6.6

Time to Maturity and Bond Values
Relationship among time to maturity, required returns, and bond values (Mills Company's 6% coupon rate, 10-year maturity, $1,000 par, January 1, 2018, issue date, paying annual interest)

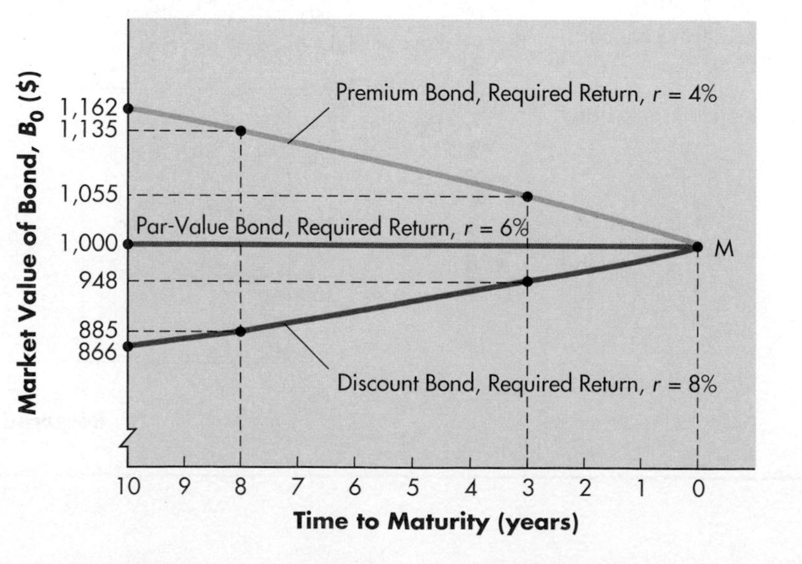

6%, and 4%—remains constant throughout the bond's 10-year life. The bond's value at both 8% and 4% approaches and ultimately equals the bond's $1,000 par value at its maturity, as the discount (at 8%) or premium (at 4%) declines with the passage of time.

interest rate risk
The chance that interest rates will change and thereby change the required return and bond value. Rising rates, which result in decreasing bond values, are of greatest concern.

Changing Required Returns The chance that a bond's required return will change and thereby alter the bond's price is called **interest rate risk**. Bondholders are typically more concerned with rising interest rates because an increase in a bond's required return causes a decrease in its price. The shorter the time until a bond's maturity, the less responsive is its market value to a given change in the required return. In other words, *short maturities have less interest rate risk than long maturities when all other features (coupon interest rate, par value, and interest payment frequency) are the same.* This statement proves true because of the mathematics of time value; the present values of cash flows arriving in the near future change far less than the present values of cash flows that come in the more distant future, in response to a change in the discount rate.

EXAMPLE 6.12

MyLab Finance Solution Video

The effect of changing required returns on bonds with differing maturities can be illustrated by using Mills Company's bond and Figure 6.6. If the required return rises from 6% to 8% when the bond has 8 years to maturity (see the vertical dashed line at 8 years), the bond's value decreases from $1,000 to $885.07, which is an 11.5% decrease. If the same change in required return had occurred with only 3 years to maturity (see the vertical dashed line at 3 years), the bond's value would have dropped to just $948.46, only a 5.1% decrease. Similar types of responses can be seen for the change in bond value associated with decreases in required returns. The shorter the time to maturity, the less the impact on bond value caused by a given change in the required return.

YIELD TO MATURITY (YTM)

Earlier in this chapter we discussed several different measures of a bond's return. The best of these is the bond's yield to maturity (YTM), which is the compound annual rate of return earned on a bond purchased on a given day and held to maturity. Mathematically, a bond's YTM is the discount rate that equates the bond's market price to the present value of the cash flows paid by the bond to investors. Remember that in Equations 6.5 and 6.5a we referred to the discount rate as the bond's required return, so a bond's YTM is really a measure of its required return. The YTM calculation assumes that the bond makes all scheduled interest and principal payments as promised.[4] The yield to maturity on a bond with a current price equal to its par value (i.e., $B_0 = M$) will always equal the coupon rate. When the bond value differs from par, the YTM will differ from the coupon rate.

To calculate a bond's YTM, you must know its current market price, the number of years to maturity, its par value, and its coupon rate. In principle, you

4. Many bonds have a *call feature,* which means they may not reach maturity if the issuer, after a specified time, calls them back. Because the call feature typically cannot be exercised until a specific future date, investors often calculate the *yield to call (YTC)*. The yield to call represents the rate of return that investors earn if they buy a callable bond at a specific price and hold it until it is called back and they receive the *call price,* which would be set at or above the bond's par value. Here our focus is solely on the more general measure of yield to maturity.

could find the YTM for a bond making annual coupon payments by solving Equation 6.5 or 6.5a for r. Solving for r algebraically is extremely difficult, so usually we find the YTM by using a calculator or spreadsheet, or by trial and error. The calculator and spreadsheet provide accurate YTM values with minimal effort.

IRF PERSONAL FINANCE EXAMPLE 6.13 Earl Washington wishes to find the YTM on Mills Company's bond. The bond currently sells for $929.76, has a 6% coupon rate and $1,000 par value, pays interest annually, and has 10 years to maturity.

MyLab Finance Financial Calculator

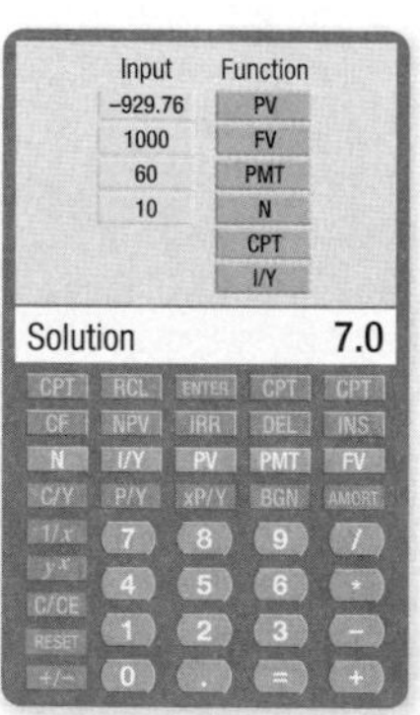

Calculator use Most calculators require either the present value (B_0 in this case) or the future values (I and M in this case) to be input as negative numbers to calculate yield to maturity. We take that approach here. Using the inputs shown at the left, you should find the YTM to be 7.0%.

Spreadsheet use The yield to maturity of Mills Company's bond also can be calculated as shown in the Excel spreadsheet below. First, enter all the bond's cash flows. Note that you begin with the bond's price as an outflow (a negative number). In other words, an investor has to pay the price up front to receive the cash flows over the next 10 years. Next, use Excel's *internal rate of return* function. This function calculates the discount rate that makes the present value of a series of cash flows equal to zero. In this case, when the present value of all cash flows is zero, the present value of the inflows (coupon payments and principal) equals the present value of the outflows (the bond's initial price). In other words, the internal rate of return function is giving us the bond's YTM, the discount rate that equates the bond's price to the present value of its cash flows.

Since the typical bond's interest payments form an annuity stream, you can further reduce the work necessary to solve for a bond's yield to maturity using Excel. The second screenshot on the next page shows how to use the RATE function in Excel to determine a bond's yield to maturity.

	A	B
1	YIELD TO MATURITY	
2	Year	Cash Flow
3	0	–$929.76
4	1	$60
5	2	$60
6	3	$60
7	4	$60
8	5	$60
9	6	$60
10	7	$60
11	8	$60
12	9	$60
13	10	$1,060
14	YTM	7.0%

Entry in Cell B14 is =IRR(B3:B13)

	A	B
1	YIELD TO MATURITY	
2	Par value	$1,000
3	Coupon interest rate	6%
4	Interest payments per year	1
5	Interest payment	$60
6	Number of years to maturity	10
7	Bond current value	–$929.76
8	Bond yield to maturity	7.0%
	Entry in Cell B14 is =RATE(B6*B4,B5,B7,B2,0).	

→ REVIEW QUESTIONS MyLab Finance Solutions

6–16 What procedure is used to value a bond that pays annual interest? Semiannual interest?

6–17 What relationship between the required return and the coupon rate will cause a bond to sell at a discount? At a premium? At its par value?

6–18 If the required return on a bond differs from its coupon rate, describe the behavior of the bond price over time as the bond moves toward maturity.

6–19 As a risk-averse investor, would you prefer bonds with short or long periods until maturity? Why?

6–20 What is a bond's yield to maturity (YTM)? Briefly describe the use of a financial calculator and the use of an Excel spreadsheet for finding YTM. Why is the YTM a good measure of the required return on a bond?

→ EXCEL REVIEW QUESTIONS MyLab Finance Solutions

6–21 Spreadsheet models can be used to determine the value of a bond based on its provisions and the required rate of return. Using the information provided at MyLab Finance find the value of an annual coupon bond using a spreadsheet model.

6–22 Some bonds make interest payments more than once per year. Using the information provided at MyLab Finance develop a spreadsheet capable of comparing bond values for differing payment frequencies.

6–23 As a financial manager it is often helpful to know the yield to maturity of outstanding bonds. Using the information provided at MyLab Finance use a spreadsheet to compute the yield to maturity for a bond.

SUMMARY

FOCUS ON VALUE

Interest rates and required returns embody the real cost of money, inflationary expectations, and issuer and issue risk. They reflect the return required by market participants as compensation for the risk perceived in a specific investment. The interest rate or required return on a bond varies with the bond's maturity, and typically rates are higher on longer term bonds. The yield curve plots the relation between the required return and the maturity of bonds with similar risk profiles.

The value of an asset equals the present value of its expected cash flows, using the required return as the discount rate. Bonds are the easiest financial assets to value; both the amounts and the timing of their cash flows are contractual and therefore known with near certainty (at least for high-grade bonds). The financial manager needs to understand how to apply valuation techniques to bonds, stocks, and tangible assets (as we will demonstrate in the following chapters) to make decisions that are consistent with the firm's **share price maximization goal.**

REVIEW OF LEARNING GOALS

LG1 **Describe interest rate fundamentals, the term structure of interest rates, and risk premiums.** Equilibrium in the flow of funds between savers and borrowers produces the interest rate or required return. Most interest rates are expressed in nominal terms. The nominal interest rate represents the rate at which money grows over time, whereas the real interest rate represents the rate at which purchasing power grows over time. The difference between the nominal rate and the real rate is (approximately) the inflation rate (or the expected inflation rate). For risky assets, the nominal interest rate is the sum of the risk-free rate and a risk premium reflecting issuer and issue characteristics. The risk-free rate is the real rate of interest plus an inflation premium.

For any class of similar-risk bonds, the term structure of interest rates reflects the relation between the interest rate or required return and the time to maturity. Yield curves plot this relation on a graph and can be downward sloping (inverted), upward sloping (normal), or flat. The expectations theory, liquidity preference theory, and market segmentation theory are cited to explain the shape of the yield curve. Risk premiums for non-Treasury debt issues result from business risk, financial risk, interest rate risk, liquidity risk, tax risk, default risk, maturity risk, and contractual provision risk.

LG2 **Review the legal aspects of bond financing and bond cost.** Corporate bonds are long-term debt instruments indicating that a corporation has borrowed an amount that it promises to repay in the future under clearly defined terms. Most bonds are issued with maturities of 10 to 30 years and a par value of $1,000. The bond indenture, enforced by a trustee, states all conditions of the bond issue. It contains both standard debt provisions and restrictive covenants, which may include a sinking-fund requirement and/or a security interest. The cost of a bond to an issuer depends on its maturity, offering size, and issuer risk and on the basic cost of money.

LG3 **Discuss the general features, yields, prices, ratings, popular types, and international issues of corporate bonds.** A bond issue may include a conversion feature, a call feature, or stock purchase warrants. The return on a bond can be measured by its current yield, yield to maturity (YTM), or yield to call (YTC). Bond prices are typically reported along with their coupon, maturity date, and yield to maturity (YTM). Bond ratings by independent agencies indicate the risk of a bond issue. Various types of traditional and contemporary bonds are available.

Eurobonds and foreign bonds enable established creditworthy companies and governments to borrow large amounts internationally.

LG 4 **Understand the key inputs and basic model used in the bond valuation process.** Key inputs to the valuation process include cash flows, timing, risk, and the required return. The value of any asset is equal to the present value of all future cash flows it is expected to provide over the relevant time period.

LG 5 **Apply the basic valuation model to bonds, and describe the impact of required return and time to maturity on bond values.** The value of a bond is the present value of its coupon payments plus the present value of its par value. The discount rate used to determine bond value is the required return, which may differ from the bond's coupon rate. A bond can sell at a discount, at par, or at a premium, depending on whether the required return is greater than, equal to, or less than its coupon rate. The amount of time to maturity affects bond prices. The price of a bond will approach its par value as the bond moves closer to maturity. The chance that interest rates will change and thereby alter the required return and bond value is called interest rate risk. The shorter the amount of time until a bond's maturity, the less responsive is its market value to a given change in the required return.

LG 6 **Explain yield to maturity (YTM), its calculation, and the procedure used to value bonds that pay interest semiannually.** Yield to maturity is the rate of return investors earn if they buy a bond at a specific price and hold it until maturity. YTM can be calculated by using a financial calculator or by using an Excel spreadsheet. Bonds that pay interest semiannually are valued by using the same procedure used to value bonds paying annual interest except that the interest payments are one-half of the annual interest payments, the number of periods is twice the number of years to maturity, and the required return is one-half of the stated annual required return on similar-risk bonds.

OPENER-IN-REVIEW

In the chapter opener, you learned about new bonds issued by Aston Martin in 2017. Assume that those bonds paid interest semiannually.

a. How much cash would a bondholder receive every 6 months given that the bonds have a coupon rate of 5.75%?

b. Suppose that when they were first issued, Aston Martin bonds were set to mature in 20 years and that the required return in the market on those bonds was 6% per year. What was the market price of an Aston Martin bond? Did the bond sell at par, at a premium, or at a discount? Why?

c. Given your answer to part **b**, what was the current yield of Aston Martin bonds when they were first issued? Suppose the bonds are now worth $1,075 each. What is the current yield on the bonds now?

d. The chapter opener also discussed bonds that Aston Martin originally issued in 2011 with a 10.25% coupon rate. Assume for simplicity that these bonds paid interest annually, were originally issued at par value ($1,000), and were set to mature 8 years after they were issued. A year after they were issued, the bonds were trading at a price that was 39% below par value due to Aston Martin's deteriorating financial condition. What was the YTM on Aston Martin's bonds at that time?

SELF-TEST PROBLEMS (Solutions in Appendix)

IRF

ST6–1 **Bond valuation** Lahey Industries has outstanding a $1,000 par-value bond with an 8% coupon rate. The bond has 12 years remaining to its maturity date.

a. If interest is paid annually, find the value of the bond when the required return is (1) 7%, (2) 8%, and (3) 10%.

b. Indicate for each case in part **a** whether the bond is selling at a discount, at a premium, or at its par value.

c. Using the 10% required return, find the bond's value when interest is paid semiannually.

IRF

ST6–2 **Bond yields** Elliot Enterprises' bonds currently sell for $1,026.57, have a 6.5% coupon rate and a $1,000 par value, pay interest annually, and have 18 years to maturity.

a. Calculate the bonds' current yield.

b. Calculate the bonds' yield to maturity (YTM).

c. Compare the YTM calculated in part **b** to the bonds' coupon rate and current yield (calculated in part **a**). Use a comparison of the bonds' current price and par value to explain these differences.

WARM-UP EXERCISES All problems are available in MyLab Finance.

E6–1 The nominal, risk-free rate on T-bills is 1.23%. If the real rate of interest is 0.80%, what is the expected inflation rate?

E6–2 The yields for Treasuries with differing maturities on a recent day were as shown in the table below.

Maturity	Yield
3 months	1.41%
6 months	1.71
2 years	2.68
3 years	3.01
5 years	3.70
10 years	4.51
30 years	5.25

a. Use the information to plot a yield curve for this date.
b. If the expectations hypothesis is true, approximately what rate of return do investors expect a 5-year Treasury note to pay 5 years from now?
c. If the expectations hypothesis is true, approximately what rate of return do investors expect a 1-year Treasury security to pay starting 2 years from now?
d. Is it possible that even though the yield curve slopes up in this problem, investors do not expect rising interest rates? Explain.

LG1

E6–3 The YTMs for Treasuries with differing maturities (with each rate expressed as an annual rate) on a recent day were as shown in the following table.

Maturity	YTM
3 months	1.41%
6 months	1.71
2 years	2.68
3 years	3.01
5 years	3.70
10 years	4.51
30 years	5.25

The real rate of interest is 0.8% per year. Use the information in the preceding table to calculate the approximate inflation expectation for each maturity.

LG1

E6–4 Assume that the rate of inflation expected over the coming year is 3.3%. Explain how a 1-year T-bill could earn a negative real rate of return over the next year. How could it have a zero real rate of return? What minimum rate of return must the T-bill earn to meet your requirement of a 2% real rate of return?

LG1

E6–5 Calculate the risk premium for each of the following rating classes of long-term securities, assuming that the yield to maturity (YTM) for comparable Treasuries is 4.51%.

Rating class	Nominal interest rate
AAA	5.12%
BBB	5.78
B	7.82

LG4

E6–6 You have two assets and must calculate their values today based on their payment streams and required returns. Asset 1 has a required return of 9% and will produce a stream of $300 starting in 1 year and continuing indefinitely. Asset 2 has a required return of 7% and will produce a cash flow of $1,400 in 1 year, $1,300 in 2 years, and $850 in 3 years.

LG5

E6–7 A bond with 5 years to maturity and a coupon rate of 6% has a par, or face, value of $20,000. Interest is paid annually. If the required return on this bond is 8%, what is the price of the bond?

E6–8 Assume a 5-year Treasury bond has a coupon rate of 4.5%.

a. Give examples of required rates of return that would make the bond sell at a discount, at a premium, and at par.

b. If this bond's par value is $10,000, calculate the differing values for this bond given the required rates you chose in part **a.**

PROBLEMS

All problems are available in MyLab Finance. The MyLab icon indicates problems in Excel format available in MyLab Finance.

P6–1 **Interest rate fundamentals: The real rate of return** Carl Foster, a trainee at an investment banking firm, is trying to get an idea of what real rate of return investors are expecting in today's marketplace. He has looked up the rate paid on 3-month U.S. Treasury bills and found it to be 1.5%. He has decided to use the recent rate of change in the Consumer Price Index as a proxy for the inflationary expectations of investors. That annualized rate now stands at 0.5%. On the basis of the information that Carl has collected, what estimate can he make of the real rate of return?

P6–2 **Equilibrium rate of interest** To estimate the equilibrium rate of interest, the economics division of Mountain Banks—a major bank holding company—has gathered the data summarized in the following table. Because the likelihood is high that new tax legislation will be passed in the near future, the table also includes current data as well as data reflecting the probable impact of passage of the legislation on the demand for funds. (*Note:* The proposed legislation will not affect the supply schedule of funds. Assume a perfect world in which inflation is expected to be zero, funds suppliers and demanders have no liquidity preference, and all outcomes are certain.)

	Currently		With passage of tax legislation
Amount of funds supplied/demanded ($ billion)	Interest rate required by funds suppliers	Interest rate required by funds demanders	Interest rate required by funds demanders
$ 1	2%	7%	9%
5	3	6	8
10	4	4	7
20	6	3	6
50	7	2	4
100	9	1	3

a. Draw the supply curve and the demand curve for funds using the current data. (*Note:* Unlike the functions in Figure 6.1, the functions here will not appear as straight lines.)

b. Using your graph, label and note the equilibrium rate of interest using the current data.

c. Add to the graph, drawn in part **a**, the new demand curve expected in the event that the proposed tax legislation is passed.
d. What is the new equilibrium rate of interest? Compare and analyze this finding in light of your analysis in part **b**.

Personal Finance Problem

LG1

P6–3 **Real and nominal rates of interest** Zane Perelli currently has $100 that he can spend today on socks costing $2.50 each. Alternatively, he could invest the $100 in a risk-free U.S. Treasury security that is expected to earn a 9% nominal rate of interest. The consensus forecast of leading economists is a 5% rate of inflation over the coming year.
a. How many socks can Zane purchase today?
b. How much money will Zane have at the end of 1 year if he forgoes purchasing the socks today and invests his money instead?
c. How much would you expect the socks to cost at the end of 1 year in light of the expected inflation?
d. Use your findings in parts **b** and **c** to determine how many socks (fractions are OK) Zane can purchase at the end of 1 year. In percentage terms, how many more or fewer socks can Zane buy at the end of 1 year?
e. What is Zane's real rate of return over the year? How is it related to the percentage change in Zane's buying power found in part **d**? Explain.

P6–4 **Yield curve** A firm wishing to evaluate interest rate behavior has gathered yield data on five U.S. Treasury securities, each having a different maturity and all measured at the same point in time. The summarized data follow.

U.S. Treasury security	Time to maturity	Yield
A	1 year	12.6%
B	10 years	11.2
C	6 months	13.0
D	20 years	11.0
E	5 years	11.4

a. Draw the yield curve associated with these data.
b. Describe the resulting yield curve in part **a**, and explain what it says about the direction of future interest rates under the expectations theory.

P6–5 **Nominal interest rates and yield curves** Economic forecasters predict that the rate of inflation will hold steady at 2% per year indefinitely. The table below shows the nominal interest rate paid on Treasury securities having different maturities.

Maturity	Nominal rate of return
3 months	5%
2 years	6
5 years	8
10 years	8.5
20 years	9

a. Approximately what real interest rate do Treasury securities offer investors at each maturity?

b. If the nominal rate of interest paid by every Treasury security above suddenly dropped by 1.5% without any change in inflationary expectations, what effect, if any, would it have on your answers in part **a**? Explain.

c. Using your findings in part **a**, draw a yield curve for U.S. Treasury securities. Describe the general shape of the curve and explain what it says about the future direction of interest rates under the expectations theory.

d. What would a follower of the liquidity preference theory say about how the preferences of lenders and borrowers tend to affect the shape of the yield curve drawn in part **c**?

e. What would a follower of the market segmentation theory say about the supply and demand for long-term loans versus the supply and demand for short-term loans given the yield curve constructed for part **c** of this problem?

P6–6 **Nominal and real rates** Tyra loves to shop at her favorite store, Dollar Barrel, where she can find hundreds of items priced at exactly $1. Tyra has $200 to spend and is thinking of going on a shopping spree at Dollar Barrel, but she is also thinking of investing her money.

a. Suppose the expected rate of inflation is 1% (so next year, everything at Dollar Barrel will cost $1.01) and Tyra can earn 5% on money that she invests. Approximately what real rate of interest could Tyra earn if she invests her money? How many items can she buy at Dollar Barrel today, and how many can she buy a year from now if she invests her money and goes shopping later? What is the percentage increase in Tyra's purchasing power if she waits a year to go shopping? Compare your answer to the approximate real interest rate on Tyra's investment.

b. Now suppose that the expected inflation rate is 10% and Tyra can earn 20% on money that she invests over the year. What is the approximate real rate of interest that Tyra will earn? Calculate the number of items that Tyra could buy next year from Dollar Barrel if she invests her money. What is the percentage increase in her purchasing power if she waits a year to go shopping? Relate your answer back to Tyra's real rate of return.

P6–7 **Term structure of interest rates** The following yield data for a number of highest-quality corporate bonds existed at each of the three points in time noted.

	Yield		
Time to maturity (years)	5 years ago	2 years ago	Today
1	9.1%	14.6%	9.3%
3	9.2	12.8	9.8
5	9.3	12.2	10.9
10	9.5	10.9	12.6
15	9.4	10.7	12.7
20	9.3	10.5	12.9
30	9.4	10.5	13.5

a. On the same set of axes, draw the yield curve at each of the three given times.
b. Label each curve in part **a** with its general shape (downward sloping, upward sloping, flat).
c. Describe the general interest rate expectation existing at each of the three times, assuming the expectations theory holds.
d. Examine the data from 5 years ago. According to the expectations theory, what approximate return did investors expect a 5-year bond to pay as of today?

LG1

P6–8 **Term structure** A 1-year Treasury bill currently offers a 5% rate of return. A 2-year Treasury note offers a 5.5% rate of return. Under the expectations theory, what rate of return do investors expect a 1-year Treasury bill to pay next year?

LG1

P6–9 **Risk premiums** In January 2016, Anheuser-Busch issued an outstanding bond that pays a 3.3% coupon rate, matures in January 2023, and has a yield to maturity of 2.82%. In January 2017, Santander Holdings issued an outstanding bond that pays a 3.571% coupon rate, matures in January 2023, and has a yield to maturity of 3.341%.

a. Does the Anheuser-Busch bond sell at a premium, at par, or at a discount? How do you know? What about the Santander bond?
b. Which bond would you guess has a higher rating? Why?
c. Can you draw any conclusion about the shape of the yield curve, either now or when these bonds were first issued, from the information given in the problem? Why or why not?

LG2

P6–10 **Bond interest payments before and after taxes** Charter Corp. has issued 2,500 debentures with a total principal value of $2,500,000. The bonds have a coupon rate of 7%.

a. What dollar amount of interest per bond can an investor expect to receive each year from Charter?
b. What is Charter's total interest expense per year associated with this bond issue?
c. Assuming that Charter is in a 35% corporate tax bracket, what is the company's net after-tax interest cost associated with this bond issue?

LG4

P6–11 **Bond prices and yields** Assume that the Financial Management Corporation's $1,000-par-value bond had a 5.700% coupon, matures on May 15, 2027, has a current price quote of 97.708, and has a yield to maturity (YTM) of 6.034%. Given this information, answer the following questions:

a. What was the dollar price of the bond?
b. What is the bond's current yield?
c. Is the bond selling at par, at a discount, or at a premium? Why?
d. Compare the bond's current yield calculated in part **b** to its YTM and explain why they differ.

Personal Finance Problem

P6–12 **Valuation fundamentals** Imagine that you are trying to evaluate the economics of purchasing a condominium to live in during college rather than renting an apartment. If you buy the condo, during each of the next 4 years you will have to pay property taxes and maintenance expenditures of about $6,000 per year, but you will avoid paying rent of $10,000 per year. When you graduate 4 years from now, you expect to sell the condo for $125,000. If you buy the condo, you will use money you have saved that is currently invested and earning a 4% annual rate of return. Assume for simplicity that all cash flows (rent, maintenance, etc.) would occur at the end of each year.

a. Draw a timeline showing the cash flows, their timing, and the required return applicable to valuing the condo.

b. What is the maximum price you would be willing to pay to acquire the condo? Explain.

P6–13 **Valuation of assets** Using the information provided in the following table, find the value of each asset today.

Asset	Cash flow Year	Cash flow Amount	Appropriate required return
A	1	$ 3,000	8%
	2	3,000	
	3	3,000	
B	1 through ∞	$ 500	5%
C	1	$ 0	6%
	2	0	
	3	0	
	4	0	
	5	45,000	
D	1 through 5	$ 1,500	4%
	6	8,500	
E	1	$ 2,000	7%
	2	3,000	
	3	5,000	
	4	7,000	
	5	4,000	
	6	1,000	

Personal Finance Problem

P6–14 **Asset valuation and risk** Laura Drake wishes to estimate the value of an asset expected to provide cash inflows of $3,000 per year for each of the next 4 years and $15,000 in 5 years. Her research indicates that she must earn 4% on low-risk assets, 7% on average-risk assets, and 14% on high-risk assets.

a. Determine what is the most Laura should pay for the asset if it is classified as (1) low-risk, (2) average-risk, and (3) high-risk.

b. Suppose that Laura is unable to assess the risk of the asset and wants to be certain she's making a good deal. On the basis of your findings in part **a**, what is the most she should pay? Why?

c. All else being the same, what effect does increasing risk have on the value of an asset? Explain your answer in light of your findings in part **a**.

P6–15 Basic bond valuation Complex Systems has an outstanding issue of $1,000-par-value bonds with a 12% coupon rate. The issue pays interest *annually* and has 16 years remaining to its maturity date.

a. If bonds of similar risk are currently earning a 10% rate of return, how much should the Complex Systems bonds sell for today?

b. Describe the *two* possible reasons why the rate on similar-risk bonds is below the coupon rate on the Complex Systems bonds.

c. If the required return were at 12% instead of 10%, what would the current value of Complex Systems' bonds be? Contrast this finding with your findings in part **a** and discuss.

P6–16 Bond valuation: Annual interest Calculate the value of each of the bonds shown in the following table, all of which pay interest *annually*.

Bond	Par value	Coupon rate	Years to maturity	Required return
A	$1,000	11%	20	12%
B	1,000	8	16	8
C	100	9	8	7
D	500	6	13	8
E	1,000	7	10	5

LG5 **P6–17 Bond value and changing required returns** Midland Utilities has a bond issue outstanding that will mature to its $1,000 par value in 12 years. The bond has a coupon rate of 11% and pays interest annually.

a. Find the value of the bond if the required return is (1) 11%, (2) 15%, and (3) 8%.

b. Plot your findings in part **a** on a set of "required return (x-axis)–market value of bond (y-axis)" axes.

c. Use your findings in parts **a** and **b** to discuss the relationship between the coupon rate on a bond and the required return and the market value of the bond relative to its par value.

d. What two possible reasons could cause the required return to differ from the coupon rate?

LG5 **P6–18 Bond value and time: Constant required returns** Pecos Manufacturing has just issued a 15-year, 12% coupon rate, $1,000-par bond that pays interest annually. The required return is currently 14%, and the company is certain it will remain at 14% until the bond matures in 15 years.

a. Assuming that the required return does remain at 14% until maturity, find the value of the bond with (1) 15 years, (2) 12 years, (3) 9 years, (4) 6 years, (5) 3 years, and (6) 1 year to maturity.

b. Plot your findings on a set of "time to maturity (x-axis)–market value of bond (y-axis)" axes constructed similarly to Figure 6.6.

c. All else remaining the same, when the required return differs from the coupon rate and is assumed to be constant to maturity, what happens to the bond value as time moves toward maturity? Explain your answer in light of the graph in part **b**.

Personal Finance Problem

P6–19 Bond value and time: Changing required returns Lynn Parsons is considering investing in either of two outstanding bonds. The bonds both have $1,000 par values and 11% coupon rates and pay annual interest. Bond A has exactly 5 years to maturity, and bond B has 15 years to maturity.

a. Calculate the value of bond A if the required return is (1) 8%, (2) 11%, and (3) 14%.

b. Calculate the value of bond B if the required return is (1) 8%, (2) 11%, and (3) 14%.

c. From your findings in parts **a** and **b**, complete the following table, and discuss the relationship between time to maturity and changing required returns.

Required return	Value of bond A	Value of bond B
8%	?	?
11	?	?
14	?	?

d. If Lynn wants to minimize interest rate risk, which bond should she purchase? Why?

P6–20 Yield to maturity The relationship between a bond's yield to maturity and coupon rate can be used to predict its pricing level. For each of the bonds listed, state whether the price of the bond will be at a premium to par, at par, or at a discount to par.

Bond	Coupon rate	Yield to maturity	Price
A	6%	10%	______
B	8	8	______
C	9	7	______
D	7	9	______
E	12	10	______

P6–21 Yield to maturity The Salem Company bond currently sells for $867.59, has a 6% coupon rate and a $1,000 par value, pays interest annually, and has 15 years to maturity.

a. Calculate the yield to maturity (YTM) on this bond.

b. Explain the relationship that exists between the coupon rate and yield to maturity and the par value and market value of a bond.

P6–22 Yield to maturity Each of the bonds shown in the following table pays interest *annually*.

Bond	Par value	Coupon rate	Years to maturity	Current value
A	$1,000	9%	8	$ 820
B	1,000	12	16	1,000
C	500	12	12	560
D	1,000	15	10	1,120
E	1,000	5	3	900

a. Calculate the yield to maturity (YTM) for each bond.
b. What relationship exists between the coupon rate and yield to maturity and the par value and market value of a bond? Explain.

Personal Finance Problem

P6–23 **Bond valuation and yield to maturity** Mark Goldsmith's broker has shown him two bonds issued by different companies. Each has a maturity of 5 years, a par value of $1,000, and a yield to maturity of 7.5%. The first bond is issued by Crabbe Waste Disposal Corporation and has a coupon rate of 6.324% paid annually. The second bond, issued by Malfoy Enterprises, has a coupon rate of 8.8% paid annually.
a. Calculate the selling price for each bond.
b. Mark has $20,000 to invest. If he wants to invest only in bonds issued by Crabbe Waste Disposal, how many of those bonds could he buy? What if he wants to invest only in bonds issued by Malfoy Enterprises? Round your answers to the nearest integer.
c. What is the total interest income that Mark could earn each year if he invested only in Crabbe bonds? How much interest would he earn each year if he invested only in Malfoy bonds?
d. Assume that Mark will reinvest all the interest he receives as it is paid, and his rate of return on reinvested interest will be 10%. Calculate the total dollars that Mark will accumulate over 5 years if he invests in Crabbe bonds or Malfoy bonds. Your total dollar calculation will include the interest Mark gets, the principal he receives when the bonds mature, and all the additional interest he earns from reinvesting the coupon payments that he receives.
e. The bonds issued by Crabbe and Malfoy might appear to be equally good investments because they offer the same yield to maturity of 7.5%. Notice, however, that your answers to part **d** are not the same for each bond, suggesting that one bond is a better investment than the other. Why is that the case?

P6–24 **Bond valuation: Semiannual interest** Find the value of a bond maturing in 6 years, with a $1,000 par value and a coupon rate of 10% (5% paid semiannually) if the required return on similar-risk bonds is 14% per year (7% paid semiannually).

P6–25 **Bond valuation: Semiannual interest** Calculate the value of each of the bonds shown in the following table, all of which pay interest semiannually.

Bond	Par value	Coupon rate	Years to maturity	Required stated annual return
A	$1,000	10%	12	8%
B	1,000	12	20	12
C	500	12	5	14
D	1,000	14	10	10
E	100	6	4	14

P6–26 **Bond valuation: Quarterly interest** Calculate the value of a $5,000-par-value bond paying quarterly interest at an annual coupon rate of 10% and having 10 years until maturity if the required return on similar-risk bonds is currently a 12% annual rate paid quarterly.

P6–27 **ETHICS PROBLEM** Bond-rating agencies have invested significant sums of money in an effort to determine which quantitative and nonquantitative factors best predict bond defaults. Furthermore, some of the raters invest time and money to meet privately with corporate personnel to get information used in assigning the issue's bond rating. To recoup those costs, some bond-rating agencies have tied their ratings to the purchase of additional services. Do you believe this is an acceptable practice? Defend your position.

SPREADSHEET EXERCISE

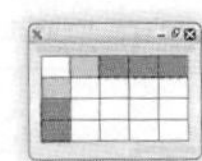

CSM Corporation has a bond issue outstanding that has 15 years remaining to maturity and carries a coupon rate of 6%. Interest on the bond is paid on a semiannual basis. The par value of the CSM bond is $1,000, and it is currently selling for $874.42.

TO DO

a. Create a spreadsheet similar to the Excel spreadsheet examples in the chapter to solve for the yield to maturity.
b. Create a spreadsheet similar to the Excel spreadsheet examples in the chapter to solve for the price of the bond if the yield to maturity is 2% higher.
c. Create a spreadsheet similar to the Excel spreadsheet examples in the chapter to solve for the price of the bond if the yield to maturity is 2% lower.
d. What can you summarize about the relationship between the price of the bond, the par value, the yield to maturity, and the coupon rate?

MyLab Finance Visit www.pearson.com/mylab/finance for **Chapter Case: *Evaluating Annie Hegg's Proposed Investment in Atilier Industries Bonds,*** Group Exercises, and other numerous resources.

CHAPTER 7

Stock Valuation

LEARNING GOALS

LG1 Differentiate between debt and equity.

LG2 Discuss the features of both common and preferred stock.

LG3 Apply the basic valuation model to stocks, and describe the relevant cash flows and the impact of required return.

LG4 Understand the concept of market efficiency and how to value stocks using zero-growth, constant-growth, and variable-growth dividend models.

LG5 Discuss the free cash flow valuation model and the book value, liquidation value, and price/earnings (P/E) multiple approaches.

LG6 Explain the relationships among financial decisions, return, risk, and the firm's value.

MyLab Finance Chapter Introduction Video

WHY THIS CHAPTER MATTERS TO YOU

In your *professional* life

ACCOUNTING You need to understand the difference between debt and equity in terms of tax treatment; the ownership claims of capital providers, including venture capitalists and stockholders; and the differences between book value per share and other market-based valuations.

INFORMATION SYSTEMS You need to understand the procedures used to issue common stock, the information needed to value stock, how to collect and process the necessary information from each functional area, and how to disseminate information to investors.

MANAGEMENT You need to understand the difference between debt and equity capital, the rights and claims of stockholders, the process of issuing common stock, and the effects each functional area has on the value of the firm's stock.

MARKETING You need to understand that the firm's ideas for products and services will greatly affect investors' beliefs regarding the likely success of the firm's projects and that projects viewed as more likely to succeed are also viewed as more valuable and therefore lead to a higher stock value.

OPERATIONS You need to understand that the evaluations of venture capitalists and other would-be investors will in part depend on the efficiency of the firm's operations and that more cost-efficient operations lead to better growth prospects and therefore higher stock valuations.

In your *personal* life

At some point, you are likely to hold stocks as an asset in your retirement program. You may want to estimate a stock's value. If the stock is selling below its estimated value, you may buy the stock; if its market price is above its value, you may sell it. Some individuals rely on financial advisors for such buy or sell recommendations. Regardless of how you approach investment decisions, it will be helpful to understand how stocks are valued.

Brian Kersey/UP/Newscom

TESLA INC.

Stock Prices Are All About the Future

One of the most "hotly" debated topics of our day has been global warming and the benefits and costs of lower emissions. Many companies are investing in radical new technologies with the hope of capitalizing on the going-green movement. On June 29, 2010, Tesla Motors raised $226 million in its initial public offering (IPO) of common stock. Tesla, whose shares trade on the Nasdaq stock exchange, was the first automaker to use lithium ion batteries to produce an all-electric vehicle with a range of more than 200 miles. Even though Tesla racked up losses of $279 million in the years preceding its IPO and had never been profitable, investors were enthusiastic about the company, and Tesla's stock price rose from $17 to $24 on its first day of trading.

Excitement about Tesla's prospects was fueled in part by its mission to reduce carbon emissions and in part by its charismatic cofounder, Elon Musk, who had previously started several successful companies, including PayPal. It also helped that the federal government offered a tax subsidy of $7,500 to anyone who purchased an electric vehicle, and some states offered additional tax incentives. In its first 7 years as a public company, Tesla posted a quarterly profit just 8 times against 20 quarters charged with losses. Even so, the stock surged from its $17 IPO price to an all-time high of $385 in September 2017. The same year, the company changed its name from Tesla Motors to Tesla Inc. to highlight its product offerings outside the automotive business. Tesla's stock met some resistance in November 2017 when it reported larger-than-expected losses and production delays on its mass-market electric sedan, the Model 3. Still, at a price exceeding $300 per share, Tesla's stock was grounded by investors' beliefs that in the long run the company would generate positive cash flows, perhaps even without government subsidies.

7.1 Differences Between Debt and Equity

debt
Includes all borrowing incurred by a firm, including bonds, and is repaid according to a fixed schedule of payments.

equity
Funds provided by the firm's owners (investors or stockholders) that are repaid subject to the firm's performance.

Although debt and equity capital are both sources of external financing used by firms, they are very different in several important respects. Most importantly, debt financing is obtained from creditors, and equity financing is obtained from stockholders whose investment makes them part owners of the firm. Creditors (lenders or debtholders) have a legal right to be repaid, whereas stockholders have only an expectation of being repaid. **Debt** includes all borrowing incurred by a firm, including bonds, and is repaid according to a fixed schedule of payments. **Equity** consists of funds provided by the firm's owners (investors or stockholders), and the stockholders earn a return that is not guaranteed but is tied to the firm's performance. A firm can obtain equity either *internally*, by retaining earnings rather than paying them out as dividends to its stockholders, or *externally*, by selling common or preferred stock. The key differences between debt and equity capital are summarized in Table 7.1 and discussed in the following pages.

VOICE IN MANAGEMENT

Unlike creditors, stockholders are owners of the firm. Stockholders generally have voting rights that permit them to select the firm's directors and vote on special issues. In contrast, debtholders do not receive voting privileges but instead rely on the firm's contractual obligations to be their voice.

CLAIMS ON INCOME AND ASSETS

Stockholders' claims on income and assets are secondary to the claims of creditors. Their claims on income cannot be paid until all the creditors' claims, including both interest and scheduled principal payments, have been satisfied. After satisfying creditor's claims, the firm's board of directors decides whether to distribute dividends to the owners.

MATTER OF FACT

How Are Assets Divided in Bankruptcy?

According to the U.S. Securities and Exchange Commission, in bankruptcy assets are divided up as follows:

1. **Secured creditors:** Secured bank loans or secured bonds are paid first.
2. **Unsecured creditors:** Unsecured bank loans or unsecured bonds, suppliers, or customers have the next claim.
3. **Equityholders:** Equityholders or the owners of the company have the last claim on assets, and they may not receive anything if the secured and unsecured creditors' claims are not fully repaid.

Stockholders' claims on assets also are secondary to the claims of creditors. If the firm fails, its assets are sold, and the proceeds are distributed in this order: secured creditors, unsecured creditors, and equityholders. Because equityholders are the last to receive any distribution of assets, their investment is relatively risky, and they expect greater returns from their investment in the firm's stock than the returns creditors require on the firm's borrowings. The greater rate of

TABLE 7.1 Key Differences Between Debt and Equity

	Type of capital	
Characteristic	Debt	Equity
Voice in management[a]	No	Yes
Claims on income and assets	Senior to equity	Subordinate to debt
Maturity	Stated	None
Tax treatment	Interest deduction	No deduction

[a]Debtholders do not have voting rights, but instead they rely on the firm's contractual obligations to them to be their voice.

return expected by stockholders means that the cost of equity financing is higher relative to the cost of debt financing for the firm.

MATURITY

Unlike debt, equity is a permanent form of financing for the firm. It does not "mature," so repayment is not required. When they purchase shares, stockholders must recognize that, although a ready market may exist for their shares, the price of the shares will fluctuate over time, and there is no way to know what the share price will be when an investor is ready to sell. This fluctuation of the market price of equity makes the overall returns to a firm's stockholders even more risky.

TAX TREATMENT

Interest payments to debtholders are treated as tax-deductible expenses by the issuing firm, whereas dividend payments to a firm's stockholders are not tax deductible. The tax deductibility of interest lowers the corporation's cost of debt financing—yet another reason the cost of debt financing is lower than that of equity financing.

→ **REVIEW QUESTION** MyLab Finance Solution

7–1 What are the key differences between debt and equity?

LG2

7.2 Common and Preferred Stock

A firm can obtain equity capital by selling either common or preferred stock. All corporations initially issue common stock to raise equity capital. Some later issue either additional common stock or preferred stock to raise more equity capital. Although both common and preferred stock are forms of equity capital, preferred stock has some similarities to debt that significantly differentiate it from common stock. Here we first consider the features of both common and preferred stock and then describe the process of issuing common stock, including the use of venture capital.

COMMON STOCK

The true owners of a corporate business are the common stockholders. Common stockholders are sometimes referred to as *residual owners* because they receive what is left—the residual—after all other claims on the firm's income and assets have been satisfied. They are assured of only one thing: They cannot lose any more than they have invested in the firm. As a result of their generally uncertain position, common stockholders expect to earn relatively high returns. Those returns may come in the form of dividends, capital gains, or both.

Ownership

The common stock of a firm can be **privately owned** by private investors or **publicly owned** by public investors. Private companies are usually smaller than public companies and they are often **closely owned** by an individual investor or a small group of private investors (such as a family). Public companies are **widely owned** by many unrelated individual and institutional investors. The shares of privately owned firms generally do not trade actively in the stock market. If they do trade, the transactions are among private investors and often require the firm's consent. Large corporations, emphasized in the following discussions, are publicly owned, and their shares are generally actively traded in the stock markets described in Chapter 2.

privately owned (stock)
The common stock of a firm is owned by private investors; this stock is not publicly traded.

publicly owned (stock)
The common stock of a firm is owned by public investors; this stock is publicly traded.

closely owned (stock)
The common stock of a firm is owned by an individual or a small group of investors (such as a family); they are usually privately owned companies.

widely owned (stock)
The common stock of a firm is owned by many unrelated individual and institutional investors.

Par Value

The market value of common stock is completely unrelated to its par value. The **par value** of common stock is an arbitrary value established for legal purposes in the firm's corporate charter and is generally set quite low, often $1 or less. Recall that when a firm sells new shares of common stock, the firm records the par value of the shares sold in the capital section of the balance sheet as part of common stock. One benefit of this recording is that at any time the total number of shares of common stock outstanding can be found by dividing the book value of common stock by the par value.

Setting a low par value is advantageous in states where certain corporate taxes are based on the par value of stock. A low par value is also beneficial in states that have laws against selling stock at a discount to par. For example, a company whose common stock has a par value of $20 per share might be unable to issue stock if investors are unwilling to pay more than $16 per share.

par-value common stock
An arbitrary value that is established for legal purposes in the firm's corporate charter and that can be used to find the total number of shares outstanding by dividing it into the book value of common stock.

Preemptive Rights

The **preemptive right** allows common stockholders to purchase shares in any new stock sale that the firm undertakes, thus maintaining their proportionate ownership in the corporation. Without the preemptive right, new share issues could dilute the ownership of existing stockholders. A **dilution of ownership** is a reduction in each previous shareholder's fractional ownership resulting from the sale of new common shares. Preemptive rights allow preexisting shareholders to maintain their preissuance voting control and protects them against the **dilution of earnings**: a reduction in their fractional claim on earnings that could occur when the firm sells new shares of common stock.

In a *rights offering,* the firm grants **rights** to its shareholders. These financial instruments allow stockholders to purchase additional shares at a price below

preemptive right
Allows common stockholders to maintain their proportionate ownership in the corporation when new shares are issued, thus protecting them from dilution of ownership.

dilution of ownership
A reduction in each previous shareholder's fractional ownership resulting from the sale of new common shares.

dilution of earnings
A reduction in each previous shareholder's fractional claim on the firm's earnings resulting from the sale of new common shares.

rights
Financial instruments that allow stockholders to purchase additional shares at a price below the market price, in direct proportion to their fractional ownership.

the market price, in direct proportion to their fractional ownership. In these situations, rights are an important financing tool that simultaneously allow the firm to raise new equity capital while providing stockholders an incentive to maintain their ownership stake by participating in the offering.

authorized shares
Shares of common stock that a firm's corporate charter allows it to issue.

outstanding shares
Issued shares of common stock held by investors, including both private and public investors.

treasury stock
Issued shares of common stock held by the firm; often these shares have been repurchased by the firm.

issued shares
Shares of common stock that have been put into circulation; the sum of *outstanding shares* and *treasury stock*.

Authorized, Outstanding, and Issued Shares

The corporate charter of a firm indicates how many **authorized shares** it can issue. The firm cannot sell more shares than the charter authorizes without obtaining approval through a shareholder vote. To avoid later amendment of the charter, firms generally attempt to authorize more shares than they initially plan to issue.

Authorized shares become **outstanding shares** when they are issued or sold to investors. If the firm repurchases any of its outstanding shares, these are recorded as **treasury stock** and are no longer considered outstanding shares. **Issued shares** are the shares of common stock that have been put into circulation; they represent the sum of outstanding shares and treasury stock.

EXAMPLE 7.1

Golden Enterprises, a producer of medical pumps, has the following stockholders' equity account on December 31:

Stockholders' Equity	
Common stock—$0.80 par value:	
Authorized 35,000,000 shares; issued 15,000,000 shares	$ 12,000,000
Paid-in capital in excess of par	63,000,000
Retained earnings	31,000,000
	$106,000,000
Less: Cost of treasury stock (1,000,000 shares)	4,000,000
Total stockholders' equity	$102,000,000

How many shares of additional common stock can Golden sell without gaining approval from its shareholders? The firm has 35 million authorized shares, 15 million issued shares, and 1 million shares of treasury stock. Thus, 14 million shares are outstanding (15 million issued shares minus 1 million shares of treasury stock), and Golden can issue 21 million additional shares (35 million authorized shares minus 14 million outstanding shares) without seeking shareholder approval. This total includes the treasury shares currently held, which the firm can reissue to the public without obtaining shareholder approval.

Voting Rights

Generally, each share of common stock entitles its holder to one vote in the election of directors and on special issues. Votes are generally assignable and may be cast at the annual stockholders' meeting.

proxy statement
A statement transferring the votes of a stockholder to another party.

Because most stockholders do not attend the annual meeting to vote, they may sign a **proxy statement** transferring their votes to another party. The solicitation of proxies from shareholders is closely controlled by the Securities and Exchange Commission to ensure that proxies are not being solicited on the basis of false or misleading information. Management usually receives the stockholders' proxies because it can solicit them at company expense.

proxy battle
The attempt by a nonmanagement group to gain control of the management of a firm by soliciting a sufficient number of proxy votes.

Occasionally, when the firm is widely owned, outsiders may wage a **proxy battle** to unseat the existing management and gain control of the firm. Winning a corporate election requires votes from a majority of the shares voted. Historically, the odds of an outside group winning a proxy battle were generally slim, but that has changed in recent years. Investors such as Carl Icahn have had repeated success gaining seats on boards of directors and affecting corporate policies in other ways through proxy fights.

Rather than trying to gain control of the firm through a proxy fight, shareholders can simply make proposals that may be voted on at a shareholders meeting. Even in very large firms, these proposals can sometimes prove effective. In 2016, for instance, shareholders of the largest 250 U.S. public companies, as ranked by *Fortune* magazine, put forward 580 proposals, of which 47.1% received majority support.

supervoting shares
Stock that carries with it multiple votes per share rather than the single vote per share typically given on regular shares of common stock.

nonvoting common stock
Common stock that carries no voting rights; issued when the firm wishes to raise capital through the sale of common stock but does not want to give up its voting control.

In recent years, many firms, including household names like Google and Facebook, have issued two or more classes of common stock with unequal voting rights. A firm can use different classes of stock as a defense against a *hostile takeover* in which an outside group, without management support, tries to gain voting control of the firm by buying its shares in the marketplace. **Supervoting shares**, which have multiple votes per share, allow "insiders" to maintain control against an outside group whose shares have only one vote each. At other times, a class of **nonvoting common stock** is issued when the firm wishes to raise capital through the sale of common stock but does not want to give up its voting control.

When firms issue different classes of common stock on the basis of unequal voting rights, class A common typically—but not universally—has one vote per share, and class B common has supervoting rights. In most cases, the multiple share classes are equal with respect to all other aspects of ownership, although some exceptions do apply to this general rule. In particular, there is usually no difference in the distribution of earnings (dividends) and assets. Treasury stock, which is held within the corporation, generally *does not* have voting rights, *does not* earn dividends, and *does not* have a claim on assets in liquidation.

Dividends

The payment of dividends to the firm's shareholders is at the discretion of the company's board of directors. Most corporations that pay dividends distribute them quarterly. Dividends may be paid in cash, stock, or merchandise. Cash dividends are the most common, merchandise dividends the least.

Common stockholders are not promised a dividend, but they come to expect certain payments on the basis of the firm's dividend payment history. Before firms pay dividends to common stockholders, they must pay any past due dividends owed to preferred stockholders. The ability to pay dividends can be affected by restrictive debt covenants designed to ensure that the firm can repay its creditors.

Since passage of the *Jobs and Growth Tax Relief Reconciliation Act of 2003*, many firms now pay larger dividends to shareholders, who are subject to a maximum tax rate of 20% on dividends rather than the maximum tax rate of 39.6% on other forms of income. Chapter 14 explores the important aspects of firms' dividend decisions in greater depth.

MATTER OF FACT

Did Tax Cuts Stimulate Dividends?

A careful analysis of how firms responded to the dividend tax cuts contained in the 2003 Jobs and Growth Tax Relief Reconciliation Act found that firms dramatically increased dividends soon after that law was passed. One interesting comparison involved the tendency of firms that had never paid dividends to start paying them. In the quarters leading up to the tax cut, only about 4 firms per quarter began paying dividends, but in the quarters immediately following the passage of the new tax law, 29 firms per quarter announced they would start paying dividends. Similar increases occurred in firms already paying dividends, with nearly 50% of all dividend-paying firms announcing they would increase their dividend payments by 20% or more after the tax cut became law. An important confounding factor arose, however: Corporate earnings jumped at the same time, so whether dividends rose due to tax policy or due to improving corporate profits remains a matter of debate.

International Stock Issues

Although the international market for common stock is not as large as the international market for bonds, cross-border issuance and trading of common stock have increased dramatically in the past 30 years.

Some corporations issue stock in foreign markets. For example, the stock of General Electric trades in Frankfurt, London, Paris, and Tokyo; the stocks of Time Warner and Microsoft trade in Frankfurt and London; and the stock of McDonald's trades in Frankfurt, London, and Paris. The Frankfurt, London, and Tokyo markets are the most popular. Issuing stock internationally broadens the ownership base and helps a company integrate into the local business environment. Having locally traded stock can facilitate corporate acquisitions because firms can use their own shares as a method of payment.

Foreign corporations have also discovered the benefits of trading their stock in the United States. The disclosure and reporting requirements mandated by the U.S. Securities and Exchange Commission have historically discouraged all but the largest foreign firms from directly listing their shares on the New York Stock Exchange or the American Stock Exchange.

American depositary shares (ADSs)
Dollar-denominated receipts for the stocks of foreign companies that are held by a U.S. financial institution overseas.

American depositary receipts (ADRs)
Securities, backed by *American depositary shares (ADSs)*, that permit U.S. investors to hold shares of non-U.S. companies and trade them in U.S. markets.

As an alternative, most foreign companies choose to tap the U.S. market through **American depositary shares (ADSs)**. These shares are dollar-denominated receipts for the stocks of foreign companies that are held by a U.S. financial institution overseas. They serve as backing for **American depositary receipts (ADRs)**, which are securities that permit U.S. investors to hold shares of non-U.S. companies and trade them in U.S. markets. Because ADRs are issued, in dollars, to U.S. investors, they are subject to U.S. securities laws. At the same time, they give investors the opportunity to diversify their portfolios internationally.

PREFERRED STOCK

par-value preferred stock
Preferred stock with a stated face value that is used with the specified dividend percentage to determine the annual dollar dividend.

Most corporations do not issue preferred stock, but preferred shares are common in some industries such as financial services. *Preferred stock* gives its holders privileges that make them senior to common stockholders. Preferred stockholders are promised a fixed periodic dividend, stated either as a percentage or as a dollar amount. How the dividend is specified depends on whether the preferred stock has a *par value*. **Par-value preferred stock** has a stated face value, and its

no-par preferred stock
Preferred stock with no stated face value but with a stated annual dollar dividend.

annual dividend is specified as a percentage of this value. **No-par preferred stock** has no stated face value, but its annual dividend is stated in dollars. Preferred stock is most often issued by public utilities, by financial institutions such as banks and insurance companies, by acquiring firms in merger transactions, and by young firms receiving investment funds from venture capital firms. Preferred dividends are not tax deductible for the firm that pays them.

Basic Rights of Preferred Stockholders

The basic rights of preferred stockholders are somewhat stronger than those of common stockholders. Preferred stock is often considered *quasi-debt* because, much like interest on debt, it specifies a fixed periodic payment (dividend). Unlike debt, however, preferred stock has no maturity date. Because they have a fixed claim on the firm's income that takes precedence over the claim of common stockholders, preferred stockholders are exposed to less risk.

Preferred stockholders are also given preference over common stockholders in the liquidation of assets in a legally bankrupt firm, although they must "stand in line" behind creditors. The amount of the claim of preferred stockholders in liquidation normally equals the par or stated value of the preferred stock. Preferred stockholders are not normally given a voting right, although preferred stockholders are sometimes allowed to elect one member of the board of directors.

Features of Preferred Stock

A preferred stock issue generally includes a number of features. Along with the stock's par value, the amount of dividend payments, the dividend payment dates, and any restrictive covenants, such features are specified in an agreement similar to a bond indenture.

Restrictive Covenants The restrictive covenants in a preferred stock issue focus on ensuring the firm's continued existence and regular payment of the dividend. These covenants include provisions about passing (i.e., skipping) dividends, the sale of senior securities, mergers, sales of assets, minimum liquidity requirements, and repurchases of common stock. The violation of preferred stock covenants usually permits preferred stockholders either to obtain representation on the firm's board of directors or to force the retirement of their stock at or above its par or stated value.

cumulative (preferred stock)
Preferred stock for which all passed (unpaid) dividends in arrears, along with the current dividend, must be paid before dividends can be paid to common stockholders.

noncumulative (preferred stock)
Preferred stock for which passed (unpaid) dividends do not accumulate.

Cumulation Most preferred stock is **cumulative** with respect to any dividends passed. That is, all dividends in arrears, along with the current dividend, must be paid before dividends can be paid to common stockholders. If preferred stock is **noncumulative**, passed (unpaid) dividends do not accumulate. In this case, only the current dividend must be paid before dividends can be paid to common stockholders. Because common stockholders can receive dividends only after the dividend claims of preferred stockholders have been satisfied, paying preferred dividends when they are due is in the firm's best interest.

callable feature (preferred stock)
A feature of *callable preferred stock* that allows the issuer to retire the shares within a certain period of time and at a specified price.

Other Features Preferred stock can be *callable* or *convertible*. Preferred stock with a **callable feature** allows the issuer to retire outstanding shares within a certain period of time at a specified price. The call price is normally set at or above the initial issuance price, but it may decrease as time passes. Making preferred stock callable provides the issuer with a way to bring the fixed-payment commitment of the preferred issue to an end if conditions favor it.

conversion feature (preferred stock)
A feature of *convertible preferred stock* that allows holders to change each share into a stated number of shares of common stock.

Preferred stock with a **conversion feature** allows holders to change each share into a stated number of shares of common stock, usually anytime after a predetermined date. The number of shares of common stock for which the preferred stock can be exchanged may be fixed, or it may change through time according to a predetermined formula.

→ **REVIEW QUESTIONS** MyLab Finance Solutions

7–2 What risks do common stockholders take that other suppliers of capital do not?

7–3 How does a rights offering protect a firm's stockholders against the dilution of ownership?

7–4 Explain the relationships among authorized shares, outstanding shares, treasury stock, and issued shares.

7–5 What are the advantages to both U.S.-based and foreign corporations of issuing stock outside their home markets? What are American depositary receipts (ADRs)? What are American depositary shares (ADSs)?

7–6 What claims do preferred stockholders have with respect to distribution of earnings (dividends) and assets?

7–7 Explain the cumulative feature of preferred stock. What is the purpose of a call feature in a preferred stock issue?

7.3 Common Stock Valuation

Common stockholders expect rewards through periodic cash flows, such as cash dividends, or an increasing share value. Some investors decide which stocks to buy and sell based on a strategy to hold a broadly diversified portfolio of stocks. Other investors have a more speculative motive for trading only specific stocks. These investors try to spot companies whose shares are *misvalued,* meaning that the true value of the shares is different from the current market price. These investors buy shares they believe to be *undervalued* (i.e., the market price is less than the true value) and sell shares they think are *overvalued* (i.e., the market price is greater than the true value). Regardless of one's motive for trading, understanding how to value common stocks is an important part of the investment process. Stock valuation is also an important tool for financial managers. How can they work to maximize the stock price without understanding the factors that determine the value of the stock? In this section, we will describe specific stock valuation techniques. First, we will consider the relationship between market efficiency and stock valuation.

MARKET EFFICIENCY AND STOCK VALUATION

Rational buyers and sellers use their assessment of an asset's risk and return to determine its value. To a buyer, the asset's value represents the maximum purchase price, and to a seller, it represents the minimum sale price. In competitive markets with many active participants, such as a stock exchange, the interactions of many buyers and sellers result in an equilibrium price—the *market value*—for each security. This price reflects the collective actions that buyers and sellers take on the basis of all available information. Buyers and sellers digest new information quickly as it becomes available and, through their purchase and sale activities, create a new

MATTER OF FACT

The Value of Speed

The University of Michigan produces a monthly survey measuring consumer confidence, and that survey routinely causes stock prices to move when it is released. In June 2013, various news organizations reported that Thomson Reuters had a contract allowing it to distribute information about the monthly consumer confidence survey to its clients, via a conference call, 5 minutes before the survey results were posted on the university's website. The contract contained another provision that allowed Thomson Reuters to distribute survey results electronically to an elite group of clients at 9:54:58 a.m., 2 seconds prior to the conference call. The 2 seconds of lead time over the rest of the market could allow these clients to trade stocks before most market participants learned about the new information in the survey.

market equilibrium price. Because the flow of new information is continual and the content of that information is unpredictable (otherwise, it would not be *new* information), stock prices fluctuate, always moving toward a new equilibrium that reflects the most recent information available. This general concept, introduced in Chapter 2, is known as *market efficiency*.

Not all market participants are believers in the efficient-market hypothesis. Some think it is worthwhile to search for undervalued or overvalued securities and then trade them to profit from market inefficiencies. Others argue that only mere luck allows market participants to anticipate new information correctly and as a result earn *abnormal returns*, that is, actual returns greater than should be expected given the risk of the investment. They believe that market participants are unlikely to earn abnormal returns over the long run. Contrary to this belief, some well-known investors such as Warren Buffett and Bill Gross have managed to earn abnormal returns on their portfolios for extended periods. It is unclear whether their success is the result of good fortune, or their superior ability to anticipate new information, or of some form of market inefficiency.

The Behavioral Finance Challenge

Although considerable evidence supports the concept of market efficiency, a growing body of academic evidence has begun to cast doubt on the validity of this notion. The research documents various *anomalies*—outcomes that are inconsistent with efficient markets—in stock returns. A number of academics and practitioners have also recognized that emotions and other subjective factors play a role in investment decisions.

behavioral finance
A growing body of research that focuses on investor behavior and its impact on investment decisions and stock prices. Advocates are commonly referred to as "behaviorists."

This focus on investor behavior has resulted in a significant body of research, collectively referred to as **behavioral finance**. Advocates of behavioral finance are commonly referred to as "behaviorists." Daniel Kahneman was awarded the 2002 Nobel Prize in economics for his work in behavioral finance, specifically for integrating insights from psychology and economics. More recently, Richard Thaler received the 2017 Nobel Prize in Economics for his work on the tendency of the stock market to overreact to trends, the economic consequences of consumers failing to exert self control, and the role of investor sentiment in the pricing of certain types of mutual funds. Ongoing research into the psychological factors that can affect investor behavior and the resulting effects on stock prices will likely result in growing acceptance of behavioral finance. The *Focus on Practice* box further explains some findings of behavioral finance.

Although challenges to the efficient-market hypothesis, such as those presented by advocates of behavioral finance, are interesting and worthy of study, in this text we generally take the position that markets are efficient. We will use the terms *expected return* and *required return* interchangeably because they should be equal in an efficient market. In other words, we will operate under the assumption that a stock's market price at any point in time is the best estimate of its value. We're now ready to look closely at the mechanics of common stock valuation.

COMMON STOCK DIVIDEND VALUATION MODEL

Like the value of a bond, discussed in Chapter 6, the value of a share of common stock is equal to the present value of all future cash flows it is expected to provide. So Equation 6.4 can be used to find the value of a share of stock by discounting stock's expected cash flows back to their present value, using the required return commensurate with the stock's risk as the appropriate discount rate.

Although a stockholder can earn capital gains by selling stock at a price above that originally paid, what the buyer really pays for is the right to all future dividends. What about stocks that do not currently pay dividends? Such stocks have a value attributable to a future dividend stream or to the proceeds from the sale of the company.

The basic dividend valuation model for common stock is given by

$$P_0 = \frac{D_1}{(1+r)^1} + \frac{D_2}{(1+r)^2} + \ldots + \frac{D_\infty}{(1+r)^\infty} \quad (7.1)$$

where

P_0 = value today of common stock
D_t = dividend *expected* at the end of year t
r = required return on common stock

The equation can be simplified somewhat by redefining each year's dividend, D_t, in terms of anticipated growth. We will consider three models here: zero growth, constant growth, and variable growth.

Zero-Growth Dividend Model

zero-growth dividend model
An approach to dividend valuation that assumes a constant, nongrowing dividend stream.

The simplest approach to dividend valuation, the **zero-growth dividend model**, assumes a constant, nongrowing dividend stream. Mature, steady-income-producing firms that have already made and cultivated their long-term strategic investments exemplify firms that pay a constant dividend over time; these firms are sometimes referred to as "cash cows." In terms of the notation already introduced,

$$D_1 = D_2 = \ldots = D_\infty$$

When we let D_1 represent the amount of the annual dividend, Equation 7.1 under zero growth reduces to

$$P_0 = D_1 \times \sum_{t=1}^{\infty} \frac{1}{(1+r)^t} = D_1 \times \frac{1}{r} = \frac{D_1}{r} \quad (7.2)$$

FOCUS ON PRACTICE *in practice*

Understanding Human Behavior Helps Us Understand Investor Behavior

Market anomalies are patterns inconsistent with the efficient-market hypothesis. Behavioral finance has a number of theories to help explain how human emotions influence people in their investment decision-making processes.

Regret theory deals with the emotional reaction people experience after realizing they have made an error in judgment. When deciding whether to sell a stock, investors become emotionally affected by the price at which they purchased the stock. A sale at a loss would confirm that the investor miscalculated the value of the stock when it was purchased. The correct approach when considering whether to sell a stock is, "Would I buy this stock today if it were already liquidated?" If the answer is no, it is time to sell. Regret theory also holds true for investors who passed up buying a stock that now is selling at a much higher price. Again, the correct approach is to value the stock today without regard to its prior value.

Herding is another market behavior affecting investor decisions. Some investors rationalize their decision to buy certain stocks with "everyone else is doing it." Investors may feel less embarrassment about losing money on a popular stock than about losing money on an unknown or unpopular stock.

People have a tendency to place particular events into *mental accounts*, and the difference between these compartments sometimes influences behavior more than the events themselves. Researchers have asked people the following question: "Would you purchase a $20 ticket at the local theater if you realize after you get there that you have lost a $20 bill?" Roughly 88% of people would do so. Under another scenario, people were asked whether they would buy a second $20 ticket if they arrived at the theater and realized they had left at home a ticket purchased in advance for $20. Only 40% of respondents would buy another. In both scenarios, the person is out $40, but mental accounting leads to a different outcome. In investing, compartmentalization is best illustrated by the hesitation to sell an investment that once had monstrous gains and now has a modest gain. During bull markets, people get accustomed to paper gains. When a market correction deflates investors' net worth, they are hesitant to sell, causing them to wait for the return of that gain.

Other investor behaviors are prospect theory and anchoring. According to *prospect theory*, people express a different degree of emotion toward gains than losses. Individuals are stressed more by prospective losses than they are buoyed by the prospect of equal gains. *Anchoring* is the tendency of investors to place more value on recent information. People tend to give too much credence to recent market opinions and events and mistakenly extrapolate recent trends that differ from historical, long-term averages and probabilities. Anchoring is a partial explanation for the longevity of some bull markets.

Most stock valuation techniques require that all relevant information be available to properly determine a stock's value and potential for future gain. Behavioral finance may explain the connection between valuation and an investor's actions based on that valuation.

► *Theories of behavioral finance can apply to other areas of human behavior as well as investing. Think of a situation in which you may have demonstrated one of these behaviors. Share your situation with a classmate.*

The equation shows that with zero growth, the value of a share of common stock would equal the present value of a perpetuity of D_1 dollars discounted at a required rate of return for common stock, r. (Perpetuities were introduced in Chapter 5; see Equation 5.14 and the related discussion.)

IRF PERSONAL FINANCE EXAMPLE 7.2

MyLab Finance Solution Video

Chuck Swimmer estimates that the dividend paid on the common stock of Denham Company, an established textile producer, is expected to remain constant at $3 per share indefinitely. If his required return on its common stock is 15%, then using Equation 7.2 we find the stock's value is $20 ($3 ÷ 0.15) per share.

Preferred Stock Valuation Because preferred stock typically provides its holders with a fixed annual dividend and because it never matures, Equation 7.2 can be used to find the value of preferred stock. The value of preferred stock can be estimated by inserting the dividend on the preferred stock for D_1 and the required return for preferred stock, r, in Equation 7.2. For example, a preferred stock paying a $5 annual dividend and having a required return of 13% would have a value of $38.46 ($5 ÷ 0.13) per share.

Constant-Growth Dividend Model

constant-growth dividend model
A widely cited dividend valuation approach that assumes dividends will grow at a constant rate, but a rate less than the required return.

The **constant-growth dividend model** assumes that dividends will grow at a constant rate, but a rate less than the required return. (The assumption that the constant dividend growth rate, g, is less than the required return, r, is a necessary mathematical condition for deriving this model.[1]) Firms that are relatively mature but have not yet exhausted all of their investment opportunities may exhibit a relatively constant dividend growth rate. If the firm's policy is to pay out only a portion of earnings while reinvesting the rest, then as the firm's earnings grow from returns earned on reinvested earnings, dividends will grow, too. By letting D_0 represent the most recent dividend, we can rewrite Equation 7.1 as

$$P_0 = \frac{D_0 \times (1+g)^1}{(1+r)^1} + \frac{D_0 \times (1+g)^2}{(1+r)^2} + \ldots + \frac{D_0 \times (1+g)^\infty}{(1+r)^\infty} \quad (7.3)$$

If we simplify Equation 7.3 and let $D_1 = D_0 \times (1 + g)$, it can be rewritten as

Gordon growth dividend model
A common name for the *constant-growth dividend model* that is widely cited in dividend valuation.

$$P_0 = \frac{D_1}{r - g} \quad (7.4)$$

The constant-growth dividend model in Equation 7.4 is commonly called the **Gordon growth dividend model**. An example will show how it works.

IRF EXAMPLE 7.3

MyLab Finance Solution Video

Lamar Company, a small cosmetics company, from 2014 through 2019 paid the following per-share dividends on its common stock:

Year	Dividend per share
2019	$1.40
2018	1.29
2017	1.20
2016	1.12
2015	1.05
2014	1.00

1. Another assumption of the constant-growth dividend model as presented is that earnings and dividends grow at the same rate. This assumption is true only in cases in which a firm pays out a fixed percentage of its earnings each year (has a fixed payout ratio). In the case of a declining industry, a negative growth rate ($g < 0\%$) might exist. In such a case, the constant-growth dividend model, as well as the variable-growth dividend model presented in the next section, remains fully applicable to the valuation process.

We assume that the historical average annual growth rate of dividends is an accurate estimate of the future constant annual dividend growth rate, g. To find the historical average annual growth rate of dividends, we must solve the following for g:

$$D_{2019} = D_{2014} \times (1 + g)^5$$

$$\frac{D_{2019}}{D_{2014}} = (1 + g)^5$$

$$\frac{\$1.40}{\$1.00} = (1 + g)^5$$

$$\left(\frac{\$1.40}{\$1.00}\right)^{\frac{1}{5}} - 1 = g$$

$$0.0696 = g$$

$$7\% = g$$

MyLab Finance Financial Calculator

Input	Function
−1.00	PV
1.40	FV
5	N
	CPT
	I/Y

Solution 6.96

We can also use a financial calculator to quickly find that the historical average annual growth rate of Lamar Company dividends equals approximately 7%. (*Note:* Most calculators require *either* the PV or FV value to be input as a negative number to calculate an unknown interest or growth rate. That approach is used here.) We estimate that Lamar's dividend in 2020, D_1, will equal \$1.50 (about 7% more than the 2019 dividend). Assume the required return, r, is 15%. By substituting these values into Equation 7.4, we estimate the value of the stock to be

$$P_0 = \frac{\$1.50}{0.15 - 0.07} = \frac{\$1.50}{0.08} = \underline{\underline{\$18.75}} \text{ per share}$$

Given the estimated values of D_1, r, and g, Lamar Company's stock value is \$18.75 per share.

As you can see, the constant-growth model makes quick work of finding the present value of an infinite stream of dividends. However, keep in mind that the accuracy of the stock valuation found using this model largely depends on the assumed growth rate. Consider that changing the assumed dividend growth rate from 7% to 8% for Lamar causes the calculated valuation to increase by more than 15%, to \$21.57.

Variable-Growth Dividend Model

variable-growth dividend model
A dividend valuation approach that allows for a change in the dividend growth rate.

The zero- and constant-growth common stock models do not allow for any shift in expected growth rates. Because future growth rates might shift up or down as a result of changing business conditions, we find it useful to consider a **variable-growth dividend model** that allows for a change in the dividend growth rate.[2] For example, reflect on a young firm that experiences rapid growth in sales and earnings in its early years as its products take off, but after some time the rate of growth levels off, causing dividend growth to follow the same pattern. We will assume that a single shift in growth rates occurs at the end of year n, and we will use g_1 to represent the initial growth rate and g_2 for the growth rate after the

2. More than one change in the growth rate can be incorporated into the model, but to simplify the discussion we will consider only a single growth-rate change. Although this model can incorporate an unlimited number of changes in the growth rate, building in a large number of different growth rates probably does not improve the model's accuracy a great deal.

shift. To determine the value of a share of stock in the case of variable growth, we use a four-step procedure:

Step 1 Find the value of the cash dividends at the end of *each year*, D_t, during the initial growth period, years 1 through n. This step may require adjusting the most recent dividend, D_0, using the initial growth rate, g_1, to calculate the dividend amount for each year. Therefore, for the first n years,

$$D_t = D_0 \times (1 + g_1)^t$$

Step 2 Find the present value of the dividends expected during the initial growth period. Using the notation presented earlier, we can give this value as

$$\sum_{t=1}^{n} \frac{D_0(1 + g_1)^t}{(1 + r)^t} = \sum_{t=1}^{n} \frac{D_t}{(1 + r)^t}$$

Step 3 Find the value of the stock *at the end of the initial growth period,* by applying the constant-growth model (Equation 7.4) to the dividends expected from year $n + 1$ to infinity. That is, $P_n = (D_{n+1})/(r - g_2)$ is the present value in year n of all dividends expected from year $n + 1$ to infinity, assuming a constant dividend growth rate, g_2. To express this value in today's dollars (rather than in year n dollars), we need to discount P_n for an additional n periods using the required return r as follows

$$\frac{1}{(1 + r)^n} \times \frac{D_{n+1}}{r - g_2}$$

Step 4 Add the present value components found in Steps 2 and 3 to find the value of the stock, P_0, given in Equation 7.5:

$$P_0 = \underbrace{\sum_{t=1}^{n} \frac{D_0 \times (1 + g_1)^t}{(1 + r)^t}}_{\substack{\textit{Present value of}\\ \textit{dividends}\\ \textit{during initial}\\ \textit{growth period}}} + \underbrace{\left[\frac{1}{(1 + r)^n} \times \frac{D_{n+1}}{r - g_2}\right]}_{\substack{\textit{Present value of}\\ \textit{price of stock}\\ \textit{at end of initial}\\ \textit{growth period}}} \qquad (7.5)$$

The following example illustrates the application of these steps to a variable-growth situation with only one change in the growth rate.

IRF PERSONAL FINANCE EXAMPLE 7.4 Victoria Robb is thinking about purchasing the common stock of Warren Industries, a rapidly growing boat manufacturer. She finds that the firm's most recent (2019) annual dividend payment was \$1.50 per share. Victoria estimates that these dividends will increase at a 10% annual rate, g_1, over the next 3 years (2020, 2021, and 2022) because of the introduction of a hot new boat. Beyond 2022, she expects the firm's mature product line to result in a slowing of the dividend growth rate to 5% per year, g_2, for the foreseeable future. Victoria's required return, r, is 15%. To estimate the current value of Warren's common stock, P_0, she applies the four-step procedure to these data.

TABLE 7.2 **Calculation of Present Value of Warren Industries Dividends (2020–2022)**

t	Year	$D_0 = D_{2019}$ (1)	$(1 + g_1)^t$ (2)	D_t [(1) × (2)] (3)	$(1 + r)^t$ (4)	Present value of dividends [(3) ÷ (4)] (5)
1	2020	$1.50	1.100	$1.65	1.150	$1.43
2	2021	1.50	1.210	1.82	1.323	1.37
3	2022	1.50	1.331	2.00	1.521	1.32

$$\text{Sum of present value of dividends} = \sum_{t=1}^{3} \frac{D_0 \times (1 + g_1)^t}{(1 + r_s)^t} = \underline{\underline{\$4.12}}$$

Step 1 Columns 1, 2, and 3 of Table 7.2 calculate the value of the cash dividends in each of the next 3 years, which are $1.65, $1.82, and $2.00.

Step 2 The present value in 2019 of the next three dividends is calculated in columns 3, 4, and 5 of Table 7.2. The sum of the present values of the three dividends is $4.12.

Step 3 To find the value of the stock at the end of the initial growth period $n =$ 2022, first calculate $D_{n+1} = D_{2023}$:

$$D_{2023} = D_{2022} \times (1 + 0.05) = \$2.00 \times (1.05) = \$2.10$$

Based on $D_{2023} = \$2.10$, a 15% required return, and a 5% dividend growth rate, the value in 2022 of all dividends paid in 2023 and beyond, or equivalently the price of the stock in 2022, is

$$P_{2022} = \frac{D_{2023}}{r - g_2} = \frac{\$2.10}{0.15 - 0.05} = \frac{\$2.10}{0.10} = \$21.00$$

Finally, convert the $21 share value in 2022 into a present (end-of-2019) value by discounting it at 15% for three years as follows

$$\frac{P_{2022}}{(1 + r)^3} = \frac{\$21}{(1 + 0.15)^3} = \$13.81$$

Step 4 As specified in Equation 7.5, add the present value of the initial dividend stream (found in Step 2) to the present value of the stock at the end of the initial growth period (found in Step 3) to obtain the current value of Warren Industries stock

$$P_0 = \$4.12 + \$13.81 = \underline{\underline{\$17.93}} \text{ per share}$$

Victoria's calculations indicate that the stock is currently worth $17.93 per share.

FREE CASH FLOW STOCK VALUATION MODEL

As an alternative to the dividend valuation models presented earlier in this chapter, analysts sometimes estimate a firm's value by using projected *free cash flows (FCFs)*. This approach is appealing when valuing firms that have no dividend history or are startups, or when valuing an operating unit or division of a larger public company.

Although dividend valuation models are widely used and accepted, in these situations a more general free cash flow valuation model is preferred.

free cash flow valuation model
A model that determines the value of an entire company as the present value of its expected *free cash flows* discounted at the firm's *weighted average cost of capital,* which is its expected average future cost of funds over the long run.

The **free cash flow valuation model** is based on the same premise as dividend valuation models: The value of a share of common stock is the present value of all future cash flows it is expected to provide over an infinite time horizon. However, in the free cash flow valuation model, instead of valuing the firm's expected dividends, we value the firm's expected *free cash flows,* defined in Chapter 4 (on page 154, Equation 4.4). Free cash flow represents the amount of cash flow available to investors—the providers of debt (creditors) and equity (owners)—after the firm meets all its other obligations.

The free cash flow valuation model estimates the value of the entire company by finding the present value of its expected free cash flows discounted at its *weighted average cost of capital,* r_{WACC}, which is a blend of the firm's cost of debt and equity financing (we'll say more about this in Chapter 9), as specified in Equation 7.6:

$$V_C = \frac{FCF_1}{(1 + r_{WACC})^1} + \frac{FCF_2}{(1 + r_{WACC})^2} + \ldots + \frac{FCF_\infty}{(1 + r_{WACC})^\infty} \tag{7.6}$$

where

V_C = value of the entire company
FCF_t = free cash flow expected at the end of year t
r_{WACC} = the firm's weighted average cost of capital

Note the similarity between Equations 7.6 and 7.1, the general stock valuation equation.

Because the value of the entire company, V_C, is the market value of the entire enterprise (i.e., of all assets), to find common stock value, V_S, we must subtract the market value of all the firm's debt, V_D, and the market value of preferred stock, V_P, from V_C:

$$V_S = V_C - V_D - V_P \tag{7.7}$$

Because it is difficult to accurately forecast a firm's free cash flow far into the future, specific annual free cash flows are typically forecast for only short horizons, beyond which a constant growth rate is assumed. Here we assume that the first 5 years of free cash flows are explicitly forecast and that a constant rate of free cash flow growth occurs beyond the end of year 5 to infinity. This model is methodologically similar to the variable-growth dividend model presented earlier in this chapter. An example demonstrates how to use the model.

EXAMPLE 7.5

It is currently December 31, 2019, and Dewhurst Inc. wishes to determine the value of its common stock by using the free cash flow valuation model. To apply the model, the firm's CFO developed the free cash flow estimates and other data given in Table 7.3. We can now apply the model in four steps.

Step 1 First calculate the present value of each cash flow that Dewhurst produces in the years 2020 through 2024. The first several rows of Table 7.4

TABLE 7.3 **Dewhurst Inc.'s Data for the Free Cash Flow Valuation Model**

Free cash flow		
Year (t)	(FCF_t)	Other data
2020	$400,000	Growth rate of FCF, beyond 2024 to infinity, $g_{FCF} = 3\%$
2021	450,000	Weighted average cost of capital, $r_{WACC} = 9\%$
2022	520,000	Market value of all debt, V_D = $3,100,000
2023	560,000	Market value of preferred stock, V_P = $800,000
2024	600,000	Number of shares of common stock outstanding = 300,000

list those present values. For example, the present value of the $400,000 cash flow that comes in 2020 is $366,972.

Step 2 Use the constant growth model to calculate the present value, as of 2024, of all cash flows that arrive in years 2025 and beyond. Because cash flows grow at a steady 3% clip over that time horizon, the free cash flow in 2025 is $618,000 (3% more than the 2024 cash flow of $600,000). Therefore, we can calculate the present value in 2024 of all cash flows from 2025 to infinity as follows:

$$\begin{aligned} PV_{2024} &= FCF_{2025} \div (r_{WACC} - g) \\ &= \$618{,}000 \div (0.09 - 0.03) \\ &= \$10{,}300{,}000 \end{aligned}$$

Finally, since we are valuing Dewhurst in 2019, we need to discount the $10,300,000 figure an additional 5 years to calculate its present value today (not in 2024). Table 7.4 shows that the present value is $6,692,658.

Step 3 Add up the present values of the individual cash flows from 2020 to 2024 as well as the present value of cash flows that arrive in 2025 and beyond to get the total value, V_c, of Dewhurst in 2019. Table 7.4 shows that the company's total value is $8,626,426.

TABLE 7.4 **Calculation of the Value of the Entire Company for Dewhurst Inc.**

t	Year	FCF_t (1)	$(1 + r_{WACC})^t$ (2)	Present value of FCF_t [(1) ÷ (2)] (3)
1	2020	$ 400,000	1.090	$ 366,972
2	2021	450,000	1.188	378,788
3	2022	520,000	1.295	401,544
4	2023	560,000	1.412	396,601
5	2024	600,000	1.539	389,864
5	2024	10,300,000	1.539	6,692,658
			Value of entire company, V_C =	$8,626,426[a]

[a]This value of the entire company is based on the rounded values that appear in the table. The precise value found without rounding is $8,628,234.

Step 4 Calculate the value of the common stock using Equation 7.7. Substituting into Equation 7.7 the value of the entire company, V_C, calculated in Step 3, and the market values of debt, V_D, and preferred stock, V_P, given in Table 7.3, yields the value of the common stock, V_S:

$$V_S = \$8{,}626{,}426 - \$3{,}100{,}000 - \$800{,}000 = \underline{\underline{\$4{,}726{,}426}}$$

The value of Dewhurst's common stock is therefore estimated to be \$4,726,426. By dividing this total by the 300,000 shares of common stock that the firm has outstanding, we get a common stock value of \$15.75 per share (\$4,726,426 ÷ 300,000).

The free cash flow valuation model is similar to the dividend valuation models presented earlier. The appeal of this approach is its focus on free cash flow estimates rather than on forecasted dividends, which are far more difficult to estimate for firms that have not yet started paying dividends. The more general nature of the free cash flow model is responsible for its growing popularity, particularly with CFOs and other financial managers.

OTHER APPROACHES TO COMMON STOCK VALUATION

Many other approaches to common stock valuation exist. Some approaches that see widespread use focus on book value, liquidation value, and some type of price/earnings multiple.

book value per share
The amount per share of common stock that would be received if all of the firm's assets were *sold for their exact book (accounting) value* and the proceeds remaining after paying all liabilities (including preferred stock) were divided among the common stockholders.

Book Value

Book value per share is simply the amount per share of common stock that would be received if all the firm's assets were sold for their exact book (accounting) value, if its liabilities (including preferred stock) were paid at book value, and if the proceeds remaining were divided among the common stockholders. This method is not particularly sophisticated because it relies on historical balance sheet data. It ignores the firm's expected earnings potential and generally falls far short of the firm's value in the marketplace. Let us look at an example.

EXAMPLE 7.6

At year-end 2019, Lamar Company's balance sheet shows total assets of \$6 million, total liabilities and preferred stock of \$4.5 million, and 100,000 shares of common stock outstanding. Its book value per share would therefore be

$$\frac{\$6{,}000{,}000 - \$4{,}500{,}000}{100{,}000 \text{ shares}} = \underline{\underline{\$15}} \text{ per share}$$

For many firms, the book value of assets is quite a bit less than the market value, so the book value per share is usually a conservative estimate of a stock's value. However, if investors believe that the book value of a firm's assets is overstated or the value of its liabilities is understated, the stock's market value may fall short of its book value.

liquidation value per share
The *actual amount* per share of common stock that would be received if all the firm's assets were *sold for their market value,* liabilities (including preferred stock) were paid, and any remaining money were divided among the common stockholders.

Liquidation Value

Liquidation value per share is the actual amount per share of common stock that would be received if all the firm's assets were sold for their market value, liabilities and preferred stock were paid, and any remaining money were divided among the common stockholders. This measure is more realistic than book value—because it is based on the current market value of the firm's assets—but it still may not fully account for the earning power of those assets. An example will illustrate.

EXAMPLE 7.7

Lamar Company found on investigation that it could obtain \$6.25 million if it sold its assets today. The firm's liquidation value per share would therefore be

$$\frac{\$6{,}250{,}000 - \$4{,}500{,}000}{100{,}000 \text{ shares}} = \underline{\underline{\$17.50}} \text{ per share}$$

Ignoring liquidation expenses, this amount would be the firm's minimum value.

Price/Earnings (P/E) Multiples

The *price/earnings (P/E) ratio*, introduced in Chapter 3, reflects the amount investors are willing to pay for each dollar of earnings. The average P/E ratio in a particular industry can be used as a guide to a firm's value, if we can assume that investors value the earnings of that firm in the same way they do the "average" firm in the industry. The **price/earnings multiple approach** is a popular technique used to estimate the firm's share value; it is calculated by multiplying the firm's expected earnings per share (EPS) by the average price/earnings (P/E) ratio for the industry.

price/earnings multiple approach
A popular technique used to estimate the firm's share value; calculated by multiplying the firm's expected earnings per share (EPS) by the average price/earnings (P/E) ratio for the industry.

Figure 7.1 plots the yearly Shiller P/E ratio for the S&P 500 Stock Index and several industry sectors, as reported by multpl.com for the years 2010 through 2017. These yearly P/E ratios are the price-to-average earnings from the preceding 10 years and are, therefore, less prone to large earnings swings that can be caused by variation of profit margins across business cycles. A useful starting point for evaluating the P/E ratio is the *market P/E ratio*. A common proxy for the market P/E ratio shown in Figure 7.1 is the average P/E ratio of all the stocks in a given market index, like the S&P 500. The market P/E ratio indicates the general state of

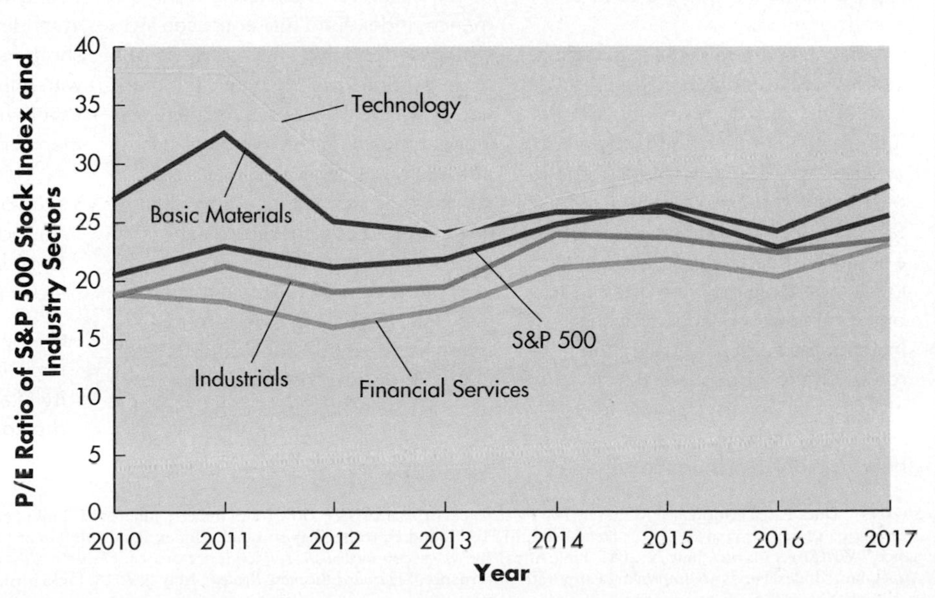

P/E Ratio of S&P 500 Stock Index and Industry Sectors
The yearly average price-to-earnings ratio for stocks in the S&P 500 fluctuated around a mean of 24 from 2010 to 2017. The yearly average price-to-earnings ratio for various industry sectors had means that ranged from 15 for the energy sector to 51 for the real estate sector.
(*Source:* Data from http://www.multpl.com)

the market and gives an idea of how aggressively investors are pricing earning. Other things being equal, the higher the market P/E ratio, the more optimistic investors are regarding the future performance of the average stock. From 2010 to 2017, the yearly P/E ratio for the S&P 500 stock index averaged 24, and Figure 7.1 shows that it was generally rising as the United States continued to rebound from the Great Recession and businesses ramped up investing in growth opportunities. Not surprisingly, the yearly P/E ratios for individual industry sectors can differ from the market P/E ratio. Other things being equal, an industry that is less risky will have a higher P/E as will an industry with higher expected earnings growth. In Figure 7.1 you can observe that the yearly P/E ratios for both the

FOCUS ON ETHICS *in practice*

Index Funds and Corporate Governance

The Efficient Markets Hypothesis implies it is tough for investors to outperform the market consistently. Consider the performance of mutual funds run by managers who buy stocks thought to be undervalued and sell those thought overvalued—so-called active funds. Active funds that post great returns seldom stay on top. For example, of the 585 active funds ranked among the top 25% for annual returns as of March 2013, only 0.34% remained in the top performance quartile each of the next four years.

Because the record suggests successful stock picking may be more luck than skill, investors have increasingly funneled their money into index funds, which simply buy and hold a portfolio of stocks in a particular index like the S&P 500. Index-fund managers follow a so-called passive approach to investing—they make no attempt to buy winning stocks and sell losers. Instead, they aim at equaling the return on the index while charging investors the lowest possible fees. From 1998 to 2014, the share of assets held by index funds tripled. To some, this trend has a dark side—index funds, the argument goes, are "lazy investors" with little interest in policing the companies they partially own.

Corporate management's job is to maximize shareholder wealth. If the CEO leaves value on the table, stockholders can vote her out. Disgruntled stockholders can also sell, which drives down the share price and makes it easier for a large investor or another firm to buy control and force a change. But unlike investors who buy or sell based on expected firm performance, index-fund managers see individual stocks only as a small piece of a large portfolio built to mimic the market. Moreover, because passive funds work at matching the market return, not finding under- or overvalued stocks, they lack the means to identify firms in need of a shake-up. Vanguard—a pioneer among index funds with more than $4 trillion in assets—had only 15 analysts assessing management at 13,000 companies in late 2016. Finally, even if an index fund were to identify an underperformer, it might still balk at voting against management for fear of losing a chance to handle the firm's employee-retirement funds. Such concerns have led to calls for index funds to abstain from voting at shareholder meetings, which would strengthen the voice of more informed, engaged investors.

New research suggests, however, that firms largely owned by index funds have some excellent governance practices. Such firms are more likely to have directors on their board willing to hold management accountable and less likely to issue shares with unequal voting rights (which aid management in fending off hostile takeovers). In short, fear that index funds might ally with unhappy shareholders contributes to a framework for keeping management focused on share price.

► *If you were the CEO of a publicly traded company, would you want a large bloc of your shares held by index funds? Why or why not?*

► *Now, suppose you manage a large index fund, what responsibility (if any) do you have for ensuring the companies in your portfolio maximize shareholder wealth?*

Sources: "Does Past Performance Matter?" *The Persistence Scorecard,* S&P Dow Jones Indices, June 2017. Link: https://us.spindices.com/documents/spiva/persistence-scorecard-june-2017.pdf; Henderson, M. Todd, and Dorothy Shapiro Lund, "Index Funds are Great for Investors, Risky for Corporate Governance," *Wall Street Journal,* June 22, 2017. Link: https://www.wsj.com/articles/index-funds-are-great-for-investors-risky-for-corporate-governance-1498170623; Appel, Ian. "Index Funds are Improving Corporate Governance," *Harvard Business Review,* May 9, 2016. Link: https://hbr.org/2016/05/research-index-funds-are-improving-corporate-governance.

financial services and industrial sectors are running somewhat in parallel and below that of the P/E ratio for the S&P 500, and from this you might discern that either the riskiness is higher or the growth prospects are lower for firms in these sectors relative to the average stock in the market. Historically, the former has been the case. In contrast, the technology sector generally has both faster-growing and riskier earnings than the market average. However, since the technology sector's P/E ratio is consistently above that of the market, we can conclude that in comparison to the average stock, the relative difference in earning growth is greater than the relative difference in risk. The yearly P/E ratio for the basic materials sector initially runs above the P/E ratio for the S&P 500 and then falls below that of the market in 2015. Given that this industry sector tends to be relatively riskier than the market, we might conclude from Figure 7.1 that investors had anticipated sufficiently larger earnings growth for the sector relative to the average stock in the market for the period leading up to 2015.

The P/E ratio valuation technique is a simple method of determining a stock's value. Because it is based on a firm's expected earnings, the widespread use of the P/E ratio as a valuation tool has increased the demand for more frequent announcements or "guidance" regarding future earnings. Some firms have been caught pushing ethical boundaries to boost investors' earnings expectations, while other firms avoid providing any earnings guidance at all.

The use of P/E multiples is especially helpful in valuing firms that are not publicly traded, but analysts use this approach for public companies, too. In any case, the price/earnings multiple approach is forward looking because it considers expected earnings, and it usually produces higher valuations than the book value or liquidation value approaches.

PERSONAL FINANCE EXAMPLE 7.8

MyLab Finance Solution Video

Ann Perrier plans to use the price/earnings multiple approach to estimate the value of Lamar Company's stock, which she currently holds in her retirement account. She estimates that Lamar Company will earn $1.90 per share next year (2020). This expectation is based on an analysis of the firm's historical earnings trend and on expected economic and industry conditions. She finds the price/earnings (P/E) ratio for firms in the same industry to average 14. Multiplying Lamar's expected earnings per share (EPS) of 1.90 by this ratio gives her a value for the firm's shares of $26.60, assuming that investors will continue to value the average firm at 14 times its earnings.

So how much is Lamar Company's stock really worth? That's a trick question because there's no one right answer. It is important to recognize that the answer depends on the assumptions made and the techniques used. Professional securities analysts typically use a variety of models and techniques to value stocks. For example, an analyst might use the constant-growth dividend model, liquidation value, and a P/E multiple to estimate the worth of a given stock. If the analyst feels comfortable with his or her estimates, the stock would be valued at no more than the largest estimate. Of course, should the firm's estimated liquidation value per share exceed its "going concern" value per share, estimated by using one of the valuation models (zero-, constant-, or variable-growth or free cash flow) or the P/E multiple approach, the firm would be viewed as "worth more dead than alive." In such an event, the firm would lack sufficient earning power to justify its existence and should probably be liquidated.

MATTER OF FACT

Problems with P/E Valuation

The P/E multiple approach is a fast and easy way to estimate a stock's value. However, P/E ratios vary widely over time. In 1980, the average stock had a P/E ratio below 9, but by the year 2000, the ratio had risen above 40. Therefore, analysts using the P/E approach in the 1980s would have come up with much lower estimates of value than analysts using the model 20 years later. By 2012, the average stock had a P/E ratio of about 20, which is close to the long-run average; however, at the start of 2017 the average was back up to around 28. When using this approach to estimate stock values, the estimate will depend more on whether stock market valuations generally are high or low rather than on whether the particular company is doing well or not.

→ **REVIEW QUESTIONS** MyLab Finance Solutions

7–8 Describe the events that occur in an efficient market in response to new information that cause the expected return to exceed the required return. What happens to the market value?

7–9 What does the efficient-market hypothesis (EMH) say about (**a**) securities prices, (**b**) their reaction to new information, and (**c**) investor opportunities to profit? What is the behavioral finance challenge to this hypothesis?

7–10 Describe, compare, and contrast the following common stock dividend valuation models: (**a**) zero-growth, (**b**) constant-growth, and (**c**) variable-growth.

7–11 Describe the free cash flow valuation model, and explain how it differs from the dividend valuation models. What is the appeal of this model?

7–12 Explain each of the three other approaches to common stock valuation: (**a**) book value, (**b**) liquidation value, and (**c**) P/E multiples. Which of them is considered the best?

LG6

7.4 Decision Making and Common Stock Value

Valuation equations measure the stock value at a point in time based on expected return and risk. Any decisions of the financial manager that affect these variables can cause change in the value of the firm. Figure 7.2 depicts the relationship among financial decisions, return, risk, and stock value.

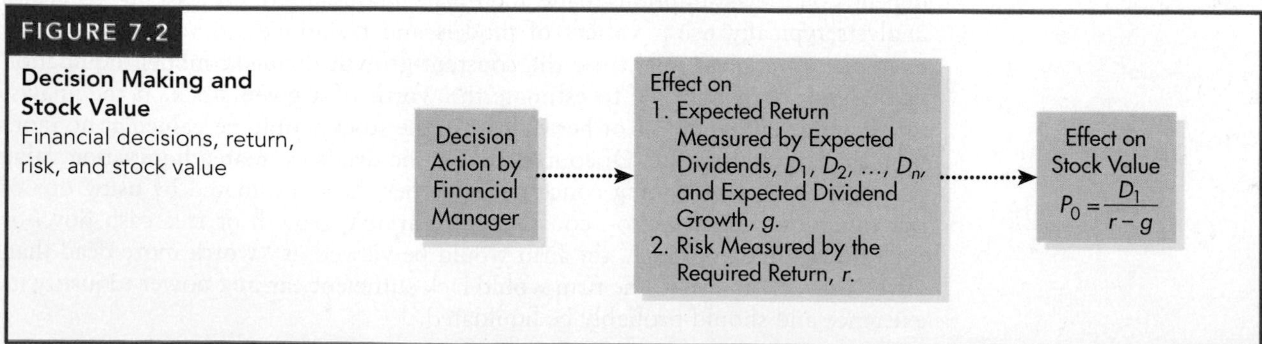

FIGURE 7.2

Decision Making and Stock Value

Financial decisions, return, risk, and stock value

CHANGES IN EXPECTED DIVIDENDS

Any management action that would cause stockholders to raise their dividend expectations should increase the firm's value (as long as stockholders perceive no increase in the risk of the future dividend stream). In Equation 7.4, we can see that P_0 will increase for any rise in D_1 or g. Any action by the financial manager that will increase the level of expected dividends without changing risk (the required return) should be undertaken because it will positively affect owners' wealth.

EXAMPLE 7.9

Using the constant-growth dividend model given earlier in Example 7.3, we found Lamar Company to have a share value of $18.75. On the following day, the firm announced a major technological breakthrough that would revolutionize its industry. Current and prospective stockholders would not be expected to adjust their required return of 15%, but they would expect that future dividends will increase. Specifically, they expect that although the dividend next year, D_1, will remain at $1.50, the expected growth rate thereafter will increase from 7% to 9%. If we substitute $D_1 = \$1.50$, $r = 0.15$, and $g = 0.09$ into Equation 7.4, the resulting share value is $25 [$1.50 ÷ (0.15 − 0.09)]. The increased value therefore resulted from the higher expected future dividends reflected in the increase in growth rate.

CHANGES IN RISK

Although the required return, r, is the focus of Chapters 8 and 9, at this point we can reconsider its fundamental components. Any measure of required return consists of two components, a risk-free rate and a risk premium. We expressed this relationship as Equation 6.3 in Chapter 6, which we repeat here:

$$r = \underbrace{r^* + i}_{\substack{\text{risk-free} \\ \text{rate, } R_F}} + \underbrace{RP}_{\substack{\text{risk} \\ \text{premium}}}$$

In Chapter 8, you will learn that the real challenge in finding the required return is determining the appropriate risk premium. In Chapters 8 and 9, we will discuss how investors and managers can estimate the risk premium for any particular asset. For now, recognize that r represents the minimum return that the firm's stock must provide to shareholders to compensate them for bearing the risk of holding the firm's equity.

Any action taken by the financial manager that increases the risk shareholders must bear will also raise the risk premium required by shareholders and hence the required return. Additionally, the required return can be affected by changes in the risk-free rate, even if the risk premium remains constant. For example, if the risk-free rate increases due to a rise in expected inflation, the required return goes up, too. In Equation 7.1, we can see that an increase in the required return, r, will reduce share value, P_0, and that a decrease in the required return will increase share value. Thus, any action by the financial manager that increases risk contributes to a reduction in value, and any action that decreases risk contributes to an increase in value.

EXAMPLE 7.10

Assume that Lamar Company's 15% required return resulted from a risk-free rate of 4% and a risk premium of 11%. With this return, the firm's share value was calculated in Example 7.3 to be $18.75.

Now imagine the financial manager makes a decision that, without changing expected dividends, causes the firm's risk premium to increase to 12%. Assuming that the risk-free rate remains at 4%, the new required return on Lamar stock will be 16% (4% + 12%), and substituting $D_1 = \$1.50$, $r = 0.16$, and $g = 0.07$ into the valuation equation (Equation 7.3) results in a new share value of \$16.67 [\$1.50 ÷ (0.16 − 0.07)]. As expected, raising the required return, without any corresponding increase in expected dividends, makes the firm's stock value decline. Clearly, the financial manager's action was not in the owners' best interest.

COMBINED EFFECT

A financial decision rarely affects dividends and risk independently; most decisions affect both factors, often in the same direction. As firms take on more risk, their shareholders expect to see higher dividends. The net effect on value depends on the relative size of the changes in these two variables.

EXAMPLE 7.11

If we assume that the two changes illustrated for Lamar Company in the preceding examples occur simultaneously, the key variable values would be $D_1 = \$1.50$, $r = 0.16$, and $g = 0.09$. Substituting into the valuation model, we obtain a share price of \$21.43 [\$1.50 ÷ (0.16 − 0.09)]. The net result of the decision, which increased dividend growth (g, from 7% to 9%) as well as required return (r, from 15% to 16%), is positive. The share price increased from \$18.75 to \$21.43. Even with the combined effects, the decision appears to be in the best interest of the firm's owners because it increases their wealth.

→ REVIEW QUESTIONS MyLab Finance Solutions

7–13 Explain the linkages among financial decisions, return, risk, and stock value.

7–14 Assuming that all other variables remain unchanged, what effect would each of the following have on stock price? (**a**) The firm's risk premium increases. (**b**) The firm's required return decreases. (**c**) The dividend expected next year decreases. (**d**) The growth rate of dividends is expected to increase.

SUMMARY

FOCUS ON VALUE

The price of each share of a firm's common stock is the value of each ownership interest. Although common stockholders typically have voting rights, which indirectly give them a say in management, their most significant right is their claim on the residual cash flows of the firm. This claim is subordinate to those of vendors, employees, customers, lenders, the government (for taxes), and preferred stockholders. The value of the common stockholders' claim is embodied in the future cash flows they are entitled to receive. The present value of those expected cash flows is the firm's share value.

To determine this present value, forecast cash flows are discounted at a rate that reflects their risk. Riskier cash flows are discounted at higher rates, resulting in lower present values than less risky expected cash flows, which are discounted at lower rates. The value of the firm's common stock is therefore driven by its expected cash flows (returns) and risk (certainty of the expected cash flows).

In pursuing the firm's goal of **maximizing the stock price**, the financial manager must carefully consider the balance of return and risk associated with each proposal and must undertake only those actions that create value for owners. By focusing on value creation and by managing and monitoring the firm's cash flows and risk, the financial manager should be able to achieve the firm's goal of share price maximization.

REVIEW OF LEARNING GOALS

LG 1 **Differentiate between debt and equity.** Holders of equity capital (common and preferred stock) are owners of the firm. Typically, only common stockholders have a voice in management. Equityholders' claims on income and assets are secondary to creditors' claims, there is no maturity date, and dividends paid to stockholders are not tax deductible.

LG 2 **Discuss the features of both common and preferred stock.** The common stock of a firm can be privately owned, closely owned, or publicly owned. It can be sold with or without a par value. Preemptive rights allow common stockholders to avoid dilution of ownership when new shares are issued. Not all shares authorized in the corporate charter are outstanding. If a firm has treasury stock, it will have issued more shares than are outstanding. Some firms have two or more classes of common stock that differ mainly in having unequal voting rights. Proxies transfer voting rights from one party to another. The decision to pay dividends to common stockholders is made by the firm's board of directors. Firms can issue stock in foreign markets. The stock of many foreign corporations is traded in U.S. markets in the form of American depositary receipts (ADRs), which are backed by American depositary shares (ADSs).

Preferred stockholders have preference over common stockholders with respect to the distribution of earnings and assets. They do not normally have voting privileges. Preferred stock issues may have certain restrictive covenants, cumulative dividends, a call feature, and a conversion feature.

LG 3 **Apply the basic valuation model to stocks, and describe the relevant cash flows and the impact of required return.** Like the value of a bond, which we discussed in Chapter 6, the value of a share of common stock is equal to the present value of all future cash flows it is expected to provide. So, Equation 6.4 can be used to find the value of a share of stock by discounting stock's expected cash flows back to their present value, using the required return commensurate with the stock's risk as the appropriate discount rate.

Although a stockholder can earn capital gains by selling stock at a price above that originally paid, what the buyer really pays for is the right to all future dividends. What about stocks that do not currently pay dividends? Such stocks have a value attributable to a future dividend stream or to the proceeds from the sale of the company. Therefore, from a valuation viewpoint, future dividends are relevant.

LG4 Understand the concept of market efficiency and how to value stocks using zero-growth, constant-growth, and variable-growth dividend models. Market efficiency assumes that the quick reactions of rational investors to new information cause the market value of common stock to adjust upward or downward quickly. The efficient-market hypothesis (EMH) suggests that securities are fairly priced, that they reflect fully all publicly available information, and that investors should therefore not waste time trying to find and capitalize on mispriced securities. Behavioral finance advocates challenge this hypothesis by arguing that emotion and other factors play a role in investment decisions.

The value of a share of stock is the present value of all future dividends it is expected to provide over an infinite time horizon. Three dividend growth dividend models—zero-growth, constant-growth, and variable-growth—can be considered in common stock valuation. The most widely cited model is the constant-growth dividend model.

LG5 Discuss the free cash flow valuation model and the book value, liquidation value, and price/earnings (P/E) multiple approaches. The free cash flow valuation model values firms that have no dividend history, startups, or an operating unit or division of a larger public company. The model finds the value of the entire company by discounting the firm's expected free cash flow at its weighted average cost of capital. The common stock value is found by subtracting the market values of the firm's debt and preferred stock from the value of the entire company.

Book value per share is the amount per share of common stock that would be received if all the firm's assets were sold for their exact book (accounting) value and the proceeds remaining after paying all liabilities (including preferred stock) were divided among the common stockholders. Liquidation value per share is the actual amount per share of common stock that would be received if all the firm's assets were sold for their market value, liabilities (including preferred stock) were paid, and the remaining money were divided among the common stockholders. The P/E multiple approach estimates stock value by multiplying the firm's expected earnings per share (EPS) by the average P/E ratio for the industry.

LG6 Explain the relationships among financial decisions, return, risk, and the firm's value. In a stable economy, any action by the financial manager that increases the level of expected dividends without changing risk should increase share value; any action that reduces the level of expected dividends without changing risk should reduce share value. Similarly, any action that increases risk (required return) will reduce share value; any action that reduces risk will increase share value. An assessment of the combined effect of return and risk on stock value must be part of the financial decision-making process.

OPENER-IN-REVIEW

Tesla Motors shares were offered to IPO investors at $17. Exactly 7 years later, the price was $360.75 per share. What was the compound annual return that Tesla investors earned over this period? Given that Tesla paid no dividends and was not expected to start paying them soon, what method might analysts have used to value the company's shares in 2017? The company sold 13.3 million shares in its IPO, with a par value of $0.001 per share. How much paid-in capital did Tesla record on its balance sheet as a result of the IPO? Do you think that a highly favorable 2013 *Consumer Reports* review of the Model S boosted Tesla's stock primarily because the review reduced the company's risk or because it boosted expected cash flows?

SELF-TEST PROBLEMS (Solutions in Appendix)

IRF

ST7–1 Common stock valuation Perry Motors' common stock just paid its annual dividend of $1.80 per share. The required return on the common stock is 12%. Estimate the value of the common stock under each of the following assumptions about the dividend:

a. Dividends are expected to grow at an annual rate of 0% to infinity.
b. Dividends are expected to grow at a constant annual rate of 5% to infinity.
c. Dividends are expected to grow at an annual rate of 5% for each of the next 3 years, followed by a constant annual growth rate of 4% in year 4 to infinity.

IRF

ST7–2 Free cash flow valuation Erwin Footwear wishes to assess the value of its Active Shoe Division. This division has debt with a market value of $12,500,000 and no preferred stock. Its weighted average cost of capital is 10%. The Active Shoe Division's estimated free cash flow each year from 2020 through 2023 is given in the following table. Beyond 2023 to infinity, the firm expects its free cash flow to grow at 4% annually.

Year (t)	Free cash flow (FCF_t)
2020	$ 800,000
2021	1,200,000
2022	1,400,000
2023	1,500,000

a. Use the free cash flow valuation model to estimate the value of Erwin's entire Active Shoe Division.
b. Use your finding in part **a** along with the data provided to find this division's common stock value.
c. If the Active Shoe Division as a public company will have 500,000 shares outstanding, use your finding in part **b** to calculate its value per share.

WARM-UP EXERCISES All problems are available in MyLab Finance.

E7–1 A balance sheet balances assets with their sources of debt and equity financing. If a corporation has assets equal to $5.2 million and a debt ratio of 75.0%, how much debt does the corporation have on its books?

LG2 **E7–2** Angina Inc. has 5 million shares outstanding. The firm is considering issuing an additional 1 million shares. After selling these shares at their $20 per share offering price and netting 95% of the sale proceeds, the firm is obligated by an earlier agreement to sell an additional 250,000 shares at 90% of the offering price. In total, how much cash will the firm net from these stock sales?

LG2 **E7–3** Figurate Industries has 750,000 shares of cumulative preferred stock outstanding. It has passed the last three quarterly dividends of $2.50 per share and now (at the end of the current quarter) wishes to distribute a total of $12 million to its shareholders. If Figurate has 3 million shares of common stock outstanding, how large a per-share common stock dividend will it be able to pay?

LG3 **E7–4** Today the common stock of Gresham Technology closed at $24.60 per share, down $0.35 from yesterday. If the company has 4.6 million shares outstanding and annual earnings of $11.2 million, what is its P/E ratio today? What was its P/E ratio yesterday?

LG4 **E7–5** Stacker Weight Loss currently pays an annual year-end dividend of $1.20 per share. It plans to increase this dividend by 5% next year and maintain it at the new level for the foreseeable future. If the required return on this firm's stock is 8%, what is the value of Stacker's stock?

LG6 **E7–6** Brash Corporation initiated a new corporate strategy that fixes its annual dividend at $2.25 per share forever. If the risk-free rate is 4.5% and the risk premium on Brash's stock is 10.8%, what is the value of Brash's stock?

PROBLEMS

All problems are available in MyLab Finance. The MyLab icon indicates problems in Excel format available in MyLab Finance.

LG2 **P7–1** **Authorized and available shares** Aspin Corporation's charter authorizes issuance of 2,000,000 shares of common stock. Currently, 1,400,000 shares are outstanding, and 100,000 shares are being held as treasury stock. The firm wishes to raise $48,000,000 for a plant expansion. Discussions with its investment bankers indicate that the sale of new common stock will net the firm $60 per share.

a. What is the maximum number of new shares of common stock the firm can sell without receiving further authorization from shareholders?

b. Judging by the data given and your finding in part **a**, do you think the firm will be able to raise the needed funds without receiving further authorization?

c. What must the firm do to obtain authorization to issue more than the number of shares found in part **a**?

LG2 **P7–2** **Preferred dividends** Acura Labs Inc. has an outstanding issue of preferred stock with a $40 par value and an 8% annual dividend.

a. What is the annual dollar dividend? If it is paid quarterly, how much will be paid each quarter?

b. If the preferred stock is noncumulative and the board of directors has passed the preferred dividend for the last three quarters, how much must be paid to preferred stockholders in the current quarter before dividends are paid to common stockholders?

c. If the preferred stock is cumulative and the board of directors has passed the preferred dividend for the last three quarters, how much must be paid to preferred stockholders in the current quarter before dividends are paid to common stockholders?

P7–3 **Preferred dividends** In each case in the following table, how many dollars of preferred dividends per share must be paid to preferred stockholders in the current period before common stock dividends are paid?

Case	Type	Par value	Dividend per share per period	Periods of dividends passed
A	Cumulative	$ 80	$4	3
B	Noncumulative	110	2.0%	2
C	Noncumulative	100	$3	1
D	Cumulative	60	1.5%	4
E	Cumulative	70	3.0%	0

P7–4 **Convertible preferred stock** Valerian Corp. convertible preferred stock has a fixed conversion ratio of five common shares per one share of preferred stock. The preferred stock pays a dividend of $10.00 per share per year. The common stock currently sells for $20.00 per share and pays a dividend of $1.00 per share per year.

a. On the basis of the conversion ratio and the price of the common shares, what is the current conversion value of each preferred share?

b. If the preferred shares are selling at $96.00 each, should an investor convert the preferred shares to common shares?

c. What factors might cause an investor not to convert from preferred to common stock?

P7–5 **Preferred stock valuation** TXS Manufacturing has an outstanding preferred stock issue with a par value of $65 per share. The preferred shares pay dividends annually at a rate of 10%.

a. What is the annual dividend on TXS preferred stock?

b. If investors require a return of 8% on this stock and the next dividend is payable 1 year from now, what is the price of TXS preferred stock?

c. Suppose that TXS has not paid dividends on its preferred shares in the past 2 years, but investors believe it will start paying dividends again in 1 year. What is the value of TXS preferred stock if it is cumulative and if investors require an 8% rate of return?

Personal Finance Problem

P7–6 **Common stock value: Zero growth** Kelsey Drums Inc. is a well-established supplier of fine percussion instruments to orchestras all over the United States. The company's class A common stock has paid a dividend of $2.80 per share per year for the last 12 years. Management expects to continue to pay at that amount for the foreseeable future. Kim Arnold purchased 200 shares of Kelsey class A common stock 10 years ago at a time when the required return for the stock was 7.6%. She wants to sell her shares today. The current required rate of return for the stock is 9.25%. How much capital gain or loss will Kim have on her shares?

P7–7 Preferred stock valuation Jones Design wishes to estimate the value of its outstanding preferred stock. The preferred issue has an $80 par value and pays an annual dividend of $6.40 per share. Similar-risk preferred stocks are currently earning a 9.3% annual rate of return.

a. What is the market value of the outstanding preferred stock?

b. If an investor purchases the preferred stock at the value calculated in part **a**, how much does she gain or lose per share if she sells the stock when the required return on similar-risk preferred stocks has risen to 10.5%? Explain.

P7–8 Common stock value: Constant growth Use the constant-growth dividend model (Gordon growth model) to find the value of each firm shown in the following table.

Firm	Dividend expected next year	Dividend growth rate	Required return
A	$1.20	8%	13%
B	4.00	5	15
C	0.65	10	14
D	6.00	8	9
E	2.25	8	20

P7–9 Common stock value: Constant growth McCracken Roofing Inc. common stock paid a dividend of $1.20 per share last year. The company expects earnings and dividends to grow at a rate of 5% per year for the foreseeable future.

a. What required rate of return for this stock would result in a price per share of $28?

b. If McCracken expects both earnings and dividends to grow at an annual rate of 10%, what required rate of return would result in a price per share of $28?

LG4

P7–10 Common stock value: Constant growth Seagate Technology is a global leader in data storage solutions and a high-yield dividend payer. From 2015 through 2019, Seagate paid the following per-share dividends:

Year	Dividend per share
2019	$2.52
2018	2.25
2017	1.83
2016	1.19
2015	1.52

Assume that the historical annual growth rate of Seagate dividends is an accurate estimate of the future constant annual dividend growth rate. Use a 20% required rate of return to find the value of Seagate's stock immediately after it paid its 2019 dividend of $2.52.

P7–11 Common stock value: Constant growth The common stock of Barr Labs Inc. trades for $114 per share. Investors expect the company to pay a $1.35 dividend next year, and they expect that dividend to grow at a constant rate forever. If investors require a 15.8% return on this stock, what dividend growth rate do they anticipate?

Personal Finance Problem

P7–12 **Common stock value: Constant growth** Over the past 6 years, Elk County Telephone has paid the dividends shown in the following table.

Year	Dividend per share
2019	$2.87
2018	2.76
2017	2.60
2016	2.46
2015	2.37
2014	2.25

The firm's dividend per share in 2020 is expected to be $3.02.

a. If you can earn 13% on similar-risk investments, what is the most you would be willing to pay per share in 2019, just after the $2.87 dividend?

b. If you can earn only 10% on similar-risk investments, what is the most you would be willing to pay per share?

c. Compare and contrast your findings in parts **a** and **b**, and discuss the impact of changing risk on share value.

MyLab

P7–13 **Common stock value: Variable growth** Newman Manufacturing is considering a cash purchase of the stock of Grips Tool. During the year just completed, Grips earned $4.25 per share and paid cash dividends of $2.55 per share ($D_0 = 2.55$). Grips' earnings and dividends are expected to grow at 25% per year for the next 3 years, after which they are expected to grow at 10% per year to infinity. What is the maximum price per share that Newman should pay for Grips if it has a required return of 15% on investments with risk characteristics similar to those of Grips?

Personal Finance Problem

P7–14 **Common stock value: Variable growth** Home Place Hotels Inc. is entering into a 3-year remodeling and expansion project. The construction will have a limiting effect on earnings during that time, but when completed, it should allow the company to enjoy much improved growth in earnings and dividends. Last year, the company paid a dividend of $3.40. It expects zero growth in the next year. In years 2 and 3, 5% growth is expected, and in year 4, 15% growth. In year 5 and thereafter, growth should be a constant 10% per year. What is the maximum price per share that an investor who requires a return of 14% should pay for Home Place Hotels common stock?

P7–15 **Common stock value: Variable growth** Lawrence Industries' most recent annual dividend was $1.80 per share ($D_0 = \$1.80$), and the firm's required return is 11%. Find the market value of Lawrence's shares when:

a. Dividends are expected to grow at 8% annually for 3 years, followed by a 5% constant annual growth rate in year 4 to infinity.

b. Dividends are expected to grow at 8% annually for 3 years, followed by a 0% constant annual growth rate in year 4 to infinity.

c. Dividends are expected to grow at 8% annually for 3 years, followed by a 10% constant annual growth rate in year 4 to infinity.

Personal Finance Problem

LG4

P7–16 **Free cash flow valuation** You are evaluating the potential purchase of a small business with no debt or preferred stock that is currently generating $42,500 of free cash flow (FCF_0 = $42,500). On the basis of a review of similar-risk investment opportunities, you must earn an 18% rate of return on the proposed purchase. Because you are relatively uncertain about future cash flows, you decide to estimate the firm's value using several possible assumptions about the growth rate of cash flows.

a. What is the firm's value if cash flows are expected to grow at an annual rate of 0% from now to infinity?

b. What is the firm's value if cash flows are expected to grow at a constant annual rate of 7% from now to infinity?

c. What is the firm's value if cash flows are expected to grow at an annual rate of 12% for the first 2 years, followed by a constant annual rate of 7% from year 3 to infinity?

P7–17 **Free cash flow valuation** Nabor Industries is considering going public but is unsure of a fair offering price for the company. Before hiring an investment banker to assist in making the public offering, managers at Nabor have decided to make their own estimate of the firm's common stock value. The firm's CFO has gathered data for performing the valuation using the free cash flow valuation model.

The firm's weighted average cost of capital is 11%, and it has $1,500,000 of debt and $400,000 of preferred stock in terms of market value. The estimated free cash flows over the next 5 years, 2020 through 2024, are given below. Beyond 2024 to infinity, the firm expects its free cash flow to grow by 3% annually.

Year (t)	Free cash flow (FCF_t)
2020	$200,000
2021	250,000
2022	310,000
2023	350,000
2024	390,000

a. Estimate the value of Nabor Industries' entire company by using the free cash flow valuation model.

b. Use your finding in part **a**, along with the data provided above, to find Nabor Industries' common stock value.

c. If the firm plans to issue 200,000 shares of common stock, what is its estimated value per share?

Personal Finance Problem

P7–18 **Using the free cash flow valuation model to price an IPO** Assume that you have an opportunity to buy the stock of CoolTech Inc., an IPO being offered for $12.50 per share. Although you are very much interested in owning the company, you are concerned about whether it is fairly priced. To determine the value of the shares, you have decided to apply the free cash flow valuation model to the firm's financial data that you've accumulated from a variety of data sources. The key values you have compiled are summarized in the following table.

Free cash flow		Other data
Year (t)	FCF_t	
2020	$ 700,000	Growth rate of FCF, beyond 2023 to infinity = 2%
2021	800,000	Weighted average cost of capital = 8%
2022	950,000	Market value of all debt = $2,700,000
2023	1,100,000	Market value of preferred stock = $1,000,000
		Number of shares of common stock outstanding = 1,100,000

a. Use the free cash flow valuation model to estimate CoolTech's common stock value per share.
b. Judging by your finding in part **a** and the stock's offering price, should you buy the stock?
c. On further analysis, you find that the growth rate of FCF beyond 2023 will be 3% rather than 2%. What effect would this finding have on your responses in parts **a** and **b**?

LG5

P7–19 **Book and liquidation value** The balance sheet for Gallinas Industries is as follows.

Gallinas Industries Balance Sheet as of December 31			
Assets		**Liabilities and stockholders' equity**	
Cash	$ 40,000	Accounts payable	$100,000
Marketable securities	60,000	Notes payable	30,000
Accounts receivable	120,000	Accrued wages	30,000
Inventories	160,000	Total current liabilities	$160,000
Total current assets	$380,000	Long-term debt	$180,000
Land and buildings (net)	$150,000	Preferred stock	$ 80,000
Machinery and equipment	250,000	Common stock (10,000 shares)	260,000
Total fixed assets (net)	$400,000	Retained earnings	100,000
Total assets	$780,000	Total liabilities and stockholders' equity	$780,000

Additional information with respect to the firm is available:
(1) Preferred stock can be liquidated at book value.
(2) Accounts receivable and inventories can be liquidated at 90% of book value.
(3) The firm has 10,000 shares of common stock outstanding.
(4) All interest and dividends are currently paid up.
(5) Land and buildings can be liquidated at 130% of book value.
(6) Machinery and equipment can be liquidated at 70% of book value.
(7) Cash and marketable securities can be liquidated at book value.

Given this information, answer the following:
a. What is Gallinas Industries' book value per share?
b. What is its liquidation value per share?
c. Compare, contrast, and discuss the values found in parts **a** and **b**.

P7–20 **Valuation with price/earnings multiples** For each of the firms shown in the following table, use the data given to estimate its common stock value employing price/earnings (P/E) multiples.

Firm	Expected EPS	Price/earnings multiple
A	$3.00	6.2
B	4.50	10.0
C	1.80	12.6
D	2.40	8.9
E	5.10	15.0

P7–21 **Management action and stock value** REH Corporation's most recent dividend was $3 per share, its expected annual rate of dividend growth is 5%, and the required return is now 15%. A variety of proposals are being considered by management to redirect the firm's activities. Determine the impact on share price for each of the following proposed actions, and indicate the best alternative.

a. Do nothing, which will leave the key financial variables unchanged.
b. Invest in a new machine that will increase the dividend growth rate to 6% and lower the required return to 14%.
c. Eliminate an unprofitable product line, which will increase the dividend growth rate to 7% and raise the required return to 17%.
d. Merge with another firm, which will reduce the growth rate to 4% and raise the required return to 16%.
e. Acquire a subsidiary operation from another manufacturer. The acquisition should increase the dividend growth rate to 8% and increase the required return to 17%.

P7–22 **Integrative: Risk and valuation** Given the following information for the stock of Foster Company, calculate the risk premium on its common stock.

Current price per share of common	$50.00
Expected dividend per share next year	$ 3.00
Constant annual dividend growth rate	6.5%
Risk-free rate of return	4.5%

P7–23 **Integrative: Risk and valuation** Giant Enterprises' stock has a required return of 14.8%. The company, which plans to pay a dividend of $2.60 per share in the coming year, anticipates that its future dividends will increase at an annual rate consistent with that experienced over the 2013–2019 period, when the following dividends were paid.

Year	Dividend per share
2019	$2.45
2018	2.28
2017	2.10
2016	1.95
2015	1.82
2014	1.80
2013	1.73

a. If the risk-free rate is 4%, what is the risk premium on Giant's stock?
b. Using the constant-growth dividend model, estimate the value of Giant's stock.
c. Explain what effect, if any, a decrease in the risk premium would have on the value of Giant's stock.

P7–24 **Integrative: Risk and valuation** Hamlin Steel Company wishes to determine the value of Craft Foundry, a firm that it is considering acquiring for cash. Hamlin wishes to determine the applicable discount rate to use as an input to the constant-growth valuation model. Craft's stock is not publicly traded. After studying the required returns of firms similar to Craft that are publicly traded, Hamlin believes that an appropriate risk premium on Craft stock is about 9%. The risk-free rate is currently 5%. Craft's dividend per share for each of the past 6 years is shown in the following table.

Year	Dividend per share
2019	$3.44
2018	3.28
2017	3.15
2016	2.90
2015	2.75
2014	2.45

a. Given that Craft is expected to pay a dividend of $3.68 next year, determine the maximum cash price that Hamlin should pay for each share of Craft.
b. Describe the effect on the resulting value of Craft of
   (1) A decrease in its dividend growth rate of 2% from that exhibited over the 2014–2019 period.
   (2) A decrease in its risk premium to 4%.

P7–25 **ETHICS PROBLEM** Melissa is trying to value the stock of Generic Utility Inc., which is clearly not growing at all. Generic declared and paid a $5 dividend last year. The required return for utility stocks is 11%, but Melissa is unsure about the financial reporting integrity of Generic's finance team. She decides to add an extra 1% "credibility" risk premium to the required return as part of her valuation analysis.
a. What is the value of Generic's stock, assuming that the financials are trustworthy?
b. What is the value of Generic's stock, assuming that Melissa includes the extra 1% "credibility" risk premium?
c. What is the difference between the values found in parts **a** and **b**, and how might one interpret that difference?

SPREADSHEET EXERCISE

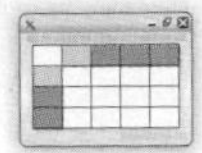

You are interested in purchasing the common stock of Azure Corporation. The firm recently paid a dividend of $3 per share. It expects its earnings—and hence its dividends—to grow at a rate of 7% for the foreseeable future. Currently, similar-risk stocks have required returns of 10%.

TO DO

a. Given the data above, calculate the present value of this security. Use the constant-growth dividend model (Equation 7.4) to find the stock value.

b. One year later, your broker offers to sell you additional shares of Azure at $73. The most recent dividend paid was $3.21, and the expected growth rate for earnings remains at 7%. If you determine that the appropriate risk premium is 6.74% and you observe that the risk-free rate, R_F, is currently 5.25%, what is the firm's current required return?

c. Applying Equation 7.4, determine the value of the stock using the new dividend and required return from part **b.**

d. Given your calculation in part **c**, would you buy the additional shares from your broker at $73 per share? Explain.

e. Given your calculation in part **c**, would you sell your old shares for $73? Explain.

MyLab Finance Visit www.pearson.com/mylab/finance for **Chapter Case:** ***Assessing the Impact of Suarez Manufacturing's Proposed Risky Investment on Its Stock Value,*** Group Exercises, and numerous online resources.

Encore International

In the world of trendsetting fashion, instinct and marketing savvy are prerequisites to success. Jordan Ellis had both. During 2019, his international casual-wear company, Encore, rocketed to $300 million in sales after 10 years in business. His fashion line covered young women from head to toe with hats, sweaters, dresses, blouses, skirts, pants, sweatshirts, socks, and shoes. In Manhattan, an Encore shop was found every five or six blocks, each featuring a different color. Some shops showed the entire line in lapis blue, and others featured it in grenadine.

Encore had made it. The company's historical growth was so spectacular that no one could have predicted it. However, securities analysts speculated that Encore could not keep up the pace. They warned that competition is fierce in the fashion industry and that the firm might encounter little or no growth in the future. They estimated that stockholders also should expect no growth in future dividends.

Contrary to the conservative securities analysts, Jordan Ellis believed that the company could maintain a constant annual growth rate in dividends per share of 6% in the future, or possibly 8% for the next 2 years and 6% thereafter. Ellis based his estimates on an established long-term expansion plan into European and Latin American markets. Venturing into these markets was expected to cause the risk of the firm, as measured by the risk premium on its stock, to increase immediately from 8.8% to 10%. Currently, the risk-free rate is 6%.

In preparing the long-term financial plan, Encore's chief financial officer has assigned a junior financial analyst, Marc Scott, to evaluate the firm's current stock price. He has asked Marc to consider the conservative predictions of the securities analysts and the aggressive predictions of the company founder, Jordan Ellis.

Marc has compiled the following 2019 financial data to aid his analysis.

Data item	2019 value
Earnings per share (EPS)	$6.25
Price per share of common stock	$40.00
Book value of common stock equity	$60,000,000
Total common shares outstanding	2,500,000
Common stock dividend per share	$4.00

TO DO

a. What is the firm's current book value per share?

b. What is the firm's current P/E ratio?

c. (1) What is the current required return for Encore stock?

(2) What will be the new required return for Encore stock, assuming that the firm expands into European and Latin American markets as planned?

d. If the securities analysts are correct and there is no growth in future dividends, what will be the value per share of the Encore stock? (*Note:* Use the new required return on the company's stock here.)

e. (1) If Jordan Ellis's predictions are correct, what will be the value per share of Encore stock if the firm maintains a constant annual 6% growth rate in future dividends? (*Note:* Continue to use the new required return here.)

(2) If Jordan Ellis's predictions are correct, what will be the value per share of Encore stock if the firm maintains a constant annual 8% growth rate in dividends per share over the next 2 years and 6% thereafter?

f. Compare the current (2019) price of the stock and the stock values found in parts **a**, **d**, and **e**. Discuss why these values may differ. Which valuation method do you believe most clearly represents the true value of the Encore stock?

PART FOUR

Risk and the Required Rate of Return

CHAPTERS IN THIS PART

Most people intuitively understand the principle that risk and return are linked. After all, as the old saying goes, "Nothing ventured, nothing gained." In the next two chapters, we'll explore how investors and financial managers quantify risk and how they determine what amount of additional return is appropriate compensation for taking extra risk.

Chapter 8 lays the groundwork, defining the terms risk and return and explaining why investors think about risk in different ways, depending on whether they want to understand the risk of a specific investment or the risk of a broad portfolio of investments. Perhaps the most famous and widely applied theory in all finance, the capital asset pricing model (or CAPM), is introduced here. The CAPM tells investors and managers alike what return they should expect given the risk of the asset they want to invest in.

Chapter 9 applies these lessons in a managerial finance setting. Firms raise money from two broad sources, owners and lenders. Owners provide equity financing and lenders provide debt. To maximize the value of the firm, managers have to satisfy both groups, and doing so means earning returns high enough to meet investors' expectations. Chapter 9 focuses on the cost of capital or, more precisely, the weighted average cost of capital (WACC). The WACC tells managers exactly what return their investments in plant and equipment, advertising, and human resources have to earn if the firm is to satisfy its investors. Essentially, the WACC is a hurdle rate, the minimum acceptable return that a firm should earn on any investment it makes.

CHAPTER 8

Risk and Return

LEARNING GOALS

LG 1 Understand the meaning and fundamentals of risk, return, and risk preferences.

LG 2 Describe procedures for assessing and measuring the risk of a single asset.

LG 3 Discuss the measurement of return and standard deviation for a portfolio and the concept of correlation.

LG 4 Understand the risk and return characteristics of a portfolio in terms of correlation and diversification and the impact of international assets on a portfolio.

LG 5 Review the two types of risk and the derivation and role of beta in measuring the relevant risk of both a security and a portfolio.

LG 6 Explain the capital asset pricing model (CAPM), its relationship to the security market line (SML), and the major forces causing shifts in the SML.

MyLab Finance Chapter Introduction Video

WHY THIS CHAPTER MATTERS TO YOU

In your *professional* life

ACCOUNTING You need to understand the relationship between risk and return because of the effect that riskier projects will have on the firm's financial statements.

INFORMATION SYSTEMS You need to understand how to do scenario and correlation analyses to build decision packages that help management analyze the risk and return of various business opportunities.

MANAGEMENT You need to understand the relationship between risk and return and how to measure that relationship to evaluate data that come from finance personnel and translate those data into decisions that increase the value of the firm.

OPERATIONS You need to understand why investments in plant, equipment, and systems need to be evaluated in light of their impact on the firm's risk and return, which together will affect the firm's value.

In your *personal* life

The tradeoff between risk and return enters into numerous personal financial decisions. You will use these two concepts when you invest your savings, buy real estate, finance major purchases, purchase insurance, invest in securities, and implement retirement plans. Deepening your quantitative and qualitative understanding of risk and return will help you make decisions based on the tradeoffs between risk and return in light of your personal disposition toward risk.

Matthew Staver/Bloomberg/Getty Images

LEGG MASON GLOBAL ASSET MANAGEMENT

Miller's Time

For more than a decade, Bill Miller stood at the top of the investment world. The mutual fund that he managed, the Legg Mason Value Trust, had outperformed the Standard & Poor's 500 Stock Composite Index for 15 consecutive years, a record still unmatched by any other portfolio manager. From 1991 to 2005, the S&P 500 earned an average return of 12.7%, while Miller's fund averaged 16.4%. That performance attracted lots of new investors, and Miller's fund grew to more than $20 billion under management.

Whether that string was due to skill or luck, it ended in 2006. Miller trailed the index in 4 of the next 5 years, sometimes by a wide margin. During that period, Miller ranked in the bottom 1% of all stock fund managers, and investors left in droves. Even worse, Miller faced thinly veiled ridicule in the film *The Big Short*, in which a character named Bruce Miller displayed comic overconfidence in the belief that the housing market and the financial sector would not falter in 2008. By the time Miller handed over management of the Value Trust to his successor in April 2012, assets under management had fallen to $2.8 billion.

Just 1 year later, however, Miller was on top again. In the 12 months ended on March 31, 2013, the Legg Mason Opportunity fund that Miller managed with Samantha McLemore was the top-performing fund in its category. One reason was that Miller and McLemore placed a large bet on a recovery in financial stocks, the same kind of bet that cost Miller dearly during the financial crisis. More than 34% of the Opportunity fund's assets were invested in financial stocks such as Bank of America, and this time the bet paid off.

Source: Peter DeMarzo

Unfortunately for his investors, Miller trailed the market for the next 3 years, prompting his employer, Legg Mason, to cut ties with the company's most famous portfolio manager after 35 years. Miller's career reveals several important lessons related to risk and return, the subject of this chapter. First, with an investment that offers very high returns (whether that investment is a fund or a stock or anything else), high risk is usually lurking somewhere. Second, the risk of an undiversified (or poorly diversified) portfolio is higher than that of a well-diversified portfolio. Third, it is extremely difficult to earn abnormal (i.e., above average) returns for an extended period, even if you are a professional investor.

LG1

8.1 Risk and Return Fundamentals

portfolio
A collection or group of assets.

Most important business decisions entail two key financial considerations: risk and return. Each financial decision presents certain risk and return characteristics, and the combination of these characteristics can increase or decrease a firm's share price. Analysts use different methods to quantify risk, depending on whether they are looking at a single asset or a **portfolio**—a collection or group of assets. We will look at both, beginning with the risk of a single asset. First, though, it is important to introduce some fundamental ideas about risk, return, and risk preferences.

WHAT IS RISK?

risk
A measure of the uncertainty surrounding the return that an investment will earn.

In the most basic sense, **risk** is a measure of the uncertainty surrounding the return that an investment will earn. Investments whose returns are more uncertain are generally riskier. A $1,000 government bond that guarantees its holder $5 interest after 30 days has no risk because there is no uncertainty associated with the return. A $1,000 investment in a firm's common stock is very risky because the value of that stock may move up or down substantially over the same 30 days.

WHAT IS RETURN?

total rate of return
The total gain or loss experienced on an investment over a given period expressed as a percentage of the investment's value; calculated by dividing the asset's cash distributions during the period, plus change in value, by its beginning-of-period value.

If risk is related to the uncertainty surrounding an investment's return, we must be certain we know how to measure an investment's return. The **total rate of return** is the total gain or loss experienced on an investment over a given period expressed as a percentage of the investment's value at the beginning of the period. Mathematically, an investment's total return is the sum of any cash distributions (e.g., dividends or interest payments) plus the change in the investment's value, divided by the beginning-of-period value. The expression for calculating the total rate of return earned on any asset over period t, r_t, is commonly defined as

$$r_t = \frac{C_t + P_t - P_{t-1}}{P_{t-1}} \quad (8.1)$$

where

$$r_t = \text{total return during period } t$$
$$C_t = \text{cash (flow) received from the asset investment in period } t$$
$$P_t = \text{price (value) of asset at time } t$$
$$P_{t-1} = \text{price (value) of asset at time } t - 1$$

The return, r_t, reflects the combined effect of cash flow, C_t, and changes in value, $P_t - P_{t-1}$, over the period.[1]

FOCUS ON ETHICS *in practice*

If It Seems Too Good to Be True, It Probably Is

For years, investors clamored to put their money with Bernard Madoff. They may not have understood his secret trading system, but they loved his double-digit returns. Madoff's impeccable credentials—he once chaired the board of directors of the NASDAQ Stock Market—silenced the few skeptics, but beating the market consistently for your clients usually requires taking more risk or committing fraud. Bernie's investors learned the hard way about fraud when authorities closed Madoff's operation and arrested him in December 2008. He ultimately admitted his wealth-management business was a giant Ponzi scheme.

Such a scheme— named for its most notorious practitioner, Charles Ponzi—involves promising initial investors eye-popping, low-risk returns, then fraudulently paying them off with money from new investors. Two ingredients make it work—a plausible explanation for the returns and investors greedy enough not to ask questions. In December 1919, Ponzi launched a Boston company to buy postage coupons in Europe that, presumably, could be traded in the United States for American stamps worth much more. He boasted this strategy would generate enough profit to pay investors a 50% return at a time when bank deposits offered only 5% annually. Eight months later, the scam ended as all Ponzi schemes do—when new investors stopped wanting in, and current investors started wanting out. The trigger was newspaper stories with skeptical questions like, where were the 160 million in postage coupons needed to deliver promised returns? For costing his investors over $240 million in today's dollars, Ponzi spent nearly 11 years in prison.

Madoff's scheme ran much longer and on a much bigger scale. He credited mysterious, complex trades for great performance year after year, even when markets tanked. To his investors, dependably high returns with low risk were plausible given Madoff's history and stature on Wall Street. Rival fund managers grew skeptical, however, when attempts to reverse engineer and replicate Bernie's trading strategies fell far short of matching his results. In November 2005, Harry Markopolos submitted a detailed report to the Securities and Exchange Commission titled, "The World's Largest Hedge Fund Is a Fraud," but after a cursory investigation Madoff was cleared. The scam began unraveling in fall 2008 when Bernie's investors tried to cash in—ironically not fearing fraud but as part of general flight to safe assets during the financial crisis.

For costing his investors an estimated $17.5 *billion*, Madoff received a 150-years prison sentence. But the ripple effects went far beyond his fleeced clients. Recent research indicates, for example, other investors with social connections to Madoff clients started transferring funds from professionally managed accounts to insured bank deposits soon after the scandal broke. The large sums transferred ultimately forced a number of investment advisors to close up shop.

▶ *What are warning signs that an investment advisor's activities may be suspect? Both Ponzi and Madoff claimed later they knew what they were doing was wrong, but they expected to earn enough eventually to deliver on their promises. Do you believe them?*

Sources: www.sec.gov/news/studies/2009/oig-509/exhibit-0293.pdf and https://corpgov.law.harvard.edu/2016/02/18/trust-busting-the-effect-of-fraud-on-investor-behavior/

1. This expression does not imply that an investor necessarily buys the asset at time $t - 1$ and sells it at time t. Rather, it represents the increase (or decrease) in wealth that the investor has experienced during the period by holding a particular investment.

Equation 8.1 is used to determine the rate of return over a time period as short as 1 day or as long as 10 years or more. In the most common situation, t is 1 year, and r therefore represents an annual rate of return.

EXAMPLE 8.1

MyLab Finance Solution Video

Robin wishes to determine the return on two stocks she owned during 2016, Apple Inc. and Wal-Mart. At the beginning of the year, Apple stock traded for $105.35 per share, and Wal-Mart stock was valued at $61.46. During the year, Apple paid $2.37 per share in dividends, and Wal-Mart shareholders received dividends of $2.00 per share. At the end of the year, Apple stock was worth $115.82, and Wal-Mart stock sold for $69.12. Substituting into Equation 8.1, we can calculate the annual rate of return, r, for each stock:

$$\text{Apple: } (\$2.37 + \$115.82 - \$105.35) \div \$105.35 = 12.2\%$$
$$\text{Wal-Mart: } (\$2.00 + \$69.12 - \$61.46) \div \$61.46 = 15.7\%$$

Robin made money on both stocks in 2016. On a percentage basis, her return was higher on Wal-Mart stock, though her profit in dollar terms was greater with Apple stock.

expected return
The return that an asset is expected to generate in the future, composed of a risk-free rate plus a risk premium.

The preceding example focused on the historical returns actually earned (also called *realized returns*) on two investments. This chapter concentrates on *expected returns* and the relationship between expected returns and risk. When corporate financial managers are making investment decisions, they need a way to estimate the expected returns their investment opportunities might earn. As the name implies, an asset's **expected return** is the return that the asset is expected to generate in some future time period, and it is composed of a risk-free rate plus a risk premium. Fundamentally, expected returns are driven by risk in the sense that riskier investments tend to produce higher returns. Even though the goal of this chapter is to understand the link between expected returns and risk, looking at historical returns is still instructive because it provides insights about the past behavior of different types of assets, especially how the returns produced by those assets are related to their risks.

Investment returns vary both over time and between different types of investments. By averaging historical returns over a long period, we can focus on the returns that different kinds of investments tend to generate. Table 8.1 shows both the nominal and real (i.e., after inflation) average annual rates of return from 1900 to 2016 for three different types of investments: Treasury bills, Treasury bonds, and common stocks. Although bills and bonds are both issued by the U.S. government and are therefore relatively safe investments, bills have maturities of 1 year or less, whereas bonds have maturities ranging up to 30 years. Consequently, the interest rate risk associated with Treasury bonds is much higher than with bills. Over the past 117 years, bills earned the lowest returns, just 3.8% per year

TABLE 8.1 Historical Returns on Selected Investments (1900–2016)

Investment	Average nominal return	Average real return
Treasury bills	3.8%	0.9%
Treasury bonds	5.3	2.5
Common stocks	11.4	8.4

Source: Elroy Dimson, Paul Marsh, Mike Staunton, *Credit Suisse Global Investment Returns Yearbook 2017*.

on average in nominal terms and only 0.9% annually in real terms. The latter number means that the average Treasury bill return barely exceeded the average rate of inflation. Bond returns were higher at 5.3% in nominal terms and 2.5% in real terms. Clearly, though, stocks outshone the other types of investments, earning average annual nominal returns of 11.4% and average real returns of 8.4%.

In light of these statistics, you might wonder why anyone would invest in bonds or bills if the returns on stocks are so much higher. The answer, as you will soon see, is that stocks are much riskier than either bonds or bills and that risk leads some investors to prefer the safer, albeit lower, returns on Treasury securities.

RISK PREFERENCES

Different people react to risk in different ways. Economists use three categories to describe how investors respond to risk. First, investors who are **risk seeking** prefer investments with higher risk, so much so that they may choose investments with very low expected returns for the thrill of taking extra risk. Although most individuals do not exhibit this behavior most of the time, it is not difficult to find examples of risk-seeking behavior, particularly in the realm of gambling. By design, the average person who buys a lottery ticket or gambles in a casino loses money. After all, state governments and casinos make money from these endeavors, which implies that individuals lose on average and the expected return is negative. People nonetheless buy lottery tickets and visit casinos, and in doing so they exhibit risk-seeking behavior.

risk seeking
The attitude toward risk in which investors prefer investments with greater risk, perhaps even if they have lower expected returns.

A second attitude toward risk is risk neutrality. Investors who are **risk neutral** choose investments based solely on their expected returns, disregarding the risks. When choosing between two investments, *risk-neutral investors will always select the investment with the higher expected return regardless of its risk.*

risk neutral
The attitude toward risk in which investors choose the investment with the higher expected return regardless of its risk.

The third category of behavior with respect to risk, *and the one that describes the behavior of most people most of the time,* is risk aversion. Investors who are **risk averse** prefer less risky over more risky investments, holding the expected rate of return fixed. A risk-averse investor who believes that two different investments have the same expected return will choose the investment whose returns are more certain. However, note that it is not correct to say that a risk-averse investor always shies away from risk. Risk-averse investors merely require compensation (in the form of a higher return) to induce them to purchase riskier assets. Stated another way, when choosing between two investments, *a risk-averse investor will not make the riskier investment unless it offers a higher expected return to compensate the investor for bearing the additional risk.*

risk averse
The attitude toward risk in which investors require an increased expected return as compensation for an increase in risk.

Most people have an intuitive understanding that stocks are riskier than bonds. If we take that as a given, then Table 8.1 provides direct evidence that the market is dominated by risk-averse investors. In equilibrium, stocks *must* pay higher returns (on average) than bonds; otherwise, risk-averse investors would not buy stocks. However, even among risk-averse investors, the degree to which individuals can tolerate risk varies a great deal. One investor, observing in Table 8.1 that stocks pay an average annual return that is 6.1% higher than the average return on bonds, might decide that a risk premium of that magnitude is more than enough justification for investing in stocks. Another person might prefer to invest in bonds, even though they offer much lower returns, because they are not as risky as stocks. Both investors are risk averse, but they differ in terms of their *risk tolerance.* Investors with a low risk tolerance (or a high degree of risk aversion) require a very large risk premium to induce them to hold riskier assets. Investors with a high risk tolerance will invest in riskier assets for a much lower risk premium.

→ **REVIEW QUESTIONS** MyLab Finance Solutions

8–1 What is risk in the context of financial decision making?

8–2 Define return, and describe how to find the total rate of return on an investment.

8–3 Compare the following risk preferences: (a) risk averse, (b) risk neutral, and (c) risk seeking. Which risk preference is most common among financial managers? What is the difference between risk aversion and risk tolerance?

8.2 Risk of a Single Asset

In this section, we refine our understanding of risk. Surprisingly, the concept of risk changes when the focus shifts from the risk of a single asset held in isolation to the risk of a portfolio of assets. Here, we examine different statistical methods to quantify risk; later, we apply those methods to portfolios.

RISK ASSESSMENT

The notion that risk is somehow connected to uncertainty is intuitive. The more uncertain you are about how an investment will perform, the riskier that investment seems. Scenario analysis provides a simple way to quantify that intuition, and probability distributions offer a more sophisticated method for analyzing the risk of an investment.

scenario analysis
An approach for assessing risk that uses several possible alternative outcomes (scenarios) to obtain a sense of the variability among returns.

range
A measure of an asset's risk, which is found by subtracting the return associated with the pessimistic (worst) outcome from the return associated with the optimistic (best) outcome.

Scenario Analysis

Scenario analysis uses several possible alternative outcomes (scenarios) to obtain a sense of the variability of returns. One common method involves considering pessimistic (worst), most likely (expected), and optimistic (best) outcomes and the returns associated with them for a given asset. Given these scenarios, one way to quantify risk is to measure the range of possible outcomes. The **range** is the difference between the return provided by the optimistic and pessimistic scenarios. Intuitively, an asset with a greater range of possible returns seems more risky.

EXAMPLE 8.2

Norman Company, a manufacturer of custom golf equipment, wants to choose the better of two investments, A and B. Each requires an initial outlay of \$10,000, and each has a most likely annual rate of return of 15%. Management has estimated returns associated with each investment's pessimistic and optimistic outcomes. The three estimates for each asset, along with its range, are given in Table 8.2. Asset A appears to be less risky than asset B; its range of 4% (17% − 13%) is less than the range of 16% (23% − 7%) for asset B. The risk-averse

TABLE 8.2 Assets A and B

	Asset A	Asset B
Initial investment	\$10,000	\$10,000
Annual rate of return		
Pessimistic	13%	7%
Most likely	15%	15%
Optimistic	17%	23%
Range	4%	16%

decision maker would prefer asset A over asset B, because A offers the same most likely return as B (15%), with lower risk (smaller range).

It's not unusual for financial managers to think about the best and worst possible outcomes when they are in the early stages of analyzing a new investment project. No matter how great the intuitive appeal of this approach, looking at the range of outcomes that an investment might produce is a highly unsophisticated way of measuring its risk. More refined methods require some basic statistical tools.

Probability Distributions

probability
The *chance* that a given outcome will occur.

Probability distributions provide a more quantitative insight into an asset's risk. The **probability** of a given outcome is its *chance* of occurring. We would expect that an outcome with an 80% probability would occur 8 out of 10 times. An outcome with a probability of 100% is certain to occur. Outcomes with a probability of zero will never occur.

EXAMPLE 8.3

Norman Company's past estimates indicate that the probabilities of the pessimistic, most likely, and optimistic outcomes are 25%, 50%, and 25%, respectively. Note that the sum of these probabilities must equal 100%; that is, the probability distribution must assign a probability to every possible outcome such that no other outcomes are possible.

MATTER OF FACT

Beware of the Black Swan

Is it ever possible to know for sure that a particular outcome can never happen–that the chance of its occurrence is 0%? In the 2007 bestseller *The Black Swan: The Impact of the Highly Improbable*, Nassim Nicholas Taleb argues that seemingly improbable or even impossible events are more likely to occur than most people think, especially in the area of finance. The book's title refers to a long-held belief that all swans were white, a belief held by many people until a black variety was discovered in Australia. Taleb reportedly earned a large fortune during the 2007–2008 financial crisis by betting that financial markets would plummet.

probability distribution
A model that relates probabilities to the associated outcomes.

bar chart
The simplest type of probability distribution; shows only a limited number of outcomes and associated probabilities for a given event.

A **probability distribution** is a model that relates probabilities to the associated outcomes. The simplest type of probability distribution is the **bar chart**. The bar charts for Norman Company's assets A and B are shown in Figure 8.1. Although both assets have the same average return, the range of return is much greater, or more dispersed, for asset B than for asset A: 16% versus 4%.

FIGURE 8.1

Bar Charts
Bar charts for asset A's and asset B's returns

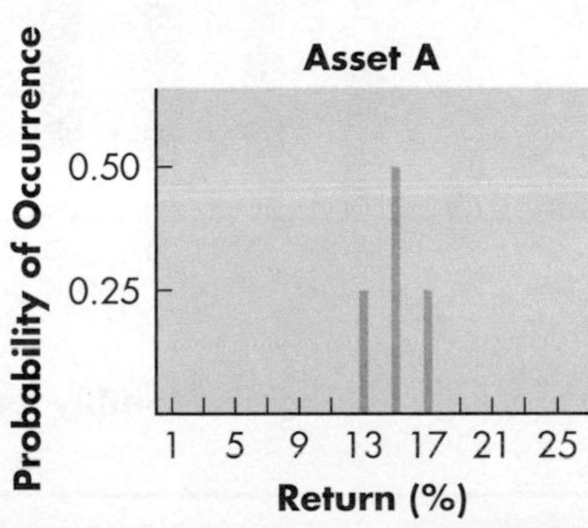

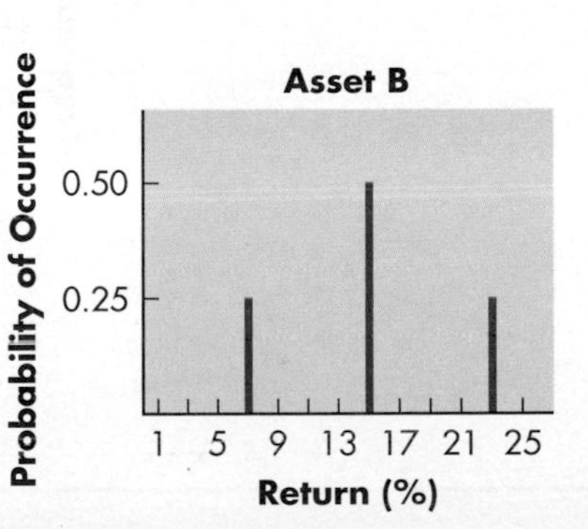

Most investments have more than two or three possible outcomes, and in most cases the probability of each outcome is unknown. One way to deal with such problems is to create a bar chart using historical data on actual returns. Figure 8.2 shows two such charts, one for Google and one for Coca-Cola, which use historical monthly returns on these two stocks from 2007 to 2017. The charts group monthly returns into bins or ranges and then show the relative frequency with which returns fell into each bin historically. For example, in the bottom part of Figure 8.2, we can see that

FIGURE 8.2

Bar Charts for Coca-Cola and Google

The bar charts use monthly returns from 2007 to 2017 on Coca-Cola and Google stock to illustrate the historical likelihood of each stock generating a return of a given magnitude.

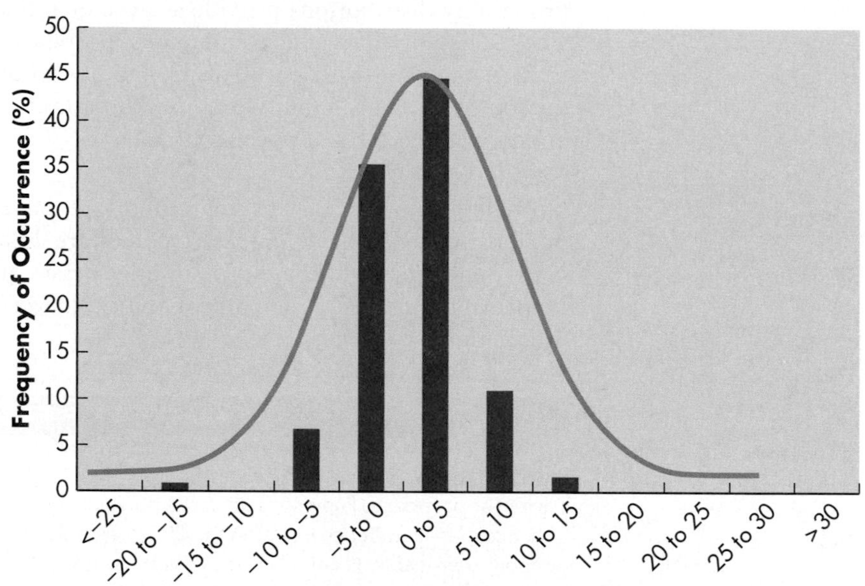

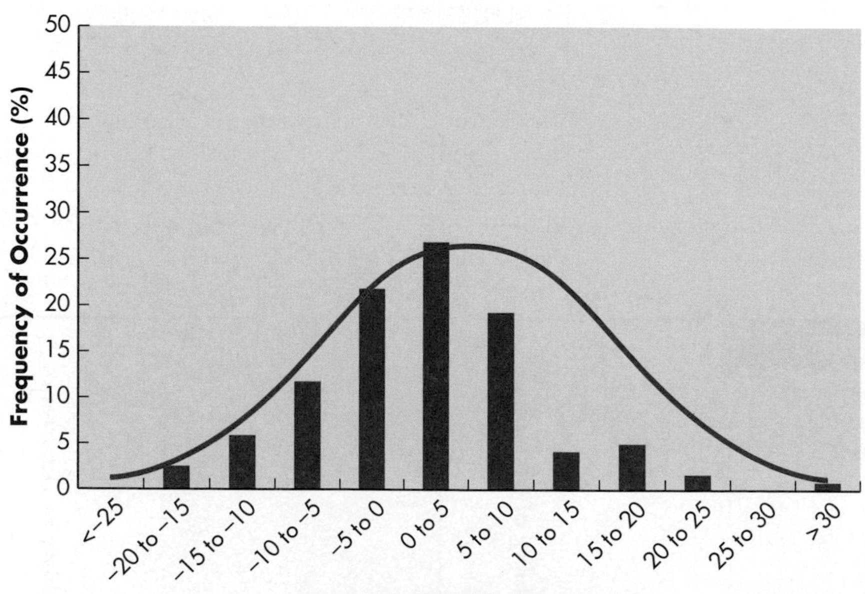

about 27% of the time the monthly return on Google stock was between 0% and 5%. Coca-Cola's monthly return was between 0% and 5% much more often, about 45% of the time over that decade. Google's returns were far more likely to be very high or low than were Coca-Cola's. For example, Google stock achieved a monthly return of between 15% and 20% about 5% of the time, whereas Coca-Cola stock never performed that well in a single month between 2007 and 2017. In principle, we could use these historical frequencies to form estimates of the probabilities of different return outcomes for Google and Coca-Cola on a forward-looking basis.

If we had many more data points for Google and Coca-Cola monthly stock returns, the bar charts in Figure 8.2 would begin to look more and more like smooth curves representing a **continuous probability distribution**. This type of distribution can be thought of as a bar chart for a very large number of outcomes. Figure 8.2 superimposes continuous probability distributions on the bar charts for Google and Coca-Cola. It should be evident from the figure that Google stock returns have much greater dispersion than the distribution for Coca-Cola. Intuitively, Google seems more risky than Coca-Cola.

continuous probability distribution
A probability distribution showing all the possible outcomes and associated probabilities for a given event.

RISK MEASUREMENT

In addition to considering the range of returns that an investment might produce, the risk of an asset can be measured quantitatively with statistics. The most common statistical measure used to describe an investment's risk is its standard deviation.

Standard Deviation

standard deviation (σ)
The most common statistical indicator of an asset's risk; it measures the dispersion around the average.

The **standard deviation**, σ, measures the dispersion or volatility of an investment's return around the average return. We can think about an investment's average return in two ways. First, if we know all the different returns that an investment might generate, along with their associated probabilities, we define the average return, $\bar{r}$, as follows:

$$\bar{r} = \sum_{j=1}^{n} r_j \times Pr_j \tag{8.2}$$

where

r_j = return for the jth outcome
Pr_j = probability of occurrence of the jth outcome
n = number of outcomes considered

As we have already noted, in most situations we do not know every possible outcome, nor do we know the probabilities of each outcome. In that case, we estimate an investment's average return simply by taking the arithmetic mean from a series of historical returns

$$\bar{r} = \frac{\sum_{j=1}^{n} r_j}{n} \tag{8.2a}$$

where n is the number of historical returns over which we are taking the average.[2]

2. Note that if there are n outcomes and each outcome has the same probability, $1/n$, then Equations 8.2 and 8.2a are identical.

EXAMPLE 8.4

Table 8.3 presents the average returns for Norman Company's assets A and B. Column 1 gives the Pr_j's, and column 2 gives the r_j's. In each case, $n = 3$. Each asset's average return is 15%.

TABLE 8.3 Average Returns for Assets A and B

Possible outcomes	Probability Pr_j	Returns r_j	$Pr_j \times r_j$
Asset A			
Pessimistic	0.25	13%	3.25%
Most likely	0.50	15	7.50
Optimistic	0.25	17	4.25
Total	1.00		Average return 15.00%
Asset B			
Pessimistic	0.25	7%	1.75%
Most likely	0.50	15	7.50
Optimistic	0.25	23	5.75
Total	1.00		Average 15.00%

Once we determine an investment's average return, then we can calculate the standard deviation. As before, the formula we use to calculate the standard deviation depends on whether we know each possible return outcome and its associated probability or whether we do not have that information. When outcomes and their probabilities are known, the expression for the *standard deviation of returns*, σ, is

$$\sigma = \sqrt{\sum_{j=1}^{n} (r_j - \bar{r})^2 \times Pr_j} \tag{8.3}$$

In the more common situation of knowing neither the full list of possible outcomes nor their associated probabilities, we estimate the standard deviation using n observations of historical data, using the following formula:

$$\sigma = \sqrt{\frac{\sum_{j=1}^{n} (r_j - \bar{r})^2}{n - 1}} \tag{8.3a}$$

An asset with a high standard deviation has returns that fluctuate more than does an asset with a low standard deviation.

EXAMPLE 8.5

Table 8.4 presents the standard deviations for Norman Company's assets A and B, based on the data in Table 8.3. The standard deviation for asset A is 1.41%, and the standard deviation for asset B is 5.66%. The higher volatility of asset B's returns is clearly reflected in the higher standard deviation.

TABLE 8.4 Calculating the Standard Deviation of the Returns for Assets A and B

Asset A	Squared deviation	Probability	
j	$(r_j - \bar{r})^2$	Pr_j	$(r_j - \bar{r})^2 \times Pr_j$
1	$(13\% - 15\%)^2 = 4\%^2$	0.25	$4\%^2 \times 0.25 = 1\%^2$
2	$(15\% - 15\%)^2 = 0\%^2$	0.50	$0\%^2 \times 0.25 = 0\%^2$
3	$(17\% - 15\%)^2 = 4\%^2$	0.25	$4\%^2 \times 0.25 = 1\%^2$

$$\sum_{j=1}^{3}(r_j - \bar{r})^2 \times Pr_j = 1\%^2 + 0\%^2 + 1\%^2 = 2\%^2$$

$$\sigma = \sqrt{\sum_{j=1}^{3}(r_j - \bar{r})^2 \times Pr_j} = \sqrt{2\%^2} = \underline{\underline{1.41\%}}$$

Asset B			
1	$(\ 7\% - 15\%)^2 = 64\%^2$	0.25	$64\%^2 \times 0.25 = 16\%^2$
2	$(15\% - 15\%)^2 = \ 0\%^2$	0.50	$0\%^2 \times 0.25 = \ 0\%^2$
3	$(23\% - 15\%)^2 = 64\%^2$	0.25	$64\%^2 \times 0.25 = 16\%^2$

$$\sum_{j=1}^{3}(r_j - \bar{r})^2 \times Pr_j = 16\%^2 + 0\%^2 + 16\%^2 = 32\%^2$$

$$\sigma = \sqrt{\sum_{j=1}^{3}(r_j - \bar{r})^2 \times Pr_j} = \sqrt{32\%^2} = \underline{\underline{5.66\%}}$$

Historical Returns and Risk We can now use the standard deviation as a measure of risk to assess the historical (1900–2016) investment return data in Table 8.1. Table 8.5 repeats the historical nominal average returns in column 1 and shows the standard deviations associated with each of them in column 2. A close relationship is evident between the investment returns and the standard deviations: Investments with higher returns have higher standard deviations. For example, stocks have the highest average return at 11.4%, which is nearly 4 times the average return on Treasury bills. At the same time, stocks are much more volatile, with a standard deviation of 19.8%, nearly 7 times greater than the 2.9% standard deviation of Treasury bills. If we accept the idea that the standard deviation is a valid way to quantify an investment's risk, the historical data confirm the existence of a positive relationship between risk and return. That relationship reflects *risk aversion* by market participants, who require higher returns as compensation for greater risk. The historical

MATTER OF FACT

All Stocks Are Not Created Equal

Table 8.5 shows that stocks are riskier than bonds, but are some stocks riskier than others? The answer is emphatically *yes*. A recent study examined the historical returns of large stocks and small stocks and found that the average annual return on large stocks from 1926 through 2016 was 12.0%, while small stocks earned 16.6% per year on average. The higher returns on small stocks came with a cost, however. The standard deviation of small stock returns was a whopping 31.9%, whereas the standard deviation on large stocks was just 19.9%.

TABLE 8.5 Historical Returns and Standard Deviations on Selected Investments (1900–2016)

Investment	Average nominal return	Standard deviation	Coefficient of variation
Treasury bills	3.8%	2.9%	0.76
Treasury bonds	5.3	9.0	1.70
Common stocks	11.4	19.8	1.74

Source: Elroy Dimson, Paul Marsh, Mike Staunton, *Credit Suisse Global Investment Returns Yearbook 2017.*

data in columns 1 and 2 of Table 8.5 clearly show that during the 1900–2016 period, investors were, on average, rewarded with higher returns on higher-risk investments.

normal probability distribution
A symmetrical probability distribution whose shape resembles a "bell-shaped" curve.

Normal Distribution A **normal probability distribution**, depicted in Figure 8.3, resembles a symmetrical "bell-shaped" curve. The symmetry of the curve means that half the probability is associated with the values to the left of the peak and half with the values to the right. As noted on the figure, for normal probability distributions, 68% of possible outcomes will lie between ± 1 standard deviation from the expected return, 95% of all outcomes will lie between ± 2 standard deviations from the expected return, and 99.7% of all outcomes will lie between ± 3 standard deviations from the expected return.

EXAMPLE 8.6

Using the data in Table 8.5 and assuming that the probability distributions of returns for common stocks and bonds are normal, we can surmise that 68% of the possible outcomes would have a return ranging between −8.4% and 31.2% for stocks and between −3.7% and 14.3% for bonds; 95% of the possible return outcomes would range between −28.2% and 51.0% for stocks and between −12.7% and 23.3% for bonds. The greater volatility of stock returns is clearly reflected in the much wider range of possible returns for each level of confidence (68% or 95%).

FIGURE 8.3

Bell-Shaped Curve
Normal probability distribution, with percentage of return outcomes for standard deviation ranges

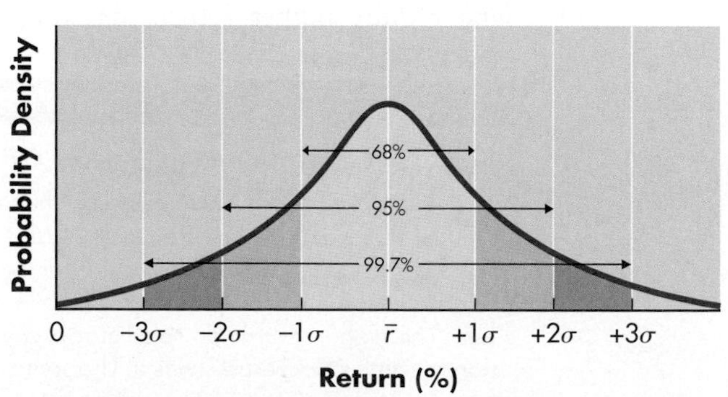

Coefficient of Variation: Trading Off Risk and Return

coefficient of variation (*CV*) A measure of relative dispersion that is useful in comparing the risks of assets with differing expected returns.

The **coefficient of variation, *CV*,** is a measure of relative dispersion that is useful in comparing the risks of assets with differing expected returns. The equation for the coefficient of variation is

$$CV = \frac{\sigma}{\bar{r}} \tag{8.4}$$

A higher coefficient of variation means that an investment has more volatility relative to its expected return. Because investors prefer higher returns and less risk, one might intuitively expect investors to gravitate toward investments with a low coefficient of variation. However, this logic doesn't always apply for reasons that will emerge in the next section. For now, consider the coefficients of variation in column 3 of Table 8.5. That table reveals that Treasury bills have the lowest coefficient of variation and therefore the lowest risk relative to their return. Does that mean that investors should load up on Treasury bills and divest themselves of stocks? Not necessarily.

EXAMPLE 8.7

Substituting the standard deviations (from Table 8.4) and the expected returns (from Table 8.3) for assets A and B into Equation 8.4, we find that the coefficients of variation for A and B are 0.094 (1.41% ÷ 15%) and 0.377 (5.66% ÷ 15%), respectively. Asset B has the higher coefficient of variation.

PERSONAL FINANCE EXAMPLE 8.8

Marilyn Ansbro is reviewing stocks for inclusion in her investment portfolio. The stock she wishes to analyze is Danhaus Industries Inc. (DII), a diversified manufacturer of pet products. One of her key concerns is risk; as a rule, she will invest only in stocks with a coefficient of variation below 0.75. She has gathered price and dividend data (shown in the accompanying table) for DII over the past 3 years, 2017–2019, and she plans to calculate DII's coefficient of variation using this admittedly limited historical sample.

	Stock Price		
Year	Beginning	End	Dividend paid
2017	$35.00	$36.50	$3.50
2018	36.50	34.50	3.50
2019	34.50	35.00	4.00

Substituting the price and dividend data for each year into Equation 8.1, we get the following information:

Year	Returns
2017	[$3.50 + ($36.50 − $35.00)] ÷ $35.00 = $5.00 ÷ $35.00 = 14.3%
2018	[$3.50 + ($34.50 − $36.50)] ÷ $36.50 = $1.50 ÷ $36.50 = 4.1%
2019	[$4.00 + ($35.00 − $34.50)] ÷ $34.50 = $4.50 ÷ $34.50 = 13.0%

Substituting into Equation 8.2a we get the average return, $\bar{r}_{2017\text{–}2019}$:

$$\bar{r}_{2017\text{–}2019} = (14.3\% + 4.1\% + 13.0\%) \div 3 = 10.5\%$$

Substituting the average return and annual returns into Equation 8.3a, we get the standard deviation, $\sigma_{2017\text{–}2019}$:

$$\sigma_{2017\text{–}2019} = \sqrt{[(14.3\% - 10.5\%)^2 + (4.1\% - 10.5\%)^2 + (13.0\% - 10.5\%)^2] \div (3-1)}$$

$$= \sqrt{(14.44\%^2 + 40.96\%^2 + 6.25\%^2) \div 2} = \sqrt{30.825\%^2} = 5.6\%$$

Finally, substituting the standard deviation of returns and the average return into Equation 8.4, we get the coefficient of variation, CV:

$$CV = 5.6\% \div 10.5\% = 0.53$$

Because the coefficient of variation of returns on the DII stock over the 2017–2019 period of 0.53 is well below Marilyn's maximum coefficient of variation of 0.75, she concludes that the DII stock would be an acceptable investment.

→ REVIEW QUESTIONS MyLab Finance Solutions

8–4 Explain how the range is used in scenario analysis.

8–5 What does a plot of the probability distribution of outcomes show a decision maker about an asset's risk?

8–6 What relationship exists between the size of the standard deviation and the degree of asset risk?

8–7 What does the coefficient of variation reveal about an investment's risk that the standard deviation does not?

8.3 Risk of a Portfolio

In real-world situations, the risk of any single investment would not be viewed independently of other assets. New investments must be considered in light of their impact on the risk and return of an investor's *portfolio* of assets. The financial manager's goal is to create an **efficient portfolio**, one that provides the maximum return for a given level of risk. We therefore need a way to measure the return and the standard deviation of a portfolio of assets. As part of that analysis, we will look at the statistical concept of *correlation,* which underlies the process of diversification used to develop an efficient portfolio.

efficient portfolio
A portfolio that maximizes return for a given level of risk.

PORTFOLIO RETURN AND STANDARD DEVIATION

The *return on a portfolio* is a weighted average of the returns on the individual assets from which it is formed. We can use Equation 8.5 to find the portfolio return, r_p:

$$r_p = (w_1 \times r_1) + (w_2 \times r_2) + \ldots (w_n \times r_n) = \sum_{j=1}^{n} w_j \times r_j \qquad (8.5)$$

Where

w_j = percentage of the portfolio's total dollar value invested in asset j

r_j = return on asset j

Of course, $\sum_{j=1}^{n} w_j = 1$, which means that 100% of the portfolio's assets must be included in this computation.

EXAMPLE 8.9

MyLab Finance Solution Video

James purchases 100 shares of Wal-Mart at a price of \$80 per share, so his total investment in Wal-Mart is \$8,000. He also buys 100 shares of Cisco Systems at \$32 per share, so the total investment in Cisco stock is \$3,200. Combining these two holdings, James's total portfolio is worth \$11,200. Of the total, 71.43% is invested in Wal-Mart (\$8,000 ÷ \$11,200), and 28.57% is invested in Cisco Systems (\$3,200 ÷ \$11,200). Thus, $w_1 = 0.7143$, $w_2 = 0.2857$, and $w_1 + w_2 = 1.0$.

The *standard deviation of a portfolio's returns* is found by applying the formula for the standard deviation of a single asset. Specifically, apply Equation 8.3 when you know the probabilities of every possible return, and apply Equation 8.3a when using historical data to estimate the standard deviation.

EXAMPLE 8.10

Assume that we wish to determine the historical average return and the standard deviation of returns for portfolio XY, created by combining equal portions (50% each) of assets X and Y. Historical returns generated by assets X and Y during the period 2014–2018 appear in part A of Table 8.6. Before focusing on the average return and standard deviation of the portfolio, we will consider those statistics for

TABLE 8.6 Historical Returns, Average Return, and Standard Deviation for Portfolio XY

A. Historical portfolio returns

Year	Asset X return, r_x	Asset Y return, r_y	Portfolio return[a]
2014	8%	16%	(0.50 × 8%) + (0.50 × 16%) = 12%
2015	10	14	(0.50 × 10%) + (0.50 × 14%) = 12%
2016	12	12	(0.50 × 12%) + (0.50 × 12%) = 12%
2017	14	10	(0.50 × 14%) + (0.50 × 10%) = 12%
2018	16	8	(0.50 × 16%) + (0.50 × 8%) = 12%

B. Average portfolio return, 2014–2018

$$\bar{r}_p = \frac{12\% + 12\% + 12\% + 12\% + 12\%}{5} = 12\%$$

C. Standard deviation of portfolio returns[b]

$$\sigma_p = \sqrt{\frac{(12\% - 12\%)^2 + (12\% - 12\%)^2 + (12\% - 12\%)^2 + (12\% - 12\%)^2 + (12\% - 12\%)^2}{5 - 1}} = 0\%$$

[a]Using Equation 8.5.
[b]Using Equation 8.3a.

each asset individually. Using Equations 8.2a and 8.3a, we can calculate the average return and standard deviation for each asset as follows:

$$\bar{r}_X = \frac{8\% + 10\% + 12\% + 14\% + 16\%}{5} = 12\%$$

$$\bar{r}_Y = \frac{16\% + 14\% + 12\% + 10\% + 8\%}{5} = 12\%$$

$$\sigma_X = \sqrt{\frac{(8\% - 12\%)^2 + (10\% - 12\%)^2 + (12\% - 12\%)^2 + (14\% - 12\%)^2 + (16\% - 12\%)^2}{5-1}} = 3.16\%$$

$$\sigma_Y = \sqrt{\frac{(16\% - 12\%)^2 + (14\% - 12\%)^2 + (12\% - 12\%)^2 + (10\% - 12\%)^2 + (8\% - 12\%)^2}{5-1}} = 3.16\%$$

Assets X and Y are quite similar in that both have an average return of 12% and a standard deviation of 3.16% during the 2014 to 2018 period. Now let us see what happens when we put the two assets together in a portfolio.

The latter columns of part A show what return a portfolio consisting of assets X and Y would have earned in each year. Notice that a rather strange outcome occurs for the portfolio. Even though the returns of assets X and Y fluctuate from year to year, the portfolio produces the same 12% return every single year. Parts B and C show the calculations behind the rather obvious conclusion that portfolio XY's average historical return is 12% and its standard deviation is 0%.

If you look carefully at the historical returns on assets X and Y, you can see they are moving in opposite directions. In other words, Asset X's return is lowest in 2014 and highest in 2018, whereas the opposite is true for Asset Y. As a result, movements in the returns of Asset X are always exactly offset by opposite movements in Asset Y's return, so the 50-50 portfolio earns the same return year after year. This result is a very special case of a crucial concept in portfolio theory called correlation, to which we now turn.

correlation
A statistical measure of the relationship between any two series of numbers.

positively correlated
Describes two series that move in the same direction.

negatively correlated
Describes two series that move in opposite directions.

correlation coefficient
A measure of the degree of correlation between two series.

perfectly positively correlated
Describes two *positively correlated* series that have a *correlation coefficient* of +1.

CORRELATION

Correlation is a statistical measure of the relationship between any two series of numbers. The numbers may represent data of any kind, from investment returns to test scores. If two series tend to vary in the same direction, they are **positively correlated.** If the series vary in opposite directions, they are **negatively correlated.** For example, suppose that we gathered data on the retail price and weight of new cars. It is likely we would find that larger cars cost more than smaller ones, so we would say that among new cars, weight and price are positively correlated. If we also measured the fuel efficiency of these vehicles (as measured by the number of miles they can travel per gallon of gasoline), we would find that lighter cars are more fuel efficient than heavier cars. In that case, we would say that fuel economy and vehicle weight are negatively correlated.[3]

The degree of correlation is measured by the **correlation coefficient,** which ranges from +1 for **perfectly positively correlated** series to −1 for

3. Note here that we are talking about general tendencies. For instance, a large hybrid SUV might have better fuel economy than a smaller sedan powered by a conventional gasoline engine, but that does not change the general tendency that lighter cars achieve better fuel economy.

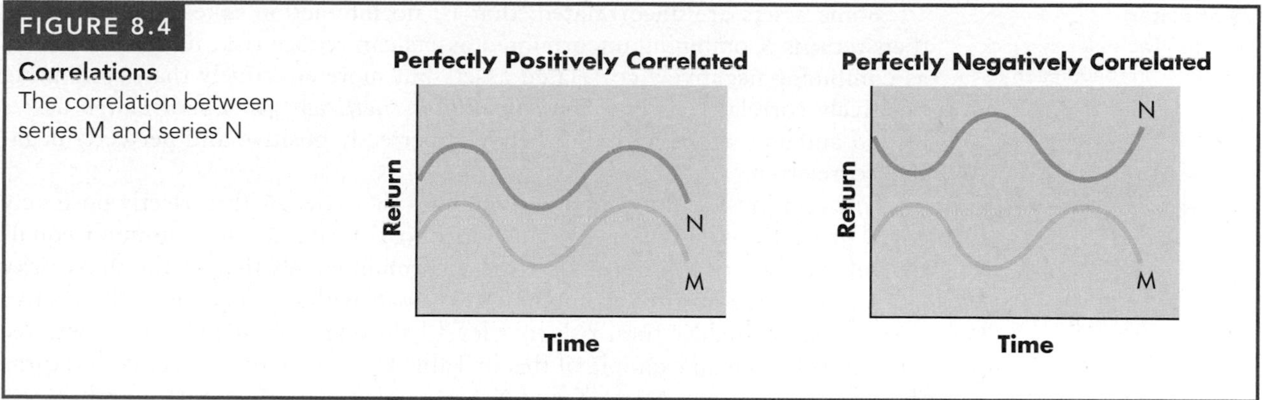

FIGURE 8.4
Correlations
The correlation between series M and series N

perfectly negatively correlated
Describes two *negatively correlated* series that have a *correlation coefficient* of −1.

perfectly negatively correlated series. These two extremes are depicted for series M and N in Figure 8.4. The perfectly positively correlated series move exactly together without exception; the perfectly negatively correlated series move in exactly opposite directions.

DIVERSIFICATION

The concept of correlation is essential to developing an efficient portfolio. To reduce overall risk, it is best to *diversify* by combining, or adding to the portfolio, assets that have the lowest possible correlation. Combining assets that have a low correlation with each other can reduce the overall variability of a portfolio's returns. Figure 8.5 shows the returns that two assets, F and G, earn over time. Both assets earn the same average or expected return, $\bar{r}$, but note that when F's return is above average, the return on G is below average and vice versa. In other words, returns on F and G are negatively correlated, and when these two assets are combined in a portfolio, the risk of that portfolio falls without reducing the average return (i.e., the portfolio's average return is also $\bar{r}$). For risk-averse investors, that is very good news. They get rid of something they don't like (risk) without having to sacrifice what they do like (return). Even if assets are positively correlated, the lower the correlation between them the greater will be the risk reduction achieved through diversification.

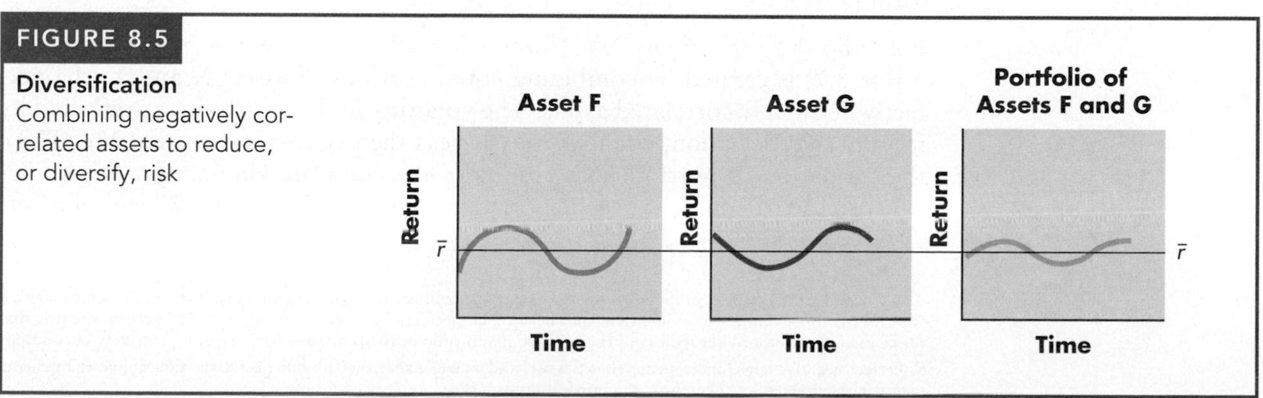

FIGURE 8.5
Diversification
Combining negatively correlated assets to reduce, or diversify, risk

uncorrelated
Describes two series that lack any interaction and therefore have a *correlation coefficient* of zero.

Some assets are **uncorrelated**; that is, no interaction takes place between their returns. Combining uncorrelated assets can reduce risk, not as effectively as combining negatively correlated assets but more effectively than combining positively correlated assets. The *correlation coefficient for uncorrelated assets is zero* and acts as the midpoint between perfectly positive and perfectly negative correlation.

The creation of a portfolio that combines two assets with perfectly positively correlated returns results in overall portfolio risk that at the minimum equals that of the least risky asset and at the maximum equals that of the most risky asset. However, a portfolio combining two assets with less than perfectly positive correlation *can* reduce total risk to a level below that of either component. We have already seen an example of this in Table 8.6, where two assets with returns that varied over time, Assets X and Y, were combined into a portfolio that produced returns that did not vary at all. For a more realistic example, assume that you buy stock in a company that manufactures machine tools. The business is very *cyclical,* so the stock will do well when the economy is expanding, and it will do poorly during a recession. If you bought shares in another machine-tool company, with sales positively correlated with those of your firm, the combined portfolio would still be cyclical, and risk would not be reduced a great deal. Alternatively, however, you could buy stock in a discount retailer, whose sales are *countercyclical.* It typically performs worse during economic expansions than it does during recessions (when consumers are trying to save money on every purchase). A portfolio that contained both of these stocks might be less volatile than either stock on its own.

EXAMPLE 8.11

Table 8.7 presents historical returns from three different assets—X, Y, and Z—from 2014 to 2018, along with their average returns and standard deviations. You encountered Assets X and Y previously in Table 8.6, so here we are just adding data for a third asset, Z. Each of the assets has an expected return of 12% and a standard deviation of 3.16%. The assets therefore have equal return and equal volatility. The return patterns of assets X and Y are perfectly negatively correlated. When X enjoys its highest return, Y experiences its lowest return and vice versa. The returns of assets X and Z are perfectly positively correlated. They move in precisely the same direction, so when the return on X is high, so is the return on Z. (*Note:* The returns for X and Z are identical.)[4] Now let's consider what happens when we combine these assets in different ways to form portfolios.

Portfolio XY Portfolio XY (shown initially in Table 8.6 and repeated in Table 8.7) is created by combining equal portions of assets X and Y, the perfectly negatively correlated assets. The volatility in this portfolio, as reflected by its standard deviation, equals 0%, whereas the expected return is 12%. Thus, the formation of portfolio XY results in the complete elimination of risk because in each and every year the portfolio earns a 12% return.[5] *Whenever assets*

4. We use identical returns in this example to permit clear illustration of the concepts, but it is not necessary for the returns on X and Z to be identical for them to be perfectly positively correlated. Any return streams that move exactly together—regardless of the relative magnitude of the returns—are perfectly positively correlated.

5. Perfect negative correlation means that the ups and downs experienced by one asset are exactly offset by movements in the other asset. Therefore, the portfolio return does not vary over time.

ABLE 8.7 **Average Returns and Standard Deviations for Portfolios XY and XZ**

	Asset Returns			Portfolio Returns[a]	
Year	r_X	r_Y	r_Z	r_{XY}	r_{XZ}
2014	8%	16%	8%	(0.50 × 8%) + (0.50 × 16%) = 12%	(0.50 × 8%) + (0.50 × 8%) = 8%
2015	10	14	10	(0.50 × 10%) + (0.50 × 14%) = 12%	(0.50 × 10%) + (0.50 × 10%) = 10%
2016	12	12	12	(0.50 × 12%) + (0.50 × 12%) = 12%	(0.50 × 12%) + (0.50 × 12%) = 12%
2017	14	10	14	(0.50 × 14%) + (0.50 × 10%) = 12%	(0.50 × 14%) + (0.50 × 14%) = 14%
2018	16	8	16	(0.50 × 16%) + (0.50 × 8%) = 12%	(0.50 × 16%) + (0.50 × 16%) = 16%
Statistic					
Average[b]	12%	12%	12%	12%	12%
Standard deviation[c]	3.16%	3.16%	3.16%	0%	3.16%

[a]Portfolio XY, which consists of 50% of asset X and 50% of asset Y, illustrates *perfect negative correlation*. Portfolio XZ, which consists of 50% of asset X and 50% of asset Z, illustrates *perfect positive correlation*.

[b]Using Equation 8.2a.

[c]Using Equation 8.3a. Note that for any portfolio consisting of two assets, you could also calculate the portfolio standard deviation directly by using the standard deviations of the assets in the portfolio as well as the correlation coefficient between them using the following formula:

$$\sigma_p = \sqrt{w_1^2\sigma_1^2 + w_2^2\sigma_2^2 + 2w_1w_2\rho_{12}\sigma_1\sigma_2}$$

where w_1 and w_2 are the fractions of the portfolio invested in assets 1 and 2, σ_1 and σ_2 are the standard deviations of each asset, and ρ_{12} is the correlation coefficient between assets 1 and 2. So, for portfolio XY the correlation coefficient would be –1.0, and for portfolio XZ the correlation coefficient would be 1.0.

are perfectly negatively correlated, some combination of the two assets exists such that the resulting portfolio's returns are risk free.

Portfolio XZ Portfolio XZ (shown in Table 8.7) is created by combining equal portions of assets X and Z, the perfectly positively correlated assets. Individually, assets X and Z have the same standard deviation, 3.16%, and because they always move together, combining them in a portfolio does nothing to reduce risk; the portfolio standard deviation is also 3.16%. As was the case with portfolio XY, the expected return of portfolio XZ is 12%. Because both portfolios provide the same expected return, but portfolio XY achieves that expected return with no risk, portfolio XY is clearly preferred by risk-averse investors over portfolio XZ.

CORRELATION, DIVERSIFICATION, RISK, AND RETURN

In general, the lower the correlation between asset returns, the greater the risk reduction that investors can achieve by diversifying. The following example illustrates how correlation influences the risk of a portfolio but not the portfolio's expected return.

EXAMPLE 8.12

MyLab Finance Solution Video

Consider two assets—Lo and Hi—with the characteristics described in the following table.

Asset	Expected return, $\bar{r}$	Risk (standard deviation), σ
Lo	6%	3%
Hi	8	8

FIGURE 8.6

Possible Correlations
Range of portfolio return ($\bar{r}_p$) and risk (σ_{r_p}) for combinations of assets Lo and Hi for various correlation coefficients

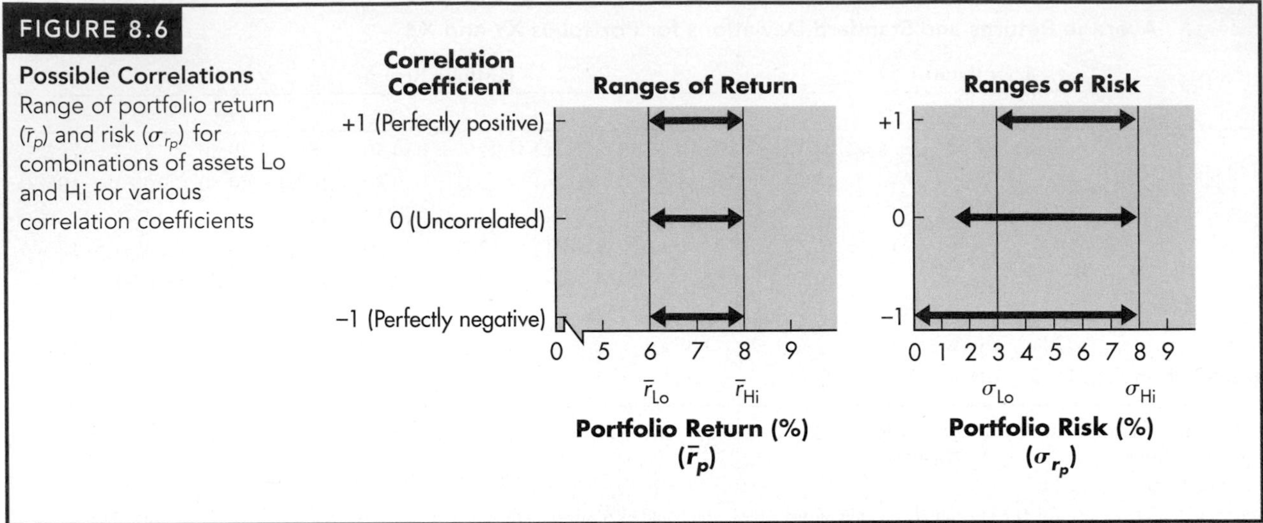

Clearly, asset Lo offers a lower return than Hi does, but Lo is also less risky than Hi. It is natural to think that a portfolio combining Lo and Hi would offer a return between 6% and 8% and that the portfolio's risk would also fall between the risk of Lo and Hi (between 3% and 8%). That intuition is only partly correct.

The performance of a portfolio consisting of assets Lo and Hi depends not only on the expected return and standard deviation of each asset (given above) but also on how the returns on the two assets are correlated. We will illustrate the results of three specific scenarios: (1) returns on Lo and Hi are perfectly positively correlated, (2) returns on Lo and Hi are uncorrelated, and (3) returns on Lo and Hi are perfectly negatively correlated.

The results of the analysis appear in Figure 8.6. Whether the correlation between Lo and Hi is +1, 0, or −1, a portfolio of those two assets must have an expected return between 6% and 8%. That is why the line segments at the left in Figure 8.6 all range between 6% and 8%. If a portfolio is mostly invested in Lo with only a little money invested in Hi, the portfolio's return will be close to 6%. If more money is invested in Hi, the portfolio return will be closer to 8%. However, the standard deviation of a portfolio depends critically on the correlation between Lo and Hi. Only when Lo and Hi are perfectly positively correlated can it be said that the portfolio standard deviation must fall between 3% (Lo's standard deviation) and 8% (Hi's standard deviation). As the correlation between Lo and Hi becomes weaker (i.e., as the correlation coefficient falls), investors may find they can form portfolios of Lo and Hi with standard deviations that are even less than 3% (i.e., portfolios that are less risky than holding asset Lo by itself). That is why the line segments at the right in Figure 8.6 vary. In the special case when Lo and Hi are perfectly negatively correlated, it is possible to diversify away all the risk and form a portfolio that is risk free.

INTERNATIONAL DIVERSIFICATION

One excellent practical example of portfolio diversification involves including foreign assets in a portfolio. The inclusion of assets from countries with business cycles that are not perfectly correlated with the U.S. business cycle reduces the portfolio's responsiveness to market movements. The ups and the downs of different markets around the world offset one another, at least to some extent, and the result is a portfolio that is less risky than one invested entirely in the U.S. market.

Returns from International Diversification

Over long periods, internationally diversified portfolios tend to perform better (meaning that they earn higher returns relative to the risks taken) than purely domestic portfolios. However, over shorter periods, such as 1 or 2 years, internationally diversified portfolios may perform better or worse than domestic portfolios. For example, consider what happens when the U.S. economy is performing rather poorly and the dollar is depreciating in value against most foreign currencies. At such times, the dollar returns to U.S. investors on a portfolio of foreign assets can be very attractive. However, international diversification can yield subpar returns, particularly when the dollar is appreciating in value relative to other currencies. When the value of U.S. currency appreciates, the U.S. dollar value of a foreign-currency-denominated portfolio of assets declines. Even if this portfolio yields a satisfactory return in foreign currency, the return to U.S. investors will be reduced when foreign profits are translated into dollars. Subpar local currency portfolio returns, coupled with an appreciating dollar, can yield truly dismal dollar returns to U.S. investors.

Overall, though, the logic of international portfolio diversification assumes that these fluctuations in currency values and relative performance will average out over long periods. Compared to similar, purely domestic portfolios, an internationally diversified portfolio will tend to yield a comparable return at a lower level of risk.

political risk
Risk that arises from the possibility that a host government will take actions harmful to foreign investors or that political turmoil will endanger investments.

Risks of International Diversification

In addition to the risk induced by currency fluctuations, several other financial risks are unique to international investing. Most important is **political risk**, which arises from the possibility that a host government will take actions harmful to

GLOBAL FOCUS *in practice*

An International Flavor to Risk Reduction

Earlier in this chapter (see Table 8.5), we learned that from 1900 through 2016, the U.S. stock market produced an average annual nominal return of 11.4%, but that return was associated with a relatively high standard deviation: 19.8% per year. Could U.S. investors have done better by diversifying globally? The answer is somewhat mixed. Elroy Dimson, Paul Marsh, and Mike Staunton calculated the historical returns on a portfolio that included U.S. stocks as well as stocks from 22 other countries. This diversified portfolio produced returns that were not quite as high as the U.S. average, just 9.5% per year. However, the globally diversified portfolio was also less volatile, with an annual standard deviation of 17.0%. Dividing the standard deviation by the annual return produces a coefficient of variation for the globally diversified portfolio of 1.79, nearly identical to the 1.74 coefficient of variation reported for U.S. stocks in Table 8.5.

► *International mutual funds do not include any domestic assets, whereas global mutual funds include both foreign and domestic assets. How might this difference affect their correlation with U.S. equity mutual funds?*

Source: Elroy Dimson, Paul Marsh, and Mike Staunton, *Credit Suisse Global Investment Returns Yearbook 2017.*

foreign investors or that political turmoil will endanger investments. Political risks are particularly acute in developing countries, where unstable or ideologically motivated governments may attempt to block return of profits by foreign investors or even seize (nationalize) their assets in the host country. For example, reflecting former President Hugo Chavez's desire to broaden the country's socialist revolution, Venezuela maintained a list of priority goods for import that excluded a large percentage of the necessary inputs to the automobile production process. As a result, Toyota halted auto production in Venezuela, and three other auto manufacturers temporarily closed or deeply cut their production there. Chavez also forced most foreign energy firms to reduce their stakes and give up control of oil projects in Venezuela.

For more discussion of reducing risk through international diversification, see the *Global Focus* box.

→ REVIEW QUESTIONS MyLab Finance Solutions

8–8 What is an efficient portfolio? How can the return and standard deviation of a portfolio be determined?

8–9 Why is the correlation between asset returns important? How does diversification allow risky assets to be combined so that the risk of the portfolio is less than the risk of the individual assets in it?

8–10 How does international diversification enhance risk reduction? When might international diversification result in subpar returns? What are political risks, and how do they affect international diversification?

8.4 Risk and Return: The Capital Asset Pricing Model (CAPM)

Thus far, we have observed a tendency for riskier investments to earn higher returns, and we have learned that investors can reduce risk through diversification. Now we want to quantify the relationship between risk and return. In other words, we wish to measure how much additional return an investor should expect from taking a little extra risk. The classic theory that links risk and return for all assets is the **capital asset pricing model (CAPM)**. We will use the CAPM to understand the basic risk–return tradeoffs involved in all types of financial decisions.

capital asset pricing model (CAPM)
The classic theory that links risk and return for all assets.

TYPES OF RISK

In the last section, we saw that the standard deviation of a portfolio may be less than the standard deviation of the individual assets in the portfolio. That's the power of diversification. To see this concept more clearly, consider what happens to the risk of a portfolio consisting of a single security (asset) to which we add securities randomly selected from, say, the population of all actively traded securities. Using the standard deviation of return, σ_{rp}, to measure the total portfolio risk, Figure 8.7 depicts the behavior of the total portfolio risk (*y*-axis) as more securities are added (*x*-axis). With the addition of securities, the total portfolio risk declines as a result of diversification, and tends to approach a lower limit.

FIGURE 8.7

Risk Reduction
Portfolio risk and diversification

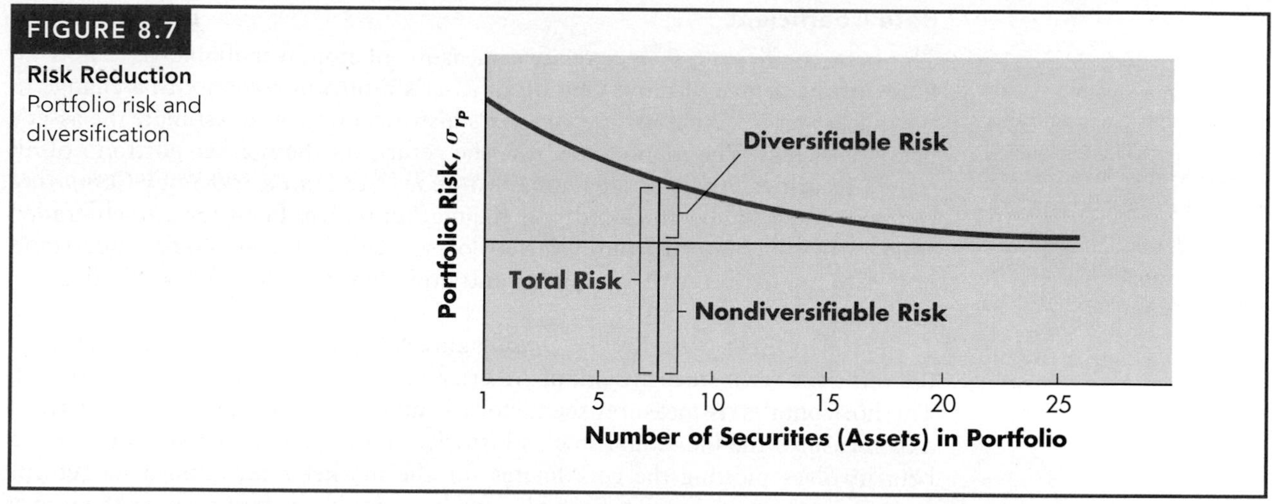

total risk
The combination of a security's *nondiversifiable risk* and *diversifiable risk.*

diversifiable risk
The portion of an asset's risk that is attributable to firm-specific, random causes; can be eliminated through diversification. Also called *unsystematic risk.*

nondiversifiable risk
The relevant portion of an asset's risk attributable to market factors that affect all firms; cannot be eliminated through diversification. Also called *systematic risk.*

The **total risk** of a security can be viewed as consisting of two parts:

$$\text{Total security risk} = \text{Nondiversifiable risk} + \text{Diversifiable risk} \quad (8.6)$$

Diversifiable risk (sometimes called *unsystematic risk*) represents the portion of an asset's risk that is associated with random causes that can be eliminated through diversification. It is attributable to firm-specific events, such as strikes, lawsuits, regulatory actions, or the loss of key accounts. Figure 8.7 shows that diversifiable risk gradually disappears as the number of stocks in the portfolio increases. **Nondiversifiable risk** (also called *systematic risk*) the portion of an asset's risk that is attributable to market factors that affect all firms; it cannot be eliminated through diversification. Factors such as war, inflation, the overall state of the economy, international incidents, and political events account for nondiversifiable risk. In Figure 8.7, nondiversifiable risk is represented by the horizontal black line below which the blue curve can never go, no matter how diversified the portfolio becomes.

Because any investor can easily create a portfolio of assets that will eliminate virtually all diversifiable risk, *the only relevant risk is nondiversifiable risk.* Any investor or firm therefore must be concerned solely with nondiversifiable risk. The measurement of nondiversifiable risk is thus of primary importance in selecting assets with the most desired risk–return characteristics.

THE MODEL: CAPM

The capital asset pricing model (CAPM) links nondiversifiable risk to expected returns. We will discuss the model in five sections. The first section deals with the beta coefficient, which is a measure of nondiversifiable risk. The second section presents an equation of the model itself, and the third section graphically describes the relationship between risk and return. The fourth section discusses the effects of changes in inflationary expectations and risk aversion on the relationship between risk and return. The fifth section offers some comments on the CAPM.

Beta Coefficient

beta coefficient (β)
A relative measure of nondiversifiable risk. An *index* of the degree of movement of an asset's return in response to a change in the *market return.*

market return
The return on the market portfolio of all traded securities.

The **beta coefficient, β,** is a relative measure of nondiversifiable risk. It is an index of the degree of movement of an asset's return in response to a change in the market return. Analysts use an asset's historical returns to estimate the asset's beta coefficient. The **market return** is the return on the market portfolio of all traded securities. Analysts often use the *Standard & Poor's 500 Stock Composite Index* or some similar stock index as the market return. Betas for actively traded stocks can be obtained from a variety of sources, but you should understand how they are derived and interpreted and how they are applied to portfolios.

Deriving Beta from Return Data Figure 8.8 plots the relationship between the returns of two stocks (Bank of America and Pepsico) and the market return. The horizontal axis measures the historical market returns and that the vertical axis measures the individual stock's historical returns. The first step in deriving beta involves plotting the coordinates for the market return and asset returns from various points in time. Each blue (yellow) dot in the figure shows the return on Pepsico (Bank of America) and the return on the overall market for a particular month drawn from the period October 2014 to October 2017. By use of statistical techniques, the "characteristic line" that best explains the relationship between the asset return and the market return coordinates is fit to the data

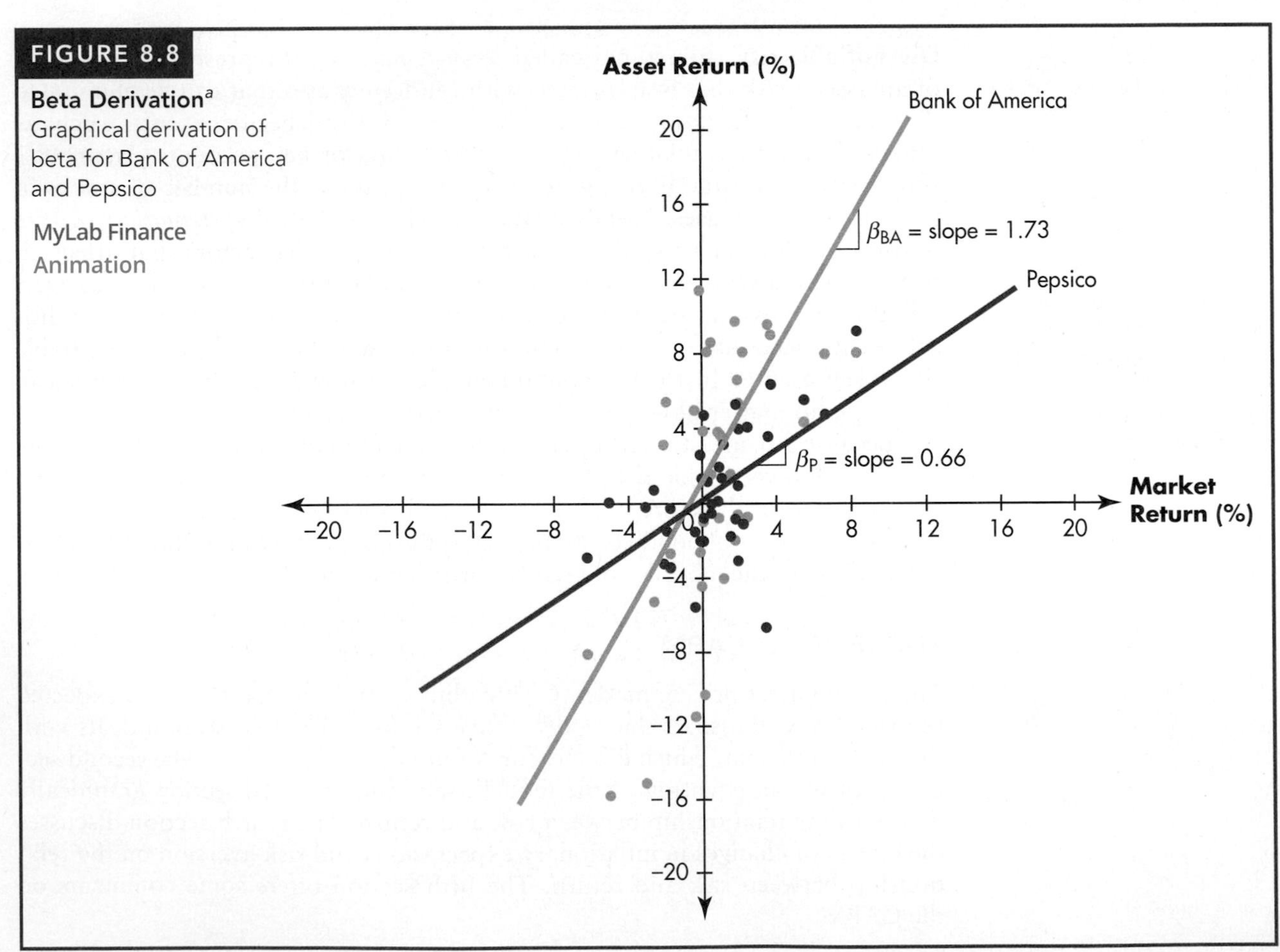

FIGURE 8.8

Beta Derivation[a]
Graphical derivation of beta for Bank of America and Pepsico

MyLab Finance Animation

TABLE 8.8 Selected Beta Coefficients and Their Interpretations

Beta	Direction of response	Magnitude of response
2.0	Move in same direction as market	Twice as responsive as the market
1.0		Same response as the market
0.5		Only half as responsive as the market
0		Unaffected by market movements
−0.5	Move in opposite direction to market	Only half as responsive as the market
−1.0		Same response as the market
−2.0		Twice as responsive as the market

points.[6] The slope of this line is *beta*. The characteristic lines tell us that the betas for Bank of America and Pepsico are 1.73 and 0.66 respectively. Because Bank of America's stock returns are very sensitive to changing market returns, it is a riskier stock than Pepsi.

Interpreting Betas The beta coefficient for the entire market (and the average beta across all stocks) equals 1.0. All other betas are viewed in relation to this value. Asset betas may be positive or negative, but positive betas are the norm. The majority of beta coefficients fall between 0.5 and 2.0. The return of a stock that is half as responsive as the market ($\beta = 0.5$) should change by 0.5% for each 1% change in the return of the market portfolio. A stock that is twice as responsive as the market ($\beta = 2.0$) should experience a 2% change in its return for each 1% change in the return of the market portfolio. Table 8.8 provides various beta values and their interpretations. Beta coefficients for actively traded stocks can be obtained from published sources such as *Value Line Investment Survey*, via the Internet, or through brokerage firms. Betas for some selected stocks are given in Table 8.9.

MyLab Finance Animation

TABLE 8.9 Beta Coefficients for Selected Stocks (September 12, 2017)

Stock	Beta	Stock	Beta
Anheuser-Busch	0.96	Int'l Business Machines	0.95
Apple	1.38	JP Morgan Chase & Co.	1.24
Bank of America	1.73	Microsoft	1.48
Costco	0.89	Newmont Mining	0.20
Disney	1.27	PepsiCo, Inc.	0.66
eBay	1.68	Qualcomm	1.49
ExxonMobil Corp.	0.63	Sempra Energy	0.54
Gap (The), Inc.	0.38	Verizon	0.69
General Electric	1.01	Wal-Mart Stores	0.05
Intel	1.31	Xerox	0.94

Source: Data from Yahoo Finance, www.finance.yahoo.com

6. The empirical measurement of beta is approached by using *least-squares regression analysis*.

Portfolio Betas We can easily estimate the beta of a portfolio by using the betas of the individual assets it includes. Letting w_j represent the proportion of the portfolio's total dollar value represented by asset j and letting β_j equal the beta of asset j, we can use Equation 8.7 to find the portfolio beta, β_p:

$$\beta_p = (w_1 \times \beta_1) + (w_2 \times \beta_2) + \ldots + (w_n \times \beta_n) = \sum_{j=1}^{n} w_j \times \beta_j \quad (8.7)$$

Of course, $\sum_{j=1}^{n} w_j = 1$, which means that 100% of the portfolio's assets must be included in this computation.

Portfolio betas are interpreted in the same way as the betas of individual assets. They indicate the degree of responsiveness of the *portfolio's* return to changes in the market return. For example, when the market return increases by 10%, a portfolio with a beta of 0.75 will experience a 7.5% increase in its return ($0.75 \times 10\%$); a portfolio with a beta of 1.25 will experience a 12.5% increase in its return ($1.25 \times 10\%$). Clearly, a portfolio containing mostly low-beta assets will have a low beta, and one containing mostly high-beta assets will have a high beta.

PERSONAL FINANCE EXAMPLE 8.13 Mario Austino, an individual investor, wishes to assess the risk of two small portfolios he is considering, V and W. Both portfolios contain five assets, with the proportions and betas shown in Table 8.10. The betas for the two portfolios, β_V and β_W, can be calculated by substituting data from the table into Equation 8.7:

$$\beta_V = (0.10 \times 1.65) + (0.30 \times 1.00) + (0.20 \times 1.30) + (0.20 \times 1.10) + (0.20 \times 1.25)$$
$$= 0.165 + 0.300 + 0.260 + 0.220 + 0.250 = \underline{\underline{1.20}}$$

$$\beta_W = (0.10 \times 0.80) + (0.10 \times 1.00) + (0.20 \times 0.65) + (0.10 \times 0.75) + (0.50 \times 1.05)$$
$$= 0.080 + 0.100 + 0.130 + 0.075 + 0.525 = \underline{\underline{0.91}}$$

Portfolio V's beta is about 1.20, and portfolio W's is 0.91. These values make sense because portfolio V contains relatively high-beta assets, and portfolio W contains relatively low-beta assets. Mario's calculations show that portfolio V's returns are more responsive to changes in market returns and are therefore more

TABLE 8.10 Mario Austino's Portfolios V and W

	Portfolio V		Portfolio W	
Asset	Proportion	Beta	Proportion	Beta
1	0.10	1.65	0.10	0.80
2	0.30	1.00	0.10	1.00
3	0.20	1.30	0.20	0.65
4	0.20	1.10	0.10	0.75
5	0.20	1.25	0.50	1.05
Totals	1.00		1.00	

risky than portfolio W's. He must now decide which, if either, portfolio he feels comfortable adding to his existing investments.

The Equation

Using the beta coefficient to measure nondiversifiable risk, the *capital asset pricing model (CAPM)* is given by

$$r_j = R_F + [\beta_j \times (r_m - R_F)] \tag{8.8}$$

where

r_j = expected return or required return on asset j

R_F = risk-free rate of return, commonly measured by the return on a U.S. Treasury bill

β_j = beta coefficient or index of nondiversifiable risk for asset j

r_m = market return; expected return on the market portfolio of assets

risk-free rate of return (R_F)
The required return on a *risk-free asset,* typically a 3-month *U.S. Treasury bill.*

U.S. Treasury bills (T-bills)
Short-term IOUs issued by the U.S. Treasury; considered the *risk-free asset.*

Equation 8.8 shows that the CAPM has two parts: (1) the **risk-free rate of return,** R_F, which is the required return on a *risk-free asset,* typically a 3-month **U.S. Treasury bill (T-bill)**, a short-term IOU issued by the U.S. Treasury; and (2) the *risk premium.* These parts are, respectively, the two elements on either side of the plus sign in Equation 8.8. The $(r_m - R_F)$ portion of the risk premium is called the *market risk premium* because it represents the premium that the investor must receive for taking the average amount of risk associated with holding the market portfolio of assets.

Historical Risk Premiums Using the historical return data for stocks, bonds, and Treasury bills for the 1900–2016 period shown in Table 8.1, we can calculate the risk premiums for each investment category. The calculation (consistent with Equation 8.8) involves merely subtracting the historical U.S. Treasury bill's average return from the historical average return for a given investment:

Investment	Risk premium[a]
Stocks	11.4% − 3.8% = 7.6%
Treasury bonds	5.3% − 3.8% = 1.5%

[a]Historical average returns obtained from Table 8.1.

Reviewing the risk premiums calculated above, we can see that the risk premium is higher for stocks than for bonds. This outcome makes sense intuitively because stocks are riskier than bonds (equity is riskier than debt).

EXAMPLE 8.14

Benjamin Corporation, a growing computer software developer, wishes to determine the required return on an asset Z, which has a beta of 1.5. The risk-free rate of return is 2%; the expected return on the market portfolio of assets is 6%. Substituting $\beta_Z = 1.5$, $R_F = 2\%$, and $r_m = 6\%$ into the capital asset pricing model given in Equation 8.8 yields a required return of

$$r_Z = 2\% + [1.5 \times (6\% - 2\%)] = 2\% + 6\% = 8\%$$

The market risk premium of 4% (6% − 2%), when adjusted for the asset's index of risk (beta) of 1.5, results in a risk premium for asset Z of 6% (1.5 × 4%). That risk premium, when added to the 2% risk-free rate, results in an 8% required return.

Other things being equal, *the higher the beta, the higher the required return, and the lower the beta, the lower the required return.*

The Graph: The Security Market Line (SML)

security market line (SML) The depiction of the *capital asset pricing model (CAPM)* as a graph that reflects the required return in the marketplace for each level of nondiversifiable risk (beta).

If we depict the capital asset pricing model (Equation 8.8) graphically, it is called the **security market line (SML)**. The SML is a straight line that shows the required return in the marketplace for each level of nondiversifiable risk (beta). In the graph, we plot risk as measured by beta, β, on the x-axis, and we plot required returns, r, on the y-axis. If you know the beta of any asset, you can use the SML to find that asset's expected or required return.

EXAMPLE 8.15

In the preceding example for Benjamin Corporation, the risk-free rate, R_F, was 2%, and the market return, r_m, was 6%. We can plot the SML by using the two sets of coordinates for the betas associated with R_F and r_m, β_{R_F} and β_m (i.e., $\beta_{R_F} = 0$,[7] $R_F = 2\%$; and $\beta_m = 1.0$, $r_m = 6\%$). Figure 8.9 presents the resulting security market line. The line has an intercept of 2%, meaning that a security with no risk earns a 2% return. The slope of the line is 4%, equal to the risk premium on the market portfolio (6% − 2%). The figure highlights that there

FIGURE 8.9

Security Market Line
Security market line (SML) with Benjamin Corporation's asset Z data shown

MyLab Finance Animation

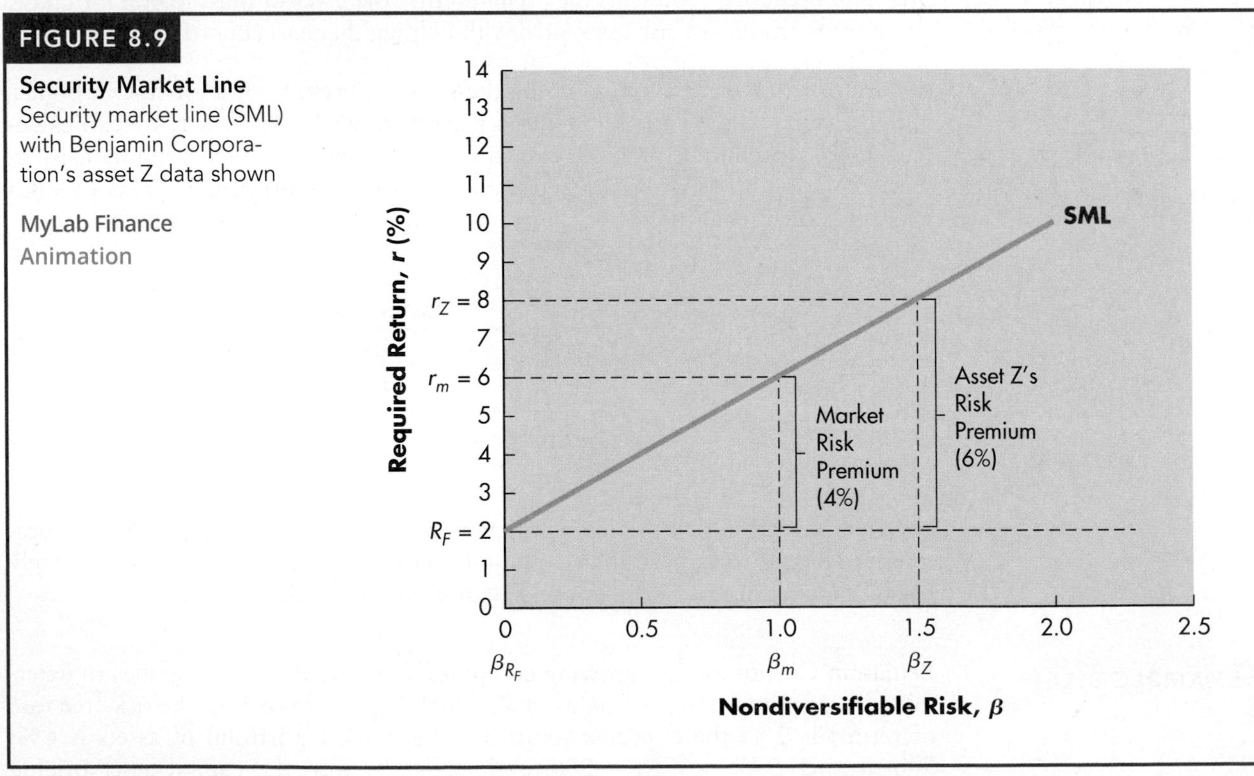

7. Because R_F is the rate of return on a risk-free asset, the beta associated with the risk-free asset, β_{rf}, would equal 0. The zero beta on the risk-free asset reflects not only its absence of risk but also that the asset's return is unaffected by movements in the market return.

is a tradeoff between a security's nondiversifiable risk and its required return. Notice that asset Z, which has a beta of 1.5, has a required return of 8%. Thus, asset Z's risk premium is 6% (8% − 2%), which is higher than the market's risk premium. The general principle illustrated in the figure is that the risk premium for an asset with a beta greater than 1.0 will be greater than the risk premium of the market, whereas an asset with a beta below 1.0 will have a risk premium that is less than the market's risk premium.

Shifts in the Security Market Line

The security market line is not stable over time, and shifts in the security market line can result in a change in required return. The position and slope of the SML are affected by two major forces—inflationary expectations and risk aversion—which we analyze next.[8]

Changes in Inflationary Expectations Changes in inflationary expectations affect the risk-free rate of return, R_F. The equation for the risk-free rate of return is

$$R_F = r^* + i \tag{8.9}$$

This equation shows that, assuming a constant real rate of interest, r^*, changes in inflationary expectations, reflected in an inflation premium, i, will result in corresponding changes in the risk-free rate. Therefore, a change in inflationary expectations that results from events such as international trade embargoes or major alterations in Federal Reserve policy will produce a shift in the SML. Because the risk-free rate is a basic component of all rates of return, any change in R_F will be reflected in *all* required rates of return.

Changes in inflationary expectations result in parallel shifts in the SML in direct response to the magnitude and direction of the change. This effect can best be illustrated by an example.

EXAMPLE 8.16

In the preceding example, using the CAPM, the required return for asset Z, r_Z, was 8%. Assuming that the risk-free rate of 2% includes a 1% real rate of interest, r^*, and a 1% inflation premium, *IP*, then Equation 8.9 confirms that

$$R_F = 1\% + 1\% = 2\%$$

Now assume that recent economic events have resulted in an *increase of 3% in inflationary expectations, raising the inflation premium* to 4% (i_1). As a result, all returns likewise rise by 3%. In this case, the new returns (noted by subscript 1) are

$$R_{F_1} = 5\% \text{ (rises from 2\% to 5\%)}$$
$$r_{m_1} = 9\% \text{ (rises from 6\% to 9\%)}$$

Substituting these values, along with asset Z's beta (β_Z) of 1.5, into the CAPM (Equation 8.8), we find that asset Z's new required return (r_{Z_1}) can be calculated:

$$r_{Z_1} = 5\% + [1.5 \times (9\% - 5\%)] = 5\% + 6\% = \underline{\underline{11\%}}$$

8. A firm's beta can alter over time as a result of changes in the firm's asset mix, in its financing mix, or in external factors not within management's control, such as natural disasters or shifts in consumer tastes.

FIGURE 8.10

Inflation Shifts SML
Impact of increased inflationary expectations on the SML

MyLab Finance Animation

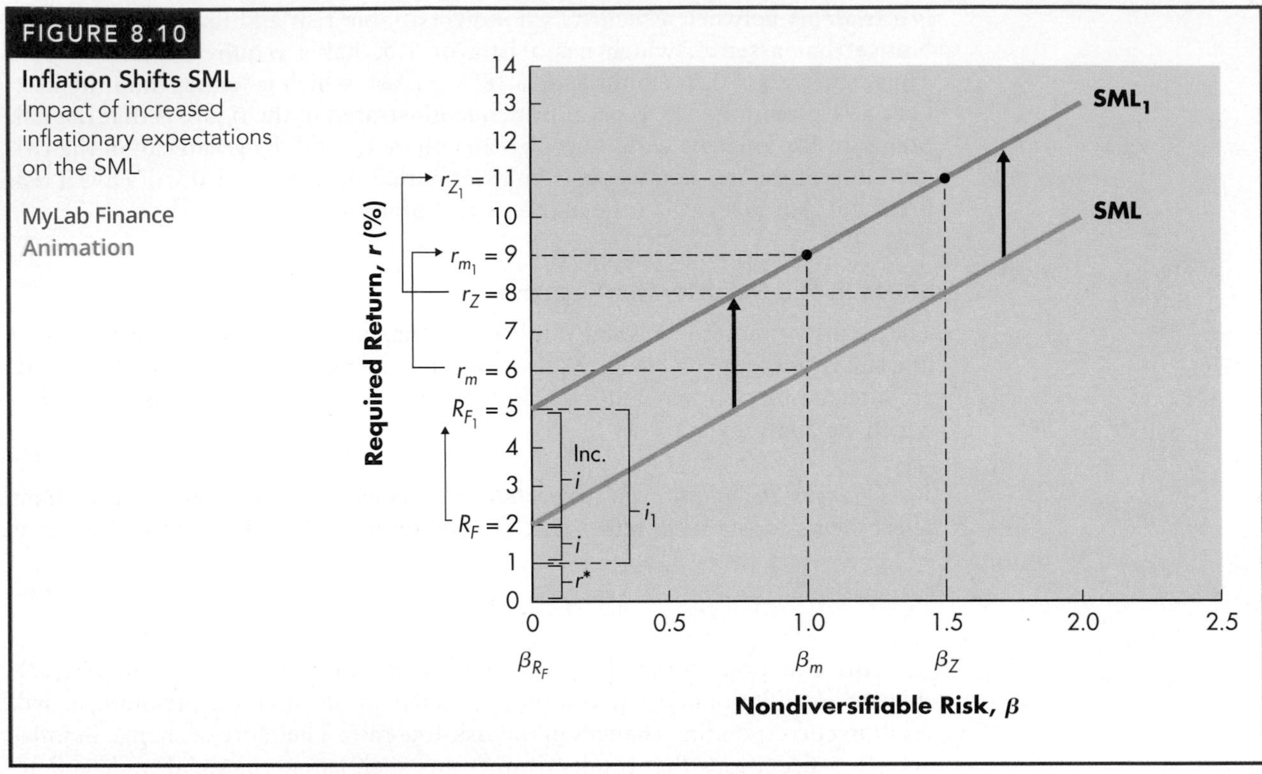

Comparing r_{Z_1} of 11% to r_Z of 8%, we see that the change of 3% in asset Z's required return exactly equals the change in the inflation premium. The same 3% increase results for all assets.

Figure 8.10 depicts the situation just described. It shows that the 3% increase in inflationary expectations results in a parallel shift upward of 3% in the SML. Clearly, the required returns on all assets rise by 3%. Note that the rise in the inflation premium from 5% to 8% (i to i_1) causes the risk-free rate to rise from 2% to 5% (R_F to R_{F_1}) and the market return to increase from 6% to 9% (r_m to r_{m_1}). The security market line therefore shifts upward by 3% (SML to SML_1), causing the required return on all risky assets, such as asset Z, to rise by 3%. The important lesson here is that *a given change in inflationary expectations will be fully reflected in a corresponding change in the returns of all assets, as reflected graphically in a parallel shift of the SML.*

Changes in Risk Aversion The slope of the security market line reflects the general risk preferences of investors in the marketplace. As discussed earlier, most investors are *risk averse;* that is, they require increased returns for increased risk. If investors become more risk averse, then the slope of the SML becomes steeper. In other words, when investors are more risk averse, they demand a higher return for any risk level, which means that the slope of the SML is steeper. This also means that risk premiums increase with greater risk aversion.

Changes in risk aversion and the slope of the SML result from changing preferences of investors, which generally stem from economic, political, or social events. Examples of events that *increase* risk aversion include a stock market crash, assassination of a key political leader, and the outbreak of war. In general, widely shared expectations of hard times ahead tend to cause investors to become more risk averse, requiring higher returns as compensation for accepting a given level of risk. The following examples demonstrate the impact of increased risk aversion on the SML.

EXAMPLE 8.17

In the preceding examples, the SML in Figure 8.9 reflected a risk-free rate (R_F) of 2%, a market return (r_m) of 6%, a market risk premium ($r_m - R_F$) of 4%, and a required return on asset Z (r_Z) of 8% with a beta (β_Z) of 1.5. Assume that recent economic events have made investors more risk averse, causing a new higher market return (r_{m_1}) of 9%. Graphically, this change would cause the SML to pivot upward as shown in Figure 8.11, causing a new market risk premium ($r_{m_1} - R_F$) of 7%. As a result, the required return on all risky assets will increase. We can calculate the new required return for asset Z, with a beta of 1.5, by using the CAPM (Equation 8.8):

$$r_{Z_1} = 2\% + [1.5 \times (9\% - 2\%)] = 2\% + 10.5\% = \underline{\underline{12.5\%}}$$

This value appears on the new security market line (SML_1) in Figure 8.11. Note that although asset Z's risk, as measured by beta, did not change, its required return has increased because of the increased risk aversion reflected in the market

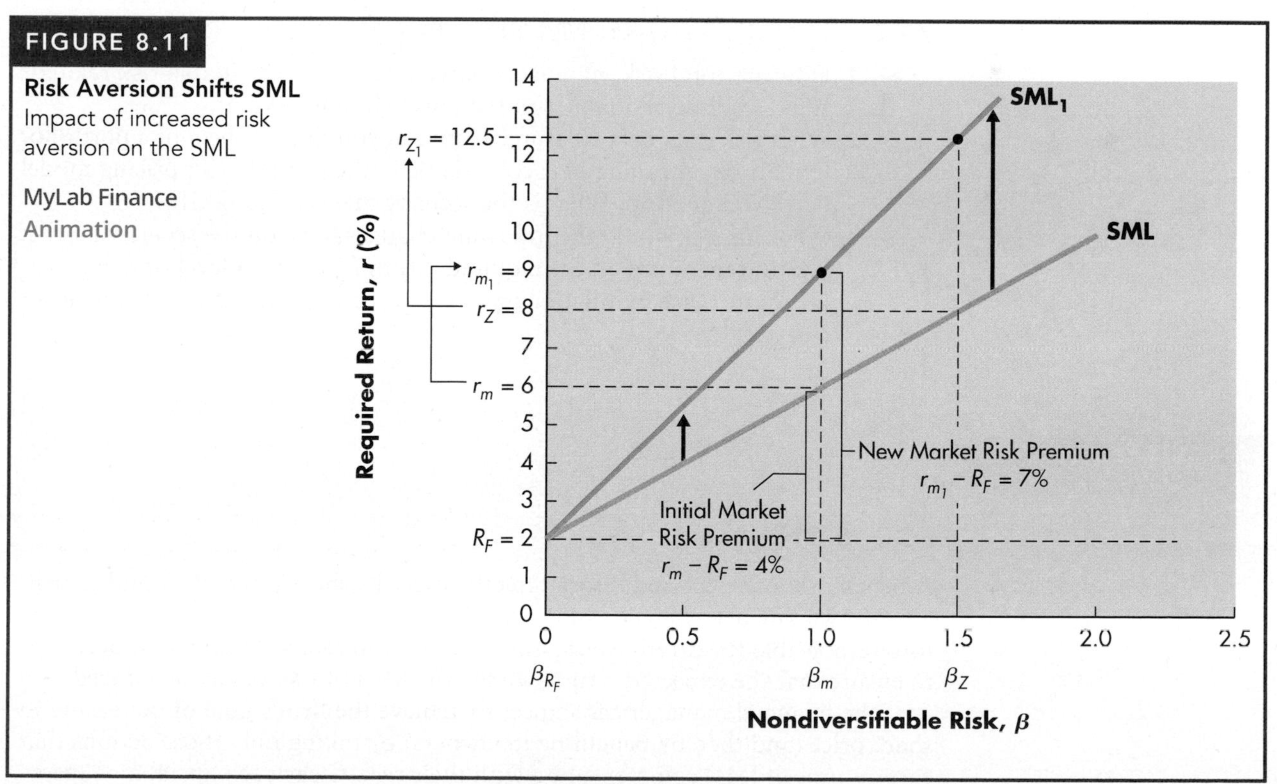

FIGURE 8.11

Risk Aversion Shifts SML
Impact of increased risk aversion on the SML

MyLab Finance Animation

risk premium. To summarize, *greater risk aversion results in higher required returns for each level of risk. Similarly, a reduction in risk aversion causes the required return for each level of risk to decline.*

Some Comments on the CAPM

To estimate a stock's beta, analysts generally use historical data. The estimated beta may or may not actually indicate the *future* variability of returns. Therefore, the required returns specified by the model can be viewed only as rough approximations. Users of betas commonly make subjective adjustments to the historically determined betas to reflect their expectations of the future.

The CAPM was developed to explain the behavior of security prices and provide a mechanism whereby investors could assess the impact of a proposed security investment on their portfolio's overall risk and return. The CAPM assumes that markets are efficient and have the following characteristics: many small investors, all having the same information and expectations with respect to securities; no restrictions on investment, no taxes, and no transaction costs; and rational investors, who view securities similarly and are risk averse, preferring higher returns and lower risk.

Although the perfect world described in the preceding paragraph appears unrealistic, studies have supported the CAPM's main prediction that stocks with higher betas should have higher returns on average. The CAPM also sees widespread application in corporations that use the model to assess the required returns their shareholders demand (and therefore the returns the firms' managers need to achieve when they invest shareholders' money).

→ REVIEW QUESTIONS MyLab Finance Solutions

8–11 How are total risk, nondiversifiable risk, and diversifiable risk related? Why is nondiversifiable risk the only relevant risk?

8–12 What risk does beta measure? How can you find the beta of a portfolio?

8–13 Explain the meaning of each variable in the capital asset pricing model (CAPM) equation. What is the security market line (SML)?

8–14 What impact would the following changes have on the security market line and therefore on the required return for a given level of risk? (**a**) An increase in inflationary expectations. (**b**) Investors become less risk averse.

SUMMARY

FOCUS ON VALUE

A firm's risk and expected return directly affect its share price. Risk and return are the two key determinants of the firm's value. The financial manager is therefore responsible for carefully assessing the risk and return of all major decisions to ensure that the expected returns justify the level of risk being introduced.

The financial manager can expect to achieve **the firm's goal of increasing its share price** (and thereby benefiting its owners) by taking only those actions that earn returns at least commensurate with their risk. Clearly, financial managers must recognize, measure, and evaluate risk–return tradeoffs to ensure that their decisions contribute to the creation of value for owners.

REVIEW OF LEARNING GOALS

LG1 **Understand the meaning and fundamentals of risk, return, and risk preferences.** Risk is a measure of the uncertainty surrounding the return that an investment will produce. The total rate of return is the sum of cash distributions, such as interest or dividends, plus the change in the asset's value over a given period, divided by the investment's beginning-of-period value. Investment returns vary both over time and between different types of investments. Investors may be risk averse, risk neutral, or risk seeking. Most financial decision makers are risk averse. A risk-averse decision maker requires a higher expected return on a more risky investment alternative.

LG2 **Describe procedures for assessing and measuring the risk of a single asset.** The risk of a single asset is measured in much the same way as that of a portfolio of assets. Scenario analysis and probability distributions can be used to assess risk. The range, the standard deviation, and the coefficient of variation can measure risk quantitatively.

LG3 **Discuss the measurement of return and standard deviation for a portfolio and the concept of correlation.** The return of a portfolio is calculated as the weighted average of returns on the individual assets from which it is formed. The portfolio standard deviation is found by using the formula for the standard deviation of a single asset.

Correlation—the statistical relationship between any two series of numbers—can be positively correlated, negatively correlated, or uncorrelated. At the extremes, the series can be perfectly positively correlated or perfectly negatively correlated.

LG4 **Understand the risk and return characteristics of a portfolio in terms of correlation and diversification and the impact of international assets on a portfolio.** Diversification involves combining assets with low correlation to reduce the risk of the portfolio. The range of risk in a two-asset portfolio depends on the correlation between the two assets. If they are perfectly positively correlated, the portfolio's risk will be between the individual assets' risks. If they are perfectly negatively correlated, the portfolio's risk will be between the risk of the riskier asset and zero.

International diversification can further reduce a portfolio's risk. Foreign assets have the risk of currency fluctuation and political risks.

LG5 **Review the two types of risk and the derivation and role of beta in measuring the relevant risk of both a security and a portfolio.** The total risk of a security consists of nondiversifiable and diversifiable risk. Diversifiable risk can be eliminated through diversification. Nondiversifiable risk is the only relevant risk. Nondiversifiable risk is measured by the beta coefficient, a relative measure of the relationship between an asset's return and the market return. Beta is derived by finding the slope of the "characteristic line" that best explains the historical relationship between the asset's return and the market return. The beta of a portfolio is a weighted average of the betas of the individual assets that it includes.

LG6 **Explain the capital asset pricing model (CAPM), its relationship to the security market line (SML), and the major forces causing shifts in the SML.** In the CAPM, beta relates an asset's risk relative to the market to the asset's required return. The graphical depiction of the CAPM is the SML, which shifts over time in response to changing inflationary expectations and/or changes in investor risk aversion. Changes in inflationary expectations result in parallel shifts in the SML. Increasing risk aversion results in the slope of the SML becoming steeper. Decreasing risk aversion reduces the slope of the SML. Although it has some shortcomings, the CAPM provides a useful conceptual framework for evaluating and linking risk and return.

OPENER-IN-REVIEW

In the chapter opener, you learned that Bill Miller's investment performance was alternating between the very top and the very bottom of his profession. What aspect of his investment strategy would lead you to expect that his performance might exhibit greater volatility than that of managers of other mutual funds? The following table shows the annual performance from 2009 to 2012 of Miller's fund and the S&P 500 index.

Opportunity Year	S&P 500 Return on Miller's Fund	Return on S&P 500
2009	76.0%	26.5%
2010	16.6	15.1
2011	−34.9	2.1
2012	39.6	16.0

Calculate the average annual return of the Opportunity fund and the S&P 500. Which performed better over this period? If you had put $1,000 in each investment at the beginning of 2009, how much money would you have in each investment at the end of 2012? Calculate the standard deviation of the Opportunity fund's return and those of the S&P 500. Which is more volatile?

SELF-TEST PROBLEMS (Solutions in Appendix)

ST8–1 **Portfolio analysis** You have been asked for your advice in selecting a portfolio of assets and have been given the following data:

Year	Expected return Asset A	Asset B	Asset C
2019	12%	16%	12%
2020	14	14	14
2021	16	12	16

You have been told that you can create two portfolios—one consisting of assets A and B and the other consisting of assets A and C—by investing equal proportions (50%) in each of the two component assets.

a. What is the expected return for each asset over the 3-year period?

b. What is the standard deviation for each asset's return?

c. What is the expected return for each of the two portfolios?

d. How would you characterize the correlations of returns of the two assets making up each of the two portfolios identified in part **c**?

e. What is the standard deviation for each portfolio?

f. Which portfolio do you recommend? Why?

LG5 LG6

ST8–2 **Beta and CAPM** Currently under consideration is an investment with a beta, b, of 1.50. At this time, the risk-free rate of return, R_F, is 3%, and the return on the market portfolio of assets, r_m, is 10%. You believe this investment will earn an annual rate of return of 11%.

a. If the return on the market portfolio were to increase by 10%, what would you expect to happen to the investment's return? What if the market return were to decline by 10%?

b. Use the capital asset pricing model (CAPM) to find the required return on this investment.

c. On the basis of your calculation in part **b**, would you recommend this investment? Why or why not?

d. Assume that as a result of investors becoming less risk averse, the market return drops by 3% to 8%. What effect would this change have on your responses in parts **b** and **c**?

WARM-UP EXERCISES

All problems are available in MyLab Finance.

LG1

E8–1 An analyst predicted last year that the stock of Logistics Inc. would offer a total return of at least 10% in the coming year. At the beginning of the year, the firm had a total stock market capitalization of $10 million. At the end of the year, its market cap was $12 million even though it experienced a loss, or negative net income, of $2.5 million. Logistics paid no dividends during the year. Did the analyst's prediction prove correct? Explain using the values for total annual return.

LG2

E8–2 Four analysts cover the stock of Fluorine Chemical. One forecasts a 5% return for the coming year. The second expects the return to be –5%. The third predicts a 10% return. The fourth expects a 3% return in the coming year. You are relatively confident that the return will be positive but not large, so you arbitrarily assign probabilities of 35%, 5%, 20%, and 40%, respectively, to the analysts' forecasts. Given these probabilities, what is Fluorine Chemical's expected return for the coming year?

LG2

E8–3 The expected annual returns are 15% for investment 1 and 12% for investment 2. The standard deviation of the first investment's return is 10%; the second investment's return has a standard deviation of 5%. Which investment is less risky based solely on its standard deviation? Which investment is less risky based on its coefficient of variation?

E8–4 Your portfolio has three asset classes. U.S. government T-bills account for 45% of the portfolio, large-company stocks constitute another 40%, and small-company stocks make up the remaining 15%. If the expected returns are 2% for the T-bills, 10% for the large-company stocks, and 15% for the small-company stocks, what is the expected return of the portfolio?

E8–5 You wish to calculate the risk level of your portfolio based on its beta. The five stocks in the portfolio with their respective weights and betas are shown in the accompanying table. Calculate the beta of your portfolio.

Stock	Portfolio weight	Beta
Alpha	20%	1.15
Centauri	10	0.85
Zen	15	1.60
Wren	20	1.35
Yukos	35	1.85

E8–6
a. Calculate the required rate of return for an asset that has a beta of 1.8, given a risk-free rate of 5% and a market return of 10%.
b. If investors have become more risk averse due to recent geopolitical events and the market return rises to 13%, what is the required rate of return for the same asset?
c. Use your findings in part **a** to graph the initial security market line (SML), and then use your findings in part **b** to graph (on the same set of axes) the shift in the SML.

PROBLEMS

All problems are available in MyLab Finance. The MyLab icon indicates problems in Excel format available in MyLab Finance.

P8–1 **Rate of return** Douglas Keel, a financial analyst for Orange Industries, wishes to estimate the rate of return for two similar-risk investments, X and Y. Douglas's research indicates that the immediate past returns will serve as reasonable estimates of future returns. A year earlier, investment X had a market value of $20,000, and investment Y had a market value of $55,000. During the year, investment X generated cash flow of $1,500, and investment Y generated cash flow of $6,800. The current market values of investments X and Y are $21,000 and $55,000, respectively.
a. Calculate the expected rate of return on investments X and Y using the most recent year's data.
b. Assuming the two investments are equally risky, which one should Douglas recommend? Why?

P8–2 **Return calculations** For each of the investments shown in the following table, calculate the rate of return earned over the period.

Investment	Cash flow during period	Beginning-of-period value	End-of-period value
A	−$ 800	$ 1,100	$ 100
B	15,000	120,000	118,000
C	7,000	45,000	48,000
D	80	600	500
E	1,500	12,500	12,400

LG1

P8–3 **Risk preferences** Sharon Smith, the financial manager for Barnett Corporation, wishes to select one of three prospective investments: X, Y, and Z. Assume that the measure of risk Sharon cares about is an asset's standard deviation. The expected returns and standard deviations of the investments are as follows:

Investment	Expected return	Standard deviation
X	14%	7%
Y	14	8
Z	14	9

a. If Sharon were risk neutral, which investment would she select? Explain why.
b. If she were risk averse, which investment would she select? Why?
c. If she were risk seeking, which investment would she select? Why?
d. Suppose a fourth investment, W, is available. It offers an expected return of 15%, and it has a standard deviation of 9%. If Sharon is risk averse, can you say which investment she will choose? Why or why not? Are there any investments that you are certain she will not choose?

LG2

P8–4 **Risk analysis** Solar Designs is considering an investment in an expanded product line. Two possible types of expansion are under review. After investigating the possible outcomes, the company made the estimates shown in the following table. The pessimistic and optimistic outcomes occur with a probability of 25%, and the most likely outcome occurs with a probability of 50%.

	Expansion A	Expansion B
Initial investment	$12,000	$12,000
Annual rate of return		
Pessimistic	16%	10%
Most likely	20%	20%
Optimistic	24%	30%

a. Determine the range of the rates of return for each of the two projects.
b. Which project seems less risky? Why?
c. If you were making the investment decision, which one would you choose? Why? What does this decision imply about your feelings toward risk?
d. Assume that expansion B's most likely outcome is 21% per year and that all other facts remain the same. Does your answer to part c now change? Why?

P8–5 Risk and probability Micro-Pub Inc. is considering the purchase of one of two microfilm cameras, R and S. Both should provide benefits over a 10-year period, and each requires an initial investment of $4,000. Management has constructed the accompanying table showing estimates of rates of return and probabilities for pessimistic, most likely, and optimistic results.

a. Determine the range for the rate of return for each of the two cameras.
b. Determine the average return for each camera.
c. The purchase of which camera is riskier? Why?

	Camera R		Camera S	
	Amount	Probability	Amount	Probability
Initial investment	$4,000	1.00	$4,000	1.00
Annual rate of return				
Pessimistic	20%	0.25	15%	0.20
Most likely	25%	0.50	25%	0.55
Optimistic	30%	0.25	35%	0.25

P8–6 Bar charts and risk Swan's Sportswear is thinking about bringing out a line of designer jeans. Currently, it is negotiating with two well-known designers. Because of the highly competitive nature of the industry, the two lines of jeans have been given code names. After market research, the firm has established the expectations shown in the following table about the annual rates of return.

		Annual rate of return	
Market acceptance	Probability	Line J	Line K
Very poor	0.05	0.0075	0.010
Poor	0.15	0.0125	0.025
Average	0.60	0.0850	0.080
Good	0.15	0.1475	0.135
Excellent	0.05	0.1625	0.150

Use the table to:

a. Construct a bar chart for each line's annual rate of return.
b. Calculate the average return for each line.
c. Evaluate the relative riskiness for each jeans line's rate of return using the bar charts.

P8–7 Coefficient of variation Metal Manufacturing has isolated four alternatives for meeting its need for increased production capacity. The following table summarizes data gathered relative to each alternative.

Alternative	Expected return	Standard deviation of return
A	20%	7.0%
B	22	9.5
C	19	6.0
D	16	5.5

a. Calculate the coefficient of variation for each alternative.
b. If the firm wishes to minimize risk, which alternative do you recommend? Why?

LG2

P8–8 Standard deviation versus coefficient of variation as measures of risk Greengage Inc., a successful nursery, is considering several expansion projects. All the alternatives promise to produce an acceptable return. Data on four possible projects follow.

Project	Expected return	Range	Standard deviation
A	12.0%	4.0%	2.9%
B	12.5	5.0	3.2
C	13.0	6.0	3.5
D	12.8	4.5	3.0

a. Which project is least risky, judging on the basis of range?
b. Which project has the lowest standard deviation? Explain why standard deviation may not be an entirely appropriate measure of risk for purposes of this comparison.
c. Calculate the coefficient of variation for each project. Which project do you think Greengage's owners should choose? Explain why.

Personal Finance Problem

P8–9 Rate of return, standard deviation, and coefficient of variation Mike is searching for a stock to include in his current stock portfolio. He is interested in Hi-Tech Inc.; he has been impressed with the company's computer products and believes that Hi-Tech is an innovative market player. However, Mike realizes that any time you consider a technology stock, risk is a major concern. The rule he follows is to include only securities with a coefficient of variation of returns below 0.90.

Mike has obtained the following price information for the period 2015 through 2018. Hi-Tech stock, being growth oriented, did not pay any dividends during these 4 years.

	Stock price	
Year	Beginning	End
2015	$14.36	$21.55
2016	21.55	64.78
2017	64.78	72.38
2018	72.38	91.80

a. Calculate the rate of return for each year, 2015 through 2018, for Hi-Tech stock.
b. Calculate the average return over this time period.
c. Calculate the standard deviation of returns over the past 4 years.
d. Based on parts **b** and **c**, determine the coefficient of variation of returns for the security.
e. Given the calculation in part **d**, what should be Mike's decision regarding the inclusion of Hi-Tech stock in his portfolio?

P8–10 Assessing return and risk Swift Manufacturing must choose between two asset purchases. The annual rate of return and the related probabilities given in the following table summarize the firm's analysis to this point.

Project 257		Project 432	
Rate of return	Probability	Rate of return	Probability
−10%	0.01	10%	0.05
10	0.04	15	0.10
20	0.05	20	0.10
30	0.10	25	0.15
40	0.15	30	0.20
45	0.30	35	0.15
50	0.15	40	0.10
60	0.10	45	0.10
70	0.05	50	0.05
80	0.04		
100	0.01		

a. For each project, compute:
   (1) The range of possible rates of return.
   (2) The average return.
   (3) The standard deviation of the returns.
   (4) The coefficient of variation of the returns.

b. Construct a bar chart of each distribution of rates of return.

c. Which project would you consider less risky? Why?

P8–11 Integrative: Expected return, standard deviation, and coefficient of variation Three assets—F, G, and H—are currently under consideration by Perth Industries. The probability distributions of expected returns for these assets are shown in the following table.

	Asset F		Asset G		Asset H	
j	Pr_j	Return, r_j	Pr_j	Return, r_j	Pr_j	Return, r_j
1	0.10	40%	0.40	35%	0.10	40%
2	0.20	10	0.30	10	0.20	20
3	0.40	0	0.30	−20	0.40	10
4	0.20	−5			0.20	0
5	0.10	−10			0.10	−20

a. Calculate the average return, $\bar{r}$, for each of the three assets. Which provides the largest average return?

b. Calculate the standard deviation, σ_r, for each asset's returns. Which appears to have the greatest risk?

c. Calculate the coefficient of variation, CV, for each asset's returns. Which appears to have the greatest relative risk?

P8–12 Normal probability distribution Answer the following questions, assuming that the rates of return associated with a given asset investment are normally distributed; that the expected return, $\bar{r}$, is 18.9%; and that the coefficient of variation, CV, is 0.75.

a. Find the standard deviation of returns, σ.

b. Calculate the range of expected return outcomes associated with the following probabilities of occurrence: (1) 68%, (2) 95%, (3) 99.7%.

c. Draw the probability distribution associated with your findings in parts **a** and **b**.

Personal Finance Problem

P8–13 Portfolio return and standard deviation Jamie Wong is thinking of building an investment portfolio containing two stocks, L and M. Stock L will represent 40% of the dollar value of the portfolio, and stock M will account for the other 60%. The historical returns over the last 6 years, 2013–2018, for each of these stocks are shown in the following table.

	Expected return	
Year	Stock L	Stock M
2013	14%	20%
2014	14	18
2015	16	16
2016	17	14
2017	17	12
2018	19	10

a. Calculate the actual portfolio return, r_p, for each of the 6 years.

b. Calculate the average return for each stock and for the portfolio over the 6-year period.

c. Calculate the standard deviation of returns for each asset and for the portfolio. How does the portfolio standard deviation compare to the standard deviations of the individual assets?

d. How would you characterize the correlation of returns of the two stocks L and M?

e. Discuss any benefits of diversification achieved by Jamie through creation of the portfolio.

P8–14 Portfolio analysis You have been given the historical return data shown in the first table on three assets—F, G, and H—over the period 2016–2019.

	Historical return		
Year	Asset F	Asset G	Asset H
2016	16%	17%	14%
2017	17	16	15
2018	18	15	16
2019	19	14	17

Using these assets, you have isolated the three investment alternatives shown in the following table.

Alternative	Investment
1	100% of asset F
2	50% of asset F and 50% of asset G
3	50% of asset F and 50% of asset H

a. Calculate the average return over the 4-year period for each of the three alternatives.

b. Calculate the standard deviation of returns over the 4-year period for each of the three alternatives.

c. Use your findings in parts **a** and **b** to calculate the coefficient of variation for each of the three alternatives.

d. On the basis of your findings, which of the three investment alternatives do you think performed better over this period? Why?

P8–15 Correlation, risk, and return Matt Peters wishes to evaluate the risk and return behaviors associated with various combinations of assets V and W under three assumed degrees of correlation: perfectly positive, uncorrelated, and perfectly negative. The expected returns and standard deviations calculated for each of the assets are shown in the following table.

Asset	Expected return, $\bar{r}$	Standard deviation, σ
V	8%	5%
W	13	10

a. If the returns of assets V and W are perfectly positively correlated (correlation coefficient = +1), describe the range of (1) expected return and (2) risk associated with all possible portfolio combinations.

b. If the returns of assets V and W are uncorrelated (correlation coefficient = 0), describe the approximate range of (1) expected return and (2) risk associated with all possible portfolio combinations.

c. If the returns of assets V and W are perfectly negatively correlated (correlation coefficient = −1), describe the range of (1) expected return and (2) risk associated with all possible portfolio combinations.

Personal Finance Problem

P8–16 International investment returns Joe Martinez, a U.S. citizen living in Brownsville, Texas, invested in the common stock of Telmex, a Mexican corporation. He purchased 1,000 shares at 20.50 pesos per share. Twelve months later, he sold them at 24.75 pesos per share. He received no dividends during that time.

a. What was Joe's investment return (in percentage terms) for the year, on the basis of the peso value of the shares?

b. The exchange rate for pesos was 9.21 pesos per US$1.00 at the time of the purchase. At the time of the sale, the exchange rate was 9.85 pesos per US$1.00. Translate the purchase and sale prices into US$.

c. Calculate Joe's investment return on the basis of the US$ value of the shares.
d. Explain why the two returns are different. Which one is more important to Joe? Why?

P8–17 **Total, nondiversifiable, and diversifiable risk** David Talbot randomly selected securities from all those listed on the New York Stock Exchange for his portfolio. He began with a single security and added securities one by one until a total of 20 securities were held in the portfolio. After each security was added, David calculated the portfolio standard deviation, σ. The calculated values are shown in the following table.

Number of securities	Std. dev., σ	Number of securities	Std. dev., σ
1	14.50%	11	7.00%
2	13.30	12	6.80
3	12.20	13	6.70
4	11.20	14	6.65
5	10.30	15	6.60
6	9.50	16	6.56
7	8.80	17	6.52
8	8.20	18	6.50
9	7.70	19	6.48
10	7.30	20	6.47

a. Plot the data from the table above on a graph that has the number of securities on the x-axis and the portfolio standard deviation on the y-axis.
b. Divide the total portfolio risk in the graph into its nondiversifiable and diversifiable risk components, and label each of these on the graph.
c. Describe which of the two risk components is the relevant risk, and explain why it is relevant. How much of this risk exists in David Talbot's portfolio?

P8–18 **Graphical derivation of beta** A firm wishes to estimate graphically the betas for two assets, A and B. It has gathered the return data shown in the following table for the market portfolio and for both assets over the past 10 years, 2009–2018.

	Actual return		
Year	Market portfolio	Asset A	Asset B
2009	6%	11%	16%
2010	2	8	11
2011	−13	−4	−10
2012	−4	3	3
2013	−8	0	−3
2014	16	19	30
2015	10	14	22
2016	15	18	29
2017	8	12	19
2018	13	17	26

a. On a set of "market return (x-axis)–asset return (y-axis)" axes, use the data given to draw the characteristic line for asset A and for asset B.
b. Use the characteristic lines from part **a** to estimate the betas for assets A and B.
c. Use the betas found in part **b** to comment on the relative risks of assets A and B.

P8–19 **Graphical derivation and interpreting beta** You are analyzing the performance of two stocks. The first, shown in Panel A, is Cyclical Industries Incorporated. Cyclical Industries makes machine tools and other heavy equipment, the demand for which rises and falls closely with the overall state of the economy. The second stock, shown in Panel B, is Biotech Cures Corporation. Biotech Cures uses biotechnology to develop new pharmaceutical compounds to treat incurable diseases. Biotech's fortunes are driven largely by the success or failure of its scientists to discover new and effective drugs. Each data point on the graph shows the monthly return on the stock of interest and the monthly return on the overall stock market. The lines drawn through the data points represent the characteristic lines for each security.

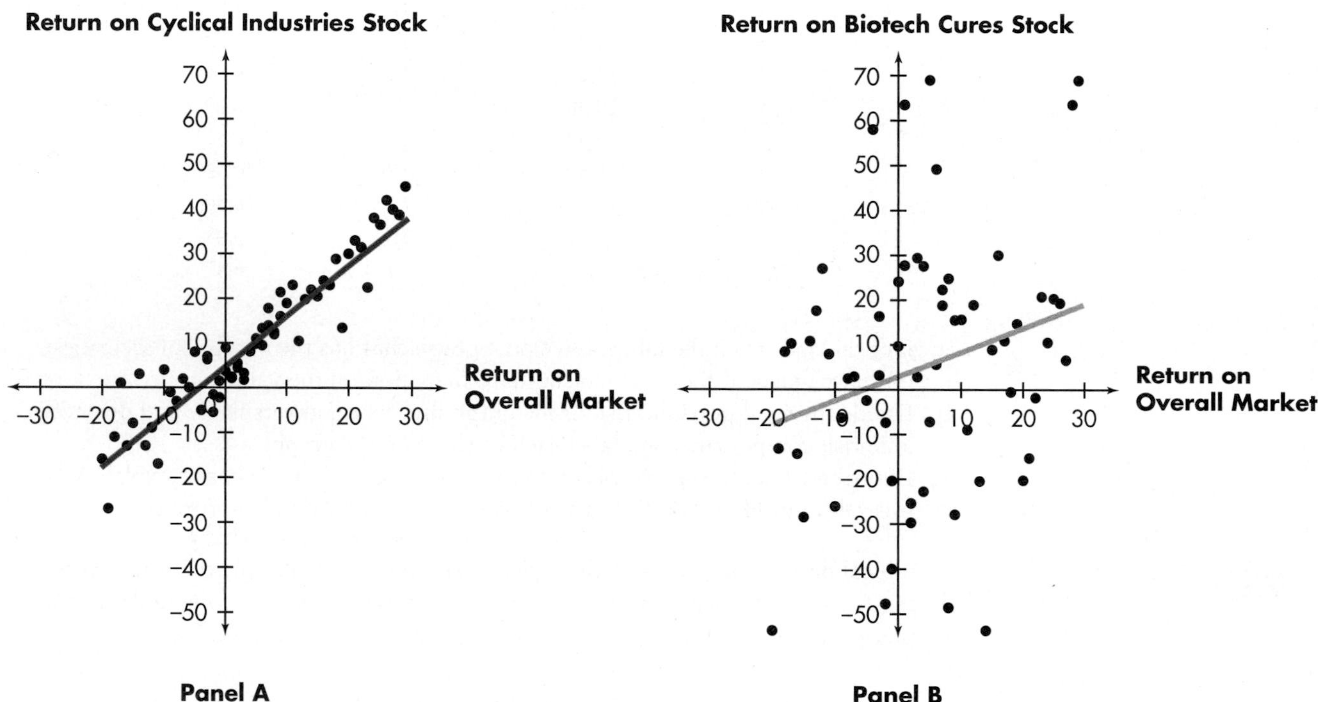

a. Which stock do you think has a higher standard deviation? Why?
b. Which stock do you think has a higher beta? Why?
c. Which stock do you think is riskier? What does the answer to this question depend on?

P8–20 **Interpreting beta** A firm wishes to assess the impact of changes in the market return on an asset that has a beta of 1.20.

a. If the market return increased by 15%, what impact would this change be expected to have on the asset's return?
b. If the market return decreased by 8%, what impact would this change be expected to have on the asset's return?
c. If the market return did not change, what impact, if any, would be expected on the asset's return?
d. Would this asset be considered more or less risky than the market? Explain.

Asset	Beta
A	0.50
B	1.60
C	−0.20
D	0.90

LG5

P8–21 Betas Answer the questions below for assets A to D shown in the table.

a. What impact would a 10% increase in the market return be expected to have on each asset's return?

b. What impact would a 10% decrease in the market return be expected to have on each asset's return?

c. If you believed that the market return would increase in the near future, which asset would you prefer? Why?

d. If you believed that the market return would decrease in the near future, which asset would you prefer? Why?

Personal Finance Problem

LG5

P8–22 Betas and risk rankings You are considering three stocks—A, B, and C—for possible inclusion in your investment portfolio. Stock A has a beta of 0.80, stock B has a beta of 1.40, and stock C has a beta of −0.30.

a. Rank these stocks from the most risky to the least risky.

b. If the return on the market portfolio increased by 12%, what change would you expect in the return for each stock?

c. If the return on the market portfolio decreased by 5%, what change would you expect in the return for each stock?

d. If you believed that the stock market was getting ready to experience a significant decline, which stock would you probably add to your portfolio? Why?

e. If you anticipated a major stock market rally, which stock would you add to your portfolio? Why?

Personal Finance Problem

P8–23 Portfolio betas Rose Berry is attempting to evaluate two possible portfolios, which consist of the same five assets held in different proportions. She is particularly interested in using beta to compare the risks of the portfolios, so she has gathered the data shown in the following table.

		Portfolio weights	
Asset	Asset beta	Portfolio A	Portfolio B
1	1.30	10%	30%
2	0.70	30	10
3	1.25	10	20
4	1.10	10	20
5	0.90	40	20
Totals		100%	100%

a. Calculate the betas for portfolios A and B.

b. Compare the risks of these portfolios to the market as well as to each other. Which portfolio is more risky?

P8–24 Capital asset pricing model (CAPM) For each case in the following table, use the capital asset pricing model to find the required return.

Case	Risk-free rate, R_F	Market return, r_m	Beta, β
A	1%	8%	1.30
B	2	6	0.90
C	5	13	−0.20
D	6	12	1.00
E	4	10	0.60

Personal Finance Problem

P8–25 Beta coefficients and the capital asset pricing model Katherine Wilson is wondering how much risk she must undertake to generate an acceptable return on her portfolio. The risk-free return currently is 5%. The return on the overall stock market is 16%. Use the CAPM to calculate how high the beta coefficient of Katherine's portfolio would have to be to achieve each of the following expected portfolio returns.

a. 10%
b. 15%
c. 18%
d. 20%
e. Katherine is risk averse. What is the highest return she can expect if she is unwilling to take more than an average risk?

P8–26 Manipulating CAPM Use the basic equation for the capital asset pricing model (CAPM) to work each of the following problems.

a. Find the required return for an asset with a beta of 0.90 when the risk-free rate and market return are 8% and 12%, respectively.
b. Find the risk-free rate for a firm with a required return of 15% and a beta of 1.25 when the market return is 14%.
c. Find the market return for an asset with a required return of 16% and a beta of 1.10 when the risk-free rate is 9%.
d. Find the beta for an asset with a required return of 15% when the risk-free rate and market return are 10% and 12.5%, respectively.

Personal Finance Problem

P8–27 Portfolio return and beta Jamie Peters invested $100,000 to set up the following portfolio 1 year ago.

Asset	Cost	Beta at purchase	Yearly income	Value today
A	$20,000	0.80	$1,600	$20,000
B	35,000	0.95	1,400	36,000
C	30,000	1.50	—	34,500
D	15,000	1.25	375	16,500

a. Calculate the portfolio beta on the basis of the original cost figures.
b. Calculate the percentage return of each asset in the portfolio for the year.
c. Calculate the percentage return of the portfolio on the basis of original cost, using income and gains during the year.
d. At the time Jamie made his investments, investors were estimating that the market return for the coming year would be 10%. The estimate of the risk-free rate of return averaged 4% for the coming year. Calculate an expected rate of return for each stock on the basis of its beta and the expectations of market and risk-free returns.
e. On the basis of the actual results, explain how each stock in the portfolio performed relative to those CAPM-generated expectations of performance. What factors could explain these differences?

LG6

P8–28 **Security market line (SML)** Assume that the risk-free rate, R_F, is currently 9% and that the market return, r_m, is currently 13%.
a. Draw the security market line (SML) on a set of "nondiversifiable risk (x-axis)–required return (y-axis)" axes.
b. Calculate and label the market risk premium on the axes in part **a.**
c. Given the previous data, calculate the required return on asset A having a beta of 0.80 and asset B having a beta of 1.30.
d. Draw in the betas and required returns from part **c** for assets A and B on the axes in part **a.** Label the risk premium associated with each asset, and discuss them.

LG6

P8–29 **Shifts in the security market line** Assume that the risk-free rate, R_F, is currently 8%; the market return, r_m, is 12%; and asset A has a beta, β_A, of 1.10.
a. Draw the security market line (SML) on a set of "nondiversifiable risk (x-axis)–required return (y-axis)" axes.
b. Use the CAPM to calculate the required return, r_A, on asset A, and depict asset A's beta and required return on the SML drawn in part **a.**
c. Assume that as a result of recent economic events, inflationary expectations have declined by 2%, lowering R_F and r_m to 6% and 10%, respectively. Draw the new SML on the axes in part **a,** and calculate and show the new required return for asset A.
d. Assume that as a result of recent events, investors have become more risk averse, causing the market return to rise by 1%, to 13%. Ignoring the shift in part **c,** draw the new SML on the same set of axes that you used before, and calculate and show the new required return for asset A.
e. From the previous changes, what conclusions can be drawn about the impact of (1) decreased inflationary expectations and (2) increased risk aversion on the required returns of risky assets?

LG6

P8–30 **Integrative: Risk, return, and CAPM** Wolff Enterprises must consider several investment projects, A through E, using the capital asset pricing model (CAPM) and its graphical representation, the security market line (SML). Relevant information is presented in the following table.

Item	Rate of return	Beta, β
Risk-free asset	9%	0.00
Market portfolio	14	1.00
Project A	—	1.50
Project B	—	0.75
Project C	—	2.00
Project D	—	0.00
Project E	—	−0.50

a. Calculate (1) the required rate of return and (2) the risk premium for each project, given its level of nondiversifiable risk.
b. Use your findings in part **a** to draw the security market line (required return relative to nondiversifiable risk).
c. Discuss the relative nondiversifiable risk of projects A through E.
d. Assume that recent economic events have caused investors to become less risk averse, causing the market return to decline by 2%, to 12%. Calculate the new required returns for assets A through E, and draw the new security market line on the same set of axes that you used in part **b.**
e. Compare your findings in parts **a** and **b** with those in part **d.** What conclusion can you draw about the impact of a decline in investor risk aversion on the required returns of risky assets?

P8–31 **ETHICS PROBLEM** Risk is a major concern of almost all investors. When shareholders invest their money in a firm, they expect managers to take risks with those funds. What ethical limits should managers observe when taking risks with other people's money?

SPREADSHEET EXERCISE

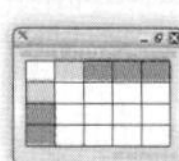

Jane is considering investing in three different stocks or creating three distinct two-stock portfolios. Jane views herself as a rather conservative investor. She is able to obtain historical returns for the three securities for the years 2012 through 2018. The data are given in the following table.

Year	Stock A	Stock B	Stock C
2012	10%	10%	12%
2013	13	11	14
2014	15	8	10
2015	14	12	11
2016	16	10	9
2017	14	15	9
2018	12	15	10

In any of the possible two-stock portfolios, the weight of each stock in the portfolio will be 50%. The three possible portfolio combinations are AB, AC, and BC.

TO DO

Create a spreadsheet similar to Tables 8.6 and 8.7 to answer the following:

a. Calculate the average return for each individual stock.
b. Calculate the standard deviation for each individual stock.
c. Calculate the average returns for portfolios AB, AC, and BC.
d. Calculate the standard deviations for portfolios AB, AC, and BC.
e. Would you recommend that Jane invest in the single stock A or the portfolio consisting of stocks A and B? Explain your answer from a risk–return viewpoint.
f. Would you recommend that Jane invest in the single stock B or the portfolio consisting of stocks B and C? Explain your answer from a risk–return viewpoint.

MyLab Finance Visit www.pearson.com/mylab/finance for **Chapter Case: *Analyzing Risk and Return on Chargers Products' Investments,*** Group Exercises, and numerous online resources.

CHAPTER 9

The Cost of Capital

LEARNING GOALS

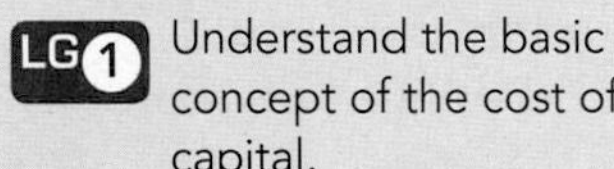

LG 1 Understand the basic concept of the cost of capital.

LG 2 List the primary sources of capital available to firms.

LG 3 Determine the cost of long-term debt, and explain why the after-tax cost of debt is the relevant cost of debt.

LG 4 Determine the cost of preferred stock.

LG 5 Calculate the required return on a company's common stock, and explain how it relates to the cost of retained earnings and the cost of new issues of common stock.

LG 6 Calculate the weighted average cost of capital (WACC), and discuss alternative weighting schemes.

MyLab Finance Chapter Introduction Video

WHY THIS CHAPTER MATTERS TO YOU

In your *professional* life

ACCOUNTING You need to understand the various sources of capital and how their costs are calculated to provide the data necessary to determine the firm's overall cost of capital.

INFORMATION SYSTEMS You need to understand the various sources of capital and how their costs are calculated to develop systems that will estimate the costs of those sources of capital as well as the overall cost of capital.

MANAGEMENT You need to understand the cost of capital to select long-term investments after assessing their acceptability and relative rankings.

MARKETING You need to understand the firm's cost of capital because proposed projects must earn returns in excess of it to be acceptable.

OPERATIONS You need to understand the firm's cost of capital to assess the economic viability of investments in plant and equipment needed to improve or grow the firm's capacity.

In your *personal* life

Knowing your *personal cost of capital* will allow you to make informed decisions about your personal consuming, borrowing, and investing. Managing personal wealth is a lot like managing the wealth of a business because you need to understand the tradeoffs between consuming wealth and growing wealth and how growing wealth can be accomplished by investing your own monies or borrowed monies. Understanding the cost of capital concepts will allow you to make better long-term decisions and maximize the value of your personal wealth.

JOHNSON & JOHNSON

Exceeding Expectations

Photo Central/Alamy Stock Photo

Listed at number 13 on the 2017 *Fortune* list of the World's Most Admired Companies, Johnson & Johnson manages a portfolio of widely recognized consumer products ranging from over-the-counter drugs to beauty products. J&J is one of only a handful of companies to increase its dividend payments to shareholders for 55 consecutive years, and from 2007 to 2017, J&J stock outperformed the S&P 500 by more than 2% per year. The company's CEO, Alex Gorsky, received a 95% approval rating from employees who filled out surveys on Glassdoor in 2016. All signs indicate that J&J is a well-run company.

What financial factors account for J&J's success? A May 2017 report at SeekingAlpha.com highlighted one of the key elements responsible for J&J's outstanding stock performance over the prior decade. The report noted that J&J generated after-tax operating profits equal to almost 17% of the capital invested in the business. In other words, J&J managers used the money that stockholders and lenders invested in the company to generate a return (in terms of profits) of almost 17%, a rate of return that far exceeded investors' expectations. To understand what rate of return their investors require, managers at J&J and most other large companies rely on the concept of *weighted average cost of capital, or WACC*. To calculate the WACC, managers must ascertain what returns their lenders and stockholders require and weight those returns based on the amount of debt and equity capital used by the firm. In J&J's case, the SeekingAlpha.com article estimated that the company's WACC was about 6%, so the profits generated by J&J were nearly three times greater than what their investors required. Performance like that results in a rising stock price.

Source: From "Johnson & Johnson: Own This Fairly Priced Stock Of Vulnerable Healthcare Products Managed By Happy Employees" by David J. Waldron. Published by *Seeking Alpha*. https://seekingalpha.com/article/4070718-johnson-and-johnson-fairly-priced-stock-vulnerable-healthcare-products-managed-happy.

9.1 Overview of the Cost of Capital

Chapter 1 established that the firm's goal is to maximize shareholder wealth. To do so, managers must make investments that are worth more than they cost. That is, investments need to have positive net present values (NPVs). In this chapter, you will learn about the cost of capital, which is (usually) the rate of return that financial managers use in determining which investment opportunities add value to the firm. The **cost of capital** represents the firm's cost of financing and is the minimum rate of return that a project must earn to increase firm value. When investors (i.e., stockholders and lenders) provide funding to a firm, they do so with the expectation that the firm will pay them a return. The returns that investors require constitute a cost of capital the firm must pay to investors. Investments that produce returns above the cost of capital will have positive

cost of capital
Represents the firm's cost of financing and is the minimum rate of return that a project must earn to increase the firm's value.

FOCUS ON ETHICS *in practice*

The Cost of Capital Also Rises

Gertrude Stein—who shaped 20th century art and literature through discussions in her 1920s Paris home with the likes of Pablo Picasso and Ernest Hemingway—famously wrote of Oakland, California, "There is no there, there." Had she lived until September 2016, she might have said the same about consumer accounts in the mega bank across the bay in San Francisco.

Wells Fargo entered 2016 in an enviable position. The bank easily weathered the 2008 financial crisis by remaining focused on its core business—retail banking in bricks-and-mortar branches. In July 2015, *U.S. News and World Report* touted Wells as the "best bank stock today," and in February 2016, *The Banker* awarded the distinction of "most valuable brand in banking" for the fourth consecutive year. Shrewd acquisitions and a knack for cross-selling vaulted Wells into the company of the world's largest banks—a long way from its start as part bank, part stagecoach in the 1850s.

Then, on September 8, 2016, the stagecoach threw a wheel—news broke that aggressive sales quotas had driven Wells employees to open millions of unauthorized accounts. When the dust settled, CEO John Stumpf was out, and the bank faced a $185 million fine from the Consumer Financial Protection Bureau in addition to $110 million in civil settlements with wronged customers. Even worse, consumer faith earned over 164 years was badly shaken. Wells Fargo became the largest business to ever lose accreditation with the Better Business Bureau.

The account scandal had broader financial consequences. In the month following disclosure, the price of Wells's stock tumbled 13.5% as damaging details emerged. Then on October 18, in an uncommon move for an investment-grade firm, Wells Fargo postponed its planned issue of new 10-year bonds when S&P Global Ratings raised the likelihood of a downgrade in the bank's credit rating. At the time, comparable Wells's debt offered a yield 162 basis points (100 bps = 1 percentage point) over Treasuries—up from 151 before the scandal broke.

The bank's weighted average cost of capital rose as well, reflecting a higher beta on common stock on top of the higher risk premium on debt. Going into 2016, Wells had not reported a loss in 45 years—a record in part traceable to emphasis on consumer financial products and services, which rank among the most steady business lines for commercial banks. This emphasis helps account for the low beta on Wells Fargo common stock, 0.9 in August 2016—meaning Wells stock was less risky than the average stock (beta = 1) as well as the stocks of other mega banks like Bank of America (beta = 1.6). But bad publicity from the scandal together with Wells' decision to end sales quotas produced a 40% drop in new checking accounts in 2016 and a 43% falloff in credit-card applications. Such declines go far to explain why Wells' beta climbed to 1.0 by year-end 2016.

► *Many feel only muscular government regulation—supported by severe punishment for transgressions—can deter corporations from unethical acts. How did markets punish Wells Fargo? In your opinion, how much of a role should markets play in policing corporate ethics?*

NPVs and will increase the value of the firm, because these investments are worth more than they cost. In contrast, projects with returns below the cost of capital will have negative NPVs and will decrease firm value.

The cost of capital is an extremely important financial concept. It acts as a major link between the firm's long-term investment decisions and the wealth of the firm's owners as determined by the market value of their shares. Managers use the cost of capital in a variety of ways. First, the cost of capital is usually the discount rate that managers apply to NPV calculations in deciding whether to undertake a particular investment. Second, as was highlighted in the chapter opener, managers use the cost of capital as a kind of benchmark against which they can judge their performance. To be specific, managers assess whether the returns they are earning on capital investments exceed or fall short of the firm's cost of capital. Third, managers use the cost of capital to value entire companies, as is necessary when a firm engages in mergers and acquisitions.

Many factors affect a firm's cost of capital, not the least of which is the ethical conduct of senior managers; read the *Focus on Ethics* box to see how an ethical lapse increased the cost of capital at Wells Fargo.

THE BASIC CONCEPT

capital
A firm's long-term sources of financing, which include both debt and equity.

capital structure
The mix of debt and equity financing that a firm employs.

Firms need money to pay for their investments. The term **capital** refers to a firm's long-term sources of financing, which include both debt and equity. Firms raise capital by selling securities such as common stock, preferred stock, and bonds to investors and by reinvesting profits back into the firm. A firm's **capital structure** refers to the mixture of debt and equity financing it employs. Some firms prefer capital structures that are close to 100% equity, while other firms borrow heavily. Table 9.1 shows the percentages of debt and equity financing in place at a number of well-known firms in 2017.

Table 9.1 shows that in 2017 General Electric's total capital had a market value of $494.5 billion. The company had debt outstanding with a market value of $250.2 billion and equity outstanding with a market value of $244.3 billion. Thus, debt accounted for about 51% of the company's long-term financing, and equity accounted for the remaining 49%. As another way to look at this, investors entrusted GE's managers with $494.5 billion, and to be successful, GE's managers need to invest that money in assets producing sufficient cash flows to provide both GE bondholders and stockholders the returns they expect. Whatever returns GE's assets produce ultimately flow back to its investors.

TABLE 9.1 Capital Structures of Well-Known Companies in 2017

Company	Value of Outstanding Debt ($ billions)	% Debt	Value of Outstanding Equity ($ billions)	% Equity	Total Capital ($ billions)
Alphabet	$ 3.9	1%	$643.5	99%	$647.40
Johnson & Johnson	23.5	6	341.6	94	365.10
Procter & Gamble	30.5	12	220.4	88	250.90
Dow Chemical	19.3	20	75.0	80	94.30
General Electric	250.2	51	244.3	49	494.50
General Motors	55.0	53	49.6	47	104.60

Now consider this thought experiment. Suppose you want to purchase a tiny fraction, say, 1/10,000,000, of GE's debt and the same fraction of its equity. To do this, you must buy $25,020 worth of GE bonds and $24,430 worth of GE stock. Your total portfolio is worth $49,450, and 51% of your portfolio consists of GE debt, with the other 49% consisting of GE equity, the very same percentages in GE's overall capital structure. What would your expected return on this portfolio be?

The answer is that the expected return on your portfolio would be the same as the overall expected return earned by GE.[1] By purchasing the same fraction (1/10,000,000) of GE's debt and equity, you have created a portfolio earning a return that mimics the overall return earned by debt and equity investors at GE, a return known as the **weighted average cost of capital (WACC)**. The WACC is a weighted average of the firm's cost of debt capital and its cost of equity capital, where the weights correspond to the percentage of each type of financing used by the firm. The WACC reflects the overall cost of financing to the firm, not just the cost of one financing source.

weighted average cost of capital (WACC)
A weighted average of a firm's cost of debt and equity financing, where the weights reflect the percentage of each type of financing used by the firm.

Managers must take into account the costs of both forms of capital when they make investment decisions because the cash flows produced by investments must be sufficient to satisfy the expectations of both types (debt and equity) of investors. As Table 9.1 illustrates, most firms do finance their activities with a blend of equity and debt. In Chapter 13, we will explore the factors that determine what mix of debt and equity is optimal for any particular firm. For now, we will simply say that most firms have a desired mix of financing, and the cost of capital must reflect the cost of each type of financing used. To capture all the relevant financing costs, assuming some desired mix of financing, we need to look at the overall cost of capital rather than just the cost of any single source of financing.

EXAMPLE 9.1

MyLab Finance Solution Video

A firm is currently considering two investment opportunities. Two financial analysts, working independently of each other, are evaluating these opportunities. Assume the following information about investments A and B.

Investment A

Cost	$100,000
Life	20 years
Expected Return	7%

The analyst studying this investment recalls that the company recently issued bonds paying a 6% rate of return. He reasons that because the investment project earns 7% while the firm can issue debt at 6%, the project must be worth doing, so he recommends that the company undertake this investment.

Investment B

Cost	$100,000
Life	20 years
Expected Return	12%

1. From the basic accounting equation, we know that assets equal debt plus equity, $A = D + E$. Divide both sides of this equation by 10,000,000 to obtain $0.0000001A = 0.0000001D + 0.0000001E$. By purchasing 1/10,000,000 of GE's debt and equity (which is the right side of the previous equation), you have created a claim against 1/10,000,000 of GE's assets. Thus, the return on your portfolio is the same as the return produced by GE's assets.

The analyst assigned to this project knows that the firm has common stock outstanding and that investors who hold the company's stock expect a 14% return on their investment. The analyst decides that the firm should not undertake this investment because it produces only a 12% return while the company's shareholders expect a 14% return.

In this example, each analyst is making a mistake by focusing on one source of financing rather than on the overall financing mix. What if instead the analysts used a combined cost of financing? By weighting the cost of each source of financing by its relative proportion in the firm's capital structure, the firm can obtain a *weighted average cost of capital (WACC)*. Assuming this firm desires a 50–50 mix of debt and equity, the WACC is 10%[(0.50 × 6% debt) + (0.50 × 14% equity)]. With this average cost of financing, the firm should reject the first opportunity (7% expected return < 10% WACC) and accept the second (12% expected return > 10% WACC).

SOURCES OF LONG-TERM CAPITAL

In this chapter, our concern is only with the long-term sources of capital available to a firm because they are the sources that supply the financing necessary to support the firm's major investments. The process by which firms make investment decisions designed to maximize shareholders' wealth is called capital budgeting. We study capital budgeting in Part Five, but at this point it is sufficient to say that capital budgeting activities are chief among the responsibilities of financial managers and that they cannot be carried out without knowing the appropriate cost of capital with which to judge the firm's investment opportunities.

Long-term capital for firms derives from four basic sources: long-term debt, preferred stock, common stock, and retained earnings. All entries on the right-hand side of the balance sheet, other than current liabilities, represent these sources:

Balance Sheet		
Assets	Current liabilities	
	Long-term debt	Sources of long-term capital
	Stockholders' equity Preferred stock Common stock equity Common stock Retained earnings	Sources of long-term capital

Not every firm will use all of these financing sources. In particular, the number of firms that issue preferred stock is relatively small. Even so, most firms will have some mix of funds from these sources in their capital structures. Although a firm's existing mix of financing sources may reflect its target capital structure, ultimately the marginal cost of capital necessary to raise the next marginal dollar of financing is most relevant for evaluating the firm's future investment opportunities.

→ **REVIEW QUESTIONS** MyLab Finance Solutions

9–1 What is the cost of capital?

9–2 What role does the cost of capital play in the firm's long-term investment decisions? How does it relate to the firm's ability to maximize shareholder wealth?

9–3 What does the firm's capital structure represent?

9–4 What are the typical sources of long-term capital available to the firm?

LG3

9.2 Cost of Long-Term Debt

Firms that borrow money pay interest to lenders. That interest is a cost to the borrower, but interest alone does not fully reflect a firm's borrowing cost. If a firm borrows money by issuing bonds, it will incur costs specifically tied to the process of issuing new securities, separate from the interest payments made on those securities. In addition, in the United States, the tax laws allow firms to treat interest payments as a tax-deductible expense.[2] That deduction reduces a firm's taxes, and thereby reduces the cost of debt. The **cost of long-term debt**, r_d, is the financing cost associated with new funds raised through long-term borrowing, taking into account the firm's interest payments and other borrowing costs. Typically, firms raise long-term debt by issuing corporate bonds, though they may also borrow on a long-term basis from banks or other financial institutions.

cost of long-term debt
The financing cost associated with new funds raised through long-term borrowing.

NET PROCEEDS

net proceeds
Funds actually received by the firm from the sale of a security.

flotation costs
The total costs of issuing and selling a security.

The **net proceeds** from the sale of a bond, or any security, are the funds that the firm receives from the sale. Net proceeds are less than total proceeds due to **flotation costs,** which represent the total costs of issuing and selling securities. These costs apply to all public offerings of securities: debt, preferred stock, and common stock. They include two components: (1) *underwriting costs,* or compensation earned by investment bankers for selling the security; and (2) *administrative costs,* or issuer expenses such as legal and accounting costs.

When firms sell bonds, they usually set the coupon rate so that the bonds will sell close to par value, but often by the time the bond sale occurs, interest rates have moved slightly and the bond may sell slightly above par (at a premium) or slightly below par (at a discount). The total proceeds from a bond sale equal the market price of the bond (which may not equal par value) times the number of bonds sold.

EXAMPLE 9.2

Duchess Corporation, a major hardware manufacturer, is contemplating selling \$10 million worth of 20-year, 6% coupon bonds, each with a par value of \$1,000. Because bonds with similar risk earn returns equal to 6%, Duchess's bonds will sell in the market at par value, and they will have a yield to maturity (YTM) equal to the coupon rate, 6%. However, Duchess will incur flotation costs equal to 2% of the par value of the bond ($0.02 \times \$1,000$), or \$20. The *net proceeds* to the firm from the sale of each bond are therefore \$980.

2. The Tax Cuts and Jobs Act of 2017 placed a limit on how much interest firms can deduct. The limit is based on a complex formula that changes over time, but roughly firms cannot deduct interest that exceeds 30% of their EBIT. In this chapter, we will usually assume that firms are below this limit and can fully deduct all interest payments.

BEFORE-TAX COST OF DEBT

The before-tax cost of debt, r_d, is simply the rate of return the firm must pay on new borrowing. If a firm could issue bonds without incurring flotation costs, then the firm's before-tax cost of debt would equal the return required by bondholders. Flotation costs mean that a firm's before-tax cost of debt is slightly higher than the bondholders' required return. You can find a firm's before-tax cost of debt for bonds in any of three ways: quotation, calculation, or approximation.

Using Market Quotations

A relatively quick method for finding the before-tax cost of debt is to observe the *yield to maturity (YTM)* on the firm's existing bonds or bonds of similar risk issued by other companies. The YTM of existing bonds reflects the rate of return required by the market. For example, if the market requires a YTM of 6% for a similar-risk bond, managers can use this value as an estimate of the before-tax cost of debt, r_d, for new bonds. You can find bond yields in sources such as the *Wall Street Journal*.

Calculating the Cost

Managers can calculate the cost of debt associated with a particular bond issue by calculating the bond's YTM. To calculate the YTM, remember that managers must know the cash flows the bond will provide as well as its market price. Taking the costs of issuing the bonds into account requires managers to use the net proceeds from the bond issue rather than the market price.[3] This approach finds the before-tax cost of debt by calculating the YTM generated by the bond's cash flows, given the net proceeds that the firm receives when it issues the bonds. The YTM represents the annual before-tax percentage cost of the debt.

EXAMPLE 9.3

In the preceding example, Duchess receives proceeds of $980 by issuing a 20-year bond with a $1,000 par value and 6% coupon interest rate. To calculate the before-tax cost of debt, begin by writing down the cash flows associated with this bond issue. The cash flow pattern consists of an initial inflow (the net proceeds) followed by a series of annual outflows (the interest payments). In the final year, when the debt is retired, an outflow representing the repayment of the principal also occurs. The cash flows associated with Duchess Corporation's bond issue are as follows:

End of year(s)	Cash flow
0	$ 980
1–20	−60
20	−1,000

3. As an alternative, managers can account for flotation costs by treating them as cash outflows associated with the investment that the bonds are being issued to fund. In this approach, the cost of debt is the YTM calculated using the bond's market price rather than the net proceeds.

Duchess can determine the before-tax cost of debt by finding the YTM, which is the discount rate that equates the present value of the bond outflows to the initial inflow.

MyLab Finance Financial Calculator

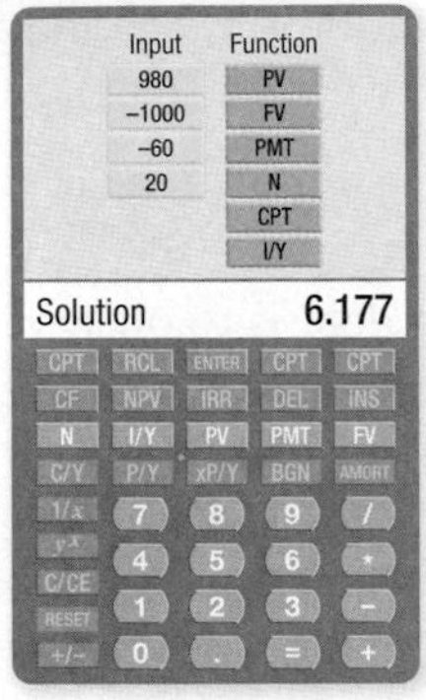

Calculator use (*Note:* Most calculators require either the present value [net proceeds] or the future value [annual interest payments and repayment of principal] to be input as negative numbers when we calculate yield to maturity. That approach is used here.) Using the calculator and the inputs shown at the left, you should find the before-tax cost of debt (yield to maturity) to be 6.177%.

Spreadsheet use The before-tax cost of debt on the Duchess Corporation bond can be calculated using an Excel spreadsheet. The following Excel spreadsheet shows that by referencing the cells containing the bond's net proceeds, coupon payment, years to maturity, and par value as part of Excel's RATE function, you can quickly determine that the appropriate before-tax cost of debt for Duchess Corporation's bond is 6.177%.

	A	B
1	FINDING THE BEFORE-TAX COST OF DEBT	
2	Par value	–$1,000
3	Coupon interest rate	6.0%
4	Interest payments per year	1
5	Interest payment	–$60
6	Number of years to maturity	20
7	Net proceeds from sale of bond	$980
8	Before-tax cost of debt	6.177%

Entry in Cell B8 =RATE(B6*B4,B5,B7,B2,0).
The minus sign appears before the $1,000 in B2 and the $60 in B5 because these values are cash outflows for the corporation.

Approximating the Cost

Although not as precise as using a calculator, there is a method for approximating the before-tax cost of debt. The before-tax cost of debt, r_d, for a bond with a $1,000 par value can be approximated by

$$r_d = \frac{I + \dfrac{\$1{,}000 - N_d}{n}}{\dfrac{N_d + \$1{,}000}{2}} \tag{9.1}$$

Where

I = annual interest in dollars
N_d = net proceeds from the sale of debt (bond)
n = number of years to the bond's maturity

EXAMPLE 9.4

Substituting the appropriate values from the Duchess Corporation example into the approximation formula given in Equation 9.1, we get

$$r_d = \frac{\$60 + \dfrac{\$1{,}000 - \$980}{20}}{\dfrac{\$980 + \$1{,}000}{2}} = \frac{\$60 + \$1}{\$990}$$

$$= \frac{\$61}{\$990} = 0.06162 \text{ or } 6.162\%$$

This approximate value of before-tax cost of debt is close to the 6.177%, but it lacks the precision of the value derived using the calculator or spreadsheet.

AFTER-TAX COST OF DEBT

Unlike the dividends paid to common and preferred stockholders, the interest payments paid to bondholders are tax deductible, so the interest expense on debt reduces taxable income (as long as interest does not exceed 30% of EBIT) and, therefore, the firm's tax liability. In effect, this means the after-tax cost of debt to the firm will be less than the stated rate of return paid to bondholders on their bonds. To find the firm's net cost of debt, we must account for the tax savings created by debt and solve for the cost of long-term debt on an after-tax basis. The after-tax cost of debt equals the product of the before-tax cost, r_d, and the term, 1 minus the tax rate, T:

$$\text{After-tax cost of debt} = r_d \times (1 - T) \qquad (9.2)$$

EXAMPLE 9.5

MyLab Finance Solution Video

Duchess Corporation has a 21% tax rate. Using the 6.177% before-tax debt cost calculated above and applying Equation 9.2, we find an after-tax cost of debt of 4.88% [6.177% × (1 − 0.21)]. If Duchess' interest expense reaches 30% of EBIT, then any *additional* interest expense is not deductible and for any additional borrowing the before- and after-tax cost of debt are equal. Recall that when bondholders purchase a Duchess bond at par value, they expect to earn a 6% YTM. Incorporating the issuance costs and the tax benefit of debt, the firm's after-tax cost of debt is just 4.88%, quite a bit less than the 6% return offered to bondholders. In most cases, debt is the least expensive form of financing available to a firm. Debt is a relatively inexpensive form of financing for two main reasons. First, debt is less risky than preferred or common stock. That alone makes debt a low-cost form of financing because investors accept lower returns on bonds than on stock. Second, the firm enjoys a tax benefit from issuing debt that it does not receive when it uses equity capital.

PERSONAL FINANCE EXAMPLE 9.6

MyLab Finance Solution Video

Kait and Kasim Sullivan, a married couple in the 28% income-tax bracket, wish to borrow $60,000 to pay for a new luxury car. To finance the purchase, either they can borrow the $60,000 through the auto dealer at an annual interest rate of 4.5%, or they can take a $60,000 second mortgage on their home. The best annual rate they can get on the second mortgage is 5.5%. They already have qualified for both loans being considered.

If they borrow from the auto dealer, the interest on this loan will not be deductible for federal tax purposes. However, the interest on the second mortgage would be tax deductible because the tax law allows individuals to deduct interest paid on a home mortgage. To choose the least-cost financing, the Sullivans calculated the after-tax cost of both sources of long-term debt. Because interest on the auto loan is not tax deductible, its after-tax cost equals its before-tax cost of 4.5%. Because the interest on the second mortgage is tax deductible, its after-tax cost can be found using Equation 9.2:

$$\text{After-tax cost of debt} = 5.5\% \times (1 - 0.28) = 5.5\% \times 0.72 = 3.96\%$$

Because the 3.96% after-tax cost of the second mortgage is less than the 4.5% cost of the auto loan, the Sullivans may decide to use the second mortgage to finance the auto purchase.

Considered in isolation, a firm's least expensive after-tax source of financing is usually debt. However, even if debt is cheaper than other forms of financing, this does not imply that firms should always finance their investments with debt. Financing with debt puts the firm's existing shareholders in a riskier position because the firm must repay lenders regardless of whether it is profitable. Therefore, if a firm chooses to borrow more, its existing shareholders will demand a higher rate of return, thus raising the firm's cost of equity financing. The increase in cost of equity could partially or fully offset the benefit of using low-cost debt as a financing source, so firms must carefully weigh the tradeoffs they face when using different sources of capital. Finding the optimal mix of debt and equity capital is a problem that we will explore in depth in a later chapter.

→ REVIEW QUESTIONS MyLab Finance Solutions

9–5 What are the net proceeds from the sale of a bond? What are flotation costs, and how do they affect a bond's net proceeds?

9–6 What methods can be used to find the before-tax cost of debt?

9–7 How is the before-tax cost of debt converted into the after-tax cost?

→ EXCEL REVIEW QUESTION MyLab Finance Solutions

9–8 The interest expense on debt provides a tax deduction for the issuer, so any calculation of a firm's net cost of debt should reflect this benefit. Using the information provided at MyLab Finance, compute a firm's after-tax cost of debt with a spreadsheet model.

9.3 Cost of Preferred Stock

Preferred stock represents a special type of ownership interest in the firm. It gives preferred stockholders the right to receive dividends before the firm can distribute any earnings to common stockholders. The key characteristics of preferred stock were described in Chapter 7, but we provide a brief review here.

PREFERRED STOCK DIVIDENDS

When companies issue preferred shares, the shares usually pay a fixed dividend and have a fixed par value. When discussing the features of a particular preferred stock issue, investors may refer to the fixed dividend either in dollar terms or as a percentage of the stock's par value. For example, suppose a company issues preferred stock that promises an annual $4 dividend in perpetuity and has a par value of $50. The dividend equals 8% of the preferred's par value, so investors might refer to this stock as a "$4 preferred share" or an "8% preferred share."

CALCULATING THE COST OF PREFERRED STOCK

cost of preferred stock, r_p
The ratio of the preferred stock dividend to the firm's net proceeds from the sale of preferred stock.

The **cost of preferred stock, r_p,** is the ratio of the preferred stock dividend to the firm's net proceeds from the sale of the preferred stock. As with bonds, net proceeds equal the total proceeds minus any flotation costs. The following equation gives the cost of preferred stock, r_p, in terms of the annual dollar dividend, D_p, and the net proceeds from the sale of the stock, N_p:

$$r_p = \frac{D_p}{N_p} \tag{9.3}$$

EXAMPLE 9.7

Duchess Corporation is contemplating issuance of an 8% preferred stock they expect to sell at par value for $80 per share. The cost of issuing and selling the stock will be $2.50 per share. The first step in finding the cost of the stock is to calculate the dollar amount of the annual preferred dividend, which is $6.40 (0.08 × $80). The net proceeds per share from the proposed sale of stock equals the sale price minus the flotation costs ($80 − $2.50 = $77.50). Substituting the annual dividend, D_p, of $6.40 and the net proceeds, N_p, of $77.50 into Equation 9.3 gives the cost of preferred stock, 8.258% ($6.4 ÷ $77.50).

The cost of Duchess's preferred stock (8.258%) is slightly greater than the 8% return that preferred stockholders require because of the issuance costs that Duchess must pay. The cost of preferred stock is much greater than the after-tax cost of its long-term debt (3.706%). This difference exists both because interest payments are tax deductible, whereas preferred dividends are not, and because preferred stock is riskier than long-term debt and therefore must pay a higher return.

→ **REVIEW QUESTION** MyLab Finance Solution

9–9 How would you calculate the cost of preferred stock?

LG 5

9.4 Cost of Common Stock

The cost of common stock is the return required on the stock by investors in the marketplace, possibly adjusted to account for costs of issuing new shares of stock. There are two forms of common stock financing: (1) retained earnings and (2) new issues of common stock. As a first step in finding each of these costs, we must estimate the required return on common stock.

FINDING THE COST OF COMMON STOCK EQUITY

cost of common stock equity
The costs associated with using common stock equity financing. The cost of common stock equity is equal to the required return on the firm's common stock in the absence of flotation costs. Thus, the cost of common stock equity is the same as the cost of retained earnings, but the cost of issuing new common equity is higher.

The **cost of common stock equity** reflects the costs that firms incur to utilize common stock financing. Just as the costs of debt and preferred stock were influenced by the required returns of bondholders and preferred stockholders, the cost of common stock equity will reflect the return required by the firm's stockholders. However, calculating the required return for common stock is more difficult than finding the required return on bonds or preferred shares. With bonds, the YTM provides an easy-to-calculate estimate of the return that bondholders expect, and likewise with preferred stock—the ratio of the preferred share's dividend to its market price indicates the return that preferred shareholders expect. Dividends on common shares, however, are not fixed, as are bond interest payments and preferred dividends. Moreover, for most common stocks, a significant component of the return that investors receive comes in the form of a capital gain resulting from reinvestment of the firm's earnings in the business. Therefore, managers require a different approach to calculate the required return on common stock. Two techniques are used for this calculation. One relies on the constant-growth valuation model, while the other makes use of the capital asset pricing model (CAPM).

Using the Constant-Growth Valuation (Gordon Growth) Model

constant-growth valuation (Gordon growth) model
A model that calculates the value of common stock as the present value of an infinite dividend stream that grows at a constant rate.

In Chapter 7, we found that the value of a share of common stock equals the present value of all future dividends paid to shareholders. Valuing common stock therefore requires estimates of future dividend payments. One simple way to derive such estimates is to assume that dividends will grow at a constant rate forever. The **constant-growth valuation model**, also known as the **Gordon growth model**, values common stock by making that very assumption. The key expression derived for this model is

$$P_0 = \frac{D_1}{r_s - g} \tag{9.4}$$

where

P_0 = current value of common stock
D_1 = dividend expected in 1 year
r_s = required return on common stock
g = constant rate of growth in dividends

Solving Equation 9.4 for r_s results in the following expression for the required return on common stock:

$$r_s = \frac{D_1}{P_0} + g \tag{9.5}$$

Equation 9.5 indicates that the required return on common stock equals the ratio of the dividend expected in 1 year to the current market price, plus the dividend growth rate. The first term captures the rate of return that shareholders expect to earn from dividends, and the second term captures the return they expect to earn from capital gains.

EXAMPLE 9.8

Duchess Corporation wishes to determine the required return on its common stock, r_s. The market price, P_0, of its common stock is \$50 per share. Duchess recently paid a \$3.80 dividend. The company has increased its dividend for several consecutive years. Just 5 years ago, Duchess paid a dividend of \$2.98 on its common stock.

Using a financial calculator or electronic spreadsheet, in conjunction with the technique described earlier in this text for finding growth rates, we can calculate the average annual dividend growth rate, g, over the past 5 years. The average dividend growth rate is about 5%. If Duchess continues to increase the dividend at this rate, then next year's dividend will be 5% more than the \$3.80 dividend that it just paid, or \$3.99. Substituting $D_1 = \$3.99$, $P_0 = \$50$, and $g = 5\%$ into Equation 9.5 yields the cost of common stock equity:

$$r_s = \frac{\$3.99}{\$50} + 0.05 = 0.0798 + 0.05 = 0.1298 = 12.98\%$$

Because this estimate depends on a somewhat imprecise forecast of the company's long-run dividend growth rate, a kind of false precision arises in concluding that the required return on equity is 12.98%, so we will just round up to 13%.

Using the Capital Asset Pricing Model (CAPM)

capital asset pricing model (CAPM)
Describes the relationship between the required return, r_s, and the nondiversifiable risk of the firm as measured by the beta coefficient, β.

Recall from Chapter 8 that the **capital asset pricing model (CAPM)** describes the relationship between the required or expected return on some asset j, r_j, and the nondiversifiable risk of the asset as measured by the beta coefficient, β_j. The basic CAPM is

$$r_j = R_F + [\beta_j \times (r_m - R_F)] \tag{9.6}$$

where

R_F = risk-free rate of return

r_m = market return; return on the market portfolio of assets

If Duchess wants to use the CAPM to estimate the required return on its common stock, it needs three pieces of information: the risk-free rate, the return on the overall stock market, and the beta of its common shares.

EXAMPLE 9.9

Duchess Corporation now wishes to calculate the required return on its common stock, r_s, by using the CAPM. The firm's investment advisors and its own analysts indicate that the risk-free rate, R_F, equals 3%; the firm's beta, β, equals 1.5; and the market return, r_m, equals 9%. Substituting these values into Equation 9.6, the company estimates that the required return on its common stock, r_s, is 12%:

$$r_s = 3.0\% + [1.5 \times (9.0\% - 3.0\%)] = 3.0\% + 9\% = 12.0\%$$

Notice that this estimate of the required return on Duchess stock does not line up exactly with the estimate obtained from the constant-growth model. That is to be expected because the two models rely on different assumptions. In practice, analysts at Duchess might average the two figures to arrive at a final estimate for the required return on common stock.

Comparing Constant-Growth and CAPM Techniques

The CAPM technique differs from the constant-growth valuation model in that it directly considers the firm's risk, as reflected by beta, in determining the required return on common stock equity. The constant-growth model does not look at risk directly; it uses an indirect approach to infer what return shareholders expect based upon the price they are willing to pay for the stock today, P_0, given estimates of the firm's future dividends. Using the constant-growth model to find the required return on a stock is somewhat analogous to finding the required return on a bond by calculating its YTM. Both calculations rely on a security's current market price and its future cash flows to arrive at a required return. With bonds, the future cash flows are relatively easy to predict, whereas with common stock, the long-run dividend stream is much harder to estimate.

Flotation Costs and the Cost of Common Equity

Recall that for debt and preferred stock, the firm may face flotation costs, which increase the cost of capital to the firm. Thus far we have ignored these costs related to common equity, so the estimates we have obtained for Duchess reflect only the required return on the company's stock. If Duchess issues new shares of common stock, its cost of equity will exceed the return that its shareholders require due to flotation costs. The firm could treat those costs as cash outflows associated with the specific project that prompts the firm to issue new shares in the first place, or it could make an adjustment to the required return on equity to reflect flotation costs. Unlike the CAPM, the constant-growth model offers a relatively easy way to adjust for flotation costs in finding the cost of common stock.

When a firm issues new common stock, a variety of costs reduce the net proceeds the firm receives. These costs include the underwriting fees and administrative costs discussed earlier. In addition, investment bankers usually sell new shares of common stock at a slight discount to their current market value, a phenomenon known as *underpricing*. Underpricing represents a cost to issuers because it requires them to sell a greater number of shares (which will over time receive a greater amount of dividends) than would be the case if shares were sold at full market value.

cost of a new issue of common stock, r_n
The cost of common stock, net of underpricing and associated flotation costs.

Our purpose in finding the firm's overall cost of capital is to determine the after-tax cost of *new* funds required for financing projects. The **cost of a new issue of common stock, r_n,** is determined by calculating the cost of common stock, net of underpricing and associated flotation costs. We can use the constant-growth valuation model expression for the required return on common stock, r_s, as a starting point. If we let N_n represent the net proceeds from the sale of new common stock after subtracting underpricing and flotation costs, the cost of the new issue, r_n, can be expressed as:[4]

$$r_n = \frac{D_1}{N_n} + g \tag{9.7}$$

4. An alternative form of this equation is

$$r_n = \frac{D_1}{P_0 \times (1 - f)} + g \tag{9.7a}$$

where f represents the *percentage* reduction in current market price expected as a result of underpricing and flotation costs. Simply stated, N_n in Equation 9.7 is equivalent to $p_0 \times (1 - f)$ in Equation 9.7a.

The net proceeds from the sale of new common stock, N_n, will be less than the current market price, P_0. Therefore, the cost of new issues, r_n, will always be greater than the return that stockholders require, r_s. The cost of new common stock is normally greater than any other long-term financing cost because common stock is riskier, and therefore must pay a higher return, than any other security that firms issue.

EXAMPLE 9.10

In the constant-growth valuation example, we found that Duchess Corporation's required return on common stock, r_s, was 13%, using the following values: an expected dividend, D_1, of \$3.99; a current market price, P_0, of \$50; and an expected growth rate of dividends, g, of 5%.

To determine its cost of new common stock, r_n, Duchess Corporation has estimated that on average, new shares can be sold for \$48. Thus, Duchess's shares will be underpriced by \$2 per share. A second cost associated with a new issue is flotation costs of \$1.50 per share that would be paid to issue and sell the new shares. The total underpricing and flotation costs per share are therefore \$3.50.

Subtracting the \$3.50-per-share underpricing and flotation cost from the current \$50 share price results in expected net proceeds of \$46.50 per share. Substituting $D_1 = \$3.99$, $N_n = \$46.50$, and $g = 5\%$ into Equation 9.7 results in a cost of new common stock, r_n:

$$r_n = \frac{\$3.99}{\$46.50} + 0.05 = 0.0858 + 0.05 = 0.1358 = 13.58\%$$

Duchess Corporation's cost of new common stock is therefore between 13% and 14%.

COST OF RETAINED EARNINGS

In our discussion of the cost of equity financing so far, we have assumed that firms would raise equity by issuing new shares of common stock, but they may also use earnings they have retained to reinvest in the business. If firms use retained earnings to finance new investment, they incur no incremental flotation costs. This does not mean that retained earnings are free for the firm to use, however. Retained earnings have an opportunity cost, meaning that if the firm did not use them to reinvest in investment projects, it could distribute them to shareholders as dividends, and the shareholders could make other investments with them. Thus, the **cost of retained earnings,** r_r, to the firm is the same as the required return on the firm's common stock, r_s.

cost of retained earnings, r_r
The cost of using retained earnings as a financing source. The cost of retained earnings is equal to the required return on a firm's common stock, r_s.

$$r_r = r_s \tag{9.8}$$

It is not necessary to adjust the cost of retained earnings for flotation costs because by retaining earnings the firm "raises" equity capital without incurring these costs.

EXAMPLE 9.11

The cost of retained earnings for Duchess Corporation equals the required return on equity. Recall that we calculated the required return using two methods. With the constant-growth model, we estimated the required return on equity to be 13% (before accounting for flotation costs and underpricing), and with the CAPM, the required return on equity was 12%. Thus, the cost for Duchess

MATTER OF FACT

Retained Earnings, the Preferred Source of Financing

In the United States and most other countries, firms rely more heavily on retained earnings than any other financing source. For example, a 2016 survey of U.K. firms conducted by the Bank of England found that about 80% of the companies surveyed listed retained earnings as one of their primary sources of funds. Bank loans were a distant second choice, mentioned as a primary source of funds by roughly 58% of the companies.[5]

Corporation to finance investments through retained earnings, r_r, falls somewhere in the range of 12.0% to 13.0%. Both estimates are lower than the cost of a new issue of common stock because by using retained earnings the firm avoids the additional costs associated with issuing new equity.

→ REVIEW QUESTIONS MyLab Finance Solutions

9–10 What premise about share value underlies the constant-growth valuation (Gordon growth) model that we use to measure the cost of common stock equity, r_s?

9–11 How do the constant-growth valuation model and capital asset pricing model methods for finding the cost of common stock differ?

9–12 Why is the cost of financing a project with retained earnings less than the cost of financing it with a new issue of common stock?

LG6

9.5 Weighted Average Cost of Capital

As noted earlier, the *weighted average cost of capital (WACC)*, r_{wacc}, reflects the expected average cost of the different forms of capital used by a company. It equals the weighted average cost of each specific type of capital, where the weights equal the proportion of each capital source in the firm's capital structure.

CALCULATING THE WEIGHTED AVERAGE COST OF CAPITAL (WACC)

Calculating the WACC is straightforward: Multiply the individual cost of each form of financing by its proportion in the firm's capital structure and sum the weighted values. As an equation, the weighted average cost of capital, r_{wacc}, can be specified as

$$r_{wacc} = (w_d \times r_d)(1 - T) + (w_p \times r_p) + (w_s \times r_{s \text{ or } n}) \qquad (9.9)$$

5. Jumana Salehee, Iren Levina, and Srdan Tatomir, "The financial system and productive investment: new survey evidence," *Bank of England Quarterly Bulletin*, Q1 2017.

where

w_d = proportion of long-term debt in capital structure

w_p = proportion of preferred stock in capital structure

w_s = proportion of common stock equity in capital structure

$w_d + w_p + w_s = 1.0$

We want to highlight four important points related to Equation 9.9:

1. The weights must be nonnegative and sum to 1.0. Simply stated, the WACC must account for all financing costs within the firm's capital structure.
2. The weights are based on the market value of each capital source as a percentage of the market value of the firm's total capital. For example, w_s is based on the market value of the firm's stock, not on its par value or the value of equity shown on the firm's balance sheet.
3. We multiply the firm's common stock equity weight, w_s, by either the required return on the firm's stock, r_s, or the cost of new common stock, r_n. Remember that when firms finance investments with retained earnings, the cost of retained earnings, r_r, is the same as the required return on the firm's stock. However, when the firm issues new shares, the cost of equity is higher due to flotation costs, so the firm may use r_n in Equation 9.9.
4. We multiply the firm's cost of debt by $(1 - T)$ to capture the tax deduction tied to interest payments.

EXAMPLE 9.12

In earlier examples, we found the costs of the various types of capital for Duchess Corporation to be as follows:

$$r_d(1 - T) = 4.880\% = 4.88\%$$
$$r_p = 8.258\% = 8.26\%$$
$$r_s = 13.00\%$$

Duchess has total capital with a market value of \$1 billion. The market value of the firm's outstanding long-term debt is \$400 million, the value of its preferred stock is \$100 million, and the market value of its common stock is \$500 million. Thus, the weights for the weighted average cost of capital (WACC) calculation are as follows:

Source of capital	Weight
Long-term debt	40%
Preferred stock	10
Common stock equity	50
Total	100%

Because the firm expects to have a sizable amount of retained earnings available, it plans to use the required return on equity, r_s (or, equivalently, the cost of retained earnings, r_r), as the cost of common stock equity. The calculation for Duchess Corporation's WACC appears in Table 9.2. The resulting WACC for Duchess is 9.28%. This establishes a hurdle rate for Duchess, meaning that the company should accept investment opportunities that promise returns above 9.28% as long as those investment opportunities are not riskier than the firm's current investments.

TABLE 9.2 Calculation of the Weighted Average Cost of Capital for Duchess Corporation

Source of capital	Weight w	Cost r	Weighted cost $w \times r$
Long-term debt	0.40	4.88%	1.95%
Preferred stock	0.10	8.26	0.83
Common stock equity	0.50	13.00	6.50
Totals	1.00		WACC = 9.28%

FOCUS ON PRACTICE *in practice*

Uncertain Times Make for an Uncertain Weighted Average Cost of Capital

As U.S. financial markets experienced and recovered from the 2008 financial crisis, firms struggled to keep track of their weighted average cost of capital. The individual component costs were moving rapidly in response to the financial market turmoil. Volatile financial markets can make otherwise manageable cost-of-capital calculations exceedingly complex and inherently error prone, possibly wreaking havoc with investment decisions. If a firm underestimates its cost of capital, it risks making investments that are not economically justified, and if a firm overestimates its financing costs, it risks forgoing value-maximizing investments.

Although the WACC computation does not change when markets become unstable, the uncertainty surrounding the components that constitute the WACC increases dramatically. The financial crisis pushed interest rates on long-term corporate bonds to historically high levels. Other things being equal, high borrowing costs put upward pressure on the WACC. But at the same time that rates on corporate bonds increased, yields on Treasury securities fell to historic lows. The risk-free rate is a key input to the cost of equity calculation for firms that use the CAPM to calculate the cost of equity, so falling Treasury rates seemed to be putting downward pressure on the cost of equity. These and other factors made it difficult for firms to gain a genuine understanding of what capital costs they actually faced during the financial crisis.

Since then, Treasury rates have remained low, and corporate borrowing rates have fallen substantially. Central banks around the world have taken actions to keep interest rates low to reduce capital costs for firms, which in theory should encourage firms to make new investments and help spur economic recovery. After all, if capital is less expensive, then the rate of return that an investment must earn to create value for shareholders, the so-called hurdle rate, should be lower, too. However, a 2016 report by JP Morgan noted that since the financial crisis, firms had maintained high hurdle rates for new investments. In its survey of more than 100 financial executives, JP Morgan discovered that executives understood that the costs of both equity and debt had fallen since the financial crisis, and that the WACC had fallen as a consequence. Even so, these executives maintained hurdle rates for new investments at the same levels that had been in place years earlier. JP Morgan estimated that the WACC for a typical company had fallen to about 7.5% by 2016, but even so, the report suggested that the average hurdle rate used by companies in deciding whether to accept or decline investment opportunities remained "stuck" at close to 12%. In principle, this meant that firms were passing up investment opportunities that might have created value for their investors. The Morgan report speculated that managers might have maintained high hurdle rates because they expected significant near-term increases in interest rates.

► *Why is having a hurdle rate above the cost of capital bad for shareholders? Is there a flaw in the argument that if interest rates may rise in the near term, the hurdle rate for an investment should be above the WACC?*

Source: Marc Zenner, Evan Junek, and Ram Chivukula, "It's time to reassess your hurdle rates," JP Morgan Chase and Co., November 2016.

CAPITAL STRUCTURE WEIGHTS

market value weights
Weights that use market values to measure the proportion of each type of capital in the firm's financial structure.

We noted earlier that when calculating a firm's WACC, analysts should use **market value weights** for the percentages of each type of financing, rather than book or par values. This is because the market value better reflects the value of the funds that investors have placed in the hands of managers and on which investors expect to earn a return. For debt, the difference between market value and book value is usually not extremely large, but for equity the difference can be enormous. For example, on its March 2017 balance sheet, Netflix reported common stock equity of about $3 billion and a similar value for long-term debt. Those numbers would suggest that Netflix was financed with a 50-50 mix of debt and equity. However, the market value of Netflix stock was about $70 billion! The market value of equity was vastly greater than its book value because market values are inherently forward looking, whereas book values take a more historical perspective. Investors expected Netflix to generate much more cash flow in the future than it had in the past, and that view was reflected in the market value of the company's stock, but not in the value of equity on its books. Of course, the investors who held Netflix debt could earn only a fixed return (i.e., the interest payments they were promised) no matter how well the company performed in the future, so although the market value of the company's debt might rise and fall somewhat as market interest rates move, the market value of debt could never exceed its book value to the same degree that was true for equity. The notion that Netflix was financed with a 50-50 mix of debt and equity was grossly incorrect—based on market values, equity investors provided about 96% of the firm's capital with debt, accounting for just 4% of total capital.

The preceding example raises another subtle point about the weights in the WACC calculation. In 2016, equity accounted for 96% of the total financing used by Netflix. But in the 5-year period from 2012 to 2016, the return on Netflix common stock averaged almost 66% per year. Thus, the market value of Netflix equity was increasing very rapidly, and an almost unavoidable consequence of such an increase was that the capital structure at Netflix became heavily tilted toward equity. Even if managers at Netflix had desired to maintain a capital structure that had more of a balance between debt and equity, it might have been difficult for them to borrow money rapidly enough to maintain that balance given how fast the company's stock price was increasing. Suppose that Netflix managers determined that the optimal capital structure for their company should contain 25% debt and 75% equity. In other words, imagine that a 25-75 mixture of debt and equity was the **target capital structure** for the company. In that case, an alternative to using the actual market value weights in the WACC calculation (4% debt and 96% equity) would be to use the *target capital structure weights* (25% debt and 75% equity). Doing so would be a way to anticipate how the company's capital structure might evolve in the near term as managers take actions to move their actual capital structure to the desired target.

target capital structure
The mix of debt and equity financing that a firm desires over the long term. The target capital structure should reflect the optimal mix of debt and equity for a particular firm.

→ REVIEW QUESTIONS MyLab Finance Solutions

9–13 What is the weighted average cost of capital (WACC), and how is it calculated?

9–14 What is the relationship between the firm's target capital structure and the weighted average cost of capital (WACC)?

9–15 Describe the logic underlying the use of target weights to calculate the WACC, and compare and contrast this approach with the use of historical weights. What is the preferred weighting scheme?

SUMMARY

FOCUS ON VALUE

The cost of capital is an extremely important rate of return, particularly in capital budgeting decisions. It is an overall cost that blends the costs of the firm's debt and equity financing sources. Because the cost of capital is the pivotal rate of return used in the investment decision process, its accuracy can significantly affect the quality of these decisions.

Underestimation of the cost of capital can make poor projects look attractive; overestimation can make good projects look unattractive. By applying the techniques presented in this chapter to estimate the firm's cost of capital, the financial manager will improve the likelihood that the firm's long-term decisions will be consistent with its overall goal of **maximizing shareholder wealth.**

REVIEW OF LEARNING GOALS

LG1 **Understand the basic concept of the cost of capital.** The cost of capital is the minimum rate of return that a firm must earn on its investments to increase the firm's value. The weighted average cost of capital is a number that blends the costs of each type of capital that a firm uses and establishes a minimum rate of return that the firm's investment should earn.

LG2 **List the primary sources of capital available to firms.** The primary sources of capital for most firms include debt, preferred stock, common stock, and retained earnings.

LG3 **Determine the cost of long-term debt, and explain why the after-tax cost of debt is the relevant cost of debt.** Managers can find the before-tax cost of long-term debt by using cost quotations, calculations (either by calculator or spreadsheet), or an approximation. The after-tax cost of debt is the product of the before-tax cost of debt and 1 minus the tax rate. The after-tax cost of debt is the relevant cost of debt because it is the lowest possible cost of debt for the firm due to the deductibility of interest expenses.

LG4 **Determine the cost of preferred stock.** The cost of preferred stock is the ratio of the preferred stock dividend to the firm's net proceeds from the sale of preferred stock.

LG5 **Calculate the required return on a company's common stock, and explain how it relates to the cost of retained earnings and the cost of new issues of common stock.** The required return on the firm's stock can be calculated by using the constant-growth valuation (Gordon growth) model or the

CAPM. The cost of retained earnings is equal to the required return on common stock equity. An adjustment to the required return on common stock equity to reflect underpricing and flotation costs is necessary to find the cost of new issues of common stock.

LG6 **Calculate the weighted average cost of capital (WACC), and discuss alternative weighting schemes.** The firm's WACC is a weighted average of the firm's cost of debt and equity capital, where the weights are based on the market values of each type of financing relative to the total market value of all financing used by the firm.

OPENER-IN-REVIEW

In the chapter opener you learned that Johnson & Johnson's weighted average cost of capital was around 6% but its investments were earning returns closer to 17%. In 2016, J&J invested about $3.2 billion in capital expenditures. Suppose J&J spends the same amount this year to expand its manufacturing facilities, and that investment produces a net cash flow of $544 million (17% of $3.2 billion) every year in perpetuity. Calculate the NPV of that investment using a 6% discount rate. How much value does the $3.2 billion investment create or destroy? Does it seem that J&J should be pursuing growth in this market?

SELF-TEST PROBLEM (Solutions in Appendix)

ST9–1 **Individual financing costs and WACC** Humble Manufacturing is interested in measuring its overall cost of capital. The firm is in the 21% tax bracket. The company's financial analysts have gathered the following data:

Debt The firm can raise debt by selling $1,000-par-value, 10% coupon interest rate, 10-year bonds on which annual interest payments will be made. When these bonds are issued, their market price will be $970. The firm must also pay flotation costs of $20 per bond.

Preferred stock The firm can sell 11% (annual dividend) preferred stock at its $100-per-share par value. Analysts expect that the cost of issuing and selling the preferred stock will be $4 per share.

Common stock The firm's common stock is currently selling for $80 per share. The firm expects to pay cash dividends of $6 per share next year. The firm's dividends have been growing at an annual rate of 6%, and this growth will continue in the future. The stock will have to be underpriced by $4 per share, and flotation costs amount to $4 per share.

Retained earnings The firm expects to have $225,000 of retained earnings available in the coming year. Once the firm exhausts these retained earnings, it will use new common stock as the form of common stock equity financing.

a. Calculate the individual cost of each source of financing. (Round to the nearest 0.1%.)
b. Calculate the firm's weighted average cost of capital (WACC) using the weights shown in the following table, which are based on the firm's target capital structure proportions. (Round to the nearest 0.1%.)

Source of capital	Weight
Long-term debt	40%
Preferred stock	15
Common stock equity	45
Total	100%

c. In which, if any, of the investments shown in the following table do you recommend that the firm invest? Explain your answer. How much new financing is required?

Investment opportunity	Expected rate of return	Initial investment
A	11.2%	$100,000
B	9.7	500,000
C	12.9	150,000
D	16.5	200,000
E	11.8	450,000
F	10.1	600,000
G	10.5	300,000

WARM-UP EXERCISES

All problems are available in MyLab Finance

LG3 **E9–1** A firm raises capital by selling $20,000 worth of debt with flotation costs equal to 2% of its par value. If the debt matures in 10 years and has a coupon interest rate of 8% (paid annually), what is the bond's YTM?

LG4 **E9–2** Your firm, People's Consulting Group, has been asked to consult on a potential preferred stock offering by Brave New World. This 9% preferred stock issue would be sold at its par value of $55 per share. Flotation costs would total $3 per share. Calculate the cost of this preferred stock.

LG5 **E9–3** Duke Energy has been paying dividends steadily for 20 years. During that time, dividends have grown at a compound annual rate of 3%. If Duke Energy's current stock price is $78 and the firm plans to pay a dividend of $6.50 next year, what is the required return on Duke's common stock?

E9–4 Weekend Warriors Inc. has 35% debt and 65% equity in its capital structure. The firm's estimated after-tax cost of debt is 8% and its estimated cost of equity is 13%. Determine the firm's weighted average cost of capital (WACC).

E9–5 Oxy Corporation uses debt, preferred stock, and common stock to raise capital. The firm's capital structure targets the following proportions: debt, 55%; preferred stock, 10%; and common stock, 35%. If the cost of debt is 6.7%, preferred stock costs 9.2%, and common stock costs 10.6%, what is Oxy's weighted average cost of capital (WACC)?

PROBLEMS

All problems are available in MyLab Finance. The MyLab icon indicates problems in Excel format available in MyLab Finance.

P9–1 **Concept of cost of capital and WACC** Mace Manufacturing is in the process of analyzing its investment decision-making procedures. Two projects evaluated by the firm recently involved building new facilities in different regions, North and South. The basic variables surrounding each project analysis and the resulting decision actions are summarized in the following table.

Basic variables	North	South
Initial cost	−\$6 million	−\$5 million
Life	15 years	15 years
Expected return	8%	15%
Least-cost financing		
Source	Debt	Equity
Cost (after-tax)	7%	16%
Decision		
Action	Invest	Don't invest
Reason	8% > 7% cost	15% < 16% cost

a. An analyst evaluating the North facility expects that the project will be financed by debt that costs the firm 7%. What recommendation do you think this analyst will make regarding the investment opportunity?

b. Another analyst assigned to study the South facility believes that funding for that project will come from the firm's retained earnings at a cost of 16%. What recommendation do you expect this analyst to make regarding the investment?

c. Explain why the decisions in parts **a** and **b** may not be in the best interests of the firm's investors.

d. If the firm maintains a capital structure containing 40% debt and 60% equity, find its weighted average cost of capital (WACC) using the data in the table.

e. If both analysts had used the WACC calculated in part **d**, what recommendations would they have made regarding the North and South facilities?

f. Compare and contrast the analyst's initial recommendations with your findings in part **e**. Which decision method seems more appropriate? Explain why.

P9–2 **Cost of debt using both methods** Currently, Warren Industries can sell 15-year, \$1,000-par-value bonds paying annual interest at a 7% coupon rate. Because current market rates for similar bonds are just under 7%, Warren can sell its bonds for \$1,010 each; Warren will incur flotation costs of \$30 per bond in this process. The firm is in the 21% tax bracket.

a. Find the net proceeds from sale of the bond, N_d.

b. Show the cash flows from the firm's point of view over the maturity of the bond.

c. Calculate the before-tax and after-tax costs of debt.

d. Use the approximation formula to estimate the before-tax and after-tax costs of debt.

e. Compare and contrast the costs of debt calculated in parts **c** and **d.** Which approach do you prefer? Why?

Personal Finance Problem

P9–3 **Before-tax cost of debt and after-tax cost of debt** David Abbot is buying a new house, and he is taking out a 30-year mortgage. David will borrow \$200,000 from a bank, and to repay the loan he will make 360 monthly payments (principal and interest) of \$1,199.10 per month over the next 30 years. David can deduct interest payments on his mortgage from his taxable income, and based on his income, David is in the 30% tax bracket.

a. What is the before-tax interest rate (per year) on David's loan?

b. What is the after-tax interest rate that David is paying?

P9–4 **Cost of debt using the approximation formula** For each of the following \$1,000-par-value bonds, assuming annual interest payment and a 21% tax rate, calculate the after-tax cost to maturity, using the approximation formula.

Bond	Life (years)	Underwriting fee	Discount (−) or premium (+)	Coupon interest rate
A	20	\$25	−\$20	9%
B	16	40	+10	10
C	15	30	−15	12
D	25	15	par	9
E	22	20	−60	11

P9–5 **The cost of debt** Gronseth Drywall Systems Inc. is in discussions with its investment bankers regarding the issuance of new bonds. The investment banker has informed the firm that different maturities will carry different coupon rates and sell at different prices. The firm must choose among several alternatives. In each case, the bonds will have a \$1,000 par value and flotation costs will be \$30 per bond. The company is taxed at a rate of 21%. Calculate the after-tax cost of financing with each of the following alternatives.

Alternative	Coupon rate	Time to maturity (years)	Premium or discount
A	9%	16	\$250
B	7	5	50
C	6	7	par
D	5	10	−75

Personal Finance Problem

LG3 **P9–6** **After-tax cost of debt** Bella Wans is interested in buying a new motorcycle. She has decided to borrow money to pay the $25,000 purchase price of the bike. She is in the 25% income tax bracket. She can either borrow the money at an interest rate of 5% from the motorcycle dealer or take out a second mortgage on her home. That mortgage would come with an interest rate of 6%. Interest payments on the mortgage would be tax deductible for Bella, but interest payments on the loan from the motorcycle dealer could not be deducted on Bella's federal tax return.

a. Calculate the after-tax cost of borrowing from the motorcycle dealership.
b. Calculate the after-tax cost of borrowing through a second mortgage on Bella's home.
c. Which source of borrowing is less costly for Bella?
d. Should Bella consider any other factors when deciding which loan to take out?

LG4 **P9–7** **Cost of preferred stock** Taylor Systems has just issued preferred stock. The stock has an 8% annual dividend and a $100 par value and was sold at $99.50 per share. In addition, flotation costs of $1.50 per share must be paid.

a. Calculate the cost of the preferred stock.
b. If the firm sells the preferred stock with a 10% annual dividend and nets $90.00 after flotation costs, what is its cost?

LG4 MyLab **P9–8** **Cost of preferred stock** Determine the cost for each of the following preferred stocks.

Preferred stock	Par value	Sale price	Flotation cost	Annual dividend
A	$100	$101	$9.00	11%
B	40	38	$3.50	8%
C	35	37	$4.00	$5.00
D	30	26	5% of par	$3.00
E	20	20	$2.50	9%

LG5 **P9–9** **Cost of common stock equity: CAPM** Netflix common stock has a beta, β, of 0.8. The risk-free rate is 3%, and the market return is 10%.

a. Determine the risk premium on Netflix common stock.
b. Determine the required return that Netflix common stock should provide.
c. Determine Netflix's cost of common stock equity using the CAPM.

LG5 **P9–10** **Cost of common stock equity** Ross Textiles wishes to measure its cost of common stock equity. The firm's stock is currently selling for $70.67. The firm just recently paid a dividend of $4. The firm has been increasing dividends regularly. Five years ago, the dividend was just $2.99.

After underpricing and flotation costs, the firm expects to net $69 per share on a new issue.

a. Determine average annual dividend growth rate over the past 5 years. Report your answer to the nearest whole percentage. Using that growth rate, what dividend would you expect the company to pay next year?
b. Determine the net proceeds, N_n, that the firm will actually receive.

c. Using the constant-growth valuation model, determine the required return on the company's stock, r_s, which should equal the cost of retained earnings, r_r.
d. Using the constant-growth valuation model, determine the cost of new common stock, r_n.

P9–11 **Retained earnings versus new common stock** Using the data for each firm shown in the following table, calculate the cost of retained earnings and the cost of new common stock using the constant-growth valuation model.

Firm	Current market price per share	Dividend growth rate	Projected dividend per share next year	Underpricing per share	Flotation cost per share
A	$50.00	8%	$2.25	$2.00	$1.00
B	20.00	4	1.00	0.50	1.50
C	42.50	6	2.00	1.00	2.00
D	19.00	2	2.10	1.30	1.70

P9–12 **The effect of tax rate on WACC** K. Bell Jewelers wishes to explore the effect on its cost of capital of the rate at which the company pays taxes. The firm wishes to maintain a capital structure of 40% debt, 10% preferred stock, and 50% common stock. The cost of financing with retained earnings is 10%, the cost of preferred stock financing is 8%, and the before-tax cost of debt financing is 6%. Calculate the weighted average cost of capital (WACC) given the tax rate assumptions in parts **a** to **c**.

a. Tax rate = 40%
b. Tax rate = 35%
c. Tax rate = 25%
d. Describe the relationship between changes in the rate of taxation and the WACC.

P9–13 **WACC: Market value weights** The market values and after-tax costs of various sources of capital used by Ridge Tool are shown in the following table.

Source of capital	Market value	Individual cost
Long-term debt	$700,000	5.3%
Preferred stock	50,000	12.0
Common stock equity	650,000	16.0

a. Calculate the firm's WACC.
b. Explain how the firm can use this cost in the investment decision-making process.

P9–14 **WACC: Book weights and market weights** Webster Company has compiled the information shown in the following table.

Source of capital	Book value	Market value	After-tax cost
Long-term debt	$4,000,000	$3,840,000	6.0%
Preferred stock	40,000	60,000	13.0
Common stock equity	1,060,000	3,000,000	17.0
Totals	$5,100,000	$6,900,000	

a. Calculate the WACC using book value weights.
b. Calculate the WACC using market value weights.
c. Compare the answers obtained in parts **a** and **b**. Explain the differences.

P9–15 **WACC and target weights** After careful analysis, Dexter Brothers has determined that its optimal capital structure is composed of the sources and target market value weights shown in the following table.

Source of capital	Target market value weight
Long-term debt	30%
Preferred stock	15
Common stock equity	55
Total	100%

The cost of debt is 4.2%, the cost of preferred stock is 9.5%, the cost of retained earnings is 13.0%, and the cost of new common stock is 15.0%. All are after-tax rates. The company's debt represents 25%, the preferred stock represents 10%, and the common stock equity represents 65% of total capital on the basis of the current market values of the three components. The company expects to have a significant amount of retained earnings available and does not expect to sell any new common stock.

a. Calculate the WACC on the basis of historical market value weights.
b. Calculate the WACC on the basis of target market value weights.
c. Compare the answers obtained in parts **a** and **b**. Explain the differences.

P9–16 **Cost of capital** Edna Recording Studios Inc. reported earnings available to common stock of $4,200,000 last year. From those earnings, the company paid a dividend of $1.26 on each of its 1,000,000 common shares outstanding. The capital structure of the company includes 40% debt, 10% preferred stock, and 50% common stock. It is taxed at a rate of 21%.

a. If the market price of the common stock is $40 and dividends are expected to grow at a rate of 6% per year for the foreseeable future, what is the required return on the company's common stock, and thus the company's cost of retained earnings financing?
b. If underpricing and flotation costs on new shares of common stock amount to $7.00 per share, what is the company's cost of new common stock financing?
c. The company can issue a $2.00 dividend preferred stock for a market price of $25.00 per share. Flotation costs would amount to $3.00 per share. What is the cost of preferred stock financing?
d. The company can issue $1,000-par-value, 10% coupon, 5-year bonds that can be sold for $1,200 each. Flotation costs would amount to $25.00 per bond. Use the estimation formula to figure the approximate cost of debt financing.
e. What is the WACC?

P9–17 **Calculation of individual costs and WACC** Dillon Labs has asked its financial manager to measure the cost of each specific type of capital as well as the weighted average cost of capital (WACC). The WACC is to be measured by using the following weights: 40% long-term debt, 10% preferred stock, and 50% common stock equity (retained earnings, new common stock, or both). The firm's tax rate is 21%.

Debt The firm can sell for $1,020 a 10-year, $1,000-par-value bond paying annual interest at a 7% coupon rate. A flotation cost of 3% of the par value is required.

Preferred stock An 8% (annual dividend) preferred stock having a par value of $100 can be sold for $98. An additional fee of $2 per share must be paid to the underwriters.

Common stock The firm's common stock is currently selling for $59.43 per share. The stock has paid a dividend that has gradually increased for many years, rising from $2.70 ten years ago to the $4 dividend payment that the company just recently made. If the company wants to issue new common shares, it will sell them $1.50 below the current market value to attract investors, and the company will pay $2 per share in flotation costs.

a. Calculate the after-tax cost of debt.
b. Calculate the cost of preferred stock.
c. Calculate the cost of common stock (both retained earnings and new common stock).
d. Calculate the WACC for Dillon Labs.

Personal Finance Problem

P9–18 **Weighted average cost of capital (WACC)** John Dough has just been awarded his degree in business. He has three education loans outstanding. They all mature in 5 years, and he can repay them without penalty any time before maturity. The amounts owed on each loan and the annual interest rate associated with each loan are given in the following table.

Loan	Balance due	Annual interest rate
1	$20,000	6%
2	12,000	9
3	32,000	5

John can also combine the total of his three debts (i.e., $64,000) and create a consolidated loan from his bank. His bank will charge a 7.2% annual interest rate for a period of 5 years.

Should John do nothing (leave the three individual loans as is) or create a consolidated loan (the $64,000 question)?

LG3 LG4 LG5 LG6

P9–19 **Calculation of individual costs and WACC** Lang Enterprises is interested in measuring its overall cost of capital. Current investigation has gathered the following data. The firm is in the 21% tax bracket.

Debt The firm can raise debt by selling $1,000-par-value, 8% coupon interest rate, 20-year bonds on which annual interest payments will be made. To sell the issue, an average discount of $30 per bond would have to be given. The firm also must pay flotation costs of $30 per bond.

Preferred stock The firm can sell 8% preferred stock at its $95-per-share par value. The cost of issuing and selling the preferred stock is expected to be $5 per share. Preferred stock can be sold under these terms.

Common stock The firm's common stock is currently selling for $90 per share. The firm expects to pay cash dividends of $7 per share next year. The firm's dividends have been growing at an annual rate of 6%, and this growth is expected to continue into the future. The stock must be underpriced by $7 per share, and flotation costs are expected to amount to $5 per share. The firm can sell new common stock under these terms.

Retained earnings When measuring this cost, the firm does not concern itself with the tax bracket or brokerage fees of owners. It expects to have available $100,000 of retained earnings in the coming year; once these retained earnings are exhausted, the firm will use new common stock as the form of common stock equity financing.

a. Calculate the after-tax cost of debt.
b. Calculate the cost of preferred stock.
c. Calculate the cost of common stock.
d. Calculate the firm's WACC using the capital structure weights shown in the following table. (Round answer to the nearest 0.1%.)

Source of capital	Weight
Long-term debt	30%
Preferred stock	20
Common stock equity	50
Total	100%

LG 6

P9–20 **Weighted average cost of capital (WACC)** American Exploration Inc., a natural gas producer, is trying to decide whether to revise its target capital structure. Currently, it targets a 50-50 mix of debt and equity, but it is considering a target capital structure with 70% debt. American Exploration currently has 6% after-tax cost of debt and a 12% cost of common stock. The company does not have any preferred stock outstanding.

a. What is American Exploration's current WACC?
b. Assuming that its cost of debt and equity remain unchanged, what will be American Exploration's WACC under the revised target capital structure?
c. Do you think that shareholders are affected by the increase in debt to 70%? If so, how are they affected? Are their common stock claims riskier now?
d. Suppose that in response to the increase in debt, American Exploration's shareholders increase their required return so that the cost of common equity is 16%. What will its new WACC be in this case?
e. What does your answer in part **b** suggest about the tradeoff between financing with debt versus equity?

LG 1

P9–21 **ETHICS PROBLEM** During the 1990s, General Electric put together a long string of consecutive quarters in which the firm managed to meet or beat the earnings forecasts of Wall Street stock analysts. Some skeptics wondered if GE "managed" earnings to meet Wall Street's expectations, meaning that GE used accounting gimmicks to conceal the true volatility in its business. How do you think GE's long-run track record of meeting or beating earnings forecasts affected its cost of capital? If investors learn that GE's performance was achieved largely through accounting gimmicks, how do you think they would respond?

SPREADSHEET EXERCISE

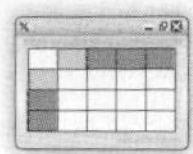

Nova Corporation is interested in measuring the cost of each specific type of capital as well as the weighted average cost of capital (WACC). Historically, the firm has raised capital in the following manner:

Source of capital	Weight
Long-term debt	35%
Preferred stock	12
Common stock equity	53

The tax rate of the firm is currently 21%. The needed financial information and data are as follows:

Debt Nova can raise debt by selling $1,000-par-value, 6.5% coupon interest rate, 10-year bonds on which annual interest payments will be made. To sell the issue, an average discount of $20 per bond needs to be given. There is an associated flotation cost of 2% of par value.

Preferred stock Preferred stock can be sold under the following terms: The security has a par value of $100 per share, the annual dividend rate is 6% of the par value, and the flotation cost is expected to be $4 per share. The preferred stock is expected to sell for $102 before cost considerations.

Common stock The current price of Nova's common stock is $35 per share. The cash dividend is expected to be $3.25 per share next year. The firm's dividends have grown at an annual rate of 5%, and it is expected that the dividend will continue at this rate for the foreseeable future. The flotation costs are expected to be approximately $2 per share. Nova can sell new common stock under these terms.

Retained earnings The firm expects to have available $100,000 of retained earnings in the coming year. Once these retained earnings are exhausted, the firm will use new common stock as the form of common stock equity financing. (*Note:* When measuring this cost, the firm does not concern itself with the tax bracket or brokerage fees of owners.)

TO DO

Create a spreadsheet to answer the following questions:

a. Calculate the after-tax cost of debt.
b. Calculate the cost of preferred stock.
c. Calculate the cost of retained earnings.
d. Calculate the cost of new common stock.
e. Calculate the firm's WACC using retained earnings and the capital structure weights shown in the table above.
f. Calculate the firm's WACC using new common stock and the capital structure weights shown in the table above.

MyLab Finance Visit www.pearson.com/mylab/finance for **Chapter Case: *Making Star Products' Financing/Investment Decision*,** Group Exercises, and numerous online resources.

Integrative Case 4

Eco Plastics Company

Since its inception, Eco Plastics Company has been revolutionizing plastic and trying to do its part to save the environment. Eco's founder, Marion Cosby, developed a biodegradable plastic that her company is marketing to manufacturing companies throughout the southeastern United States. After operating as a private company for 6 years, Eco went public in 2012 and is listed on the Nasdaq stock exchange.

As the chief financial officer of a young company with lots of investment opportunities, Eco's CFO closely monitors the firm's cost of capital. The CFO keeps tabs on each of the individual costs of Eco's three main financing sources: long-term debt, preferred stock, and common stock. The target capital structure for Eco is given by the weights in the following table:

Source of capital	Weight
Long-term debt	30%
Preferred stock	20
Common stock equity	50
Total	100%

At the present time, Eco can raise debt by selling 20-year bonds with a $1,000 par value and a 10.5% annual coupon interest rate. Eco's corporate tax rate is 21%, and its bonds generally require an average discount of $45 per bond and flotation costs of $32 per bond when being sold. Eco's outstanding preferred stock pays a 9% dividend and has a $95-per-share par value. The cost of issuing and selling additional preferred stock is expected to be $7 per share. Because Eco is a young firm that requires lots of cash to grow, it does not currently pay a dividend to common stockholders. To track the cost of common stock, the CFO uses the capital asset pricing model (CAPM). The CFO and the firm's investment advisors believe that the appropriate risk-free rate is 4% and that the market's expected return equals 13%. Using data from 2012 through 2018, Eco's CFO estimates the firm's beta to be 1.3.

Although Eco's current target capital structure includes 20% preferred stock, the company is considering using debt financing to retire the outstanding preferred stock, thus shifting their target capital structure to 50% long-term debt and 50% common stock. If Eco shifts its capital mix from preferred stock to debt, its financial advisors expect its beta to increase to 1.5.

TO DO

a. Calculate Eco's current after-tax cost of long-term debt.
b. Calculate Eco's current cost of preferred stock.
c. Calculate Eco's current cost of common stock.
d. Calculate Eco's current weighted average cost capital (WACC).

e. (1) Assuming that the debt financing costs do not change, what effect would a shift to a more highly leveraged capital structure consisting of 50% long-term debt, 0% preferred stock, and 50% common stock have on the risk premium for Eco's common stock? What would be Eco's new cost of common equity?
(2) What would be Eco's new weighted average cost of capital (WACC)?
(3) Which capital structure—the original one or this one—seems better? Why?

PART FIVE

Long-Term Investment Decisions

CHAPTERS IN THIS PART

Probably nothing that financial managers do contributes more to the firm's goal of maximizing shareholder value than making good investment decisions. The term *capital budgeting* describes the process for evaluating and selecting investment projects. Often, investment projects can be very large, such as building a new plant or launching a new product line. These endeavors can create enormous value for shareholders, but they can also bankrupt the company. In Part Five, you'll learn how financial managers decide which investment opportunities to pursue.

Chapter 10 discusses the capital budgeting tools that financial managers and analysts use to evaluate the merits of an investment. Some of these techniques are quite intuitive and simple to use, such as payback analysis. Others are a little more complex, such as the net present value and internal rate of return approaches. In general, the more complex techniques provide more comprehensive evaluations, but the simpler approaches often lead to the same value-maximizing decisions.

Chapter 11 illustrates how to develop the capital budgeting cash flows required by the techniques covered in Chapter 10. After studying this chapter, you will understand the inputs that are necessary to build the relevant cash flows needed to determine whether a particular investment is likely to create or destroy value for shareholders.

Chapter 12 introduces additional techniques for evaluating the risks inherent in capital investment projects. Because of the huge scale that capital investments often involve and their importance to the firm's financial well-being, managers invest a tremendous amount of time and energy trying to understand the risks associated with these projects.

CHAPTER

10

Capital Budgeting Techniques

LEARNING GOALS

LG 1 Understand the key elements of the capital budgeting process.

LG 2 Calculate, interpret, and evaluate the payback period.

LG 3 Calculate, interpret, and evaluate the net present value (NPV) and economic value added (EVA).

LG 4 Calculate, interpret, and evaluate the internal rate of return (IRR).

LG 5 Use net present value profiles to compare NPV and IRR techniques.

LG 6 Discuss NPV and IRR in terms of conflicting rankings and the strengths of each approach.

MyLab Finance Chapter Introduction Video

WHY THIS CHAPTER MATTERS TO YOU

In your *professional* life

ACCOUNTING You need to understand capital budgeting techniques to help determine the relevant cash flows associated with proposed capital expenditures.

INFORMATION SYSTEMS You need to understand capital budgeting techniques to design decision modules that help reduce the amount of work required to analyze proposed capital expenditures.

MANAGEMENT You need to understand capital budgeting techniques to correctly analyze the relevant cash flows of proposed projects and decide whether to accept or reject them.

MARKETING You need to understand capital budgeting techniques to grasp how the firm's decision makers will evaluate proposals for new marketing programs, for new products, and for the expansion of existing product lines.

OPERATIONS You need to understand capital budgeting techniques to know how the firm's decision makers will evaluate proposals for the acquisition of new equipment and plants.

In your *personal* life

You can apply the capital budgeting techniques used by financial managers to measure either the value of a given asset purchase or its compound rate of return. The IRR technique is widely applied in personal finance to measure both the actual and the forecast rate of returns on investment securities, real estate, credit card debt, consumer loans, and leases.

MARITIME RESOURCES CORP.

The Gold Standard for Evaluating Gold Mines

Michael DeFreitas/Robertharding/Alamy Stock Photo

On March 2, 2017, Maritime Resources Corp., a Canadian mining firm, announced the results of a preliminary economic assessment of a proposal to reopen an old gold mine that had ceased operations in 2004 due to low gold prices. At the time the mine was closed, engineers were aware that gold deposits remained in the mine, but the costs of extracting those deposits were too high relative to gold's then-current market price. Since the mine's closure, gold prices had risen threefold, from just under $400 to more than $1,200 per ounce, suggesting that the deposits that were once too expensive to mine might be worth extracting. Maritime hired an independent engineering firm, WSP Canada Inc., to assess the financial feasibility of reopening the mine.

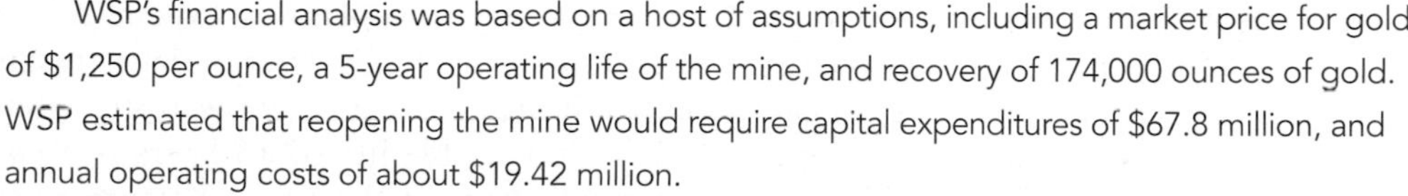

WSP's financial analysis was based on a host of assumptions, including a market price for gold of $1,250 per ounce, a 5-year operating life of the mine, and recovery of 174,000 ounces of gold. WSP estimated that reopening the mine would require capital expenditures of $67.8 million, and annual operating costs of about $19.42 million.

On the basis of those assumptions, WSP calculated several metrics suggesting that reopening the gold mine would create value for Maritime's shareholders. First, WSP estimated that the mine's *payback period* was about 2 years, meaning that the mine would generate cash flows sufficient for Maritime Resources to recoup its $67.8 million up-front investment in roughly 2 years. Second, WSP's analysis suggested that over its 5-year life the mine generated cash inflows that exceed its outflows by $44.2 million on a present value basis. That is, the mine's *net present value* was $44.2 million. Third, WSP calculated that reopening and operating the mine would generate a compound annual *internal rate of return* of 34.8%. The news that Maritime had identified a valuable investment opportunity was greeted warmly by the stock market, as Maritime's stock rose almost 6% when the WSP feasibility study was released to the public.

Payback, internal rate of return, and net present value are all methods that companies use to evaluate potential investment projects. Each of these techniques has advantages and disadvantages, but the net present value method has become the gold standard for analyzing investments. This chapter explains why.

Source: From "Maritime's Prefeasibility Study on Hammerdown Gold Mine Returns an IRR of 46.8% and NPV (8%) of $71.2M" by Douglas Fulcher. Published by Junior Mining Network LLC. https://www.juniorminingnetwork.com/junior-miner-news/press-releases/1227-tsx-venture/mae/29879-maritime-s-prefeasibility-study-on-hammerdown-gold-mine-returns-an-irr-of-46-8-and-npv-8-of-71-2m.html.

LG 1

10.1 Overview of Capital Budgeting

capital budgeting
The process of evaluating and selecting long-term investments that contribute to the firm's goal of maximizing owners' wealth.

Long-term investments represent sizable outlays of funds that commit a firm to some course of action. Consequently, the firm needs procedures to analyze and select its long-term investments. **Capital budgeting** is the process of evaluating and selecting long-term investments that contribute to the firm's goal of maximizing owners' wealth. Firms typically make a variety of long-term investments, such as investments in fixed assets, which include property (land), plant, and equipment, and investments in research and development. These assets, often referred to as earning assets, generally provide the basis for the firm's earning power and value.

When undertaking large investments, firms typically have to answer two separate questions. First, is the investment a good one, meaning does it create value for shareholders? Second, where will the money to pay for the investment come from? Will the firm pay the up-front costs using equity, debt, or a mixture of the two? For now we focus exclusively on the first decision, the investment decision. Chapters 10 through 12 concentrate on the tools that financial managers use to make good investment decisions without regard to the specific method of financing used. We begin by discussing the motives for capital expenditure.

MOTIVES FOR CAPITAL EXPENDITURE

capital expenditure
An outlay of funds by the firm that the firm expects to produce benefits over a period of time greater than 1 year.

operating expenditure
An outlay of funds by the firm resulting in benefits received within 1 year.

A **capital expenditure** is an outlay of funds that the firm expects to produce benefits over a period of time greater than 1 year. An **operating expenditure** is an outlay resulting in benefits received within 1 year. Fixed-asset outlays are capital expenditures, but not all capital expenditures are classified as fixed assets. A \$600,000 outlay for a new machine with a usable life of 15 years is a capital expenditure that would appear as a fixed asset on the firm's balance sheet. A \$6 million outlay for an advertising campaign that produces benefits over a long period is also a capital expenditure, but it would rarely be shown as a fixed asset. In either case, the potential expenditure of funds to generate benefits over a long time period is an investment project that the firm's analysts should evaluate to determine whether it is likely to increase or decrease shareholder value.

Companies invest large sums in many different kinds of projects. Some of the more common investment projects are capital expenditures to expand operations, to replace or renew fixed assets, and to obtain some other, less tangible benefit over a long period.

STEPS IN THE PROCESS

capital budgeting process
Consists of five distinct but interrelated steps: *proposal generation, review and analysis, decision making, implementation, and follow-up.*

The **capital budgeting process** consists of five distinct but interrelated steps:

1. *Proposal generation.* Managers at all levels in a business make proposals for new investment projects that are reviewed by finance personnel. Proposals that require large outlays receive greater scrutiny than less costly ones.
2. *Review and analysis.* Financial managers perform formal review and analysis to assess the merits of investment proposals.
3. *Decision making.* Firms typically delegate capital expenditure decisions on the basis of dollar limits. Generally, the board of directors or a team of very senior executives must authorize expenditures beyond a certain amount. Often, plant managers have authority to make decisions necessary to keep the production line moving.

4. *Implementation.* Following approval, firms make expenditures and implement projects. Expenditures for a large project often occur in phases.
5. *Follow-up.* Managers monitor results and compare actual costs and benefits to the projections that they originally used to justify making the investment. Managers may take actions to expand, contract, or shut down investments when actual outcomes differ from projected ones.

Each step in the process is important. Review and analysis and decision making (Steps 2 and 3) consume the majority of time and effort, however. Follow-up (Step 5) is an important but often ignored step aimed at allowing the firm to improve the accuracy of its cash flow estimates and increase the value of its investments on an ongoing basis. Our focus here and in the next two chapters is on project review and analysis (Step 2) and decision making (Step 3).

BASIC TERMINOLOGY

Before developing the concepts, techniques, and practices related to the capital budgeting process, we need to explain some basic terminology. In addition, we will present some key assumptions that simplify the discussion in the remainder of this chapter and in Chapters 11 and 12.

Independent versus Mutually Exclusive Projects

independent projects
Projects whose cash flows are unrelated to (or independent of) one another; accepting or rejecting one project does not change the desirability of other projects.

mutually exclusive projects
Projects that compete with one another so that the acceptance of one eliminates from further consideration all other projects that serve a similar function.

Most investments fall into one of two categories: (1) independent projects, or (2) mutually exclusive projects. **Independent projects** are those with cash flows unrelated to (or independent of) one another; accepting or rejecting one project does not change the desirability of other projects. **Mutually exclusive projects** are those that have essentially the same function and therefore compete with one another. Accepting one project eliminates from further consideration all other projects that serve a similar function. For example, a firm in need of increased production capacity could obtain it by (1) expanding its plant, (2) acquiring another company, or (3) contracting with another company for production. Clearly, accepting any one option eliminates the immediate need for either of the others.

Unlimited Funds versus Capital Rationing

unlimited funds
The financial situation in which a firm is able to accept all independent projects that provide an acceptable return.

capital rationing
The financial situation in which a firm has only a fixed number of dollars available for capital expenditures and numerous projects compete for these dollars.

The availability of funds for capital expenditures affects the firm's decisions. If a firm has **unlimited funds** for investment (or if it can raise as much money as it needs by borrowing or issuing stock), making capital budgeting decisions is quite simple: The firm should invest in all projects that will provide an acceptable return. Often, though, firms operate under **capital rationing** instead, which means that they have a fixed budget available for capital expenditures and that numerous projects will compete for these dollars. We present procedures for dealing with capital rationing in Chapter 12. For now, we will assume that if a firm identifies an investment project that will make its shareholders better off, the firm can either use its existing financial resources or raise external funding to pay for the investment.

Accept–Reject versus Ranking Approaches

accept–reject approach
The evaluation of capital expenditure proposals to determine whether they meet the firm's minimum acceptance criterion.

Two standard approaches to capital budgeting decisions are available. The **accept–reject approach** involves evaluating capital expenditure proposals to determine whether they meet the firm's minimum acceptance criterion.

Managers might use this approach if they have sufficient funds to invest in every project that creates value for shareholders, or they might use it to narrow down a large list of investment opportunities, only some of which will receive additional scrutiny.

ranking approach
The ranking of capital expenditure projects on the basis of some predetermined measure, such as how much value the project creates for shareholders.

The second method, the **ranking approach**, involves ranking projects on the basis of some predetermined measure, such as how much value the project creates for shareholders. The purpose of ranking projects is to ensure that if the firm cannot invest in every worthwhile project, it invests in the combination of projects that maximize shareholder wealth. In other words, ranking is useful in selecting the "best" of a group of acceptable projects and in evaluating projects when firms have limited capital.

CAPITAL BUDGETING TECHNIQUES

Large firms evaluate dozens, perhaps even hundreds, of different ideas for new investments each year. To ensure that the investment projects selected have the best chance of increasing the value of the firm, financial managers need tools to help them evaluate the merits of individual projects and to rank competing investments. A number of techniques are available for performing such analyses. The best techniques take into account the time value of money as well as the tradeoff between risk and return. Project evaluation methods that fail to account for money's time value or for risk may not lead to shareholder value maximization.

Bennett Company's Relevant Cash Flows

We will use one basic problem to illustrate all the techniques described in this chapter. The problem concerns Bennett Company, a medium-sized metal fabricator that is currently contemplating two projects with conventional cash flow patterns:[1] Project A requires an initial investment of $420,000, and project B requires an initial investment of $450,000. The projected cash flows for the two projects appear in Table 10.1 and on the timelines in Figure 10.1. Both projects

TABLE 10.1 Capital Expenditure Data for Bennett Company

	Project A	Project B
Initial investment	−$420,000	−$450,000
Year	Operating cash inflows	
1	$140,000	$280,000
2	140,000	120,000
3	140,000	100,000
4	140,000	100,000
5	140,000	100,000

1. A conventional cash flow pattern is one in which the up-front cash flow is negative and all subsequent cash flows are positive. A nonconventional pattern occurs if the up-front cash flow is positive and subsequent cash flows are negative (e.g., when a firm sells extended warranties and pays benefits later) or when the cash flows fluctuate between positive and negative (as might occur when firms have to reinvest in a project to extend its life).

FIGURE 10.1

Bennett Company's Projects A and B

Timelines depicting the conventional cash flows of projects A and B

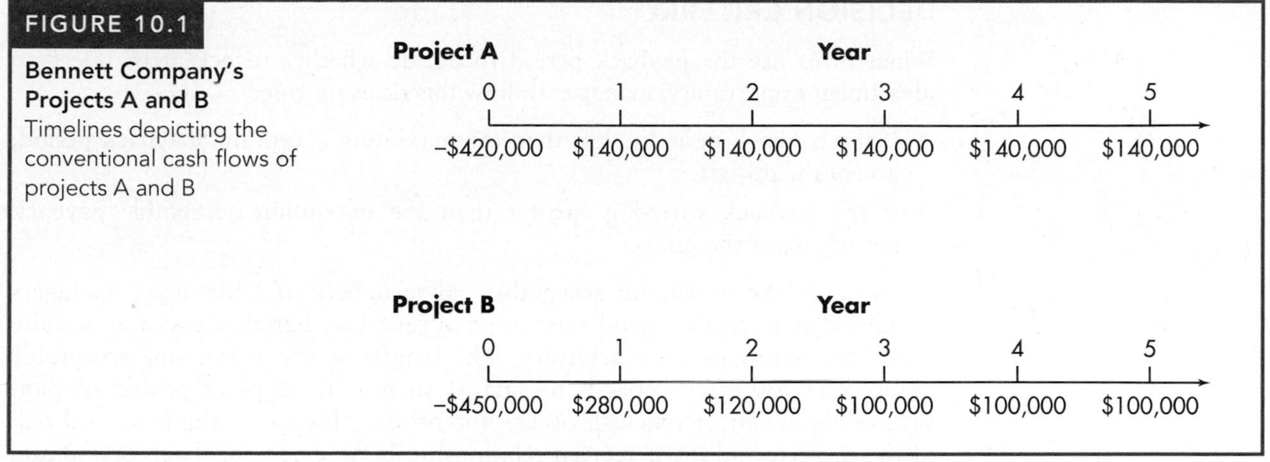

involve one initial cash outlay followed by annual cash inflows, a fairly typical pattern for new investments. We begin with a look at the three most widely used capital budgeting techniques: payback period, net present value, and internal rate of return.

→ **REVIEW QUESTION** MyLab Finance Solution

10–1 What is the financial manager's goal in selecting investment projects for the firm? Define the capital budgeting process, and explain how it helps managers achieve their goal.

10.2 Payback Period

payback period
The time it takes an investment to generate cash inflows sufficient to recoup the initial outlay required to make the investment.

Small and medium-sized firms often use the payback period approach to evaluate proposed investments. The **payback period** is the time it takes an investment to generate cash inflows sufficient to recoup the initial outlay required to make the investment. In the case of an annuity (such as the Bennett Company's project A), you can calculate the payback period by dividing the initial investment by the annual cash inflow. For a mixed stream of cash inflows (such as project B), simply add up the yearly cash inflows until the accumulated sum equals (or exceeds) the initial investment.

Many firms use the payback period because it is simple to calculate and to understand. Unfortunately, the payback method has some serious flaws, which we will discuss shortly, and because of those flaws making investment decisions based on the payback period may not accomplish the firm's goal of maximizing shareholder wealth.

DECISION CRITERIA

When firms use the payback period to decide whether to accept or reject an investment opportunity, managers follow this decision rule:

- If the payback period is less than the maximum acceptable payback period, accept the project.
- If the payback period is greater than the maximum acceptable payback period, reject the project.

What is the maximum acceptable payback period? Ultimately, managers decide what payback period they deem acceptable, but that decision is quite subjective—perhaps even arbitrary. The length of the maximum acceptable payback period often depends on factors such as the type of project (expansion, replacement or renewal, other), the product life cycle, the perceived risk of the project, and the perceived relationship between the payback period and the share value.

EXAMPLE 10.1

We can calculate the payback period for Bennett Company's projects A and B, using the data in Table 10.1. For project A, which is an annuity, the payback period is 3.0 years ($420,000 initial investment ÷ $140,000 annual cash inflow). Because project B generates a mixed stream of cash inflows, the calculation of its payback period is not as clear-cut. In year 1, the firm will recover $280,000 of its $450,000 initial investment. By the end of year 2, $400,000 ($280,000 from year 1 + $120,000 from year 2) will have been recovered. At the end of year 3, $500,000 will have been recovered. Only 50% of the year-3 cash inflow of $100,000 is needed to complete the payback of the initial $450,000. The payback period for project B is therefore 2.5 years (2 years + 50% of year 3).

If Bennett's maximum acceptable payback period were 2.75 years, project A would be rejected and project B would be accepted. If the maximum acceptable payback period were 2.25 years, both projects would be rejected. If the projects were being ranked, B would be preferred over A because it has a shorter payback period. Note, however, that no matter what payback period Bennett requires, it is unclear from payback analysis which investment will do the most to increase shareholder wealth. All we can say is that project B recoups the initial investment more rapidly than does project A.

MATTER OF FACT

Payback in India

A 2017 survey of firms in India found that two-thirds of those firms always or almost always conducted payback analysis when they made major investment decisions. Similar to results found in U.S. firms, small companies in India were more likely than large firms to use the payback approach. For all its flaws, the payback approach still sees widespread use around the world.

PROS AND CONS OF PAYBACK ANALYSIS

Large firms sometimes use the payback approach to evaluate small projects (or as one of several metrics used to judge a larger project's merits), and small firms use it to evaluate most projects. The payback method's popularity results from its simplicity and intuitive appeal. By measuring how quickly the firm recovers its initial investment, the payback period also gives at least some consideration to the timing of cash flows. Likewise, the payback approach offers a crude way to adjust for project risk if managers require a faster payback on riskier endeavors.

The major weakness of the payback period is that the appropriate payback period is merely a subjectively determined number. No firm connection exists between the payback period and the goal of shareholder wealth maximization. To make that point another way, it is easy to think of an investment project that takes a long time to pay off (and hence would be rejected for having a very slow payback period) but creates enormous value for shareholders. For example, almost any research and development project conducted by a pharmaceutical firm would fit this description. It takes years for a drug to progress through the initial discovery phase and a series of clinical trials before the firm can sell it to patients. That process can cost drug companies millions or even hundreds of millions of dollars, and almost no drug compound can recover those costs within a few years. However, a successful drug creates enormous value for shareholders in the long run. The *Focus on Practice* box offers more information about the pros and cons of the payback approach.

PERSONAL FINANCE EXAMPLE 10.2 Gabriela Perez is considering investing \$20,000 to obtain a 5% interest in a rental property. Her good friend and real estate agent, Josh Williams, put the deal together, and he estimates that Gabriela should receive between \$4,000 and \$6,000 per year in cash from her 5% interest in the property. Gabriela expects to remain in the 25% income-tax bracket for quite a while, and she will not make an investment unless the after-tax cash flows pay back the initial cost in fewer than 7 years.

Gabriela's calculation of the payback period on this deal begins with computing the range of annual after-tax cash flow:

$$\begin{aligned}\text{After-tax cash flow} &= (1 - \text{tax rate}) \times \text{Pre-tax cash flow}\\ &= (1 - 0.25) \times \$4{,}000 = \$3{,}000\\ &= (1 - 0.25) \times \$6{,}000 = \$4{,}500\end{aligned}$$

The after-tax cash flow ranges from \$3,000 to \$4,500. Dividing the \$20,000 initial investment by each of the estimated after-tax cash flows, we get the payback period:

$$\begin{aligned}\text{Payback period} &= \text{Initial investment} \div \text{After-tax cash flow}\\ &= \$20{,}000 \div \$3{,}000 = 6.67 \text{ years}\\ &= \$20{,}000 \div \$4{,}500 = 4.44 \text{ years}\end{aligned}$$

Because Gabriela's proposed rental property investment will pay itself back in either scenario in fewer than 7 years, the investment is acceptable.

In addition to lacking a firm connection to the shareholder value maximization goal, the payback approach suffers from a second weakness—payback calculations fail to fully account for the time value of money.[2] An example illustrates this weakness.

2. To consider differences in timing explicitly in applying the payback method, some firms use the *discounted payback approach*. To find the discounted payback period, managers first calculate the present value of the cash inflows at the appropriate discount rate and then find the payback period by using those cash flows rather than undiscounted cash flows.

FOCUS ON PRACTICE *in practice*

Limits on Payback Analysis

In tough economic times, the standard for a payback period is often reduced. Chief information officers (CIOs) are apt to reject projects with payback periods of more than 2 years. "We start with payback period," says Ron Fijalkowski, CIO at Strategic Distribution, Inc., in Bristol, Pennsylvania. "For sure, if the payback period is over 36 months, it's not going to get approved. But our rule of thumb is we'd like to see 24 months. And if it's close to 12, it's probably a no-brainer."

Although easy to compute and to understand, the payback period brings with it some drawbacks. "Payback gives you an answer that tells you a bit about the beginning stage of a project, but it doesn't tell you much about the full lifetime of the project," says Chris Gardner, a cofounder of iValue LLC, an IT valuation consultancy in Barrington, Illinois. "The simplicity of computing payback may encourage sloppiness, especially the failure to include all costs associated with an investment, such as training, maintenance, and hardware upgrade costs," says Douglas Emond, senior vice president and chief technology officer at Eastern Bank in Lynn, Massachusetts. For example, he says, "you may be bringing in a hot new technology, but uh-oh, after implementation you realize that you need a .Net guru in-house, and you don't have one."

The payback method's emphasis on the short term, however, has a special appeal for IT managers. "That's because the history of IT projects that take longer than 3 years is disastrous," says Gardner. Indeed, Ian Campbell, chief research officer at Nucleus Research, Inc., in Wellesley, Massachusetts, says the payback period is an absolutely essential metric for evaluating IT projects—even more important than discounted cash flow (NPV and IRR)—because it spotlights the risks inherent in lengthy IT projects. "It should be a hard-and-fast rule to never take an IT project with a payback period greater than 3 years, unless it's an infrastructure project you can't do without," Campbell says.

Whatever the weaknesses of the payback period method of evaluating capital projects, the simplicity of the method does allow it to be used in conjunction with other, more sophisticated measures. It can be used to screen potential projects and winnow them down to the few that merit more careful scrutiny with, for example, net present value (NPV).

► *In your view, if the payback period method is used in conjunction with the NPV method, should it be used before or after the NPV evaluation?*

Source: Gary Anthes, "ROI guide: Payback period," Computerworld.com (February 17, 2003), www.computerworld.com/s/article/78529/ROI_Guide_Payback_Period?taxono

EXAMPLE 10.3

DeYarman Enterprises, a small medical appliance manufacturer, is considering two mutually exclusive projects named Gold and Silver (i.e., DeYarman can invest in only one project, not both). The firm uses the payback period to choose projects, and it requires any investment to recover its initial cost within 4 years. The cash flows and payback period for each project appear in Table 10.2. Both projects have 3-year payback periods, which would suggest that they are equally desirable. But comparing the cash flow patterns of each investment immediately reveals that Silver produces more cash flow sooner than Gold. In year 1, Silver generates \$40,000 in cash inflow compared to just \$5,000 for Gold. We know that because money has a time value, it is preferable to receive cash flow sooner rather than later. The payback approach fails to recognize that benefit. Any capital budgeting tool that properly accounts for the time value of money would suggest that project Silver is better for shareholders than project Gold.

TABLE 10.2 Relevant Cash Flows and Payback Periods for DeYarman Enterprises' Projects

	Project Gold	Project Silver
Initial investment	−$50,000	−$50,000
Year	Operating cash inflows	
1	$ 5,000	$40,000
2	5,000	2,000
3	40,000	8,000
4	10,000	10,000
5	10,000	10,000
Payback period	3 years	3 years

A third weakness of the payback method is that it places no value on (i.e., totally ignores) cash flows that arrive after the payback period. Thus, the payback method will fail to recognize the true value of investments that deliver cash flow in the more distant future.

EXAMPLE 10.4

Rashid Company, a software developer, has two investment opportunities, X and Y. Data for X and Y appear in Table 10.3. The payback period for project X is 2 years; for project Y, it is 3 years. Strict adherence to the payback approach suggests that project X is preferable to project Y. However, if we look beyond the payback period, we see that project X returns only an additional $1,200 ($1,000 in year 3 + $100 in year 4 + $100 in year 5), whereas project Y returns an additional $7,000 ($4,000 in year 4 + $3,000 in year 5). On the basis of this information, project Y appears preferable to X. The payback approach ignored the cash inflows occurring after the end of the payback period.

TABLE 10.3 Calculation of the Payback Period for Rashid Company's Two Alternative Investment Projects

	Project X	Project Y
Initial investment	−$10,000	−$10,000
Year	Operating cash inflows	
1	$5,000	$3,000
2	5,000	4,000
3	1,000	3,000
4	100	4,000
5	100	3,000
Payback period	2 years	3 years

→ REVIEW QUESTIONS MyLab Finance Solutions

10–2 What is the payback period? How is it calculated?

10–3 What weaknesses are commonly associated with the use of the payback period to evaluate a proposed investment?

10.3 Net Present Value (NPV)

The method used by most large companies to evaluate investment projects is called *net present value (NPV)*. The intuition behind the NPV method is simple. When firms make investments, they are spending money that they obtained, in one form or another, from investors. Investors expect a return on the money that they give to firms, so a firm should undertake an investment only if the present value of the cash flow that the investment generates is greater than the cost of making the investment in the first place. Because the *NPV* method takes into account the time value of investors' money, it is more likely to identify value-increasing investments than is the payback rule. The NPV method discounts the investment's cash flows at a rate that reflects the investment's risk—cash flows from riskier investments are discounted at higher rates. The discount rate in an NPV calculation is the minimum return that a project must earn to satisfy the firm's investors. Projects with lower returns fail to meet investors' expectations and therefore decrease the firm's value, and projects with higher returns increase the firm's value.

net present value (NPV)
A capital budgeting technique that measures an investment's value by calculating the present value of its cash inflows and outflows.

In many cases, an investment project begins with a cash outflow that is then followed by a series of cash inflows over several years. In this instance, the **net present value (NPV)** is found by subtracting a project's initial investment (CF_0) from the present value of its cash inflows (CF_t) discounted at a rate that is appropriate given the investment's risk (r):

$$\text{NPV} = \text{Present value of cash inflows} - \text{Initial investment}$$

$$NPV = \sum_{t=1}^{n} \frac{CF_t}{(1 + r)^t} - CF_0 \tag{10.1}$$

Of course, not every investment opportunity has this kind of standard cash flow pattern. Sometimes firms receive money up front and have to pay out cash in later years. Other times a project requires several years of cash outflows before inflows begin. Therefore, a more general equation for an investment's NPV is

$$NPV = \sum_{t=0}^{n} \frac{CF_t}{(1 + r)^t} \tag{10.1a}$$

where CF_t in any period (including period 0) can be positive or negative.

Even though the investments that firms make are not equally risky, in practice some firms apply the same discount rate to every investment project. When that is the case, firms typically use their weighted average cost of capital (WACC) as the discount rate, r, in Equations 10.1 and 10.1a.

DECISION CRITERIA

When managers use the NPV method to decide whether to accept or reject an investment proposal, the decision rule they follow is:

- If the NPV is greater than \$0, accept the project.
- If the NPV is less than \$0, reject the project.

If the NPV is greater than \$0, the firm will earn a return greater than its cost of capital. Such action should increase the market value of the firm, and therefore the wealth of its owners, by an amount equal to the NPV.

EXAMPLE 10.5

MyLab Finance Solution Video

MyLab Finance Financial Calculator

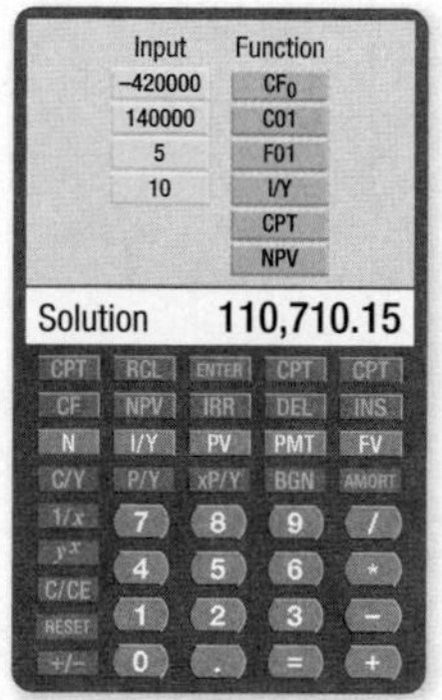

Project A

We can illustrate the NPV approach by using the Bennett Company data presented in Table 10.1. Figure 10.2 shows the calculation of the NPV for projects A and B, assuming that Bennett discounts project cash flows at 10%. These calculations result in net present values for projects A and B of \$110,710 and \$109,244, respectively. Both projects are acceptable because the net present value of each is greater than \$0. If the projects were being ranked, however, project A would be considered superior to B because its net present value is higher than that of B.

Calculator use We can use the cash flow register CF and preprogrammed NPV function in a financial calculator to perform the NPV calculation. The keystrokes for project A begin with entering the investment amount as a cash outflow at time 0, $CF_0 = -420{,}000$, then enter the first annuity cash inflow, $CF_1 = 140{,}000$, and then indicate the frequency of the annuity's cash inflow, $F01 = 5$. After entering the discount rate, $I/Y = 10$, compute the NPV.

The keystrokes for project B—the mixed stream—appear in the left margin on the next page. Because the last three cash inflows for project B are the same ($CF_3 = CF_4 = CF_5 = 100{,}000$), after inputting the first of these cash inflows, CF_3, we merely input its frequency, $F03 = 3$.

The calculated NPVs for projects A and B of \$110,710 and \$109,244, respectively, agree with the NPVs already cited.

FIGURE 10.2

Calculation of NPVs for Bennett Company's Capital Expenditure Alternatives

Timelines depicting the cash flows and NPV calculations for projects A and B

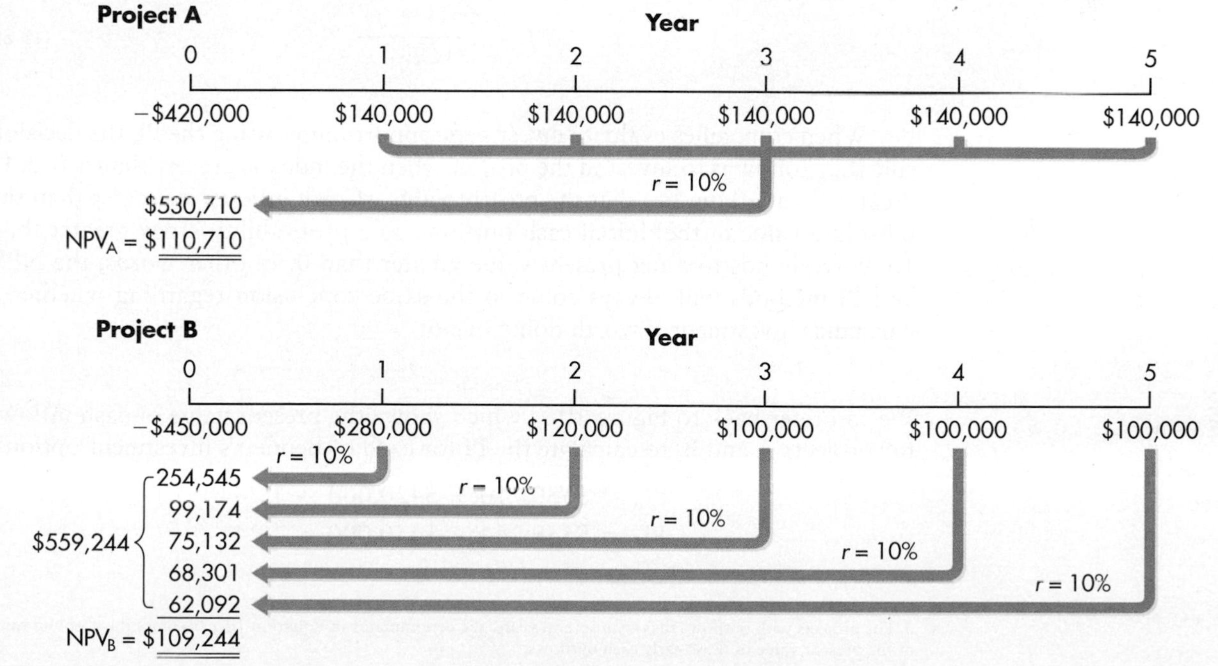

Project A

Year

0	1	2	3	4	5
–\$420,000	\$140,000	\$140,000	\$140,000	\$140,000	\$140,000

r = 10%

\$530,710

NPV$_A$ = \$110,710

Project B

Year

0	1	2	3	4	5
–\$450,000	\$280,000	\$120,000	\$100,000	\$100,000	\$100,000

r = 10%

\$559,244 { 254,545; 99,174; 75,132; 68,301; 62,092 }

NPV$_B$ = \$109,244

MyLab Finance Financial Calculator

Input	Function
−450000	CF_0
280000	C01
120000	C02
100000	C03
3	F03
10	I/Y
	CPT
	NPV

Solution 109,243.97

Project B

Spreadsheet use The following Excel screenshot illustrates how to calculate the NPVs using a spreadsheet.

	A	B	C
1	DETERMINING THE NET PRESENT VALUE		
2	Firm's cost of capital		10%
3		Year-End Cash Flow	
4	Year	Project A	Project B
5	0	$ −420,000	$ −450,000
6	1	$ 140,000	$ 280,000
7	2	$ 140,000	$ 120,000
8	3	$ 140,000	$ 100,000
9	4	$ 140,000	$ 100,000
10	5	$ 140,000	$ 100,000
11	NPV	$ 110,710	$ 109,244
12	Choice of project		Project A

Entry in Cell B11 is
=NPV(C2,B6:B10)+B5
Copy the entry in Cell B11 to Cell C11.
Entry in Cell C12 is =IF(B11>C11,B4,C4).

NPV AND THE PROFITABILITY INDEX

A variation of the NPV rule is called the profitability index (PI). For a project that has an initial cash outflow followed by cash inflows, the profitability index (PI) is simply equal to the present value of cash inflows divided by the absolute value of the initial cash outflow:[3]

$$PI = \frac{\sum_{t=1}^{n} \frac{CF_t}{(1+r)^t}}{|CF_0|} \tag{10.2}$$

When companies evaluate investment opportunities using the PI, the decision rule they follow is to invest in the project when the index is greater than 1.0. A PI greater than 1.0 implies that the present value of cash inflows is greater than the (absolute value of the) initial cash outflow, so a profitability index greater than 1.0 corresponds to a net present value greater than 0. In other words, the NPV and PI methods will always come to the same conclusion regarding whether a particular investment is worth doing or not.

EXAMPLE 10.6

MyLab Finance Solution Video

We can refer back to Figure 10.2, which shows the present value of cash inflows for projects A and B, to calculate the PI for each of Bennett's investment options:

$$PI_A = \$530{,}710 \div \$420{,}000 = 1.26$$

$$PI_B = \$559{,}244 \div \$450{,}000 = 1.24$$

3. For projects with outflows that span several years, the denominator in Equation 10.2 becomes the absolute value of the present value of those early cash outflows.

According to the profitability index, both projects are acceptable (because PI > 1.0 for both), which shouldn't be surprising because we already know that both projects have positive NPVs. Furthermore, in this particular case, the NPV rule and the PI both indicate that project A is preferred over project B. It is not always true that the NPV and PI methods will rank projects in exactly the same order. Different rankings can occur when alternative projects require initial outlays that have very different magnitudes.

NPV AND ECONOMIC VALUE ADDED

Economic Value Added (EVA), a registered trademark of the consulting firm Stern Stewart & Co., is another close cousin of the NPV method. Whereas the NPV approach calculates the value of an investment over its entire life, the EVA approach gives managers a tool to measure an investment's performance on a year-by-year basis. The EVA method begins the same way that NPV does: by calculating a project's net cash flows. However, the EVA approach subtracts from those cash flows a charge that is designed to capture the return that the firm's investors demand on the project. That is, the EVA calculation asks whether a project generates positive cash flows above and beyond what investors demand. If so, the project is worth undertaking.

The EVA method determines whether a project earns a *pure economic profit.* When accountants say that a firm has earned a profit, they mean that revenues are greater than expenses. But the term **pure economic profit** refers to a profit that is higher than expected given the competitive rate of return on a particular line of business. A firm that shows a positive profit on its income statement may or may not earn a pure economic profit, depending on how large the profit is relative to the capital invested in the business. For instance, in the four quarters ending on March 31, 2017, Exxon Mobile Corporation, the oil-producing giant, reported that it had earned a net profit of $10 billion. Does that seem like a large profit? Perhaps it doesn't when you consider that Exxon's balance sheet showed total assets of more than $344 billion. In other words, Exxon's profit represented a return of 2.9% on the firm's assets. That return was slightly less than the return offered by a 30-year Treasury bond at that time. Exxon shareholders surely expect a risk premium above Treasury rates, so the company's performance fell below the expectations of their investors. Thus, the company earned a *pure economic loss* over those four quarters. Stated differently, Exxon's EVA during that period was negative because it did not earn a return greater than its cost of capital.

pure economic profit
A profit above and beyond the normal competitive rate of return in a line of business.

EXAMPLE 10.7

Suppose that a certain project costs $1,000,000 up front, but after that it will generate net cash inflows each year (in perpetuity) of $120,000. To calculate the NPV of this project, we would simply discount the cash flows and add them up. If the firm's cost of capital is 10%, the project's NPV is:[4]

$$\text{NPV} = -\$1{,}000{,}000 + (\$120{,}000 \div 0.10) = \$200{,}000$$

To calculate the investment's economic value added in any particular year, we start with the annual $120,000 cash flow. Next, we assign a charge that accounts for the return that investors demand on the capital invested by the firm

4. We are using Equation 5.7 to calculate the present value of the perpetual stream of $120,000 cash flows.

in the project. In this case, the firm invested \$1,000,000, and investors expect a 10% return. This means that the project's annual capital charge is \$100,000 (\$1,000,000 × 10%), and its EVA is \$20,000 per year:

$$\text{EVA} = \text{project cash flow} - [(\text{cost of capital}) \times (\text{invested capital})]$$
$$= \$120{,}000 - \$100{,}000 = \$20{,}000$$

In other words, this project earns more than its cost of capital each year, so the project is clearly worth doing. To calculate the EVA for the project over its entire life, we would simply discount the annual EVA figures using the firm's cost of capital. In this case, the project produces an annual EVA of \$20,000 in perpetuity. Discounting at 10% gives a project EVA of \$200,000 (\$20,000 ÷ 0.10), identical to the NPV. In this example, both the NPV and EVA methods reach the same conclusion, namely, that the project creates \$200,000 in value for shareholders. If the cash flows in our example had fluctuated through time rather than remaining fixed at \$120,000 per year, an analyst would calculate the investment's EVA every year and then discount those figures to the present, using the firm's cost of capital. If the resulting figure is positive, the project generates a positive EVA and is worth doing.

→ REVIEW QUESTIONS MyLab Finance Solutions

10–4 How is the net present value (NPV) calculated for a project with a conventional cash flow pattern?

10–5 What decision rule do managers follow when they use NPV to accept or reject investment ideas? How is an investment's NPV related to the firm's market value?

10–6 Explain the similarities and differences between NPV, PI, and EVA.

→ EXCEL REVIEW QUESTION MyLab Finance Solutions

10–7 Almost all firms have to deal with limited financial resources and therefore cannot undertake all positive NPV projects. With the information provided at MyLab Finance, use a spreadsheet to rank various projects based on their NPVs.

LG 4

10.4 Internal Rate of Return (IRR)

internal rate of return (IRR)
The discount rate that equates the NPV of an investment opportunity with \$0 (because the present value of cash inflows equals the initial investment); it is the rate of return that the firm will earn if it invests in the project and receives the given cash inflows.

The **internal rate of return (IRR)** is the discount rate that makes the NPV of an investment opportunity equal to \$0. In other words, the IRR is the discount rate that equates the present value of a project's cash inflows to the present value of its cash outflows. The IRR has another interpretation, similar to the yield to maturity (YTM) on a bond. The IRR is the average annual compound rate of return that a company earns on an investment project, assuming that project inflows and outflows occur as projected. Mathematically, the IRR is the value of r in Equation 10.1 that causes the NPV to equal \$0. Replacing r in Equation 10.1 with IRR, we have

$$\$0 = \sum_{t=1}^{n} \frac{CF_t}{(1 + IRR)^t} - CF_0 \qquad (10.3)$$

Or, recognizing that projects may have cash inflows or outflows in any time period (including period 0), we can define the IRR more generally as

$$0 = \sum_{t=0}^{n} \frac{CF_t}{(1 + IRR)^t} \tag{10.3a}$$

DECISION CRITERIA

When managers rely on the IRR approach to accept or reject proposed investments, the decision rule they apply is:

- If the IRR is greater than the cost of capital, accept the project.
- If the IRR is less than the cost of capital, reject the project.

By following this rule, managers accept only investments expected to earn a rate of return that meets or exceeds the firm's required rate of return. Investing in those projects should increase the market value of the firm and therefore the wealth of its owners.

CALCULATING THE IRR

With most financial calculators, you merely punch in all cash flows as if to calculate an NPV and then depress IRR to find the internal rate of return. Spreadsheets also have preprogrammed functions that allow you to calculate a project's IRR very quickly.

EXAMPLE 10.8

MyLab Finance Solution Video

MyLab Finance Financial Calculator

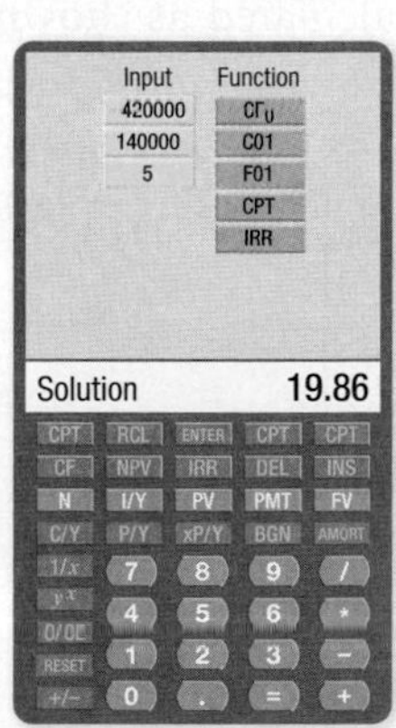

Project A

We can demonstrate the internal rate of return (IRR) approach by using the Bennett Company data presented in Table 10.1. Algebraically, the IRR for project A is the number that solves this equation:

$$0 = -420{,}000 + \frac{\$140{,}000}{(1+IRR)^1} + \frac{\$140{,}000}{(1+IRR)^2} + \frac{\$140{,}000}{(1+IRR)^3} + \frac{\$140{,}000}{(1+IRR)^4} + \frac{\$140{,}000}{(1+IRR)^5}$$

Again, we are looking for the discount rate that makes the NPV of project A's cash flows equal to zero. One way to solve this equation is to use a trial-and-error approach, trying different values for the IRR until reaching a solution. Likewise, the IRR for project B is the discount rate that makes the NPV of that project's cash flows equal zero.

Figure 10.3 uses timelines to depict the framework for finding the IRRs for Bennett's projects A and B. We can see in the figure that the IRR is the unknown discount rate that causes the NPV to equal \$0.

Calculator use To find the IRR using the preprogrammed function in a financial calculator, the keystrokes for each project are the same as those shown on pages 441 and 442 for the NPV calculation, except that you don't enter a value for I/Y or compute NPV. Instead, once the cash flows have been entered you push CPT and IRR as shown here and on page 446.

Comparing the IRRs of projects A and B given in Figure 10.3 to Bennett Company's 10% cost of capital, we can see that both projects are acceptable because the return on each project is greater than the cost of capital:

$$IRR_A = 19.9\% > 10.0\%$$

$$IRR_B = 21.7\% > 10.0\%$$

FIGURE 10.3

Calculation of IRRs for Bennett Company's Capital Expenditure Alternatives
Timelines depicting the cash flows and IRR calculations for projects A and B

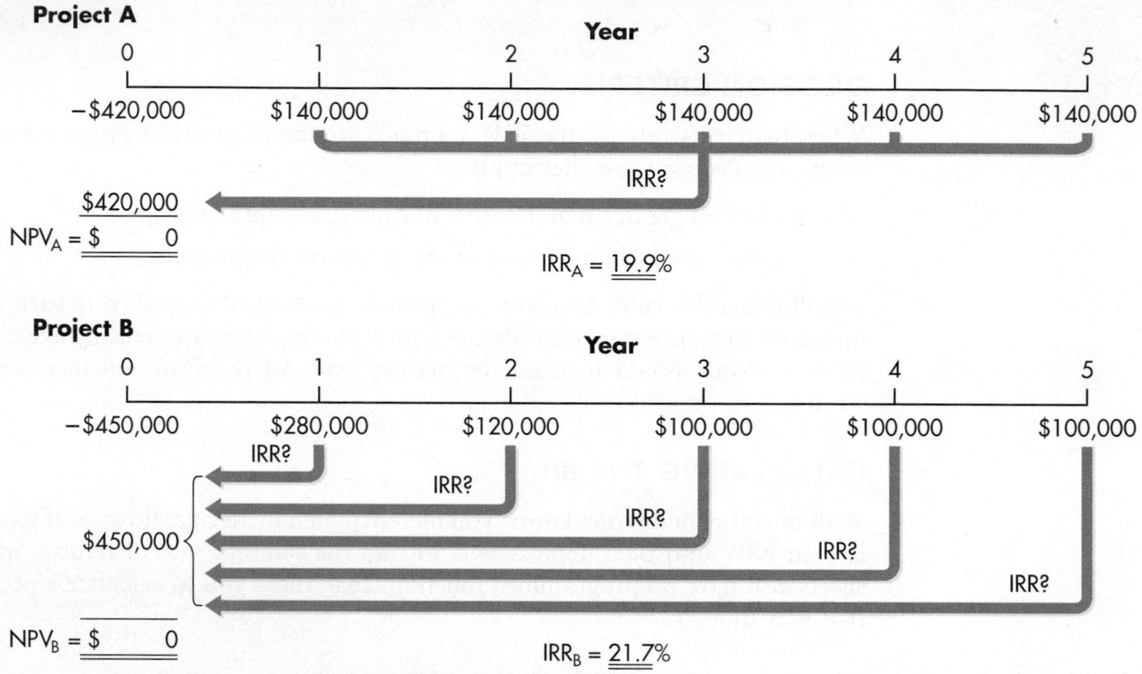

MyLab Finance Financial Calculator

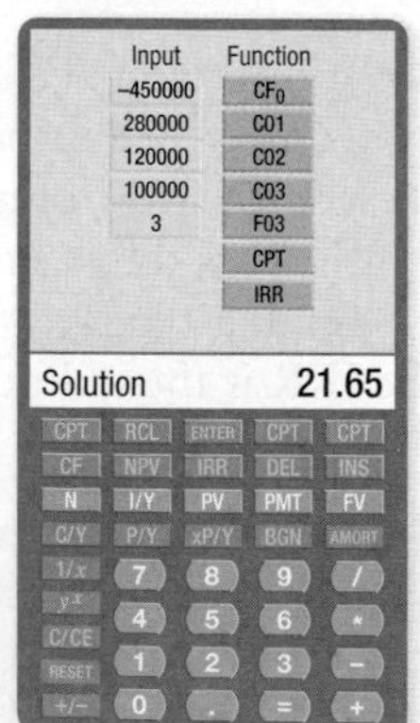

Project B

Comparing the two projects' IRRs, Bennett's managers rank project B over project A because project B delivers a higher IRR ($IRR_B = 21.7\% > IRR_A = 19.9\%$). If these projects are mutually exclusive, meaning that Bennett can choose one project or the other but not both, the IRR decision technique would recommend project B.

Spreadsheet use The internal rate of return also can be calculated as shown on the following Excel spreadsheet.

	A	B	C
1	DETERMINING THE INTERNAL RATE OF RETURN		
2		Year-End Cash Flow	
3	Year	Project A	Project B
4	0	$ −420,000	$ −450,000
5	1	$ 140,000	$ 280,000
6	2	$ 140,000	$ 120,000
7	3	$ 140,000	$ 100,000
8	4	$ 140,000	$ 100,000
9	5	$ 140,000	$ 100,000
10	IRR	19.9%	21.7%
11	Choice of project		Project B

Entry in Cell B10 is =IRR(B4:B9).
Copy the entry in Cell B10 to Cell C10.
Entry in Cell C11 is =IF(B10>C10,B3,C3).

In the preceding example, the IRR suggests that project B, which has an IRR of 21.7%, is preferable to project A, which has an IRR of 19.9%. This ranking conflicts with the NPV ranking obtained previously—project A had a higher NPV than project B. Such conflicts are not unusual. There is no guarantee that NPV and IRR will rank projects in the same order. However, both methods usually reach the same conclusion about whether a single project, considered in isolation, is acceptable or not.

PERSONAL FINANCE EXAMPLE 10.9 Tony DiLorenzo is evaluating an investment opportunity. He is comfortable with the investment's level of risk. On the basis of competing investment opportunities, he believes this investment must earn a minimum compound annual after-tax return of 9% to be acceptable. Tony's initial investment would be $7,500, and he expects to receive annual after-tax cash flows of $500 per year in each of the first 4 years, followed by $700 per year at the end of years 5 through 8. He plans to sell the investment at the end of year 8 and net $9,000, after taxes.

To calculate the investment's IRR, Tony first summarizes the after-tax cash flows as shown in the following table:

Year	Cash flow
0	−$7,500 (Initial investment)
1	500
2	500
3	500
4	500
5	700
6	700
7	700
8	9,700 ($700 + $9,000)

Substituting the after-tax cash flows for years 0 through 8 into a financial calculator or spreadsheet, he finds the investment's IRR of 9.54%. Given that the projected IRR of 9.54% exceeds Tony's required minimum return of 9%, the investment is acceptable.

→ REVIEW QUESTIONS MyLab Finance Solutions

10–8 What is the internal rate of return (IRR) on an investment? How is it determined?

10–9 What is the decision rule that managers follow when they use the IRR method to accept or reject investment proposals? How is that decision rule related to the firm's market value?

10–10 Do the net present value (NPV) and internal rate of return (IRR) agree with respect to accept–reject decisions? With respect to ranking decisions? Explain.

→ EXCEL REVIEW QUESTION MyLab Finance Solutions

10–11 In addition to using NPV to evaluate projects, most firms also use IRR. With the information provided at MyLab Finance, use a spreadsheet to rank various projects based on their IRRs.

10.5 Comparing NPV and IRR Techniques

The NPV and IRR decision rules do not always agree on which projects managers should undertake, especially when projects are mutually exclusive (but not only then). In this section, we discuss why these disagreements between methods arise and how to resolve them.

NET PRESENT VALUE PROFILES

net present value profile
Graph that depicts a project's NPVs calculated at different discount rates.

As we will discuss later in this text, managers are typically not satisfied to do a simple NPV or IRR calculation and accept or reject an investment idea based solely on that calculation. Instead, managers want to see how sensitive an investment's NPV is to changes in the assumptions used to generate the NPV. One example of this type of sensitivity analysis is called a **net present value profile**, which is simply a graph showing a project's NPV calculated at different discount rates. Managers use these profiles not only to see how changes in discount rates affect project NPVs but also to compare different projects, especially when the NPV and IRR methods provide conflicting rankings.

EXAMPLE 10.10

To prepare net present value profiles for Bennett Company's two projects, A and B, the first step is to develop a number of "discount rate–net present value" coordinates. Three coordinates are easy to obtain for each project; they are at a discount rate of 0%, at a discount rate of 10% (the cost of capital, r), and the IRR. The net present value at a 0% discount rate is the sum of all the cash inflows minus the initial investment. Using the data in Table 10.1 and assuming a 0% discount rate, we get

For project A:

($140,000 + $140,000 + $140,000 + $140,000 + $140,000) − $420,000 = $280,000

For project B:

($280,000 + $120,000 + $100,000 + $100,000 + $100,000) − $450,000 = $250,000

The net present values for projects A and B at the 10% cost of capital are $110,710 and $109,244, respectively (from Figure 10.2). Because the IRR is the discount rate for which net present value equals zero, the IRRs (from Figure 10.3) of 19.9% for project A and 21.7% for project B result in $0 NPVs. Table 10.4 summarizes the three sets of coordinates for each of the projects.

TABLE 10.4 Discount Rate–NPV Coordinates for Projects A and B

	Net present value	
Discount rate	Project A	Project B
0%	$280,000	$250,000
10	110,710	109,244
19.9	0	—
21.7	—	0

FIGURE 10.4

NPV Profiles
Net present value profiles for Bennett Company's projects A and B

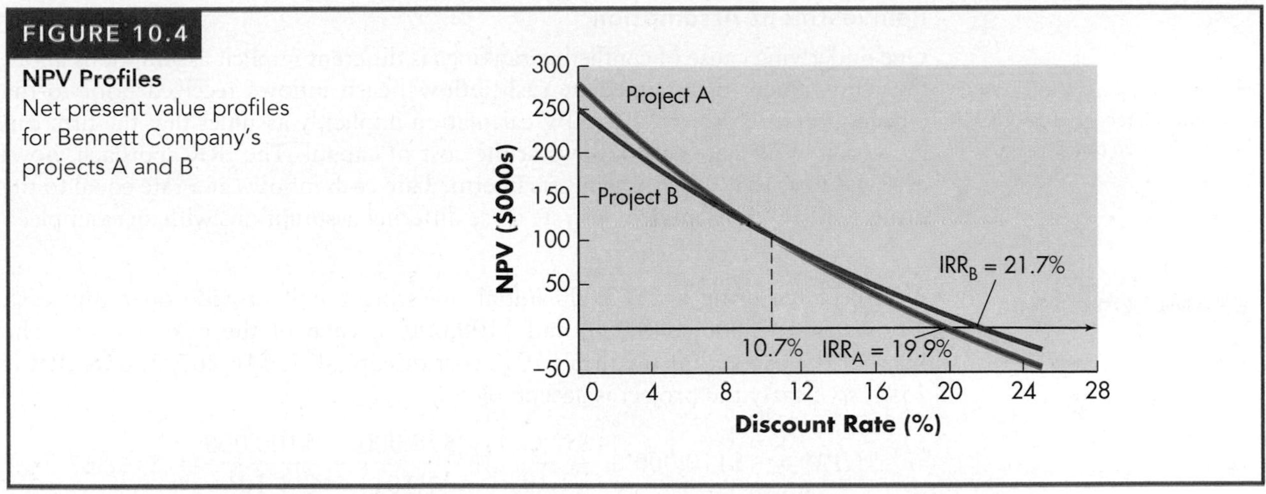

Of course, it is easy to generate more coordinates by simply calculating the NPV for each project at other discount rates. Plotting all of those coordinates results in the net present value profiles for projects A (the blue curve) and B (the red curve) shown in Figure 10.4. The figure reveals three important facts:

1. The IRR of project B is greater than that of project A, so managers using the IRR method to rank projects will choose B over A if both projects are acceptable.
2. The NPV of project A is sometimes higher and sometimes lower than that of project B, depending on the discount rate; thus, the NPV method will not consistently rank A above B or vice versa. The NPV ranking will depend on the firm's cost of capital.
3. When the cost of capital is approximately 10.7%, projects A and B have identical NPVs.

The cost of capital for Bennett Company is 10%; at that rate, project A has a higher NPV than project B (the blue line is above the red line in Figure 10.4 when the discount rate is 10%). Therefore, the NPV and IRR methods rank the two projects differently. If Bennett's cost of capital were a little higher, say 12%, the NPV method would rank project B over project A and there would be no conflict in the rankings provided by the NPV and IRR approaches.

CONFLICTING RANKINGS

Ranking different investment opportunities is an important consideration when projects are mutually exclusive or when capital rationing is necessary. When projects are mutually exclusive, ranking enables the firm to determine which project is best from a financial standpoint. When capital rationing is necessary, ranking projects will provide a logical starting point for determining which group of projects to accept. As we'll see, **conflicting rankings** using NPV and IRR result from *differences in the reinvestment rate assumption, the timing of each project's cash flows, and the magnitude of the initial investment.*

conflicting rankings
Conflicts in the ranking given a project by NPV and IRR, resulting from differences in the magnitude and timing of cash flows.

Reinvestment Assumption

intermediate cash inflows
Cash inflows received prior to the termination of a project.

One underlying cause of conflicting rankings is different implicit assumptions about the reinvestment of **intermediate cash inflows,** cash inflows received prior to the termination of a project. The NPV calculation implicitly assumes that the firm can reinvest intermediate cash inflows at the cost of capital. The IRR approach, however, assumes that the firm reinvests intermediate cash inflows at a rate equal to the project's IRR.[5] We can demonstrate these differing assumptions with an example.

EXAMPLE 10.11

A project requiring a \$170,000 initial investment will provide operating cash inflows of \$52,000, \$78,000, and \$100,000 in each of the next 3 years. The NPV of the project (at the firm's 10% cost of capital) is \$16,867, and its IRR is 15%, so clearly the project is acceptable.

$$NPV = -\$170{,}000 + \frac{\$52{,}000}{1.10} + \frac{\$78{,}000}{1.10^2} + \frac{\$100{,}000}{1.10^3} = \$16{,}867$$

$$0 = -\$170{,}000 + \frac{\$52{,}000}{1 + IRR} + \frac{\$78{,}000}{(1 + IRR)^2} + \frac{\$100{,}000}{(1 + IRR)^3}$$

$$IRR = 15\%$$

Now let's see what happens if we assume that the firm reinvests cash flows as they come in. Table 10.5 shows how much the firm can earn by reinvesting each intermediate cash flow at either 10% (the cost of capital) or 15% (the project's IRR). If we assume that the firm earns 10% on reinvested cash flows, the firm could accumulate \$248,720 in 3 years. Now suppose we discount that value back to the present, using the 10% cost of capital. In doing so, we are asking the question, what is the project worth today if it costs \$170,000 and the firm can reinvest cash flows at 10%? We have

$$PV = \frac{\$248{,}720}{(1.10)^3} = \$186{,}867$$

$$NPV = \$186{,}867 - \$170{,}000 = \$16{,}867$$

The project's NPV calculated this way is \$16,867, which matches the number stated at the beginning of this example. This confirms what we said earlier, namely, that the NPV approach assumes that the firm reinvests cash flows at the cost of capital. It is interesting that if the firm invests \$170,000 today and 3 years later has accumulated \$248,720, then its average annual return over that period is 13.5%, not the 15% figure obtained in the IRR calculation.

$$\$170{,}000(1 + r)^3 = \$248{,}720$$

$$r = 0.135 = 13.5\%$$

5. To eliminate the reinvestment rate assumption of the IRR, some practitioners calculate the *modified internal rate of return (MIRR)*. The MIRR is found by converting each cash inflow to its future value measured at the end of the project's life and then summing the future values of all inflows to get the project's *terminal value*. Each future value is found by using the cost of capital, thereby eliminating the reinvestment rate criticism of the traditional IRR. The MIRR represents the discount rate that causes the terminal value just to equal the initial investment. Because it uses the cost of capital as the reinvestment rate, the MIRR is generally viewed as a better measure of a project's true profitability than the IRR. Although this technique is frequently used in commercial real estate valuation and is a preprogrammed function on some financial calculators, its failure to resolve the issue of conflicting rankings and its theoretical inferiority to NPV have resulted in the MIRR receiving only limited attention and acceptance in the financial literature.

TABLE 10.5 Reinvestment Rate Comparisons for a Project

			Reinvestment rate	
			10%	15%
Year	Operating cash inflows	Number of years earning interest (t)	Future value	Future value
1	$ 52,000	2	$ 62,920	$ 68,770
2	78,000	1	85,800	89,700
3	100,000	0	100,000	100,000
		Future value end of year	$248,720	$258,470

NPV @ 10% = $16,867

IRR = 15%

Note: Initial investment in this project is $170,000.

Next, assume that the firm reinvests intermediate cash flows at 15%. Table 10.5 shows that the firm can accumulate $258,470 in 3 years by reinvesting cash flows as they arrive. If undertaking this project costs $170,000 and the firm can reinvest cash flows at 15%, what is the project worth today, assuming a 10% cost of capital? Discounting $258,470 back to the present, we obtain

$$PV = \frac{\$258{,}470}{(1.10)^3} = \$194{,}192$$

$$NPV = \$194{,}192 - \$170{,}000 = \$24{,}192$$

This time the NPV is larger than it was before, and that difference is driven entirely by the 15% reinvestment rate assumption. Table 10.6 summarizes the important lessons from this example. The project's NPV is $16,867, but if the firm can reinvest cash flows only at the cost of capital, the project effectively earns a 13.5% annual return. The project's IRR is 15%, but that assumes the firm can reinvest cash flows at 15%. If the firm could do so, the project would be even more valuable than the NPV calculation indicates.

TABLE 10.6 Project Cash Flows after Reinvestment

	Reinvestment rate	
	10%	15%
Initial investment	−$170,000	
Year	Operating cash inflows	
1	$ 0	$ 0
2	0	0
3	248,720	258,470
NPV @ 10%	$16,867	$24,192
IRR	13.5%	15.0%

Timing of the Cash Flow

Another reason the IRR and NPV methods may provide different rankings for investment options has to do with differences in the timing of cash flows. Go back to the timelines for investments A and B in Figure 10.1. The up-front investment required by each investment is similar, but after that, the timing of each project's cash flows is quite different. Project B has a large cash inflow almost immediately (in year 1), whereas project A provides cash flows that are distributed evenly across time. Because so much of project B's cash flows arrive early in its life (especially compared to the timing for project A), the NPV of project B will not be particularly sensitive to changes in the discount rate. Project A's NPV, in contrast, will fluctuate more as the discount rate changes. In essence, project B is somewhat akin to a short-term bond, whose price doesn't change much when interest rates move, and project A is more like a long-term bond, whose price fluctuates a great deal when rates change.

You can see this pattern if you review the NPV profiles for projects A and B in Figure 10.4. The blue line representing project A is considerably steeper than the red line representing project B. At very low discount rates, project A has a higher NPV, but as the discount rate increases, the NPV of project A declines rapidly. When the discount rate is high enough, the NPV of project B overtakes that of project A.

We can summarize this discussion as follows. Because project A's cash flows arrive later than project B's cash flows do, when the firm's cost of capital is relatively low (to be specific, below about 10.7%), the NPV method will rank project A ahead of project B. At a higher cost of capital, the early arrival of project B's cash flows becomes more advantageous, and the NPV method will rank project B over project A. The differences in the timing of cash flows between the two projects do not affect the ranking provided by the IRR method, which always puts project B ahead of project A. Table 10.7 illustrates how the conflict in rankings between the NPV and IRR approaches depends on the firm's cost of capital.

Magnitude of the Initial Investment

Suppose that someone offered you the following two investment options. You could invest $2 today and receive $3 tomorrow, or you could invest $1,000 today and receive $1,100 tomorrow. The first investment provides a return (an IRR) of 50% in just 1 day, a return that surely would surpass any reasonable hurdle rate. But after making this investment, you're only better off by $1. On

TABLE 10.7 Ranking Projects A and B Using IRR and NPV Methods

Method	Project A	Project B
IRR		✓
NPV		
if $r < 10.7\%$	✓	
if $r > 10.7\%$		✓

the other hand, the second choice offers a return of 10% in a single day. That's far less than the first opportunity, but earning 10% in a single day is still a very high return. In addition, if you accept this investment, you will be $100 better off tomorrow than you were today.

Most people would choose the second option presented above, even though the rate of return on that option (10%) is far less than the rate offered by the first option (50%). They reason (correctly) that it is sometimes better to accept a lower return on a larger investment than to accept a very high return on a small investment. Said differently, most people know that they are better off taking the investment that pays them a $100 profit in just 1 day rather than the investment that generates just a $1 profit.[6]

The preceding example illustrates what is known as the scale (or magnitude) problem. The scale problem occurs when two projects are very different in terms of how much money is required to invest in each project. In these cases, the IRR and NPV methods may rank projects differently. The IRR approach (and the PI method) may favor small projects with high returns (like the $2 loan that turns into $3), whereas the NPV approach favors the investment that makes the investor the most money (like the $1,000 investment that yields $1,100 in 1 day). In the case of the Bennett Company's projects, the scale problem is not likely to be the cause of the conflict in project rankings because the initial investment required to fund each project is quite similar.

To summarize, it is important for financial managers to watch for conflicts in project rankings provided by the NPV and IRR methods, but differences in the magnitude and timing of cash inflows do not guarantee conflicts in ranking. In general, the greater the difference between the magnitude and timing of cash inflows, the greater the likelihood of conflicting rankings. Conflicts based on NPV and IRR can be reconciled computationally; to do so, we create and analyze an incremental project reflecting the difference in cash flows between the two mutually exclusive projects.

WHICH APPROACH IS BETTER?

Many companies use both the NPV and IRR techniques because current technology makes them easy to calculate. Although the IRR approach suffers from several problems that do not befall the NPV method, both techniques see widespread use. The IRR technique is popular despite its theoretical shortcomings, so clearly firms find value in both methods.

Theoretical View

On a theoretical basis, NPV is the better approach to capital budgeting for several reasons. Most importantly, the NPV measures how much wealth a project creates (or destroys if the NPV is negative) for shareholders. Given that the financial manager's objective is to maximize shareholder wealth, the NPV approach has the clearest link to this objective and therefore is the "gold standard" for evaluating investment opportunities.

6. Note that the profitability index also provides an incorrect ranking in this example. The first option has a PI of 1.5 ($3 ÷ $2), and the second option's PI equals 1.1 ($1,100 ÷ $1,000). Just like the IRR, the PI suggests that the first option is better, but we know that the second option makes more money.

multiple IRRs
More than one IRR resulting from a capital budgeting project with a *nonconventional cash flow pattern;* the maximum number of IRRs for a project is equal to the number of sign changes in its cash flows.

For an investment project, the NPV calculation always provides a single answer, but sometimes the IRR calculation has more than one solution. A project with a nonconventional cash flow pattern may have **multiple IRRs.** Mathematically, the maximum number of real roots to an equation is equal to its number of sign changes. Take an equation like $x^2 - 5x + 6 = 0$, which has two sign changes in its coefficients—from positive ($+x^2$) to negative ($-5x$) and then from negative ($-5x$) to positive ($+6$). If we factor the equation (remember factoring from high school math?), we get $(x - 2) \times (x - 3)$, which means that two different values solve the equation: x can equal either 2 or 3. Substitute either number back into the equation, and you'll see that the equation is valid.

This same outcome can occur when finding the IRR for projects with nonconventional cash flows because they have more than one sign change in the stream of cash flows. When a project has multiple IRRs, analysts face a problem in trying to implement the IRR decision rule. Suppose that a certain investment has two IRRs, 7% and 14%, and suppose that the firm considering the investment has a cost of capital of 10%. The IRR rule says that the firm should accept the investment if the IRR exceeds the cost of capital, but in this case one IRR is greater than the cost of capital and one IRR is below it. In such a situation, it is not clear whether to accept or reject the project. That such a challenge does not exist when using NPV enhances its theoretical superiority.

Practical View

Evidence suggests that despite the theoretical superiority of NPV, financial managers use the IRR approach just as often as the NPV method. The appeal of the IRR technique is due to the general disposition of business people to think in terms of rates of return rather than actual dollar returns. Because interest rates, profitability, and so on are most often expressed as annual rates of return, the use of IRR makes sense to financial decision makers. They tend to find NPV less intuitive because it does not measure benefits relative to the amount invested. Firms that analyze investments using the IRR technique also calculate project NPVs as well, so the theoretical shortcomings of the IRR most likely do not often lead managers to make suboptimal decisions.

MATTER OF FACT

Which Methods Do Companies Actually Use?

Researchers surveyed chief financial officers (CFOs) about what methods they used to evaluate capital investment projects. One interesting finding was that many companies use more than one of the approaches we've covered in this chapter. The most popular approaches by far were IRR and NPV, used by 76% and 75% (respectively) of the CFOs responding to the survey. These techniques enjoy wider use in larger firms, with the payback approach more common in smaller firms.[7]

7. John R. Graham and Campbell R. Harvey, "The theory and practice of corporate finance: Evidence from the field," *Journal of Financial Economics* 60 (2001), pp. 187–243.

FOCUS ON ETHICS *in practice*

Baby You Can Drive My Car—Just Not a VW Diesel

Volkswagen had come a long way. In 1934, Hitler challenged German industry to come up with an inexpensive vehicle for ordinary families—"a People's Car." Ferdinand Porsche's design got the nod, and construction began on a factory to produce Beetles in modern-day Wolfsburg, Germany—still the corporate headquarters. By 2015, VW was the world's second largest automaker, producing 10.2 million cars annually. Not content with second, CEO Martin Winterkorn announced plans to pass Toyota and lead the industry "economically and ecologically" by 2018.

Then, on September 18, 2015, Volkswagen's fortunes changed. The U.S. Environmental Protection Agency (EPA) charged the company with deliberately programming diesel engines on eight passenger models to fool emissions tests. Allegedly, "defeat devices" enabled the cars to meet government standards during testing, despite spewing up to 40 times permissible levels of nitrogen-oxide pollutants in ordinary driving. VW later conceded that roughly 11 million cars worldwide contained such devices.

Volkswagen paid a big price immediately. Within days, the EPA ordered VW to recall nearly 500,000 diesel cars, and the company suspended U.S. sales of all 2015 and 2016 models alleged to have defeat devices. Within a week, VW stock plummeted 33%, the yield on its outstanding five-year debt doubled, and Winterkorn resigned. Within a month, Standard & Poor's downgraded the company's short- and long-term debt from A to A- and indicated further downgrades were possible.

By November, it was clear the scandal wasn't going away. On top of the cost of recalls, Volkswagen faced staggering government fines and civil settlements. Even worse, the scandal was damaging the brand—sales of VW-group cars worldwide fell 5.3% in October 2015. The capital budget took the first hit. Net present value was under assault from two directions—a higher cost of capital and lower expected cash flows. With lower credit ratings, VW would now pay more for debt financing. Declining sales meant lower expected cash flows from R&D and new factories. Accordingly, VW forgot about burying Toyota and cut the capital budget roughly 8%—the first reduction since global auto sales crashed during the Great Recession.

In March 2017, Volkswagen pled guilty in U.S. court to conspiracy and obstruction of justice. The record fine pushed the cost of the emissions scandal in the U.S. alone to roughly 1.3 times the entire company's net income for 2014. For its ethical transgressions, VW saw not only current earnings but also growth opportunities squashed like a bug.

► *The U.S. boasts the world's largest auto market but also the toughest emissions standards. Volkswagen believed boosting U.S. sales with "clean diesel" cars was key to overtaking Toyota. What role did VW's desire to be top automaker play in the emissions scandal?*

► *Ferdinand Piëch, grandson of Ferdinand Porsche, served as Volkswagen's CEO from 1993 to 2002 and board chairman until 2015. He also selected the next two CEOs (including Winterkorn). What role did insider succession play in the scandal?*

Environmental Protection Agency, "EPA, California Notify Volkswagen of Clean Air Act Violations/Carmaker Allegedly Used Software that Circumvents Emissions Testing for Certain Air Pollutants," *Press Release*, September 18, 2015. Ewing, Jack and Jad Mouawad. "VW Cuts Its R&D Budget in Face of Costly Emissions Scandal," *New York Times*, November 20, 2015.

The *Focus on Ethics* box recounts how an ethical lapse at Volkswagen dramatically reduced the NPVs (and IRRs) of its investment opportunities, at least for a few years.

→ REVIEW QUESTIONS MyLab Finance Solutions

10–12 How is a net present value profile used to compare projects? What causes conflicts in the ranking of projects via net present value and internal rate of return?

10–13 Does the assumption concerning the reinvestment of intermediate cash inflow tend to favor NPV or IRR? In practice, which technique is preferred and why?

SUMMARY

FOCUS ON VALUE

The financial manager must apply appropriate decision techniques to assess whether proposed investment projects create value. Most large companies use the net present value (NPV) or the internal rate of return (IRR) method for capital budgeting. Both the NPV and IRR approaches indicate whether a proposed investment creates or destroys shareholder value.

The NPV method clearly indicates the expected dollar amount of wealth creation from a proposed project, whereas an IRR calculation does not measure the wealth created by an investment. For several reasons, NPV and IRR do not necessarily rank projects in the same way. NPV is the theoretically preferred approach. In practice, however, IRR enjoys widespread use because of its intuitive appeal. Regardless, the application of NPV and IRR to good estimates of cash flows should enable the financial manager to recommend projects that are consistent with the firm's goal of **maximizing shareholder wealth.**

REVIEW OF LEARNING GOALS

LG 1 **Understand the key elements of the capital budgeting process.** Managers use capital budgeting techniques to make investment decisions that maximize the value of the firm. Applied to each project's cash flows, they indicate which capital expenditures are consistent with the firm's goal of maximizing owners' wealth.

LG 2 **Calculate, interpret, and evaluate the payback period.** The payback period is the amount of time required for the firm to recover its initial investment. Shorter payback periods are preferred. The payback period is relatively easy to calculate, has simple intuitive appeal, focuses on a project's cash flows, and is at least a crude way of adjusting for a project's risk. However, the payback method does not have a strong connection to the wealth maximization goal. It offers only crude adjustments for the time value of money and for project risk.

LG 3 **Calculate, interpret, and evaluate the net present value (NPV) and economic value added (EVA).** The NPV method measures the wealth generated by a project; positive NPV projects create value, while negative NPV projects destroy value. The rate at which cash flows are discounted in calculating NPV is called the discount rate, required return, cost of capital, or opportunity cost. Projects that earn returns exceeding this rate create value for shareholders. The EVA method begins the same way that NPV does: by calculating a project's net cash flows. However, the EVA approach subtracts from those cash flows a charge that is designed to capture the return that the firm's investors demand on the project. That is, the EVA calculation asks whether a project generates positive cash flows above and beyond what investors demand. If so, the project is worth undertaking.

LG 4 **Calculate, interpret, and evaluate the internal rate of return (IRR).** The IRR is the compound annual rate of return that the firm will earn by investing in a project and receiving the projected cash inflows, assuming that the firm can reinvest intermediate cash flows at a rate equal to the project's IRR. By accepting only those projects with IRRs in excess of the firm's cost of capital, the firm should enhance its market value and the wealth of its owners. Both NPV and IRR yield the same accept–reject decisions, but they often provide conflicting rankings.

LG 5 **Use net present value profiles to compare NPV and IRR techniques.** A net present value profile is a graph that depicts projects' NPVs for various discount rates. The NPV profile is prepared by developing a number of "discount rate–net present value" coordinates (including discount rates of 0%, the cost of capital, and the IRR for each project) and then plotting them on the same set of discount rate–NPV axes.

LG 6 **Discuss NPV and IRR in terms of conflicting rankings and the strengths of each approach.** Conflicting rankings of projects frequently emerge from NPV and IRR as a result of differences in the reinvestment rate assumption as well as the magnitude and timing of cash flows. NPV assumes reinvestment of intermediate cash inflows at the more conservative cost of capital; IRR assumes reinvestment at the project's IRR. Theoretically speaking, the NPV approach is superior because it does a better job of ranking projects and because it does not suffer from some of the mathematical quirks that occasionally affect IRR calculations. Even so, many firms use the IRR approach because it has a very intuitive interpretation and is easy for managers to understand and to communicate to others.

OPENER-IN-REVIEW

The following is some additional information regarding the Maritime Resources mining opportunity mentioned in the chapter opener.

Initial cost	$67.8 million
Project life	5 years
Cash flow in years 1–5	$30.45 million (in Canadian dollars)

a. The chapter opener reported that the project had an NPV of $44.2 million and an internal rate of return of 34.8%. From those two facts alone, what can you conclude about Maritime's cost of capital?

b. Given the information above about the project's NPV, its initial cost, and the subsequent cash flows that it generates, can you estimate Maritime's cost of capital?

c. What is the project's payback period?

SELF-TEST PROBLEM (Solutions in Appendix)

IRF

ST10–1 **All techniques with NPV profile: Mutually exclusive projects** Fitch Industries is in the process of choosing the better of two equal-risk, mutually exclusive capital expenditure projects, M and N. The relevant cash flows for each project are shown in the following table. The firm's cost of capital is 9%.

	Project M	Project N
Initial investment (CF_0)	−$40,000	−$40,000
Year (t)	**Cash inflows (CF_t)**	
1	$14,000	$23,000
2	14,000	12,000
3	14,000	10,000
4	14,000	9,000

a. Calculate each project's payback period.
b. Calculate the net present value (NPV) for each project.
c. Calculate the internal rate of return (IRR) for each project.
d. Summarize the preferences dictated by each measure you calculated, and indicate which project you would recommend. Explain why.
e. Draw the net present value profiles for these projects on the same set of axes, and explain the circumstances under which a conflict in rankings might exist.

WARM-UP EXERCISES All problems are available in MyLab Finance

E10–1 Elysian Fields Inc. uses a maximum payback period of 6 years and currently must choose between two mutually exclusive projects. Project Hydrogen requires an initial outlay of $25,000; project Helium requires an initial outlay of $35,000. Using the expected cash inflows given for each project in the following table, calculate each project's payback period. Which project meets Elysian's standards?

	Expected cash inflows (CF_t)	
Year	Hydrogen	Helium
1	$6,000	$7,000
2	6,000	7,000
3	8,000	8,000
4	4,000	5,000
5	3,500	5,000
6	2,000	4,000

LG3

E10–2 Herky Foods is considering acquisition of a new wrapping machine. By purchasing the machine, Herky will save money on packaging in each of the next 5 years, producing the series of cash inflows shown below. The initial investment (CF_0) is estimated at $1.25 million. Using a 6% discount rate, determine the net present value (NPV) of the machine given its expected operating cash inflows shown in the following table. Based on the project's NPV, should Herky make this investment?

Year	Cash inflow (CF_t)
1	$400,000
2	375,000
3	300,000
4	350,000
5	200,000

LG3

E10–3 Axis Corp. is considering investment in the best of two mutually exclusive projects. Project Kelvin involves an overhaul of the existing system; it will cost $52,500 and generate cash inflows of $24,500 per year for the next 3 years. Project Thompson involves replacement of the existing system; it will cost $265,000 and generate cash inflows of $61,000 per year for 6 years. Using an 8.75% cost of capital, calculate each project's NPV, and make a recommendation based on your findings.

LG4

E10–4 Billabong Tech uses the internal rate of return (IRR) to select projects. Calculate the IRR for each of the following projects and recommend the best project based on this measure. Project T-Shirt requires an initial investment of $15,000 and generates cash inflows of $8,000 per year for 4 years. Project Board Shorts requires an initial investment of $25,000 and produces cash inflows of $12,000 per year for 5 years.

LG4 LG5

E10–5 Cooper Electronics uses NPV profiles to visually evaluate competing projects. Key data for the two projects under consideration are given in the following table. Using these data, graph, on the same set of axes, the NPV profiles for each project, using discount rates of 0%, 8%, and the IRR.

	Terra	Firma
Initial investment (CF_0)	−$30,000	−$25,000
Year	Operating cash inflows (CF_t)	
1	$ 7,000	$6,000
2	10,000	9,000
3	12,000	9,000
4	10,000	8,000

PROBLEMS

All problems are available in MyLab Finance. The MyLab icon indicates problems in Excel format available in MyLab Finance.

LG 2

P10–1 Payback period The Ball Shoe Company is considering an investment project that requires an initial investment of $542,000 and returns after-tax cash inflows of $75,000 per year for 10 years. The firm has a maximum acceptable payback period of 8 years.

a. Determine the payback period for this project.
b. Should the company accept the project? Why or why not?

LG 2

P10–2 Payback comparisons Nova Products has a 5-year maximum acceptable payback period. The firm is considering the purchase of a new machine and must choose between two alternative ones. The first machine requires an initial investment of $14,000 and generates annual after-tax cash inflows of $3,000 for each of the next 7 years. The second machine requires an initial investment of $21,000 and provides an annual cash inflow after taxes of $4,000 for 20 years.

a. Determine the payback period for each machine.
b. Comment on the acceptability of the machines, assuming they are independent projects.
c. Which machine should the firm accept? Why?
d. Do the machines in this problem illustrate any of the weaknesses of using payback? Discuss.

LG 2

P10–3 Choosing between two projects with acceptable payback periods Shell Camping Gear Inc. is considering two mutually exclusive projects. Each requires an initial investment (CF_0) of $100,000. John Shell, president of the company, has set a maximum payback period of 4 years. The after-tax cash inflows associated with each project are shown in the following table.

	Cash inflows (CF_t)	
Year	Project A	Project B
1	$10,000	$40,000
2	20,000	30,000
3	30,000	20,000
4	40,000	10,000
5	20,000	20,000

a. Determine the payback period of each project.
b. Because they are mutually exclusive, Shell must choose one. Which should the company invest in?
c. Explain why one of the projects is a better choice than the other.

Personal Finance Problem

LG 2

P10–4 Long-term investment decision, payback method Bill Williams has the opportunity to invest in project A, which costs $9,000 today and promises to pay $2,200, $2,500, $2,500, $2,000, and $1,800 over the next 5 years. Or Bill can invest $9,000 in project B, which promises to pay $1,500, $1,500, $1,500, $3,500, and $4,000 over the next 5 years.

a. How long will it take for Bill to recoup his initial investment in project A?
b. How long will it take for Bill to recoup his initial investment in project B?

c. Using the payback period, which project should Bill choose?
d. Do you see any problems with his choice?

LG3 **P10–5** **NPV** Calculate the net present value (NPV) for the following 15-year projects. Comment on the acceptability of each. Assume that the firm has a cost of capital of 9%.

a. Initial investment is $1,000,000; cash inflows are $150,000 per year.
b. Initial investment is $2,500,000; cash inflows are $320,000 per year.
c. Initial investment is $3,000,000; cash inflows are $365,000 per year.

LG3 **P10–6** **NPV for varying costs of capital** Le Pew Cosmetics is evaluating a new fragrance-mixing machine. The machine requires an initial investment of $360,000 and will generate after-tax cash inflows of $62,650 per year for 8 years. For each of the costs of capital listed, (1) calculate the net present value (NPV), (2) indicate whether to accept or reject the machine, and (3) explain your decision.

a. The cost of capital is 6%.
b. The cost of capital is 8%.
c. The cost of capital is 10%.

P10–7 **Net present value: Independent projects** Using a 10% cost of capital, calculate the net present value for each of the independent projects shown in the following table, and indicate whether each is acceptable.

	Cash flows (CF_t) in thousands				
Year	A	B	C	D	E
0	–$250	–$375	–$550	–$750	–$1,150
1	50	45	350	200	80
2	90	55	210	235	135
3	140	65	165	250	190
4	80	55	55	265	255
5		45	45	100	315
6		35	10	50	380
7		25			275
8		15			100
9		5			15
10					25

LG3 **P10–8** **NPV** Simes Innovations Inc. is negotiating to purchase exclusive rights to manufacture and market a solar-powered toy car. The car's inventor has offered Simes the choice of either a one-time payment of $1,500,000 today or a series of five year-end payments of $385,000.

a. If Simes has a cost of capital of 9%, which form of payment should it choose?
b. What yearly payment would make the two offers identical in value at a cost of capital of 9%?
c. Would your answer to part **a** of this problem be different if the yearly payments were made at the beginning of each year? Show what difference, if any, that change in timing would make to the present value calculation.
d. The after-tax cash inflows associated with this purchase are projected to amount to $250,000 per year for 15 years. Will this factor change the firm's decision about how to fund the initial investment?

P10–9 **NPV and maximum return** A firm can purchase new equipment for a $150,000 initial investment. The equipment generates an annual after-tax cash inflow of $44,400 for 4 years.

a. Determine the net present value (NPV) of the equipment, assuming the firm has a 10% cost of capital. Is the project acceptable?

b. If the firm's cost of capital is lower than 10%, does the investment in equipment become more or less desirable? What is the highest cost of capital (closest whole-percentage rate) that the firm can have and still find that purchasing the equipment is worthwhile? Discuss this finding in light of your response in part **a.**

P10–10 **NPV: Mutually exclusive projects** Hook Industries is considering the replacement of one of its old metal stamping machines. Three alternative replacement machines are under consideration. The relevant cash flows associated with each are shown in the following table. The firm's cost of capital is 15%.

	Machine A	Machine B	Machine C
Initial investment (CF_0)	−$85,000	−$60,000	−$130,000
Year (t)	Cash inflows (CF_t)		
1	$18,000	$12,000	$50,000
2	18,000	14,000	30,000
3	18,000	16,000	20,000
4	18,000	18,000	20,000
5	18,000	20,000	20,000
6	18,000	25,000	30,000
7	18,000	—	40,000
8	18,000	—	50,000

a. Calculate the net present value (NPV) of each press.

b. Using NPV, evaluate the acceptability of each press.

c. Rank the presses from best to worst, using NPV.

d. Calculate the profitability index (PI) for each press.

e. Rank the presses from best to worst, using PI.

Personal Finance Problem

P10–11 **Long-term investment decision, NPV method** Jenny Jenks has researched the financial pros and cons of entering into a 1-year MBA program at her state university. The tuition and books for the master's program will have an up-front cost of $50,000. If she enrolls in an MBA program, Jenny will quit her current job, which pays $50,000 per year after taxes (for simplicity, treat any lost earnings as part of the up-front cost). On average, a person with an MBA degree earns an extra $20,000 per year (after taxes) over a business career of 40 years. Jenny believes that her opportunity cost of capital is 6%. Given her estimates, find the net present value (NPV) of entering this MBA program. Are the benefits of further education worth the associated costs?

P10–12 **Payback and NPV** Neil Corporation has three projects under consideration. The cash flows for each project are shown in the following table. The firm has a 16% cost of capital.

	Project A	Project B	Project C
Initial investment (CF_0)	−\$40,000	−\$40,000	−\$40,000
Year (t)	Cash inflows (CF_t)		
1	\$13,000	\$ 7,000	\$19,000
2	13,000	10,000	16,000
3	13,000	13,000	13,000
4	13,000	16,000	10,000
5	13,000	19,000	7,000

a. Calculate each project's payback period. Which project is preferred according to this method?
b. Calculate each project's net present value (NPV). Which project is preferred according to this method?
c. Comment on your findings in parts **a** and **b**, and recommend the best project. Explain your recommendation.

P10–13 **NPV and EVA** A project costs \$2,500,000 up front and will generate cash flows in perpetuity of \$240,000. The firm's cost of capital is 9%.
a. Calculate the project's NPV.
b. Calculate the annual EVA in a typical year.
c. Calculate the overall project EVA and compare to your answer in part **a.**

P10–14 **Internal rate of return** For each of the projects shown in the following table, calculate the internal rate of return (IRR). Then indicate, for each project, the maximum cost of capital that the firm could have and still find the IRR acceptable.

	Project A	Project B	Project C	Project D
Initial investment (CF_0)	−\$90,000	−\$490,000	−\$20,000	−\$240,000
Year (t)	Cash inflows (CF_t)			
1	\$20,000	\$150,000	\$7,500	\$120,000
2	25,000	150,000	7,500	100,000
3	30,000	150,000	7,500	80,000
4	35,000	150,000	7,500	60,000
5	40,000	—	7,500	—

P10–15 **Internal rate of return** Peace of Mind Inc. (PMI) sells extended warranties for durable consumer goods such as washing machines and refrigerators. When PMI sells an extended warranty, it receives cash up front from the customer, but later PMI must cover any repair costs that arise. An analyst working for PMI is considering a warranty for a new line of big-screen TVs. A consumer who purchases the 2-year warranty will pay PMI \$200. On average, the repair costs that PMI must cover will average \$106 for each of the warranty's 2 years. If PMI has a cost of capital of 7%, should it offer this warranty for sale?

P10–16 **IRR: Mutually exclusive projects** Bell Manufacturing is attempting to choose the better of two mutually exclusive projects for expanding the firm's warehouse capacity. The relevant cash flows for the projects are shown in the following table. The firm's cost of capital is 15%.

	Project X	Project Y
Initial investment (CF_0)	−$500,000	−$325,000
Year (t)	Cash inflows (CF_t)	
1	$100,000	$140,000
2	120,000	120,000
3	150,000	95,000
4	190,000	70,000
5	250,000	50,000

a. Calculate the IRR to the nearest whole percent for each of the projects.
b. Assess the acceptability of each project on the basis of the IRRs found in part **a**.
c. Which project, on this basis, is preferred?

Personal Finance Problem

P10–17 **Problems with the IRR method** Acme Oscillators is considering an investment project that has the following rather unusual cash flow pattern.

Year	CF_t
0	$100.0
1	−460.0
2	791.0
3	−602.6
4	171.6

a. Calculate the project's NPV at each of the following discount rates: 0%, 5%, 10%, 20%, 30%, 40%, 50%.
b. What do the calculations tell you about this project's IRR? The IRR rule tells managers to invest if a project's IRR is greater than the cost of capital. If Acme Oscillators' cost of capital is 8%, should the company accept or reject this investment?
c. Notice that this project's greatest NPVs come at very high discount rates. Can you provide an intuitive explanation for that pattern?

P10–18 **IRR, investment life, and cash inflows** Oak Enterprises accepts projects earning more than the firm's 15% cost of capital. Oak is currently considering a 10-year project that provides annual cash inflows of $10,000 and requires an initial investment of $61,450. (*Note:* All amounts are after taxes.)
a. Determine the IRR of this project. Is it acceptable?
b. Assuming that the cash inflows remain at $10,000 per year, how many additional years would the flows have to continue to make the project acceptable (i.e., to make it have an IRR of 15%)?
c. With a 10-year life, an initial investment of $61,540, and a cost of capital of 15%, what is the minimum annual cash inflow the investment would have to provide in order for this project to make sense for Oak's shareholders?

P10–19 **NPV and IRR** Benson Designs has prepared the following estimates for a long-term project it is considering. The initial investment is $18,250, and the project is expected to yield after-tax cash inflows of $4,000 per year for 7 years. The firm has a 10% cost of capital.

a. Determine the net present value (NPV) for the project.
b. Determine the internal rate of return (IRR) for the project.
c. Would you recommend that the firm accept or reject the project? Explain your answer.

P10–20 **NPV, with rankings** Botany Bay Inc., a maker of casual clothing, is considering four projects. Because of past financial difficulties, the company has a high cost of capital at 15%.

	Project A	Project B	Project C	Project D
Initial investment (CF_0)	−$50,000	−$100,000	−$80,000	−$180,000
Year (t)	Cash inflows (CF_t)			
1	$20,000	$35,000	$20,000	$100,000
2	20,000	50,000	40,000	80,000
3	20,000	50,000	60,000	60,000

a. Calculate the NPV of each project, using a cost of capital of 15%.
b. Rank acceptable projects by NPV.
c. Calculate the IRR of each project, and use it to determine the highest cost of capital at which all the projects would be acceptable.

P10–21 **All techniques, conflicting rankings** Nicholson Roofing Materials Inc. is considering two mutually exclusive projects, each with an initial investment of $150,000. The company's board of directors has set a maximum 4-year payback requirement and has set its cost of capital at 9%. The cash inflows associated with the two projects are shown in the following table.

	Cash inflows (CF_t)	
Year	Project A	Project B
1	$45,000	$75,000
2	45,000	60,000
3	45,000	30,000
4	45,000	30,000
5	45,000	30,000
6	45,000	30,000

a. Calculate the payback period for each project.
b. Calculate the NPV of each project at 0%.
c. Calculate the NPV of each project at 9%.
d. Derive the IRR of each project.
e. Rank the projects by each of the techniques used. Make and justify a recommendation.
f. Go back one more time and calculate the NPV of each project using a cost of capital of 12%. Does the ranking of the two projects change compared to your answer in part e? Why?

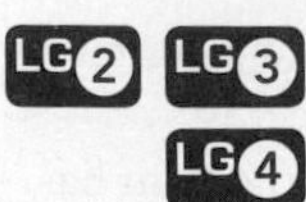

P10–22 Payback, NPV, and IRR Rieger International is evaluating the feasibility of investing $95,000 in a piece of equipment that has a 5-year life. The firm has estimated the cash inflows associated with the proposal, as shown in the following table. The firm has a 12% cost of capital.

Year (t)	Cash inflows (CF_t)
1	$20,000
2	25,000
3	30,000
4	35,000
5	40,000

a. Calculate the payback period for the proposed investment.
b. Calculate the net present value (NPV) for the proposed investment.
c. Calculate the internal rate of return (IRR), rounded to the nearest whole percent, for the proposed investment.
d. Evaluate the acceptability of the proposed investment using NPV and IRR. What recommendation would you make relative to implementation of the project? Why?

P10–23 NPV, IRR, and NPV profiles Thomas Company is considering two mutually exclusive projects. The firm, which has a 12% cost of capital, has estimated its cash flows as shown in the following table.

	Project A	Project B
Initial investment (CF_0)	−$130,000	−$85,000
Year (t)	Cash inflows (CF_t)	
1	$25,000	$40,000
2	35,000	35,000
3	45,000	30,000
4	50,000	10,000
5	55,000	5,000

a. Calculate the NPV of each project, and assess its acceptability.
b. Calculate the IRR for each project, and assess its acceptability.
c. Draw the NPV profiles for both projects on the same set of axes.
d. Evaluate and discuss the rankings of the two projects on the basis of your findings in parts **a**, **b**, and **c**.
e. Explain your findings in part **d** in light of the pattern of cash inflows associated with each project.

P10–24 All techniques: Decision among mutually exclusive investments Pound Industries is attempting to select the best of three mutually exclusive projects. The initial investment and after-tax cash inflows associated with these projects are shown in the following table.

Cash flows	Project A	Project B	Project C
Initial investment (CF_0)	−$60,000	−$100,000	−$110,000
Cash inflows (CF_t), $t = 1$ to 5	20,000	31,500	32,500

a. Calculate the payback period for each project.
b. Calculate the net present value (NPV) of each project, assuming that the firm has a cost of capital equal to 13%.
c. Calculate the internal rate of return (IRR) for each project.
d. Draw the net present value profiles for both projects on the same set of axes, and discuss any conflict in ranking that may exist between NPV and IRR.
e. Summarize the preferences dictated by each measure, and indicate which project you would recommend. Explain why.

P10–25 **All techniques with NPV profile: Mutually exclusive projects** Projects A and B, of equal risk, are alternatives for expanding Rosa Company's capacity. The firm's cost of capital is 13%. The cash flows for each project are shown in the following table.
a. Calculate each project's payback period.
b. Calculate the net present value (NPV) for each project.
c. Calculate the internal rate of return (IRR) for each project.
d. Draw the net present value profiles for both projects on the same set of axes, and discuss any conflict in ranking that may exist between NPV and IRR.
e. Summarize the preferences dictated by each measure, and indicate which project you would recommend. Explain why.

	Project A	Project B
Initial investment (CF_0)	−$80,000	−$50,000
Year (t)	Cash inflows (CF_t)	
1	$15,000	$15,000
2	20,000	15,000
3	25,000	15,000
4	30,000	15,000
5	35,000	15,000

P10–26 **Integrative: Multiple IRRs** Froogle Enterprises is evaluating an unusual investment project. What makes the project unusual is the stream of cash inflows and outflows shown in the following table.

Year	Cash flow
0	$ 200,000
1	−920,000
2	1,582,000
3	−1,205,200
4	343,200

a. Why is it difficult to calculate the payback period for this project?
b. Calculate the investment's net present value at each of the following discount rates: 0%, 5%, 10%, 15%, 20%, 25%, 30%, 35%.
c. What does your answer to part **b** tell you about this project's IRR?
d. Should Froogle invest in this project if its cost of capital is 5%? What if the cost of capital is 15%?
e. In general, when faced with a project like this one, how should a firm decide whether to invest in the project or reject it?

P10–27 **Integrative: Conflicting Rankings** The High-Flying Growth Company (HFGC) has been expanding very rapidly in recent years, making its shareholders rich in the process. The average annual rate of return on the stock in the past few years has been 20%, and HFGC managers believe that 20% is a reasonable figure for the firm's cost of capital. To sustain a high growth rate, HFGC's CEO argues that the company must continue to invest in projects that offer the highest rate of return possible. Two projects are currently under review. The first is an expansion of the firm's production capacity, and the second involves introducing one of the firm's existing products into a new market. Cash flows from each project appear in the following table.

a. Calculate the NPV, IRR, and PI for both projects.
b. Rank the projects based on their NPVs, IRRs, and PIs.
c. Do the rankings in part **b** agree or not? If not, why not?
d. The firm can afford to undertake only one of these investments, and the CEO favors the product introduction because it offers a higher rate of return (i.e., a higher IRR) than the plant expansion. What do you think the firm should do? Why?

Year	Plant expansion	Product introduction
0	−$3,500,000	−$500,000
1	1,500,000	250,000
2	2,000,000	350,000
3	2,500,000	375,000
4	2,750,000	425,000

P10-28 **Problems with IRR** White Rock Services Inc. has an opportunity to make an investment with the following projected cash flows.

Year	Cash Flow
0	$1,690,000
1	−3,887,000
2	2,225,025

a. Calculate the NPV at the following discount rates and plot an NPV profile for this investment: 0%, 5%, 7.5%, 10%, 15%, 20%, 22.5%, 25%, 30%.
b. What does the NPV profile tell you about this investment's IRR?
c. If the company follows the IRR decision rule and their cost of capital is 15%, should they accept or reject the opportunity? Why is it hard to make a decision on this investment based solely on the IRR rule?
d. If the company's cost of capital is 15%, should they reject or accept the investment based on its NPV?

P10–29 **ETHICS PROBLEM** Diane Dennison is a financial analyst working for a large chain of discount retail stores. Her company is looking at the possibility of replacing the existing fluorescent lights in all of its stores with LED lights. The main advantage of making this switch is that the LED lights are much more efficient and will cost less to operate. In addition, the LED lights last much longer and will have to be replaced after 10 years, whereas the existing lights have to be replaced after 5 years. Of course, making this change will require a large investment to purchase new LED lights and to pay for the labor of switching out tens of thousands of bulbs. Diane plans to use a 10-year horizon to analyze this proposal, figuring that changes to lighting technology will eventually make this investment obsolete.

Diane's friend and coworker, David, has analyzed another energy-saving investment opportunity that involves replacing outdoor lighting with solar-powered fixtures in a few of the company's stores. David also used a 10-year horizon to conduct his analysis. Cash flow forecasts for each project appear below. The company uses a 10% discount rate to analyze capital budgeting proposals.

Year	LED project	Solar project
0	–$4,200,000	–$500,000
1	700,000	60,000
2	700,000	60,000
3	700,000	60,000
4	700,000	60,000
5	1,000,000	60,000
6	700,000	60,000
7	700,000	60,000
8	700,000	60,000
9	700,000	60,000
10	700,000	60,000

a. What is the NPV of each investment? Which investment (if either) should the company undertake?
b. David approaches Diane for a favor. David says that the solar lighting project is a pet project of his boss, and David really wants to get the project approved to curry favor with his boss. He suggests to Diane that they roll their two projects into a single proposal. The cash flows for this combined project would simply equal the sum of the two individual projects. Calculate the NPV of the combined project. Does it appear to be worth doing? Would you recommend investing in the combined project?
c. What is the ethical issue that Diane faces? Is any harm done if she does the favor for David as he asks?

SPREADSHEET EXERCISE

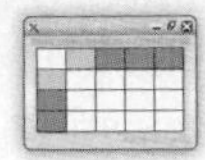

The Drillago Company is involved in searching for locations in which to drill for oil. The firm's current project requires an initial investment of $15 million and has an estimated life of 10 years. The expected future cash inflows for the project appear in the following table.

Year	Cash inflows
1	$ 600,000
2	1,000,000
3	1,000,000
4	2,000,000
5	3,000,000
6	3,500,000
7	4,000,000
8	6,000,000
9	8,000,000
10	12,000,000

The firm's current cost of capital is 13%.

TO DO

Create a spreadsheet to answer the following questions.

a. Calculate the project's net present value (NPV). Is the project acceptable under the NPV technique? Explain.

b. Calculate the project's internal rate of return (IRR). Is the project acceptable under the IRR technique? Explain.

c. In this case, did the two methods produce the same results? Generally, is there a preference between the NPV and IRR techniques? Explain.

d. Calculate the payback period for the project. If the firm usually accepts projects that have payback periods between 1 and 7 years, is this project acceptable?

MyLab Finance Visit www.pearson.com/mylab/finance for **Chapter Case: *Making Norwich Tool's Lathe Investment Decision,*** Group Exercises, and numerous online resources.

CHAPTER

11

Capital Budgeting Cash Flows

LEARNING GOALS

LG 1 Discuss net and incremental cash flows, and describe the three major types of net cash flows.

LG 2 Discuss replacement versus expansion decisions, sunk costs and opportunity costs, and international capital budgeting.

LG 3 Calculate the initial investment associated with a proposed investment project.

LG 4 Discuss the tax implications associated with the sale of an old asset.

LG 5 Find the operating cash flows associated with a proposed investment project.

LG 6 Determine the terminal cash flow associated with a proposed investment project.

MyLab Finance Chapter Introduction Video

WHY THIS CHAPTER MATTERS TO YOU

In your *professional* life

ACCOUNTING You need to understand capital budgeting cash flows to provide revenue, cost, depreciation, and tax data for use both in monitoring existing projects and in developing cash flows for proposed investment projects.

INFORMATION SYSTEMS You need to understand capital budgeting cash flows to maintain and facilitate the retrieval of cash flow data for both completed and existing projects.

MANAGEMENT You need to understand capital budgeting cash flows so that you will know which cash flows are relevant in making decisions about proposals for acquiring additional production facilities, for new marketing programs, for new products, and for the expansion of existing product lines.

MARKETING You need to understand capital budgeting cash flows so that you can make revenue and cost estimates for proposals for new marketing programs, for new products, and for the expansion of existing product lines.

OPERATIONS You need to understand capital budgeting cash flows so that you can make revenue and cost estimates for proposals for the acquisition of new equipment and production facilities.

In your *personal* life

You are not mandated to provide financial statements prepared using generally accepted accounting principles, so you naturally focus on cash flows. When considering a major outflow of funds (e.g., purchase of a house, funding of a college education), you can project the associated cash flows and use these estimates to determine the value and affordability of the assets and any associated future outlays.

Kristoffer Tripplaar/Alamy Stock Photo

MOLSON COORS BREWING COMPANY

Brewing Up a Deal

In late 2015, the Denver-based brewing company Molson Coors announced that it would acquire the remaining 58% ownership stake it did not already own in MillerCoors, a joint venture created in 2008 between Molson Coors and SABMiller. Taking full ownership of the joint venture would give Molson Coors complete control of the Miller brand outside the United States, as well as brands controlled by the joint venture within the United States. Molson agreed to pay $12 billion for the acquisition with a combination of cash on hand plus additional funds raised by issuing new debt and equity securities.

What justified the deal's $12 billion price tag? According to Molson Coors senior management, the acquisition would create billions in incremental revenue, $250 million per year for 15 years in incremental tax savings (worth $2.4 billion in present value terms), and at least $200 million per year in incremental cost savings, achieved by making improvements to the company's procurement processes and implementing other operational enhancements.

A little more than a year later, in early 2017, Molson Coors reported that in 2016 it had generated $1.1 billion in operating cash flow, an increase of $411 million from the prior year, driven mostly by the MillerCoors acquisition. In terms of free cash flow, the company generated $864 million, up $140 million from the prior year. Although the company had a long way to go in realizing all the benefits envisioned from the MillerCoors acquisition, 1 year after the deal it appeared that the company was on track to create value for its shareholders through the purchase of MillerCoors.

Every firm must evaluate the costs and returns of projects for asset renewal, replacement, or expansion; research and development; advertising; and other major investments, such as mergers and acquisitions, that require a long-term commitment of funds in expectation of future returns. This chapter explains how to identify the incremental cash outflows and inflows that managers must identify and value when making major investment decisions.

Sources: (1) http://www.businesswire.com/news/home/20170214005479/en/Molson-Coors-Reports-2016-Fourth-Quarter-Full; (2) http://www.molsoncoors.com/en/news/molson%20coors%20to%20acquire%20millercoors%20and%20global%20miller%20brand%20portfolio

LG1 LG2

11.1 Project Cash Flows

net cash flows
The net (or the sum of) incremental after-tax cash flows over a project's life.

incremental cash flows
The additional after-tax cash flows—outflows or inflows—that will occur only if the investment is made.

Chapter 10 introduced the capital budgeting process and the techniques financial managers use for evaluating and selecting long-term investment projects. To evaluate these opportunities, financial managers must identify the net cash flows associated with the investment opportunity. A project's **net cash flows** are the net (or the sum of) incremental after-tax cash flows over a project's life. The **incremental cash flows** represent the additional after-tax cash flows—outflows or inflows—that will occur only if the firm makes the investment. As noted in Chapter 4, we focus on cash flows rather than accounting figures because cash flows directly affect the firm's ability to pay bills and purchase assets. Once they have estimates of incremental cash flows in place, managers can evaluate the investment project using the valuation techniques introduced in Chapter 10. The *Focus on Ethics* box on page 476 discusses what can go wrong when managers fail to make investment decisions based on *incremental* cash flows.

The remainder of this chapter is devoted to the procedures that managers use to estimate the incremental cash flows associated with an investment project and the ways managers apply those cash flow estimates to make investment decisions.

MAJOR CASH FLOW TYPES

The cash flows of any project may include (1) an initial investment, (2) operating cash flows, and (3) a terminal cash flow. In the typical pattern, the initial investment is a net cash outflow that occurs at the beginning (time zero) of the project, the operating cash flows occur over the life of the project and tend to be net cash inflows, and the terminal cash flow occurs at the end of the project. In most situations, the terminal cash flow will be a net inflow. However, for any particular investment, any of these net cash flows could be inflows or outflows, since each is a function of the sum of incremental cash inflows and outflows that take place for a particular period during the project's life.

initial investment
The incremental cash flows for a project at time zero.

Figure 11.1 depicts on a timeline the net cash flows for a proposed investment project. The **initial investment** for the project is a $50,000 cash outflow at time zero. The incremental cash flows that make up the initial investment

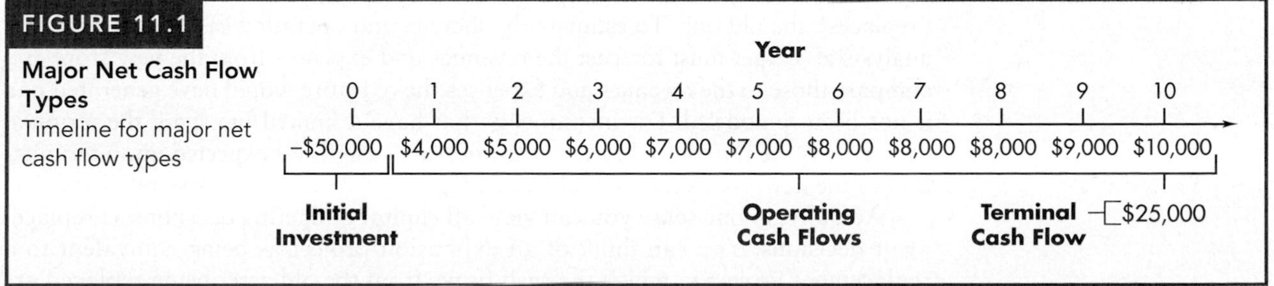

FIGURE 11.1
Major Net Cash Flow Types
Timeline for major net cash flow types

operating cash flows
The net incremental after-tax cash flows occurring each period during the project's life.

terminal cash flows
The net after-tax cash flow occurring in the final year of the project.

typically include the cost of acquiring new assets, the proceeds from the disposal of the old assets, and cash flows resulting from up-front changes to net working capital. The **operating cash flows,** which are the sum of incremental after-tax cash flows occurring each period during the project's life, gradually increase from $4,000 in the first year to $10,000 in the 10th year. For this project, the operating cash flows are all cash inflows, but that is not always the case. The **terminal cash flow** is a net after-tax cash flow occurring in the project's final year. It is often attributable to liquidation. In this case, the terminal cash flow is an inflow of $25,000, received at the end of the project's 10-year life. Note that the terminal cash flow does not include the $10,000 operating cash inflow for year 10; in other words, total cash flows in year 10 are $35,000.

REPLACEMENT VERSUS EXPANSION DECISIONS

Many common investments that firms undertake involve a decision to expand the firm's activities. Expansion decisions include investments designed to increase the capacity of a factory, to launch a product in a new market, or to open a new location. Identifying incremental cash flows along with developing net cash flow estimates is relatively straightforward in these sorts of projects. The initial investment, operating cash flows, and terminal cash flow are merely the net after-tax cash flows associated with the proposed expansion project. For example, if Target Corporation opens a new retail store in a town that previously had no Target stores, the initial investment would include the cost of opening the new store and stocking it with inventory. Operating cash flows would include all the cash inflows and outflows associated with running a Target store in a typical year. All cash flows are incremental because if Target does not open a store in this location, it has no cash outflows or inflows.

Perhaps an even more common situation occurs when a firm must decide whether to replace some asset that it already owns with a new asset. Such decisions include replacing old equipment, upgrading computers and software, or remodeling facilities. Identifying incremental cash flows for these sorts of investment projects is more complicated because the firm must compare the cash flows that result from the new investment to the cash flows that would have occurred if no investment had been made. For instance, if a company buys new equipment to replace existing machinery, the initial investment includes the cost of the new equipment as well as any cash flows associated with the removal and sale of the old equipment. Similarly, identifying incremental operating cash flows is more complex for replacement decisions than for expansion decisions. If Target Corporation remodels one of its existing stores, that is a kind of replacement decision because the remodeled store "replaces" the old one. To estimate the incremental operating cash flows, financial analysts at Target must forecast the revenues and expenses from the new store and compare those to the revenues and expenses the old store would have generated had it not been remodeled. For investments that have a limited life span, the terminal cash flow is the difference between the after-tax cash flows expected upon termination of the new asset versus the old asset. Figure 11.2 illustrates these relationships.

Actually, in one sense you can view all capital budgeting decisions as replacement decisions. You can think of an expansion project as being equivalent to a replacement project in which the cash flows from the old asset being replaced are zero. In light of this and the fact that replacement decisions are so common in business, we will focus on these decisions in most of our examples here.

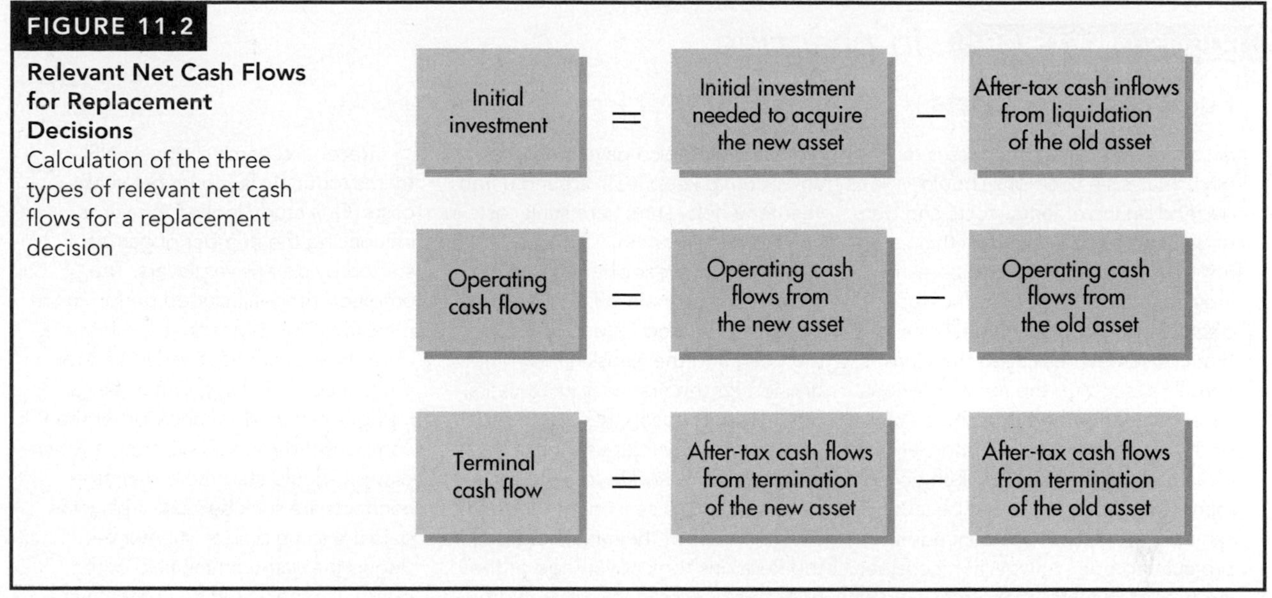

FIGURE 11.2

Relevant Net Cash Flows for Replacement Decisions
Calculation of the three types of relevant net cash flows for a replacement decision

SUNK COSTS AND OPPORTUNITY COSTS

When estimating the incremental cash flows associated with a proposed investment opportunity, the firm must take care to treat sunk costs and opportunity costs properly. These costs are easy to mishandle, classifying costs as incremental when they are not or ignoring costs that should be counted as part of a project's incremental cash flows. **Sunk costs** are cash outlays that have already been made (past outlays) and cannot be recovered, whether or not the firm follows through and makes an investment. Suppose that before building a new store, managers at Target first invest a lot of time and money to assess the market for the proposed store. This analysis might look at the population and average income in the surrounding community, the local cost of labor, taxes, and many other factors. The process may cost tens of thousands of dollars. However, once it is completed, those costs are sunk and should not influence the company's decision to open a new store. Whether Target opens a new store or not, it cannot recover the costs of analyzing the investment opportunity in the local market. Sunk costs are irrelevant and should not be included in a project's incremental cash flows.

sunk costs
Cash outlays that have already been made (past outlays) and cannot be recovered, whether or not the firm follows through and makes an investment.

Opportunity costs are cash flows that the firm could have realized from the best alternative use of assets already in place. When a firm undertakes a replacement project, it repurposes or replaces some portion of its existing assets to generate a new cash flow stream and, in doing so, forgoes any of the future cash inflows that the existing assets would have provided had they not been replaced. Thus, the incremental operating cash flows for a replacement project will be the difference between the new operating cash flows and the forgone operating cash flows. Opportunity costs therefore represent cash flows that the firm will not realize as a result of using that asset in the proposed project. Thus, any opportunity costs are relevant and should be included as part of the cash flow projections when determining a project's net cash flows.

opportunity costs
Cash flows that could have been realized from the best alternative use of an owned asset.

FOCUS ON ETHICS *in practice*

Fumbling Sunk Costs

A core concept in economics is marginal analysis—decisions should depend on incremental costs and benefits. Costs already incurred that cannot be recovered—*sunk costs*—are irrelevant. Surprisingly, businesses often wrongly consider sunk costs, a practice sometimes called the *Concorde Fallacy* after the most notorious case. Long after the Supersonic Transport Aircraft proved a commercial disaster, the British and French governments continued funding it because no senior official wanted to concede the project had been folly. When considering project renewal, managers have an ethical duty to focus on net present value and avoid letting emotional factors or concerns about their own reputations distort investment decisions.

Professional sports offer the best-known example of the Concorde Fallacy—a team signs a marquee player to an expensive long-term contract, then sticks with him no matter what. Consider the case of Robert Griffin III (RGIII), the 2011 Heisman Trophy-winning quarterback drafted second by the National Football League (NFL) Washington Redskins. Griffin cost the Redskins plenty—a four-year guaranteed contract worth $21.1 million as well as numerous draft picks traded to obtain the second overall pick in the draft. The deal also gave the Redskins an option to keep RGIII around a fifth year for a hefty sum; here sunk costs entered the equation.

In the first year of the contract, the investment paid off handsomely—Griffin was named Offensive Rookie of the Year, and the Redskins won their division for the first time in 13 years. But late that season, RGIII suffered the first of many injuries that kept him from regaining rookie form. Just before the 2015 season (the fourth and final year of the initial contract) the Redskins took advantage of their right to sign Griffin for 2016, promising a cool $16.2 million. At the time, the move was called "the biggest blunder in NFL history" because of the injury risk. The Redskins tried to hedge by not guaranteeing the salary—meaning the full amount would be owed only if RGIII stayed healthy the entire 2016 season. But under the terms of the initial contract, the team was on the hook if a 2015 injury prevented him from playing in 2016. Sure enough, in the 2015 preseason, Griffin suffered a concussion—forcing the Redskins to bench him to prevent further injury that could carry over and cost $16.2 million. The team owned up to the mistake by releasing a now-healthy RGIII after the 2015 season.

Recent research suggests NFL teams routinely fail to ignore sunk costs. One study looked at factors influencing the number of games started by defensive players. The empirical model included performance measures like solo tackles for linebackers as well as contract size to test for the Concorde Fallacy. Other things being equal, performance rather than compensation should determine which players should start more games—contracts are sunk because a player is paid the same dollars whether he begins the game on the field or the bench. Contracts turned out to have a large impact—a 15% increase in a defensive player's compensation boosted the number of starts as much as nine extra solo tackles would. In other words, more expensive players were more likely to start even if they did not perform better than players on the bench. From an economic perspective, choosing starters based on sunk costs deserves a flag for illegal procedure.

► *Recommitting to a losing project for emotional or reputational reasons can destroy shareholder wealth. What safeguards could a firm use to remove such bias from recommitment decisions?*

Sources: Isidore, Chris. "Redskins' RG3 Contract May Be Biggest Blunder in NFL History," *CNN Money*, September 1, 2015. Keefer, Quinn A. W. "Performance Feedback Does Not Eliminate Sunk Cost Fallacy." *Journal of Labor Research* 36 (2015): 409–426.

EXAMPLE 11.1

MyLab Finance Solution Video

Jankow Equipment is considering enhancing its drill press X12, which it purchased 3 years earlier for $237,000, by retrofitting it with the computerized control system from an obsolete piece of equipment it owns. The obsolete equipment could be sold today for $42,000, but without its computerized control system, it would be worth nothing. Jankow is in the process of estimating the labor and materials costs of retrofitting the system to drill press X12 and the benefits expected from the retrofit. The $237,000 cost of drill press X12 is a sunk cost because it represents an earlier cash outlay. It would not be included as a cash outflow when determining the cash flows relevant to the retrofit decision. However, if Jankow uses the computerized control system of the obsolete machine, then Jankow will have an opportunity cost of $42,000, which is the cash the company could have received by selling the obsolete equipment in its current condition. By retrofitting the drill press, Jankow gives up the opportunity to sell the old equipment for $42,000. This opportunity cost would be included as a cash outflow associated with using the computerized control system.

INTERNATIONAL CAPITAL BUDGETING AND LONG-TERM INVESTMENTS

Although managers use the same basic capital budgeting principles for domestic and international projects, they must address several additional factors when evaluating foreign investment opportunities. International capital budgeting differs from the domestic version because (1) cash outflows and inflows occur in a foreign currency and (2) foreign investments entail potentially significant political risk. Firms can minimize both risks through careful planning.

Companies face long-term and short-term currency risks related to both the invested capital and the cash flows resulting from it. Firms can mitigate long-term currency risk by financing the foreign investment, at least partly, in local capital markets. This step ensures that the project's revenues, operating costs, and financing costs will be in the local currency. Likewise, firms can protect the dollar value of short-term, local-currency cash flows by using special securities such as futures, forwards, and options.

Firms mitigate political risks by using both operating and financial strategies. For example, by structuring an investment as a joint venture and selecting a well-connected local partner, a U.S. company can minimize the risk that foreign governments will seize its operations. Further, by structuring the financing of such investments as debt rather than as equity, companies also can protect themselves from having their investment returns blocked by local governments. Debt-service payments are legally enforceable claims, whereas equity returns (such as dividends) are not. Even if local courts do not support the claims of the U.S. company, the company can threaten to pursue its case in U.S. courts.

foreign direct investment (FDI)
The transfer of capital, managerial, and technical assets to a foreign country.

Despite the preceding difficulties, **foreign direct investment (FDI)**, which involves the transfer of capital, managerial, and technical assets to a foreign country, has surged in recent years. Such investment is evident in the growing

MATTER OF FACT

Who Receives the Most FDI?

FDI plays an important role in the U.S. economy. According to the 2016 *World Investment Report*, global flows of FDI totaled $1.8 trillion, the highest level since the global economic and financial crisis began in 2008 and within 10% of the 2007 peak.

As tends to be the case, the United States was the world's largest recipient of FDI, receiving $380 billion in FDI, and the largest provider, investing $300 billion in countries around the world. Hong Kong and mainland China were the second and third largest recipients of FDI, receiving $175 billion and $136 billion, respectively.

market values of foreign assets owned by U.S.–based companies and of foreign direct investment in the United States, particularly by British, Canadian, Chinese, Dutch, German, and Japanese companies. Furthermore, foreign direct investment by U.S. companies seems to be accelerating. See the *Global Focus* box for a discussion of recent foreign direct investment in China.

→ REVIEW QUESTIONS MyLab Finance Solutions

11–1 Why is it important to evaluate capital budgeting projects on the basis of incremental cash flows?

11–2 What three types of net cash flows may exist for a given project? How can expansion decisions be treated as replacement decisions? Explain.

11–3 What effect do sunk costs and opportunity costs have on a project's net cash flows?

11–4 How can firms mitigate currency risk and political risk when investing in a foreign country?

GLOBAL FOCUS *in practice*

Changes May Influence Future Investments in China

Foreign direct investment in China has been growing rapidly for many years. From 2001 to 2015, FDI in China grew from $47 billion to $136 billion, a compound annual growth rate of 7.9%. China allows three types of foreign investments: a wholly foreign-owned enterprise (WFOE), in which the firm is entirely funded with foreign capital; a joint venture, in which the foreign partner must provide at least 25% of initial capital; and a representative office (RO), the most common and easily established entity, which cannot perform business activities that directly result in profits. Generally, an RO is the first step in establishing a China presence and includes mechanisms for upgrading to a WFOE or joint venture. More than three-fourths of the dollar value of Chinese FDI takes the form of wholly-owned foreign enterprises operating in China, and most of the rest consists of joint ventures.

China has run a trade surplus for many years, although recently the surplus has been shrinking, and some outsiders believe that the Chinese government artificially inflates its surplus figures. With the trade surplus, China is no longer desperate for capital from overseas, but is now primarily interested in foreign skills and technologies. Prime Minister Li Keqiang wants to steer investments toward science and technology. Li is giving tax breaks and promising speedy approvals for investments in the country's western and central regions.

Typical of foreign investors in China is Intel Capital, a subsidiary of Intel Corporation. From 1998 to 2015, Intel Capital invested more than $1.9 billion in more than 140 companies in China. Intel Capital focuses its investments in projects such as data centers and cloud computing, smartphones and tablets, and semiconductor design and manufacturing. Intel Capital is no beginner at foreign investment; it has invested more than $11.8 billion in 1,473 companies in 57 countries around the world.

As with any foreign investment, investing in China is not without risk. One potential risk facing foreign investors in China is that the government could decide to nationalize private companies. Many public companies in China are firms once owned by the communist government, such as China Life Insurance Company, and it is always possible that the government may decide to own and control these companies again. The list of governments similar to China's that have nationalized private companies is fairly long. Although no evidence indicates that this will happen in China, companies should consider it a risk.

► *Although China has been actively campaigning for foreign investment, how do you think that having a communist government affects its foreign investment?*

11.2 Finding the Initial Investment

The term *initial investment* as used here refers to the relevant, up-front net cash flow that managers should consider when evaluating a prospective investment opportunity. Our discussion of capital budgeting will focus on projects with initial investments that occur at time zero, the time at which a firm makes the capital expenditure. We calculate the initial investment by netting all of the incremental cash flows that occur at time zero: subtracting all the cash outflows occurring at time zero from all the cash inflows that occur at that time.

The basic format for determining the initial investment appears in Table 11.1. The cash flows that make up a project's initial investment include the installed cost of the new asset, the after-tax proceeds (if any) from the sale of the old asset that the firm is replacing, and the change (if any) in net working capital. Note that for expansion projects there will be no after-tax proceeds from the sale of an old asset, so the initial investment is simply the installed cost of the new asset and any change in net working capital.

cost of the new asset
The cash outflow necessary to acquire a new asset.

installation costs
Any added costs that are necessary to place the new asset into operation.

installed cost of the new asset
The cost of the new asset plus its installation costs; equals the asset's depreciable value.

after-tax proceeds from the sale of the old asset
The difference between the old asset's sale proceeds and any applicable tax liability or refund related to its sale.

proceeds from the sale of the old asset
The before-tax cash inflow net of any removal costs that results from the sale of the old asset and is normally subject to some type of tax treatment.

INSTALLED COST OF THE NEW ASSET

As Table 11.1 shows, managers calculate the installed cost of a new asset by adding the cost of the new asset to its installation costs. The **cost of the new asset** is the cash outflow necessary to acquire the new asset, which is usually simply its purchase price. **Installation costs** are any added costs necessary to place the new asset into operation. The IRS requires the firm to add installation costs to the purchase price of an asset to determine its depreciable value, which is expensed over a period of years. The **installed cost of the new asset,** calculated by adding the cost of the new asset to its installation costs, equals its depreciable value.

AFTER-TAX PROCEEDS FROM THE SALE OF THE OLD ASSET

Table 11.1 shows that the *after-tax proceeds from the sale of the old asset* decrease the firm's initial investment. The **after-tax proceeds from the sale of the old asset** include the old asset's sale proceeds and any applicable tax liability or refund related to its sale.

The **proceeds from the sale of the old asset** represent the before-tax cash inflow net of any removal costs that result from selling the old asset. Normally,

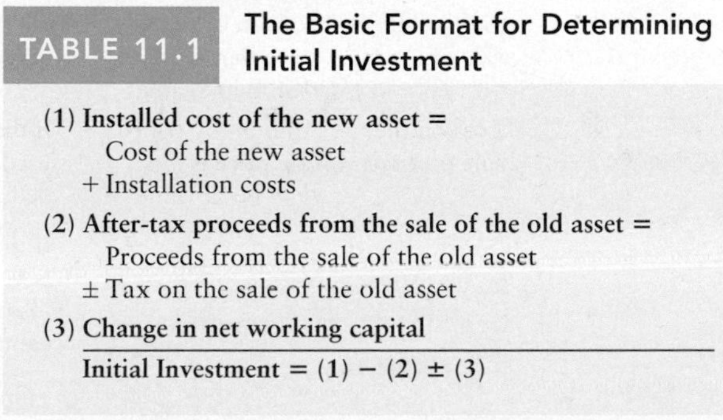

TABLE 11.1 The Basic Format for Determining Initial Investment

(1) **Installed cost of the new asset =**
  Cost of the new asset
  + Installation costs
(2) **After-tax proceeds from the sale of the old asset =**
  Proceeds from the sale of the old asset
  ± Tax on the sale of the old asset
(3) **Change in net working capital**

Initial Investment = (1) − (2) ± (3)

tax on the sale of the old asset
Tax that depends on the relationship between the old asset's sale price and its book value and on existing government tax rules.

selling an old asset triggers a tax-related cash flow, either additional tax payments or a tax refund. The **tax on the sale of the old asset** depends on the relationship between the asset's sale price and its book value and on existing government tax rules.

Book Value

book value
The asset's value on the firm's balance sheet as determined by accounting principles. The difference between what an asset cost (including installation costs) and the accumulated depreciation on the asset.

The **book value** of an asset is the asset's value on the firm's balance sheet as determined by accounting principles.[1] An asset's book value is usually just the difference between what the asset cost (including installation costs) and the accumulated depreciation on the asset.

$$\text{Book value} = \text{Installed cost of asset} - \text{Accumulated depreciation} \quad (11.1)$$

EXAMPLE 11.2

Hudson Industries, a small electronics company, acquired a machine tool 2 years ago with an installed cost of \$100,000. The asset was not eligible for 100% bonus depreciation under current tax law, so it was being depreciated under MACRS, using a 5-year recovery period. Table 4.2 shows that under MACRS for a 5-year recovery period, 20% and 32% of the installed cost would be depreciated in years 1 and 2, respectively. In other words, 52% (20% + 32%) of the \$100,000 cost, or \$52,000 (0.52 × \$100,000), would be the accumulated depreciation after 2 years. Substituting into Equation 11.1, we get

$$\text{Book value} = \$100{,}000 - \$52{,}000 = \underline{\underline{48{,}000}}$$

The book value of Hudson's asset at the end of year 2 is therefore \$48,000.

Three tax treatments are possible and depend on the asset's selling price: The asset may be sold for (1) more than its book value, (2) its book value, or (3) less than its book value. In the first case, the firm generates a gain on the sale of the asset, in the second case it breaks even, and in the third case it realizes a loss on the sale of the asset. In the breakeven case, there is no tax consequence related to the asset sale; however, the other two cases have associated tax consequences. The tax treatments for the sale of an asset for more or less than book value are defined and summarized in Table 11.2. We will use an example to illustrate.

TABLE 11.2 Tax Treatments for the Sales of Assets

Tax case	Definition	Tax treatment	Tax consequence
Gain on the sale of asset	Portion of the sale price that is *greater than* book value	All gains above book value are taxed as ordinary income.	21% of gain is a tax liability.
Loss on the sale of asset	Amount by which sale price is *less than* book value	If the asset is depreciable and used in business, then loss is deducted from ordinary income.	21% of loss is a tax savings.
		If the asset is *not* depreciable or is *not* used in business, then loss is deductible only against capital gains.	21% of loss is a tax savings.

1. Recall that firms can keep one set of books for financial reporting purposes and another set for tax purposes. The book value we refer to here is the value on the books for tax purposes, also known as the asset's *tax basis*.

EXAMPLE 11.3

MyLab Finance Solution Video

The old asset purchased 2 years ago for $100,000 by Hudson Industries has a current book value of $48,000. What will happen if the firm now decides to sell the asset and replace it? The tax consequences depend on the sale price. Figure 11.3 depicts the taxable income resulting from four possible sale prices in light of the asset's initial purchase price of $100,000 and its current book value of $48,000. The tax consequences of each of these sale prices are described in the following paragraphs.

recaptured depreciation
The portion of an asset's sale price that is above its book value and below its initial purchase price.

The sale of the asset for more than its book value If Hudson sells the old asset for $110,000, it realizes a gain of $62,000 ($110,000 – $48,000). Technically, this gain is made up of two parts: a capital gain and **recaptured depreciation,** which is the portion of the sale price that is above book value and below the initial purchase price. For Hudson, the capital gain is $10,000 ($110,000 sale price – $100,000 initial purchase price); recaptured depreciation is $52,000 (the $100,000 initial purchase price – $48,000 book value).

The tax treatment of capital gains can be quite complex, so to keep things simple we assume that the total gain above book value of $62,000 is taxed at Hudson's ordinary corporate income tax rate of 21%, resulting in taxes of $13,020 (0.21 × $62,000). Hudson would not have paid these taxes had they not replaced the old equipment, so the taxes are part of the incremental cash flows at time zero. That is, the taxes constitute a portion of the replacement project's initial investment. In effect, the taxes raise the amount of the firm's initial investment in the new asset by reducing the proceeds from the sale of the old asset.

If Hudson instead sells the old asset for $70,000, it experiences a gain above book value (in the form of recaptured depreciation) of $22,000 ($70,000 – $48,000), as shown under the $70,000 sale price in Figure 11.3. This gain is taxed as ordinary income. Because the firm is in the 21% tax bracket, the taxes on the $22,000 gain are $4,620 (0.21 × $22,000). This amount in taxes should be used in calculating the initial investment in the new asset.

FIGURE 11.3

Tax Consequences from the Sale of an Asset
Tax consequences from the sale of an asset at various sale prices for Hudson Industries

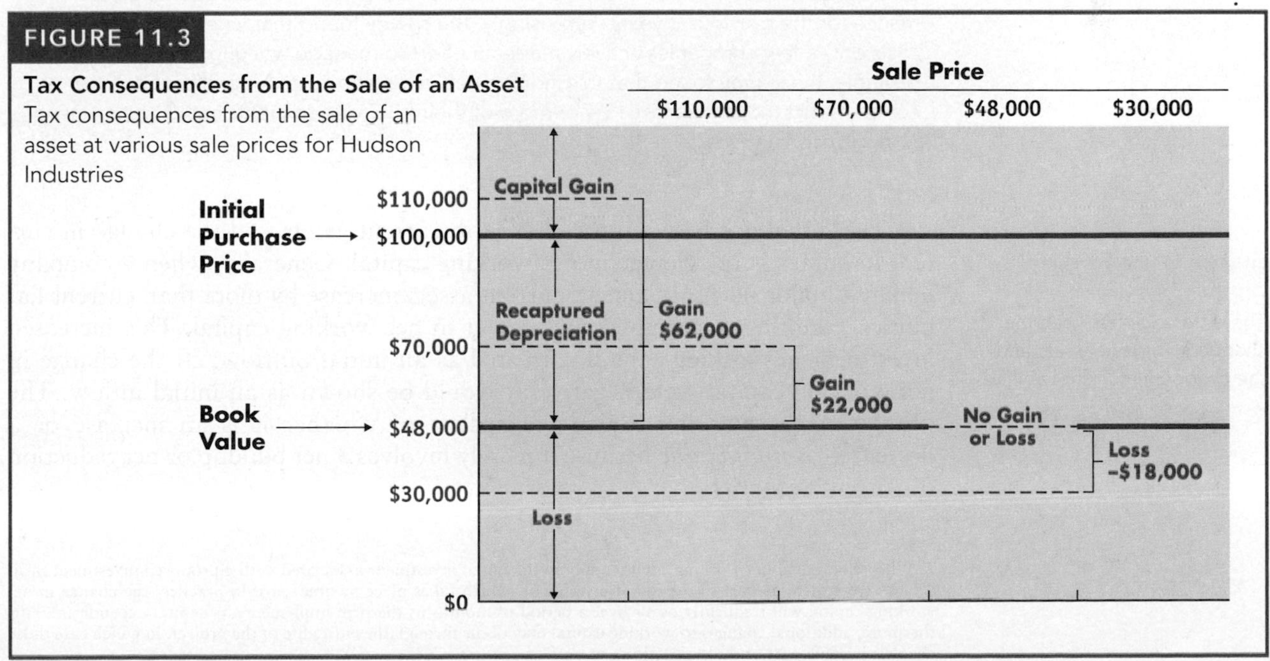

The sale of the asset for its book value If Hudson sells the old asset for $48,000, there is no gain or loss on the sale, as Figure 11.3 shows. Because there is no gain or loss, there is no incremental tax effect of the sale.

The sale of the asset for less than its book value If Hudson sells the asset for $30,000, it experiences a loss of $18,000 ($48,000 − $30,000), as shown under the $30,000 sale price in Figure 11.3. The firm may use the loss to offset ordinary operating income, which saves the firm $3,780 (0.21 × $18,000) in taxes. And, if current operating earnings are not sufficient to offset the loss, the firm may be able to apply these losses to prior or future years' taxes.

CHANGE IN NET WORKING CAPITAL

net working capital
The difference between the firm's current assets and its current liabilities.

Net working capital is the difference between the firm's current assets and its current liabilities. Changes in net working capital often accompany capital budgeting decisions. If a firm acquires new machinery to expand its production output, it will experience an increase in levels of cash, accounts receivable, inventories, accounts payable, and expense accruals. These increases result from the need for more cash to support expanded operations, more accounts receivable and inventories to support increased sales, and more accounts payable and expense accruals to support increased outlays made to meet expanded product demand. As noted in Chapter 4, increases in cash, accounts receivable, and inventories are *outflows of cash,* whereas increases in accounts payable and expense accruals are *inflows of cash.*

MATTER OF FACT

Ignoring Working Capital Can Kill the Bottom Line

The REL 2015 Working Capital Survey of the top 1000 companies in North America and Europe found that only 1% of companies had improved their working capital performance for the previous 3 years. Surprisingly, the survey found that when not facing a crisis only a few companies actively made an effort to manage working capital. Not surprisingly, the survey found that this indifference came at a cost: A significant number of companies in the survey lost 15% or more of their EBIT due to inefficient or nonexistent working capital management.

change in net working capital
The difference between the change in current assets and the change in current liabilities.

The difference between the change in current assets and the change in current liabilities is the **change in net working capital.** Generally, when a company makes a major new investment, current assets increase by more than current liabilities, resulting in a greater investment in net working capital. This increased investment in working capital is treated as an initial outflow.[2] If the change in net working capital were negative, it would be shown as an initial inflow. The change in net working capital—regardless of whether it is an increase or a decrease—*is not taxable* because it merely involves a net buildup or net reduction of current accounts.

2. When changes in net working capital apply to the initial investment associated with a proposed investment project, we treat them as part of the initial investment, which takes place at time zero. In practice, the change in net working capital will frequently occur over a period of months as the firm implements its capital expenditure. Furthermore, additional changes to working capital may occur through the entire life of the project, in which case those changes become part of the cash inflows or outflows in subsequent years.

EXAMPLE 11.4

Danson Company is expanding. Analysts expect that the changes summarized in Table 11.3 will occur and will be maintained over the life of the expansion. Current assets will increase by $22,000, and current liabilities will increase by $9,000, resulting in a $13,000 increase in net working capital. This increase in net working capital is part of the initial cash outflow required to begin the expansion project, so we treat it as a cash outflow in calculating the initial investment.

TABLE 11.3 Calculation of Change in Net Working Capital for Danson Company

Current account	Change in balance	
Cash	+$ 4,000	
Accounts receivable	+ 10,000	
Inventories	+ 8,000	
(1) Current assets		+ $22,000
Accounts payable	+$ 7,000	
Expense accruals	+ 2,000	
(2) Current liabilities		+$ 9,000
Change in net working capital = (1) − (2)		+ $13,000

CALCULATING THE INITIAL INVESTMENT

A variety of tax and other considerations enter into the initial investment calculation. The following example illustrates calculation of the initial investment according to the format in Table 11.1.[3]

EXAMPLE 11.5

Powell Corporation is trying to determine the initial investment required to replace an old machine with a new one. The new machine costs $380,000, and an additional $20,000 will be necessary to install it. It will be depreciated under MACRS, using a 5-year recovery period.[4] The old machine was purchased 3 years ago at a cost of $240,000 and was being depreciated under MACRS, using a 5-year recovery period. The firm can sell the old machine for $280,000. The firm expects that a $35,000 increase in current assets and an $18,000 increase in current liabilities will accompany the replacement, resulting in a $17,000 ($35,000 − $18,000) increase in net working capital. The firm's tax rate is 21%.

The only component of the initial investment calculation that is difficult to obtain is taxes. The tax consequences of the sale of the old machine depend on the selling price relative to the asset's book value. To find the book value of the

3. For simplicity, throughout the discussions of capital budgeting, we assume that all assets evaluated as candidates for replacement have usable lives that are equal to the lives of the assets they replace. This assumption enables us to avoid the problem of unequal lives, which is discussed in Chapter 12.

4. Were the machine eligible for 100% bonus depreciation under the tax law, the initial investment would be reduced by an immediate $84,000 (0.21 × $400,000) tax savings.

old machine, use the depreciation percentages from Table 4.2 of 20%, 32%, and 19% for years 1, 2, and 3, respectively. The book value is the difference between the original $240,000 purchase price and the accumulated depreciation over the 3 years that the asset was in use. The resulting book value is

$$\$240{,}000 - [(0.20 + 0.32 + 0.19) \times \$240{,}000] = \$69{,}600$$

Powell Corporation realizes a gain of $210,400 ($280,000 – $69,600) on the sale. The total taxes on the gain are $44,184 (0.21 × $210,400). Powell's financial analysts must subtract these taxes from the $280,000 sale price of the old machine to calculate the after-tax proceeds from its sale.

Substituting the relevant amounts into the format in Table 11.1 results in an initial investment of $181,184, which represents the net cash outflow required at time zero.

Installed cost of new machine		
Cost of new machine	$380,000	
+ Installation costs	20,000	
Total installed cost		$400,000
– After-tax proceeds from the sale of the old machine		
Proceeds from the sale of the old machine	$280,000	
– Tax on the sale of the old machine	44,184	
Total after-tax proceeds		235,816
+ Change in net working capital		17,000
Initial investment		181,184

→ **REVIEW QUESTIONS** MyLab Finance Solutions

11–5 Explain how to use each of the following inputs to calculate the initial investment: (a) cost of the new asset, (b) installation costs, (c) proceeds from the sale of the old asset, (d) tax on the sale of the old asset, and (e) change in net working capital.

11–6 How do you calculate the book value of an asset?

11–7 What three tax situations may result from the sale of an asset that is being replaced?

11–8 Referring to the basic format for calculating an initial investment, explain how a firm would determine the depreciable value of the new asset.

LG5

11.3 Finding the Operating Cash Flows

Operating cash flows are the net incremental after-tax cash flows that occur after a firm makes a new investment and begins operating with the new investment in place. Finding the operating cash flows requires identifying all the incremental cash flows related to the firm's operations that will be affected by the investment decision; this includes any current incremental cash flows that will be forgone and any new incremental cash flows that will be created. In this section, we use the income statement format to clarify what we mean by incremental, after-tax cash flows.

INTERPRETING THE TERM *CASH FLOWS*

All costs and benefits expected from a proposed project must be measured on a cash flow basis. Cash outflows represent costs incurred by the firm, and cash inflows represent dollars that the firm receives and can then spend. Cash flows generally are not equal to accounting profits. This is so in part because accounting rules do not allow firms to fully deduct or expense the cost of fixed assets at the time of purchase. Instead, firms expense a portion of this cost through depreciation deductions each year over the useful life of the fixed asset. As a result, when a firm pays cash for a fixed asset, the firm's profits will not fully reflect the cost of the asset in the year of purchase. In subsequent years, firms reduce their profits by taking depreciation expenses, even though no cash outlays are tied to those depreciation charges.

INTERPRETING THE TERM *AFTER-TAX*

Cash flows that result from investment projects must be measured on an after-tax basis because the firm will not have the use of any cash flows until it has both satisfied the government's tax claims and captured the government's tax refunds, credits, or other tax breaks. Firms can use only the after-tax cash flows to pay returns to lenders and shareholders, so when making investment decisions, analysts must take care to measure incremental cash flows after taxes.

A simple technique can convert after-tax net profits into operating cash flows. The calculation requires adding depreciation and any other noncash charges (amortization and depletion) deducted as expenses on the firm's income statement back to net profits after taxes. Recognize that depreciation expenses are not actually cash inflows themselves. Adding depreciation to profit simply recognizes that the profit calculation requires firms to deduct an expense not tied to a specific cash outlay. Adding depreciation to after-tax profit "corrects" this issue and provides a number that better matches the actual cash inflows and outflows.

EXAMPLE 11.6

Powell Corporation's estimates of its revenue and expenses (excluding depreciation and interest), with and without the proposed new machine described in Example 11.5, are given in Table 11.4. Note that both the expected usable life of the new machine and the remaining usable life of the old machine are 5 years. The new machine's depreciable value is the sum of the $380,000 purchase price and the $20,000 installation cost. The firm calculates annual depreciation

TABLE 11.4 Powell Corporation's Revenue and Expenses (Excluding Depreciation and Interest) for New and Old Machines

With new machine			With old machine		
Year	Revenue	Expenses (excl. depr. and int.)	Year	Revenue	Expenses (excl. depr. and int.)
1	$2,520,000	$2,300,000	1	$2,200,000	$1,990,000
2	2,520,000	2,300,000	2	2,300,000	2,110,000
3	2,520,000	2,300,000	3	2,400,000	2,230,000
4	2,520,000	2,300,000	4	2,400,000	2,250,000
5	2,520,000	2,300,000	5	2,250,000	2,120,000

TABLE 11.5 **Depreciation Expense for New and Old Machines for Powell Corporation**

Year	Cost	Applicable MACRS depreciation percentages (from Table 4.2)	Depreciation
With new machine			
1	$400,000	20%	$400,000 × 20% = $ 80,000
2	400,000	32	$400,000 × 32% = $128,000
3	400,000	19	$400,000 × 19% = $ 76,000
4	400,000	12	$400,000 × 12% = $ 48,000
5	400,000	12	$400,000 × 12% = $ 48,000
6	400,000	5	$400,000 × 5% = $ 20,000
Totals		100%	$400,000
With old machine			
1	$240,000	12% (year-4 depreciation)	$240,000 × 12% = $28,800
2	240,000	12 (year-5 depreciation)	$240,000 × 12% = $28,800
3	240,000	5 (year-6 depreciation)	$240,000 × 5% = $12,000
4	Because the old machine is at the end of the third year of its cost recovery at the time the analysis is performed, it has only the final 3 years of depreciation (as noted above) still applicable.		0
5			0
6			0
Total			$69,600[a]

[a]The total $69,600 represents the book value of the old machine at the end of the third year, as calculated in Example 11.5.

deductions on the new machine, using the MACRS percentages based on a 5-year recovery period.[5] The resulting depreciation on this machine for each of the 6 years, as well as the remaining 3 years of depreciation (years 4, 5, and 6) on the old machine, are calculated in Table 11.5.[6]

The income statement format in Table 11.6 illustrates how to calculate the operating cash flows each year. Note that we exclude interest because we are focusing purely on the "investment decision." The interest is relevant to the "financing decision," which we will address later in this text. Because we exclude interest expense, "earnings before interest and taxes" (EBIT) is equivalent to "net profits before taxes," and the calculation of "operating cash flow" (OCF) in Table 11.6 is identical to the definition that we provided in Chapter 4 (defined in Equation 4.3).

Substituting the data from Tables 11.4 and 11.5 into this format and assuming a 21% tax rate, we get Table 11.7, which demonstrates the calculation of operating cash flows for each year for both the new and the old machines. Because the new machine is depreciated over 6 years, the analysis must be

5. Were the new machine eligible for 100% bonus depreciation under the tax law, there would be no depreciation deductions for the *new machine* in years 1–6 because Powell would deduct the entire cost in year 0.

6. It is important to recognize that although both machines will provide 5 years of use, the new machine will be depreciated over the 6-year period, whereas the old machine, as noted in the preceding example, has been depreciated over 3 years and therefore has remaining only its final 3 years (years 4, 5, and 6) of depreciation (12%, 12%, and 5%, respectively, under MACRS).

TABLE 11.6 Calculation of Operating Cash Flows Using the Income Statement Format

Revenue
− Expenses (excluding depreciation and interest)
Earnings before interest, taxes, depreciation, and amortization (EBITDA)
− Depreciation
Earnings before interest and taxes (EBIT)
− Taxes (rate = T)
Net operating profit after taxes [NOPAT = EBIT × $(1 - T)$]
+ Depreciation
Operating cash flows (OCF) (same as OCF in Equation 4.3)

TABLE 11.7 Calculation of Operating Cash Flows for Powell Corporation's New and Old Machines

	Year 1	Year 2	Year 3	Year 4	Year 5	Year 6
With new machine						
Revenue[a]	$2,520,000	$2,520,000	$2,520,000	$2,520,000	$2,520,000	$ 0
− Expenses (excluding depreciation and interest)[b]	2,300,000	2,300,000	2,300,000	2,300,000	2,300,000	0
Earnings before interest, taxes, depreciation, and amortization	$ 220,000	$ 220,000	$ 220,000	$ 220,000	$ 220,000	$ 0
− Depreciation[c]	80,000	128,000	76,000	48,000	48,000	20,000
Earnings before interest and taxes	$ 140,000	$ 92,000	$ 144,000	$ 172,000	$ 172,000	−$20,000
− Taxes (rate, $T = 21\%$)	29,400	19,320	30,240	36,120	36,120	− 4,200
Net operating profit after taxes	$ 110,600	$ 72,680	$ 113,760	$ 135,880	$ 135,880	−$15,800
+ Depreciation[c]	80,000	128,000	76,000	48,000	48,000	20,000
Operating cash flows	$ 190,600	$ 200,680	$ 189,760	$ 183,880	$ 183,880	$ 4,200
With old machine						
Revenue[a]	$2,200,000	$2,300,000	$2,400,000	$2,400,000	$2,250,000	$ 0
− Expenses (excluding depreciation and interest)[b]	1,990,000	2,110,000	2,230,000	2,250,000	2,120,000	0
Earnings before interest, taxes, depreciation, and amortization	$ 210,000	$ 190,000	$ 170,000	$ 150,000	$ 130,000	$ 0
− Depreciation[c]	28,800	28,800	12,000	0	0	0
Earnings before interest and taxes	$ 181,200	$ 161,200	$ 158,000	$ 150,000	$ 130,000	$ 0
− Taxes (rate, $T = 21\%$)	38,052	33,852	33,180	31,500	27,300	0
Net operating profit after taxes	$ 143,148	$ 127,348	$ 124,820	$ 118,500	$ 102,700	$ 0
+ Depreciation[c]	28,800	28,800	12,000	0	0	0
Operating cash flows	$ 171,948	$ 156,148	$ 136,820	$ 118,500	$ 102,700	$ 0

[a]From column 1 of Table 11.4.
[b]From column 2 of Table 11.4.
[c]From column 3 of Table 11.5.

performed over the 6-year period to account for all the tax benefits of depreciation. The resulting operating cash flows appear in the final row of Table 11.7 for each machine. The $4,200 year-6 operating cash inflow for the new machine results solely from the tax benefit of its year-6 depreciation deduction.[7]

INTERPRETING THE TERM *INCREMENTAL*

The final step in estimating the net operating cash flows for a proposed replacement project is to calculate the incremental cash flows. The differences in cash flows that occur with the new machines compared to cash flows that occurred with the old machine are incremental cash flows.

EXAMPLE 11.7

Table 11.8 demonstrates the calculation of Powell Corporation's net operating cash flows for each year of the replacement project. The estimates of operating cash flows developed in Table 11.7 for the new and old machines appear in columns 1 and 2, respectively. Column 2 values represent the amount of operating cash flows that Powell Corporation will receive if it does not replace the old machine. If the new machine replaces the old machine, the firm's operating cash flows for each year will be those shown in column 1. Subtracting the old machine's operating cash flows from the new machine's operating cash flows, we get the net operating cash flows for the replacement project for each year, shown in column 3. These net operating cash flows represent the amounts by which each respective year's operating cash flow will change as a result of the replacement project. For example, in year 1, Powell Corporation's operating cash flow would increase by $18,652 if the proposed project were undertaken. These are the relevant cash flows that analysts should consider when evaluating the benefits of making a capital budgeting decision regarding the replacement of the old machine with the new machine.[8]

---

7. Although here we have calculated the year-6 operating cash flow for the new machine, this cash flow will later be eliminated as a result of the assumed sale of the machine at the end of year 5.

8. We can use the following equation to calculate the net operating cash flow for a replacement project in year t, $NOCF_t$:

$$NOCF_t = [\Delta EBITDA_t \times (1 - T)] + (\Delta D_t \times T)$$

where

$\Delta EBITDA_t$ = change in earnings before interest, taxes, depreciation, and amortization [revenues − expenses (excl. depr. and int.)] in year t

T = firm's marginal tax rate

ΔD_t = change in depreciation expense in year t

Applying this formula to the Powell Corporation data given in Tables 11.4 and 11.5 for year 3, we get the following values of variables:

$$\begin{aligned}\Delta EBITDA_3 &= (\$2{,}520{,}000 - \$2{,}300{,}000) - (\$2{,}400{,}000 - \$2{,}230{,}000)\\ &= \$220{,}000 - \$170{,}000 = \$50{,}000\\ \Delta D_3 &= \$76{,}000 - \$12{,}000 = \$64{,}000\\ T &= 0.21\end{aligned}$$

Substituting into the equation yields

$$\begin{aligned}NOCF_3 &= [\$50{,}000 \times (1 - 0.21)] + (\$64{,}000 \times 0.21)\\ &= \$39{,}500 + \$13{,}440 = \underline{\underline{\$52{,}940}}\end{aligned}$$

The $52,940 of net cash inflow for year 3 is the same value as that calculated for year 3 in column 3 of Table 11.8.

TABLE 11.8 Operating Cash Flows for Powell Corporation

	Operating cash flows		
Year	New machine[a]	Old machine[a]	Net OCF
1	$190,600	$171,948	$190,600 − $171,948 = $18,652
2	200,680	156,148	$200,680 − $156,148 = $44,532
3	189,760	136,820	$189,760 − $136,820 = $52,940
4	183,880	118,500	$183,880 − $118,500 = $65,380
5	183,880	102,700	$183,880 − $102,700 = $81,180
6	4,200	0	$ 4,200 − $ 0 = $ 4,200

[a]From final row for respective machine in Table 11.7.

→ REVIEW QUESTIONS MyLab Finance Solutions

11–9 How does depreciation enter into the calculation of operating cash flows? How does the income statement format in Table 11.6 relate to Equation 4.3 for finding operating cash flow (OCF)?

11–10 How are the net operating cash flows that are associated with a replacement decision calculated?

LG6

11.4 Finding the Terminal Cash Flow

A project's terminal cash flow is the cash flow resulting from termination and liquidation of a project at the end of its economic life. It represents the after-tax cash flow, exclusive of operating cash flows, that occurs in the final year of the project. For replacement projects, analysts must take into account the proceeds from both the new asset and the old asset. The proceeds from the sale of the new and the old asset, often called "salvage value," represent the amount net of any removal costs expected on termination of the project. For expansion types of investment projects, the proceeds from the old asset are zero. Regardless of the project type, a change in new working capital often takes place at the end of a project life, so this incremental cash flow, too, must be included in the terminal cash flow. Table 11.9 shows a basic format for calculating an investment project's terminal cash flow.

TABLE 11.9 The Basic Format for Determining Terminal Cash Flow

(1) After-tax proceeds from the sale of the new asset =

Proceeds from the sale of the new asset

± Tax on the sale of the new asset

(2) After-tax proceeds from the sale of the old asset =

Proceeds from the sale of the old asset

± Tax on the sale of the old asset

(3) Change in net working capital

Terminal cash flow = (1) − (2) ± (3)

AFTER-TAX PROCEEDS FROM THE SALE OF NEW AND OLD ASSETS

When the investment being analyzed involves replacing an old asset with a new one, two elements are key in finding the terminal cash flow. First, at the end of the project's life, the firm will dispose of the new asset, possibly by selling it, so the after-tax proceeds from selling the new asset represent an incremental cash inflow. However, remember that if the firm had not replaced the old asset, the firm would have received proceeds from the sale of the old asset at the end of the project (rather than counting those after-tax proceeds at the beginning of the project timeline as part of the initial investment). Because the firm no longer has the opportunity to obtain the proceeds from selling the old machine at the end of the project's life, we must count as an incremental cash outflow the after-tax proceeds that the firm would have received from disposal of the old asset.

Recall that taxes come into play whenever an asset sells for a value different from its book value. If the net proceeds from the sale exceed book value, a tax payment shown as an outflow (deduction from sale proceeds) will occur. When the net proceeds from the sale fall short of book value, a tax benefit shown as a cash inflow (addition to sale proceeds) will result. Table 11.2 summarizes the tax treatments and consequences when assets sell for a price other than book value. For assets sold to net exactly book value, no taxes will be due.

CHANGE IN NET WORKING CAPITAL

When we calculated the initial investment, we took into account any change in net working capital that is attributable to the new asset. Now, when we calculate the terminal cash flow, the change in net working capital represents the reversion of any initial net working capital investment. Most often, this will show up as a cash inflow due to the reduction in net working capital; with termination of the project, the need for the increased net working capital investment usually ends. As long as no changes in working capital occur after the initial investment, the amount recovered at termination will equal the amount shown in the calculation of the initial investment. If working capital changes year to year as a firm expands or contracts operations, then those changes should be incorporated into the yearly operating cash flows. Changes to working capital by themselves do not trigger incremental taxes, so there are no tax consequences to consider.

Calculating the terminal cash flow involves the same procedures used to find the initial investment. In the following example, we calculate the terminal cash flow for a replacement decision.

EXAMPLE 11.8

Continuing with the Powell Corporation example, assume that the firm expects to liquidate the new machine at the end of its 5-year usable life, to net $50,000 after paying removal and cleanup costs. Had the new machine not replaced the old machine, the old machine would have been liquidated after 5 years to net $10,000. The firm expects to recover its $17,000 net working capital investment upon termination of the project. The firm pays taxes at a rate of 21%.

From the analysis of the operating cash flows presented earlier, we can see that the new machine will have a book value of $20,000 (equal to the year-6 depreciation) after 5 years. The old machine would have been fully depreciated and therefore would have a book value of zero after 5 years. Because the sale price of $50,000 for the new machine is below its initial installed cost of $400,000, but greater than its book value of $20,000, the firm will pay taxes only on the recaptured depreciation of $30,000 ($50,000 sale proceeds − $20,000 book value). Applying the ordinary tax rate of 21% to this $30,000 results in a tax of $6,300 (0.21 × $30,000) on the sale of the new machine. Its after-tax sale proceeds would therefore equal $43,700 ($50,000 sale proceeds − $6,300 taxes). Because the old machine would have been sold for $10,000 at termination, which is less than its original purchase price of $240,000 and above its book value of zero, it would have experienced a taxable gain of $10,000 ($10,000 sale price − $0 book value). Applying the 21% tax rate to the $10,000 gain, the firm would have owed a tax of $2,100 (0.21 × $10,000) on the sale of the old machine at the end of year 5. The firm's after-tax sale proceeds from the old machine would have equaled $7,900 ($10,000 sale price − $2,100 taxes). Substituting the appropriate values into the format in Table 11.9 results in the terminal cash inflow of $52,800.

After-tax proceeds from the sale of the new machine		
Proceeds from the sale of the new machine	$50,000	
− Tax on sale of the new machine	6,300	
Total after-tax proceeds: new machine		$43,700
− After-tax proceeds from the sale of the old machine		
Proceeds from the sale of the old machine	$10,000	
− Tax on the sale of the old machine	2,100	
Total after-tax proceeds: old machine		7,900
+ Change in net working capital		17,000
Terminal cash flow		$52,800

→ **REVIEW QUESTION** MyLab Finance Solution

11–11 Explain how the terminal cash flow is calculated for replacement projects.

LG3 LG5 LG6

11.5 Summarizing the Net Cash Flows

The initial investment, operating cash flows, and terminal cash flow together represent a project's net cash flows. We can view these cash flows as the net after-tax cash flows attributable to the proposed project. They represent, in a cash flow sense, how much better or worse off the firm will be if it chooses to implement the proposal.

EXAMPLE 11.9

MyLab Finance Solution Video

Below we depict the relevant net cash flows for Powell Corporation's proposed replacement project on a timeline. Note that because Powell plans to sell the new asset at the end of its 5-year usable life, the $4,200 year-6 operating cash inflow calculated in Table 11.8 has no relevance; the terminal cash flow effectively replaces this value in the analysis.

Timeline for Powell Corporation's replacement project net cash flows

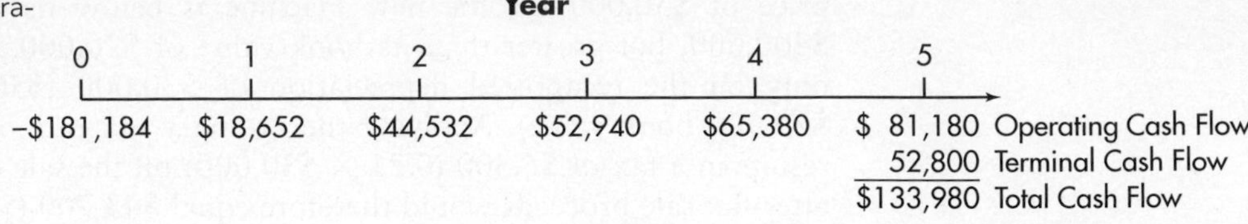

With these cash flow estimates in hand, a financial manager could then calculate the investment's NPV or IRR using the techniques covered in Chapter 10.

PERSONAL FINANCE EXAMPLE 11.10 After receiving a sizable bonus from her employer, Tina Taylor is contemplating the purchase of a new car. She believes that by estimating and analyzing the cash flows, she could make a more rational decision about whether to make this large purchase. Tina's cash flow estimates for the car purchase are as follows:

Negotiated price of new car	$33,500
Taxes and fees on new car purchase	$ 1,650
Proceeds from the sale of her old car	$ 9,750
Estimated value of new car in 3 years	$10,500
Estimated value of old car in 3 years	$ 5,700
Estimated annual repair costs on new car	0 (in warranty)
Estimated annual repair costs on old car	$ 400

Using the cash flow estimates, Tina calculates the initial investment, operating cash flows, terminal cash flow, and a summary of all cash flows for the car purchase.

Initial Investment

Total cost of new car		
Cost of car	$33,500	
+ Taxes and fees	1,650	$35,150
− Proceeds from the sale of old car		9,750
Initial investment		$25,400

Operating Cash Flows	**Year 1**	**Year 2**	**Year 3**
Cost of repairs on new car	$ 0	$ 0	$ 0
− Cost of repairs on old car	400	400	400
Operating cash flows (savings)	$400	$400	$400

Terminal Cash Flow: End of Year 3

Proceeds from the sale of new car	$15,500
− Proceeds from the sale of old car	5,700
Terminal cash flow	$ 9,800

Summary of Cash Flows

End of Year	**Cash Flow**
0	−$25,400
1	+ 400
2	+ 400
3	+ 10,200 ($400 + $9,800)

The cash flows associated with Tina's car purchase decision reflect her net costs of the new car over the assumed 3-year ownership period, but they ignore the many intangible benefits of owning a car. Whereas the fuel cost and basic transportation service provided are assumed to be the same with the new car as with the old car, Tina will have to decide if the cost of moving up to a new car can be justified in terms of other factors, such as the improved safety technology on the new car.

→ REVIEW QUESTION MyLab Finance Solution

11–12 Diagram and describe the three types of net cash flows for a capital budgeting project.

SUMMARY

FOCUS ON VALUE

A key responsibility of financial managers is to review and analyze proposed investment decisions to make sure the firm undertakes only those that contribute positively to the value of the firm. Using a variety of tools and techniques, financial managers estimate the cash flows that a proposed investment will generate and then apply decision techniques to assess the investment's impact on the firm's value. The most difficult and important aspect of this capital budgeting process is developing good estimates of the relevant cash flows.

The relevant cash flows are the net after-tax incremental cash flows resulting from a proposed investment. These estimates represent the cash flow benefits that are likely to accrue to the firm as a result of implementing the investment. By applying to the cash flows decision techniques that capture the time value of money and risk factors, the financial manager can estimate how the investment will affect the firm's share price. Consistent application of capital budgeting procedures to proposed long-term investments should therefore allow the firm to **maximize its stock price.**

REVIEW OF LEARNING GOALS

LG 1 Discuss net and incremental cash flows, and describe the three major types of net cash flows. A project's net cash flows are the net (or the sum of) incremental after-tax cash flows over a project's life. The incremental cash flows represent the additional after-tax cash flows—outflows or inflows—that will occur only if the investment is made. The three major net cash flow types of any project include (1) an initial investment, (2) operating cash flows, and (3) terminal cash flow. The initial investment occurs at time zero, the operating cash flows occur during the project's life, and the terminal cash flow occurs at the end of the project.

LG2 **Discuss replacement versus expansion decisions, sunk costs and opportunity costs, and international capital budgeting.** For replacement decisions, the differences between the cash flows of the new asset and the old asset are incremental cash flows. Expansion decisions are viewed as replacement decisions in which all cash flows from the old asset are zero. When estimating relevant cash flows, ignore sunk costs and include opportunity costs as cash outflows. In international capital budgeting, currency risks and political risks can be minimized through careful planning.

LG3 **Calculate the initial investment associated with a proposed investment project.** The initial investment is the initial cash flow required, taking into account the installed cost of the new asset, the after-tax proceeds from the sale of the old asset, and any change in net working capital. The after-tax proceeds from the sale of the old asset reduce the initial investment required to launch an investment project. Taxes on the sale of the old asset depend on the selling price relative to the asset's book value. A gain or a loss can result from sale of an asset, depending on whether the asset sells for (1) more than book value, (2) book value, or (3) less than book value. The change in net working capital is the difference between the change in current assets and the change in current liabilities expected to accompany a given investment decision.

LG4 **Discuss the tax implications associated with the sale of an old asset.** There is typically a tax implication from the sale of an old asset. The tax implication depends on the relationship between its sale price and book value and on existing government tax rules. Generally, if the old asset sells for more than its book value, the difference is subject to a capital gains tax, and if the old asset sells for less than its book value, the company is entitled to a tax deduction equal to the difference.

LG5 **Find the operating cash flows associated with a proposed investment project.** The operating cash flows are the sum of incremental after-tax cash flows occurring each period during the project's life. The income statement format adds depreciation back to net operating profit after taxes to calculate an investment's annual operating cash inflows. The net cash flows for a replacement project are the difference between the operating cash flows of the new project and those of the old project.

LG6 **Determine the terminal cash flow associated with a proposed investment project.** The terminal cash flow represents the after-tax cash flow (exclusive of operating cash inflows) that is expected from liquidation of a project. It is calculated for replacement projects by finding the difference between the after-tax proceeds from the sale of the new and the old asset at termination and then adjusting this difference for any change in net working capital. Sale price and depreciation data are used to find the taxes and the after-tax sale proceeds on the new and old assets. The change in net working capital typically represents the reversion of any initial net working capital investment.

OPENER-IN-REVIEW

The chapter opener talked about the $12 billion acquisition by Molson Coors of the MillerCoors joint venture. According to Molson, the acquisition provided 15 years' worth of tax savings in the amount of $250 million per year. These tax benefits had a present value at the time of the acquisition of $2.4 billion. Assume that the tax benefit stream is an annuity due, meaning that the first year of benefits comes immediately. What is the discount rate that Molson Coors is applying to this deal?

SELF-TEST PROBLEMS (Solutions in Appendix)

ST11–1 **Book value, taxes, and initial investment** Irvin Enterprises, a sole proprietorship, is purchasing of a new piece of equipment to replace the old equipment. The new version costs $75,000 and requires $5,000 in installation costs. It will be depreciated under MACRS, using a 5-year recovery period. The old piece of equipment was purchased 4 years ago for an installed cost of $50,000; it was being depreciated under MACRS, using a 5-year recovery period. The old equipment can be sold today for $55,000 net of any removal or cleanup costs. As a result of the proposed replacement, the firm's investment in net working capital is expected to increase by $15,000. The firm pays taxes at a rate of 40%. (Table 4.2 contains the applicable MACRS depreciation percentages.)

a. Calculate the book value of the old piece of equipment.
b. Determine the taxes, if any, attributable to the sale of the old equipment.
c. Find the initial investment associated with the proposed equipment replacement.

ST11–2 **Determining net cash flows** A machine in use by a partnership was purchased 2 years ago for $40,000. The machine is being depreciated under MACRS, using a 5-year recovery period. It has 3 years of life remaining, and it can be sold today to net $42,000. A new machine, using a 3-year MACRS recovery period, can be purchased at a price of $140,000. It requires $10,000 to install and has a 3-year usable life. If the new machine is acquired, the investment in accounts receivable will be expected to rise by $10,000, the inventory investment will increase by $25,000, and accounts payable will increase by $15,000. Earnings before interest, taxes, depreciation, and amortization are expected to be $70,000 for each of the next 3 years with the old machine and to be $120,000 in the first year and $130,000 in the second and third years with the new machine. At the end of 3 years, the market value of the old machine will equal zero, but the new machine could be sold to net $35,000 before taxes. The firm is subject to a 40% tax rate. (Table 4.2 contains the applicable MACRS depreciation percentages.)

a. Determine the initial investment associated with the proposed replacement decision.
b. Calculate the operating cash flows for years 1 to 4 associated with the proposed replacement. (*Note:* Only depreciation cash flows must be considered in year 4.)
c. Calculate the terminal cash flow associated with the proposed replacement decision. (*Note:* This decision is made at the end of year 3.)
d. Depict on a timeline the net cash flows found in parts **a**, **b**, and **c** that are associated with the proposed replacement decision, assuming it is terminated at the end of year 3.

WARM-UP EXERCISES

All problems are available in MyLab Finance.

LG2 **E11–1** If Halley Industries reimburses employees who earn master's degrees and who agree to remain with the firm for an additional 3 years, should the expense of the tuition reimbursement be categorized as a capital expenditure or an operating expenditure?

LG2 **E11–2** Iridium Corp. has spent $3.5 billion over the past decade developing a satellite-based telecommunication system. It is currently trying to decide whether to spend an additional $350 million on the project. The firm expects that this outlay will finish the project and will generate cash flow of $15 million per year over the next 5 years. A competitor has offered $450 million for the satellites already in orbit. Classify the firm's outlays as sunk costs *or* opportunity costs, and specify the incremental cash flows.

LG3 **E11–3** Landscapes Unlimited has spent $2,200 evaluating a new service area for expanding its business territory. The expansion will require the purchase of a new truck for $35,000, and fitting the truck with a flatbed that will cost $6,500 to install. The company would realize $8,250 in after-tax proceeds from the sale of an old truck. If Landscapes' working capital is unaffected by this project, what is the initial investment amount for this project?

LG3 LG4 **E11–4** A few years ago, Largo Industries implemented an inventory auditing system at an installed cost of $175,000. Since then, it has taken depreciation deductions totaling $124,250. What is the system's current book value? If Largo sold the system for $110,000, how much recaptured depreciation would result?

LG3 LG4 **E11–5** Bryson Sciences is planning to purchase a high-powered microscopy machine for $385,000 and incur an additional $31,300 in installation expenses. It is replacing older microscopy equipment that can be sold for $116,500, resulting in taxes from a gain on the sale of $42,600. Because of this transaction, current assets will increase by $11,000, and current liabilities will increase by $5,200. Calculate the initial investment in the high-powered microscopy machine.

PROBLEMS

All problems are available in MyLab Finance. The MyLab icon indicates problems in Excel format available in MyLab Finance.

LG2 **P11–1** **Classification of expenditures** Given the following list of outlays, indicate whether each is normally considered a capital expenditure or an operating expenditure. Explain your answers.

a. An outlay of $27,600 for a marketing research report
b. A $275 outlay for an office machine
c. An outlay of $1,750,000 to purchase copyrights from an author
d. A $175,000 investment in a portfolio of marketable securities
e. An outlay of $4,000,000 for a major research and development program
f. An outlay of $3,200 for a new machine tool
g. An outlay of $3,450,000 for a new building
h. An initial lease payment of $12,575 for electronic point-of-sale cash register systems

P11–2 Net cash flow and timeline depiction For each of the following projects, determine the net cash flows, and depict the cash flows on a timeline.

a. A project that requires an initial investment of $120,000 and will generate annual operating cash inflows of $25,000 for the next 18 years. In each of the 18 years, maintenance of the project will require a $5,000 cash outflow.

b. A new machine with an installed cost of $85,000. Sale of the old machine will yield $30,000 after taxes. Operating cash inflows generated by the replacement will exceed the operating cash inflows of the old machine by $20,000 in each year of a 6-year period. At the end of year 6, liquidation of the new machine will yield $20,000 after taxes, which is $10,000 greater than the after-tax proceeds expected from the old machine had it been retained and liquidated at the end of year 6.

c. An asset that requires an initial investment of $2 million and will yield annual operating cash inflows of $300,000 for each of the next 10 years. Operating cash outlays will be $20,000 for each year except year 6, when an overhaul requiring an additional cash outlay of $500,000 will be required. The asset's liquidation value at the end of year 10 is expected to be zero.

P11–3 Replacement versus expansion cash flows Tesla Systems has estimated the cash flows over the 5-year lives for two projects, A and B. These cash flows are summarized in the table below.

	Project A	Project B
Initial investment	−$4,650,000	$1,550,000
Year	Operating cash inflows	
1	$ 560,000	$380,000
2	925,000	380,000
3	1,350,000	380,000
4	2,225,000	380,000
5	3,400,000	380,000

a. If project A, which requires an initial investment of $4,650,000, is a replacement for project B and the $1,550,000 initial investment shown for project B is the after-tax cash inflow expected from liquidating project B, what would be the net cash flows for this replacement decision?

b. Instead, if project A is an expansion decision, what would be the net cash flows and how can it be viewed as a special form of a replacement decision? Explain.

LG2

P11–4 Sunk costs and opportunity costs Masters Golf Products Inc. spent 3 years and $1,000,000 to develop its new line of club heads to replace a line that is becoming obsolete. To begin manufacturing them, the company will have to invest $1,800,000 in new equipment. The new clubs are expected to generate an increase in operating cash inflows of $750,000 per year for the next 10 years. The company has determined that the existing line could be sold to a competitor for $250,000.

a. How should the $1,000,000 in development costs be classified?

b. How should the $250,000 sale price for the existing line be classified?

c. Depict all the known incremental cash flows on a timeline.

P11–5 **Sunk costs and opportunity costs** Gen-X Industries is developing the incremental cash flows associated with the proposed replacement of an existing machine tool with a new, technologically advanced one. Given the following costs related to the proposed project, explain whether each would be treated as a sunk cost or an opportunity cost in developing the incremental cash flows associated with the proposed replacement decision.

a. Gen-X would be able to use the same tooling, which had a book value of $40,000, on the new machine tool as it had used on the old one.

b. Gen-X would be able to use its existing computer system to develop programs for operating the new machine tool. The old machine tool did not require these programs. Although the firm's computer has excess capacity available, the capacity could be leased to another firm for an annual fee of $17,000.

c. Gen-X would have to obtain additional floor space to accommodate the larger new machine tool. The space that would be used is currently being leased to another company for $10,000 per year.

d. Gen-X would use a small storage facility to store the increased output of the new machine tool. The storage facility was built by Gen-X 3 years earlier at a cost of $120,000. Because of its unique configuration and location, it is currently of no use to either Gen-X or any other firm.

e. Gen-X would retain an existing overhead crane, which it had planned to sell for its $180,000 market value. Although the crane was not needed with the old machine tool, it would be used to position raw materials on the new machine tool.

Personal Finance Problem

P11–6 **Sunk and opportunity cash flows** Dave and Ann Stone have been living at their current home for the past 6 years. During that time, they have replaced the water heater for $375, have replaced the dishwasher for $599, and have had to make miscellaneous repair and maintenance expenditures of approximately $1,500. They have decided to move out and rent the house for $975 per month. Newspaper advertising will cost $75. Dave and Ann intend to paint the interior of the home and power-wash the exterior. They estimate that will run about $900.

The house should be ready to rent after that. In reviewing the financial situation, Dave views all the expenditures as being relevant, so he plans to net out the estimated expenditures discussed above from the rental income.

a. Do Dave and Ann understand the difference between sunk costs and opportunity costs? Explain the two concepts to them.

b. Which of the expenditures should be classified as sunk cash flows, and which should be viewed as opportunity cash flows?

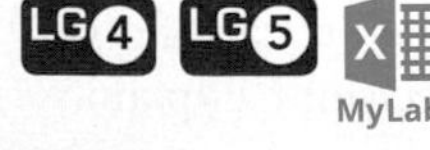

P11–7 **Book value** Find the book value for each of the assets shown in the accompanying table, assuming that MACRS depreciation is being used. (See Table 4.2 for the applicable depreciation percentages.)

Asset	Installed cost	Recovery period (years)	Elapsed time since purchase (years)
A	$ 950,000	5	3
B	40,000	3	1
C	96,000	5	4
D	350,000	5	1
E	1,500,000	7	5

P11–8 **Book value and taxes on sale of assets** Troy Industries purchased a new machine 3 years ago for $80,000. It is being depreciated under MACRS with a 5-year recovery period. Assume a 21% tax rate.

a. Use Table 4.2 to calculate the book value of the machine.

b. Calculate the firm's tax liability if it sold the machine for each of the following amounts: $100,000; $56,000; $23,200; and $15,000.

P11–9 **Tax calculations** For each of the following cases, determine the total taxes resulting from the transaction. Assume a 40% tax rate. The asset was purchased 2 years ago for $200,000 and is being depreciated under MACRS, using a 5-year recovery period. (See Table 4.2 for the applicable depreciation percentages.)

a. The asset sells for $220,000.

b. The asset sells for $150,000.

c. The asset sells for $96,000.

d. The asset sells for $80,000.

P11–10 **Change in net working capital calculation** Samuels Manufacturing is considering the purchase of a new machine to replace one it believes is obsolete. The firm has total current assets of $920,000 and total current liabilities of $640,000. As a result of the proposed replacement, the following changes are anticipated in the levels of the current asset and current liability accounts noted.

Account	Change
Expense accruals	+$ 40,000
Marketable securities	0
Inventories	− 10,000
Accounts payable	+ 90,000
Notes payable	0
Accounts receivable	+ 150,000
Cash	+ 15,000

a. Using the information given, calculate any change in net working capital that is expected to result from the proposed replacement action.

b. Explain why a change in these current accounts would be relevant in determining the initial investment for the proposed investment project.

c. Would the change in net working capital enter into any of the other cash flow types that make up the project's net cash flows? Explain.

P11–11 **Calculating initial investment** Vastine Medical Inc. is replacing its computer system, which was purchased 2 years ago at a cost of $325,000. The system can be sold today for $200,000. It is being depreciated using MACRS and a 5-year recovery period. A new computer system will cost $500,000 to purchase and install. Replacement of the computer system would not involve any change in net working capital. Assume a 21% tax rate.

a. Calculate the book value of the existing computer system (see Table 4.2).

b. Calculate the after-tax proceeds of its sale for $200,000.

c. Calculate the initial investment associated with the replacement project. What would the initial investment be if the new computer qualified for 100% bonus depreciation?

P11–12 **Initial investment: Basic calculation** Cushing Partners is considering the purchase of a new grading machine to replace the existing one. The existing machine was purchased 3 years ago at an installed cost of $20,000; it was being depreciated under MACRS, using a 5-year recovery period. (See Table 4.2 for the applicable depreciation percentages.) The existing machine is expected to have a usable life of at least 5 more years. The new machine costs $35,000 and requires $5,000 in installation costs; it will be depreciated using a 5-year recovery period under MACRS. The existing machine can currently be sold for $25,000 without incurring any removal or cleanup costs. The firm is subject to a 40% tax rate. Calculate the initial investment associated with the proposed purchase of a new grading machine.

P11–13 **Initial investment at various sale prices** Ed Mann, sole owner of Edward Mann Consulting (EMC) is replacing one machine with another. The old machine was purchased 3 years ago for an installed cost of $10,000. The firm is depreciating the machine under MACRS, using a 5-year recovery period (see Table 4.2). The new machine costs $24,000 and requires $2,000 in installation costs. The firm is subject to a 40% tax rate. In each of the following cases, calculate the initial investment for the replacement.

a. EMC sells the old machine for $11,000.
b. EMC sells the old machine for $7,000.
c. EMC sells the old machine for $2,900.
d. EMC sells the old machine for $1,500.

P11–14 **Calculating initial investment** DuPree Coffee Roasters Inc. wishes to expand and modernize its facilities. The installed cost of a proposed computer-controlled automatic-feed roaster will be $130,000. The firm has a chance to sell its 4-year-old roaster for $35,000. The existing roaster originally cost $60,000 and was being depreciated using MACRS and a 7-year recovery period. (See Table 4.2 for the applicable depreciation percentages.) DuPree is subject to a 21% tax rate.

a. What is the book value of the existing roaster?
b. Calculate the after-tax proceeds of the sale of the existing roaster.
c. Calculate the change in net working capital using the figures in the following table.

Anticipated Changes in Current Assets and Current Liabilities	
Expense accruals	−$20,000
Inventory	+ 50,000
Accounts payable	+ 40,000
Accounts receivable	+ 70,000
Cash	0
Notes payable	+ 15,000

d. Calculate the initial investment associated with the new roaster.

P11–15 **Depreciation** A firm is evaluating the acquisition of an asset that costs $64,000 and requires $4,000 in installation costs. If the firm depreciates the asset under MACRS, using a 5-year recovery period (see Table 4.2 for the applicable depreciation percentages), determine the depreciation charge for each year.

P11–16 **Operating cash inflows** A partnership is considering renewing its equipment to meet increased demand for its product. The cost of equipment modifications is $1.9 million plus $100,000 in installation costs. The firm will depreciate the equipment modifications under MACRS, using a 5-year recovery period. (See Table 4.2 for the applicable depreciation percentages.) Additional sales revenue from the renewal should amount to $1,200,000 per year, and additional operating expenses and other costs (excluding depreciation and interest) will amount to 40% of the additional sales. The firm is subject to a tax rate of 40%. (*Note:* Answer the following questions for each of the next 6 years.)

a. What incremental earnings before interest, taxes, depreciation, and amortization will result from the renewal?

b. What incremental net operating profits after taxes will result from the renewal?

c. What operating cash flows will result from the renewal?

Personal Finance Problem

P11–17 **Operating cash flows** Richard and Linda Thomson operate a lawn maintenance service for commercial property. They have been using a John Deere riding mower for the past several years and believe it is time to buy a new one. They would like to know the operating cash flows associated with the replacement of the old riding mower. The following data are available:

There are 5 years of remaining useful life on the old mower.

The old mower has a zero book value.

The new mower is expected to last 5 years.

The Thomsons will follow a 5-year MACRS recovery period for the new mower.

Depreciable value of the new mower is $1,800.

They are subject to a 40% tax rate.

The new mower is expected to be more fuel efficient, maneuverable, and durable than previous models and can result in reduced operating expenses of $500 per year.

The Thomsons will buy a maintenance contract that calls for annual payments of $120.

Create an operating cash flow statement for the replacement of Richard and Linda's John Deere riding mower. Show the operating cash flow for the next 6 years. How would the schedule change if the new mower is eligible for 100% bonus depreciation under the tax law?

P11–18 **Operating cash flows: Expense reduction** Miller Corporation is considering replacing a machine. The replacement will reduce operating expenses (i.e., increase earnings before interest, taxes, depreciation, and amortization) by $16,000 per year for each of the 5 years the new machine is expected to last. Although the old machine has zero book value, it can be used for 5 more years. The depreciable value of the new machine is $48,000. The firm will depreciate the machine under MACRS, using a 5-year recovery period (see Table 4.2 for the applicable depreciation percentages), and is subject to a 21% tax rate. Estimate the operating cash flows generated by the replacement. (*Note:* Be sure to consider the depreciation in year 6.)

P11–19 **Operating cash flows** Strong Tool Partners has been considering purchasing a new lathe to replace a fully depreciated lathe that would otherwise last 5 more years. The new lathe is expected to have a 5-year life and depreciation charges of $2,000 in year 1; $3,200 in year 2; $1,900 in year 3; $1,200 in both year 4 and year 5; and $500 in year 6. The firm estimates the revenues and expenses (excluding depreciation and interest) for the new and the old lathes to be as shown in the table below. The firm is subject to a 40% tax rate.

	New lathe		Old lathe	
Year	Revenue	Expenses (excluding depreciation and interest)	Revenue	Expenses (excluding depreciation and interest)
1	$40,000	$30,000	$35,000	$25,000
2	41,000	30,000	35,000	25,000
3	42,000	30,000	35,000	25,000
4	43,000	30,000	35,000	25,000
5	44,000	30,000	35,000	25,000

a. Calculate the operating cash flows associated with each lathe. (*Note:* Be sure to consider the depreciation in year 6.)

b. Calculate the operating cash flows resulting from the proposed lathe replacement.

c. Depict on a timeline the operating cash flows calculated in part **b.**

P11–20 **Operating cash inflows** Scenic Tours Inc. is a provider of bus tours throughout New England. The corporation is considering the replacement of 10 of its older buses. The existing buses were purchased 4 years ago at a total cost of $2,700,000 and are being depreciated using MACRS and a 5-year recovery period (see Table 4.2). The new buses would have larger passenger capacity and better fuel efficiency as well as lower maintenance costs. The total cost for 10 new buses is $3,000,000. Like the older buses, the new ones would be depreciated using MACRS and a 5-year recovery period. Scenic is subject to a tax rate of 21%. The accompanying table presents revenues and cash expenses (excluding depreciation and interest) for the proposed purchase as well as the current fleet. Use all the information given to calculate operating cash flows for the proposed bus replacement.

	Year					
	1	2	3	4	5	6
With the proposed new buses						
Revenue	$1,850,000	$1,850,000	$1,830,000	$1,825,000	$1,815,000	$1,800,000
Expenses (excluding depreciation and interest)	460,000	460,000	468,000	472,000	485,000	500,000
With the current buses						
Revenue	$1,800,000	$1,800,000	$1,790,000	$1,785,000	$1,775,000	$1,750,000
Expenses (excluding depreciation and interest)	500,000	510,000	520,000	520,000	530,000	535,000

LG6 **P11–21 Terminal cash flow: Various lives and sale prices** Looner Industries is currently analyzing the purchase of a new machine that costs $160,000 and requires $20,000 in installation costs. Net working capital will increase immediately by $30,000, but those funds will be recovered at the end of the machine's life. The firm plans to depreciate the machine under MACRS, using a 5-year recovery period (see Table 4.2), and expects to sell it to net $10,000 before taxes at the end of its usable life. The firm is subject to a 40% tax rate.

a. Calculate the terminal cash flow for a usable life of (1) 3 years, (2) 5 years, and (3) 7 years.

b. Discuss the effect of usable life on terminal cash flows, using your findings in part **a.**

c. Assuming a 5-year usable life, calculate the terminal cash flow if the machine were sold to net (1) $9,000 or (2) $170,000 (before taxes) at the end of 5 years.

d. Discuss the effect of sale price on terminal cash flow, using your findings in part **c.**

LG6 **P11–22 Terminal cash flow: Replacement decision** Russell Industries is considering replacing a fully depreciated machine that has a remaining useful life of 10 years with a newer, more sophisticated machine. The new machine will cost $200,000 and will require $30,000 in installation costs. It will be depreciated under MACRS, using a 5-year recovery period (see Table 4.2 for the applicable depreciation percentages). A $25,000 increase in net working capital will be required to support the new machine. The firm's managers plan to evaluate the potential replacement over a 4-year period. They estimate that the old machine could be sold at the end of 4 years to net $15,000 before taxes; the new machine at the end of 4 years will be worth $75,000 before taxes. Calculate the terminal cash flow at the end of year 4 that is relevant to the proposed purchase of the new machine. The firm is subject to a 40% tax rate.

LG3 LG4 LG5 LG6 **P11–23 Net cash flows for a marketing campaign** Dan Marcus is the sole proprietor of Marcus Tube, a manufacturer of high-quality aluminum tubing, has maintained stable sales and profits over the past 10 years. Although the market for aluminum tubing has been expanding by 3% per year, Marcus has been unsuccessful in sharing this growth. To increase its sales, the firm is considering an aggressive marketing campaign that centers on regularly running ads in all relevant trade journals and websites and exhibiting products at all major regional and national trade shows. The campaign is expected to require an annual tax-deductible expenditure of $150,000 over the next 5 years. Sales revenue, as shown in the accompanying income statement for 2018, totaled $20,000,000. If the proposed marketing campaign is not initiated, sales are expected to remain at this level in each of the next 5 years, 2019 through 2023. With the marketing campaign, sales are expected to rise to the levels shown in the accompanying table for each of the next 5 years; cost of goods sold is expected to remain at 80% of sales; general and administrative expense (exclusive of any marketing campaign outlays) is expected to remain at 10% of sales; and annual depreciation expense is expected to remain at $500,000. Assuming a 40% tax rate, find the net cash flows over the next 5 years associated with the proposed marketing campaign.

Marcus Tube Income Statement for the Year Ended December 31, 2018	
Sales revenue	$20,000,000
Less: Cost of goods sold (80%)	16,000,000
Gross profits	$ 4,000,000
Less: Operating expenses	
General and administrative expense (10%)	$ 2,000,000
Depreciation expense	500,000
Total operating expense	$ 2,500,000
Earnings before interest and taxes	$ 1,500,000
Less: Taxes (rate = 40%)	600,000
Net operating profit after taxes	$ 900,000

Marcus Tube Sales Forecast	
Year	Sales revenue
2019	$20,500,000
2020	21,000,000
2021	21,500,000
2022	22,500,000
2023	23,500,000

P11–24 **Net cash flows: No terminal value** Central Laundry is replacing an existing piece of machinery with a new model. The old machine was purchased 3 years ago for $50,000 and was being depreciated under MACRS, using a 5-year recovery period. The machine has 5 years of usable life remaining. The new machine costs $76,000, requires $4,000 in installation costs, and will be depreciated under MACRS, using a 5-year recovery period (see Table 4.2). The firm can currently sell the old machine for $55,000 without incurring any removal or cleanup costs. The firm's tax rate is 21%. The revenues and expenses (excluding depreciation and interest) for the new and old machines for the next 5 years appear in the table below.

	New machine		Old machine	
Year	Revenue	Expenses (excl. depr. and int.)	Revenue	Expenses (excl. depr. and int.)
1	$750,000	$720,000	$674,000	$660,000
2	750,000	720,000	676,000	660,000
3	750,000	720,000	680,000	660,000
4	750,000	720,000	678,000	660,000
5	750,000	720,000	674,000	660,000

a. Calculate the initial investment associated with replacement of the old machine by the new one.

b. Determine the operating cash flows associated with the proposed replacement. (*Note:* Be sure to consider the depreciation in year 6.)

c. Depict on a timeline the net cash flows found in parts **a** and **b** associated with the proposed replacement decision.)

d. How would your answers change if the new machine is eligible for 100% bonus depreciation?

P11–25 **Integrative: Determining net cash flows** Lombard Company is contemplating the purchase of a new high-speed widget grinder to replace the existing grinder. The existing grinder was purchased 2 years ago at an installed cost of $60,000; it was being depreciated under MACRS, using a 5-year recovery period. The existing grinder is expected to have a usable life of 5 more years. The new grinder costs $105,000 and requires $5,000 in installation costs; it has a 5-year usable life and would be depreciated under MACRS, using a 5-year recovery period. Lombard can currently sell the existing grinder for $70,000 without incurring any removal or cleanup costs. To support the increased business resulting from purchase of the new grinder, accounts receivable would increase by $40,000, inventories by $30,000, and accounts payable by $58,000. At the end of 5 years, the existing grinder would have a market value of zero; the new grinder would be sold to net $29,000 after removal and cleanup costs and before taxes. The firm is subject to a 40% tax rate. The estimated earnings before interest, taxes, depreciation, and amortization over the 5 years for both the new and the existing grinder are shown in the following table. (See Table 4.2 for the applicable depreciation percentages.)

	Earnings before interest, taxes, depreciation, and amortization	
Year	**New grinder**	**Existing grinder**
1	$43,000	$26,000
2	43,000	24,000
3	43,000	22,000
4	43,000	20,000
5	43,000	18,000

a. Calculate the initial investment associated with the replacement of the existing grinder by the new one.
b. Determine the operating cash flows associated with the proposed grinder replacement. (*Note:* Be sure to consider the depreciation in year 6.)
c. Determine the terminal cash flow expected at the end of year 5 from the proposed grinder replacement.
d. Depict on a timeline the net cash flows associated with the proposed grinder replacement decision.

Personal Finance Problem

LG3 LG4 LG5 LG6

P11–26 **Determining net cash flows for a new boat** Jan and Deana have been dreaming about owning a boat for some time and have decided that estimating its cash flows will help them in their decision process. They expect to have a disposable annual income of $24,000. Their cash flow estimates for the boat purchase are as follows:

Negotiated price of the new boat	$70,000
Sales tax rate (applicable to purchase price)	6.5%
Boat trade-in	$ 0
Estimated value of new boat in 4 years	$40,000
Estimated monthly repair and maintenance	$ 800
Estimated monthly docking fee	$ 500

Using these cash flow estimates, calculate the following:
a. The initial investment
b. Operating cash flow
c. Terminal cash flow
d. Summary of annual cash flow
e. On the basis of their disposable annual income, what advice would you give Jan and Deana regarding the proposed boat purchase?

P11–27 Integrative: Determining net cash flows Atlantic Drydock is considering replacing an existing hoist with one of two newer, more efficient pieces of equipment. The existing hoist is 3 years old, cost $32,000, and is being depreciated under MACRS, using a 5-year recovery period. Although the existing hoist has only 3 years (years 4, 5, and 6) of depreciation remaining under MACRS, it has a remaining usable life of 5 years. Hoist A, one of the two possible replacement hoists, costs $40,000 to purchase and $8,000 to install. It has a 5-year usable life and will be depreciated under MACRS, using a 5-year recovery period. Hoist B costs $54,000 to purchase and $6,000 to install. It also has a 5-year usable life and will be depreciated under MACRS, using a 5-year recovery period.

Increased investments in net working capital will accompany the decision to acquire hoist A or hoist B. Purchase of hoist A would result in a $4,000 increase in net working capital; hoist B would result in a $6,000 increase in net working capital. The projected earnings before interest, taxes, depreciation, and amortization with each alternative hoist and the existing hoist are given in the following table.

	Earnings before interest, taxes, depreciation, and amortization		
Year	With hoist A	With hoist B	With existing hoist
1	$21,000	$22,000	$14,000
2	21,000	24,000	14,000
3	21,000	26,000	14,000
4	21,000	26,000	14,000
5	21,000	26,000	14,000

The existing hoist can currently be sold for $18,000 and will not incur any removal or cleanup costs. At the end of 5 years, the existing hoist can be sold to net $1,000 before taxes. Hoists A and B can be sold to net $12,000 and $20,000 before taxes, respectively, at the end of the 5-year period. The firm is subject to a 40% tax rate. (See Table 4.2 for the applicable depreciation percentages.)

a. Calculate the initial investment associated with each alternative.

b. Calculate the incremental operating cash flows associated with each alternative. (*Note:* Be sure to consider the depreciation in year 6.)

c. Calculate the terminal cash flow at the end of year 5 associated with each alternative.

d. Depict on a timeline the relevant cash flows associated with each alternative.

LG1 LG2 LG3 LG4 LG5 LG6 MyLab

P11–28 Integrative: Complete investment decision With the market price of gold at C$1,562.50 per ounce (C$ stands for Canadian dollars), Maritime Resources Corp., a Canadian mining firm, would like to assess the financial feasibility of reopening an old gold mine that had ceased operations in the past due to low gold prices. Reopening the mine would require an up-front capital expenditure of C$67.8 million and annual operating expenses of C$19.42 million. Maritime expects that over a 5-year operating life it can recover 174,000 ounces of gold from the mine and that the project will have no terminal value. Maritime uses straight-line depreciation, has a 21.04% corporate tax rate, and has an 11.2% cost of capital.

a. Calculate the operating cash flows for the gold mine project.

b. Depict on a timeline the net cash flows for the gold mine project.

c. Calculate the internal rate of return (IRR) for the gold mine project.

d. Calculate the net present value (NPV) for the gold mine project.
e. Make a recommendation to accept or reject the gold mine project, and justify your answer.

P11–29 **Integrative: Complete investment decision** Wells Printing is considering the purchase of a new printing press. The total installed cost of the press is $2.2 million. This outlay would be partially offset by the sale of an existing press. The old press has zero book value, cost $1 million 10 years ago, and can be sold currently for $1.2 million before taxes. As a result of acquisition of the new press, sales in each of the next 5 years are expected to be $1.6 million higher than with the existing press, but product costs (excluding depreciation) will represent 50% of sales. The new press will not affect the firm's net working capital requirements. The new press will be depreciated under MACRS, using a 5-year recovery period. The firm is subject to a 40% tax rate. Wells Printing's cost of capital is 11%. (*Note:* Assume that the old and the new presses will each have a terminal value of $0 at the end of year 6.)

a. Determine the initial investment required by the new press.
b. Determine the operating cash flows attributable to the new press. (*Note:* Be sure to consider the depreciation in year 6.)
c. Determine the payback period.
d. Determine the net present value (NPV) and the internal rate of return (IRR) related to the proposed new press.
e. Make a recommendation to accept or reject the new press, and justify your answer.

P11–30 **Integrative: Investment decision** Holliday Manufacturing is considering the replacement of an existing machine. The new machine costs $1,200,000 and requires installation costs of $150,000. The existing machine can be sold currently for $185,000 before taxes. It is 2 years old, cost $800,000 new, and has a $384,000 book value and a remaining useful life of 5 years. It was being depreciated under MACRS, using a 5-year recovery period (see Table 4.2), and therefore has the final 4 years of depreciation remaining. If it is held for 5 more years, the machine's market value at the end of year 5 will be $0. Over its 5-year life, the new machine should reduce operating costs by $350,000 per year. The new machine will be depreciated under MACRS, using a 5-year recovery period. The new machine can be sold for $200,000 net of removal and cleanup costs at the end of 5 years. An increased investment in net working capital of $25,000 will be needed to support operations if the new machine is acquired. Assume that the firm has adequate operating income against which to deduct any loss experienced on the sale of the existing machine. The firm has a 9% cost of capital and is subject to a 40% tax rate.

a. Develop the net cash flows needed to analyze the proposed replacement.
b. Determine the net present value (NPV) of the proposal.
c. Determine the internal rate of return (IRR) of the proposal.
d. Make a recommendation to accept or reject the replacement proposal, and justify your answer.
e. What is the highest cost of capital that the firm could have and still accept the proposal? Explain.

P11–31 **ETHICS PROBLEM** Cash flow projections are a central component to the analysis of new investment ideas. In most firms, the person responsible for making these projections is not the same person who generated the investment idea in the first place. Why?

SPREADSHEET EXERCISE

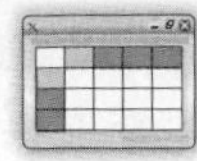

Damon Corporation, a sports equipment manufacturer, has a machine currently in use that was originally purchased 3 years ago for $120,000. The firm depreciates the machine under MACRS, using a 5-year recovery period. Once removal and cleanup costs are taken into consideration, the expected net selling price for the old machine will be $70,000.

Damon can buy a new machine for a net price of $160,000 (including installation costs of $15,000). The new machine will be depreciated under MACRS, using a 5-year recovery period. If the firm acquires the new machine, its working capital needs will change: Accounts receivable will increase $15,000, inventory will increase $19,000, and accounts payable will increase $16,000.

Earnings before interest, taxes, depreciation, and amortization (EBITDA) for the old machine are expected to be $95,000 for each of the successive 5 years. For the new machine, the expected EBITDA for each of the next 5 years are $105,000, $110,000, $120,000, $120,000, and $120,000, respectively. The corporate tax rate (*T*) for the firm is 21%. (Table 4.2 contains the applicable MACRS depreciation percentages.)

Damon expects to liquidate the new machine after 5 years for $24,000. The old machine should net $8,000 upon liquidation at the end of the same period, when Damon also expects to recover its net working capital investment. The firm is subject to a tax rate of 21%.

TO DO

Create a spreadsheet similar to Tables 11.1, 11.5, 11.7, and 11.9 to answer the following:

a. Create a spreadsheet to calculate the initial investment.

b. Create a spreadsheet to prepare a depreciation schedule for both the new and the old machine. Both machines are depreciated under MACRS, using a 5-year recovery period. Remember that the old machine has only 3 years of depreciation remaining.

c. Create a spreadsheet to calculate the operating cash flows for Damon Corporation for both the new and the old machine.

d. Create a spreadsheet to calculate the terminal cash flow associated with the project.

e. Repeat all of the calculations above assuming that the new machine qualifies for 100% bonus depreciation.

MyLab Finance Visit www.pearson.com/mylab/finance for **Chapter Case: *Developing Net Cash Flows for Clark Upholstery Company's Machine Renewal or Replacement Decision,*** Group Exercises, and numerous online resources.

CHAPTER 12

Risk and Refinements in Capital Budgeting

LEARNING GOALS

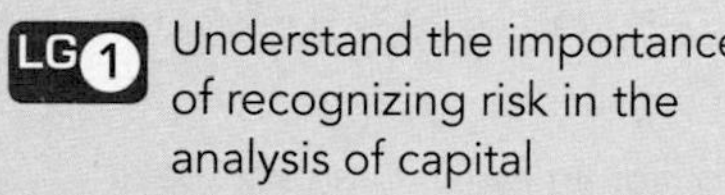

LG 1 Understand the importance of recognizing risk in the analysis of capital budgeting projects.

LG 2 Discuss breakeven analysis, scenario analysis, and simulation as behavioral approaches for dealing with risk.

LG 3 Review the unique risks that multinational companies face.

LG 4 Describe the determination and use of risk-adjusted discount rates (RADRs), portfolio effects, and the practical aspects of RADRs.

LG 5 Select the best of a group of unequal-lived, mutually exclusive projects using annualized net present values (ANPVs).

LG 6 Explain the role of real options and the objective and procedures for selecting projects under capital rationing.

MyLab Finance Chapter Introduction Video

WHY THIS CHAPTER MATTERS TO YOU

In your *professional* life

ACCOUNTING You need to understand the risk caused by the variability of cash flows, how to compare projects with unequal lives, and how to measure project returns when capital is being rationed.

INFORMATION SYSTEMS You need to understand how risk is incorporated into capital budgeting techniques and how those techniques may be refined for special circumstances so as to design decision modules for analyzing proposed capital projects.

MANAGEMENT You need to understand behavioral approaches for dealing with risk, including international risk, in capital budgeting decisions; how to risk-adjust discount rates; how to refine capital budgeting techniques when projects have unequal lives or when capital must be rationed; and how to recognize real options embedded in capital projects.

MARKETING You need to understand how the risk of proposed projects is measured in capital budgeting, how projects with unequal lives will be evaluated, how to recognize and treat real options embedded in proposed projects, and how projects will be evaluated when capital must be rationed.

OPERATIONS You need to understand how the firm's decision makers will evaluate proposals for the acquisition of new equipment and plants, especially projects that are risky, have unequal lives, or may need to be abandoned or slowed, or when capital is limited.

In your *personal* life

All long-term decisions entail risk. When making personal financial decisions, you should consider risk in the decision-making process. Simply put, you should demand higher returns for greater risk. Failing to incorporate risk into your financial decision-making process will likely result in poor decisions and reduced wealth.

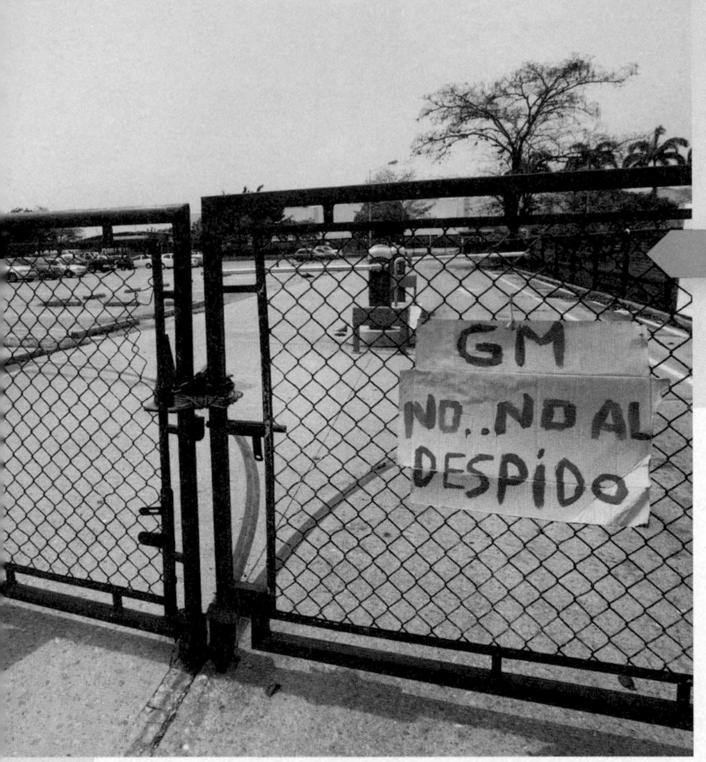

Juan Carlos Hernandez/ZUMA Wire/Alamy Live News

GENERAL MOTORS

Venezuelan Government Seizes Factory Owned by GM

The fortunes of General Motors had been looking up since the company emerged from its 2009 bankruptcy. Revenues had been creeping up, increasing from $105 billion in 2010 to $152 billion in 2016. Even so, the company's stock price in early 2017 was no higher than it had been in 2010, when the company sold stock to investors in its post-bankruptcy IPO. The company faced intense pressure from activist investors to do something about delivering higher returns to shareholders.

In that environment, more unwelcome news arrived in April 2017, when the government of Venezuela abruptly seized the company's factory. Car production had fallen for several years under the socialist government of President Nicholas Maduro. Auto production in the entire country was just 2,849 vehicles in 2016, down from 172,218 cars in 2007. GM itself had stopped producing cars in 2015, and the factory it owned in Venezuela produced nothing but spare parts. General Motors was just the latest in a long string of dozens of foreign companies whose assets were seized by the Venezuelan government.

GM executives had decided to remain in Venezuela rather than withdrawing entirely, in the hope that a more business-friendly government might be elected. Instead, the company's remaining assets were lost, and the prospect for any compensation from President Maduro's administration seemed dim. In remaining in Venezuela, GM demonstrated its willingness to take on not only the inherent risks associated with auto production but also the political risks of doing business in Venezuela.

When firms undertake major investments, they cannot avoid taking risks. These risks may arise from the nature of the business that a company operates in, such as the risks of oil exploration, but political factors can also create risks that may diminish the value of a company's investments. This chapter focuses on the tools available to managers that help them better understand the risks of major investments.

12.1 Introduction to Risk in Capital Budgeting

In our discussion of capital budgeting thus far, we have assumed that a firm's investment projects all have the same risk, which implies that the acceptance of any project would not change the firm's overall risk. In actuality, these assumptions often do not hold: Projects are not equally risky, and undertaking a major new investment can increase or decrease the firm's overall risk. We begin this chapter by relaxing these assumptions and focusing on how managers evaluate the risks of different projects. Naturally, we will use many of the risk concepts developed in Chapter 8.

We continue the Bennett Company example from Chapter 10. The relevant cash flows and NPVs for Bennett Company's two mutually exclusive projects—A and B—appear in Table 12.1.

TABLE 12.1 Relevant Cash Flows and NPVs for Bennett Company's Projects

	Project A	Project B
A. Relevant cash flows		
Initial investment	−$420,000	−$450,000
Year	Operating cash inflows	
1	$140,000	$280,000
2	140,000	120,000
3	140,000	100,000
4	140,000	100,000
5	140,000	100,000
B. Decision technique		
NPV @ 10% cost of capital[a]	$110,710	$109,244

[a]From Figure 10.2 on page 441; calculated using a financial calculator.

In the following three sections, we use the basic risk concepts presented in Chapter 8 to demonstrate behavioral approaches for dealing with risk, international risk considerations, and the use of risk-adjusted discount rates to explicitly recognize risk in the analysis of capital budgeting projects.

→ REVIEW QUESTION MyLab Finance Solution

12–1 Are most mutually exclusive capital budgeting projects equally risky? If you think about a firm as a portfolio of many different kinds of investments, how can the acceptance of a project change a firm's overall risk?

12.2 Behavioral Approaches for Dealing with Risk

Firms use behavioral approaches to get a "feel" for a project's risk, whereas other approaches try to quantify and measure project risk. Here we present a few behavioral approaches to dealing with risk in capital budgeting: breakeven analysis, scenario analysis, and simulation.

MATTER OF FACT

What Does Your Gut Say?

A survey of more than 1,000 U.S. CEOs asked business leaders what tools they used to allocate capital within their firms. The leading answer, given by almost 80% of the survey respondents, was that CEOs use the NPV method to decide how to invest the firm's money. But nearly half the CEOs also said that their "gut feel" for a project was an important factor in their decisions.

Source: John Graham and Campbell Harvey, 2015, "Capital allocation and delegation of decision-making authority within firms," *Journal of Financial Economics*, Vol. 115, pp. 449–470.

BREAKEVEN ANALYSIS

risk (in capital budgeting) The uncertainty surrounding the cash flows that a project will generate or, more formally, the degree of variability of cash flows.

In the context of capital budgeting, the term **risk** refers to the uncertainty surrounding the cash flows that a project will generate. More formally, risk in capital budgeting is related to the degree of variability of cash flows. Projects with a broad range of possible cash flows are usually more risky than projects that have a narrow range of possible cash flows.

In many projects, risk stems almost entirely from the cash flows that a project will generate several years in the future because managers generally know with relative certainty how much the project's initial investment will cost. The subsequent cash flows, of course, derive from a number of variables related to revenues, expenditures, and taxes. Forecasts of an investment project's cash flow rely on many assumptions about sales, the cost of raw materials, labor rates, utility costs, tax rates, and many other factors. We will concentrate on the risk in the cash flows, but remember that this risk actually results from the interaction of these underlying variables. Therefore, to assess the risk of a proposed capital expenditure, the analyst must evaluate the probability that the cash inflows will be large enough to produce a positive NPV.

EXAMPLE 12.1

MyLab Finance Solution Video

Treadwell Tire Company, a tire retailer with a 10% cost of capital, is considering investing in either of two mutually exclusive projects, A and B. Each requires a \$10,000 initial investment, and both are expected to provide constant annual cash inflows over their 15-year lives. For either project to be acceptable, its NPV must be greater than zero. In other words, the present value of the annuity (i.e., the project's cash inflows) must be greater than the initial cash outflow. If we let CF equal the annual cash inflow and CF_0 equal the initial investment, an investment project with an annuity-like cash flow pattern (such as projects A and B) will have a positive NPV if the following condition holds:[1]

$$\text{NPV} = \left(\frac{CF}{r}\right) \times \left[1 - \frac{1}{(1+r)^n}\right] - CF_0 > \$0 \qquad (12.1)$$

breakeven cash inflow The minimum level of cash inflow necessary for a project to be acceptable, that is, NPV > \$0.

By substituting $r = 10\%$, $n = 15$ years, and $CF_0 = \$10{,}000$, we can find the **breakeven cash inflow,** the minimum annual cash inflow necessary for Treadwell's projects to create value for shareholders.

1. This equation makes use of the algebraic shortcut for the present value of an annuity, introduced in Personal Finance Example 5.7.

MyLab Finance Financial Calculator

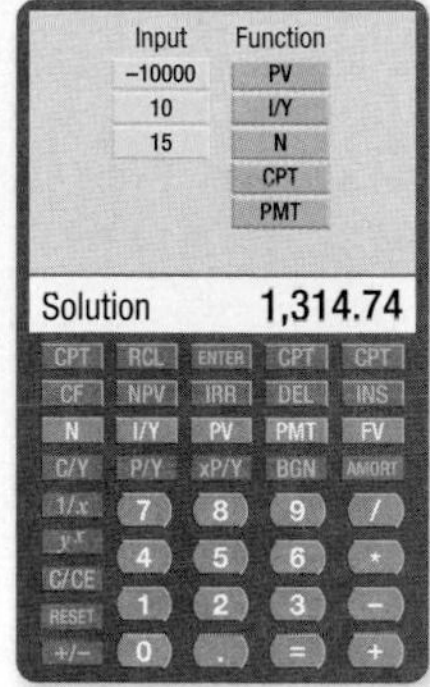

Calculator use Recognizing that the initial investment (CF_0) is the present value (PV), we can use the calculator inputs shown at the left to find the breakeven cash inflow (CF), which is an ordinary annuity (PMT).

Spreadsheet use The breakeven cash inflow also can be calculated as shown on the following Excel spreadsheet.

	A	B
1	BREAKEVEN CASH INFLOW	
2	Initial investment	–$10,000
3	Cost of capital	10%
4	Number of years	15
5	Breakeven cash inflow	$1,314.74
	Entry in Cell B5 is =PMT(B3,B4,B2,0,0). The minus sign appears before the initial investment in B4 because it is a cash outflow.	

The calculator and spreadsheet values indicate that, for the projects to be acceptable, they must have annual cash inflows of at least $1,315. Given this breakeven level of cash inflows, managers can assess the risk of each project by determining the probability that the project's cash inflows will equal or exceed this level. Analysts can obtain estimates of that probability using various statistical techniques, but often managers make judgments about the likelihood of a project generating enough cash flow to break even based on their experience with other similar projects. For now, let us suppose that managers have estimated the probability that projects A and B will generate at least $1,315 in annual cash flow as follows:

$$\text{Probability of } CF_A > \$1{,}315 \rightarrow 100\%$$
$$\text{Probability of } CF_B > \$1{,}315 \rightarrow 65\%$$

Because project A is certain (100% probability) to have a positive net present value, whereas project B will have only a 65% chance of having a positive NPV, project A seems less risky than project B.

The example clearly identifies risk as it relates to the chance that a project is acceptable, but it does not address the issue of cash flow variability. Even though project B has a greater chance of loss than project A, it might result in higher potential NPVs. Recall that the combination of risk and return is what determines value. Similarly, the benefit of a capital expenditure and its impact on the firm's value must be viewed in light of both risk and return. The analyst must therefore consider the variability of cash inflows and NPVs to assess project risk and return fully.

SCENARIO ANALYSIS

In dealing with project risk, financial analysts use scenario analysis to capture the variability of cash inflows and NPVs. *Scenario analysis* is a behavioral approach that uses several possible alternative outcomes (scenarios) to obtain a sense of the variability of returns, measured here by NPV. This technique often proves useful in getting a feel for the variability of return in response to changes

TABLE 12.2 Scenario Analysis of Treadwell's Projects A and B

	Project A	Project B
Initial investment	**−$10,000**	**−$10,000**
	Annual cash inflows	
Outcome		
Pessimistic	$1,500	$ 0
Most likely	2,000	2,000
Optimistic	2,500	4,000
Range	1,000	4,000
	Net present values[a]	
Outcome		
Pessimistic	$1,409	−$10,000
Most likely	5,212	5,212
Optimistic	9,015	20,424
Range	7,606	30,424

[a]These values were calculated by using the corresponding annual cash inflows. A 10% cost of capital and a 15-year life for the annual cash inflows were used.

in a key outcome. In capital budgeting, one of the most common scenario approaches is to estimate the NPVs associated with pessimistic (worst), most likely (expected), and optimistic (best) estimates of cash inflow. The range can be determined by subtracting the pessimistic-outcome NPV from the optimistic-outcome NPV.

EXAMPLE 12.2

Continuing with Treadwell Tire Company, assume that the financial manager created three scenarios for each project: pessimistic, most likely, and optimistic. Table 12.2 summarizes the cash inflows and resulting NPVs in each case. Comparing the ranges of cash inflows ($1,000 for project A and $4,000 for B) and, more important, the ranges of NPVs ($7,606 for project A and $30,424 for B) suggests that project A is less risky than project B. Given that both projects have the same most likely NPV of $5,212, a risk-averse decision maker would likely take project A because it has less risk (smaller NPV range) and no possibility of loss (all NPVs > $0).

The widespread availability of computers and spreadsheets has greatly enhanced the use of scenario analysis because technology allows analysts to create a wide range of different scenarios quickly.

simulation
A statistics-based behavioral approach that applies predetermined probability distributions and random numbers to estimate risky outcomes.

SIMULATION

Simulation is a statistics-based behavioral approach that applies predetermined probability distributions and random numbers to estimate risky outcomes. By tying the various cash flow components together in a mathematical model and

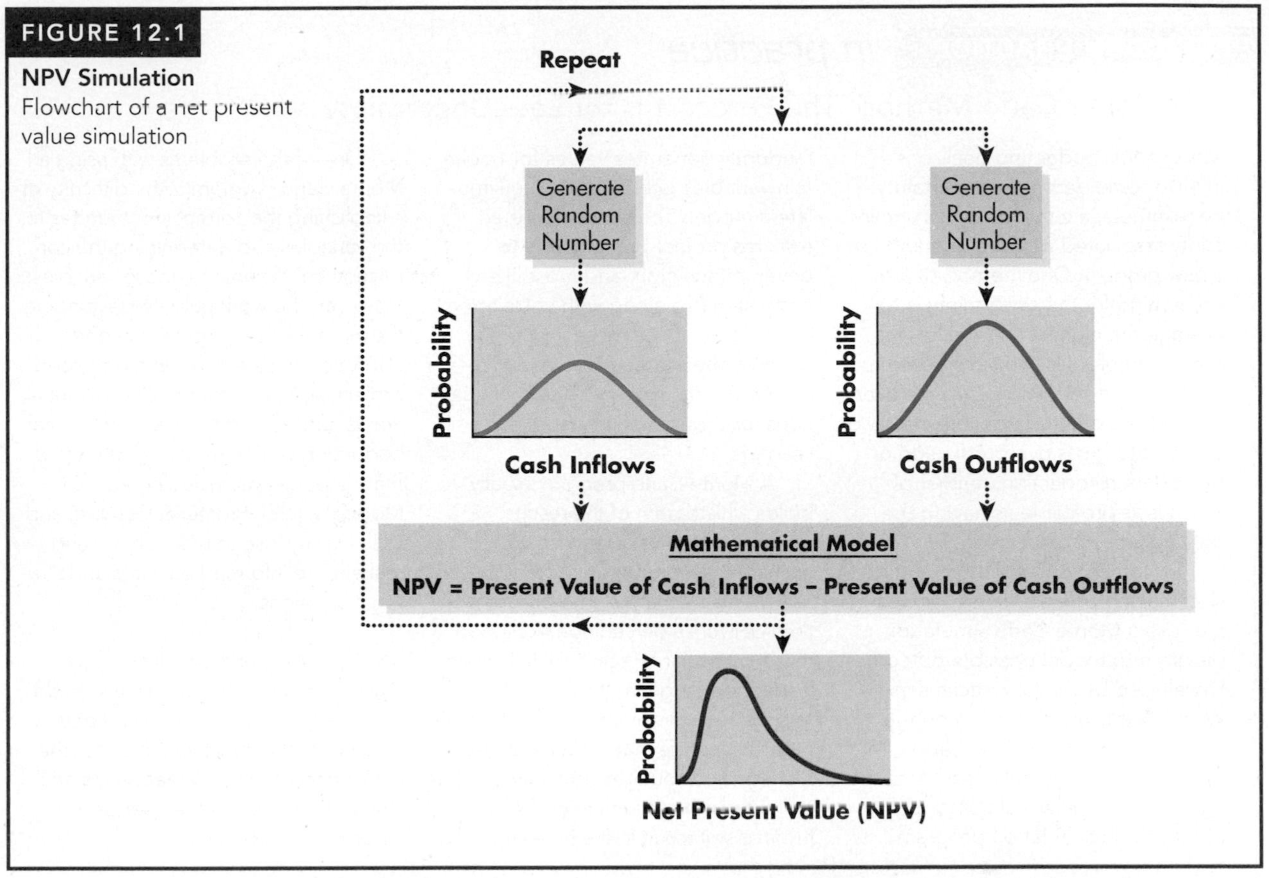

FIGURE 12.1

NPV Simulation
Flowchart of a net present value simulation

repeating the process numerous times, the financial manager can develop a probability distribution of project returns.

Figure 12.1 presents a flowchart of the simulation of the net present value of a project. The process of generating random numbers and using the probability distributions for cash inflows and cash outflows enables the financial manager to determine values for each of these variables. Substituting these values into the mathematical model results in an NPV. By repeating this process perhaps a thousand times, managers can create a probability distribution of net present values.

Although Figure 12.1 simulates only gross cash inflows and cash outflows, more sophisticated simulations using individual inflow and outflow components, such as sales volume, sale price, raw material cost, labor cost, and maintenance expense, are quite common. From the distribution of returns, the decision maker can determine not only the expected value of the return but also the probability of achieving or surpassing a given return. The use of computers has made the simulation approach feasible. Monte Carlo simulation programs, made popular by widespread use of personal computers, are described in the *Focus on Practice* box.

The output of simulation provides an excellent basis for decision making because it enables the decision maker to view a continuum of risk–return tradeoffs rather than a single-point estimate.

FOCUS ON PRACTICE *in practice*

The Monte Carlo Method: The Forecast Is for Less Uncertainty

Most capital budgeting decisions involve some degree of uncertainty. For example, a company faces uncertainty associated with the demand for a new product. One method of accounting for this uncertainty is to average the highest and the lowest prediction of sales. However, such a method is flawed. Producing the average of the expected possible demand can lead to gross overproduction or gross underproduction, neither of which is as profitable as having the right volume of production.

To combat uncertainty in the decision-making process, some companies use a Monte Carlo simulation program to model possible outcomes. Developed by mathematicians in World War II while working on the atomic bomb, the *Monte Carlo method* was not widely used until the advent of the personal computer. A Monte Carlo simulation program randomly generates values for uncertain variables over and over to simulate a model. The simulation then requires project practitioners to develop low, high, and most likely cost estimates along with correlation coefficients. Once these inputs are derived, the Monte Carlo program can be run through just a few simulations, or thousands, in just a few seconds.

A Monte Carlo program usually builds a histogram of the results, referred to as a frequency chart, for each forecast or output cell that the user wants to analyze. The program then delivers a percentage likelihood that a particular forecast will fall within a specified range, much like a weather forecast. The program also has an optimization feature that allows a project manager with budget constraints to figure out which combination of possible projects will result in the highest profit.

One of the problems with using a Monte Carlo program is the difficulty of establishing the correct input ranges for the variables and determining the correlation coefficients for those variables. However, the work put into developing the input for the program can often clarify some uncertainty in a proposed project. Although Monte Carlo simulation is not the perfect answer to capital budgeting problems, it is another tool that corporations, including ALCOA, Motorola, Intel, Procter & Gamble, and Walt Disney, use to manage risk and make more informed business and strategic decisions.

► *A Monte Carlo simulation program requires the user to first build an Excel spreadsheet model that captures the input variables for the proposed project. What issues and what benefits can the user derive from this process?*

→ REVIEW QUESTIONS MyLab Finance Solutions

12–2 Define risk in terms of the cash flows from a capital budgeting project. How can determination of the breakeven cash inflow be used to gauge project risk?

12–3 Describe how each of the following behavioral approaches can be used to deal with project risk: (**a**) scenario analysis and (**b**) simulation.

→ EXCEL REVIEW QUESTION MyLab Finance Solution

12–4 To judge the sensitivity of a project's NPV, financial managers will often compare a project's forecasted cash inflows to the breakeven cash flows. Using the information provided at MyLab Finance, develop a spreadsheet to compare forecasted and breakeven cash inflows.

12.3 International Risk Considerations

Although the basic techniques of capital budgeting are the same for multinational companies (MNCs) as for purely domestic firms, firms that operate in several countries face risks unique to the international arena. Two types of risk—exchange rate risk and political risk—are particularly important.

exchange rate risk
The danger that an unexpected change in the exchange rate between the dollar and the currency in which a project's cash flows are denominated will reduce the market value of that project's cash flow.

Exchange rate risk reflects the danger that an unexpected change in the exchange rate between the dollar and the currency in which a project's cash flows are denominated will reduce the market value of that project's cash flow. The dollar value of future cash inflows can be dramatically altered if the local currency depreciates against the dollar. In the short term, specific cash flows can be hedged by using financial instruments such as currency futures and options. Long-term exchange rate risk can best be minimized by financing the project, in whole or in part, in local currency.

Political risk is much harder to protect against. Firms that make investments abroad may find that the host-country government can limit the firm's ability to return profits back home. Governments can seize the firm's assets or otherwise interfere with a project's operation. The difficulties of managing political risk after the fact underscore the importance of accounting for political risks before making an investment. Managers can do so either by adjusting a project's expected cash inflows to account for the probability of political interference or by using risk-adjusted discount rates (discussed later in this chapter) in capital budgeting formulas. In general, it is much better to adjust individual project cash flows for political risk subjectively than to use a blanket adjustment for all projects.

MATTER OF FACT

Adjusting for Currency Risk

A survey of chief financial officers (CFOs) found that more than 40% of the CFOs believed it was important to adjust an investment project's cash flows or discount rates to account for foreign exchange risk.

In addition to unique risks that MNCs must face, several other special issues are relevant only for international capital budgeting. One of these special issues is taxes. Because only after-tax cash flows are relevant for capital budgeting, financial managers must carefully account for taxes paid to foreign governments on profits earned within their borders. They must also assess the impact of these tax payments on the parent company's U.S. tax liability.

Another special issue in international capital budgeting is *transfer pricing.* Much of the international trade involving MNCs is, in reality, simply the shipment of goods and services from one of a parent company's subsidiaries to another subsidiary located abroad. The parent company therefore has some discretion in setting **transfer prices**, the prices that subsidiaries charge each other for the goods and services traded between them. The widespread use of transfer pricing in international trade makes capital budgeting in MNCs very difficult unless the transfer prices that are used accurately reflect actual costs and incremental cash flows.

transfer prices
Prices that subsidiaries charge each other for the goods and services traded between them.

Finally, MNCs often must approach international capital projects from a strategic, rather than strictly financial, point of view. For example, an MNC may feel compelled to invest in a country to ensure continued access, even if the project itself may not have a positive net present value. This motivation was important for Japanese automakers that set up assembly plants in the United States in the early 1980s. For much the same reason, U.S. investment in Europe surged during the years before the market integration of the European Community in 1992. MNCs often invest in production facilities in the home country of major rivals to deny these competitors an uncontested home market. MNCs also may feel compelled to invest in certain industries or countries to achieve a broad corporate objective, such as completing a product line or diversifying raw material sources, even when the project's cash flows may not be sufficiently profitable.

→ REVIEW QUESTION MyLab Finance Solution

12–5 Briefly explain how the following items affect the capital budgeting decisions of multinational companies: (a) exchange rate risk; (b) political risk; (c) tax law differences; (d) transfer pricing; and (e) a strategic, rather than a strictly financial, viewpoint.

LG 4

12.4 Risk-Adjusted Discount Rates

The approaches for dealing with risk that have been presented so far enable the financial manager to get a "feel" for project risk. Unfortunately, they do not explicitly recognize project risk. We will now illustrate the most popular risk-adjustment technique that uses the net present value (NPV) decision method. The NPV decision rule of accepting only those projects with NPVs > \$0 will continue to hold. Close examination of the basic equation for NPV, Equation 10.1, should make it clear that because the initial investment (CF_0) is known with certainty, a project's risk is embodied in the present value of its cash inflows:

$$NPV = \sum_{t=1}^{n} \frac{CF_t}{(1 + r)^t} - CF_0$$

Two opportunities to adjust the present value of cash inflows for risk exist: (1) The cash inflows (CF_t) can be adjusted, or (2) the discount rate (r) can be adjusted. Adjusting the cash inflows is highly subjective, so here we describe the more common process of adjusting the discount rate. In addition, we consider the portfolio effects of project analysis as well as the practical aspects of the risk-adjusted discount rate.

DETERMINING RISK-ADJUSTED DISCOUNT RATES (RADRS)

A popular approach for risk adjustment involves the use of risk-adjusted discount rates (RADRs). This approach uses Equation 10.1 but employs a risk-adjusted discount rate, as noted in the following expression:[2]

$$NPV = \sum_{t=1}^{n} \frac{CF_t}{(1 + RADR)^t} - CF_0 \tag{12.2}$$

risk-adjusted discount rate (RADR)
The rate of return that must be earned on a given project to compensate the firm's owners adequately, that is, to maintain or improve the firm's share price.

The **risk-adjusted discount rate (RADR)** is the rate of return that must be earned on a given project to compensate the firm's owners adequately (i.e., to maintain or improve the firm's share price). The higher the risk of a project, the higher the RADR and therefore the lower the net present value for a given stream of cash inflows.

PERSONAL FINANCE EXAMPLE 12.3 Talor Namtig is considering investing \$1,000 in either of two stocks, A or B. She plans to hold the stock for exactly 5 years and expects both stocks to pay \$80 in annual end-of-year cash dividends. After 5 years, she estimates that she will sell stock A for \$1,200 and stock B for \$1,500. Talor has carefully researched the two stocks and believes that although stock A has average risk, stock B is considerably riskier. Her research indicates that she should earn an annual return on an average-risk stock of 11%. Because stock B is considerably riskier, she will require a 14%

2. The risk-adjusted discount rate approach can be applied in using the internal rate of return as well as the net present value. When the IRR is used, the risk-adjusted discount rate becomes the hurdle rate that the IRR must exceed for acceptance of the project. When NPV is used, the projected cash inflows are merely discounted at the risk-adjusted discount rate.

return from it. Talor makes the following calculations to find the risk-adjusted net present values (NPVs) for the two stocks:

$$NPV_A = \frac{\$80}{(1+0.11)^1} + \frac{\$80}{(1+0.11)^2} + \frac{\$80}{(1+0.11)^3} + \frac{\$80}{(1+0.11)^4} + \frac{\$80}{(1+0.11)^5} + \frac{\$1{,}200}{(1+0.11)^5} - \$1{,}000 = \underline{\underline{\$7.81}}$$

$$NPV_B = \frac{\$80}{(1+0.14)^1} + \frac{\$80}{(1+0.14)^2} + \frac{\$80}{(1+0.14)^3} + \frac{\$80}{(1+0.14)^4} + \frac{\$80}{(1+0.14)^5} + \frac{\$1{,}500}{(1+0.14)^5} - \$1{,}000 = \underline{\underline{\$53.70}}$$

Although Talor's calculations indicate that both stock investments are acceptable (NPVs $> \$0$) on a risk-adjusted basis, she should invest in Stock B because it has a higher NPV.

Because the logic underlying the use of RADRs is closely linked to the capital asset pricing model (CAPM) developed in Chapter 8, here we review that model and discuss its use in finding RADRs.

Review of CAPM

In Chapter 8, we used the capital asset pricing model (CAPM) to link the relevant risk and return for all assets traded in efficient markets. In the development of the CAPM, the total risk of an asset was defined as

$$\text{Total risk} = \text{Nondiversifiable risk} + \text{Diversifiable risk} \quad (12.3)$$

For assets traded in an efficient market, the diversifiable risk, which results from uncontrollable or random events, can be eliminated through diversification. The relevant risk is therefore the nondiversifiable risk, the risk for which owners of these assets are rewarded. Nondiversifiable risk for securities is commonly measured by using beta, which is an index of the degree of movement of an asset's return in response to a change in the market return.

Using beta, β_j, to measure the relevant risk of any asset j, the CAPM is

$$r_j = R_F + [\beta_j \times (r_m - R_F)] \quad (12.4)$$

where

r_j = required return on asset j
R_F = risk-free rate of return
β_j = beta coefficient for asset j
r_m = return on the market portfolio of assets

In Chapter 8, we demonstrated that the required return on any asset could be determined by substituting values of R_F, β_j, and r_m into the CAPM (Equation 12.4). Any security expected to earn in excess of its required return would be acceptable, and those expected to earn an inferior return would be rejected.

FIGURE 12.2

CAPM and SML
CAPM and SML in capital budgeting decision making

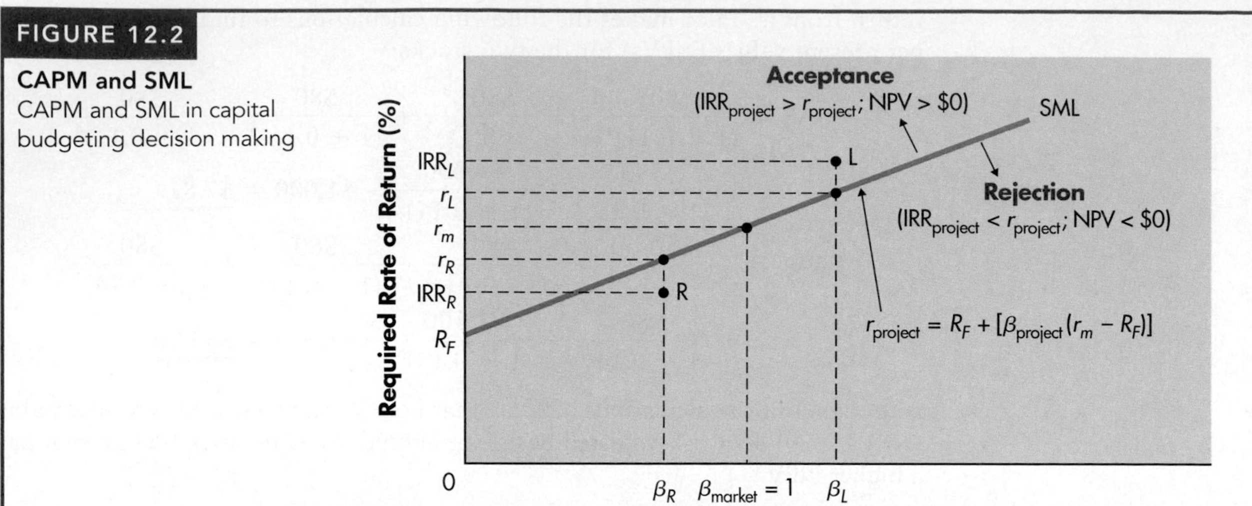

Using CAPM to Find RADRs

If we assume for a moment that real corporate assets such as computers, machine tools, and special-purpose machinery are traded in efficient markets, the CAPM can be redefined as

$$r_{\text{project } j} = R_F + [\beta_{\text{project } j} \times (r_m - R_F)] \tag{12.5}$$

The *security market line* (SML)—the graphical depiction of the CAPM—is shown for Equation 12.5 in Figure 12.2. Any project having an IRR above the SML would be acceptable because its IRR would exceed the required return, r_{project}; any project with an IRR below r_{project} would be rejected. In terms of NPV, any project falling above the SML would have a positive NPV, and any project falling below the SML would have a negative NPV.[3]

EXAMPLE 12.4

Figure 12.2 shows two projects, L and R. Project L has a beta, β_L, and generates an internal rate of return, IRR$_L$. The required return for a project with risk β_L is r_L. Because project L generates a return greater than that required (IRR$_L > r_L$), this project is acceptable. Project L will have a positive NPV when its cash inflows are discounted at its required return, r_L. Project R, in contrast, generates an IRR below that required for its risk, β_R (IRR$_R < r_R$). This project will have a negative NPV when its cash inflows are discounted at its required return, r_R. Project R should be rejected.

3. Whenever the IRR is above the cost of capital or required return (IRR > r), the NPV is positive, and whenever the IRR is below the cost of capital or required return (IRR < r), the NPV is negative. Because by definition the IRR is the discount rate that causes NPV to equal zero and the IRR and NPV always agree on accept–reject decisions, the relationship noted in Figure 12.2 logically follows.

FOCUS ON ETHICS *in practice*

Remain Calm—All is Well

Legend holds that Nathan Meyer Rothschild, who got rich speculating on British government bonds after the battle of Waterloo, once said, "Buy when there's blood in the streets, even if it's your own." The image is unsettling, but his larger point—which was not about buying or selling *per se*—was sound. Rothschild meant to keep your head when others lose theirs. For a capital budgeter, this means remaining coolly focused on shareholder wealth, even when markets go berserk. Brexit offers a case in point.

The United Kingdom (U.K.) made history on Thursday, June 23, 2016 by voting to leave the European Union (E.U.). Britain's departure from the E.U., dubbed "Brexit" in the press, immediately roiled financial markets. Friday, the pound plunged to a 31-year low against the U.S. dollar. By Monday, the FTSE 100—a widely followed British stock index—was down nearly 6%. Then a miracle occurred; the FTSE rallied. By Wednesday the 29th, British stocks had more than erased all losses, and the financial press was touting "the Brexit Bounce." What's a British capital budgeter to do?

The answer is to look past market volatility to Net Present Value (NPV), calmly analyzing the implications of Brexit for project cash flows and discount rates. For U.K. firms dependent on trade with the other 27 E.U. countries (which collectively take 45% of British exports), Brexit probably means a decline in expected project cash flows. In addition, because Brexit is unprecedented, greater uncertainty attaches to any cash-flow forecast. This means hiking risk-adjusted discount rates. Together, lower expected cash flows and higher discount rates imply fewer positive NPV projects—as appears to have been the case for mergers under consideration. In the 11 weeks following the Brexit vote, the number of deals involving U.K companies fell by one-third (compared with 2015).

For British firms not as dependent on E.U. trade, assessing the impact of Brexit on project NPVs is trickier but starts with the British economy and the British pound. Other things equal, a stronger economy implies larger cash flows on U.K. projects. A weaker pound could also boost cash flows over the longer run by making British goods cheap enough to offset the loss of privileged access to E.U. markets. In the wake of the Brexit vote, some economists began predicting recession, but real growth in the U.K—while far from robust—remained positive, at least through 2017. A full year after Brexit, the pound was still weak against both the Euro and U.S. dollar compared with pre-June 2016 levels. These factors may explain why the FTSE 100 gained 17% the year following the historic vote. Whatever the reason, capital budgeters in and outside Britain would do well to recall the implications of Rothschild's advice—when markets gyrate, stay focused on cash flows and discount rates.

► *Suppose you are a CEO and market turmoil from a shock unrelated to your company has your shareholders nervous. Nonetheless, you believe everything will blow over, leaving the company unaffected. What is your responsibility to shareholders?*

Faulconbridge, Guy; Kate Holton; and Andrew MacAskill. "Brexit Chills M&A Activity Despite Some Big Deals, Data Say," *Reuters*, September 12, 2016.

The *Focus on Ethics* box above describes a situation in which a political event in the United Kingdom prompted many firms in that country to rethink their project discount raters.

APPLYING RADRs

Because the CAPM is based on an assumed efficient market, which does not always exist for real corporate (nonfinancial) assets such as plant and equipment, managers sometimes argue that the CAPM is not directly applicable in calculating RADRs. Instead, financial managers sometimes assess the total risk of a project and use it to determine the risk-adjusted discount rate (RADR), which can be used in Equation 12.2 to find the NPV.

To avoid damaging its market value, a firm must use the correct discount rate to evaluate a project. If a firm fails to incorporate all relevant risks in its decision-making process, it may discount a risky project's cash inflows at too low a rate and accept an otherwise unacceptable project. The firm's market price may drop later as investors recognize that the firm itself has become more risky. Conversely, if the firm discounts a project's cash inflows at too high a rate, it may reject an otherwise acceptable project. In this case, the firm's market price may drop because investors who believe that the firm is being overly conservative will sell their stock, applying downward pressure on the firm's market value.

Unfortunately, no formal mechanism is available for linking total project risk to the level of required return. As a result, most firms subjectively determine the RADR by adjusting their existing required return. They adjust it up or down, depending on whether the proposed project is more or less risky, respectively, than the average risk of the firm. This CAPM type of approach provides a "rough estimate" of the project risk and required return because both the project risk measure and the linkage between risk and required return are estimates.

EXAMPLE 12.5

Bennett Company wishes to use the risk-adjusted discount rate approach to determine, according to NPV, whether to implement project A or project B. In addition to the data presented in part A of Table 12.1, Bennett's management, after much analysis, subjectively assigned "risk indexes" of 1.6 to project A and 1.0 to project B. The risk index is merely a numerical scale used to classify project risk: Higher index values are assigned to higher-risk projects and vice versa. The CAPM-type relationship used by the firm to link risk (measured by the risk index) and the required return (RADR) are shown in the following table. Management developed this relationship after analyzing CAPM and the risk–return relationships of the projects they considered and implemented during the past few years.

	Risk index	Required return (RADR)
	0.0	6% (risk-free rate, R_F)
	0.2	7
	0.4	8
	0.6	9
	0.8	10
Project B →	1.0	11
	1.2	12
	1.4	13
Project A →	1.6	14
	1.8	16
	2.0	18

MyLab Finance Financial Calculator

Input	Function
−420000	CF_0
140000	C01
5	F01
14	I/Y
	CPT
	NPV

Solution 60,631

Input	Function
−450000	CF_0
280000	C01
120000	C02
100000	C03
3	F03
11	I/Y
	CPT
	NPV

Solution 97,984

Because project A is riskier than project B, its RADR of 14% is greater than project B's 11%. The net present value of each project, calculated using its RADR, is found as shown on the timelines in Figure 12.3. The results clearly show that project B is preferable because its risk-adjusted NPV of $97,984 is greater than the $60,631 risk-adjusted NPV for project A. As reflected by the NPVs in part B of Table 12.1, if the discount rates were not adjusted for risk, project A would be preferred to project B.

Calculator use We can again use the preprogrammed NPV function in a financial calculator to simplify the NPV calculation. The keystrokes for project A—the annuity—are as shown at the left. The keystrokes for project B—the mixed stream—are also shown at the left. The calculated NPVs for projects A and B of $60,631 and $97,984, respectively, agree with those shown in Figure 12.3.

Spreadsheet use Analysis of projects using risk-adjusted discount rates (RADRs) also can be performed as shown on the following Excel spreadsheet.

MyLab

	A	B	C	D
1	ANALYSIS OF PROJECTS USING RISK-ADJUSTED DISCOUNT RATES			
2	Year(s)	Cash Inflow	Present Value	Formulas for Calculated Values in Column C
3		Project A		
4	5	$140,000	$480,631	=–PV(C7,A4,B4,0,0)
5	Initial Investment		–$420,000	
6	Net Present Value		$60,631	=SUM(C4:C5)
7	Required Return (RADAR)		14%	
8		Project B		
9	1	$280,000	$252,252	=–PV(C17,A9,0,B9,0)
10	2	$120,000	$97,395	=–PV(C17,A10,0,B10,0)
11	3	$100,000	$73,119	=–PV(C17,A11,0,B11,0)
12	4	$100,000	$65,873	=–PV(C17,A12,0,B12,0)
13	5	$100,000	$59,345	=–PV(C17,A13,0,B13,0)
14	Initial Investment		–$450,000	
15	Net Present Value		$97,984	=SUM(C9:C14)
16	Required Return (RADAR)		11%	
17	Choice of project		B	=IF(C6>=C16,"A","B")

The minus signs appear before the entries in Cells C4 and C9:C13 to convert the results to positive values.

FIGURE 12.3

Calculation of NPVS for Bennett Company's Capital Expenditure Alternatives Using RADRs
Timelines depicting the cash flows and NPV calculations using RADRs for projects A and B

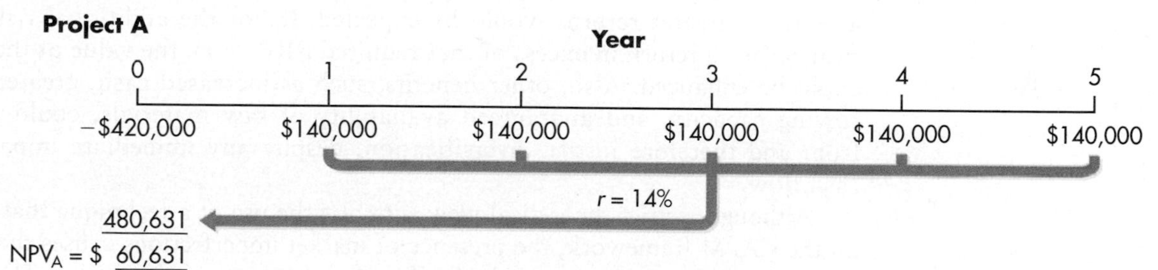

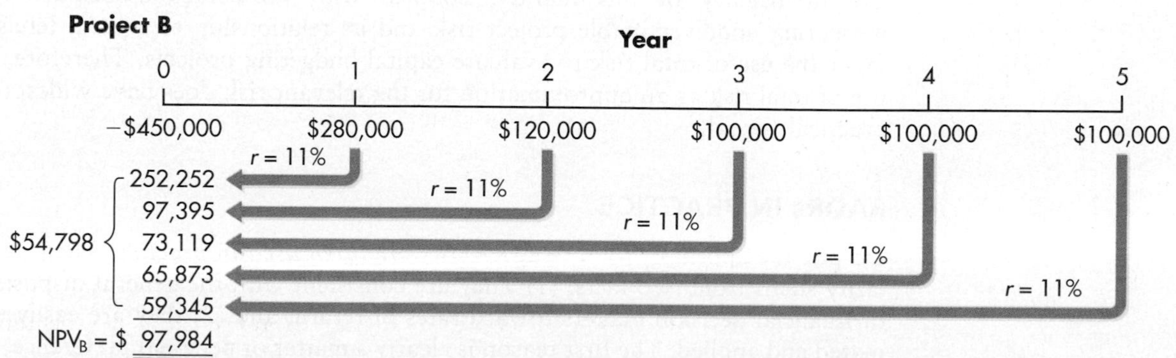

Note: When we use the risk indexes of 1.6 and 1.0 for projects A and B, respectively, along with the table above, a risk-adjusted discount rate (RADR) of 14% results for project A and an RADR of 11% results for project B.

The usefulness of risk-adjusted discount rates should now be clear. The real difficulty lies in estimating project risk and linking it to the required return (RADR).

PORTFOLIO EFFECTS

As noted in Chapter 8, because investors are not rewarded for taking diversifiable risk, they should hold a diversified portfolio of securities to eliminate that risk. Because a business firm can be viewed as a portfolio of assets, is it similarly important that the firm maintain a diversified portfolio of assets?

It seems logical that the firm could reduce the variability of its cash flows by holding a diversified portfolio. By combining two projects with negatively correlated cash inflows, the firm could reduce the combined cash inflow variability and therefore the risk.

Are firms rewarded for diversifying risk in this fashion? If they are, the value of the firm could be enhanced through diversification into other lines of business. Surprisingly, the value of the stock of firms whose shares are traded publicly in an efficient marketplace is generally not affected by diversification. In other words, diversification is not normally rewarded and therefore is generally not necessary.

Why are firms not rewarded for diversification? It is because investors themselves can diversify by holding securities in a variety of firms; they do not need the firm to do it for them. Investors can also diversify more readily. They can make transactions more easily and at a lower cost because of the greater availability of information and trading mechanisms.

Of course, if a firm acquires a new line of business and its cash flows tend to respond more to changing economic conditions (i.e., greater nondiversifiable risk), greater returns would be expected. If, for the additional risk, the firm earned a return in excess of that required ($\text{IRR} > r$), the value of the firm could be enhanced. Also, other benefits, such as increased cash, greater borrowing capacity, and guaranteed availability of raw materials, could result from and therefore justify diversification, despite any immediate impact on cash flow.

Although a strict theoretical view supports the use of a technique that relies on the CAPM framework, the presence of market imperfections causes the market for real corporate assets to be inefficient at least some of the time. The relative inefficiency of this market, coupled with difficulties associated with measuring nondiversifiable project risk and its relationship to return, tends to favor the use of total risk to evaluate capital budgeting projects. Therefore, the use of total risk as an approximation for the relevant risk does have widespread practical appeal.

RADRs IN PRACTICE

Despite the appeal of total risk, *RADRs are often used in practice.* Their popularity stems from two facts: (1) They are consistent with the general disposition of financial decision makers toward rates of return, and (2) they are easily estimated and applied. The first reason is clearly a matter of personal preference, but the second is based on the computational convenience and well-developed procedures involved in the use of RADRs.

TABLE 12.3 **Bennett Company's Risk Classes and RADRs**

Risk class	Description	Risk-adjusted discount rate, RADR
I	*Below-average risk:* Projects with low risk. Typically involve routine replacement without renewal of existing activities.	8%
II	*Average risk:* Projects similar to those currently implemented. Typically involve replacement or renewal of existing activities.	10%[a]
III	*Above-average risk:* Projects with higher than normal, but not excessive, risk. Typically involve expansion of existing or similar activities.	14%
IV	*Highest risk:* Projects with very high risk. Typically involve expansion into new or unfamiliar activities.	20%

[a]This RADR is actually the firm's cost of capital, which is discussed in detail in Chapter 9. It represents the firm's required return on its existing portfolio of projects, which is assumed to be unchanged with acceptance of the "average-risk" project.

In practice, firms often establish a number of *risk classes,* with a RADR assigned to each. Like the CAPM-type risk–return relationship described earlier, management develops the risk classes and RADRs based on both CAPM and the risk–return behaviors of past projects. The financial manager then subjectively places each new project in the appropriate risk class and uses the corresponding RADR to evaluate it. This evaluation is sometimes done on a division-by-division basis, in which case each division has its own set of risk classes and associated RADRs, similar to those for Bennett Company in Table 12.3. The use of *divisional costs of capital* and associated risk classes enables a large multidivisional firm to incorporate differing levels of divisional risk into the capital budgeting process and still recognize differences in the levels of individual project risk.

EXAMPLE 12.6

Assume that the management of Bennett Company decided to use risk classes to analyze projects and so placed each project in one of four risk classes according to its perceived risk. The classes ranged from I for the lowest-risk projects to IV for the highest-risk projects. Associated with each class was an RADR appropriate to the risk level of projects in the class, as given in Table 12.3. Bennett classified as lower-risk those projects that tend to involve routine replacement or renewal activities; higher-risk projects involve expansion, often into new or unfamiliar activities.

The financial manager of Bennett has assigned project A to class III and project B to class II. The cash flows for project A would be evaluated using a 14% RADR, and project B's would be evaluated using a 10% RADR.[4] The NPV of

4. Note that the 10% RADR for project B using the risk classes in Table 10.3 differs from the 11% RADR used in the preceding example for project B. This difference is attributable to the less precise nature of the use of risk classes.

project A at 14% was calculated in Figure 12.3 to be $60,631, and the NPV for project B at a 10% RADR was shown in Table 12.1 to be $109,244. Clearly, with RADRs based on the use of risk classes, project B is preferred over project A. As noted earlier, this result is contrary to the preferences shown in Table 12.1, where differing risks of projects A and B were not taken into account.

→ **REVIEW QUESTIONS** MyLab Finance Solutions

12–6 Describe the basic procedures involved in using risk-adjusted discount rates (RADRs). How is this approach related to the capital asset pricing model (CAPM)?

12–7 Explain why a firm whose stock is actively traded in the securities markets need not concern itself with diversification. Despite this reason, how is the risk of capital budgeting projects frequently measured? Why?

12–8 How are risk classes often used to apply RADRs?

12.5 Capital Budgeting Refinements

The manager must often make refinements in the analysis of capital budgeting projects to accommodate special circumstances. These adjustments permit the relaxation of certain simplifying assumptions presented earlier. Three areas frequently requiring special forms of analysis include (1) comparison of mutually exclusive projects having unequal lives, (2) recognition of real options, and (3) capital rationing caused by a binding budget constraint.

COMPARING PROJECTS WITH UNEQUAL LIVES

The financial manager must often select the best of a group of unequal-lived projects. If the projects are independent, the length of the project lives is not critical. But when unequal-lived projects are mutually exclusive, the impact of differing lives must be considered because the projects do not provide service over comparable time periods. This step is especially important when continuing service is needed from the project under consideration. The discussions that follow assume that the unequal-lived, mutually exclusive projects being compared are ongoing. If they were not, the project with the highest NPV would be selected.

The Problem

A simple example will demonstrate the general problem of noncomparability caused by the need to select the best of a group of mutually exclusive projects with differing usable lives.

EXAMPLE 12.7

The AT Company, a regional cable television company, is evaluating two projects, X and Y. The following table gives relevant cash flows for each project. The applicable cost of capital for use in evaluating these equally risky projects is 10%.

	Project X	Project Y
Initial investment	−$70,000	−$85,000
Year	Annual cash inflows	
1	$28,000	$35,000
2	33,000	30,000
3	38,000	25,000
4	–	20,000
5	–	15,000
6	–	10,000

MyLab Finance Financial Calculator

Input	Function
−70000	CF_0
28000	C01
33000	C02
38000	C03
10	I/Y
	CPT
	NPV

Solution 11,277.24

Input	Function
−85000	CF_0
35000	C01
30000	C02
25000	C03
20000	C04
15000	C05
10000	C06
10	I/Y
	CPT
	NPV

Solution 19,013.27

Calculator use With the preprogrammed NPV function in a financial calculator, we use the keystrokes shown at the left for project X and for project Y to find their respective NPVs of $11,277.24 and $19,013.27.

Spreadsheet use The net present values of two projects with unequal lives also can be compared as shown on the following Excel spreadsheet.

MyLab

	A	B	C
1	COMPARISON OF NET PRESENT VALUES OF TWO PROJECTS WITH UNEQUAL LIVES		
2		Cost of Capital	10%
3		Cash Flows	
4	Year	Project X	Project Y
5	0	−$70,000	−$85,000
6	1	$28,000	$35,000
7	2	$33,000	$30,000
8	3	$38,000	$25,000
9	4		$20,000
10	5		$15,000
11	6		$10,000
12	NPV	$11,277.24	$19,013.27
13	Choice of project		Project Y

Entry in Cell B12 is =NPV(C2,B6:B11)+B5.
Copy the entry in Cell B12 to Cell C12.
Entry in Cell C13 is
=IF(B12>C12,B4,IF(C12>B12,C4,"Indifferent")).

Ignoring the differences in project lives, we can see that both projects are acceptable (both NPVs are greater than zero) and that project Y is preferred over project X. If the projects were independent and only one could be accepted, project Y—with the larger NPV—would be preferred. If the projects were mutually exclusive, their differing lives would have to be considered. Project Y provides 3 more years of service than project X.

The analysis in the preceding example is incomplete if the projects are mutually exclusive (which will be our assumption throughout the remaining discussions). To compare these unequal-lived, mutually exclusive projects correctly, we must consider the differing lives in the analysis; an incorrect decision could result from simply using NPV to select the better project. Although a number of approaches are available for dealing with unequal lives, here we present the most efficient technique: the *annualized net present value (ANPV) approach*.

Annualized Net Present Value (ANPV) Approach

annualized net present value (ANPV) approach
An approach to evaluating unequal-lived projects that converts the net present value of unequal-lived, mutually exclusive projects into an equivalent annual amount (in NPV terms).

The **annualized net present value (ANPV) approach**[5] converts the net present value of unequal-lived, mutually exclusive projects into an equivalent annual amount (in NPV terms) that can help in selecting the best project.[6] This net present value–based approach can be applied to unequal-lived, mutually exclusive projects by using the following steps:

Step 1 Calculate the net present value of each project j, NPV_j, over its life, n_j, using the appropriate cost of capital, r.

Step 2 Convert the NPV_j into an annuity having life n_j. That is, find an annuity that has the same life and the same NPV as the project.

Step 3 Select the project that has the highest ANPV.

EXAMPLE 12.8

MyLab Finance Solution Video

MyLab Finance Financial Calculator

Input	Function
11277.24	PV
10	I/Y
3	N
	CPT
	PMT

Solution −4,534.74

Input	Function
19013.27	PV
10	I/Y
6	N
	CPT
	PMT

Solution −4,365.59

By using the AT Company data presented earlier for projects X and Y, we can apply the three-step ANPV approach as follows:

Step 1 The net present values of projects X and Y discounted at 10%—as calculated in the preceding example for a single purchase of each asset—are

$$NPV_X = \$11{,}277.24$$
$$NPV_Y = \$19{,}013.27$$

Step 2 In this step, we want to convert the NPVs from Step 1 into annuities. For project X, we are trying to find the answer to the question, what 3-year annuity (equal to the life of project X) has a present value of $11,277.24 (the NPV of project X)? Likewise, for project Y we want to know what 6-year annuity has a present value of $19,013.27. Once we have these values, we can determine which project, X or Y, delivers a higher annual cash flow on a present value basis.

Calculator use The keystrokes required to find the ANPV on a financial calculator are identical to those demonstrated in Chapter 5 for finding the annual payments on an installment loan. These keystrokes are shown at the left for project X and for project Y. The resulting ANPVs for projects X and Y are $4,534.74 and $4,365.59, respectively. (Note that the calculator solutions are shown as negative values because the PV inputs were entered as positive values.)

Spreadsheet use The annualized net present values of two projects with unequal lives also can be compared as shown on the following Excel spreadsheet.

---

5. This approach is also called the "equivalent annual annuity (EAA)" or the "equivalent annual cost." The term "annualized net present value" (ANPV) is used here due to its descriptive clarity.

6. The theory underlying this as well as other approaches for comparing projects with unequal lives assumes that each project can be replaced in the future for the same initial investment and that each will provide the same expected future cash inflows. Although changing technology and inflation will affect the initial investment and expected cash inflows, the lack of specific attention to them does not detract from the usefulness of this technique.

	A	B	C
1	COMPARISON OF ANNUALIZED NET PRESENT VALUES OF TWO PROJECTS WITH UNEQUAL LIVES		
2		Cost of Capital	10%
3		Cash Flows	
4	Year	Project X	Project Y
5	0	–$70,000	–$85,000
6	1	$28,000	$35,000
7	2	$33,000	$30,000
8	3	$38,000	$25,000
9	4		$20,000
10	5		$15,000
11	6		$10,000
12	NPV	$11,277.24	$19,013.27
13	ANPV	$4,534.74	$4,365.59
14	Choice of project		Project X

Entry in Cell B12 is =NPV(C2,B6:B11)+B5.
Copy the entry in Cell B12 to Cell C12.
Entry in Cell B13 is =–PMT(C2,A8,B12,0,0).
Entry in Cell C13 is =–PMT(C2,A11,C12,0,0).
Entry in Cell C14 is
=IF(B13>C13,B4,IF(C13>B13,C4,“Indifferent”)).

Step 3 Reviewing the ANPVs calculated in Step 2, we can see that project X would be preferred over project Y. Given that projects X and Y are mutually exclusive, project X would be the recommended project because it provides the higher annualized net present value.

RECOGNIZING REAL OPTIONS

real options
Opportunities that are embedded in capital projects and that enable managers to alter their cash flows and risk in a way that affects project acceptability (NPV). Also called *strategic options.*

The procedures described in Chapters 10 and 11 and thus far in this chapter suggest that to make capital budgeting decisions, we must (1) estimate relevant cash flows, (2) apply an appropriate decision technique such as NPV or IRR to those cash flows, and (3) recognize and adjust the decision technique for project risk. Although this traditional procedure is believed to yield good decisions, a more strategic approach has emerged in recent years. This more modern view considers any **real options**, opportunities embedded in capital projects (“real,” rather than financial, asset investments) that enable managers to alter their cash flows and risk in a way that affects project acceptability (NPV). Because these opportunities are more likely to exist in, and be more important to, large “strategic” capital budgeting projects, they are sometimes called strategic options.

Table 12.4 briefly describes some of the more common types of real options—abandonment, flexibility, growth, and timing. It should be clear from their descriptions that each of these option types could be embedded in a capital budgeting decision and that explicit recognition of them would probably alter the cash flow and risk of a project and change its NPV.

By explicitly recognizing real options when making capital budgeting decisions, managers can make improved, more strategic decisions that consider in advance the economic impact of certain contingent actions on project cash flow

TABLE 12.4 Major Types of Real Options

Option type	Description
Abandonment option	The option to abandon or terminate a project prior to the end of its planned life. This option allows management to avoid or minimize losses on projects that turn bad. Explicitly recognizing the abandonment option when evaluating a project often increases its NPV.
Flexibility option	The option to incorporate flexibility into the firm's operations, particularly production. It generally includes the opportunity to design the production process to accept multiple inputs, to use flexible production technology to create a variety of outputs by reconfiguring the same plant and equipment, and to purchase and retain excess capacity in capital-intensive industries subject to wide swings in output demand and long lead time in building new capacity from scratch. Recognition of this option embedded in a capital expenditure should increase the NPV of the project.
Growth option	The option to develop follow-on projects, expand markets, expand or retool plants, and so on that would not be possible without implementation of the project being evaluated. If a project being considered has the measurable potential to open new doors if successful, recognition of the cash flows from such opportunities should be included in the initial decision process. Growth opportunities embedded in a project often increase the NPV of the project in which they are embedded.
Timing option	The option to determine when various actions with respect to a given project are taken. This option recognizes the firm's opportunity to delay acceptance of a project for one or more periods, to accelerate or slow the process of implementing a project in response to new information, or to shut down a project temporarily in response to changing product market conditions or competition. As in the case of the other option types, the explicit recognition of timing opportunities can improve the NPV of a project that fails to recognize this option in an investment decision.

and risk. Such recognition will cause the project's strategic NPV to differ from its traditional NPV, as indicated by Equation 12.6.

$$NPV_{strategic} = NPV_{traditional} + \text{Value of real options} \tag{12.6}$$

Application of this relationship is illustrated in the following example.

EXAMPLE 12.9

Assume that a strategic analysis of Bennett Company's projects A and B (see cash flows and NPVs in Table 12.1) finds no real options embedded in project A and two real options embedded in project B. The two real options in project B are as follows: (1) The project would have, during the first 2 years, some downtime resulting in unused production capacity that could be applied to contract manufacturing for another firm; and (2) the project's computerized control system could, with some modification, control two other machines, thereby reducing labor cost, without affecting operation of the new project.

Bennett's management estimated the NPV of the contract manufacturing over the 2 years following implementation of project B to be \$27,000 and the NPV of the computer control sharing to be \$22,000. Management believed there was a 60% chance that the contract manufacturing option would be exercised and only a 30% chance that the computer control sharing option would be exercised. The combined value of these two real options would be the sum of their expected values:

$$\begin{aligned}\text{Value of real options for project B} &= (0.60 \times \$27{,}000) + (0.30 \times \$22{,}000)\\ &= \$16{,}200 + \$6{,}600 = \$22{,}800\end{aligned}$$

Substituting the $22,800 real options value along with the traditional NPV of $109,244 for project B (from Table 12.1) into Equation 12.6, we get the strategic NPV for project B:

$$NPV_{strategic} = \$109,244 + \$22,800 = \underline{\underline{\$132,044}}$$

Bennett Company's project B therefore has a strategic NPV of $132,044, which is above its traditional NPV and now exceeds project A's NPV of $110,710. Clearly, recognition of project B's real options improved its NPV (from $109,244 to $132,044) and causes it to be preferred over project A (NPV of $132,044 for B > NPV of $110,710 for A), which has no real options embedded in it.

It is important to realize that recognition of attractive real options when determining NPV could cause an otherwise unacceptable project ($NPV_{traditional} < \$0$) to become acceptable ($NPV_{strategic} > \$0$). The failure to recognize the value of real options could therefore cause management to reject acceptable projects. Although discerning embedded real options requires more strategic thinking and analysis, it is important for the financial manager to identify and incorporate real options in the NPV process. The procedures for doing so efficiently are emerging, and the use of the strategic NPV that incorporates real options is expected to become more commonplace in the future.

CAPITAL RATIONING

Firms commonly operate under *capital rationing* in that they have more acceptable independent projects than they can fund. In theory, capital rationing should not exist. Firms should accept all projects that have positive NPVs (or IRRs > the cost of capital). However, in practice, most firms operate under capital rationing. Generally, firms attempt to isolate and select the best acceptable projects subject to a capital expenditure budget set by management. Research has found that management internally imposes capital expenditure constraints to avoid what it deems to be "excessive" levels of new financing, particularly debt. Although failing to fund all acceptable independent projects is theoretically inconsistent with the goal of maximizing owner wealth, here we will discuss capital rationing procedures because they are widely used in practice.

The objective of capital rationing is to select the group of projects that provides the highest overall net present value and does not require more dollars than are budgeted. As a prerequisite to capital rationing, the best of any mutually exclusive projects must be chosen and placed in the group of independent projects. Next we discuss two basic approaches to project selection under capital rationing.

internal rate of return approach
An approach to capital rationing that involves graphing project IRRs in descending order against the total dollar investment to determine the group of acceptable projects.

investment opportunities schedule (IOS)
The graph that plots project IRRs in descending order against the total dollar investment.

Internal Rate of Return Approach

The **internal rate of return approach** involves graphing project IRRs in descending order against the total dollar investment. This graph is called the **investment opportunities schedule (IOS)**. By drawing the cost-of-capital line and then imposing a budget constraint, the financial manager can determine the group of acceptable projects. The problem with this technique is that it does not guarantee the maximum dollar return to the firm. It merely provides an intuitively appealing solution to capital rationing problems.

EXAMPLE 12.10

MyLab Finance Solution Video

Tate Company, a fast-growing plastics company, is confronted with six projects competing for its fixed budget of $250,000. The initial investment and IRR for each project are as follows:

Project	Initial investment	IRR
A	–$ 80,000	12%
B	–70,000	20
C	–100,000	16
D	–40,000	8
E	–60,000	15
F	–110,000	11

The firm has a cost of capital of 10%. Figure 12.4 presents the IOS that results from ranking the six projects in descending order on the basis of their IRRs. According to the schedule, only projects B, C, and E should be accepted. Together they will absorb $230,000 of the $250,000 budget. Projects A and F are acceptable but cannot be chosen because of the budget constraint. Project D is not worthy of consideration; its IRR is less than the firm's 10% cost of capital.

The drawback of this approach is that it offers no guarantee that the acceptance of projects B, C, and E will maximize total dollar returns and therefore owners' wealth.

net present value approach
An approach to capital rationing that is based on the use of present values to determine the group of projects that will maximize owners' wealth.

Net Present Value Approach

The **net present value approach** is based on the use of present values to determine the group of projects that will maximize owners' wealth. It is implemented by ranking projects on the basis of IRRs and then evaluating the present value of the

FIGURE 12.4

Investment Opportunities Schedule
Investment opportunities schedule (IOS) for Tate Company projects

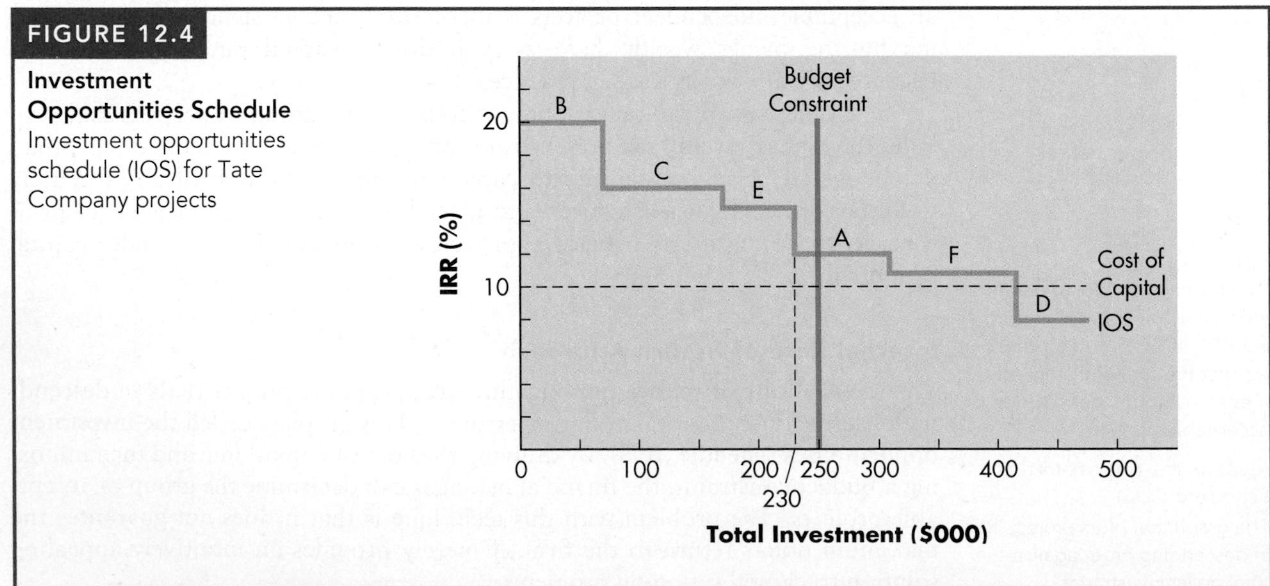

TABLE 12.5 **Rankings for Tate Company Projects**

Project	Initial investment	IRR	Present value of inflows at 10%	
B	−$ 70,000	20%	$112,000	
C	−100,000	16	145,000	
E	−60,000	15	79,000	
A	−80,000	12	100,000	
F	−110,000	11	126,500	Cutoff point
D	−40,000	8	36,000	(IRR < 10%)

benefits from each potential project to determine the combination of projects with the highest overall present value. This method is the same as maximizing net present value because the entire budget is viewed as the total initial investment. Any portion of the firm's budget that is not used does not increase the firm's value. At best, the unused money can be invested in marketable securities or returned to the owners in the form of cash dividends. In either case, the wealth of the owners is not likely to be enhanced.

EXAMPLE 12.11

The projects described in the preceding example are ranked in Table 12.5 on the basis of IRRs. The present value of the cash inflows associated with the projects is also included in the table. Projects B, C, and E, which together require $230,000, yield a present value of $336,000. However, if projects B, C, and A were implemented, the total budget of $250,000 would be used, and the present value of the cash inflows would be $357,000, which is greater than the return expected from selecting the projects on the basis of the highest IRRs. Implementing B, C, and A is preferable because they maximize the present value for the given budget. The firm's objective is to use its budget to generate the highest present value of inflows. Assuming that any unused portion of the budget does not gain or lose money, the total NPV for projects B, C, and E would be $106,000 ($336,000 − $230,000), whereas the total NPV for projects B, C, and A would be $107,000 ($357,000 − $250,000). Selection of projects B, C, and A will therefore maximize NPV.

→ **REVIEW QUESTIONS** MyLab Finance Solutions

12–9 Explain why a mere comparison of the NPVs of unequal-lived, ongoing, mutually exclusive projects is inappropriate. Describe the annualized net present value (ANPV) approach for comparing unequal-lived, mutually exclusive projects.

12–10 What are real options? What are some major types of real options?

12–11 What is the difference between the strategic NPV and the traditional NPV? Do they always result in the same accept–reject decisions?

12–12 What is capital rationing? In theory, should capital rationing exist? Why does it frequently occur in practice?

12–13 Compare and contrast the internal rate of return approach and the net present value approach to capital rationing. Which is better? Why?

→ EXCEL REVIEW QUESTION MyLab Finance Solution

12–14 Comparing projects with unequal lives is often done by comparing the projects' annualized net present value. With the information provided at MyLab Finance, use a spreadsheet to compare projects based on their ANPV.

SUMMARY

FOCUS ON VALUE

Not all capital budgeting projects have the same risk as the firm's existing portfolio of projects. The financial manager must adjust projects for differences in risk when evaluating their acceptability. Without such an adjustment, management could mistakenly accept projects that destroy shareholder value or could reject projects that create shareholder value. To ensure that neither of these outcomes occurs, the financial manager must make certain that only those projects creating shareholder value are recommended.

Risk-adjusted discount rates (RADRs) provide a mechanism for adjusting the discount rate to make it consistent with the risk–return preferences of market participants. Procedures for comparing projects with unequal lives, for explicitly recognizing real options embedded in capital projects, and for selecting projects under capital rationing enable the financial manager to refine the capital budgeting process further. These procedures, along with risk-adjustment techniques, should enable the financial manager to make capital budgeting decisions that are consistent with the firm's goal of **maximizing stock price.**

REVIEW OF LEARNING GOALS

LG 1 **Understand the importance of recognizing risk in the analysis of capital budgeting projects.** The cash flows associated with capital budgeting projects typically have different levels of risk, and the acceptance of a project generally affects the firm's overall risk. Thus, it is important to incorporate risk considerations in capital budgeting. Various behavioral approaches can help the manager to get a "feel" for the level of project risk. Other approaches explicitly recognize project risk in the analysis of capital budgeting projects.

LG 2 **Discuss breakeven analysis, scenario analysis, and simulation as behavioral approaches for dealing with risk.** Risk in capital budgeting is the degree of variability of cash flows, which for conventional capital budgeting projects stems almost entirely from net cash flows. Finding the breakeven cash inflow and estimating the probability that it will be realized make up one behavioral approach for assessing capital budgeting risk. Scenario analysis is another behavioral approach for capturing the variability of cash inflows and NPVs. Simulation is a statistically based approach that results in a probability distribution of project returns.

LG 3 **Review the unique risks that multinational companies face.** Although the basic capital budgeting techniques are the same for multinational and purely domestic companies, firms that operate in several countries must also deal with exchange rate and political risks, tax law differences, transfer pricing, and strategic issues.

LG 4 **Describe the determination and use of risk-adjusted discount rates (RADRs), portfolio effects, and the practical aspects of RADRs.** The risk of a project whose initial investment is known with certainty is embodied in the present value of its cash inflows, using NPV. There are two opportunities to adjust the present value of cash inflows for risk: (1) adjust the cash inflows or (2) adjust the discount rate. Because adjusting the cash inflows is highly subjective, adjusting discount rates is more popular. RADRs use a market-based adjustment of the discount rate to calculate NPV. The RADR is closely linked to CAPM, but because real corporate assets are generally not traded in an efficient market, the CAPM cannot be applied directly to capital budgeting. Instead, firms develop some CAPM-type relationship to link a project's risk to its required return, which is used as the discount rate. Often, for convenience, firms will rely on total risk as an approximation for relevant risk when estimating required project returns. RADRs are commonly used in practice because decision makers find rates of return easy to estimate and apply.

LG 5 **Select the best of a group of unequal-lived, mutually exclusive projects using annualized net present values (ANPVs).** The ANPV approach is the most efficient method of comparing ongoing, mutually exclusive projects that have unequal usable lives. It converts the NPV of each unequal-lived project into an equivalent annual amount, its ANPV. The ANPV can be calculated using equations, a financial calculator, or a spreadsheet. The project with the highest ANPV is best.

LG 6 **Explain the role of real options and the objective and procedures for selecting projects under capital rationing.** Real options are opportunities that are embedded in capital projects and that allow managers to alter their cash flow and risk in a way that affects project acceptability (NPV). By explicitly recognizing real options, the financial manager can find a project's strategic NPV. Some of the more common types of real options are abandonment, flexibility, growth, and timing options. The strategic NPV improves the quality of the capital budgeting decision.

Capital rationing exists when firms have more acceptable independent projects than they can fund. Capital rationing commonly occurs in practice. Its objective is to select from all acceptable projects the group that provides the highest overall net present value and does not require more dollars than are budgeted. The two basic approaches for choosing projects under capital rationing are the internal rate of return approach and the net present value approach. The NPV approach better achieves the objective of using the budget to generate the highest present value of inflows.

OPENER-IN-REVIEW

The chapter opener describes the expropriation of a General Motors investment in a Venezuelan factory. If you were a financial analyst at GM, how might you use scenario analysis to evaluate the risk of investing in a plant in Venezuela?

SELF-TEST PROBLEM (Solutions in Appendix)

IRF

ST12–1 Risk-adjusted discount rates CBA Company is considering two mutually exclusive projects, A and B. The following table shows the CAPM-type relationship between a risk index and the required return (RADR) applicable to CBA Company.

Risk index	Required return (RADR)
0.0	7.0% (risk-free rate, R_F)
0.2	8.0
0.4	9.0
0.6	10.0
0.8	11.0
1.0	12.0
1.2	13.0
1.4	14.0
1.6	15.0
1.8	16.0
2.0	17.0

Project data are as follows:

	Project A	Project B
Initial investment (CF_0)	−\$15,000	−\$20,000
Project life	3 years	3 years
Annual cash inflow (CF)	\$7,000	\$10,000
Risk index	0.4	1.8

a. Ignoring any differences in risk and assuming that the firm's cost of capital is 10%, calculate the net present value (NPV) of each project.

b. Use NPV to evaluate the projects, using risk-adjusted discount rates (RADRs) to account for risk.

c. Compare, contrast, and explain your findings in parts **a** and **b**.

WARM-UP EXERCISES All problems are available in MyLab Finance.

E12–1 Birkenstock is considering an investment in a nylon-knitting machine. The machine requires an initial investment of \$27,000, has a 5-year life, and has no residual value at the end of the 5 years. The company's cost of capital is 10.87%. Known with less certainty are the actual after-tax cash inflows for each of the 5 years. The company has estimated expected cash inflows for three scenarios: pessimistic, most likely, and optimistic. These expected cash inflows are listed in the following table. Calculate the range for the NPV given each scenario.

	Expected cash inflows		
Year	Pessimistic	Most likely	Optimistic
1	$6,750	$ 9,250	$11,750
2	7,250	10,250	13,250
3	8,750	11,750	15,750
4	7,750	10,750	12,750
5	5,750	7,750	8,750

LG2 **E12–2** You wish to evaluate a project requiring an initial investment of $59,500 and having a useful life of 7 years. What minimum amount of annual cash inflow do you need if your firm has an 8.7% cost of capital? If the project is forecast to earn $11,400 per year over the 7 years, what is its IRR? Is the project acceptable?

LG4 **E12–3** Like most firms in its industry, Culinary Cafe uses a subjective risk assessment tool of its own design. The tool is a simple index by which projects are ranked by level of perceived risk on a scale of 0 to 10. The scale is re-created in the following table.

Risk index	Required return
0	4.0% (current risk-free rate)
1	4.5
2	5.0
3	5.5
4	6.0
5	6.5 (current IRR)
6	7.0
7	7.5
8	8.0
9	8.5
10	9.0

The firm is analyzing two projects based on their RADRs. Project Pita requires an initial investment of $12,500 and is assigned a risk index of 6. Project Grape Leaf requires an initial investment of $7,500 and is assigned a risk index of 8. The two projects have 7-year lives. Pita is projected to generate cash inflows of $5,500 per year. Grape Leaf is projected to generate cash inflows of $4,000 per year. Use each project's RADR to select the better project.

LG5 **E12–4** Fiftycent Inc. has hired you to advise the firm on a capital budgeting issue involving two unequal-lived, mutually exclusive projects, S and T. The cash flows for each project are presented in the following table. Calculate the NPV and the annualized net present value (ANPV) for each project, using the firm's cost of capital of 9%. Which project would you recommend?

	Project S	Project T
Initial investment	−$42,000	−$67,500
Year	Cash inflows	
1	$17,750	$26,400
2	24,600	22,600
3	36,800	37,000
4	–	19,700
5	–	10,900
6	–	15,350
7	–	9,780

E12–5 Powerswitch Electric is faced with a capital budget of $150,000 for the coming year. It is considering six investment projects and has a cost of capital of 7%. The six projects along with their initial investments and their IRRs are listed in the following table. Using the data given, prepare an investment opportunities schedule (IOS). Which projects does the IOS suggest should be funded? Does this group of projects maximize NPV? Explain.

Project	Initial investment	IRR
1	−$75,000	8%
2	−40,000	10
3	−35,000	7
4	−50,000	11
5	−45,000	9
6	−20,000	6

PROBLEMS

All problems are available in MyLab Finance. The MyLab icon indicates problems in Excel format available in MyLab Finance.

P12–1 **Recognizing risk** Spin Corp., a media services firm with net earnings of $3,200,000 in the past year, is considering the following projects.

Project	Initial investment	Details
A	−$ 35,000	Replace existing office furnishings.
B	−500,000	Purchase digital video editing equipment for use with several existing accounts.
C	−450,000	Develop proposal to bid for a $2,000,000 per year 10-year contract with the U.S. Navy, not now an account.
D	−685,000	Purchase the exclusive rights to market a quality educational television program in syndication to local markets in the European Union, a part of the firm's existing business activities.

The media services business is cyclical and highly competitive. The board of directors has asked you, as chief financial officer, to do the following:

a. Evaluate the risk of each proposed project and rank it "low," "medium," or "high."
b. Comment on why you chose each ranking.

LG2

P12–2 Breakeven cash inflows The Sleek Ring Company, a leading producer of fine cast silver jewelry, is considering the purchase of new casting equipment that will allow it to expand its product line. The up-front cost of the equipment is $690,000. The company expects the equipment to produce steady income throughout its 15-year life.

a. If Sleek Ring requires an 8% return on its investment, what minimum yearly cash inflow will be necessary for the company to go forward with this project?
b. How would the minimum yearly cash inflow change if the company required an 11% return on its investment?

LG2

P12–3 Breakeven cash inflows and risk Boardman Gasses and Chemicals is a supplier of highly purified gases to semiconductor manufacturers. A large chip producer has asked Boardman to build a new gas production facility close to an existing semiconductor plant. Once the new gas plant is in place, Boardman will be the exclusive supplier for that semiconductor fabrication plant for the subsequent 10 years. Boardman is considering one of two plant designs. The first is for Boardman's "standard" plant, which will cost $38.5 million to build. The second is for a "custom" plant, which will cost $53.5 million to build. The custom plant will allow Boardman to produce the highly specialized gases required for an emerging semiconductor manufacturing process. Boardman estimates that its client will order $12.5 million of product per year if the standard plant is constructed, but if the custom design is put in place, Boardman expects to sell $17.5 million worth of product annually to its client. Boardman has enough money to build either type of plant, and, in the absence of risk differences, accepts the project with the highest NPV. The cost of capital is 16.9%.

a. Find the NPV for each project. Are the projects acceptable?
b. Find the breakeven cash inflow for each project.
c. The firm has estimated the probabilities of achieving various ranges of cash inflows for the two projects as shown in the following table. What is the probability that each project will achieve at least the breakeven cash inflow found in part **b**?

	Probability of achieving cash inflow in given range	
Range of cash inflow ($ millions)	**Standard Plant**	**Custom Plant**
$0–$5	0%	5%
$5–$8	10	10
$8–$11	60	15
$11–$14	25	25
$14–$17	5	20
$17–$20	0	15
Above $20	0	10

d. Which project is more risky? Which project has the potentially higher NPV? Discuss the risk–return tradeoffs of the two projects.
e. If the firm wished to minimize losses (i.e., NPV < $0), which project would you recommend? Which would you recommend if the goal were to achieve a higher NPV?

P12–4 Basic scenario analysis Prime Paints is in the process of evaluating two mutually exclusive additions to its processing capacity. The firm's financial analysts have developed pessimistic, most likely, and optimistic estimates of the annual cash inflows associated with each project. The following table shows these estimates.

	Project A	Project B
Initial investment (CF_0)	−$12,200	−$12,200
Outcome	Annual cash inflows (CF)	
Pessimistic	$ 850	$1,550
Most likely	1,650	1,650
Optimistic	2,450	1,750

a. Determine the range of annual cash inflows for each project.
b. Assume that the firm's cost of capital is 9.3% and that both projects have 15-year lives. Construct a table similar to this one for the NPVs for each project. Include the range of NPVs for each project.
c. Do parts **a** and **b** provide consistent views of the two projects? Explain.
d. Which project do you recommend? Why?

P12–5 Scenario analysis Kiosk Corp. produces vending machines and places them in public buildings. The company has obtained permission to place one of its machines in a local library. The company makes two types of machines. One distributes soft drinks, and the other distributes snack foods. Kiosk expects both machines to provide benefits over a 12-year period, and each has a required investment of $5,200. The firm uses a 6.35% cost of capital. Management has constructed the following table of estimates of annual cash inflows for pessimistic, most likely, and optimistic results.

	Soft drinks	Snack foods
Initial investment (CF_0)	−$5,200	−$5,200
Outcome	Annual cash inflows (CF)	
Pessimistic	$ 500	$ 400
Most likely	750	750
Optimistic	1,000	1,200

a. Determine the range of annual cash inflows for each of the two vending machines.
b. Construct a table similar to this one for the NPVs associated with each outcome for both machines.
c. Find the range of NPVs, and subjectively compare the risks associated with these machines.
d. Which project do you recommend? Why?

P12–6 Scenario analysis Recall from P11-28 that when the market price of gold is C$1,562.50 per ounce (C$ stands for Canadian dollars) the NPV for Maritime Resources Corp.—a Canadian mining firm that was reopening an old gold mine that had ceased operations in the past due to low gold prices—is C$44,188,992. Reopening the mine would require an up-front capital expenditure of C$67.8 million and annual operating expenses of C$19.42 million. Maritime expects that over a 5-year operating life it can recover 174,000 ounces of gold from the mine and that the project will have no terminal value. Maritime uses straight-line depreciation, has a 21.04% corporate tax rate, and has an 11.2% cost of capital. Before moving forward with the project, Maritime would like to determine the sensitivity of its capital budgeting decision to the market price of gold, which could fluctuate over the 5-year project life.

a. Calculate the internal rate of return (IRR) for the gold mine project if the price of gold drops 10%.
b. Calculate the net present value (NPV) for the gold mine project if the price of gold drops 10%.
c. Calculate the internal rate of return (IRR) for the gold mine project if the price of gold drops 20%.
d. Calculate the net present value (NPV) for the gold mine project if the price of gold drops 20%.
e. Below what price per ounce of gold is Maritime's reopening of its old gold mine no longer acceptable?

Personal Finance Problem

P12–7 **Impact of inflation on investments** You are interested in an investment project that costs $40,000 initially. The investment has a 5-year horizon and promises future end-of-year cash inflows of $12,000, $12,500, $11,500, $9,000, and $8,500, respectively. Your current opportunity cost is 6.5% per year. However, the Fed has stated that inflation may rise by 1.5% or may fall by the same amount over the next 5 years.

Assume a direct positive impact of inflation on the prevailing rates (Fisher effect) and answer the following questions. (Assume that inflation has an impact on the opportunity cost, but that the cash flows are contractually fixed and are not affected by inflation).

a. What is the net present value (NPV) of the investment under the current required rate of return?
b. What is the net present value (NPV) of the investment under a period of rising inflation?
c. What is the net present value (NPV) of the investment under a period of falling inflation?
d. From your answers in **a**, **b**, and **c**, what relationship do you see emerge between changes in inflation and asset valuation?

P12–8 **Simulation** Ogden Corporation has compiled the following information on a capital expenditure proposal:

(1) The projected cash inflows are normally distributed with a mean of $36,000 and a standard deviation of $9,000.
(2) The projected cash outflows are normally distributed with a mean of $30,000 and a standard deviation of $6,000.
(3) The firm has an 11% cost of capital.
(4) The probability distributions of cash inflows and cash outflows are not expected to change over the project's 10-year life.

a. Describe how the foregoing data can be used to develop a simulation model for finding the net present value of the project.
b. Discuss the advantages of using a simulation to evaluate the proposed project.

P12–9 Risk-adjusted discount rates: Basic Country Wallpapers is considering investing in one of three mutually exclusive projects, E, F, and G. The firm's cost of capital, r, is 15%, and the risk-free rate, R_F, is 10%. The firm has gathered the basic cash flow and risk index data for each project as shown in the following table.

	Project (j)		
	E	F	G
Initial investment (CF_0)	− \$15,000	− \$11,000	− \$19,000
Year (t)	Cash inflows (CF_t)		
1	\$6,000	\$6,000	\$ 4,000
2	6,000	4,000	6,000
3	6,000	5,000	8,000
4	6,000	2,000	12,000
Risk index (RI_j)	1.80	1.00	0.60

a. Find the net present value (NPV) of each project, using the firm's cost of capital. Which project is preferred in this situation?
b. The firm uses the following equation to determine the risk-adjusted discount rate, $RADR_j$, for each project j:

$$RADR_j = R_F + [RI_j \times (r - R_F)]$$

where

R_F = risk-free rate of return
RI_j = risk index for project j
r = cost of capital

Substitute each project's risk index into this equation to determine its RADR.
c. Use the RADR for each project to determine its risk-adjusted NPV. Which project is preferable in this situation?
d. Compare and discuss your findings in parts **a** and **c**. Which project do you recommend that the firm accept?

P12–10 Risk-adjusted discount rates: Tabular After a careful evaluation of investment alternatives and opportunities, Masters School Supplies has developed a CAPM-type relationship linking a risk index to the required return (RADR), as shown in the following table.

Risk index	Required return (RADR)
0.0	7.0% (risk-free rate, R_F)
0.2	8.0
0.4	9.0
0.6	10.0
0.8	11.0
1.0	12.0
1.2	13.0
1.4	14.0
1.6	15.0
1.8	16.0
2.0	17.0

The firm is considering two mutually exclusive projects, A and B. Following are the data that the firm has been able to gather about the projects.

	Project A	Project B
Initial investment (CF_0)	−\$20,000	−\$30,000
Project life	5 years	5 years
Annual cash inflow (CF)	\$7,000	\$10,000
Risk index	0.2	1.4

All the firm's cash inflows have already been adjusted for taxes.

a. Evaluate the projects using risk-adjusted discount rates.

b. Discuss your findings in part **a**, and recommend the preferred project.

Personal Finance Problem

P12–11 **Mutually exclusive investments and risk** Lara Fredericks is interested in two mutually exclusive investments. Both investments cover the same time horizon of 6 years. The cost of the first investment is \$10,000, and Lara expects equal and consecutive year-end payments of \$3,000. The second investment promises equal and consecutive payments of \$3,800, with an initial outlay of \$12,000 required. The current required return on the first investment is 8.5%, and the second carries a required return of 10.5%.

a. What is the net present value of the first investment?

b. What is the net present value of the second investment?

c. Being mutually exclusive, which investment should Lara choose? Explain.

d. Which investment was relatively more risky? Explain.

P12–12 **Risk-adjusted rates of return using CAPM** Centennial Catering Inc. is considering two mutually exclusive investments. The company wishes to use a CAPM-type risk-adjusted discount rate (RADR) in its analysis. Centennial's managers believe that the appropriate market rate of return is 12%, and they observe that the current risk-free rate of return is 7%. Cash flows associated with the two projects are shown in the following table.

	Project X	Project Y
Initial investment (CF_0)	**− \$70,000**	**− \$78,000**
Year (t)	**Cash inflows (CF_t)**	
1	\$30,000	\$22,000
2	30,000	32,000
3	30,000	38,000
4	30,000	46,000

a. Use a risk-adjusted discount rate approach to calculate the net present value of each project, given that project X has an RADR factor of 1.20 and project Y has an RADR factor of 1.40. The RADR factors are similar to project betas. (Use Equation 12.5 to calculate the required project return for each.)

b. Discuss your findings in part **a**, and recommend the preferred project.

P12–13 **Risk classes and RADR** Moses Manufacturing is attempting to select the best of three mutually exclusive projects, X, Y, and Z. Although all the projects have 5-year lives, they possess differing degrees of risk. Project X is in class V, the highest-risk class; project Y is in class II, the below-average-risk class; and project Z is in class III, the average-risk class. The basic cash flow data for each project and the risk classes and risk-adjusted discount rates (RADRs) used by the firm are shown in the following tables.

	Project X	Project Y	Project Z
Initial investment (CF_0)	– \$180,000	– \$235,000	– \$310,000
Year (t)		Cash inflows (CF_t)	
1	\$80,000	\$50,000	\$90,000
2	70,000	60,000	90,000
3	60,000	70,000	90,000
4	60,000	80,000	90,000
5	60,000	90,000	90,000

Risk Classes and RADRs

Risk class	Description	Risk-adjusted discount rate (RADR)
I	Lowest risk	10%
II	Below-average risk	13
III	Average risk	15
IV	Above-average risk	19
V	Highest risk	22

a. Find the risk-adjusted NPV for each project.
b. Which project, if any, would you recommend that the firm undertake?

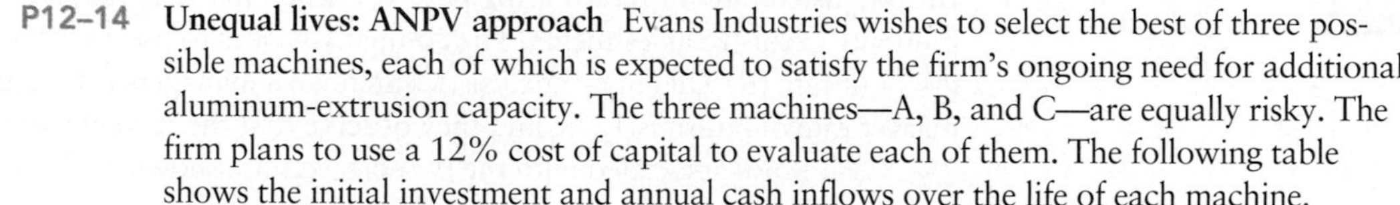

P12–14 Unequal lives: ANPV approach Evans Industries wishes to select the best of three possible machines, each of which is expected to satisfy the firm's ongoing need for additional aluminum-extrusion capacity. The three machines—A, B, and C—are equally risky. The firm plans to use a 12% cost of capital to evaluate each of them. The following table shows the initial investment and annual cash inflows over the life of each machine.

	Machine A	Machine B	Machine C
Initial investment (CF_0)	– \$92,000	– \$65,000	– \$100,500
Year (t)		Cash inflows (CF_t)	
1	\$12,000	\$10,000	\$30,000
2	12,000	20,000	30,000
3	12,000	30,000	30,000
4	12,000	40,000	30,000
5	12,000	–	30,000
6	12,000	–	–

a. Calculate the NPV for each machine over its life. Rank the machines in descending order on the basis of NPV.
b. Use the annualized net present value (ANPV) approach to evaluate and rank the machines in descending order on the basis of ANPV.
c. Compare and contrast your findings in parts **a** and **b**. Which machine would you recommend that the firm acquire? Why?

P12–15 **Unequal lives: ANPV approach** Portland Products is considering the purchase of one of three mutually exclusive projects for increasing production efficiency. The firm plans to use a 14% cost of capital to evaluate these equal-risk projects. The initial investment and annual cash inflows over the life of each project are given in the following table.

	Project X	Project Y	Project Z
Initial investment (CF_0)	– $78,000	– $52,000	– $66,000
Year (t)		Cash inflows (CF_t)	
1	$17,000	$28,000	$15,000
2	25,000	38,000	15,000
3	33,000	–	15,000
4	41,000	–	15,000
5	–	–	15,000
6	–	–	15,000
7	–	–	15,000
8	–	–	15,000

a. Calculate the NPV for each project over its life. Rank the projects in descending order on the basis of NPV.

b. Use the annualized net present value (ANPV) approach to evaluate and rank the projects in descending order on the basis of ANPV.

c. Compare and contrast your findings in parts **a** and **b.** Which project would you recommend that the firm purchase? Why?

LG5

P12–16 **Unequal lives: ANPV approach** JBL Co. has designed a new conveyor system. Management must choose among three alternative courses of action: (1) The firm can sell the design outright to another corporation with payment over 2 years; (2) it can license the design to another manufacturer for a period of 5 years, its likely product life; or (3) it can manufacture and market the system itself, an alternative that will result in 6 years of cash inflows. The company has a cost of capital of 12%. Cash flows associated with each alternative are as presented in the following table.

Alternative	Sell	License	Manufacture
Initial investment (CF_0)	– $200,000	– $200,000	– $450,000
Year (t)		Cash inflows (CF_t)	
1	$200,000	$250,000	$200,000
2	250,000	100,000	250,000
3	–	80,000	200,000
4	–	60,000	200,000
5	–	40,000	200,000
6	–	–	200,000

a. Calculate the net present value of each alternative and rank the alternatives on the basis of NPV.

b. Calculate the annualized net present value (ANPV) of each alternative, and rank them accordingly.

c. Why is ANPV preferred over NPV when ranking projects with unequal lives?

Personal Finance Problem

LG5

P12–17 NPV and ANPV decisions Richard and Linda Butler decide that it is time to purchase a high-definition (HD) television because the technology has improved and prices have fallen over the past 3 years. From their research, they narrow their choices to two sets, the Samsung 64-inch plasma with 1080p capability and the Sony 64-inch plasma with 1080p features. The price of the Samsung is $2,350, and the Sony will cost $2,700. They expect to keep the Samsung for 3 years; if they buy the more expensive Sony unit, they will keep the Sony for 4 years. They expect to sell the Samsung for $400 by the end of 3 years; they expect to sell the Sony for $350 at the end of year 4. Richard and Linda estimate the end-of-year entertainment benefits (i.e., not going to movies or events and watching at home) from the Samsung to be $900 and from the Sony to be $1,000. Both sets can be viewed as quality units and are equally risky purchases. They estimate their opportunity cost to be 9%.

The Butlers wish to choose the better alternative from a purely financial perspective. To perform this analysis they wish to do the following:

a. Determine the NPV of the Samsung HD plasma TV.
b. Determine the ANPV of the Samsung HD plasma TV.
c. Determine the NPV of the Sony HD plasma TV.
d. Determine the ANPV of the Sony HD plasma TV.
e. Which set should the Butlers purchase? Why?

LG6

P12–18 Real options and the strategic NPV Jenny Rene, the CFO of Asor Products Inc., has just completed an evaluation of a proposed capital expenditure for equipment that would expand the firm's manufacturing capacity. Using the traditional NPV methodology, she found the project unacceptable because

$$\text{NPV}_{\text{traditional}} = -\$1,700 < \$0$$

Before recommending rejection of the proposed project, she has decided to assess whether real options might be embedded in the firm's cash flows. Her evaluation uncovered three options:

Option 1: Abandonment. The project could be abandoned at the end of 3 years, resulting in an addition to NPV of $1,200.

Option 2: Growth. If the projected outcomes occurred, an opportunity to expand the firm's product offerings further would become available at the end of 4 years. Exercise of this option is estimated to add $3,000 to the project's NPV.

Option 3: Timing. Certain phases of the proposed project could be delayed if market and competitive conditions caused the firm's forecast revenues to develop more slowly than planned. Such a delay in implementation at that point has an NPV of $10,000.

Jenny estimated that there was a 25% chance that the abandonment option would need to be exercised, a 30% chance that the growth option would be exercised, and only a 10% chance that the implementation of certain phases of the project would affect timing.

a. Use the information provided to calculate the strategic *NPV*, $NPV_{\text{strategic}}$, for Asor Products' proposed equipment expenditure.
b. On the basis of your findings in part **a**, what action should Jenny recommend to management with regard to the proposed equipment expenditure?
c. In general, how does this problem demonstrate the importance of considering real options when making capital budgeting decisions?

P12–19 **Capital rationing: IRR and NPV approaches** Valley Corporation is attempting to select the best of a group of independent projects competing for the firm's fixed capital budget of $4.5 million. The firm recognizes that any unused portion of this budget will earn less than its 15% cost of capital, thereby resulting in a present value of inflows that is less than the initial investment. The firm has summarized, in the following table, the key data for selecting the best group of projects.

Project	Initial investment	IRR	Present value of inflows at 15%
A	−$5,000,000	17%	$5,400,000
B	−800,000	18	1,100,000
C	−2,000,000	19	2,300,000
D	−1,500,000	16	1,600,000
E	−800,000	22	900,000
F	−2,500,000	23	3,000,000
G	−1,200,000	20	1,300,000

a. Use the internal rate of return (IRR) approach to select the best group of projects.
b. Use the net present value (NPV) approach to select the best group of projects.
c. Compare, contrast, and discuss your findings in parts **a** and **b**.
d. Which projects should the firm implement? Why?

LG 6

P12–20 **Capital rationing: NPV approach** A firm with a 13% cost of capital must select the optimal group of projects from those shown in the following table, given its capital budget of $1 million.

Project	Initial investment	NPV at 13% cost of capital
A	−$300,000	$ 84,000
B	−200,000	10,000
C	−100,000	25,000
D	−900,000	90,000
E	−500,000	70,000
F	−100,000	50,000
G	−800,000	160,000

a. Calculate the present value of cash inflows associated with each project.
b. Select the optimal group of projects, keeping in mind that unused funds are costly.

LG 4

P12–21 **ETHICS PROBLEM** The Environmental Protection Agency sometimes imposes penalties on firms that pollute the environment. But did you know there is a legal market for pollution? For example, a mechanism developed to limit excessive air pollution is the use of carbon credits. Carbon credits are a tradable permit scheme allowing businesses that cannot meet their greenhouse-gas-emissions limits to purchase carbon credits from businesses that are below their quota. By allowing credits to be bought and sold, a business for which reducing its emissions would be expensive or prohibitive can pay another business to make the reduction for it. Do you agree with this arrangement? How would you feel as an investor in a company that uses carbon credits to legally exceed its pollution limits?

SPREADSHEET EXERCISE

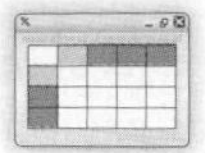

Dyno Corporation has two projects that it would like to undertake. However, due to capital restraints, the two projects—Alpha and Beta—must be treated as mutually exclusive. Both projects are equally risky, and the firm plans to use a 10% cost of capital to evaluate each. Project Alpha has an estimated life of 12 years, and project Beta has an estimated life of 9 years. The cash flow data have been prepared as given in the following table.

	Cash flows	
	Project Alpha	Project Beta
CF_0	−$5,500,000	−$6,500,000
CF_1	300,000	400,000
CF_2	500,000	600,000
CF_3	500,000	800,000
CF_4	550,000	1,100,000
CF_5	700,000	1,400,000
CF_6	800,000	2,000,000
CF_7	950,000	2,500,000
CF_8	1,000,000	2,000,000
CF_9	1,250,000	1,000,000
CF_{10}	1,500,000	
CF_{11}	2,000,000	
CF_{12}	2,500,000	

TO DO

Create a spreadsheet to answer the following questions.

a. Calculate the NPV for each project over its respective life. Rank the projects in descending order on the basis of NPV. Which one would you choose?
b. Use the annualized net present value (ANPV) approach to evaluate and rank the projects in descending order on the basis of ANPV. Which one would you choose?
c. Compare and contrast your findings in parts **a** and **b**. Which project would you recommend that the firm choose? Explain.

MyLab Finance Visit www.pearson.com/mylab/finance for **Chapter Case: *Evaluating Cherone Equipment's Risky Plans for Increasing Its Production Capacity,*** Group Exercises, and numerous online resources.

Integrative Case 5

Lasting Impressions Company

Lasting Impressions (LI) Company is a medium-sized, privately owned commercial printer of promotional advertising brochures, booklets, and other direct-mail pieces. The firm's major clients are ad agencies based in New York and Chicago. The typical job is characterized by high quality and production runs of more than 50,000 units. LI has not been able to compete effectively with larger printers because of its existing older, inefficient presses. The firm is currently having problems meeting run length requirements as well as meeting quality standards in a cost-effective manner.

The general manager has proposed the purchase of one of two large, six-color presses designed for long, high-quality runs. The purchase of a new press would enable LI to reduce its cost of labor and therefore the price to the client, putting the firm in a more competitive position. The key financial characteristics of the old press and of the two proposed presses are summarized as follows.

Old press Originally purchased 3 years ago at an installed cost of $400,000, it is being depreciated under MACRS, using a 5-year recovery period. The old press has a remaining economic life of 5 years. It can be sold today to net $420,000 before taxes; if it is retained, it can be sold to net $150,000 before taxes at the end of 5 years.

Press A This highly automated press can be purchased for $830,000 and will require $40,000 in installation costs. It will be depreciated under MACRS, using a 5-year recovery period. At the end of the 5 years, the machine could be sold to net $400,000 before taxes. If this machine is acquired, it is anticipated that the current account changes shown in the following table would result.

Cash	+ $ 25,400
Accounts receivable	+ 120,000
Inventories	− 20,000
Accounts payable	+ 35,000

Press B This press is not as sophisticated as press A. It costs $640,000 and requires $20,000 in installation costs. It will be depreciated under MACRS, using a 5-year recovery period. At the end of 5 years, it can be sold to net $330,000 before taxes. Acquisition of this press will have no effect on the firm's net working capital investment.

The firm estimates that its earnings before depreciation, interest, and taxes with the old press and with press A or press B for each of the 5 years would be as shown in the table at the top of the next page. The firm is subject to a 40% tax rate. The firm's cost of capital, r, applicable to the proposed replacement is 14%.

Earnings before Depreciation, Interest, and Taxes for Lasting Impressions Company's Presses

Year	Old press	Press A	Press B
1	$120,000	$250,000	$210,000
2	120,000	270,000	210,000
3	120,000	300,000	210,000
4	120,000	330,000	210,000
5	120,000	370,000	210,000

TO DO

a. For each of the two proposed replacement presses, determine:
(1) Initial investment.
(2) Operating cash inflows. (*Note:* Be sure to consider the depreciation in year 6.)
(3) Terminal cash flow. (*Note:* This is at the end of year 5.)

b. Using the data developed in part **a**, find and depict on a timeline the relevant cash flow stream associated with each of the two proposed replacement presses, assuming that each is terminated at the end of 5 years.

c. Using the data developed in part **b**, apply each of the following decision techniques:
(1) Payback period. (*Note:* For year 5, use only the operating cash inflows—that is, exclude terminal cash flow—when making this calculation.)
(2) Net present value (NPV).
(3) Internal rate of return (IRR).

d. Draw net present value profiles for the two replacement presses on the same set of axes, and discuss conflicting rankings of the two presses, if any, resulting from use of NPV and IRR decision techniques.

e. Recommend which, if either, of the presses the firm should acquire if the firm has (1) unlimited funds or (2) capital rationing.

f. The operating cash inflows associated with press A are characterized as very risky, in contrast to the low-risk operating cash inflows of press B. What impact does that have on your recommendation?

PART SIX

Long-Term Financial Decisions

CHAPTERS IN THIS PART

Chapters 10 through 12 focused on how firms should invest money, but those chapters were silent on where firms obtained the money to invest in the first place. In Chapters 13 and 14, we examine firms' long-term financial decisions. Broadly speaking, these chapters focus on the tradeoffs associated with different sources of investment capital.

Chapter 13 looks at the firm's most basic long-term financial decision: whether to raise money by selling stock (equity) or by borrowing money (debt). We call a firm's mix of debt and equity financing its capital structure. Some firms choose a capital structure that contains no debt at all, whereas other firms rely more heavily on debt financing than on equity. The capital structure choice is extremely important because how much debt a firm uses influences the returns a firm can provide to its investors as well as the risks associated with those returns. More debt generally means higher returns, but also higher risks. Chapter 13 illustrates how firms balance that tradeoff.

Chapter 14 focuses on payout policy. Payout policy refers to the decisions that firms make about whether and how to distribute cash to shareholders via dividends and share repurchases. In terms of decision making, we can observe a similarity between capital structure and payout policy. Some firms choose to distribute no cash at all, preferring instead to reinvest cash in the business or to build up large cash reserves for possible use in strategic investments like acquisitions. Other firms pay billions in dividends and stock buybacks each year. Chapter 14 explains the factors that firms consider when forming their payout policies.

CHAPTER

13

Leverage and Capital Structure

LEARNING GOALS

LG1 Discuss leverage, capital structure, breakeven analysis, the operating breakeven point, and the effect of changing costs on the breakeven point.

LG2 Understand operating, financial, and total leverage and the relationships among them.

LG3 Describe the types of capital, external assessment of capital structure, the capital structure of non–U.S. firms, and capital structure theory.

LG4 Explain the optimal capital structure using a graphical view of the firm's cost-of-capital functions and a zero-growth valuation model.

LG5 Discuss the EBIT–EPS approach to capital structure.

LG6 Review the return and risk of alternative capital structures, their linkage to market value, and other important considerations related to capital structure.

MyLab Finance Chapter Introduction Video

WHY THIS CHAPTER MATTERS TO YOU

In your *professional* life

ACCOUNTING You need to understand how to calculate and analyze operating and financial leverage and to be familiar with the tax and earnings effects of various capital structures.

INFORMATION SYSTEMS You need to understand the types of capital and what capital structure is because you will provide much of the information needed in management's determination of the best capital structure for the firm.

MANAGEMENT You need to understand leverage so that you can control risk and magnify returns for the firm's owners and to understand capital structure theory so that you can make decisions about the firm's optimal capital structure.

MARKETING You need to understand breakeven analysis, which you will use in pricing and product feasibility decisions.

OPERATIONS You need to understand the impact of fixed and variable operating costs on the firm's breakeven point and its operating leverage because these costs will have a major effect on the firm's risk and return.

In your *personal* life

Like corporations, you routinely incur debt, using both credit cards for short-term needs and negotiated long-term loans. When you borrow over the long term, you experience the benefits and consequences of leverage. Also, the level of your outstanding debt relative to net worth is conceptually the same as a firm's capital structure. It reflects your financial risk and affects the availability and cost of borrowing.

APPLE INC.

Apple Leverages Its Brand

Deposit Photos/Glow Images

Responding to historically low interest rates in the United States and several other countries, Apple Inc. sold $7 billion in bonds to investors in July 2016, its third bond sale in just a few months. The company said it planned to use the proceeds from its bond sales to repurchase its common stock. That was just the latest move in Apple's long-term program to buy back huge quantities of its own shares and thereby reduce the number of shares outstanding. Between 2012 and 2017, Apple repurchased a staggering $144 billion of its own stock. To put that number in perspective, with the money it spent buying back its own stock, Apple could have purchased *all* the outstanding shares of any number of well-known companies such as McDonald's, Qualcomm, Boeing, Goldman Sachs, or Starbucks.

In buying back its own stock, Apple accomplished two objectives. First, it distributed cash to shareholders. A firm's *payout policy*, which is the subject of Chapter 14, describes how much cash the firm distributes to its stockholders and the manner in which it moves cash from the firm to investors. In 2017, Apple distributed money to shareholders in two ways—it paid dividends and repurchased shares. Apple paid roughly $13 billion in dividends to shareholders, a figure dwarfed by the company's share repurchase program.

The second objective Apple had in mind when it issued bonds to fund shareholders' payments was to alter the firm's *capital structure*, or its mix of debt and equity financing. With more of its financing coming from debt, Apple was adding financial leverage to its business, meaning that if the firm succeeded in selling its products, the returns to shareholders would be magnified. However, if Apple instead experienced a decline in its business, financial leverage could magnify its losses, too. Even after its share buybacks and bond issues, Apple's capital structure was still heavily tilted toward equity, with just 10% of the company's funding coming from debt. Recognizing that Apple used only a modest amount of debt and had billions of cash reserves on its balance sheet, bond-rating agencies assigned a rating of AA+ to Apple's bonds, one step below the highest possible AAA rating.

Source: "Apple Inc. Gears Up to Distribute $3.1 billion in Dividends to shareholders" by Daniel Eran Dilger. Published by appleinsider. http://appleinsider.com/articles/17/02/08/apple-inc-gears-up-to-distribute-31-billion-in-dividends-to-shareholders

13.1 Leverage

leverage
Refers to the effects that fixed costs have on the returns that shareholders earn; higher leverage generally results in higher but more volatile returns.

Leverage refers to the effects that fixed costs have on the returns that shareholders earn. By "fixed costs," we mean costs that do not rise and fall with changes in a firm's sales. Firms have to pay fixed costs whether business conditions are good or bad. These costs may be operating costs, such as those incurred by purchasing and operating plant and equipment, or they may be financial costs, such as the fixed costs of making debt payments. We say that a firm with higher fixed costs has greater leverage. Generally, leverage magnifies both returns and risks. A firm with more leverage may earn higher returns on average than a firm with less leverage, but the returns on the more leveraged firm will also be more volatile.

Many business risks are beyond the control of managers, but not those associated with leverage. Managers can either increase or decrease leverage by adopting strategies that rely more heavily on fixed or variable costs. For example, a choice that many firms confront is whether to make their own products or to outsource manufacturing to another firm. A company that does its own manufacturing may invest billions in factories around the world. These factories generate costs whether they are running or not, so a firm that manufactures its own products will tend to have higher leverage. In contrast, a company that outsources production can quickly reduce its costs when demand is low simply by not placing orders. Therefore, such a firm will generally have lower leverage compared to a firm that manufactures in house.

capital structure
The mix of long-term debt and equity maintained by a firm.

Managers also influence leverage by choosing a specific **capital structure**, which is the mix of long-term debt and equity maintained by a firm. The more debt a firm issues, the higher are its debt repayment costs, and those costs must be paid regardless of how the firm's products are selling. Because leverage can have such a large impact on a firm, the financial manager must understand how to measure and evaluate leverage, particularly when making capital structure decisions.

Table 13.1 uses an income statement to highlight where different sources of leverage come from.

- *Operating leverage* relates to the relationship between the firm's sales revenue and its earnings before interest and taxes (EBIT) or *operating profits*. When costs of operations (such as cost of goods sold and operating expenses) are largely fixed, small changes in revenue will lead to much larger changes in EBIT.

TABLE 13.1 General Income Statement Format and Types of Leverage

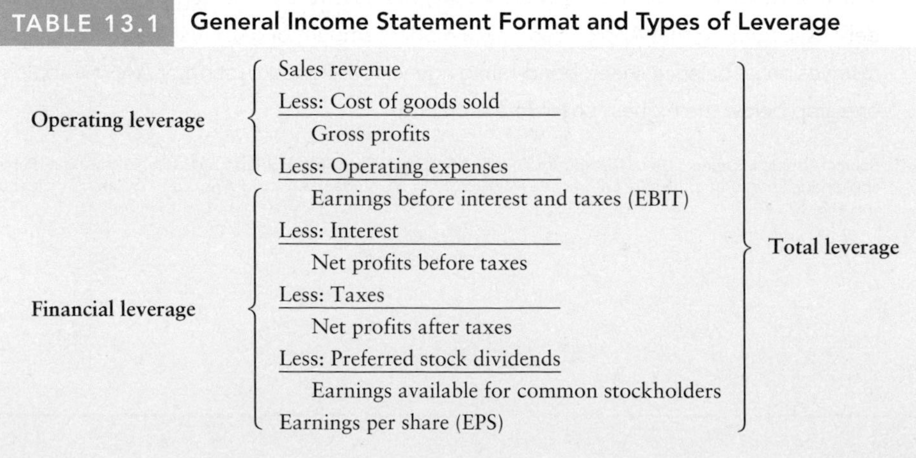

Type of leverage	Income statement item	
Operating leverage	Sales revenue	Total leverage
	Less: Cost of goods sold	
	Gross profits	
	Less: Operating expenses	
Financial leverage	Earnings before interest and taxes (EBIT)	
	Less: Interest	
	Net profits before taxes	
	Less: Taxes	
	Net profits after taxes	
	Less: Preferred stock dividends	
	Earnings available for common stockholders	
	Earnings per share (EPS)	

- *Financial leverage* relates to the relationship between the firm's EBIT and its common stock earnings per share (EPS). On the income statement, you can see that the deductions taken from EBIT to get to EPS include interest, taxes, and preferred dividends. Taxes are clearly variable, rising and falling with the firm's profits, but interest expense and preferred dividends are usually fixed. When these fixed items are large (i.e., when the firm has a lot of financial leverage), small changes in EBIT produce larger changes in EPS.
- *Total leverage* is the combined effect of operating and financial leverage. It relates to the relationship between the firm's sales revenue and EPS.

We will examine the three types of leverage concepts in detail. First, though, we look at breakeven analysis, which lays the foundation for leverage concepts by demonstrating how fixed costs affect the firm's operations.

BREAKEVEN ANALYSIS

breakeven analysis
Used to determine the level of operations necessary to cover all costs and to evaluate the profitability associated with various levels of sales; also called *cost-volume-profit analysis.*

operating breakeven point
The level of sales necessary to cover all *operating costs;* the point at which EBIT = \$0.

Firms use **breakeven analysis,** also called *cost-volume-profit analysis,* (1) to determine the level of operations necessary to cover all costs and (2) to evaluate the profitability associated with various levels of sales. The firm's **operating breakeven point** is the level of sales necessary to cover all operating costs. At that point, earnings before interest and taxes (EBIT) equal \$0.[1]

The first step in finding the operating breakeven point is to divide the cost of goods sold and operating expenses into fixed and variable operating costs. Fixed costs are costs that the firm must pay in a given period regardless of the sales volume achieved during that period. These costs are typically contractual; rent, for example, is a fixed cost. Because fixed costs do not vary with sales, we typically measure them relative to time. For instance, we would typically measure rent as the amount due per month. Variable costs vary directly with sales volume. Shipping costs, for example, are a variable cost.[2] We typically measure variable costs in dollars per unit sold.

Algebraic Approach

Using the following variables, we can recast the operating portion of the firm's income statement given in Table 13.1 into the algebraic representation shown in Table 13.2, where

$$P = \text{sale price per unit}$$
$$Q = \text{sales quantity in units}$$
$$FC = \text{fixed operating cost per period}$$
$$VC = \text{variable operating cost per unit}$$

Rewriting the algebraic calculations in Table 13.2 as a formula for earnings before interest and taxes yields Equation 13.1:

$$\text{EBIT} = (P \times Q) - FC - (VC \times Q) \tag{13.1}$$

1. Quite often, managers calculate the breakeven point so that it represents the point at which all costs—both operating and financial—are covered. For now, we focus on the operating breakeven point as a way to introduce the concept of operating leverage. We will discuss financial leverage later.

2. Some costs, commonly called semifixed or semivariable, are partly fixed and partly variable. An example is sales commissions that are fixed for a certain volume of sales and then increase to higher levels for higher volumes. For convenience and clarity, we assume that all costs can be classified as either fixed or variable.

TABLE 13.2 Operating Leverage, Costs, and Breakeven Analysis

	Item	Algebraic representation
Operating leverage	Sales revenue	$(P \times Q)$
	Less: Fixed operating costs	$-\quad FC$
	Less: Variable operating costs	$-(VC \times Q)$
	Earnings before interest and taxes	EBIT

Simplifying Equation 13.1 yields

$$\text{EBIT} = Q \times (P - VC) - FC \tag{13.2}$$

As noted above, the operating breakeven point is reached when sales just cover all fixed and variable operating costs, which means that EBIT equals \$0. Setting EBIT equal to \$0 and solving Equation 13.2 for Q yields

$$Q = \frac{FC}{P - VC} \tag{13.3}$$

where Q is the firm's operating breakeven point.[3]

EXAMPLE 13.1

MyLab Finance Solution Video

Assume that Cheryl's Posters, a small poster retailer, has fixed operating costs of \$2,500. Its sale price is \$10 per poster, and its variable operating cost is \$5 per poster. Applying Equation 13.3 to these data yields

$$Q = \frac{\$2{,}500}{\$10 - \$5} = \frac{\$2{,}500}{\$5} = 500 \text{ units}$$

At sales of 500 units, the firm's EBIT should just equal \$0. The firm will have positive EBIT for sales greater than 500 units and negative EBIT, or a loss, for sales less than 500 units. We can confirm this conclusion by substituting values above and below 500 units, along with the other values given, into Equation 13.1.

Graphical Approach

Figure 13.1 presents in graphical form the breakeven analysis of the data in the preceding example. The firm's operating breakeven point is the point at which its total operating cost—the sum of its fixed and variable operating costs—equals sales revenue. At this point, EBIT equals \$0. The figure shows that for sales

3. Because the firm is assumed to be a single-product firm, its operating breakeven point is found in terms of unit sales, Q. For multiproduct firms, the operating breakeven point is generally found in terms of dollar sales, S. We can find S by substituting the contribution margin, which is 100% minus total variable operating costs as a percentage of total sales, denoted $VC\%$, into the denominator of Equation 13.3. The result is Equation 13.3a:

$$S = \frac{FC}{1 - VC\%} \tag{13.3a}$$

This multiproduct-firm breakeven point assumes that the firm's product mix remains the same at all levels of sales.

FIGURE 13.1

Breakeven Analysis
Graphical operating breakeven analysis

MyLab Finance Animation

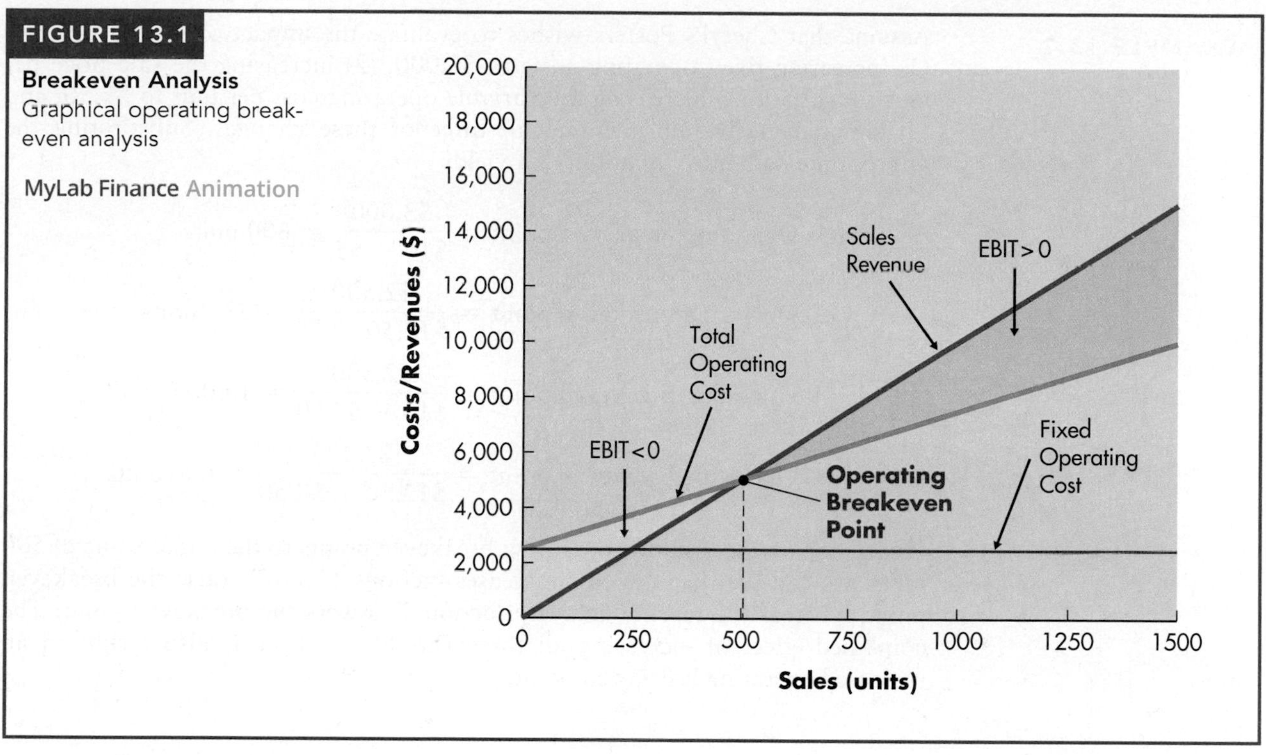

below 500 units, total operating cost exceeds sales revenue, and EBIT is less than \$0 (a loss). For sales above the breakeven point of 500 units, sales revenue exceeds total operating cost, and EBIT is greater than \$0.

Changing Costs and the Operating Breakeven Point

A firm's operating breakeven point is sensitive to a number of variables: the fixed operating cost (*FC*), the sale price per unit (*P*), and the variable operating cost per unit (*VC*). Refer to Equation 13.3 to see how increases or decreases in these variables affect the breakeven point. The sensitivity of the breakeven sales volume (*Q*) to an increase in each of these variables is summarized in Table 13.3. As might be expected, an increase in cost (*FC* or *VC*) tends to increase the operating breakeven point, whereas an increase in the sale price per unit (*P*) decreases the operating breakeven point.

TABLE 13.3 Sensitivity of Operating Breakeven Point to Increases in Key Breakeven Variables

Increase in variable	Effect on operating breakeven point
Fixed operating cost (*FC*)	Increase
Sale price per unit (*P*)	Decrease
Variable operating cost per unit (*VC*)	Increase

Note: Decreases in each of the variables shown would have the opposite effect on the operating breakeven point.

EXAMPLE 13.2

Assume that Cheryl's Posters wishes to evaluate the impact of several options: (1) increasing fixed operating costs to \$3,000; (2) increasing the sale price per unit to \$12.50; (3) increasing the variable operating cost per unit to \$7.50; and (4) simultaneously implementing all three of these changes. Substituting the appropriate data into Equation 13.3 yields

$$\text{(1) Operating breakeven point} = \frac{\$3{,}000}{\$10 - \$5} = 600 \text{ units}$$

$$\text{(2) Operating breakeven point} = \frac{\$2{,}500}{\$12.50 - \$5} = 333\tfrac{1}{3}\text{units}$$

$$\text{(3) Operating breakeven point} = \frac{\$2{,}500}{\$10 - \$7.50} = 1{,}000 \text{ units}$$

$$\text{(4) Operating breakeven point} = \frac{\$3{,}000}{\$12.50 - \$7.50} = 600 \text{ units}$$

If we compare the resulting operating breakeven points to the initial value of 500 units, we can see that the cost increases (actions 1 and 3) raise the breakeven point, whereas the revenue increase (action 2) lowers the breakeven point. The combined effect of increasing all three variables (action 4) also results in an increased operating breakeven point.

PERSONAL FINANCE EXAMPLE 13.3

Rick Polo is considering having a new fuel-saving device installed in his car. The installed cost of the device is \$240 paid up front plus a monthly fee of \$15. He can terminate use of the device any time without penalty. Rick estimates that the device will reduce his average monthly gas consumption by 20%, which, assuming no change in his monthly mileage, translates into a savings of about \$28 per month. He is planning to keep the car for 2 more years and wishes to determine whether he should have the device installed in his car.

To assess the financial feasibility of purchasing the device, Rick calculates the number of months it will take to break even. Letting the installed cost of \$240 represent the fixed cost (*FC*), the monthly savings of \$28 represent the benefit (*P*), and the monthly fee of \$15 represent the variable cost (*VC*), and substituting these values into the breakeven point equation, Equation 13.3, we get

$$\begin{aligned}\text{Breakeven point (in months)} &= \$240 \div (\$28 - \$15) = \$240 \div \$13\\ &= \underline{\underline{18.5 \text{ months}}}\end{aligned}$$

Because the fuel-saving device pays itself back in 18.5 months, which is less than the 24 months that Rick is planning to continue owning the car, he should have the fuel-saving device installed in his car.

OPERATING LEVERAGE

operating leverage
The use of *fixed operating costs* to magnify the effects of changes in sales on the firm's earnings before interest and taxes.

Operating leverage results from the existence of fixed costs that the firm must pay to operate. Using the structure presented in Table 13.2, we can define **operating leverage** as the use of fixed operating costs to magnify the effects of changes in sales on the firm's earnings before interest and taxes.

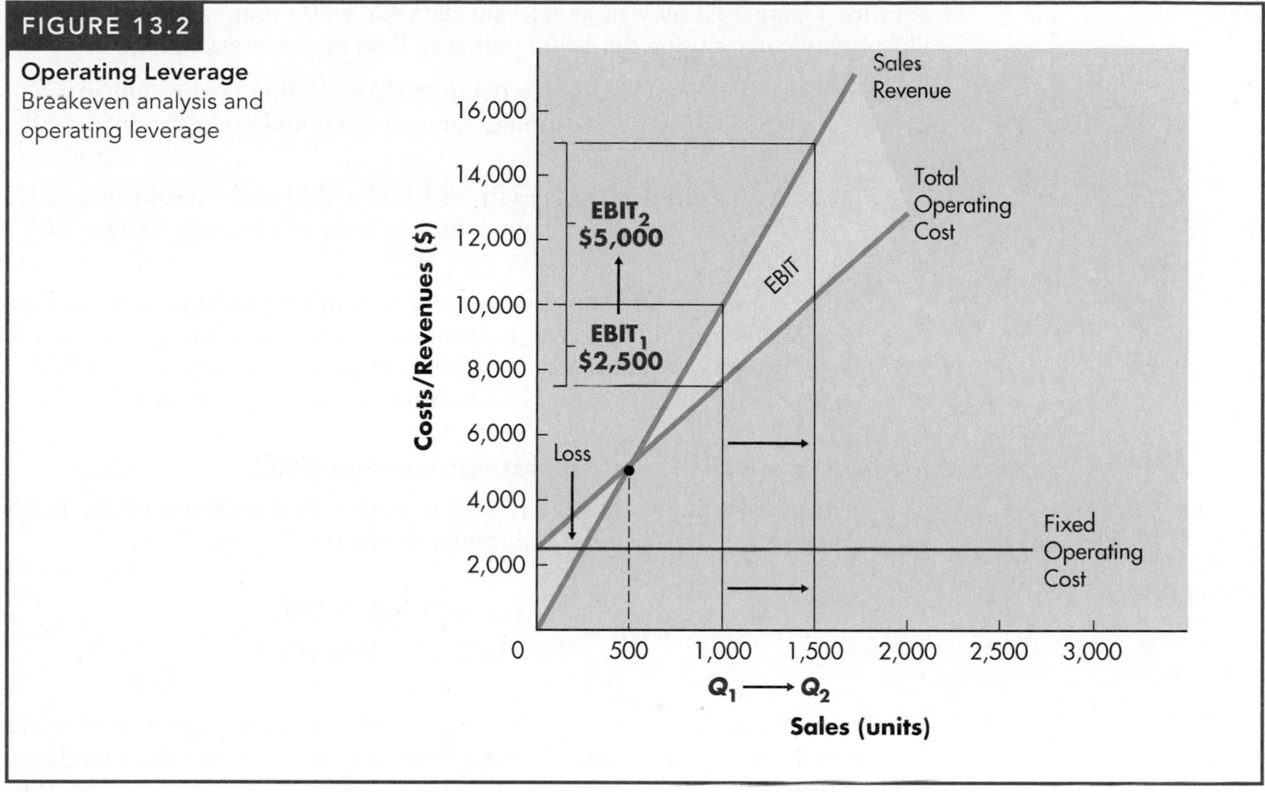

FIGURE 13.2

Operating Leverage
Breakeven analysis and operating leverage

EXAMPLE 13.4

Using the data for Cheryl's Posters (sale price, P = \$10 per unit; variable operating cost, VC = \$5 per unit; fixed operating cost, FC = \$2,500), Figure 13.2 presents the operating breakeven graph originally shown in Figure 13.1. The additional notations on the graph indicate that as the firm's sales increase from 1,000 to 1,500 units (Q_1 to Q_2), its EBIT increases from \$2,500 to \$5,000 ($EBIT_1$ to $EBIT_2$). In other words, a 50% increase in sales (1,000 to 1,500 units) results in a 100% increase in EBIT (\$2,500 to \$5,000). Table 13.4 includes the

TABLE 13.4 **The EBIT for Various Sales Levels**

	Case 2		Case 1
	−50% ←		→ +50%
Sales (in units)	500	1,000	1,500
Sales revenue[a]	\$5,000	\$10,000	\$15,000
Less: Variable operating costs[b]	2,500	5,000	7,500
Less: Fixed operating costs	2,500	2,500	2,500
Earnings before interest and taxes (EBIT)	\$ 0	\$ 2,500	\$ 5,000
	−100%		+100%

[a]Sales revenue = \$10/unit × sales in units.
[b]Variable operating costs = \$5/unit × sales in units.

data for Figure 13.2 as well as relevant data for a 500-unit sales level. We can illustrate two cases using the 1,000-unit sales level as a reference point:

Case 1 A 50% increase in sales (from 1,000 to 1,500 units) results in a 100% increase in earnings before interest and taxes (from \$2,500 to \$5,000).

Case 2 A 50% decrease in sales (from 1,000 to 500 units) results in a 100% decrease in earnings before interest and taxes (from \$2,500 to \$0).

From the preceding example, we see that operating leverage works in both directions. When a firm has fixed operating costs, operating leverage is present. An increase in sales results in a more-than-proportional increase in EBIT; a decrease in sales results in a more-than-proportional decrease in EBIT.

Measuring the Degree of Operating Leverage (DOL)

degree of operating leverage (DOL)
The numerical measure of the firm's operating leverage.

The **degree of operating leverage** (DOL) is a numerical measure of the firm's operating leverage. It can be derived using the equation[4]

$$\text{DOL} = \frac{\text{Percentage change in EBIT}}{\text{Percentage change in sales}} \tag{13.4}$$

Whenever the percentage change in EBIT resulting from a given percentage change in sales is greater than the percentage change in sales, operating leverage exists. In other words, as long as DOL is greater than 1, there is operating leverage.

EXAMPLE 13.5

MyLab Finance Solution Video

Applying Equation 13.4 to cases 1 and 2 in Table 13.4 yields the following results:

$$\text{Case 1} \quad \frac{+100\%}{+50\%} = 2.0$$

$$\text{Case 2} \quad \frac{-100\%}{-50\%} = 2.0$$

These calculations show that Cheryl's Posters' EBIT changes twice as much (on a percentage basis) as its sales. For a given base level of sales, the higher the value resulting from applying Equation 13.4, the greater the degree of operating leverage.

A more direct formula for calculating the degree of operating leverage at a base sales level, Q, is[5]

$$\text{DOL at base sales level } Q = \frac{Q \times (P - VC)}{Q \times (P - VC) - FC} \tag{13.5}$$

4. The degree of operating leverage also depends on the base level of sales used as a point of reference. The closer the base sales level is to the operating breakeven point, the greater the operating leverage. Comparison of the degree of operating leverage of two firms is valid only when using the same base level of sales for both firms.

5. Technically, the formula for DOL given in Equation 13.5 should include absolute value signs because it is possible to get a negative DOL when the EBIT for the base sales level is negative. Because we assume that the EBIT for the base level of sales is positive, we do not use the absolute value signs.

EXAMPLE 13.6

Substituting $Q = 1{,}000$, $P = \$10$, $VC = \$5$, and $FC = \$2{,}500$ into Equation 13.5 gives us

$$\text{DOL at 1,000 units} = \frac{1{,}000 \times (\$10 - \$5)}{1{,}000 \times (\$10 - \$5) - \$2{,}500} = \frac{\$5{,}000}{\$2{,}500} = 2.0$$

As before, the DOL value of 2.0 means that at Cheryl's Posters a change in sales volume results in an EBIT change that is twice as large in percentage terms.[6]

See the *Focus on Practice* box for a discussion of operating leverage at the semiconductor company Qualcomm.

FOCUS ON PRACTICE *in practice*

Qualcomm's Leverage

Qualcomm Inc., one of the largest semiconductor companies in the United States, designs and sells wireless telecommunications chips. Unlike some other chip manufacturers, such as Intel, Qualcomm is largely a *fabless* company, meaning that it does not own and operate its own fabrication (i.e., manufacturing) plants, but rather outsources the production of the devices it sells to third parties. This strategy makes Qualcomm's fixed costs lower than those of other firms that manufacture their own products.

Even so, some of Qualcomm's costs are fixed. The company invests heavily in research and development, and it incurs those costs well before it knows what the demand for new devices will be. In addition, Qualcomm's labor force, numbering roughly 30,000 employees, is highly skilled. Many of the company's workers have advanced degrees in technical fields such as electrical engineering. Although we often think of labor as a variable cost, most companies do not lay off their most skilled workers due to a temporary decline in sales. Thus, at least some of Qualcomm's payroll is best considered a fixed cost, at least in the short run.

To what extent do Qualcomm's fixed costs give the company operating leverage? As demonstrated in the following table, the company experienced sales increases in every year from 2011 to 2014, but the percentage increase in EBIT was significantly greater than the gain in sales only in 2011. From 2012 to 2014, Qualcomm's degree of operating leverage hovered at or below 1.0, prompting some Wall Street analysts to question why the company was not able to increase its profits faster during a period of rapid sales gains. In 2015 and 2016, Qualcomm fell behind the leading edge of technology, and some of its core chips for cell phones were no longer competitive. As a result, sales fell in 2 consecutive years, and EBIT fell even faster. In 2015 and 2016, Qualcomm's degree of operating leverage roughly doubled what it had been in the previous 4 years. Qualcomm experienced the downside of operating leverage in 2015 and 2016 without benefiting from it in the previous years when sales were on the rise.

► *Summarize the pros and cons of operating leverage.*

Item	FY2011	FY2012	FY2013	FY2014	FY2015	FY2016
Sales revenue (millions)	$14,566	$19,121	$24,866	$26,487	$25,281	$23,554
EBIT (millions)	$4,882	$5,705	$7,561	$8,034	$7,212	$6,269
(1) Percent change in sales	32.4%	31.4%	30.0%	6.5%	−4.6%	−6.8%
(2) Percent change in EBIT	48.6%	16.8%	32.5%	6.2%	−10.2%	−13.1%
DOL [(2) ÷ (1)]	1.5	0.5	1.1	1.0	2.2	1.9

6. When total revenue in dollars from sales—instead of unit sales—is available, the following equation, in which TR = total revenue in dollars at a base level of sales and TVC = total variable operating costs in dollars, can be used:

$$\text{DOL at base dollar sales } TR = \frac{TR - TVC}{TR - TVC - FC}$$

This formula is especially useful for finding the DOL for multiproduct firms. It should be clear that because in the case of a single-product firm, $TR = Q \times P$ and $TVC = Q \times VC$, substitution of these values into Equation 13.5 results in the equation given here.

Fixed Costs and Operating Leverage

Changes in fixed operating costs affect operating leverage significantly. Firms sometimes can alter the mix of fixed and variable costs in their operations. For example, a firm could compensate sales representatives with a fixed salary and bonus rather than on a pure percent-of-sales commission basis. Or it could outsource some of its activities, such as manufacturing, paying manufacturing costs only when sales volume justifies doing so. To best illustrate the effects of changes in fixed operating costs on operating leverage, we will continue our example.

EXAMPLE 13.7

MyLab Finance Solution Video

Assume that Cheryl's Posters eliminates sales commissions and increases salaries. This exchange results in a reduction in the variable cost per unit from \$5 to \$4.50 and an increase in the fixed costs from \$2,500 to \$3,000. Table 13.5 presents an analysis like that in Table 13.4, but using the new costs. Although the EBIT of \$2,500 at the 1,000-unit sales level is the same as before the shift in cost structure, Table 13.5 shows that the firm has increased its operating leverage by increasing fixed costs and lowering variable costs.

With the substitution of the appropriate values into Equation 13.5, the degree of operating leverage at the 1,000-unit base level of sales becomes

$$\text{DOL at 1,000 units} = \frac{1{,}000 \times (\$10 - \$4.50)}{1{,}000 \times (\$10 - \$4.50) - \$3{,}000} = \frac{\$5{,}500}{\$2{,}500} = 2.2$$

Comparing this value to the DOL of 2.0 before the shift to more fixed costs makes it clear that the higher the firm's fixed operating costs relative to variable operating costs, the greater the degree of operating leverage. Under the new cost structure, a 50% change in sales would lead to a 110% (50% × 2.2) change in EBIT.

FINANCIAL LEVERAGE

Financial leverage results from the presence of fixed financial costs that the firm must pay. Using the framework in Table 13.1, we can define **financial leverage**

financial leverage
The use of *fixed financial costs* to magnify the effects of changes in earnings before interest and taxes on the firm's earnings per share.

TABLE 13.5 Operating Leverage and Increased Fixed Costs

	Case 2		Case 1
	−50% ←		→ +50%
Sales (in units)	500	1,000	1,500
Sales revenue[a]	\$5,000	\$10,000	\$15,000
Less: Variable operating costs[b]	2,250	4,500	6,750
Less: Fixed operating costs	3,000	3,000	3,000
Earnings before interest and taxes (EBIT)	−\$ 250	\$ 2,500	\$ 5,250
	−110% ←		→ +110%

[a]Sales revenue was calculated as indicated in Table 13.4.
[b]Variable operating costs = \$4.50/unit × sales in units.

as the use of fixed financial costs to magnify the effects of changes in earnings before interest and taxes on the firm's earnings per share. The two most common fixed financial costs are (1) interest on debt and (2) preferred stock dividends. Firms must pay these expenses regardless of the amount of EBIT available to pay them.[7]

EXAMPLE 13.8

Green Foods, a small organic food company, expects EBIT of $10,000 in the current year. It has a $20,000 bond with a 7% (annual) coupon rate of interest and an issue of 600 shares of $4 (annual dividend per share) preferred stock outstanding. It also has 1,000 shares of common stock outstanding. The annual interest on the bond issue is $1,400 (0.07 × $20,000). The annual dividends on the preferred stock are $2,400 ($4.00/share × 600 shares). Table 13.6 presents the earnings per share (EPS) corresponding to levels of EBIT of $6,000, $10,000, and $14,000, assuming that the firm is in the 21% tax bracket. The table illustrates two situations:

Case 1 A 40% increase in EBIT (from $10,000 to $14,000) results in an 72% increase in earnings per share (from $4.39 to $7.55).

Case 2 A 40% decrease in EBIT (from $10,000 to $6,000) results in an 72% decrease in earnings per share (from $4.39 to $1.23).

TABLE 13.6 The EPS for Various EBIT Levels[a]

	Case 2 −40%		Case 1 +40%
EBIT	$6,000	$10,000	$14,000
Less: Interest (*I*)	1,400	1,400	1,400
Net profits before taxes	$4,600	$ 8,600	$12,600
Less: Taxes ($T = 0.21$)	966	1,806	2,646
Net profits after taxes	$3,634	$ 6,794	$ 9,954
Less: Preferred stock dividends (*PD*)	2,400	2,400	2,400
Earnings available for common (EAC)	$1,234	$ 4,394	$ 7,554
Earnings per share (EPS)	= $1.23	= $4.39	= $7.55
	−72%		+72%

[a]As noted in Chapter 2, for accounting and tax purposes, interest is a *tax-deductible expense,* whereas dividends must be paid from after-tax cash flows.

The effect of financial leverage is such that an increase in the firm's EBIT results in a more-than-proportional increase in the firm's earnings per share, whereas a decrease in the firm's EBIT results in a more-than-proportional decrease in EPS.

7. Although a firm's board of directors can elect to stop paying preferred stock dividends, the firm typically cannot pay dividends on common stock until the preferred shareholders receive all the dividends they are owed. Although failure to pay preferred dividends cannot force the firm into bankruptcy, it increases the common stockholders' risk because they cannot receive dividends until the claims of preferred stockholders are satisfied.

Measuring the Degree of Financial Leverage (DFL)

degree of financial leverage (DFL)
The numerical measure of the firm's financial leverage.

The **degree of financial leverage** (DFL) is a numerical measure of the firm's financial leverage. Computing it is much like computing the degree of operating leverage. One approach for obtaining the DFL is[8]

$$\text{DFL} = \frac{\text{Percentage change in EPS}}{\text{Percentage change in EBIT}} \tag{13.6}$$

Whenever the percentage change in EPS resulting from a given percentage change in EBIT is greater than the percentage change in EBIT, financial leverage exists. In other words, whenever DFL is greater than 1, there is financial leverage.

EXAMPLE 13.9

Applying Equation 13.6 to cases 1 and 2 in Table 13.6 yields the following two cases:

$$\text{Case 1} \quad \frac{+72\%}{+40\%} = 1.8$$

$$\text{Case 2} \quad \frac{-72\%}{-40\%} = 1.8$$

These calculations show that when Green Foods' EBIT changes, its EPS changes 1.8 times as fast on a percentage basis due to the firm's financial leverage. The higher this value is, the greater the degree of financial leverage.

PERSONAL FINANCE EXAMPLE 13.10

Shanta and Ravi Shandra wish to assess the impact effect of additional long-term borrowing on their degree of financial leverage (DFL). The Shandras currently have $4,200 available after meeting all their monthly living (operating) expenses, before making monthly loan payments. They currently have monthly loan payment obligations of $1,700 and are considering the purchase of a new car, which would result in a $500 per month increase (to $2,200) in their total monthly loan payments. Because a large portion of Ravi's monthly income represents commissions, the Shandras believe that the $4,200 per month currently available for making loan payments could vary by 20% above or below that amount.

To assess the potential impact of the additional borrowing on their financial leverage, the Shandras calculate their DFL for both current ($1,700) and proposed ($2,200) loan payments, as shown on the next page, using the currently available $4,200 as a base and a 20% change.

Based on their calculations, the amount the Shandras will have available after loan payments with their current debt changes by 1.68% for every 1% change in the amount they will have available for making the loan payments. This change is considerably less responsive—and therefore less risky—than the 2.10% change in the amount available after loan payments for each 1% change in the amount available for making loan payments with the proposed additional $500 in monthly debt payments. Although it appears that the Shandras can afford the additional

8. This approach is valid only when the same base level of EBIT is used to calculate and compare these values. In other words, the base level of EBIT must be held constant to compare the financial leverage associated with different levels of fixed financial costs.

loan payments, they must decide if, given the variability of Ravi's income, they are comfortable with the increased financial leverage and risk.

	Current DFL			Proposed DFL		
Available for making loan payments	\$4,200	(+20%)	\$5,040	\$4,200	(+20%)	\$5,040
Less: Loan payments	1,700		1,700	2,200		2,200
Available after loan payments	\$2,500	(+33.6%)	\$3,340	\$2,000	(+42%)	\$2,840
		$\text{DFL} = \frac{+33.6\%}{+20\%} = 1.68$			$\text{DFL} = \frac{+42\%}{+20\%} = 2.10$	

A more direct formula for calculating the degree of financial leverage at a base level of EBIT is given by Equation 13.7, where we use the notation from Table 13.6.[9] Note that in the denominator the term $1/(1 - T)$ converts the after-tax preferred stock dividend to a before-tax amount for consistency with the other terms in the equation.

$$\text{DFL at base level EBIT} = \frac{\text{EBIT}}{\text{EBIT} - I - \left(PD \times \frac{1}{1 - T}\right)} \qquad (13.7)$$

EXAMPLE 13.11

Entering EBIT = \$10,000, I = \$1,400, PD = \$2,400, and the tax rate (T = 0.21) from Table 13.6 into Equation 13.7 yields

$$\text{DFL at \$10,000 EBIT} = \frac{\$10,000}{\$10,000 - \$1,400 - \left(\$2,400 \times \frac{1}{1 - 0.21}\right)}$$

$$= \frac{\$10,000}{\$5,562} = 1.8$$

Note that the formula given in Equation 13.7 provides a more direct method for calculating the degree of financial leverage than does the approach using Table 13.6 and Equation 13.6.

TOTAL LEVERAGE

total leverage
The use of *fixed costs, both operating and financial,* to magnify the effects of changes in sales on the firm's earnings per share.

We also can assess the combined effect of operating and financial leverage on the firm's risk by using a framework similar to that used in developing the individual concepts of leverage. This combined effect, or **total leverage,** can be defined as the use of *fixed costs, both operating and financial,* to magnify the effects of changes in sales on the firm's earnings per share. Total leverage can therefore be viewed as the total impact of the fixed costs in the firm's operating and financial structure.

9. By using the formula for DFL in Equation 13.7, it is possible to get a negative value for the DFL if the EPS for the base level of EBIT is negative. Rather than show absolute value signs in the equation, we instead assume that the base-level EPS is positive.

EXAMPLE 13.12

Cables Inc., a computer cable manufacturer, expects sales of 20,000 units at $5 per unit in the coming year and must meet the following obligations: variable operating costs of $2 per unit, fixed operating costs of $10,000, interest of $20,000, and preferred stock dividends of $12,000. The firm is in the 21% tax bracket and has 5,000 shares of common stock outstanding. Table 13.7 presents the levels of earnings per share associated with the expected sales of 20,000 units and with sales of 30,000 units.

Table 13.7 illustrates that as a result of a 50% increase in sales (from 20,000 to 30,000 units), the firm would experience a 203% increase in earnings per share (from $2.34 to $7.08). Although not shown in the table, a 50% decrease in sales would, conversely, result in a 203% decrease in earnings per share. In this example, the impact of total leverage is considerable, resulting in a percentage change in earnings per share that is 4.1 times the percentage change in sales, whether sales are increasing or decreasing.

Measuring the Degree of Total Leverage (DTL)

degree of total leverage (DTL)
The numerical measure of the firm's total leverage.

The **degree of total leverage (DTL)** is a numerical measure of the firm's total leverage. It can be computed much like operating and financial leverage are computed. One approach for measuring DTL is[10]

$$\text{DTL} = \frac{\text{Percentage change in EPS}}{\text{Percentage change in sales}} \quad (13.8)$$

TABLE 13.7 The Total Leverage Effect

		+50% →			
Sales (in units)	20,000	30,000			
Sales revenue[a]	$100,000	$150,000	$\text{DOL} = \frac{+60\%}{+50\%} = 1.2$		
Less: Variable operating costs[b]	40,000	60,000			
Less: Fixed operating costs	10,000	10,000			
Earnings before interest and taxes (EBIT)	$ 50,000	$ 80,000			
		+60% →			$\text{DTL} = \frac{+203\%}{+50\%} = 4.1$
Less: Interest	20,000	20,000			
Net profits before taxes	$ 30,000	$ 60,000			
Less: Taxes ($T = 0.21$)	6,300	12,600	$\text{DFL} = \frac{+203\%}{+60\%} = 3.4$		
Net profits after taxes	$ 23,700	$ 47,400			
Less: Preferred stock dividends	12,000	12,000			
Earnings available for common stockholders	$ 11,700	$ 35,400			
Earnings per share (EPS)	$\frac{\$11,700}{5,000} = \$2.34$	$\frac{\$35,400}{5,000} = \$7.08$			
		+203% →			

[a]Sales revenue = $5/unit × sales in units.
[b]Variable operating costs = $2/unit × sales in units.

10. This approach is valid only when the same base level of sales is used to calculate and compare these values. In other words, the base level of sales must be held constant if we are to compare the total leverage associated with different levels of fixed costs.

Whenever the percentage change in EPS resulting from a given percentage change in sales is greater than the percentage change in sales, total leverage exists. In other words, as long as the DTL is greater than 1, there is total leverage.

EXAMPLE 13.13

Applying Equation 13.8 to the data in Table 13.7 yields

$$\text{DTL} = \frac{+203\%}{+50\%} = 4.1$$

Because this result is much greater than 1, Cables Inc. has a great deal of total leverage that is arising from operating leverage, financial leverage, or both. The higher the value is, the greater the degree of total leverage.

A more direct formula for calculating the degree of total leverage at a given base level of sales, Q, is provided by the following equation,[11] which uses the same notation presented earlier:

$$\text{DTL at base sales level } Q = \frac{Q \times (P - VC)}{Q \times (P - VC) - FC - I - \left(PD \times \frac{1}{1-T}\right)} \qquad (13.9)$$

EXAMPLE 13.14

Substituting $Q = 20{,}000$, $P = \$5$, $VC = \$2$, $FC = \$10{,}000$, $I = \$20{,}000$, $PD = \$12{,}000$, and the tax rate ($T = 0.21$) into Equation 13.9 yields

DTL at 20,000 units

$$= \frac{20{,}000 \times (\$5 - \$2)}{20{,}000 \times (\$5 - \$2) - \$10{,}000 - \$20{,}000 - \left(\$12{,}000 \times \frac{1}{1 - 0.21}\right)}$$

$$= \frac{\$60{,}000}{\$14{,}810} = 4.1$$

Clearly, the formula used in Equation 13.9 provides a more direct method for calculating the degree of total leverage than does the approach using Table 13.7 and Equation 13.8.

Relationship of Operating, Financial, and Total Leverage

Total leverage reflects the combined impact of operating and financial leverage on the firm. High operating leverage and high financial leverage will cause total leverage to be high. The opposite will also be true. The relationship between operating leverage and financial leverage is multiplicative rather than additive. The relationship between the degree of total leverage (DTL) and the degrees of operating leverage (DOL) and financial leverage (DFL) is given by

$$\text{DTL} = \text{DOL} \times \text{DFL} \qquad (13.10)$$

11. By using the formula for DTL in Equation 13.9, it is possible to get a negative value for the DTL if the EPS for the base level of sales is negative. For our purposes, rather than show absolute value signs in the equation, we instead assume that the base-level EPS is positive.

EXAMPLE 13.15

Substituting the values calculated for DOL and DFL, shown on the right-hand side of Table 13.7, into Equation 13.10 yields

$$DTL = 1.2 \times 3.4 = 4.1$$

The resulting degree of total leverage is the same value that we calculated directly in the preceding examples.

The *Focus on Ethics* box considers some ethical issues relating to the topic of leverage.

FOCUS ON ETHICS *in practice*

Repo 105 Man

On September 15, 2008, Lehman Brothers filed for Chapter 11—the largest such bankruptcy in American history. The move stunned global financial markets and, many argue, triggered the ensuing financial crisis. Founded in 1850, Lehman had weathered many financial panics and recessions (including the Great Depression) to grow into the nation's fourth largest investment bank. The firm was also a major player in subprime mortgages; therein lay its doom.

From 2000 to 2008, U.S. investment banks borrowed heavily to grow, and Lehman was no exception. In February 2008, Lehman held $786 billion in assets with only $24.8 billion in stockholder equity—a debt-to-equity ratio of nearly 32-to-1. With that much leverage, it would take only a small drop in asset values to wipe out the firm, and the meltdown of the subprime-mortgage market obliged. During the preceding housing boom, lenders scrambled to give mortgages to applicants with less than "prime" credit—such borrowers accounted for nearly one-third of 2005 originations. Many qualified only because of low "teaser" interest rates and expected home-price appreciation. When teaser rates expired and housing prices peaked, defaults on subprime mortgages began to climb. And firms top-heavy with securities backed by those mortgages—like Lehman Brothers—found themselves in trouble.

As its finances deteriorated, Lehman turned to "Repo 105s" to mask its leverage (and vulnerability to the falling prices of subprime-backed securities). Financial institutions commonly use repurchase agreements, or repos, to borrow short-term—a firm wanting cash sells securities with a promise to buy them back a short time later at a higher price. Lehman had something else in mind—executing repos just prior to releasing quarterly financial statements, using the cash to temporarily pay down debt, and then unwinding everything shortly after the statements were public. To the public, these transactions made Lehman's leverage ratio appear much smaller than it really was. Securities were repurchased at 105% of initial sales price because of an accounting rule requiring repos at 102% or less to be reported as loans on the balance sheet. Through Repo 105s, Lehman "removed" between $39 and $50 billion in assets and debt from its reported balance sheets the last three quarters before bankruptcy. No reputable American law firm would bless the legality of these transactions, so the firm found one in the U.K. and did the deals through its London office.

The fallout continued long after Lehman Brothers' demise. In 2013, the firm's auditors, Ernst & Young (E&Y), agreed to pay $99 million to investors and in 2015 another $10 million to the State of New York for not blowing the whistle on the shady repos. Allegedly, E&Y kept mum because Lehman was its eighth largest U.S. auditing client, forgetting Warren Buffett's wise counsel: "It takes 20 years to build a reputation and five minutes to ruin it. If you think about that, you'll do things differently."

► *Because the Repo 105 deals took place in London, Lehman executives hid behind the legal blessing from a U.K. law firm to escape U.S. prosecution. Does "legal" make the transactions ethical?*

► *What ethical duty did E&Y have as Lehman's auditor to go public with the intent of the Repo 105 transactions?*

See *Knowledge@Wharton*, "Lehman's Demise and Repo 105: No Accounting for Deception," Wharton Business School, University of Pennsylvania, March 31, 2010 (http://knowledge.wharton.upenn.edu/article/lehmans-demise-and-repo-105-no-accounting-for-deception/) for an overview of the scandal.

→ **REVIEW QUESTIONS** MyLab Finance Solutions

13–1 What does the term leverage mean? How are operating leverage, financial leverage, and total leverage related to the income statement?

13–2 What is the operating breakeven point? How do changes in fixed operating costs, the sale price per unit, and the variable operating cost per unit affect it?

13–3 What is operating leverage? What causes it? How do you measure the degree of operating leverage (DOL)?

13–4 What is financial leverage? What causes it? How do you measure the degree of financial leverage (DFL)?

13–5 What is the general relationship among operating leverage, financial leverage, and the total leverage of the firm? Do these types of leverage complement one another? Why or why not?

13.2 The Firm's Capital Structure

MyLab Finance Video

Capital structure is one of the most complex areas of financial decision making because of its interrelationship with other financial decision variables. Poor capital structure decisions can reduce the value of the firm by increasing the cost of capital, thereby lowering the NPVs of investment projects and making more of them unacceptable. Effective capital structure decisions can increase the value of the firm by lowering the cost of capital, resulting in higher NPVs and more acceptable investment opportunities.

TYPES OF CAPITAL

All the items on the right-hand side of the firm's balance sheet, excluding current liabilities, are sources of capital. The following simplified balance sheet illustrates the basic breakdown of total capital into its two components, debt and equity:

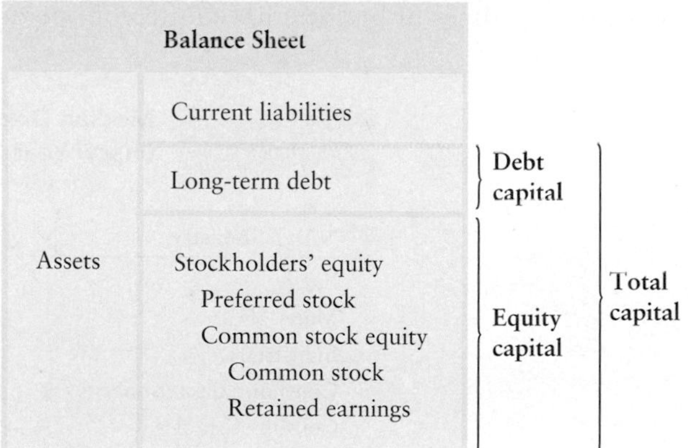

The cost of debt is lower than the cost of other forms of financing. Lenders demand relatively lower returns because they take the least risk of any contributors of long-term capital. Lenders have a higher priority of claim against any earnings or assets available for payment, and they can exert far greater legal pressure against the company to make payment than can owners of preferred or common stock. The tax deductibility of interest payments also lowers the debt cost to the firm substantially, though less so since the Tax Cuts and Jobs Act of 2017 lowered the corporate tax rate to a flat 21%.

Unlike debt capital, which the firm must eventually repay, equity capital remains invested in the firm indefinitely. The two main sources of equity are (1) preferred stock and (2) common stock and retained earnings. Common stock is typically the most expensive form of equity, followed by retained earnings and then preferred stock. Our concern here is the relationship between debt and equity. The more debt a firm uses, the greater will be the firm's financial leverage. That leverage makes stockholders' claims more risky, increasing the cost of equity. In addition, as a firm borrows more its cost of debt may rise as lenders question the firm's ability to repay debts. Whether the firm borrows very little or a great deal, it is always true that stockholders' claims are riskier than those of lenders, so the cost of equity always exceeds the cost of debt.

EXTERNAL ASSESSMENT OF CAPITAL STRUCTURE

We saw earlier that *financial leverage* results from the use of fixed-cost financing, such as debt and preferred stock, to magnify return and risk. The amount of leverage in the firm's capital structure can influence its value by affecting return and risk. Those outside the firm can make a rough assessment of capital structure by using measures found in the firm's financial statements. Some of these important debt ratios were presented in Chapter 3. For example, a direct measure of the degree of indebtedness is the *debt ratio* (total liabilities ÷ total assets). The higher this ratio is, the greater the relative amount of debt (or financial leverage) in the firm's capital structure. Measures of the firm's ability to meet contractual payments associated with debt include the *times interest earned ratio* (EBIT ÷ interest) and the *fixed-payment coverage ratio* (see page 103). These ratios provide indirect information on financial leverage. Generally, the smaller these ratios are, the greater the firm's financial leverage is, and the less able it is to meet payments as they come due.

The level of debt (financial leverage) that is acceptable for one industry or line of business can be highly risky in another, because different industries and lines of business have different operating characteristics. Table 13.8 presents the

TABLE 13.8 Median Debt Ratios for Key Economic Sectors (Fiscal Year 2016)

NAICS Industry	Debt ratio	Times interest earned ratio
Energy	48%	0.3
Materials	27	10.1
Industrials	52	6.8
Consumer discretionary	55	8.5
Consumer staples	55	7.0
Healthcare	38	6.0
Financial	87	NA
Information technology	46	19.2
Telecommunications	55	5.1
Utilities	46	1.5

debt and times interest earned ratios for selected industries and lines of business. Significant industry differences are evident in these data. Differences in debt positions also likely exist within an industry or line of business.

PERSONAL FINANCE EXAMPLE 13.16 Those who lend to individuals, like lenders to corporations, typically use ratios to assess the applicant's ability to meet the contractual payments associated with the requested debt. The lender, after obtaining information from a loan application and other sources, calculates ratios and compares them to predetermined allowable values. Typically, if the applicant's ratio values are within an acceptable range, the lender will make the requested loan.

The best example of this process is a real estate mortgage loan application. The mortgage lender usually invokes the following two requirements:

1. Monthly mortgage payments may not exceed 25% to 30% of monthly gross (before-tax) income
2. Total monthly installment payments (including the mortgage payment) may not exceed 33% to 38% of monthly gross (before-tax) income

Assume that the Loo family is applying for a mortgage loan. The family's monthly gross (before-tax) income is \$5,380, and they currently have monthly installment loan obligations that total \$560. The \$275,000 mortgage loan they are applying for will require monthly payments of \$1,400. The lender requires (1) the monthly mortgage payment to be less than 28% of monthly gross income and (2) total monthly installment payments (including the mortgage payment) to be less than 37% of monthly gross income. The lender calculates and evaluates these ratios for the Loos, as shown below.

1. Mortgage payment ÷ Gross income = \$1,400 ÷ \$5,380
   = 26% < 28% maximum, therefore **OK**
2. Total installment payments ÷ Gross income = (\$560 + \$1,400) ÷ \$5,380
   = \$1,960 ÷ \$5,380
   = 36.4% < 37% maximum, therefore **OK**

The Loos' ratios meet the lender's standards. So, assuming they have adequate funds for the down payment and meet other lender requirements, the Loos will be granted the loan.

CAPITAL STRUCTURE OF NON–U.S. FIRMS

In general, non–U.S. companies have much higher degrees of indebtedness than their U.S. counterparts. This is largely because U.S. capital markets are more developed than those elsewhere and have played a greater role in corporate financing than has been the case in other countries. In most European countries, and especially in Japan and other Pacific Rim nations, large commercial banks are more actively involved in the financing of corporate activity than has been true in the United States. Furthermore, in many of these countries, banks are allowed to make large equity investments in nonfinancial corporations, a practice prohibited for U.S. banks. Finally, share ownership tends to be more tightly controlled among founding-family, institutional, and even public investors in Europe and Asia than is the case for most large U.S. corporations. Tight ownership enables owners to understand the firm's financial condition better, resulting in their willingness to tolerate a higher degree of indebtedness.

MATTER OF FACT

Leverage Around the World

A study of the use of long-term debt in 42 countries found that firms in Argentina used more long-term debt than firms in any other country. Relative to their assets, firms in Argentina used almost 60% more long-term debt than did U.S. companies. Indian firms were heavy users of long-term debt as well. At the other end of the spectrum, companies from Italy, Greece, and Poland used very little long-term debt. In those countries, firms used only about 40% as much long-term debt as did their U.S. counterparts.

Nonetheless, similarities do exist between U.S. corporations and those in other countries. First, the same industry patterns of capital structure tend to be found all around the world. For example, in nearly all countries, pharmaceutical and other high-growth industrial firms usually have lower debt ratios than do steel companies, airlines, and electric utility companies. In part, it has to do with the nature of the assets held by these firms. High-growth firms whose main assets are intangibles (such as patents and rights to intellectual property) tend to borrow less than firms having tangible assets that can be pledged as collateral for loans. Second, the capital structures of the largest U.S.-based multinational companies, which have access to capital markets around the world, typically resemble the capital structures of multinational companies from other countries more than they resemble those of smaller U.S. companies. In other words, in most countries larger firms tend to borrow more than smaller firms do. Third, companies that are riskier and have more volatile income streams tend to borrow less, as do firms that are highly profitable. Finally, the worldwide trend is away from reliance on banks for financing and toward greater reliance on security issuance. Over time, the differences in the capital structures of U.S. and non–U.S. firms will probably lessen.

CAPITAL STRUCTURE THEORY

Although it is difficult to provide financial managers with a precise methodology for determining a firm's optimal capital structure, research suggests that optimal capital structure lies within a range. In this regard, financial theory does offer help in understanding the factors that influence a firm's optimal capital structure and how capital structure affects the firm's value.

In 1958, Franco Modigliani and Merton H. Miller[12] (commonly known as "M and M") demonstrated mathematically that, in a world with perfect markets,[13] the capital structure that a firm chooses does not affect its value. Many researchers,

12. Franco Modigliani and Merton H. Miller, "The cost of capital, corporation finance, and the theory of investment," *American Economic Review* (June 1958), pp. 261–297.

13. In perfect markets (1) there are no taxes, (2) there are no brokerage or flotation costs for securities, (3) there are no information asymmetries (i.e., investors and managers have the same information about the firm's investment prospects), and (4) investors can borrow at the same rate as corporations.

including M and M, have examined whether capital structure may affect firm value in imperfect, real-world markets. The consensus is that there is an optimal capital structure that balances the benefits and costs of debt financing. The major benefit of debt is the tax savings that arise because firms can deduct interest expense from taxable income. The costs of debt are related to (1) the increased probability of bankruptcy associated with heavier borrowing, (2) the *agency costs* of the lender's constraining the firm's actions, and (3) the costs associated with managers having more information about the firm's prospects than do investors.

Tax Benefits

When interest expense is tax-deductible, borrowing reduces firms' taxes, lowering the government's share of earnings and increasing the share going to investors. Interest deductibility essentially subsdizes a firm's cost of debt. Letting r_d equal the before-tax cost of debt and letting T equal the tax rate, the after-tax cost of debt is $r_d \times (1 - T)$.[14]

Bankruptcy Costs and the Probability of Bankruptcy

What happens when a firm is unable to pay its debts and goes bankrupt? In theory, because lenders have a higher priority claim than shareholders, when a firm cannot repay its lenders in full, the shareholders walk away empty handed and lenders receive whatever assets remain. In that situation, lenders might liquidate the firm's remaining assets, or they might hire a new management team to run the firm in the hope that this team can make the firm profitable again. In essence, after bankruptcy, ownership of the firm transfers from its former stockholders to its lenders.

In practice, the ownership transition just described can be slow, contentious, and expensive. A firm in or approaching bankruptcy incurs a variety of costs that siphon cash flows away from the firm's investors. These *bankruptcy costs* reduce the value of the firm relative to what it would be in the absence of those costs. Bankruptcy costs may include *direct costs,* such as the fees paid to lawyers to negotiate with lenders, or the costs may be *indirect*, such as missed investment opportunities the firm does not undertake because managers are too distracted by the bankruptcy process to focus on running the business. Because these costs reduce the cash flows that investors receive and thereby lower the value of the firm, managers must exercise care in taking any actions that could increase the probability of bankruptcy with its attendant costs. Bankruptcy risk depends on how much exposure the firm has to business risk and financial risk.

Business Risk We define *business risk* as the risk that is reflected in fluctuations of the firm's cash flows before considering any debt financing. Business risk varies across industries and across firms within an industry, no matter what capital structures those firms choose. A number of factors influence whether business risk is high or low in a particular industry or firm. In general, firms with more operating leverage are exposed to greater business risk than firms with less operating leverage. We have already seen that greater operating leverage leads to more volatility in the cash flows generated by a firm. Although operating leverage is an important factor influencing business risk, two other factors—revenue stability

14. Current tax law prohibits firms from deducting interest that exceeds 30% of EBIT. However, firms can carry forward interest expense that is nondeductible in one year to subsequent years. Furthermore, the 30% limitation does not apply to small firms such as Cooke Company in the examples to follow.

and cost stability—also affect it. *Revenue stability* reflects the variability of the firm's sales revenues. Because revenue is simply the product of the quantity of goods and services sold by a firm times the price charged by the firm, a firm with relatively stable revenues is one that has steady demand for what it produces and that can sell its output for a price that does not fluctuate a great deal. Such a firm has low business risk. Firms with highly volatile product demand and prices have unstable revenues that result in high levels of business risk. *Cost stability* reflects the relative predictability of input prices such as those for labor and materials. The more predictable and stable these input prices are, the lower the business risk.

Business risk varies among firms, regardless of their lines of business, and is not affected by capital structure decisions. The higher a firm's business risk, the more cautious the firm must be in establishing its capital structure. Firms with high business risk therefore tend toward less highly leveraged capital structures, and firms with low business risk tend toward more highly leveraged capital structures. We will hold business risk constant throughout the discussions that follow.

EXAMPLE 13.17

Cooke Company, a soft drink manufacturer, is preparing to make a capital structure decision. It has obtained estimates of sales and the associated levels of earnings before interest and taxes (EBIT) from its forecasting group. There is a 25% chance that sales will total \$400,000, a 50% chance that sales will total \$600,000, and a 25% chance that sales will total \$800,000. Fixed operating costs total \$200,000, and variable operating costs equal 50% of sales. Table 13.9 summarizes this information and calculates the EBIT for each scenario.

Table 13.9 shows that there is a 25% chance that the EBIT will be \$0, a 50% chance that it will be \$100,000, and a 25% chance that it will be \$200,000. These EBIT data effectively reflect a certain level of business risk that captures the firm's operating leverage, sales revenue variability, and cost predictability. When developing the firm's capital structure, the financial manager must be mindful of the degree of business risk the firm faces.

Financial Risk In addition to the business risk that a firm faces, if the firm uses debt in its capital structure, it also bears financial risk. *Financial risk* refers to fluctuations in the cash flows that a firm generates for its shareholders that result from financing the firm's activities with debt or other fixed-cost forms of financing. The more fixed-cost financing—debt (including financial leases) and preferred stock—a firm has in its capital structure, the greater its financial leverage and risk. Financial risk depends on the capital structure decision made by the management, and that decision should be influenced by the business risk the firm faces.

TABLE 13.9 Sales and Associated EBIT Calculations for Cooke Company (\$000)

Probability of sales	0.25	0.50	0.25
Sales revenue	\$400	\$600	\$800
Less: Fixed operating costs	200	200	200
Less: Variable operating costs (50% of sales)	200	300	400
Earnings before interest and taxes (EBIT)	\$ 0	\$100	\$200

Total Risk The *total risk* of a firm—business and financial risk combined—determines the likelihood that the firm could go bankrupt when cash flows fall so much that the firm is unable to meet its financial obligations. A continuation of the Cooke Company example demonstrates financial risk, its relationship to business risk, and their combined impact.

EXAMPLE 13.18

Cooke Company's current capital structure is as follows:

Current capital structure	
Long-term debt	$ 0
Common stock equity (25,000 shares at $20)	500,000
Total capital (assets)	$500,000

For simplicity we assume that the firm has no current liabilities, which means that its total capital equals total assets. Suppose Cooke is considering seven alternative capital structures corresponding to different amounts of debt and equity. Currently, the company has a debt ratio of 0%, but it may increase that ratio to any of the following values: 10%, 20%, 30%, 40%, 50%, and 60%. If the company decides to use at least some long-term debt financing, it will use the proceeds from borrowing to retire equity, leaving total capital and total assets at $500,000.[15] In other words, Cooke has no plans to borrow money to finance new investment. Table 13.10 shows the mix of debt and equity associated with

TABLE 13.10 Capital Structures Associated with Alternative Debt Ratios for Cooke Company

	Capital structure ($000)			
Debt ratio (1)	Total assets[a] (2)	Debt [(1) × (2)] (3)	Equity [(2) − (3)] (4)	Shares of common stock outstanding (000) [(4) ÷ $20][b] (5)
0%	$500	$ 0	$500	25.00
10	500	50	450	22.50
20	500	100	400	20.00
30	500	150	350	17.50
40	500	200	300	15.00
50	500	250	250	12.50
60	500	300	200	10.00

[a]Because the firm has no current liabilities, its total assets equal its total capital of $500,000.
[b]The $20 value represents the value per share of common stock equity noted earlier.

15. This assumption is needed so that we can assess alternative capital structures without having to consider the returns associated with the investment of additional funds raised. Attention here is given only to the mix of capital, not to its investment.

the seven possible capital structures as well as the number of shares of common stock outstanding under each alternative.

If Cooke Company decides to borrow money, the interest rate it will pay on its debt depends in part on how much the firm borrows. Lenders generally charge higher rates on loans to more heavily indebted borrowers. Table 13.11 shows the interest rate that Cooke will have to pay (on all of its debt) for each proposed capital structure. The table also indicates how much interest expense Cooke will pay at each debt level.

Table 13.12 demonstrates how Cooke can increase its financial risk by using more debt in its capital structure. The table calculates the expected value of Cooke's EPS, the standard deviation of EPS, and the coefficient of variation of EPS for each of three debt levels: 0%, 30%, and 60%.[16] For each capital structure, Table 13.12 shows the values of EBIT that Cooke might generate (as well as their associated probabilities from Table 13.9), the interest expense that Cooke must pay (from Table 13.11), and the resulting EPS figures (using the number of outstanding shares from Table 13.10).

Table 13.12 shows that with no debt at all, Cooke's earnings per share has an expected value of $2.40, with a standard deviation of $1.70 and a coefficient of variation of 0.71. Those figures indicate that even if Cooke borrows no money, its EPS is still risky, and that is because of Cooke's business risk. If Cooke decides to borrow money, its risk will increase due to financial risk. With 30% debt, the expected EPS rises to $3.12, but risk increases, too. The standard deviation of EPS is $2.42 at a 30% debt level, and the coefficient of variation rises to 0.78. With 60% debt, expected EPS is at its highest level, $4.65, but its standard deviation is $4.24, which is more than twice the standard deviation of EPS in the no-debt capital structure. Likewise, the coefficient of variation is highest at 60% debt, reaching 0.86.

TABLE 13.11 Level of Debt, Interest Rate, and Dollar Amount of Annual Interest Associated with Cooke Company's Alternative Capital Structures

Capital structure debt ratio	Debt ($000)	Interest rate on *all* debt	Interest ($000)
0%	$ 0	0.0%	$0.00 × 0.0 = $ 0.00
10	50	5.0	$ 50 × 0.05 = $ 2.50
20	100	5.5	$100 × 0.055 = $ 5.50
30	150	6.0	$150 × 0.06 = $ 9.00
40	200	6.5	$200 × 0.065 = $13.00
50	250	7.0	$250 × 0.07 = $17.50
60	300	7.5	$300 × 0.075 = $22.50

16. We use the coefficient of variation here to assess the risk of Cooke's EPS relative to its expected value. As Cooke increases the percentage of debt in its capital structure, earnings become more volatile, so stockholders will demand a higher rate of return. To know exactly how much higher the required return on equity would be as debt increases, we would need an estimate of the beta of Cooke's stock at each debt level. We show the coefficient of variation here only to convey the idea that the risk of the company's earnings, even relative to the expected EPS figure, is increasing as debt is rising.

TABLE 13.12 **Calculation of EPS for Selected Debt Ratios ($000) for Cooke Company**

Probability of EBIT		0.25	0.50	0.25
Debt ratio = 0%				
EBIT (Table 13.9)		$ 0.00	$100.00	$200.00
Less: Interest (Table 13.11)		0.00	0.00	0.00
Net profits before taxes		$ 0.00	$100.00	$200.00
Less: Taxes ($T = 0.40$)		0.00	40.00	80.00
Net profits after taxes		$ 0.00	$ 60.00	$120.00
EPS (25.0 shares, Table 13.10)		$ 0.00	$ 2.40	$ 4.80
Expected EPS[a]	$2.40			
Standard deviation of EPS[a]	$1.70			
Coefficient of variation of EPS[a]	0.71			
Debt ratio = 30%				
EBIT (Table 13.9)		$ 0.00	$100.00	$200.00
Less: Interest (Table 13.11)		9.00	9.00	9.00
Net profits before taxes		–$ 9.00	$ 91.00	$191.00
Less: Taxes ($T = 0.40$)		–3.60[b]	36.40	76.40
Net profits after taxes		–$ 5.40	$ 54.60	$114.60
EPS (17.50 shares, Table 13.10)		–0.31	$ 3.12	$ 6.55
Expected EPS[a]	$3.12			
Standard deviation of EPS[a]	$2.42			
Coefficient of variation of EPS[a]	0.78			
Debt ratio = 60%				
EBIT (Table 13.9)		$ 0.00	$100.00	$200.00
Less: Interest (Table 13.11)		22.50	22.50	22.50
Net profits before taxes		–$22.50	$ 77.50	$177.50
Less: Taxes ($T = 0.40$)		–9.00[b]	31.00	71.00
Net profits after taxes		–$13.50	$ 46.50	$106.50
EPS (10.00 shares, Table 13.10)		–$ 1.35	$ 4.65	$ 10.65
Expected EPS[a]	$4.65			
Standard deviation of EPS[a]	$4.24			
Coefficient of variation of EPS[a]	0.91			

[a]Chapter 8 presented the procedures required to calculate the expected value, standard deviation, and coefficient of variation.

[b]We assume that when the firm earns a net loss, it can deduct that loss against past earnings, and thereby obtain a tax benefit equal to 40% times the current period's net loss.

Table 13.13 summarizes the pertinent data for all seven alternative capital structures.[17] As the firm's financial leverage increases, the expected EPS rises,

17. The values for expected EPS, the standard deviation of EPS, and the coefficient of variation for the 0%, 30%, and 60% debt levels come directly from Table 13.12. We do not show the step-by-step calculations to produce those figures for the 10%, 20%, and 50% debt levels, but the process is the same, as shown in Table 13.12.

TABLE 13.13 **Expected EPS, Standard Deviation, and Coefficient of Variation for Alternative Capital Structures for Cooke Company**

Capital structure debt ratio	Expected EPS	Standard deviation of EPS	Coefficient of variation of EPS
0%	$2.40	$1.70	$1.70 ÷ $2.40 = 0.71
10	2.60	1.88	$1.88 ÷ $2.60 = 0.73
20	2.84	2.12	$2.12 ÷ $2.84 = 0.75
30	3.12	2.42	$2.42 ÷ $3.12 = 0.78
40	3.48	2.83	$2.83 ÷ $3.48 = 0.81
50	3.96	3.39	$3.39 ÷ $3.96 = 0.86
60	4.65	4.24	$4.24 ÷ $4.65 = 0.91

demonstrating that by borrowing more money, Cooke can deliver higher returns to shareholders. However, as leverage increases, so does risk, as reflected in both the standard deviation of EPS and the coefficient of variation. Cooke's shareholders will not be indifferent to the increase in risk they face as the firm borrows more money. In fact, they will demand a higher return as compensation for bearing that additional risk. Cooke's managers must decide how to weigh the higher EPS that borrowing helps the company deliver against the higher risk that debt imposes on shareholders.

Figure 13.3 illustrates the nature of the risk–return tradeoff associated with the seven capital structures under consideration by plotting the data from Table 13.13. The figure shows that as debt is substituted for equity (as the debt ratio increases), the level of EPS rises (graph **a**). If we look at risk as measured by the coefficient of variation (graph **b**), we can see that risk increases with increasing leverage. A portion of the risk simply reflects Cooke's business risk, but the portion that changes in response to increasing financial leverage is financial risk.

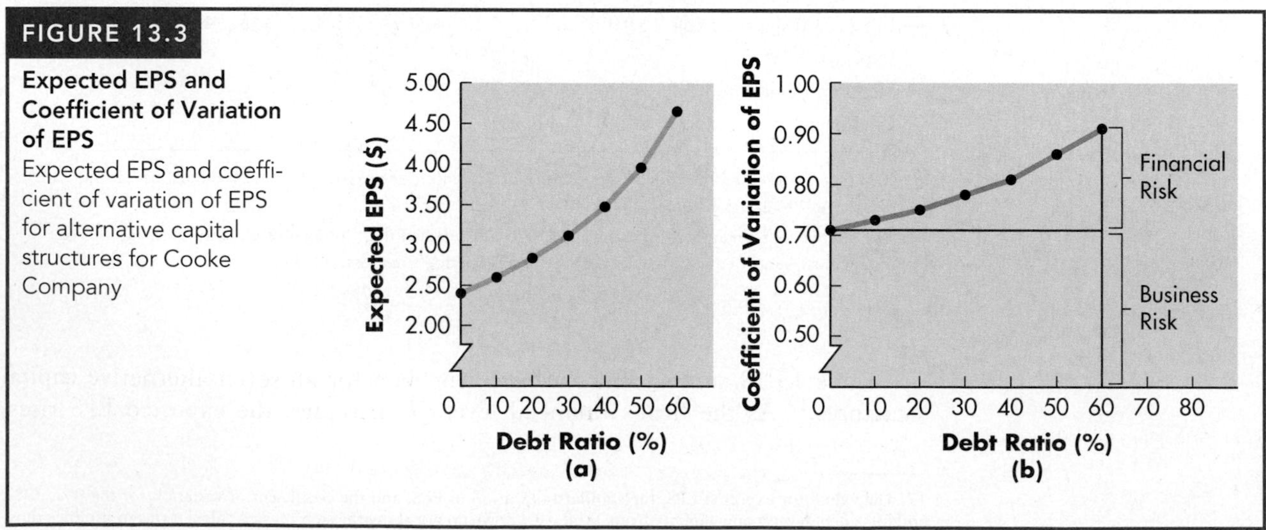

FIGURE 13.3

Expected EPS and Coefficient of Variation of EPS

Expected EPS and coefficient of variation of EPS for alternative capital structures for Cooke Company

Clearly, a risk–return tradeoff exists relative to the use of financial leverage. Later in the chapter, we will address how to combine these factors into a valuation framework. The key point here is that as a firm introduces more leverage into its capital structure, it will typically experience increases in both the expected return and the associated risk.

Agency Costs Imposed by Lenders

As noted in Chapter 1, the managers of firms typically act as *agents* of the owners (stockholders). The owners give the managers the authority to manage the firm for the owners' benefit. The *agency problem* created by this relationship extends not only to the relationship between owners and managers but also to that between owners and lenders.

When a lender provides funds to a firm, the interest rate charged is based on the lender's assessment of the firm's risk. The lender–borrower relationship therefore depends on the lender's expectations for the firm's subsequent behavior. The borrowing rates are, in effect, locked in when the loans are negotiated. After obtaining a loan at a certain rate, the firm could increase its risk by investing in risky projects or by incurring additional debt. Such action could weaken the lender's position in terms of its claim on the cash flow of the firm. From another point of view, if these risky investment strategies paid off, the stockholders would benefit. Because payment obligations to the lender remain unchanged, the excess cash flows generated by a positive outcome from the riskier action would enhance the value of the firm to its owners. In other words, if the risky investments pay off, the owners receive all the benefits; if the risky investments do not pay off, the lenders share in the costs if the firm cannot fully repay its debts.

Managers acting on behalf of stockholders therefore have an incentive to take advantage of lenders. To avoid this situation, lenders impose certain constraints on borrowers, who as a result incur *agency costs*. Lenders typically protect themselves by including provisions in the loan agreement limiting the firm's ability to alter its business and financial risk. These loan provisions may require firms to maintain a minimum level of liquidity, or they may restrict how the firm can spend money—for example, by restricting dividend payments.

By including appropriate provisions in the loan agreement, the lender limits management's ability to take actions that increase the firm's risk and thus protects itself against the adverse consequences of this agency problem. Of course, in exchange for incurring agency costs by agreeing to the operating and financial constraints placed on it by the loan provisions, the firm should benefit by obtaining funds at a lower cost.

Asymmetric Information

asymmetric information
The situation in which managers of a firm have more information about operations and future prospects than do investors.

When two or more parties in an economic transaction have different information, we say that there is **asymmetric information.** In the context of capital structure decisions, asymmetric information simply means that managers of the firm have more information about the firm's operations and future prospects than investors have. To understand how asymmetric information between managers and investors could have implications for a firm's capital structure, consider the following illustrations of the *pecking order and signaling theories*.

Pecking Order Theory Suppose that managers of a firm have a highly profitable investment opportunity that requires financing. Managers would like to tell investors about this great investment opportunity, but investors are skeptical. After all, managers always have incentives to claim that their investment decisions will lead to fabulous profits, but investors have no way to verify these claims. If managers try to sell stock to finance the investments, investors are only willing to pay a price reflecting the verifiable information they have, which means that managers must sell stock at a discount (relative to the price they could get if there were no asymmetric information). This situation makes raising new equity very costly, and sometimes managers may decide to pass up positive NPV investments to avoid having to sell equity to investors at a discount.

As one solution to this problem, managers can maintain financial slack, cash reserves from retained earnings that they can use to finance new investments. When firms do not have enough financial slack to finance their profitable investment opportunities, managers will prefer to raise external financing by issuing debt rather than equity. Providers of debt financing receive a fixed return, so when the new investment begins to generate high returns for the firm, those cash flows will largely go to the firm's existing stockholders.

pecking order theory
A hierarchy of financing that begins with retained earnings, which is followed by debt financing and finally external equity financing.

The consequence is a financial **pecking order,** meaning a hierarchy of financing that begins with retained earnings, followed by debt, and finally new stock issues. When managers want to finance a new project, they will first do so using retained earnings. If internally generated cash is insufficient to fund new investments, managers will raise external financing through the debt markets. Issuing new equity is their last resort.

This pecking order theory is consistent with several facts about firms' financing decisions. First, companies fund the vast majority of new investments through retained earnings, raising external financing infrequently. Second, firms do raise debt with greater frequency than equity, as the pecking order theory predicts. Third, as we have already noted, profitable companies (who have plenty of financial slack) generally tend to borrow less than unprofitable firms.

Signaling Theory An old saying goes, "Put your money where your mouth is." The idea is that anyone can brag, but only those who are willing to put real dollars at stake behind their claims are credible. How does this aphorism relate to capital structure decisions? Suppose, for example, that management has information that the prospects for the firm's future are very good. Managers could issue a press release trying to convince investors that the firm's future is bright, but investors will want tangible evidence for the claims. Furthermore, providing that evidence has to be costly to the firm; otherwise, other firms with less rosy prospects will just mimic the actions of the firm with truly excellent prospects. One thing that managers might do is to borrow a lot of money by issuing debt. In so doing, they are demonstrating to the market their faith that the firm will generate sufficient cash flows in the future to retire the outstanding debt. Firms whose prospects are not as good will hesitate to issue a lot of debt because they may have difficulty repaying the debt and may even go bankrupt. In other words, issuing debt is a credible **signal** that managers believe the firm's performance will be very good in the future. Debt financing is a *positive*

signal
A financing action by management that is believed to reflect its view of the firm's stock value; generally, debt financing is viewed as a *positive signal* that management believes the stock is "undervalued," and a stock issue is viewed as a *negative signal* that management believes the stock is "overvalued."

signal suggesting management's belief that the stock is "undervalued" and therefore a bargain.

By the same token, when firms decide to issue stock, investors worry that this move could be a *negative signal*, indicating the managers' belief that the firm's future profitability may be rather poor and that the stock price is currently overvalued. Therefore, investors often interpret the announcement of a stock issue as bad news, and the stock price declines.

Most research casts doubt on the importance of signaling as a primary determinant of firms' capital structure choices. For instance, we have already seen that the most profitable firms tend to borrow less, whereas the signaling theory says that profitable firms should borrow more as a way to convince investors of just how high the firm's future profits will be. Furthermore, in surveys that ask managers to describe how they choose between debt and equity financing, managers rarely say they choose debt as a way to convey information to investors. Still, the signaling theory predicts that a firm's stock price should rise when it issues debt and fall when it issues equity, and this is exactly what happens in the real world much of the time.

OPTIMAL CAPITAL STRUCTURE

What, then, is the optimal capital structure? To provide insight into an answer, we will examine some basic financial relationships. Because the value of a firm equals the present value of its future cash flows, it follows that *managers can maximize the value of the firm by minimizing the cost of capital, holding cash flows constant.* In other words, the present value of future cash flows is at its highest when the discount rate (the cost of capital) is at its lowest. By using a modification of the simple zero-growth valuation model (see Equation 7.2 in Chapter 7), we can define the value of the firm, V, as

$$V = \frac{\text{EBIT} \times (1 - T)}{r_{wacc}} = \frac{\text{NOPAT}}{r_{wacc}} \tag{13.11}$$

where

EBIT = earnings before interest and taxes

T = tax rate

NOPAT = net operating profits after taxes, which are the after-tax operating earnings available to the debt and equity holders, EBIT $\times$ $(1-T)$

r_{wacc} = weighted average cost of capital

If we hold NOPAT (and therefore EBIT) constant, the value of the firm, V, reaches a maximum when the weighted average cost of capital, r_{wacc}, is at a minimum.

Cost Functions

Figure 13.4(a) plots three cost functions—the after-tax cost of debt, the cost of equity, and the weighted average cost of capital (WACC)—as a function of financial leverage measured by the debt ratio (debt to total assets). The after-tax *cost of debt*, $r_d(1 - \text{T})$ is relatively low at low debt levels, but it slowly increases as

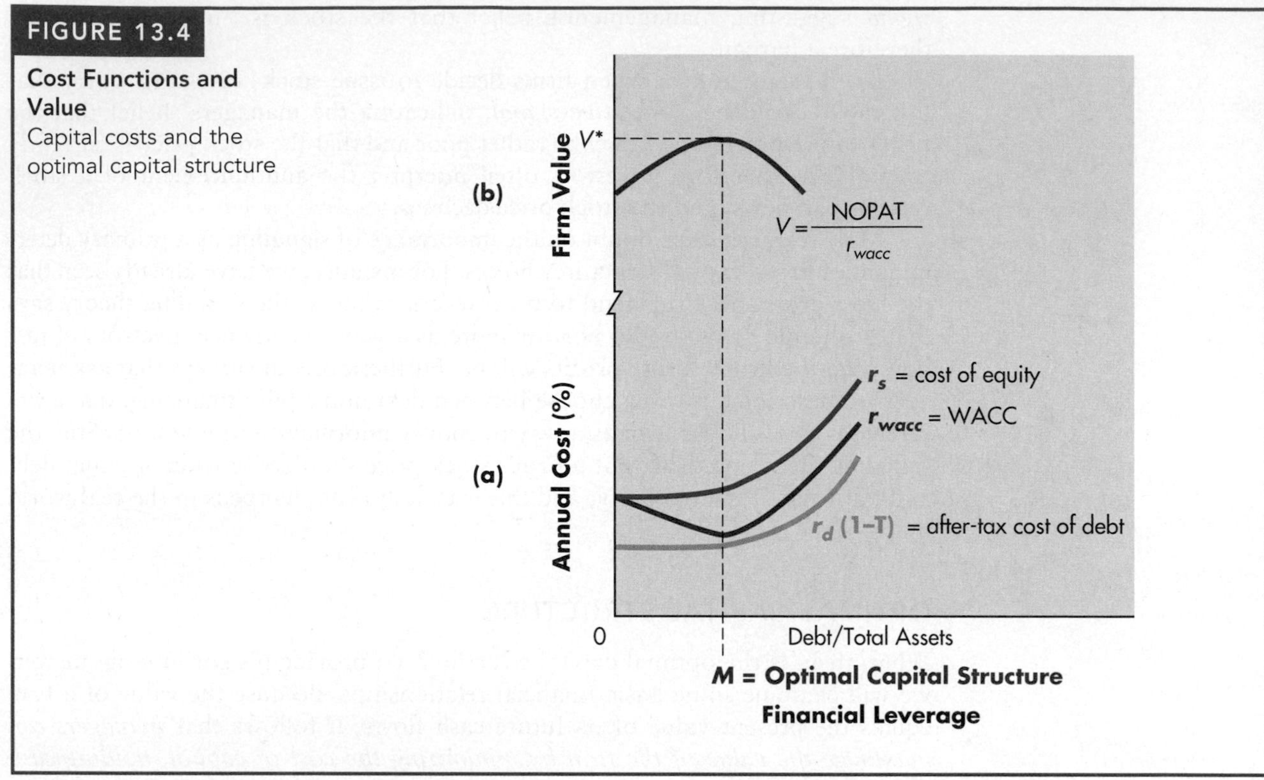

FIGURE 13.4

Cost Functions and Value
Capital costs and the optimal capital structure

leverage increases to compensate lenders for rising risk. The *cost of equity,* r_s, is greater than the cost of debt. It increases as financial leverage increases, but it generally rises more rapidly than the cost of debt. The cost of equity rises because the stockholders require a higher return as leverage increases to compensate for the higher degree of financial risk.

The *weighted average cost of capital,* r_{wacc}, results from a weighted average of the firm's debt and equity capital costs. At a debt ratio of zero, the firm is 100% equity financed. As managers substitute debt for equity and the debt ratio increases, the WACC declines because the savings from using low-cost, tax-deductible debt offset the increased cost of equity that occurs as leverage increases. In this range, the tax benefits of additional debt outweigh the costs of borrowing more. However, as the debt ratio continues to increase, the increased debt and equity costs eventually cause the WACC to rise, which occurs after point *M* in Figure 13.4(*a*). In other words, the bankruptcy costs, agency costs, and other costs associated with higher debt levels eventually outweigh the additional tax benefits the firm could generate by borrowing even more. This behavior results in a U-shaped weighted average cost-of-capital function.

Graphical View of Optimal Structure

optimal capital structure
The capital structure at which the weighted average cost of capital is minimized, thereby maximizing the firm's value.

The **optimal capital structure** is the mixture of debt and equity that minimizes the WACC and maximizes the value of the firm. In Figure 13.4(*a*), point *M* represents the *minimum weighted average cost of capital,* the point of optimal financial leverage and hence of optimal capital structure for the firm. Figure 13.4(*b*) is a graph of the value of the firm that results from substitution of r_{wacc} in Figure 13.4(*a*) for various levels of financial leverage into the zero-growth valuation model in Equation 13.11. As shown in Figure 13.4(*b*), at the optimal capital structure, point *M*, the value of the firm reaches a maximum at V^*.

As a practical matter, finding the precise mix of debt and equity that maximizes the firm's value is very difficult. The costs and benefits of debt are not always easy to quantify. For example, when managers decide to rely more heavily on debt, they know the probability that the firm could go bankrupt (and incur bankruptcy costs) increases, but exactly how much it increases is uncertain. Likewise, managers have no way to obtain precise estimates of the bankruptcy costs that the firm will incur if bankruptcy occurs. Accordingly, firms generally try to operate in a range that places them near what they believe to be the optimal capital structure. In other words, firms usually manage toward a *target capital structure*.

→ REVIEW QUESTIONS MyLab Finance Solutions

13–6 What is a firm's capital structure? What ratios assess the degree of financial leverage in a firm's capital structure?

13–7 In what ways are the capital structures of U.S. firms and non–U.S. firms different? How are they similar?

13–8 What is the major benefit of debt financing? How does it affect the firm's cost of debt?

13–9 What are business risk and financial risk? How does each influence the firm's capital structure decisions?

13–10 Briefly describe the agency problem that exists between owners and lenders. How do lenders cause firms to incur agency costs to resolve this problem?

13–11 How does asymmetric information affect the firm's capital structure decisions? How do the firm's financing actions give investors signals that reflect management's view of stock value?

13–12 How do the cost of debt, the cost of equity, and the weighted average cost of capital (WACC) behave as the firm's financial leverage increases from zero? Where is the optimal capital structure? What is its relationship to the firm's value at that point?

LG5

13.3 EBIT–EPS Approach to Capital Structure

It should be clear from earlier chapters that the goal of the financial manager is to maximize the value of the firm. One of the widely followed variables affecting the firm's value is its earnings, which represent the returns earned on behalf of owners. Even though focusing exclusively on earnings ignores risk (the other key variable affecting the firm's stock price), we can gain some useful insights into the merits of alternative capital structures by studying how changing debt levels impact earnings. The **EBIT–EPS approach** to capital structure involves selecting the capital structure that maximizes EPS over the expected range of earnings before interest and taxes (EBIT).

EBIT–EPS approach
An approach for selecting the capital structure that maximizes earnings per share (EPS) over the expected range of earnings before interest and taxes (EBIT).

PRESENTING A FINANCING PLAN GRAPHICALLY

To analyze the effects of a firm's capital structure on the owners' returns, we consider the relationship between earnings before interest and taxes (EBIT) and earnings per share (EPS). In other words, we want to see how changes in EBIT lead to changes in EPS under different capital structures. In all our examples, we will assume that business risk remains constant. That is, the firm's basic operational risks remain constant, and only financial risk varies as capital structures change. EPS is a measure of the owners' returns that is closely related to the firm's share price.[18]

Data Required

To draw a graph illustrating how changes in EBIT lead to changes in EPS, we simply need to find two coordinates and plot a straight line between them. On our graph, we will plot EBIT on the horizontal axis and EPS on the vertical axis. The following example illustrates the approach for constructing the graph.

EXAMPLE 13.19

We can plot coordinates on the EBIT–EPS graph by assuming specific EBIT values and calculating the EPS associated with them.[19] Such calculations for three capital structures—debt ratios of 0%, 30%, and 60%—for Cooke Company appear in Table 13.12. For EBIT values of \$100,000 and \$200,000, the associated EPS values calculated there are summarized in the table below the graph in Figure 13.5.

Plotting the Data

financial breakeven point
The level of EBIT necessary to just cover all *fixed financial costs;* the level of EBIT for which EPS = \$0.

Figure 13.5 shows the relationship between EBIT and EPS for three possible capital structures for the Cooke Company. Each line in the figure represents a different capital structure, and where the lines cross the horizontal axis defines a financial breakeven point. The **financial breakeven point** is the point at which EPS equals \$0, which means that the firm generates just enough EBIT to cover its fixed financial costs, which in this case include only interest expense. You can see that for the capital structure with 0% debt, EPS does not fall below \$0 unless

18. The relationship between EPS and owner wealth is not necessarily one of cause and effect. As indicated in Chapter 1, maximizing profits is not the same as maximizing owners' wealth. Nevertheless, changes in earnings per share often have an impact on owners' wealth because earnings are usually positively correlated with cash flows, and they provide investors with useful information about how a firm is likely to perform going forward.

19. A convenient method for finding one EBIT–EPS coordinate is to calculate the financial breakeven point, the level of EBIT for which the firm's EPS just equals \$0. It is the level of EBIT needed just to cover all fixed financial costs: annual interest (I) and preferred stock dividends (PD). The equation for the financial breakeven point is

$$\text{Financial breakeven point} = I + \frac{PD}{1 - T}$$

where T is the tax rate. It can be seen that when $PD = \$0$, the financial breakeven point is equal to I, the annual interest payment.

FIGURE 13.5

EBIT–EPS Approach
A comparison of selected capital structures for Cooke Company (data from Table 13.12)

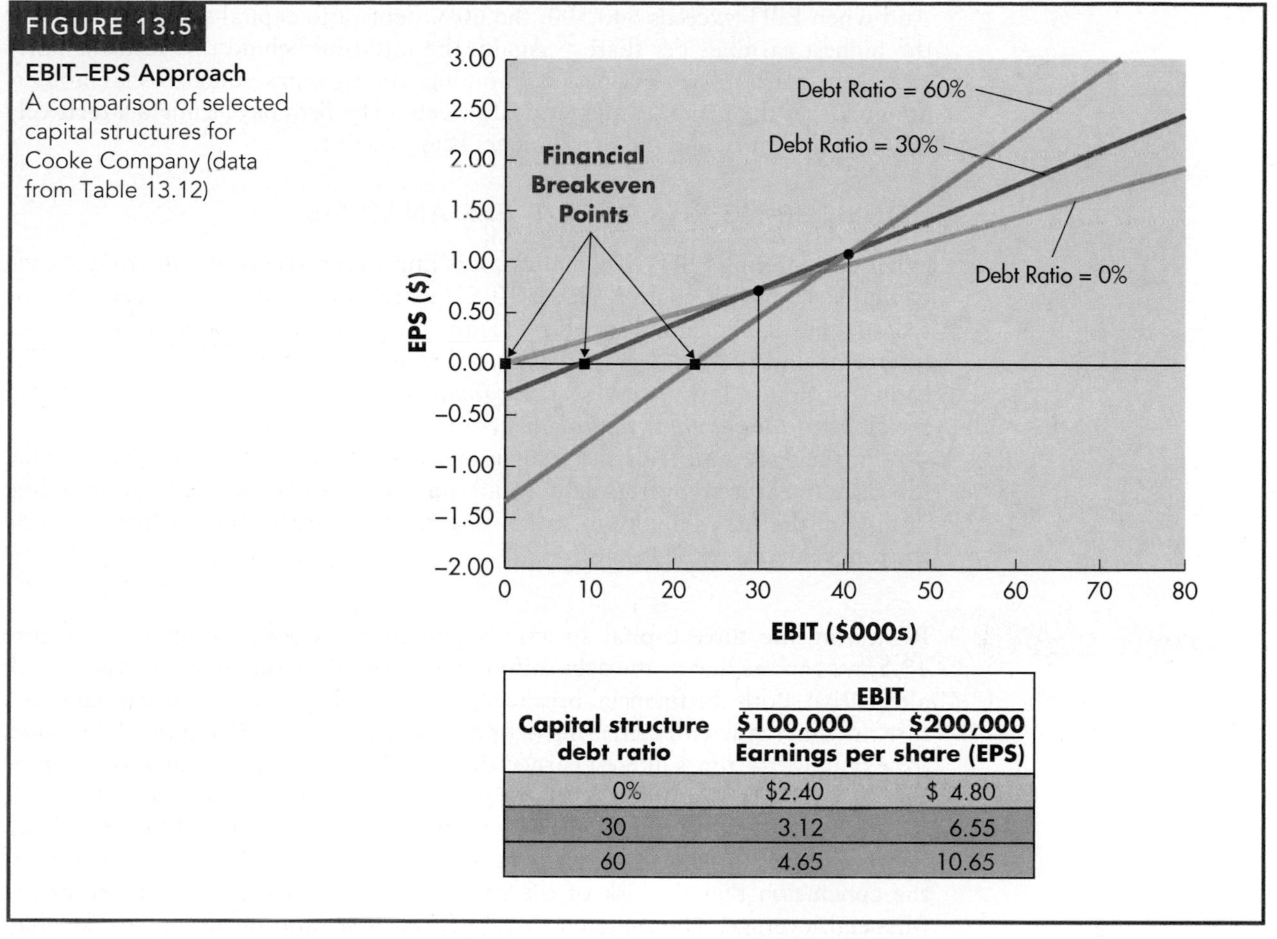

Capital structure debt ratio	EBIT $100,000	$200,000
	Earnings per share (EPS)	
0%	$2.40	$ 4.80
30	3.12	6.55
60	4.65	10.65

EBIT does. In contrast, for the 30% and 60% capital structures, EPS will be negative unless the firm earns sufficient EBIT to cover its interest expense.

COMPARING ALTERNATIVE CAPITAL STRUCTURES

In addition to identifying the financial breakeven point for each capital structure, Figure 13.5 identifies the ranges of EBIT over which each possible capital structure produces the highest EPS.

EXAMPLE 13.20

Cooke Company's capital structure alternatives appear on the EBIT–EPS axes in Figure 13.5. This figure shows that each capital structure is superior to the others in terms of maximizing EPS over certain ranges of EBIT. Having no debt at all (debt ratio = 0%) is best for levels of EBIT between $0 and $30,000. That conclusion makes sense because when business conditions are relatively weak, Cooke would have difficulty meeting its financial obligations if it had any debt. Between $30,000 and $40,500 of EBIT, the capital structure associated with a debt ratio of 30% produces higher EPS than either of the other two capital structures.

And when EBIT exceeds \$40,500, the 60% debt ratio capital structure provides the highest earnings per share.[20] Again, the intuition behind this result is fairly straightforward. When business is booming, the earnings going to shareholders are greater if the firm uses a great deal of debt. The firm pays lenders a relatively low rate of return, and the shareholders keep the rest.

CONSIDERING RISK IN EBIT–EPS ANALYSIS

When interpreting EBIT–EPS analysis, it is important to consider the risk of each capital structure alternative. Figure 13.5 illustrates two aspects that relate to the risk of a particular capital structure: (1) the *financial breakeven point* (EBIT–axis intercept) and (2) the *degree of financial leverage* reflected in the slope of the capital structure line. *The higher the financial breakeven point and the steeper the slope of the capital structure line, the greater the financial risk.*[21]

Further assessment of risk can be performed by using ratios. As financial leverage (measured by the debt ratio) increases, we expect a corresponding decline in the firm's ability to make scheduled interest payments (measured by the times interest earned ratio).

EXAMPLE 13.21

Reviewing the three capital structures plotted for Cooke Company in Figure 13.5, we can see that as the debt ratio increases, so does the financial risk of each alternative. Both the financial breakeven point and the slope of the capital structure lines increase with increasing debt ratios. If we use the \$100,000 EBIT value, for example, the times interest earned ratio (EBIT ÷ interest) for the zero-leverage capital structure is infinity (\$100,000 ÷ \$0); for the 30% debt case, it is 11.1 (\$100,000 ÷ \$9,000); and for the 60% debt case, it is 4.4 (\$100,000 ÷ \$22,500). Because lower times interest earned ratios reflect higher risk, these ratios support the conclusion that the risk of the capital structures increases with increasing financial leverage. The capital structure for a debt ratio of 60% is riskier than that for a debt ratio of 30%, which in turn is riskier than the capital structure for a debt ratio of 0%.

---

20. An algebraic technique helps to identify the indifference points between the capital structure alternatives. This technique involves expressing each capital structure as an equation stated in terms of earnings per share, setting the equations for two capital structures equal to each other, and solving for the level of EBIT that causes the equations to be equal. When we use the notation from footnote 18 and let n equal the number of shares of common stock outstanding, the general equation for the earnings per share from a financing plan is

$$\text{EPS} = \frac{(1 - T) \times (\text{EBIT} - I) - PD}{n}$$

Comparing Cooke Company's 0% and 30% capital structures, we get

$$\frac{(1 - 0.40) \times (\text{EBIT} - \$0) - \$0}{25.00} = \frac{(1 - 0.40) \times (\text{EBIT} - \$9.00) - \$0}{17.50}$$

$$\frac{0.60 \times \text{EBIT}}{25.00} = \frac{0.60 \times \text{EBIT} - \$5.40}{17.50}$$

$$10.50 \times \text{EBIT} = 15.00 \times \text{EBIT} - \$135.00$$

$$\$135.00 = 4.50 \times \text{EBIT}$$

$$\text{EBIT} = \$30$$

The calculated value of the indifference point between the 0% and 30% capital structures is therefore \$30,000, as can be seen in Figure 13.5.

21. The degree of financial leverage (DFL) is reflected in the slope of the EBIT–EPS function. The steeper the slope, the greater the degree of financial leverage, because the change in EPS (y-axis) that results from a given change in EBIT (x-axis) increases with increasing slope and decreases with decreasing slope.

BASIC SHORTCOMING OF EBIT–EPS ANALYSIS

The most important point to recognize when using EBIT–EPS analysis is that this technique tends to concentrate on maximizing earnings rather than maximizing owner wealth as reflected in the firm's stock price. The EPS-maximizing approach generally ignores risk. If investors did not require risk premiums (additional returns) as the firm increased the proportion of debt in its capital structure, a strategy involving maximizing EPS would also maximize stock price. But because risk premiums rise with increases in financial leverage, maximizing EPS does not necessarily maximize the value of the firm. To select the best capital structure, firms must integrate both return (EPS) and risk (via the required return, r_s) into a valuation framework consistent with the capital structure theory presented earlier.

→ REVIEW QUESTION MyLab Finance Solutions

13–13 Explain the EBIT–EPS approach to capital structure. Include in your explanation a graph indicating the financial breakeven point; label the axes. Is this approach consistent with maximization of the owners' wealth?

13.4 Choosing the Optimal Capital Structure

This section describes the procedures for linking to market value the return and risk associated with alternative capital structures.

LINKAGE

To determine the firm's value under alternative capital structures, the firm must find the level of return that it must earn to compensate owners for the risk being incurred. This approach is consistent with the overall valuation framework developed in Chapters 6 and 7 and applied to capital budgeting decisions in Chapters 10 through 12.

Financial analysts can estimate the required return associated with a given level of financial risk in a number of ways. Theoretically, the preferred approach would be first to estimate the beta associated with each alternative capital structure and then to use the CAPM framework presented in Equation 8.8 to calculate the required return, r_s. A more operational approach involves linking the financial risk associated with each capital structure alternative directly to the required return. Such an approach is similar to the CAPM-type approach demonstrated in Chapter 12 for linking project risk and required return (RADR). Here it involves estimating the required return associated with each level of financial risk as measured by a statistic such as the coefficient of variation of EPS. Regardless of the approach used, one would expect the required return to increase as the financial risk increases.

EXAMPLE 13.22

Cooke Company, using as risk measures the coefficients of variation of EPS associated with each of the seven alternative capital structures, estimated the associated required returns, which are shown in Table 13.14. As expected, the estimated required return of owners, r_s, increases with increasing risk, as measured by the coefficient of variation of EPS.

TABLE 13.14 Required Returns for Cooke Company's Alternative Capital Structures

Capital structure debt ratio	Coefficient of variation of EPS (from Table 13.13)	Estimated required return, r_s
0%	0.71	8.50%
10	0.73	8.75
20	0.75	9.00
30	0.78	9.50
40	0.81	11.00
50	0.86	13.00
60	0.91	15.50

ESTIMATING VALUE

The value of the firm's stock associated with alternative capital structures can be estimated using one of the standard valuation models. If, for simplicity, we assume that all earnings are paid out as dividends, we can use a standard zero-growth valuation model such as that developed in Chapter 7. The model, originally stated in Equation 7.2, is restated here with EPS substituted for dividends (because in each year the dividends would equal EPS):

$$P_0 = \frac{\text{EPS}}{r_s} \tag{13.12}$$

By substituting the expected level of EPS and the associated required return, r_s, into Equation 13.12, we can estimate the per-share value of the firm, P_0.

EXAMPLE 13.23

We can now estimate the value of Cooke Company's stock under each of the alternative capital structures. Substituting the expected EPS (from Table 13.13) and the required returns, r_s (from Table 13.14), into Equation 13.12 for each capital structure, we obtain the share values given in the last column of Table 13.15. Plotting the resulting share values against the associated debt ratios, as

TABLE 13.15 Calculation of Share Value Estimates Associated with Alternative Capital Structures for Cooke Company

Capital structure debt ratio	Expected EPS (from Table 13.13)	Estimated required return, r_s (from Table 13.14)	Estimated share value
0%	$2.40	8.50%	$2.40 ÷ 0.085 = $28.24
10	2.60	8.75	$2.60 ÷ 0.0875 = $29.71
20	2.84	9.00	$2.84 ÷ 0.09 = $31.56
30	3.12	9.50	$3.12 ÷ 0.095 = $32.84
40	3.48	11.00	$3.48 ÷ 0.11 = $31.64
50	3.96	13.00	$3.96 ÷ 0.13 = $30.46
60	4.65	15.50	$4.65 ÷ 0.155 = $30.00

FIGURE 13.6

Estimating Value
Estimated share value and EPS for alternative capital structures for Cooke Company

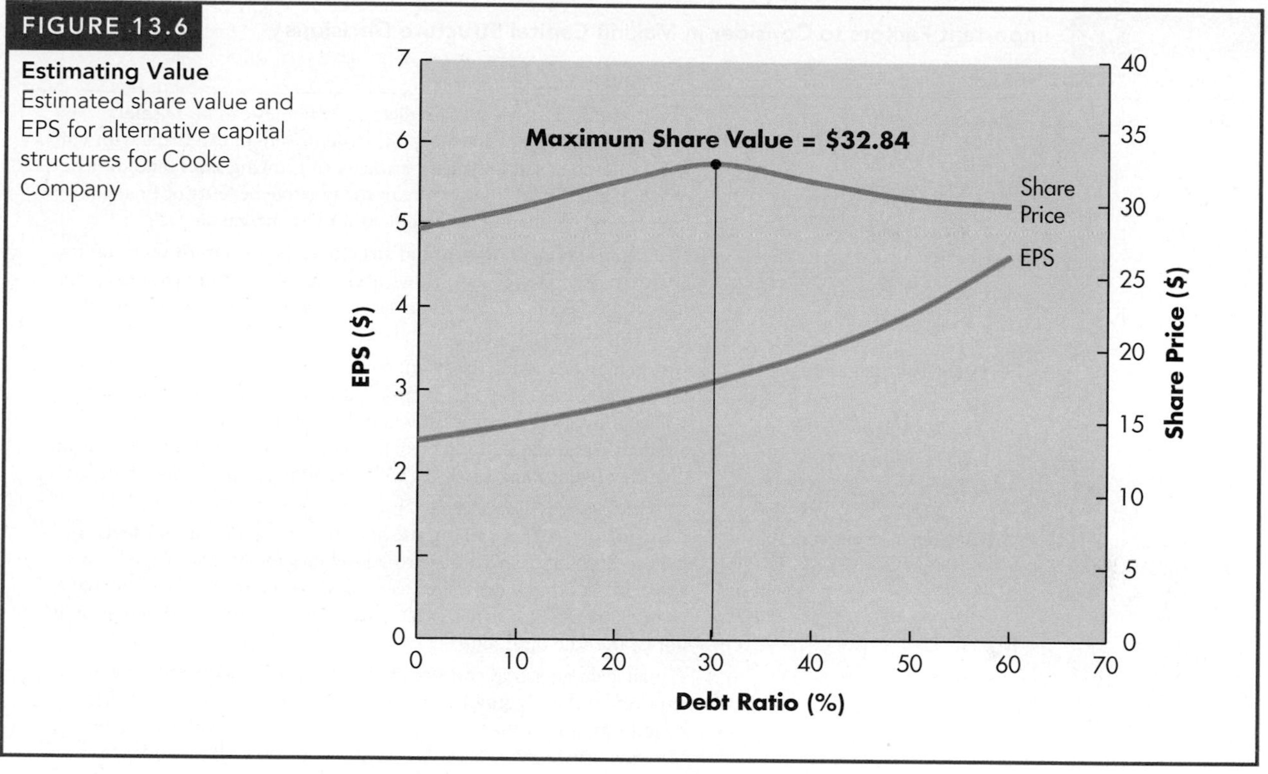

shown in Figure 13.6, clearly illustrates that the maximum share value occurs at the capital structure associated with a debt ratio of 30%.

MAXIMIZING VALUE VERSUS MAXIMIZING EPS

Throughout this text, we have specified the goal of the financial manager as maximizing owner wealth, not profit. Although some relationship exists between expected profit and value, there is no reason to believe that profit-maximizing strategies necessarily result in wealth maximization. It is therefore the wealth of the owners as reflected in the estimated share value that should serve as the criterion for selecting the best capital structure. A final look at Cooke Company will highlight this point.

EXAMPLE 13.24

Further analysis of Figure 13.6 clearly shows that although the firm's profits (EPS) are maximized at a debt ratio of 60%, share value is maximized at a 30% debt ratio. Therefore, the preferred capital structure would be the 30% debt ratio. The two approaches provide different conclusions because EPS maximization does not account for risk.

SOME OTHER IMPORTANT CONSIDERATIONS

Because finding the optimal capital structure involves a great deal of uncertainty, managers must temper any quantitative analysis of capital structure with other important considerations. Table 13.16 summarizes some of the more important additional factors involved in capital structure decisions.

TABLE 13.16 Important Factors to Consider in Making Capital Structure Decisions

Concern	Factor	Description
Business risk	Revenue stability	Firms that have stable and predictable revenues can more safely undertake highly leveraged capital structures than can firms with volatile patterns of sales revenue. Firms with growing sales tend to benefit from added debt; they can reap the positive benefits of financial leverage, which magnifies the effect of these increases.
	Cash flow	When considering a new capital structure, the firm must focus on its ability to generate the cash flows necessary to meet obligations. Cash forecasts reflecting an ability to service debts (and preferred stock) must support any shift in capital structure.
Agency costs	Contractual obligations	A firm may be contractually constrained with respect to the type of funds that it can raise. For example, a firm might be prohibited from selling additional debt except when the claims of holders of such debt are made subordinate to the existing debt. Contractual constraints on the sale of additional stock, as well as on the ability to distribute dividends on stock, might also exist.
	Management preferences	Occasionally, a firm will impose an internal constraint on the use of debt to limit its risk exposure to a level deemed acceptable to management. In other words, because of risk aversion, the firm's management constrains the firm's capital structure at a level that may or may not be the true optimum.
	Control	A management group concerned about control may prefer to issue debt rather than (voting) common stock. Under favorable market conditions, a firm that wanted to sell equity could make a *preemptive offering* or issue *nonvoting shares*, allowing each shareholder to maintain proportionate ownership. Generally, only in closely held firms or firms threatened by takeover does control become a major concern in the capital structure decision.
Asymmetric information	External risk assessment	The firm's ability to raise funds quickly and at favorable rates depends on the external risk assessments of lenders and bond raters. The firm must consider the impact of capital structure decisions both on share value and on published financial statements from which lenders and raters assess the firm's risk.
	Timing	At times when interest rates are low, debt financing might be more attractive; when interest rates are high, the sale of stock may be more appealing. Sometimes both debt and equity capital become unavailable at reasonable terms. General economic conditions—especially those of the capital market—can thus significantly affect capital structure decisions.

→ **REVIEW QUESTIONS** MyLab Finance Solutions

13–14 Why do maximizing EPS and maximizing value not necessarily lead to the same conclusion about the optimal capital structure?

13–15 What important factors in addition to quantitative factors should a firm consider when it is making a capital structure decision?

SUMMARY

FOCUS ON VALUE

The amount of leverage (fixed-cost assets or funds) used by a firm directly affects its risk, return, and share value. Generally, higher leverage raises risk and return, and lower leverage reduces risk and return. Operating leverage concerns the level of fixed operating costs; financial leverage focuses on fixed financial costs, particularly interest on debt, lease payments, and any preferred stock dividends. The firm's capital structure determines its financial leverage. Because of its fixed interest payments, the more debt a firm uses relative to its equity, the greater its financial leverage.

The value of the firm is clearly affected by its degree of operating leverage and by the composition of its capital structure. The financial manager must therefore carefully consider the types of operating and financial costs the firm will incur, recognizing that higher risk comes with greater fixed costs. Major decisions with regard to both operating cost structure and capital structure must therefore focus on their impact on the firm's value. The firm should implement only those leverage and capital structure decisions that are consistent with its goal of **maximizing its stock price.**

REVIEW OF LEARNING GOALS

LG 1 **Discuss leverage, capital structure, breakeven analysis, the operating breakeven point, and the effect of changing costs on the breakeven point.** Leverage results from the use of fixed costs to magnify returns to a firm's owners. Capital structure, the firm's mix of long-term debt and equity, affects leverage and therefore the firm's value. Breakeven analysis measures the level of sales necessary to cover total operating costs. The operating breakeven point may be calculated algebraically by dividing fixed operating costs by the difference between the sale price per unit and variable operating cost per unit, or it may be determined graphically. The operating breakeven point increases with increased fixed and variable operating costs and decreases with an increase in sale price, and vice versa.

LG 2 **Understand operating, financial, and total leverage and the relationships among them.** Operating leverage is the use of fixed operating costs by the firm to magnify the effects of changes in sales on EBIT. The higher the fixed operating costs, the greater the operating leverage. Financial leverage is the use of fixed financial costs by the firm to magnify the effects of changes in EBIT on EPS. The higher the fixed financial costs, the greater the financial leverage. The total leverage of the firm is the use of fixed costs—both operating and financial—to magnify the effects of changes in sales on EPS.

LG 3 **Describe the types of capital, external assessment of capital structure, the capital structure of non–U.S. firms, and capital structure theory.** Debt capital and equity capital make up a firm's capital structure. Capital structure can be externally assessed by using financial ratios: debt ratio, times interest earned ratio, and fixed-payment coverage ratio. Non–U.S. companies tend to have much higher degrees of indebtedness than do their U.S. counterparts, primarily because U.S. capital markets are more developed.

Research suggests there is an optimal capital structure that balances the firm's benefits and costs of debt financing. The major benefit of debt financing is the tax shield. The costs of debt financing include the probability of bankruptcy, agency costs imposed by lenders, and asymmetric information, which typically causes firms to raise funds in a pecking order so as to send positive signals to the market and thereby enhance shareholder wealth.

LG 4 **Explain the optimal capital structure using a graphical view of the firm's cost-of-capital functions and a zero-growth valuation model.** The zero-growth valuation model defines the firm's value as its net operating profits after taxes (NOPAT), or after-tax EBIT, divided by its weighted average cost of capital. Assuming that NOPAT is constant, the value of the firm is maximized by minimizing its weighted average cost of capital (WACC). The optimal capital structure minimizes the WACC. Graphically, the firm's WACC exhibits a U-shaped curve whose minimum value defines the optimal capital structure that maximizes owner wealth.

LG 5 **Discuss the EBIT–EPS approach to capital structure.** The EBIT–EPS approach evaluates capital structures in light of the returns they provide the firm's owners and their degree of financial risk. Under the EBIT–EPS approach, the preferred capital structure is the one expected to provide maximum EPS over the firm's expected range of EBIT. Graphically, this approach reflects risk in terms of the financial breakeven point and the slope of the capital structure line. The major shortcoming of EBIT–EPS analysis is that it concentrates on maximizing earnings (returns) rather than owners' wealth, which considers risk as well as return.

LG 6 **Review the return and risk of alternative capital structures, their linkage to market value, and other important considerations related to capital structure.** The best capital structure can be selected by using a valuation model to link return and risk factors. The preferred capital structure is the one that results in the highest estimated share value, not the highest EPS. Other important nonquantitative factors must also be considered when making capital structure decisions.

OPENER-IN-REVIEW

The chapter opener describes a shift in Apple's financial strategy that began in 2012. Specifically, Apple took actions that (modestly) increased its reliance on debt. The following table shows Apple's annual revenues (in millions) and its earnings per share (EPS) for a few years before and a few years after the company began changing its capital structure. Use these figures to answer the questions.

	2010	2011	2012
Revenues	$ 65,225	$108,249	$156,508
EPS	$ 2.16	$ 3.95	$ 6.31
	2014	**2015**	**2016**
Revenues	$182,795	$233,715	$215,091
EPS	$ 6.49	$ 9.28	$ 8.35

a. Now that the company has decided to use the proceeds from a bond issue to repurchase shares, what would you expect the effect of that decision to be on Apple's degree of total leverage?

b. Calculate the percentage change in revenues and in EPS from 2010 to 2011 and from 2011 to 2012 (before Apple altered its capital structure). What was Apple's degree of total leverage at this time?

c. Calculate the percentage changes in revenues and EPS from 2014 to 2015 and from 2015 to 2016 (after Apple had been altering its capital structure for a few years). What was Apple's degree of total leverage at this time?

d. Do your findings in questions **b** and **c** align with your expectations from question **a**?

e. What do you think happened to the beta of Apple's common stock from 2010 to 2016?

SELF-TEST PROBLEMS (Solutions in Appendix)

ST13–1 **Breakeven point and all forms of leverage** TOR most recently sold 100,000 units at \$7.50 each; its variable operating costs are \$3.00 per unit, and its fixed operating costs are \$250,000. Annual interest charges total \$80,000, and the firm has 8,000 shares of \$5 (annual dividend) preferred stock outstanding. It currently has 20,000 shares of common stock outstanding. Assume that the firm is subject to a 40% tax rate.

a. At what level of sales (in units) would the firm break even on operations (i.e., EBIT = \$0)?

b. Calculate the firm's earnings per share (EPS) in tabular form at (1) the current level of sales and (2) a 120,000-unit sales level.

c. Using the current \$750,000 level of sales as a base, calculate the firm's degree of operating leverage (DOL).

d. Using the EBIT associated with the \$750,000 level of sales as a base, calculate the firm's degree of financial leverage (DFL).

e. Use the degree of total leverage (DTL) concept to determine the effect (in percentage terms) of a 50% increase in TOR's sales from the \$750,000 base level on its earnings per share.

ST13–2 **EBIT–EPS analysis** Newlin Electronics is considering additional financing of \$10,000. It currently has \$50,000 of 12% (annual interest) bonds and 10,000 shares of common stock outstanding. The firm can obtain the financing through a 12% (annual interest) bond issue or through the sale of 1,000 shares of common stock. The firm has a 21% tax rate.

a. Calculate two EBIT–EPS coordinates for each plan by selecting any two EBIT values and finding their associated EPS values.

b. Plot the two financing plans on a set of EBIT–EPS axes.

c. On the basis of your graph in part **b**, at what level of EBIT does the bond plan become superior to the stock plan?

ST13–3 **Optimal capital structure** Hawaiian Macadamia Nut Company has collected the data in the following table with respect to its capital structure, expected earnings per share, and required return.

Capital structure debt ratio	Expected earnings per share	Required return, r_s
0%	$3.12	13%
10	3.90	15
20	4.80	16
30	5.44	17
40	5.51	19
50	5.00	20
60	4.40	22

a. Compute the estimated share value associated with each of the capital structures, using the simplified method described in this chapter (see Equation 13.12).

b. Determine the optimal capital structure on the basis of (1) maximization of expected earnings per share and (2) maximization of share value.

c. Which capital structure do you recommend? Why?

WARM-UP EXERCISES

All problems are available in MyLab Finance

LG 1 **E13–1** Canvas Reproductions has fixed operating costs of $12,500 and variable operating costs of $10 per unit and sells its paintings for $25 each. At what level of unit sales will the company break even in terms of EBIT?

LG 1 **E13–2** The Great Fish Taco Corporation currently has fixed operating costs of $15,000, sells its premade tacos for $6 per box, and incurs variable operating costs of $2.50 per box. If the firm has a potential investment that would simultaneously raise its fixed costs to $16,500 and allow it to charge a per-box sale price of $6.50 due to better-textured tacos, what will the impact be on its operating breakeven point in boxes?

LG 2 **E13–3** Chico's has sales of 15,000 units at a price of $20 per unit. The firm incurs fixed operating costs of $30,000 and variable operating costs of $12 per unit. What is Chico's degree of operating leverage (DOL) at a base level of sales of 15,000 units?

LG 2 **E13–4** Parker Investments has EBIT of $20,000, interest expense of $3,000, and preferred dividends of $4,000. If it pays taxes at a rate of 38%, what is Parker's degree of financial leverage (DFL) at a base level of EBIT of $20,000?

LG 4 **E13–5** Cobalt Industries had sales of 150,000 units at a price of $10 per unit. It faced fixed operating costs of $250,000 and variable operating costs of $5 per unit. The company is subject to a tax rate of 21% and has a weighted average cost of capital of 8.5%. Calculate Cobalt's net operating profits after taxes (NOPAT), and use them to estimate the value of the firm.

PROBLEMS

All problems are available in MyLab Finance. The MyLab icon indicates problems in Excel format available in MyLab Finance.

P13–1 **Breakeven point: Algebraic** Kate Rowland wishes to estimate the number of flower arrangements she must sell at $24.95 to break even. She has estimated fixed operating costs of $12,350 per year and variable operating costs of $15.45 per arrangement. How many flower arrangements must Kate sell to break even on operating costs?

P13–2 **Breakeven comparisons: Algebraic** Given the price and cost data shown in the accompanying table for each of the three firms, F, G, and H, answer the questions that follow.

Firm	F	G	H
Sale price per unit	$ 18.00	$ 21.00	$ 30.00
Variable operating cost per unit	6.75	13.50	12.00
Fixed operating cost	45,000	30,000	90,000

a. What is the operating breakeven point in units for each firm?
b. How would you rank these firms in terms of their risk?

P13–3 **Breakeven point: Algebraic and graphical** Fine Leather Enterprises sells its single product for $129.00 per unit. The firm's fixed operating costs are $473,000 annually, and its variable operating costs are $86.00 per unit.
a. Find the firm's operating breakeven point in units.
b. Label the x-axis "Sales (units)" and the y-axis "Costs/Revenues ($)," and then graph the firm's sales revenue, total operating cost, and fixed operating cost functions on these axes. In addition, label the operating breakeven point and the areas of loss and profit (EBIT).

P13–4 **Breakeven analysis** Barry Carter is considering opening a used-book store. He wants to estimate the number of books he must sell to break even. The books will be sold for $13.98 each, variable operating costs are $10.48 per book, and annual fixed operating costs are $73,500.
a. Find the operating breakeven point in number of books.
b. Calculate the total operating costs at the breakeven volume found in part **a**.
c. If Barry estimates that at a minimum he can sell 2,000 books per month, should he go into the business?
d. How much EBIT will Barry realize if he sells the minimum 2,000 books per month noted in part **c**?

Personal Finance Problem

P13–5 **Breakeven analysis** Paul Scott has a 2014 Cadillac that he wants to update with a satellite-based emergency response system so that he will have access to roadside assistance should he need it. Adding this feature to his car requires a flat fee of $500, and the service provider requires monthly charges of $20. In his line of work as a traveling salesperson, he estimates that this device can save him time and money, about $35 per month. He plans to keep the car for another 3 years.

a. Calculate the breakeven point for the device in months.
b. Based on **a,** should Paul have the system installed in his car?

LG1 P13–6 **Breakeven point: Changing costs/revenues** JWG Company publishes *Creative Crosswords.* Last year, the book of puzzles sold for $10, with a variable operating cost of $8 per book and a fixed operating cost of $40,000.

a. How many books must JWG sell this year to achieve the breakeven point for the stated operating costs if all figures remain the same as for last year?
b. How many books must JWG sell this year to achieve the breakeven point for the stated operating costs if fixed operating costs increase to $44,000 and all other figures remain the same?
c. How many books must JWG sell this year to achieve the breakeven point for the stated operating costs if the selling price increases to $10.50 and all costs remain the same as for last year?
d. How many books must JWG sell this year to achieve the breakeven point for the stated operating costs if the variable operating cost per book increases to $8.50 and all other figures remain the same?
e. What conclusions about the operating breakeven point can be drawn from your answers?

LG1 P13–7 **Breakeven analysis** Molly Jasper and her sister, Caitlin Peters, got into the novelties business almost by accident. Molly, a talented sculptor, often made little figurines as gifts for friends. Occasionally, she and Caitlin would set up a booth at a crafts fair and sell a few of the figurines along with jewelry that Caitlin made. Little by little, demand for the figurines, now called Mollycaits, grew, and the sisters began to reproduce some of the favorites in resin, using molds of the originals. The day came when a buyer for a major department store offered them a contract to produce 1,500 figurines of various designs for $10,000. Molly and Caitlin realized that it was time to get down to business. To make bookkeeping simpler, Molly had priced all the figurines at $8.00 each. Variable operating costs amounted to an average of $6.00 per unit. To produce the order, Molly and Caitlin would have to rent industrial facilities for a month, which would cost them $4,000.

a. Calculate Mollycaits' operating breakeven point.
b. Calculate Mollycaits' EBIT on the department store order.
c. If Molly renegotiates the contract at a price of $10.00 per figurine, what will the EBIT be?
d. If the store refuses to pay more than $8.00 per unit but is willing to negotiate quantity, what quantity of figurines will result in an EBIT of $4,000?
e. At this time, Mollycaits come in 15 different varieties. Whereas the average variable cost per unit is $6.00, the actual cost varies from unit to unit. What recommendation would you have for Molly and Caitlin with regard to pricing and the numbers and types of units that they offer for sale?

LG2 P13–8 **EBIT sensitivity** Stewart Industries sells its finished product for $9 per unit. Its fixed operating costs are $20,000, and the variable operating cost per unit is $5.

a. Calculate the firm's earnings before interest and taxes (EBIT) for sales of 10,000 units.
b. Calculate the firm's EBIT for sales of 8,000 and 12,000 units, respectively.
c. Calculate the percentage changes in sales (from the 10,000-unit base level) and associated percentage changes in EBIT for the shifts in sales indicated in part **b.**

d. On the basis of your findings in part **c**, comment on the sensitivity of changes in EBIT in response to changes in sales.

LG2 MyLab

P13–9 **Degree of operating leverage** Grey Products has fixed operating costs of $380,000, variable operating costs of $16 per unit, and a selling price of $63.50 per unit.

a. Calculate the operating breakeven point in units.
b. Calculate the firm's EBIT at 9,000, 10,000, and 11,000 units, respectively.
c. With 10,000 units as a base, what are the percentage changes in units sold and EBIT as sales move from the base to the other sales levels used in part **b**?
d. Use the percentages computed in part **c** to determine the degree of operating leverage (DOL).
e. Use the formula for degree of operating leverage to determine the DOL at 10,000 units.

LG2

P13–10 **Degree of operating leverage: Graphical** Levin Corporation has fixed operating costs of $72,000, variable operating costs of $6.75 per unit, and a selling price of $9.75 per unit.

a. Calculate the operating breakeven point in units.
b. Compute the degree of operating leverage (DOL) using the following unit sales levels as a base: 25,000, 30,000, 40,000. Use the formula given in the text.
c. Graph the DOL figures that you computed in part **b** (on the y-axis) against base sales levels (on the x-axis).
d. Compute the degree of operating leverage at 24,000 units; add this point to your graph.
e. What principle do your graph and figures illustrate?

P13–11 **EPS calculations** Southland Industries has $60,000 of 6% (annual interest) bonds outstanding, 1,500 shares of preferred stock paying an annual dividend of $5 per share, and 4,000 shares of common stock outstanding. Assuming that the firm has a 40% tax rate, compute earnings per share (EPS) for the following levels of EBIT:

a. $24,600
b. $30,600
c. $35,000

LG2

P13–12 **Degree of financial leverage** Northwestern Savings and Loan has a current capital structure consisting of $250,000 of 16% (annual interest) debt and 2,000 shares of common stock. The firm pays taxes at the rate of 21%.

a. Using EBIT values of $80,000 and $120,000, determine the associated earnings per share (EPS).
b. Using $80,000 of EBIT as a base, calculate the degree of financial leverage (DFL).
c. Rework parts **a** and **b**, assuming that the firm has $100,000 of 16% (annual interest) debt and 3,000 shares of common stock.

Personal Finance Problem

LG2

P13–13 **Financial leverage** Max Small has outstanding school loans that require a monthly payment of $1,000. He needs to buy a new car for work and estimates that this purchase will add $350 per month to his existing monthly obligations. Max will have $3,000 available after meeting all his monthly living (operating) expenses. This amount could vary by plus or minus 10%.

a. To assess the potential impact of the additional borrowing on his financial leverage, calculate the DFL in tabular form for both the current and proposed loan payments, using Max's available $3,000 as a base and a 10% change.

b. Can Max afford the additional loan payment?
c. Should Max take on the additional loan payment?

LG2 LG5 **P13–14** **DFL and graphical display of financing plans** Wells and Associates has an EBIT of $67,500. Interest costs are $22,500, and the firm has 15,000 shares of common stock outstanding. Assume a 40% tax rate.

a. Use the degree of financial leverage (DFL) formula to calculate the DFL for the firm.
b. Using a set of EBIT–EPS axes, plot Wells and Associates' financing plan.
c. If the firm also has 1,000 shares of preferred stock paying a $6.00 annual dividend per share, what is the DFL?
d. Plot the financing plan, including the 1,000 shares of $6.00 preferred stock, on the axes used in part **b.**
e. Briefly discuss the graph of the two financing plans.

LG1 LG2 MyLab **P13–15** **Integrative: Multiple leverage measures** Play-More Toys produces inflatable beach balls, selling 400,000 balls per year. Each ball produced has a variable operating cost of $0.84 and sells for $1.00. Fixed operating costs are $28,000. The firm has annual interest charges of $6,000, preferred dividends of $2,000, and a 21% tax rate.

a. Calculate the operating breakeven point in units.
b. Use the degree of operating leverage (DOL) formula to calculate DOL.
c. Use the degree of financial leverage (DFL) formula to calculate DFL.
d. Use the degree of total leverage (DTL) formula to calculate DTL. Compare this answer with the product of DOL and DFL calculated in parts **b** and **c.**

LG2 **P13–16** **Integrative: Leverage and risk** Firm R has sales of 100,000 units at $2.00 per unit, variable operating costs of $1.70 per unit, and fixed operating costs of $6,000. Interest is $10,000 per year. Firm W has sales of 100,000 units at $2.50 per unit, variable operating costs of $1.00 per unit, and fixed operating costs of $62,500. Interest is $17,500 per year. Assume that both firms are in the 40% tax bracket.

a. Compute the degree of operating, financial, and total leverage for firm R.
b. Compute the degree of operating, financial, and total leverage for firm W.
c. Compare the relative risks of the two firms.
d. Discuss the principles of leverage that your answers illustrate.

LG1 LG2 **P13–17** **Integrative: Multiple leverage measures and prediction** Carolina Fastener Inc. makes a patented marine bulkhead latch that wholesales for $6.00. Each latch has variable operating costs of $3.50. Fixed operating costs are $50,000 per year. The firm pays $13,000 interest and preferred dividends of $7,000 per year. At this point, the firm is selling 30,000 latches per year and is taxed at a rate of 21%.

a. Calculate Carolina Fastener's operating breakeven point.
b. On the basis of the firm's current sales of 30,000 units per year and its interest and preferred dividend costs, calculate its EBIT and earnings available for common.
c. Calculate the firm's degree of operating leverage (DOL).
d. Calculate the firm's degree of financial leverage (DFL).
e. Calculate the firm's degree of total leverage (DTL).
f. Carolina Fastener has entered into a contract to produce and sell an additional 15,000 latches in the coming year. Use the DOL, DFL, and DTL to predict and calculate the changes in EBIT and earnings available for common. Check your work by a simple calculation of Carolina Fastener's EBIT and earnings available for common, using the basic information given.

Personal Finance Problem

LG3

P13–18 Capital structure Kirsten Neal is interested in purchasing a new house, given that mortgage rates are low. Her bank has specific rules regarding an applicant's ability to meet the contractual payments associated with the requested debt. Kirsten must submit personal financial data for her income, expenses, and existing installment loan payments. The bank then calculates and compares certain ratios to predetermined allowable values to determine if it will make the requested loan. The requirements are as follows:

(1) Monthly mortgage payments $< 28\%$ of monthly gross (before-tax) income.

(2) Total monthly installment payments (including the mortgage payments) $< 37\%$ of monthly gross (before-tax) income.

Kirsten submits the following personal financial data:

Monthly gross (before-tax) income	$ 4,500
Monthly installment loan obligations	375
Requested mortgage	150,000
Monthly mortgage payments	1,100

a. Calculate the ratio for requirement 1.

b. Calculate the ratio for requirement 2.

c. Assuming that Kirsten has adequate funds for the down payment and meets other lender requirements, will she be granted the loan?

LG3

P13–19 Various capital structures Charter Enterprises currently has $1 million in total assets and is totally equity financed. It is contemplating a change in its capital structure. Compute the amount of debt and equity that would be outstanding if the firm were to shift to each of the following debt ratios: 10%, 20%, 30%, 40%, 50%, 60%, and 90%. (*Note:* The amount of total assets would not change.) Is there a limit to the debt ratio's value?

P13–20 Debt and financial risk John Tower is the sole owner of Tower Interiors, and he has made the forecast of sales shown in the following table.

Sales	Probability
$200,000	0.20
300,000	0.60
400,000	0.20

The firm has fixed operating costs of $75,000 and variable operating costs equal to 70% of the sales level. The company pays $12,000 in interest per period. The tax rate is 40%.

a. Compute the earnings before interest and taxes (EBIT) for each level of sales.

b. Compute the earnings per share (EPS) for each level of sales, the expected EPS, the standard deviation of the EPS, and the coefficient of variation of EPS, assuming that there are 10,000 shares of common stock outstanding.

c. Tower has the opportunity to reduce its leverage to zero and pay no interest. This change will require that the number of shares outstanding be increased to 15,000. Repeat part **b** under this assumption.

d. Compare your findings in parts **b** and **c**, and comment on the effect of the reduction of debt to zero on the firm's financial risk.

P13–21 **EPS and optimal debt ratio** Williams Glassware has estimated, at various debt ratios, the expected earnings per share and the standard deviation of the earnings per share, as shown in the following table.

Debt ratio	Earnings per share (EPS)	Standard deviation of EPS
0%	$2.30	$1.15
20	3.00	1.80
40	3.50	2.80
60	3.95	3.95
80	3.80	5.53

a. Estimate the optimal debt ratio on the basis of the relationship between earnings per share and the debt ratio. You will probably find it helpful to graph the relationship.
b. Graph the relationship between the coefficient of variation and the debt ratio. Label the areas associated with business risk and financial risk.

P13–22 **EBIT–EPS and capital structure** Data-Check is considering two capital structures. The key information is shown in the following table. Assume a 21% tax rate.

Source of capital	Structure A	Structure B
Long-term debt	$100,000 at 16% coupon rate	$200,000 at 17% coupon rate
Common stock	4,000 shares	2,000 shares

a. Calculate two EBIT–EPS coordinates for each of the structures by selecting any two EBIT values and finding their associated EPS values.
b. Plot the two capital structures on a set of EBIT–EPS axes.
c. Indicate over what EBIT range, if any, each structure is preferred.
d. Discuss the leverage and risk aspects of each structure.
e. If the firm is fairly certain that its EBIT will exceed $75,000, which structure would you recommend? Why? What if the tax rate is higher, say 40%?

P13–23 **EBIT–EPS and preferred stock** Litho-Print is considering two possible capital structures, A and B, shown in the following table. Assume a 40% tax rate.

Source of capital	Structure A	Structure B
Long-term debt	$75,000 at 16% coupon rate	$50,000 at 15% coupon rate
Preferred stock	$10,000 with an 18% annual dividend	$15,000 with an 18% annual dividend
Common stock	8,000 shares	10,000 shares

a. Calculate two EBIT–EPS coordinates for each of the structures by selecting any two EBIT values and finding their associated EPS values.
b. Graph the two capital structures on the same set of EBIT–EPS axes.

c. Discuss the leverage and risk associated with each of the structures.
d. Over what range of EBIT is each structure preferred?
e. Which structure do you recommend if the firm expects its EBIT to be $35,000? Explain. What if the tax rate is just 21%?

LG3 LG4 LG6

P13–24 **Integrative: Optimal capital structure** Medallion Cooling Systems has total assets of $10,000,000, EBIT of $2,000,000, and preferred dividends of $200,000 and is taxed at a rate of 40%. In an effort to determine the optimal capital structure, the firm has assembled data on the cost of debt, the number of shares of common stock for various levels of indebtedness, and the overall required return on investment:

Capital structure debt ratio	Cost of debt, r_d	Number of common stock shares	Required return, r_s
0%	0%	200,000	12%
15	8	170,000	13
30	9	140,000	14
45	12	110,000	16
60	15	80,000	20

a. Calculate earnings per share for each level of indebtedness.
b. Use Equation 13.12 and the earnings per share calculated in part **a** to calculate a price per share for each level of indebtedness.
c. Choose the optimal capital structure. Justify your choice.

LG3 LG4 LG6

P13–25 **Integrative: Optimal capital structure** Nelson Law Partners has made the following forecast of sales, with the associated probabilities of occurrence noted.

Sales	Probability
$200,000	0.20
300,000	0.60
400,000	0.20

The company has fixed operating costs of $100,000 per year, and variable operating costs represent 40% of sales. The existing capital structure consists of 25,000 shares of common stock that have a $10 per share book value. No other capital items are outstanding. The marketplace has assigned the following required returns to risky earnings per share.

Coefficient of variation of EPS	Estimated required return, r_s
0.43	15%
0.47	16
0.51	17
0.56	18
0.60	22
0.64	24

The company is contemplating shifting its capital structure by substituting debt in the capital structure for common stock. The three different debt ratios under consideration are shown in the following table, along with an estimate, for each ratio, of the corresponding required interest rate on all debt.

Debt ratio	Interest rate on *all* debt
20%	10%
40	12
60	14

The tax rate is 40%. The market value of the equity for a leveraged firm can be found by using the simplified method (see Equation 13.12).

a. Calculate the expected earnings per share (EPS), the standard deviation of EPS, and the coefficient of variation of EPS for the three proposed capital structures.

b. Determine the optimal capital structure, assuming (1) maximization of earnings per share and (2) maximization of share value.

c. Construct a graph (similar to Figure 13.6) showing the relationships in part **b.** (*Note:* You will probably have to sketch the lines because you have only three data points.)

P13–26 **Integrative: Optimal capital structure** The board of directors of Morales Publishing Inc. has commissioned a capital structure study. The company has total assets of $40,000,000. It has earnings before interest and taxes of $8,000,000 and is taxed at a rate of 21%.

a. Create a spreadsheet like the one in Table 13.10 showing values of debt and equity as well as the total number of shares, assuming a book value of $25 per share.

% Debt	Total assets	$ Debt	$ Equity	Number of shares @ $25
0%	$40,000,000	$____	$____	____
10	40,000,000	____	____	____
20	40,000,000	____	____	____
30	40,000,000	____	____	____
40	40,000,000	____	____	____
50	40,000,000	____	____	____
60	40,000,000	____	____	____

b. Given the before-tax cost of debt at various levels of indebtedness, calculate the yearly interest expenses.

% Debt	$ Total debt	Before-tax cost of debt, r_d	$ Interest expense
0%	$____	0.0%	$____
10	____	7.5	____
20	____	8.0	____
30	____	9.0	____
40	____	11.0	____
50	____	12.5	____
60	____	15.5	____

c. Using EBIT of $8,000,000, a 21% tax rate, and the information developed in parts **a** and **b**, calculate the most likely earnings per share for the firm at various levels of indebtedness. Mark the level of indebtedness that maximizes EPS.

% Debt	EBIT	Interest expense	EBT	Taxes	Net income	Number of shares	EPS
0%	$8,000,000	$____	$____	$____	$____	____	$____
10	8,000,000	____	____	____	____	____	____
20	8,000,000	____	____	____	____	____	____
30	8,000,000	____	____	____	____	____	____
40	8,000,000	____	____	____	____	____	____
50	8,000,000	____	____	____	____	____	____
60	8,000,000	____	____	____	____	____	____

d. Using the EPS developed in part **c**, the estimates of required return, r_s, and Equation 13.12, estimate the value per share at various levels of indebtedness. Mark the level of indebtedness in the following table that results in the maximum price per share, P_0.

Debt	EPS	r_s	P_0
0%	$____	10.0%	$____
10	____	10.3	____
20	____	10.9	____
30	____	11.4	____
40	____	12.6	____
50	____	14.8	____
60	____	17.5	____

e. Prepare a recommendation to the board of directors of Morales Publishing that specifies the degree of indebtedness that will accomplish the firm's goal of optimizing shareholder wealth. Use your findings in parts **a** through **d** to justify your recommendation.

P13–27 **Integrative: Optimal capital structure** Country Textiles, which has fixed operating costs of \$300,000 and variable operating costs equal to 40% of sales, has made the following three sales estimates, with their probabilities noted.

Sales	Probability
\$ 600,000	0.30
900,000	0.40
1,200,000	0.30

The firm wishes to analyze five possible capital structures: 0%, 15%, 30%, 45%, and 60% debt ratios. The firm's total assets of \$1 million are assumed to be constant. Its common stock has a book value of \$25 per share, and the firm is in the 40% tax bracket. The following additional data have been gathered for use in analyzing the five capital structures under consideration.

Capital structure debt ratio	Before-tax cost of debt, r_d	Required return, r_s
0%	0.0%	10.0%
15	8.0	10.5
30	10.0	11.6
45	13.0	14.0
60	17.0	20.0

a. Calculate the level of EBIT associated with each of the three levels of sales.

b. Calculate the amount of debt, the amount of equity, and the number of shares of common stock outstanding for each of the five capital structures being considered.

c. Calculate the annual interest on the debt under each of the five capital structures being considered. (*Note:* The before-tax cost of debt, r_d, is the interest rate applicable to all debt associated with the corresponding debt ratio.)

d. Calculate the EPS associated with each of the three levels of EBIT calculated in part **a** for each of the five capital structures being considered.

e. Calculate (1) the expected EPS, (2) the standard deviation of EPS, and (3) the coefficient of variation of EPS for each of the five capital structures, using your findings in part **d**.

f. Plot the expected EPS and coefficient of variation of EPS against the capital structures (x-axis) on separate sets of axes, and comment on the return and risk relative to capital structure.

g. Using the EBIT–EPS data developed in part **d**, plot the 0%, 30%, and 60% capital structures on the same set of EBIT–EPS axes, and discuss the ranges over which each is preferred. What is the major problem with the use of this approach?

h. Using the valuation model given in Equation 13.12 and your findings in part **e**, estimate the share value for each of the capital structures being considered.

i. Compare and contrast your findings in parts **f** and **h**. Which structure is preferred if the goal is to maximize EPS? Which structure is preferred if the goal is to maximize share value? Which capital structure do you recommend? Explain.

P13–28 **ETHICS PROBLEM** "Information asymmetry lies at the heart of the ethical dilemma that managers, stockholders, and bondholders confront when companies initiate management buyouts or swap debt for equity." Comment on this statement. What steps might a board of directors take to ensure that the company's actions are ethical with regard to all parties?

SPREADSHEET EXERCISE

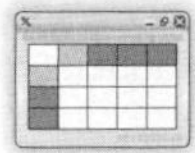

Starstruck Company would like to determine its optimal capital structure. Several of its managers believe that the best method is to rely on the estimated earnings per share (EPS) of the firm because they believe that profits and stock price are closely related. The financial managers have suggested another method that uses estimated required returns to estimate the share value of the firm. The following financial data are available.

Capital structure debt ratio	Estimated EPS	Estimated required return
0%	$1.75	11.40%
10	1.90	11.80
20	2.25	12.50
30	2.55	13.25
40	3.18	18.00
50	3.06	19.00
60	3.10	25.00

TO DO

a. Based on the given financial data, create a spreadsheet to calculate the estimated share values associated with the seven alternative capital structures. Refer to Table 13.15.

b. Use Excel to graph the relationship between capital structure and the estimated EPS of the firm. What is the optimal debt ratio? Refer to Figure 13.6.

c. Use Excel to graph the relationship between capital structure and the estimated share value of the firm. What is the optimal debt ratio? Refer to Figure 13.6.

d. Do both methods lead to the same optimal capital structure? Which method do you favor? Explain.

e. What is the major difference between the EPS and share value methods?

MyLab Finance Visit www.pearson.com/mylab/finance for **Chapter Case: *Evaluating Tampa Manufacturing's Capital Structure,*** Group Exercises, and numerous online resources.

CHAPTER

14

Payout Policy

LEARNING GOALS

LG 1 Understand cash payout procedures, their tax treatment, and the role of dividend reinvestment plans.

LG 2 Describe the residual theory of dividends and the key arguments with regard to dividend irrelevance and relevance.

LG 3 Discuss the key factors involved in establishing a dividend policy.

LG 4 Review and evaluate the three basic types of dividend policies.

LG 5 Evaluate stock dividends from accounting, shareholder, and company points of view.

LG 6 Explain stock splits and the firm's motivation for undertaking them.

MyLab Finance Chapter Introduction Video

WHY THIS CHAPTER MATTERS TO YOU

In your *professional* life

ACCOUNTING You need to understand the types of dividends and payment procedures for them because you will have to record and report the declaration and payment of dividends; you also will provide the financial data that management must have to make dividend decisions.

INFORMATION SYSTEMS You need to understand types of dividends, payment procedures, and the financial data the firm must have to make and implement dividend decisions.

MANAGEMENT To make appropriate dividend decisions for the firm, you need to understand types of dividends, arguments about the relevance of dividends, the factors that affect dividend policy, and types of dividend policies.

MARKETING You need to understand factors affecting dividend policy because you may want to argue that the firm would fare better by retaining funds for use in new marketing programs or products, rather than paying them out as dividends.

OPERATIONS You need to understand factors affecting dividend policy because you may find that the firm's dividend policy imposes limitations on planned expansion, replacement, or renewal projects.

In your *personal* life

Many individual investors buy common stock for the anticipated cash dividends. From a personal finance perspective, you should understand why and how firms pay dividends, as well as the informational and financial implications of receiving them. Such understanding will help you select common stocks that have dividend-paying patterns consistent with your long-term financial goals.

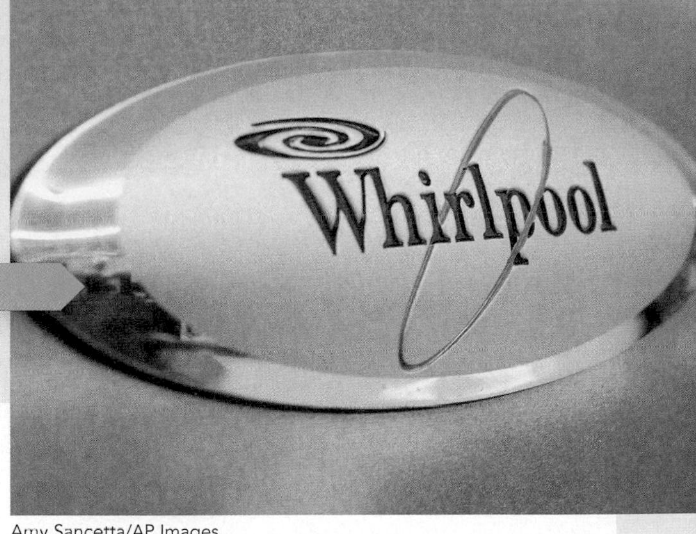

Amy Sancetta/AP Images

WHIRLPOOL CORPORATION

Increasing Dividends

In April 2017, after a period of improving performance, Whirlpool Corporation, the worldwide appliance manufacturer, announced that it would increase the quarterly dividend it paid to its stockholders by 10%, up to $1.10 per share from $1.00 in the previous quarter. Whirlpool's CEO, Jeff Fettig, explained, "This dividend increase represents our continuing commitment to enhance returns for shareholders and our confidence in the strength of our business. We remain focused on creating long-term value and returning strong levels of cash to our shareholders while funding our brands and innovation programs."

Why does Whirlpool pay dividends? Fettig's press release suggests two possibilities. One is that by paying dividends the company can "enhance returns" to shareholders. In other words, Whirlpool believes that returns to shareholders will be higher if the firm pays a dividend (and increases it) than if the firm does not pay a dividend. That sounds logical, but consider that when a firm pays a dividend, it is simply taking cash out of its bank account and putting that cash in the hands of shareholders. Presumably, after a firm pays a dividend, its share price will reflect that it no longer holds as much cash as it did prior to the dividend payment. In other words, paying a dividend may be simply switching money from one pocket (the company's) to another (the shareholder's). Supporting this idea, on the day that Whirlpool's shareholders actually earned the $1.10 dividend, the company's stock price dropped by exactly $1.10.

The second part of Fettig's statement reveals another reason that Whirlpool may pay a dividend. Whirlpool increased its dividend to show "confidence in the strength of our business." In other words, Whirlpool executives are telling the market that the firm's financial position is strong enough and its prospects bright enough that managers are confident they can afford to increase the dividend by 10% and still run the company effectively. Indeed, Whirlpool's history suggests that managers use the dividend policy strategically. From 1957 to 2017, Whirlpool maintained its annual per-share dividend 50% of the time and increased the payout 48.3% of the time. Compare that record with the dividend history of Emerson Electric Co., a company that as of 2016 had increased its dividend per share for 60 consecutive years. Although Emerson and Whirlpool adopt different policies with respect to dividend increases, both companies clearly avoid decreasing dividends.

14.1 The Basics of Payout Policy

payout policy
Decisions that a firm makes regarding whether to distribute cash to shareholders, how much cash to distribute, and the means by which cash should be distributed.

The term **payout policy** refers to the decisions that firms make about whether to distribute cash to shareholders, how much cash to distribute, and by what means the cash should be distributed. Although these decisions might seem less important than the investment decisions covered in Chapters 10 through 12 and the financing choices discussed in Chapter 13, they are important decisions that managers and boards of directors face routinely. Investors monitor firms' payout policies carefully, and unexpected changes in those policies can have significant effects on firms' stock prices. The recent history of Whirlpool Corporation, briefly outlined in the chapter opener, demonstrates many important dimensions of payout policy.

ELEMENTS OF PAYOUT POLICY

Dividends are not the only means by which firms can distribute cash to shareholders. Firms can also conduct share repurchases, in which they typically buy back some of their outstanding common stock through purchases in the open market. Whirlpool Corporation, like many other companies, uses both methods to put cash in the hands of its stockholders. In addition to increasing its dividend payout, Whirlpool repurchased \$525 million worth of its common stock in 2016 and pledged to continue share buybacks in 2017, even though the company's total free cash flow in 2016 was just \$543 million. In other words, counting the combined value of Whirlpool's dividends and share repurchases, the company paid out more than 100% of its free cash flow in 2016 to stockholders. To do so, Whirlpool had to take on additional long-term debt.

When we observe the decisions that companies make regarding payouts to shareholders, some common patterns emerge:

1. Rapidly growing firms generally do not pay out cash to shareholders.
2. Slowing growth, positive cash flow generation, and favorable tax conditions can prompt firms to initiate cash payouts to investors. The ownership base of the company can also figure importantly in the decision to distribute cash.
3. Firms can make cash payouts through dividends or share repurchases. Many companies use both methods. In some years, more cash is paid out via dividends, but sometimes share repurchases are larger than dividend payments.
4. When business conditions are weak, firms are more willing to reduce share buybacks than to cut dividends. Firms may even be willing to borrow money temporarily to avoid cutting dividends.

TRENDS IN EARNINGS AND DIVIDENDS

Figure 14.1 illustrates both long-term trends and cyclical movements in earnings and dividends paid by large U.S. firms that are part of the Standard & Poor's 500 Stock Composite Index. The figure plots monthly earnings and dividend payments from 1950 through 2016. The top line represents the earnings per share of firms in the S&P 500 index, and the bottom line represents dividends

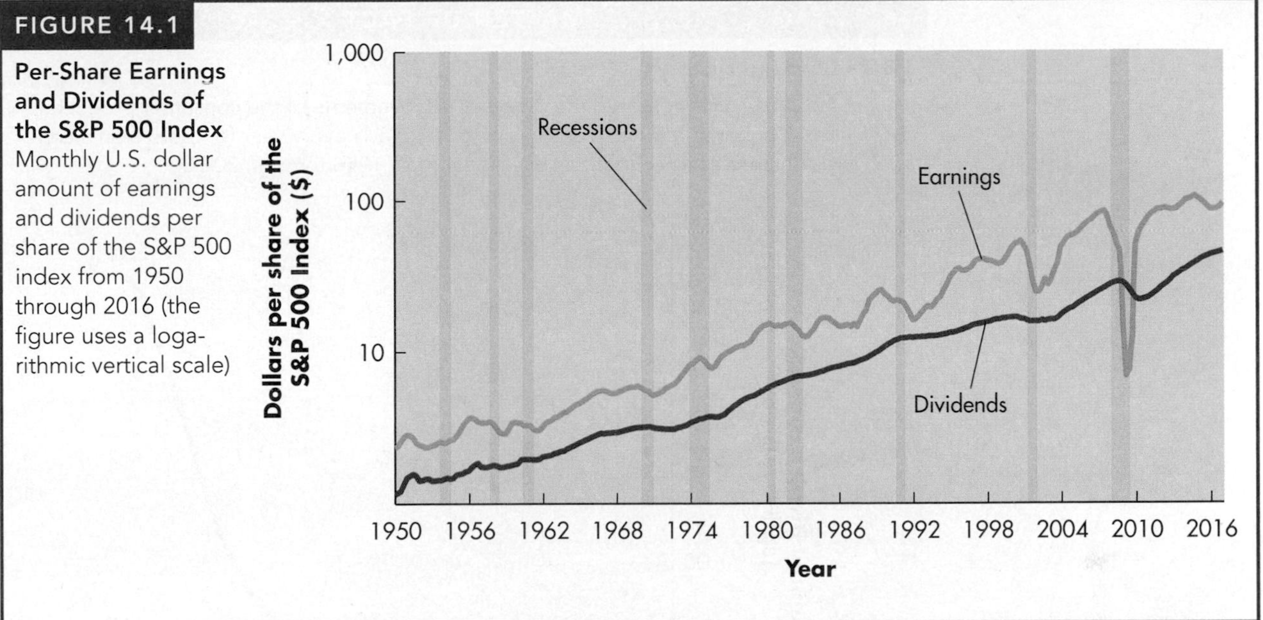

FIGURE 14.1

Per-Share Earnings and Dividends of the S&P 500 Index
Monthly U.S. dollar amount of earnings and dividends per share of the S&P 500 index from 1950 through 2016 (the figure uses a logarithmic vertical scale)

per share. The vertical bars highlight 10 periods during which the U.S. economy was in recession. The figure yields several important lessons. First, observe that over the long term the earnings and dividends lines tend to move together. Figure 14.1 uses a logarithmic scale, so the slope of each line represents the growth rate of earnings or dividends. Over the 67 years shown in the figure, the two lines tend to have about the same slope, meaning that earnings and dividends grow at about the same rate when you take a long-term perspective. It makes perfect sense: Firms pay dividends out of earnings, so for dividends to grow over the long-term, earnings must grow, too.

Second, the earnings series is much more volatile than the dividends series. That is, the line plotting earnings per share is quite bumpy, but the dividend line is much smoother, which suggests that firms do not adjust their dividend payments each time earnings move up or down. Instead, firms tend to smooth dividends, increasing them slowly when earnings are growing rapidly and maintaining dividend payments, rather than cutting them, when earnings decline.

To see this second point more clearly, look closely at the vertical bars in Figure 14.1. It is apparent that during recessions corporate earnings usually decline, but dividends either do not decline at all or do not decline as sharply as earnings. In 6 of the last 10 recessions, dividends were actually higher when the recession ended than just before it began, although the last two recessions are notable exceptions to this pattern. Note also that, just after the end of a recession, earnings typically increase quite rapidly. Dividends increase, too, but not as fast.

A third lesson from Figure 14.1 is that the effect of the most recent recession on both corporate earnings and dividends was large by historical standards. An enormous earnings decline occurred from 2007 to 2009. This decline forced

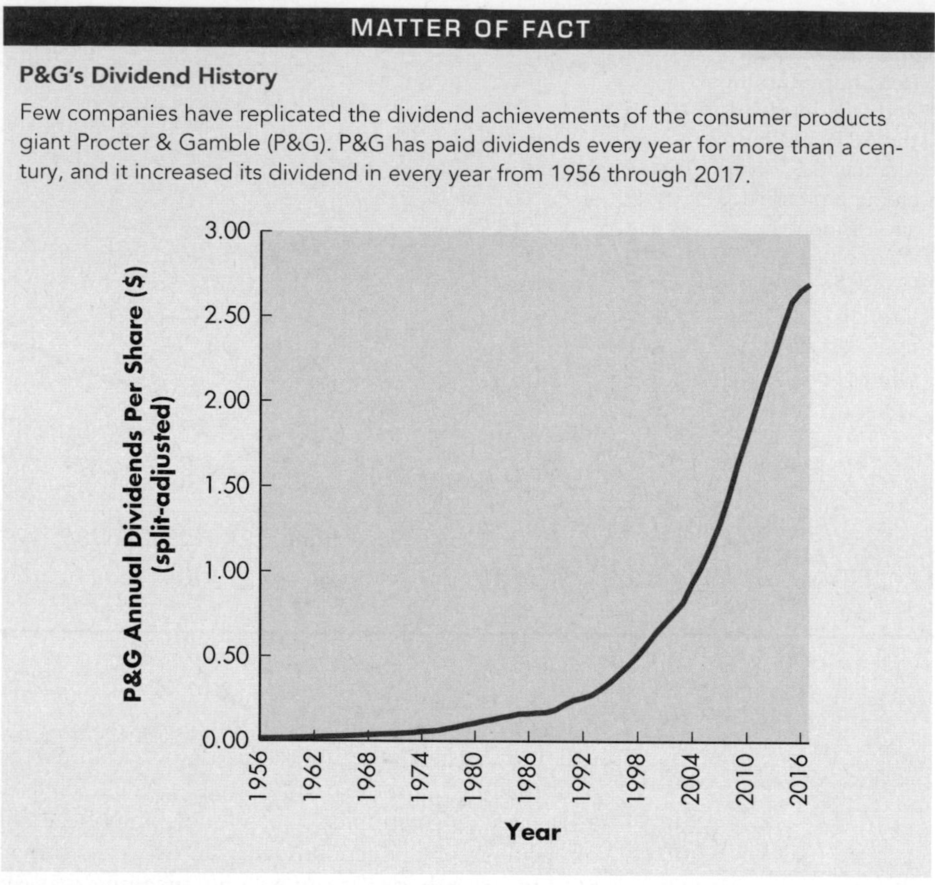

MATTER OF FACT

P&G's Dividend History

Few companies have replicated the dividend achievements of the consumer products giant Procter & Gamble (P&G). P&G has paid dividends every year for more than a century, and it increased its dividend in every year from 1956 through 2017.

firms to cut dividends more drastically than they had in years; nonetheless, the drop in dividends was slight compared with the earnings decrease.

TRENDS IN DIVIDENDS AND SHARE REPURCHASES

When firms want to distribute cash to shareholders, they can either pay dividends or repurchase outstanding shares. Figure 14.2 plots aggregate dividends and share repurchases from 1971 through 2016 for all U.S. firms listed on U.S. stock exchanges (again, the figure uses a logarithmic vertical scale). A quick glance at the figure reveals that share repurchases played a relatively minor role in firms' payout practices in the 1970s. In 1971, for example, aggregate dividends totaled nearly \$21.8 billion, but share repurchases that year were just \$1.1 billion. In the 1980s, share repurchases began to grow rapidly and then slowed again in the early 1990s. The value of aggregate share repurchases first eclipsed total dividend payments in 2006. That year, firms paid \$421 billion in dividends, but they repurchased \$565 billion worth of stock. Share repurchases continued to outpace dividends for 2 more years, peaking at \$678 billion in 2007. Repurchases retreated for the next 3 years, but then began to pick up again in 2011, along with dividends.

FIGURE 14.2

Aggregate Dividends and Repurchases for All U.S. Publicly Listed Companies
Aggregate U.S. dollar amount of dividends and share repurchases for all U.S. companies listed on U.S. stock exchanges in each year from 1971 through 2016 (the figure uses a logarithmic vertical scale)

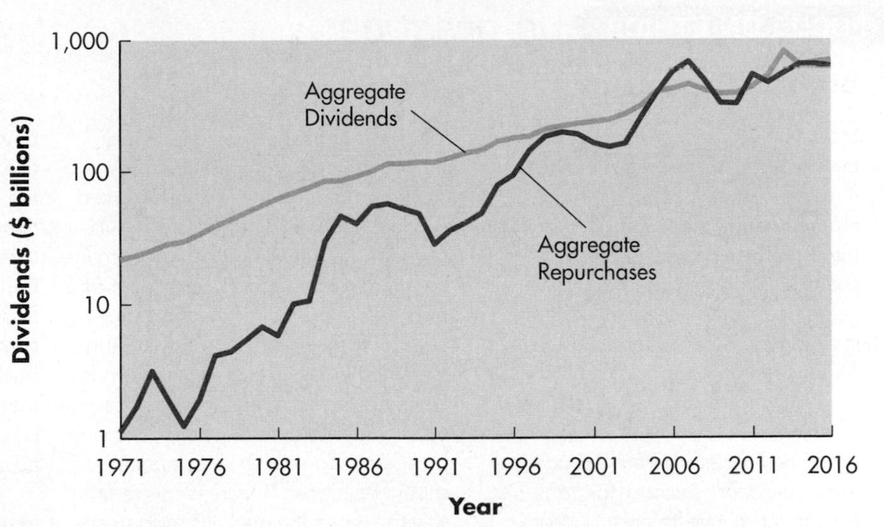

Whereas aggregate dividends rise smoothly over time, Figure 14.2 shows that share repurchases display much more volatility. The largest drops in repurchase activity occurred in 1974–1975, 1981, 1986, 1989–1991, 2000–2002, and 2008–2011. All these drops correspond to periods when the U.S. economy was mired in or just emerging from a recession. During most of these periods, dividends continued to grow modestly. Only during the most recent, severe recession did both share repurchases and dividends fall.

Combining the lessons from Figures 14.1 and 14.2, we can draw three broad conclusions about firms' payout policies. First, firms exhibit a strong desire to maintain modest, steady growth in dividends that is roughly consistent with the long-run growth in earnings. Second, share repurchases have accounted for a growing fraction of total cash payouts over time. If dividends have grown in step with earnings while share repurchases have grown more rapidly, then the implication is that the total cash paid out by firms, relative to earnings, has been rising over time. Third, when earnings fluctuate, firms adjust their short-term payouts primarily by adjusting share repurchases (rather than dividends), cutting buybacks during recessions, and increasing them rapidly during economic expansions.

MATTER OF FACT

Share Repurchases Gain Worldwide Popularity

The growing importance of share repurchases in corporate payout policy is not confined to the United States. In most of the world's largest economies, repurchases have been on the rise in recent years, eclipsing dividend payments at least some of the time in countries as diverse as Belgium, Denmark, Finland, Hungary, Ireland, Japan, Netherlands, South Korea, and Switzerland. A study of payout policy at firms from 25 different countries found that share repurchases rose at an annual rate of 19% from 1999 through 2008.

FOCUS ON ETHICS *in practice*

Buyback Mountain

Stock repurchases, or buybacks, have become the preferred way for large firms to shuttle cash to shareholders. From the end of the Great Recession through 2016, S&P 500 companies spent $3.3 trillion repurchasing shares—compared with paying just $2.3 trillion in dividends. Finance theory offers two reasons shareholders love repurchases. First, buybacks are "tax efficient"—meaning the typical investor pays less tax on cash received from a repurchase than a dividend. Second, for firms with few attractive investments, buybacks reduce management's temptation to waste available cash.

Two other motives for repurchasing stock are potentially less kind to shareholders—earnings management and market timing. Other things equal, repurchases reduce the number of outstanding shares, thereby increasing earnings per share (EPS). This gambit is attractive because the market often wallops firms that miss their earnings targets. Dangling from this stick, there is a carrot—CEO compensation is often tied to EPS. But repurchasing stock just to magnify earnings could harm shareholders. A recent study looked at firms that would have just missed their EPS forecast but for a stock repurchase; these firms reduced capital expenditures and R&D in subsequent quarters. In other words, management repurchased stock to get EPS over the hump, rather than use the cash to invest in the company's future.

Another justification often given for buybacks is market timing. Suppose management's assessment of company prospects suggests the stock price should be higher. If there is no credible way to correct the market's misperception, a stock buyback may offer the best alternative for enhancing shareholder value. Repurchasing undervalued shares means remaining stockholders will profit when the market comes to its senses. The only problem is management's view may be wishful thinking. Indeed, *The Economist* recently observed, "managers in aggregate are about as good at predicting share prices as dart-throwing simians."

But managers who repurchase "undervalued" stock may not just be monkeying around with shareholder value. Recent research found more than half of repurchasing firms were able to buy stock back at small discounts relative to the average market price during the repurchase month—the median discount was 0.88%. Furthermore, firms that repurchased infrequently got even better deals. The median discount for firms buying just once a year was 5.9%, compared with 1.5% for monthly buybacks—presumably because less frequent repurchasers have more flexibility to "time the market" to take advantage of undervaluation.

Recent data point to a slowdown in the repurchase boom. Through March 2017, buyback volume of S&P 500 companies was off 1.6% from the prior quarter and 17.5% from first quarter 2016. Even with the decline, the $133.1 billion in stock repurchased from January through March exceeded buybacks in 24 of the last 31 quarters. Going forward, it appears firms sitting on mountains of cash are unlikely to quit buying back shares.

► *Given the market generally punishes firms that miss their EPS forecast, do you believe it is ethical to use stock repurchases just to hit the target?*

Sources: Almeida, Heitor; Vyacheslav Fos; and Mathias Kronlund. "The Real Effect of Share Repurchases," *Journal of Financial Economics 119* (2016): 168–185. *The Economist*. "Share Buy-Backs: The Repurchase Revolution," September 12, 2014. Ditmar, Amy, and Laura Casares Field. "Do Corporate Managers Know When Their Shares are Undervalued? New Evidence Based on Actual (and Not Just Announced) Stock Buybacks," *Journal of Applied Corporate Finance 28* (Fall 2016): 73–84.

→ **REVIEW QUESTIONS** MyLab Finance Solutions

14–1 What two ways can firms distribute cash to shareholders?

14–2 Why do rapidly growing firms generally pay no dividends?

14–3 The dividend payout ratio equals dividends paid divided by earnings. How would you expect this ratio to behave during a recession? What about during an economic boom?

14.2 The Mechanics of Payout Policy

At quarterly or semiannual meetings, a firm's board of directors decides whether and in what amount to pay cash dividends. If the firm has already established a precedent of paying dividends, the decision facing the board is usually whether to maintain or increase the dividend, and that decision is based

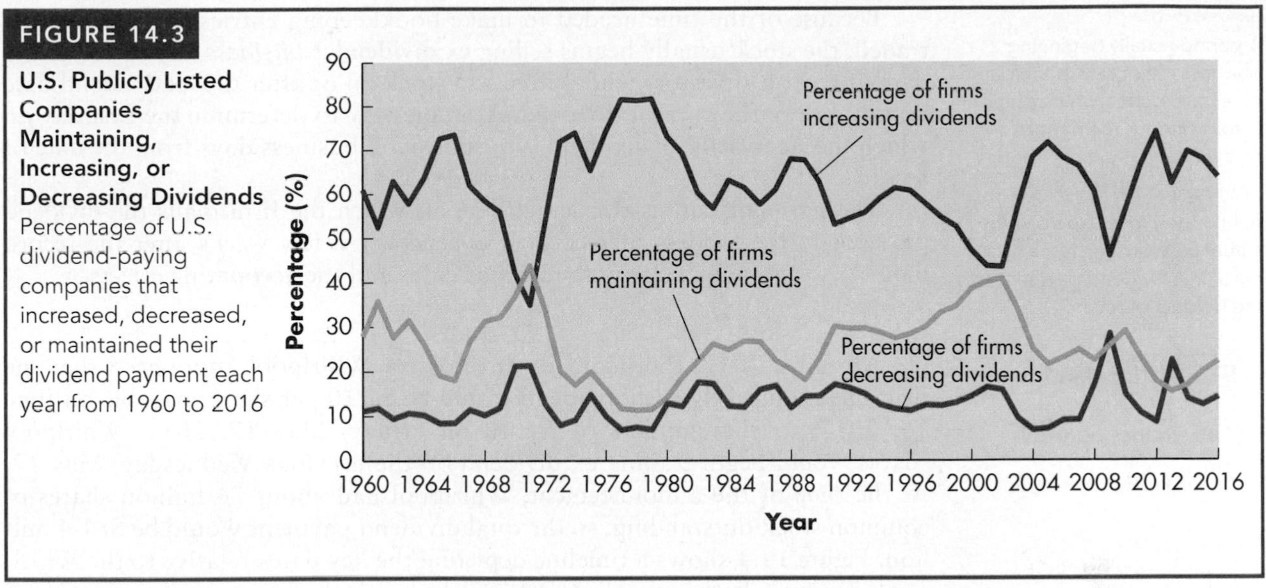

FIGURE 14.3

U.S. Publicly Listed Companies Maintaining, Increasing, or Decreasing Dividends
Percentage of U.S. dividend-paying companies that increased, decreased, or maintained their dividend payment each year from 1960 to 2016

primarily on the firm's recent performance and its ability to generate cash flow in the future. Boards rarely cut dividends unless they believe that the firm's ability to generate cash is in serious jeopardy. Figure 14.3 shows the percentage of U.S. dividend-paying companies that increased, decreased, or maintained their dividend payment each year from 1960 to 2016. The figure excludes dividend-payers from the financial services and regulated utility industries because regulators heavily influence the dividend decisions of those firms. Figure 14.3 shows that most firms that pay dividends increase their payments over time. In a typical year about 62% of dividend payers raise their dividend, which is about 5 times greater than the percentage of firms cutting dividends. Notice, however, that the percentage of firms increasing their dividend was particularly low in 1971, 2001, 2002, and 2009. In each of those years the U.S. economy was in or just emerging from a recession.

Cutting the dividend payment is clearly something that firms try to avoid, as fewer than 13% of firms reduce the dividend in an average year. But dividend cuts tend to rise when recessions occur. Just over 28% of dividend-paying firms actually cut their dividend in 2009 as the U.S. economy swooned. The percentage of firms just maintaining their dividend also tends to rise when business conditions are weak. In an average year about 25% of firms hold their dividend steady, but in 1971 almost 44% of firms chose to pay the same dividend that they paid in 1970. In fact, during the period 1960 to 2016, there were just three episodes in which the percentage of firms maintaining or cutting their dividend was greater than the percentage of firms increasing the dividend: 1970 to 1971, 2000 to 2002, and 2009. All three periods correspond to recessions.

CASH DIVIDEND PAYMENT PROCEDURES

date of record (dividends)
Set by the firm's directors, the date on which all persons whose names are recorded as stockholders receive a declared dividend at a specified future time.

When a firm's directors declare a dividend, they issue a statement indicating the dividend amount and setting three important dates: the *date of record,* the *ex-dividend date,* and the *payment date.* All persons whose names are recorded as stockholders on the **date of record** receive the dividend. These stockholders are often referred to as *holders of record.*

ex dividend
A period usually beginning 2 *business days* prior to the date of record, during which a stock is sold without the right to receive the current dividend.

payment date
Set by the firm's directors, the actual date on which the firm mails the dividend payment to the holders of record.

Because of the time needed to make bookkeeping entries when a stock is traded, the stock usually begins selling **ex dividend** 2 *business days* prior to the date of record. Investors who purchase a stock on or after the ex dividend date do not receive the current dividend. A simple way to determine the first day on which the stock sells ex dividend is to subtract 2 business days from the date of record.

The **payment date** is the actual date on which the firm mails the dividend payment to the holders of record. It is generally a few weeks after the record date. An example will clarify the various dates and the accounting effects.

EXAMPLE 14.1

MyLab Finance Solution Video

On April 17, 2017, the board of directors of Whirlpool announced that the firm's next quarterly cash dividend would be $1.10 per share, payable on June 15, 2017, to shareholders of record on Friday, May 19, 2017. Whirlpool shares would begin trading ex dividend on the previous Wednesday, May 17. At the time of the announcement, Whirlpool had about 74 million shares of common stock outstanding, so the total dividend payment would be $81.4 million. Figure 14.4 shows a timeline depicting the key dates relative to the Whirlpool dividend. Before the dividend was declared, the key accounts of the firm were as follows (dollar values quoted in thousands):[1]

Cash	$951,000	Dividends payable	$0
		Retained earnings	$7,394,000

When the dividend was announced by the directors, $81.4 million of the retained earnings ($1.10 per share × 74 million shares) was transferred to the dividends payable account. The key accounts thus became

Cash	$951,000	Dividends payable	$81,400
		Retained earnings	$7,312,600

FIGURE 14.4

Dividend Payment Timeline
Timeline for the announcement and payment of a cash dividend for Whirlpool

Declaration Date
Monday, April 17
Ex Dividend Date
Wednesday, May 17
Date of Record
Friday, May 19
Payment Date
Thursday, June 15
Board of directors declares $1.10 per share dividend, payable to holders of record on Friday, May 19, payable on Thursday, June 15.
Stock begins to sell ex dividend on Wednesday, May 17, which is 2 days before the Friday, May 19, date of record.
Checks of $1.10 per share are mailed on Thursday, June 15, to all holders of record on Friday, May 19.
Time

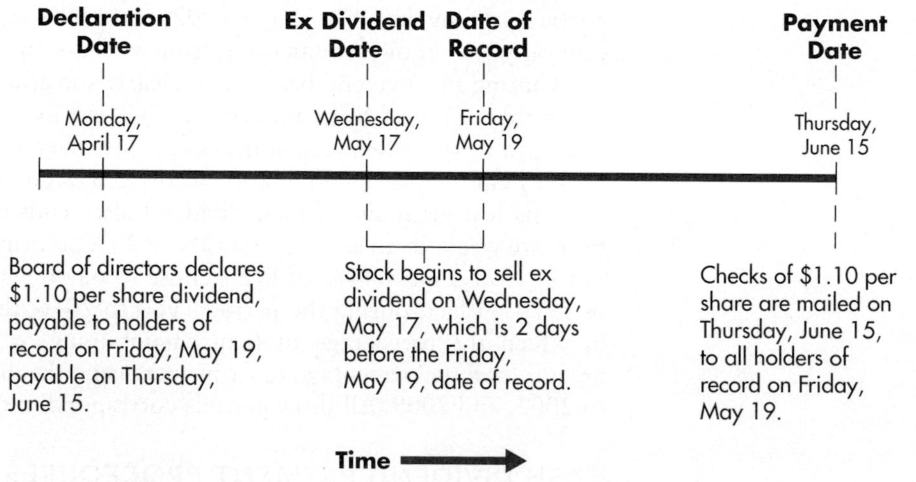

1. The accounting transactions described here reflect only the effects of the dividend. Whirlpool's actual financial statements during this period will reflect many other transactions.

When Whirlpool actually paid the dividend on June 15, this produced the following balances in the key accounts of the firm:

Cash	$869,600	Dividends payable	$0
		Retained earnings	$7,312,600

The net effect of declaring and paying the dividend was to reduce the firm's total assets (and stockholders' equity) by almost $81.4 million.

SHARE REPURCHASE PROCEDURES

The mechanics of cash dividend payments are virtually the same for every dividend paid by every public company. With share repurchases, firms can use at least two different methods to get cash into the hands of shareholders. The most common method of executing a share repurchase program is called an open-market share repurchase. In an **open-market share repurchase,** as the name suggests, firms simply buy back some of their outstanding shares on the open market. Firms have a great deal of latitude regarding when and how they execute these open-market purchases. Some firms make purchases in fixed amounts at regular intervals, whereas other firms try to behave more opportunistically, buying back more shares when they think the share price is relatively low and fewer shares when they think the price is high.

open-market share repurchase
A share repurchase program in which firms simply buy back some of their outstanding shares on the open market.

In contrast, firms sometimes repurchase shares through a *self-tender offer* or simply a *tender offer*. In a **tender offer share repurchase,** a firm announces the price it is willing to pay to buy back shares and the quantity of shares it wishes to repurchase. The tender offer price is usually set at a significant premium above the current market price. Shareholders who want to participate let the firm know how many shares they would like to sell back to the firm at the stated price. If shareholders do not offer to sell back as many shares as the firm wants to repurchase, the firm may either cancel or extend the offer. If the offer is oversubscribed, meaning that shareholders want to sell more shares than the firm wants to repurchase, the firm typically repurchases shares on a pro rata basis. For example, if the firm wishes to buy back 10 million shares, but investors offer to sell 20 million shares back to the firm, the firm would repurchase exactly half of the shares tendered by each shareholder.

tender offer share repurchase
A repurchase program in which a firm offers to repurchase a fixed number of shares, usually at a premium relative to the market value, and shareholders decide whether or not they want to sell back their shares at that price.

Dutch auction share repurchase
A repurchase method in which the firm specifies how many shares it wants to buy back and a range of prices at which it is willing to repurchase shares. Investors specify how many shares they will sell at each price in the range, and the firm determines the minimum price required to repurchase its target number of shares. All investors who tender receive the same price.

A third method of buying back shares is called a **Dutch auction share repurchase.** In a Dutch auction, the firm specifies a range of prices at which it is willing to repurchase shares and the quantity of shares that it desires. Investors can tender their shares to the firm at any price in the specified range, which allows the firm to trace out a demand curve for their stock. That is, the demand curve specifies how many shares investors will sell back to the firm at each price in the offer range. This analysis allows the firm to determine the minimum price required to repurchase the desired quantity of shares, and every shareholder receives that price.

EXAMPLE 14.2

In June 2017, Lifeway Foods announced a Dutch auction repurchase for 6 million common shares at prices ranging from $8.50 to $9.50 per share. Lifeway shareholders were instructed to contact the company to indicate how many shares they would be willing to sell at different prices in this range. Suppose that after accumulating this information from investors, Lifeway constructed the following demand schedule:

Offer price	Shares tendered	Cumulative total
$8.50	1,000,000	1,000,000
8.75	1,500,000	2,500,000
9.00	3,500,000	6,000,000
9.25	4,000,000	10,000,000
9.50	4,500,000	14,500,000

At a price of $9, shareholders are willing to tender a total of 6 million shares, exactly the amount that Lifeway wants to repurchase. Each shareholder who expressed a willingness to tender shares at a price of $9 *or less* receives $9, and Lifeway repurchases all 6 million shares at a cost of roughly $54 million.

TAX TREATMENT OF DIVIDENDS AND REPURCHASES

For many years, dividends and share repurchases had very different tax consequences. The dividends that investors received were generally taxed at ordinary income tax rates. Therefore, if a firm paid $10 million in dividends, that payout would trigger significant tax liabilities for the firm's shareholders (at least those subject to personal income taxes). However, when firms repurchased shares, the taxes triggered by that type of payout were generally much lower. Several reasons accounted for this difference. Only those shareholders who sold their shares as part of the repurchase program had any immediate tax liability. Shareholders who did not participate did not owe any taxes. Furthermore, some shareholders who did participate in the repurchase program might not owe any taxes on the funds they received if they were tax-exempt institutions or if they sold their shares at a loss. Finally, even those shareholders who participated in the repurchase program and sold their shares for a profit paid taxes only at the (usually lower) capital gains tax rate (assuming the shares were held for at least 1 year) and even that tax applied only to the gain, not to the entire value of the shares repurchased. Consequently, investors could generally expect to pay far less in taxes on money that a firm distributed through a share repurchase compared to money paid out as dividends. That differential tax treatment in part explains the growing popularity of share repurchase programs in recent decades.

The *Jobs and Growth Tax Relief Reconciliation Act of 2003* significantly changed the tax treatment of corporate dividends for most taxpayers. Prior to passage of the 2003 law, dividends received by investors were taxed as ordinary income at rates as high as 35%. The 2003 act reduced the tax rate on corporate dividends for most taxpayers to the tax rate applicable to capital gains, which was a maximum rate of 15%. This change significantly diminished the degree of "double taxation" of dividends, which results when the corporation is first taxed on its income and then shareholders pay taxes on the dividends they receive. After-tax cash flow to dividend recipients was much greater at the lower dividend tax rate; the result was noticeably higher dividend payouts by corporations after the passage of the 2003 legislation.

Several tax changes have been enacted since 2003. Under current tax law, stockholders face tax rates on dividends and capital gains as low as 0% or as high as 23.8%, depending on their income level. (For more details on the taxation of dividends and capital gains, see the Focus on Practice box.)

PERSONAL FINANCE EXAMPLE 14.3

MyLab Finance Solution Video

The board of directors of Espinoza Industries Inc., on October 4 of the current year, declared a quarterly dividend of $0.46 per share payable to all holders of record on Friday, October 26, with a payment date of November 19. Rob and Kate Heckman, who purchased 500 shares of Espinoza's common stock on Thursday, October 15, wish to determine whether they will receive the recently declared dividend and, if so, when and how much they would net after taxes from the dividend given that the dividends would be subject to a 15% federal income tax.

Given the Friday, October 26, date of record, the stock would begin selling *ex dividend* 2 business days earlier on Wednesday, October 24. Purchasers of the stock on or before Tuesday, October 23, would receive the right to the dividend. Because the Heckmans purchased the stock on October 15, they would be

FOCUS ON PRACTICE *in practice*

Capital Gains and Dividend Tax Treatment Extended to 2012 and Beyond for Some

In 1980, the percentage of firms paying monthly, quarterly, semiannual, or annual dividends stood at 60%. By the end of 2002, this number had declined to 20%. In May 2003, President George W. Bush signed into law the *Jobs and Growth Tax Relief Reconciliation Act of 2003* (JGTRRA). Prior to that new law, dividends were taxed once as part of corporate earnings and again as the personal income of the investor, in both cases with a potential top rate of 35%. The result was an effective tax rate of 57.75% on some dividends. Although the 2003 tax law did not completely eliminate the double taxation of dividends, it reduced the maximum possible effect of the double taxation of dividends to 44.75%. For taxpayers in the lower tax brackets, the combined effect was a maximum of 38.25%. Both the number of companies paying dividends and the amount of dividends spiked following the lowering of tax rates on dividends. For example, total dividends paid rose almost 14% in the first quarter after the new tax law was enacted, and the percentage of firms initiating dividends rose by nearly 40% the same quarter.

The tax rates under JGTRRA were originally programmed to expire at the end of 2008. However, in May 2006, Congress passed the *Tax Increase Prevention and Reconciliation Act of 2005* (TIPRA), extending the beneficial tax rates for 2 more years. Taxpayers in tax brackets above 15% paid a 15% rate on dividends paid before December 31, 2008. For taxpayers with a marginal tax rate of 15% or lower, the dividend tax rate was 5% until December 31, 2007, and 0% from 2008 to 2010. Long-term capital gains tax rates were reduced to the same rates as the new dividend tax rates through 2010. Although JGTRRA expired at the end of 2010, Congress extended the law until 2012 by passing the Tax Relief, Unemployment Insurance Reauthorization, and Job Creation Act of 2010.

At the onset of 2012, the pre-JGTRRA taxation of dividends would reappear unless further legislation made the law permanent. Those arguing to make the JGTRRA permanent pointed toward the weak economy and suggested that taxes needed to remain low to stimulate business investment and job creation. Others noted that the U.S. budget deficit was at an all-time high, so some combination of higher taxes and reduced spending was necessary to avoid economic problems associated with too much debt.

In early 2012, Congress passed the American Taxpayer Relief Act of 2012. For individuals in the 25%, 28%, 33%, and 35% income tax brackets, qualified dividends as well as capital gains continued to be taxed at 15%. However, for individuals with more than $418,400 in taxable income—and couples with more than $470,701—the rate was increased to 20%. As was the case under JGTRRA, people in the 10% and 15% brackets, as before, will have a zero tax rate on dividends and capital gains.

Today, most individuals still face tax rates on dividends and capital gains of 0%, 15%, or 20% depending on their income level, but high-income taxpayers face an additional 3.8% tax on investment income (dividends or capital gains). However, the corporate income tax rate has been cut from 35% to 21%, so the highest possible effective tax rate on dividends, combining corporate and individual taxes, is 39.8% compared to 57.75% prior to 2003.

► *How might the expected future reappearance of higher tax rates on individuals receiving dividends affect corporate dividend payout policies?*

eligible to receive the dividend of $0.46 per share. Thus, the Heckmans will receive $230 in dividends ($0.46 per share × 500 shares), which will be mailed to them on the November 19 payment date. Because they are subject to a 15% federal income tax on the dividends, the Heckmans will net $195.50 [(1 − 0.15) × $230] after taxes from the Espinoza Industries dividend.

DIVIDEND REINVESTMENT PLANS

dividend reinvestment plans (DRIPs)
Plans that enable stockholders to use dividends received on the firm's stock to acquire additional shares—even fractional shares—at little or no transaction cost.

Today, many firms offer **dividend reinvestment plans** (**DRIPs**), which enable stockholders to use dividends received on the firm's stock to acquire additional shares—even fractional shares—at little or no transaction cost. Some companies even allow investors to make their initial purchases of the firm's stock directly from the company without going through a broker. With DRIPs, plan participants typically can acquire shares at about 5% below the prevailing market price. From its point of view, the firm can issue new shares to participants more economically, avoiding the underpricing and flotation costs that would accompany the public sale of new shares. The existence of a DRIP may enhance the market appeal of a firm's shares.

STOCK PRICE REACTIONS TO CORPORATE PAYOUTS

What happens to the stock price when a firm pays a dividend or repurchases shares? In theory, the answers to those questions are straightforward. Take a dividend payment, for example. Suppose that a firm has $1 billion in assets, financed entirely by 10 million shares of common stock. Each share should be worth $100 ($1 billion ÷ 10,000,000 shares). Now suppose that the firm pays a $1 per share cash dividend, for a total dividend payout of $10 million. The assets of the firm fall to $990 million. Because shares outstanding remain at 10 million, each share should be worth $99. In other words, the stock price should fall by $1, exactly the amount of the dividend. The reduced share price simply reflects that cash formerly held by the firm is now in the hands of investors. To be precise, this reduction in share price should occur not when the dividend checks are mailed but rather when the stock begins trading ex dividend.

For share repurchases, the intuition is that "you get what you pay for." In other words, if the firm buys back shares at the going market price, the reduction in cash is exactly offset by the reduction in the number of shares outstanding, so the market price of the stock should remain the same. Once again, consider the firm with $1 billion in assets and 10 million shares outstanding worth $100 each. Let's say that the firm decides to distribute $10 million in cash by repurchasing 100,000 shares of stock. After the repurchase is completed, the firm's assets will fall by $10 million to $990 million, but the shares outstanding will fall by 100,000 to 9,900,000. The new share price is therefore $990,000,000 ÷ 9,900,000, or $100, as before.

In practice, taxes and a variety of other market imperfections may cause the actual change in share price in response to a dividend payment or share repurchase to deviate from what we expect in theory. In the case of dividends, stock prices do fall, on average, on ex dividend dates, but the decline in the stock price is usually less than the dividend payment. Furthermore, the stock price reaction to a cash payout may be different than the reaction to an announcement about an upcoming payout. For example, when a firm announces that it will increase its dividend, the share price usually rises on that news, even though the share price will fall when the dividend is actually paid. The next section discusses in greater depth the impact of payout policy on the value of the firm.

→ **REVIEW QUESTIONS** MyLab Finance Solutions

14–4 Who are holders of record? When does a stock sell ex dividend?

14–5 What effect did the *Jobs and Growth Tax Relief Reconciliation Act of 2003* have on the taxation of corporate dividends? On corporate dividend payouts?

14–6 What benefit is available to participants in a dividend reinvestment plan? How might the firm benefit from such a plan?

LG 2

14.3 Relevance of Payout Policy

The financial literature has reported numerous theories and empirical findings concerning payout policy. Although this research provides some interesting insights about payout policy, capital budgeting and capital structure decisions are generally considered more important than payout decisions. In other words, firms should not sacrifice good investment and financing decisions for a payout policy of questionable importance.

The most important question about payout policy is this one: Does payout policy have a significant effect on the value of a firm? A number of theoretical and empirical answers to this question have been proposed, but as yet there is no widely accepted rule to help a firm find its "optimal" payout policy. Most theories that have been proposed to explain the consequences of payout policy have focused on dividends. From here on, we will use the terms *dividend policy* and *payout policy* interchangeably, meaning that we make no distinction between dividend payouts and share repurchases in terms of the theories that try to explain whether these policies have an effect on the firm's value.

RESIDUAL THEORY OF DIVIDENDS

residual theory of dividends
A school of thought suggesting that the dividend paid by a firm should be viewed as a *residual,* that is, the amount left over after all acceptable investment opportunities have been undertaken.

The **residual theory of dividends** is a school of thought suggesting that the dividend paid by a firm should be viewed as a *residual*, that is, the amount left over after all acceptable investment opportunities have been undertaken. This view of dividends is echoed in the comments from Jeff Fettig, CEO of Whirlpool, in the chapter opener. In announcing a dividend increase, Mr. Fettig said that his company was focused on returning cash to shareholders, "while funding our brands and innovation programs." In other words, Whirlpool would first fund the investments it needed to make in its business, and then it would return remaining cash to shareholders through dividends.

Using this residual approach, the firm would treat the dividend decision in three steps, as follows:

Step 1 Determine its optimal level of capital expenditures, which would be the level that exploits all a firm's positive NPV projects.

Step 2 Using the optimal capital structure proportions (see Chapter 13), estimate the total amount of equity financing needed to support the expenditures generated in Step 1.

Step 3 Because the cost of retained earnings, r_r, is less than the cost of new common stock, r_n, use retained earnings to meet the equity requirement determined in Step 2. If retained earnings are inadequate to meet this need, sell new common stock. If the available retained earnings are in excess of this need, distribute the surplus amount—the residual—as dividends.

According to this approach, as long as the firm's equity need exceeds the amount of retained earnings, no cash dividend is paid. The argument for this approach is that sound management includes making certain the company has the money it needs to compete effectively. This view of dividends suggests that the required return of investors, r_s, is *not* influenced by the firm's dividend policy, a premise that in turn implies that dividend policy is irrelevant in the sense that it does not affect the firm's value.

THE DIVIDEND IRRELEVANCE THEORY

dividend irrelevance theory
Miller and Modigliani's theory that, in a perfect world, the firm's value is determined solely by the earning power and risk of its assets (investments) and that the manner in which it splits its earnings stream between dividends and internally retained (and reinvested) funds does not affect this value.

The residual theory of dividends implies that if the firm cannot invest its earnings to receive a return exceeding the cost of capital, it should distribute the earnings by paying dividends to stockholders. This approach suggests that dividends represent an earnings residual rather than an active decision variable that affects the firm's value. Such a view is consistent with the **dividend irrelevance theory** put forth by Merton H. Miller and Franco Modigliani.[2] They argue that the firm's value is determined solely by the earning power and risk of its assets (investments) and that the manner in which it splits its earnings stream between dividends and internally retained (and reinvested) funds does not affect this value. Miller and Modigliani's theory suggests that in a perfect world (certainty, no taxes, no transactions costs, and no other market imperfections), the value of the firm is unaffected by the distribution of dividends.

Of course, real markets do not satisfy the "perfect markets" assumptions of Miller and Modigliani's original theory. One market imperfection that may be important is taxation. Historically, dividends have usually been taxed at higher rates than capital gains. A firm that pays out its earnings as dividends may trigger higher tax liabilities for its investors than a firm that retains earnings. As a firm retains earnings, its share price should rise, and investors enjoy capital gains. Investors can defer paying taxes on these gains indefinitely simply by not selling their shares. Even if they do sell their shares, they may pay a relatively low tax rate on the capital gains. In contrast, when a firm pays dividends, investors receive cash immediately and pay taxes at the rates dictated by then-current tax laws.

Even though this discussion makes it seem that retaining profits rather than paying them out as dividends may be better for shareholders on an after-tax basis, Miller and Modigliani argue that this assumption may not be the case. They observe that not all investors are subject to income taxation. Some institutional investors, such as pension funds, do not pay taxes on the dividends and

2. Merton H. Miller and Franco Modigliani, "Dividend policy, growth and the valuation of shares," *Journal of Business* 34 (October 1961), pp. 411–433.

capital gains they earn. The payout policies of different firms, then, have no impact on the taxes such investors have to pay. Therefore, Miller and Modigliani argue, a **clientele effect** can exist in which different types of investors are attracted to firms with different payout policies due to tax effects. Tax-exempt investors may invest more heavily in firms that pay dividends because they are not affected by the typically higher tax rates on dividends. Investors who would have to pay higher taxes on dividends may prefer to invest in firms that retain more earnings rather than paying dividends. If a firm changes its payout policy, the value of the firm will not change; instead, what will change is the type of investor who holds the firm's shares. According to this argument, tax clienteles mean that payout policies cannot affect the firm's value, but they can affect the ownership base of the company.

clientele effect
The argument that different payout policies attract different types of investors but still do not change the value of the firm.

In summary, Miller and Modigliani and other proponents of dividend irrelevance argue that, all else being equal, an investor's required return—and therefore the value of the firm—is unaffected by dividend policy. In other words, there is no "optimal" dividend policy for a particular firm.

ARGUMENTS FOR DIVIDEND RELEVANCE

Miller and Modigliani's assertion that dividend policy was irrelevant sounded radical when first proposed. The prevailing wisdom at the time was that payout policy could improve the value of the firm and therefore had relevance. The key argument in support of **dividend relevance theory** is attributed to Myron J. Gordon and John Lintner,[3] who suggest that there is, in fact, a direct relationship between the firm's dividend policy and its market value. Fundamental to this proposition is their **bird-in-the-hand argument**, which suggests that investors see current dividends as less risky than future dividends or capital gains: "A bird in the hand is worth two in the bush." Gordon and Lintner argue that current dividend payments reduce investor uncertainty, causing investors to discount the firm's earnings at a lower rate and, all else being equal, to place a higher value on the firm's stock. Conversely, if firms reduce or do not pay dividends, investor uncertainty will increase, raising the required return and lowering the stock's value.

dividend relevance theory
The theory, advanced by Gordon and Lintner, that there is a direct relationship between a firm's dividend policy and its market value.

bird-in-the-hand argument
The belief, in support of dividend relevance theory, that investors see current dividends as less risky than future dividends or capital gains.

Miller and Modigliani argued that the bird-in-the-hand theory was a fallacy. They said that investors who want immediate cash flow from a firm that did not pay dividends could simply sell off a portion of their shares. Remember that the stock price of a firm that retains earnings should rise over time as cash builds up inside the firm. By selling a few shares every quarter or every year, investors could, according to Miller and Modigliani, replicate the same cash flow stream that they would have received if the firm had paid dividends rather than retaining earnings. In other words, investors could create their own "homemade dividends" if firms chose not to pay dividends.

Studies have shown that large changes in dividends do affect share price. Increases in dividends result in higher share price, and decreases in dividends result in lower share price. One interpretation of this evidence is that what matters is not the dividends per se but rather the **informational content** of dividends

informational content
The information provided by the dividends of a firm with respect to future earnings, which causes owners to bid up or down the price of the firm's stock.

3. Myron J. Gordon, "Optimal investment and financing policy," *Journal of Finance* 18 (May 1963), pp. 264–272; and John Lintner, "Dividends, earnings, leverage, stock prices, and the supply of capital to corporations," *Review of Economics and Statistics* 44 (August 1962), pp. 243–269.

with respect to future earnings. In other words, investors view a change in dividends, up or down, as a *signal* that management expects future earnings to change in the same direction. Investors view an increase in dividends as a *positive signal,* and they bid up the share price. They view a decrease in dividends as a *negative signal* that causes investors to sell their shares, resulting in the share price decreasing.

Another argument supporting the idea that dividends can affect the value of the firm is the *agency cost theory*. Recall that agency costs are costs that arise due to the separation between the firm's owners and its managers. Managers sometimes have different interests than owners do. Managers may want to retain earnings simply to increase the size of the firm's asset base. Greater prestige and perhaps higher compensation are associated with running a larger firm. Shareholders are aware of the temptations that managers face, and they worry that retained earnings may not be invested wisely. The *agency cost theory* says that a firm that commits to paying dividends is reassuring shareholders that managers will not waste their money. Given this reassurance, investors will pay higher prices for firms promising regular dividend payments.

Although many other arguments related to dividend relevance have been put forward, empirical studies have not provided evidence that conclusively settles the debate about whether and how payout policy affects the firm's value. As we have already said, even if dividend policy really matters, it may be less important than other decisions that financial managers make, such as the decision to invest in a large new project or the decision about what combination of debt and equity the firm should use to finance its operations. Still, most financial managers today, especially those running large corporations, believe that payout policy can affect the value of the firm.

→ REVIEW QUESTIONS MyLab Finance Solutions

14–7 Does following the residual theory of dividends lead to a stable dividend? Is this approach consistent with dividend relevance?

14–8 Contrast the basic arguments about dividend policy advanced by Miller and Modigliani and by Gordon and Lintner.

LG3

14.4 Factors Affecting Dividend Policy

dividend policy
The plan of action to be followed whenever the firm makes a dividend decision.

The **dividend policy** represents a plan of action to be followed whenever the firm makes a dividend decision. Firms develop policies consistent with their goals. Before we review some popular types of dividend policies, we discuss five factors that firms consider in establishing a dividend policy. They are legal constraints, contractual constraints, the firm's growth prospects, owner considerations, and market considerations.

LEGAL CONSTRAINTS

Most states prohibit corporations from paying out as cash dividends any portion of the firm's "legal capital," which is typically measured by the par value of common stock. Other states define legal capital to include not only the par value of the common stock but also any paid-in capital in excess of par. These *capital impairment restrictions* are generally established to provide a sufficient equity base to protect creditors' claims. An example will clarify the differing definitions of capital.

EXAMPLE 14.4

The stockholders' equity account of Miller Flour Company, a large grain processor, is presented in the following table.

Miller Flour Company Stockholders' Equity	
Common stock at par	$100,000
Paid-in capital in excess of par	200,000
Retained earnings	140,000
Total stockholders' equity	$440,000

In states where the firm's legal capital is defined as the par value of its common stock, the firm could pay out $340,000 ($200,000 + $140,000) in cash dividends without impairing its capital. In states where the firm's legal capital includes all paid-in capital, the firm could pay out only $140,000 in cash dividends.

Firms sometimes impose an earnings requirement limiting the amount of dividends. With this restriction, the firm cannot pay more in cash dividends than the sum of its most recent and past retained earnings. However, *the firm is not prohibited from paying more in dividends than its current earnings.*[4]

EXAMPLE 14.5

Assume that Miller Flour Company, from the preceding example, in the year just ended has $30,000 in earnings available for common stock dividends. As the table in Example 14.4 indicates, the firm has past retained earnings of $140,000. Thus, it can legally pay dividends of up to $170,000.

If a firm has overdue liabilities or is legally insolvent or bankrupt, most states prohibit it from paying cash dividends. In addition, the Internal Revenue Service prohibits firms from accumulating earnings to reduce the owners' taxes. If the IRS can determine that a firm has accumulated an excess of earnings to allow owners to delay paying ordinary income taxes on dividends received, it may levy an **excess earnings accumulation tax** on any retained earnings above $250,000 for most businesses.

excess earnings accumulation tax
The tax the IRS levies on retained earnings above $250,000 for most businesses when it determines that the firm has accumulated an excess of earnings to allow owners to delay paying ordinary income taxes on dividends received.

During the recent financial crisis, a number of financial institutions received federal financial assistance. Those firms had to agree to restrictions on dividend payments to shareholders until they repaid the money they received from the government. Bank of America, for example, had more than 30 years of consecutive dividend increases before accepting federal bailout money. As part of its

4. A firm that has an operating loss in the current period can still pay cash dividends as long as sufficient retained earnings against which to charge the dividend are available and, of course, as long as it has the cash with which to make the payments.

bailout, Bank of America had to cut dividends to $0.01 per share. Even in the absence of a crisis, financial institutions may face limits on dividend payments if regulators deem that such payments would reduce an institution's equity capital below an acceptable level. Utility companies also face regulatory constraints on their dividend payouts.

CONTRACTUAL CONSTRAINTS

Often, the firm's ability to pay cash dividends is constrained by restrictive provisions in a loan agreement. Generally, these constraints prohibit the payment of cash dividends until the firm achieves a certain level of earnings, or they may limit dividends to a certain dollar amount or percentage of earnings. Constraints on dividends help to protect creditors from losses due to the firm's insolvency.

GROWTH PROSPECTS

The firm's financial requirements are directly related to how much it expects to grow and what assets it will need to acquire. It must evaluate its profitability and risk to develop insight into its ability to raise capital externally. In addition, the firm must determine the cost and speed with which it can obtain financing. Generally, a large, mature firm has adequate access to new capital, whereas a rapidly growing firm may not have sufficient funds available to support its acceptable projects. A growth firm likely has to depend heavily on internal financing through retained earnings, so it is likely to pay out only a very small percentage of its earnings as dividends. A more established firm is in a better position to pay out a large proportion of its earnings, particularly if it has ready sources of financing.

OWNER CONSIDERATIONS

The firm must establish a policy that has a favorable effect on the wealth of its owners. One consideration is the tax status of a firm's owners. If a firm has a large percentage of wealthy stockholders who have sizable incomes, it may decide to pay out a lower percentage of its earnings to allow the owners to delay the payment of taxes until they sell the stock. Because cash dividends are taxed at the same rate as capital gains (as a result of the 2003 and 2012 Tax Acts), this strategy benefits owners through the tax deferral rather than as a result of a lower tax rate. Lower-income shareholders, however, who need dividend income, will prefer a higher payout of earnings.

A second consideration is the owners' investment opportunities. A firm should not retain funds for investment in projects yielding lower returns than the owners could obtain from external investments of equal risk. If it appears that the owners have better opportunities externally, the firm should pay out a higher percentage of its earnings. If the firm's investment opportunities are at least as good as similar-risk external investments, a lower payout is justifiable.

A final consideration is the potential dilution of ownership. If a firm pays out a high percentage of earnings, new equity capital will have to be raised with common stock. The result of a new stock issue may be dilution of both control and earnings for the existing owners. By paying out a low percentage of its earnings, the firm can minimize the possibility of such dilution.

MARKET CONSIDERATIONS

catering theory
A theory that says firms cater to the preferences of investors, initiating or increasing dividend payments during periods in which high-dividend stocks are particularly appealing to investors.

One of the more recent theories proposed to explain firms' payout decisions is called the *catering theory*. According to the **catering theory**, investors' demands for dividends fluctuate over time. For example, during an economic boom accompanied by a rising stock market, investors may be more attracted to stocks that offer prospects of large capital gains. When the economy is in recession and the stock market is falling, investors may prefer the security of a dividend. The catering theory suggests that firms are more likely to initiate dividend payments or to increase existing payouts when investors exhibit a strong preference for dividends. Firms *cater to* the preferences of investors.

→ **REVIEW QUESTION** MyLab Finance Solution

14–9 What five factors do firms consider in establishing dividend policy? Briefly describe each of them.

14.5 Types of Dividend Policies

The firm must formulate its dividend policy with two objectives in mind: providing for sufficient financing and maximizing the wealth of the firm's owners. Three different dividend policies are described in the following sections. A particular firm's dividend policy may incorporate elements of each.

dividend payout ratio
Indicates the percentage of each dollar earned that a firm distributes to the owners in the form of cash. It is calculated by dividing the firm's cash dividend per share by its earnings per share.

constant-payout-ratio dividend policy
A dividend policy based on the payment of a certain percentage of earnings to owners in each dividend period.

CONSTANT-PAYOUT-RATIO DIVIDEND POLICY

One type of dividend policy involves the use of a constant payout ratio. The **dividend payout ratio** indicates the percentage of each dollar earned that the firm distributes to the owners in the form of cash. It equals the firm's cash dividend per share divided by its earnings per share. With a **constant-payout-ratio dividend policy,** the firm pays a certain percentage of earnings to owners in each dividend period.

The problem with this policy is that if the firm's earnings drop or if a loss occurs in a given period, the dividends may be low or even nonexistent. Because dividends are often considered an indicator of the firm's future condition and status, the firm's stock price may be adversely affected.

EXAMPLE 14.6

Peachtree Industries, a miner of potassium, has a policy of paying out 40% of earnings in cash dividends. In periods when a loss occurs, the firm's policy is to pay no cash dividends. Data on Peachtree's earnings, dividends, and average stock prices for the past 6 years follow.

Year	Earnings/share	Dividends/share	Average price/share
2019	−$0.50	$0.00	$42.00
2018	3.00	1.20	52.00
2017	1.75	0.70	48.00
2016	−1.50	0.00	38.00
2015	2.00	0.80	46.00
2014	4.50	1.80	50.00

Dividends increased in 2017 and in 2018 but decreased in the other years. In years of decreasing dividends, the firm's stock price dropped; when dividends increased, the price of the stock increased. Peachtree's sporadic dividend payments appear to make its owners uncertain about the returns they can expect.

REGULAR DIVIDEND POLICY

regular dividend policy
A dividend policy based on the payment of a fixed-dollar dividend in each period.

The **regular dividend policy** is based on the payment of a fixed-dollar dividend in each period. Often, firms that use this policy increase the regular dividend once a *sustainable* increase in earnings has occurred. Under this policy, dividends are almost never decreased.

EXAMPLE 14.7

The dividend policy of Woodward Laboratories, a producer of a popular artificial sweetener, is to pay annual dividends of $1.00 per share until per-share earnings have exceeded $4.00 for 3 consecutive years. At that point, the annual dividend is raised to $1.50 per share, and a new earnings plateau is established. The firm does not anticipate decreasing its dividend unless its liquidity is in jeopardy. Data for Woodward's earnings, dividends, and average stock prices for the past 12 years follow.

Year	Earnings/share	Dividends/share	Average price/share
2019	$4.50	$1.50	$47.50
2018	3.90	1.50	46.50
2017	4.60	1.50	45.00
2016	4.20	1.00	43.00
2015	5.00	1.00	42.00
2014	2.00	1.00	38.50
2013	6.00	1.00	38.00
2012	3.00	1.00	36.00
2011	0.75	1.00	33.00
2010	0.50	1.00	33.00
2009	2.70	1.00	33.50
2008	2.85	1.00	35.00

Whatever the level of earnings, Woodward Laboratories paid dividends of $1.00 per share through 2016. In 2017, the dividend increased to $1.50 per share because earnings in excess of $4.00 per share had been achieved for 3 years. In 2017, the firm also had to establish a new earnings plateau for further dividend increases. Woodward Laboratories' average price per share exhibited a stable, increasing behavior in spite of a somewhat volatile pattern of earnings.

target dividend-payout ratio
A dividend policy under which the firm attempts to pay out a certain percentage of earnings as a stated dollar dividend and adjusts that dividend toward a target payout as proven earnings increases occur.

Often, a regular dividend policy is built around a **target dividend-payout ratio.** Under this policy, the firm attempts to pay out a certain *percentage* of earnings, but rather than let dividends fluctuate, it pays a stated dollar dividend and adjusts that dividend toward the target payout as proven earnings increases occur. For instance, Woodward Laboratories appears to have a target payout ratio of around 35%. The payout was about 35% ($1.00 ÷ $2.85) when the dividend policy was set in 2008, and when the dividend was raised to $1.50 in 2017, the payout ratio was about 33% ($1.50 ÷ $4.60).

LOW-REGULAR-AND-EXTRA DIVIDEND POLICY

low-regular-and-extra dividend policy
A dividend policy based on paying a low regular dividend, supplemented by an additional ("extra") dividend when earnings are higher than normal in a given period.

extra dividend
An additional dividend optionally paid by the firm when earnings are higher than normal in a given period.

Some firms establish a **low-regular-and-extra dividend policy,** paying a low regular dividend, supplemented by an additional ("extra") dividend when earnings are higher than normal in a given period. By calling the additional dividend an **extra dividend,** the firm avoids setting expectations that the dividend increase will be permanent. This policy is especially common among companies that experience cyclical shifts in earnings.

By establishing a low regular dividend that is paid each period, the firm gives investors the stable income necessary to build confidence in the firm, and the extra dividend permits them to share in the earnings from an especially good period. Firms using this policy may raise the level of the regular dividend once proven increases in earnings have been achieved. The extra dividend should not be a regular event; otherwise, investors will begin to see it as part of the regular dividend paid by the firm and react to cuts in the extra dividend by reducing the share price.

→ REVIEW QUESTION MyLab Finance Solution

14–10 Describe a constant-payout-ratio dividend policy, a regular dividend policy, and a low-regular-and-extra dividend policy. What are the effects of these policies?

LG5 LG6

14.6 Other Forms of Dividends

Two common transactions that bear some resemblance to cash dividends are stock dividends and stock splits. Although the stock dividends and stock splits are closely related to each other, their economic effects are quite different from those of cash dividends or share repurchases. Whereas cash dividends and repurchases fundamentally transfer money from the firm to investors, the effects of stock dividends and stock splits are mostly cosmetic.

STOCK DIVIDENDS

stock dividend
The payment, to existing owners, of a dividend in the form of stock.

A **stock dividend** is the payment, to existing owners, of a dividend in the form of stock. Often firms pay stock dividends as a replacement for or a supplement to cash dividends. In a stock dividend, investors simply receive additional shares in proportion to the shares they already own. No cash is distributed, and no real value is transferred from the firm to investors. Instead, because the number of outstanding shares increases, the stock price declines roughly in line with the amount of the stock dividend.

Accounting Aspects

small (ordinary) stock dividend
A stock dividend representing less than 20% to 25% of the common stock outstanding when the dividend is declared.

In an accounting sense, the payment of a stock dividend is a shifting of funds between stockholders' equity accounts rather than an outflow of funds. When a firm declares a stock dividend, the procedures for announcement and distribution are the same as those described earlier for a cash dividend. The accounting entries associated with the payment of a stock dividend vary depending on its size. A **small (ordinary) stock dividend** is a stock dividend that represents less than 20% to 25% of the common stock outstanding when the dividend is declared. Small stock dividends are most common.

EXAMPLE 14.8

The current stockholders' equity on the balance sheet of Garrison Corporation, a distributor of prefabricated cabinets, is as shown in the following accounts.

Preferred stock	$300,000
Common stock (100,000 shares at $4 par)	$400,000
Paid-in capital in excess of par	$600,000
Retained earnings	$700,000
Total stockholders' equity	$2,000,000

Garrison, which has 100,000 shares of common stock outstanding, declares a 10% stock dividend when the market price of its stock is $15 per share. When Garrison issues 10,000 new shares (10% of 100,000) at the prevailing market price of $15 per share, it shifts $150,000 ($15 per share × 10,000 shares) from retained earnings to the common stock and paid-in capital accounts. Garrison adds a total of $40,000 ($4 par × 10,000 shares) to common stock, and it adds the remaining $110,000 [($15 − $4) × 10,000 shares] to the paid-in capital in excess of par. The resulting account balances are as follows:

Preferred stock	$300,000
Common stock (110,000 shares at $4 par)	$440,000
Paid-in capital in excess of par	$710,000
Retained earnings	$550,000
Total stockholders' equity	$2,000,000

The firm's total stockholders' equity has not changed; the company has merely shifted funds among stockholders' equity accounts.

Shareholder's Viewpoint

The shareholder receiving a stock dividend typically receives nothing of value. After the firm pays the dividend, the per-share value of the shareholder's stock decreases in proportion to the dividend in such a way that the market value of his or her total holdings in the firm remains unchanged. Therefore, stock dividends are usually non-taxable. The shareholder's proportion of ownership in the firm also remains the same, and *as long as the firm's earnings remain unchanged,* so does the dollar value of his or her share of total earnings. (However, if the firm's earnings and cash dividends increase when the stock dividend is issued, an increase in share value is likely to result.)

EXAMPLE 14.9

Ms. Xu owned 10,000 shares of Garrison Corporation's stock. The company's recent earnings were $220,000, and they are not expected to change in the near future. Before the stock dividend, Ms. Xu owned 10% (10,000 shares ÷ 100,000 shares) of the firm's stock, which was selling for $15 per share. Earnings per share were $2.20 ($220,000 ÷ 100,000 shares). Because Ms. Xu owned 10,000 shares, her stock represented a claim against Garrison's earnings of $22,000 ($2.20 per share × 10,000 shares). After receiving the 10% stock dividend, Ms. Xu has 11,000 shares, which again is 10% of the ownership (11,000 shares ÷ 110,000 shares). The market price of the stock should drop to $13.64 per share [$15 × (1.00 ÷ 1.10)], which means that the market value of Ms. Xu's holdings is $150,000 (11,000 shares × $13.64 per share). This is the same as the initial value of her holdings (10,000 shares × $15 per share). The future earnings per share drops to $2 ($220,000 ÷ 110,000 shares) because the same $220,000 in earnings must now be divided among 110,000 shares. Because Ms. Xu still owns 10% of the stock, her share of total earnings is still \$22,000 (\$2 per share × 11,000 shares).

In summary, if the firm's earnings remain constant and total cash dividends do not increase, a stock dividend results in a lower per-share market value for the firm's stock.

The Company's Viewpoint

Stock dividends are more costly to issue than cash dividends, but certain advantages may outweigh these costs. Firms find the stock dividend to be a way to give owners something without having to use cash. Generally, when a firm needs to preserve cash to finance rapid growth, it uses a stock dividend. When the stockholders recognize that the firm is reinvesting the cash flow to maximize future earnings, the market value of the firm should at least remain unchanged. However, if the stock dividend is paid to retain cash for satisfying past-due bills, a decline in market value may result.

STOCK SPLITS

stock split
A method commonly used to lower the market price of a firm's stock by increasing the number of shares belonging to each shareholder.

Although not a type of dividend, *stock splits* have an effect on a firm's share price similar to that of stock dividends. A **stock split** is a method firms use to lower the market price of their stock by increasing the number of shares belonging to each shareholder. In a 2-for-1 split, for example, the firm exchanges two new shares for each old share. The result is that each new share is worth about half the value of each old share. A stock split has no effect on the firm's capital structure and is usually nontaxable.

Quite often, a firm believes that its stock is priced too high and that lowering the market price will enhance trading activity. Stock splits are often made prior to issuing additional stock to enhance that stock's marketability and stimulate market activity. Firms often increase dividends and announce other important news at the same time that they split their stock, so the total market value of the firm may rise slightly after a split.[5]

EXAMPLE 14.10

MyLab Finance Solution Video

Delphi Company, a forest products concern, had 200,000 shares of \$2-par-value common stock and no preferred stock outstanding. Because the stock is selling at a high market price, the firm has declared a 2-for-1 stock split. The total before- and after-split stockholders' equity is shown in the following table.

Before split		After 2-for-1 split	
Common stock		Common stock	
(200,000 shares at \$2 par)	\$ 400,000	(400,000 shares at \$1 par)	\$ 400,000
Paid-in capital in excess of par	4,000,000	Paid-in capital in excess of par	4,000,000
Retained earnings	2,000,000	Retained earnings	2,000,000
Total stockholders' equity	\$6,400,000	Total stockholders' equity	\$6,400,000

The insignificant effect of the stock split on the firm's books is obvious.

5. Eugene F. Fama, Lawrence Fisher, Michael C. Jensen, and Richard Roll, "The adjustment of stock prices to new information," *International Economic Review* 10 (February 1969), pp. 1–21, found that the stock price increases before the split announcement and that the increase in stock price is maintained if dividends per share are increased but is lost if dividends per share are *not* increased, following the split.

reverse stock split
A method used to raise the market price of a firm's stock by exchanging a certain number of outstanding shares for one new share.

Usually firms splitting their stock increase the number of shares outstanding, but sometimes firms engage in a **reverse stock split** in which more than one outstanding share is exchanged for one new share. For example, in a 1-for-3 split, a firm replaces three outstanding shares with one new share. In a reverse stock split, the firm's stock price rises due to the reduction in shares outstanding. Firms may conduct a reverse split if their stock price is getting so low that the exchange where the stock trades threatens to delist the stock. For example, the New York Stock Exchange requires that the average closing price of a listed security must be no less than $1 over any consecutive 30-day trading period. In June 2017, Xerox conducted a 1-for-4 reverse split of its stock, largely because the company had divested a large part of its existing business in a spinoff—a transaction that used significant assets of Xerox to create a new, independent company called Conduent. That transaction essentially divided the prior value of Xerox into two pieces, and the result was a sharp decline in the price of Xerox stock (which for Xerox shareholders was offset by the value of the new shares in Conduent that they received after the spinoff). Xerox managers believed that by conducting a reverse split, they would increase the price of Xerox stock to a level that would make it more liquid and therefore more attractive to investors.

PERSONAL FINANCE EXAMPLE 14.11 Shakira Washington, a single investor in the 24% federal income tax bracket, owns 260 shares of Advanced Technology Inc., common stock. She originally bought the stock 2 years ago at its initial public offering (IPO) price of $9 per share. The stock of this fast-growing technology company is currently trading for $60 per share, so the current value of her Advanced Technology stock is $15,600 (260 shares × $60 per share). Because the firm's board believes that the stock would trade more actively in the $20 to $30 price range, it just announced a 3-for-1 stock split. Shakira wishes to determine the impact of the stock split on her holdings and taxes.

Because the stock will split 3 for 1, after the split Shakira will own 780 shares (3 × 260 shares). She should expect the market price of the stock to drop to $20 (1/3 × $60) immediately after the split; the value of her after-split holding will be $15,600 (780 shares × $20 per share). Because the $15,600 value of her after-split holdings in Advanced Technology stock exactly equals the before-split value of $15,600, Shakira has experienced neither a gain nor a loss on the stock as a result of the 3-for-1 split. Even if there were a gain or loss attributable to the split, Shakira would not have any tax liability unless she actually sold the stock and realized that (or any other) gain or loss.

→ REVIEW QUESTIONS MyLab Finance Solutions

14–11 Why do firms issue stock dividends? Comment on the following statement: "I have a stock that promises to pay a 20% stock dividend every year, and therefore it guarantees that I will break even in 5 years."

14–12 Compare a stock split with a stock dividend.

SUMMARY

FOCUS ON VALUE

Payout policy refers to the cash flows that a firm distributes to its common stockholders through share repurchases and dividends. A share of common stock gives its owner the right to receive all future dividends. The present value of all those future dividends determines the firm's stock value.

Corporate payouts not only represent cash flows to shareholders but also contain useful information about the firm's current and future performance. Such information affects the shareholders' perception of the firm's risk. A firm can also pay stock dividends or initiate stock splits. Although those transactions are largely cosmetic, they can influence a firm's value if they convey new information about the firm to investors.

Although the theory of relevance of dividends is still evolving, the behavior of most firms and stockholders suggests that dividend policy affects share prices. Therefore, financial managers try to develop and implement dividend policy that is consistent with the firm's goal of **maximizing stock price.**

REVIEW OF LEARNING GOALS

LG1 **Understand cash payout procedures, their tax treatment, and the role of dividend reinvestment plans.** The board of directors makes the cash payout decision and, for dividends, establishes the record and payment dates. As a result of tax-law changes, investors pay taxes on corporate dividends at a maximum rate of 23.8%. Some firms offer dividend reinvestment plans that allow stockholders to acquire shares in lieu of cash dividends.

LG2 **Describe the residual theory of dividends and the key arguments with regard to dividend irrelevance and relevance.** The residual theory suggests that dividends should be viewed as the earnings left after all acceptable investment opportunities have been undertaken. Miller and Modigliani argue in favor of dividend irrelevance, using a perfect world in which market imperfections such as transaction costs and taxes do not exist. Gordon and Lintner advance the theory of dividend relevance, basing their argument on the uncertainty-reducing effect of dividends, supported by their bird-in-the-hand argument. Empirical studies fail to provide clear support of dividend relevance. Even so, the actions of financial managers and stockholders tend to support the belief that dividend policy does affect stock value.

LG3 **Discuss the key factors involved in establishing a dividend policy.** A firm's dividend policy should provide for sufficient financing and maximize stockholders' wealth. Dividend policy is affected by legal and contractual constraints, by growth prospects, and by owner and market considerations. Legal constraints prohibit corporations from paying out as cash dividends any portion of the firm's "legal capital," nor can firms with overdue liabilities and legally insolvent or bankrupt firms pay cash dividends. Contractual constraints result from restrictive provisions in the firm's loan agreements. Growth prospects affect the relative importance of retaining earnings rather than paying them out in dividends. The tax status of owners, the owners' investment opportunities, and the potential dilution of ownership are important owner considerations. Finally, market considerations are related to the stockholders' preference for the continuous payment of fixed or increasing streams of dividends.

LG4 **Review and evaluate the three basic types of dividend policies.** With a constant-payout-ratio dividend policy, the firm pays a fixed percentage of earnings to the owners each period; dividends move up and down with earnings, and no dividend is paid when a loss occurs. Under a regular dividend policy, the firm pays a fixed-dollar dividend each period; it increases the amount of dividends only after a proven increase in earnings. The low-regular-and-extra dividend policy is similar to the regular dividend policy except that it pays an extra dividend when the firm's earnings are higher than normal.

LG5 **Evaluate stock dividends from accounting, shareholder, and company points of view.** Firms may pay stock dividends as a replacement for or supplement to cash dividends. The payment of stock dividends involves a shifting of funds between capital accounts rather than an outflow of funds. Stock dividends do not change the market value of stockholders' holdings, proportion of ownership, or share of total earnings. Therefore, stock dividends are usually nontaxable. However, stock dividends may satisfy owners and enable the firm to preserve its market value without having to use cash.

LG6 **Explain stock splits and the firm's motivation for undertaking them.** Stock splits are used to enhance trading activity of a firm's shares by lowering or raising their market price. A stock split merely involves accounting adjustments; it has no effect on the firm's cash or on its capital structure and is usually nontaxable.

To retire outstanding shares, firms can repurchase stock in lieu of paying a cash dividend. Reducing the number of outstanding shares increases earnings per share and the market price per share. Stock repurchases also defer the tax payments of stockholders.

OPENER-IN-REVIEW

The chapter opener described Whirlpool's decision to dramatically increase its dividend in early 2017 to $1.10 per share. In the previous quarter, Whirlpool paid a dividend of $1 on March 15 to shareholders of record on March 3. When do you think the stock began trading ex dividend? The market price of Whirlpool stock just before the ex dividend date was $178.59. Immediately after the stock went ex dividend, the market price was $178.14. Is that price change surprising? Calculate the return that an investor might have earned if she had purchased the stock before the ex dividend date, sold the stock immediately afterward, and received the dividend a few weeks later.

SELF-TEST PROBLEM (Solutions in Appendix)

ST14–1 **Stock repurchase** The Off-Shore Steel Company has earnings available for common stockholders of $2 million and has 500,000 shares of common stock outstanding at $60 per share. The firm is currently contemplating the payment of $2 per share in cash dividends.

a. Calculate the firm's current earnings per share (EPS) and price/earnings (P/E) ratio.
b. If the firm can repurchase stock at $62 per share, how many shares can be purchased in lieu of making the proposed cash dividend payment?
c. How much will the EPS be after the proposed repurchase? Why?
d. If the stock sells at the old P/E ratio, what will the market price be after repurchase?
e. Compare and contrast the earnings per share before and after the proposed repurchase.
f. Compare and contrast the stockholders' position under the dividend and repurchase alternatives.

WARM-UP EXERCISES All problems are available in MyLab Finance

E14–1 Bristol's Bistro, Inc., has declared a dividend of $1.25 per share for shareholders of record on Tuesday, December 3. The firm has 350,000 shares outstanding and will pay the dividend on December 28. How much cash will be needed to pay the dividend? When will the stock begin selling ex dividend?

E14–2 Chancellor Industries has retained earnings available of $1.2 million. The firm plans to make two investments that require financing of $950,000 and $1.75 million, respectively. Chancellor uses a target capital structure with 60% debt and 40% equity. Apply the residual theory to determine what dividends, if any, can be paid out, and calculate the resulting dividend payout ratio.

LG3

E14–3 Ashkenazi Companies has the following stockholders' equity account:

Common stock (350,000 shares at $3 par)	$1,050,000
Paid-in capital in excess of par	$2,500,000
Retained earnings	$750,000
Total stockholders' equity	$4,300,000

Assuming that state laws define legal capital solely as the par value of common stock, how much of a per-share dividend can Ashkenazi pay? If legal capital were more broadly defined to include all paid in capital, how much of a per-share dividend could Ashkenazi pay?

E14–4 The board of Kopi Industries is considering a new dividend policy that would set dividends at 60% of earnings. The recent past has witnessed earnings per share (EPS) and dividends paid per share as shown in the following table.

Year	EPS	Dividend/share
2016	$1.75	$0.95
2017	1.95	1.20
2018	2.05	1.25
2019	2.25	1.30

Based on Kopi's historical dividend payout ratio, discuss whether a constant payout ratio of 60% would benefit shareholders.

LG5

E14–5 The current stockholders' equity account for Hilo Farms is as follows:

Common stock (50,000 shares at $3 par)	$150,000
Paid-in capital in excess of par	$250,000
Retained earnings	$450,000
Total stockholders' equity	$850,000

Hilo has announced plans to issue an additional 5,000 shares of common stock as part of its stock dividend plan. The current market price of Hilo's common stock is $20 per share. Show how the proposed stock dividend would affect the stockholder's equity account.

PROBLEMS

All problems are available in MyLab Finance. The MyLab icon indicates problems in Excel format available in MyLab Finance.

P14–1 **Dividend payment procedures** At the quarterly dividend meeting, Wood Shoes declared a cash dividend of $1.10 per share for holders of record on Monday, July 10. The firm has 300,000 shares of common stock outstanding and has set a payment date of July 31. Prior to the dividend declaration, the firm's key accounts were as follows:

Cash	$500,000	Dividends payable	$0
		Retained earnings	$2,500,000

a. Show the entries after the meeting adjourned.
b. When is the ex dividend date?
c. What values would the key accounts have after the July 31 payment date?
d. What effect, if any, will the dividend have on the firm's total assets?
e. Ignoring general market fluctuations, what effect, if any, will the dividend have on the firm's stock price on the ex dividend date?

Personal Finance Problem

P14–2 **Dividend payment** Kathy Snow wishes to purchase shares of Countdown Computing Inc. The company's board of directors has declared a cash dividend of $0.80 to be paid to holders of record on Wednesday, May 12.

a. What is the last day that Kathy can purchase the stock (trade date) and still receive the dividend?
b. What day does this stock begin trading ex dividend?

c. What change, if any, would you expect in the price per share when the stock begins trading on the ex dividend day?

d. If Kathy held the stock for less than one quarter and then sold it for \$39 per share, would she achieve a higher investment return by (1) buying the stock prior to the ex dividend date at \$35 per share and collecting the \$0.80 dividend or (2) buying it on the ex dividend date at \$34.20 per share but not receiving the dividend?

P14–3 **Residual dividend policy** As president of Young's of California, a large clothing chain, you have just received a letter from a major stockholder. The stockholder asks about the company's dividend policy. In fact, the stockholder has asked you to estimate the amount of the dividend that you are likely to pay next year. You have not yet collected all the information about the expected dividend payment, but you do know the following:

(1) The company follows a residual dividend policy.

(2) The total capital budget for next year is likely to be one of three amounts, depending on the results of capital budgeting studies that are currently under way. The capital expenditure amounts are \$2 million, \$3 million, and \$4 million.

(3) The forecasted level of potential retained earnings next year is \$2 million.

(4) The target or optimal capital structure is a debt ratio of 40%.

You have decided to respond by sending the stockholder the best information available to you.

a. Describe a residual dividend policy.

b. Compute the amount of the dividend (or the amount of new common stock needed) and the dividend payout ratio for each of the three capital expenditure amounts.

c. Compare, contrast, and discuss the amount of dividends (calculated in part **b**) associated with each of the three capital expenditure amounts.

LG3

P14–4 **Dividend constraints** The Howe Company's stockholders' equity account follows:

Common stock (400,000 shares at \$4 par)	\$1,600,000
Paid-in capital in excess of par	\$1,000,000
Retained earnings	\$1,900,000
Total stockholders' equity	\$4,500,000

The earnings available for common stockholders from this period's operations are \$100,000, which have been included as part of the \$1.9 million retained earnings.

a. What is the maximum dividend per share that the firm can pay? (Assume that legal capital includes all paid-in capital.)

b. If the firm has \$160,000 in cash, what is the largest per-share dividend it can pay without borrowing?

c. Indicate the accounts and changes, if any, that will result if the firm pays the dividends indicated in parts **a** and **b**.

d. Indicate the effects of an \$80,000 cash dividend on stockholders' equity.

P14–5 **Dividend constraints** A firm has \$800,000 in paid-in capital, retained earnings of \$40,000 (including the current year's earnings), and 25,000 shares of common stock outstanding. In the current year, it has $29,000 of earnings available for the common stockholders.

a. What is the most the firm can pay in cash dividends to each common stockholder? (Assume that legal capital includes all paid-in capital.)
b. What effect would a cash dividend of $0.80 per share have on the firm's balance sheet entries?
c. If the firm cannot raise any new funds from external sources, what do you consider the key constraint with respect to the magnitude of the firm's dividend payments? Why?

P14–6 **Low-regular-and-extra dividend policy** Bennett Farm Equipment Sales Inc. is in a highly cyclical business. Although the firm has a target payout ratio of 25%, its board realizes that strict adherence to that ratio would result in a fluctuating dividend and create uncertainty for the firm's stockholders. Therefore, the firm has declared a regular dividend of $0.50 per share per year with extra cash dividends to be paid when earnings justify them. Earnings per share for the past several years are shown in the following table.

Year	EPS	Year	EPS
2019	$3.00	2016	$2.80
2018	2.40	2015	2.15
2017	2.20	2014	1.97

a. Calculate the payout ratio for each year on the basis of the regular $0.50 dividend and the cited EPS.
b. Calculate the difference between the regular $0.50 dividend and a 25% payout for each year.
c. Bennett has established a policy of paying an extra dividend of $0.25 only when the difference between the regular dividend and a 25% payout amounts to $1.00 or more. Show the regular and extra dividends in those years when an extra dividend would be paid. What would be done with the "extra" earnings that are not paid out?
d. The firm expects that future earnings per share will continue to cycle but will remain above $2.20 per share in most years. What factors should be considered in making a revision to the amount paid as a regular dividend? If the firm revises the regular dividend, what new amount should it pay?

LG4

P14–7 **Alternative dividend policies** Over the past 10 years, a firm has had the earnings per share shown in the following table.

Year	Earnings per share	Year	Earnings per share
2019	$4.00	2014	$2.40
2018	3.80	2013	1.20
2017	3.20	2012	1.80
2016	2.80	2011	−0.50
2015	3.20	2010	0.25

a. If the firm's dividend policy were based on a constant payout ratio of 40% for all years with positive earnings and 0% otherwise, what would be the annual dividend for each year?
b. If the firm had a dividend payout of $1.00 per share, increasing by $0.10 per share whenever the dividend payout fell below 50% for 2 consecutive years, what annual dividend would the firm pay each year?
c. If the firm's policy were to pay $0.50 per share each period except when earnings per share exceed $3.00, when an extra dividend equal to 80% of earnings beyond $3.00 would be paid, what annual dividend would the firm pay each year?
d. Discuss the pros and cons of each dividend policy described in parts **a** through **c**.

P14–8 **Alternative dividend policies** Given the earnings per share over the period 2012–2019 shown in the following table, determine the annual dividend per share under each of the policies set forth in parts **a** through **d**.

Year	Earnings per share
2019	$1.40
2018	1.56
2017	1.20
2016	−0.85
2015	1.05
2014	0.60
2013	1.00
2012	0.44

a. Pay out 50% of earnings in all years with positive earnings.
b. Pay $0.50 per share and increase to $0.60 per share whenever earnings per share rise above $0.90 per share for 2 consecutive years.
c. Pay $0.50 per share except when earnings exceed $1.00 per share, in which case pay an extra dividend of 60% of earnings above $1.00 per share.
d. Combine the policies described in parts **b** and **c**. When the dividend is raised (in part **b**), raise the excess dividend base (in part **c**) from $1.00 to $1.10 per share.
e. Compare and contrast each of the dividend policies described in parts **a** through **d**.

LG5

P14–9 **Stock dividend: Firm** Columbia Paper has the following stockholders' equity account. The firm's common stock has a current market price of $30 per share.

Preferred stock	$100,000
Common stock (10,000 shares at $2 par)	$20,000
Paid-in capital in excess of par	$280,000
Retained earnings	$100,000
Total stockholders' equity	$500,000

a. Show the effects on Columbia of a 5% stock dividend.
b. Show the effects of (1) a 10% and (2) a 20% stock dividend.
c. In light of your answers to parts **a** and **b**, discuss the effects of stock dividends on stockholders' equity.

P14–10 **Cash versus stock dividend** Milwaukee Tool has the following stockholders' equity account. The firm's common stock currently sells for $4 per share.

Preferred stock	$100,000
Common stock (400,000 shares at $1 par)	$400,000
Paid-in capital in excess of par	$200,000
Retained earnings	$320,000
Total stockholders' equity	$1,020,000

a. Show the effects on the firm of a cash dividend of $0.01, $0.05, $0.10, and $0.20 per share.
b. Show the effects on the firm of a 1%, 5%, 10%, and 20% stock dividend.
c. Compare the effects in parts **a** and **b**. What are the significant differences between the two methods of paying dividends?

Personal Finance Problem

P14–11 **Stock dividend: Investor** Sarah Warren currently holds 400 shares of Nutri-Foods. The firm has 40,000 shares outstanding. The firm most recently had earnings available for common stockholders of $80,000, and its stock has been selling for $22 per share. The firm intends to retain its earnings and pay a 10% stock dividend.
a. How much does the firm currently earn per share?
b. What proportion of the firm does Sarah currently own?
c. What proportion of the firm will Sarah own after the stock dividend? Explain your answer.
d. At what market price would you expect the stock to sell after the stock dividend?
e. Discuss what effect, if any, the payment of stock dividends will have on Sarah's share of the ownership and earnings of Nutri-Foods.

Personal Finance Problem

P14–12 **Stock dividend: Investor** Security Data Company has outstanding 50,000 shares of common stock currently selling at $40 per share. The firm most recently had earnings available for common stockholders of $120,000, but it has decided to retain these funds and is considering either a 5% or a 10% stock dividend in lieu of a cash dividend.
a. Determine the firm's current earnings per share.
b. If Sam Waller currently owns 500 shares of the firm's stock, determine his proportion of ownership currently and under each of the proposed stock dividend plans. Explain your findings.
c. Calculate and explain the market price per share under each of the stock dividend plans.
d. For each of the proposed stock dividends, calculate the earnings per share after payment of the stock dividend.
e. What is the value of Sam's holdings under each of the plans? Explain.
f. Should Sam have any preference with respect to the proposed stock dividends? Why or why not?

P14–13 **Stock split: Firm** Growth Industries' current stockholders' equity account is as follows:

Preferred stock	$400,000
Common stock (600,000 shares at $3 par)	$1,800,000
Paid-in capital in excess of par	$200,000
Retained earnings	$800,000
Total stockholders' equity	$3,200,000

a. Indicate the change, if any, expected if the firm declares a 2-for-1 stock split.
b. Indicate the change, if any, expected if the firm declares a 1-for-$1\frac{1}{2}$ reverse stock split.
c. Indicate the change, if any, expected if the firm declares a 3-for-1 stock split.
d. Indicate the change, if any, expected if the firm declares a 6-for-1 stock split.
e. Indicate the change, if any, expected if the firm declares a 1-for-4 reverse stock split.

Personal Finance Problem

P14–14 **Stock splits** Nathan Detroit owns 400 shares of the drink company Monster Beverage Corp., which he purchased for $122 per share. Nathan read in the *Wall Street Journal* that the company's board of directors had voted to split the stock 3-for-1. Just before the stock split, Monster Beverage shares were trading for $132.59.

Answer the following questions about the impact of the stock split on his holdings and taxes. Nathan is in the 24% federal income tax bracket.

a. How many shares of Monster Beverage will Nathan own after the stock split?
b. Immediately after the split, what do you expect the value of Monster Beverage to be?
c. Compare the total value of Nathan's stock holdings before and after the split, given that the price of Monster Beverage stock immediately after the split was $44.78. What do you find?
d. Does Nathan experience a gain or loss on the stock as a result of the 2-for-1 split?
e. What is Nathan's tax liability from the event?

P14–15 **Stock split versus stock dividend: Firm** Mammoth Corporation is considering a 3-for-2 stock split. It currently has the stockholders' equity position as shown. The current stock price is $120 per share. The most recent period's earnings available for common stock are included in retained earnings.

Preferred stock	$1,000,000
Common stock (100,000 shares at $3 par)	$300,000
Paid-in capital in excess of par	$1,700,000
Retained earnings	$10,000,000
Total stockholders' equity	$13,000,000

a. What effects on Mammoth would result from the stock split?
b. What change in stock price would you expect to result from the stock split?
c. What is the maximum cash dividend per share that the firm could pay on common stock before and after the stock split? (Assume that legal capital includes all paid-in capital.)

d. Contrast your answers to parts a through c with the circumstances surrounding a 50% stock dividend.
e. Explain the differences between stock splits and stock dividends.

LG5 LG6

P14–16 Stock dividend versus stock split: Firm The board of Wicker Home Health Care Inc. is exploring ways to expand the number of shares outstanding in an effort to reduce the market price per share to a level that the firm considers more appealing to investors. The options under consideration are a 20% stock dividend and, alternatively, a 5-for-4 stock split. At the present time, the firm's equity account and other per-share information are as follows:

Preferred stock	$0
Common stock (100,000 shares at $1 par)	$100,000
Paid-in capital in excess of par	$900,000
Retained earnings	$700,000
Total stockholders' equity	$1,700,000

Price per share	$30.00
Earnings per share	$3.60
Dividend per share	$1.08

a. Show the effect on the equity accounts and per-share data of a 20% stock dividend.
b. Show the effect on the equity accounts and per-share data of a 5-for-4 stock split.
c. Which option will accomplish Wicker's goal of reducing the current stock price while maintaining a stable level of retained earnings?
d. What legal constraints might encourage the firm to choose a stock split over a stock dividend?

LG6

P14–17 Stock repurchase The following financial data on the Bond Recording Company are available:

Earnings available for common stockholders	$800,000
Number of shares of common stock outstanding	400,000
Earnings per share ($800,000 ÷ 400,000)	$2
Market price per share	$20
Price/earnings (P/E) ratio ($20 ÷ $2)	10

The firm is currently considering whether it should use $400,000 of its earnings to pay cash dividends of $1 per share or to repurchase stock at $21 per share.
a. Approximately how many shares of stock can the firm repurchase at the $21-per-share price, using the funds that would have gone to pay the cash dividend?
b. Calculate the EPS after the repurchase. Explain your calculations.
c. If the stock still sells at 10 times earnings, what will the market price be after the repurchase?
d. Compare the pre- and post-repurchase earnings per share.
e. Compare and contrast the stockholders' positions under the dividend and repurchase alternatives. What are the tax implications under each alternative?

LG6

P14–18 Stock repurchase Harte Textiles Inc., a maker of custom upholstery fabrics, is concerned about preserving the wealth of its stockholders during a cyclical downturn in the home furnishings business. The company has maintained a constant dividend payout of $2.00 tied to a target payout ratio of 40%. Management is preparing a share repurchase recommendation to present to the firm's board of directors. The following data have been gathered from the past 2 years.

	2018	2019
Earnings available for common stockholders	$1,260,000	$1,200,000
Number of shares outstanding	300,000	300,000
Earnings per share	$ 4.20	$ 4.00
Market price per share	$ 23.50	$ 20.00
Price/earnings ratio	5.6	5.0

a. How many shares should the company have outstanding in 2019 if its earnings available for common stockholders in that year are $1,200,000 and it pays a dividend of $2.00, given that its desired payout ratio is 40%?

b. How many shares would Harte have to repurchase to have the level of shares outstanding calculated in part a?

P14–19 **ETHICS PROBLEM** Assume that you are the CFO of a company contemplating a stock repurchase next quarter. You know that there are several methods of reducing the current quarterly earnings, which may cause the stock price to fall prior to the announcement of the proposed stock repurchase. What course of action would you recommend to your CEO? If your CEO came to you first and recommended reducing the current quarter's earnings, what would be your response?

SPREADSHEET EXERCISE

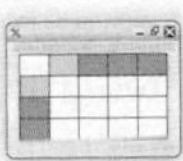

One way to lower the market price of a firm's stock is via a stock split. Rock-O Corporation finds itself in a different situation: Its stock has been selling at relatively low prices. To increase the market price of the stock, the company chooses to use a reverse stock split of 2-for-3.

The company currently has 700,000 common shares outstanding and no preferred stock. The common stock carries a par value of $1. At this time, the paid-in capital in excess of par is $7,000,000, and the firm's retained earnings are $3,500,000.

TO DO

Create a spreadsheet to determine the following:

a. The stockholders' equity section of the balance sheet before the reverse stock split.

b. The stockholders' equity section of the balance sheet after the reverse stock split.

MyLab Finance Visit www.pearson.com/mylab/finance **for Chapter Case: *Establishing General Access Company's Dividend Policy and Initial Dividend,*** Group Exercises, and numerous online resources.

Integrative Case 6

O'Grady Apparel Company

The O'Grady Apparel Company was founded nearly 160 years ago when an Irish merchant named Garrett O'Grady landed in Los Angeles with an inventory of heavy canvas, which he hoped to sell for tents and wagon covers to miners headed for the California goldfields. Instead, he turned to the sale of harder-wearing clothing.

Today, O'Grady Apparel Company is a small manufacturer of fabrics and clothing whose stock is traded in the OTC market. In 2019, the Los Angeles–based company experienced sharp increases in both domestic and European markets, resulting in record earnings. Sales rose from $15.9 million in 2018 to $18.3 million in 2019, with earnings per share of $3.28 and $3.84, respectively.

European sales represented 29% of total sales in 2019, up from 24% the year before and only 3% in 2014, 1 year after foreign operations were launched. Although foreign sales represent nearly one-third of total sales, the growth in the domestic market is expected to affect the company most markedly. Management expects sales to surpass $21 million in 2020, and earnings per share are expected to rise to $4.40. (Selected income statement items are presented in Table 1.)

Because of the recent growth, Margaret Jennings, the corporate treasurer, is concerned that available funds are not being used to their fullest potential. The projected $1,300,000 of internally generated 2020 funds is expected to be insufficient to meet the company's expansion needs. Management has set a policy of maintaining the current capital structure proportions of 25% long-term debt, 10% preferred stock, and 65% common stock equity for at least the next 3 years. In addition, it plans to continue paying out 40% of its earnings as dividends. Total capital expenditures are yet to be determined.

Jennings has been presented with several competing investment opportunities by division and product managers. However, because funds are limited, choices of which projects to accept must be made. A list of investment opportunities is shown in Table 2. To analyze the effect of the increased financing requirements on the weighted average cost of capital (WACC), Jennings contacted a leading investment banking firm that provided the financing cost data given in Table 3. O'Grady is in the 21% tax bracket.

TABLE 1

Selected Income Statement Items

	2017	2018	2019	Projected 2020
Net sales	$13,860,000	$15,940,000	$18,330,000	$21,080,000
Net profits after taxes	$ 1,520,000	$ 1,750,000	$ 2,020,000	$ 2,323,000
Earnings per share (EPS)	2.88	3.28	3.84	4.40
Dividends per share	1.15	1.31	1.54	1.76

TABLE 2

Investment Opportunities

Investment opportunity	Internal rate of return (IRR)	Initial investment
A	13%	$400,000
B	11	200,000
C	16	700,000
D	19	500,000
E	10	300,000
F	14	600,000
G	9	500,000

TABLE 3

Financing Cost Data

Long-term debt: The firm can raise $700,000 of additional debt by selling 10-year, $1,000, 6% annual interest rate bonds to net $970 after flotation costs. Any debt in excess of $700,000 will have a before-tax cost, r_d, of 9%.

Preferred stock: Preferred stock, regardless of the amount sold, can be issued with a $60 par value and a 8% annual dividend rate. It will net $57 per share after flotation costs.

Common stock equity: The firm expects its dividends and earnings to grow at a constant rate of 10% per year. The firm's stock is currently selling for $20 per share. The firm expects to have $1,300,000 of available retained earnings. Once the retained earnings have been exhausted, the firm can raise additional funds by selling new common stock, netting $16 per share after underpricing and flotation costs.

TO DO

a. Over the relevant ranges noted in the following table, calculate the after-tax cost of each source of financing needed to complete the table.

Source of capital	Range of new financing	After-tax cost (%)
Long-term debt	$0–$700,000	______
	$700,000 and above	______
Preferred stock	$0 and above	______
Common stock equity	$0–$1,300,000	______
	$1,300,000 and above	______

b. (1) Determine the break point associated with common equity. A break point represents the total amount of financing that the firm can raise before it triggers an increase in the cost of a particular financing source. For example, O'Grady plans to use 25% long-term debt in its capital structure. So, for every $1 in debt that the firm uses, it will use $3 from other financing sources (total financing is then $4, and because $1 comes from long-term debt, its share in the total is the desired 25%). From Table 3, we see that after the firm raises $700,000 in long-term debt, the cost of this financing source begins to rise. Therefore, the firm can raise total capital of $2.8 million before the cost of debt will rise ($700,000 in debt plus $2.1 million in other sources to maintain the 25% proportion for debt), and $2.8 million is the break point for debt. If the firm wants to maintain a capital structure with 25% long-term debt and it also wants to raise more than $2.8 million in total financing, it will require more than $700,000 in long-term debt, and it will trigger the higher cost of the additional debt it issues beyond $700,000.

(2) Using the break points developed in part (1), determine each of the ranges of *total* new financing over which the firm's weighted average cost of capital (WACC) remains constant.

(3) Calculate the weighted average cost of capital for each range of total new financing. Draw a graph with the WACC on the vertical axis and total money raised on the horizontal axis, and show how the firm's WACC increases in "steps" as the amount of money raised increases.

c. (1) Sort the investment opportunities described in Table 2 from highest to lowest return, and plot a line on the graph you drew in part (3) above, showing how much money is required to fund the investments, starting with the highest return and going to the lowest. In other words, this line will plot the relationship between the IRR on the firm's investments and the total financing required to undertake those investments.

(2) Which, if any, of the available investments would you recommend that the firm accept? Explain your answer.

d. (1) Assuming that the specific financing costs do not change, what effect would a shift to a more highly leveraged capital structure consisting of 50% long-term debt, 10% preferred stock, and 40% common stock have on your previous findings? (*Note:* Rework parts **b** and **c** using these capital structure weights.)

(2) Which capital structure—the original one or this one—seems better? Why?

e. (1) What type of dividend policy does the firm appear to employ? Does it seem appropriate given the firm's recent growth in sales and profits and given its current investment opportunities?

(2) Would you recommend an alternative dividend policy? Explain. How would this policy affect the investments recommended in part **c**(2)?

PART SEVEN

Short-Term Financial Decisions

CHAPTERS IN THIS PART

Short-term financial decisions are guided by the same financial management principles as long-term financial decisions, but the time frame is different: days, weeks, and months rather than years. Working capital management focuses on managing short-term cash flows by evaluating their timing, risk, and impact on firm value. Although long-term financial decisions ultimately determine the firm's ability to maximize shareholder wealth, long-term outcomes may not even be realized if financial managers fail to make effective short-term financial decisions.

Chapter 15 discusses the techniques and strategies for managing working capital and current assets. The chapter also introduces the fundamentals of net working capital and the importance of the cash conversion cycle. Chapter 16 discusses the importance of controlling accounts payable expenses and managing other current liabilities. You will learn how some companies finance current assets by using current liabilities, including accounts payable, accruals, lines of credit, commercial paper, and short-term loans. Successful adherence to the fundamentals of working capital management will help ensure that the firm can meet its operating obligations and maximize its long-term investments.

CHAPTER 15

Working Capital and Current Assets Management

LEARNING GOALS

LG 1 Understand working capital management, net working capital, and the related tradeoff between profitability and risk.

LG 2 Describe the cash conversion cycle, its funding requirements, and the key strategies for managing it.

LG 3 Discuss inventory management: differing views, common techniques, and international concerns.

LG 4 Explain the credit selection process and the quantitative procedure for evaluating changes in credit standards.

LG 5 Review the procedures for quantitatively considering early payment discount changes, other aspects of credit terms, and credit monitoring.

LG 6 Understand the management of receipts and disbursements, including float, speeding up collections, slowing down payments, cash concentration, zero-balance accounts, and investing in marketable securities.

MyLab Finance Chapter Introduction Video

WHY THIS CHAPTER MATTERS TO YOU

In your *professional* life

ACCOUNTING You need to understand the cash conversion cycle and the management of inventory, accounts receivable, and receipts and disbursements of cash.

INFORMATION SYSTEMS You need to understand the cash conversion cycle, inventory, accounts receivable, and receipts and disbursements of cash to design financial information systems that facilitate effective working capital management.

MANAGEMENT You need to understand the management of working capital so that you can efficiently manage current assets and decide whether to finance the firm's funds requirements aggressively or conservatively.

MARKETING You need to understand credit selection and monitoring because sales will be affected by the availability of credit to purchasers; sales will also be affected by inventory management.

OPERATIONS You need to understand the cash conversion cycle because you will be responsible for reducing the cycle through the efficient management of production, inventory, and costs.

In your *personal* life

You often will face short-term purchasing decisions, which tend to focus on consumable items. Many involve tradeoffs between quantity and price: Should you buy large quantities to pay a lower unit price, hold the items, and use them over time? Or should you buy smaller quantities more frequently and pay a slightly higher unit price? Analyzing these types of short-term purchasing decisions will help you make the most of your money.

THE HACKETT GROUP SURVEY

Are CFOs Afraid of the Ghost of the Financial Crisis Past?

Koya979/Fotolia

In a 2016 survey of the largest U.S. firms, The Hackett Group, a strategic consulting firm, found that companies were taking advantage of low interest rates to increase debt, while at the same time paying little attention to another low-cost source of funds—their own working capital. The survey found that corporate debt was up 9.3% in 2016, and that in the years since the financial crisis corporations had increased their debt every year, raising total debt levels by 58% since 2009.

With money available at historically low interest rates, companies were perhaps paying less attention to managing their current assets and liabilities than was advisable. For example, the Hackett survey discovered that the average company's cash conversion cycle—a measure of how quickly firms generate cash by turning over inventory, collecting receivables, and paying their suppliers—had increased by 7% to 35.6 days, which was the longest (i.e., slowest) cash conversion cycle since the 2008 recession. Hackett estimated that if all firms increased their working capital management at least to the level of the top quartile of firms in their industries, they would free up more than $1 trillion in cash that they could invest elsewhere or use to pay dividends to shareholders or to retire debt. The survey indicated that firms could free up more than $400 billion through better inventory management practices and more than $300 billion by managing receivables more effectively.

The issues that firms must balance when deciding how much inventories and receivables to hold also arise in the management of other working capital items such as cash and accounts payable. This chapter explains the tradeoffs involved in managing working capital and how managers should evaluate those tradeoffs.

15.1 Net Working Capital Fundamentals

The balance sheet provides information about the structure of a firm's investments on the one hand and the structure of its financing sources on the other hand. In previous chapters we studied capital budgeting, which focuses on the long-term assets on the left-hand side of a firm's balance sheet, and capital structure, which focuses on the long-term liabilities and equity on the balance sheet. In this chapter and the next we turn our focus to the choices that confront financial analysts as they manage the firm's short-term assets and liabilities. As with all other financial decisions, the object is to manage current assets and liabilities in a way that maximizes the value of the firm.

WORKING CAPITAL MANAGEMENT

In chapter 4 you learned that changes in a firm's net working capital directly impact free cash flow, and in chapter 7 you saw that a firm's value depends on its free cash flow. Thus, managers can increase firm value by managing working capital accounts such as receivables, inventories, and payables efficiently. The goal of **working capital (or short-term financial) management** is to manage each of the firm's current assets and current liabilities to achieve a balance between profitability and risk that contributes positively to the firm's value.

working capital (or short-term financial) management
Management of current assets and current liabilities.

Firms reduce financing costs or increase the funds available for expansion by minimizing the amount of funds tied up in working capital. Therefore, it should not be surprising to learn that working capital is one of the financial manager's most important and time-consuming activities. Surveys by *CFO* magazine and Duke University have found that corporate CFOs spend almost 30 hours per month engaged in working capital and cash management, which is more time than they spend on any other single activity. Similar surveys have revealed that CFOs believe their efforts to manage working capital effectively add as much value to the firm as any of their other activities.

MATTER OF FACT

CFOs Value Working Capital Management

A survey of CFOs from firms around the world suggests that working capital management sits at the top of the list of most valued finance functions. Among 19 different finance functions, CFOs viewed working capital management as equally important as capital structure, debt issuance and management, bank relationships, and tax management. Their satisfaction with the performance of working capital management was quite the opposite, however. CFOs viewed the performance of working capital management as better only than that of pension management. Consistent with their view that working capital management is a high-value but low-satisfaction activity, CFOs identified working capital as the finance function second most in need of additional resources.[1]

1. Henri Servaes and Peter Tufano, "CFO views on the importance and execution of the finance function," *CFO Views* (January 2006), pp. 1–104.

NET WORKING CAPITAL

working capital
The portion of the firm's assets used in day-to-day transactions. The primary elements of working capital circulate from one form to another in the ordinary course of business.

Working capital consists of the portion of the firm's assets used in day-to-day transactions. The primary elements of working capital circulate from one form to another in the ordinary course of business. This idea embraces the recurring transition from cash (and marketable securities) to inventories to accounts receivable and back to cash.

Current liabilities represent the firm's short-term financing, because they include all debts that come due in 1 year or less. These debts usually include amounts owed to suppliers (accounts payable), employees and governments (accruals), and banks (notes payable), among others. (You can refer to Chapter 3 for a full discussion of balance sheet items.)

Net working capital is the difference between the firm's current assets and its current liabilities. When current assets exceed current liabilities, the firm has positive net working capital. When current assets are less than current liabilities, the firm has negative net working capital.

The conversion of current assets from inventory to accounts receivable to cash provides an important source of funds that firms use to pay current liabilities. The cash outlays for current liabilities are relatively predictable. When the firm incurs an obligation, managers generally know when the corresponding payment will be due. More difficult to predict are the cash inflows: the conversion of the current assets to more liquid forms. The more predictable its cash inflows, the less net working capital a firm needs. Because most firms are unable to match cash inflows to cash outflows with certainty, they usually need current assets that more than cover outflows for current liabilities. In general, the greater the margin by which a firm's current assets cover its current liabilities, the greater the firm's ability to pay its bills as they come due.

TRADEOFF BETWEEN PROFITABILITY AND RISK

insolvent
Describes a firm that is unable to pay its bills as they come due.

A tradeoff exists between a firm's profitability and its risk. Profitability, in this context, is the relationship between revenues and costs generated by using the firm's assets—both current and fixed—in productive activities. A firm can increase its profits by (1) increasing revenues or (2) decreasing costs. Risk, in the context of working capital management, is the probability that a firm will be unable to pay its bills as they come due. A firm that cannot pay its bills as they come due is **insolvent.** Other things being equal, the greater the firm's net working capital, the lower its risk of insolvency. In other words, the more net working capital, the more liquid the firm and therefore the lower its risk of becoming insolvent. Using these definitions of profitability and risk, we can demonstrate the tradeoff between them by considering changes in current assets and current liabilities separately.

Changes in Current Assets

To understand how changing the level of the firm's current assets affects its profitability–risk tradeoff, consider the ratio of current assets to total assets. This ratio indicates the percentage of total assets that is current. The upper portion of Table 15.1 summarizes the effects on both profitability and risk of an increase or decrease in this ratio, holding total assets constant. When the ratio increases—that is, when current assets increase—profitability decreases. Why? The answer

TABLE 15.1 Effects of Changing Ratios on Profits and Risk

Ratio	Change in ratio	Effect on profit	Effect on risk
$\frac{\text{Current assets}}{\text{Total assets}}$	Increase Decrease	Decrease Increase	Decrease Increase
$\frac{\text{Current liabilities}}{\text{Total assets}}$	Increase Decrease	Increase Decrease	Increase Decrease

is because for most firms current assets are less profitable than fixed assets. Fixed assets add more value to a firm's products than do current assets.

The upper line in Figure 15.1 shows the median ratio of current assets divided by total assets among all U.S. public companies (excluding financial firms) from 1950 to 2016. The figure clearly shows that over time firms have been cutting their investments in current assets, consistent with the view that current assets provide lower returns to shareholders.[2] The middle line in Figure 15.1 shows that most of the reduction in that ratio has been driven by reductions in inventory as a percentage of assets. Improvements in information technology over the past half-century allowed firms to manage their inventories much more efficiently, ordering and holding goods in inventory only when needed.

Other things being equal, if firms cut back on current assets, they tend to increase risk. However, note the behavior of the bottom line in Figure 15.1. That line tracks the ratio of cash and marketable securities divided by total assets. That ratio, after reaching a low point in 1979, has been increasing for more than

FIGURE 15.1
Yearly Medians for All U.S.–Listed Nonfinancial Companies

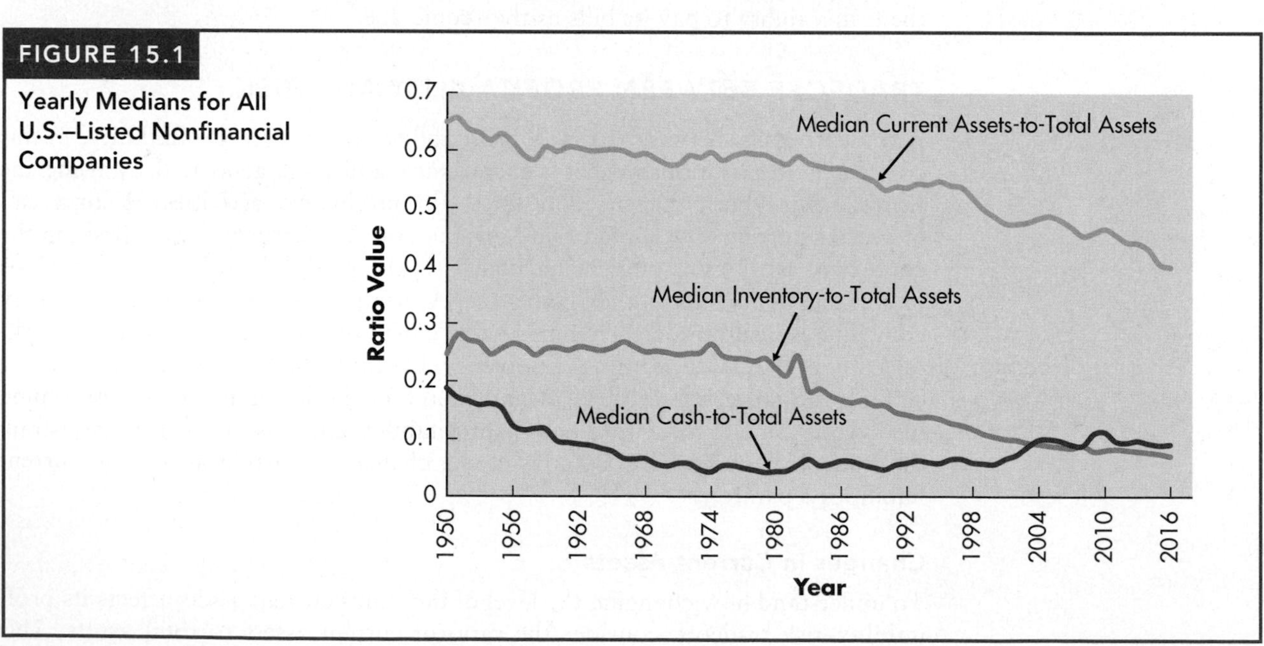

2. In part, the decline in the ratio of current assets to total assets is due to a shift in the mix of public companies operating in the United States. Since 1950, the economy has shifted away from manufacturing and toward service-oriented companies. To the extent that many service providers carry little or no inventory, an increasing number of such firms would tend to lower the current assets to total assets ratio. If we focused only on manufacturing firms, we would see that this ratio remained relatively steady over this period, but the inventory-to-assets ratio also dropped for these firms.

three decades. Increasing cash holdings tends to offset the rise in risk associated with a lower investment in working capital. In other words, while firms are increasing their risk by cutting back on their holdings of current assets, they are increasing their holdings of the *least risky current asset*—cash. Remember that as you go down the asset side of the balance sheet, the risk associated with the assets increases. Cash and marketable securities are less risky than accounts receivable. Receivables in turn are less risky than inventories, which are less risky than fixed assets. The nearer an asset is to cash, the less risky it is, and companies are holding more cash today than they have since the early 1960s. At the same time that companies are trying to limit their investments in current assets to earn higher returns, they are increasing their cash holdings to mitigate the risk associated with a less liquid balance sheet.

Changes in Current Liabilities

We also can demonstrate how changing the level of the firm's current liabilities affects its profitability–risk tradeoff by using the ratio of current liabilities to total assets. This ratio indicates the percentage of total assets that has been financed with current liabilities. Again, assuming that total assets remain unchanged, the effects on both profitability and risk of an increase or decrease in the ratio are summarized in the lower portion of Table 15.1. When the ratio increases, profitability increases. Why? Here it is because the firm uses more of the less-expensive current liabilities financing and less long-term financing. Current liabilities are less expensive because they bear no interest (with the exception of notes payable). However, when the ratio of current liabilities to total assets increases, the risk of insolvency also rises because the increase in current liabilities in turn decreases net working capital. The opposite effects on profit and risk result from a reduction in the ratio of current liabilities to total assets.

→ REVIEW QUESTIONS MyLab Finance Solutions

15–1 Why is working capital management one of the most important and time-consuming activities of the financial manager? What is net working capital?

15–2 What is the relationship between the predictability of a firm's cash inflows and its required level of net working capital? How are net working capital, liquidity, and risk of insolvency related?

15–3 Why does an increase in the ratio of current assets to total assets decrease both profits and risk as measured by net working capital? How do changes in the ratio of current liabilities to total assets affect profitability and risk?

LG2

15.2 Cash Conversion Cycle

cash conversion cycle (CCC)
The length of time between when a firm pays cash for raw materials and when it receives cash from collecting receivables.

Central to working capital management is an understanding of the firm's *cash conversion cycle*. The **cash conversion cycle (CCC)** is the length of time between when a firm pays cash for its raw materials and when it receives cash from collecting its receivables. Companies with a long cash conversion cycle must wait a long time after they pay their suppliers before they receive payment from customers, and the gap between when a firm pays and when it receives payment creates a need for financing to sustain the firm's operations. This cycle frames discussion of the management of the firm's current assets in this chapter and that of the management of current liabilities in Chapter 16. We begin by demonstrating the calculation and application of the cash conversion cycle.

CALCULATING THE CASH CONVERSION CYCLE

operating cycle (OC)
The time from the beginning of the production process to collection of cash from the sale of the finished product.

A firm's **operating cycle** (OC) is the time from the beginning of the production process to collection of cash from the sale of the finished product. The operating cycle encompasses two major short-term asset categories, inventory and accounts receivable. The OC equals the sum of the *average age of inventory (AAI)* and the *average collection period (ACP)*:

$$OC = AAI + ACP \tag{15.1}$$

MATTER OF FACT

Increasing Speed Lowers Working Capital

A firm can lower its working capital if it can speed up its operating cycle. For example, if a firm accepts bank credit (like a Visa card), it will receive cash sooner after the sale is transacted than if it has to wait until the customer pays its accounts receivable.

However, the process of producing and selling a product also includes the purchase of production inputs (raw materials) on account, which results in accounts payable. Accounts payable reduce the number of days a firm's resources are tied up in the operating cycle. The time it takes to pay the accounts payable, measured in days, is the *average payment period (APP)*. The operating cycle less the average payment period yields the cash conversion cycle. The formula for the cash conversion cycle is

$$CCC = OC - APP \tag{15.2}$$

Substituting the relationship in Equation 15.1 into Equation 15.2, we can see that the cash conversion cycle has three main components—(1) average age of the inventory, (2) average collection period, and (3) average payment period.

$$CCC = AAI + ACP - APP \tag{15.3}$$

If a firm can pay its suppliers at the same time that it collects payment from customers, its cash conversion cycle is zero days. However, most firms must pay their bills before they collect on their sales, meaning that the cash conversion cycle is greater than zero. Furthermore, each day of the cash conversion cycle represents a day for which the firm needs financing (other than money collected from sales) to sustain its operations. The longer the cash conversion cycle, the greater a firm's financing need. If a firm changes any of the components of the cash conversion cycle, it changes the financial resources tied up in the day-to-day operation of the firm.

EXAMPLE 15.1

MyLab Finance Solution Video

In its 2017 annual report, Best Buy reported that it had revenues of \$39.40 billion, cost of goods sold of \$29.96 billion, accounts receivable of \$1.34 billion, inventory of \$4.86 billion, and accounts payable of \$4.98 billion. From this information (and assuming for simplicity that cost of goods sold equals purchases), we can determine that the company's average age of inventory was 59 days, its average collection period was 12 days, and its average payment period was 61 days. Thus, the cash conversion cycle for Best Buy was just 10 days ($59 + 12 - 61 = 10$). Figure 15.2 presents Best Buy's cash conversion cycle as a timeline.

FIGURE 15.2

Timeline for Best Buy's Cash Conversion Cycle
Best Buy's operating cycle in 2017 was 71 days, and its cash conversion cycle was 12 days.

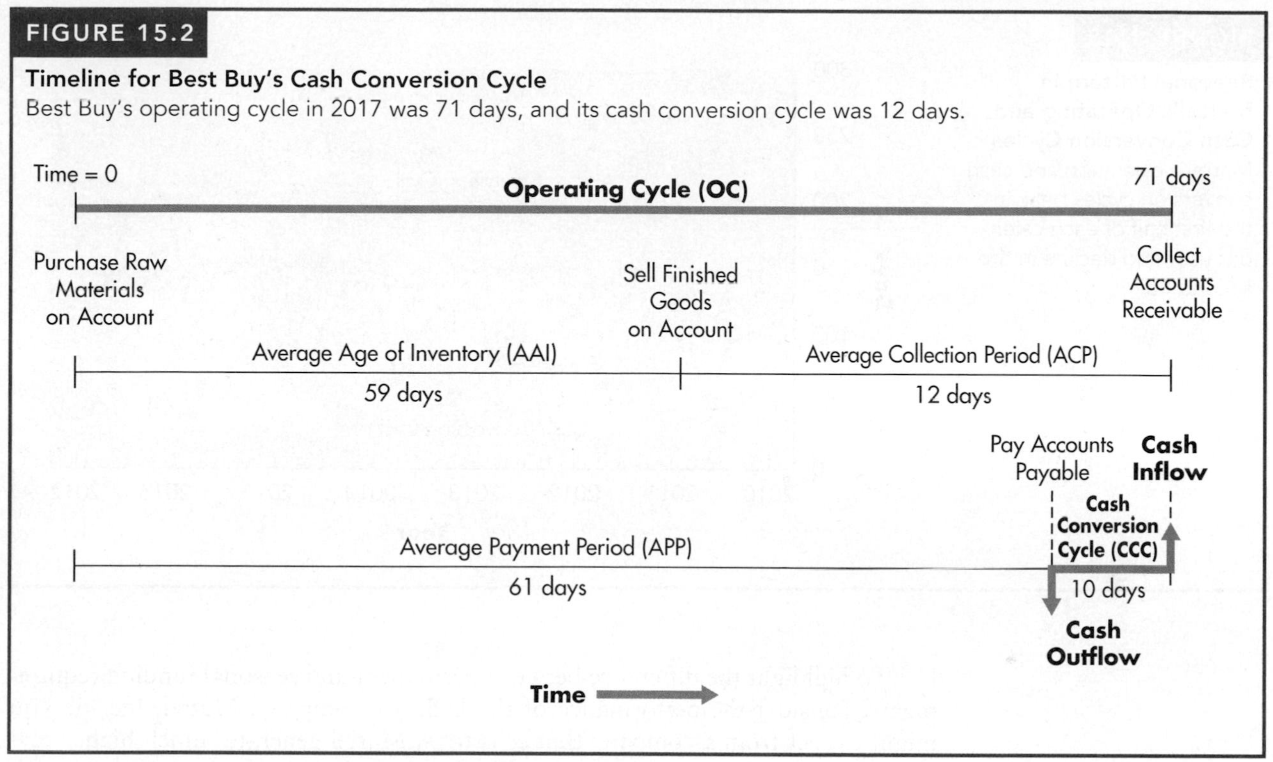

If we add Best Buy's inventory and receivables balances and subtract accounts payable, we find that the company has $1.22 billion invested in the working capital components of this cash conversion cycle. That gives the company plenty of motivation to make improvements. Changes in any of the component cycles will change the resources tied up in Best Buy's operations. For example, if Best Buy could reduce its inventory from 59 days to 50 days, holding all else equal, its working capital requirement would fall by more than $750 million, illustrating why companies pay close attention to working capital management.

FUNDING REQUIREMENTS OF THE CASH CONVERSION CYCLE

We can use the cash conversion cycle as a basis for discussing how the firm funds its required investment in operating assets. We first differentiate between permanent and seasonal funding needs and then describe aggressive and conservative seasonal funding strategies.

permanent funding requirement
A constant investment in operating assets resulting from constant sales over time.

seasonal funding requirement
An investment in operating assets that varies over time as a result of cyclical sales.

Permanent versus Seasonal Funding Needs

If the firm's sales are constant, its investment in operating assets should also be constant, and the firm will have only a **permanent funding requirement.** If the firm's sales are seasonal, its investment in operating assets will vary over time with its sales cycles, and the firm will have **seasonal funding requirements** in addition to the permanent funding required for its minimum investment in operating assets.

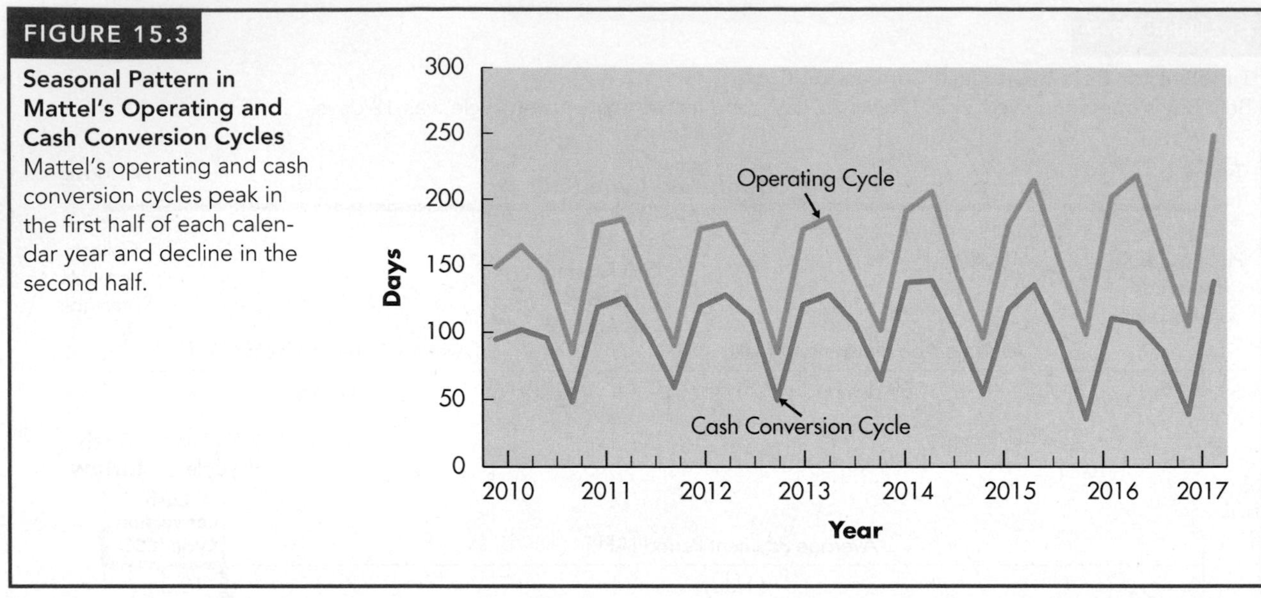

FIGURE 15.3

Seasonal Pattern in Mattel's Operating and Cash Conversion Cycles
Mattel's operating and cash conversion cycles peak in the first half of each calendar year and decline in the second half.

To highlight the difference between permanent and seasonal funding requirements, consider the performance of the U.S. toy company, Mattel, Inc. As you might expect from a company that sells toys, Mattel generates much higher revenue in the last three months of the calendar year than during any other quarter. For example, the company's sales from October to December in any given year are typically more than 2 times greater than sales from January to March. As a consequence, by December 31 each year, the company's inventory (in terms of days of inventory on hand) is at a low point for the year, and the firm spends the next 6 months building inventory back up to be ready for the next busy season. Payables track inventory closely, while receivables follow with a short lag, usually peaking the quarter after inventory does.

Figure 15.3 shows the implications of this seasonal pattern for Mattel's operating and cash conversion cycles from 2010 through early 2017. Both cycles tend to rise during the first six months of the calendar year and fall in the last two quarters. The gap between the high and low points is significant. From 2010 to 2017, the peak cash conversion cycle averaged about 125 days, whereas the cycle's low point was typically about 50 days. At a minimum, we can say that Mattel needed financing sufficient to cover a 50-day cash conversion cycle. Hence, that determines the size of Mattel's permanent funding requirement. However, the 75-day difference between Mattel's longest and shortest cash conversion cycle means that the company has a significant seasonal funding need during the first half of each year.

EXAMPLE 15.2

MyLab Finance Solution Video

Nicholson Company holds, on average, \$50,000 in cash and marketable securities, \$1,250,000 in inventory, and \$750,000 in accounts receivable. Nicholson's business is very stable over time, so its operating assets can be viewed as permanent. In addition, Nicholson's accounts payable of \$425,000 are stable over time. Thus, Nicholson has a permanent investment in operating assets of \$1,625,000 (\$50,000 + \$1,250,000 + \$750,000 − \$425,000). That amount would also equal its permanent funding requirement.

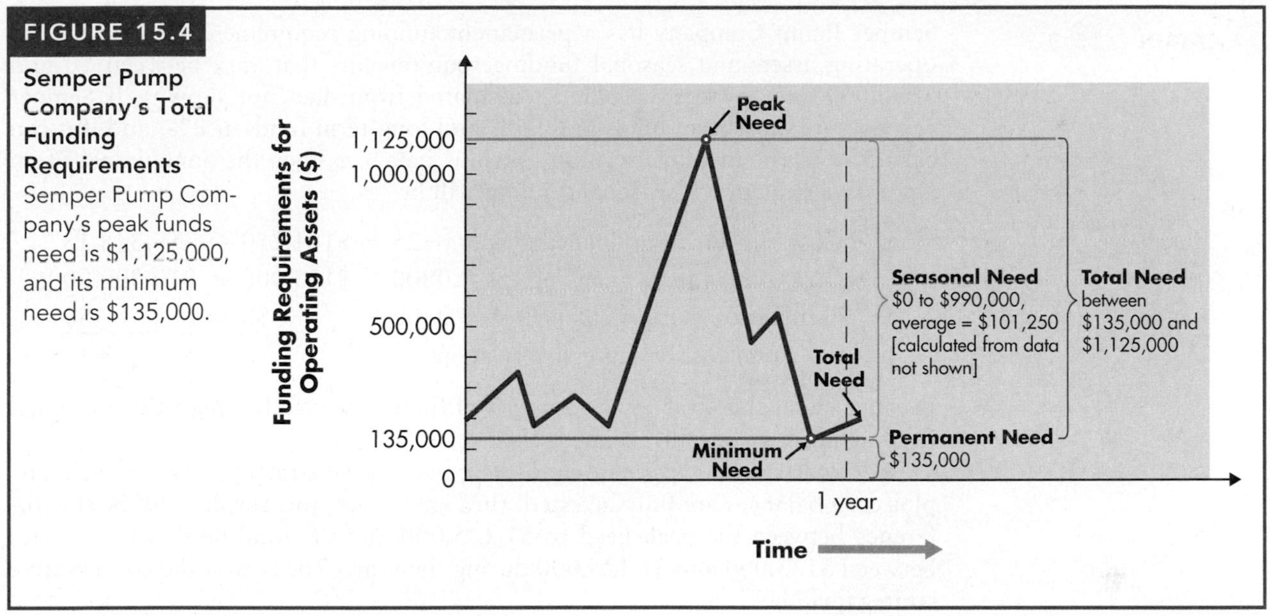

FIGURE 15.4

Semper Pump Company's Total Funding Requirements
Semper Pump Company's peak funds need is $1,125,000, and its minimum need is $135,000.

In contrast, Semper Pump Company, which produces bicycle pumps, has seasonal funding needs. Semper has seasonal sales; its peak sales are driven by the summertime purchases of bicycle pumps. Semper holds, at minimum, $25,000 in cash and marketable securities, $100,000 in inventory, and $60,000 in accounts receivable. At peak times, Semper's inventory increases to $750,000, and its accounts receivable increase to $400,000. To capture production efficiencies, Semper produces pumps at a constant rate throughout the year. Thus, accounts payable remain at $50,000 throughout the year. Accordingly, Semper has a permanent funding requirement for its minimum level of operating assets of $135,000 ($25,000 + $100,000 + $60,000 − $50,000) and peak seasonal funding requirements (in excess of its permanent need) of $990,000 [($25,000 + $750,000 + $400,000 − $50,000) − $135,000]. Semper's total funding requirements for operating assets vary from a minimum of $135,000 (permanent) to a seasonal peak of $1,125,000 ($135,000 + $990,000). Figure 15.4 depicts these needs over time.

Aggressive versus Conservative Seasonal Funding Strategies

aggressive funding strategy
A funding strategy under which the firm funds its seasonal requirements with short-term debt and its permanent requirements with long-term debt or equity.

conservative funding strategy
A funding strategy under which the firm funds both its seasonal and its permanent requirements with long-term debt or equity.

Short-term funds are typically less expensive than long-term funds. That is, interest rates on short-term loans are typically lower than rates on long-term loans (or equity) because the yield curve is typically upward sloping. However, long-term funds allow the firm to lock in its cost of funds over a period of time and thus avoid the risk of increases in short-term interest rates. Also, long-term funding ensures that the required funds are available to the firm when needed. Short-term funding entails the risk that the firm may not be able to obtain the funds needed to cover its seasonal peaks. Under an **aggressive funding strategy,** the firm funds its seasonal requirements with short-term debt and its permanent requirements with long-term debt or equity. Under a **conservative funding strategy,** the firm funds both its seasonal and its permanent requirements with long-term debt or equity.

EXAMPLE 15.3

Semper Pump Company has a permanent funding requirement of $135,000 in operating assets and seasonal funding requirements that vary between $0 and $990,000 and average $101,250 (calculated from data not shown). If Semper can borrow short-term funds at 6.25% and long-term funds at 8%, and if it can earn 5% on the investment of any surplus balances, then the annual cost of an aggressive strategy for seasonal funding will be

Cost of short-term financing	= 0.0625 ×	$101,250 =	$6,328.13
+ Cost of long-term financing	= 0.0800 ×	$135,000 =	$10,800.00
− Earnings on surplus balances	= 0.0500 ×	$0 =	$0
Total cost of aggressive strategy			$17,128.13

Because under this strategy the amount of financing exactly equals the estimated funding need, no surplus balances exist.

Alternatively, Semper can choose a conservative strategy, under which surplus cash balances are fully invested. (In Figure 15.4, this surplus will be the difference between the peak need of $1,125,000 and the total need, which varies between $135,000 and $1,125,000 during the year.) The cost of the conservative strategy will be

Cost of short-term financing	= 0.0625 ×	$0 =	$0
+ Cost of long-term financing	= 0.0800 ×	$1,125,000 =	$90,000.00
− Earnings on surplus balances	= 0.0500 ×	$888,750 =	$44,437.50
Total cost of conservative strategy			$45,562.50

The average surplus balance would be calculated by subtracting the sum of the permanent need ($135,000) and the average seasonal need ($101,250) from the seasonal peak need ($1,125,000) to get $888,750 ($1,125,000 − $135,000 − $101,250). This represents the surplus amount of financing that Semper could invest, on average, in short-term assets that earn a 5% annual return.

These calculations demonstrate that for Semper, the aggressive strategy is far less expensive than the conservative strategy. However, it is equally clear that Semper has substantial peak-season operating-asset needs and that it must have adequate funding available to meet the peak needs and ensure ongoing operations.

The aggressive strategy's heavy reliance on short-term financing makes it riskier than the conservative strategy because of interest rate swings and possible difficulties in obtaining needed short-term financing quickly when seasonal peaks occur. The conservative strategy avoids these risks through the locked-in interest rate and long-term financing, but it is more costly because of the negative spread between the earnings rate on surplus funds (5% in the example) and the cost of the long-term funds that create the surplus (8% in the example). Where the firm operates, between the extremes of the aggressive and conservative seasonal funding strategies, depends on management's disposition toward risk and the strength of its banking relationships.

STRATEGIES FOR MANAGING THE CASH CONVERSION CYCLE

Some firms establish a target cash conversion cycle and then monitor and manage the actual cash conversion cycle toward the targeted value. A positive cash conversion cycle, as was the case for Best Buy in 2017, means the firm must use debt or equity to support its operating assets. Those sources of funds are costly, so the firm benefits by minimizing their use in supporting operating assets. In other words, to maximize shareholder wealth, managers should work to minimize the length of the cash conversion cycle (subject to a variety of constraints mentioned below), which minimizes the need for costly financing. Managers can achieve this goal by implementing a combination of the following strategies:

1. Turn over inventory as quickly as possible without stockouts that result in lost sales.
2. Collect accounts receivable as quickly as possible without losing sales from high-pressure collection techniques or from credit terms that are not competitive in the market.
3. Manage mail, processing, and clearing time to reduce them when collecting from customers and to increase them when paying suppliers.
4. Pay accounts payable as slowly as possible without damaging the firm's credit rating or its relationships with suppliers.

Techniques for implementing these four strategies are the focus of the remainder of this chapter and the following chapter.

→ REVIEW QUESTIONS MyLab Finance Solutions

15–4 What is the difference between the firm's operating cycle and its cash conversion cycle?

15–5 Why is it helpful to divide the funding needs of a seasonal business into its permanent and seasonal funding requirements when developing a funding strategy?

15–6 What are the benefits, costs, and risks of an aggressive funding strategy and of a conservative funding strategy? Under which strategy is the borrowing often in excess of the actual need?

15–7 Why is it important for a firm to minimize the length of its cash conversion cycle?

15.3 Inventory Management

The first component of the cash conversion cycle is the average age of inventory. The objective for managing inventory, as noted earlier, is to turn over inventory as quickly as possible (or equivalently, to minimize the average age of inventory) without losing sales from stockouts. The financial manager tends to act as an advisor or "watchdog" in matters concerning inventory. He or she does not have direct control over inventory but does provide input to the inventory management process.

DIFFERING VIEWPOINTS ABOUT INVENTORY LEVEL

Viewpoints about appropriate inventory levels commonly differ among a firm's finance, marketing, manufacturing, and purchasing managers. Each views inventory levels in light of his or her own objectives. The financial manager's general disposition toward inventory levels is to keep them low, to ensure that the firm's money is not being unwisely invested in excess resources. The marketing manager, in contrast, would like to have large inventories of the firm's finished products. This would ensure that all orders could be filled quickly, eliminating the need for backorders due to stockouts.

The manufacturing manager's major responsibility is to implement the production plan so that it results in the desired amount of finished goods of acceptable quality available on time at a low cost. In fulfilling this role, the manufacturing manager would keep raw materials inventories high to avoid production delays. He or she also would favor large production runs for the sake of lower unit production costs, which would result in high finished goods inventories.

The purchasing manager is concerned solely with the raw materials inventories. He or she must have on hand, in the correct quantities at the desired times and at a favorable price, whatever raw materials are required by production. Without proper control, in an effort to get quantity discounts or in anticipation of rising prices or a shortage of certain materials, the purchasing manager may purchase larger quantities of resources than are actually needed at the time.

COMMON TECHNIQUES FOR MANAGING INVENTORY

Numerous techniques are available for effectively managing the firm's inventory. Here we briefly consider four commonly used techniques.

ABC System

ABC inventory system
Inventory management technique that divides inventory into three groups—A, B, and C, in descending order of importance and level of monitoring—on the basis of the dollar investment in each.

A firm using the **ABC inventory system** divides its inventory into three groups: A, B, and C. The A group includes those items with the largest dollar investment. Typically, this group consists of 20% of the firm's inventory items but 80% of its investment in inventory. The B group consists of items that account for the next largest investment in inventory. The C group comprises a large number of items that require a relatively small investment.

The inventory group of each item determines the item's level of monitoring. The A group items receive the most intense monitoring because of the high dollar investment. Typically, managers track A group items on a perpetual inventory system that allows daily verification of each item's inventory level. B group items are frequently controlled through periodic, perhaps weekly, checking of their levels. Managers monitor C group items with unsophisticated techniques, such as the two-bin method. With the **two-bin method,** the item is stored in two bins. As an item is needed, inventory is removed from the first bin. When that bin is empty, an order is placed to refill the first bin while inventory is drawn from the second bin. The second bin is used until empty, and so on.

two-bin method
Unsophisticated inventory-monitoring technique that is typically applied to C group items and involves reordering inventory when one of two bins is empty.

The large dollar investment in A and B group items suggests the need for a better method of inventory management than the ABC system. The EOQ model, discussed next, is an appropriate model for managing A and B group items.

Economic Order Quantity (EOQ) Model

economic order quantity (EOQ) model
Inventory management technique for determining an item's optimal order size, which is the size that minimizes the total of its order costs and carrying costs.

One technique for determining the optimal order size for inventory items is the **economic order quantity (EOQ) model.** The EOQ model considers various costs of inventory and then determines what order size minimizes total inventory cost.

order costs
The fixed clerical costs of placing and receiving an inventory order.

carrying costs
The variable costs per unit of holding an item in inventory for a specific period of time.

The EOQ model works by trading off two categories of inventory costs: *order costs* and *carrying costs*. **Order costs** include the fixed clerical costs of placing and receiving orders: the cost of writing a purchase order, of processing the resulting paperwork, and of receiving an order and checking it against the invoice. The more orders a firm places, the higher are order costs. In the EOQ model, we measure order costs in dollars per order. **Carrying costs** are the variable costs per unit of holding an item of inventory for a specific period of time. Carrying costs include storage costs, insurance costs, the costs of deterioration and obsolescence, and the opportunity cost of investing funds in inventory rather than in other assets that earn a return. A firm can push carrying costs down by placing many small orders rather than a few large ones. In the EOQ model, we measure carrying costs in dollars per unit per period.

Order costs decrease as the size of the order increases and the number of orders falls. Carrying costs, however, increase with increases in the order size. The EOQ model analyzes the tradeoff between order costs and carrying costs to determine the order quantity that minimizes the total inventory cost.

Mathematical Development of EOQ A formula can be developed for determining the firm's EOQ for a given inventory item, where

$$S = \text{usage in units per period}$$
$$O = \text{cost per order}$$
$$Q = \text{order quantity in units}$$
$$C = \text{carrying cost per unit per period}$$

The first step is to derive the cost functions for order cost and carrying cost. Total order cost equals the cost per order (O) times the number of orders. The number of orders equals $S \div Q$, the usage in units per period (S) divided by the order quantity in units (Q), so the order cost equals

$$\text{Order cost} = O \times (S \div Q) \quad (15.4)$$

The carrying cost is the cost of carrying a unit of inventory per period (C) multiplied by the firm's average inventory. The average inventory is $Q \div 2$ because EOQ model assumes that a firm's inventory is drawn down at a steady rate between orders. That is, the average inventory is the order quantity (Q) divided by 2. Thus, carrying cost equals

$$\text{Carrying cost} = C \times (Q \div 2) \quad (15.5)$$

total cost of inventory
The sum of order costs and carrying costs of inventory.

The firm's **total cost of inventory** equals the sum of the order cost and the carrying cost. Thus, the total cost function is

$$\text{Total cost} = [O \times (S \div Q)] + [C \times (Q \div 2)] \quad (15.6)$$

Because the EOQ is the order quantity that minimizes the total cost function, we must solve the total cost function for the EOQ.[3] The resulting equation is

$$\text{EOQ} = \sqrt{\frac{2 \times S \times O}{C}} \quad (15.7)$$

3. In this simple model, the EOQ occurs at the point where the order cost $[O \times (S \div Q)]$ just equals the carrying cost $[C \times (Q \div 2)]$. To demonstrate, we set the two costs equal and solve for Q:

$$[O \times (S \div Q)] = [C \times (Q \div 2)]$$

Then cross-multiplying, we get

$$2 \times O \times S = C \times Q^2$$

Dividing both sides by C, we get

$$Q^2 = (2 \times O \times S) \div C$$

so

$$Q = \sqrt{(2 \times O \times S) \div C}$$

Remember that the EOQ as defined by Equation 15.7 is simply the size of the order that the firm should place to minimize costs. Think intuitively about what Equation 15.7 says regarding the optimal order quantity. If the rate at which the firm uses inventory, S, increases, then the order quantity should be higher. That makes sense because if a firm uses inventory very rapidly and if it places small orders, it will have to place many of them and order costs will be very high. Similarly, Equation 15.7 says that if the carrying cost per unit (C) is high, the order quantity should be smaller. That makes sense, too, because if inventory is costly to hold (perhaps because it spoils or because its value declines rapidly), a firm does not want to hold a large inventory balance.

PERSONAL FINANCE EXAMPLE 15.4 Individuals sometimes are confronted with personal finance decisions involving cost tradeoffs similar to the tradeoff between the fixed order costs and variable carrying costs of inventory that corporations face. Take the case of the von Dammes, who supplement the income they earn from their primary jobs by painting houses in their spare time.

The von Dammes estimate that over the course of a year they will buy 250 gallons of paint at an average cost of \$20 per gallon. For every trip they make to the paint store, the von Dammes spend about \$10 in fuel and other costs related to the wear and tear on their personal vehicle. They store the paint in a self-storage unit and estimate that they spend about \$2 per gallon of paint in storage costs. How often should they visit the paint store, and how much paint should they purchase on each visit?

Applying the EOQ model to this problem, we have:

$$S = 250 \text{ gallons per year} \qquad O = \$10 \text{ per order} \qquad C = \$2 \text{ per gallon}$$

$$EOQ = \sqrt{\frac{2 \times 250 \times \$10}{\$2}} = 50$$

The von Dammes should purchase 50 gallons of paint each time they visit the store. Given their annual use of 250 gallons, they will make 5 trips to the store per year.

reorder point
The point at which to reorder inventory, expressed as days of lead time × daily usage.

Reorder Point Once the firm has determined its economic order quantity, it must determine when to place an order. The **reorder point** reflects the number of days of lead time the firm needs to place and receive an order and the firm's daily usage of the inventory item. Assuming that the firm uses inventory at a constant rate, the formula for the reorder point is

$$\text{Reorder point} = \text{Days of lead time} \times \text{Daily usage} \tag{15.8}$$

safety stock
Extra inventory that is held to prevent stockouts of important items.

For example, if a firm knows it takes 3 days to place and receive an order and if it uses 15 units per day of the inventory item, the reorder point is 45 units of inventory (3 days × 15 units/day). Thus, as soon as the item's inventory level falls to the reorder point (45 units, in this case), the firm places an order for the item's EOQ. If the estimates of lead time and usage are correct, the order will arrive exactly as the inventory level reaches zero. However, lead times and usage rates are not precise, so most firms hold **safety stock** (extra inventory) to prevent stockouts of important items.

EXAMPLE 15.5

MyLab Finance Solution Video

MAX Company, a producer of dinnerware, has an A group inventory item that is vital to the production process. This item costs \$1,500, and MAX uses 1,100 units of the item per year. MAX wants to determine its optimal order strategy for the item. To calculate the EOQ, we need the following inputs:

$$\text{Order cost per order} = \$150$$
$$\text{Carrying cost per unit per year} = \$200$$

Substituting into Equation 15.7, we get

$$\text{EOQ} = \sqrt{\frac{2 \times 1{,}100 \times \$150}{\$200}} \approx \underline{\underline{41}} \text{ units}$$

The reorder point for MAX depends on the number of days MAX operates per year. Assuming that MAX operates 250 days per year and uses 1,100 units of this item, its daily usage is 4.4 units (1,100 ÷ 250). If its lead time is 2 days and MAX wants to maintain a safety stock of 4 units, the reorder point for this item is [(2 × 4.4) + 4], or 12.8 units. However, orders are made only in whole units, so MAX places the order when the inventory falls to 13 units.

The firm's goal for inventory is to turn it over as quickly as possible without stockouts. Inventory turnover is best calculated by dividing cost of goods sold by average inventory. The EOQ model determines the optimal order size and, indirectly, through the assumption of constant usage, the average inventory. Thus, the EOQ model determines the firm's optimal inventory turnover rate, given the firm's specific costs of inventory.

Just-in-Time (JIT) System

just-in-time (JIT) system
Inventory management technique that minimizes inventory investment by having materials arrive at exactly the time they are needed for production.

Firms use the **just-in-time (JIT) system** to minimize inventory investment. The philosophy is that materials should arrive at exactly the time they are needed for production. Ideally, the firm would have only work-in-process inventory. Because its objective is to minimize inventory investment, a JIT system uses no (or very little) safety stock. Extensive coordination among the firm's employees, its suppliers, and shipping companies must exist to ensure that material inputs arrive on time. Failure of materials to arrive on time results in a shutdown of the production line until the materials do arrive. Likewise, a JIT system requires high-quality parts from suppliers. When quality problems arise, production must be stopped until the problems are resolved.

The goal of the JIT system is manufacturing efficiency. It uses inventory as a tool for attaining efficiency by emphasizing quality of the materials used and their timely delivery. When JIT is working properly, it forces process inefficiencies to surface.

Knowing the level of inventory is, of course, an important part of any inventory management system. As described in the *Focus on Practice* box, radio frequency identification technology may be the "next new thing" in improving inventory and supply chain management.

FOCUS ON PRACTICE *in practice*

In Bed with RFID

When you think about a company's inventory, you may envision pallets full of boxes stacked high in a warehouse. But for high-end hotels, an important inventory category is the high-thread-count linens in every guest room. Luxury bedding can cost hundreds of dollars, so hotel managers need to closely track every sheet and pillowcase. At the recently opened LUMA Hotel Times Square, managers use radio frequency identification (RFID) technology to do just that. The hotel installed a system created by InvoTech Systems that tracks each of the hotel's 15,000 linen items using RFID-enabled laundry carts. The system allows LUMA to eliminate the daily task of sorting and hand counting all the different types of linens. Each piece of linen the hotel orders comes with a washable RFID tag that allows the hotel to track every item to and from its laundry. Making sure that it has just the right amount of linen in stock helps LUMA hold down costs while delighting its guests.

► *What problem might occur with the full implementation of RFID technology in retail industries? Specifically, consider the amount of data that might be collected.*

Source: https://www.hospitalitynet.org/news/4082782.html

materials requirement planning (MRP) system
Inventory management technique that applies EOQ concepts and uses a computer to compare production needs to available inventory balances and determine when orders should be placed for various items on a product's bill of materials.

manufacturing resource planning II (MRP II)
An extension of MRP that uses a sophisticated computerized system to integrate data from numerous areas such as finance, accounting, marketing, engineering, and manufacturing and generate production plans as well as numerous financial and management reports.

enterprise resource planning (ERP)
A computerized system that electronically integrates external information about the firm's suppliers and customers with the firm's departmental data so that information on all available resources—human and material—can be instantly obtained in a fashion that eliminates production delays and controls costs.

Computerized Systems for Resource Control

Today, a number of systems are available for controlling inventory and other resources. One of the most basic is the **materials requirement planning (MRP) system.** Firms use that system to determine what materials to order and when to order them. MRP applies EOQ concepts to determine how much to order. Using a computer, MRP simulates each product's bill of materials, inventory status, and manufacturing process. The *bill of materials* is simply a list of all parts and materials that go into making the finished product. For a given production plan, the computer simulates material requirements by comparing production needs to available inventory balances. On the basis of the time it takes for a product that is in process to move through the various production stages and the lead time to get materials, the MRP system determines when orders should be placed for various items on the bill of materials. The objective of this system is to lower the firm's inventory investment without impairing production. If the firm's pretax cost of capital for investments of equal risk is 10%, every dollar of investment released from inventory will increase before-tax profits by $0.10.

An extension of MRP is **manufacturing resource planning II (MRP II)**, which integrates data from numerous areas such as finance, accounting, marketing, engineering, and manufacturing, using a sophisticated computer system. This system generates production plans as well as numerous financial and management reports. In essence, it models the firm's processes so that the firm can assess and monitor the effects of changes in one area of operations on other areas. For example, the MRP II system would allow the firm to determine the effect of an increase in labor costs on sales and profits.

Whereas MRP and MRP II tend to focus on internal operations, **enterprise resource planning (ERP)** systems expand the focus to the external environment by including information about suppliers and customers. ERP electronically integrates all of a firm's departments so that, for example, production can call up sales information and immediately know how much must be produced to fill customer orders. Because all available resources—human and material—are known, the system can eliminate production delays and control costs. ERP systems automatically note changes, such as a supplier's inability to meet a scheduled delivery date, so that production can make necessary adjustments.

INTERNATIONAL INVENTORY MANAGEMENT

International inventory management is typically much more complicated for exporters in general, and for multinational companies in particular, than for purely domestic firms. The production and manufacturing economies of scale that might be expected from selling products globally may prove elusive if products must be tailored for individual local markets, as frequently happens, or if actual production takes place in factories around the world. When raw materials, intermediate goods, or finished products must be transported over long distances—particularly by ocean shipping—there will be more delays, confusion, damage, and theft than occur in a one-country operation. The international inventory manager therefore puts a premium on flexibility. He or she is usually less concerned about ordering the economically optimal quantity of inventory than about making sure that sufficient quantities of inventory are delivered where they are needed, when they are needed, and in a condition to be used as planned.

→ REVIEW QUESTIONS MyLab Finance Solutions

15–8 What are likely to be the viewpoints of each of the following managers about the levels of the various types of inventory: finance, marketing, manufacturing, and purchasing? Why is inventory an investment?

15–9 Briefly describe the following techniques for managing inventory: (1) ABC system, economic order quantity (EOQ) model, (2) just-in-time (JIT) system, and (3) three computerized systems for resource control, MRP, MRP II, and ERP.

15–10 What factors make managing inventory more difficult for exporters and multinational companies?

15.4 Accounts Receivable Management

The second component of the cash conversion cycle is the average collection period. This period is the average length of time from a sale on credit until the payment becomes usable funds for the firm. The average collection period has two parts. The first part is the time from the sale until the customer mails the payment. The second part is the time from when the payment is mailed until the firm has the collected funds in its bank account. The first part of the average collection period involves managing the credit available to the firm's customers, and the second part involves collecting and processing payments. This section of the chapter discusses the firm's accounts receivable credit management.

The objective for managing accounts receivable is to collect accounts receivable as quickly as possible without losing sales from high-pressure collection techniques or by offering credit terms that are not competitive in the industry. Accomplishing this goal encompasses three topics: (1) credit selection and standards, (2) credit terms, and (3) credit monitoring.

CREDIT SELECTION AND STANDARDS

Credit selection involves application of techniques for determining which customers should receive credit. This process involves evaluating the customer's creditworthiness and comparing it to the firm's **credit standards,** its minimum requirements for extending credit to a customer.

credit standards
The firm's minimum requirements for extending credit to a customer.

Five C's of Credit

five C's of credit
The five key dimensions—character, capacity, capital, collateral, and conditions—used by credit analysts to provide a framework for in-depth credit analysis.

One credit selection technique is known as the **five C's of credit,** which provides a framework for in-depth credit analysis. Because of the time and expense involved, this credit selection method is used for large-dollar credit requests. The five C's are as follows:

1. *Character:* The applicant's record of meeting past obligations.
2. *Capacity:* The applicant's ability to repay the requested credit, as judged in terms of financial statement analysis focused on cash flows available to repay debt obligations.
3. *Capital:* The applicant's debt relative to equity.
4. *Collateral:* The amount of assets the applicant has available for use in securing the credit. The larger the amount of available assets, the greater the chance that a firm will recover funds if the applicant defaults.
5. *Conditions:* Current general and industry-specific economic conditions and any unique conditions surrounding a specific transaction.

Analysis via the five C's of credit does not yield a routine accept/reject decision, so its use requires an analyst experienced in reviewing and granting credit requests. Application of this framework tends to ensure that the firm's credit customers will pay, without being pressured, within the stated credit terms.

Credit Scoring

credit scoring
A credit selection method commonly used with high-volume/small-dollar credit requests; relies on a credit score determined by applying statistically derived weights to a credit applicant's scores on key financial and credit characteristics.

Credit scoring is a method of credit selection that firms commonly use with high-volume/small-dollar credit requests. **Credit scoring** applies statistically derived weights to a credit applicant's scores on key financial and credit characteristics to predict whether he or she will pay the requested credit in a timely fashion. The procedure results in a score that measures the applicant's overall credit strength, and the score is used to make the accept/reject decision for granting the applicant credit. Credit scoring is most commonly used by large credit card operations, such as those of banks, oil companies, and department stores. The purpose of credit scoring is to make a relatively informed credit decision quickly and inexpensively, recognizing that the cost of a single bad scoring decision is small. However, if bad debts from scoring decisions increase, managers must reevaluate the scoring system. The *Focus on Ethics* box discusses a case in which a customer stole millions of dollars of merchandise from a national retail chain through fraudulent credit applications.

FOCUS ON ETHICS in practice

If You Can Bilk It, They Will Come

For many non-financial firms, extending trade credit is an important part of doing business. A challenge for these firms is that, unlike banks, they often lack long experience managing such accounts—thereby opening the door to employee or customer fraud.

A recent survey by the Association of Certified Fraud Examiners indicates the typical firm loses 5% of revenues annually to internal fraud. Companies with fewer than 100 employees are most at risk. The typical fraudster has 1 to 5 years employment tenure and no criminal history. "Lapping" is the most common type of internal accounts-receivable fraud—a clerk pockets payments to customer A's account, then uses payments from customer B to keep A's account current, credits customer B's account with payments from customer C, and so on.

A few simple safeguards can go a long way toward preventing internal fraud or catching it early (which cuts losses dramatically):

- Segregating and rotating duties that involve receiving or disbursing payments.
- Requiring all employees to take annual vacations.
- Training managers to review subordinate work with an eye for possible fraud.
- Creating internal "hotlines" for employees to report suspected impropriety.

The last safeguard is particularly important as internal fraud is mostly commonly exposed by employee tips.

Large companies are less vulnerable because they can invest more in prevention and detection. But even big firms can get hurt when they leave an opening. Consider a recent case of customer fraud at Lowe's—a home-improvement retailer with over 1,800 stores in the U.S., Canada, and Mexico. In January 2017, federal authorities arrested Kenneth Cassidy of Brooklyn, New York for allegedly opening at least 173 "pre-funded" trade-credit accounts at individual stores throughout the U.S.—each with a different fake company name and counterfeit check. Individual stores sent the applications and checks to corporate headquarters in North Carolina for processing, so up to 10 days could elapse before a check bounced. But, in the interim, Lowe's extended credit to the bogus company for the full "pre-funding" of the account. By not making sure the checks cleared first, Lowe's allowed Cassidy to steal over $2.6 million in merchandise.

Interestingly, the fraud appears to have relied on marginal analysis. Cassidy recognized Lowe's had a materiality threshold for investigating scams, so he kept the pre-funding checks under $1,600 to reduce the chance of discovery. Keeping the fake checks small, however, had a "shoe-leather" cost—the time and energy necessary to apply for accounts in hundreds of stores. By trading off capture risk and shoe-leather costs, Cassidy was able to bilk Lowes from June 2012 to December 2016.

The moral: If accounts-receivable policies leave an opening for fraud, some bad guy will find it.

▶ *Small firms are frequent victims of internal fraud because (i) the owner knows and trusts all employees and (ii) size makes segregating duties difficult. Careful monitoring through micromanagement, audits, and cameras can reduce vulnerability but at the risk of losing the "family feel" of a small business. How should small firms weigh the benefits of reducing fraud losses against the costs of lower employee morale?*

"Report to the Nations on Occupational Fraud and Abuse," *2014 Global Fraud Study*. Fairbanks, Phil. "Feds Say Man Used 173 Accounts to Scam Lowe's of $2.6 million." Additional facts obtained from court documents.

Changing Credit Standards

Financial analysts sometimes contemplate changing the firm's credit standards to improve returns and create greater value for owners. To demonstrate, consider the following changes and effects on profits that should result from the *relaxation* of credit standards.

Effects of Relaxation of Credit Standards

Variable	Direction of change	Effect on profits
Sales volume	Increase	Positive
Investment in accounts receivable	Increase	Negative
Bad-debt expenses	Increase	Negative

If managers tighten credit standards, the opposite effects would likely occur.

EXAMPLE 15.6

Dodd Tool, a manufacturer of lathe tools, is currently selling a product for \$10 per unit. Sales (all on credit) for last year were 60,000 units. The variable cost per unit is \$6. The firm's total fixed costs are \$120,000.

The firm is currently contemplating a relaxation of credit standards that should result in the following: a 5% increase in unit sales to 63,000 units; an increase in the average collection period from 30 days (the current level) to 45 days; an increase in bad-debt expenses from 1% of sales (the current level) to 2%. The firm determines that its cost of tying up funds in receivables is 10% before taxes.

To determine whether to relax its credit standards, Dodd Tool must calculate its effect on the firm's additional profit contribution from sales, the cost of the marginal investment in accounts receivable, and the cost of marginal bad debts.

Additional Profit Contribution from Sales Because fixed costs are "sunk" and therefore unaffected by a change in the sales level, the only cost relevant to a change in sales is variable costs. Sales are expected to increase by 5%, or 3,000 units. The profit contribution per unit will equal the difference between the sale price per unit (\$10) and the variable cost per unit (\$6). The profit contribution per unit therefore will be \$4. The total additional profit contribution from sales will be \$12,000 (3,000 units × \$4 per unit).

Cost of the Marginal Investment in Accounts Receivable To determine the cost of the marginal investment in accounts receivable, Dodd must find the difference between the cost of carrying receivables under the two credit standards. Because its concern is only with the out-of-pocket costs, the relevant cost is the variable cost. The average investment in accounts receivable can be calculated by using the formula

$$\text{Average investment in accounts receivable} = \frac{\text{Total variable cost of annual sales}}{\text{Turnover of accounts receivable}} \tag{15.9}$$

where

$$\text{Turnover of accounts receivable} = \frac{365}{\text{Average collection period}}$$

The total variable cost of annual sales under the present and proposed plans can be found as follows, using the variable cost per unit of \$6.

Total variable cost of annual sales

$$\text{Under present plan: } (\$6 \times 60{,}000 \text{ units}) = \$360{,}000$$
$$\text{Under proposed plan: } (\$6 \times 63{,}000 \text{ units}) = \$378{,}000$$

The turnover of accounts receivable is the number of times each year that the firm's accounts receivable are actually turned into cash. It equals 365 (the number of days per year) divided by the average collection period.

Turnover of accounts receivable

$$\text{Under present plan: } \frac{365}{30} = 12.2$$

$$\text{Under proposed plan: } \frac{365}{45} = 8.1$$

By substituting the cost and turnover data just calculated into Equation 15.9 for each case, we get the following average investments in accounts receivable:

Average investment in accounts receivable

$$\text{Under present plan: } \frac{\$360{,}000}{12.2} = \$29{,}508$$

$$\text{Under proposed plan: } \frac{\$378{,}000}{8.1} = \$46{,}667$$

We calculate the marginal investment in accounts receivable and its cost as follows:

Cost of marginal investment in accounts receivable

Average investment under proposed plan	$46,667
− Average investment under present plan	$29,508
Marginal investment in accounts receivable	$17,159
× Cost of funds tied up in receivables	0.10
Cost of marginal investment in A/R	$ 1,716

The resulting value of $1,716 is a cost because it represents the maximum amount that could have been earned before taxes on the $17,159 had it been placed in an equally risky investment earning 10% before taxes.

Cost of Marginal Bad Debts We find the cost of marginal bad debts by taking the difference between the levels of bad debts before and after the proposed relaxation of credit standards.

Cost of marginal bad debts

Under proposed plan: (0.02 × $10/unit × 63,000 units)	=	$12,600
− Under present plan: (0.01 × $10/unit × 60,000 units)	=	$ 6,000
Cost of marginal bad debts		$ 6,600

Note that the bad-debt costs are calculated by using the sale price per unit ($10) to deduct not just the true loss of variable cost ($6) that results when a customer fails to pay its account but also the profit contribution per unit (in this case, $4) that is included in the "additional profit contribution from sales." Thus, the resulting cost of marginal bad debts is $6,600.

Making the Credit Standard Decision To decide whether to relax its credit standards, the firm must compare the additional profit contribution from sales to the added costs of the marginal investment in accounts receivable and marginal bad debts. If the additional profit contribution is greater than marginal costs, the firm should relax credit standards.

EXAMPLE 15.7

The results and key calculations related to Dodd Tool's decision whether to relax its credit standards are summarized in Table 15.2. The net addition to total profits resulting from such an action will be $3,684 per year. Therefore, the firm *should* relax its credit standards as proposed.

TABLE 15.2 Effects on Dodd Tool of a Relaxation of Credit Standards

Additional profit contribution from sales		
[3,000 units × ($10 − $6)]		$12,000
Cost of marginal investment in A/R[a]		
Average investment under proposed plan:		
$\frac{\$6 \times 63{,}000}{8.1} = \frac{\$378{,}000}{8.1}$	$46,667	
− Average investment under present plan:		
$\frac{\$6 \times 60{,}000}{12.2} = \frac{\$360{,}000}{12.2}$	29,508	
Marginal investment in A/R	$17,159	
Cost of marginal investment in A/R (0.10 × $17,159)		−1,716
Cost of marginal bad debts		
Bad debts under proposed plan (0.02 × $10 × 63,000)	$12,600	
− Bad debts under present plan (0.01 × $10 × 60,000)	6,000	
Cost of marginal bad debts		−6,600
Net profit from implementation of proposed plan		$ 3,684

[a]The denominators 8.1 and 12.2 in the calculation of the average investment in accounts receivable under the proposed and present plans are the accounts receivable turnovers for each of these plans (365 ÷ 45 = 8.1 and 365 ÷ 30 = 12.2).

The procedure described here for evaluating a proposed change in credit standards is also commonly used to evaluate other changes in the management of accounts receivable. If Dodd Tool had been contemplating tightening its credit standards, for example, the cost would have been a reduction in the profit contribution from sales, and the return would have been from reductions in the cost of the investment in accounts receivable and in the cost of bad debts. Another application of this procedure is demonstrated later in this chapter.

Managing International Credit

Credit management is difficult enough for managers of purely domestic companies, and these tasks become much more complex for companies that operate internationally. It is partly because (as we have seen before) international operations typically expose a firm to exchange rate risk. It is also due to the dangers and delays involved in shipping goods long distances and in having to cross international borders.

Exports of finished goods are usually priced in the currency of the importer's local market; most commodities, in contrast, are priced in dollars. Therefore, a U.S. company that sells a product in Japan, for example, would have to price that product in Japanese yen and extend credit to a Japanese wholesaler in the local currency (yen). If the yen depreciates against the dollar before the U.S. exporter collects on its account receivable, the U.S. company experiences an exchange rate loss; the yen collected are worth fewer dollars than at the time the sale was made. Of course, the yen could just as easily appreciate against the dollar, yielding an exchange rate gain to the U.S. exporter.

For a major currency such as the Japanese yen, the exporter can *hedge* against this risk by using the currency futures, forward, or options markets, but it is costly to do so, particularly for relatively small amounts. If the exporter is selling to a customer in a developing country, probably no effective instrument will be available for protecting against exchange rate risk at any price. This risk may be further magnified because credit standards may be much lower (and acceptable collection techniques much different) in developing countries than in the United States. Although it may seem tempting to just "not bother" with exporting, U.S. companies no longer can concede foreign markets to international rivals. These export sales, if carefully monitored and (where possible) effectively hedged against exchange rate risk, often prove very profitable.

CREDIT TERMS

credit terms
The terms of sale for customers who have been extended credit by the firm.

early payment discount
A percentage deduction from the purchase price; available to the credit customer that pays its account within a specified time.

Credit terms are the terms of sale for customers who have been extended credit by the firm. Terms of *net 30* mean the customer has 30 days from the beginning of the credit period (typically the end of month or the date of invoice) to pay the full invoice amount. Some firms offer **early payment discounts,** percentage deductions from the purchase price for paying within a specified time. For example, terms of *2/10 net 30* mean the customer can take a 2% discount from the invoice amount if the customer pays within 10 days of the beginning of the credit period. Otherwise, the customer owes the full invoice within 30 days.

A firm's business strongly influences its regular credit terms. For example, a firm selling perishable items will have very short credit terms because its items have little long-term collateral value; a firm in a seasonal business may tailor its terms to fit the industry cycles. A firm wants its regular credit terms to conform to its industry's standards. If its terms are more restrictive than its competitors', it may lose business; if its terms are less restrictive than its competitors', it may attract poor-quality customers that probably could not pay under the standard industry terms. Accordingly, the firm's regular credit terms should match the industry standards, but individual customer terms should reflect the riskiness of the customer.

Early Payment Discount

Including an early payment discount in the credit terms is an effective way to speed up collections without putting pressure on customers. The discount provides an incentive for customers to pay sooner. By speeding collections, the discount decreases the firm's investment in accounts receivable, but it also decreases the per-unit profit. Additionally, initiating a discount should reduce bad debts because customers will pay sooner, and it should increase sales volume because customers who take the discount pay a lower price for the product. Accordingly, firms that consider offering a discount must perform a benefit–cost analysis to determine whether extending a discount is profitable.

EXAMPLE 15.8

MAX Company has annual sales of $10 million and an average collection period of 40 days (turnover = 365 ÷ 40 = 9.1). That period has two main components. First, consistent with the firm's credit terms of net 30, MAX finds that it takes customers 32 days to mail payments on average (not everyone pays within 30 days). Second, it takes 8 days for MAX to receive, process, and collect payments once they are mailed. MAX is considering initiating an early payment discount by changing its credit terms from net 30 to 2/10 net 30. The firm expects this change to reduce the amount of time until the payments are placed in the mail, resulting in an average collection period of 25 days (turnover = 365 ÷ 25 = 14.6).

TABLE 15.3 Analysis of Initiating an Early Payment Discount for MAX Company

Additional profit contribution from sales		
[50 units × ($3,000 − $2,300)]		$ 35,000
Cost of marginal investment in A/R[a]		
Average investment presently (without discount):		
$\frac{\$2,300 \times 1,100 \text{ units}}{9.1} = \frac{\$2,530,000}{9.1}$	$278,022	
− Average investment with proposed discount:[b]		
$\frac{\$2,300 \times 1,150 \text{ units}}{14.6} = \frac{\$2,645,000}{14.6}$	181,164	
Reduction in accounts receivable investment	$ 96,858	
Cost savings from reduced investment in accounts receivable (0.10 × $96,858)[c]		9,686
Cost of discount (0.02 × 0.80 × 1,150 × $3,000)		−55,200
Net profit from initiation of proposed discount		−$ 10,514

[a]In analyzing the investment in accounts receivable, we use the variable cost of the product sold ($1,500 raw materials cost + $800 production cost = $2,300 per unit variable cost) instead of the sale price because the variable cost is a better indicator of the firm's investment.

[b]The average investment in accounts receivable with the proposed discount is estimated to be tied up for an average of 25 days instead of the 40 days under the original terms.

[c]MAX's opportunity cost of funds is 14%.

As noted earlier in Example 15.5, MAX has a raw material with current annual usage of 1,100 units. Each finished product produced requires one unit of this raw material at a variable cost of $1,500 per unit, incurs another $800 of variable cost in the production process, and sells for $3,000 on terms of net 30. Variable costs therefore total $2,300 ($1,500 + $800). MAX estimates that 80% of its customers will take the 2% discount and that offering the discount will increase sales of the finished product by 50 units (from 1,100 to 1,150 units) per year but will not alter its bad-debt percentage. MAX's opportunity cost of funds invested in accounts receivable is 10%. Should MAX offer the proposed discount? An analysis similar to that demonstrated earlier for the credit standard decision, presented in Table 15.3, shows a net loss from the discount of $10,514. Thus, MAX should not initiate the proposed discount. However, other discounts may be advantageous.

Early Payment Discount Period

early payment discount period
The number of days after the beginning of the credit period during which the discount is available.

The financial manager can change the **early payment discount period,** the number of days after the beginning of the credit period during which the discount is available. The net effect of changes in this period is difficult to analyze because of the nature of the forces involved. For example, if a firm were to increase its discount period by 10 days (e.g., changing its credit terms from 2/10 net 30 to 2/20 net 30), the following changes could occur: (1) Sales would increase, positively affecting profit; (2) bad-debt expenses would decrease, positively affecting profit; and (3) the profit per unit would decrease as a result of more people taking the discount, negatively affecting profit.

The difficulty for the financial manager lies in assessing what impact an increase in the discount period would have on the firm's investment in accounts receivable. This investment will decrease because some customers not currently taking advantage of the discount may now do so. However, the investment in accounts receivable will increase for two reasons: (1) Customers who are already taking the discount will continue to do so but will pay later, and (2) new customers attracted by the new policy will result in new accounts receivable. If the firm were to decrease the discount period, the effects would be the opposite of those just described.

Credit Period

credit period
The number of days after the beginning of the credit period until full payment of the account is due.

Changes in the **credit period,** the number of days after the beginning of the credit period until full payment of the account is due, also affect a firm's profitability. For example, increasing a firm's credit period from net 30 days to net 45 days should increase sales, positively affecting profit. But both the investment in accounts receivable and bad-debt expenses would also increase, negatively affecting profit. The increased investment in accounts receivable would result from both more sales and generally slower receivables turnover, on average, as a result of the longer credit period. The increase in bad-debt expenses results because the longer the credit period, the more time available for a firm to fail, making it unable to pay its accounts payable. A decrease in the length of the credit period is likely to have the opposite effects. Note that the variables affected by an increase in the credit period behave in the same way they would have if the credit standards had been relaxed, as demonstrated earlier in Table 15.2.

CREDIT MONITORING

credit monitoring
The ongoing review of a firm's accounts receivable to determine whether customers are paying according to the stated credit terms.

The final issue a firm should consider in its accounts receivable management is credit monitoring. **Credit monitoring** is an ongoing review of the firm's accounts receivable to determine whether customers are paying according to the stated credit terms. If they are not paying in a timely manner, credit monitoring will alert the firm to the problem. Slow payments are costly to a firm because they lengthen the average collection period and thus increase the firm's investment in accounts receivable. Firms usually monitor the credits by watching the average collection period and by constructing an aging schedule for their accounts receivable.

Average Collection Period

The average collection period is the second component of the cash conversion cycle. As noted in Chapter 3, it is the average number of days that credit sales are outstanding. The average collection period has two components: (1) the time from sale until the customer places the payment in the mail and (2) the time to receive, process, and collect the payment once it has been mailed by the customer. The formula for finding the average collection period is

$$\text{Average collection period} = \frac{\text{Accounts receivable}}{\text{Average sales per day}} \tag{15.10}$$

Assuming receipt, processing, and collection time is constant, the average collection period tells the firm, on average, when its customers pay their accounts.

Knowing its average collection period enables the firm to determine whether there is a general problem with accounts receivable. For example, a firm that has credit terms of net 30 would expect its average collection period (minus receipt, processing, and collection time) to equal about 30 days. If the actual collection period is significantly greater than 30 days, the firm has reason to review its credit operations. If the firm's average collection period is increasing over time, it has cause for concern about its accounts receivable management. A first step in analyzing an accounts receivable problem is to "age" the accounts receivable. By this process, the firm can determine whether the problem exists in its accounts receivable in general or is attributable to a few specific accounts.

aging schedule
A credit-monitoring technique that breaks down accounts receivable into groups on the basis of their time of origin; it indicates the percentages of the total accounts receivable balance that have been outstanding for specified periods of time.

Aging of Accounts Receivable

An **aging schedule** breaks down accounts receivable into groups on the basis of their time of origin. The breakdown is typically made on a month-by-month basis, going back 3 or 4 months. The resulting schedule indicates the percentages of the total accounts receivable balance that have been outstanding for specified periods of time. The purpose of the aging schedule is to enable the firm to pinpoint problems. A simple example will illustrate the form and evaluation of an aging schedule.

EXAMPLE 15.9

The accounts receivable balance on the books of Dodd Tool on December 31, 2018, was $200,000. The firm extends net 30-day credit terms to its customers. To gain insight into the firm's relatively lengthy—51.3-day—average collection period, Dodd prepared the following aging schedule.

Age of account	Balance outstanding	Percentage of total balance outstanding
0–30 days	$ 80,000	40%
31–60 days	36,000	18
61–90 days	52,000	26
91–120 days	26,000	13
Over 120 days	6,000	3
Totals at 12/31/15	$200,000	100%

Because Dodd extends 30-day credit terms to its customers, they have 30 days after the end of the month of sale to remit payment. Therefore, we see that 40% of the accounts are current (age $<$ 30 days) and the remaining 60% are overdue (age $>$ 30 days). Eighteen percent of the balance outstanding is 1–30 days overdue, 26% is 31–60 days overdue, 13% is 61–90 days overdue, and 3% is more than 90 days overdue. Although the collections seem generally slow, a noticeable irregularity in these data is the high percentage of the balance outstanding that is 31–60 days overdue (ages of 61–90 days). Clearly, a problem must have occurred 61–90 days ago. Investigation may reveal that the problem can be attributed to the hiring of a new credit manager, the acceptance of a new account that made a large credit purchase but has not yet paid for it, or an ineffective collection policy. When this type of discrepancy is found in the aging schedule, the analyst should determine, evaluate, and remedy its cause.

TABLE 15.4 Common Collection Techniques

Technique[a]	Brief description
Letters	After a certain number of days, the firm sends a polite letter reminding the customer of the overdue account. If the account is not paid within a certain period after this letter has been sent, a second, more demanding letter is sent.
Telephone calls	If letters prove unsuccessful, a telephone call may be made to the customer to request immediate payment. If the customer has a reasonable excuse, arrangements may be made to extend the payment period. A call from the seller's attorney may be used.
Personal visits	This technique is much more common at the consumer credit level, but it may also be effectively employed by industrial suppliers. Sending a local salesperson or a collection person to confront the customer can be very effective. Payment may be made on the spot.
Collection agencies	A firm can turn uncollectible accounts over to a collection agency or an attorney for collection. The fees for this service are typically quite high; the firm may receive less than 50¢ on the dollar from accounts collected in this way.
Legal action	Legal action is the most stringent step, an alternative to the use of a collection agency. Not only is direct legal action expensive, but it may force the debtor into bankruptcy without guaranteeing the ultimate receipt of the overdue amount.

[a]The techniques are listed in the order in which they are typically followed in the collection process.

Common Collection Techniques

Firms use a number of collection techniques, ranging from letters to legal action. As an account becomes more and more overdue, the collection effort becomes more intense. Table 15.4 lists and describes several common techniques in the order that firms would typically implement them in the collection process.

→ REVIEW QUESTIONS MyLab Finance Solutions

15–11 What is the role of the five C's of credit in the credit selection activity?

15–12 Explain why credit scoring is typically applied to consumer credit decisions rather than to mercantile credit decisions.

15–13 What are the basic tradeoffs in a tightening of credit standards?

15–14 Why are the risks involved in international credit management more complex than those associated with purely domestic credit sales?

15–15 Why do a firm's regular credit terms typically conform to those of its industry?

15–16 Why should a firm actively monitor the accounts receivable of its credit customers? How are the average collection period and an aging schedule used for credit monitoring?

15.5 Management of Receipts and Disbursements

The third component of the cash conversion cycle, the average payment period, also has two parts: (1) the time from purchase of goods on account until the firm mails its payment and (2) the receipt, processing, and collection time required by the firm's suppliers. The receipt, processing, and collection time for the firm, both from its customers and to its suppliers, is the focus of receipts and disbursements management.

FLOAT

float
Funds that have been sent by the payer but are not yet usable funds to the payee.

mail float
The time delay between when payment is placed in the mail and when it is received.

processing float
The time between receipt of a payment and its deposit into the firm's account.

clearing float
The time between deposit of a payment and when spendable funds become available to the firm.

Float refers to funds that have been sent by the payer but are not yet usable funds to the payee. Float is important in the cash conversion cycle because its presence lengthens both the firm's average collection period and its average payment period. However, the goal of the firm should be to shorten its average collection period and lengthen its average payment period. Both can be accomplished by managing float.

Float has three component parts:

1. **Mail float** is the time delay between when payment is placed in the mail and when it is received.
2. **Processing float** is the time between receipt of the payment and its deposit into the firm's account.
3. **Clearing float** is the time between deposit of the payment and when spendable funds become available to the firm. This component of float is attributable to the time required for a check to clear the banking system.

Some common techniques for managing the component parts of float to speed up collections and slow down payments are described here.

SPEEDING UP COLLECTIONS

Speeding up collections reduces customer collection float time and thus reduces the firm's average collection period, which decreases the investment the firm must make in its cash conversion cycle. In our earlier examples, MAX Company had annual sales of $10 million and 8 days of total collection float (receipt, processing, and collection time). If MAX can reduce its float time by 3 days, it will reduce its investment in the cash conversion cycle by $82,192 [$\$10,000,000 \times (3 \div 365)$].

lockbox system
A collection procedure in which customers mail payments to a post office box that is emptied regularly by the firm's bank, which processes the payments and deposits them in the firm's account. This system speeds up collection time by reducing processing time as well as mail and clearing time.

One technique for speeding up collections is a lockbox system. A **lockbox system** works as follows: Rather than mailing payments to the company, customers mail payments to a post office box. The firm's bank empties the post office box regularly, processes each payment, and deposits the payments in the firm's account. The bank sends (or transmits electronically) deposit slips, along with payment enclosures, to the firm so it can properly credit customers' accounts. Lockboxes are geographically dispersed to match the locations of the firm's customers. A lockbox system affects all three components of float. Lockboxes reduce mail time and often clearing time by being near the firm's customers. Lockboxes reduce processing time to nearly zero because the bank deposits payments before the firm processes them. Obviously, a lockbox system reduces collection float time, but not without a cost; therefore, a firm must perform an economic analysis to determine whether to implement a lockbox system.

MATTER OF FACT

U.S.P.S. Problems Create Opportunities for Banks

For decades, the United States Postal Service has been struggling financially. In 2012, the USPS announced that to cut costs it would dramatically reduce the number of mail-processing facilities that it operated. For companies, this change meant an increase in mail float. For Fifth Third Bank, it was an opportunity. The bank announced a new remote lockbox capture program in which business-to-business payments would be retrieved at local post offices around the country. Next, Fifth Third would make electronic images of those payments, and the images would be processed at the bank's Cincinnati processing hub. Fifth Third promised customers that it would reduce mail float and speed up the collection process for its clients.

Large firms with geographically dispersed customers are the primary users of lockbox systems. However, a firm does not have to be large to benefit from a lockbox. Smaller firms can also benefit, primarily from transferring the processing of payments to the bank.

SLOWING DOWN PAYMENTS

controlled disbursing
The strategic use of mailing points and bank accounts to lengthen mail float and clearing float, respectively.

Float is also a component of the firm's average payment period. In this case, the float is in favor of the firm. The firm may benefit by increasing all three components of its payment float. One popular technique for increasing payment float is **controlled disbursing,** which involves the strategic use of mailing points and bank accounts to lengthen mail float and clearing float, respectively. Firms must use this approach carefully, though, because longer payment periods may strain supplier relations.

In summary, a reasonable overall policy for float management is (1) to collect payments as quickly as possible because once the payment is in the mail the funds belong to the firm and (2) to delay making payment to suppliers because once the payment is mailed the funds belong to the supplier.

CASH CONCENTRATION

cash concentration
The process used by the firm to bring lockbox and other deposits together into one bank, often called the *concentration bank*.

Cash concentration is the process used by the firm to bring lockbox and other deposits together into one bank, often called the *concentration bank*. Cash concentration has three main advantages. First, it creates a large pool of funds for use in making short-term cash investments. Because there is a fixed-cost component in the transaction cost associated with such investments, investing a single pool of funds reduces the firm's transaction costs. The larger investment pool also allows the firm to choose from a greater variety of short-term investment vehicles. Second, concentrating the firm's cash in one account improves the tracking and internal control of the firm's cash. Third, having one concentration bank enables the firm to implement payment strategies that reduce idle cash balances. Of course, a downside is that pooling all of a firm's cash at one bank could create a major problem if that institution were to fail.

depository transfer check (DTC)
An unsigned check drawn on one of a firm's bank accounts and deposited in another.

A variety of mechanisms are available for transferring cash from the lockbox bank and other collecting banks to the concentration bank. One mechanism is a **depository transfer check** (DTC), which is an unsigned check drawn on one of the firm's bank accounts and deposited in another. For cash concentration, a DTC is drawn on each lockbox or other collecting bank account and deposited in the concentration bank account. Once the DTC has cleared the bank on which it is drawn (which may take several days), the transfer of funds is completed. Most firms currently provide deposit information by telephone to the concentration bank, which then prepares and deposits into its account the DTC drawn on the lockbox or other collecting bank account.

ACH (automated clearinghouse) transfer
Preauthorized electronic withdrawal from the payer's account and deposit into the payee's account via a settlement among banks by the automated clearinghouse, or ACH.

A second mechanism is an **ACH (automated clearinghouse) transfer,** which is a preauthorized electronic withdrawal from the payer's account. A computerized clearing facility (called the *automated clearinghouse,* or *ACH*) makes a paperless transfer of funds between the payer and payee banks. An ACH settles accounts among participating banks. Individual accounts are settled by respective bank balance adjustments. ACH transfers clear in 1 day. For cash concentration, an ACH transfer is made from each lockbox bank or other collecting bank to the concentration bank. An ACH transfer can be thought of as an electronic

DTC, but because the ACH transfer clears in 1 day, it provides benefits over a DTC; however, both banks in the ACH transfer must be members of the clearinghouse.

wire transfer
An electronic communication that, via bookkeeping entries, removes funds from the payer's bank and deposits them in the payee's bank.

A third cash concentration mechanism is a **wire transfer.** A wire transfer is an electronic communication that, via bookkeeping entries, removes funds from the payer's bank and deposits them in the payee's bank. Wire transfers can eliminate mail and clearing float and may reduce processing float as well. For cash concentration, the firm moves funds using a wire transfer from each lockbox or other collecting account to its concentration account. Wire transfers are a substitute for DTC and ACH transfers, but they are more expensive.

Firms must balance the costs and benefits of concentrating cash to determine the type and timing of transfers from its lockbox and other collecting accounts to its concentration account. The transfer mechanism selected should be the most profitable one. (The profit per period of any transfer mechanism equals earnings on the increased availability of funds minus the cost of the transfer system.)

ZERO-BALANCE ACCOUNTS

zero-balance account (ZBA)
A disbursement account that always has an end-of-day balance of zero because the firm deposits money to cover checks drawn on the account only as they are presented for payment each day.

Zero-balance accounts (ZBAs) are disbursement accounts that always have an end-of-day balance of zero. The purpose is to eliminate nonearning cash balances in corporate checking accounts. A ZBA works well as a disbursement account under a cash concentration system.

ZBAs work as follows: Once all a given day's checks are presented for payment from the firm's ZBA, the bank notifies the firm of the total amount of checks, and the firm transfers funds into the account to cover the amount of that day's checks. This transfer leaves an end-of-day balance of $0 (zero dollars). The ZBA enables the firm to keep all its operating cash in an interest-earning account, thereby eliminating idle cash balances. Thus, a firm that used a ZBA in conjunction with a cash concentration system would need two accounts. The firm would concentrate its cash from the lockboxes and other collecting banks into an interest-earning account and would write checks against its ZBA. The firm would cover the exact dollar amount of checks presented against the ZBA with transfers from the interest-earning account, leaving the end-of-day balance in the ZBA at $0.

A ZBA is a disbursement-management tool. As we discussed earlier, the firm would prefer to maximize its payment float. However, some cash managers believe that actively attempting to increase float time on payments is unethical. A ZBA enables the firm to maximize the use of float on each check without altering the float time of payments to its suppliers. Keeping all the firm's cash in an interest-earning account enables the firm to maximize earnings on its cash balances by capturing the full float time on each check it writes.

PERSONAL FINANCE EXAMPLE 15.10 Megan Laurie, a 25-year-old nurse, works at a hospital that pays her every 2 weeks by direct deposit into her checking account, which pays no interest and has no minimum balance requirement. She takes home about $1,800 every 2 weeks, or about $3,600 per month. She maintains a checking account balance of around $1,500. Whenever it exceeds that amount, she transfers the excess into her savings account, which currently pays 1.0% annual interest. She currently has a savings account balance of $17,000 and estimates that she transfers about $600 per month from her checking account into her savings account.

Megan pays her bills immediately when she receives them. Her monthly bills average about $1,900, and her monthly cash outlays for food and gas total about $900. An analysis of Megan's bill payments indicates that on average she pays her bills 8 days early. Megan could also invest money in a mutual fund that invests in short-term, low-risk investments paying 2.0% annual interest. Megan is interested in learning how she might better manage her cash balances.

Megan talks with her sister, who has had a finance course, and they come up with three ways for Megan to better manage her cash balance:

1. **Invest current balances.** Megan can transfer her current savings account balances into the low-risk mutual fund, thereby increasing the rate of interest earned from 1.0% to about 2.0%. On her current $17,000 balance, she will immediately increase her annual interest earnings by about $170 [(0.02 − 0.01) × $17,000].
2. **Invest monthly surpluses.** Megan can transfer monthly the $600 from her checking account to the mutual fund, thereby increasing the annual earnings on each monthly transfer by about $6 [(0.02 − 0.01) × $600], which for the 12 transfers would generate additional annual earnings of about $72 (12 months × $6).
3. **Slow down payments.** Rather than paying her bills immediately on receipt, Megan can pay her bills nearer their due date. By doing so, she can gain 8 days of disbursement float each month, or 96 days per year (8 days per month × 12 months), on an average of $1,900 of bills. Assuming that she can earn 2.0% annual interest on the $1,900, slowing down her payments would save about $10 annually [(96 ÷ 365) × 0.02 × $1,900].

On the basis of these three recommendations, Megan would increase her annual earnings by a total of about $252 ($170 + $72 + $10).

INVESTING IN MARKETABLE SECURITIES

Marketable securities are short-term, interest-earning, money market instruments that can easily be converted into cash. Marketable securities are part of the firm's liquid assets. The firm uses them to earn a return on temporarily idle funds. To be truly marketable, a security must have (1) a ready market to minimize the amount of time required to convert it into cash and (2) safety of principal, which means that it experiences little or no loss in value over time.

The securities most commonly held as part of the firm's marketable-securities portfolio are divided into two groups: (1) government issues, which have relatively low yields as a consequence of their low risk; and (2) nongovernment issues, which have slightly higher yields than government issues with similar maturities because of the slightly higher risk associated with them. Table 15.5 summarizes the key features of popular marketable securities.

TABLE 15.5 Features of Marketable Securities

Security	Issuer	Description	Initial maturity	Risk and return
Government issues				
Treasury bills	U.S. Treasury	Issued weekly at auction; sold at a discount; strong secondary market	4, 13, and 26 weeks	Lowest, virtually risk-free
Treasury notes	U.S. Treasury	Stated interest rate; interest paid semiannually; strong secondary market	1–10 years	Low, but higher than U.S. Treasury bills
Treasury bonds	U.S. Treasury	Stated interest rate; interest paid semiannually; strong secondary market	11–30 years	Less than corporate bonds, but higher than U.S. Treasury bills and notes
Federal agency issues	Agencies of federal government	Not an obligation of U.S. Treasury; strong secondary market	9 months to 30 years	Slightly higher than U.S. Treasury issues
Nongovernment issues				
Negotiable certificates of deposit (CDs)	Commercial banks	Represent specific cash deposits in commercial banks; amounts and maturities tailored to investor needs; large denominations; good secondary market	1 month to 3 years	Higher than U.S. Treasury issues and comparable to commercial paper
Commercial paper	Corporation with a high credit standing	Unsecured note of issuer; large denominations	3–270 days	Higher than U.S. Treasury issues and comparable to negotiable CDs
Banker's acceptances	Banks	Results from a bank guarantee of a business transaction; sold at discount from maturity value	30–180 days	About the same as negotiable CDs and commercial paper but higher than U.S. Treasury issues
Eurodollar deposits	Foreign banks	Deposits of currency not native to the country in which the bank is located; large denominations; active secondary market	1 day to 3 years	High, due to less regulation of depository banks and some foreign exchange risk
Money market mutual funds	Professional portfolio management companies	Professionally managed portfolios of marketable securities; provide instant liquidity	None—depends on wishes of investor	Vary, but generally higher than U.S. Treasury issues and comparable to negotiable CDs and commercial paper
Repurchase agreements	Bank or securities dealer	Bank or securities dealer sells specific securities to firm and agrees to repurchase them at a specific price and time	Customized to purchaser's needs	Generally slightly below that associated with the outright purchase of the security

→ **REVIEW QUESTIONS** MyLab Finance Solutions

15–17 What is float, and what are its three components?

15–18 What are the firm's objectives with regard to collection float and to payment float?

15–19 What are the three main advantages of cash concentration?

15–20 What are three mechanisms of cash concentration? What is the objective of using a zero-balance account (ZBA) in a cash concentration system?

15–21 What two characteristics make a security marketable? Why are the yields on nongovernment marketable securities generally higher than the yields on government issues with similar maturities?

SUMMARY

FOCUS ON VALUE

It is important for a firm to maintain a reasonable level of net working capital. To do so, it must balance the high profit and high risk associated with low levels of current assets and high levels of current liabilities against the low profit and low risk that result from high levels of current assets and low levels of current liabilities. A strategy that achieves a reasonable balance between profits and risk should positively contribute to the firm's value.

Similarly, the firm should manage its cash conversion cycle by turning inventory quickly; collecting accounts receivable quickly; managing mail, processing, and clearing time; and paying accounts payable slowly. These strategies should enable the firm to manage its current accounts efficiently and to minimize the amount of resources invested in operating assets.

The financial manager can manage inventory, accounts receivable, and cash receipts to minimize the firm's operating cycle investment, thereby reducing the amount of resources needed to support its business. Using these strategies, as well as managing accounts payable and cash disbursements to shorten the cash conversion cycle, should minimize the additional funds needed to support the firm's resource requirements. Active management of the firm's net working capital and current assets should positively contribute to the firm's goal of **maximizing its stock price.**

REVIEW OF LEARNING GOALS

LG 1 **Understand working capital management, net working capital, and the related tradeoff between profitability and risk.** Working capital (or short-term financial) management focuses on managing each of the firm's current assets (inventory, accounts receivable, cash, and marketable securities) and current liabilities (accounts payable, accruals, and notes payable) in a manner that positively contributes to the firm's value. Net working capital is the difference between current assets and current liabilities. Risk, in the context of short-term financial decisions, is the probability that a firm will be unable to pay its bills as they come due. Assuming a constant level of total assets, the higher a firm's ratio of current assets to total assets, the less profitable the firm and the less risky it is. The converse is also true. With constant total assets, the higher a firm's ratio of current liabilities to total assets, the more profitable and the more risky the firm is. The converse of this statement is also true.

LG 2 **Describe the cash conversion cycle, its funding requirements, and the key strategies for managing it.** The cash conversion cycle has three components: (1) average age of inventory, (2) average collection period, and (3) average payment period. The length of the cash conversion cycle determines the amount of time resources are tied up in the firm's day-to-day operations. The firm's investment in short-term assets often consists of both permanent and seasonal funding requirements. The seasonal requirements can be financed using either an aggressive (low-cost, high-risk) financing strategy or a conservative (high-cost, low-risk) financing strategy. The firm's funding decision for its cash conversion cycle ultimately depends on management's disposition toward risk and the strength of the firm's banking relationships. To minimize its reliance on negotiated liabilities, the financial manager seeks to (1) turn over inventory as quickly as possible; (2) collect accounts receivable as quickly as possible; (3) manage mail, processing, and clearing time; and (4) pay accounts payable as slowly as possible. Use of these strategies should minimize the length of the cash conversion cycle.

LG 3 **Discuss inventory management: differing views, common techniques, and international concerns.** The viewpoints of marketing, manufacturing, and purchasing managers about the appropriate levels of inventory tend to cause higher inventories than those deemed appropriate by the financial manager. Four techniques for effectively managing inventory are (1) the ABC system, (2) the economic order quantity (EOQ) model, (3) the just-in-time (JIT) system, and (4) computerized systems for resource control: MRP, MRP II, and ERP. International inventory managers place greater emphasis on making sure that sufficient quantities of inventory are delivered where and when needed, and in the right condition, than on ordering the economically optimal quantities.

LG 4 **Explain the credit selection process and the quantitative procedure for evaluating changes in credit standards.** Credit selection techniques determine which customers' creditworthiness is consistent with the firm's credit standards. Two common credit selection techniques are the five C's of credit and credit scoring. Changes in credit standards can be evaluated mathematically by assessing the effects of a proposed change on profits from sales, the cost of accounts receivable investment, and bad-debt costs.

LG 5 **Review the procedures for quantitatively considering early payment discount changes, other aspects of credit terms, and credit monitoring.** Changes in credit terms—the discount, the discount period, and the credit period—can be quantified similarly to changes in credit standards. Credit monitoring, the ongoing review of accounts receivable, frequently involves use of the average collection period and an aging schedule.

LG 6 **Understand the management of receipts and disbursements, including float, speeding up collections, slowing down payments, cash concentration, zero-balance accounts, and investing in marketable securities.** Float refers to funds that have been sent by the payer but are not yet usable funds to the payee. The components of float are mail time, processing time, and clearing time. Float occurs in both the average collection period and the average payment period. One technique for speeding up collections is a lockbox system. A popular technique for slowing payments is controlled disbursing.

The goal for managing operating cash is to balance the opportunity cost of nonearning balances against the transaction cost of temporary investments. Firms commonly use depository transfer checks (DTCs), ACH transfers, and wire transfers to transfer lockbox receipts to their concentration banks quickly. Zero-balance accounts (ZBAs) can be used to eliminate nonearning cash balances in corporate checking accounts. Marketable securities are short-term, interest-earning, money market instruments used by the firm to earn a return on temporarily idle funds. They may be government or nongovernment issues.

OPENER-IN-REVIEW

In the chapter opener, you learned that U.S. companies had been building up their inventory and receivables balances after the financial crisis while simultaneously borrowing at low interest rates. In this chapter you also learned that the opportunity cost of funds is an important consideration when firms make changes to their policies that alter the balances of working capital accounts such as inventory and receivables. Suppose that firms are managing their working capital assets to maximize shareholder value. If market interest rates drop, reflecting a lower opportunity cost of funds for firms, how should they change working capital account balances?

SELF-TEST PROBLEMS (Solutions in Appendix)

LG2 ST15–1 **Cash conversion cycle** Hurkin Manufacturing Company pays accounts payable on the 10th day after purchase. The average collection period is 30 days, and the average age of inventory is 40 days. The firm currently has annual sales of about $18 million and purchases of $14 million. The firm is considering a plan that would stretch its accounts payable by 20 days. If the firm pays 6% per year for its resource investment, what annual savings can it realize by this plan? Assume a 360-day year.

LG3 ST15–2 **EOQ analysis** Thompson Paint Company uses 60,000 gallons of pigment per year. The cost of ordering pigment is $200 per order, and the cost of carrying the pigment in inventory is $1 per gallon per year. The firm uses pigment at a constant rate every day throughout the year.

a. Calculate the EOQ.

b. Assuming that it takes 20 days to receive an order once it has been placed, determine the reorder point in terms of gallons of pigment. (*Note:* Use a 365-day year.)

LG4 ST15–3 **Relaxing credit standards** Regency Rug Repair Company is trying to decide whether it should relax its credit standards. The firm repairs 72,000 rugs per year at an average price of $32 each. Bad-debt expenses are 1% of sales, the average collection period is 40 days, and the variable cost per unit is $28. Regency expects that if it does relax its credit standards, the average collection period will increase to 48 days and that bad debts will increase to $1^1/_2$% of sales. Sales will increase by 4,000 repairs per year. If the firm has a required rate of return on equal-risk investments of 7%, what recommendation would you give the firm? Use your analysis to justify your answer. (*Note:* Use a 365-day year.)

WARM-UP EXERCISES All problems are available in MyLab Finance

LG2 **E15–1** Everdeen Inc. has a 90-day operating cycle. If its average age of inventory is 35 days, how long is its average collection period? If its average payment period is 30 days, what is its cash conversion cycle? Place all this information on a timeline similar to Figure 15.2.

LG2 **E15–2** Icy Treats Inc. is a seasonal business that sells frozen desserts. At the peak of its summer selling season, the firm has $35,000 in cash, $125,000 in inventory, $70,000 in accounts receivable, and $65,000 in accounts payable. During the slow winter period, the firm holds $10,000 in cash, $55,000 in inventory, $40,000 in accounts receivable, and $35,000 in accounts payable. Calculate Icy Treats' minimum and peak funding requirements.

LG3 **E15–3** Mama Leone's Frozen Pizzas uses 50,000 pounds of cheese per year. Each pound costs $5.50. The ordering cost for the cheese is $250 per order, and its carrying cost is $1.50 per pound per year. Calculate the firm's economic order quantity (EOQ) for the cheese. Mama Leone's operates 250 days per year and maintains a minimum inventory level of 2 days' worth of cheese as a safety stock. Assuming that the lead time to receive orders of cheese is 3 days, calculate the reorder point.

LG4 **E15–4** Forrester Fashions has annual credit sales of 250,000 units with an average collection period of 70 days. The company has a per-unit variable cost of $20 and a per-unit sale price of $30. Bad debts currently are 5% of sales. The firm estimates that a proposed relaxation of credit standards would not affect its 70-day average collection period but would increase bad debts to 7.5% of sales, which would rise to 300,000 units per year. Forrester requires a 12% return on investments. Show all necessary calculations needed to evaluate Forrester's proposed relaxation of credit standards.

LG5 **E15–5** Klein's Tools is considering offering a discount to speed up the collection of accounts receivable. Currently, the firm has an average collection period of 65 days, annual sales are 35,000 units, the per-unit price is $40, and the per-unit variable cost is $29. A 2% discount is being considered. Klein's Tools estimates that 80% of its customers will take the 2% discount. If sales are expected to rise to 37,000 units per year and the firm has a 15% required rate of return, what minimum average collection period is necessary to approve the discount plan?

PROBLEMS

All problems are available in MyLab Finance. The MyLab icon indicates problems in Excel format available in MyLab Finance.

LG2 **P15–1** **Cash conversion cycle** American Products is concerned about managing cash efficiently. On average, inventories have an age of 80 days, and accounts receivable are collected in 40 days. Accounts payable are paid approximately 30 days after they arise. The firm has annual sales of about $30 million. Goods sold total $20 million, and purchases are $15 million.

a. Calculate the firm's operating cycle.
b. Calculate the firm's cash conversion cycle.
c. Calculate the amount of resources needed to support the firm's cash conversion cycle.
d. Discuss how management might be able to reduce the cash conversion cycle.

LG2 **P15–2** **Changing cash conversion cycle** Camp Manufacturing turns over its inventory 5 times each year, has an average payment period of 35 days, and has an average collection period of 60 days. The firm has annual sales of $3.5 million and cost of goods sold of $2.4 million.

a. Calculate the firm's operating cycle and cash conversion cycle.
b. What is the dollar value of inventory held by the firm?
c. If the firm could reduce the average age of its inventory from 73 days to 63 days, by how much would it reduce its dollar investment in working capital?

LG2 **P15–3** **Multiple changes in cash conversion cycle** Garrett Industries turns over its inventory 6 times each year; it has an average collection period of 45 days and an average payment period of 30 days. The firm's annual sales are $3 million. Assume there is no difference in the investment per dollar of sales in inventory, receivables, and payables, and assume a 365-day year.

a. Calculate the firm's cash conversion cycle, its daily cash operating expenditure, and the amount of resources needed to support its cash conversion cycle.
b. Find the firm's cash conversion cycle and resource investment requirement if it makes the following changes simultaneously.
   (1) Shortens the average age of inventory by 5 days.
   (2) Speeds the collection of accounts receivable by an average of 10 days.
   (3) Extends the average payment period by 10 days.
c. If the firm pays 13% for its resource investment, by how much, if anything, could it increase its annual profit as a result of the changes in part **b**?
d. If the annual cost of achieving the profit in part **c** is $35,000, what action would you recommend to the firm? Why?

P15–4 **Aggressive versus conservative seasonal funding strategy** Dynabase Tool has forecast its total funds requirements for the coming year as shown in the following table.

Month	Amount	Month	Amount
January	$2,000,000	July	$12,000,000
February	2,000,000	August	14,000,000
March	2,000,000	September	9,000,000
April	4,000,000	October	5,000,000
May	6,000,000	November	4,000,000
June	9,000,000	December	3,000,000

a. Divide the firm's monthly funds requirement into (1) a permanent component and (2) a seasonal component, and find the monthly average for each of these components.

b. Describe the amount of long-term and short-term financing used to meet the total funds requirement under (1) an aggressive funding strategy and (2) a conservative funding strategy. Assume that, under the aggressive strategy, long-term funds finance permanent needs and short-term funds are used to finance seasonal needs.

c. Assuming that short-term funds cost 5% annually and that the cost of long-term funds is 10% annually, use the averages found in part **a** to calculate the total cost of each of the strategies described in part **b.** Assume that the firm can earn 3% on any excess cash balances.

d. Discuss the profitability–risk tradeoffs associated with the aggressive strategy and those associated with the conservative strategy.

P15–5 **EOQ analysis** Tiger Corporation purchases 1,400,000 units per year of one component. The fixed cost per order is $55. The annual carrying cost of the item is 27% of its $10 cost.

a. Determine the EOQ if (1) the conditions stated above hold, (2) the order cost is $1 rather than $55, and (3) the order cost is $55 but the carrying cost is $0.01.

b. What do your answers illustrate about the EOQ model? Explain.

P15–6 **EOQ, reorder point, and safety stock** Alexis Company uses 800 units of a product per year on a continuous basis. The product has a fixed cost of $50 per order, and its carrying cost is $2 per unit per year. It takes 5 days to receive a shipment after an order is placed, and the firm wishes to hold 10 days' usage in inventory as a safety stock.

a. Calculate the EOQ.

b. Determine the average level of inventory. (*Note:* Use a 365-day year to calculate daily usage.)

c. Determine the reorder point.

d. Indicate which of the following variables change if the firm does not hold the safety stock: (1) order cost, (2) carrying cost, (3) total inventory cost, (4) reorder point, (5) economic order quantity. Explain.

Personal Finance Problem

LG3

P15–7 **Marginal costs** Jimmy Johnson is interested in buying a new Jeep SUV. Two options are available, a V-6 model and a V-8 model. Whichever model he chooses, he plans to drive it for a period of 5 years and then sell it. Assume that the trade-in value of the two vehicles at the end of the 5-year ownership period will be identical.

The two models have definite differences, and Jimmy needs to make a financial comparison. The manufacturer's suggested retail price (MSRP) of the V-6 and V-8 are $30,260 and $44,320, respectively. Jimmy believes the difference of $14,060 to be the marginal cost difference between the two vehicles. However, many more data are available, and you suggest to Jimmy that his analysis may be too simple and will lead him to a poor financial decision. Assume that the prevailing discount rate for both vehicles is 5.5% annually. Other pertinent information on this purchase is shown in the following table.

3	V-6	V-8
MSRP	$30,260	$44,320
Engine (liters)	3.7	5.7
Cylinders	6	8
Depreciation over 5 years	$17,337	$25,531
Finance charges[a] over entire 5-year period	$ 5,171	$ 7,573
Insurance over 5 years	$ 7,546	$ 8,081
Taxes and fees over 5 years	$ 2,179	$ 2,937
Maintenance/repairs over 5 years	$ 5,600	$ 5,600
Average miles per gallon	19	14
Ownership period in years	5	5
Miles driven per year over 5 years	15,000	15,000
Cost per gallon of gas over 5-year ownership	$ 3.15	$ 3.15

[a] The finance charges are the difference between the total principal and interest paid over the entire 5-year period less the actual cost of the SUV. Assuming an annual 5.5% discount rate over each of the 5 years and the respective present values of $30,260 for the V-6 and $44,320 for the V-8, the annual annuity payments are $7,086.20 and $10,379.70, respectively. [*V-6:* (5 × $7,086.20) − ($30,260) = $5,171; and *V-8:* (5 × $10,379.70) − $44,320 = $7,573.]

a. Calculate the total "true" cost for each vehicle over the 5-year ownership period.
b. Calculate the total fuel cost for each vehicle over the 5-year ownership period.
c. What is the marginal fuel cost from purchasing the larger V-8 SUV?
d. What is the marginal cost of purchasing the larger and more expensive V-8 SUV?
e. What is the total marginal cost associated with purchasing the V-8 SUV? How does this figure compare with the $14,060 that Jimmy calculated?

P15–8 Accounts receivable changes without bad debts Tara's Textiles currently has credit sales of $360 million per year and an average collection period of 60 days. Assume that the price of Tara's products is $60 per unit and that the variable costs are $55 per unit. The firm is considering an accounts receivable change that will result in a 20% increase in sales and a 20% increase in the average collection period. No change in bad debts is expected. The firm's equal-risk opportunity cost on its investment in accounts receivable is 14%. (*Note:* Use a 365-day year.)

a. Calculate the additional profit contribution from sales that the firm will realize if it makes the proposed change.
b. What marginal investment in accounts receivable will result?
c. Calculate the cost of the marginal investment in accounts receivable.
d. Should the firm implement the proposed change? What other information would be helpful in your analysis?

LG4

P15–9 Accounts receivable changes with bad debts A firm is evaluating an accounts receivable change that would increase bad debts from 2% to 4% of sales. Sales are currently 50,000 units, the selling price is $20 per unit, and the variable cost per unit is $15. As a result of the proposed change, sales are forecast to increase to 60,000 units.

a. What are bad debts in dollars currently and under the proposed change?
b. Calculate the cost of the marginal bad debts to the firm.

c. Ignoring the additional profit contribution from increased sales, if the proposed change saves $3,500 and causes no change in the average investment in accounts receivable, would you recommend it? Explain.
d. Considering all changes in costs and benefits, would you recommend the proposed change? Explain.
e. Compare and discuss your answers in parts **c** and **d**.

LG4

P15–10 **Relaxation of credit standards** Lewis Enterprises is considering relaxing its credit standards to increase its currently sagging sales. As a result of the proposed relaxation, sales are expected to increase by 10% from 10,000 to 11,000 units during the coming year, the average collection period is expected to increase from 45 to 60 days, and bad debts are expected to increase from 1% to 3% of sales. The sale price per unit is $40, and the variable cost per unit is $31. The firm's required return on equal-risk investments is 10%. Evaluate the proposed relaxation, and make a recommendation to the firm. (*Note:* Assume a 365-day year.)

LG5

P15–11 **Initiating an early payment discount** Gardner Company currently makes all sales on credit and offers no discount. The firm is considering offering a 2% discount for payment within 15 days. The firm's current average collection period is 60 days, sales are 40,000 units, selling price is $45 per unit, and variable cost per unit is $36. The firm expects that the change in credit terms will result in an increase in sales to 42,000 units, that 70% of the sales will take the discount, and that the average collection period will fall to 30 days. If the firm's required rate of return on equal-risk investments is 10%, should the proposed discount be offered? (*Note:* Assume a 365-day year.)

LG5

P15–12 **Shortening the credit period** A firm is contemplating shortening its credit period from 40 to 30 days and believes that, as a result of this change, its average collection period will decline from 45 to 36 days. Bad-debt expenses are expected to decrease from 1.5% to 1% of sales. The firm is currently selling 12,000 units but believes that sales will decline to 10,000 units as a result of the proposed change. The sale price per unit is $56, and the variable cost per unit is $45. The firm has a required return on equal-risk investments of 12%. Evaluate this decision, and make a recommendation to the firm. (*Note:* Assume a 365-day year.)

LG5

P15–13 **Lengthening the credit period** Parker Tool is considering lengthening its credit period from 30 to 60 days. All customers will continue to pay on the net date. The firm currently bills $450,000 for sales and has $345,000 in variable costs. The change in credit terms is expected to increase sales to $510,000. Bad-debt expenses will increase from 1% to 1.5% of sales. The firm has a required rate of return on equal-risk investments of 20%. (*Note:* Assume a 365-day year.)

a. What additional profit contribution from sales will be realized from the proposed change?
b. What is the cost of the marginal investment in accounts receivable?
c. What is the cost of the marginal bad debts?
d. Do you recommend this change in credit terms? Why or why not?

LG6

P15–14 **Float** Simon Corporation has daily cash receipts of $65,000. A recent analysis of its collections indicated that customers' payments were in the mail an average of 3.0 days. Once received, the payments are processed in 2.0 days. After payments are deposited, it takes an average of 2.5 days for these receipts to clear the banking system.

a. How much collection float (in days) does the firm currently have?
b. If the firm's opportunity cost is 9%, would it be economically advisable for the firm to pay an annual fee of $16,500 to reduce collection float by 2 days? Explain why or why not.
c. What would the company's opportunity cost have to be to make the $16,500 fee worthwhile?

LG6

P15–15 **Lockbox system** Eagle Industries believes that a lockbox system can shorten its accounts receivable collection period by 3 days. Credit sales are $3,240,000 per year, billed on a continuous basis. The firm has other equally risky investments that earn a return of 15%. The cost of the lockbox system is $9,000 per year. (*Note:* Assume a 365-day year.)
a. What amount of cash will be made available for other uses under the lockbox system?
b. What net benefit (cost) will the firm realize if it adopts the lockbox system? Should it adopt the proposed lockbox system?

LG6

P15–16 **Zero-balance account** Union Company is considering establishment of a zero-balance account. The firm currently maintains an average balance of $420,000 in its disbursement account. As compensation to the bank for maintaining the zero-balance account, the firm will have to pay a monthly fee of $1,000 and maintain a $300,000 non-interest-earning deposit in the bank. The firm currently has no other deposits in the bank. Evaluate the proposed zero-balance account, and make a recommendation to the firm, assuming it has a 12% opportunity cost.

Personal Finance Problem

LG6

P15–17 **Management of cash balance** Alexis Morris, an assistant manager at a local department store, gets paid every 2 weeks by direct deposit into her checking account. This account pays no interest and has no minimum balance requirement. Her monthly income is $4,200. Alexis has a "target" cash balance of around $1,200, and whenever it exceeds that amount, she transfers the excess into her savings account, which currently pays 2.0% annual interest. Her current savings balance is $15,000, and Alexis estimates that she transfers about $500 per month from her checking account into her savings account. Alexis doesn't waste any time in paying her bills, and her monthly bills average about $2,000. Her monthly cash outlay for food, gas, and other sundry items totals about $850. Reviewing her payment habits indicates that on average she pays her bills 9 days early. At this time, most marketable securities are yielding about 4.75% annual interest.

Show how Alexis can better manage her cash balance.
a. What can Alexis do regarding the handling of her current balances?
b. What do you suggest that she do with her monthly surpluses?
c. What do you suggest Alexis do about the manner in which she pays her bills?
d. Can Alexis grow her earnings by better managing her cash balances? Show your work.

LG6

P15–18 **ETHICS PROBLEM** A group of angry shareholders has placed a corporate resolution before all shareholders at a company's annual stockholders' meeting. The resolution demands that the company stretch its accounts payable because these shareholders have determined that all the company's competitors do so, and the firm operates in a highly competitive industry. How could management at the annual stockholders' meeting defend the firm's practice of paying suppliers on time?

SPREADSHEET EXERCISE

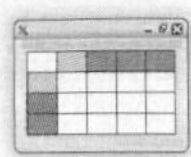

The current balance in accounts receivable for Eboy Corporation is $443,000. This level was achieved with annual (365 days) credit sales of $3,544,000. The firm offers its customers credit terms of net 30. However, in an effort to help its cash flow position and to follow the actions of its rivals, the firm is considering changing its credit terms from net 30 to 2/10 net 30. The objective is to speed up the receivable collections and thereby improve the firm's cash flows. Eboy would like to increase its accounts receivable turnover to 12.0.

The firm works with a raw material whose current annual usage is 1,450 units. Each finished product requires one unit of this raw material at a variable cost of $2,600 per unit and sells for $4,200 on terms of net 30. It is estimated that 70% of the firm's customers will take the 2% discount and that, with the discount, sales of the finished product will increase by 50 units per year. The firm's opportunity cost of funds invested in accounts receivable is 12.5%.

In analyzing the investment in accounts receivable, use the variable cost of the product sold instead of the sale price because the variable cost is a better indicator of the firm's investment.

TO DO

Create a spreadsheet similar to Table 15.3 to analyze whether the firm should initiate the proposed discount. What is your advice? Make sure that you calculate the following:

a. Additional profit contribution from sales.
b. Average investment in accounts receivable at present (without the early payment discount).
c. Average investment in accounts receivable with the proposed discount.
d. Reduction in investment in accounts receivable.
e. Cost savings from reduced investment in accounts receivable.
f. Cost of the discount.
g. Net profit (loss) from initiation of proposed discount.

MyLab Finance Visit www.pearson.com/mylab/finance for **Chapter Case: *Assessing Roche Publishing Company's Cash Management Efficiency,*** Group Exercises, and numerous online resources.

CHAPTER

16

Current Liabilities Management

LEARNING GOALS

LG 1 Review accounts payable, the key components of credit terms, and the procedures for analyzing those terms.

LG 2 Understand the effects of stretching accounts payable on their cost and the use of accruals.

LG 3 Describe interest rates and the basic types of unsecured bank sources of short-term loans.

LG 4 Discuss the basic features of commercial paper and the key aspects of international short-term loans.

LG 5 Explain the characteristics of secured short-term loans and the use of accounts receivable as short-term-loan collateral.

LG 6 Describe the various ways in which inventory can be used as short-term-loan collateral.

MyLab Finance Chapter Introduction Video

WHY THIS CHAPTER MATTERS TO YOU

In your *professional* life

ACCOUNTING You need to understand how to analyze supplier credit terms to decide whether the firm should take or give up discounts for early payment; you also need to understand the various types of short-term loans, both unsecured and secured, that you will be required to record and report.

INFORMATION SYSTEMS You need to understand what data the firm will need to process accounts payable, track accruals, and meet bank loans and other short-term debt obligations in a timely manner.

MANAGEMENT You need to know the sources of short-term loans so that, if short-term financing is needed, you will understand its availability and cost.

MARKETING You need to understand how accounts receivable and inventory can be used as loan collateral; the procedures used by the firm to secure short-term loans with such collateral could affect customer relationships.

OPERATIONS You need to understand the use of accounts payable as a form of short-term financing and the effect on one's suppliers of stretching payables; you also need to understand the process by which a firm uses inventory as collateral.

In your *personal* life

Managing current liabilities is an important part of your financial strategy. It takes discipline to avoid viewing cash and credit purchases equally. You need to borrow for a purpose, not convenience. You also need to repay credit purchases in a timely fashion. Excessive use of short-term credit, particularly with credit cards, can create personal liquidity problems and, at the extreme, personal bankruptcy.

Ringo Chiu/Zuma Press, Inc/Alamy Stock Photo

FASTPAY

Getting Cash into the Hands of Online Media Companies

Digital advertising revenues hit $72.5 billion in 2016, a 21.8% increase over 2015, which was itself a record-breaking year. Online ads are everywhere, from Google search pages to YouTube videos to your Facebook News Feed. A challenge for the publishers of online ads is collecting money for those ads. The industry standard calls for publishers of online ads to send invoices within 30 days after an ad campaign is complete, and the advertiser then has 30 days or more to pay for the ad. Thus, companies that sell online advertising can accumulate large receivables balances, and collecting cash can be a slow process.

That's where the company FastPay comes in. FastPay makes loans to publishers, ad-tech companies, and other digital media businesses based on those firms' accounts receivable. FastPay lends up to $20 million per borrower, with the terms of the loan based on the quality of the receivable. For example, if Pepsi were to enter into an agreement with YouTube to place online ads in videos, FastPay would grant a loan to YouTube on relatively favorable terms because it views Pepsi as a good credit risk. One area of rapid expansion for FastPay is in making loans to Facebook Preferred Marketing Developers, a network of small and medium-sized businesses that builds advertising apps on Facebook, manages ad campaigns, and helps Facebook develop new marketing strategies.

Firms rely on a wide array of short-term financing vehicles. In this chapter, you'll learn about the ways companies can use short-term finance to help maximize the wealth of their shareholders.

16.1 Spontaneous Liabilities

spontaneous liabilities
Financing that arises from the normal course of business; the two major short-term sources of such liabilities are accounts payable and accruals.

Spontaneous liabilities arise from the normal course of business. For example, when a retailer orders goods for inventory, the manufacturer of those goods usually does not demand immediate payment but instead extends a short-term loan to the retailer that appears on the retailer's balance sheet under accounts payable. The more goods the retailer orders, the greater will be the accounts payable balance. Also in response to increasing sales, the firm's accruals increase as wages and taxes rise because of greater labor requirements and the higher taxes on the firm's increased earnings. No explicit cost is normally attached to either of these current liabilities (i.e., they do not bear interest), although they do have certain implicit costs. In addition, both are forms of **unsecured short-term financing,** short-term financing obtained without pledging specific assets as collateral. The firm should take advantage of these "interest-free" sources of unsecured short-term financing whenever possible.

unsecured short-term financing
Short-term financing obtained without pledging specific assets as collateral.

ACCOUNTS PAYABLE MANAGEMENT

Accounts payable are the major source of unsecured short-term financing for business firms. They result from transactions in which the firm purchases merchandise without signing a formal note to show the firm's liability to the seller. The firm in effect agrees to pay the supplier the amount required in accordance with credit terms normally stated on the supplier's invoice. We present the discussion of accounts payable here from the viewpoint of the purchaser.

Role in the Cash Conversion Cycle

The average payment period is the final component of the *cash conversion cycle* introduced in Chapter 15. The average payment period has two parts: (1) the time from the purchase of raw materials until the firm mails the payment and (2) payment float time (the time it takes after the firm mails its payment until the supplier has withdrawn spendable funds from the firm's account). In Chapter 15, we discussed issues related to payment float time. Here we discuss the firm's management of the time that elapses between its purchase of raw materials and its mailing payment to the supplier. This activity is **accounts payable management.**

accounts payable management
Management by the firm of the time that elapses between its purchase of raw materials and its mailing payment to the supplier.

When the seller of goods charges no interest and offers no discount to the buyer for early payment, the buyer's goal is to pay as slowly as possible without damaging its credit rating or its relationship with the supplier. In other words, firms should pay their accounts payable on the last day possible, given the supplier's stated credit terms. For example, if the terms are net 30, the firm should pay no sooner than 30 days from the *beginning of the credit period,* which is typically either the *date of invoice* or the *end of the month (EOM)* in which the firm made the purchase. This timing allows for the maximum use of an interest-free loan from the supplier and will not damage the firm's credit rating (because the firm pays within the stated credit terms). In addition, some firms offer an explicit or implicit "grace period" that extends a few days beyond the stated payment date. If taking advantage of that grace period does no harm to the buyer's relationship with the seller, the buyer will typically take advantage of the grace period.

EXAMPLE 16.1

In 2016, Brown-Forman Corporation (BF), manufacturer of alcoholic beverage brands such as Jack Daniels, had annual revenue of \$4.011 billion, cost of goods sold of \$1.867 billion, and purchases of \$1.347 billion. BF had an average age of inventory (AAI) of 206 days, an average collection period (ACP) of 51 days, and an average payment period (APP) of 141 days. Thus, the cash conversion cycle for BF was 116 days (206 + 51 − 141).

The resources BF had invested in this cash conversion cycle (assuming a 365-day year) were

Inventory	= \$1.867 billion × (206 ÷ 365)	=	\$1.054 billion
+ Accounts receivable	= \$4.011 billion × (51 ÷ 365)	=	\$0.559 billion
− Accounts payable	= \$1.347 billion × (141 ÷ 365)	=	\$0.52 billion
	= Resources invested	=	\$1.093 billion

Based on BF's APP and average accounts payable, the daily accounts payable generated by BF is about \$3.69 million (\$0.52 billion ÷ 141). If BF were to increase its average payment period by 5 days, its accounts payable would increase by about \$18.452 million (5 × \$3.69 million). As a result, BF's cash conversion cycle would decrease by 5 days, and the firm would reduce its investment in operations by \$18.452 million. If this action did not damage BF's credit rating, it would be in the company's best interest.

Analyzing Credit Terms

The credit terms offered to a firm by its suppliers enable it to delay payments for its purchases. Because the supplier's cost of having its money tied up in merchandise after it is sold is probably reflected in the purchase price, the purchaser is already indirectly paying for this benefit. Sometimes a supplier will offer a discount for early payment. In that case, the purchaser should carefully analyze credit terms to determine the best time to repay the supplier. The purchaser must weigh the benefits of paying the supplier as late as possible against the costs of passing up the discount for early payment.

Taking the Discount If a firm intends to take an early payment discount, it should pay on the last day of the discount period. There is no added benefit from paying earlier than that date.

EXAMPLE 16.2

Lawrence Industries, operator of a small chain of video stores, purchased \$1,000 worth of merchandise on February 27 from a supplier extending terms of 2/10 net 30 EOM. If the firm takes the discount, it must pay \$980 [\$1,000 − (0.02 × \$1,000)] by March 10, thereby saving \$20.

cost of giving up an early payment discount
The implied rate of interest paid to delay payment of an account payable for an additional number of days.

Giving Up the Discount If the firm chooses to give up the discount, it should pay on the final day of the credit period, or at the end of the grace period. Giving up a discount carries an implicit cost. The **cost of giving up an early payment discount** is the implied rate of interest paid to delay payment of an account payable for an additional number of days. In other words, when a firm gives up a discount, it pays a higher cost for the goods that it orders. The higher cost the firm pays is like interest on a loan, and the length of this loan is the number of additional days that the purchaser can delay payment to the seller. A simple example illustrates this cost. The example assumes that payment will be made on the last possible day (either the final day of the discount period or the final day of the credit period).

EXAMPLE 16.3

MyLab Finance Solution Video

In Example 16.2, we saw that Lawrence Industries could take the discount on its February 27 purchase by paying \$980 on March 10. If Lawrence gives up the discount, it can pay on March 30. To keep its money for an extra 20 days, the firm must pay an extra \$20, or \$1,000 rather than \$980. In other words, if the firm pays on March 30, it will pay \$980 (what it could have paid on March 10) plus \$20. The extra \$20 is like interest on a loan, and in this case the \$980 is like the loan principal. Lawrence Industries owes \$980 to its supplier on March 10, but the supplier is willing to accept \$980 plus \$20 in interest on March 30. Figure 16.1 shows the payment options that are open to the company.

To calculate the implied interest rate associated with giving up the discount, we simply treat \$980 as the loan principal, \$20 as the interest, and 20 days (the time from March 10 to March 30) as the term of the loan. The interest rate that Lawrence pays by giving up the discount is 2.04% (\$20 ÷ \$980). Keep in mind that the 2.04% interest rate applies to a 20-day loan. To calculate an annualized interest rate, we multiply the interest rate on this transaction times the number of 20-day periods during a year. The general expression for calculating the annual percentage cost of giving up an early payment discount is[1]

$$\text{Cost of giving up early payment discount} = \frac{CD}{100\% - CD} \times \frac{365}{N} \quad (16.1)$$

FIGURE 16.1

Payment Options
Payment options for Lawrence Industries

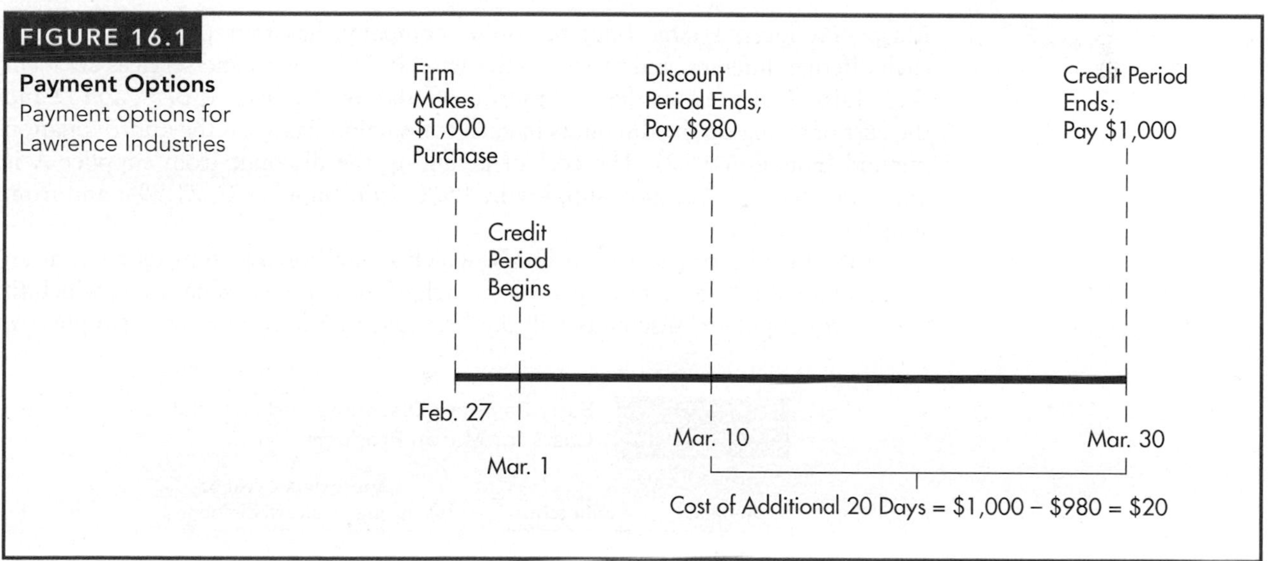

1. Equation 16.1 and the related discussions are based on the assumption that only one discount is offered. In the event that the supplier offers multiple discounts, the cost of giving up the discount must be calculated for each alternative. Furthermore, the interest rate calculation in Equation 16.1 is a simple-interest calculation.

Where

CD = stated discount in percentage terms

N = number of days that payment can be delayed by giving up the discount

Substituting the values for CD (2%) and N (20 days) into Equation 16.1 results in an annualized cost of giving up the early payment discount of 37.24%

$$37.24\% = \frac{2\%}{100\% - 2\%} \times \frac{365}{20}$$

A simple way to *approximate* the cost of giving up a discount is to use the stated discount percentage, CD, in place of the first term of Equation 16.1:

$$\text{Approximate early payment of giving up early payment discount} = CD \times \frac{365}{N} \qquad (16.2)$$

The smaller the discount, the closer the approximation to the actual cost of giving it up. Using this approximation, the cost of giving up the discount for Lawrence Industries is 36.5% [2% × (365 ÷ 20)].

Using the Cost of Giving Up an Early Payment Discount in Decision Making The financial manager must determine whether it is advisable to take a discount. A primary consideration influencing this decision is the cost of other short-term sources of funding. When a firm can obtain financing from a bank or other institution at a lower cost than the implicit interest rate offered by its suppliers, the firm is better off borrowing from the bank and taking the discount offered by the supplier.

EXAMPLE 16.4

Mason Products, a large building-supply company, has four possible suppliers, each offering different credit terms. Otherwise, their products and services are identical. Table 16.1 presents the credit terms offered by suppliers A, B, C, and D and the cost of giving up the discounts in each transaction based on the approximation method (Equation 16.2). The cost of giving up the discount from supplier A is approximately 36.5%; from supplier B, 4.9%; from supplier C, 21.9%; and from supplier D, 29.2%.

If the firm needs short-term funds, which it can borrow from its bank at an interest rate of 6%, and if the firm views each of the suppliers separately, which (if any) of the suppliers' discounts will the firm give up? In dealing with supplier A,

TABLE 16.1 Early-Payment Discounts and Associated Costs for Mason Products

Supplier	Credit terms	Approximate cost of giving up a cash discount
A	2/10 net 30 EOM	36.5%
B	1/10 net 85 EOM	4.9
C	3/20 net 70 EOM	21.9
D	4/10 net 60 EOM	29.2

the firm takes the discount, because the cost of giving it up is 36.5%, and then borrows the funds it requires from its bank at 6% interest. With supplier B, the firm would do better to give up the discount, because the cost of this action is less than the cost of borrowing money from the bank (4.9% versus 6%). With either supplier C or supplier D, the firm should take the discount, because in both cases the cost of giving up the discount is greater than the 6% cost of borrowing from the bank.

The example shows that the cost of giving up a discount is relevant when we are comparing a single supplier's credit terms to the cost of borrowing from a bank or other short-term lender. However, not all firms follow the practice suggested here. For example, some firms, particularly small firms and poorly managed firms, routinely give up all discounts because they either lack alternative sources of unsecured short-term financing or fail to recognize the implicit costs of their actions.

Effects of Stretching Accounts Payable

stretching accounts payable
Paying bills as late as possible without damaging the firm's credit rating.

Firms sometimes attempt to reduce the implicit costs they pay on accounts payable by **stretching accounts payable**, that is, paying bills as late as possible without damaging their credit rating. Such a strategy can reduce the cost of giving up an early payment discount.

EXAMPLE 16.5

Lawrence Industries was extended credit terms of 2/10 net 30 EOM. The cost of giving up the discount, assuming payment on the last day of the credit period, was approximately 36.5% [2% × (365 ÷ 20)]. If the firm were able to stretch its account payable to 70 days without damaging its credit rating, the approximate cost of giving up the discount would be just 12.2% [2% × (365 ÷ 60)]. Stretching accounts payable reduces the implicit cost of giving up a discount.

Although stretching accounts payable may be financially attractive, it raises an important ethical issue: It may cause the firm to violate the agreement it entered into with its supplier when it purchased merchandise. Clearly, a supplier would not look kindly on a customer that regularly and purposely postponed paying for purchases.

PERSONAL FINANCE EXAMPLE 16.6

Jack and Mary Nobel, a young married couple, are in the process of purchasing a 55-inch OLED TV at a cost of $1,900. The electronics dealer currently has a special financing plan that would allow them to either (1) put $200 down and finance the balance of $1,700 at 3% annual interest over 24 months, resulting in payments of $73 per month; or (2) receive an immediate $150 cash rebate, thereby paying only $1,750 cash. The Nobels, who have saved enough to pay cash for the TV, can currently earn 5% annual interest on their savings. They wish to determine whether borrowing or paying cash is the better payment option for the TV.

The upfront outlay for the financing alternative is the $200 down payment, whereas the Nobels will pay out $1,750 up front under the cash purchase alternative. So, the cash purchase will require an initial outlay that is $1,550 ($1,750 − $200) greater than under the financing alternative. Assuming they can earn a simple interest rate of 5% on savings, the cash purchase will cause the Nobels to give up an opportunity to earn $155 (2 years × 0.05 × $1,550) over the 2 years.

If they choose the financing alternative, the $1,550 would grow to $1,705 ($1,550 + $155) at the end of 2 years. But under the financing alternative, the Nobels will pay out a total of $1,752 (24 months × $73 per month) over the 2-year loan term. The cost of the financing alternative can be viewed as $1,752, and the cost of the cash payment (including forgone interest earnings) would be $1,705. Because it is less expensive, *the Nobels should pay cash for the TV*. The lower cost of the cash alternative is largely the result of the $150 cash rebate.

ACCRUALS

accruals
Liabilities for services received for which payment has yet to be made.

The second spontaneous source of short-term business financing is accruals. **Accruals** are liabilities for services received for which payment has yet to be made. The most common items accrued by a firm are wages and taxes. Firms have little flexibility in manipulating the timing of payments made to the government. However, firms can manipulate accrual of wages to some extent by delaying payment of wages, thereby receiving an interest-free loan from employees who receive payment sometime after they have performed the work. Note that state or federal law or union regulations often govern the pay period for employees who earn an hourly rate. However, in other cases, firms have discretion over the frequency of wage payments.

EXAMPLE 16.7

Tenney Company, a large janitorial service company, currently pays its employees at the end of each work week. The weekly payroll totals $400,000. If the firm were to extend the pay period by paying its employees 1 week later throughout an entire year, the employees would in effect be lending the firm $400,000 for a year. If the firm could earn 10% annually on invested funds, such a strategy would be worth $40,000 per year (0.10 × $400,000).

→ REVIEW QUESTIONS MyLab Finance Solutions

16–1 What are the two major sources of spontaneous short-term financing for a firm? How do their balances behave relative to the firm's sales?

16–2 Is there a cost associated with taking an early payment discount? Is there any cost associated with giving up a discount? How do borrowing costs affect the decision to take or forego an early payment discount?

16–3 What is "stretching accounts payable"? What effect does this action have on the cost of giving up a discount?

LG3 LG4

16.2 Unsecured Sources of Short-Term Loans

Businesses obtain unsecured short-term loans from two major sources, banks and sales of commercial paper. Unlike the spontaneous sources of unsecured short-term financing, bank loans and commercial paper carry an explicit interest rate (rather than the implicit rate tied to early payment discounts). Bank loans are more widespread because banks lend to firms of all sizes; only large firms can issue commercial paper. As the *Focus on Ethics* box explains, bank loans offer additional benefits to shareholders beyond the capital they provide to firms. In addition, firms can use international loans to finance international transactions.

FOCUS ON ETHICS *in practice*

Bank Loans and Shareholder Wealth

Companies finance investment projects with internal and external funds. Although the specific mix differs across industries, one theme emerges—most companies borrow from banks, even when they have grown large enough to access public debt and equity markets easily. Understanding why is essential to a manager's duty to maximize shareholder wealth.

Commercial banks create value for firm shareholders by solving adverse-selection and moral-hazard problems in financing. Solving adverse-selection problems means sorting good borrowers from bad—that is, determining which firms have the means to repay their loans. Solving moral-hazard problems means monitoring borrowers after loans are made—that is, ensuring firms with the means to repay actually do so. Firm shareholders benefit when banks offer attractive funding by sorting and monitoring efficiently.

For publicly traded companies, bank loans also benefit shareholders by conferring "seals of approval." Because banks specialize in originating and monitoring loans, their lending decisions convey information to financial markets about borrowers. When, for example, a bank lends to firm X, the market learns firm X has projects with cash flows sufficient to cover the principal and interest, and firm X's management is likely to use some of those cash flows to pay off the loan. The positive signal enhances shareholder wealth by (i) credibly revealing good news about the prospects and management of firm X and (ii) lowering firm X's cost of funding from non-bank sources. Studies in the 1980s and 1990s confirmed the value of bank lending to shareholders––announcements of extension or renewal of bank credit typically boosted the stock prices of borrowing firms.

Since the 1990s, financial innovation has changed bank lending. Traditionally, originating banks had trouble selling business loans because buyers assumed the motivation was negative inside information about borrowers. But then Wall Street discovered business loans could be securitized like mortgages—that is, the loans could be purchased from originators and bundled, with cash flows from the bundle used to make principal and interest payments on newly issued debt securities. Driven by securitization, U.S. loan sales soared from well under $50 billion per year in the early 1990s to over $400 billion per year since 2007. Banks love the new flexibility—existing business loans can easily be sold for cash to make new loans. But there is a potential downside—dilution of the signal from the original loan. Prior to securitization, markets saw extension of credit as good news about borrowers because banks were stuck with the loans to maturity.

To assess the impact of securitization, a recent study re-examined the market's reaction to bank lending decisions—but with a twist. This research looked at movement in the stock prices of borrowing firms when originating banks (i) first announced loans and (ii) later announced sales of those loans. Interestingly, both events were good for shareholders. The jump in a borrower's stock price for initial loans was comparable to earlier studies, but the bump for subsequent sales was even larger. Evidently, loan sales emit a positive signal because banks value the flexibility enough to avoid dumping "lemons" on securitizers.

▶ *Does the value of bank loans as seals of approval vary across different types of firms (i.e., new vs. established, larger vs. smaller, robust financial shape vs. distressed)?*

For example, see Billett, Matthew; Mark J. Flannery; and Jon A. Garfinkel. "The Effect of Lender Identity on a Borrowing Firm's Equity Return," *Journal of Finance* 50 (1995): 699–718. Gande, Amar and Anthony Saunders. "Are Banks Still Special When There is a Secondary Market for Loans?" *Journal of Finance* 67 (2012): 1649–1684.

BANK LOANS

Banks are a major source of unsecured short-term loans to businesses. The major type of loan made by banks to businesses is the **short-term, self-liquidating loan.** These loans are intended merely to carry the firm through seasonal peaks in financing needs that are due primarily to buildups of inventory and accounts receivable. As the firm converts inventories and receivables into cash, it generates the funds needed to retire these loans. In other words, the use to which the borrowed money is put provides the mechanism through which the loan is repaid, hence the term *self-liquidating*.

short-term, self-liquidating loan
An unsecured short-term loan in which the use to which the borrowed money is put provides the mechanism through which the loan is repaid.

Banks lend unsecured, short-term funds in three basic ways: through single-payment notes, through lines of credit, and through revolving credit agreements. Before we look at these types of loans, we examine loan interest rates.

Loan Interest Rates

The interest rate on a bank loan can be a fixed or a floating rate, and the interest rate is often based on a market benchmark rate such as the prime rate, the federal funds rate, or the London Interbank Offered Rate. The **prime rate of interest (prime rate)** is an interest rate charged by leading U.S. banks on business loans to creditworthy borrowers. The **federal funds rate** is the rate at which U.S. financial institutions make overnight loans to each other. The **London Interbank Offered Rate (LIBOR)** is a rate at which banks around the world make short-term loans to each other, and as an international interest rate benchmark, LIBOR may be associated with loans in different currencies at different maturities. The LIBOR rate most often used as a benchmark in commercial loans is the 3-month LIBOR in U.S. dollars.

prime rate of interest (prime rate)
An interest rate charged by leading U.S. banks on business loans to creditworthy borrowers.

federal funds rate
The rate at which U.S. banks make overnight loans to each other.

London Interbank Offered Rate (LIBOR)
The rate at which international banks make short-term loans to each other. There are many different LIBOR rates corresponding to different currencies and maturities.

These benchmark interest rates fluctuate with changing supply-and-demand relationships for short-term funds. Banks generally determine the rate they offer to a borrower by adding a risk premium or "spread" to the benchmark rate. The magnitude of the spread depends on the borrower's risk profile—banks charge higher spreads on loans to borrowers that are more likely to have difficulty paying back what they owe. The size of the spread also depends on overall market conditions. Spreads tend to widen during economic recessions, and they narrow during expansions. For example, during the recession that lasted from December 2007 to June 2009, the average spread on commercial loans was 2.74% above the federal funds rate. The period 1996 to 1999 saw the most rapid 4-year growth spurt in the U.S. economy since the mid 1980s, and during that stretch the spread on commercial loans averaged just 1.80% above federal funds. More recently, the spread averaged 2.34% in 2016 and 2017.

Fixed- and Floating-Rate Loans Loans can have either fixed or floating interest rates. On a **fixed-rate loan,** the rate of interest is set at or above the prime rate (or some other benchmark interest rate) on the date of the loan and remains at that fixed rate until maturity. On a **floating-rate loan,** the spread above the benchmark rate is fixed initially, but the loan interest rate varies or "floats," as the benchmark rate varies. Floating-rate loans may have provisions that allow the interest rate to vary at any time that the benchmark rate changes, or the loan rate may change only at fixed increments such as quarterly or yearly, and only then in response to a change in the benchmark rate. Generally, the spread will be lower on a floating-rate loan than on a fixed-rate loan of equivalent risk because the lender bears less risk with a floating-rate loan. Most business loans are floating-rate loans.

fixed-rate loan
A loan with a rate of interest that is determined at a set increment above the prime rate and remains unvarying until maturity.

floating-rate loan
A loan with a rate of interest initially set at an increment above the prime rate and allowed to "float," or vary, above prime *as the prime rate varies* until maturity.

Method of Computing Interest Once the *nominal (or stated) annual rate* is established, the method of computing interest is determined. Interest may be due either when a loan matures or in advance. If interest is due at maturity, the *effective (or true) annual rate*—the actual rate of interest paid—for a 1-year loan is equal to

$$\frac{\text{Interest}}{\text{Amount borrowed}} \tag{16.3}$$

Most bank loans to businesses require the interest payment at maturity.

When the borrower pays interest *in advance,* the bank deducts the interest payment from the loan principal, so that the borrower actually receives less money than the loan's face value (and less than the borrower must repay). Loans on which borrowers pay interest in advance are called **discount loans.** The effective annual rate for a 1-year discount loan is calculated as

discount loan
Loan on which interest is paid in advance by being deducted from the amount borrowed.

$$\frac{\text{Interest}}{\text{Amount borrowed} - \text{Interest}} \tag{16.4}$$

Paying interest in advance raises the effective annual rate above the stated annual rate.

EXAMPLE 16.8

Wooster Company, a manufacturer of athletic apparel, wants to borrow \$10,000 for 1 year at a stated annual interest rate of 10%. If Wooster pays the interest on the loan at maturity, the firm will pay \$1,000 (0.10 × \$10,000) for the use of the \$10,000 for the year. At the end of the year, Wooster will write a check to the lender for \$11,000, consisting of the \$1,000 interest as well as the return of the \$10,000 principal. Substituting into Equation 16.3 reveals that the effective annual rate is therefore

$$\frac{\$1{,}000}{\$10{,}000} = 10.0\%$$

If Wooster borrows the money at the same 10% stated annual rate, but it pays the interest in advance, the firm still pays \$1,000 in interest, but it receives only \$9,000 (\$10,000 − \$1,000). The effective annual rate in this case is

$$\frac{\$1{,}000}{\$10{,}000 - \$1{,}000} = \frac{\$1{,}000}{\$9{,}000} = 11.1\%$$

At the end of the year, Wooster writes a check to the lender for \$10,000, having "paid" the \$1,000 in interest up front by borrowing just \$9,000. Paying interest in advance thus makes the effective annual rate (11.1%) greater than the stated annual rate (10.0%).

Single-Payment Notes

single-payment note
A short-term, one-time loan made to a borrower who needs funds for a specific purpose for a short period.

A creditworthy business borrower can obtain a **single-payment note** from a commercial bank. This type of loan is usually a one-time loan made to a borrower who needs funds for a specific purpose for a short period. The resulting instrument is a note, signed by the borrower, which states the terms of the loan, including the length of the loan and the interest rate. This type of short-term note generally has a maturity of 30 days to 9 months or more. The interest charged is usually tied in some way to the prime rate or another benchmark interest rate.

EXAMPLE 16.9

Gordon Manufacturing, a producer of rotary mower blades, recently borrowed \$100,000 from each of two banks, bank A and bank B. The loans were incurred on the same day, when the prime rate of interest was 4.25%. Each loan involved a 90-day note with interest due in 90 days. The interest rate was set at 1.50% above the prime rate on bank A's fixed-rate note. Over the 90-day period, the rate of interest on this note will remain at 5.75% (4.25% prime rate + 1.50% increment) regardless of fluctuations in the prime rate. The total interest cost on this loan is $1,417.81 [$100,000 × (5.75% × 90 ÷ 365)], which means that the 90-day rate on this loan is about 1.42% ($1,417.81 ÷ $100,000).

Assuming that the loan from bank A is rolled over each 90 days throughout the year under the same terms and circumstances, we can find its effective annual interest rate, or *EAR*, by using Equation 5.10. Because the loan costs 1.42% for 90 days, it is necessary to compound (1 + 0.0142) for 4.06 periods in the year (i.e., 365 ÷ 90) and then subtract 1:

$$EAR = (1 + 0.0142)^{4.06} - 1$$
$$= 1.0589 - 1 = 0.0589 = \underline{\underline{5.89\%}}$$

The effective annual rate of interest on the fixed-rate, 90-day note is 5.89%.

Bank B set the interest rate at 1% above the prime rate on its floating-rate note. The rate charged over the 90 days will vary directly with the prime rate. Initially, the rate will be 5.25% (4.25% + 1%), but when the prime rate changes, so will the rate of interest on the note. For instance, if after 30 days the prime rate rises to 4.5% and after another 30 days it drops back to 4.25%, the firm will be paying 0.432% for the first 30 days (5.25% × 30 ÷ 365), 0.452% for the next 30 days (5.5% × 30 ÷ 365), and 0.432% for the last 30 days (5.25% × 30 ÷ 365). Its total interest cost will be $1,315 [$100,000 × (0.432% + 0.452% + 0.432%)], resulting in a 90-day rate of about 1.32% ($1,315 ÷ $100,000).

Again, assuming the loan is rolled over each 90 days throughout the year under the same terms and circumstances, its effective annual rate is 5.47%:

$$EAR = (1 + 0.0132)^{4.06} - 1$$
$$= 1.0547 - 1 = 0.0547 = \underline{\underline{5.47\%}}$$

Clearly, in this case the floating-rate loan would have been less expensive than the fixed-rate loan as indicated by its lower effective annual rate.

PERSONAL FINANCE EXAMPLE 16.10 Megan Schwartz has been approved by Clinton National Bank for a 180-day loan of $30,000 that will allow her to make the down payment and close the loan on her new condo. She needs the funds to bridge the time until the sale of her current condo, from which she expects to receive $42,000.

Clinton National offered Megan the following two financing options for the $30,000 loan: (1) a fixed-rate loan at 2% above the prime rate or (2) a variable-rate loan at 1% above the prime rate. Currently, the prime rate of interest is 5%, and the consensus forecast of a group of mortgage economists for changes in the prime rate over the next 180 days is as follows:

60 days from today the prime rate will rise by 1.0%.

90 days from today the prime rate will rise another 0.5%.

150 days from today the prime rate will drop by 1.0%.

Using the forecast prime rate changes, Megan wishes to determine the lowest interest-cost loan for the next 6 months.

Fixed-Rate Loan: Total interest cost over 180 days

$$= \$30{,}000 \times (0.05 + 0.02) \times (180 \div 365)$$
$$= \$30{,}000 \times 0.03452 \approx \underline{\underline{\$1{,}036}}$$

Variable-Rate Loan: The applicable interest rate would begin at 6% (5% + 1%) and remain there for 60 days. Then the applicable rate would rise to 7% (6% + 1%) for the next 30 days and then to 7.5% (6.5% + 0.5%) for the next 60 days. Finally, the applicable rate would drop to 6.5% (7.5% − 1%) for the final 30 days.

Total interest cost over 180 days

$$\begin{aligned} &= \$30{,}000 \times [(0.06 \times 60 \div 365) + (0.07 \times 30 \div 365) \\ &\quad + (0.075 \times 60 \div 365) + (0.065 \times 30 \div 365)] \\ &= \$30{,}000 \times (0.00986 + 0.00575 + 0.01233 + 0.00534) \\ &= \$30{,}000 \times 0.03328 \approx \underline{\underline{\$988}} \end{aligned}$$

The estimated total interest cost on the variable-rate loan of $988 is less than the total interest cost of $1,036 on the fixed-rate loan, so Megan might be tempted to take the variable-rate loan. However, the estimated interest cost on that loan depends on the interest rate forecast. Megan's actual interest cost could be higher or lower than $988 if she takes out the variable-rate loan, whereas the $1,036 interest cost from the fixed-rate loan is locked in. Megan has to decide whether the expected $48 ($1,036 − $988) savings in interest cost over the 180 days is worth the risk of accepting the variable rate loan.

Lines of Credit

line of credit
An agreement between a commercial bank and a business specifying the amount of unsecured short-term borrowing the bank will make available to the firm over a given period of time.

A **line of credit** is an agreement between a commercial bank and a business, specifying the amount of unsecured short-term borrowing the bank will make available to the firm over a given period. It is similar to the agreement under which issuers of bank credit cards, such as MasterCard, Visa, and Discover, extend preapproved credit to cardholders. A line-of-credit agreement is typically made for a period of 1 year and often places certain constraints on the borrower. It is not a guaranteed loan; rather, it indicates that if the bank has sufficient funds available, it will allow the firm to borrow up to a certain amount of money. The amount of a line of credit is the maximum amount the firm can borrow from the bank at any point in time during the year.

When applying for a line of credit, the borrower may be required to submit such documents as its cash budget, pro forma income statement and balance sheet, and recent audited financial statements. If the bank finds the customer acceptable, it will extend the line of credit. The major attraction of a line of credit from the bank's point of view is that it eliminates the need to examine the creditworthiness of a customer each time it borrows money within the year.

Interest Rates The interest rate on a line of credit is normally a floating rate: the prime rate plus a premium. If the prime rate changes, the interest rate charged on new as well as outstanding borrowing automatically changes. The amount a borrower is charged in excess of the prime rate depends on creditworthiness. The more creditworthy the borrower, the lower the premium (interest increment) above prime and vice versa.

Operating-Change Restrictions In a line-of-credit agreement, a bank may impose **operating-change restrictions**, which give it the right to revoke the line if any major changes occur in the firm's financial condition or operations. The bank usually requires the firm to submit up-to-date, and preferably audited, financial statements for periodic review. In addition, the firm must inform the bank about shifts in key managerial personnel or in the firm's operations before changes take place. Such changes may affect the future success and debt-paying ability of the firm and thus could alter its credit status. If the bank does not agree with the proposed changes and the firm makes them anyway, the bank has the right to revoke the line of credit.

operating-change restrictions
Contractual restrictions that a bank may impose on a firm's financial condition or operations as part of a line-of-credit agreement.

Compensating Balances To ensure that the borrower will be a "good customer," many short-term unsecured bank loans—single-payment notes and lines of credit—require the borrower to maintain, in a checking account, a **compensating balance** equal to a certain percentage of the amount borrowed. Banks frequently require compensating balances of 10% to 20%. A compensating balance not only forces the borrower to be a good customer of the bank but may also raise the interest cost to the borrower.

compensating balance
A required checking account balance equal to a certain percentage of the amount borrowed from a bank under a line-of-credit or revolving credit agreement.

EXAMPLE 16.11

MyLab Finance Solution Video

Estrada Graphics, a graphic design firm, has borrowed $1 million under a line-of-credit agreement. It must pay a stated interest rate of 8% and maintain, in its checking account, a compensating balance equal to 20% of the amount borrowed, or $200,000. Thus, it actually receives the use of only $800,000. To use that amount for a year, the firm pays interest of $80,000 (0.08 × $1,000,000). The effective annual rate on the funds is therefore 10% ($80,000 ÷ $800,000), which is 2% more than the stated rate of 8%.

If the firm normally maintains a balance of $200,000 or more in its checking account, the effective annual rate equals the stated annual rate of 8% because none of the $1 million borrowed is needed to satisfy the compensating-balance requirement. If the firm normally maintains a $100,000 balance in its checking account, only an additional $100,000 will have to be tied up, leaving it with $900,000 of usable funds. The effective annual rate in this case would be 8.89% ($80,000 ÷ $900,000). Thus, a compensating balance raises the cost of borrowing only if it is larger than the firm's normal cash balance.

Annual Cleanups To ensure that firms use money lent under a line-of-credit agreement to finance seasonal needs, many banks require an **annual cleanup.** In these cases, the borrower must have a loan balance of zero—that is, owe the bank nothing—for a certain number of days during the year. Insisting that the borrower carry a zero loan balance for a certain period ensures that short-term loans do not turn into long-term loans.

annual cleanup
The requirement that for a certain number of days during the year borrowers under a line of credit carry a zero loan balance (i.e., owe the bank nothing).

All the characteristics of a line-of-credit agreement are negotiable to some extent. Today, banks bid competitively to attract large, well-known firms. A prospective borrower should attempt to negotiate a line of credit with the most favorable interest rate, for an optimal amount of funds, and with a minimum of restrictions. Borrowers today frequently pay fees to lenders instead of maintaining deposit balances as compensation for loans and other services. The lender attempts to get a return commensurate with the risk it takes when lending to the borrower. Negotiations should produce a line of credit that is suitable to both borrower and lender.

Revolving Credit Agreements

revolving credit agreement
A line of credit *guaranteed* to a borrower by a commercial bank regardless of the scarcity of money.

commitment fee
The fee that is normally charged on a *revolving credit agreement;* it often applies to the *average unused portion* of the borrower's credit line.

A **revolving credit agreement** is nothing more than a guaranteed line of credit. It is guaranteed in the sense that the commercial bank promises to make available a certain amount of money to the borrower regardless of the scarcity of money. The interest rate and other requirements of a revolving credit agreement are similar to those for a line of credit. It is not uncommon for a revolving credit agreement to cover a period greater than 1 year.[2] Because the bank guarantees the availability of funds, it normally charges a **commitment fee** on a revolving credit agreement. This fee often applies to the average unused balance of the borrower's credit line. It is normally about 0.5% of the average unused portion of the line.

EXAMPLE 16.12

REH Company, a major real estate developer, has a $2 million revolving credit agreement with its bank. Its average borrowing under the agreement for the past year was $1.5 million. The bank charges a commitment fee of 0.5% on the average unused balance. Because the average unused portion of the committed funds was $500,000 ($2 million − $1.5 million), the commitment fee for the year was $2,500 (0.005 × $500,000). Of course, REH also had to pay interest on the actual $1.5 million borrowed under the agreement. Assuming that REH paid $112,500 interest on the $1.5 million borrowed, the effective cost of the agreement was 7.67% [($112,500 + $2,500) ÷ $1,500,000]. Although more expensive than a line of credit, a revolving credit agreement can be less risky from the borrower's viewpoint because the availability of funds is guaranteed.

COMMERCIAL PAPER

commercial paper
A form of financing consisting of short-term, unsecured promissory notes issued by firms with a high credit standing.

Commercial paper is a short-term, unsecured promissory note issued by a firm with a high credit standing. Generally, only large, financially sound firms issue commercial paper. Like bonds, commercial paper issues are often rated by rating agencies, and to attain a high rating (and a low interest rate), many commercial paper issues have a "back up" line of credit from a commercial bank. Most commercial paper issues have maturities ranging from 3 to 270 days. Although there is no set denomination, firms usually issue commercial paper in multiples of $100,000 or more. Finance companies issue a large portion of the commercial paper today; manufacturing firms account for a smaller portion. Businesses purchase commercial paper to provide an interest-earning reserve of liquidity. For further information on recent use of commercial paper, see the *Focus on Practice* box.

Interest on Commercial Paper

Commercial paper sells at a discount from its par, or face value. The size of the discount and the length of time to maturity determine the interest rate paid by the issuer of commercial paper, as illustrated by the following example.

2. Many authors classify the revolving credit agreement as a form of intermediate-term financing, defined as having a maturity of 1 to 7 years, but we do not use the intermediate-term financing classification; only short-term and long-term classifications are made. Because many revolving credit agreements cover more than 1 year, they can be classified as a form of long-term financing; however, they are discussed here because of their similarity to line-of-credit agreements.

FOCUS ON PRACTICE *in practice*

The Ebb and Flow of Commercial Paper

The difficult economic and credit environment in the post–September 11 era, combined with historically low interest rates and a deep desire by corporate issuers to reduce exposure to refinancing risk, had a depressing effect on commercial paper volumes from 2001 through 2003. According to the Federal Reserve, U.S. nonfinancial commercial paper declined 68% over the 3-year period, from $315.8 billion outstanding at the beginning of 2001 to $101.4 billion by December 2003. In addition to lower volume, credit quality of commercial paper declined over the same period, with the ratio of downgrades outpacing upgrades 17 to 1 in 2002.

In 2004, signs emerged that the volume and rating contraction in commercial paper was finally coming to an end. The most encouraging of them was the pickup in economic growth, which spurs the need for short-term debt to finance corporate working capital. Although commercial paper is typically used to fund working capital, it is often boosted by a sudden surge of borrowing activity for other strategic activities, such as mergers and acquisitions and long-term capital investments. According to Federal Reserve Board data, at the end of July 2004, total U.S. commercial paper outstanding was $1.33 trillion.

By 2006, commercial paper surged to $1.98 trillion, an increase of 21.5% over 2005 levels. However, after peaking at $2.22 trillion, the tide changed in response to the credit crisis that began in August 2007. According to Federal Reserve data, as of October 1, 2008, the commercial paper market had contracted to $1.6 trillion, a reduction of nearly 28%, and new issues virtually dried up for several weeks. With much of the commercial paper outstanding at the start of the credit crisis coming up for renewal, the Federal Reserve began operating the Commercial Paper Funding Facility (CPFF) on October 27, 2008. The CPFF was intended to provide a liquidity backstop to U.S. issuers of commercial paper and, thereby, increase the availability of credit in short-term capital markets. CPFF allowed for the Federal Reserve Bank of New York to finance the purchase of highly rated unsecured and asset-backed commercial paper from eligible issuers.

Even with the CPFF up and running, companies that were worried about their ability to roll over their outstanding commercial paper every few weeks turned to long-term debt to meet their liquidity needs. Merrill Lynch & Co. and Bloomberg data showed that to manage short-term liability risk, companies were paying as much as $75 million in additional annual interest to swap long-term debt for $1 billion of 30-day commercial paper.

With the recession in the rearview mirror and short-term credit markets working again, the CPFF was closed on February 1, 2010. But 7 years later, the commercial paper market was still far smaller than it had been before the financial crisis. In February 2017, the Federal Reserve reported that the total amount of commercial paper outstanding was only $950 billion, less than half the size of the market in 2007, before the crisis.

► *What factors contribute to an expansion of the commercial paper market? What factors cause a contraction in the commercial paper market?*

EXAMPLE 16.13

MyLab Finance Solution Video

Bertram Corporation, a large shipbuilder, has just issued $1 million worth of commercial paper that has a 90-day maturity and sells for $995,000. At the end of 90 days, the purchaser of this paper will receive $1 million for its $995,000 investment. The interest paid on the financing is therefore $5,000 on a principal of $995,000. The 90-day interest rate on the paper is 0.502% ($5,000 ÷ $995,000). Assuming that the paper is rolled over each 90 days throughout the year (i.e., $365 \div 90 = 4.06$ times per year), the effective annual rate for Bertram's commercial paper, found by using Equation 5.10, is 2.054% $[(1 + 0.00502)^{4.06} - 1]$.

An interesting characteristic of commercial paper is that its interest cost is normally below the prime rate. In other words, firms are able to raise funds more cheaply by selling commercial paper than by borrowing from a commercial bank (although commercial banks sometimes offer very large borrowers loans at a rate that is below prime). The reason is that many suppliers of short-term funds do not have the option, as banks do, of making low-risk business loans at the prime rate. They can invest safely only in marketable securities such as Treasury bills and commercial paper.

Although the stated interest cost of borrowing through the sale of commercial paper is normally lower than the prime rate, the overall cost of commercial paper may not be less than that of a bank loan. Additional costs include various fees and flotation costs. Also, even if it is slightly more expensive to borrow from a commercial bank, it may at times be advisable to do so to establish a good working relationship with a bank. This strategy increases the chances that when money is tight, firms can obtain funds promptly and at a reasonable interest rate.

MATTER OF FACT

Lending Limits

Commercial banks are legally prohibited from lending amounts in excess of 15% (plus an additional 10% for loans secured by readily marketable collateral) of the bank's unimpaired capital and surplus to any one borrower. This restriction is intended to protect depositors by forcing the commercial bank to spread its risk across a number of borrowers. In addition, smaller commercial banks do not have many opportunities to lend to large, high-quality business borrowers.

INTERNATIONAL LOANS

In some ways, arranging short-term financing for international trade is no different from financing purely domestic operations. In both cases, producers must finance production and inventory and then continue to finance accounts receivable before collecting any cash payments from sales. In other ways, however, the short-term financing of international sales and purchases is fundamentally different from that of strictly domestic trade.

International Transactions

The important difference between international and domestic transactions is that payments are often made or received in a foreign currency. Not only must a U.S. company pay the costs of doing business in the foreign exchange market, but it also is exposed to exchange rate risk. A U.S.-based company that exports goods and has accounts receivable denominated in a foreign currency faces the risk that the U.S. dollar will appreciate in value relative to the foreign currency. The risk to a U.S. importer with foreign-currency-denominated accounts payable is that the dollar will depreciate. Although exchange rate risk can often be hedged by using currency forward, futures, or options markets, doing so is costly and is not possible for all foreign currencies.

Typical international transactions are large and have long maturity dates. Therefore, companies involved in international trade generally have to finance larger dollar amounts for longer time periods than companies that operate domestically. Furthermore, because foreign companies are rarely well known in the United States, some financial institutions are reluctant to lend to U.S. exporters or importers, particularly smaller firms.

Financing International Trade

letter of credit
A letter written by a company's bank to the company's foreign supplier, stating that the bank guarantees payment of an invoiced amount if all the underlying agreements are met.

Several specialized techniques have evolved for financing international trade. Perhaps the most important financing vehicle is the **letter of credit,** a letter written by a company's bank to the company's foreign supplier, stating that the bank guarantees payment of an invoiced amount if all the underlying agreements are met. The letter of credit essentially substitutes the bank's reputation and creditworthiness for that of its commercial customer. A U.S. exporter is more willing to sell goods to a foreign buyer if the transaction is covered by a letter of credit issued by a well-known bank in the buyer's home country.

Firms that do business in foreign countries on an ongoing basis often finance their operations, at least in part, in the local market. A company that has an assembly plant in Mexico, for example, might choose to finance its purchases of Mexican goods and services with peso funds borrowed from a Mexican bank. This practice not only minimizes exchange rate risk but also improves the company's business ties to the host community. Multinational companies, however, sometimes finance their international transactions through dollar-denominated loans from international banks. The Eurocurrency loan markets allow creditworthy borrowers to obtain financing on attractive terms.

Transactions Between Subsidiaries

Much international trade involves transactions between corporate subsidiaries. A U.S. company might, for example, manufacture one part in an Asian plant and another part in the United States, assemble the product in Brazil, and sell it in Europe. The shipment of goods back and forth between subsidiaries creates accounts receivable and accounts payable, but the parent company has considerable discretion about how and when payments are made. In particular, the parent company can minimize foreign exchange fees and other transaction costs by "netting" what affiliates owe each other and paying only the net amount due rather than having both subsidiaries pay each other the gross amounts due.

→ REVIEW QUESTIONS MyLab Finance Solutions

16–4 How is the prime rate of interest relevant to the cost of short-term bank borrowing? What is a floating-rate loan?

16–5 How does the effective annual rate differ between a loan requiring interest payments at maturity and another, similar loan requiring interest in advance?

16–6 What are the basic terms and characteristics of a single-payment note? How is the effective annual rate on such a note found?

16–7 What is a line of credit? Describe each of the following features that are often included in these agreements: (**a**) operating-change restrictions, (**b**) compensating balance, and (**c**) annual cleanup.

16–8 What is a revolving credit agreement? How does this arrangement differ from the line-of-credit agreement? What is a commitment fee?

16–9 How do firms use commercial paper to raise short-term funds? Who can issue commercial paper? Who buys commercial paper?

16–10 What is the important difference between international and domestic transactions? How is a letter of credit used in financing international trade transactions? How is "netting" used in transactions between subsidiaries?

16.3 Secured Sources of Short-Term Loans

When a firm has exhausted its sources of unsecured short-term financing, it may be able to obtain additional short-term loans on a secured basis. **Secured short-term financing** has specific assets pledged as collateral. The collateral commonly takes the form of an asset, such as accounts receivable or inventory. The lender obtains a security interest in the collateral through the execution of a **security agreement** with the borrower that specifies the collateral held against the loan. In addition, the terms of the loan against which the security is held form part of the security agreement. A copy of the security agreement is filed in a public office within the state, usually a county or state court. Filing provides subsequent lenders with information about which assets of a prospective borrower are unavailable for use as collateral. The filing requirement protects the lender by legally establishing the lender's security interest.

secured short-term financing
Short-term financing (loan) that has specific assets pledged as collateral.

security agreement
The agreement between the borrower and the lender that specifies the collateral held against a secured loan.

CHARACTERISTICS OF SECURED SHORT-TERM LOANS

Although many people believe that holding collateral as security reduces the risk that a loan will default, lenders do not usually view loans in this way. Lenders recognize that holding collateral can reduce losses if the borrower defaults, but the presence of collateral has no impact on default risk. A lender requires collateral to ensure recovery of some portion of the loan in default. What the lender wants above all, however, is repayment as scheduled. In general, lenders prefer to make less risky loans at lower rates of interest than to find themselves in a position requiring liquidation of collateral.

Collateral and Terms

Lenders of secured short-term funds prefer collateral that has a duration closely matched to the term of the loan. Current assets are the most desirable short-term-loan collateral because they can normally be converted into cash much sooner than fixed assets. Thus, the short-term lender of secured funds generally accepts only liquid current assets as collateral.

Typically, the lender determines the desirable **percentage advance** to make against the collateral. This percentage advance constitutes the principal of the secured loan and is normally between 30% and 100% of the book value of the collateral. It varies according to the type and liquidity of collateral.

percentage advance
The percentage of the book value of the collateral that constitutes the principal of a secured loan.

Other things being equal, for an individual firm the interest rate charged on secured short-term loans is typically lower than the rate on unsecured short-term loans. Lenders require the riskiest borrowers to provide collateral and pay higher interest rates. The riskiest borrowers that only have access to secured lending often pay higher interest rates than the typical less risky, unsecured borrower. In addition, negotiating and administering secured loans is more costly for the lender than negotiating and administering unsecured loans. The lender therefore normally requires added compensation in the form of a service charge, a yet higher interest rate, or both.

Institutions Extending Secured Short-Term Loans

The primary sources of secured short-term loans to businesses are commercial banks and commercial finance companies. Both institutions deal in short-term loans secured primarily by accounts receivable and inventory. We have already described the operations of commercial banks. **Commercial finance companies** are lending

commercial finance companies
Lending institutions that make *only* secured loans—both short-term and long-term—to businesses.

institutions that make only secured loans—both short-term and long-term—to businesses. Unlike banks, finance companies are not permitted to hold deposits.

If its unsecured and secured short-term borrowing power from the commercial bank is exhausted, a borrower may turn to the commercial finance company for additional secured borrowing. Because the finance company generally ends up with higher-risk borrowers, its interest charges on secured short-term loans are usually higher than those of commercial banks. The leading U.S. commercial finance companies include the CIT Group and General Electric Corporate Financial Services.

USE OF ACCOUNTS RECEIVABLE AS COLLATERAL

Two commonly used means of obtaining short-term financing with accounts receivable are *pledging accounts receivable* and *factoring accounts receivable.* Actually, only a pledge of accounts receivable creates a secured short-term loan; factoring really entails the sale of accounts receivable at a discount. Although factoring is not actually a form of secured short-term borrowing, it does involve the use of accounts receivable to obtain needed short-term funds.

Pledging Accounts Receivable

pledge of accounts receivable
The use of a firm's accounts receivable as security, or collateral, to obtain a short-term loan.

A **pledge of accounts receivable** is often used to secure a short-term loan. Because accounts receivable are normally quite liquid, they are an attractive form of short-term-loan collateral.

The Pledging Process When a firm requests a loan against accounts receivable, the lender first evaluates the firm's accounts receivable to determine their desirability as collateral. The lender makes a list of the acceptable accounts, along with the billing dates and amounts. If the borrowing firm requests a loan for a fixed amount, the lender needs to select only enough accounts to secure the funds requested. If the borrower wants the maximum loan available, the lender evaluates all the accounts to select the maximum amount of acceptable collateral.

After selecting the acceptable accounts, the lender normally adjusts the dollar value of these accounts for expected returns on sales and other allowances. If a customer whose account has been pledged returns merchandise or receives some type of allowance, such as an early payment discount for early payment, the amount of the collateral is automatically reduced. For protection from such occurrences, the lender normally reduces the value of the acceptable collateral by a fixed percentage.

lien
A publicly disclosed legal claim on loan collateral.

non-notification basis
The basis on which a borrower, having pledged an account receivable, continues to collect the account payments without notifying the account customer.

notification basis
The basis on which an account customer whose account has been pledged (or factored) is notified to remit payment directly to the lender (or factor).

Next, the lender must determine the percentage to be advanced against the collateral. The lender evaluates the quality of the acceptable receivables and the expected cost of their liquidation. This percentage represents the principal of the loan and typically ranges between 50% and 90% of the face value of acceptable accounts receivable. To protect its interest in the collateral, the lender files a **lien,** which is a publicly disclosed legal claim on the collateral.

Notification Pledges of accounts receivable are normally made on a **non-notification basis,** meaning that a customer whose account has been pledged as collateral is not notified. Under the non-notification arrangement, the borrower still collects the pledged account receivable, and the lender trusts the borrower to remit these payments as they are received. If a pledge of accounts receivable is made on a **notification basis,** the customer is notified to remit payment directly to the lender.

MATTER OF FACT

Receivables Trading

Founded in 2007, the Receivables Exchange is an online marketplace where organizations such as hedge funds and commercial banks looking for short-term investments can bid on receivables pledged by large companies from a wide range of industries. Companies that need cash put their receivables up for auction on the Receivables Exchange, and investors bid on them. In its first few years of operation, the Receivables Exchange provided funding of more than $1 billion to companies selling their receivables. The Receivables Exchange attracted the attention of the NYSE Euronext, which purchased a minority stake in the company in 2011, and eventually the exchange was rebranded as LiquidX. Auction-based trading in receivables is still a niche business and in the aggregate does not provide a large volume of financing for businesses.

Pledging Cost The stated cost of a pledge of accounts receivable is normally 1% to 4% above the prime rate. In addition to the stated interest rate, a service charge of up to 3% may be levied by the lender to cover its administrative costs. Clearly, pledges of accounts receivable are a high-cost source of short-term financing.

Factoring Accounts Receivable

factoring accounts receivable
The outright sale of accounts receivable at a discount to a *factor* or other financial institution.

factor
A financial institution that specializes in purchasing accounts receivable from businesses.

nonrecourse basis
The basis on which accounts receivable are sold to a factor with the understanding that the factor accepts all credit risks on the purchased accounts.

Factoring accounts receivable involves selling them outright, at a discount, to a financial institution. A **factor** is a financial institution that specializes in purchasing accounts receivable from businesses. Although it is not the same as obtaining a short-term loan, factoring accounts receivable is similar to borrowing with accounts receivable as collateral.

Factoring Agreement A factoring agreement normally states the exact conditions and procedures for the purchase of an account. The factor, like a lender against a pledge of accounts receivable, chooses accounts for purchase, selecting only those that appear to be acceptable credit risks. Where factoring occurs on a continuing basis, the factor will actually make the firm's credit decisions because this will guarantee the acceptability of accounts. Factoring is normally done on a *notification basis,* and the factor receives payment of the account directly from the customer. In addition, most sales of accounts receivable to a factor are made on a **nonrecourse basis,** meaning that the factor agrees to accept all credit risks. Thus, if a purchased account turns out to be uncollectible, the factor must absorb the loss.

MATTER OF FACT

Quasi Factoring

The use of credit cards such as MasterCard, Visa, and Discover by consumers has some similarity to factoring because the vendor that accepts the card is reimbursed at a discount for purchases made with the card. The difference between factoring and credit cards is that cards are nothing more than a line of credit extended by the issuer, which charges the vendors a fee for accepting the cards. In factoring, the factor does not analyze credit until after the sale has been made; in many cases (except when factoring is done on a continuing basis), the initial credit decision is the responsibility of the vendor, not the factor that purchases the account.

Typically, the factor is not required to pay the firm until the account is collected or until the last day of the credit period, whichever occurs first. The factor sets up an account similar to a bank deposit account for each customer. As payment is received or as due dates arrive, the factor deposits money into the seller's account, from which the seller is free to make withdrawals as needed.

In many cases, if the firm leaves the money in the account, a surplus will exist on which the factor will pay interest. In other instances, the factor may make advances to the firm against uncollected accounts that are not yet due. These advances represent a negative balance in the firm's account, on which interest is charged.

Factoring Cost Factoring costs include commissions, interest levied on advances, and interest earned on surpluses. The factor deposits in the firm's account the book value of the collected or due accounts purchased by the factor, less the commissions. The commissions are typically stated as a 1% to 3% discount from the book value of factored accounts receivable. The interest levied on advances is generally a few percentage points above the prime rate. It is levied on the actual amount advanced. The interest paid on surpluses is generally between 0.2% and 0.5% per month.

Although its costs may seem high, factoring has certain advantages that make it attractive to many firms. One is the ability it gives the firm to turn accounts receivable immediately into cash without having to worry about repayment. Another advantage is that it ensures a known pattern of cash flows. In addition, if factoring is undertaken on a continuing basis, the firm can eliminate or scale back its credit and collection departments.

USE OF INVENTORY AS COLLATERAL

Inventory is generally second to accounts receivable in desirability as short-term loan collateral. Inventory normally has a market value greater than its book value, which is used to establish its value as collateral. A lender whose loan is secured with inventory will probably be able to sell that inventory for at least book value if the borrower defaults on its obligations.

The most important characteristic of inventory being evaluated as loan collateral is marketability. A warehouse of perishable items, such as fresh peaches, may be quite marketable, but if the cost of storing and selling the peaches is high, they may not be desirable collateral. Specialized items, such as moon-roving vehicles, are also not desirable collateral because finding a buyer for them could be difficult. When evaluating inventory as possible loan collateral, the lender looks for items with very stable market prices that have ready markets and that lack undesirable physical properties.

Floating Inventory Liens

floating inventory lien
A secured short-term loan against inventory under which the lender's claim is on the borrower's inventory in general.

A lender may be willing to secure a loan under a **floating inventory lien,** which is a claim on inventory in general. This arrangement is most attractive when the firm has a stable level of inventory that consists of a diversified group of relatively inexpensive merchandise. Inventories of items such as auto tires, screws and bolts, and shoes are candidates for floating-lien loans. Because it is difficult for a lender to verify the presence of the inventory, the lender generally advances less than 50% of the book value of the average inventory. The interest charge on a floating lien is 3% to 5% above the prime rate. Commercial banks often require floating liens as extra security on what would otherwise be an unsecured loan. Floating-lien inventory loans may also be available from commercial finance companies.

Trust Receipt Inventory Loans

trust receipt inventory loan
A secured short-term loan against inventory under which the lender advances 80% to 100% of the cost of the borrower's relatively expensive inventory items in exchange for the borrower's promise to repay the lender, with accrued interest, immediately after the sale of each item of collateral.

A **trust receipt inventory loan** often can be made against relatively expensive automotive, consumer durable, and industrial goods that can be identified by serial number. Under this agreement, the borrower keeps the inventory, and the lender may advance 80% to 100% of its cost. The lender files a *lien* on all the items financed. The borrower is free to sell the merchandise but is trusted to remit the amount lent, along with accrued interest, to the lender immediately after the sale. The lender then releases the lien on the item. The lender makes periodic checks of the borrower's inventory to make sure the required collateral remains in the hands of the borrower. The interest charge to the borrower is normally 2% or more above the prime rate.

Trust receipt loans are often made by manufacturers' wholly owned financing subsidiaries, known as captive finance companies, to their customers. Captive finance companies are especially popular in industries that manufacture consumer durable goods because they provide the manufacturer with a useful sales tool. For example, Ford Motor Credit Company, the financing subsidiary of Ford Motor Company, grants these types of loans to its dealers. Trust receipt loans are also available through commercial banks and commercial finance companies.

Warehouse Receipt Loans

warehouse receipt loan
A secured short-term loan against inventory under which the lender receives control of the pledged inventory collateral, which is stored by a designated warehousing company on the lender's behalf.

A **warehouse receipt loan** is an arrangement whereby the lender, which may be a commercial bank or finance company, receives control of the pledged inventory collateral, which is stored by a designated agent on the lender's behalf. After selecting acceptable collateral, the lender hires a warehousing company to act as its agent and take possession of the inventory.

Two types of warehousing arrangements are possible. A *terminal warehouse* is a central warehouse used to store the merchandise of various customers. The lender normally uses such a warehouse when the inventory is easily transported and can be delivered to the warehouse relatively inexpensively. Under a *field warehouse* arrangement, the lender hires a field-warehousing company to set up a warehouse on the borrower's premises or to lease part of the borrower's warehouse to store the pledged collateral. Regardless of the type of warehouse, the warehousing company places a guard over the inventory. Only on written approval of the lender can the warehousing company release any portion of the secured inventory.

The actual lending agreement specifically states the requirements for the release of inventory. As with other secured loans, the lender accepts only collateral that it believes to be readily marketable and advances only a portion—generally 75% to 90%—of the collateral's value. The specific costs of warehouse receipt loans are generally higher than those of any other secured lending arrangements because of the need to hire and pay a warehousing company to guard and supervise the collateral. The basic interest charged on warehouse receipt loans is higher than that charged on unsecured loans, generally ranging from 3% to 5%

above the prime rate. In addition to the interest charge, the borrower must absorb the costs of warehousing by paying the warehouse fee, which is generally between 1% and 3% of the amount of the loan. The borrower is normally also required to pay the insurance costs on the warehoused merchandise.

→ REVIEW QUESTIONS MyLab Finance Solutions

16–11 Are secured short-term loans viewed as more risky or less risky than unsecured short-term loans? Why?

16–12 In general, what interest rates and fees are levied on secured short-term loans? Why are these rates generally higher than the rates on unsecured short-term loans?

16–13 Describe and compare the basic features of the following methods of using accounts receivable to obtain short-term financing: (**a**) pledging accounts receivable and (**b**) factoring accounts receivable. Be sure to mention the institutions that offer each of them.

16–14 For the following methods of using inventory as short-term loan collateral, describe the basic features of each, and compare their use: (**a**) floating lien, (**b**) trust receipt loan, and (**c**) warehouse receipt loan.

SUMMARY

FOCUS ON VALUE

Current liabilities represent an important and generally inexpensive source of financing for a firm. The level of short-term (current liabilities) financing used by a firm affects its profitability and risk. Accounts payable and accruals are spontaneous liabilities that should be carefully managed because they represent free financing (in the absence of discounts for early payments). Notes payable, which represent negotiated short-term financing, should be obtained at the lowest cost under the best possible terms. Large, well-known firms can obtain unsecured short-term financing through the sale of commercial paper. On a secured basis, the firm can obtain loans from banks or commercial finance companies, using either accounts receivable or inventory as collateral.

The financial manager must obtain the right quantity and form of current liabilities financing to provide the lowest-cost funds with the least risk. Such a strategy should positively contribute to the firm's goal of **maximizing the stock price.**

REVIEW OF LEARNING GOALS

LG1 **Review accounts payable, the key components of credit terms, and the procedures for analyzing those terms.** The major spontaneous source of short-term financing is accounts payable. They are the primary source of short-term funds. Credit terms may differ with respect to the credit period, early payment discount, discount period, and beginning of the credit period. Discounts should be given up only when a firm in need of short-term funds must pay an interest rate on borrowing that is greater than the cost of giving up the discount.

LG 2 **Understand the effects of stretching accounts payable on their cost and the use of accruals.** Stretching accounts payable can lower the cost of giving up an early payment discount. Accruals, which result primarily from wage and tax obligations, are virtually free.

LG 3 **Describe interest rates and the basic types of unsecured bank sources of short-term loans.** Banks are the major source of unsecured short-term loans to businesses. The interest rate on these loans is tied to the prime rate of interest or another benchmark rate by a risk premium and may be fixed or floating. It should be evaluated by using the effective annual rate. Whether interest is paid when the loan matures or in advance affects the rate. Bank loans may take the form of a single-payment note, a line of credit, or a revolving credit agreement.

LG 4 **Discuss the basic features of commercial paper and the key aspects of international short-term loans.** Commercial paper is an unsecured IOU issued by firms with a high credit standing. International sales and purchases expose firms to exchange rate risk. Such transactions are larger and of longer maturity than domestic transactions, and they can be financed by using a letter of credit, by borrowing in the local market, or through dollar-denominated loans from international banks. On transactions between subsidiaries, "netting" can be used to minimize foreign exchange fees and other transaction costs.

LG 5 **Explain the characteristics of secured short-term loans and the use of accounts receivable as short-term-loan collateral.** Secured short-term loans are those for which the lender requires collateral, which are usually current assets such as accounts receivable or inventory. Only a percentage of the book value of acceptable collateral is advanced by the lender. These loans are more expensive than unsecured loans. Commercial banks and commercial finance companies make secured short-term loans. Both pledging and factoring involve the use of accounts receivable to obtain needed short-term funds.

LG 6 **Describe the various ways in which inventory can be used as short-term-loan collateral.** Inventory can be used as short-term-loan collateral under a floating lien, a trust receipt arrangement, or a warehouse receipt loan.

OPENER-IN-REVIEW

In the chapter opener, you learned about FastPay, a company that lends to online ad publishers based on advertising receivables. Suppose you are running a business that relies on online ad revenues. It typically takes 60 days to collect from your customers and convert receivables into cash. FastPay offers you $150,000 in cash in exchange for the right to collect $155,000 in receivables from a particular customer. You have a bank line of credit that allows you to borrow on a short-term basis at an annual interest rate of 7%. Should you borrow on the credit line or accept the offer from FastPay?

SELF-TEST PROBLEM (Solutions in Appendix)

ST16–1 **Early payment discount decisions** The credit terms for each of three suppliers are shown in the following table. (*Note:* Assume a 365-day year.)

Supplier	Credit terms
X	1/10 net 55 EOM
Y	2/10 net 30 EOM
Z	2/20 net 60 EOM

a. Determine the approximate cost of giving up the early payment discount from each supplier.

b. Assuming that the firm needs short-term financing, indicate whether it would be better to give up the discount or take the discount and borrow from a bank at 15% annual interest. Evaluate each supplier separately using your findings in part **a.**

c. Now assume that the firm could stretch its accounts payable (net period only) by 20 days from supplier Z. What impact, if any, would that have on your answer in part **b** relative to this supplier?

WARM-UP EXERCISES All problems are available in MyLab Finance

LG1 E16–1 Lyman Nurseries purchased seeds costing $25,000 with terms of 3/15 net 30 EOM on January 12. How much will the firm pay if it takes the discount? What is the approximate cost of giving up the discount, using the simplified formula?

LG2 E16–2 Cleaner's Inc. is switching to paying employees every 2 weeks rather than weekly and will therefore "skip" 1 week's pay. The firm has 25 employees who work a 60-hour week and earn an average wage of $12.50 per hour. Using a 10% rate of interest, how much will this change save the firm annually?

LG3 E16–3 Jasmine Scents has been given two competing offers for short-term financing. Both offers are for borrowing $15,000 for 1 year. The first offer is a discount loan at 8%, and the second offer is for interest to be paid at maturity at a stated interest rate of 9%. Calculate the effective annual rates for each loan, and indicate which loan offers the better terms.

LG3 E16–4 Jackson Industries has borrowed $125,000 under a line-of-credit agreement. Although the company normally maintains a checking account balance of $15,000 in the lending bank, this credit line requires a 20% compensating balance. The stated interest rate on the borrowed funds is 10%. What is the effective annual rate of interest on the line of credit?

E16–5 Horizon Telecom sold $300,000 worth of 120-day commercial paper for $298,000. What is the dollar amount of interest paid on the commercial paper? What is the effective 120-day rate on the paper?

PROBLEMS

All problems are available in MyLab Finance. The MyLab icon indicates problems in Excel format available in MyLab Finance.

P16–1 **Payment dates** Determine the date when a firm must pay for purchases made and invoices dated on June 19 under each of the following credit terms:

a. Net 30 date of invoice.
b. Net 30 EOM.
c. Net 45 date of invoice.
d. Net 60 EOM.

P16–2 **Cost of giving up early payment discounts** Determine the cost of giving up the discount under each of the following terms of sale. (*Note:* Assume a 365-day year.)

a. 2/10 net 30.
b. 1/10 net 30.
c. 1/10 net 45.
d. 3/10 net 90.
e. 1/10 net 60.
f. 3/10 net 30.
g. 4/10 net 180.

P16–3 **Credit terms** Purchases made on credit are due in full by the end of the billing period. Many firms extend a discount for payment made in the first part of the billing period. The original invoice contains a type of shorthand notation that explains the credit terms that apply. (*Note:* Assume a 365-day year.)

a. Write the shorthand expression of credit terms for each of the following:

Discount	Discount period	Credit period	Beginning of credit period
1%	15 days	45 days	date of invoice
2	10	30	end of month
2	7	28	date of invoice
1	10	60	end of month

b. For each of the sets of credit terms in part **a**, calculate the number of days until full payment is due for invoices dated March 12.

c. For each of the sets of credit terms, calculate the cost of giving up the early payment discount.

d. If the firm's cost of short-term financing is 8%, what would you recommend in regard to taking the discount or giving it up in each case?

P16–4 **Early payment discount versus loan** Joanne Germano works in an accounts payable department of a major retailer. She has attempted to convince her boss to take the discount on the 1/15 net 65 credit terms most suppliers offer, but her boss argues that giving up the 1% discount is less costly than a short-term loan at 7%. Prove to whoever is wrong that the other is correct. (*Note:* Assume a 365-day year.)

Personal Finance Problem

P16–5 **Borrow or pay cash for an asset** Mark and Stacy McCoy are set to move into their first apartment. They visited Levin Furniture, looking for a dining room table and buffet. Dining room sets are typically one of the more expensive home furnishing items, and the store offers financing arrangements to customers. Mark and Stacy have the cash to pay for the furniture, but it would definitely deplete their savings, so they want to look at all their options.

The dining room set costs $14,500, and Levin Furniture offers a financing plan that would allow them to either (1) put 20% down and finance the balance at 5% annual interest compounded monthly over 48 months or (2) receive an immediate $500 cash rebate.

Mark and Stacy currently earn 1.7% annual interest compounded monthly on their savings.

a. Calculate the cash down payment for the loan.

b. Calculate the monthly payment on the available loan. (*Hint:* Treat the current loan as an annuity and solve for the monthly payment.)

c. Calculate the net cash outlay under the cash purchase option.

d. Assuming Mark and Stacy can earn a monthly compound interest rate of 1.7% on savings, what will they give up (opportunity cost) over the 4 years if they pay cash?

e. What is the cost of the cash alternative at the end of 4 years?

f. Should Mark and Stacy choose the financing or the cash alternative?

P16–6 **Early payment discount decisions** Prairie Manufacturing has four possible suppliers, all of which offer different credit terms. Except for the differences in credit terms, their products and services are virtually identical. The credit terms offered by these suppliers are shown in the following table. (*Note:* Assume a 365-day year.)

Supplier	Credit terms
J	1/5 net 30 EOM
K	2/20 net 80 EOM
L	1/15 net 60 EOM
M	3/10 net 90 EOM

a. Calculate the approximate cost of giving up the early payment discount from each supplier.

b. If the firm needs short-term funds, which are currently available from its commercial bank at 9%, and if each of the suppliers is viewed separately, which, if any, of the suppliers' early payment discounts should the firm give up? Explain why.

c. Now assume that the firm could stretch by 30 days its accounts payable (net period only) from supplier M. What impact, if any, would that have on your answer in part **b** relative to this supplier?

LG2 P16–7 **Changing payment cycle** On accepting the position of chief executive officer and chairman of Muse Inc., Dominic Howard changed the firm's weekly payday from Monday afternoon to the following Friday afternoon. The firm's weekly payroll was $100 million, and the cost of short-term funds was 5%. If the effect of this change was to delay check clearing by 1 week, what annual savings, if any, were realized?

LG2 P16–8 **Spontaneous sources of funds, accruals** When Waverly Wear Inc. merged with Southerly Inc., Waverly's employees were switched from a weekly to a biweekly pay period. Waverly's weekly payroll amounted to $389,500. The annual cost of funds for the combined firms is 8.76%. What annual savings, if any, are realized by this change of pay period?

LG3 P16–9 **Cost of bank loan** Data Back-Up Systems has obtained a $10,000, 90-day bank loan at an annual interest rate of 15%, payable at maturity. (*Note:* Assume a 365-day year.)

a. How much interest (in dollars) will the firm pay on the 90-day loan?
b. Find the 90-day rate on the loan.
c. Annualize your result in part **b** to find the effective annual rate for this loan, assuming it is rolled over every 90 days throughout the year under the same terms and circumstances.

Personal Finance Problem

LG3 P16–10 **Unsecured sources of short-term loans** John Savage has obtained a short-term loan from First Carolina Bank. The loan matures in 180 days and is in the amount of $45,000. John needs the money to cover start-up costs in a new business. He hopes to have sufficient backing from other investors in 6 months. First Carolina Bank offers John two financing options for the $45,000 loan: a fixed-rate loan at 2.5% above prime rate or a variable-rate loan at 1.5% above prime.

Currently, the prime rate of interest is 6.5%, and the consensus interest rate forecast of a group of economists is as follows: Sixty days from today the prime rate will rise by 0.5%; 90 days from today the prime rate will rise another 1%; 180 days from today the prime rate will drop by 0.5%.

Using the forecast prime rate changes, answer the following questions.

a. Calculate the total interest cost over 180 days for a fixed-rate loan.
b. Calculate the total interest cost over 180 days for a variable-rate loan.
c. Which is the lower-interest-cost loan for the next 180 days?

LG3 P16–11 **Effective annual rate** A financial institution made a $4 million, 1-year discount loan at 6% interest, requiring a compensating balance equal to 5% of the face value of the loan. Determine the effective annual rate associated with this loan. (*Note:* Assume that the firm currently maintains $0 on deposit in the financial institution.)

LG3 P16–12 **Compensating balances and effective annual rates** Lincoln Industries has a line of credit at Bank Two that requires it to pay 11% interest on its borrowing and to maintain a compensating balance equal to 15% of the amount borrowed. The firm has borrowed $800,000 during the year under the agreement.

a. Calculate the effective annual rate on the firm's borrowing if the firm normally maintains no deposit balances at Bank Two.

b. Calculate the effective annual rate on the firm's borrowing if the firm normally maintains $70,000 in deposit balances at Bank Two.

c. Calculate the effective annual rate on the firm's borrowing if the firm normally maintains $150,000 in deposit balances at Bank Two.

d. Compare, contrast, and discuss your findings in parts **a**, **b**, and **c**.

LG3

P16–13 **Compensating balance versus discount loan** Weathers Catering Supply Inc. needs to borrow $150,000 for 6 months. State Bank has offered to lend the funds at a 9% annual rate subject to a 10% compensating balance. (*Note:* Weathers currently maintains $0 on deposit in State Bank.) Frost Finance Co. has offered to lend the funds at a 9% annual rate with discount-loan terms. The principal of both loans would be payable at maturity as a single sum.

a. Calculate the effective annual rate of interest on each loan.

b. What could Weathers do that would reduce the effective annual rate on the State Bank loan?

LG3

P16–14 **Integrative: Comparison of loan terms** Cumberland Furniture wishes to establish a prearranged borrowing agreement with a local commercial bank. The bank's terms for a line of credit are 3.30% over the prime rate, and each year the borrowing must be reduced to zero for a 30-day period. For an equivalent revolving credit agreement, the rate is 2.80% over prime with a commitment fee of 0.50% on the average unused balance. With both loans, the required compensating balance is equal to 20% of the amount borrowed. (*Note:* Cumberland currently maintains $0 on deposit at the bank.) The prime rate is currently 8%. Both agreements have $4 million borrowing limits. The firm expects on average to borrow $2 million during the year no matter which loan agreement it decides to use.

a. What is the effective annual rate under the line of credit?

b. What is the effective annual rate under the revolving credit agreement? (*Hint:* Compute the ratio of the dollars that the firm will pay in interest and commitment fees to the dollars that the firm will effectively have use of.)

c. If the firm does expect to borrow an average of half the amount available, which arrangement would you recommend for the borrower? Explain why.

LG4

P16–15 **Cost of commercial paper** Commercial paper is usually sold at a discount. Fan Corporation has just sold an issue of 90-day commercial paper with a face value of $1 million. The firm has received initial proceeds of $978,000. (*Note:* Assume a 365-day year.)

a. What effective annual rate will the firm pay for financing with commercial paper, assuming it is rolled over every 90 days throughout the year?

b. If a brokerage fee of $9,612 was paid from the initial proceeds to an investment banker for selling the issue, what effective annual rate will the firm pay, assuming the paper is rolled over every 90 days throughout the year?

LG5

P16–16 **Accounts receivable as collateral** Kansas City Castings (KCC) is attempting to obtain the maximum loan possible using accounts receivable as collateral. The firm extends net-30-day credit. The amounts that are owed KCC by its 12 credit customers, the average age of each account, and the customer's average payment period are as shown in the following table.

Customer	Account receivable	Average age of account	Average payment period of customer
A	$37,000	40 days	30 days
B	42,000	25	50
C	15,000	40	60
D	8,000	30	35
E	50,000	31	40
F	12,000	28	30
G	24,000	30	70
H	46,000	29	40
I	3,000	30	65
J	22,000	25	35
K	62,000	35	40
L	80,000	60	70

a. If the bank will accept all accounts that can be collected in 45 days or less as long as the customer has a history of paying within 45 days, which accounts will be acceptable? What is the total dollar amount of accounts receivable collateral? (*Note:* Accounts receivable that have an average age greater than the customer's average payment period are also excluded.)

b. In addition to the conditions in part **a**, the bank recognizes that 5% of credit sales will be lost to returns and allowances. Also, the bank will lend only 80% of the acceptable collateral (after adjusting for returns and allowances). What level of funds would be made available through this lending source?

P16–17 **Accounts receivable as collateral** Springer Products wishes to borrow $80,000 from a local bank using its accounts receivable to secure the loan. The bank's policy is to accept as collateral any accounts that are normally paid within 30 days of the end of the credit period as long as the average age of the account is not greater than the customer's average payment period. Springer's accounts receivable, their average ages, and the average payment period for each customer are shown in the following table. The company extends terms of net 30 days.

Customer	Account receivable	Average age of account	Average payment period of customer
A	$20,000	10 days	40 days
B	6,000	40	35
C	22,000	62	50
D	11,000	68	65
E	2,000	14	30
F	12,000	38	50
G	27,000	55	60
H	19,000	20	35

a. Calculate the dollar amount of acceptable accounts receivable collateral held by Springer Products.
b. The bank reduces collateral by 10% for returns and allowances. What is the level of acceptable collateral under this condition?
c. The bank will advance 75% against the firm's acceptable collateral (after adjusting for returns and allowances). What amount can Springer borrow against these accounts?

LG3 LG5

P16–18 **Accounts receivable as collateral, cost of borrowing** Maximum Bank has analyzed the accounts receivable of Scientific Software, Inc. The bank has chosen eight accounts totaling $134,000 that it will accept as collateral. The bank's terms include a lending rate set at prime plus 3% and a 2% commission charge. The prime rate currently is 8.5%.

a. The bank will adjust the accounts by 10% for returns and allowances. It then will lend up to 85% of the adjusted acceptable collateral. What is the maximum amount that the bank will lend to Scientific Software?
b. What is Scientific Software's effective annual rate of interest if it borrows $100,000 for 12 months? For 6 months? For 3 months? (*Note:* Assume a 365-day year and a prime rate that remains at 8.5% during the life of the loan.)

LG5

P16–19 **Factoring** Blair Finance factors the accounts of the Holder Company. All eight factored accounts are shown in the following table, with the amount factored, the date due, and the status on May 30. Indicate the amounts that Blair should have remitted to Holder as of May 30 and the dates of those remittances. Assume that the factor's commission of 2% is deducted as part of determining the amount of the remittance.

Account	Amount	Date due	Status on May 30
A	$200,000	May 30	Collected May 15
B	90,000	May 30	Uncollected
C	110,000	May 30	Uncollected
D	85,000	June 15	Collected May 30
E	120,000	May 30	Collected May 27
F	180,000	June 15	Collected May 30
G	90,000	May 15	Uncollected
H	30,000	June 30	Collected May 30

LG1 LG6

P16–20 **Inventory financing** Raymond Manufacturing faces a liquidity crisis: It needs a loan of $100,000 for 1 month. Having no source of additional unsecured borrowing, the firm must find a secured short-term lender. The firm's accounts receivable are quite low, but its inventory is considered liquid and reasonably good collateral. The book value of the inventory is $300,000, of which $120,000 is finished goods. (*Note:* Assume a 365-day year.)

(1) City-Wide Bank will make a $100,000 trust receipt loan against the finished goods inventory. The annual interest rate on the loan is 12% on the outstanding loan balance plus a 0.25% administration fee levied against the $100,000 initial loan amount. Because it will be liquidated as inventory is sold, the average amount owed over the month is expected to be $75,000.

(2) Sun State Bank will lend $100,000 against a floating lien on the book value of inventory for the 1-month period at an annual interest rate of 13%.
(3) Citizens' Bank and Trust will lend $100,000 against a warehouse receipt on the finished goods inventory and charge 15% annual interest on the outstanding loan balance. A 0.5% warehousing fee will be levied against the average amount borrowed. Because the loan will be liquidated as inventory is sold, the average loan balance is expected to be $60,000.

a. Calculate the dollar cost of each of the proposed plans for obtaining an initial loan amount of $100,000.
b. Which plan do you recommend? Why?
c. If the firm had made a purchase of $100,000 for which it had been given terms of 2/10 net 30, would it increase the firm's profitability to give up the discount and not borrow as recommended in part **b**? Why or why not?

P16–21 **ETHICS PROBLEM** Rancco Inc. reported total sales of $73 million last year, including $13 million in revenue (labor, sales to tax-exempt entities) exempt from sales tax. The company collects sales tax at a rate of 5%. In reviewing its information as part of its loan application, you notice that Rancco's sales tax payments show a total of $2 million in payments over the same time period. What are your conclusions regarding the financial statements that you are reviewing? How might you verify any discrepancies?

SPREADSHEET EXERCISE

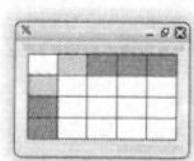

Your company is considering manufacturing protective cases for a popular new smartphone. Management decides to borrow $200,000 from each of two banks, First American and First Citizen. On the day that you visit both banks, the quoted prime interest rate is 7%. Each loan is similar in that each involves a 60-day note, with interest to be paid at the end of 60 days.

The interest rate was set at 2% above the prime rate on First American's fixed-rate note. Over the 60-day period, the rate of interest on this note will remain at the 2% premium over the prime rate regardless of fluctuations in the prime rate.

First Citizen sets its interest rate at 1.5% above the prime rate on its floating-rate note. The rate charged over the 60 days will vary directly with the prime rate.

TO DO

Create a spreadsheet to calculate and analyze the following for the First American loan:

a. Calculate the total dollar interest cost on the loan. Assume a 365-day year.
b. Calculate the 60-day rate on the loan.
c. Assume that the loan is rolled over each 60 days throughout the year under identical conditions and terms. Calculate the effective annual rate of interest on the fixed-rate, 60-day First American note.

Next, create a spreadsheet to calculate the following for the First Citizen loan:

d. Calculate the initial interest rate.
e. Assuming that the prime rate immediately jumps to 7.5% and after 30 days it drops to 7.25%, calculate the interest rate for the first 30 days and the second 30 days of the loan.
f. Calculate the total dollar interest cost.
g. Calculate the 60-day rate of interest.
h. Assume that the loan is rolled over each 60 days throughout the year under the same conditions and terms. Calculate the effective annual rate of interest.
i. Which loan would you choose, and why?

MyLab Finance Visit www.pearson.com/mylab/finance for **Chapter Case: *Selecting Kanton Company's Financing Strategy and Unsecured Short-Term Borrowing Arrangement,*** Group Exercises, and numerous online resources.

Integrative Case 7

Casa de Diseño

In January 2019, Teresa Leal was named treasurer of Casa de Diseño. She decided that she could best orient herself by systematically examining each area of the company's financial operations. She began by studying the firm's short-term financial activities.

Casa de Diseño, located in southern California, specializes in a furniture line called "Ligne Moderna." Of high quality and contemporary design, the furniture appeals to the customer who wants something unique for his or her home or apartment. Most Ligne Moderna furniture is built by special order because a wide variety of upholstery, accent trimming, and colors is available. The product line is distributed through exclusive dealership arrangements with well-established retail stores. Casa de Diseño's manufacturing process virtually eliminates the use of wood. Plastic and metal provide the basic framework, and wood is used only for decorative purposes.

Casa de Diseño entered the plastic-furniture market in late 2007. The company markets its plastic-furniture products as indoor–outdoor items under the brand name "Futuro." Futuro plastic furniture emphasizes comfort, durability, and practicality and is distributed through wholesalers. The Futuro line has been very successful, accounting for nearly 40% of the firm's sales and profits in 2018. Casa de Diseño anticipates some additions to the Futuro line and also some limited change of direction in its promotion, in an effort to expand the applications of the plastic furniture.

Leal has decided to study the firm's cash management practices. To assess the effects of these practices, she must first determine the current operating and cash conversion cycles. In her investigations, she found that Casa de Diseño purchases all its raw materials and production supplies on open account. The company is operating at production levels that preclude volume discounts. Most suppliers do not offer early payment discounts, and Casa de Diseño usually receives credit terms of net 30. An analysis of Casa de Diseño's accounts payable showed that its average payment period is 30 days. Leal consulted industry data and found that the industry average payment period was 39 days. Investigation of six California furniture manufacturers revealed that their average payment period was also 39 days.

Next, Leal studied the production cycle and inventory policies. Casa de Diseño tries not to hold any more inventory than necessary in either raw materials or finished goods. The average inventory age was 110 days. Leal determined that the industry standard, as reported in a survey done by *Furniture Age*, the trade association journal, was 83 days.

Casa de Diseño sells to all its customers on a net-60 basis, in line with the industry trend to grant such credit terms on specialty furniture. Leal discovered, by aging the accounts receivable, that the average collection period for the firm was 75 days. Investigation of the trade association's and California manufacturers' averages showed that the same collection period existed where net-60 credit terms were given. Where discounts were offered, the collection period was significantly shortened. Leal believed that if Casa de Diseño were to offer credit terms of 3/10 net 60, the average collection period could be reduced by 40%.

Casa de Diseño was spending an estimated $26,500,000 per year on operating-cycle investments. Leal considered this expenditure level to be the minimum she could expect the firm to disburse during 2019. Her concern was whether the firm's cash management was as efficient as it could be. She knew that the company paid 15% annual interest for its resource investment. For this reason, she was concerned about the financing cost resulting from any inefficiencies in the management of Casa de Diseño's cash conversion cycle. (*Note:* Assume a 365-day year, and assume that the operating-cycle investment per dollar of payables, inventory, and receivables is the same.)

TO DO

a. Assuming a constant rate for purchases, production, and sales throughout the year, what are Casa de Diseño's existing operating cycle (OC), cash conversion cycle (CCC), and resource investment requirement?

b. If Leal can optimize Casa de Diseño's operations according to industry standards, what will Casa de Diseño's operating cycle (OC), cash conversion cycle (CCC), and resource investment need to be under these more efficient conditions?

c. In terms of resource investment requirements, what is the cost of Casa de Diseño's operational inefficiency?

d. (1) If, in addition to achieving industry standards for payables and inventory, the firm can reduce the average collection period by offering credit terms of 3/10 net 60, what additional savings in resource investment costs will result from the shortened cash conversion cycle, assuming the level of sales remains constant?

(2) If the firm's sales (all on credit) are $40,000,000 and 45% of the customers are expected to take the discount, by how much will the firm's annual revenues be reduced as a result of the discount?

(3) If the firm's variable cost of the $40,000,000 in sales is 80%, determine the reduction in the average investment in accounts receivable and the annual savings that will result from this reduced investment, assuming that sales remain constant.

(4) If the firm's bad-debts expenses decline from 2% to 1.5% of sales, what annual savings will result, assuming that sales remain constant?

(5) Use your findings in parts (2) through (4) to assess whether offering the early payment discount can be justified financially. Explain why or why not.

e. On the basis of your analysis in parts **a** through **d**, what recommendations would you offer Teresa Leal?

f. Review for Teresa Leal the key sources of short-term financing, other than accounts payable, that she may consider for financing Casa de Diseño's resource investment need calculated in part **b**. Be sure to mention both unsecured and secured sources.

PART EIGHT

Special Topics in Managerial Finance

CHAPTERS IN THIS PART

It has become a cliché to say that business is becoming more complex and more global over time, but, like all clichés, the statement has a ring of truth. In this final part, we examine three special topics that are among the most challenging and exciting topics in finance.

Chapter 17 introduces hybrid and derivative securities. A hybrid is a security that has characteristics similar to other securities. For example, preferred stock is a hybrid because it has some debt-like and some equity-like features. Just as many bonds pay a fixed interest rate, preferred stock pays a fixed dividend. However, preferred stock is more like equity in that investors who hold preferred shares cannot force a firm into bankruptcy if it stops paying preferred dividends. A derivative is a security that derives its value from some other security. For example, a call option is a derivative because its value depends on the price of an underlying asset such as a share of common stock. Perhaps surprisingly, investors can use derivatives to either speculate on price changes in the stock market or protect themselves against such movements.

Chapter 18 focuses on mergers, leveraged buyouts, and bankruptcy. They are three of the biggest "events" that can happen in the life of a corporation, and certainly most large companies acquire other companies from time to time. Chapter 18 explains the techniques that firms use to execute various types of mergers and acquisitions and highlights the motivations behind those transactions. The chapter also discusses a significant event that firms generally want to avoid: business failure. We discuss the different types and causes of business failures as well as several mechanisms used to resolve these failures.

Chapter 19 emphasizes global dimensions of financial management, starting with an overview of trading blocs and other international institutions that have a significant impact on multinational businesses. The chapter offers in-depth coverage of the financial risks associated with doing business internationally, especially risks related to movements in exchange rates, and the techniques that firms use to manage those risks. Finally, Chapter 19 provides a glimpse into the wide range of options available to multinational firms for raising money in markets around the world.

CHAPTER

17

Hybrid and Derivative Securities

LEARNING GOALS

LG1 Differentiate between hybrid and derivative securities and their roles in the corporation.

LG2 Review the types of leases, leasing arrangements, the lease-versus-purchase decision, the effects of leasing on future financing, and the advantages and disadvantages of leasing.

LG3 Describe the types of convertible securities, their general features, and financing with convertibles.

LG4 Demonstrate the procedures for determining the straight bond value, the conversion (or stock) value, and the market value of a convertible bond.

LG5 Explain the key characteristics of stock purchase warrants, the implied price of an attached warrant, and the values of warrants.

LG6 Define options, and discuss calls and puts, options markets, options trading, the role of call and put options in fund raising, and hedging foreign-currency exposures with options.

MyLab Finance Chapter Introduction Video

WHY THIS CHAPTER MATTERS TO YOU

In your *professional* life

ACCOUNTING You need to understand the types of leasing arrangements and the general features of convertible securities, stock purchase warrants, and options, which you will be required to record and report.

INFORMATION SYSTEMS You need to understand types of leasing arrangements and the general features of convertible securities to design systems that will track data used to make lease-or-purchase and conversion decisions.

MANAGEMENT You need to understand when and why it may make better sense to lease assets rather than to purchase them. You need to understand how convertible securities and stock purchase warrants work to decide when the firm would benefit from their use. You also need to understand the impact of call and put options on the firm.

MARKETING You need to understand leasing as a way to finance a new project proposal. You also should understand how hybrid securities can be used to raise funds for new projects.

OPERATIONS You need to understand the role of leasing in financing new equipment. You also need to understand the maintenance obligations associated with leased equipment.

In your *personal* life

Understanding hybrid and derivative securities will benefit your investment activities. Even more useful is an understanding of leasing, which you may use to finance certain long-lived assets such as housing or cars. Knowing how to analyze and compare leasing to the alternative of purchasing should help you better manage your personal finances.

Sam Yeh/AFP/Getty Images

ADVANCED MICRO DEVICES

AMD Taps the Bond Market for Cash

For 50 years, two U.S. companies competed in the lucrative market for producing computer Central Processing Units (CPUs). The larger of the two firms, Intel, dominated the market for the brains of desktop and laptop computers, but Intel's smaller competitor, Advanced Micro Devices (AMD) carved out a niche as a less expensive provider of chips to PC manufacturers and makers of gaming systems.

In September 2016, AMD announced its intention to sell $700 million in 10-year bonds to investors. The bonds offered a coupon rate of 2.125% on a $1,000 par value. Of particular interest to investors, however, was the provision that investors could convert one AMD bond into 125 shares of AMD common stock. Naturally, investors would be willing to exchange their bonds for stock only if the value of the stock they received was greater than the value of the bonds. In other words, the convertible bond structure allowed investors to benefit if AMD's stock price increased. Because of that potential benefit, investors were willing to accept a lower interest rate on AMD's bonds than they otherwise would have demanded. AMD said it would use the proceeds from the bond sale to retire some of its existing debt, on which the company was paying much higher interest rates.

Convertible bonds are one example of a hybrid security. Convertibles have some features similar to ordinary bonds, such as a fixed principal amount, periodic interest payments, and a specific maturity date. Convertibles also behave a little like stock, however, because investors who hold convertible bonds can earn higher returns than ordinary bonds provide if the issuing company's common stock rises. In this chapter, you'll learn about convertibles and other hybrid securities used in corporate finance.

Source: News Release,Advanced Micro Devices, http://ir.amd.com/phoenix.zhtml?c=74093&p=irol-newsArticle&ID=2200801.

LG1

17.1 Overview of Hybrids and Derivatives

Chapters 6 and 7 described the characteristics of the key securities—corporate bonds, common stock, and preferred stock—used by corporations to raise long-term funds. In their simplest form, bonds are pure debt, and common stock is pure equity. Preferred stock, on the other hand, is a form of equity that promises to pay fixed periodic dividends that are similar to the fixed contractual interest payments on bonds. Because it blends the characteristics of both debt (a fixed dividend payment) and equity (ownership), preferred stock is considered a **hybrid security**. Other popular hybrid securities include financial leases, convertible securities, and stock purchase warrants. Each of these hybrid securities is described in the sections that follow.

hybrid security
A security that possesses characteristics of both debt and equity financing.

The final section of this chapter focuses on a type of **derivative security** known as *options*. Derivatives are securities that are neither debt nor equity but derive their value from an underlying asset that is often another security, such as a share of common stock. As you'll learn, derivatives are not used by corporations to raise funds but rather serve as a useful tool for managing certain aspects of the firm's risk.

derivative security
A security that is neither debt nor equity but derives its value from an underlying asset that is often another security.

→ **REVIEW QUESTION** MyLab Finance Solutions

17–1 Differentiate between a hybrid security and a derivative security.

LG2

17.2 Leasing

Leasing enables the firm to obtain the use of certain fixed assets for which it must make a series of contractual, periodic, tax-deductible payments. The **lessee** is the receiver of the services of the assets under the lease contract, and the **lessor** is the owner of the assets. Leasing can take a number of forms.

leasing
The process by which a firm can obtain the use of certain fixed assets for which it must make a series of contractual, periodic, tax-deductible payments.

lessee
The receiver of the services of the assets under a lease contract.

lessor
The owner of assets that are being leased.

TYPES OF LEASES

The two basic types of leases available to a business are *operating leases* and *financial leases* (often called *capital leases* by accountants).

Operating Leases

An **operating lease** is normally a contractual arrangement whereby the lessee agrees to make periodic payments to the lessor, often for 5 or fewer years, to obtain an asset's services. Such leases are generally *cancelable* at the option of the lessee, who may be required to pay a penalty for cancellation. Assets that are leased under operating leases have a usable life that is longer than the term of the lease. Usually, however, they would become less efficient and technologically obsolete if leased for a longer period. Computer systems are prime examples of assets whose relative efficiency is expected to diminish as the technology changes. The operating lease is therefore a common arrangement for obtaining such systems, as well as for other relatively short-lived assets such as automobiles.

operating lease
A cancelable contractual arrangement whereby the lessee agrees to make periodic payments to the lessor, often for 5 or fewer years, to obtain an asset's services; generally, the total payments over the term of the lease are less than the lessor's initial cost of the leased asset.

If an operating lease is held to maturity, the lessee at that time returns the leased asset to the lessor, who may lease it again or sell the asset. Normally, the asset still has a positive market value at the termination of the lease. In some instances, the lease contract gives the lessee the opportunity to purchase the leased asset. Generally, the total payments made by the lessee to the lessor are less than the lessor's initial cost of the leased asset.

Financial (or Capital) Leases

financial (or capital) lease
A longer-term lease than an operating lease that is noncancelable and obligates the lessee to make payments for the use of an asset over a predefined period of time; the total payments over the term of the lease are greater than the lessor's initial cost of the leased asset.

A **financial (or capital) lease** is a longer-term lease than an operating lease. Financial leases are *noncancelable* and obligate the lessee to make payments for the use of an asset over a predefined period. Businesses commonly enter into financial leases when they need land, buildings, and large pieces of equipment. The noncancelable feature of the financial lease makes it similar to certain types of long-term debt. When a firm leases an asset under a capital lease, the asset appears on the firm's balance sheet and is depreciated over time, almost as if the firm actually owned the asset. As with debt, failure to make the contractual lease payments can result in bankruptcy for the lessee.

With a financial lease, the total payments over the term of the lease are greater than the lessor's initial cost of the leased asset. In other words, the lessor must receive more than the asset's purchase price to earn its required return on the investment. Technically, under *FASB* (Financial Accounting Standards Board) *Statement No. 13*, "Accounting for Leases," a financial (or capital) lease is defined as one that has *any* of the following elements:[1]

1. The lease transfers ownership of the property to the lessee by the end of the lease term.
2. The lease contains an option to purchase the property at a "bargain price."
3. The lease term is equal to 75% or more of the estimated economic life of the property (exceptions exist for property leased toward the end of its usable economic life).
4. At the beginning of the lease, the present value of the lease payments is equal to 90% or more of the fair market value of the leased property.

This chapter emphasizes financial leases, because they result in inescapable long-term financial commitments by the firm.

The *Focus on Practice* box discusses leasing by Seritage Growth Properties that did not have a happy ending.

LEASING ARRANGEMENTS

direct lease
A lease under which a lessor owns or acquires the assets that are leased to a given lessee.

sale-leaseback arrangement
A lease under which the lessee sells an asset to a prospective lessor and then leases back the same asset, making fixed periodic payments for its use.

Lessors use three primary techniques for obtaining assets to be leased. The method depends largely on the desires of the prospective lessee.

1. A **direct lease** results when a lessor owns or acquires the assets that are leased to a given lessee. In other words, the lessee did not previously own the assets that it is leasing.
2. In a **sale-leaseback arrangement**, lessors acquire leased assets by purchasing assets already owned by the lessee and leasing them back. This technique is

1. In early 2016, FASB published new standards for lease accounting under *Accounting Standards Update (ASU) 842*. The new rules do not go into effect until 2019, so we cover the rules prevailing prior to that year in this chapter.

FOCUS ON PRACTICE *in practice*

I'd Like to Return This (Entire Store), Please

Once upon a time, Sears was the undisputed king of American retailers, but in 2017 the company's proud history seemed to be approaching its end. In its 10-K filing that year, Sears acknowledged that "our historical operating results indicate substantial doubt exists related to the Company's ability to continue as a going concern."* From 2010 to 2017, the number of Sears retail locations shrank from roughly 3,500 to barely 600, and in 2017 the company lost more than $2 billion.

Amidst the free fall in Sears' performance, the company decided to enter into a sale-leaseback transaction in 2014 with Seritage Growth Properties, a real estate investment trust (REIT) created specifically to purchase Sears physical stores and lease them back to the company. Under the agreement that governed the sale-leaseback deal, Seritage retained the right to close some Sears locations, redevelop them, and lease them to other tenants. The deal appealed to Sears because it provided the company with a much-needed cash infusion of $2.7 billion. For Seritage, the agreement offered a stream of rental revenues, either from Sears or from other retailers who might occupy the spaces that Sears vacated. The terms of the arrangement were so favorable to Seritage that legendary investor Warren Buffett announced that he had purchased an 8% stake in Seritage in December 2015. News of Buffett's investment boosted Seritage's stock price by almost 17% in a single day, and the REIT's shares rose another 38% over the subsequent 4 months. In early 2016, it seemed that Warren Buffett had once again made a savvy investment.

However, the cash infusion that Sears received from Seritage proved insufficient to revive the company. Sears closed another 20 stores in June 2017, and the company's Canadian arm filed for bankruptcy that same month. Unfortunately for Seritage, Sears' woes came during a major downturn for brick-and-mortar retailers facing intense competition from Amazon and other online retailers. More than 300 retailers went under in the first half of 2017, making it more difficult for Seritage to lease the spaces that Sears left behind. As Sears' fortunes turned darker, Seritage's stock price fell, losing 24% of its value in just over a year.

► *Describe the ways in which the transaction between Seritage and Sears is similar to Seritage's buying long-term bonds from Sears.*

*"Lauren Gensler, Sears Admits It Has 'Substantial Doubt' About Its Ability To Survive"

leveraged lease
A lease under which the lessor acts as an equity participant, supplying only about 20% of the cost of the asset, while a lender supplies the balance.

maintenance clauses
Provisions normally included in an operating lease that require the lessor to maintain the assets and to make insurance and tax payments.

renewal options
Provisions especially common in operating leases that grant the lessee the right to re-lease assets at the expiration of the lease.

purchase options
Provisions frequently included in both operating and financial leases that allow the lessee to purchase the leased asset at maturity, typically for a prespecified price.

normally initiated by a firm that needs funds for operations. By selling an existing asset to a lessor and then *leasing it back*, the lessee receives cash for the asset immediately while obligating itself to make fixed periodic payments for use of the leased asset.

3. Leasing arrangements that include one or more third-party lenders are **leveraged leases.** Under a leveraged lease, the lessor acts as an equity participant, supplying only about 20% of the cost of the asset, and a lender supplies the balance. Leveraged leases are especially popular in structuring leases of very expensive assets.

A lease agreement typically specifies whether the lessee is responsible for maintenance of the leased assets. Operating leases may include **maintenance clauses** requiring the lessor to maintain the assets and to make insurance and tax payments. Financial leases nearly always require the lessee to pay maintenance and other costs.

The lessee is usually given the option to renew a lease at its expiration. **Renewal options,** which grant lessees the right to re-lease assets at expiration, are especially common in operating leases because their term is generally shorter than the usable life of the leased assets. **Purchase options,** allowing the lessee to purchase the leased asset at maturity, typically for a prespecified price, are frequently included in both operating and financial leases.

The lessor can be one of a number of parties. In operating leases, the lessor is likely to be the manufacturer's leasing subsidiary or an independent leasing company. Financial leases are frequently handled by independent leasing companies or by the leasing subsidiaries of large financial institutions such as commercial banks and life insurance companies. Life insurance companies are especially active in real estate leasing. Pension funds, like commercial banks, have also been increasing their leasing activities.

LEASE-VERSUS-PURCHASE DECISION

lease-versus-purchase (or lease-versus-buy) decision
The decision facing firms needing to acquire new fixed assets: whether to lease the assets or to purchase them, using borrowed funds or available liquid resources.

Firms that are contemplating the acquisition of new fixed assets commonly confront the **lease-versus-purchase (or lease-versus-buy) decision.** The alternatives available are (1) lease the assets, (2) borrow funds to purchase the assets, or (3) purchase the assets using available liquid resources. Alternatives 2 and 3, although they differ, are analyzed in a similar fashion; even if the firm has the liquid resources with which to purchase the assets, the use of these funds is viewed as equivalent to borrowing. Therefore, we need to compare only the leasing and purchasing alternatives.

The lease-versus-purchase decision involves application of the capital budgeting methods presented in Chapters 10 through 12. First, we determine the relevant cash flows and then we apply present value techniques. The following steps are involved in the analysis:

Step 1 Find the *after-tax cash outflows for each year under the lease alternative.* This step generally involves a fairly simple tax adjustment of the annual lease payments. In addition, the cost of exercising a purchase option in the final year of the lease term must frequently be included.[2]

Step 2 Find the *after-tax cash outflows for each year under the purchase alternative.* This step involves adjusting the sum of the scheduled loan payment and maintenance cost outlay for the tax shields resulting from the tax deductions attributable to maintenance, depreciation, and interest.

Step 3 Calculate the *present value of the cash outflows* associated with the lease (from Step 1) and purchase (from Step 2) alternatives using the *after-tax cost of debt* as the discount rate. The after-tax cost of debt is used to evaluate the lease-versus-purchase decision because the decision itself involves the choice between two *financing* techniques—leasing and borrowing—that have very low risk.

Step 4 Choose the alternative with the *lower present value* of cash outflows from Step 3. It will be the *least-cost* financing alternative.

The application of each of these steps is demonstrated in the following example.

EXAMPLE 17.1

Roberts Company, a small machine shop, is contemplating acquiring a new machine that costs $24,000. Arrangements can be made to lease or purchase the machine. The firm is in the 40% tax bracket.

2. Including the cost of exercising a purchase option in the cash flows for the lease alternative ensures that under both lease and purchase alternatives the firm owns the asset at the end of the relevant time horizon. The other approach would be to include the cash flows from sale of the asset in the cash flows for the purchase alternative at the end of the lease term. These strategies guarantee avoidance of unequal lives, which were discussed in Chapter 12. In addition, they make any subsequent cash flows irrelevant because these would be either identical or nonexistent, respectively, under each alternative.

Lease The firm would obtain a 5-year lease requiring annual end-of-year lease payments of \$6,000. All maintenance costs would be paid by the lessor, and insurance and other costs would be borne by the lessee. The lessee would exercise its option to purchase the machine for \$1,200 at termination of the lease.[3]

Purchase The firm would finance the purchase of the machine with a 9%, 5-year loan requiring end-of-year installment payments of \$6,170.[4] The machine would be depreciated under MACRS using a 5-year recovery period. The firm would pay \$1,500 per year for a service contract that covers all maintenance costs; insurance and other costs would be borne by the firm. The firm plans to keep the machine and use it beyond its 5-year recovery period.

Using these data, we can apply the steps presented earlier:

Step 1 The after-tax cash outflow from the lease payments can be found by multiplying the before-tax payment of \$6,000 by 1 minus the tax rate, T, of 40%.

$$\begin{aligned}\text{After-tax cash outflow from lease} &= \$6{,}000 \times (1 - T)\\ &= \$6{,}000 \times (1 - 0.40) = \$3{,}600\end{aligned}$$

Therefore, the lease alternative results in annual cash outflows over the 5-year lease of \$3,600. In the final year, the \$1,200 cost of the purchase option would be added to the \$3,600 lease outflow to get a total cash outflow in year 5 of \$4,800 (\$3,600 + \$1,200).

Step 2 The after-tax cash outflow from the purchase alternative is a bit more difficult to find. First, the interest component of each annual loan payment must be determined because the Internal Revenue Service allows the deduction of interest only—not principal—from income for tax purposes.[5] Table 17.1 presents the calculations necessary to split the loan payments into their interest and principal components. Columns 3 and 4 show the annual interest and principal paid. Column 5 subtracts the principal payment made each year from the beginning-of-year principal balance to determine how much principal is owed at the end of each year.

---

3. Lease payments are generally made at the beginning of the year. To simplify the following discussions, we assume end-of-year lease payments. We are assuming that the machine's market value and book value are both \$1,200 at the end of 5 years.

4. The annual loan payment on the 9%, 5-year loan of \$24,000 is calculated by using the loan amortization technique described in Chapter 5. To calculate the loan payment in Excel, you would use the "pmt" function, entering into any blank cell, = pmt(0.09,5,24000,0,0). In the terms inside the parentheses, 0.09 is the interest rate, 5 is the term of the lease in years, and 24,000 is the amount being borrowed (or, equivalently, the cost of the new machine). The final two zeros inside the parentheses tell Excel that after 5 years the loan is totally paid off (zero remaining balance) and that payments are made at the end of each year. The exact loan payment is \$6,170.22, but in the example we round down to the nearest dollar.

5. When the rate of interest on the loan used to finance the purchase just equals the cost of debt, the present value of the after-tax loan payments (annual loan payments − interest tax shields) discounted at the after-tax cost of debt just equals the initial loan principal. In such a case, it is unnecessary to amortize the loan to determine the payment amount and the amounts of interest when finding after-tax cash outflows. The loan payments and interest payments (columns 1 and 4 in Table 17.2) can be ignored, and, in their place, the initial loan principal (\$24,000) is shown as an outflow occurring at time zero. To allow for a loan interest rate that is different from the firm's cost of debt and for easier understanding, here we isolate the loan payments and interest payments rather than use this computationally more efficient approach.

TABLE 17.1 Determining the Interest and Principal Components of the Roberts Company Loan Payments

End of year	Loan payments (1)	Beginning-of-year principal (2)	Payments: Interest [0.09 × (2)] (3)	Payments: Principal [(1) − (3)] (4)	End-of-year principal [(2) − (4)] (5)
1	$6,170	$24,000	$2,160	$4,010	$19,990
2	6,170	19,990	1,799	4,371	15,619
3	6,170	15,619	1,406	4,764	10,855
4	6,170	10,855	977	5,193	5,662
5	6,170	5,662	510	5,660	—[a]

[a]The values in this table have been rounded to the nearest dollar, which results in a slight difference ($2) between the beginning-of-year-5 principal (in column 2) and the year-5 principal payment (in column 4).

In Table 17.2, the annual loan payment is shown in column 1, and the annual maintenance cost, which is a tax-deductible expense, is shown in column 2. Next, we find the annual depreciation write-off resulting from the $24,000 machine. Using the applicable MACRS 5-year recovery period depreciation percentages—20% in year 1, 32% in year 2, 19% in year 3, and 12% in years 4 and 5—given in Table 4.2 results in the annual depreciation for years 1 through 5 given in column 3 of Table 17.2.[6]

Table 17.2 presents the calculations required to determine the cash outflows[7] associated with borrowing to purchase the new machine. Column 7 of the table presents the after-tax cash outflows associated with the purchase alternative. A few points should be clarified with respect to the calculations in Table 17.2. The

TABLE 17.2 After-Tax Cash Outflows Associated with Purchasing for Roberts Company

End of year	Loan payments (1)	Maintenance costs (2)	Depreciation (3)	Interest[a] (4)	Total deductions [(2) + (3) + (4)] (5)	Tax shields [(0.40 × (5)] (6)	After-tax cash outflows [(1) + (2) − (6)] (7)
1	$6,170	$1,500	$4,800	$2,160	$ 8,460	$3,384	$4,286
2	6,170	1,500	7,680	1,799	10,979	4,392	3,278
3	6,170	1,500	4,560	1,406	7,466	2,986	4,684
4	6,170	1,500	2,880	977	5,357	2,143	5,527
5	6,170	1,500	2,880	510	4,890	1,956	5,714

[a]From Table 17.1, column 3.

6. We are ignoring depreciation in year 6 because regardless of which option the company selects there will be $1,200 worth of depreciation remaining.

7. Although other cash outflows such as insurance and operating expenses may be relevant here, they would be the same under the lease and purchase alternatives and therefore would cancel out in the final analysis.

TABLE 17.3 Comparison of Cash Outflows Associated with Leasing versus Purchasing for Roberts Company

	Leasing		Purchasing	
	After-tax cash outflows	Present value of outflows	After-tax cash outflows[a]	Present value of outflows
End of year	(1)	(2)	(3)	(4)
1	$3,600	$ 3,396	$4,286	$ 4,043
2	3,600	3,204	3,278	2,917
3	3,600	3,023	4,684	3,933
4	3,600	2,852	5,527	4,378
5	4,800[b]	3,587	5,714	4,270
	PV of cash outflows	$16,062	PV of cash outflows	$19,541

[a]From column 7 of Table 17.2.
[b]After-tax lease payment outflow of $3,600 plus the $1,200 cost of exercising the purchase option.

major cash outflows are the total loan payment for each year given in column 1 and the annual maintenance cost in column 2. The sum of these two outflows is reduced by the tax savings from writing off the maintenance, depreciation, and interest expenses associated with the new machine and its financing. The resulting cash outflows are the after-tax cash outflows associated with the purchase alternative.

Step 3 The present values of the cash outflows associated with the lease (from Step 1) and purchase (from Step 2) alternatives are calculated in Table 17.3 using the firm's 6% after-tax cost of debt.[8] The table also shows the sum of the present values of the cash outflows for the leasing alternative and the sum of those for the purchasing alternative.

Step 4 Because the present value of cash outflows for leasing ($16,062) is lower than that for purchasing ($19,541), the leasing alternative is preferred. Leasing results in an incremental savings of $3,479 ($19,541 − $16,062) and is therefore the less costly alternative.

The techniques described here for comparing lease and purchase alternatives may be applied in different ways. The approach illustrated by the Roberts Company data is one of the most straightforward. It is important to recognize that the lower cost of one alternative over the other results from factors such as the differing tax brackets of the lessor and lessee, different tax treatments of leases versus purchases, and differing risks and borrowing costs for lessor and lessee. Therefore, when making a lease-versus-purchase decision, the firm will find that inexpensive borrowing opportunities, high required lessor returns, and

8. If we ignore any flotation costs, the firm's after-tax cost of debt would be 5.4% [9% debt cost × (1 − 0.40 tax rate)]. To reflect both the flotation costs associated with selling new debt and the possible need to sell the debt at a discount, we use an after-tax debt cost of 6% as the applicable discount rate. A more detailed discussion of techniques for calculating the after-tax cost of debt is found in Chapter 9.

a low risk of obsolescence increase the attractiveness of purchasing. Subjective factors must also be included in the decision-making process. Like most financial decisions, the lease-versus-purchase decision requires some judgment or intuition.

PERSONAL FINANCE EXAMPLE 17.2 Jake Jiminez is considering either leasing or purchasing a new Honda Fit that will cost $15,000. The 3-year lease requires an initial payment of $1,800 and monthly payments of $300. Purchasing requires a $2,500 down payment, sales tax of 5% ($750), and 36 monthly payments of $392. He estimates the trade-in value of the new car will be $8,000 at the end of 3 years. Assuming that Jake can earn 4% annual interest on his savings and is subject to a 5% sales tax on purchases, we can make a reasonable recommendation to Jake using the following analysis (for simplicity, ignoring the time value of money).

Lease cost	
Down payment	$ 1,800
Total lease payments (36 months × $300/month)	10,800
Opportunity cost of initial payment (3 years × 0.04 × $1,800)	216
Total cost of leasing	$12,816

Purchase cost	
Down payment	$ 2,500
Sales tax (0.05 × $15,000)	750
Total loan payments (36 months × $392/month)	14,112
Opportunity cost of down payment (3 years × 0.04 × $2,500)	300
Less: Estimated trade-in value of car at end of loan	– 8,000
Total cost of purchasing	$ 9,662

Because the total cost of leasing of $12,816 is greater than the $9,662 total cost of purchasing, Jake should purchase rather than lease the car.

EFFECTS OF LEASING ON FUTURE FINANCING

Because leasing is considered a type of financing, it affects the firm's future financing, just as carrying existing debt has an impact on a firm's ability to borrow even more. Lease payments are shown as a tax-deductible expense on the firm's income statement. Anyone analyzing the firm's income statement would probably recognize that an asset is being leased, although the amount and term of the lease would be unclear.

capitalized lease
A financial (capital) lease that has the present value of all its payments included as an asset and corresponding liability on the firm's balance sheet, as required by the Financial Accounting Standards Board (FASB) in *FASB Statement No. 13.*

The Financial Accounting Standards Board (FASB), in *FASB Statement No. 13,* "Accounting for Leases," requires explicit disclosure of financial (capital) lease obligations on the firm's balance sheet. Such a lease must be shown as a **capitalized lease,** meaning that the present value of all its payments is included as an asset and corresponding liability on the firm's balance sheet. An operating lease, on the other hand, need not be capitalized, but its basic features must be disclosed in a footnote to the financial statements. *FASB Statement No. 13*, of course, establishes detailed guidelines to be used in capitalizing leases. Subsequent standards have further refined lease capitalization and disclosure procedures.

EXAMPLE 17.3

Jeffrey Company, a manufacturer of water purifiers, is leasing an asset under a 10-year lease requiring annual end-of-year payments of $15,000. The lease can be capitalized merely by calculating the present value of the lease payments over the life of the lease. However, the rate at which the payments should be discounted is difficult to determine.[9] If 10% were used, the present, or capitalized, value of the lease would be $92,169. This value would be shown as an asset and corresponding liability on the firm's balance sheet, which should result in an accurate reflection of the firm's true financial position.

Because the consequences of missing a financial lease payment are the same as those of missing an interest or principal payment on debt, a financial analyst must view the lease as a long-term financial commitment of the lessee. With *FASB Statement No. 13*, the inclusion of each financial (capital) lease as an asset and corresponding liability (i.e., long-term debt) provides for a balance sheet that more accurately reflects the firm's financial status. It thereby permits various types of financial ratio analyses to be performed directly on the statement by any interested party.

ADVANTAGES AND DISADVANTAGES OF LEASING

Leasing has a number of commonly cited advantages and disadvantages that managers should consider when making a lease-versus-purchase decision. It is not unusual for a number of them to apply in a given situation. Table 17.4 describes the commonly cited advantages and disadvantages of leasing.

→ REVIEW QUESTIONS MyLab Finance Solutions

17–2 What is leasing? Define, compare, and contrast operating leases and financial (or capital) leases. How does the Financial Accounting Standards Board's *Statement No. 13* define a financial (or capital) lease? Describe three methods used by lessors to acquire assets to be leased.

17–3 Describe the four basic steps involved in the lease-versus-purchase decision process. How are capital budgeting methods applied in this process?

17–4 What type of lease must be treated as a capitalized lease on the balance sheet? How does the financial manager capitalize a lease?

17–5 List and discuss the commonly cited advantages and disadvantages that should be considered when deciding whether to lease or purchase.

9. The Financial Accounting Standards Board in *Statement No. 13* established certain guidelines for the appropriate discount rate to use when capitalizing leases. Most commonly, the rate that the lessee would have incurred to borrow the funds to buy the asset with a secured loan under terms similar to the lease repayment schedule is used. It simply represents the *before-tax cost of a secured debt*.

TABLE 17.4 Advantages and Disadvantages of Leasing

Advantages

- The firm may *avoid the cost of obsolescence.* This advantage is especially true in the case of operating leases, which generally have relatively short lives.
- A lessee *avoids many of the restrictive covenants* (such as minimum liquidity, subsequent borrowing, and cash dividend payments) that are normally included as part of a long-term loan but are *not* normally found in a lease agreement.
- In the case of low-cost assets that are infrequently acquired, leasing—especially operating leases—may provide the firm with needed *financing flexibility.* The firm does not have to arrange other financing for these assets.
- Sale-leaseback arrangements may permit the firm to *increase its liquidity* by converting an *existing* asset into cash. This conversion can benefit a firm that is short of working capital or in a liquidity bind.
- Leasing allows the lessee, in effect, to *depreciate land,* which would be prohibited if the land were purchased. Because the lessee who leases land is permitted to deduct the *total lease payment* as an expense for tax purposes, the effect is the same as if the firm had purchased the land and then depreciated it.
- Because leasing may not increase the assets or liabilities on the firm's balance sheet, leasing may result in misleading *financial ratios.* Understating assets and liabilities can cause certain ratios, such as the total asset turnover, to look better than they might be. With the adoption of *FASB Statement No. 13,* this advantage no longer applies to financial leases, although it remains a potential advantage for operating leases.
- Leasing provides *100% financing.* Most loan agreements for the purchase of fixed assets require a down payment; thus the borrower is able to borrow only 90% to 95% of the purchase price of the asset.
- In the case of *bankruptcy* or *reorganization,* the maximum claim of lessors against the corporation is 3 years of lease payments. If debt is used to purchase an asset, the creditors have a claim that is equal to the total outstanding loan balance.

Disadvantages

- In many leases, the *return to the lessor is quite high;* the firm might be better off borrowing to purchase the asset.
- The *terminal value* of an asset, if any, is realized by the lessor. If the lessee had purchased the asset, it could have claimed its terminal value. Of course, an expected terminal value, when recognized by the lessor, results in lower lease payments.
- The lessee is generally *prohibited from making improvements* on the leased property or asset without the lessor's approval. However, lessors generally encourage leasehold improvements when these are expected to enhance the asset's salvage value.
- If a lessee leases an *asset that subsequently becomes obsolete,* it still must make lease payments over the remaining term of the lease. This condition is true even if the asset is unusable.

LG3 LG4

17.3 Convertible Securities

conversion feature
An option that is included as part of a bond or a preferred stock issue and allows its holder to change the security into a stated number of shares of common stock.

A **conversion feature** is an option that is included as part of a bond or a preferred stock issue and allows its holder to change the security into a stated number of shares of common stock. The conversion feature typically enhances the marketability of an issue.

TYPES OF CONVERTIBLE SECURITIES

Corporate bonds and preferred stocks may be convertible into common stock. The most common type of convertible security is the bond. Convertibles normally have an accompanying *call feature,* which permits the issuer to retire or encourage conversion of outstanding convertibles when appropriate.

Convertible Bonds

convertible bond
A bond that can be changed into a specified number of shares of common stock.

A **convertible bond** can be changed into a specified number of shares of common stock. Firms nearly always issue convertible bonds as *debentures*—unsecured bonds—with a call feature. From the bondholder's perspective, convertibles offer more upside potential than ordinary bonds. That's because if the bond issuer's stock performs very well, bondholders can convert their bonds into shares and earn capital gains on the issuer's stock. Because the conversion feature offers the prospect of higher returns, firms usually pay lower interest rates on convertible bonds than on similar-risk nonconvertible or **straight bonds.** The conversion feature adds a degree of speculation to a bond issue, although the issue still maintains its value as a bond. Usually, the right to convert bonds into shares rests with the bondholder, which is to say that the bondholder may choose to receive the cash flows that the bond provides or forgo those cash flows by exchanging the bond for stock. In some cases, however, firms issue *mandatory convertible bonds*, which specify that the bonds must convert from bonds to shares at a specified date.

straight bond
A bond that is nonconvertible, having no conversion feature.

Convertible Preferred Stock

Convertible preferred stock is preferred stock that can be changed into a specified number of shares of common stock. Like convertible bonds, convertible preferred stock offers the potential for higher returns than would be offered by nonconvertible or **straight preferred stock**, and therefore convertible preferred shares usually pay lower dividends. Convertible preferred stock behaves much like convertible bonds. The following discussions will concentrate on the more widespread convertible bonds.

convertible preferred stock
Preferred stock that can be changed into a specified number of shares of common stock.

straight preferred stock
Preferred stock that is nonconvertible, having no conversion feature.

MATTER OF FACT

Convertible Bonds Dominate the Convertible Securities Market

Although convertible bonds and convertible preferred stocks both offer investors the opportunity to earn a fixed interest (or dividend) payment with additional upside potential if the underlying stock performs well, convertible bonds are far more common than convertible preferreds. As of December 2016, the total market value of all outstanding convertible securities in the United States was $207.5 billion, with convertible bonds accounting for 74% of that total. Mandatory convertible bonds make up 17% of the market, leaving just 9% of the market for convertible preferred stock.

GENERAL FEATURES OF CONVERTIBLES

Convertible securities are nearly always convertible at any time during the life of the security. Occasionally, conversion is permitted only for a limited number of years, such as for 5 or 10 years after issuance of the convertible.

Conversion Ratio

The **conversion ratio** is the ratio at which investors can exchange a convertible security for common stock. The conversion ratio can be stated in two ways:

1. Sometimes the conversion ratio is stated in terms of a given number of shares of common stock. To find the **conversion price,** which is the per-share price that is effectively paid for common stock as the result of conversion, divide the par value (not the market value) of the convertible security by the conversion ratio.

conversion ratio
The ratio at which a convertible security can be exchanged for common stock.

conversion price
The per-share price that is effectively paid for common stock as the result of conversion of a convertible security.

EXAMPLE 17.4

MyLab Finance Solution Video

In 2017, the global semiconductor firm STMicroelectronics issued 7-year convertible bonds with a par value of $1,000 that was convertible into 49 shares of the company's common stock. Thus, the conversion ratio for these bonds was 49, and the conversion price was about $20.41 ($1,000 ÷ 49).

2. Sometimes, instead of the conversion ratio, the conversion price is given. The conversion ratio can be obtained by dividing the par value of the convertible by the conversion price.

EXAMPLE 17.5

In the spring of 2017, Tesla Motors announced that it would issue 5-year convertible bonds that carried a conversion price of $359.87. Given a $1,000 par value, that conversion price translated into a conversion rate of 2.7788 shares ($1,000 ÷ $359.87). In other words, each bond could be converted into just under 3 shares of Tesla stock. At the time of the bond issue, Tesla's stock was trading for about $252 per share, so purchasers of the Tesla's convertible bonds would not choose to convert their bonds into shares unless Tesla's stock price increased dramatically.

The issuer of a convertible security normally establishes a conversion ratio or conversion price that *sets the conversion price per share at the time of issuance above the current market price of the firm's stock.* If the prospective purchasers do not expect conversion ever to be feasible, they will purchase a straight security or some other convertible issue.

conversion (or stock) value
The value of a convertible security measured in terms of the market price of the common stock into which it can be converted.

Conversion (or Stock) Value

The **conversion (or stock) value** is the value of the convertible measured in terms of the market price of the common stock into which it can be converted. We can find the conversion value simply by multiplying the conversion ratio by the current market price of the firm's common stock.

EXAMPLE 17.6

McNamara Industries, a petroleum processor, has a $1,000 bond outstanding that is convertible into common stock at $62.50 per share. The conversion ratio is therefore 16 ($1,000 ÷ $62.50). Because the current market price of the common stock is $65 per share, the conversion value is $1,040 (16 × $65). Because the conversion value is above the bond value of $1,000, conversion is a viable option for the owner of the convertible security.

contingent securities
Convertibles, warrants, and stock options. Their presence affects the reporting of a firm's earnings per share (EPS).

basic EPS
Earnings per share (EPS) calculated without regard to any contingent securities.

Effect on Earnings per Share

The presence of **contingent securities,** which include convertibles as well as warrants and stock options (described later in this chapter), affects the reporting of the firm's earnings per share (EPS). Firms with contingent securities, which, if converted or exercised would dilute (i.e., lower) earnings per share, are required to report earnings in two ways—*basic EPS* and *diluted EPS.*

Accountants calculate **basic EPS** without regard to any contingent securities that might be converted into common shares in the future. Basic EPS equals earnings available for common stockholders divided by the number of shares of common stock outstanding. We use this standard method of calculating EPS throughout this book.

diluted EPS
Earnings per share (EPS) calculated under the assumption that all contingent securities that would have dilutive effects are converted and exercised and are therefore common stock.

Accountants calculate **diluted EPS** under the assumption that *all* contingent securities that might be converted into stock will be converted. In other words, diluted EPS takes into account the maximum number of common shares that would result if all of a firm's convertible securities are converted into shares. Diluted EPS equals earnings available for common stockholders divided by the number of common shares that would be outstanding after investors have swapped out all of the firm's convertible securities for common stock. Suffice it to say that firms with outstanding convertibles, warrants, and/or stock options must report basic and diluted EPS on their income statements.

FINANCING WITH CONVERTIBLES

Using convertible securities to raise long-term funds can help the firm achieve its cost-of-capital and capital structure goals. There also are a number of more specific motives and considerations involved in evaluating convertible financing.

Motives for Convertible Financing

Firms issue convertibles for a variety of reasons. Managers often view issuing convertible securities as a form of *deferred common stock financing.* When a firm issues a convertible bond, both the firm and the bondholders expect the security to be converted into common stock at some future point. Because the firm initially sells the bond with a conversion price above the current market price of the firm's stock, immediate conversion is not attractive. The issuer of a convertible could alternatively sell common stock, but only at or below its current market price. By selling the convertible, the issuer in effect makes a *deferred sale* of common stock. As the market price of the firm's common stock rises to a higher level, conversion may occur. Deferring the issuance of new common stock until the market price of the stock has increased means that fewer shares will have to be issued, thereby decreasing the dilution of both ownership and earnings.

Another motive for convertible financing is its *use as a "sweetener" for financing.* Because the purchaser of the convertible is given the opportunity to become a common stockholder and share in the firm's future success, convertibles normally pay lower interest rates than nonconvertibles. Therefore, from the firm's viewpoint, including a conversion feature reduces the interest cost of debt. The purchaser of the issue sacrifices a portion of interest return for the potential opportunity to become a common stockholder. Another important motive for issuing convertibles is that, generally speaking, convertible securities can be issued with far fewer restrictive covenants than nonconvertibles. Because many investors view convertibles as equity, the covenant issue is not as important to them.

A final motive for using convertibles is to *raise cheap funds temporarily.* By using convertible bonds, the firm can temporarily raise debt, which is typically less expensive than common stock, to finance projects. Once such projects are under way, the firm may wish to shift its capital structure to a less highly leveraged position. A conversion feature gives the issuer the opportunity, through actions of convertible holders, to shift its capital structure at a future time.

Other Considerations

When the price of the firm's common stock rises above the conversion price, the market price of the convertible security will normally rise, too. When that happens, many convertible holders will not convert because the prices of their bonds already reflect the value of the common stock they would receive if the bonds converted. Furthermore, if bondholders do not trade in their bonds for common shares, they can still receive fixed periodic interest payments. Because of this behavior, virtually all convertible securities have a call feature that enables the issuer to encourage or *"force" conversion*. The call price of the security generally exceeds the security's par value by an amount equal to 1 year's stated interest on the security. Although the issuer must pay a premium for calling a security, the call privilege is generally not exercised until the conversion value of the security is 10% to 15% above the call price. This type of premium above the call price helps to assure the issuer that the holders of the convertible will convert it when the call is made, instead of accepting the call price.

Unfortunately, instances arise when the market price of a security does not reach a level sufficient to stimulate the conversion of associated convertibles. A convertible security that cannot be forced into conversion by using the call feature is known as an **overhanging issue.** An overhanging issue can be quite detrimental to a firm. If the firm were to call the issue, the bondholders would accept the call price rather than convert the bonds. In this case, the firm not only would have to pay the call premium but would also require additional financing to pay off the bonds at their par value. If the firm raised these funds through the sale of equity, a large number of shares would have to be issued because of their low market price, which, in turn, could result in the dilution of existing ownership. Another means of financing the call would be the use of debt or preferred stock, but this use would leave the firm's capital structure no less leveraged than before the call.

overhanging issue
A convertible security that cannot be forced into conversion by using the call feature.

DETERMINING THE VALUE OF A CONVERTIBLE BOND

The key characteristic of convertible securities that enhances their marketability is their ability to minimize the possibility of a loss while providing a possibility of capital gains. Here we discuss the three values of a convertible bond: (1) the straight bond value, (2) the conversion value, and (3) the market value.

Straight Bond Value

The **straight bond value** of a convertible bond is the price at which it would sell in the market without the conversion feature. We find this value by determining the value of a nonconvertible bond with similar payments issued by a firm with the same risk. The straight bond value is typically the floor, or minimum, price at which the convertible bond would be traded. The straight bond value equals the present value of the bond's interest and principal payments discounted at the interest rate the firm would have to pay on a nonconvertible bond.

straight bond value
The price at which a convertible bond would sell in the market without the conversion feature.

EXAMPLE 17.7

Duncan Company, a southeastern discount store chain, has just sold a $1,000-par-value, 20-year convertible bond with a 6.5% coupon rate. The bond interest will be paid at the end of each year, and the principal will be repaid at maturity. A straight bond could have been sold at par with a 7.8% coupon rate, so that is the discount rate we use to calculate the straight bond value of Duncan's convertible. We can calculate the straight bond value of the convertible as follows:

Year(s)	Payments	Present value
1–20	$ 65[a]	$647.79
20	1,000	222.65
	Straight bond value	$870.44

[a]$1,000 at 6.5% = $65 interest per year.

This value, $870.44, is the minimum price at which the convertible bond is expected to sell. Generally, only in certain instances in which the stock's market price is below the conversion price can we expect the bond to sell at this level.

Conversion (or Stock) Value

Recall that the *conversion (or stock) value* of a convertible security is the value of the convertible measured in terms of the market price of the common stock into which the security can be converted. When the market price of the common stock exceeds the conversion price, the conversion (or stock) value exceeds the par value. An example will clarify the point.

EXAMPLE 17.8

Duncan Company's convertible bond, described in Example 17.7, is convertible at $50 per share. Each bond can be converted into 20 shares because each bond has a $1,000 par value. The conversion values of the bond when the stock is selling at $30, $40, $50, $60, $70, and $80 per share are shown in the following table:

Market price of stock	Conversion value
$30	$ 600
40	800
50 (conversion price)	1,000 (par value)
60	1,200
70	1,400
80	1,600

When the market price of the common stock exceeds the $50 conversion price, the conversion value exceeds the $1,000 par value. Because the straight bond value of $870.44 (calculated in Example 17.7) is a function of the interest rate and not the stock price, the bond will not sell for less than this amount, regardless of its conversion value as long as the market interest rate on similar nonconvertible bonds remains at 7.8%. If the market price per share were $30, the bond would still sell for $870.44—not $600—because its value as a bond would dominate.

market premium
The amount by which the market value exceeds the straight or conversion value of a convertible security.

Market Value

The market value of a convertible is likely to be greater than its straight value or its conversion value. The amount by which the market value exceeds its straight or conversion value is called the **market premium.** The general relationships

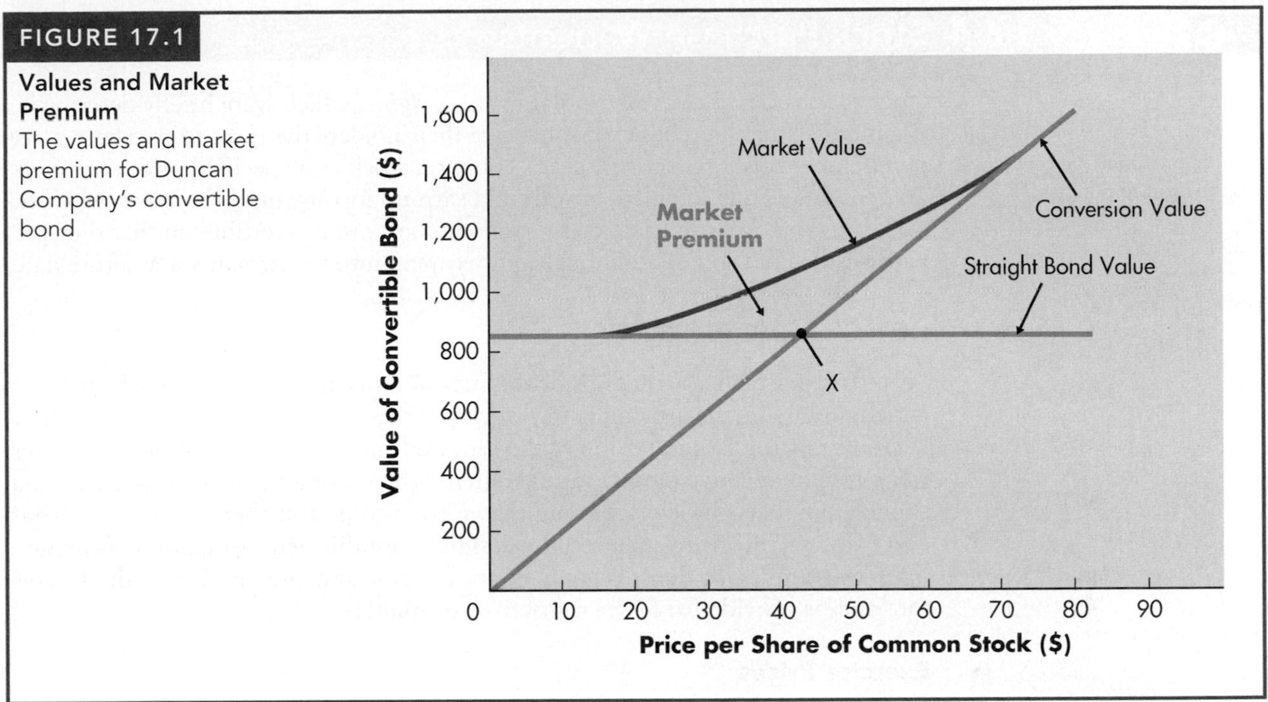

FIGURE 17.1

Values and Market Premium
The values and market premium for Duncan Company's convertible bond

among the straight bond value, conversion value, market value, and market premium for Duncan Company's convertible bond are shown in Figure 17.1. The straight bond value acts as a floor for the security's value up to the point X, where the stock price is high enough to cause the conversion value to exceed the straight bond value. The market premium is attributed to the convertible, giving investors a chance to experience attractive capital gains from increases in the stock price while taking less risk. The floor (straight bond value) provides protection against losses resulting from a decline in the stock price caused by falling profits or other factors. The market premium tends to be greatest when the straight bond value and conversion (or stock) value are nearly equal. Investors perceive the benefits of these two sources of value to be greatest at this point.

→ REVIEW QUESTIONS MyLab Finance Solutions

17–6 What is the conversion feature? What is a conversion ratio? How do convertibles and other contingent securities affect EPS? Briefly describe the motives for convertible financing.

17–7 When the market price of the stock rises above the conversion price, why may a convertible security not be converted? How can the call feature be used to force conversion in this situation? What is an overhanging issue?

17–8 Define the straight bond value, conversion (or stock) value, market value, and market premium associated with a convertible bond, and describe the general relationships among them.

17.4 Stock Purchase Warrants

stock purchase warrants
Instruments that give their holders the right to purchase a certain number of shares of the issuer's common stock at a specified price over a certain period of time.

Stock purchase warrants are similar to stock *rights*, which were briefly described in Chapter 7. **Stock purchase warrants** give their holders the right to purchase a certain number of shares of the issuer's common stock at a specified price over a certain period of time. Holders of warrants earn no income until they exercise or sell their warrants. Warrants also bear some similarity to convertibles in that they provide for the injection of additional equity capital into the firm at some future date.

KEY CHARACTERISTICS

Firms often attach warrants to debt issues as "sweeteners." When a firm sells a large bond issue, the attachment of stock purchase warrants may add to the marketability of the issue and lower the required interest rate. As sweeteners, warrants resemble conversion features. Often, when a new firm is raising its initial capital, suppliers of debt will require warrants to permit them to share in whatever success the firm achieves. In addition, established companies sometimes offer warrants with debt to compensate for risk and thereby lower the interest rate and/or provide for fewer restrictive covenants.

Exercise Prices

exercise (or option) price
The price at which holders of warrants can purchase a specified number of shares of common stock.

The price at which holders of warrants can purchase a specified number of shares of common stock is normally referred to as the **exercise (or option) price.** This price is usually set at 10% to 20% above the market price of the firm's stock at the time of issuance. Until the market price of the stock exceeds the exercise price, holders of warrants will not exercise them because they can purchase the stock more inexpensively in the marketplace.

Warrants normally have a life of no more than 10 years, although some have infinite lives. Unlike convertible securities, warrants cannot be called, but their limited life stimulates holders to exercise their warrants when the exercise price is below the market price of the firm's stock.

Warrant Trading

A warrant is usually *detachable,* which means that the bondholder may sell the warrant without selling the security to which it is attached. Many detachable warrants are actively traded in both broker and dealer markets. Warrants often provide investors with better opportunities for gain (with increased risk) than the underlying common stock.

Comparison of Warrants to Rights and Convertibles

The similarity between a warrant and a right should be clear: Both result in new equity capital flowing into the firm, although the warrant provides for deferred equity financing. The life of a right is typically not more than a few months; a warrant is generally exercisable for a period of years. Firms issue rights at a subscription price below the prevailing market price of the stock; they generally issue warrants at an exercise price 10% to 20% above the prevailing market price.

Warrants and convertibles also have similarities. The exercise of a warrant shifts the firm's capital structure to a less highly leveraged position because new common stock is issued without any change in debt. If a convertible bond were converted, the reduction in leverage would be even more pronounced because common stock would be issued in exchange for a reduction in debt. In addition, the exercise of a warrant provides an influx of new capital; with convertibles, the new capital is raised when the securities are originally issued rather than when they are converted. The influx of new equity capital resulting from the exercise of a warrant does not occur until the firm has achieved a certain degree of success that is reflected in an increased price for its stock. In this case, the firm conveniently obtains needed funds.

IMPLIED PRICE OF AN ATTACHED WARRANT

implied price of a warrant
The price effectively paid for each warrant attached to a bond.

When warrants are attached to a bond, the **implied price of a warrant**—the price that is effectively paid for each attached warrant—can be found by using the following equation:

$$\text{Implied price of } \textit{all} \text{ warrants} = \text{Price of bond with warrants attached} - \text{Straight bond value} \quad (17.1)$$

We find the straight bond value in a fashion similar to that used in valuing convertible bonds. Dividing the implied price of *all* warrants by the number of warrants attached to each bond results in the implied price of *each* warrant.

EXAMPLE 17.9

Martin Marine Products, a manufacturer of marine drive shafts and propellers, just issued a 7%-coupon-rate, $1,000-par, 20-year bond paying annual interest and having 20 warrants attached for the purchase of the firm's stock. The bonds were initially sold for their $1,000 par value. When issued, similar-risk straight bonds were selling to yield an 8.5% rate of return. The straight value of the bond would be the present value of its payments discounted at the 8.5% yield on similar-risk straight bonds:

Year(s)	Payments	Present value
1–20	$ 70[a]	$662.43
20	1,000	195.62
	Straight bond value	$858.05

[a]$1,000 at 7% = $70 interest per year.

Substituting the $1,000 price of the bond with warrants attached and the $858.05 straight bond value into Equation 17.1, we get an implied price of *all* warrants of $141.95:

$$\text{Implied price of } \textit{all} \text{ warrants} = \$1{,}000 - \$858.05 = \underline{\underline{\$141.95}}$$

Dividing the implied price of *all* warrants by the number of warrants attached to each bond—20 in this case—we find the implied price of *each* warrant:

$$\text{Implied price of } \textit{each} \text{ warrant} = \$141.95 \div 20 = \underline{\underline{\$7.10}}$$

Therefore, by purchasing Martin Marine Products' bond with warrants attached for $1,000, one is effectively paying about $7.10 for each warrant.

The implied price of each warrant is meaningful only when compared to the specific features of the warrant, that is, the number of shares that can be purchased and the specified exercise price. These features can be analyzed in light of the prevailing common stock price to estimate the true *market value* of each warrant. Clearly, if the implied price is above the estimated market value, the price of the bond with warrants attached may be too high. If the implied price is below the estimated market value, the bond may be quite attractive. Firms must therefore price their bonds with warrants attached in a way that causes the implied price of its warrants to fall slightly below their estimated market value. Such an approach allows the firm to sell the bonds more easily at a lower coupon rate than would apply to straight debt, thereby reducing its debt service costs.

VALUES OF WARRANTS

warrant premium
The difference between the market value and the theoretical value of a warrant.

Like a convertible security, a warrant has both a market value and a theoretical value. The difference between these values, or the **warrant premium,** depends largely on investor expectations and on the ability of investors to get more leverage from the warrants than from the underlying stock.

Theoretical Value of a Warrant

The *theoretical value* of a stock purchase warrant is the amount one would expect the warrant to sell for in the marketplace. The equation for the theoretical value of a warrant is

$$TVW = (P_0 - E) \times N \quad (17.2)$$

where

TVW = theoretical value of a warrant
P_0 = current market price of a share of common stock
E = exercise price of the warrant
N = number of shares of common stock obtainable with one warrant

The use of Equation 17.2 can be illustrated by the following example.

EXAMPLE 17.10

Dustin Electronics, a major producer of transistors, has outstanding warrants that are exercisable at \$40 per share and entitle holders to purchase three shares of common stock. The warrants were initially attached to a bond issue to sweeten the bond. The common stock of the firm is currently selling for \$45 per share. Substituting P_0 = \$45, E = \$40 and N = 3 into Equation 17.2 yields a theoretical warrant value of (\$45 − \$40) × 3, or \$15.

Market Value of a Warrant

The market value of a stock purchase warrant is generally above the theoretical value of the warrant. Only when the theoretical value of the warrant is very high or the warrant is near its expiration date are the market and theoretical values converge. The general relationship between the theoretical and market values of Dustin Electronics' warrants is presented graphically in Figure 17.2. The market

FIGURE 17.2

Values and Warrant Premium
The value and warrant premium for Dustin Electronics' stock purchase warrants

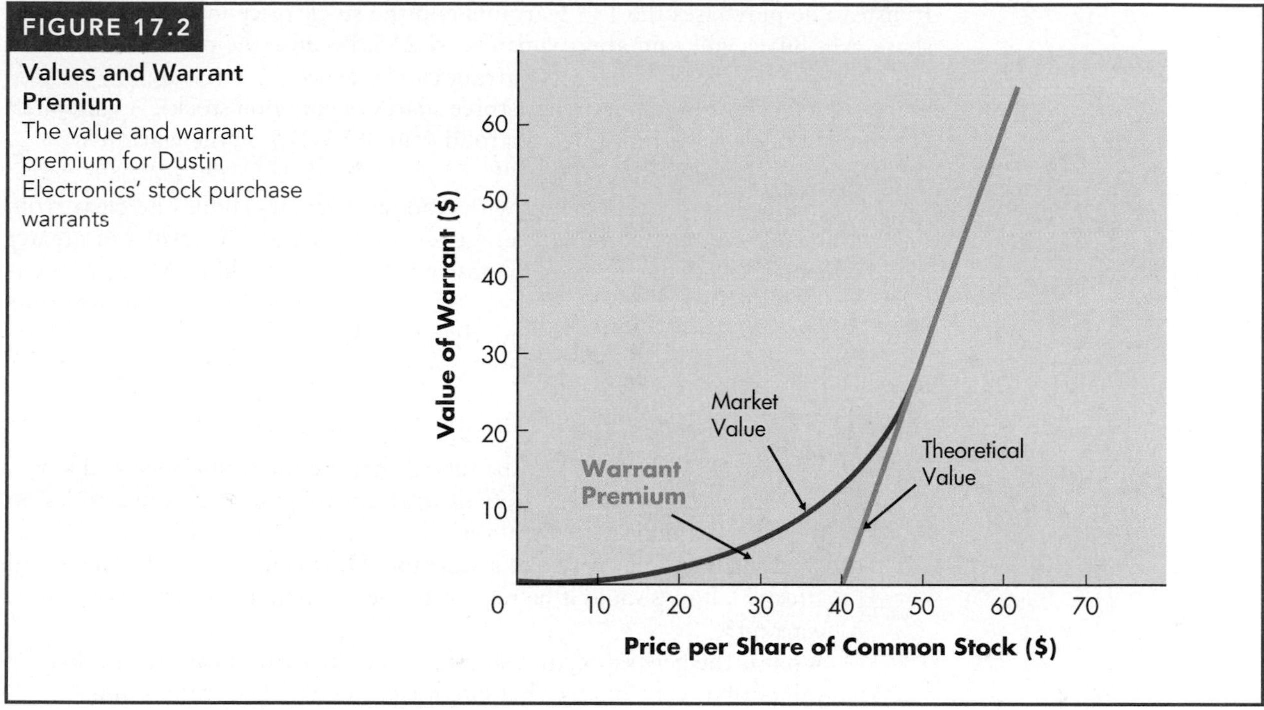

value of warrants generally exceeds the theoretical value by the greatest amount when the stock's market price is close to the warrant exercise price per share. The amount of time until expiration also affects the market value of the warrant. Generally speaking, the closer the warrant is to its expiration date, the more likely that its market value will equal its theoretical value.

Warrant Premium

The *warrant premium,* or the amount by which the market value of Dustin Electronics' warrants exceeds the theoretical value of these warrants, is also shown in Figure 17.2. This premium results from a combination of positive investor expectations and the ability of the investor with a fixed sum to invest to obtain much larger potential returns (and risk) by trading in warrants rather than the underlying stock.

PERSONAL FINANCE EXAMPLE 17.11 Stan Buyer has $2,430, which he is interested in investing in Dustin Electronics. The firm's stock is currently selling for $45 per share, and its warrants are selling for $18 per warrant. Each warrant entitles the holder to purchase three shares of Dustin's common stock at $40 per share. Because the stock is selling for $45 per share, the theoretical warrant value, calculated in the preceding example, is $15 [($45 − $40) × 3].

The warrant premium results from positive investor expectations and leverage opportunities. Mr. Buyer could spend his $2,430 in either of two ways: He could purchase 54 shares of common stock at $45 per share or 135 warrants at $18 per warrant, ignoring brokerage fees. If Mr. Buyer purchases the stock and its price rises to $48, he will gain $162 ($3 per share × 54 shares) by selling the stock.

If instead he purchases the 135 warrants and the stock price increases by $3 per share, Mr. Buyer will gain approximately $1,215. Because the price of a share of stock rises by $3, the price of each warrant can be expected to rise by $9 (because each warrant can be used to purchase three shares of common stock). A gain of $9 per warrant on 135 warrants means a total gain of $1,215 on the warrants.

The greater leverage associated with trading warrants should be clear from the example. Of course, because leverage works both ways, it results in greater risk. If the market price fell by $3, the loss on the stock would be $162, whereas the loss on the warrants would be close to $1,215. Clearly, investing in warrants is more risky than investing in the underlying stock.

→ **REVIEW QUESTIONS** MyLab Finance Solutions

17–9 What are stock purchase warrants? What are the similarities and key differences between the effects of warrants and those of convertibles on the firm's capital structure and its ability to raise new capital?

17–10 What is the implied price of a warrant? How is it estimated? To be effective, how should it be related to the estimated market value of a warrant?

17–11 What is the general relationship between the theoretical and market values of a warrant? In what circumstances are these values quite close? What is a warrant premium?

LG6

17.5 Options

option
An instrument that provides its holder with an opportunity to purchase or sell a specified asset at a stated price on or before a set expiration date.

An **option** is an instrument that provides its holder with an opportunity to purchase or sell a specified asset at a stated price on or before a set *expiration date.* Options are probably the most popular type of *derivative security.* The development of organized options exchanges has created markets in which to trade these securities. Three basic forms of options are rights, warrants, and calls and puts. Rights are discussed in Chapter 7, and warrants were described in the preceding section.

CALLS AND PUTS

call option
An option to purchase a specified number of shares of a stock (typically 100) on or before a specified future date at a stated price.

strike price
The price at which the holder of a call option can buy (or the holder of a put option can sell) a specified amount of stock at any time prior to the option's expiration date.

The two most common types of options are calls and puts. A **call option** is an option to *purchase* a specified number of shares of a stock (typically 100) on or before a specified future date at a stated price. The stock that the option holder has the right to buy is called the *underlying asset,* and the call option derives its value from the value of the underlying stock (hence the term derivative security). Call options usually expire in a few months, although some call options have much longer lives. The **strike price** is the price at which the holder of the option can buy the underlying stock at any time prior to the option's expiration date. A call option is most valuable when its strike price is well below the market price of the underlying stock (hence, the option gives the holder the right to buy the stock at a bargain price). When the strike price of a call option is less than the market price of the stock, the option is *in the money.* When a call option's strike price is above the market price of the underlying stock, the option is *out of the money.*

The exchange where the option trades generally sets option strike prices at or near the prevailing market price of the stock at the time the option is listed for trading. For example, if a firm's stock is currently selling for $50 per share, an option exchange might list option contracts for trading with strike prices of $45, $50, and $55. Like other securities, the value of a call option is determined by the interactions of buyers and sellers trading options in the market. A call option's market price is called the *option premium,* and it represents the price one must pay to acquire the right to buy the stock at the strike price.

put option
An option to sell a specified number of shares of a stock (typically 100) on or before a specified future date at a stated price.

A **put option** is an option to *sell* a specified number of shares of a stock (typically 100) on or before a specified future date at a stated strike price. Like the call option, the strike price of the put is set close to the market price of the underlying stock at the time of issuance. The lives and costs of puts are similar to those of calls. A put option is *in the money* when the market price of the underlying stock is below the strike price, and it is *out of the money* when the underlying stock's market price is above the strike price. When a put option is in the money, the option holder can sell the stock at an above-market price.

OPTIONS MARKETS

There are two ways of making options transactions. The first involves making a transaction through 1 of 20 or so call and put options dealers with the help of a stockbroker. The other, more popular mechanism is the organized options exchanges. The dominant exchange is the *Chicago Board Options Exchange (CBOE),* which was established in 1973, though options trade at several other exchanges. The options traded on these exchanges are standardized and thus are considered registered securities. Each option is for 100 shares of the underlying stock. The forces of supply and demand determine option prices.

MATTER OF FACT

Flat Options Trading since the Recession

After experiencing explosive growth in its first 35 years of options trading, the Chicago Board Options Exchange saw a decline in its business in 2009 due to the recession. The CBOE reported total options trading volume that year of 1.135 billion option contracts, down from 1.193 billion in 2008. Since the recession ended, trading volume in options has barely changed. In fact, in 2015 a total of 1.04 billion contracts were traded on the CBOE, a figure that was more than 12.5% below the CBOE's pre-recession peak.

OPTIONS TRADING

The most obvious motive for purchasing call options is the expectation that the market price of the underlying stock will rise by more than enough to cover the cost of the option, thereby allowing the purchaser of the call to profit.

PERSONAL FINANCE EXAMPLE 17.12

MyLab Finance Solution Video

Assume that Cindy Peters pays $250 for a 3-month call option on Wing Enterprises, a maker of aircraft components, at a strike price of $50. By paying $250, Cindy is guaranteed that she can purchase 100 shares of Wing at $50 per share at any time during the next 3 months. If Wing's stock price rises above $50, Cindy could exercise her option to buy the stock at $50 and then immediately sell it in the open market at the higher market price. The stock price must climb $2.50 per share ($250 ÷ 100 shares) to $52.50 per share to cover the $250 cost of the option (ignoring any brokerage fees). If the stock price rises more than that, Cindy earns a net profit from buying and exercising the option. For example, if the stock price were to rise to $60 per share during the period, Cindy's net profit would be $750. She could make a $10 profit per share by exercising her right to buy shares at $50 and then immediately selling them in the open market for $60 each. Because she has the right to buy 100 shares, Cindy's gross profit on this transaction would be $1,000, but because she spent $250 to acquire the option in the first place, her net profit would be $750.

Because this $750 profit would be earned on a $250 initial investment, it illustrates the high potential return on investment that options offer (a 300% gain in this example). Of course, had the stock price not risen above $50 per share, Cindy would have lost the $250 she invested because there would have been no reason to exercise the option, and her return on that investment would have been –100%. Had the stock price risen to between $50 and $52.50 per share, Cindy would have exercised the option, though the gain from exercising would not have been large enough to completely offset the original $250 purchase price of the option.

Put options are often purchased in the expectation that the share price of a given security will decline over the life of the option. Investors gain from put options when the price of the underlying stock declines by more than the per-share cost of the option. The logic underlying the purchase of a put is exactly the opposite of that underlying the use of call options.

PERSONAL FINANCE EXAMPLE 17.13

MyLab Finance Solution Video

Assume that Don Kelly pays $325 for a 6-month put option on Dante United, a baked goods manufacturer, at a strike price of $40. Don purchased the put option in expectation that the stock price would drop because of the introduction of a new product line by Dante's chief competitor. By paying $325, Don is assured that he can sell 100 shares of Dante at $40 per share at any time during the next 6 months. If the stock price drops below $40, Don can purchase 100 shares at the prevailing market price and then exercise his option to sell them for $40 each. The stock price must drop by $3.25 per share ($325 ÷ 100 shares) to $36.75 per share to cover the cost of the option (ignoring any brokerage fees). If the stock price falls more than that, Don can make a profit from buying and exercising the option. For example, if the stock price were to drop to $30 per share during the period, Don could buy 100 shares on the open market for $3,000 and then exercise his right to sell those shares for $40 each (or $4,000 total). Don's net profit would be $675 [(100 shares × $40/share) − (100 shares × $30/share) − $325].

Because that $675 return would be earned on only a $325 investment, it illustrates the high potential return on investment that options offer. Of course, had the stock price risen above $40 per share, Don would have lost the $325 he invested because he would have had no reason to exercise the option. Had the stock price fallen to between $36.75 and $40.00 per share, Don would have exercised the option to reduce his loss to an amount less than $325.

Some investors buy puts not to speculate on a potential price decline but to protect themselves from that event. Purchasers of puts commonly own the underlying shares, and buying puts provides a way to protect the value of the shares that the investor already owns. For example, an investor who owns 100 shares of Intel Corp. stock, selling for $34 per share, could buy put options on Intel stock with a $30 strike price. This option would guarantee that even if the price of Intel stock plummets, the investor would be able to sell her shares for $30 each.

ROLE OF CALL AND PUT OPTIONS IN FUND RAISING

Although call and put options are extremely popular investments, they play no direct role in the fund-raising activities of the firm. These options are issued by investors and options exchanges, not businesses. They are not a source of financing to the firm because the firm does not receive the proceeds when investors buy options, nor do firms receive funds when investors exercise options to buy shares. Buyers of options have no say in the firm's management, and they do not have voting rights; only stockholders are given these privileges. Despite the popularity of options as investments, the financial manager has very little need to deal with them, especially as part of fund-raising activities.

In addition to the ordinary call and put options that trade on exchanges, many types of financial contracts and agreements contain option-like features that influence the behavior of parties to those agreements. One such arrangement is deposit insurance, in which the government promises to protect bank depositors in the event that a bank goes under. The *Focus on Ethics* box explains why deposit insurance is like an option and how that option can affect the behavior of bank managers.

HEDGING FOREIGN-CURRENCY EXPOSURES WITH OPTIONS

The Chicago Mercantile Exchange (CME) and the Philadelphia Stock Exchange (PHLX) offer exchange-traded options contracts on the Canadian dollar, the euro, the Japanese yen, the Swiss franc, and several other important currencies. *Currency options* are used by a wide range of traders, from the largest multinational companies to small exporters and importers, as well as by individual investors and speculators. Options allow **hedging** by companies, which involves offsetting or protecting against the risk of adverse price movements, while simultaneously preserving the possibility of profiting from favorable price movements. Using options to hedge risk is similar to purchasing insurance. The firm pays a premium (the cost of the option), and in exchange it receives a cash inflow if the event that the firm is hedging against actually occurs. If the event does not occur, the option expires as worthless, and the money spent to acquire the option is lost, just as would be the case if you purchased auto insurance and never had an accident.

hedging
Offsetting or protecting against the risk of adverse price movements.

EXAMPLE 17.14

Assume that a U.S. exporter just booked a sale denominated in Swiss francs with payment due upon delivery in 3 months. The exporter is exposed to currency risk because when it receives francs in payment, it will sell those francs in exchange for dollars, but the exchange rate at which that transaction will occur is unknown. If the Swiss franc declines in value, the dollar value of the payment that the exporter will receive in 3 months is reduced (because each franc buys fewer dollars on the foreign exchange market). The company could hedge the risk of depreciation in the franc by purchasing a Swiss franc put option, which would give the company

FOCUS ON ETHICS *in practice*

Banking on Options

Options may not provide funding for non-financial firms, but they are central to modern finance. Not only are millions traded daily, the valuation framework yields insight into corporate decisions with option-like dimensions. A good example is guarantees of bank deposits, which the Federal Deposit Insurance Corporation (FDIC) has offered since 1934.

To see the option in deposit insurance, recall a "put" gives the holder the right, but not the obligation, to sell an asset at the strike price. Suppose, for example, you hold a put option on XYZ stock with a strike of $10. Should the stock price fall to $2, the put would be valuable because you could buy XYZ in the market, sell through the option contract, and pocket $8 on every share. If the price rises to $18, however, you would do better selling XYZ stock on the market (i.e., not exercising the put). This asymmetry—exercise in-the-money options but ignore out-of-the-money options—has an important implication: An increase in the riskiness of the underlying asset can make an option more valuable. In the example above, the put is more valuable if the price of XYZ stock varies from $2 to $18 rather than from $9 to $11. Why? Because at any price above the strike—$11 or $18—the option is out of the money while exercising the put earns $8 per share when stock price falls to $2 but only $1 when it dips to $9.

Deposit insurance offers the right, but not the obligation, to turn an underwater bank over to the FDIC. As long as the value of assets (mostly loans) exceeds liabilities (mostly insured deposits)—the CEO will not "put" the bank because shareholders would lose their equity (also called capital). But if loan losses drag the value of assets below liabilities—capital is negative—shareholders are wiped out, so the banker will hand the mess to the FDIC and walk away.

The option to dump losses on the FDIC can affect a bank's appetite for risk. Banks with healthy capital approach risky loans with caution because shareholders bear all the gains and losses. But when capital is nearly gone, risky loans become appealing because shareholders keep all the upside while the FDIC bears most of the downside—another example of moral hazard (as explored in *Focus on Ethics* for chapter 16). This framework explains why U.S. bank failures were rare prior to the 1980s—government limitations on bank competition contained moral hazard by keeping profits high and capital strong. Then, deregulation and financial innovation ate away capital, spurring bankers to take more risk. Between 1934 and 1981, on average 13 U.S. banks failed each year—compared with 255 per year from 1982 to 1992.

Regulators try to keep bankers from playing "heads I win, tails the FDIC loses" with capital requirements (including "stress testing" the preparedness of large banks for a serious recession or financial crisis), risk-based deposit-insurance premiums, and regular examinations. When asked why he robbed banks, Willie Sutton is said to have answered, "because that's where the money is." Bank regulators keep a close eye on capital and asset risk because that's where the value of the put is.

► *How should a bank manager weigh her ethical duty to shareholders to "game" regulations to increase value of the put option in deposit insurance against her duty as a citizen not to saddle taxpayers with the losses?*

► *Outside the financial services industry, debt and the limited liability structure of a corporation give managers a put option similar to the one the FDIC gives banks. If a firm's investments turn out poorly, managers, on behalf of shareholders, can "put" the firm's asset in the hands of lenders and walk away by going bankrupt. How does this influence the risk-taking incentives of managers, and what can bondholders do about it?*

the right to sell Swiss francs at a fixed price (say, 1 franc in exchange for $1.04). This option would become valuable if the value of the Swiss franc was less than $1.04 when the payment in francs arrives in 3 months. On the other hand, if 1 Swiss franc was worth more than $1.04 when the exporter received payment, the firm would allow the put option to expire unexercised and would instead convert the Swiss francs received in payment into dollars at the new, higher dollar price. The exporter would be protected from adverse price risk but would still be able to profit from favorable price movements.

→ **REVIEW QUESTIONS** MyLab Finance Solutions

17–12 What is an option? Define calls and puts. What role, if any, do call and put options play in the fund-raising activities of the firm?

17–13 How can the firm use currency options to hedge foreign-currency exposures resulting from international transactions?

SUMMARY

FOCUS ON VALUE

In addition to basic corporate securities like stocks and bonds, the firm can use hybrid securities in its fund-raising activities. These securities, which possess characteristics of both debt and equity, enable the firm to raise funds at less cost or to provide for desired future changes in the firm's capital structure.

Leasing, particularly financial (capital) leases, may enable the firm to use the lease as a substitute for the debt-financed purchase of an asset, with more attractive risk–return tradeoffs. Similarly, by issuing convertible rather than straight debt or by attaching stock purchase warrants to a bond issue or debt financing, the firm may provide lenders with the potential to benefit from stock price movements in exchange for a lower interest rate or less restrictive covenants in the bond or debt agreement. Although options are not a source of financing to the firm, this derivative security can help provide incentives to employees. Currency options can be used to hedge adverse currency movements in international transactions.

Clearly, the financial manager should use hybrid and derivative securities to increase return (often by lowering financing costs) and reduce risk. By taking only those actions believed to result in attractive risk–return tradeoffs, the financial manager can positively contribute to the firm's goal of maximizing the stock price.

REVIEW OF LEARNING GOALS

LG 1 **Differentiate between hybrid and derivative securities and their roles in the corporation.** Hybrid securities are forms of debt or equity financing that possess characteristics of both debt and equity. Common hybrid securities include preferred stock, financial leases, convertible securities, and stock purchase warrants. Derivatives are securities that are neither debt nor equity but derive their value from an underlying asset that is often another security, such as a share of common stock. Options are a popular derivative security.

LG 2 **Review the types of leases, leasing arrangements, the lease-versus-purchase decision, the effects of leasing on future financing, and the advantages and disadvantages of leasing.** A lease enables the firm to make contractual, tax-deductible payments to obtain the use of fixed assets. Operating leases are generally 5 or fewer years in term, cancelable, and renewable, and they provide for maintenance by the lessor. Financial leases are longer term, noncancelable, and not renewable, and they nearly always require the lessee to maintain the asset. *FASB Statement No. 13* provides specific guidelines for defining a financial (capital) lease. A lessor can obtain assets to be leased through a direct lease, a sale-leaseback arrangement, or a leveraged lease. The lease-versus-purchase decision can be evaluated by calculating the after-tax cash outflows associated with the leasing and purchasing alternatives. The more desirable alternative is the one that has the lower present value of after-tax cash outflows. *FASB Statement No. 13* requires firms to show financial leases as assets and corresponding liabilities on their balance sheets; operating leases must be shown in footnotes to the financial statements. The firm should consider advantages and disadvantages when making lease-versus-purchase decisions.

LG3 **Describe the types of convertible securities, their general features, and financing with convertibles.** Corporate bonds and preferred stock may both be convertible into common stock. The conversion ratio indicates the number of shares for which a convertible can be exchanged and determines the conversion price. A conversion privilege is nearly always available at any time in the life of the security. The conversion value is the value of the convertible measured in terms of the market price of the common stock into which it can be converted. The presence of convertibles and other contingent securities (warrants and stock options) often requires the firm to report both basic and diluted earnings per share (EPS). Convertibles are used to obtain deferred common stock financing, to "sweeten" bond issues, to minimize restrictive covenants, and to raise cheap funds temporarily. The call feature is sometimes used to encourage or "force" conversion; occasionally, an overhanging issue results.

LG4 **Demonstrate the procedures for determining the straight bond value, the conversion (or stock) value, and the market value of a convertible bond.** The straight bond value of a convertible is the price at which it would sell in the market without the conversion feature. It typically represents the minimum value at which a convertible bond trades. The conversion value is found by multiplying the conversion ratio by the current market price of the underlying common stock. The market value of a convertible generally exceeds both its straight and conversion values, resulting in a market premium. The premium is largest when the straight and conversion values are nearly equal.

LG5 **Explain the key characteristics of stock purchase warrants, the implied price of an attached warrant, and the values of warrants.** Stock purchase warrants enable their holders to purchase a certain number of shares of common stock at the specified exercise price. Warrants are often attached to debt issues as "sweeteners," generally have limited lives, are detachable, and may be traded in broker and dealer markets. Warrants are similar to stock rights except that the exercise price of a warrant is initially set above the underlying stock's current market price. Warrants are similar to convertibles, but exercising them has a less pronounced effect on the firm's leverage and brings in new funds. The implied price of an attached warrant can be found by dividing the difference between the bond price with warrants attached and the straight bond value by the number of warrants attached to each bond. The market value of a warrant usually exceeds its theoretical value, creating a warrant premium. Investors generally get more leverage from trading warrants than from trading the underlying stock.

LG6 **Define options, and discuss calls and puts, options markets, options trading, the role of call and put options in fund raising, and hedging foreign-currency exposures with options.** An option provides its holder with an opportunity to purchase or sell a specified asset at a stated price on or before a set expiration date. Rights, warrants, and calls and puts are all options. Calls are options to purchase common stock, and puts are options to sell common stock. Options exchanges provide organized marketplaces in which purchases and sales of call and put options can be made. The options traded on the exchanges are standardized, and the prices at which they trade are determined by the forces of supply and demand. Call and put options do not play a direct role in the fund-raising activities of the financial manager. Currency options can be used to hedge the firm's foreign-currency exposures resulting from international transactions.

OPENER-IN-REVIEW

The chapter opener described an AMD 10-year convertible bond issue in which each investor could exchange his or her $1,000 par value bond for 125 shares of AMD common stock. When these bonds were issued, AMD's stock was trading for $6 per share.

a. What is the conversion ratio of AMD's convertible bonds?
b. What is the conversion price associated with AMD's convertible bonds?
c. What was the conversion value of AMD's convertible bonds at the time they were issued?
d. By how much did AMD's stock price have to increase (from its starting value of $6 per share) before it would make sense for investors to exchange their bonds for common stock?
e. If AMD had attempted to issue nonconvertible bonds, the company would have had to pay an interest rate of 3.5%. What was the straight bond value of AMD's convertible bonds when they were issued? (For simplicity, assume annual interest payments.)

SELF-TEST PROBLEMS (Solutions in Appendix)

IRF

ST17–1 **Lease versus purchase** The Hot Bagel Shop wishes to evaluate two plans for financing an oven: leasing and borrowing to purchase. The firm is in the 40% tax bracket.

Lease The shop can lease the oven under a 5-year lease requiring annual end-of-year payments of $5,000. All maintenance costs will be paid by the lessor, and insurance and other costs will be borne by the lessee. The lessee will exercise its option to purchase the asset for $4,000 at termination of the lease.

Purchase The oven costs $20,000 and will have a 5-year life. It will be depreciated under MACRS using a 5-year recovery period. (See Table 4.2 for the applicable depreciation percentages.) The total purchase price will be financed by a 5-year, 15% loan requiring equal annual end-of-year payments of $5,967. The firm will pay $1,000 per year for a service contract that covers all maintenance costs; insurance and other costs will be borne by the firm. The firm plans to keep the equipment and use it beyond its 5-year recovery period.

a. For the leasing plan, calculate the following:
   (1) The after-tax cash outflow each year.
   (2) The present value of the cash outflows, using a 9% discount rate.
b. For the purchasing plan, calculate the following:
   (1) The annual interest expense deductible for tax purposes for each of the 5 years.
   (2) The after-tax cash outflow resulting from the purchase for each of the 5 years.
   (3) The present value of the cash outflows, using a 9% discount rate.
c. Compare the present values of the cash outflow streams for these two plans, and determine which plan would be preferable. Explain your answer.

IRF

ST17–2 **Finding convertible bond values** Mountain Mining Company has an outstanding issue of convertible bonds with a $1,000 par value. These bonds are convertible into 40 shares of common stock. They have a 5% annual coupon rate and a 25-year maturity. The interest rate on a straight bond of similar risk is currently 6.5%.

a. Calculate the straight bond value of the bond.
b. Calculate the conversion (or stock) value of the bond when the market price of the common stock is $20, $25, $28, $35, and $50 per share.
c. For each of the stock prices given in part **b**, at what price would you expect the bond to sell? Why?
d. What is the least you would expect the bond to sell for, regardless of the common stock price behavior?

WARM-UP EXERCISES

All problems are available in MyLab Finance

E17–1 N and M Corp. is considering leasing a new machine for $25,000 per year. The lease arrangement calls for a 5-year lease with an option to purchase the machine at the end of the lease for $3,500. The firm is in the 21% tax bracket. What is the present value of the lease outflows, including the purchase option, if lease payments are made at the end of each year and if the after-tax cost of debt is 7%?

E17–2 During the past 2 years Meacham Industries issued three separate convertible bonds. For each of them, calculate the conversion price:

a. A $1,000-par-value bond that is convertible into 10 shares of common stock.
b. A $1,000-par-value bond that is convertible into 20 shares of common stock.
c. A $1,500-par-value bond that is convertible into 50 shares of common stock.

LG3 **E17–3** Newcomb Company has a bond outstanding with a $1,000 par value and convertible at $30 per share. What is the bond's conversion ratio? If the underlying stock currently trades at $25 per share, what is the bond's conversion value? Would it be advisable for a bondholder to exercise the conversion option?

LG4 **E17–4** Crystal Cafes recently sold a $1,000-par-value, 10-year convertible bond with a 7% coupon rate. The interest payments will be paid annually at the end of each year and the principal will be repaid at maturity. A similar bond without a conversion feature would have sold with an 8.5% coupon rate. What is the minimum price that the Crystal Cafes' convertible bond should sell for?

LG6 **E17–5** A 6-month call option on 100 shares of SRS Corp. stock is selling for $320. The strike price for the option is $80. The stock is currently selling at $79 per share. Ignoring brokerage fees, what price must the stock achieve to just cover the expense of the option? If the stock price rises to $85, what will the net profit on the option contract be?

PROBLEMS

All problems are available in MyLab Finance. The MyLab icon indicates problems in Excel format available in MyLab Finance.

LG2 **P17–1** **Lease cash flows** Given the lease payments and terms shown in the following table, determine the yearly after-tax cash outflows for each firm, assuming that lease payments are made at the end of each year and that the firm is in the 21% tax bracket. Assume that no purchase option exists.

Firm	Annual lease payment	Term of lease
A	$100,000	4 years
B	80,000	14
C	150,000	8
D	60,000	25
E	20,000	10

LG2 **P17–2** **Loan interest** For each of the loan amounts, interest rates, annual payments, and loan terms shown in the following table, calculate the annual interest paid each year over the term of the loan, assuming that the payments are made at the end of each year.

Loan	Amount	Interest rate	Annual payment	Term
A	$14,000	10%	$ 4,416	4 years
B	17,500	12	10,355	2
C	2,400	13	1,017	3
D	49,000	14	14,273	5
E	26,500	16	7,191	6

P17–3 **Loan payments and interest** Schuyler Company wishes to purchase an asset costing $117,000. The full amount needed to finance the asset can be borrowed at 14% interest. The terms of the loan require equal end-of-year payments for the next 6 years. Determine the total annual loan payment, and break it into the amount of interest and the amount of principal paid for each year. (*Hint:* Use the techniques presented in Chapter 5 to find the loan payment.)

P17–4 **Lease versus purchase** JLB Corporation is attempting to determine whether to lease or purchase research equipment. The firm is in the 21% tax bracket, and its after-tax cost of debt is currently 8%. The terms of the lease and of the purchase are as follows:

Lease Annual end-of-year lease payments of $25,200 are required over the 3-year life of the lease. All maintenance costs will be paid by the lessor; insurance and other costs will be borne by the lessee. The lessee will exercise its option to purchase the asset for $5,000 at termination of the lease.

Purchase The research equipment, costing $60,000, can be financed entirely with a 14% loan requiring annual end-of-year payments of $25,844 for 3 years. The firm in this case will depreciate the equipment under MACRS using a 3-year recovery period. (See Table 4.2 for the applicable depreciation percentages.) The firm will pay $1,800 per year for a service contract that covers all maintenance costs; insurance and other costs will be borne by the firm. The firm plans to keep the equipment and use it beyond its 3-year recovery period.

a. Calculate the after-tax cash outflows associated with each alternative.
b. Calculate the present value of each cash outflow stream, using the after-tax cost of debt.
c. Which alternative—lease or purchase—would you recommend? Why?

P17–5 **Lease versus purchase** Northwest Lumber Company needs to expand its facilities. To do so, the firm must acquire a machine costing $80,000. The machine can be leased or purchased. The firm is in the 21% tax bracket, and its after-tax cost of debt is 9%. The terms of the lease and purchase plans are as follows:

Lease The leasing arrangement requires end-of-year payments of $19,800 over 5 years. All maintenance costs will be paid by the lessor; insurance and other costs will be borne by the lessee. The lessee will exercise its option to purchase the asset for $24,000 at termination of the lease.

Purchase If the firm purchases the machine, its cost of $80,000 will be financed with a 5-year, 14% loan requiring equal end-of-year payments of $23,302. The machine will be depreciated under MACRS using a 5-year recovery period. (See Table 4.2 for the applicable depreciation percentages.) The firm will pay $2,000 per year for a service contract that covers all maintenance costs; insurance and other costs will be borne by the firm. The firm plans to keep the equipment and use it beyond its 5-year recovery period.

a. Determine the after-tax cash outflows of Northwest Lumber under each alternative.
b. Find the present value of each after-tax cash outflow stream, using the after-tax cost of debt.
c. Which alternative—lease or purchase—would you recommend? Why?

Personal Finance Problem

LG2

P17–6 **Lease-versus-purchase decision** Joanna Browne is considering either leasing or purchasing a new Chrysler Sebring convertible that has a manufacturer's suggested retail price (MSRP) of $33,000. The dealership offers a 3-year lease that requires a capital payment of $3,300 ($3,000 down payment + $300 security deposit) and monthly payments of $494. Purchasing requires a $2,640 down payment, sales tax of 6.5% ($2,145), and 36 monthly payments of $784. Joanna estimates that the value of the car will be $17,000 at the end of 3 years. She can earn 5% annual interest on her savings and is subject to a 6.5% sales tax on purchases.

Make a reasonable recommendation to Joanna, using a lease-versus-purchase analysis that, for simplicity, ignores the time value of money.

a. Calculate the total cost of leasing.
b. Calculate the total cost of purchasing.
c. Which should Joanna do?

LG2

P17–7 **Capitalized lease values** Given the lease payments, terms remaining until the leases expire, and discount rates shown in the following table, calculate the capitalized value of each lease, assuming that lease payments are made annually at the end of each year.

Lease	Lease payment	Remaining term	Discount rate
A	$ 40,000	12 years	10%
B	120,000	8	12
C	9,000	18	14
D	16,000	3	9
E	47,000	20	11

LG3 

P17–8 **Conversion price** Calculate the conversion price for each of the following convertible bonds:

a. A $1,000-par-value bond that is convertible into 40 shares of common stock.
b. A $1,000-par-value bond that is convertible into 25 shares of common stock.
c. A $1,000-par-value bond that is convertible into 125 shares of common stock.

LG3

P17–9 **Conversion ratio** What is the conversion ratio for each of the following bonds?

a. A $1,000-par-value bond that is convertible into common stock at $43.75 per share.
b. A $1,000-par-value bond that is convertible into common stock at $25 per share.
c. A $600-par-value bond that is convertible into common stock at $30 per share.

LG3

P17–10 **Conversion (or stock) value** What is the conversion (or stock) value of each of the following convertible bonds?

a. A $1,000-par-value bond that is convertible into 25 shares of common stock. The common stock is currently selling for $50 per share.
b. A $1,000-par value bond that is convertible into 12.5 shares of common stock. The common stock is currently selling for $42 per share.
c. A $1,000-par-value bond that is convertible into 100 shares of common stock. The common stock is currently selling for $10.50 per share.

LG3 MyLab

P17–11 Conversion (or stock) value Find the conversion (or stock) value for each of the $1,000-par-value convertible bonds described in the following table.

Convertible	Conversion ratio	Current market price of stock
A	22.50	$42.25
B	18	50.00
C	20	44.00
D	45	19.50

LG4

P17–12 Straight bond value Calculate the straight bond value for each of the bonds shown in the table below.

Bond	Par value	Coupon rate (paid annually)	Interest rate on equal-risk straight bond	Years to maturity
A	$1,000	6%	7.0%	20
B	1,000	7	8.5	14
C	1,000	8	10.0	30
D	1,000	9	10.5	25

LG4

P17–13 Determining values: Convertible bond Eastern Clock Company has an outstanding issue of convertible bonds with a $1,000 par value. These bonds are convertible into 50 shares of common stock. They have a 10% annual coupon rate and a 20-year maturity. The interest rate on a straight bond of similar risk is currently 12%.

a. Calculate the straight bond value of the bond.

b. Calculate the conversion (or stock) value of the bond when the market price of the common stock is $15, $20, $23, $30, and $45 per share.

c. For each of the stock prices given in part **b,** at what price would you expect the bond to sell? Why?

d. What is the least you would expect the bond to sell for, regardless of the common stock price behavior?

LG4

P17–14 Determining values: Convertible bond Craig's Cake Company has an outstanding issue of 15-year convertible bonds with a $1,000 par value. These bonds are convertible into 80 shares of common stock. They have an 8% annual coupon rate, whereas the interest rate on straight bonds of similar risk is 10%.

a. Calculate the straight bond value of this bond.

b. Calculate the conversion (or stock) value of the bond when the market price is $9, $12, $13, $15, and $20 per share of common stock.

c. For each of the common stock prices given in part **b,** at what price would you expect the bond to sell? Why?

d. Make a graph of the straight value and conversion value of the bond for each common stock price given. Plot the per-share common stock prices on the x-axis and the bond values on the y-axis. Use this graph to indicate the minimum market value of the bond associated with each common stock price.

P17–15 Implied prices of attached warrants Calculate the implied price of each warrant for each of the bonds shown in the following table.

Bond	Price of bond with warrants attached	Par value	Coupon rate (paid annually)	Interest rate on equal-risk straight bond	Years to maturity	Number of warrants attached to bond
A	$1,000	$1,000	12.0%	13%	15	10
B	1,100	1,000	9.5	12	10	30
C	500	500	10.0	11	20	5
D	1,000	1,000	10.0	12	20	20

P17–16 Evaluation of the implied price of an attached warrant Dinoo Mathur wishes to determine whether the $1,000 price asked for Stanco Manufacturing's bond is fair in light of the theoretical value of the attached warrants. The $1,000-par-value, 30-year, 11.5%-interest-rate bond pays annual interest and has 10 warrants attached for purchase of common stock. The theoretical value of each warrant is $12.50. The interest rate on an equal-risk straight bond is currently 13%.

a. Find the straight value of Stanco Manufacturing's bond.
b. Calculate the implied price of all warrants attached to Stanco's bond.
c. Calculate the implied price of each warrant attached to Stanco's bond.
d. Compare the implied price for each warrant calculated in part c to its theoretical value. On the basis of this comparison, what assessment would you give Dinoo with respect to the fairness of Stanco's bond price? Explain.

P17–17 Warrant values Kent Hotels has warrants that allow the purchase of three shares of its outstanding common stock at $50 per share. The common stock price per share and the market value of the warrant associated with that stock price are shown in the table.

Common stock price per share	Market value of warrant
$42	$ 2
46	8
48	9
54	18
58	28
62	38
66	48

a. For each of the common stock prices given, calculate the theoretical warrant value.
b. Graph the theoretical and market values of the warrant on a set of axes with per-share common stock price on the x-axis and warrant value on the y-axis.
c. Assume that the warrant value is $12 when the market price of common stock is $50. Does that contradict or support the graph you have constructed? Explain.
d. Specify the area of warrant premium. Why does this premium exist?
e. If the expiration date of the warrants is quite close, would you expect your graph to look different? Explain.

Personal Finance Problem

P17–18 **Common stock versus warrant investment** Susan Michaels is evaluating the Burton Tool Company's common stock and warrants to choose the better investment. The firm's stock is currently selling for $16 per share; its warrants to purchase three shares of common stock at $15 per share are selling for $8. Ignoring transaction costs, Ms. Michaels has $8,000 to invest. She is quite optimistic with respect to Burton because she believes the firm is about to land a new, large government contract.

a. How many shares of stock and how many warrants can Ms. Michaels purchase?

b. Suppose that Ms. Michaels purchased the stock, held it 1 year, and then sold it for $26 per share. What total gain would she realize, ignoring brokerage fees and taxes?

c. Suppose that Ms. Michaels purchased warrants and held them for 1 year and the market price of the stock increased to $26 per share. Ignoring brokerage fees and taxes, what would be her total gain if the market value of the warrants increased to $35 and she sold out?

d. What benefit, if any, would the warrants provide? Are there any differences in the risk of these two alternative investments? Explain.

Personal Finance Problem

P17–19 **Common stock versus warrant investment** Tom Baldwin can invest $6,300 in the common stock or the warrants of Lexington Life Insurance. The common stock is currently selling for $30 per share. Its warrants, which provide for the purchase of two shares of common stock at $28 per share, are currently selling for $7. The stock is expected to rise to a market price of $32 within the next year, so the expected theoretical value of a warrant over the next year is $8. The expiration date of the warrant is 1 year from the present.

a. If Mr. Baldwin purchases the stock, holds it for 1 year, and then sells it for $32, what is his total gain? (Ignore brokerage fees and taxes.)

b. If Mr. Baldwin purchases the warrants and converts them to common stock in 1 year, what is his total gain if the market price of common shares is actually $32? (Ignore brokerage fees and taxes.)

c. Repeat parts **a** and **b**, assuming that the market price of the stock in 1 year is (1) $30 and (2) $28.

d. Discuss the two alternatives and the tradeoffs associated with them.

P17–20 **Options profits and losses** For each of the 100-share options shown in the following table, use the underlying stock price at expiration and other information to determine the amount of profit or loss an investor would have had, ignoring brokerage fees.

Option	Type of option	Cost of option	Strike price per share	Underlying stock price per share at expiration
A	Call	$200	$50	$55
B	Call	350	42	45
C	Put	500	60	50
D	Put	300	35	40
E	Call	450	28	26

Personal Finance Problem

LG6

P17–21 Call option Carol Krebs is considering buying 100 shares of Sooner Products Inc. at $62 per share. Because she has read that the firm will probably soon receive certain large orders from abroad, she expects the price of Sooner to increase to $70 per share. As an alternative, Carol is considering purchase of a call option for 100 shares of Sooner at a strike price of $60. The 90-day option will cost $600. Ignore any brokerage fees or dividends.

a. What will Carol's profit be on the stock transaction if its price does rise to $70 and she sells?

b. How much will Carol earn on the option transaction if the underlying stock price rises to $70?

c. How high must the stock price rise for Carol to break even on the option transaction?

d. Compare, contrast, and discuss the relative profit and risk associated with the stock and the option transactions.

Personal Finance Problem

P17–22 Put option Ed Martin, the pension fund manager for Stark Corporation, is considering purchase of a put option in anticipation of a price decline in the stock of Carlisle Inc. The option to sell 100 shares of Carlisle at any time during the next 90 days at a strike price of $45 can be purchased for $380. The stock of Carlisle is currently selling for $46 per share.

a. Ignoring any brokerage fees or dividends, what profit or loss will Ed make if he buys the option and the lowest price of Carlisle stock during the 90 days is $46, $44, $40, and $35?

b. What effect would the price of Carlisle's stock slowly rising from its initial $46 level to $55 at the end of 90 days have on Ed's purchase?

c. In light of your findings, discuss the potential risks and returns from using put options to attempt to profit from an anticipated decline in share price.

P17–23 ETHICS PROBLEM A hedge fund charged with managing part of Harvard University's endowment purchased more than 1 million put options on Enron stock not long before the company went bankrupt, making tens of millions of dollars in the process. Some members of the university argued that profiting on the collapse of Enron was unethical. What do you say?

SPREADSHEET EXERCISE

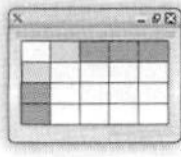

Morris Company, a small manufacturing firm, wants to acquire a new machine that costs $30,000. Arrangements can be made to lease or purchase the machine. The firm is in the 21% tax bracket. The firm has gathered the following information about the two alternatives:

Lease Morris would obtain a 5-year lease requiring annual end-of-year lease payments of $10,000. The lessor would pay all maintenance costs; insurance and other costs would be borne by the lessee. Morris would be given the right to exercise its option to purchase the machine for $3,000 at the end of the lease term.

Purchase Morris can finance the purchase of the machine with an 8.5%, 5-year loan requiring annual end-of-year installment payments. The machine would be depreciated under MACRS using a 5-year recovery period. The exact depreciation rates over the next six periods would be 20%, 32%, 19%, 12%, 12%, and 5%, respectively. Morris would pay $1,200 per year for a service contract that covers all maintenance costs. The firm plans to keep the machine and use it beyond its 5-year recovery period.

TO DO

Create a spreadsheet similar to Tables 17.1, 17.2, and 17.3 to answer the following:

a. Calculate the after-tax cash outflow from the lease for Morris Company.
b. Calculate the annual loan payment.
c. Determine the interest and principal components of the loan payments.
d. Calculate the after-tax cash outflows associated with the purchasing option.
e. Calculate and compare the present values of the cash outflows associated with both the leasing and purchasing options.
f. Which alternative is preferable? Explain.

MyLab Finance Visit www.pearson.com/mylab/finance for **Chapter Case: *Financing L. Rashid Company's Chemical Waste Disposal System*,** Group Exercises, and numerous online resources.

CHAPTER

18

Mergers, LBOs, Divestitures, and Business Failure

LEARNING GOALS

LG 1 Understand merger fundamentals, including terminology, motives for merging, and types of mergers.

LG 2 Describe the objectives and procedures used in leveraged buyouts (LBOs) and divestitures.

LG 3 Demonstrate the procedures used to value the target company and discuss the effect of stock swap transactions on earnings per share.

LG 4 Discuss the merger negotiation process, holding companies, and international mergers.

LG 5 Understand the types and major causes of business failure and the use of voluntary settlements to sustain or liquidate the failed firm.

LG 6 Explain bankruptcy legislation and the procedures involved in reorganizing or liquidating a bankrupt firm.

MyLab Finance Chapter Introduction Video

WHY THIS CHAPTER MATTERS TO YOU

In your *professional* life

ACCOUNTING You need to understand mergers, leveraged buyouts, and divestitures of assets to record and report these organizational changes; you also need to understand bankruptcy procedures because you will play a large part in any reorganization or liquidation.

INFORMATION SYSTEMS You need to understand what data must be tracked in the case of mergers, leveraged buyouts, divestitures of assets, or bankruptcy so as to devise the systems needed to effect these organizational changes.

MANAGEMENT You need to understand the motives for mergers so that you will know when and why a merger is a good idea. Also, you may need to know how to fend off an unwelcome takeover attempt, when to divest the firm of assets for strategic reasons, and what options are available in the case of business failure.

MARKETING You need to understand mergers and divestitures, which may enable the firm to grow, diversify, or achieve synergy and therefore require changes in the firm's marketing organization, plans, and goals.

OPERATIONS You need to understand mergers and divestitures because ongoing operations will be significantly affected by these organizational changes. Also, you should know that business failure may result in reorganization of the firm to provide adequate financing for ongoing operations.

In your *personal* life

As an investor, you should understand corporate mergers, leveraged buyouts, and divestitures. More important, though, is an understanding of the causes and remedies associated with corporate bankruptcy. Clearly, an unstated personal financial goal is to avoid bankruptcy, an outcome that those who develop and implement reasonable personal financial plans are not likely to experience.

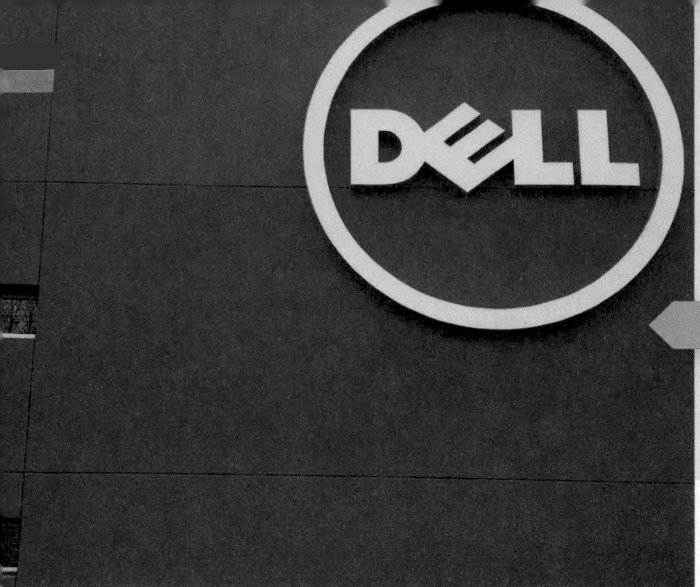

Kristoffer Tripplaar/Alamy Stock Photo

DELL INC.

Carl Icahn and Founder Michael Dell Fight for Computer Maker

Founded in 1984 by a 19-year-old college dropout, Dell Inc. was one of the largest and best-known computer manufacturers during the 1990s. In March 2000, just before the "technology bubble" burst, Dell's stock price hit an all-time high of almost $59 per share, making the company's shareholders very happy and the founder, Michael Dell, one of the world's richest men. Dell's fortunes were changing, however. As consumers began to spend less on new computers and more on smartphones and other mobile devices such as tablets, Dell was slow to innovate, and its products lagged market trends. By November 2012, the stock price had lost almost 85% of its value, falling all the way to $9 per share.

By late 2012, Michael Dell thought that he had a solution to his company's woes. Along with the private equity firm Silver Lake Partners, he planned to take the company private in a transaction known as a leveraged buyout (LBO). In a typical LBO, a small group of investors invest their own money as well as substantial funds borrowed from banks and other lenders to buy up a company's outstanding shares, usually at a price that reflects a premium above the current stock price. In its bid for Dell shares, Silver Lake made a sequence of offers, starting at $11.22 per share and rising to $13.65 by February 2013. Some shareholders, though, believed that Michael Dell was trying to buy the stock at a bargain price. Among them was the famous "corporate raider" Carl Icahn, who aggressively bought Dell shares while the company was forming its plans to go private. Icahn accumulated more than $2 billion worth of Dell stock, becoming its largest stockholder in the process. Icahn proposed a new slate of directors to replace Dell's existing board, and he argued that the firm should bring a tender offer to repurchase more than 1 billion of its own shares at $14 each. Michael Dell countered that Icahn's offer was risky and would jeopardize the company's future. In the end, Michael Dell and Silver Lake increased the total value of their offer to $25 billion and completed the buyout of public shareholders.

The colorful battle between Michael Dell and Carl Icahn is not unusual. When companies get into trouble, especially when a longtime founder is in charge, disagreements arise about how to move forward, and outside investors may attempt to gain control of the firm. The firm's board of directors has a duty to act in the interests of shareholders when a takeover contest occurs, but it is not always clear what action is in the shareholders' best interest. In this case, shareholders would receive a premium from Michael Dell and Silver Lake if the company went private, but Icahn believed that under his leadership the company's stock price would go even higher.

18.1 Merger Fundamentals

Firms sometimes use mergers to expand externally by acquiring control of another firm. Whereas the overriding objective for a merger should be to improve the firm's share value, a number of more immediate motivations such as diversification, tax considerations, and increasing owner liquidity frequently exist. Sometimes mergers are pursued to acquire specific assets owned by the target rather than by a desire to run the target as a going concern. Here we discuss merger fundamentals: terminology, motives, and types. In the following sections, we will describe the related topics of leveraged buyouts (LBOs) and divestitures and will review the procedures used to analyze and negotiate mergers.

TERMINOLOGY

corporate restructuring
The activities involving expansion or contraction of a firm's operations or changes in its asset or financial (ownership) structure.

In the broadest sense, activities involving expansion or contraction of a firm's operations or changes in its asset or financial (ownership) structure are called **corporate restructuring.** The topics addressed in this chapter—mergers, LBOs, and divestitures—are some of the most common forms of corporate restructuring. We begin our discussion of these topics by defining some basic merger terminology.

Mergers, Consolidations, and Holding Companies

merger
The combination of two or more firms, in which the resulting firm maintains the identity of one of the firms, usually the larger.

consolidation
The combination of two or more firms to form a completely new corporation.

holding company
A corporation that has voting control of one or more other corporations.

subsidiaries
The companies controlled by a holding company.

A **merger** occurs when two or more firms combine and the resulting firm maintains the identity of one of the firms. Usually, the assets and liabilities of the smaller firm are merged into those of the larger firm. **Consolidation**, by contrast, involves the combination of two or more firms to form a completely new corporation. The new corporation normally absorbs the assets and liabilities of the companies from which it is formed. Because of the similarity of mergers and consolidations, we use the term *merger* throughout this chapter to refer to both.

A **holding company** is a corporation that has voting control of one or more other corporations. The companies controlled by a holding company are normally referred to as its **subsidiaries.** Control of a subsidiary is typically obtained by purchasing a sufficient number of shares of its stock, usually 50% or more, although sometimes control of a large, widely held company can be obtained with an ownership stake much lower than 50%.

Acquiring Versus Target Companies

acquiring company
The firm in a merger transaction that attempts to acquire another firm.

target company
The firm in a merger transaction that the acquiring company is pursuing.

The firm in a merger transaction that attempts to acquire another firm is commonly called the **acquiring company.** The firm that the acquiring company seeks to buy is the **target company.** Generally, the acquiring company identifies, evaluates, and negotiates with the management and/or shareholders of the target company. Occasionally, the management of a target company initiates its acquisition by seeking out potential acquirers.

Friendly Versus Hostile Takeovers

Mergers can occur on either a friendly or a hostile basis. Typically, after identifying the target company, the acquirer initiates discussions. If the target management is receptive to the acquirer's proposal, it may endorse the merger and recommend shareholder approval. If the stockholders approve the merger, the transaction is typically consummated either through a cash purchase of shares by the acquirer or through an exchange of the acquirer's stock, or some combination of stock and cash for the target firm's shares. This type of negotiated transaction is known as a **friendly merger**.

friendly merger
A merger transaction endorsed by the target firm's management, approved by its stockholders, and easily consummated.

If the takeover target's management does not support the proposed takeover, it can fight the acquirer's actions. In this case, the acquirer can attempt to gain control of the firm by buying sufficient shares of the target firm in the marketplace. This move is typically accomplished by using a *tender offer,* which, as noted in Chapter 14, is a formal offer to purchase a given number of shares at a specified price. This type of unfriendly transaction is commonly referred to as a **hostile merger.** Clearly, hostile mergers are more difficult to consummate because the target firm's management acts to deter rather than facilitate the acquisition. Regardless, hostile takeovers are sometimes successful.

hostile merger
A merger transaction that the target firm's management does not support, forcing the acquiring company to try to gain control of the firm by buying shares in the marketplace.

Strategic Versus Financial Mergers

strategic merger
A merger transaction undertaken to achieve economies of scale.

Mergers occur for either strategic or financial reasons. **Strategic mergers** seek to achieve various economies of scale by eliminating redundant functions, increasing market share, improving raw material sourcing and finished product distribution, and so on.[1] In these mergers, the operations of the acquiring and target firms are combined to achieve synergies, thereby causing the performance of the merged firm to exceed that of the premerged firms. The 2017 mergers of Qualcomm and NXP Semiconductors (both high-tech firms) and Dow Chemical and DuPont (both chemical companies) are examples of strategic mergers. An interesting variation of the strategic merger involves the purchase of specific product lines (rather than the whole company) for strategic reasons. The 2016 $80 million acquisition of Broadcom Ltd.'s wireless infrastructure unit by MaxLinear Inc. is an example of such a merger.

financial merger
A merger transaction undertaken with the goal of restructuring the acquired company to improve its cash flow and unlock its unrealized value.

Financial mergers are based on the acquisition of companies that can be restructured to improve their cash flow. These mergers involve the acquisition of the target firm by an acquirer, which may be another company or a group of investors that may even include the target firm's existing management. The objective of the acquirer is to cut costs drastically and sell off certain unproductive assets or other assets that are not compatible with the target firm's core business to increase the target firm's cash flow. The acquirer uses increased cash flow to service the sizable debt incurred to finance the transaction. Financial mergers are based not on the combined firm's ability to achieve economies of scale but rather on the acquirer's belief that it can enhance the target's value through restructuring.

The ready availability of *junk bond* financing throughout the 1980s fueled the financial merger wave during that period. With the temporary collapse of the junk bond market in the early 1990s, the bankruptcy filings of a number of prominent financial mergers of the 1980s, and the rising stock market of

---

1. A somewhat similar nonmerger arrangement is the strategic alliance, an agreement typically between a large company with established products and channels of distribution and an emerging technology company with a promising research and development program in areas of interest to the larger company. In exchange for its financial support, the larger, established company obtains a stake in the technology being developed by the emerging company. Today, strategic alliances are commonplace in the biotechnology, information technology, and software industries.

MATTER OF FACT

Limits on Growth

Certain legal constraints on mergers and acquisitions exist, especially when a proposed acquisition will lead to reduced competition. The various antitrust laws, which are enforced by the Federal Trade Commission (FTC) and the Justice Department, prohibit business combinations that eliminate competition. In 2015, a U.S. court blocked the proposed merger between Anthem and Cigna on grounds that combining those two businesses would significantly reduce competition in the healthcare industry.

the later 1990s, financial mergers lost some of their luster. As a result, the strategic merger, which does not rely so heavily on debt, continues to dominate today.

MOTIVES FOR MERGING

Firms merge to fulfill certain objectives. The overriding goal for merging is maximization of the owners' wealth as reflected in the acquirer's share price. More specific motives include growth or diversification, synergy, fund raising, increased managerial skill or technology, tax considerations, increased ownership liquidity, and defense against takeover. These motives should be pursued when they lead to owner wealth maximization.

Growth or Diversification

Companies that desire rapid growth in *size* or *market share* or diversification in *the range of their products* may find that a merger can fulfill this objective. Instead of relying entirely on internal or "organic" growth, the firm may achieve its growth or diversification objectives much faster by merging with an existing firm. Such a strategy is often less costly than the alternative of developing the necessary production capacity. If a firm that wants to expand operations can find a suitable going concern, it may avoid many of the risks associated with the design, manufacture, and sale of additional or new products. Moreover, when a firm expands or extends its product line by acquiring another firm, it may remove a potential competitor.

Synergies

Synergies are financial benefits from a merger such as economies of scale gained from the merged firms' lower overhead, or increased power in the marketplace from an enhanced product portfolio. Synergies contribute to revenue growth and profit margin gains. Synergies are easier to capture when firms merge with other firms in the same line of business because many redundant functions and employees can be eliminated. Staff functions, such as purchasing and sales, are probably most greatly affected by this type of combination.

Fund Raising

Often, firms combine to enhance their fund-raising ability. A firm may be unable to obtain funds for its own internal expansion but able to obtain funds for external business combinations. Quite often, one firm may combine with another that has high liquid assets and low levels of liabilities. The acquisition of this type of "cash-rich" company immediately increases the firm's borrowing power by decreasing its financial leverage, which should allow funds to be raised externally at lower cost.

Increased Managerial Skill or Technology

Occasionally, a firm will have good potential that it finds itself unable to develop fully because of deficiencies in certain areas of management or an absence of needed product or production technology. If the firm cannot hire the management or develop the technology it needs, it might combine with a compatible

FOCUS ON ETHICS *in practice*

Is There Any Good in Greed?

Teldar Paper has 33 different vice presidents, each earning over $200,000 a year. I have spent the last two months analyzing what all these guys do, and I still can't figure it out. One thing I do know is [Teldar] lost $110 million last year, and I'll bet half … was spent on … paperwork going back and forth between all these vice presidents… …[I]n my book you either do it right, or you get eliminated. In [my] last seven deals … 2.5 million stockholders … made a pretax profit of $12 billion… …I am not a destroyer of companies; I am a liberator of them!

Gordon Gekko

Gekko, the takeover artist in the 1987 film *Wall Street*, ranks 24th on the American Film Institute's list of top movie villains. His next words—"Greed is good"—put him there. But notice Gekko was not talking up materialism; he wanted Teldar's management to put shareholders first.

Michael Jensen of Harvard University argues the U.S. is undergoing a "modern industrial revolution." Changes in productive technology, global competition, regulatory/tax policy, and management technique have created excess capacity, which necessitates movement of land, labor, and physical capital from overproducing industries to firms with growth potential. Four forces can make this happen: (i) the capital markets (by financing mergers, acquisitions, and leveraged buy-outs); (ii) the legal, political, and regulatory system; (iii) the market for final products, and (iv) internal control systems, starting with the board of directors.

Jensen sees the capital markets as the most effective, in part by providing growing firms with the funds to boost capacity through strategic acquisitions. Capital markets also underwrite financial mergers or leveraged buyouts, which force troubled companies to cut production and costs. Absent such pressure, management in declining industries can hold off needed change because the legal/political/regulatory system is too blunt to force restructuring while product markets and internal-control systems take too long.

But why is it important to reallocate resources quickly? Economic history provides a big-picture answer. Income per capita around the world was stagnant before 1800; since then advances in technology have raised Western living standards by well over 10 times, with unskilled labor reaping most of the benefits. For per-capita output and income to continue growing, scarce land, labor, and physical capital must migrate from low- to high-value uses following disruptive shocks. Put another way, firms benefiting from technological breakthroughs cannot grow, creating income and jobs, unless industries disadvantaged by those breakthroughs release resources.

From a narrower perspective, stockholders profit when resources are liberated in the wake of economic shocks. Owners of firms in expanding industries will see their wealth rise as additional land, labor, and capital are used to boost output, profit, and dividends. In declining industries, slowing the outflow of resources punishes shareholders because maintaining unprofitable business lines—a negative NPV investment—causes further declines in stock prices. Better to scale back operations, so owners can invest the savings in companies that can create jobs and pay dividends.

► *Technological change may raise average living standards over the long run, but in the short run, workers in declining industries with firm-specific skills will lose jobs and income. How should a CEO view the tradeoff between the shareholder and worker interests?*

"The Modern Industrial Revolution, Exit, and the Failure of Internal Control Systems." *Journal of Applied Corporate Finance* 22 (Winter 2010): 43–58. Clark, Gregory. *A Farewell to Alms: A Brief Economic History of the World.* Princeton, NJ: Princeton University Press, 2007.

firm that has the needed managerial personnel or technical expertise. Of course, any merger should contribute to maximizing the owners' wealth.

tax loss carryforward
In a merger, the tax loss of one of the firms that can be applied against a limited amount of future income of the merged firm over 20 years or until the total tax loss has been fully recovered, whichever comes first.

Tax Considerations

Tax considerations are often a key motive for merging. In such a case, the tax benefit generally stems from one of the firms having a **tax loss carryforward.** In other words, the company's tax loss can be applied against future income of the merged firm over an unlimited number of future tax years. There are, however, some limitations on the dollar amount of tax loss carryforwards.[2] Two situations could create an incentive for firms to merge to take advantage of tax loss carryforwards. A company with a tax loss could acquire a profitable company to use the tax loss. In this case, the acquiring firm would boost the combination's after-tax earnings by reducing the taxable income of the acquired firm. A tax loss may also be useful when a profitable firm acquires a firm that has such a loss. In either situation, however, the merger must be justified not only on the basis of the tax benefits but also on grounds consistent with the goal of owner wealth maximization. Moreover, the tax benefits described can be used only in mergers—not in the formation of holding companies—because only in the case of mergers are operating results reported on a consolidated basis. An example will clarify the use of the tax loss carryforward.

EXAMPLE 18.1

MyLab Finance Solution Video

Bergen Company, a wheel bearing manufacturer, has a total of $450,000 in tax loss carryforwards resulting from operating tax losses of $150,000 per year in each of the past 3 years. To use these losses and to diversify its operations, Hudson Company, a molder of plastics, has acquired Bergen through a merger. Hudson expects to have *earnings before taxes* of $300,000 per year. We assume that these earnings are realized, that loss carryforwards are deductible up to 80% of pre-tax earnings in any given year, that the Bergen portion of the merged firm just breaks even, and that Hudson is in the 21% tax bracket. The total taxes paid by the two firms and their after-tax earnings without and with the merger are as shown in Table 18.1.

TABLE 18.1 **Total Taxes and After-Tax Earnings for Hudson Company without and with Merger**

	Year			Total for
	1	2	3	3 years
Total taxes and after-tax earnings without merger				
(1) Earnings before taxes	$300,000	$300,000	$300,000	$900,000
(2) Taxes [0.21 × (1)]	63,000	63,000	63,000	189,000
(3) Earnings after taxes [(1) − (2)]	$237,000	$237,000	$237,000	$711,000
Total taxes and after-tax earnings with merger				
(4) Earnings before losses	$300,000	$300,000	$300,000	$900,000
(5) Tax loss carryforward	240,000	210,000	0	450,000
(6) Earnings before taxes [(4) − (5)]	$ 60,000	$90,000	$300,000	$450,000
(7) Taxes [0.21 × (6)]	12,600	18,900	63,000	94,500
(8) Earnings after taxes [(4) − (7)]	$287,400	$281,100	$237,000	$805,500

2. There are some limits on loss carryforwards. For example, the Tax Cuts and Jobs Act of 2017 does not allow a firm to deduct a loss from a previous tax year if that loss is greater than 80% of a subsequent year's pre-tax income. Older provisions of the tax code impose additional limits on the deductibility of prior losses on firms that are merging.

With the merger, the total tax payments are less: $94,500 (total of line 7) versus $189,000 (total of line 2). With the merger, the total after-tax earnings are more: $805,500 (total of line 8) versus $711,000 (total of line 3). Note that the tax loss deducted in year 1 is just 80% of pre-tax earnings that year. If the loss had been larger, the merged firm might have had to carry losses beyond year 2, but eventually the $450,000 in losses would be written off entirely.

Increased Ownership Liquidity

The merger of two small firms or of a small and a larger firm may provide the owners of the small firm(s) with greater liquidity due to the higher marketability associated with the shares of larger firms. Instead of holding shares in a small firm that has a very "thin" market, the owners will receive shares that are traded in a broader market and can thus be liquidated more readily. Also, owning shares for which market price quotations are readily available provides owners with a better sense of the value of their holdings. Especially in the case of small, closely held firms, the improved liquidity of ownership obtainable through a merger with an acceptable firm may have considerable appeal.

Defense Against Takeover

Occasionally, when a firm becomes the target of an unfriendly takeover, it will acquire another company as a defensive tactic. Typically, in such a strategy, the original target firm takes on additional debt to finance its defensive acquisition; because of the debt load, the target firm becomes too highly leveraged financially to be of any further interest to its suitor. To be effective, a defensive takeover must create greater value for shareholders than they would have realized had the firm been merged with its suitor.

TYPES OF MERGERS

horizontal merger
A merger of two firms in the same line of business.

vertical merger
A merger in which a firm acquires a supplier or a customer.

congeneric merger
A merger in which one firm acquires another firm that is in the same general industry but is neither in the same line of business nor a supplier or customer.

conglomerate merger
A merger combining firms in unrelated businesses.

The four types of mergers are the (1) horizontal merger, (2) vertical merger, (3) congeneric merger, and (4) conglomerate merger. A **horizontal merger** results when two firms *in the same line of business* merge. An example is the 2017 merger of British American Tobacco and R. J. Reynolds Tobacco Company. This form of merger results in the expansion of a firm's operations in a given product line and at the same time eliminates a competitor. A **vertical merger** occurs when a firm acquires *a supplier or a customer*. For example, the 2017 merger of AT&T and Time Warner is a vertical merger because Time Warner is in the business of creating media content, while AT&T is in the business of delivering content to consumers. The economic benefit of a vertical merger stems from the firm's increased control over the acquisition of raw materials or the distribution of finished goods.

A **congeneric merger** is achieved by acquiring a firm that is *in the same general industry* but is neither in the same line of business nor a supplier or customer. An example is the 2016 merger of the pharmaceutical and medical diagnostic firm Abbott Labs with the medical device company St. Jude Medical. The benefit of a congeneric merger is the resulting ability to use the same sales and distribution channels to reach customers of both businesses. A **conglomerate merger** involves the combination of firms in *unrelated businesses*. A recent example of a conglomerate merger is the 2017 acquisition by Warren Buffett's conglomerate, Berkshire

Hathaway, of the Texas-based energy company Oncor. A potential benefit of the conglomerate merger is its ability to reduce risk by merging firms that have different seasonal or cyclical patterns of sales and earnings. Of course, shareholders can easily diversify their own portfolios, so it is not clear that when businesses combine for this purpose they are really creating value for shareholders.

→ REVIEW QUESTIONS MyLab Finance Solutions

18–1 Define and differentiate among the members of each of the following sets of terms: (**a**) mergers, consolidations, and holding companies; (**b**) acquiring company and target company; (**c**) friendly merger and hostile merger; and (**d**) strategic merger and financial merger.

18–2 Briefly describe each of the following motives for merging: (**a**) growth or diversification, (**b**) synergy, (**c**) fund raising, (**d**) increased managerial skill or technology, (**e**) tax considerations, (**f**) increased ownership liquidity, and (**g**) defense against takeover.

18–3 Briefly describe each of the following types of mergers: (**a**) horizontal, (**b**) vertical, (**c**) congeneric, and (**d**) conglomerate.

18.2 LBOs and Divestitures

Before we address the mechanics of merger analysis and negotiation, you need to understand two topics that are closely related to mergers: leveraged buyouts (LBOs) and divestitures. An LBO is a method of structuring an acquisition, and divestitures involve the sale of a firm's assets.

LEVERAGED BUYOUTS (LBOs)

leveraged buyout (LBO)
An acquisition technique involving the use of a large amount of debt to purchase a firm; an example of a financial merger.

A common technique used to make acquisitions is the **leveraged buyout (LBO)**, which involves the use of a large amount of debt to purchase a firm. LBOs are a clear-cut example of a financial merger undertaken to create a high-debt private corporation with improved cash flow and value. Typically, in an LBO, 90% or more of the purchase price is financed with debt. A large part of the borrowing is secured by the acquired firm's assets, and the lenders, because of the high risk, take a portion of the firm's equity. Junk bonds have been routinely used to raise the large amounts of debt needed to finance LBO transactions. Of course, the purchasers in an LBO expect to use the improved cash flow to service the large amount of junk bond and other debt incurred in the buyout.

An attractive candidate for acquisition via a leveraged buyout should possess three key attributes:

1. It must have a good position in its industry, with a solid profit history and reasonable expectations of growth.
2. The firm should have a relatively low level of debt and a high level of "bankable" assets that can be used as loan collateral.
3. It must have stable and predictable cash flows that are adequate to meet interest and principal payments on the debt and provide adequate working capital.

Of course, a willingness on the part of existing ownership and management to sell the company on a leveraged basis is also needed.

In 1986, supermarket chain Safeway was in financial distress and on the verge of closing. Safeway was billions of dollars in debt and had too many poorly performing stores. The private equity firm Kohlberg Kravis Roberts & Co. (KKR) acquired Safeway in an LBO and proceeded to reorganize and streamline the company by closing troubled stores and laying off about 63,000 employees. Even though many of the employees initially let go were ultimately hired back, their pay was significantly reduced. Peter Magowan, then Safeway's chief executive officer, later acknowledged that many of those laid off were "very good" employees and that the cuts were done quickly. However, after KKR got the struggling grocer turned around and growing again, it took Safeway public in 1990 and eventually grew the number of employees to more than 193,000. KKR sold the last of its shares in the company in 1999, having earned $7.2 billion on its initial investment of $129 million.

Many LBOs do not live up to expectations. The largest buyout ever, one of the so-called mega buyouts that took place from 2005 to 2007, was the $45 billion LBO of TXU, the largest electric utility in Texas. Based on the expectation that an increasing demand for energy would outpace supply, causing electric prices to rise, Energy Future Holdings—backed by a consortium that included KKR, Texas Pacific Group (TPG Capital), and Goldman Sachs Capital Partners—completed the LBO in 2007. In the years that followed, the U.S. shale gas boom produced an abundance of natural gas, causing energy prices to fall and leading Energy Future Holdings to file for Chapter 11 bankruptcy in 2014, becoming one of the 10 largest nonfinancial bankruptcies in history. Berkshire Hathaway, led by investor Warren Buffett, who was convinced that the deal could not miss, lost nearly $900 million on its investment in Energy Future Holdings. Buffett later confessed to his shareholders, "that was a big mistake." As of mid-2017, the three firms that executed the LBO of TXU have written off their entire stakes in Energy Future Holdings, and creditors of the LBO are still quarreling over how to reorganize its finances. Whether and how Energy Future will emerge from bankruptcy remains to be seen; as of July 2017, Berkshire Hathaway made a $9 billion bid for the financially distressed company. However, Elliott Management Corporation, an American hedge fund managed by billionaire Paul Singer and Energy Future's biggest creditor, might make its own takeover bid.

In earlier years, other highly publicized LBOs have defaulted on the high-yield debt incurred to finance the buyout. In the 1980s, LBOs were used, often indiscriminately, for hostile takeovers; today, however, LBOs are most often used to finance management buyouts.

DIVESTITURES

operating unit
A part of a business, such as a plant, division, product line, or subsidiary, that contributes to the actual operations of the firm.

divestiture
The selling of some of a firm's assets for various strategic reasons.

Companies often achieve external expansion by acquiring an **operating unit**—plant, division, product line, subsidiary, and so on—of another company. In such a case, the seller generally believes that the value of the firm will be enhanced by converting the unit into cash or some other more productive asset. The selling of some of a firm's assets is called **divestiture.** Unlike business failure, divestiture is often undertaken for positive motives: to generate cash for expansion of other product lines, to get rid of a poorly performing operation, to streamline the corporation, or to restructure the corporation's business in a manner consistent with its strategic goals.

PERSONAL FINANCE EXAMPLE 18.2 A personal finance decision that young families with children frequently face is whether a stay-at-home parent should "divest" his or her child-care duties, hire child care, and return to work. Whereas the emotional aspects of such a decision are nonquantifiable, the economics of such a decision are measurable.

Take the case of Elena and Gino Deluca, who have two children, ages 2 and 4. They are in the process of analyzing whether it makes economic sense to hire child care and have Elena return to work as a credit analyst. They estimate that Elena will earn $5,800 per month gross, including her employer's 401(k) contributions. In addition, she expects to receive monthly employer-paid benefits that include health insurance, life insurance, and pension contributions totaling $1,800. She expects her federal and state income taxes to total about $1,900 per month. The Delucas estimate total additional expenses (child care, clothing and personal expenses, meals away from home, and transportation) related to Elena's job to total $1,500 per month. They summarized these monthly estimates as follows:

Additional gross income	$5,800	
+ Employer-paid benefits	1,800	
(1) Additional income and benefits		$7,600
Additional taxes	$1,900	
+ Additional expenses	1,500	
(2) Additional taxes and expenses		3,400
Net income (loss) [(1) − (2)]		$4,200

Because the Delucas will increase their net income by $4,200 per month, having Elena divest her child-care responsibilities and hire child care is economically justifiable.

Firms divest themselves of operating units by a variety of methods. One involves the *sale of a product line to another firm.* An example is Paramount's sale of Simon and Schuster to Pearson PLC to free up cash and allow Paramount to focus its business more advantageously on global mass consumer markets. Outright sales of operating units can be accomplished on a cash or stock swap basis via the procedures described later in this chapter. A second method that has become popular involves the *sale of the unit to existing management.* This sale is often achieved through the use of a *leveraged buyout (LBO).*

spin-off
A form of divestiture in which an operating unit becomes an independent company through the issuance of shares in it, on a pro rata basis, to the parent company's shareholders.

Sometimes firms divest assets through a **spin-off,** which results in an operating unit becoming an independent company. A firm conducts a spin-off by issuing shares in the divested operating unit on a pro rata basis to the parent company's shareholders. Such an action allows the unit to be separated from the corporation and to trade as a separate entity. In some transactions, an *equity carve-out* precedes a spin-off. In such a transaction, a parent company first sells a portion of the shares of a subsidiary in an IPO to establish a market price for the new company. Later, the parent company distributes the remaining shares of the new company to the parent-company shareholders on a pro rata basis. An example was the decision by Fiat Chrysler to spin off its Ferrari unit in 2016, a transaction that established a distinct market value for Ferrari, a luxury auto brand,

and raised additional capital for Fiat Chrysler. Like an outright sale of a business unit, a spin-off achieves the divestiture objective, although it does not bring additional cash or stock to the parent company unless it follows an equity carve-out. The final and least popular approach to divestiture involves liquidation of the operating unit's individual assets.

Regardless of the method used to divest an unwanted operating unit, the goal is to create a leaner, more focused operation that will enhance the efficiency and profitability of the enterprise and create maximum value for shareholders. Recent divestitures seem to suggest that many operating units are worth much more to others than to the firm itself. Comparisons of postdivestiture and predivestiture market values have shown that the **breakup value**—the sum of the values of a firm's operating units if each were sold separately—of many firms is significantly greater than their combined value. As a result of market valuations, divestiture often creates value in excess of the cash or stock received in the transaction. This type of thinking was behind the proposal for Brookdale Senior Living to divest its real-estate assets in the Chapter 1 opener.

breakup value
The value of a firm measured as the sum of the values of its operating units if each were sold separately.

→ REVIEW QUESTIONS MyLab Finance Solutions

18–4 What is a leveraged buyout (LBO)? What are the three key attributes of an attractive candidate for acquisition via an LBO?

18–5 What is an operating unit? What is a divestiture? What are four common methods used by firms to divest themselves of operating units? What is breakup value?

18.3 Analyzing and Negotiating Mergers

Initially, we will consider how to value the target company and how to use stock swap transactions to acquire companies. Next, we will look at the merger negotiation process. We will then review the major advantages and disadvantages of holding companies. Finally, we will discuss international mergers.

VALUING THE TARGET COMPANY

Once the acquiring company isolates a target company it wishes to acquire, it must estimate the target's value. The acquirer uses that value, along with a proposed financing scheme, to negotiate the transaction, be it on a friendly basis or a hostile basis. The value of the target is estimated by using the valuation techniques presented in Chapter 7 and applied to long-term investment decisions in Chapters 10, 11, and 12. Acquirers apply similar capital budgeting techniques whether the target firm is sought for its assets or as a going concern.

Acquisitions of Assets

Occasionally, a firm is acquired not for its income-earning potential but as a collection of assets (generally fixed assets) that the acquiring company needs. The price paid for this type of acquisition depends largely on which assets are being acquired; the value of any tax losses must also be considered. To determine whether the purchase of assets is financially justified, the acquirer must estimate both the costs and the benefits of the target assets. This estimation is a capital budgeting problem (see Chapters 10, 11, and 12) because the acquirer makes an initial cash outlay to acquire assets that it expects to generate future cash inflows.

EXAMPLE 18.3

MyLab Finance Solution Video

Clark Company, a major manufacturer of electrical transformers, is interested in acquiring certain fixed assets of Noble Company, an industrial electronics company. Noble, which has tax loss carryforwards from losses over the past 5 years, is interested in selling out, but it wishes to sell out entirely, not just get rid of certain fixed assets. A condensed balance sheet for Noble Company follows.

Noble Company Balance Sheet

Assets		Liabilities and stockholders' equity	
Cash	$ 2,000	Total liabilities	$ 80,000
Marketable securities	0	Stockholders' equity	120,000
Accounts receivable	8,000	Total liabilities and stockholders' equity	$200,000
Inventories	10,000		
Machine A	10,000		
Machine B	30,000		
Machine C	25,000		
Land and buildings	115,000		
Total assets	$200,000		

Clark Company needs only machines B and C and the land and buildings. However, it has made some inquiries and has arranged to sell the accounts receivable, inventories, and machine A for $23,000. Because there is also $2,000 in cash, Clark will get $25,000 for the excess assets. Noble wants $100,000 for the entire company, which means that Clark will have to pay the firm's creditors $80,000 and its owners $20,000. The actual outlay required of Clark after liquidating the unneeded assets will be $75,000 [($80,000 + $20,000) – $25,000].

In other words, to obtain the use of the desired assets (machines B and C and the land and buildings) and the benefits of Noble's tax losses, Clark must pay $75,000. The after-tax cash inflows that result from the new assets and applicable tax losses are $14,000 per year for the next 5 years and $12,000 per year for the following 5 years. The desirability of this asset acquisition can be determined by calculating the net present value of this outlay using Clark Company's 11% cost of capital, as shown in Table 18.2. Because the net present value of $3,063 is greater than zero, Clark's value should be increased by acquiring Noble Company's assets.

TABLE 18.2 Net Present Value of Noble Company's Assets

Year(s)	Cash inflows	Present value
1–5	$14,000	$51,743
6	12,000	6,416
7	12,000	5,780
8	12,000	5,207
9	12,000	4,691
10	12,000	4,226
	Present value of inflows	$78,063
	Less: Cash outlay required	75,000
	Net present value	$ 3,063

Acquisitions of Going Concerns

Firms analyze acquisitions of target companies that are going concerns by using capital budgeting techniques similar to those described for asset acquisitions. The methods of estimating expected cash flows from an acquisition are similar to those used in estimating capital budgeting cash flows. Typically, the acquirer prepares pro forma financial statements reflecting the postmerger cash inflows and outflows attributable to the target company (see Chapter 4). They are then adjusted to reflect the expected cash flows over the relevant time period. When discounting the cash flows expected from an acquisition, the acquirer should use a discount rate that reflects the risk of the assets it is purchasing. That discount rate could be higher or lower than its own cost of capital.

EXAMPLE 18.4

MyLab Finance Solution Video

Square Company, a major media company, is contemplating the acquisition of Circle Company, a small independent film producer that it can purchase for $60,000. Square currently has a high degree of operating leverage, which is reflected in its 13% cost of capital. Because of the low operating leverage of Circle Company, Square decides to discount the cash flows that it expects to earn as a result of the Circle Company acquisition using a 10% cost of capital. Using 10% rather than 13% recognizes that Circle's assets are less risky than Square's assets. The postmerger cash flows attributable to the target company are forecast over a 30-year time horizon. These estimated cash flows (all inflows) and the resulting net present value of the target company, Circle Company, are shown in Table 18.3.

TABLE 18.3 Net Present Value of the Circle Company Acquisition

Year(s)	Cash inflows	Present value
1–10	$ 5,000	$30,723
11–18	13,000	26,739
19–30	4,000	4,902
	Present value of inflows	$62,364
	Less: Cash purchase price	60,000
	Net present value	$ 2,364

Because the $2,364 net present value of the target company is greater than zero, the merger is acceptable. Note that if financial analysts at Square had not accounted for the difference in asset risk by discounting cash flows at 10%, they would have recommended against acquiring Circle because the NPV of the acquisition is −$11,868 using a 13% cost of capital.

STOCK SWAP TRANSACTIONS

Once the acquirer determines the value of the target company, it must decide what method of payment it wants to use to purchase the target. The simplest option is a pure cash purchase. In addition, there are virtually an infinite number of payment packages that use various combinations of cash, debt, preferred stock, and common stock.

stock swap transaction
An acquisition method in which the acquiring firm exchanges its shares for shares of the target company according to a predetermined ratio.

In contrast to a pure cash purchase, firms often pay for an acquisition by conducting a **stock swap transaction,** in which the acquirer exchanges some of its common stock for the shares of the target company. The acquirer and the target company negotiate to agree upon a *ratio of exchange*, which determines how many shares of the acquirer's stock will be exchanged for target company share. This ratio affects the various financial yardsticks that existing and prospective shareholders use to value the merged firm's shares. The use of stock as a method of payment in mergers is quite common.

Ratio of Exchange

When one firm swaps its stock for the shares of another firm, the firms must determine the number of shares of the acquiring firm to be exchanged for each share of the target firm. The first requirement, of course, is that the acquiring company have sufficient shares available to complete the transaction. Often, a firm's repurchase of shares (discussed in Chapter 14) is necessary to obtain sufficient shares for such a transaction. The acquiring firm generally offers enough of its own shares that the value of the shares given up exceeds the value of one target share. The actual **ratio of exchange** is merely the ratio of the amount paid per share of the target company to the market price per share of the acquiring firm. It is calculated in this manner because the acquiring firm pays the target firm in stock, which has a value equal to its market price.

ratio of exchange
The ratio of the amount paid per share of the target company to the market price per share of the acquiring firm.

EXAMPLE 18.5

Grand Company, a leather products concern whose stock is currently selling for $80 per share, is interested in acquiring Small Company, a producer of belts. To prepare for the acquisition, Grand has been repurchasing its own shares over the past 3 years. Small's stock is currently selling for $75 per share, but in the merger negotiations Grand has offered Small $110 per share. Because Grand does not have sufficient cash to pay $110 per share, and because it does not wish to raise that much cash by issuing new shares or by borrowing the money, Small has agreed to accept Grand's stock in exchange for its shares. As stated, Grand's stock currently sells for $80 per share, and it must pay $110 per share for Small's stock. Therefore, the ratio of exchange is 1.375 ($110 ÷ $80). So, Grand Company must exchange 1.375 shares of its stock for each share of Small's stock.

Effect on Earnings per Share

Although value creation is the primary focus of merger analysis, it is useful to consider the effects of a proposed merger on earnings per share. In the long run, an acquisition that creates value will likely produce higher earnings for the combined company, but in the short run, the resulting earnings per share differ from the premerger earnings per share for both the acquiring firm and the target firm. They depend largely on the ratio of exchange and the premerger earnings per share of each firm. It is best to view the initial and long-run effects of the ratio of exchange on earnings per share separately.

Initial Effect When the ratio of exchange is equal to 1 and both the acquiring firm and the target firm have the same premerger earnings per share, the merged firm's earnings per share will initially remain constant. In this rare instance, both the acquiring firm and the target firm would also have equal price/earnings (P/E) ratios. In most transactions, the earnings per share of the merged firm are generally above the premerger earnings per share of one firm and below the premerger earnings per share of the other, after the necessary adjustment has been made for the ratio of exchange.

EXAMPLE 18.6

As we saw in the preceding example, Grand Company is contemplating acquiring Small Company by swapping 1.375 shares of its stock for each share of Small's stock. The current financial data related to the earnings and market price for each company are given in Table 18.4.

To complete the merger and retire the 20,000 shares of Small Company stock outstanding, Grand will have to issue and (or) use treasury stock totaling 27,500 shares (1.375 × 20,000 shares). Once the merger is completed, Grand will have 152,500 shares of common stock (125,000 + 27,500) outstanding. If the earnings of each of the firms remain constant, the merged company will be expected to have earnings available for the common stockholders of $600,000 ($500,000 + $100,000). The earnings per share of the merged company therefore should equal approximately $3.93 ($600,000 ÷ 152,500 shares).

It would appear at first that Small Company's shareholders have sustained a decrease in per-share earnings from $5 to $3.93, but because each share of Small Company's original stock is equivalent to 1.375 shares of the merged company's stock, the equivalent earnings per share are actually $5.40 ($3.93 × 1.375). In other words, as a result of the merger, Grand Company's original shareholders experience a decrease in earnings per share from $4 to $3.93 to the benefit of Small Company's shareholders, whose earnings per share increase from $5 to $5.40. These results are summarized in Table 18.5.

TABLE 18.4 Grand Company's and Small Company's Financial Data

Item	Grand Company	Small Company
(1) Earnings available for common stock	$500,000	$100,000
(2) Number of shares of common stock outstanding	125,000	20,000
(3) Earnings per share [(1) ÷ (2)]	$4	$5
(4) Market price per share	$80	$75
(5) Price/earnings (P/E) ratio [(4) ÷ (3)]	20	15

TABLE 18.5 Summary of the Effects on Earnings per Share of a Merger Between Grand Company and Small Company at $110 per Share

	Earnings per share	
Stockholders	Before merger	After merger
Grand Company	$4.00	$3.93[a]
Small Company	5.00	5.40[b]

[a] $\dfrac{\$500{,}000 + \$100{,}000}{125{,}000 + (1.375 \times 20{,}000)} = \$3.93.$

[b] $3.93 × 1.375 = $5.40.

TABLE 18.6 Effect of Price/Earnings (P/E) Ratios on Earnings per Share (EPS)

	Effect on EPS	
Relationship between P/E paid and P/E of acquiring company	**Acquiring company**	**Target company**
P/E paid > P/E of acquiring company	Decrease	Increase
P/E paid = P/E of acquiring company	Constant	Constant
P/E paid < P/E of acquiring company	Increase	Decrease

The postmerger earnings per share for owners of the acquiring and target companies can be explained by comparing the price/earnings ratio paid by the acquiring company with its initial P/E ratio. Table 18.6 summarizes this relationship. By paying more than its current value per dollar of earnings to acquire each dollar of earnings (P/E paid > P/E of acquiring company), the acquiring firm transfers the claim on a portion of its premerger earnings to the owners of the target firm. Therefore, on a postmerger basis, the target firm's EPS increases, and the acquiring firm's EPS decreases. Note that this outcome is nearly always the case because the acquirer typically pays, on average, a 30% to 40% premium above the target firm's market price, which results in the P/E paid being much above its own P/E. The P/E ratios associated with the Grand–Small merger demonstrate the effect of the merger on EPS.

EXAMPLE 18.7

Grand Company's P/E ratio is 20, and the P/E ratio paid for Small Company's earnings was 22 ($110 ÷ $5). Because the P/E paid for Small Company was greater than the P/E for Grand Company (22 versus 20), the effect of the merger was to decrease the EPS for original holders of shares in Grand Company (from $4.00 to $3.93) and to increase the effective EPS of original holders of shares in Small Company (from $5.00 to $5.40).

Long-Run Effect The long-run effect of a merger on the earnings per share of the merged company depends largely on whether the earnings of the merged firm grow. Often, although an initial decrease in the per-share earnings of the stock held by the original owners of the acquiring firm is expected, the long-run effects of the merger on earnings per share are quite favorable. Because firms generally expect growth in earnings, the key factor enabling the acquiring company to experience higher future EPS than it would have without the merger is that the earnings attributable to the target company's assets grow more rapidly than those resulting from the acquiring company's premerger assets. An example will clarify this point.

EXAMPLE 18.8

In 2019, Grand Company acquired Small Company by swapping 1.375 shares of its common stock for each share of Small Company. Other key financial data and the effects of this exchange ratio were discussed in preceding examples. The total earnings of Grand Company were expected to grow at an annual rate of 3% without the merger; Small Company's earnings were expected to grow at a 7% annual rate without the merger. The same growth rates are expected to apply

FIGURE 18.1

Future EPS
Future EPS without and with the Grand–Small merger

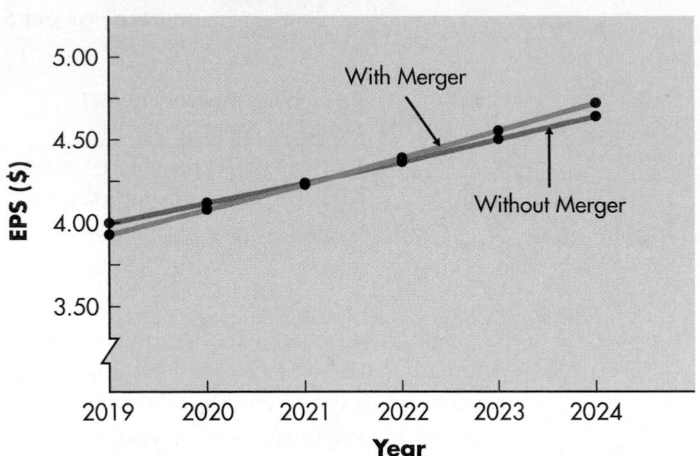

	Without merger		With merger	
Year	**Total earnings**[a]	**Earnings per share**[b]	**Total earnings**[c]	**Earnings per share**[d]
2019	$500,000	$4.00	$600,000	$3.93
2020	515,000	4.12	622,000	4.08
2021	530,450	4.24	644,940	4.23
2022	546,364	4.37	668,868	4.39
2023	562,755	4.50	693,835	4.55
2024	579,638	4.64	719,893	4.72

[a]Based on a 3% annual growth rate.
[b]Based on 125,000 shares outstanding.
[c]Based on a 3% annual growth in the Grand Company's earnings and a 7% annual growth in the Small Company's earnings.
[d]Based on 152,500 shares outstanding [125,000 shares + (1.375 × 20,000 shares)].

to the component earnings streams with the merger. The table in Figure 18.1 shows the future effects on EPS for Grand Company without and with the proposed Small Company merger on the basis of these growth rates.

The table indicates that the earnings per share without the merger will be greater than the EPS with the merger for the years 2019 through 2021. After 2021, however, the EPS will be higher than they would have been without the merger as a result of the faster earnings growth rate of Small Company (7% versus 3%). Although a few years are required for this difference in the growth rate of earnings to pay off, in the future Grand Company will receive an earnings benefit as a result of merging with Small Company at a 1.375 ratio of exchange. The long-run earnings advantage of the merger is clearly depicted in Figure 18.1.[3]

3. To discover properly whether the merger is beneficial, the earnings estimates under each alternative would have to be made over a long period—say, 50 years—and then converted to cash flows and discounted at the appropriate rate. The alternative with the higher present value would be preferred. For simplicity, only the basic intuitive view of the long-run effect is presented here.

Effect on Market Price per Share

The market price per share does not necessarily remain constant after the acquisition of one firm by another. Adjustments occur in the marketplace in response to changes in expected earnings, the dilution of ownership, changes in risk, and certain other operating and financial changes. By using the ratio of exchange, we can calculate a **ratio of exchange in market price** that indicates the market price per share of the acquiring firm *paid* for each dollar of market price per share of the target firm. This ratio, the *MPR*, is defined by

ratio of exchange in market price
Indicates the market price per share of the acquiring firm paid for each dollar of market price per share of the target firm.

$$MPR = \frac{MP_{\text{acquiring}} \times RE}{MP_{\text{target}}} \tag{18.1}$$

where

MPR = market price ratio of exchange
$MP_{\text{acquiring}}$ = market price per share of the acquiring firm
RE = ratio of exchange
MP_{target} = market price per share of the target firm

EXAMPLE 18.9

The market price of Grand Company's stock was $80 and that of Small Company's was $75. The ratio of exchange was 1.375. Substituting these values into Equation 18.1 yields a ratio of exchange in market price of 1.47 [($80 × 1.375) ÷ $75]. So, $1.47 of the market price of Grand Company is given in exchange for every $1.00 of the market price of Small Company.

The ratio of exchange in market price is normally greater than 1, which indicates that to acquire a firm, the acquirer must pay a premium above the target's market price. Even so, the original owners of the acquiring firm may still gain because the merged firm's stock may sell at a price/earnings ratio above the individual premerger ratios as a result of the improved risk–return relationship perceived by shareholders and other investors.

EXAMPLE 18.10

The financial data developed earlier for the Grand–Small merger can be used to explain the market price effects of a merger. If the earnings of the merged company remain at the premerger levels and if the stock of the merged company sells at an assumed multiple of 21 times earnings, the values in Table 18.7 can be expected. Although Grand Company's earnings per share decline from $4.00 to $3.93 (see Table 18.5), the market price of its shares will increase from $80.00 to $82.53 as a result of the merger.

TABLE 18.7 Postmerger Market Price of Grand Company Using a P/E Ratio of 21

Item	Merged company
(1) Earnings available for common stock	$600,000
(2) Number of shares of common stock outstanding	152,500
(3) Earnings per share [(1) ÷ (2)]	$3.93
(4) Price/earnings (P/E) ratio	21
(5) Expected market price per share [(3) × (4)]	$82.53

Although the behavior exhibited in the preceding example is not unusual, the financial manager must recognize that only with proper management of the merged enterprise can its market value be improved. If the merged firm cannot achieve sufficiently high earnings in view of its risk, there is no guarantee that its market price will reach the forecast value. Nevertheless, a policy of acquiring firms with low P/Es can produce favorable results for the owners of the acquiring firm. Acquisitions are especially attractive when the acquiring firm's stock price is high because fewer shares must be exchanged to acquire a given firm.

MERGER NEGOTIATION PROCESS

investment bankers
Financial intermediaries who, in addition to their role in selling new security issues, can be hired by acquirers in mergers to find suitable target companies and assist in negotiations.

Mergers are often handled by **investment bankers**, financial intermediaries who, in addition to their role in selling new security issues (described in Chapter 7), can be hired by acquirers to find suitable target companies and assist in negotiations. Once a target company is selected, the investment banker negotiates with its management or investment banker. Likewise, when management wishes to sell the firm or an operating unit of the firm, it will hire an investment banker to seek out potential buyers.

If attempts to negotiate with the management of the target company break down, the acquiring firm, often with the aid of its investment banker, can make a direct appeal to shareholders by using tender offers (as explained in the following discussion). The investment banker is typically compensated with a fixed fee, a commission tied to the transaction price, or a combination of fees and commissions.

Management Negotiations

To initiate negotiations, the acquiring firm must make an offer either in cash or based on a stock swap with a specified ratio of exchange. The target company then reviews the offer and, in light of alternative offers, accepts or rejects the terms presented. A desirable merger candidate may receive more than a single offer. Usually, it is necessary to resolve certain nonfinancial issues related to the existing management, product line policies, financing policies, and the independence of the target firm. The key factor, of course, is the per-share price offered in cash or reflected in the ratio of exchange. Sometimes negotiations break down.

Tender Offers

two-tier offer
A tender offer in which the terms offered are more attractive to those who tender shares early.

When negotiations for an acquisition fail, the acquirer may initiate a "hostile merger" by making a tender offer directly to the target firm's stockholders. As noted in Chapter 14, a tender offer is a formal offer to purchase a given number of shares of a firm's stock at a specified price. The offer is made to all the stockholders at a premium above the market price. Occasionally, the acquirer will make a **two-tier offer,** in which the terms offered are more attractive to those who tender shares early. An example of a two-tier offer is when the acquirer offers to pay $25 per share for the first 60% of the outstanding shares tendered and only $23 per share for the remaining shares. Stockholders are advised of a tender offer through announcements in financial newspapers or through direct communications from the offering firm. Sometimes a tender offer is made to add pressure to existing merger negotiations. In other cases, the tender offer may be made without warning as an attempt at an abrupt corporate takeover.

takeover defenses
Strategies for fighting hostile takeovers.

white knight
A takeover defense in which the target firm finds an acquirer more to its liking than the initial hostile acquirer and prompts the two to compete to take over the firm.

poison pill
A takeover defense in which a firm issues securities that give their holders certain rights that become effective when a takeover is attempted; these rights make the target firm less desirable to a hostile acquirer.

greenmail
A takeover defense under which a target firm repurchases, through private negotiation, a large block of stock at a premium from one or more shareholders to end a hostile takeover attempt by those shareholders.

leveraged recapitalization
A takeover defense in which the target firm pays a large debt-financed cash dividend, increasing the firm's financial leverage and thereby deterring the takeover attempt.

golden parachutes
Provisions in the employment contracts of key executives that provide them with sizable compensation if the firm is taken over; deters hostile takeovers to the extent that the cash outflows required are large enough to make the takeover unattractive.

shark repellents
Antitakeover amendments to a corporate charter that constrain the firm's ability to transfer managerial control of the firm as a result of a merger.

Fighting Hostile Takeovers

If the management of a target firm does not favor a merger or considers the price offered in a proposed merger too low, it is likely to take defensive actions to ward off the hostile takeover. The target firm generally takes such actions with the assistance of investment bankers and lawyers who help the firm develop and employ effective **takeover defenses.** There are obvious strategies, such as informing stockholders of the alleged damaging effects of a takeover, acquiring another company (discussed earlier in the chapter), or attempting to sue the acquiring firm on antitrust or other grounds. In addition, many other defenses exist (some with colorful names), such as a white knight, poison pills, greenmail, leveraged recapitalization, golden parachutes, and shark repellents.

The **white knight** strategy involves the target firm finding a more suitable acquirer (the "white knight") and prompting it to compete with the initial hostile acquirer to take over the firm. In other words, the white knight makes a competing friendly offer to acquire the target company. **Poison pills** typically involve the creation of securities that give their holders certain rights that become effective when a takeover is attempted. The "pill" allows the shareholders to receive special voting rights or securities that make the firm less desirable to the hostile acquirer. **Greenmail** is a strategy by which the firm repurchases, through private negotiation, a large block of stock at a premium from one or more shareholders to end a hostile takeover attempt by those shareholders. The name greenmail comes from the view that it is a form of corporate blackmail by the holders of a large block of shares.

Another defense against hostile takeover involves the use of a **leveraged recapitalization,** which is a strategy involving the payment of a large debt-financed cash dividend. This strategy significantly increases the firm's financial leverage, thereby deterring the takeover attempt. In addition, as a further deterrent, the recapitalization is often structured to increase the equity and control of the existing management. **Golden parachutes** are provisions in the employment contracts of key executives that provide them with sizable compensation if the firm is taken over. Golden parachutes deter hostile takeovers to the extent that the cash outflows required by these contracts are large enough to make the takeover unattractive to the acquirer, although golden parachutes may also increase the likelihood that a hostile takeover will succeed by giving managers of the target firm a financial incentive to sell out to the bidder. Another defense is the use of **shark repellents,** which are antitakeover amendments to the corporate charter that constrain the firm's ability to transfer managerial control of the firm as a result of a merger. Although this defense could entrench existing management, many firms have had these amendments ratified by shareholders.

Because takeover defenses tend to insulate management from shareholders, the potential for litigation is great when these strategies are employed. Dissident shareholders sometimes file lawsuits against management. In addition, federal and state governments frequently intervene when a proposed takeover is deemed to be in violation of federal or state law. A number of states have legislation on their books limiting or restricting hostile takeovers of companies domiciled within their boundaries.

HOLDING COMPANIES

A *holding company* is a corporation that has voting control of one or more other corporations. The holding company may need to own only a small percentage of the outstanding shares to have this voting control. In the case of companies with a relatively small number of shareholders, as much as 30% to 40% of the stock may be required. In the case of firms with a widely dispersed ownership, 10% to 20% of the shares may be sufficient to gain voting control. A holding company that wants to obtain voting control of a firm may use direct market purchases or tender offers to acquire needed shares. Although relatively few holding companies exist and they are far less important than mergers, it is still helpful to understand their key advantages and disadvantages.

Advantages of Holding Companies

The primary advantage of holding companies is the *leverage effect* that permits the firm to control a large amount of assets with a relatively small dollar investment. In other words, the owners of a holding company can *control* significantly larger amounts of assets than they could *acquire* through mergers.

EXAMPLE 18.11

Carr Company, a holding company, currently holds voting control of two subsidiaries, company X and company Y. Table 18.8 presents the balance sheets for Carr and its two subsidiaries. Carr owns approximately 17% ($10 ÷ $60) of company X and 20% ($14 ÷ $70) of company Y. These holdings are sufficient for voting control.

The owners of Carr Company's $12 worth of equity have control over $260 worth of assets (company X's $100 worth and company Y's $160 worth). Thus, the owners' equity represents only about 4.6% ($12 ÷ $260) of the total assets controlled. From the discussions of ratio analysis, leverage, and capital structure in Chapters 3 and 13, you should recognize that this is quite a high degree of leverage. If an individual stockholder or even another holding company owns $3 of Carr Company's stock, which is assumed to be sufficient for its control, it will in actuality control the whole $260 of assets. The investment itself in this case would represent only 1.15% ($3 ÷ $260) of the assets controlled.

TABLE 18.8 Balance Sheets for Carr Company and Its Subsidiaries

Assets		Liabilities and stockholders' equity	
Carr Company			
Common stock holdings		Long-term debt	$ 6
Company X	$ 10	Preferred stock	6
Company Y	14	Common stock equity	12
Total	$ 24	Total	$ 24
Company X			
Current assets	$ 30	Current liabilities	$ 15
Fixed assets	70	Long-term debt	25
Total	$100	Common stock equity	60
		Total	$100
Company Y			
Current assets	$ 20	Current liabilities	$ 10
Fixed assets	140	Long-term debt	60
Total	$160	Preferred stock	20
		Common stock equity	70
		Total	$160

pyramiding
An arrangement among holding companies wherein one holding company controls other holding companies, thereby causing an even greater magnification of earnings and losses.

The high leverage obtained through a holding company arrangement greatly magnifies earnings and losses for the holding company. Quite often, a **pyramiding** of holding companies occurs when one holding company controls other holding companies, thereby causing an even greater magnification of earnings and losses. The greater the leverage, the greater the risk involved. The risk–return tradeoff is a key consideration in the holding company decision.

Another commonly cited advantage of holding companies is that the risk protection resulting from the failure of one of the companies (such as Y in the preceding example) does not result in the failure of the entire holding company. Because each subsidiary is a separate corporation, the failure of one company should cost the holding company, at maximum, no more than its investment in that subsidiary. Other advantages include the following: (1) Certain state tax benefits may be realized by each subsidiary in its state of incorporation, (2) lawsuits or legal actions against a subsidiary do not threaten the remaining companies, and (3) it is generally easy to gain control of a firm because stockholder or management approval is not generally necessary.

Disadvantages of Holding Companies

A major disadvantage of holding companies is the increased risk resulting from the leverage effect. When general economic conditions are unfavorable, a loss by one subsidiary may be magnified. For example, if subsidiary company X in Table 18.8 experiences a loss, its inability to pay dividends to Carr Company could result in Carr Company's inability to meet its scheduled payments.

Another disadvantage is double taxation. Before paying dividends, a subsidiary must pay federal and state taxes on its earnings. Although a 50% tax exclusion is allowed on dividends received by one corporation from another, the remaining 50% received is taxable. (In the event that the holding company owns between 20% and 80% of the stock in a subsidiary, the exclusion is 80%; if it owns more than 80% of the stock in the subsidiary, 100% of the dividends are excluded.) If a subsidiary were part of a merged company, double taxation would *not* exist.

Another disadvantage is that holding companies are difficult to analyze. Security analysts and investors typically have difficulty understanding holding companies because of the complexity of such firms. As a result, these firms tend to sell at low multiples of earnings (P/Es), and the shareholder value of holding companies may suffer.

A final disadvantage of holding companies is the generally high cost of administration that results from maintaining each subsidiary company as a separate entity. A merger, in contrast, is likely to result in certain administrative economies of scale. The need for coordination and communication between the holding company and its subsidiaries may further elevate these costs.

INTERNATIONAL MERGERS

Perhaps in no other area does U.S. financial practice differ more fundamentally from practices in other countries than in the field of mergers. Outside of the United States (and, to a lesser degree, Great Britain), hostile takeovers are virtually nonexistent, and in some countries (such as Japan), takeovers of any kind are uncommon. The emphasis in the United States and Great Britain on shareholder value and reliance on public capital markets for financing is generally not shared by companies in continental Europe. Companies there are generally smaller, and other stakeholders, such as employees, bankers, and governments, are accorded greater consideration. The U.S. approach is also not the norm in Japan and other Asian nations.

Changes in Western Europe

Today, there are signs that Western Europe is moving toward a U.S.-style approach to shareholder value and public capital market financing. Since the European Union's (EU's) economic and monetary union (EMU) integration involving the introduction of a single European currency, the euro, on January 1, 2002, the cross-border European mergers have continued to grow rapidly in terms of number, size, and importance. Nationally focused companies want to achieve economies of scale in manufacturing, encourage international product development strategies, and develop distribution networks across the continent. They are also driven by the need to compete with U.S. companies, which have been operating on a continent-wide basis in Europe for decades.

These larger Europe-based companies are expected to become even more formidable competitors as more national barriers are removed. Although the vast majority of these cross-border mergers are friendly in nature, a few have been actively resisted by target firm managements. It seems clear that as European companies come to rely more on public capital markets for financing and as the market for common stock becomes more truly European in character, rather than French or British or German, active markets for European corporate equity will continue to evolve.

Foreign Takeovers of U.S. Companies

Both European and Japanese companies have been active as acquirers of U.S. companies in recent years. Foreign companies purchased U.S. firms for two major reasons: to gain access to the world's single largest, richest, and least regulated market and to acquire world-class technology. British companies have been historically the most active acquirers of U.S. firms. In the late 1980s, Japanese corporations surged to prominence with a series of very large acquisitions, including two in the entertainment industry: Sony's purchase of Columbia Pictures and Matsushita's acquisition of MCA. More recently, German firms have become especially active acquirers of U.S. companies as producing export goods in Germany has become prohibitively expensive. (German workers have some of the world's highest wages and one of the shortest workweeks.) The *Global Focus* box describes recent mergers by Australian media giant News Corp. It seems inevitable that foreign companies will continue to acquire U.S. firms even as U.S. companies continue to seek attractive acquisitions abroad.

→ REVIEW QUESTIONS MyLab Finance Solutions

18–6 Describe the procedures typically used by an acquirer to value a target company, whether it is being acquired for its assets or as a going concern.

18–7 What is the ratio of exchange? Is it based on the current market prices of the shares of the acquiring and target firms? Why may a long-run view of the merged firm's earnings per share change a merger decision?

GLOBAL FOCUS *in practice*

International Mergers

In July 2005, Australian-based media giant News Corp launched a series of acquisitions involving U.S. assets. The first was a $580 million buyout of Intermix Media, owner of Myspace.com, the fifth most viewed Internet domain in the United States at the time. Rupert Murdoch, the media mogul running News Corp, calculated that the Myspace networking site would drive traffic to his Fox TV sites.

Murdoch's next purchase came in September 2006, when News Corp acquired, from Verisign, a majority stake in Jamba, which runs Jamster, a download service for such commodities as ring tones and screen "wallpapers." News Corp's intent was to hardwire Fox's presence in the entire content life cycle, from creation, through production, to delivery on your screen. It already had a mobile content provider, Mobizzo, launched in June 2005 under the Fox Mobile Entertainment division. Among the things Mobizzo was designed to offer were 1-minute episodes derived from Fox properties such as its *American Idol* franchise.

In May 2007, News Corp set its sight on a new target, Dow Jones, publisher of the *Wall Street Journal* and *Barron's* and the owner of other financial news and content assets, including the Dow Jones Newswires, the financial website MarketWatch, and several stock market indicators (for example, the Dow Jones Industrial Average). Murdoch's News Corp bid $5 billion for Dow Jones but faced resistance from members of the Bancroft family—descendants of Clarence Barron, the "father of financial journalism"—which controls more than 50% of the voting power in the company. The News Corp bid was remarkable for its premium, which would value Dow Jones at more than double its trading value prior to the bid.

International mergers such as the ones pursued by News Corp are not as easy to execute as domestic mergers. Complicating matters are multiple legal and regulatory regimes, cultural differences, and complex timing requirements involving simultaneously closing the deal in multiple jurisdictions. Further complications may arise from a potential distrust of employees or owners from another country. In the Dow Jones case, the Dow Jones board and the Bancroft family sought to negotiate some level of independence for the *Journal* so that it might remain free of corporate interference.

Ultimately, Rupert Murdoch would have his way. On December 13, 2007, News Corp announced the completion of its acquisition of Dow Jones. The terms of the merger agreement provided that each share of Dow Jones common stock was entitled to receive, at the election of the holder, either $60.00 in cash or 2.8681 shares of Class B common units of Ruby Newco LLC, a wholly owned subsidiary of News Corp. Ruby Newco Class B common units are convertible after a period of time into a share of News Corp Class A common stock. On completion of the merger, Dow Jones became a wholly owned subsidiary of Ruby Newco, and Natalie Bancroft was appointed to the company's board of directors.

In 2010, the international tide changed for News Corp, and selling rather than buying became the norm. In 2010, Fiji's government began to require the country's media outlets to be 90% owned by Fiji nationals, resulting in the sale of Fijian newspapers (*Fiji Times, Nai Lalakai,* and *Shanti Dut*) to Motibhai Group of Companies. Then, in 2011, the struggling Myspace, after much effort to find a buyer, was sold to buyers Justin Timberlake and Specific Media. In July 2011, News Corp closed its United Kingdom *News of the World* newspaper, which was in the midst of a scandal, and withdrew its takeover bid for BSkyB.

Citing growing concerns about the recent scandals and a desire to "unlock even greater long-term shareholder value," Murdoch announced on June 28, 2012, that News Corp would be split into two new publicly traded companies. Publishing operations became the "new" News Corporation, with Robert James Thomson, editor of the *Wall Street Journal*, as CEO. Murdoch remained CEO of the media operations and properties (such as the Fox Entertainment Group and 20th Century Fox) that became 21st Century Fox. Murdoch remains chairman for both companies.

► *If you had been a shareholder of Dow Jones, what tradeoffs would you have considered when deciding whether to take the $60.00 per share or the shares in Ruby Newco?*

18–8 What role do investment bankers often play in the merger negotiation process? What is a tender offer? When and how is it used?

18–9 Briefly describe each of the following takeover defenses against a hostile merger: (**a**) white knight, (**b**) poison pill, (**c**) greenmail, (**d**) leveraged recapitalization, (**e**) golden parachutes, and (**f**) shark repellents.

18–10 What key advantages and disadvantages are associated with holding companies? What is pyramiding, and what are its consequences?

18–11 Discuss the differences in merger practices between U.S. companies and companies in other countries. What changes are occurring in international merger activity, particularly in Western Europe and Japan?

18.4 Business Failure Fundamentals

A business failure is an unfortunate circumstance. Although the majority of firms that fail do so within the first year or two of life, other firms grow, mature, and fail much later. The failure of a business can be viewed in a number of ways and can result from one or more causes.

TYPES OF BUSINESS FAILURE

A firm may fail because its returns are negative or low. A firm that consistently reports operating losses will probably experience a decline in market value, although it is common and not necessarily a sign of alarm when a young, rapidly growing firm generates losses during its growth phase. At one level we could say that a firm that generates returns below its cost of capital is failing. Negative or low returns, unless remedied, are likely to result eventually in one of the following more serious types of failure.

insolvency
Business failure that occurs when a firm is unable to pay its liabilities as they come due.

A second type of failure, **insolvency**, occurs when a firm is unable to pay its liabilities as they come due. When a firm is insolvent, its assets may still be greater than its liabilities, but it is confronted with a liquidity crisis. If some of its assets can be converted into cash within a reasonable period, the company may be able to escape complete failure. If not, the result is the third and most serious type of failure, bankruptcy.

bankruptcy
A legal process in which a court declares that a firm is unable to meet its financial obligations.

Bankruptcy refers to a legal process in which a court declares that a firm cannot meet its financial obligations and a establishes a procedure for resolving that situation. In other words, bankruptcy is a legal process that serves the purpose of resolving the state of insolvency. Depending on the specifics of the situation, the assets of a bankrupt firm might be liquidated with the firm going out of business, or a bankrupt firm might go through a restructuring process and reemerge from bankruptcy as a going concern.

MAJOR CAUSES OF BUSINESS FAILURE

The primary cause of business failure is mismanagement, which accounts for more than 50% of all cases. Numerous specific managerial faults can cause the firm to fail. Overexpansion, poor financial actions, an ineffective sales force, and high production costs can all singly or in combination cause failure. For example, poor financial actions include bad capital budgeting decisions (based on unrealistic sales and cost forecasts, failure to identify all relevant cash flows, or failure to assess risk properly), poor financial evaluation of the firm's strategic plans prior to making financial commitments, inadequate or nonexistent cash flow planning, and failure to control receivables and inventories. Because all major corporate decisions are eventually measured in terms of dollars, the financial manager may play a key role in avoiding or causing a business failure. It is the duty of the financial manager to monitor the firm's financial pulse. For example, Enron Corporation's early 2002 bankruptcy (then the largest ever) was attributed mainly to questionable partnerships set up by Enron's CFO, Andrew Fastow. Those partnerships were intended to hide Enron's debt, inflate its profits, and enrich its top management. In late 2001, these transactions lost large amounts of money, causing the corporation to file bankruptcy and resulting in criminal charges against Enron's key executives as well as its auditor, Arthur Andersen, which failed to accurately disclose Enron's financial condition.

Economic activity—especially economic downturns—can contribute to the failure of a firm.[4] If the economy goes into a recession, sales may decrease abruptly, leaving the firm with high fixed costs and insufficient revenues to cover them. Rapid rises in interest rates just prior to a recession can further contribute to cash flow problems and make it more difficult for the firm to obtain and maintain needed financing.

A final cause of business failure is deficient product development. Products (and services) go through a life cycle of birth, growth, maturity, and decline. To continue to thrive, firms must constantly reinvest cash flows generated by its existing products (or raised externally) to develop new ones. If a firm's new product pipeline remains empty for a prolonged time, the firm may eventually become uncompetitive and fail.

VOLUNTARY SETTLEMENTS

voluntary settlement
An arrangement between an insolvent or bankrupt firm and its creditors, enabling it to bypass many of the costs involved in legal bankruptcy proceedings.

When a firm becomes insolvent or bankrupt, it may arrange a **voluntary settlement** with its creditors, which enables it to bypass many of the costs involved in legal bankruptcy proceedings. The settlement is normally initiated by the debtor firm because such an arrangement may enable it to continue to exist or to be liquidated in a manner that gives the owners the greatest chance of recovering part of their investment. The debtor arranges a meeting with all its creditors. At the meeting, a committee of creditors is selected to analyze the debtor's situation and recommend a plan of action. The debtor and its creditors discuss the recommendations of the committee, and together they develop a plan for sustaining or liquidating the firm.

Voluntary Settlement to Sustain the Firm

extension
An arrangement whereby the firm's creditors receive payment in full, although not immediately.

Normally, the rationale for sustaining a firm is that creditors may recover more of what the debtor owes them if the firm continues to operate than if a liquidation occurs. Creditors and bankrupt firms use a variety of strategies in these circumstances. An **extension** is an arrangement whereby the firm's creditors receive payment in full, although not immediately. Normally, when creditors

4. The success of some firms runs countercyclical to economic activity, and other firms are unaffected by economic activity. For example, the auto repair business is likely to grow during a recession because people are less likely to buy new cars and therefore need more repairs on their unwarrantied older cars. The sales of boats and other luxury items may decline during a recession, whereas sales of staple items such as electricity are likely to be unaffected. In terms of beta—the measure of nondiversifiable risk developed in Chapter 8—a negative-beta stock would be associated with a firm whose behavior is generally countercyclical to economic activity.

grant an extension, they require the firm to make cash payments for purchases until all past debts have been paid. A second arrangement, called **composition,** is a pro rata cash settlement of creditor claims. Instead of receiving full payment of their claims, creditors receive only a partial payment. The bankrupt firms pays a uniform percentage of each dollar that it owes to satisfy each creditor's claim.

composition
A pro rata cash settlement of creditor claims by the debtor firm; a uniform percentage of each dollar owed is paid.

A third arrangement is **creditor control.** In this case, the creditor committee may decide that maintaining the firm is feasible only if the operating management is replaced. The committee may then take control of the firm and operate it until all claims have been settled. Sometimes, a plan involving some combination of extension, composition, and creditor control will result. An example of this arrangement is a settlement whereby the debtor agrees to pay a total of 75¢ on the dollar in three annual installments of 25¢ on the dollar, and the creditors agree to sell additional merchandise to the firm on 30-day terms if the existing management is replaced by new management that is acceptable to them.

creditor control
An arrangement in which the creditor committee replaces the firm's operating management and operates the firm until all claims have been settled.

Voluntary Settlement Resulting in Liquidation

After the situation of the firm has been investigated by the creditor committee, the only acceptable course of action may be liquidation of the firm. Liquidation can be carried out either privately or through the legal procedures provided by bankruptcy law. If the debtor firm is willing to accept liquidation, legal procedures may not be required. Generally, avoiding litigation enables the creditors to obtain quicker and higher settlements. However, all parties must agree to a private liquidation for it to be feasible.

The objective of the voluntary liquidation process is to recover as much per dollar owed as possible. Under voluntary liquidation, common stockholders (the firm's true owners) cannot receive any funds until the claims of all other parties have been satisfied. A common procedure is to have a meeting of the creditors at which they make an **assignment** by passing the power to liquidate the firm's assets to an adjustment bureau, a trade association, or a third party, which is designated the *assignee.* The assignee's job is to liquidate the assets, obtaining the best price possible. The assignee is sometimes referred to as the *trustee* because it is entrusted with the title to the company's assets and the responsibility to liquidate them efficiently. Once the trustee has liquidated the assets, it distributes the recovered funds to the creditors and owners (if any funds remain for the owners). The final action in a private liquidation is for the creditors to sign a release attesting to the satisfactory settlement of their claims.

assignment
A voluntary liquidation procedure by which a firm's creditors pass the power to liquidate the firm's assets to an adjustment bureau, a trade association, or a third party, which is designated the assignee.

→ REVIEW QUESTIONS MyLab Finance Solutions

18–12 What are the three types of business failure? What is the difference between insolvency and bankruptcy? What are the major causes of business failure?

18–13 Define an extension and a composition, and explain how they might be combined to form a voluntary settlement plan to sustain the firm. How is a voluntary settlement resulting in liquidation handled?

18.5 Reorganization and Liquidation in Bankruptcy

If the bankrupt firm and its creditors cannot agree on a voluntary settlement, creditors can force the firm into bankruptcy, or the firm may file for bankruptcy itself. As a result of bankruptcy proceedings, the firm may be either reorganized or liquidated. Although small businesses fail at a much higher rate than do large firms, the bankruptcies involving very large companies (some of which are featured in the *Matter of Fact* box below) sometimes lead Congress to enact legislative reforms designed to make such costly business failures less likely in the future.

MATTER OF FACT

The 10 Largest U.S. Bankruptcies

Company	Bankruptcy date	Total assets pre-bankruptcy ($ billions)	Bankruptcy outcome
Lehman Brothers Holdings, Inc.	Sept. 15, 2008	$691.0	assets liquidated
Washington Mutual	Sept. 26, 2008	327.9	reemerged as WMI Holdings Corp.
Worldcom, Inc.	July 21, 2002	103.9	reemerged as MCI Inc.
General Motors	June 1, 2009	91.0	reemerged under same name
CIT Group	Nov. 1, 2009	80.4	reemerged under same name
Enron Corp.	Dec. 2, 2001	65.5	assets liquidated
Conseco, Inc.	Dec. 17, 2002	61.4	reemerged as CNO Financial Group
MF Global	October 31, 2011	41.0	assets liquidated
Chrysler	April 30, 2009	39.3	reemerged as Chrysler Group LLC
Thornburg Mortgage	May 1, 2009	36.5	assets liquidated

BANKRUPTCY LEGISLATION

Bankruptcy Reform Act of 1978
The governing bankruptcy legislation in the United States today.

Chapter 7
The portion of the *Bankruptcy Reform Act of 1978* that details the procedures to be followed when liquidating a failed firm.

Chapter 11
The portion of the *Bankruptcy Reform Act of 1978* that outlines the procedures for reorganizing a failed (or failing) firm, whether its petition is filed voluntarily or involuntarily.

Bankruptcy in the legal sense occurs when the firm cannot pay its bills or when its liabilities exceed the fair market value of its assets. In either case, a firm may be declared legally bankrupt. However, creditors generally attempt to avoid forcing a firm into bankruptcy if they believe that they can recover more of what the firm owes by renegotiating the terms of the firm's debt.

The U.S. Constitution (Article 1, Section 8, Clause 4) governs bankruptcy in the United States and authorizes Congress to enact "uniform Laws on the subject of Bankruptcies throughout the United States." Since 1801, Congress has exercised its authority several times and in 1978 significantly modified earlier bankruptcy legislation by enacting the **Bankruptcy Reform Act of 1978,** which is commonly referred to as the "Bankruptcy Code" ("Code"). The code contains eight odd-numbered chapters (1 through 15) and one even-numbered chapter (12). A number of these chapters would apply in the instance of failure; the two key ones are Chapters 7 and 11. **Chapter 7** of the Bankruptcy Reform Act of 1978 details the procedures to be followed when liquidating a failed firm. Chapter 7 typically comes into play once a court determines that a fair, equitable, and feasible basis for the reorganization of a failed firm does not exist (although a firm may of its own accord choose not to reorganize and may instead go directly into liquidation). **Chapter 11** outlines the procedures for reorganizing a failed (or failing) firm, whether its petition is filed voluntarily or involuntarily. If a workable plan for reorganization cannot be developed, the firm will be liquidated under Chapter 7.

REORGANIZATION IN BANKRUPTCY (CHAPTER 11)

voluntary reorganization
A petition filed by a failed firm on its own behalf for reorganizing its structure and paying its creditors.

involuntary reorganization
A petition initiated by an outside party, usually a creditor, for the reorganization and payment of creditors of a failed firm.

Reorganization petitions are of two types: voluntary and involuntary. Any firm that is not a municipal or financial institution can file a petition for **voluntary reorganization** on its own behalf.[5] **Involuntary reorganization** is initiated by an outside party, usually a creditor. An involuntary petition against a firm can be filed if one of three conditions is met:

1. The firm has past-due debts of $5,000 or more.
2. Three or more creditors can prove that they have aggregate unpaid claims of $5,000 against the firm. If the firm has fewer than 12 creditors, any creditor that is owed more than $5,000 can file the petition.
3. The firm is insolvent, which means that (a) it is not paying its debts as they come due, (b) within the preceding 120 days a custodian (a third party) was appointed or took possession of the debtor's property, or (c) the fair market value of the firm's assets is less than the stated value of its liabilities.

Procedures

debtor in possession (DIP)
The term for a firm that files a reorganization petition under Chapter 11 and then develops, if feasible, a reorganization plan.

A reorganization petition under Chapter 11 must be filed in a federal bankruptcy court. On the filing of this petition, the filing firm becomes the **debtor in possession (DIP)** of the assets. If creditors object to the filing firm being the debtor in possession, they can ask the judge to appoint a trustee. After reviewing the firm's situation, the debtor in possession submits a plan of reorganization and a disclosure statement summarizing the plan to the court. A hearing is held to determine whether the plan is fair, equitable, and feasible and whether the disclosure statement contains adequate information. The court bases its approval or disapproval of the plan in light of these standards. A plan is considered fair and equitable if it maintains the priorities of the contractual claims of the creditors, preferred stockholders, and common stockholders. The court must also find the reorganization plan feasible, which means that it must be workable. The reorganized corporation must have sufficient working capital, enough funds to cover fixed charges, adequate credit prospects, and the ability to retire or refund debts as proposed by the plan.

Once approved, the plan and the disclosure statement are given to the firm's creditors and shareholders for their acceptance. Under the Bankruptcy Reform Act, creditors and owners are separated into groups with similar types of claims. In the case of creditor groups, approval of the plan is required by holders of at least two-thirds of the dollar amount of claims as well as by a numerical majority of creditors. In the case of ownership groups (preferred and common stockholders), two-thirds of the shares in each group must approve the reorganization plan for it to be accepted. Once accepted and confirmed by the court, the plan is put into effect as soon as possible.

---

5. Firms sometimes file a voluntary petition to obtain temporary legal protection from creditors or from prolonged litigation. Once they have straightened out their financial or legal affairs—prior to further reorganization or liquidation actions—they will have the petition dismissed. Although such actions are not the intent of the bankruptcy law, difficulty in enforcing the law has allowed this abuse to occur.

PERSONAL FINANCE EXAMPLE 18.12 Individuals, like corporations, sometimes fail financially. Typically, a lack of financial planning, a heavy debt load, or an economic recession can cause debtors to start missing payments and experiencing deterioration in their credit ratings. Unless they take corrective action, repossession of debt-financed property and eventually personal bankruptcy will follow. Individuals in dire financial straits have two legal options: a wage earner plan or straight bankruptcy.

A *wage earner plan,* defined under *Chapter 13* of the U.S. Bankruptcy Code, is a "work-out" procedure that involves some type of debt restructuring, typically establishing a debt-repayment schedule that is workable in light of the individual's personal income. It is similar to *reorganization* in a corporate bankruptcy. A majority of creditors must agree to this plan, under which interest payments and late fees are waived during the repayment period. If approved, the individual, who retains the use of and title to all assets, makes payments to the court, which then pays off all creditors.

Straight bankruptcy is allowed under *Chapter 7* of the bankruptcy code. It is a legal procedure, similar to *liquidation* in corporate bankruptcy, that effectively allows the debtor to "wipe the slate clean and start anew." However, straight bankruptcy does not eliminate all a debtor's obligations, nor does the debtor lose all his or her assets. For example, the debtor must make certain tax payments and keep up alimony and child-support payments but can retain certain payments from Social Security, retirement, and disability benefits. Depending on state law, the debtor can retain a certain amount of equity in a home, a car, and other assets.

The Bankruptcy Abuse Prevention and Consumer Protection Act of 2005 (BAPCPA) made several significant changes to the U.S. Bankruptcy Code. Many of the provisions are intended to make it more difficult for individuals to file for Chapter 7 bankruptcy, under which most debts are discharged. Instead, BAPCPA requires them to file for Chapter 13 bankruptcy, under which only a portion of their debts are discharged.

Role of the Debtor in Possession (DIP)

Because reorganization activities are largely in the hands of the debtor in possession (DIP), it is useful to understand the DIP's responsibilities. The DIP's first responsibility is the valuation of the firm to determine whether reorganization is appropriate. To do so, the DIP must estimate both the liquidation value of the business and its value as a going concern. If the firm's value as a going concern is less than its liquidation value, the DIP will recommend liquidation. If the opposite is found to be true, the DIP will recommend reorganization, and a plan of reorganization must be drawn up.

The key portion of the reorganization plan generally concerns the firm's capital structure. Because most firms' financial difficulties result from high fixed charges, the company's capital structure is generally recapitalized to reduce these charges. Under **recapitalization,** debts are generally exchanged for equity or the maturities of existing debts are extended. When recapitalizing the firm, the DIP seeks to build a mix of debt and equity that will allow the firm to meet its debts and provide a reasonable level of earnings for its owners.

recapitalization
The reorganization procedure under which a failed firm's debts are generally exchanged for equity or the maturities of existing debts are extended.

Once the revised capital structure has been determined, the DIP must establish a plan for exchanging outstanding obligations for new securities. The guiding principle is to observe priorities. Senior claims (those with higher legal priority) must be satisfied before junior claims (those with lower legal priority).

To comply with this principle, senior suppliers of capital must receive a claim on new capital equal to their previous claim. The common stockholders are the last to receive any new securities. (It is not unusual for them to receive nothing.) Security holders do not necessarily have to receive the same type of security they held before; often they receive a combination of securities. Once the debtor in possession has determined the new capital structure and distribution of capital, it will submit the reorganization plan and disclosure statement to the court as described.

LIQUIDATION IN BANKRUPTCY (CHAPTER 7)

The liquidation of a bankrupt firm usually occurs once the bankruptcy court has determined that reorganization is not feasible. A petition for reorganization must normally be filed by the managers or creditors of the bankrupt firm. If no petition is filed, if a petition is filed and denied, or if the reorganization plan is denied, the firm must be liquidated.

Procedures

When a firm is adjudged bankrupt, the judge may appoint a *trustee* to perform the many routine duties required in administering the bankruptcy. The trustee takes charge of the property of the bankrupt firm and protects the interest of its creditors. A meeting of creditors must be held between 20 and 40 days after the bankruptcy judgment. At this meeting, the creditors are made aware of the prospects for the liquidation. The trustee is given the responsibility to liquidate the firm, keep records, examine creditors' claims, disburse money, furnish information as required, and make final reports on the liquidation. In essence, the trustee is responsible for the liquidation of the firm. Occasionally, the court will call subsequent creditor meetings, but only a final meeting for closing the bankruptcy is required.

Priority of Claims

It is the trustee's responsibility to liquidate all the firm's assets and to distribute the proceeds to the holders of provable claims. The courts have established certain procedures for determining the provability of claims. The priority of claims, which is specified in Chapter 7 of the Bankruptcy Reform Act, must be maintained by the trustee when distributing the funds from liquidation. Any **secured creditors** have specific assets pledged as collateral and, in liquidation, receive proceeds from the sale of those assets. If these proceeds are inadequate to fully satisfy their claims, the secured creditors become **unsecured, or general, creditors** for the unrecovered amount because specific collateral no longer exists. These and all other unsecured creditors will divide up, on a pro rata basis, any funds remaining after all prior claims have been satisfied. If the proceeds from the sale of secured assets are in excess of the claims against them, the excess funds become available to meet claims of unsecured creditors.

secured creditors
Creditors who have specific assets pledged as collateral and, in liquidation of the failed firm, receive proceeds from the sale of those assets.

unsecured, or general, creditors
Creditors who have a general claim against all the firm's assets other than those specifically pledged as collateral.

The complete order of priority of claims is given in Table 18.9. Despite the priorities listed in items 1 through 7, secured creditors have first claim on proceeds from the sale of their collateral. The claims of unsecured creditors, including the unpaid claims of secured creditors, are satisfied next, and then, finally, come the claims of preferred and common stockholders.

TABLE 18.9 **Order of Priority of Claims in Liquidation of a Failed Firm**

1. The expenses of administering the bankruptcy proceedings.
2. Any unpaid interim expenses incurred in the ordinary course of business between filing the bankruptcy petition and formal action by the court in an involuntary proceeding. (This step is *not* applicable in a voluntary bankruptcy.)
3. Wages of not more than $4,650 per worker that have been earned by workers in the 90-day period immediately preceding the commencement of bankruptcy proceedings.
4. Unpaid employee benefit plan contributions that were to be paid in the 180-day period preceding the filing of bankruptcy or the termination of business, whichever occurred first. For any employee, the sum of this claim plus eligible unpaid wages (item 3) cannot exceed $4,650.
5. Claims of farmers or fishermen in a grain-storage or fish-storage facility, not to exceed $4,650 for each producer.
6. Unsecured customer deposits, not to exceed $2,100 each, resulting from purchasing or leasing a good or service from the failed firm.
7. Taxes legally due and owed by the bankrupt firm to the federal government, state government, or any other governmental subdivision.
8. Claims of secured creditors, who receive the proceeds from the sale of collateral held, regardless of the preceding priorities. If the proceeds from the liquidation of the collateral are insufficient to satisfy the secured creditors' claims, the secured creditors become unsecured creditors for the unpaid amount.
9. Claims of unsecured creditors. The claims of unsecured, or general, creditors and unsatisfied portions of secured creditors' claims (item 8) are all treated equally.
10. Preferred stockholders, who receive an amount up to the par, or stated, value of their preferred stock.
11. Common stockholders, who receive any remaining funds, which are distributed on an equal per-share basis. If different classes of common stock are outstanding, priorities may exist.

Final Accounting

After the trustee has liquidated all the bankrupt firm's assets and distributed the proceeds to satisfy all provable claims in the appropriate order of priority, he or she makes a final accounting to the bankruptcy court and creditors. Once the court approves the final accounting, the liquidation is complete.

→ REVIEW QUESTIONS MyLab Finance Solutions

18–14 What is the concern of Chapter 11 of the Bankruptcy Reform Act of 1978? How is the debtor in possession (DIP) involved in (1) the valuation of the firm, (2) the recapitalization of the firm, and (3) the exchange of obligations using the priority rule?

18–15 What is the concern of Chapter 7 of the Bankruptcy Reform Act of 1978? Under which conditions is a firm liquidated in bankruptcy? Describe the procedures (including the role of the trustee) involved in liquidating the bankrupt firm.

18–16 Indicate in which order the following claims would be settled when distributing the proceeds from liquidating a bankrupt firm: (**a**) claims of preferred stockholders; (**b**) claims of secured creditors; (**c**) expenses of administering the bankruptcy; (**d**) claims of common stockholders; (**e**) claims of unsecured, or general, creditors; (**f**) taxes legally due; (**g**) unsecured deposits of customers; (**h**) certain eligible wages; (**i**) unpaid employee benefit plan contributions; (**j**) unpaid interim expenses incurred between the time of filing and formal action by the court; and (**k**) claims of farmers or fishermen in a grain-storage or fish-storage facility.

SUMMARY

FOCUS ON VALUE

The financial manager is sometimes involved in corporate restructuring activities, which involve the expansion and contraction of the firm's operations or changes in its asset or ownership structure. A variety of motives could drive a firm toward a merger, but the overriding goal should be maximization of the owners' wealth. Occasionally, merger transactions are heavily debt-financed leveraged buyouts (LBOs). In other cases, firms attempt to improve value by divesting themselves of certain operating units that they believe constrain the firm's value, particularly when the breakup value is deemed greater than the firm's current value.

Whether the firm makes a cash purchase or uses a stock swap to acquire another firm, the risk-adjusted net present value of the transaction should be positive. In stock swap transactions, the long-run impact on the firm's earnings and risk can be evaluated to estimate the acquiring firm's postacquisition value. Only in cases where additional value is created should the transaction be undertaken.

Business failure, although unpleasant, must be treated similarly; a failing firm should be reorganized only when such an act will maximize the owners' wealth. Otherwise, liquidation should be pursued in a fashion that allows the owners the greatest amount of recovery. Regardless of whether the firm is growing, contracting, or being reorganized or liquidated in bankruptcy, the firm should take action only when that action is believed to result in a positive contribution to the **maximization of the owners' wealth.**

REVIEW OF LEARNING GOALS

LG1 **Understand merger fundamentals, including terminology, motives for merging, and types of mergers.** Mergers result from the combining of firms. Typically, the acquiring company pursues and attempts to merge with the target company, on either a friendly or a hostile basis. Mergers are undertaken either for strategic reasons to achieve economies of scale or for financial reasons to restructure the firm to improve its cash flow. The overriding goal of merging is maximization of share price. Other specific merger motives include growth or diversification, synergy, fund raising, increased managerial skill or technology, tax considerations, increased ownership liquidity, and defense against takeover. The four basic types of mergers are horizontal, vertical, congeneric, and conglomerate.

LG2 **Describe the objectives and procedures used in leveraged buyouts (LBOs) and divestitures.** LBOs involve use of a large amount of debt to purchase a firm. Divestiture involves the sale of a firm's assets, typically an operating unit; the spin-off of assets into an independent company; or the liquidation of assets. Motives for divestiture include cash generation and corporate restructuring.

LG3 **Demonstrate the procedures used to value the target company and discuss the effect of stock swap transactions on earnings per share.** The value of a target company can be estimated by applying capital budgeting techniques to the relevant cash flows. All proposed mergers with positive net present values are considered acceptable. In a stock swap transaction, a ratio of exchange must be established to measure the amount paid per share of the target company relative to the per-share market price of the acquiring firm. The resulting relationship between the price/earnings (P/E) ratio paid by the acquiring firm and its initial P/E affects the merged firm's earnings per share (EPS) and market price. If the P/E paid is greater than the P/E of the acquiring company, the EPS of the acquiring company decrease and the EPS of the target company increase.

LG4 **Discuss the merger negotiation process, holding companies, and international mergers.** Acquirers commonly hire investment bankers to find a suitable target company and assist in negotiations. A merger can be negotiated with the target firm's management or, in the case of a hostile merger, directly with the firm's shareholders by using tender offers. Management of the target firm can employ various takeover defenses, such as a white knight, poison pills, greenmail, leveraged recapitalization, golden parachutes, and shark repellents. A holding company can be created by one firm gaining control of other companies, often by owning as little as 10% to 20% of their stock. The chief advantages of holding companies are the leverage effect, risk protection, tax benefits, protection against lawsuits, and the ease of gaining control of a subsidiary. Disadvantages include increased risk due to the magnification of losses, double taxation, difficulty of analysis, and the high cost of administration. Today, mergers of companies in Western Europe have moved toward the U.S.-style approach to shareholder value and public capital market financing. Both European and Japanese companies have become active acquirers of U.S. firms.

LG5 **Understand the types and major causes of business failure and the use of voluntary settlements to sustain or liquidate the failed firm.** A firm may fail because it has negative or low returns, is insolvent, or is bankrupt. The major causes of business failure are mismanagement, downturns in economic activity, and corporate maturity. Voluntary settlements are initiated by the debtor and can result in sustaining the firm via an extension, a composition, creditor control of the firm, or a combination of these strategies. If creditors do not agree to a plan to sustain a firm, they may recommend voluntary liquidation, which bypasses many of the legal requirements and costs of bankruptcy proceedings.

LG6 **Explain bankruptcy legislation and the procedures involved in reorganizing or liquidating a bankrupt firm.** A failed firm can voluntarily or involuntarily file in federal bankruptcy court for reorganization under Chapter 11 or for liquidation under Chapter 7 of the Bankruptcy Reform Act of 1978. Under Chapter 11, the judge will appoint the debtor in possession, which develops a reorganization plan. A firm that cannot be reorganized under Chapter 11 or does not petition for reorganization is liquidated under Chapter 7. The responsibility for liquidation is placed in the hands of a court-appointed trustee, whose duties include liquidating assets, distributing the proceeds, and making a final accounting. Liquidation procedures follow a priority of claims for distribution of the proceeds from the sale of assets.

OPENER-IN-REVIEW

Just before the public learned about the potential LBO of Dell Inc., the company's stock price was trading for $10 per share. What is the size of the premium that Silver Lake and Michael Dell were offering public shareholders? In July

2013, an independent firm that advises institutional investors on how they should cast their votes at shareholders meetings issued a letter backing Michael Dell's offer. The firm argued that in the LBO transaction, shareholders would receive a premium "with certainty," whereas with Carl Icahn's offer, it was uncertain whether the value of the company would ultimately be higher than the proposed LBO price. If you were a Dell shareholder, how would that advice affect your vote?

SELF-TEST PROBLEMS (Solutions in Appendix)

IRF

ST18–1 **Cash acquisition decision** Luxe Foods is contemplating acquisition of Valley Canning Company for a cash price of $180,000. Luxe currently has high financial leverage and therefore has a cost of capital of 14%. As a result of acquiring Valley Canning, which is financed entirely with equity, the firm expects its financial leverage to be reduced and its cost of capital to drop to 11%. The acquisition of Valley Canning is expected to increase Luxe's cash inflows by $20,000 per year for the first 3 years and by $30,000 per year for the following 12 years.

a. Determine whether the proposed cash acquisition is desirable. Explain your answer.

b. If the firm's financial leverage would actually remain unchanged as a result of the proposed acquisition, would this alter your recommendation in part **a**? Support your answer with numerical data.

IRF

ST18–2 **Expected EPS: Merger decision** At the end of 2016, Lake Industries had 80,000 shares of common stock outstanding and had earnings available for common shareholders of $160,000. Butler Company, at the end of 2016, had 10,000 shares of common stock outstanding and had earned $20,000 for common shareholders. Lake's earnings are expected to grow at an annual rate of 5%, and Butler's growth rate in earnings should be 10% per year.

a. Calculate earnings per share (EPS) for Lake Industries for each of the next 5 years (2017–2021), assuming there is no merger.

b. Calculate the next 5 years' (2017–2021) earnings per share (EPS) for Lake if it acquires Butler at a ratio of exchange of 1.1.

c. Compare your findings in parts **a** and **b**, and explain why the merger looks attractive when viewed over the long run.

WARM-UP EXERCISES All problems are available in MyLab Finance

E18–1 Toni's Typesetters is analyzing a possible merger with Pete's Print Shop. Toni's has a tax loss carryforward of $200,000, which it could apply to Pete's expected earnings before taxes of $100,000 per year for the next 5 years. Using a 21% tax rate, compare the earnings after taxes for Pete's over the next 5 years both without and with the merger.

LG 3 **E18–2** Cautionary Tales Inc. is considering the acquisition of Danger Corp. at its asking price of $150,000. Cautionary would immediately sell some of Danger's assets for $15,000 if it makes the acquisition. Danger has a cash balance of $1,500 at the time of the acquisition. If Cautionary believes that it can generate after-tax cash inflows of $25,000 per year for the next 7 years from the Danger acquisition, should the firm make the acquisition? Base your recommendation on the net present value of the outlay, using Cautionary's 10% cost of capital.

LG 3 **E18–3** Willow Enterprises is considering the acquisition of Steadfast Corp. in a stock swap transaction. Currently, Willow's stock is selling for $45 per share. Although Steadfast's shares are currently trading at $30 per share, the firm's asking price is $60 per share.

a. If Willow accepts Steadfast's terms, what is the ratio of exchange?

b. If Steadfast has 15,000 shares outstanding, how many new shares must Willow issue to consummate the transaction?

c. If Willow has 110,000 shares outstanding before the acquisition and earnings for the merged company are estimated to be $450,000, what is the EPS for the merged company?

LG 3 **E18–4** Phylum Plants' stock is currently trading at a price of $55 per share. The company is considering the acquisition of Taxonomy Central, whose stock is currently trading at $20 per share. The transaction would require Phylum to swap its shares for those of Taxonomy, which would be paid $60 per share. Calculate the ratio of exchange and the ratio of exchange in market price for this transaction.

LG 4 **E18–5** All-Stores Inc. is a holding company that has voting control over both General Stores and Star Stores. All-Stores owns General Stores and Star Stores common stock valued at $15,000 and $12,000, respectively. General's balance sheet lists $130,000 of total assets, and Star has total assets of $110,000. All-Stores has total common stock equity of $20,000.

a. What percentage of the total assets controlled by All-Stores does its common stock equity represent?

b. If a stockholder holds $5,000 worth of All-Stores common stock equity and this amount gives this stockholder voting control, what percentage of the total assets controlled does this stockholder's equity investment represent?

PROBLEMS

All problems are available in MyLab Finance. The MyLab icon indicates problems in Excel format available in MyLab Finance.

LG 1 LG 3 **P18–1** **Tax effects of acquisition** Connors Shoe Company is contemplating the acquisition of Salinas Boots, a firm that has shown large operating tax losses over the past few years. As a result of the acquisition, Connors believes that the total pretax profits of the merger will not change from their present level for 15 years. The tax loss carryforward of Salinas is $800,000, and Connors projects that its annual earnings before taxes will be $280,000 per year for each of the next 15 years. These earnings are assumed to fall within the annual limit legally allowed for application of the tax loss carryforward resulting from the proposed merger (see footnote 2 earlier in this chapter). The firm is in the 21% tax bracket.

a. If Connors does not make the acquisition, what will be the company's tax liability and earnings after taxes each year over the next 15 years?
b. If the acquisition is made, what will be the company's tax liability and earnings after taxes each year over the next 15 years?
c. If Salinas can be acquired for $350,000 in cash, should Connors make the acquisition, judging on the basis of tax considerations? (Ignore present value.)

P18–2 **Tax effects of acquisition** Trapani Tool Company is evaluating the acquisition of Sussman Casting. Sussman has a tax loss carryforward of $1.8 million. Trapani can purchase Sussman for $2.1 million. It can sell the assets for $1.6 million, their book value. Trapani expects its earnings before taxes in the 5 years after the merger to be as shown in the following table.

Year	Earnings before taxes
1	$150,000
2	400,000
3	450,000
4	600,000
5	600,000

The expected earnings given are assumed to fall within the annual limit that is legally allowed for application of the tax loss carryforward resulting from the proposed merger (see footnote 2 on page 771). Trapani is in the 21% tax bracket.
a. Calculate the firm's tax payments and earnings after taxes for each of the next 5 years without the merger.
b. Calculate the firm's tax payments and earnings after taxes for each of the next 5 years with the merger.
c. What are the total benefits associated with the tax losses from the merger? (Ignore present value.)
d. Discuss whether you would recommend the proposed merger. Support your decision with figures.

P18–3 **Tax benefits and price** Hahn Textiles has a tax loss carryforward of $800,000. Two firms are interested in acquiring Hahn for the tax loss advantage. Reilly Investment Group has expected earnings before taxes of $200,000 per year for each of the next 7 years and a cost of capital of 15%. Webster Industries has expected earnings before taxes for the next 7 years as shown in the following table.

Webster Industries	
Year	Earnings before taxes
1	$ 80,000
2	120,000
3	200,000
4	300,000
5	400,000
6	400,000
7	500,000

Both Reilly's and Webster's expected earnings are assumed to fall within the annual limit legally allowed for application of the tax loss carryforward resulting from the proposed merger (see footnote 2 on page 771). Webster has a cost of capital of 15%. Both firms are subject to a 40% tax rate on ordinary income.

a. What is the tax advantage of the merger each year for Reilly?
b. What is the tax advantage of the merger each year for Webster?
c. What is the maximum cash price each interested firm would be willing to pay for Hahn Textiles? (*Hint:* Calculate the present value of the tax advantages.)
d. Use your answers in parts **a** through **c** to explain why a target company can have different values to different potential acquiring firms.

P18–4 **Asset acquisition decision** Zarin Printing Company is considering the acquisition of Freiman Press at a cash price of $60,000. Freiman Press has liabilities of $90,000. Freiman has a large press that Zarin needs; the remaining assets would be sold to net $65,000. As a result of acquiring the press, Zarin would experience an increase in cash inflow of $20,000 per year over the next 10 years. The firm has a 14% cost of capital.

a. What is the effective or net cost of the large press?
b. If that is the only way Zarin can obtain the large press, should the firm go ahead with the merger? Explain your answer.
c. If the firm could purchase a press that would provide slightly better quality and $26,000 annual cash inflow for 10 years for a price of $120,000, which alternative would you recommend? Explain your answer.

P18–5 **Cash acquisition decision** Benson Oil is being considered for acquisition by Dodd Oil. The combination, Dodd believes, would increase its cash inflows by $25,000 for each of the next 5 years and by $50,000 for each of the following 5 years. Benson has high financial leverage, and Dodd can expect its cost of capital to increase from 12% to 15% if the merger is undertaken. The cash price of Benson is $125,000.

a. Would you recommend the merger?
b. Would you recommend the merger if Dodd could use the $125,000 to purchase equipment that will return cash inflows of $40,000 per year for each of the next 10 years?
c. If the cost of capital did not change with the merger, would your decision in part **b** be different? Explain.

Personal Finance Problem

P18–6 **Divestitures** In corporate settings, it is not unusual for firms to assess the financial viability of a business unit and decide whether to retain it within the corporation or divest it. The selling of units that do not seem to "fit" should bring about greater synergy for the firm. This same logic can be applied in a personal finance situation as well. An important question that comes up for families with two working parents and young children is whether one of the working adults should stay at home or whether the family should use child-care services.

Assume that Ted and Maggie Smith have two young children who need child-care services. Currently, Maggie is a stay-at-home mother but could go back to her former job as a marketing analyst. She estimates that she could earn $3,800 per month gross, including her employer's 401(k) contributions. She will receive monthly employer-paid benefits that include health insurance, life insurance, and pension contributions totaling $1,200.

Maggie expects her federal and state income taxes to total about $1,300 per month. The Smiths have calculated that total additional expenses such as child care, clothing, personal expenses, meals away from home, and transportation related to Maggie's job could total $1,400 per month.

Does it make economic sense for the Smiths to hire child care and have Maggie return to work? To answer this question, calculate the net income or loss from her possible return to work.

LG3

P18–7 **Ratio of exchange and EPS** Marla's Cafe is attempting to acquire the Victory Club. Certain financial data on these corporations are summarized in the following table.

Item	Marla's Cafe	Victory Club
Earnings available for common stock	$20,000	$8,000
Number of shares of common stock outstanding	20,000	4,000
Market price per share	$12	$24

Marla's Cafe has sufficient authorized but unissued shares to carry out the proposed merger.

a. If the ratio of exchange is 1.8, what will be the earnings per share (EPS) based on the original shares of each firm?

b. Repeat part **a** if the ratio of exchange is 2.0.

c. Repeat part **a** if the ratio of exchange is 2.2.

d. Discuss the principle illustrated by your answers to parts **a** through **c**.

P18–8 **EPS and merger terms** Cleveland Corporation is interested in acquiring Lewis Tool Company by swapping 0.4 share of its stock for each share of Lewis stock. Certain financial data on these companies are given in the following table.

Item	Cleveland Corporation	Lewis Tool
Earnings available for common stock	$200,000	$50,000
Number of shares of common stock outstanding	50,000	20,000
Earnings per share (EPS)	$4.00	$2.50
Market price per share	$50.00	$15.00
Price/earnings (P/E) ratio	12.5	6

Cleveland has sufficient authorized but unissued shares to carry out the proposed merger.

a. How many new shares of stock will Cleveland have to issue to make the proposed merger?

b. If the earnings for each firm remain unchanged, what will the postmerger earnings per share be?

c. How much, effectively, has been earned on behalf of each of the original shares of Lewis stock?

d. How much, effectively, has been earned on behalf of each of the original shares of Cleveland Corporation's stock?

P18–9 **Ratio of exchange** Calculate the ratio of exchange (1) of shares and (2) in market price for each of the cases shown in the following table. What does each ratio signify? Explain.

	Current market price per share		
Case	Acquiring company	Target company	Price per share offered
A	$50	$25	$ 30.00
B	80	80	100.00
C	40	60	70.00
D	50	10	12.50
E	25	20	25.00

P18–10 **Expected EPS: Merger decision** Graham & Sons wishes to evaluate a proposed merger into the RCN Group. Graham had 2016 earnings of $200,000, has 100,000 shares of common stock outstanding, and expects earnings to grow at an annual rate of 7%. RCN had 2016 earnings of $800,000, has 200,000 shares of common stock outstanding, and expects its earnings to grow at 3% per year.

a. Calculate the expected earnings per share (EPS) for Graham & Sons for each of the next 5 years (2017–2021) without the merger.

b. What would Graham's stockholders earn in each of the next 5 years (2017–2021) on each of their Graham shares swapped for RCN shares at a ratio of (1) 0.6 and (2) 0.8 share of RCN for 1 share of Graham?

c. Graph the premerger and postmerger EPS figures developed in parts **a** and **b** with the year on the *x*-axis and the EPS on the *y*-axis.

d. If you were the financial manager for Graham & Sons, which would you recommend from part **b,** (1) or (2)? Explain your answer.

P18–11 **EPS and postmerger price** Data for Henry Company and Mayer Services are given in the following table. Henry Company is considering merging with Mayer by swapping 1.25 shares of its stock for each share of Mayer stock. Henry Company expects its stock to sell at the same price/earnings (P/E) multiple after the merger as before merging.

Item	Henry Company	Mayer Services
Earnings available for common stock	$225,000	$50,000
Number of shares of common stock outstanding	90,000	15,000
Market price per share	$45	$50

a. Calculate the ratio of exchange in market price.

b. Calculate the earnings per share (EPS) and price/earnings (P/E) ratio for each company.

c. Calculate the price/earnings (P/E) ratio used to purchase Mayer Services.

d. Calculate the postmerger earnings per share (EPS) for Henry Company.

e. Calculate the expected market price per share of the merged firm. Discuss this result in light of your findings in part **a.**

LG 4

P18–12 **Holding company** Scully Corporation holds enough stock in company A and company B to give it voting control of both firms. Consider the accompanying simplified balance sheets for these companies.

Assets		Liabilities and stockholders' equity	
		Scully Corporation	
Common stock holdings		Long-term debt	$ 40,000
Company A	$ 40,000	Preferred stock	25,000
Company B	60,000	Common stock equity	35,000
Total	$100,000	Total	$100,000
		Company A	
Current assets	$100,000	Current liabilities	$100,000
Fixed assets	400,000	Long-term debt	200,000
Total	$500,000	Common stock equity	200,000
		Total	$500,000
		Company B	
Current assets	$180,000	Current liabilities	$100,000
Fixed assets	720,000	Long-term debt	500,000
Total	$900,000	Common stock equity	300,000
		Total	$900,000

a. What percentage of the total assets controlled by Scully Corporation does its common stock equity represent?

b. If another company owns 15% of the common stock of Scully Corporation and, by virtue of this fact, has voting control, what percentage of the total assets controlled does the outside company's equity represent?

c. How does a holding company effectively provide a great deal of control for a small dollar investment?

d. Answer parts **a** and **b** in light of the following additional facts.

(1) Company A's fixed assets consist of $20,000 of common stock in Company C. This level of ownership provides voting control.

(2) Company C's total assets of $400,000 include $15,000 of stock in Company D, which gives Company C voting control over Company D's $50,000 of total assets.

(3) Company B's fixed assets consist of $60,000 of stock in both Company E and Company F. In both cases, this level of ownership gives it voting control. Companies E and F have total assets of $300,000 and $400,000, respectively.

P18–13 **Voluntary settlements** Classify each of the following voluntary settlements as an extension, a composition, or a combination of the two.

a. Paying all creditors 30¢ on the dollar in exchange for complete discharge of the debt.

b. Paying all creditors in full in three periodic installments.

c. Paying a group of creditors with claims of $10,000 in full over 2 years and immediately paying the remaining creditors 75¢ on the dollar.

LG5

P18–14 **Voluntary settlements** For a firm with outstanding debt of $125,000, classify each of the following voluntary settlements as an extension, a composition, or a combination of the two.

a. Paying a group of creditors in full in four periodic installments and paying the remaining creditors in full immediately.
b. Paying a group of creditors 90¢ on the dollar immediately and paying the remaining creditors 80¢ on the dollar in two periodic installments.
c. Paying all creditors 15¢ on the dollar.
d. Paying all creditors in full in 180 days.

LG5

P18–15 **Voluntary settlements: Payments** Jacobi Supply Company recently ran into certain financial difficulties that have resulted in the initiation of voluntary settlement procedures. The firm currently has $150,000 in outstanding debts and approximately $75,000 in liquidatable short-term assets. Indicate, for each of the following plans, whether the plan is an extension, a composition, or a combination of the two. Also indicate the cash payments and timing of the payments required of the firm under each plan.

a. Each creditor will be paid 50¢ on the dollar immediately, and the debts will be considered fully satisfied.
b. Each creditor will be paid 80¢ on the dollar in two quarterly installments of 50¢ and 30¢. The first installment is to be paid in 90 days.
c. Each creditor will be paid the full amount of its claims in three installments of 50¢, 25¢, and 25¢ on the dollar. The installments will be made in 60-day intervals, beginning in 60 days.
d. A group of creditors with claims of $50,000 will be immediately paid in full; the rest will be paid 85¢ on the dollar, payable in 90 days.

Personal Finance Problem

LG5

P18–16 **Bankruptcy legislation: Wage-earner plan** Jon Morgan is in a financial position where he owes more than he earns each month. Due to his lack of financial planning and a heavy debt load, Jon started missing payments and saw his credit rating plunge. Unless corrective action is taken, personal bankruptcy will follow.

Jon recently contacted his lawyer to set up a wage earner plan with his creditors and establish a debt repayment schedule that is workable in light of his personal income. His creditors have all agreed to a plan under which interest payments and late fees will be waived during the repayment period. The process would have Jon make payments to the court, which then will pay off his creditors.

Jon has outstanding debt of $28,000. His creditors have set a repayment period of 4 years during which monthly principal payments are required. They have waived all interest charges and late fees. Jon's yearly take-home income is $30,600.

a. Calculate the monthly debt repayment amount.
b. Determine how much excess income Jon will have each month after making these payments.

LG5 LG6

P18–17 **ETHICS PROBLEM** Why might employees and suppliers support management in a Chapter 11 bankruptcy declaration if they will have to wait to be paid and may never get paid? How can a CEO act ethically toward these two groups of stakeholders in the time before, during, and after the bankruptcy period?

SPREADSHEET EXERCISE

Ram Electric Company is being considered for acquisition by Cavalier Electric. Cavalier expects the combination to increase its cash flows by $100,000 for each of the next 5 years and by $125,000 for each of the following 5 years. Ram Electric has relatively high financial leverage; Cavalier expects its cost of capital to be 12% for the first 5 years and estimates that it will increase to 16% for the following 5 years if the merger is undertaken. The cash price of Ram Electric is $325,000.

TO DO

Create a spreadsheet similar to Table 18.3 to answer the following questions.

a. Determine the present value of the expected future cash inflows over the next 10 years.

b. Calculate the net present value (NPV) for the Ram Electric acquisition.

c. All else being equal, would you recommend the acquisition of Ram Electric by Cavalier Electric? Explain.

MyLab Finance Visit www.pearson.com/mylab/finance for **Chapter Case: *Deciding Whether to Acquire or Liquidate Procras Corporation,*** Group Exercises, and numerous online resources.

CHAPTER

19

International Managerial Finance

LEARNING GOALS

LG 1 Understand the major factors that influence the financial operations of multinational companies (MNCs).

LG 2 Describe the key differences between purely domestic and international financial statements: consolidation, translation of individual accounts, and international profits.

LG 3 Discuss exchange rate risk and political risk, and explain how MNCs manage them.

LG 4 Describe foreign direct investment, investment cash flows and decisions, the MNCs' capital structure, and the international debt and equity instruments available to MNCs.

LG 5 Discuss the role of the Eurocurrency market in short-term borrowing and investing (lending) and the basics of international cash, credit, and inventory management.

LG 6 Review recent trends in international mergers and joint ventures.

MyLab Finance Chapter Introduction Video

WHY THIS CHAPTER MATTERS TO YOU

In your *professional* life

ACCOUNTING You need to understand the tax rules for multinational companies, how to prepare consolidated financial statements for subsidiary companies, and how to account for international items in financial statements.

INFORMATION SYSTEMS You need to understand that if the firm undertakes foreign operations, it will need systems that track investments and operations in another currency and their fluctuations against the domestic currency.

MANAGEMENT You need to understand both the opportunities and the risks involved in international operations, the possible role of international financial markets in raising capital, and the basic hedging strategies that multinational companies can use to protect themselves against exchange rate risk.

MARKETING You need to understand the potential for expanding into international markets and the ways of doing so (exports, foreign direct investment, mergers, and joint ventures); also, you should know how investment cash flows in foreign projects will be measured.

OPERATIONS You need to understand the costs and benefits of moving operations offshore and/or buying equipment, parts, and inventory in foreign markets. Such an understanding will allow you to participate in the firm's decisions with regard to international operations.

In your *personal* life

Your direct involvement in the global marketplace is most likely to result from expenditures made during foreign travel. In addition, you may invest directly or indirectly (via mutual funds) in the stocks of foreign companies. Probably the greatest personal benefit gained from this chapter is an understanding of exchange rates, which can significantly affect foreign expenditures, purchases, and investment returns.

Philipus/Alamy Stock Photo

MAZDA MOTOR CORP.

Selling More Cars and Making Less Money

In February 2017, the Japanese automaker Mazda Motor Corp. reported a 1.6% increase in vehicle sales from the prior quarter. The company increased it sales to 387,000 cars in the quarter ending in December 2016. Despite that relatively good news, Mazda's operating profit fell a staggering 71%, down ¥33.8 billion (or $289.7 million in U.S. currency). The reason for the decline was a sharp increase in the value of the Japanese yen (¥) against the U.S. dollar. A rising yen might sound like a good thing from the perspective of a Japanese company, but in the United States, Mazda sells cars in dollars and must convert those dollars back into yen when it reports financial results. When the yen rises against the dollar, the value of Mazda's U.S. sales in terms of yen falls because each dollar of revenue is worth fewer yen. Other Japanese auto manufacturers suffered the same fate. Toyota reported a 39% operating profit decline, while Subaru's profits fell 35%.

Nearly all large companies today engage in business transactions in multiple currencies and are therefore exposed to currency risk. Most companies attempt to hedge this risk by trading financial instruments such as forward contracts, futures contracts, and options. Typically, these trades are not designed to increase or decrease a firm's profits, but rather to insulate profits from currency swings. However, to decide how many financial instruments it should buy to hedge its currency exposure, a firm must estimate the value of revenues it will receive and expenses it will pay in multiple currencies. These estimates are inevitably imperfect, so at times companies will have unexpected currency gains or losses from their hedging programs.

19.1 The Multinational Company and Its Environment

multinational companies (MNCs)
Firms that have international assets and operations in foreign markets and draw part of their total revenue and profits from such markets.

In the past few decades, as world markets have grown more interdependent, international finance has become an increasingly important element in the management of **multinational companies** (MNCs). Since World War II, a large number of firms, including many based in emerging or developing countries, have become MNCs (also referred to as *global firms* or *transnational corporations*) by developing targeted overseas markets, mainly through foreign direct investment (FDI)—that is, by establishing foreign subsidiaries or affiliates—and via mergers and acquisitions. The general principles of managerial finance apply to the management of MNCs as well as to purely domestic firms. However, certain factors unique to the international setting tend to complicate the financial management of multinational companies. A simple comparison between a domestic U.S. firm (firm A) and a U.S.-based MNC (firm B), as illustrated in Table 19.1, indicates the influence of some of the international factors on MNCs' operations.

North American Free Trade Agreement (NAFTA)
The treaty establishing free trade and open markets among Canada, Mexico, and the United States.

Central American Free Trade Agreement (CAFTA)
A trade agreement signed in 2003–2004 by the United States, the Dominican Republic, and five Central American countries (Costa Rica, El Salvador, Guatemala, Honduras, and Nicaragua).

European Union (EU)
A significant economic force currently made up of 28 nations that permit free trade within the union.

Multinationals face a variety of laws and restrictions when operating in different nation-states. The legal and economic complexities existing in this environment are significantly different from those a domestic firm would face. Here we take a brief look at that environment, starting with key trading blocs.

KEY TRADING BLOCS

In late 1992, the presidents of the United States and Mexico and the prime minister of Canada signed the **North American Free Trade Agreement** (NAFTA). The U.S. Congress ratified NAFTA in November 1993. This trade pact simply mirrors the underlying economic reality that Canada and Mexico are among the largest U.S. trading partners. In 2003 and 2004, the United States signed a bilateral trade deal with Chile and also a regional pact, known as the **Central American Free Trade Agreement (CAFTA)**, with the Dominican Republic and five Central American countries (Costa Rica, El Salvador, Guatemala, Honduras, and Nicaragua).

The **European Union, or EU**, has been in existence since 1957. It has a current membership of 28 nations, though voters in the United Kingdom voted in

TABLE 19.1 International Factors and Their Influence on MNCs' Operations

Factor	Firm A (Domestic)	Firm B (MNC)
Foreign ownership	All assets owned by domestic entities	Portions of equity of foreign investments sometimes owned by foreign partners, thus affecting foreign decision making and profits
Multinational capital markets	All debt and equity structures based on the domestic capital market	Opportunities and challenges arise from the different capital markets in which firms can issue debt and equity
Multinational accounting	All consolidation of financial statements based on one currency	Different currencies and specific translation rules influence the consolidation of financial statements into one currency
Foreign exchange risks	All operations in one currency	Fluctuations in foreign exchange markets can affect foreign revenues and profits as well as the overall value of the firm

the summer of 2016 to leave the EU. Government officials were working out exactly how and when Britain would separate itself from the EU as this book was going to press. With a total population estimated at more than 510 million (compared with the U.S. population of about 322 million) and an overall gross domestic product exceeding that of the United States, the EU is a significant global economic force. The countries of Western Europe opened a new era of free trade within the union when intraregional tariff barriers fell at the end of 1992. This transformation is commonly called the **European Open Market.** Although the EU has managed to reach agreement on most economic, monetary, financial, and legal provisions, debates continue on certain other aspects (some key), including those related to automobile production and imports, monetary union, taxes, and workers' rights.

European Open Market
The transformation of the European Union into a *single* market at year-end 1992.

As a result of the Maastricht Treaty of 1991, 12 EU nations adopted a single currency, the **euro,** as a continent-wide medium of exchange. Beginning January 1, 2002, those 12 EU nations switched to a single set of euro bills and coins, causing the national currencies of all 12 countries participating in **monetary union** to slowly disappear in the following months. As of 2017, 19 member countries were using the euro as their national currency.

euro
A single currency adopted on January 1, 1999, by 12 EU nations, which switched to a single set of euro bills and coins on January 1, 2002.

monetary union
The official melding of the national currencies of the EU nations into one currency, the *euro,* on January 1, 2002.

At the same time the European Union implemented monetary union (which also involved creating a new European Central Bank), the EU experienced a wave of new applicants, resulting in the May 1, 2004, admission of 10 and the January 1, 2007, admission of 2 new members from Eastern Europe and the Mediterranean region. The rapidly emerging new community of Europe offers both challenges and opportunities to a variety of players, including multinational firms. MNCs today face heightened levels of competition when operating inside the EU. As more of the existing restrictions and regulations are eliminated, for instance, U.S. multinationals will have to face other MNCs, some from within the EU itself.

In addition to NAFTA and the EU, a number of other bilateral or regional trading blocs have emerged. The EU itself has entered into trade accords involving at least 35 countries. In July 2017, the EU and Japan sealed a trade agreement. Latin America has several such blocs, including its largest, **Mercosur,** which is composed of Argentina, Brazil, Paraguay, Uruguay, and Venezuela (Venezuela was suspended in December 2016). It has a population of more than 270 million and a combined economic output exceeding $3 trillion. In April 2017, Mercosur and Pacific Alliance met to discuss combining trade blocs. An even larger bloc exists in the form of **ASEAN** (Association of Southeast Asian Nations), with 10 members. In 2010, the ASEAN–China Free Trade Area (ACFTA) was established among the 10 member states of the ASEAN and the People's Republic of China. ACFTA is the largest free trade area in terms of population and third largest in terms of nominal GDP. It comprises a regional free market encompassing more than 1.8 billion people. Other trading agreements involving Japan, India, South Korea, Singapore, Australia, New Zealand, and various nations in Africa either have been completed or are under negotiation.

Mercosur
A major South American trading bloc that includes countries that account for more than half of total Latin American GDP.

ASEAN
A large trading bloc that comprises 10 member nations, all in Southeast Asia. Also called the *Association of Southeast Asian Nations.*

These deals will result in an increasing share of world trade being covered by regional accords. Meanwhile, an unintended consequence is the emergence of contradictions and incompatibilities vis-à-vis the multilateral-based system embedded in WTO (discussed in the next section), all of which will force the multinationals to navigate through a rising number of trade agreements worldwide. Despite the challenges, though, U.S. companies can benefit from the formation of regional and bilateral trade pacts, but only if they are prepared to exploit them. They must offer a desirable mix of products to a collection of varied consumers and be ready to take advantage of a variety of currencies and of financial markets and instruments (such as the Euroequities discussed later in this chapter). They must staff their operations with the appropriate combination of local and foreign personnel and, when necessary, enter into joint ventures and strategic alliances.

GATT AND THE WTO

General Agreement on Tariffs and Trade (GATT)
A treaty that has governed world trade throughout most of the post-World War II era; it extends free-trading rules to broad areas of economic activity and is policed by the *World Trade Organization (WTO)*.

World Trade Organization (WTO)
International body that polices world trading practices and mediates disputes among member countries.

Although it may seem that the world is splitting into a handful of trading blocs, that scenario is less of a danger than it may appear to be because many international treaties are in force that guarantee relatively open access to at least the largest economies. The most important such treaty is the **General Agreement on Tariffs and Trade** (**GATT**). In 1994, Congress ratified the most recent version of this treaty, which has governed world trade throughout most of the post-World War II era. The current agreement extends free-trading rules to broad areas of economic activity—such as agriculture, financial services, and intellectual property rights—that had not previously been covered by international treaty and were thus effectively off-limits to foreign competition.

The 1994 GATT treaty also established a new international body, the **World Trade Organization** (**WTO**), to police world trading practices and to mediate disputes between member countries. The WTO began operating in January 1995. In 2004, preliminary approvals were granted for an eventual membership of the Russian Federation in the WTO. In December 2001, the People's Republic of China was, after years of controversy, granted membership. As of 2017, the WTO had 164 members. Given the emergence of more bilateral and regional trade accords, however, its long-term prospects and effectiveness are becoming increasingly clouded. Key evidence is the organization's inability to achieve final agreement on the global round of trade negotiations, the Doha Round, which began in 2001.

LEGAL FORMS OF BUSINESS ORGANIZATION

In many countries outside the United States, operating a foreign business as a subsidiary or affiliate can take two forms, both similar to the U.S. corporation. In German-speaking nations, the two forms are the *Aktiengesellschaft* (A.G.) and the *Gesellschaft mit beschrankter Haftung* (GmbH). In many other countries, the similar forms are a *Société Anonyme* (S.A.) and a *Société à Responsibilité Limitée* (S.A.R.L.). The A.G. and the S.A. are the most common forms, but the GmbH and the S.A.R.L. require fewer formalities for formation and operation.

joint venture
A partnership under which the participants have contractually agreed to contribute specified amounts of money and expertise in exchange for stated proportions of ownership and profit.

Establishing a business in a form such as the S.A. can involve most of the provisions that govern a U.S.-based corporation. In addition, to operate in many foreign countries it is often beneficial to enter into joint-venture business agreements with private investors or with government-based agencies of the host country. A **joint venture** is a partnership under which the participants have contractually agreed to contribute specified amounts of money and expertise in exchange for stated proportions of ownership and profit. Joint ventures are common in many emerging and developing nations.

Emerging and developing countries have varying laws and regulations regarding MNCs' subsidiary and joint-venture operations. Whereas many host countries (including Mexico, Brazil, South Korea, and Taiwan) have either completely removed or significantly liberalized their local-ownership requirements, other major economies (including China and India) have only recently relaxed these restrictions. China, for instance, has gradually opened up new economic sectors and industries to partial (and, in some cases, full) foreign participation. India continues to insist on majority local ownership in some segments of its economy. MNCs, especially those based in the United States, the EU, and Japan, will face new challenges and opportunities in the future in terms of ownership requirements, mergers, and acquisitions.

The existence of joint-venture laws and restrictions has implications for the operation of foreign-based subsidiaries. First, majority foreign ownership may result in a substantial degree of management and control by host country participants, which, in turn, can influence day-to-day operations to the detriment of the managerial policies and procedures MNCs normally pursue. Next, foreign ownership may result in disagreements among the partners as to the exact distribution of profits and the portion to be allocated for reinvestment. Moreover, operating in foreign countries, especially on a joint-venture basis, can involve problems regarding the remittance of profits. In the past, the governments of Argentina, Brazil, Venezuela, and Thailand, among others, have imposed ceilings not only on the repatriation (return) of capital by MNCs but also on profit remittances by these firms to the parent companies. These governments usually cite the shortage of foreign exchange as the motivating factor. Finally, from a "positive" point of view, it can be argued that MNCs operating in many of the less developed countries benefit from joint-venture agreements, given the potential risks stemming from political instability in the host countries. This issue will be addressed in detail in subsequent discussions.

TAXES

Multinational companies, unlike domestic firms, have financial obligations in foreign countries. One of their basic responsibilities is international taxation, a complex issue because national governments follow a variety of tax policies. In general, U.S.-based MNCs must take into account several factors.

Tax Rates and Taxable Income

First, MNCs need to examine the level of foreign taxes. Among the major industrial countries, corporate tax rates do vary. Although the rate in the United States is 21%, those in Australia, Germany, and Japan are near 30%. The United Kingdom's rate is near 20%, and Ireland has a rate of about 12%. Many less industrialized nations maintain relatively moderate rates, partly as an incentive for attracting foreign capital. Certain countries—in particular, the Bahamas, Switzerland, Liechtenstein, the Cayman Islands, and Bermuda—are known for their low tax levels. As discussed in the *Global Focus* box in Chapter 11, China has had a low rate for foreign investors, to encourage investment. These nations typically have no withholding taxes on intra-MNC dividends.

Next, a question arises regarding the definition of taxable income. Some countries tax profits as received on a cash basis, whereas others tax profits earned on an accrual basis. Differences can also exist in treatments of noncash charges, such as depreciation, amortization, and depletion. Finally, the existence of tax agreements between the United States and other governments can influence not only the total tax bill of the parent MNC but also its international operations and financial activities.

Tax Rules

Different home countries apply varying tax rates and rules to the global earnings of their own multinationals. Moreover, tax rules are subject to frequent modifications. Before 2017, the U.S. government claimed jurisdiction over all the income of an MNC, wherever earned. (Special rules applied to foreign corporations conducting business in the United States.) However, it was possible for a multinational company to take foreign income taxes as a direct credit against its U.S. tax liabilities. The following example illustrates one way that firms accomplished this objective.

EXAMPLE 19.1

MyLab Finance Solution Video

American Enterprises, a U.S.-based MNC that manufactured heavy machinery, had a foreign subsidiary that earned $100,000 before local taxes. All the after-tax funds were available to the parent in the form of dividends. The applicable taxes consisted of a 35% foreign income tax rate, a foreign dividend withholding tax rate of 10%, and a U.S. tax rate of 35%.

Subsidiary income before local taxes	$100,000
– Foreign income tax at 35%	35,000
Dividend available to be declared	$ 65,000
– Foreign dividend withholding tax at 10%	6,500
MNC's receipt of dividends	$ 58,500

Using what was called the *grossing up procedure,* the MNC added the full before-tax subsidiary income to its total taxable income. Next, the company calculated the U.S. tax liability on the grossed-up income. Finally, the related taxes paid in the foreign country were applied as a credit against the additional U.S. tax liability:

Additional MNC income		$100,000
U.S. tax liability at 35%	$35,000	
– Total foreign taxes paid, to be used as a credit ($35,000 + $6,500)	41,500	41,500
U.S. taxes due		0
Net funds available to the parent MNC		$ 58,500

Because the U.S. tax liability was less than the total taxes paid to the foreign government, no additional U.S. taxes were due on the income from the foreign subsidiary. In our example, if tax credits had not been allowed, "double taxation" by the two authorities, as shown in what follows, would have resulted in a substantial drop in the overall net funds available to the parent MNC:

Subsidiary income before local taxes	$100,000
– Foreign income tax at 35%	35,000
Dividend available to be declared	$ 65,000
– Foreign dividend withholding tax at 10%	6,500
MNC's receipt of dividends	$ 58,500
– U.S. tax liability at 35%	20,475
Net funds available to the parent MNC	$ 38,025

The preceding example clearly demonstrates that the existence of bilateral tax treaties and the subsequent application of tax credits can significantly enhance the overall net funds available to MNCs from their worldwide earnings. Consequently, in an increasingly complex and competitive international financial environment, international taxation is one of the variables that multinational corporations should fully utilize to their advantage.

The Tax Cuts and Jobs Act of 2017 made sweeping changes to how the United States taxed MNCs. Most important among these changes was the shift to a territorial tax system, meaning that profits earned by U.S. MNCs abroad were no longer subject to U.S. taxes when they were repatriated. Combined with a reduction in the top corporate tax rate from 35% to 21%, the new tax law promised a substantially lower tax burden for U.S. MNCs.

FINANCIAL MARKETS

Euromarket
The international financial market that provides for borrowing and lending currencies outside their country of origin.

Since the 1990s, the **Euromarket**—which provides for borrowing and lending currencies outside their country of origin—has grown rapidly. The Euromarket provides multinational companies with an "external" opportunity to borrow or lend funds and to do so with less government regulation.

Growth of the Euromarket

The Euromarket has grown large for several reasons. First, beginning in the early 1960s, the Russians wanted to maintain their dollar earnings outside the legal jurisdiction of the United States, mainly because of the Cold War. Second, the consistently large U.S. balance-of-payments deficits helped "scatter" dollars around the world. Third, the existence of specific regulations and controls on dollar deposits in the United States, including interest rate ceilings imposed by the government, helped send such deposits to places outside the United States.

These and other factors have combined and contributed to the creation of an "external" capital market. Its size cannot be accurately determined, mainly because of its lack of regulation and control. Several sources that periodically estimate its size are the Bank for International Settlements, Morgan Guaranty Trust, the World Bank, and the Organization for Economic Cooperation and Development. The overall size of the Euromarket is well above $4.0 trillion net international lending.

offshore centers
Certain cities or states (including London, Singapore, Bahrain, Nassau, Hong Kong, and Luxembourg) that have achieved prominence as major centers for Euromarket business.

The existence of **offshore centers** is another aspect of the Euromarket. Certain cities or states around the world—including London, Singapore, Bahrain, Nassau, Hong Kong, and Luxembourg—are considered major offshore centers for Euromarket business, although after the Brexit vote, London may drop off that list. The availability of communication and transportation facilities, language, costs, time zones, taxes, and local banking regulations are among the main reasons for the prominence of these centers.

In recent decades, various new financial instruments have appeared in the international financial markets. One is interest rate and currency swaps. Another is various combinations of forward and options contracts on different currencies. A third is new types of bonds and notes—along with an international version of U.S. commercial paper—with flexible characteristics in terms of currency, maturity, and interest rate. More details will be provided in subsequent discussions.

Major Participants

The U.S. dollar continues to dominate various segments of the global financial markets. For example, central banks worldwide maintain the major portion of their reserves in dollars. Yet, in other activities—including currency in circulation and the international bond market—the euro has surpassed the dollar, with more challenges coming from other, potential contenders such as the Chinese yuan. Similarly, although U.S. banks and other financial institutions continue to play a significant role in the global markets, financial giants from Japan and Europe have become major participants in the Euromarket.

In the three decades leading up to the new millennium, many countries in Latin America, Asia, and Africa borrowed in the global financial markets. They accumulated huge international debts, resulting in many financial and currency crises. Clearly, as the 1997 financial/currency crises of Asia, the 1998 currency collapse of Russia, and the 2001–2002 default of Argentina showed, too much international debt, along with unstable economies and currencies, can cause massive financial losses and problems for the world's MNCs. The latest data from the World Bank indicate that in developing countries around the world external debt (as a percentage of exports of goods and services) has been rising for a decade and is expected to continue to do so. Many of these nations have further liberalized their respective economies by allowing long-term capital inflows of foreign direct investments, thus reducing their exposure to foreign exchange risk.

Although nation-states may have since slowed down their official borrowings, private enterprises, including multinational companies, continue to obtain funds (and invest) in international markets. Both Eurocurrency and Eurobond markets are extensively used by MNCs.

→ REVIEW QUESTIONS MyLab Finance Solutions

19–1 What are the important international trading blocs? What is the European Union, and what is its single unit of currency? What is GATT? What is the WTO?

19–2 What is a joint venture? Why is it often essential to use this arrangement? What effect do joint-venture laws and restrictions have on the operation of foreign-based subsidiaries?

19–3 From the point of view of a U.S.-based MNC, what are the key benefits of the Tax Cuts and Job Act of 2017?

19–4 Discuss the major reasons for the growth of the Euromarket. What is an offshore center? Name the major participants in the Euromarket.

19.2 Financial Statements

Several features differentiate internationally based reports from domestically oriented financial statements. Among them are the issues of foreign subsidiary characterization, the functional currency approach of U.S. MNCs, and the translation of individual accounts.

SUBSIDIARY CHARACTERIZATION AND FUNCTIONAL CURRENCY

For a multinational company based outside the United States, its foreign subsidiaries' type of operations will determine the translation method the firm will use. For U.S.-based MNCs, the determining factor is the functional currency of each subsidiary. Table 19.2 provides further details on these points.

TRANSLATION OF INDIVIDUAL ACCOUNTS

Unlike domestic items in financial statements, international items require translation back into U.S. dollars. Since December 1982, all financial statements of U.S. multinationals (with the exceptions noted below) have had to conform to *Statement No. 52* issued by the Financial Accounting Standards Board (FASB). The basic rules of *FASB No. 52* are given in Figure 19.1.

FASB No. 52
Statement issued by the FASB requiring U.S. multinationals first to convert the financial statement accounts of foreign subsidiaries into the *functional currency* and then to translate the accounts into the parent firm's currency, using the *all-current-rate method.*

functional currency
The currency in which a subsidiary primarily generates and expends cash and in which its accounts are maintained.

FASB No. 52

Under **FASB No. 52**, the *all-current-rate method* is implemented in a two-step process. First, each subsidiary's balance sheet and income statement are measured in terms of the functional currency by using generally accepted accounting principles (GAAP). That is, each subsidiary translates foreign-currency elements into the **functional currency**, the currency in which a subsidiary primarily generates and expends cash and in which its accounts are maintained before financial statements are submitted to the parent for consolidation.

TABLE 19.2 Subsidiary/Currency Operations and Translation Method

Type of operation	Translation method
Integrated foreign entity (international practice)	Operates as an extension of the parent MNC; temporal method is the primary translation tool
Self-sustaining foreign entity (international practice)	Operates independent of the parent multinational; the all-current-rate method is the primary approach
Functional currency approach (used by U.S. MNCs)	The dominant currency in which the foreign subsidiary conducts its activities; it may be the same as the parent's (in which case, the temporal method is applied), the subsidiary's (the all-current-rate method), or a third currency (temporal, then current)

Source: David K. Eiteman, Arthur I. Stonehill, and Michael H. Moffett, *Multinational Business Finance*, 14th ed. (Boston, MA: Addison-Wesley, 2016). Reprinted and Electronically reproduced by permission of Pearson Education, Inc., New York, NY.

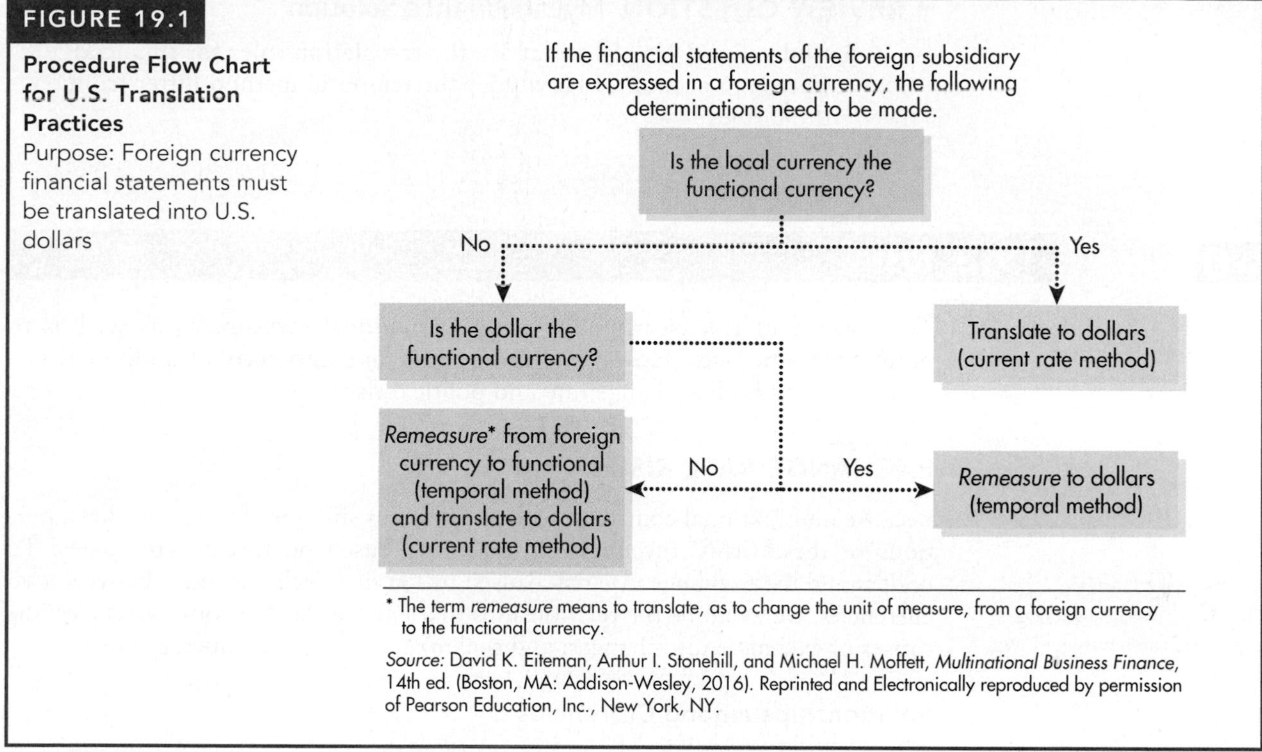
If the financial statements of the foreign subsidiary are expressed in a foreign currency, the following determinations need to be made.
Is the local currency the functional currency?
No
Yes
Is the dollar the functional currency?
Translate to dollars (current rate method)
*Remeasure** from foreign currency to functional (temporal method) and translate to dollars (current rate method)
No
Yes
Remeasure to dollars (temporal method)

FIGURE 19.1

Procedure Flow Chart for U.S. Translation Practices

Purpose: Foreign currency financial statements must be translated into U.S. dollars

* The term *remeasure* means to translate, as to change the unit of measure, from a foreign currency to the functional currency.

Source: David K. Eiteman, Arthur I. Stonehill, and Michael H. Moffett, *Multinational Business Finance*, 14th ed. (Boston, MA: Addison-Wesley, 2016). Reprinted and Electronically reproduced by permission of Pearson Education, Inc., New York, NY.

all-current-rate method
The method by which the functional-currency-denominated financial statements of an MNC's subsidiary are translated into the parent company's currency.

In the second step, the functional-currency-denominated financial statements of the foreign subsidiary are translated into the parent's currency. This process is done using the **all-current-rate method**, which requires the translation of all balance sheet items at the closing rate and all income statement items at average rates.

Each of these steps can result in certain gains or losses. The first step can lead to transaction (cash) gains or losses. Whether realized or not, these gains or losses are charged directly to current income. The completion of the second step can result in translation (accounting) adjustments, which are excluded from current income. Instead, the MNC discloses and charges these amounts to a separate component of stockholders' equity.

Temporal Method

temporal method
A method that requires specific assets and liabilities to be translated at so-called historical exchange rates and foreign-exchange translation gains or losses to be reflected in the current year's income.

The temporal method, along with a variation called *monetary/non-monetary method,* is an alternative translation approach used throughout the world. For U.S.-based multinationals, as highlighted in both Table 19.2 and Figure 19.1, the **temporal method** is used when the functional currency is the U.S. dollar or a third currency. This method requires that specific assets and liabilities be translated at so-called historical exchange rates and that foreign-exchange translation gains or losses be reflected in the current year's income. Also, if a U.S. MNC has a subsidiary in a hyperinflation country—defined as a host nation experiencing a cumulative inflation of more than 100% over a 3-year period—the temporal method is used. (In some countries, the inflation rates can be significantly higher. In Venezuela, for example, in early 2017 the inflation rate exceeded 700%.)

→ **REVIEW QUESTION** MyLab Finance Solution

19–5 Under *FASB No. 52*, what are the translation rules for financial statement accounts? How does the temporal method differ from these rules?

LG3

19.3 Risk

The concept of risk clearly applies to international investments as well as to purely domestic ones. However, MNCs must take into account additional factors, including both exchange rate and political risks.

EXCHANGE RATE RISKS

exchange rate risk
The risk caused by varying exchange rates between two currencies.

Because multinational companies operate in many different foreign markets, portions of these firms' revenues and costs are based on foreign currencies. To understand the **exchange rate risk** caused by varying exchange rates between two currencies, we examine the relationships that exist among various currencies, the causes of exchange rate changes, and the impact of currency fluctuations.

Relationships among Currencies

Since the mid-1970s, the major currencies of the world have had a *floating*—as opposed to a *fixed*—relationship with respect to the U.S. dollar and to one another. Among the currencies regarded as being major (or "hard") currencies are the British pound sterling (£), the European Union euro (€), the Japanese yen (¥), the Canadian dollar (C$), and, of course, the U.S. dollar (US$). As previously pointed out, by 2017, the euro, in circulation since 2002, had been adopted by 19 members of the EU. It has gained wide acceptance and usage in international transactions, particularly debt securities issues.

foreign exchange rate
The price of one currency in terms of another.

The price of one currency in terms of another is called the **foreign exchange rate.** For example, the exchange rate between the U.S. dollar and the Japanese yen (¥) can be expressed as

$$\text{US\$1.00} = \text{¥}98.04$$
$$\text{US\$0.01020} = \text{¥}1.00$$

The first expression indicates that 1 unit of U.S. currency is worth 98.04 units of Japanese currency. Therefore, we might say that the price (or cost) of $1 is ¥98.04. The second expression indicates that 1 unit of Japanese currency is worth 0.01020 unit of U.S. currency. In other words, the price of ¥1 is $0.01020. One number is just the reciprocal of the other:

$$\frac{1}{98.04} = 0.01020$$

$$\frac{1}{0.01020} = 98.04$$

direct quote
An exchange rate quote that indicates the number of units of foreign currency that can be purchased with one unit of domestic currency.

The two ways of quoting any exchange rate are the direct quote and the indirect quote. A **direct quote** expresses the amount of foreign currency that can be purchased with one unit of domestic currency. Thus, in the example above, a direct quote might be written as 98.04 (¥/$), assuming that we take a U.S. perspective and say that the dollar is the domestic currency. An **indirect quote** expresses the amount of domestic currency required to buy one unit of foreign currency. The indirect quote between yen and dollars might be written 0.01020($/¥).

indirect quote
An exchange rate quote that indicates the number of units of domestic currency that can be purchased with one unit of foreign currency.

Because the U.S. dollar has served as the principal currency of international finance for decades, the most common convention in foreign exchange markets is to use direct quotes to express the values of most currencies relative to the U.S. dollar. Thus, the exchange rate between the U.S. dollar and the Swiss franc (CHF) would most often appear as 0.9652(CHF/$), which indicates that $1 is worth CHF 0.9652. However, there are some exceptions to the practice of using direct quotes. For example, when quoting the exchange rate between U.S. dollars and British pounds (£), the indirect quote is more common. Thus, the exchange rate between those two currencies is most often expressed as 1.3071($/£), which means that £1 is worth $1.3071.

For the major currencies, the existence of a **floating relationship** means that the value of any two currencies with respect to each other is allowed to fluctuate on a daily basis. Conversely, some of the nonmajor currencies of the world try to maintain a **fixed (or semifixed) relationship** with respect to one of the major currencies, a combination (basket) of major currencies, or some type of international foreign exchange standard.

floating relationship
The fluctuating relationship of the values of two currencies with respect to each other.

fixed (or semifixed) relationship
The constant (or relatively constant) relationship of a currency to one of the major currencies, a combination (basket) of major currencies, or some type of international foreign exchange standard.

Every day, foreign exchange markets establish two key prices that govern trade in the world's major currencies. One price is the **spot exchange rate**, or the rate on that day. The other price is the **forward exchange rate**, or the rate at some specified future date. The foreign exchange rates given in Figure 19.2 illustrate these concepts. For instance, the figure shows that at the close on Tuesday, the spot rate for the Japanese yen was 0.01020($/¥), or equivalently, 98.04 (¥/$). The forward (future) rate was 0.01021($/¥), or 97.91(¥/$) for 6-month delivery. In other words, one could execute a contract to take delivery of Japanese yen in 6 months at a dollar price of 0.01021 ($/¥). Forward rates are also quoted for 1-month and 3-month contracts (with other, tailor-made contracts of desired maturities available to clients through the interbank market). For all such contracts, the agreements and signatures are completed on the contract purchase date, but the actual exchange of dollars and Japanese yen between buyers and sellers will take place on the future date (say, 6 months later).

spot exchange rate
The rate of exchange between two currencies on any given day.

forward exchange rate
The rate of exchange between two currencies at some specified future date.

Figure 19.2 also illustrates the differences between floating currencies and those that are either fixed or exhibit less movement over time. The middle data columns in Figure 19.2 show the 1-day and year-to-date (YTD) percentage change in each currency's movement vis-à-vis the U.S. dollar. All the major currencies previously mentioned, along with minor (or "soft") currencies such as the Russian ruble and the South African rand, experienced some changes after the beginning of the year. In contrast, the Saudi Arabian riyal and the UAE dirham underwent no change over this period.

For the floating currencies, changes in the value of foreign exchange rates are called appreciation or depreciation. For any currency that is fixed in value (with respect to the U.S. dollar or another major currency), changes in value are called official *revaluation* or *devaluation,* but these terms have the same meanings as *appreciation* and *depreciation,* respectively.

FIGURE 19.2

Exchange Rates (Monday, August 14, 2017)
Spot and forward exchange rate quotations

	In US$		US$ vs. %Change		Per US$	
	Tuesday	Monday	1-Day	Year-to-date	Tuesday	Monday
Country/currency						
Asia-Pacific						
Hong Kong dollar	0.13	0.1289	unchanged	0.1	7.7550	7.7573
India rupee	0.02	0.01687	2.60	10.6	60.81545	59.27495
Indonesia rupiah	0.0000970	0.0000973	0.36	7.0	10315	10277
Japan yen	0.01020	0.01021	0.08	13.0	98.04	97.95
1-mo forward	0.01020	0.01021	0.08	11.5	98.02	97.94
3-mo forward	0.01021	0.01021	0.08	11.5	97.98	97.91
6-mo forward	0.01021	0.01022	0.08	11.5	97.91	97.83
Pakistan rupee	0.00983	0.00982	−0.08	4.6	101.745	101.825
Taiwan dollar	0.03335	0.03339	0.13	3.2	29.983	29.945
Thailand baht	0.03199	0.03208	0.29	2.2	31.260	31.168
Vietnam dong	0.00005	0.00005	0.50	2.0	21210	21105
Europe						
Czech. Rep. koruna	0.05	0.05	−0.07	2.4	19.462	19.476
Denmark krone	0.1779	0.1779	unchanged	−0.6	5.6209	5.6209
Euro area euro	1.3263	1.3263	unchanged	−0.5	0.7540	0.7540
Russia ruble	0.03034	0.03044	0.36	8.1	32.965	32.847
Turkey lira	0.5201	0.5188	−0.24	7.8	1.09229	1.9275
UK pound	1.5237	1.5341	0.68	6.6	0.6563	0.6518
1-mo forward	1.5234	1.5338	0.68	6.2	0.6564	0.6520
3-mo forward	1.5228	1.5332	0.68	6.2	0.6567	0.6522
6-mo forward	1.5222	15.326	0.68	6.2	0.6570	0.6525
Middle East/Africa						
Egypt pound	0.14	0.14	unchanged	10.1	7.0015	7.0022
Israel shekel	0.28	0.28	unchanged	−4.2	3.5739	3.5736
Kuwait dinar	3.5156	3.5174	0.05	1.1	0.2845	0.2843
Saudi Arabia riyal	0.2666	0.2667	unchanged	unchanged	3.7504	3.7496
South Africa rand	0.1020	0.1021	0.10	15.8	9.8021	9.7921
UAE dirham	0.2722	0.2723	unchanged	unchanged	3.6732	3.6730

Data from Yahoo Finance

PERSONAL FINANCE EXAMPLE 19.2 Floyd Gonzalez, an avid cyclist, is considering a bicycling tour that for 1 week during the Tour de France will ride ahead of the actual race. The cost of the tour, which includes ground transportation, hotels, and route support in France, is 3,675 euros (€). He estimates that his round-trip airfare (including shipment of his bike) from his home in Iowa will be $1,100; in addition, he will incur another $100 in incidental U.S. travel expenses. Floyd estimates the cost of meals in France to be about €400, and he plans to take an additional $1,000 to buy gifts and other merchandise while in France. Assuming the current exchange rate is 1.3033($/€) [or, equivalently, 0.7673(€/$)], Floyd wishes to determine (1) the total dollar cost of the trip and (2) the amount in euros he will need to cover the cost of meals, gifts, and other merchandise while in France.

(1) Total cost of trip in U.S. dollars	
Cost of tour [€3,675 × 1.3033($/€)]	$4,790
Round-trip airfare	1,100
Incidental U.S. travel expenses	100
Cost of meals in France (€400 × 1.3033($/€))	521
Gifts and other merchandise	1,000
Total cost of trip in $	$7,511

(2) Amount of euros needed in France	
Cost of meals in France	€ 400
Gifts and other merchandise [$1,000 × 0.7673(€/$)]	767
Amount of €s needed in France	€1,167

The total cost of Floyd's trip would be $7,511, and he would need €1,167 to cover his cost of meals, gifts, and other merchandise while in France.

What Causes Exchange Rates to Change?

Although several economic and political factors influence foreign exchange rate movements, by far the most important explanation for long-term changes in exchange rates is a differing inflation rate between two countries. Countries that experience high inflation rates will see their currencies decline in value (depreciate) relative to the currencies of countries with lower inflation rates.

EXAMPLE 19.3

MyLab Finance Solution Video

Assume that the current exchange rate between the United States and the new nation of Farland is 2 Farland guineas (FG) per U.S. dollar, 2.00(FG/$), which is also equal to 0.50($/FG). This exchange rate means that a basket of goods worth $100 in the United States should sell for $100 × 2(FG/$) = FG200 in Farland and vice versa (goods worth FG200 in Farland should sell for $100 in the United States).

Now assume that inflation is running at a 25% annual rate in Farland but at only a 2% annual rate in the United States. In 1 year, the same basket of goods will sell for 1.25 × FG200 = FG250 in Farland and for 1.02 × $100 = $102 in the United States. These relative prices imply that in 1 year, FG250 will be worth $102 (i.e., the cost of the same basket of goods is FG250 in Farland and $102 in the United States). The exchange rate in 1 year should change to FG250/$102 = 2.45(FG/$), or 0.41($/FG). In other words, the dollar will appreciate from 2(FG/$) to 2.45(FG/$), while the Farland guinea will depreciate from 0.50($/FG) to 0.41($/FG).

The preceding simple example can also predict the level of interest rates in the two countries. To be enticed to save money, an investor must be offered a return that exceeds the country's inflation rate; otherwise, there would be no reason to forgo the pleasure of spending money (consuming) today because inflation would make that money less valuable 1 year from now. Let's assume that this *real rate of interest* is 3% per year in both Farland and the United States. Using Equation 6.1, we can now reason that the *nominal rate of interest* will be approximately equal to the real rate plus the inflation rate in each country, or 3% + 25% = 28% in Farland and 3% + 2% = 5% in the United States.[1]

Impact of Currency Fluctuations

Multinational companies face exchange rate risks under both floating and fixed arrangements. Floating currencies can be used to illustrate these risks. Consider the U.S. dollar–U.K. British pound relationship; note that the forces of international supply and demand, as well as economic and political elements, help shape both the spot and the forward rates between these two currencies. Because the MNC cannot control much (or most) of these "outside" elements, the company faces potential changes in exchange rates. These changes can, in turn, affect the MNC's revenues, costs, and profits as measured in U.S. dollars. For fixed-rate currencies, official revaluation or devaluation, like the changes brought about by the market in the case of floating currencies, can affect the MNC's operations and its dollar-based financial position.

EXAMPLE 19.4

MNC Inc., a multinational manufacturer of dental drills, has a subsidiary in Great Britain that at the end of 2019 had the financial statements shown in Table 19.3. The figures for the balance sheet and income statement are given

TABLE 19.3 Financial Statements for MNC Inc.'s British Subsidiary

Translation of balance sheet			
	12/31/19		12/31/20
Assets	£	US$[a]	US$[b]
Cash	8.00	11.43	13.33
Inventory	60.00	85.72	100.00
Plant and equipment (net)	32.00	45.71	53.34
Total	100.00	142.86	166.67
Liabilities and stockholders' equity			
Debt	48.00	68.57	80.00
Paid-in capital	40.00	57.15	66.67
Retained earnings	12.00	17.14	20.00
Total	100.00	142.86	166.67
Translation of income statement			
Sales	600.00	857.14	1,000.00
Cost of goods sold	550.00	785.71	916.67
Operating profits	50.00	71.43	83.33

[a]Foreign exchange rate assumed: US$1.00 = £0.70.
[b]Foreign exchange rate assumed: US$1.00 = £0.60.
Note: This example is simplified to show how the balance sheet and income statement are subject to foreign exchange rate fluctuations. For the applicable rules on the translation of foreign accounts, review Section 19.2 on international financial statements.

1. This rate is an approximation of the true relationship, which is actually multiplicative. The correct formula says that 1 plus the nominal rate of interest, r, is equal to the product of 1 plus the real rate of interest, r^*, and 1 plus the inflation rate, IP; that is, $(1 + r) = (1 + r^*) \times (1 + IP)$. In other words, the nominal interest rates for Farland and the United States should be 28.75% and 5.06%, respectively.

in the local currency, British pounds (£). Using an assumed foreign exchange rate of 0.70(£/$) for December 31, 2019, MNC has translated the statements into U.S. dollars. For simplicity, we assume that all the local figures remain the same during 2020. As a result, as of January 1, 2020, the subsidiary expects to show the same British pound figures on 12/31/20 as on 12/31/19. However, because of the *depreciation* in the assumed value of the dollar relative to the pound, from 0.70(£/$)to 0.60(£/$), the translated dollar values of the items on the balance sheet, along with the dollar profit value on 12/31/20, are higher than those of the previous year. The changes are due only to fluctuations in the foreign exchange rate. In this case, the British pound *appreciated* relative to the U.S. dollar, which means that the U.S. dollar *depreciated* relative to the British pound.

Additional complexities are attached to each individual account in the financial statements. For instance, it matters whether a subsidiary's debt is all in the local currency, all in U.S. dollars, or in several currencies. Moreover, it is important to determine the currency (or currencies) in which the revenues and costs are denominated. The risks shown so far relate to what is called the **accounting exposure.** In other words, foreign exchange rate fluctuations affect individual accounts in the financial statements.

accounting exposure
The risk resulting from the effects of changes in foreign exchange rates on the translated value of a firm's financial statement accounts denominated in a given foreign currency.

economic exposure
The risk resulting from the effects of changes in foreign exchange rates on the firm's value.

A different, and perhaps more important, risk element concerns **economic exposure,** which is the potential impact of foreign exchange rate fluctuations on the firm's value. Given that all future foreign revenues and thus net profits can be subject to foreign exchange rate changes, it is obvious that the present value of the net profits derived from foreign operations will have, as a part of its total diversifiable risk, an element reflecting appreciation (revaluation) or depreciation (devaluation) of various currencies with respect to the U.S. dollar.

What can the management of MNCs do about these risks? The actions will depend on the attitude of the management toward risk. This attitude, in turn, translates into how aggressively management wants to hedge (i.e., protect against) the company's undesirable positions and exposures. The firm can use the money markets, the forward (futures) markets, and the foreign-currency options markets—either individually or in combination—to hedge foreign exchange exposures. Further details on certain hedging strategies are described later.

POLITICAL RISKS

political risk
The potential discontinuity or seizure of an MNC's operations in a host country via the host's implementation of specific rules and regulations.

macro political risk
The subjection of all foreign firms to political risk (takeover) by a host country because of political change, revolution, or the adoption of new policies.

micro political risk
The subjection of an individual firm, a specific industry, or companies from a particular foreign country to political risk (takeover) by a host country.

Another important risk facing MNCs is political risk. **Political risk** refers to a host government's implementation of specific rules and regulations that can result in the discontinuity or seizure of the operations of a foreign company. Political risk is usually manifested in the form of nationalization, expropriation, or confiscation. In general, the host government takes over the assets and operations of a foreign firm, usually without proper (or any) compensation.

Political risk has two basic paths, *macro* and *micro*. **Macro political risk** refers to political change, revolution, or the adoption of new policies by a host government, which subjects *all* foreign firms in the country to political risk. In other words, no individual country or firm is treated differently; all assets and operations of foreign firms are taken over wholesale. An example of macro political risk occurred after communist regimes came to power in China in 1949 and Cuba in 1959–1960. **Micro political risk**, in contrast, refers to the case in which an individual firm, a specific industry, or companies from a particular foreign country are subjected to takeover. In the first decade of the twenty-first century—especially in the second half—Russia, Venezuela, and Bolivia were among those countries that had either nationalized the operations or suspended the long-term contractual agreements held by foreign multinationals in their respective nations. Recent years have also seen the emergence of a third path to political risk; this path encompasses "global" events such as terrorism, antiglobalization movements, and Internet-based risks, all of which affect various MNCs' operations worldwide.

Although political risk can take place in any country—even in the United States—the political instability of many developing nations generally makes the positions of multinational companies most vulnerable there. At the same time, some of these countries have the most promising markets for the goods and services MNCs offer. The main question is, therefore, how to engage in operations and foreign investment in such countries and yet avoid or minimize the potential political risk.

Table 19.4 shows some of the approaches that MNCs may be able to adopt to cope with political risk. The negative approaches are generally used by firms in extractive industries such as oil and gas and mining. The external approaches are also of limited use. The best policies MNCs can follow are the positive approaches, which have both economic and political aspects.

In recent years, MNCs have been relying on a variety of complex forecasting techniques whereby international experts, using available historical data, predict the chances for political instability in a host country and the potential effects on MNC operations. Events in Afghanistan, Venezuela, and Russia, among others, however, point to the limited use of such techniques and tend to reinforce the usefulness of the positive approaches.

TABLE 19.4 Approaches for Coping with Political Risks

Positive approaches		Negative approaches
Prior negotiation of controls and operating contracts	Direct	License or patent restrictions under international agreements
Prior agreement for sale	Direct	Control of external raw materials
Joint venture with government or local private sector	Direct	Control of transportation to (external) markets
Use of locals in management	Indirect	Control of downstream processing
Joint venture with local banks	Indirect	Control of external markets
Equity participation by middle class	Indirect	
Local sourcing	Indirect	
Local retail outlets	Indirect	

External approaches to minimize loss

International insurance or investment guarantees

Thinly capitalized firms:

- Local financing
- External financing secured only by the local operation

Source: Rita M. Rodriguez and E. Eugene Carter, *International Financial Management*, 3rd ed., 1984. Reprinted and Electronically reproduced by permission of Pearson Education, Inc., New York, NY.

national entry control systems
Comprehensive rules, regulations, and incentives introduced by host governments to regulate inflows of foreign direct investments from MNCs and at the same time extract more benefits from their presence.

A final point relates to the introduction since the 1990s by most host governments of comprehensive sets of rules, regulations, and incentives. Known as **national entry control systems**, they are aimed at regulating inflows of *foreign direct investments* involving MNCs. They are designed to extract more benefits from MNCs' presence by regulating flows of a variety of factors: local ownership, level of exportation, use of local inputs, number of local managers, internal geographic location, level of local borrowing, and the percentages of profits to be remitted and of capital to be repatriated to parent firms, for example. Host countries expect that as MNCs comply with these regulations, the potential for acts of political risk will decline, thus benefiting the MNCs as well.

FOCUS ON ETHICS *in practice*

Is Fair-Trade Coffee Fair?

"Fair trade" has caught fire; from 2004 to 2014, retail sales of fair-trade products grew an average of 26% per year. The movement has several goals, but the most important is improving the lives of the poor in developing countries. The basic strategy is for retailers in wealthy countries to erect a floor for "certified" products above the global price and pay a "social" premium for each unit produced. Most fair-trade products are commodities; coffee is the best known. In the U.S., the coffee house most strongly identified with fair trade is Starbucks. Public commitment began in 2001, when the company partnered with Transfair USA (now Fair Trade USA, a leading non-profit certifier) to sell fair-trade coffee in the U.S. and Canada.

Fair-trade certification appears to be a win-win proposition. Socially conscious consumers benefit from knowing a portion of the retail price promotes social justice. Meanwhile, higher prices for fair-trade goods boost producer incomes in developing countries, and the additional social premiums—which are invested in community infrastructure—spread benefits to the rest of the local population.

But some economists are skeptical. They argue that any social good done by fair trade pales in comparison with the real barrier to higher agricultural incomes in poor countries—massive subsidies for domestic farming in the developed world. In 2014, for example, total ag subsidies by OECD countries came to nearly $250 billion—against about $8 billion in retail sales of fair-trade products (with less than 2% of that going to participating producers). Furthermore, the weight of empirical evidence suggests little of the extra income garnered by fair-trade producers finds its way to local workers. In short, skeptics argue, fair trade is a drop in the bucket that doesn't even reach the thirstiest.

Even if the social-justice returns on fair trade prove small, companies in the developed world could end up doing well by trying to do good. Consider Starbucks. If fair trade's popularity with customers boosts demand for Starbucks products by more than fair-trade certification raises the cost of beans, then "ethically sourced coffee" (as the company puts it) is a positive net present value (NPV) investment.

Fair trade may prove to be smart politics as well. Eighty percent of fair-trade coffee comes from Latin America and the Caribbean—regions where governments have often viewed U.S. companies as exploitative, sometimes even retaliating with nationalization. By giving local producers and their communities a larger share of profits today, Starbucks could be insuring against the risk a hostile government will eliminate all profits tomorrow. Whatever its motives, the company has fared well since committing to fair trade. Since 2001, Starbucks' stock price has risen 16 times faster than the composite index of the NASDAQ.

► *Suppose market research by your company shows it would be profitable to become a fair-trade retailer. Further suppose other internal research suggests producers in developing countries and their communities would profit little from your fair-trade practices—no matter how well designed. Would it be ethical for the company to commit to fair trade just to enhance shareholder wealth?*

Narlikar, Amrita and Dan Kim. "Unfair Trade: The Fair-Trade Movement Does More Harm than Good," *Foreign Affairs*, April 4, 2013. Dragusanu, Raluca; Daniele Giovannucci; and Nathan Nunn. "The Economics of Fair Trade," *Journal of Economic Perspectives* 28 (Summer 2014): 217–236.

→ **REVIEW QUESTIONS** MyLab Finance Solutions

19–6 Define spot exchange rate and forward exchange rate. Define and compare accounting exposures and economic exposures to exchange rate fluctuations.

19–7 Explain how differing inflation rates between two countries affect their exchange rate over the long term.

19–8 Discuss macro and micro political risk. What is the emerging third path to political risk? Describe some techniques for dealing with political risk.

19.4 Long-Term Investment and Financing Decisions

Important long-term aspects of international managerial finance include foreign direct investment, investment cash flows and decisions, capital structure, long-term debt, and equity capital. Here we consider the international dimensions of these topics.

FOREIGN DIRECT INVESTMENT

foreign direct investment (FDI)
The transfer of capital, managerial, and technical assets to a foreign country by a multinational firm.

Foreign direct investment (FDI) is the transfer of capital, managerial, and technical assets to a foreign country by a multinational firm. We can explain FDI on the basis of two main approaches: the *OLI paradigm* and *strategic motives* by MNCs. The first encompasses "O" (owner-specific) advantages in an MNC's home market, "L" (location-specific) characteristics abroad, and "I" (internalization) through which the multinational controls the value chain in its industry. The second refers to companies that invest abroad as they seek markets, raw materials, production efficiency, knowledge, and/or political safety.

The equity participation on the part of an MNC can be 100% (resulting in a wholly owned foreign subsidiary) or less (leading to a joint-venture project with foreign participants). In contrast to short-term foreign portfolio investments undertaken by individuals and companies (such as internationally diversified mutual funds), FDI involves equity participation, managerial control, and day-to-day operational activities on the part of MNCs. Therefore, FDI projects will be subjected not only to business, financial, inflation, and exchange rate risks (as would foreign portfolio investments) but also to the additional element of political risk.

INVESTMENT CASH FLOWS AND DECISIONS

Measuring the amount invested in a foreign project, its resulting cash flows, and the associated risk is difficult. The returns and NPVs of such investments can significantly vary from the subsidiary's and parent's points of view. Therefore, several factors unique to the international setting need to be examined when one is making long-term investment decisions.

First, firms need to consider elements related to a parent company's investment in a subsidiary and the concept of taxes. For example, in the case of manufacturing investments, questions may arise as to the value of the equipment a parent may contribute to the subsidiary. Is the value based on market conditions in the parent country or in the local host economy? In general, the market value in the host country is the relevant "price."

The existence of different taxes—as pointed out earlier—can complicate measurement of the cash flows to be received by the parent because different definitions of taxable income can arise. Still other complications develop when it comes to measuring the actual cash flows. From a parent firm's viewpoint, the cash flows are those that are repatriated from the subsidiary. In some countries, however, such cash flows may be totally or partially blocked. Obviously, depending on the life of the project in the host country, the returns and NPVs associated with such projects can vary significantly from the subsidiary's and the parent's points of view. For instance, for a project of only 5 years' duration, if all yearly cash flows are blocked by the host government, the subsidiary may show a "normal" or even superior return and NPV, although the parent may show no return at all. For a project of longer life, even if cash flows are blocked for the first few years, the remaining years' cash flows can contribute to the parent's returns and NPV. Even so, a firm might still choose to invest in such a country if it could reinvest the cash flows in additional positive NPV projects in the same country.

Finally, the firm must consider the issue of risk attached to international cash flows. In general, the three types of risks are (1) business and financial risks, (2) inflation and exchange rate risks, and (3) political risks. The first category reflects the type of industry the subsidiary is in, as well as its financial structure. We will present more details on financial risks later. As for the other two categories, we have already discussed the risks of having investments, profits, and assets/liabilities in different currencies and the potential impacts of political risks.

The presence of the three types of risks will influence the discount rate to be used when evaluating international cash flows. The general rule is that the local cost of equity capital (applicable to the local business and financial environments within which a subsidiary operates) is the starting discount rate. To this rate the MNC would add the risks stemming from exchange rate and political factors and, from it, would subtract the benefits reflecting the parent's lower capital costs.

CAPITAL STRUCTURE

Both theory and empirical evidence indicate that the capital structures of multinational companies differ from those of purely domestic firms. Furthermore, differences are observed among the capital structures of MNCs domiciled in various countries. Several factors tend to influence the capital structures of MNCs.

International Capital Markets

MNCs, unlike smaller, domestic firms, have access to the Euromarket (discussed earlier) and the variety of financial instruments available there. Because of their access to the international bond and equity markets, MNCs may have lower long-term financing costs, which result in differences between the capital structures of MNCs and those of purely domestic companies. Similarly, MNCs based in different countries and regions may have access to different currencies and markets, resulting in variances in capital structures for these multinationals.

International Diversification

It is well established that MNCs, in contrast to domestic firms, can achieve further risk reduction in their cash flows by diversifying internationally. International diversification may lead to varying degrees of debt versus equity. Empirically, the evidence on debt ratios is mixed. Some studies have found MNCs' debt proportions to be higher than those of domestic firms. Other studies have concluded the opposite, citing imperfections in certain foreign markets, political risk factors, and complexities in the international financial environment that cause higher agency costs of debt for MNCs.

PERSONAL FINANCE EXAMPLE 19.5

MyLab Finance Solution Video

An important aspect of personal financial planning involves channeling savings into investments that can grow and fund long-term financial goals. Investors can invest in both domestic and foreign-based companies. Investing internationally offers greater diversification than investing only domestically. A number of academic studies overwhelmingly support the argument that well-structured international diversification does indeed reduce the risk of a portfolio and increase the return of portfolios of comparable risk.

To capture these diversification benefits, most individual investors buy international mutual funds. These funds take advantage of international economic developments by (1) capitalizing on changing foreign market conditions and (2) positioning their investments to benefit from devaluation of the dollar. Clearly, individuals should consider including some international investments—probably international mutual funds—in their investment portfolios.

Country Factors

A number of studies conclude that certain factors unique to each host country can cause differences in capital structures. These factors include legal, tax, political, social, and financial aspects as well as the overall relationship between the public and private sectors. Owing to these factors, differences have been found not only among MNCs based in various countries but also among the foreign subsidiaries of an MNC. However, because no one capital structure is ideal for all MNCs, each multinational has to consider a set of global and domestic factors when deciding on the appropriate capital structure for both the overall corporation and its subsidiaries. Understanding country factors can help financial managers make better-informed decisions. As discussed in the *Global Focus* box, a way to improve one's ability to understand the conduct of business in other countries is to take an overseas assignment.

LONG-TERM DEBT

As noted earlier, multinational companies have access to a variety of international financial instruments. Here we will discuss international bonds, the role of international financial institutions in underwriting such instruments, and the use of various techniques by MNCs to change the structure of their long-term debt.

international bond
A bond that is initially sold outside the country of the borrower and is often distributed in several countries.

foreign bond
A bond that is issued by a foreign corporation or government and is denominated in the investor's home currency and sold in the investor's home market.

International Bonds

In general, an **international bond** is one that is initially sold outside the country of the borrower and is often distributed in several countries. When a bond is issued by a foreign corporation or government and is denominated in the investor's home currency and sold in the investor's home market, it is called a **foreign bond**. For example, an MNC based in Germany might float a foreign bond issue in the British capital market underwritten by a British syndicate and denominated in British pounds. When an international bond is sold to investors in countries with

GLOBAL FOCUS *in practice*

Take an Overseas Assignment to Take a Step Up the Corporate Ladder

There is nothing like an extended stay in a foreign country to get a different perspective on world events, and there are sound career-enhancing reasons to work abroad. International experience can give you a competitive edge and may be vital to career advancement. Such experience goes far beyond mastering country-specific tax and accounting codes.

That's one message from the 2016 Global Mobility Trends Survey published by BGRS, a global human resources consulting company. The survey indicated that 61% of respondents said their company had communicated to employees that an international assignment was important to advance their careers. It's no wonder that companies place so much emphasis on international assignments, given that 80% of the survey respondents said the main purpose of having a globally mobile workforce was to facilitate important global business initiatives. The volume of international assignments reflected their importance to the success of a firm. The 2016 survey found that 63% of firms either increased or held steady the number of international assignments given to employees relative to the prior year, and 75% of firms said they expected the number of international assignments to remain the same or to increase through 2017.

On arrival in a foreign city, expatriates tend to live in a section of the city favored by other visitors from home. For security reasons, some executives also travel everywhere chauffeured by an English-speaking driver. It is possible for U.S. executives to live abroad for an extended period without soaking up much of the local culture. Doing so may increase one's comfort level, but at the loss of some of the valuable lessons to be learned from living abroad.

Overseas assignments do not come without some sacrifices. Long overseas postings can put stress on a family. The most common reason for turning down an international assignment (reported by 38% of survey respondents) involved family concerns, such as children's education, family adjustment, partner resistance, and language. The second most common reason (18%) for refusing an assignment was concern for a spouse's career, not unlike the same concern some employees have about a job that requires a cross-country transfer.

Yet as globalization has pushed companies across more borders, CFOs with international experience have found themselves in greater demand. Some chief executives value international experience in their CFOs more highly than either mergers and acquisitions or capital-raising experience.

► *If going abroad for a full-immersion assignment is not possible, what are some substitutes for a global assignment that may provide some—albeit limited—global experience?*

Eurobond
A bond issued by an international borrower and sold to investors in countries with currencies other than the currency in which the bond is denominated.

currencies other than the currency in which the bond is denominated, it is called a **Eurobond.** Thus, an MNC based in the United States might float a Eurobond in several European capital markets, underwritten by an international syndicate and denominated in U.S. dollars.

The U.S. dollar and the euro are the most frequently used currencies for Eurobond issues, with the euro rapidly increasing in popularity relative to the U.S. dollar. In the foreign bond category, the U.S. dollar and the euro are major choices. Low interest rates, the general stability of the currency, and the overall efficiency of the European Union's capital markets are among the primary reasons for the growing popularity of the euro.

Eurobonds are much more popular than foreign bonds. These instruments are heavily used, especially in relation to Eurocurrency loans in recent years, by major market participants, including U.S. corporations. *Equity-linked Eurobonds* (that is, Eurobonds convertible to equity), especially those offered by a number of U.S. firms, have found strong demand among Euromarket participants. It is expected that more of these innovative types of instruments will emerge on the international scene in the coming years.

A final point concerns the levels of interest rates in international markets. In the case of foreign bonds, interest rates usually directly correlate with the domestic rates prevailing in the respective countries. For Eurobonds, several interest rates may be influential. For instance, for a Eurodollar bond, the interest rate will reflect several different rates, most notably the U.S. long-term rate, the Eurodollar rate, and long-term rates in other countries.

The Role of International Financial Institutions

For foreign bonds, the underwriting institutions are those that handle bond issues in the respective countries in which such bonds are issued. For Eurobonds, a number of financial institutions in the United States, Western Europe, and Japan form international underwriting syndicates. The underwriting costs for Eurobonds are comparable to those for bond flotation in the U.S. domestic market. Although U.S. institutions once dominated the Eurobond scene, economic and financial strengths exhibited by some Western European (especially German) financial firms have led to an erosion in that dominance. For many years, a number of European firms have shared with U.S. firms the top positions in terms of acting as lead underwriters of Eurobond issues. However, U.S. investment banks continue to dominate most other international security issuance markets, such as international equity, medium-term note, syndicated loan, and commercial paper markets. U.S. corporations account for well over half of the worldwide securities issues made each year.

To raise funds through international bond issues, many MNCs establish their own financial subsidiaries. Many U.S.-based MNCs, for example, have created subsidiaries in the United States and Western Europe, especially in Luxembourg. Such subsidiaries can be used to raise large amounts of funds in "one move," the funds being redistributed wherever MNCs need them. (Special tax rules applicable to such subsidiaries also make them desirable to MNCs.)

Changing the Structure of Debt

As will be more fully explained later, MNCs can use hedging strategies to change the structure or characteristics of their long-term assets and liabilities. For instance, multinationals can use *interest rate swaps* to obtain a desired stream of interest payments (e.g., fixed rate) in exchange for another (e.g., floating rate). With *currency swaps,* they can exchange an asset/liability denominated in one currency (e.g., the U.S. dollar) for another (e.g., the British pound). The use of these tools allows MNCs to gain access to a broader set of markets, currencies, and maturities, thus leading to both cost savings and a means of restructuring the existing assets/liabilities. Growth in such use has been significant during the past few decades, and this trend is expected to continue.

EQUITY CAPITAL

Here we look at how multinational companies can raise equity capital abroad. They can sell their shares in international capital markets, or they can use joint ventures, which the host country sometimes requires.

Equity Issues and Markets

One means of raising equity funds for MNCs is to have the parent's stock distributed internationally and owned by stockholders of different nationalities. Despite some advancements made in recent years that have allowed numerous MNCs to simultaneously list their respective stocks on a number of exchanges, the world's equity markets continue to be dominated by distinct national stock exchanges (such as the New York, London, and Tokyo exchanges). At the end of 2016, for example, a rather small portion of each of the world's major stock exchanges consisted of "foreign company" listings. For example, on the NYSE, U.S. firms accounted for 78% of all listings as of early 2017. European and Canadian companies made up just 6% and 5% (respectively) of total NYSE listings. Many commentators agree that most MNCs would benefit enormously from an **international stock market** that had uniform rules and regulations governing the major stock exchanges. Unfortunately, it will likely be many years before such a market becomes a reality.

international stock market
A market with uniform rules and regulations governing major stock exchanges. MNCs would benefit greatly from such a market, which has yet to evolve.

Even with the full financial integration of the European Union, some European stock exchanges continue to compete with each other. Others have called for more cooperation in forming a single market capable of competing with the New York and Tokyo exchanges. As noted above, from the multinationals' perspective, the most desirable outcome would be to have uniform international rules and regulations with respect to all the major national stock exchanges. Such uniformity would allow MNCs unrestricted access to an international equity market paralleling the international currency and bond markets.

Joint Ventures

Earlier, we discussed the basic aspects of foreign ownership of international operations. Worth emphasizing here is that certain laws and regulations enacted by some host countries require MNCs to maintain less than 50% ownership in their subsidiaries in those countries. For a U.S.-based MNC, for example, establishing foreign subsidiaries in the form of joint ventures means that a certain portion of the firm's total international equity stock is (indirectly) held by foreign owners.

In establishing a foreign subsidiary, an MNC may wish to use as little equity and as much debt (with no recourse back to the "parent" borrower) as possible, with the debt coming from local sources in the host country or the MNC itself. Each of these actions can be supported in that the use of local debt can be a good protective measure to lessen the potential impacts of political risk and, because local sources are involved in the capital structure of a subsidiary, there may be fewer threats from local authorities in the event of changes in government or the imposing of new regulations on foreign business.

In support of the other action—having more MNC-based debt in a subsidiary's capital structure—many host governments are less restrictive toward intra-MNC interest payments than toward intra-MNC dividend remittances. The parent firm may therefore be in a better position if it has more MNC-based debt than equity in the capital structure of its subsidiaries.

→ REVIEW QUESTIONS MyLab Finance Solutions

19–9 Indicate how NPV can differ depending on whether it is measured from the parent MNC's point of view or from that of the foreign subsidiary, when cash flows may be blocked by local authorities.

19–10 Briefly discuss some of the international factors that cause the capital structures of MNCs to differ from those of purely domestic firms.

19–11 Describe the difference between foreign bonds and Eurobonds. Explain how each is sold, and discuss the determinant(s) of their interest rates.

19–12 What are the long-run advantages of having more local debt and less MNC-based equity in the capital structure of a foreign subsidiary?

LG5

19.5 Short-Term Financial Decisions

In international operations, the usual domestic sources of short-term financing, along with other sources, are available to MNCs. Included are accounts payable, accruals, bank and nonbank sources in each subsidiary's local environment, and the Euromarket. Our emphasis here is on the "foreign" sources.

The local economic market is a source of both short- and long-term financing for a subsidiary of a multinational company. Moreover, the subsidiary's borrowing and lending status, relative to a local firm in the same economy, can be superior because the subsidiary can rely on the potential backing and guarantee of its parent MNC. One drawback, however, is that most local markets and local currencies are regulated by local authorities. A subsidiary may ultimately choose to turn to the Euromarket and take advantage of borrowing and investing in an unregulated financial forum.

The Euromarket offers nondomestic long-term financing opportunities through Eurobonds, which were discussed in Chapter 6. Short-term financing opportunities are available in **Eurocurrency markets**. The forces of supply and demand are among the main factors determining exchange rates in Eurocurrency markets. Each currency's normal interest rate is influenced by economic policies pursued by the respective "home" government. For example, the interest rates offered in the Euromarket on the U.S. dollar are greatly affected by the prime rate inside the United States, and the dollar's exchange rates with other major currencies are influenced by the supply and demand forces in such markets (and in response to interest rates).

Eurocurrency markets
The portion of the Euromarket that provides short-term, foreign-currency financing to subsidiaries of MNCs.

Unlike borrowing in the domestic markets, where only one currency and a **nominal interest rate** are involved, financing activities in the Euromarket can involve several currencies and both nominal and effective interest rates. **Effective interest rates** are equal to nominal rates plus (or minus) any forecast appreciation (or depreciation) of a foreign currency relative to the currency of the MNC parent. Stated differently, the figures for effective rates are derived by adjusting the nominal interest rates for the impact of foreign-currency movements on both the principal and interest amounts. We can use Equation 19.1 to calculate the effective interest rate for a specific currency (E) given the nominal interest rate for the currency (N) and its forecast percentage change (F):

nominal interest rate
In the international context, the stated interest rate charged on financing when only the MNC parent's currency is involved.

effective interest rate
In the international context, the rate equal to the nominal rate plus (or minus) any forecast appreciation (or depreciation) of a foreign currency relative to the currency of the MNC parent.

$$E = N + F + (N \times F) \tag{19.1}$$

An example will illustrate the application and interpretation of this relationship.

EXAMPLE 19.6

A multinational plastics company, International Molding, has subsidiaries in Switzerland (local currency, Swiss franc, Sf) and Japan (local currency, Japanese yen, ¥). On the basis of each subsidiary's forecast operations, the short-term financial needs (in equivalent U.S. dollars) are as follows:

Switzerland: $80 million excess cash to be invested (lent)

Japan: $60 million funds to be raised (borrowed)

On the basis of all available information, the parent firm has provided each subsidiary with the figures given in the following table for exchange rates and interest rates. (The figures for the effective rates shown are derived using Equation 19.1.)

From the MNC's point of view, the effective rates of interest, which take into account each currency's forecast percentage change (appreciation or depreciation) relative to the U.S. dollar, are the main considerations in investment and borrowing decisions. (It is assumed here that because of local regulations, a subsidiary is not permitted to use the domestic market of any other subsidiary.) The relevant question is where funds should be invested and borrowed.

For investment purposes, the highest available effective rate of interest is 3.30% in the US$ Euromarket. Therefore, the Swiss subsidiary should invest the $80 million in Swiss francs in U.S. dollars. To raise funds, the cheapest source open to the Japanese subsidiary is the 2.01% effective rate for the Swiss franc in the Euromarket. The subsidiary should therefore raise the $60 million in Swiss francs in the Euromarket. These two transactions will result in the most revenues and least costs, respectively.

	Currency		
Item	US$	Sf	¥
Spot exchange rates		1.27(Sf/$)	108.37(¥/$)
Forecast percent change		−2.0%	+1.0%
Interest rates			
Nominal			
Euromarket	3.30%	4.10%	1.50%
Domestic	3.00%	3.80%	1.70%
Effective			
Euromarket	3.30%	2.01%	2.51%
Domestic	3.00%	1.72%	2.71%

Several points should be made with respect to the preceding example. First, it is a simplified case of the actual workings of the Eurocurrency markets. The example ignores taxes, intersubsidiary investing and borrowing, and periods longer or shorter than 1 year. Nevertheless, it shows how the existence of many currencies can provide both challenges and opportunities for MNCs. Next, the focus has been solely on accounting values; of greater importance would be the impact of these actions on market value. Finally, it is important to note the following details about the figures presented. The forecast percentage change data are those normally supplied by the MNC's international financial managers. Management may instead want a range of forecasts, from the most likely to the least likely. In addition, the company's management is likely to take a specific position in terms of its response to any remaining exchange rate exposures. If any action is to be taken, certain amounts of one or more currencies will be borrowed and then invested in other currencies in the hope of realizing potential gains to offset potential losses associated with the exposures.

CASH MANAGEMENT

In its international cash management, a multinational firm can respond to exchange rate risks by protecting (hedging) its undesirable cash and marketable securities exposures or by making certain adjustments in its operations. The former approach is more applicable in responding to accounting exposures, the latter to economic exposures. Here, we examine each approach.

hedging strategies
Techniques used to offset or protect against risk; in the international context, these include borrowing or lending in different currencies; undertaking contracts in the forward, futures, and/or options markets; and swapping assets/liabilities with other parties.

Hedging Strategies

Hedging strategies are techniques used to offset or protect against risk. In international cash management, these strategies include actions such as borrowing or lending in different currencies; undertaking contracts in the forward, futures, and/or options markets; and swapping assets/liabilities with other parties. Table 19.5 briefly outlines some of the major hedging tools

TABLE 19.5 Exchange Rate Risk-Hedging Tools

Tool	Description	Impact on risk
Borrowing or lending	Borrowing or lending in different currencies to take advantage of interest rate differentials and foreign exchange appreciation/depreciation; can be either on a certainty basis with "up-front" costs or speculative	Can be used to offset exposures in existing assets/liabilities and in expected revenues/ expenses
Forward contract	"Tailor-made" contracts representing an *obligation* to buy/sell, with the amount, rate, and maturity agreed upon between the two parties; has little up-front cost	Can eliminate downside risk but locks out any upside potential
Futures contract	Standardized contracts offered on organized exchanges; same basic tool as a forward contract but less flexible because of standardization; more flexibility because of secondary-market access; has some up-front cost	Can eliminate downside risk, plus position can be nullified, creating possible upside potential
Options	Tailor-made or standardized contracts providing the *right* to buy or to sell an amount of the currency, at a particular price, during a specified time period; has up-front cost (premium)	Can eliminate downside risk and retain unlimited upside potential
Interest rate swap	Allows the trading of one interest rate stream (e.g., on a fixed-rate U.S. dollar instrument) for another (e.g., on a floating-rate U.S. dollar instrument); fee to be paid to the intermediary	Permits firms to change the interest rate structure of their assets/liabilities and achieves cost savings via broader market access
Currency swap	Two parties exchange principal amounts of two different currencies initially; they pay each other's interest payments and then reverse principal amounts at a preagreed exchange rate at maturity; more complex than interest rate swaps	Has all the features of interest rate swaps, plus allows firms to change the currency structure of their assets/liabilities
Hybrids	A variety of combinations of some of the preceding tools; may be quite costly and/or speculative	Can create, with the right combination, a perfect hedge against certain exchange rate exposures

Note: The participants in these activities include MNCs, financial institutions, and brokers. The organized exchanges are Amsterdam, Chicago, London, New York, Philadelphia, and Zurich, among others. Although most of these tools can be used for short-term exposure management, some, such as swaps, are more appropriate for long-term hedging strategies.

available to MNCs. By far, the most commonly used technique is hedging with a forward contract.

To demonstrate how you can use a forward contract to hedge exchange rate risk, assume that you are a financial manager for Boeing Company, which has just booked a sale of three airplanes worth $360 million to Japan's All Nippon Airways. The sale is denominated in Japanese yen, and the current spot exchange rate is 108.37(¥/$). Therefore, you have priced this airplane sale at ¥39.0132 billion. If delivery were to occur today, there would be no foreign exchange risk. However, delivery and payment will not occur for 90 days. If this transaction is not hedged, Boeing will be exposed to a significant risk of loss if the Japanese yen depreciates over the next 3 months.

Suppose that the dollar appreciates against the yen from 108.37(¥/$) to 110.25(¥/$) between now and the delivery date. On delivery of the airplanes, the agreed-upon ¥39.0132 billion will then be worth only $353.861 million [¥39.0132 billion ÷ 110.25(¥/$)] rather than the $360 million you originally planned for, which is a foreign exchange loss of more than $6.1 million. If, instead of remaining unhedged, you had sold the ¥39.0132 billion forward 3 months earlier at the 90-day forward rate of 107.92(¥/$) offered by your bank, you could have locked in a net dollar sale price of $361.501 million [¥39.0132 billion ÷ 107.92(¥/$)], realizing a foreign exchange gain of more than $1.5 million. Clearly, the second option is a better alternative. Of course, if you had remained unhedged and the Japanese yen had appreciated beyond 107.92(¥/$), your firm would have experienced an even larger foreign exchange profit. Most MNCs prefer to make profits through sales of goods and services rather than by speculating on the direction of exchange rates, however.

Adjustments in Operations

In responding to exchange rate fluctuations, MNCs can give their international cash flows some protection through appropriate adjustments in assets and liabilities. Two routes are available to a multinational company. The first centers on the operating relationships that a subsidiary of an MNC maintains with other firms, or third parties. Depending on management's expectation of a local currency's position, adjustments in operations would involve the reduction of liabilities if the currency is appreciating or the reduction of financial assets if it is depreciating. For example, if a U.S.-based MNC with a subsidiary in Mexico expects the peso to appreciate in value relative to the U.S. dollar, local customers' accounts receivable would be increased and accounts payable would be reduced if at all possible. Because the dollar is the currency in which the MNC parent will have to prepare consolidated financial statements, the net result in this case would be to increase the Mexican subsidiary's resources favorably in local currency. If the peso were instead expected to depreciate, the local customers' accounts receivable would be reduced and accounts payable would be increased, thereby reducing the Mexican subsidiary's resources in the local currency.

The second route focuses on the operating relationship a subsidiary has with its parent or with other subsidiaries within the same MNC. In dealing with exchange rate risks, a subsidiary can rely on intra-MNC accounts. Specifically, undesirable exchange rate exposures can be corrected to the extent that the subsidiary can take the following steps:

1. In appreciation-prone countries, collect intra-MNC accounts receivable as soon as possible, and delay payment of intra-MNC accounts payable as long as possible.
2. In depreciation-prone countries, collect intra-MNC accounts receivable as late as possible, and pay intra-MNC accounts payable as soon as possible.

This technique is known as "leading and lagging" or simply as "leads and lags."

EXAMPLE 19.7

Assume that a U.S.-based parent company, American Computer Corporation (ACC), both buys parts from and sells parts to its wholly owned Mexican subsidiary, Tijuana Computer Company (TCC). Assume further that ACC has accounts payable of $10,000,000 that it is scheduled to pay TCC in 30 days and, in turn, has accounts receivable of (Mexican peso) MP 115.00 million due from TCC within 30 days. Because today's exchange rate is 11.50(MP/$), the accounts receivable are also worth $10,000,000. Therefore, parent and subsidiary owe each other equal amounts (although in different currencies), and both are payable in 30 days, but because TCC is a wholly owned subsidiary of ACC, the parent has complete discretion over the timing of these payments.

If ACC believes that the Mexican peso will depreciate from 11.50(MP/$) to, say, 12.75(MP/$) during the next 30 days, the combined companies can profit by collecting the weak currency (MP) debt immediately but delaying payment of the strong currency (US$) debt for the full 30 days allowed. If parent and subsidiary do so and the peso depreciates as predicted, the net result is that the MP 115.00 million payment from TCC to ACC is made immediately and is safely converted into $10,000,000 at today's exchange rate. In comparison, the delayed $10,000,000 payment from ACC to TCC will be worth MP 127.50 million [$10 million × 12.75(MP/$)]. Thus, the Mexican subsidiary will experience a foreign exchange trading profit of MP 12.50 million (MP 127.50 million − MP 115.00 million), whereas the U.S. parent receives the full amount ($10 million) due from TCC and therefore is unharmed.

As the preceding example suggests, the manipulation of an MNC's consolidated intracompany accounts by one subsidiary generally benefits one subsidiary (or the parent) while leaving the other subsidiary (or the parent) unharmed. The exact degree and direction of the actual manipulations, however, may depend on the tax status of each country. The MNC obviously would want to have the exchange rate losses in the country with the higher tax rate. Finally, changes in intra-MNC accounts can also be subject to restrictions and regulations put forward by the respective host countries of various subsidiaries.

CREDIT AND INVENTORY MANAGEMENT

Multinational firms based in different countries compete for the same global export markets. Therefore, it is essential that they offer attractive credit terms to potential customers. Increasingly, however, the maturity of developed markets is forcing MNCs to maintain and increase revenues by exporting and selling a higher percentage of their output to developing countries. Given the risks associated with these buyers, as partly evidenced by their lack of a major (hard) currency, the MNC must use a variety of tools to protect such revenues. In addition to the use of hedging and various asset and liability adjustments (described earlier), MNCs should seek the backing of their respective governments in both identifying target markets and extending credit. Multinationals based in a number of Western European nations and those based in Japan benefit from extensive involvement of government agencies that provide them with the needed service and financial support. For U.S.-based MNCs, government agencies such as the Export-Import Bank do not provide a comparable level of support.

In terms of inventory management, MNCs must consider a number of factors related to both economics and politics. In addition to maintaining the appropriate level of inventory in various locations around the world, a multinational firm must deal with exchange rate fluctuations, tariffs, nontariff barriers, integration schemes such as the EU, and other rules and regulations. Politically, inventories could be subjected to wars, expropriations, blockages, and other forms of government intervention.

→ REVIEW QUESTIONS MyLab Finance Solutions

19–13 What is the Eurocurrency market? What are the main factors determining foreign exchange rates in that market? Differentiate between the nominal interest rate and the effective interest rate in this market.

19–14 Discuss the steps to be followed in adjusting a subsidiary's accounts relative to third parties when that subsidiary's local currency is expected to appreciate in value in relation to the currency of the parent MNC.

19–15 Outline the changes to be undertaken in intra-MNC accounts if a subsidiary's currency is expected to depreciate in value relative to the currency of the parent MNC.

19.6 Mergers and Joint Ventures

The motives for domestic mergers—growth or diversification, synergy, fund raising, increased managerial skill or technology, tax considerations, increased ownership liquidity, and defense against takeover—are all applicable to MNCs' international mergers and joint ventures. We should also consider several additional points.

First, international mergers and joint ventures, especially those involving European firms acquiring assets in the United States, increased significantly beginning in the 1980s. MNCs based in Western Europe, Japan, and North America are numerous. Moreover, a fast-growing group of MNCs has emerged in the past two decades, some based in the so-called newly industrialized countries (including Singapore, South Korea, Taiwan, and China's Hong Kong) and others operating from emerging nations (such as Brazil, Argentina, Mexico, Israel, China, Malaysia, Thailand, and India). Even though many of these companies were hit hard by economic and currency crises (Asia in 1997, Russia in 1998, and Latin America in 2001–2003), top firms from these and other countries have been able to survive and even prosper. Additionally, many Western companies have taken advantage of temporary weakness in these economies to buy into companies that were previously off-limits to foreign investors, which has further added to the number and value of international mergers.

The U.S. economy is among the largest recipients of FDI inflows. Most of the foreign direct investors in the United States come from seven countries: the United Kingdom, Canada, France, the Netherlands, Japan, Switzerland, and Germany. The available data indicate that in terms of the method of entry—namely mergers and acquisitions (M&A) versus "establishments"—an overwhelming share of outlays committed by foreign multinationals in the United States between 1980 and 2006 consisted of M&A. These firms prefer M&A through which they can target U.S. companies for their advanced technology (e.g., biotechnology firms), worldwide brands (restaurant chains and food products), entertainment/media (theme parks), and financial institutions (investment banks). In contrast, in most emerging/developing nations (including China), FDI inflows take place primarily via establishments.

Although the United States remains one of the most "open" countries to FDI inflows, some of its actions in recent years have been viewed as less than welcoming. In 2005, for example, the U.S. government opposed a bid by a Chinese state-owned oil company (CNOOC) to purchase an American one (UNOCAL), which led to the ultimate withdrawal of the offer. Then, in 2005 and 2006, similar opposition, along with an identical outcome, took place in relation to a bid by a firm owned by the government of Dubai (in the United Arab Emirates) to acquire port operations in the United States.

Another trend is the current increase in the number of joint ventures between companies based in Japan and firms domiciled elsewhere in the industrialized world, especially U.S.-based MNCs. In the eyes of some U.S. corporate executives, such business ventures are viewed as a "ticket into the Japanese market" as well as a way to curb a potentially tough competitor.

Developing countries, too, have been attracting foreign direct investments in many industries. Meanwhile, a number of these nations have adopted specific policies and regulations aimed at controlling the inflows of foreign investments, a major provision being the 49% ownership limitation applied to MNCs. Of course, international competition among MNCs has benefited some developing countries in their attempts to extract concessions from the multinationals. However, an increasing number of such nations have shown greater flexibility in their recent dealings with MNCs as multinationals have become more reluctant to form joint ventures under the stated conditions. Furthermore, it is likely that as more developing countries recognize the need for foreign capital and technology, they will show even greater flexibility in their agreements with MNCs.

A final point relates to the existence of international holding companies. Places such as Liechtenstein and Panama have long been considered promising spots for forming holding companies because of their favorable legal, corporate, and tax environments. International holding companies control many business entities in the form of subsidiaries, branches, joint ventures, and other agreements. For international legal (especially tax-related) reasons as well as anonymity, such holding companies have become increasingly popular in recent years.

→ REVIEW QUESTION MyLab Finance Solutions

19–16 What are some of the major reasons for the rapid expansion in international mergers and joint ventures of firms?

SUMMARY

FOCUS ON VALUE

The growing interdependence of world markets has increased the importance of international finance in managing the multinational company (MNC). As a result, the financial manager must deal with international issues related to taxes, financial markets, accounting and profit measurement and repatriation, exchange rate risks caused by doing business in more than one currency, political risks, financing (both debt and equity) and capital structure, short-term financing, cash management issues related to hedging and adjustments in operations, and merger and joint-venture opportunities.

The complexity of each of these issues is significantly greater for the multinational firm than for a purely domestic firm. Consequently, the financial manager must approach actions and decisions in the multinational firm using both standard financial tools and techniques and additional procedures that recognize the legal, institutional, and operating differences that exist in the multinational environment. Just as in a purely domestic firm, action should be undertaken only after the financial manager has determined that it will contribute to the parent company's overall goal of **maximizing the owners' wealth** as reflected in its share price.

REVIEW OF LEARNING GOALS

LG 1 **Understand the major factors that influence the financial operations of multinational companies (MNCs).** Important international trading blocs emerged in the 1990s: one in the Americas as a result of NAFTA; the European Union (EU); and Mercosur in South America. The EU is becoming even more competitive as it achieves monetary union and many of its members use the euro as a single currency. Free trade among the largest economic powers is governed by the General Agreement on Tariffs and Trade (GATT) and is policed by the World Trade Organization (WTO).

Setting up operations in foreign countries can entail special problems related to the legal form of business organization chosen, the degree of ownership allowed by the host country, and possible restrictions and regulations on the return of capital and profits. Taxation of multinational companies is a complex issue because of the existence of varying tax rates, differing definitions of taxable income, measurement differences, and tax treaties.

The existence and expansion of dollars held outside the United States have contributed to the development of a major international financial market, the Euromarket. The large international banks, developing and industrialized nations, and multinational companies participate as borrowers and lenders in this market.

LG 2 **Describe the key differences between purely domestic and international financial statements: consolidation, translation of individual accounts, and international profits.** Regulations that apply to international operations complicate the preparation of foreign-based financial statements. Rulings in the United States require the determination for translation purposes of the functional currency used in the operations of a foreign subsidiary. Individual accounts of subsidiaries must be translated back into U.S. dollars using the procedures outlined in *FASB No. 52* and/or the temporal method. This standard also requires that only certain transactional gains or losses from international operations be included in the U.S. parent's income statement.

LG3 **Discuss exchange rate risk and political risk, and explain how MNCs manage them.** Economic exposure from exchange rate risk results from the existence of different currencies and their impact on the value of foreign operations. Long-term changes in foreign exchange rates result primarily from differing inflation rates in the two countries. The money markets, the forward (futures) markets, and the foreign-currency options markets can be used to hedge foreign exchange exposure. Political risks stem mainly from the implications of political instability for the assets and operations of MNCs. MNCs can employ negative, external, and positive approaches to cope with political risk.

LG4 **Describe foreign direct investment, investment cash flows and decisions, the MNCs' capital structure, and the international debt and equity instruments available to MNCs.** Foreign direct investment (FDI) involves an MNC's transfer of capital, managerial, and technical assets from its home country to the host country. The investment cash flows of FDIs are subject to a variety of factors, including taxes in host countries, regulations that may block the repatriation of MNCs' cash flow, various business and financial risks, and the application of a local cost of capital.

The capital structures of MNCs differ from those of purely domestic firms because of the MNCs' access to the Euromarket and the financial instruments it offers, their ability to reduce risk in their cash flows through international diversification, and the impact of factors unique to each host country. MNCs can raise long-term debt by issuing international bonds in various currencies. Foreign bonds are sold primarily in the country of the currency of issue; Eurobonds are sold primarily in countries other than the country of the issue's currency. MNCs can raise equity through sale of shares in international capital markets or through joint ventures. In establishing foreign subsidiaries, it may be more advantageous to issue debt than MNC-owned equity.

LG5 **Discuss the role of the Eurocurrency market in short-term borrowing and investing (lending) and the basics of international cash, credit, and inventory management.** Eurocurrency markets allow multinationals to invest (lend) and raise (borrow) short-term funds in a variety of currencies and to protect themselves against exchange rate risk. MNCs consider effective interest rates, which take into account currency fluctuations, in making investment and borrowing decisions. MNCs invest in the currency with the highest effective rate and borrow in the currency with the lowest effective rate. MNCs must offer competitive credit terms and maintain adequate inventories to provide timely delivery to foreign buyers. Obtaining the backing of foreign governments is helpful to MNCs in effectively managing credit and inventory.

LG6 **Review recent trends in international mergers and joint ventures.** International mergers and joint ventures, including international holding companies, increased significantly beginning in the 1980s. Special factors affecting these mergers include economic and trade conditions and various regulations imposed on MNCs by host countries.

OPENER-IN-REVIEW

In the chapter opener, you read about how appreciation of the yen against the dollar led to large currency losses at Mazda. Suppose that Mazda's quarterly operating profit in the United States averages $100 million and the exchange rate is $1 = ¥116. How much would Mazda's profit be worth in yen? What if the exchange rate is $1 = ¥100 yen?

SELF-TEST PROBLEM (Solution in Appendix)

ST19–1 **Currency movements** Today the exchange rate between U.S. dollars and Japanese yen is 97.91(¥/$). A year ago the rate was 98.91(¥/$).

a. Which currency appreciated and which currency depreciated over the course of the year?

b. Do you think that over the last year inflation was higher in the United States or in Japan?

WARM-UP EXERCISES All problems are available in MyLab Finance

E19–1 Santana Music is a U.S.-based MNC whose foreign subsidiary had pretax income of $55,000; all after-tax income is available in the form of dividends to the parent company. The local tax rate is 40%, the foreign dividend withholding tax rate is 5%, and the U.S. tax rate is 34%. Compare the net funds available to the parent corporation (a) if foreign taxes can be applied against the U.S. tax liability and (b) if they cannot.

LG3

E19–2 Assume that the Mexican peso currently trades at 12 pesos to the U.S. dollar. During the year, U.S. inflation is expected to average 3%, while Mexican inflation is expected to average 5%. What is the current value of one peso in terms of U.S. dollars? Given the relative inflation rates, what will the exchange rates be 1 year from now? Which currency is expected to appreciate and which currency is expected to depreciate over the next year?

LG5

E19–3 If Like A Lot Corp. borrows yen at a nominal annual interest rate of 2% and during the year the yen appreciates by 10%, what will the effective annual interest rate be for the loan?

LG3 LG5

E19–4 Carry Trade Inc. borrows yen when the yen is trading at ¥110/US$. If the nominal annual interest rate of the loan is 3% and at the end of the year the yen trades at ¥120/US$, what is the effective annual interest rate of the loan?

LG5

E19–5 Denim Industries can borrow its needed financing for expansion using one of two foreign lending facilities. It can borrow at a nominal annual interest rate of 8% in Mexican pesos, or it can borrow at 3% in Canadian dollars. If the peso is expected to depreciate by 10% and the Canadian dollar is expected to appreciate by 3%, which loan has the lower effective annual interest rate?

PROBLEMS

All problems are available in MyLab Finance. The MyLab icon indicates problems in Excel format available in MyLab Finance.

P19–1 **Exchange rate movements** Suppose a basket of goods in Paris costs €133 and the same basket purchased in New York costs $153.

a. At what exchange rate between euros and dollars is the cost of the basket of goods the same in each city?

b. Now suppose that over the next year inflation in France is expected to be 2% while in the U.S. the forecast is for 6% inflation. What exchange rate do you expect a year from today?

P19–2 **Translation of financial statements** A U.S.-based MNC has a subsidiary in France (local currency, euro, €). The balance sheet and income statement of the subsidiary follow. Assume that on December 31, 2019, the exchange rate is US$1.20/€. Assume that the local (euro) figures for the statements remain the same on December 31, 2020. Calculate the U.S. dollar-translated figures for the two ending time periods, assuming that between December 31, 2019, and December 31, 2020, the euro has appreciated against the U.S. dollar by 6%.

Translation of Income Statement

	December 31, 2019		December 31, 2020
	Euro	**US$**	**US$**
Sales	30,000		
Cost of goods sold	29,750	30,000	30,000
Operating profits	250	30,000	30,000

Translation of Balance Sheet

	December 31, 2019		December 31, 2020
Assets	**Euro**	**US$**	**US$**
Cash	40		
Inventory	300		
Plant and equipment (net)	160	30,000	30,000
Total	500	30,000	30,000
Liabilities and stockholders' equity			
Debt	240		
Paid-in capital	200		
Retained earnings	60	30,000	30,000
Total	500	30,000	30,000

Personal Finance Problem

P19–3 **Exchange rates** Fred Nappa is planning to take a wine-tasting tour through Italy this summer. The tour will cost 2,750 euros (€) and includes transportation, hotels, and a guide. Fred estimates that round-trip airfare from his home in North Carolina to Rome, Italy, will be $1,490; he also will incur another $300 (U.S.) in incidental travel expenses. Fred estimates the cost of meals in Italy to be about €500, and he will take an additional $1,000 to cover miscellaneous expenditures. Currently, the exchange rate is 1.3411($/€) or €.7456($/€).

a. Determine the total dollar cost of the trip to Italy.

b. Determine the amount of euros (€) Fred will need to cover meals and miscellaneous expenditures.

Personal Finance Problem

P19–4 International investment diversification The economies of the world tend to rise and fall in cycles that offset each other. International stocks can provide possible diversification for a portfolio heavy on U.S. equities. Because research on foreign companies is usually difficult for individual investors to track on their own, a foreign equity mutual fund offers the investor the expertise of a global fund manager.

Foreign-stock funds provide exposure to overseas markets at varying levels of risk. Economic and currency risk can swing in a positive or negative direction. Hence, diversification is the key to managing risk. Funds that invest overseas fall into four basic categories: global, international, emerging-market, and country-specific. The wider the reach of the fund, the less risky it is likely to be.

a. Go to http://finances-com.com/. Click on "Foreign Stock Funds Explained" under the Categories menu.

b. Briefly explain the differences between the following funds:

(1) Global fund.
(2) International fund.
(3) Emerging-market fund.
(4) Country-specific fund.

P19–5 Euromarket investment and fund raising A U.S.-based multinational company has two subsidiaries, one in Mexico (local currency, Mexican peso, MP) and one in Japan (local currency, yen, ¥). Forecasts of business operations indicate the following short-term financing position for each subsidiary (in equivalent U.S. dollars):

Mexico: $80 million excess cash to be invested (lent)
Japan: $60 million funds to be raised (borrowed)

The management gathered the following data:

	Currency		
Item	**US$**	**MP**	**¥**
Spot exchange rates		11.60(MP/$)	108.25(¥/$)
Forecast percent change		−3.0%	+1.5%
Interest rates			
Nominal			
Euromarket	4.00%	6.20%	2.00%
Domestic	3.75%	5.90%	2.15%
Effective			
Euromarket	____	____	____
Domestic	____	____	____

Determine the effective interest rates for all three currencies in both the Euromarket and the domestic market, and then indicate where the funds should be invested and raised. (*Note:* Assume that because of local regulations, a subsidiary is *not* permitted to use the domestic market of any other subsidiary.)

P19–6 **ETHICS PROBLEM** Is there a conflict between maximizing shareholder wealth and never paying bribes when doing business abroad? If so, how might you explain the firm's position to shareholders who are asking why the company does not pay bribes when its foreign competitors in various nations clearly do so?

SPREADSHEET EXERCISE

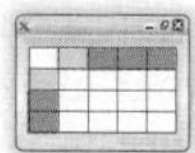

As the financial manager for a large multinational corporation (MNC), you have been asked to assess the firm's economic exposure. The two major currencies, other than the U.S. dollar, that affect the company are the Mexican peso (MP) and the British pound (£). You have been given the projected future cash flows for next year:

Currency	Total inflow	Total outflow
British pounds	£17,000,000	£11,000,000
Mexican pesos	MP 100,000,000	MP 25,000,000

The current expected exchange rate in U.S. dollars with respect to the two currencies is as follows:

Currency	Exchange rate
British pounds	1.66($/£)
Mexican pesos	0.10($/MP)

TO DO

Assume that the movements in the Mexican peso and the British pound are highly correlated. Create a spreadsheet to answer the following questions.

a. Determine the net cash flows for both the Mexican peso and the British pound.

b. Determine the net cash flow as measured in U.S. dollars. It will represent the value of the economic exposure.

c. Provide your assessment of the company's degree of economic exposure. In other words, is it high or low based on your findings in part **b**?

MyLab Finance Visit www.myfinancelab.com for **Chapter Case: *Assessing a Direct Investment in Chile by U.S. Computer Corporation,*** Group Exercises, and numerous online resources.

Integrative Case 8

Organic Solutions

Organic Solutions (OS), one of the nation's largest plant wholesalers in the southeastern United States, was poised for expansion. Through strong profitability, a conservative dividend policy, and some recent realized gains in real estate, OS had a strong cash position and was searching for a target company to acquire. The executive members on the acquisition search committee had agreed to find a firm in a similar line of business rather than one that would provide broad diversification. It would be their first acquisition, and they preferred to stay in a familiar line of business. Jennifer Morgan, director of marketing, had identified the targeted lines of business through exhaustive market research.

Ms. Morgan had determined that the servicing of plants in large commercial offices, hotels, zoos, and theme parks would complement the existing wholesale distribution business. Frequently, OS was requested by its large clients to bid on a service contract. However, the company was neither staffed nor equipped to enter this market. Ms. Morgan was familiar with the major plant service companies in the Southeast and had suggested Green Thumbs Inc. (GTI) as an acquisition target because of its significant market share and excellent reputation.

GTI had successfully commercialized a market that had been dominated by small local contractors and in-house landscaping departments. Beginning with a contract from one of the largest theme parks in the United States, GTI's growth in sales had compounded remarkably over its 8-year history. GTI had also been selected because of its large portfolio of long-term service contracts with several major *Fortune* 500 companies. These contracted clients would provide a captive customer base for the wholesale distribution of OS's plant products.

At the National Horticultural meeting in Los Angeles, Ms. Morgan and OS's chief financial officer, Jack Levine, had approached the owner of GTI (a closely held corporation) to determine whether a merger offer would be welcomed. GTI's majority owner and president, Herb Merrell, had reacted favorably and subsequently provided financial data, including GTI's earnings record and current balance sheet. These data are presented in Tables 1 and 2.

Jack Levine had estimated that the incremental cash inflow after taxes from the acquisition would be $18,750,000 for years 1 and 2; $20,500,000 for year 3; $21,750,000 for year 4; $24,000,000 for year 5; and $25,000,000 for years 6 through 30. He also estimated that the company should earn a rate of return of at least 16% on an investment of this type. Additional financial data for 2019 are given in Table 3.

TABLE 1

Green Thumbs Inc.'s Earning Record

Year	EPS	Year	EPS
2012	$2.20	2016	$2.85
2013	2.35	2017	3.00
2014	2.45	2018	3.10
2015	2.60	2019	3.30

TABLE 2

Green Thumbs Inc.'s Balance Sheet (December 31, 2019)

Assets		Liabilities and equity	
Cash	$ 2,500,000	Current liabilities	$ 5,250,000
Accounts receivable	1,500,000	Mortgage payable	3,125,000
Inventories	7,625,000	Common stock	15,625,000
Land	7,475,000	Retained earnings	9,000,000
Fixed assets (net)	13,900,000	Total liabilities and equity	$33,000,000
Total assets	$33,000,000		

TABLE 3

OS and GTI Financial Data (December 31, 2019)

Item	OS	GTI
Earnings available for common stock	$35,000,000	$15,246,000
Number of shares of common stock	10,000,000	4,620,000
Market price per share	$50	$30[a]

[a]Estimated by Organic Solutions.

TO DO

a. What is the maximum price Organic Solutions should offer GTI for a cash acquisition? (*Note:* Assume that the relevant time horizon for analysis is 30 years.)

b. If OS planned to sell bonds to finance 80% of the cash acquisition price found in part **a,** how might issuance of each of the following bonds affect the firm? Describe the characteristics and pros and cons of each bond:
   (1) Straight bonds.
   (2) Convertible bonds.
   (3) Bonds with stock purchase warrants attached.

c. (1) What is the ratio of exchange in a stock swap acquisition if OS pays $30 per share for GTI? Explain why.
   (2) What effect will this swap of stock have on the EPS of the original shareholders of (i) Organic Solutions and (ii) Green Thumbs Inc.? Explain why.
   (3) If the earnings attributed to GTI's assets grow at a much slower rate than those attributed to OS's premerger assets, what effect might this growth have on the EPS of the merged firm over the long run?

d. What other merger proposals could OS make to GTI's owners?

e. If GTI were actually a foreign-based company, what impact would that have on the foregoing analysis? Describe the added regulations, costs, benefits, and risks that are likely to be associated with such an international merger.

Appendix Solutions to Self-Test Problems

Chapter 1

ST1–1

Accounting view (accrual basis)		Financial view (cash basis)	
Worldwide Rugs income statement for the year ended 12/31		Worldwide Rugs cash flow statement for the year ended 12/31	
Sales revenue	$3,000,000	Cash inflow	$2,550,000
Less: Costs	2,500,000	Less: Cash outflow	2,500,000
Net profit	$ 500,000	Net cash flow	$ 50,000

a. $3,000,000 − $2,500,000 = $500,000

b. Yes, from an accounting perspective Worldwide Rug was profitable. It generated a 20% profit ($500,000/$2,500,000 = 0.20) on its investment.

c. The company collected 85% of its receivables in cash, so its cash inflow was $3,000,000 × 85% = $2,550,000. Net cash flow was therefore $2,550,000 − $2,500,000 = $50,000.

d. It generated a positive cash flow, but it only represents a 2% cash return on investment ($50,000/$2,500,000 = 0.02), and it may not be enough to cover operating costs incurred during the year.

e. Given the risk associated with importing and Worldwide Rug's ability to collect on its accounts receivables, a 2% cash return on investment before expenses seems unlikely to lead to long-term success. Without adequate cash inflows to meet its obligations, the firm will not survive, regardless of its level of profits.

Chapter 2

ST2–1

a. The current bid/ask spread is $0.02, the difference between $57.33 and $57.31.

b. If your sell order is routed to Nasdaq, then you will pay one-half of the bid/ask spread plus the brokerage commission. Total transactions costs will be (1/2 × $0.02 × 1,500) + $34.99 = $49.99.

c. In this case the Nasdaq dealer is taking herself out of the transaction by executing both orders at the midpoint of the bid/ask spread. So you will not have to pay one half of the bid/ask spread for every share you sell, but instead you will only pay the brokerage commission.

Total Transaction Costs = Brokerage Commission = $34.99

d. The market value of your trade is the number of shares traded (1,500) times the midpoint of the bid/ask spread ($57.32) or $85,980.

Chapter 3

ST3–1

Ratio	**Too high**	**Too low**
Current ratio = current assets/ current liabilities	May indicate that the firm is holding excessive cash, accounts receivable, or inventory.	May indicate poor ability to satisfy short-term obligations.
Inventory turnover = CGS/inventory	May indicate lower level of inventory, which may cause stockouts and lost sales.	May indicate poor inventory management, excessive or obsolete inventory, or low sales compared to competition.
Times interest earned = earnings before interest and taxes/interest	May indicate overly conservative capital structure, i.e., unwillingness to use borrowed funds even if doing so increases shareholder value.	May indicate poor ability to pay contractual interest payments.
Gross profit margin = gross profits/sales	Indicates the low cost of merchandise sold relative to the sales price; might indicate a strong competitive position in the market, as long as price is not high enough to discourage sales.	Indicates the high cost of the merchandise sold relative to the sales price; may indicate that the firm's competitive position in its market is not particularly strong.
Return on total assets = profits after taxes/ total assets	A high value is almost unambiguously a good thing, except perhaps if it indicates that the firm is not investing sufficiently in new assets to take advantage of attractive investment opportunities.	Indicates ineffective management in generating profits with the available assets.
Price/earnings (P/E) ratio = market price per share of common stock/earnings per share	Investors may have priced in a very high estimate of the firm's future growth or they may have underestimated the firm's risk.	Investors lack confidence in the firm's future outcomes or believe that the firm has an excessive level of risk.

ST3–2

O'Keefe Industries
Balance Sheet
December 31, 2019

Assets		Liabilities and stockholders' equity	
Cash	$ 32,720	Accounts payable	$ 120,000
Marketable securities	25,000	Notes payable	160,000[e]
Accounts receivable	197,280[a]	Accruals	20,000
Inventories	225,000[b]	Total current liabilities	$ 300,000[d]
Total current assets	$ 480,000	Long-term debt	$ 600,000[f]
Net fixed assets	$1,020,000[c]	Stockholders' equity	$ 600,000
Total assets	$1,500,000	Total liabilities and stockholders' equity	$1,500,000

[a]Average collection period (ACP) = 40 days
ACP = Accounts receivable/Average sales per day
40 = Accounts receivable/($1,800,000/365)
40 = Accounts receivable/$4,932
$197,280 = Accounts receivable

[b]Inventory turnover = 6.0
Inventory turnover = Cost of goods sold/Inventory
6.0 = [Sales × (1 − Gross profit margin)]/ Inventory
6.0 = [$1,800,000 × (1 − 0.25)]/Inventory
$225,000 = Inventory

[c]Total asset turnover = 1.20
Total asset turnover = Sales/ Total assets
1.20 = $1,800,000/ Total assets
$1,500,000 = Total assets
Total assets = Current assets + Net fixed assets
$1,500,000 = $480,000 + Net fixed assets
$1,020,000 = Net fixed assets

[d]Current ratio = 1.60
Current ratio = Current assets/Current liabilities
1.60 = $480,000/Current liabilities
$300,000 = Current liabilities

[e]Notes Payable = Total current liabilities − Accounts payable − Accruals
= $300,000 − $120,000 − $20,000
= $160,000

[f]Debt ratio = 0.60
Debt ratio = Total liabilities/ Total assets
0.60 = Total liabilities/$1,500,000
$900,000 = Total liabilities
Total liabilities = Current liabilities + Long-term debt
$900,000 = $300,000 + Long-term debt
$600,000 = Long-term debt

Chapter 4

ST4–1 **a.** Depreciation schedule:

Year	Cost[a] (1)	Percentages (from Table 4.2) (2)	Depreciation [(1)×(2)] (3)
1	$150,000	20%	$ 30,000
2	150,000	32	48,000
3	150,000	19	28,500
4	150,000	12	18,000
5	150,000	12	18,000
6	150,000	5	7,500
	Totals	100%	$150,000

[a]$140,000 asset cost + $10,000 installation cost.

b. Operating cash flow:

Year	EBIT (1)	NOPAT [(1) × (1 − 0.21)] (2)	Depreciation (3)	Operating cash flows [(2) + (3)] (4)
1	$160,000	$126,400	$30,000	$156,400
2	160,000	126,400	48,000	174,400
3	160,000	126,400	28,500	154,900
4	160,000	126,400	18,000	144,400
5	160,000	126,400	18,000	144,400
6	160,000	126,400	7,500	133,900

c. Change in net fixed assets in year 6 = \$0 − \$7,500 = −\$7,500
NFAI in year 6 = −\$7,500 + \$7,500 = \$0
Change in current assets in year 6 = \$110,000 − \$90,000 = \$20,000
Change in (Accounts payable + Accruals) in year 6 = (\$45,000 + \$7,000) − (\$40,000 + \$8,000) = \$52,000 − \$48,000 = \$4,000
NCAI in year 6 = \$20,000 − \$4,000 = \$16,000
For year 6
FCF = OCF − NFAI − NCAI
= \$133,900* − \$0 − \$16,000 = \$117,900
*From part **b,** column 4 value for year 6.

d. In part **b,** we can see that, in each of the 6 years, the operating cash flow is positive, which means that the firm is generating cash that it could use to invest in fixed assets or working capital, or it could distribute some of the cash flow to investors by paying interest or dividends. The free cash flow (FCF) calculated in part **c** for year 6 represents the cash flow available to investors—providers of debt and equity—after covering all operating needs and paying for net fixed asset investment (NFAI) and net current asset investment (NCAI) that occurred during the year.

ST4–2 a.

Carroll Company Cash Budget April–June						Accounts receivable at end of June	
	February	March	April	May	June	July	August
Forecast sales	$500	$600	$400	$ 200	$ 200		
Cash sales (0.30)	$150	$180	$120	$ 60	$ 60		
Collections of A/R							
Lagged 1 month [(0.7 × 0.7) = 0.49]		245	294	196	98	$ 98	
Lagged 2 months [(0.3 × 0.7) = 0.21]			105	126	84	42	$42
						$140 + $42 = $182	
Total cash receipts			$519	$ 382	$ 242		
Less: Total cash disbursements			600	500	200		
Net cash flow			−$ 81	−$ 118	$ 42		
Add: Beginning cash			115	34	− 84		
Ending cash			$ 34	−$ 84	−$ 42		
Less: Minimum cash balance			25	25	25		
Required total financing (notes payable)			—	$ 109	$ 67		
Excess cash balance (marketable securities)			$ 9	—	—		

b. Carroll Company would need a maximum of $109 in financing over the 3-month period.

c.

Account	Amount	Source of amount
Cash	$ 25	Minimum cash balance—June
Notes payable	67	Required total financing—June
Marketable securities	0	Excess cash balance—June
Accounts receivable	182	Calculation at right of cash budget statement

ST4–3 a.

Euro Designs, Inc., Pro Forma Income Statement for the Year Ended December 31, 2020	
Sales revenue (given)	$3,900,000
Less: Cost of goods sold (0.55)[a]	2,145,000
Gross profits	$1,755,000
Less: Operating expenses (0.12)[b]	468,000
Operating profits	$1,287,000
Less: Interest expense (given)	325,000
Net profits before taxes	$ 962,000
Less: Taxes (0.21 × $962,000)	202,020
Net profits after taxes	$ 759,980
Less: Cash dividends (given)	320,000
To retained earnings	$ 439,980

[a]From 2019: CGS/Sales = $1,925,000/$3,500,000 = 0.55.

[b]From 2019: Oper. Exp./Sales = $420,000/$3,500,000 = 0.12.

b. The percent-of-sales method may underestimate actual 2020 pro forma income by assuming that all costs are variable. If the firm has fixed costs, which by definition would not increase with increasing sales, the 2020 pro forma income would probably be underestimated.

Chapter 5

ST5–1 a. *Bank A:*

$FV_3 = \$10,000 \times (1 + 0.04)^3 = \$10,000 \times 1.125 = \underline{\underline{\$11,250}}$

(Calculator solution $= \$11,248.64$)

Bank B:

$FV_3 = \$10,000 \times (1 + 0.04/2)^6 = \$10,000 \times 1.126 = \underline{\underline{\$11,260}}$

(Calculator solution $= \$11,261.62$)

Bank C:

$FV_3 = \$10,000 \times (1 + 0.04/4)^{12} = \$10,000 \times 1.127 = \underline{\underline{\$11,270}}$

(Calculator solution $= \$11,268.25$)

b. *Bank A:*

$\text{EAR} = (1 + 0.04/1)^1 - 1 = (1 + 0.04)^1 - 1 = 1.04 - 1 = 0.04 = \underline{\underline{4\%}}$

Bank B:

$\text{EAR} = (1 + 0.04/2)^2 - 1 = (1 + 0.02)^2 - 1$
$= 1.0404 - 1 = 0.0404 = \underline{\underline{4.04\%}}$

Bank C:

$\text{EAR} = (1 + 0.04/4)^4 - 1 = (1 + 0.01)^4 - 1 = 1.0406 - 1$
$= 0.0406 = \underline{\underline{4.06\%}}$

c. Ms. Martin should deal with Bank C: The quarterly compounding of interest at the given 4% annual nominal rate results in the highest future value as a result of the corresponding highest effective annual rate.

d. *Bank D:*

$FV_3 = \$10,000 \times e^{0.04 \times 3} = \$10,000 \times e^{0.12}$
$= \$10,000 \times 1.127497 = \underline{\underline{\$11,274.97}}$

This alternative is better than Bank C; it results in a higher future value because of the use of continuous compounding, which with otherwise identical cash flows always results in the highest future value of any compounding period.

ST5–2 a. On the surface, annuity Y looks more attractive than annuity X because it provides $1,000 more each year than does annuity X. Of course, X being an annuity due means that the $9,000 would be received at the beginning of each year, unlike the $10,000 at the end of each year, and this fact makes annuity X more appealing than it otherwise would be.

b. *Annuity X:*

$FV_6 = \$9,000 \times \{[(1 + 0.15)^6 - 1]/0.15\} \times (1 + 0.15)$
$= \$9,000 \times 8.754 \times 1.15 = \underline{\underline{\$90,603.90}}$

(Calculator solution $= \$90,601.19$)

Annuity Y:

$FV_6 = \$10{,}000 \times \{[(1 + 0.15)^6 - 1]/0.15\}$

$= \$10{,}000 \times 8.754 = \underline{\underline{\$87{,}540.00}}$

(Calculator solution = \$87,537.38)

c. Annuity X is more attractive because its future value at the end of year 6, FV_6, of \$90,603.90 is greater than annuity Y's end-of-year-6 future value, FV_6, of \$87,540.00. The subjective assessment in part a was incorrect. The benefit of receiving annuity X's cash inflows at the beginning of each year appears to have outweighed the fact that annuity Y's annual cash inflow, which occurs at the end of each year, is \$1,000 larger (\$10,000 vs. \$9,000) than annuity X's. Notice that in each year the cash flow provided by Y is 11.11% greater than the cash flow provided by X. That is, (10,000 − 9,000)/9,000 = 0.1111. Because Ramesh can earn 15% on his investments, he would rather have \$9,000 at the start of each year and earn 15% on that as opposed to getting 11.11% more at the end of each year. If the return that Ramesh could earn on investments was less than 11.11%, he would prefer annuity Y. If the return that Ramesh could earn on investments was equal to 11.11%, he would be indifferent to the two annuities. That's easy to see because if Ramesh received \$9,000 at the start of each year and invested that at 11.11%, by the end of each year the payment that he received would have grown to \$10,000, which would just duplicate the payment that he could receive from annuity Y.

ST5–3 *Alternative A:*

Cash flow stream:

$PV_5 = \$700/0.09 \times [1 - 1/(1 + 0.09)^5]$

$= \$700/0.09 \times 0.350 = \underline{\underline{\$2{,}723}}$

(Calculator solution = \$2,722.76)

Single amount: $\underline{\underline{\$2{,}825}}$

Alternative B:

Cash flow stream:

Year (n)	Present value calculation	Present value
1	$\$1{,}100/(1 + 0.09) =$	\$1,009.17
2	$\$\ 900/(1 + 0.09)^2 =$	\$ 757.51
3	$\$\ 700/(1 + 0.09)^3 =$	\$ 540.53
4	$\$\ 500/(1 + 0.09)^4 =$	\$ 354.21
5	$\$\ 300/(1 + 0.09)^5 =$	\$ 194.98
	Present value	\$2,856.40

(Calculator solution = \$2,856.41)

Single amount: $\underline{\underline{\$2{,}800}}$

Conclusion: Alternative B in the form of a cash flow stream is preferred because its present value of \$2,856.40 is greater than the other three values.

ST5–4

$$CF = \$8{,}000/\{[(1+0.07)^5 - 1]/0.07\}$$
$$CF = \$8{,}000/5.751$$
$$CF = \$1{,}391.06$$

(Calculator solution = $1,391.13)

Judi should deposit $1,391.06 at the end of each of the 5 years to meet her goal of accumulating $8,000 at the end of the fifth year.

Chapter 6

ST6–1 a. $B_0 = I/r_d \times [1 - 1/(1+r_d)^n] + M \times 1/(1+r_d)^n$

$I = 0.08 \times \$1{,}000 = \$80$

$M = \$1{,}000$

$n = 12$ yrs

1. $r_d = 7\%$

$$B_0 = \$80/0.07 \times [1 - 1/(1+0.07)^{12}] + \$1{,}000 \times 1/(1+0.07)^{12}$$
$$= (\$1{,}142.86 \times 0.556) + (\$1{,}000 \times 0.444)$$
$$= \$635.43 + \$444.00 = \underline{\underline{\$1{,}079.43}}$$

(Calculator solution = $1,079.43)

2. $r_d = 8\%$

$$B_0 = \$80/0.08 \times [1 - 1/(1+0.08)^{12}] + \$1{,}000 \times 1/(1+0.08)^{12}$$
$$= (\$1{,}000 \times 0.603) + (\$1{,}000 \times 0.397)$$
$$= \$603.00 + \$397.00 = \underline{\underline{\$1{,}000.00}}$$

(Calculator solution = $1,000.00)

3. $r_d = 10\%$

$$B_0 = \$80/0.10 \times [1 - 1/(1+0.10)^{12}] + \$1{,}000 \times 1/(1+0.10)^{12}$$
$$= (\$800 \times 0.681) + (\$1{,}000 \times 0.319)$$
$$= \$544.80 + \$319.00 = \underline{\underline{\$863.80}}$$

(Calculator solution = $863.73)

b. 1. $r_d = 7\%$, $B_0 = \$1{,}079.43$; sells at a *premium*

2. $r_d = 8\%$, $B_0 = \$1{,}000.00$; sells at its *par value*

3. $r_d = 10\%$, $B_0 = \$863.80$; sells at a *discount*

c. $B_0 = (I/2)/r_d \times [1 - 1/(1+r_d/2)^{2n}] + M \times 1/(1+r_d/2)^{2n}$

$$= (\$80/2)/(0.10/2) \times [1 - 1/(1+0.10/2)^{24}]$$
$$+ \$1{,}000 \times 1/(1+0.10/2)^{24}$$
$$= \$800 \times 0.690 + \$1{,}000 \times 0.310$$
$$= \$552.00 + \$310.00 = \underline{\underline{\$862.00}}$$

(Calculator solution = $862.01)

ST6–2 a. $B_0 = \$1{,}026.57$

$C = 0.065 \times \$1{,}000 = \$65$

$$\text{Current yield} = \frac{\text{annual interest}}{\text{current price}} = \frac{\$65}{\$1{,}026.57} = 6.33\%$$

b. We know the bond sells for a premium, which means its YTM must be lower than its 6.5% coupon rate. We could use a trial-and-error approach to determine the bond's YTM. For example, if we plug 6% in for r in Equation 6.5, the bond price is \$1,054.14. That is a little above the bond's true market price, so we must raise the discount rate a bit. If you try 6.25%, you'll find that the bond price equals \$1,026.57, the current market price, so 6.25% is the YTM. Of course you can also find 6.25% using a calculator or Excel.

c. The YTM of 6.25% is below both the bond's 6.5% coupon interest rate and its current yield of 6.33% calculated in part **a** because the bond's market value of \$1,026.57 is above its \$1,000 par value. Whenever a bond's market value is above its par value (it sells at a *premium*), its YTM and current yield will be below its coupon interest rate; when a bond sells at *par*, the YTM and current yield will equal its coupon interest rate; and when the bond sells for less than par (at a *discount*), its YTM and current yield will be greater than its coupon interest rate. Observe also that the current yield measures the bond's coupon payment relative to its current price. When the bond sells at a premium, its YTM will be below its current yield because the YTM also takes into account that the bondholder will receive just \$1,000 back at maturity, which represents a loss relative to the bond's current market price. In other words, the YTM is measuring both the value of the coupon payment that the investor receives (just like the current yield does) and the "loss" that the bondholder endures when the bond matures.

Chapter 7

ST7–1 $D_0 = \$1.80$

$r_s = 12\%$

a. *Zero growth:*

$D_0 = D_1 = \$1.80$

$$P_0 = \frac{D_1}{r} = \frac{\$1.80}{0.12} = \underline{\underline{\$15}}$$

b. *Constant growth,* $g = 5\%$:

$D_1 = D_0 \times (1 + g) = \$1.80 \times (1 + 0.05) = \$1.89$

$$P_0 = \frac{D_1}{r_s - g} = \frac{\$1.89}{0.12 - 0.05} = \frac{\$1.89}{0.07} = \underline{\underline{\$27}}$$

c. *Variable growth*, $N=3$, $g_1=5\%$ for years 1 to 3 and $g_2=4\%$ for years 4 to ∞:

$$D_1 = D_0 \times (1+g_1)^1 = \$1.80 \times (1+0.05)^1 = \$1.89/\text{share}$$
$$D_2 = D_0 \times (1+g_1)^2 = \$1.80 \times (1+0.05)^2 = \$1.98/\text{share}$$
$$D_3 = D_0 \times (1+g_1)^3 = \$1.80 \times (1+0.05)^3 = \$2.08/\text{share}$$
$$D_4 = D_3 \times (1+g_1) = \$2.08 \times (1+0.04) = \$2.16/\text{share}$$

$$P_0 = \sum_{t=1}^{N} \frac{D_0 \times (1+g_1)^t}{(1+r)^t} + \left(\frac{1}{(1+r_s)^N} \times \frac{D_{N+1}}{r-g_2}\right)$$

First find the present value of the first 3 dividends.

$$\sum_{t=1}^{3} \frac{D_t}{(1+r)^t} = \frac{1.89}{(1+0.12)^1} + \frac{1.98}{(1+0.12)^2} + \frac{2.08}{(1+0.12)^3}$$
$$= \$1.69 + \$1.58 + \$1.48 = \$4.75$$

Next find the present value of all dividends that arrive in year 4 and beyond.

$$\left[\frac{1}{(1+r)^N} \times \frac{D_{N+1}}{r-g_2}\right] = \frac{1}{(1+0.12)^3} \times \frac{\$2.16}{0.12-0.04} = 0.712 \times \$27 = \$19.22$$

$$P_0 = \$4.75 + \$19.22 = \$23.97$$

ST7–2 a. **Step 1:** Present value in 2023 of free cash flows that arrives from 2024 to infinity:

$$FCF_{2024} = \$1{,}500{,}000 \times (1+0.04)$$
$$= \$1{,}560{,}000$$
$$\text{Present value in 2023 of } FCF_{2024\to\infty} = \frac{\$1{,}560{,}000}{0.10-0.04} = \frac{\$1{,}560{,}000}{0.06}$$
$$= \underline{\underline{\$26{,}000{,}000}}$$

Step 2: Add the value found in Step 1 to the 2023 FCF.

Total $FCF_{2023} = \$1{,}500{,}000 + \$26{,}000{,}000 = \underline{\underline{\$27{,}500{,}000}}$

Step 3: Find the sum of the present values of the FCFs for 2020 through 2023 to determine company value, VC.

Year (t)	Present value calculation	Present value in 2019 of FCF_t
2020	$ 800,000/(1 + 0.10) =	$ 727,272.73
2021	$ 1,200,000/(1 + 0.10)^2 =	$ 991,735.54
2022	$ 1,400,000/(1 + 0.10)^3 =	$ 1,051,840.72
2023	$27,500,000/(1 + 0.10)^4 =	$18,782,870.02
	Value of entire company, V_C =	$21,553,719.01

(Calculator solution = $21,553,719.01)

b. Common Stock value, $V_S = V_C - V_D - V_P$

V_C = $21,553,719.01 (calculated in part **a**)

V_D = $12,500,000 (given)

V_P = $0 (given)

V_S = $21,553,719.01 − $12,500,000 − $0 = $9,053,719.01

(Calculator solution = $9,053,719.01)

c. Price per share $= \dfrac{\$9{,}053{,}719.01}{500{,}000} = \underline{\underline{\$18.11}}/\text{share}$

(Calculator solution = \$18.11/sharc)

Chapter 8

ST8–1 a. Expected return, $\bar{r} = \dfrac{\sum \text{Returns}}{3}$

$$\bar{r}_A = \frac{12\% + 14\% + 16\%}{3} = \frac{42\%}{3} = \underline{\underline{14\%}}$$

$$\bar{r}_B = \frac{16\% + 14\% + 12\%}{3} = \frac{42\%}{3} = \underline{\underline{14\%}}$$

$$\bar{r}_C = \frac{12\% + 14\% + 16\%}{3} = \frac{42\%}{3} = \underline{\underline{14\%}}$$

b. Standard deviation, $\sigma_r = \sqrt{\dfrac{\sum_{j=1}^{3}(r_i - \bar{r})^2}{3-1}}$

$$\sigma_{r_A} = \sqrt{\frac{(12\% - 14\%)^2 + (14\% - 14\%)^2 + (16\% - 14\%)^2}{3-1}}$$

$$= \sqrt{\frac{4\%^2 + 0\%^2 + 4\%^2}{2}} = \sqrt{\frac{8\%^2}{2}} = \underline{\underline{2\%}}$$

$$\sigma_{r_B} = \sqrt{\frac{(16\% - 14\%)^2 + (14\% - 14\%)^2 + (12\% - 14\%)^2}{3-1}}$$

$$= \sqrt{\frac{4\%^2 + 0\%^2 + 4\%^2}{2}} = \sqrt{\frac{8\%^2}{2}} = \underline{\underline{2\%}}$$

$$\sigma_{r_C} = \sqrt{\frac{(12\% - 14\%)^2 + (14\% - 14\%)^2 + (16\% - 14\%)^2}{3-1}}$$

$$= \sqrt{\frac{4\%^2 + 0\%^2 + 4\%^2}{2}} = \sqrt{\frac{8\%^2}{2}} = \underline{\underline{2\%}}$$

c.

	Annual expected returns	
Year	**Portfolio AB**	**Portfolio AC**
2019	(0.50 × 12%) + (0.50 × 16%) = 14%	(0.50 × 12%) + (0.50 × 12%) = 12%
2020	(0.50 × 14%) + (0.50 × 14%) = 14%	(0.50 × 14%) + (0.50 × 14%) = 14%
2021	(0.50 × 16%) + (0.50 × 12%) = 14%	(0.50 × 16%) + (0.50 × 16%) = 16%

Over the 3-year period:

$$\bar{r}_{AB} = \frac{14\% + 14\% + 14\%}{3} = \frac{42\%}{3} = \underline{\underline{14\%}}$$

$$\bar{r}_{AC} = \frac{12\% + 14\% + 16\%}{3} = \frac{42\%}{3} = \underline{\underline{14\%}}$$

d. AB is perfectly negatively correlated.
AC is perfectly positively correlated.

e. Standard deviation of the portfolios:

$$\sigma_{r_{AB}} = \sqrt{\frac{(14\% - 14\%)^2 + (14\% - 14\%)^2 + (14\% - 14\%)^2}{3 - 1}}$$

$$= \sqrt{\frac{(0\%^2 + 0\%^2 + 0\%^2)}{2}} = \sqrt{\frac{0\%^2}{2}} = \underline{\underline{0\%}}$$

$$\sigma_{r_{AC}} = \sqrt{\frac{(12\% - 14\%)^2 + (14\% - 14\%)^2 + (16\% - 14\%)^2}{3 - 1}}$$

$$= \sqrt{\frac{4\%^2 + 0\%^2 + 4\%^2}{2}} = \sqrt{\frac{8\%^2}{2}} = \underline{\underline{2\%}}$$

f. Portfolio AB is preferred because it provides the same return (14%) as AC but with less risk $[(\sigma_{r_{AB}} = 0\%) < (\sigma_{r_{AC}} = 2\%)]$. Assets are perfectly negatively correlated eliminating all standard deviation (volatility).

ST8–2 a. When the market return increases by 10%, the investment's return would be expected to increase by 15% $(1.50 \times 10\%)$. When the market return decreases by 10%, the investment's return would be expected to decrease by 15% $[1.50 \times (-10\%)]$.

b. $r_j = R_F + [\beta_j \times (r_m - R_F)]$

$= 3\% + [1.50 \times (10\% - 3\%)] = 13.5\%$

c. No, if you believe that the investment will earn a return of 11%, you should reject it because based on its risk the required return is 13.5%.

d. $r_j = 3\% + [1.50 \times (7\% - 3\%)] = 9\%$

The investment would now be acceptable because its required return of 9% is now less than the 11% that you believe the investment will earn.

Chapter 9

ST9–1 a. Cost of debt, r_d (using approximation formula)

$$r_d = \frac{I + \dfrac{\$1{,}000 - N_d}{n}}{\dfrac{N_d + \$1{,}000}{2}}$$

$I = 0.10 \times \$1{,}000 = \$100$

$N_d = \$1{,}000 - \$30 \text{ discount} - \$20 \text{ flotation cost} = \$950$

$n = 10$ years

$$r_d = \frac{\$100 + \dfrac{\$1{,}000 - \$950}{10}}{\dfrac{\$950 + \$1{,}000}{2}} = \frac{\$100 + \$5}{\$975} = 10.8\%$$

(Calculator solution = 10.84%)

after-tax cost = $r_d \times (1 - T)$

$T = 0.21$

after-tax cost = 10.8% × (1 − 0.21) = 8.5%

Cost of preferred stock, r_p

$$r_p = \frac{D_p}{N_p}$$

$$D_p = 0.11 \times \$100 = \$11$$

$$N_p = \$100 - \$4 \text{ flotation cost} = \$96$$

$$r_p = \frac{\$11}{\$96} = \underline{\underline{11.5\%}}$$

Cost of retained earnings, r_r

$$r_r = r_s = \frac{D_1}{P_0} + g$$

$$= \frac{\$6}{\$80} + 6.0\% = 7.5\% + 6.0\% = \underline{\underline{13.5\%}}$$

Cost of new common stock, r_n

$$r_n = \frac{D_1}{N_n} + g$$

$$D_1 = \$6$$

$$N_n = \$80 - \$4 \text{ underpricing} - \$4 \text{ flotation cost} = \$72$$

$$g = 6.0\%$$

$$r_n = \frac{\$6}{\$72} + 6.0\% = 8.3\% + 6.0\% = \underline{\underline{14.3\%}}$$

b. Recognize that the firm has $225,000 in retained earnings to use. If they use that money first, and if equity constitutes 45% of total capital (the weight given in the table), then the firm can raise up to $500,000 ($225,000/0.45) without issuing new stock. Therefore, if the company plans to raise less than $500,000, the WACC for the money raised will be based on the cost of retained earnings (i.e., the required return on the firm's stock).

Source of capital	Weight (1)	Cost (2)	Weighted cost [(1) × (2)] (3)
Long-term debt	0.40	8.5%	3.4%
Preferred stock	0.15	11.5	1.7
Common stock equity	0.45	13.5	6.1
Totals	1.00		11.2%

Weighted average cost of capital = 11.2%

Now if the company wants to raise more than $500,000, it must issue new common stock, which has a higher cost than retained earnings.

Source of capital	Weight (1)	Cost (2)	Weighted cost [(1) × (2)] (3)
Long-term debt	0.40	8.5%	3.4%
Preferred stock	0.15	11.5	1.7
Common stock equity	0.45	14.3	6.4
Totals	1.00		11.5%

Weighted average cost of capital = 11.5%

c.

Investment opportunity	Internal rate of return (IRR)	Initial investment	Cumulative investment
D	16.5%	$200,000	$ 200,000
C	12.9	150,000	350,000
E	11.8	450,000	800,000
A	11.2	100,000	900,000
G	10.5	300,000	1,200,000
F	10.1	600,000	1,800,000
B	9.7	500,000	2,300,000

Projects D, C, and E should be accepted because their respective IRRs exceed the WACC. They will require $800,000 of total new financing.

Chapter 10

ST10–1 a. Payback period:

Project M: $\frac{\$40,000}{\$14,000} = \underline{\underline{2.86}}$ years

Project N:

Year (t)	Cash inflows (CF_t)	Cumulative cash inflows
1	$23,000	$23,000
2	12,000	35,000
3	10,000	45,000
4	9,000	54,000

$$2 + \frac{\$10{,}000 - \$5{,}000}{\$9{,}000} = 2.5 \text{ years}$$

b. Net present value (NPV):

Project M: $\text{NPV} = \$14{,}000/0.09 \times [1 - 1/(1+0.09)^4] - \$40{,}000$
$= (\$155{,}555.56 \times 0.2916) - \$40{,}000$
$= \$45{,}360 - \$40{,}000 = \underline{\underline{\$5{,}360}}$

(Calculator solution = \$5,356.08)

Project N:

Year (*t*)	Present value	Present values
1	$23,000/(1 + 0.09) =	$ 21,100.92
2	$12,000/(1 + 0.09)^2 =	$ 10,100.16
3	$10,000/(1 + 0.09)^3 =	$ 7,721.83
4	$ 9,000/(1 + 0.09)^4 =	$ 6,375.83
	Present value of cash inflows	$ 45,298.74
	− Initial investment	$ 40,000.00
	Net present value (NPV)	$ 5,298.74

(Calculator solution = \$5,298.74)

c. Internal rate of return (IRR):

Project M: $\text{NPV} = 0 = \$14{,}000/\text{IRR} \times [1 - 1/(1+\text{IRR})^4] - \$40{,}000$

Because a 9% discount rate results in a positive NPV of \$5,536.08, the IRR must be greater than 9%. At 10% the NPV is \$4,378. At 12% the NPV is \$2,523. Continuing to increase the discount rate, we find that at 15% the NPV is −\$30, so the IRR must be just barely below 15%. Using Excel or a calculator reveals that the IRR is 14.96%.

Project M: $\text{NPV} = \$14{,}000/0.15 \times [1 - 1/(1+0.15)^4] - \$40{,}000$
$= (\$93{,}333.33 \times 0.42825) - \$40{,}000$
$= \$39{,}970.00 - \$40{,}000 = -\$30$

$\text{IRR} \approx \underline{\underline{15\%}}$

(Calculator solution = 14.96%)

Project N: $\text{NPV} = 0 = 23{,}000/(1+\text{IRR}) + 12{,}000/(1+\text{IRR})^2 + 10{,}000/(1+\text{IRR})^3 + 9{,}000/(1+\text{IRR})^4 - 40{,}000$

Because a 9% discount rate results in a positive NPV of \$5,298.74, the IRR must be greater than 9%. Again we can use trial-and-error to try to find the IRR, or we can use a calculator or Excel. Doing the latter reveals that the

IRR is 16.19%. You can get close to a zero NPV if, using the trial-and-error approach, you try a discount rate of 16%.

$$\begin{aligned}\text{Project N: NPV} &= \$23{,}000/(1+0.16) + \$12{,}000/(1+0.16)^2 \\ &\quad + \$10{,}000/(1+0.16)^3 + \$9{,}000/(1+0.16)^4 - \$40{,}000 \\ &= \$19{,}827.59 + \$8{,}917.95 + \$6{,}406.58 + \$4{,}970.62 - \$40{,}000 \\ &= \$122.74\end{aligned}$$

Because the NPV is a small positive number when the discount rate is 16%, we know that the IRR is just a bit higher than 16%.

(Calculator solution = 16.19%)

d.

	Project	
	M	**N**
Payback period	2.86 years	2.5 years
NPV	$5,356.08	$5,298,74
IRR	14.96%	16.19%

Project M has a higher NPV, but project N has a faster payback and a higher IRR. Thus, the techniques do not agree on which project is best. However, in general when these measures conflict, it is best to go with the higher NPV, which in this case is Project M.

e. Net present value profiles:

	NPV	
Discount Rate	**Project M**	**Project N**
0%	$16,000	$14,000
2	13,308	11,821
4	10,818	9,793
6	8,511	7,903
8	6,370	6,138
10	4,378	4,487
12	2,523	2,940
14	792	1,487

From the NPV profile, you can see that Project M has a higher NPV when the discount rate is below 10%, but project N has a higher NPV at discount rates of 10% and above. More precise calculations would show that the two NPV profiles cross (i.e., the two projects have the same NPV) when the discount rate is about 9.34%. Project N's NPV is less sensitive to the discount rate (i.e., its NPV falls more slowly when the discount rate rises compared to the NPV of Project M) because it provides a great deal of cash in year 1, whereas Project M's cash flow is spread out evenly over time.

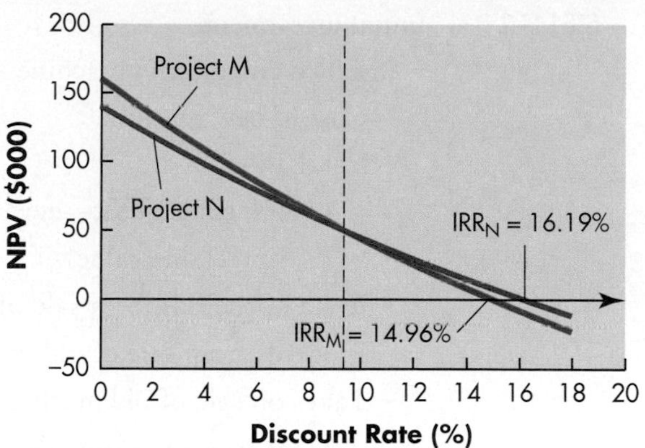

Chapter 11

ST11–1 a.

$$\text{Book value} = \text{Installed cost} - \text{Accumulated depreciation}$$
$$\text{Installed cost} = \$50{,}000$$
$$\text{Accumulated depreciation} = \$50{,}000 \times (0.20 + 0.32 + 0.19 + 0.12)$$
$$= \$50{,}000 \times 0.83 = \$41{,}500$$
$$\text{Book value} = \$50{,}000 - \$41{,}500 = \underline{\underline{\$8{,}500}}$$

b. Taxes on sale of old equipment:

$$\text{Gain on sale} = \text{Sale price} - \text{Book value}$$
$$= \$55{,}000 - \$8{,}500 = \$46{,}500$$
$$\text{Taxes} = 0.40 \times \$46{,}500 = \underline{\underline{\$18{,}600}}$$

c. Initial investment:

Installed cost of new equipment	
Cost of new equipment	$75,000
+ Installation costs	5,000
Total installed cost—new	$80,000
− After-tax proceeds from sale of old equipment	
Proceeds from sale of old equipment	55,000
− Taxes on sale of old equipment	18,600
Total after-tax proceeds—old	$36,400
+ Change in net working capital	15,000
Initial investment	$58,600

ST11–2 **a.** Initial investment:

Installed cost of new machine	
Cost of new machine	$140,000
+ Installation costs	10,000
Total installed cost—new (depreciable value)	$150,000
− After-tax proceeds from sale of old machine	
Proceeds from sale of old machine	42,000
− Taxes on sale of old machine[1]	9,120
Total after-tax proceeds—old	$ 32,880
+ Change in net working capital[2]	20,000
Initial investment	$137,120

[1]Book value of old machine = $40,000 − (0.20 + 0.32) × $40,000
= $40,000 − (0.52 × $40,000)
= $40,000 − $20,800 = $19,200

Gain on sale = $42,000 − $19,200 = $22,800

Taxes = 0.40 × $22,800 = $9,120

[2]Change in net working capital = $10,000 + $25,000 − $15,000
= $35,000 − $15,000 = $20,000

b. Incremental operating cash inflows:

Calculation of Depreciation Expense

Year	Cost (1)	Applicable MACRS depreciation percentages (from Table 4.2) (2)	Depreciation [(1) × (2)] (3)
With new machine			
1	$150,000	33%	$ 49,500
2	150,000	45	67,500
3	150,000	15	22,500
4	150,000	7	10,500
		Totals 100%	$150,000
With old machine			
1	$ 40,000	19% (year-3 depreciation)	$ 7,600
2	40,000	12 (year-4 depreciation)	4,800
3	40,000	12 (year-5 depreciation)	4,800
4	40,000	5 (year-6 depreciation)	2,000
			Total $19,200[a]

[a]The total of $19,200 represents the book value of the old machine at the end of the second year, which was calculated in part a.

Calculation of Operating Cash Inflows

	Year 1	Year 2	Year 3	Year 4
With new machine				
Earnings before depr., int., and taxes[a]	$120,000	$130,000	$130,000	$ 0
− Depreciation[b]	49,500	67,500	22,500	10,500
Earnings before int. and taxes	$ 70,500	$ 62,500	$107,500	−$10,500
− Taxes (rate, T=40%)	28,200	25,000	43,000	−4,200
Net operating profit after taxes	$ 42,300	$ 37,500	$ 64,500	−$ 6,300
+ Depreciation[b]	49,500	67,500	22,500	10,500
Operating cash inflows	$ 91,800	$105,000	$ 87,000	$ 4,200
With old machine				
Earnings before depr., int., and taxes[a]	$ 70,000	$ 70,000	$ 70,000	$ 0
− Depreciation[c]	7,600	4,800	4,800	2,000
Earnings before int. and taxes	$ 62,400	$ 65,200	$ 65,200	−$ 2,000
− Taxes (rate, T=40%)	24,960	26,080	26,080	−800
Net operating profit after taxes	$ 37,440	$ 39,120	$ 39,120	−$ 1,200
+ Depreciation[c]	7,600	4,800	4,800	2,000
Operating cash inflows	$ 45,040	$ 43,920	$ 43,920	$ 800

[a]Given in the problem.

[b]From column 3 of the preceding table, top.

[c]From column 3 of the preceding table, bottom.

Calculation of Incremental Operating Cash Inflows

	Operating cash inflows		
Year	New machine[a] (1)	Old machine[a] (2)	Incremental (relevant) [(1) − (2)] (3)
1	$ 91,800	$45,040	$46,760
2	105,000	43,920	61,080
3	87,000	43,920	43,080
4	4,200	800	3,400

[a]From the final row for the respective machine in the preceding table.

c. Terminal cash flow (end of year 3):

After-tax proceeds from sale of new machine	
Proceeds from sale of new machine	$35,000
Taxes on sale of new machine[3]	9,800
Total after-tax proceeds—new	$25,200
− After-tax proceeds from sale of old machine	
Proceeds from sale of old machine	0
− Tax on sale of old machine[4]	−800
Total after-tax proceeds—old	$ 800
+ Change in net working capital	20,000
Terminal cash flow	$44,400

[3]Book value of new machine at end of year 3

= $150,000 − [(0.33 + 0.45 + 0.15) × $150,000] = $150,000 − (0.93 × $150,000)

= $150,000 − $139,500 = $10,500

Tax on sale = 0.40 × ($35,000 sale price − $10,500 book value)

= 0.40 × $24,500 = $9,800

[4]Book value of old machine at end of year 3

= $40,000 − [(0.20 + 0.32 + 0.19 + 0.12 + 0.12) × $40,000] = $40,000 − (0.95 × $40,000)

= $40,000 − $38,000 = $2,000

Tax on sale = 0.40 × ($0 sale price − $2,000 book value)

= 0.40 × − $2,000 = −$800 (i.e., $800 tax saving)

d.

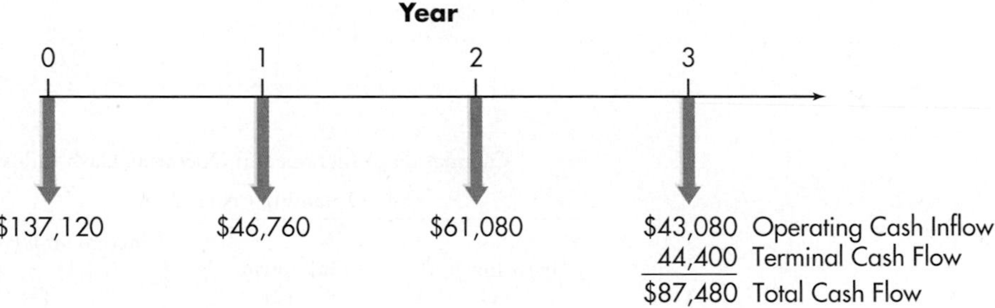

Note: The year-4 incremental operating cash inflow of $3,400 is not directly included; it is instead reflected in the book values used to calculate the taxes on sale of the machines at the end of year 3 and is therefore part of the terminal cash flow.

Chapter 12

ST12–1 **a.** Net present value (NPV) using a 10% cost of capital:

Project A: NPV $= \$7{,}000/0.10 \times [1 - 1/(1 + 0.10)^3] - \$15{,}000$
$= (\$70{,}000.00 \times 0.249) - \$15{,}000$
$= \$17{,}430.00 - \$15{,}000 = \underline{\underline{\$2{,}430}}$

(Calculator solution = \$2,407.96)

Project B:

NPV $= \$10{,}000/0.10 \times [1 - 1/(1 + 0.10)^3] - \$20{,}000$
$= (\$100{,}000.00 \times 0.249) - \$20{,}000$
$= \$24{,}900.00 - \$20{,}000 = \underline{\underline{\$4{,}900}}$*

(Calculator solution = \$4,868.52)

*Preferred project, because higher NPV.

b. Net present value (NPV) using the risk-adjusted discount rate (*RADR*) for project A of 9% and for project B of 16%.

Project A:

NPV $= \$7{,}000/0.09 \times [1 - 1/(1 + 0.09)^3] - \$15{,}000$
$= (\$77{,}777.78 \times 0.228) - \$15{,}000$
$= \$17{,}733.33 - \$15{,}000 = \underline{\underline{\$2{,}733.33}}$*

(Calculator solution = \$2,719.06)

Project B:

NPV $= \$10{,}000/0.16 \times [1 - 1/(1 + 0.16)^3] - \$20{,}000$
$= (\$62{,}500.00 \times 0.359) - \$20{,}000$
$= \$22{,}437.50 - \$20{,}000 = \underline{\underline{\$2{,}437.50}}$

(Calculator solution = \$2,458.90)

*Preferred project, because higher NPV.

c. When the differences in risk were ignored in part **a**, project B was preferred over project A, but when the higher risk of project B is incorporated into the analysis using risk-adjusted discount rates in part **b**, *project A is preferred over project B*. Clearly, project A should be implemented.

Chapter 13

ST13–1 **a.** $Q = \dfrac{FC}{P - VC}$

$$= \frac{\$250{,}000}{\$7.50 - \$3.00} = \frac{\$250{,}000}{\$4.50} = \underline{\underline{55{,}556}} \text{ units}$$

b.

	100,000 (+20%)	120,000
Sales (in units)	100,000	120,000
Sales revenue (units × \$7.50/unit)	\$750,000	\$900,000
Less: Variable operating costs (units × \$3.00/unit)	300,000	360,000
Less: Fixed operating costs	250,000	250,000
Earnings before interest and taxes (EBIT)	\$200,000	\$290,000
	+45%	
Less: Interest	80,000	80,000
Net profits before taxes	\$120,000	\$210,000
Less: Taxes ($T = 0.40$)	48,000	84,000
Net profits after taxes	\$ 72,000	\$126,000
Less: Preferred dividends (8,000 shares × \$5.00/share)	40,000	40,000
Earnings available for common	\$ 32,000	\$ 86,000

Sales: +20%; EBIT: +45%

Earnings per share (EPS) \$32,000/20,000 = \$1.60/share \$86,000/20,000 = \$4.30/share

+169%

c. $\text{DOL} = \dfrac{\%\text{ change in EBIT}}{\%\text{ change in sales}} = \dfrac{+45\%}{+20\%} = \underline{\underline{2.25}}$

d. $\text{DFL} = \dfrac{\%\text{ change in EPS}}{\%\text{ change in EBIT}} = \dfrac{+169\%}{+45\%} = \underline{\underline{3.76}}$

e. $\text{DTL} = \text{DOL} \times \text{DFL}$

$= 2.25 \times 3.76 = \underline{\underline{8.46}}$

Using the other DTL formula:

$$\text{DTL} = \frac{\%\text{ change in EPS}}{\%\text{ change in sales}}$$

$$8.46 = \frac{\%\text{ change in EPS}}{50\%}$$

$\%\text{ change in EPS} = 8.46 \times 0.50 = 4.23 = \underline{\underline{+423\%}}$

ST13–2

Data summary for alternative plans

Source of capital	Plan A (bond)	Plan B (stock)
Long-term debt	\$60,000 at 12% annual interest	\$50,000 at 12% annual interest
Annual interest =	0.12 × \$60,000 = \$7,200	0.12 × \$50,000 = \$6,000
Common stock	10,000 shares	11,000 shares

a.

	Plan A (bond)		Plan B (stock)	
EBIT[a]	$30,000	$40,000	$30,000	$40,000
Less: Interest	7,200	7,200	6,000	6,000
Net profits before taxes	$22,800	$32,800	$24,000	$34,000
Less: Taxes ($T = 0.21$)	4,788	6,888	5,040	7,140
Net profits after taxes	$18,012	$25,912	$18,960	$26,860
EPS (10,000 shares)	$1.80	$2.59		
(11,000 shares)			$1.72	$2.44

[a]Values were arbitrarily selected; other values could have been used.

Coordinates

	EBIT	
	$30,000	$40,000
Financing plan	Earnings per share (EPS)	
A (Bond)	$1.80	$2.59
B (Stock)	1.72	2.44

b.

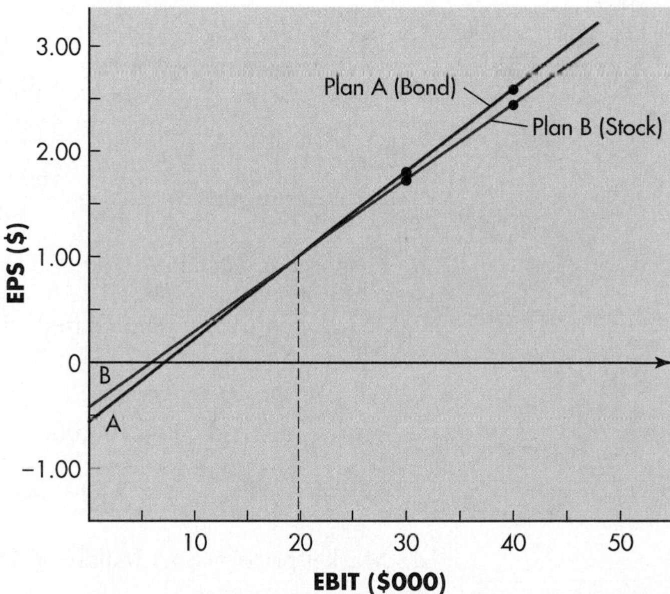

c. The bond plan (Plan A) becomes superior to the stock plan (Plan B) at *around $20,000* of EBIT, as represented by the dashed vertical line in the figure in part **b.** (*Note:* The actual point is $19,200, which was determined algebraically by using the technique described in footnote 18.)

ST13–3 a.

Capital structure debt ratio	Expected EPS (1)	Required return, r_s (2)	Estimated share value [(1) ÷ (2)] (3)
0%	$3.12	0.13	$24.00
10	3.90	0.15	26.00
20	4.80	0.16	30.00
30	5.44	0.17	32.00
40	5.51	0.19	29.00
50	5.00	0.20	25.00
60	4.40	0.22	20.00

b. Using the table in part **a**:

1. Maximization of EPS: *40% debt ratio,* EPS = $5.51/share (see column 1).
2. Maximization of share value: *30% debt ratio,* share value = $32.00 (see column 3).

c. Recommend *30% debt ratio* because it results in the maximum share value and is therefore consistent with the firm's goal of owner wealth maximization.

Chapter 14

ST14–1 **a.**

$$\text{Earnings per share (EPS)} = \frac{\$2{,}000{,}000 \text{ earnings available}}{500{,}000 \text{ shares of common outstanding}} = \underline{\underline{\$4.00}}\text{/share}$$

$$\text{Price/earnings (P/E) ratio} = \frac{\$60 \text{ market price}}{\$4.00 \text{ EPS}} = \underline{\underline{15}}$$

b. Proposed dividends = 500,000 shares × $2 per share = $1,000,000

$$\text{Shares that can be repurchased} = \frac{\$1{,}000{,}000}{\$62} = \underline{\underline{16{,}129}} \text{ shares}$$

c. *After proposed repurchase:*

Shares outstanding = 500,000 − 16,129 = 483,871

$$\text{EPS} = \frac{\$2{,}000{,}000}{483{,}871} = \underline{\underline{\$4.13}}\text{/share}$$

d. Market price = $4.13/share × 15 = $\underline{\underline{\$61.95}}$/share

e. The earnings per share (EPS) are higher after the repurchase because there are fewer shares of stock outstanding (483,871 shares versus 500,000 shares) to divide up the firm's $2,000,000 of available earnings.

f. In both cases, the stockholders would receive $2 per share: a $2 cash dividend in the dividend case or an approximately $2 increase in share price ($60.00 per share to $61.95 per share) in the repurchase case. [*Note:* The difference of $0.05 per share ($2.00 − $1.95) is due to rounding.]

Chapter 15

ST15–1

Basic data		
Time component	**Current**	**Proposed**
Average payment period (APP)	10 days	30 days
Average collection period (ACP)	30 days	30 days
Average age of inventory (AAI)	40 days	40 days

Cash conversion cycle (CCC) = AAI + ACP − APP

$CCC_{current}$ = 40 days + 30 days − 10 days = 60 days

$CCC_{proposed}$ = 40 days + 30 days − 30 days = 40 days

Reduction in CCC 20 days

Old accounts payable = 10 days × ($14,000,000 ÷ 360 days) = $388,889

New accounts payable = 30 days × ($14,000,000 ÷ 360 days) = $1,166,667

Change in accounts payable = $1,166,667 − $388,889 = $777,778

Because accounts payable has increased, the amount represents a decrease in net working capital.

Reduction in resource investment = $777,778

Annual profit increase = 0.06 × $777,778 = $46,667

ST15–2 **a.** *Data:*

S = 60,000 gallons

O = $200 per order

C = $1 per gallon per year

Calculation:

$$EOQ = \sqrt{\frac{2 \times S \times O}{C}}$$

$$= \sqrt{\frac{2 \times 60{,}000 \times \$200}{\$1}}$$

$$= \sqrt{24{,}000{,}000}$$

$$= 4{,}899 \text{ gallons}$$

b. *Data:*

Lead time = 20 days

Daily usage = 60,000 gallons/365 days

= 164.38 gallons/day

Calculation:

Reorder point = lead time in days × daily usage

= 20 days × 164.38 gallons/day

= 3,287.6 gallons

ST15–3 Tabular calculation of the effects of relaxing credit standards on Regency Rug Repair Company:

Additional profit contribution from sales		
[4,000 rugs × ($32 avg. sale price − $28 var. cost)]		$ 16,000
Cost of marginal investment in accounts receivable		
Average investment under proposed plan:		
$\frac{(\$28 \times 76{,}000 \text{ rugs})}{365/48} = \frac{\$2{,}128{,}000}{7.6}$	$280,000	
Average investment under present plan:		
$\frac{(\$28 \times 76{,}000 \text{ rugs})}{365/40} = \frac{\$2{,}016{,}000}{9.1}$	221,538	
Marginal investment in A/R	$ 58,462	
Cost of marginal investment in A/R (0.07 × $58,462)		–$ 4,092
Cost of marginal bad debts		
Bad debts under proposed plan (0.015 × $32 × 76,000 rugs)	$ 36,480	
Bad debts under present plan (0.010 × $32 × 72,000 rugs)	23,040	
Cost of marginal bad debts		–$ 13,440
Net loss from implementation of proposed plan		–$ 1,532

Recommendation: Because a net loss of $1,532 is expected to result from relaxing credit standards, *the proposed plan should not be implemented.*

Chapter 16

ST16–1 a.

Supplier	Approximate cost of giving up cash discount
X	1% × [365/(55 − 10)] = 1% × 365/45 = 1% × 8.1 = 8.1%
Y	2% × [365/(30 − 10)] = 2% × 365/20 = 2% × 18.25 = 36.5%
Z	2% × [365/(60 − 20)] = 2% × 365/40 = 2% × 9.125 = 18.25%

b.

Supplier	Recommendation
X	8.1% cost of giving up discount < 15% interest cost from bank; therefore, *give up discount.*
Y	36.5% cost of giving up discount > 15% interest cost from bank; therefore, *take discount and borrow from bank.*
Z	18.25% cost of giving up discount > 15% interest cost from bank; therefore, *take discount and borrow from bank.*

c. Stretching accounts payable for supplier Z would change the cost of giving up the cash discount to

$$2\% \times [365/(60 + 20 - 20)]) = 2\% \times 365/60 = 2\% \times 6.1 = \underline{\underline{12.2\%}}$$

In this case, in light of the 15% interest cost from the bank, the recommended strategy in part **b** would be to *give up the discount* because the 12.2% cost of giving up the discount would be less than the 15% interest cost from the bank.

Chapter 17

ST17–1 **a.** (1) and (2). In tabular form: after-tax cash outflows in column 3 and present value of the cash outflows in column 5.

End of year	Lease payment (1)	Tax adjustment [(1 − 0.40) = 0.60] (2)	After-tax cash outflows [(1) × (2)] (3)	Present value calculation (4)	Present value of outflows
1	$5,000	0.60	$3,000	$\$3{,}000/(1 + 0.09) =$	$ 2,752.29
2	5,000	0.60	3,000	$\$3{,}000/(1 + 0.09)^2 =$	$ 2,525.04
3	5,000	0.60	3,000	$\$3{,}000/(1 + 0.09)^3 =$	$ 2,316.55
4	5,000	0.60	3,000	$\$3{,}000/(1 + 0.09)^4 =$	$ 2,125.28
5	5,000	0.60	7,000[a]	$\$7{,}000/(1 + 0.09)^5 =$	$ 4,549.52
				Present value of cash outflows	$14,268.68

[a]After-tax lease payment outflow of $3,000 plus the $4,000 cost of exercising the purchase option.

(Calculator solution = $14,268.68)

b. (1) In tabular form: annual interest expense in column 3.

End of year	Loan payments (1)	Beginning-of-year principal (2)	Payments: Interest [0.15 × (2)] (3)	Payments: Principal [(1) − (3)] (4)	End-of-year principal [(2) − (4)] (5)
1	$5,967	$20,000	$3,000	$2,967	$17,033
2	5,967	17,033	2,555	3,412	13,621
3	5,967	13,621	2,043	3,924	9,697
4	5,967	9,697	1,455	4,512	5,185
5	5,967	5,185	778	5,189	—[a]

[a]The values in this table have been rounded to the nearest dollar, which results in a slight difference ($4) between the beginning-of-year-5 principal (in column 2) and the year-5 principal payment (in column 4).

(2) In tabular form: after-tax cash outflows in column 9.

End of year	Loan payments (1)	Maintenance costs (2)	Cost of oven (3)	Depreciation percentages[a] (4)	Depreciation [(3) × (4)] (5)	Interest[b] (6)	Total deductions [(2) × (5) + (6)] (7)	Tax shields [0.40 × (7)] (8)	After-tax cash outflows [(1) + (2) − (8)] (9)
1	$5,967	$1,000	$20,000	0.20	$4,000	$3,000	$8,000	$3,200	$3,767
2	5,967	1,000	20,000	0.32	6,400	2,555	9,955	3,982	2,985
3	5,967	1,000	20,000	0.19	3,800	2,043	6,843	2,737	4,230
4	5,967	1,000	20,000	0.12	2,400	1,455	4,855	1,942	5,025
5	5,967	1,000	20,000	0.12	2,400	778	4,178	1,671	5,296

[a]From Table 4.2.
[b]From column 3 of table in part b(1).

(3) In tabular form: present value of the cash outflows in column 3.

End of year	After-tax cash outflows[a] (1)	Present value calculation (2)	Present value of outflows (3)
1	$3,767	$\$3,767/(1+0.09) =$	$ 3,455.96
2	2,985	$\$2,985/(1+0.09)^2 =$	$ 2,512.41
3	4,230	$\$4,230/(1+0.09)^3 =$	$ 3,266.34
4	5,025	$\$5,025/(1+0.09)^4 =$	$ 3,559.84
5	5,296	$\$5,296/(1+0.09)^5 =$	$ 3,442.04
		Present value of cash outflows	$16,236.59

[a]From column 9 of table in part **b**(2).

(Calculator solution = $16,236.59)

c. Because the present value of the lease outflows of $14,268.68 is well below the present value of the purchase outflows of $16,236.59, *the lease is preferred.* Leasing rather than purchasing the oven should result in an incremental savings of $1,967.91 ($16,236.59 purchase cost − $14,268.68 lease cost).

ST17–2 **a.** $B_0 = \sum_{t=1}^{n} \frac{C}{(1+r)^n} + \frac{M}{(1+r)^n}$

$B_0 = C/r \times [1 - 1/(1+r)^n] + M \times 1/(1+r)^n$

$C = 0.05 \times \$1{,}000 = \$50$

$M = \$1{,}000$

$n = 25$ yrs

$r = 6.5\%$

$$B_0 = \$50/0.065 \times [1 - 1/(1+0.065)^{25}] + \$1{,}000 \times 1/(1+0.065)^{25}$$
$$= (\$769.23 \times 0.7929) + (\$1{,}000 \times 0.2071)$$
$$= \$609.92 + \$207.10 = \$817.02$$

(Calculator solution = $817.03)

b. In tabular form:

Market price of stock (1)	Conversion ratio (2)	Conversion value [(1) × (2)] (3)
$20	40	$ 800
25 (conversion price)	40	1,000 (par value)
28	40	1,120
35	40	1,400
50	40	2,000

c. The bond would be expected to sell for at least the higher of the conversion value and the straight value. In most cases (unless the stock price is very low or very high), the bond will sell for a market premium which exceeds the greater of the straight bond value or the conversion value. In no case would it be expected to sell for less than the straight value of $817.03.

d. The straight bond value of $817.03.

Chapter 18

ST18–1 **a.** Net present value at 11%:

Year(s)	Cash inflow (1)	Present value calculation at 11% (2)	Present value (3)
1–3	$20,000	$\$20,000/0.11 \times [1 - 1/(1+0.11)^3] =$	$ 48,874.29
4–15	30,000	$\$30,000/0.11 \times [1 - 1/(1+0.11)^{12}] \times 1/(1+0.11)^3 =$	$142,414.65
		Present value of inflows	$191,288.94
		Less: Cash purchase price	180,000.00
		Net present value (NPV)	$ 11,288.94

(Calculator solution = $11,288.94)

Because the NPV of $11,288.94 is greater than zero, *Luxe Foods should acquire Valley Canning.*

b. In this case, the 14% cost of capital must be used. Net present value at 14%:

Year(s)	Cash inflow (1)	Present value calculation at 14% (2)	Present value (3)
1–3	$20,000	$\$20,000/0.14 \times [1 - 1/(1+0.14)^3] =$	$ 46,432.64
4–15	30,000	$\$30,000/0.14 \times [1 - 1/(1+0.14)^{12}] \times 1/(1+0.14)^3 =$	$114,616.08
		Present value of inflows	$161,048.72
		Less: Cash purchase price	180,000.00
		Net present value (NPV)	($ 18,951.28)

(Calculator solution = −$18,951.28)

At the higher cost of capital, the *acquisition of Valley by Luxe cannot be justified.*

ST18–2 **a.** Lake Industries' EPS without merger:

	Earnings available for common				
Year	Initial value (1)	Future value calculation at 5% (2)	End-of-year value (3)	Number of shares outstanding (4)	EPS [(3) ÷ (4)] (5)
2016	$160,000	$160,000 × (1 + 0.05)^0 =	$160,000	80,000	$2.00
2017	160,000	$160,000 × (1 + 0.05)^1 =	$168,000	80,000	2.10
2018	160,000	$160,000 × (1 + 0.05)^2 =	$176,400	80,000	2.21
2019	160,000	$160,000 × (1 + 0.05)^3 =	$185,220	80,000	2.32
2020	160,000	$160,000 × (1 + 0.05)^4 =	$194,481	80,000	2.43
2021	160,000	$160,000 × (1 + 0.05)^5 =	$204,205	80,000	2.55

b. Number of postmerger shares outstanding for Lake Industries:

$$\text{Number of new shares issued} = \text{Initial number of Butler Company shares} \times \text{Ratio of exchange}$$

$$= 10{,}000 \times 1.1 = 11{,}000 \text{ shares}$$

Plus: Lake's premerger shares	80,000
Lake's postmerger shares	91,000 shares

	Earnings available for common						
	Butler Company			Lake Industries: Without merger	Lake Industries: With merger		
Year	Initial value (1)	Future value calculation at 10% (2)	End-of-year value (3)	End-of-year value[a] (4)	End-of-year value [(3) + (4)] (5)	Number of shares outstanding[b] (6)	EPS [(5) ÷ (6)] (7)
2016	$20,000	$20,000 × (1 + 0.10)^0 =	$20,000	$160,000	$180,000	91,000	$1.98
2017	20,000	$20,000 × (1 + 0.10)^1 =	$22,000	168,000	190,000	91,000	2.09
2018	20,000	$20,000 × (1 + 0.10)^2 =	$24,200	176,400	200,600	91,000	2.20
2019	20,000	$20,000 × (1 + 0.10)^3 =	$26,620	185,220	211,840	91,000	2.33
2020	20,000	$20,000 × (1 + 0.10)^4 =	$29,280	194,481	223,761	91,000	2.46
2021	20,000	$20,000 × (1 + 0.10)^5 =	$32,210	204,205	236,415	91,000	2.60

[a] From column 3 of table in part a.

[b] Calculated at beginning of this part.

c. Comparing the EPS without the proposed merger calculated in part **a** (see column 5 of table in part **a**) with the EPS with the proposed merger calculated in part **b** (see column 7 of table in part **b**), we can see that beginning in 2019, the EPS *with* the merger rises above the EPS *without* the merger. Clearly, over the long run, the EPS with the merger will exceed those without the merger. This outcome is attributed to the higher rate of growth associated with Butler's earnings (10% versus 5% for Lake).

Chapter 19

ST19–1 **a.** If the rate today is 97.91 yen per dollar and a year ago it was 98.91 yen per dollar, then today the dollar buys fewer yen than it did a year ago. The yen has appreciated and the dollar has depreciated.

b. Higher inflation tends to depreciate a nation's currency, so in this case we'd guess that inflation was higher in the U.S. because the dollar has depreciated against the yen.

Glossary

ABC inventory system
Inventory management technique that divides inventory into three groups—A, B, and C, in descending order of importance and level of monitoring—on the basis of the dollar investment in each. (Chapter 15)

ability to repay debt coverage ratios
Ratios that measure a firm's ability to make required debt payments and to pay other fixed charges such as lease payments. (Chapter 3)

accept–reject approach
The evaluation of capital expenditure proposals to determine whether they meet the firm's minimum acceptance criterion. (Chapter 10)

accounting exposure
The risk resulting from the effects of changes in foreign exchange rates on the translated value of a firm's financial statement accounts denominated in a given foreign currency. (Chapter 19)

accounts payable management
Management by the firm of the time that elapses between its purchase of raw materials and its mailing payment to the supplier. (Chapter 16)

accrual basis
In preparation of financial statements, recognizes revenue at the time of sale and recognizes expenses when they are incurred. (Chapter 1)

accruals
Liabilities for services received for which payment has yet to be made. (Chapter 16)

ACH (automated clearinghouse) transfer
Preauthorized electronic withdrawal from the payer's account and deposit into the payee's account via a settlement among banks by the automated clearinghouse, or ACH. (Chapter 15)

acquiring company
The firm in a merger transaction that attempts to acquire another firm. (Chapter 18)

activist investors
Investors who specialize in influencing management. (Chapter 1)

activity ratios
Measure the speed with which various accounts are converted into sales or cash, or inflows or outflows. (Chapter 3)

after-tax proceeds from the sale of the old asset
The difference between the old asset's sale proceeds and any applicable tax liability or refund related to its sale. (Chapter 11)

agency costs
The costs that shareholders bear due to managers' pursuit of their own interests. (Chapter 1)

aggressive funding strategy
A funding strategy under which the firm funds its seasonal requirements with short-term debt and its permanent requirements with long-term debt or equity. (Chapter 15)

aging schedule
A credit-monitoring technique that breaks down accounts receivable into groups on the basis of their time of origin; it indicates the percentages of the total accounts receivable balance that have been outstanding for specified periods of time. (Chapter 15)

all-current-rate method
The method by which the functional-currency-denominated financial statements of an MNC's subsidiary are translated into the parent company's currency. (Chapter 19)

American depositary receipts (ADRs)
Securities, backed by *American depositary shares (ADSs)*, that permit U.S. investors to hold shares of non-U.S. companies and trade them in U.S. markets. (Chapter 7)

American depositary shares (ADSs)
Dollar-denominated receipts for the stocks of foreign companies that are held by a U.S. financial institution overseas. (Chapter 7)

angel financing
Private equity financing provided to a young firm by a wealthy individual investing his or her own money. (Chapter 2)

angel investors (angels)
Wealthy individual investors who make their own investment decisions and are willing to invest in promising startups in exchange for a portion of the firm's equity. (Chapter 2)

annual cleanup
The requirement that for a certain number of days during the year borrowers under a line of credit carry a zero loan balance (i.e., owe the bank nothing). (Chapter 16)

annual percentage rate (APR)
The nominal annual rate of interest, found by multiplying the periodic rate by the number of periods in one year, that must be disclosed to consumers on credit cards and loans as a result of "truth-in-lending laws." (Chapter 5)

annual percentage yield (APY)
The effective annual rate of interest that must be disclosed to consumers by banks on their savings products as a result of "truth-in-savings laws." (Chapter 5)

annualized net present value (ANPV) approach
An approach to evaluating unequal-lived projects that converts the net present value of unequal-lived, mutually exclusive projects into an equivalent annual amount (in NPV terms). (Chapter 12)

annuity
A stream of equal periodic cash flows over a specified time period. These cash flows can be inflows or outflows of funds. (Chapter 5)

annuity due
An annuity for which the cash flow occurs at the beginning of each period. (Chapter 5)

articles of partnership
The written contract used to formally establish a business partnership. (Chapter 1)

ASEAN
A large trading bloc that comprises 10 member nations, all in Southeast Asia. Also called the *Association of Southeast Asian Nations.* (Chapter 19)

ask price
The lowest price a seller in the market is willing to accept for a security. (Chapter 2)

assignment
A voluntary liquidation procedure by which a firm's creditors pass the power to liquidate the firm's assets to an adjustment bureau, a trade association, or a third party, which is designated the assignee. (Chapter 18)

asymmetric information
The situation in which managers of a firm have more information about operations and future prospects than do investors. (Chapter 13)

authorized shares
Shares of common stock that a firm's corporate charter allows it to issue. (Chapter 7)

average age of inventory
Average number of days' sales in inventory. (Chapter 3)

average collection period
The average amount of time needed to collect accounts receivable. (Chapter 3)

average payment period
The average amount of time needed to pay accounts payable. (Chapter 3)

average tax rate
Calculated by dividing taxes paid by taxable income. (Chapter 1)

balance sheet
Summary statement of the firm's financial position at a given point in time. (Chapter 3)

bankruptcy
A legal process in which a court declares that a firm is unable to meet its financial obligations. (Chapter 18)

Bankruptcy Reform Act of 1978
The governing bankruptcy legislation in the United States today. (Chapter 18)

bar chart
The simplest type of probability distribution; shows only a limited number of outcomes and associated probabilities for a given event. (Chapter 8)

basic EPS
Earnings per share (EPS) calculated without regard to any contingent securities. (Chapter 17)

behavioral finance
A growing body of research that focuses on investor behavior and its impact on investment decisions and stock prices. Advocates are commonly referred to as "behaviorists." (Chapter 7)

benchmarking
A type of *cross-sectional analysis* in which the firm's ratio values are compared with those of a key competitor or with a group of competitors that it wishes to emulate. (Chapter 3)

beta coefficient (β)
A relative measure of nondiversifiable risk. An *index* of the degree of movement of an asset's return in response to a change in the *market return.* (Chapter 8)

bid price
The highest price a buyer in the market is willing to pay for a security. (Chapter 2)

bid/ask spread
The difference between the bid and ask prices. (Chapter 2)

bird-in-the-hand argument
The belief, in support of dividend relevance theory, that investors see current dividends as less risky than future dividends or capital gains. (Chapter 14)

board of directors
Group elected by the firm's stockholders and typically responsible for approving strategic goals and plans, setting general policy, guiding corporate affairs, and approving major expenditures. (Chapter 1)

bond
Long-term debt instrument used by business and government to raise large sums of money, generally from a diverse group of lenders. (Chapter 2)

bond indenture
A legal document that specifies both the rights of the bondholders and the duties of the issuing corporation. (Chapter 6)

book value
The asset's value on the firm's balance sheet as determined by accounting principles. The difference between what an asset cost (including installation costs) and the accumulated depreciation on the asset. (Chapter 11)

book value per share
The amount per share of common stock that would be received if all of the firm's assets were *sold for their exact book (accounting) value* and the proceeds remaining after paying all liabilities (including preferred stock) were divided among the common stockholders. (Chapter 7)

breakeven analysis
Used to indicate the level of operations necessary to cover all costs and to evaluate the profitability associated with various levels of sales; also called *cost-volume-profit analysis.* (Chapter 13)

breakeven cash inflow
The minimum level of cash inflow necessary for a project to be acceptable, that is, NPV > \$0. (Chapter 12)

breakup value
The value of a firm measured as the sum of the values of its operating units if each were sold separately. (Chapter 18)

broker market
The securities exchanges on which the two sides of a transaction, the buyer and seller, are brought together to trade securities. (Chapter 2)

business ethics
Standards of conduct or moral judgment that apply to persons engaged in commerce. (Chapter 1)

call feature
A feature included in nearly all corporate bond issues that gives the issuer the opportunity to repurchase bonds at a stated call price prior to maturity. (Chapter 6)

call option
An option to purchase a specified number of shares of a stock (typically 100) on or before a specified future date at a stated price. (Chapter 17)

call premium
The amount by which a bond's call price exceeds its par value. (Chapter 6)

call price
The stated price at which a bond may be repurchased, by use of a call feature, prior to maturity. (Chapter 6)

callable feature (preferred stock)
A feature of *callable preferred stock* that allows the issuer to retire the shares within a certain period of time and at a specified price. (Chapter 7)

capital
The money that firms raise to finance their activities. (Chapter 1)

capital
A firm's long-term sources of financing, which include both debt and equity. (Chapter 9)

capital asset pricing model (CAPM)
The classic theory that links risk and return for all assets. (Chapter 8)

capital asset pricing model (CAPM)
Describes the relationship between the required return, r_s, and the nondiversifiable risk of the firm as measured by the beta coefficient, β. (Chapter 9)

capital budgeting
A technique that helps managers decide which projects create the most value for shareholders. (Chapter 1)

capital budgeting
The process of evaluating and selecting long term investments that contribute to the firm's goal of maximizing owners' wealth. (Chapter 10)

capital budgeting process
Consists of five distinct but interrelated steps: *proposal generation, review and analysis, decision making, implementation,* and *follow-up.* (Chapter 10)

capital expenditure
An outlay of funds by the firm that the firm expects to produce benefits over a period of time *greater than* 1 year. (Chapter 10)

capital gain
Income earned by selling an asset for more than it cost. (Chapter 1)

capital market
A market that enables suppliers and demanders of long-term funds to make transactions. (Chapter 2)

capital rationing
The financial situation in which a firm has only a fixed number of dollars available for capital expenditures and numerous projects compete for these dollars. (Chapter 10)

capital structure
The mix of debt and equity financing that a firm employs. (Chapter 9)

capital structure
The mix of long-term debt and equity maintained by a firm. (Chapter 13)

capitalized lease
A financial (capital) lease that has the present value of all its payments included as an asset and corresponding liability on the firm's balance sheet, as required by the Financial Accounting Standards Board (FASB) in *FASB Statement No. 13.* (Chapter 17)

carrying costs
The variable costs per unit of holding an item in inventory for a specific period of time. (Chapter 15)

cash basis
Recognizes revenues and expenses only with respect to actual inflows and outflows of cash. (Chapter 1)

cash budget (cash forecast)
A statement of the firm's planned inflows and outflows of cash that managers use to estimate its short-term cash requirements. (Chapter 4)

cash concentration
The process used by the firm to bring lockbox and other deposits together into one bank, often called the *concentration bank.* (Chapter 15)

cash conversion cycle (CCC)
The length of time between when a firm pays cash for raw materials and when it receives cash from collecting receivables. (Chapter 15)

cash flow from financing activities
Cash flows that result from debt and equity financing transactions; includes incurrence and repayment of debt, cash inflows from the sale of stock, and cash outflows to repurchase stock or pay cash dividends. (Chapter 4)

cash flow from investment activities
Cash flows associated with purchase and sale of both fixed assets and equity investments in other firms. (Chapter 4)

cash flow from operating activities
Cash flows directly related to sale and production of the firm's products and services. (Chapter 4)

catering theory
A theory that says firms cater to the preferences of investors, initiating or increasing dividend payments during periods in which high-dividend stocks are particularly appealing to investors. (Chapter 14)

Central American Free Trade Agreement (CAFTA)
A trade agreement signed in 2003–2004 by the United States, the Dominican Republic, and five Central American countries (Costa Rica, El Salvador, Guatemala, Honduras, and Nicaragua). (Chapter 19)

change in net working capital
The difference between a change in current assets and a change in current liabilities. (Chapter 11)

Chapter 7
The portion of the *Bankruptcy Reform Act of 1978* that details the procedures to be followed when liquidating a failed firm. (Chapter 18)

Chapter 11
The portion of the *Bankruptcy Reform Act of 1978* that outlines the procedures for reorganizing a failed (or failing) firm, whether its petition is filed voluntarily or involuntarily. (Chapter 18)

clearing float
The time between deposit of a payment and when spendable funds become available to the firm. (Chapter 15)

clientele effect
The argument that different payout policies attract different types of investors but still do not change the value of the firm. (Chapter 14)

closely owned (stock)
The common stock of a firm is owned by an individual or a small group of investors (such as a family); they are usually privately owned companies. (Chapter 7)

coefficient of variation (CV)
A measure of relative dispersion that is useful in comparing the risks of assets with differing expected returns. (Chapter 13)

collateral
A specific asset against which bondholders have a claim in the event that a borrower defaults on a bond. (Chapter 6)

commercial banks
Institutions that provide savers with a secure place to invest their funds and that offer loans to individual and business borrowers. (Chapter 2)

commercial finance companies
Lending institutions that make *only* secured loans—both short-term and long-term—to businesses. (Chapter 16)

commercial paper
A form of financing consisting of short-term, unsecured promissory notes issued by firms with a high credit standing. (Chapter 16)

commitment fee
The fee that is normally charged on a *revolving credit agreement;* it often applies to the *average unused portion* of the borrower's credit line. (Chapter 16)

common stock
A unit of ownership, or equity, in a corporation. (Chapter 2)

common-size income statement
An income statement in which each item is expressed as a percentage of sales. (Chapter 3)

compensating balance
A required checking account balance equal to a certain percentage of the amount borrowed from a bank under a line-of-credit or revolving credit agreement. (Chapter 16)

composition
A pro rata cash settlement of creditor claims by the debtor firm; a uniform percentage of each dollar owed is paid. (Chapter 18)

compound interest
Interest that is earned on a given deposit and has become part of the principal at the end of a specified period. (Chapter 5)

conflicting rankings
Conflicts in the ranking given a project by NPV and IRR, resulting from *differences in the magnitude and timing of cash flows.* (Chapter 10)

congeneric merger
A merger in which one firm acquires another firm that is in the same general industry but is neither in the same line of business nor a supplier or customer. (Chapter 18)

conglomerate merger
A merger combining firms in unrelated businesses. (Chapter 18)

conservative funding strategy
A funding strategy under which the firm funds both its seasonal and its permanent requirements with long-term debt or equity. (Chapter 15)

consolidation
The combination of two or more firms to form a completely new corporation. (Chapter 18)

constant-growth dividend model
A widely cited dividend valuation approach that assumes dividends will grow at a constant rate, but a rate less than the required return. (Chapter 7)

constant-growth valuation (Gordon growth) model
A model that calculates the value of common stock as the present value of an infinite dividend stream that grows at a constant rate. (Chapter 9)

constant-payout-ratio dividend policy
A dividend policy based on the payment of a certain percentage of earnings to owners in each dividend period. (Chapter 14)

contingent securities
Convertibles, warrants, and stock options. Their presence affects the reporting of a firm's earnings per share (EPS). (Chapter 17)

continuous compounding
Compounding of interest, literally, all the time. Equivalent to compounding interest an infinite number of times per year. (Chapter 5)

continuous probability distribution
A probability distribution showing all the possible outcomes and associated probabilities for a given event. (Chapter 8)

controlled disbursing
The strategic use of mailing points and bank accounts to lengthen mail float and clearing float, respectively. (Chapter 15)

controller
The firm's chief accountant, who is responsible for the firm's accounting activities, such as corporate accounting, tax management, financial accounting, and cost accounting. (Chapter 1)

conversion (or stock) value
The value of a convertible security measured in terms of the market price of the common stock into which it can be converted. (Chapter 18)

conversion feature
A feature of convertible bonds that allows bondholders to change each bond into a stated number of shares of common stock. (Chapter 6)

conversion feature
An option that is included as part of a bond or a preferred stock issue and allows its holder to change the security into a stated number of shares of common stock. (Chapter 6)

conversion feature (preferred stock)
A feature of *convertible preferred stock* that allows holders to change each share into a stated number of shares of common stock. (Chapter 17)

conversion price
The per-share price that is effectively paid for common stock as the result of conversion of a convertible security. (Chapter 17)

conversion ratio
The ratio at which a convertible security can be exchanged for common stock. (Chapter 17)

convertible bond
A bond that can be changed into a specified number of shares of common stock. (Chapter 17)

convertible preferred stock
Preferred stock that can be changed into a specified number of shares of common stock. (Chapter 17)

corporate bond
A long-term debt instrument indicating that a corporation has borrowed a certain amount of money and promises to repay it in the future under clearly defined terms. (Chapter 6)

corporate governance
The rules, processes, and laws by which companies are operated, controlled, and regulated. (Chapter 1)

corporate restructuring
The activities involving expansion or contraction of a firm's operations or changes in its asset or financial (ownership) structure. (Chapter 18)

corporation
A legal business entity with rights and duties similar to those of individuals but with a legal identity distinct from its owners. (Chapter 1)

correlation
A statistical measure of the relationship between any two series of numbers. (Chapter 8)

correlation coefficient
A measure of the degree of correlation between two series. (Chapter 8)

cost of capital
Represents the firm's cost of financing and is the minimum rate of return that a project must earn to increase the firm's value. (Chapter 9)

cost of common stock equity
The costs associated with using common stock equity financing. The cost of common stock equity is equal to the required return on the firm's common stock in the absence of flotation costs. Thus, the cost of common stock equity is the same as the cost of retained earnings, but the cost of issuing new common equity is higher. (Chapter 9)

cost of giving up a cash discount
The implied rate of interest paid to delay payment of an account payable for an additional number of days. (Chapter 16)

cost of giving up an early payment discount
The implied rate of interest paid to delay payment of an account payable for an additional number of days. (Chapter 16)

cost of long-term debt
The financing cost associated with new funds raised through long-term borrowing. (Chapter 9)

cost of the new asset
The cash outflow necessary to acquire a new asset. (Chapter 11)

cost of a new issue of common stock, r_n
The cost of common stock, net of underpricing and associated flotation costs. (Chapter 9)

cost of preferred stock, r_p
The ratio of the preferred stock dividend to the firm's net proceeds from the sale of preferred stock. (Chapter 9)

cost of retained earnings, r_r
The cost of using retained earnings as a financing source. The cost of retained earnings is equal to the required return on a firm's common stock, r_s. (Chapter 9)

coupon rate
The percentage of a bond's par value that will be paid annually, typically in two equal semiannual payments, as interest. (Chapter 6)

credit monitoring
The ongoing review of a firm's accounts receivable to determine whether customers are paying according to the stated credit terms. (Chapter 15)

credit period
The number of days after the beginning of the credit period until full payment of the account is due. (Chapter 15)

credit scoring
A credit selection method commonly used with high-volume/small-dollar credit requests; relies on a credit score determined by applying statistically derived weights to a credit applicant's scores on key financial and credit characteristics. (Chapter 15)

credit standards
The firm's minimum requirements for extending credit to a customer. (Chapter 15)

credit terms
The terms of sale for customers who have been extended credit by the firm. (Chapter 15)

creditor control
An arrangement in which the creditor committee replaces the firm's operating management and operates the firm until all claims have been settled. (Chapter 18)

cross-sectional analysis
Comparison of different firms' financial ratios at the same point in time; involves comparing the firm's ratios with those of other firms in its industry or with industry averages. (Chapter 3)

cumulative (preferred stock)
Preferred stock for which all passed (unpaid) dividends in arrears, along with the current dividend, must be paid before dividends can be paid to common stockholders. (Chapter 7)

current assets
Short-term assets, expected to be converted into cash within 1 year. (Chapter 3)

current liabilities
Short-term liabilities, expected to be paid within 1 year. (Chapter 3)

current rate (translation) method
Technique used by U.S.–based companies to translate their foreign-currency-denominated assets and liabilities into U.S. dollars, for consolidation with the parent company's financial statements, using the year-end (current) exchange rate. (Chapter 3)

current ratio
A measure of liquidity calculated by dividing the firm's current assets by its current liabilities. (Chapter 3)

current yield
A measure of a bond's cash return for the year; calculated by dividing the bond's annual interest payment by its current price. (Chapter 6)

date of record (dividends)
Set by the firm's directors, the date on which all persons whose names are recorded as stockholders receive a declared dividend at a specified future time. (Chapter 14)

dealer market
The market in which the buyer and seller are not brought together directly but instead have their orders executed by securities dealers who "make markets" in the given security. (Chapter 2)

debt
Includes all borrowing incurred by a firm, including bonds, and is repaid according to a fixed schedule of payments. (Chapter 7)

debt ratio
Measures the proportion of total assets financed by the firm's creditors. (Chapter 3)

debt-to-equity ratio
Measures the relative proportion of total liabilities and common stock equity used to finance the firm's total assets. (Chapter 3)

debtor in possession (DIP)
The term for a firm that files a reorganization petition under Chapter 11 and then develops, if feasible, a reorganization plan. (Chapter 18)

deflation
A general trend of falling prices. (Chapter 6)

degree of financial leverage (DFL)
The numerical measure of the firm's financial leverage. (Chapter 13)

degree of indebtedness
Ratios that measure the amount of debt relative to other significant balance sheet amounts. (Chapter 3)

degree of operating leverage (DOL)
The numerical measure of the firm's operating leverage. (Chapter 13)

degree of total leverage (DTL)
The numerical measure of the firm's total leverage. (Chapter 13)

depository transfer check (DTC)
An unsigned check drawn on one of a firm's bank accounts and deposited in another. (Chapter 15)

depreciable life
Time period over which an asset is depreciated. (Chapter 4)

depreciation
A portion of the costs of fixed assets charged against annual revenues over time. (Chapter 4)

derivative security
A security that is neither debt nor equity but derives its value from an underlying asset that is often another security. (Chapter 17)

diluted EPS
Earnings per share (EPS) calculated under the assumption that all contingent securities that would have dilutive effects are converted and exercised and are therefore common stock. (Chapter 17)

dilution of earnings
A reduction in each previous shareholder's fractional claim on the firm's earnings resulting from the sale of new common shares. (Chapter 7)

dilution of ownership
A reduction in each previous shareholder's fractional ownership resulting from the sale of new common shares. (Chapter 7)

direct lease
A lease under which a lessor owns or acquires the assets that are leased to a given lessee. (Chapter 17)

direct quote
An exchange rate quote that indicates the number of units of foreign currency that can be purchased with one unit of domestic currency. (Chapter 19)

director of internal audit
Leads a team charged with making sure that all business units follow internal policies and comply with government regulations. (Chapter 1)

director of investor relations
The conduit of information between the firm and the investment community. (Chapter 1)

director of risk management
Works with the treasurer to manage risks that the firm faces related to movements in exchange rates, commodity prices, and interest rates. (Chapter 1)

discount
The amount by which a bond sells below its par value. (Chapter 6)

discount loan
Loan on which interest is paid in advance by being deducted from the amount borrowed. (Chapter 16)

discounting cash flows
The process of finding present values; the inverse of compounding interest. (Chapter 5)

diversifiable risk
The portion of an asset's risk that is attributable to firm-specific, random causes; can be eliminated through diversification. Also called *unsystematic risk*. (Chapter 8)

divestiture
The selling of some of a firm's assets for various strategic reasons. (Chapter 18)

dividend irrelevance theory
Miller and Modigliani's theory that, in a perfect world, the firm's value is determined solely by the earning power and risk of its assets (investments) and that the manner in which it splits its earnings stream between dividends and internally retained (and reinvested) funds does not affect this value. (Chapter 14)

dividend payout ratio
Indicates the percentage of each dollar earned that a firm distributes to the owners in the form of cash. It is calculated by dividing the firm's cash dividend per share by its earnings per share. (Chapter 14)

dividend per share (DPS)
The dollar amount of cash distributed during the period on behalf of each outstanding share of common stock. (Chapter 3)

dividend policy
The plan of action to be followed whenever the firm makes a dividend decision. (Chapter 14)

dividend reinvestment plans (DRIPs)
Plans that enable stockholders to use dividends received on the firm's stock to acquire additional shares—even fractional shares—at little or no transaction cost. (Chapter 14)

dividend relevance theory
The theory, advanced by Gordon and Lintner, that there is a direct relationship between a firm's dividend policy and its market value. (Chapter 14)

dividends
Periodic distributions of cash to the stockholders of a firm. (Chapter 1)

Double taxation
A situation facing corporations in which income from the business is taxed twice—once at the business level and once at the individual level when cash is distributed to shareholders. (Chapter 1)

DuPont formula
Multiplies the firm's *net profit margin* by its *total asset turnover* to calculate the firm's *return on total assets (ROA)*. (Chapter 3)

DuPont system of analysis
System used to dissect the firm's financial statements and to assess its financial condition. (Chapter 3)

Dutch auction share repurchase
A repurchase method in which the firm specifies how many shares it wants to buy back and a range of prices at which it is willing to repurchase shares. Investors specify how many shares they will sell at each price in the range, and the firm determines the minimum price required to repurchase its target number of shares. All investors who tender receive the same price. (Chapter 14)

early payment discount
A percentage deduction from the purchase price; available to the credit customer that pays its account within a specified time. (Chapter 15)

early payment discount period
The number of days after the beginning of the credit period during which the discount is available. (Chapter 15)

earnings per share (EPS)
The amount earned during the period on behalf of each outstanding share of stock, calculated by dividing the period's total earnings available for the firm's stockholders by the number of shares of stock outstanding. (Chapter 1)

EBIT–EPS approach
An approach for selecting the capital structure that maximizes earnings per share (EPS) over the expected range of earnings before interest and taxes (EBIT). (Chapter 13)

economic exposure
The risk resulting from the effects of changes in foreign exchange rates on the firm's value. (Chapter 19)

economic order quantity (EOQ) model
Inventory management technique for determining an item's optimal order size, which is the size that minimizes the total of its order costs and carrying costs. (Chapter 15)

effective (true) annual rate (EAR)
The annual rate of interest actually paid or earned. (Chapter 5)

effective interest rate
In the international context, the rate equal to the nominal rate plus (or minus) any forecast appreciation (or depreciation) of a foreign currency relative to the currency of the MNC parent. (Chapter 19)

efficient market
A market that establishes correct prices for the securities that firms sell and allocates funds to their most productive uses. (Chapter 2)

efficient market hypothesis (EMH)
Theory describing the behavior of a market in which (1) securities are in equilibrium, (2) security prices fully reflect all available information and react swiftly to new information, and (3) because stocks are fully and fairly priced, investors need not waste time looking for mispriced securities. (Chapter 2)

efficient portfolio
A portfolio that maximizes return for a given level of risk. (Chapter 8)

ending cash
The sum of the firm's beginning cash and its net cash flow for the period. (Chapter 4)

enterprise resource planning (ERP)
A computerized system that electronically integrates external information about the firm's suppliers and customers with the firm's departmental data so that information on all available resources—human and material—can be instantly obtained in a fashion that eliminates production delays and controls costs. (Chapter 15)

equipment trust certificates
See Table 6.4. (Chapter 6)

equity
Funds provided by the firm's owners (investors or stockholders) that are repaid subject to the firm's performance. (Chapter 7)

euro
A single currency adopted on January 1, 1999, by 12 EU nations, which switched to a single set of euro bills and coins on January 1, 2002. (Chapter 19)

Eurobond
A bond issued by an international borrower and sold to investors in countries with currencies other than the currency in which the bond is denominated. (Chapter 6)

Eurobond market
The market in which corporations and governments typically issue bonds denominated in dollars and sell them to investors located outside the United States. (Chapter 2)

Eurocurrency market
International equivalent of the domestic money market. (Chapter 2)

Eurocurrency markets
The portion of the Euromarket that provides short-term, foreign-currency financing to subsidiaries of MNCs. (Chapter 19)

Euromarket
The international financial market that provides for borrowing and lending currencies outside their country of origin. (Chapter 19)

European Open Market
The transformation of the European Union into a *single* market at year-end 1992. (Chapter 19)

European Union (EU)
A significant economic force currently made up of 28 nations that permit free trade within the union. (Chapter 19)

ex dividend
A period usually beginning 2 *business days* prior to the date of record, during which a stock is sold without the right to receive the current dividend. (Chapter 14)

excess cash balance
The (excess) amount available for investment by the firm if the period's ending cash is greater than the desired minimum cash balance; assumed to be invested in marketable securities. (Chapter 4)

excess earnings accumulation tax
The tax the IRS levies on retained earnings above $250,000 for most businesses when it determines that the firm has accumulated an excess of earnings to allow owners to delay paying ordinary income taxes on dividends received. (Chapter 14)

exchange rate risk
The danger that an unexpected change in the exchange rate between the dollar and the currency in which a project's cash flows are denominated will reduce the market value of that project's cash flow. (Chapter 12)

exchange rate risk
The risk caused by varying exchange rates between two currencies. (Chapter 19)

exercise (or option) price
The price at which holders of warrants can purchase a specified number of shares of common stock. (Chapter 17)

expectations theory
The theory that the yield curve reflects investor expectations about future interest rates; an expectation of rising interest rates results in an upward-sloping yield curve, and an expectation of declining rates results in a downward-sloping yield curve. (Chapter 6)

expected return
The return that an asset is expected to generate in the future, composed of a risk-free rate plus a risk premium. (Chapter 8)

extension
An arrangement whereby the firm's creditors receive payment in full, although not immediately. (Chapter 18)

external financing required ("plug" figure)
Under the judgmental approach for developing a pro forma balance sheet, the amount of external financing needed to bring the statement into balance. It can be either a positive or a negative value. (Chapter 4)

external forecast
A sales forecast based on the relationships observed between the firm's sales and certain key external economic indicators. (Chapter 4)

extra dividend
An additional dividend optionally paid by the firm when earnings are higher than normal in a given period. (Chapter 14)

factor
A financial institution that specializes in purchasing accounts receivable from businesses. (Chapter 16)

factoring accounts receivable
The outright sale of accounts receivable at a discount to a *factor* or other financial institution. (Chapter 16)

FASB No. 52
Statement issued by the FASB requiring U.S. multinationals first to convert the financial statement accounts of foreign subsidiaries into the *functional currency* and then to translate the accounts into the parent firm's currency, using the *all-current-rate method.* (Chapter 19)

Federal Deposit Insurance Corporation (FDIC)
An agency created by the Glass-Steagall Act that provides insurance for deposits at banks and monitors banks to ensure their safety and soundness. (Chapter 2)

federal funds rate
The rate at which U.S. banks make overnight loans to each other. (Chapter 16)

finance
The science and art of how individuals and firms raise, allocate, and invest money. (Chapter 1)

financial (or capital) lease
A longer-term lease than an operating lease that is noncancelable and obligates the lessee to make payments for the use of an asset over a predefined period of time; the total payments over the term of the lease are greater than the lessor's initial cost of the leased asset. (Chapter 17)

Financial Accounting Standards Board (FASB)
The accounting profession's rule-setting body, which authorizes generally accepted accounting principles (GAAP). (Chapter 3)

Financial Accounting Standards Board (FASB) Standard No. 52
Mandates that U.S.–based companies translate their foreign-currency-denominated assets and liabilities into U.S. dollars, for consolidation with the parent company's financial statements. This process is done by using the *current rate (translation) method.* (Chapter 3)

financial breakeven point
The level of EBIT necessary to just cover all *fixed financial costs;* the level of EBIT for which EPS = $0. (Chapter 13)

financial institution
An intermediary that channels the savings of individuals, businesses, and governments into loans or investments. (Chapter 2)

financial leverage
The magnification of risk and return through the use of fixed-cost financing, such as debt and preferred stock. (Chapter 3)

financial leverage
The use of *fixed financial costs* to magnify the effects of changes in earnings before interest and taxes on the firm's earnings per share. (Chapter 13)

financial leverage multiplier (FLM)
The ratio of the firm's total assets to its common stock equity. (Chapter 3)

financial markets
Forums in which suppliers of funds and demanders of funds can transact business directly. (Chapter 2)

financial merger
A merger transaction undertaken with the goal of restructuring the acquired company to improve its cash flow and unlock its unrealized value. (Chapter 18)

financial planning process
Planning that begins with long-term, or strategic, financial plans that in turn guide the formulation of short-term, or operating, plans and budgets. (Chapter 4)

financing decisions
Decisions that determine how companies raise the money they need to pursue investment opportunities. (Chapter 1)

five C's of credit
The five key dimensions—character, capacity, capital, collateral, and conditions—used by credit analysts to provide a framework for in-depth credit analysis. (Chapter 15)

fixed (or semifixed) relationship
The constant (or relatively constant) relationship of a currency to one of the major currencies, a combination (basket) of major currencies, or some type of international foreign exchange standard. (Chapter 19)

fixed-payment coverage ratio
Measures the firm's ability to meet all fixed-payment obligations. (Chapter 3)

fixed-rate loan
A loan with a rate of interest that is determined at a set increment above the prime rate and remains unvarying until maturity. (Chapter 16)

flat yield curve
A yield curve that indicates that interest rates do not vary much at different maturities. (Chapter 6)

float
Funds that have been sent by the payer but are not yet usable funds to the payee. (Chapter 15)

floating inventory lien
A secured short-term loan against inventory under which the lender's claim is on the borrower's inventory in general. (Chapter 16)

floating relationship
The fluctuating relationship of the values of two currencies with respect to each other. (Chapter 19)

floating-rate loan
A loan with a rate of interest initially set at an increment above the prime rate and allowed to "float," or vary, above prime *as the prime rate varies* until maturity. (Chapter 16)

flotation costs
The total costs of issuing and selling a security. (Chapter 9)

foreign bond
A bond that is issued by a foreign corporation or government and is denominated in the investor's home currency and sold in the investor's home market. (Chapters 2, 6 and 19)

foreign direct investment (FDI)
The transfer of capital, managerial, and technical assets to a foreign country. (Chapter 11)

foreign direct investment (FDI)
The transfer of capital, managerial, and technical assets to a foreign country by a multinational firm. (Chapter 19)

foreign exchange manager
The manager responsible for managing and monitoring the firm's exposure to loss from currency fluctuations. (Chapter 1)

foreign exchange rate
The price of one currency in terms of another. (Chapter 19)

forward exchange rate
The rate of exchange between two currencies at some specified future date. (Chapter 19)

free cash flow (FCF)
The amount of cash flow available to investors (creditors and owners) after the firm has met all operating needs and paid for investments in net fixed assets and net current assets. (Chapter 4)

free cash flow valuation model
A model that determines the value of an entire company as the present value of its expected *free cash flows* discounted at the firm's *weighted average cost of capital,* which is its expected average future cost of funds over the long run. (Chapter 7)

friendly merger
A merger transaction endorsed by the target firm's management, approved by its stockholders, and easily consummated. (Chapter 18)

functional currency
The currency in which a subsidiary primarily generates and expends cash and in which its accounts are maintained. (Chapter 19)

future value
The value on some future date of money that you invest today. (Chapter 5)

General Agreement on Tariffs and Trade (GATT)
A treaty that has governed world trade throughout most of the post-World War II era; it extends free-trading rules to broad areas of economic activity and is policed by the *World Trade Organization (WTO).* (Chapter 19)

generally accepted accounting principles (GAAP)
The practice and procedure guidelines used to prepare and maintain financial records and reports; authorized by the Financial Accounting Standards Board (FASB). (Chapter 3)

Glass-Steagall Act
An act of Congress in 1933 that created the Federal Deposit Insurance Corporation (FDIC) and separated the activities of commercial and investment banks. (Chapter 2)

golden parachutes
Provisions in the employment contracts of key executives that provide them with sizable compensation if the firm is taken over; deters hostile takeovers to the extent that the cash outflows required are large enough to make the takeover unattractive. (Chapter 18)

Gordon growth dividend model
A common name for the *constant-growth dividend model* that is widely cited in dividend valuation. (Chapter 7)

Gramm-Leach-Bliley Act
An act that allows business combinations (i.e., mergers) between commercial banks, investment banks, and insurance companies and thus permits these institutions

to compete in markets that prior regulations prohibited them from entering. (Chapter 2)

greenmail
A takeover defense under which a target firm repurchases, through private negotiation, a large block of stock at a premium from one or more shareholders to end a hostile takeover attempt by those shareholders. (Chapter 18)

gross profit margin
Measures the percentage of each sales dollar remaining after the firm has paid for its goods. (Chapter 3)

hedging
Offsetting or protecting against the risk of adverse price movements. (Chapter 17)

hedging strategies
Techniques used to offset or protect against risk; in the international context, these include borrowing or lending in different currencies; undertaking contracts in the forward, futures, and/or options markets; and swapping assets/liabilities with other parties. (Chapter 19)

holding company
A corporation that has voting control of one or more other corporations. (Chapter 18)

horizontal merger
A merger of two firms in the same line of business. (Chapter 18)

hostile merger
A merger transaction that the target firm's management does not support, forcing the acquiring company to try to gain control of the firm by buying shares in the marketplace. (Chapter 18)

hybrid security
A security that possesses characteristics of both debt and equity financing. (Chapter 17)

implied price of a warrant
The price effectively paid for each warrant attached to a bond. (Chapter 17)

income statement
Provides a financial summary of the firm's operating results during a specified period. (Chapter 3)

incremental cash flows
The additional after-tax cash flows—outflows or inflows—that will occur only if the investment is made. (Chapter 11)

independent projects
Projects whose cash flows are unrelated to (or independent of) one another; accepting or rejecting one project does not change the desirability of other projects. (Chapter 10)

indirect quote
An exchange rate quote that indicates the number of units of domestic currency that can be purchased with one unit of foreign currency. (Chapter 19)

individual investors
Investors who own relatively small quantities of shares to meet personal investment goals. (Chapter 1)

inflation
A rising trend in the prices of most goods and services. (Chapter 6)

informational content
The information provided by the dividends of a firm with respect to future earnings, which causes owners to bid up or down the price of the firm's stock. (Chapter 14)

initial investment
The incremental cash flows for a project at time zero. (Chapter 11)

initial public offering (IPO)
The first public sale of a firm's stock. (Chapter 2)

insolvency
Business failure that occurs when a firm is unable to pay its liabilities as they come due. (Chapter 18)

insolvent
Describes a firm that is unable to pay its bills as they come due. (Chapter 15)

installation costs
Any added costs that are necessary to place the new asset into operation. (Chapter 11)

installed cost of the new asset
The cost of the new asset plus its installation costs; equals the asset's depreciable value. (Chapter 11)

institutional investors
Investment professionals such as banks, insurance companies, mutual funds, and pension funds that are paid to manage and hold large quantities of securities on behalf of others. (Chapter 1)

interest rate
Usually applied to debt instruments such as bank loans or bonds; the compensation paid by the

borrower of funds to the lender; from the borrower's point of view, the cost of borrowing funds. (Chapter 6)

interest rate risk
The chance that interest rates will change and thereby change the required return and bond value. Rising rates, which result in decreasing bond values, are of greatest concern. (Chapter 6)

intermediate cash inflows
Cash inflows received prior to the termination of a project. (Chapter 10)

internal forecast
A sales forecast based on a buildup, or consensus, of sales forecasts through the firm's own sales channels. (Chapter 4)

internal rate of return (IRR)
The discount rate that equates the NPV of an investment opportunity with $0 (because the present value of cash inflows equals the initial investment); it is the rate of return that the firm will earn if it invests in the project and receives the given cash inflows. (Chapter 10)

internal rate of return approach
An approach to capital rationing that involves graphing project IRRs in descending order against the total dollar investment to determine the group of acceptable projects. (Chapter 12)

international bond
A bond that is initially sold outside the country of the borrower and is often distributed in several countries. (Chapter 19)

international equity market
A market that allows corporations to sell blocks of shares to investors in a number of different countries simultaneously. (Chapter 2)

international stock market
A market with uniform rules and regulations governing major stock exchanges. MNCs would benefit greatly from such a market, which has yet to evolve. (Chapter 19)

inventory turnover ratio
Measures the activity, or liquidity, of a firm's inventory. (Chapter 3)

inverted yield curve
A downward-sloping yield curve indicates that short-term interest rates are generally higher than long-term interest rates. (Chapter 6)

investment bank
Financial intermediary that specializes in selling new security issues and advising firms with regard to major financial transactions. (Chapter 2)

investment banks
Institutions that assist companies in raising capital, advise firms on major transactions such as mergers or financial restructurings, and engage in trading and market-making activities. (Chapter 2)

investment bankers
Financial intermediaries who, in addition to their role in selling new security issues, can be hired by acquirers in mergers to find suitable target companies and assist in negotiations. (Chapter 18)

investment decisions
Decisions that focus on how a company will spend its financial resources on long-term projects that ultimately determine whether the firm successfully creates value for its owners. (Chapter 1)

investment opportunities schedule (IOS)
The graph that plots project IRRs in descending order against the total dollar investment. (Chapter 12)

involuntary reorganization
A petition initiated by an outside party, usually a creditor, for the reorganization and payment of creditors of a failed firm. (Chapter 18)

IPO market price
The final trading price on the first day in the secondary market. (Chapter 2)

IPO offer price
The price at which the issuing firm sells its securities. (Chapter 2)

IPO underpricing
The percentage change from the final IPO offer price to the IPO market price, which is the final trading price on the first day in the secondary market; this is also called the IPO initial return. (Chapter 2)

issued shares
Shares of common stock that have been put into circulation; the sum of *outstanding shares* and *treasury stock*. (Chapter 7)

joint venture
A partnership under which the participants have contractually agreed to contribute specified amounts of money and expertise in exchange for stated proportions of ownership and profit. (Chapter 19)

judgmental approach
A simplified approach for preparing the pro forma balance sheet under which the firm estimates the values of certain balance sheet accounts and uses its external financing as a balancing, or "plug," figure. (Chapter 4)

just-in-time (JIT) system
Inventory management technique that minimizes inventory investment by having materials arrive at exactly the time they are needed for production. (Chapter 15)

lease-versus-purchase (or lease-versus-buy) decision
The decision facing firms needing to acquire new fixed assets: whether to lease the assets or to purchase them, using borrowed funds or available liquid resources. (Chapter 17)

leasing
The process by which a firm can obtain the use of certain fixed assets for which it must make a series of contractual, periodic, tax-deductible payments. (Chapter 17)

lessee
The receiver of the services of the assets under a lease contract. (Chapter 17)

lessor
The owner of assets that are being leased. (Chapter 17)

letter of credit
A letter written by a company's bank to the company's foreign supplier, stating that the bank guarantees payment of an invoiced amount if all the underlying agreements are met. (Chapter 16)

letter to stockholders
Typically, the first element of the annual stockholders' report and the primary communication from management. (Chapter 3)

leverage
Refers to the effects that fixed costs have on the returns that shareholders earn; higher leverage generally results in higher but more volatile returns. (Chapter 13)

leveraged buyout (LBO)
An acquisition technique involving the use of a large amount of debt to purchase a firm; an example of a financial merger. (Chapter 18)

leveraged lease
A lease under which the lessor acts as an equity participant, supplying only about 20% of the cost of the asset, while a lender supplies the balance. (Chapter 17)

leveraged recapitalization
A takeover defense in which the target firm pays a large debt-financed cash dividend, increasing the firm's financial leverage and thereby deterring the takeover attempt. (Chapter 18)

lien
A publicly disclosed legal claim on loan collateral. (Chapter 16)

limited liability
A legal provision that limits stockholders' liability for a corporation's debt to the amount they initially invested in the firm by purchasing stock. (Chapter 1)

line of credit
An agreement between a commercial bank and a business specifying the amount of unsecured short-term borrowing the bank will make available to the firm over a given period of time. (Chapter 16)

liquidation value per share
The *actual amount* per share of common stock that would be received if all the firm's assets were *sold for their market value,* liabilities (including preferred stock) were paid, and any remaining money were divided among the common stockholders. (Chapter 7)

liquidity
The ability to quickly buy or sell a security without having an impact on the security's price. (Chapter 2)

liquidity
A firm's ability to satisfy its short-term obligations *as they come due.* (Chapter 3)

liquidity preference
A general tendency for investors to prefer short-term (i.e., more liquid) securities. (Chapter 6)

liquidity preference theory
Theory suggesting that long-term rates are generally higher than short-term rates (hence, the yield curve is upward sloping) because investors perceive short-term investments as more liquid and less risky than long-term investments. Borrowers must offer higher rates on long-term bonds to entice investors away from their preferred short-term securities. (Chapter 6)

loan amortization
The determination of the equal periodic loan payments necessary to provide a lender with a specified interest return and to repay the loan principal over a specified period. (Chapter 5)

loan amortization schedule
A schedule of equal payments to repay a loan. It shows the allocation of each loan payment to interest and principal. (Chapter 5)

lockbox system
A collection procedure in which customers mail payments to a post office box that is emptied regularly by the firm's bank, which processes the payments and deposits them in the firm's account. This system speeds up collection time by reducing processing time as well as mail and clearing time. (Chapter 15)

London Interbank Offered Rate (LIBOR)
The rate at which international banks make short-term loans to each other. There are many different LIBOR rates corresponding to different currencies and maturities. (Chapter 16)

long-term debt
Debt for which payment is not due in the current year. (Chapter 3)

long-term (strategic) financial plans
Plans that lay out a company's financial actions and the anticipated impact of those actions over periods ranging from 2 to 10 years. (Chapter 4)

low-regular-and-extra dividend policy
A dividend policy based on paying a low regular dividend, supplemented by an additional ("extra") dividend when earnings are higher than normal in a given period. (Chapter 14)

macro political risk
The subjection of all foreign firms to political risk (takeover) by a host country because of political change, revolution, or the adoption of new policies. (Chapter 19)

MACRS recovery period
The appropriate depreciable life of an asset as determined by MACRS under pre-2018 tax law. (Chapter 4)

mail float
The time delay between when payment is placed in the mail and when it is received. (Chapter 15)

maintenance clauses
Provisions normally included in an operating lease that require the lessor to maintain the assets and to make insurance and tax payments. (Chapter 17)

managerial finance
Concerns the duties of the financial manager in a business. (Chapter 1)

manufacturing resource planning II (MRP II)
An extension of MRP that uses a sophisticated computerized system to integrate data from numerous areas such as finance, accounting, marketing, engineering, and manufacturing and generate production plans as well as numerous financial and management reports. (Chapter 15)

marginal cost–benefit analysis
Economic principle that states that financial decisions should be made and actions taken only when the marginal benefits exceed the marginal costs. (Chapter 1)

marginal tax rate
The tax rate that applies to the next dollar of income earned. (Chapter 1)

market capitalization
The total market value of a publicly traded firm's outstanding stock. Calculated as the market price times the number of shares of stock outstanding. (Chapter 2)

market makers
Securities dealers who "make markets" by offering to buy or sell certain securities at stated prices. (Chapter 2)

market order
An order to either buy or sell a security at the prevailing market prices. (Chapter 2)

market premium
The amount by which the market value exceeds the straight or conversion value of a convertible security. (Chapter 17)

market price
The price of the firm's shares as determined by the interaction of buyers and sellers in the secondary market. (Chapter 2)

market ratios
Relate a firm's market value, as measured by its current share price, to certain accounting values. (Chapter 3)

market return
The return on the market portfolio of all traded securities. (Chapter 8)

market segmentation theory
Theory suggesting that the market for loans is segmented on the basis of maturity and that the supply of and demand for loans within each segment determine its prevailing interest rate; the slope of the

yield curve is determined by the general relationship between the prevailing rates in each market segment. (Chapter 6)

market value weights
Weights that use market values to measure the proportion of each type of capital in the firm's financial structure. (Chapter 9)

market/book (M/B) ratio
Provides an assessment of how investors view the firm's performance. Firms expected to earn high returns relative to their risk typically sell at higher M/B multiples. (Chapter 3)

marketable securities
Short-term debt instruments, such as U.S. Treasury bills, commercial paper, and negotiable certificates of deposit issued by government, business, and financial institutions, respectively. (Chapter 2)

materials requirement planning (MRP) system
Inventory management technique that applies EOQ concepts and a computer to compare production needs to available inventory balances and determine when orders should be placed for various items on a product's bill of materials. (Chapter 15)

Mercosur
A major South American trading bloc that includes countries that account for more than half of total Latin American GDP. (Chapter 19)

merger
The combination of two or more firms, in which the resulting firm maintains the identity of one of the firms, usually the larger. (Chapter 18)

micro political risk
The subjection of an individual firm, a specific industry, or companies from a particular foreign country to political risk (takeover) by a host country. (Chapter 19)

mixed stream
A stream of unequal periodic cash flows that reflect no particular pattern. (Chapter 5)

modified accelerated cost recovery system (MACRS)
System used to determine the depreciation of assets for tax purposes under pre-2018 tax law. (Chapter 4)

modified DuPont formula
Relates the firm's *return on total assets (ROA)* to its *return on equity (ROE)* using the *financial leverage multiplier (FLM)*. (Chapter 3)

monetary union
The official melding of the national currencies of the EU nations into one currency, the *euro*, on January 1, 2002. (Chapter 19)

money market
A market where investors trade highly liquid securities with maturities of 1 year or less. (Chapter 2)

mortgage-backed securities
Securities that represent claims on the cash flows generated by a pool of mortgages. (Chapter 2)

multinational companies (MNCs)
Firms that have international assets and operations in foreign markets and draw part of their total revenue and profits from such markets. (Chapter 19)

multiple IRRs
More than one IRR resulting from a capital budgeting project with a *nonconventional cash flow pattern;* the maximum number of IRRs for a project is equal to the number of sign changes in its cash flows. (Chapter 10)

municipal bond
A bond issued by a state or local government body. (Chapter 6)

mutually exclusive projects
Projects that compete with one another so that the acceptance of one eliminates from further consideration all other projects that serve a similar function. (Chapter 10)

Nasdaq market
An all-electronic trading platform used to execute securities trades. (Chapter 2)

national entry control systems
Comprehensive rules, regulations, and incentives introduced by host governments to regulate inflows of foreign direct investments from MNCs and at the same time extract more benefits from their presence. (Chapter 19)

negatively correlated
Describes two series that move in opposite directions. (Chapter 8)

net cash flow
The mathematical difference between the firm's cash receipts and its cash disbursements in each period. (Chapter 4)

net cash flows
The net (or sum) of incremental after-tax cash flows over a project's life. (Chapter 11)

net operating profits after taxes (NOPAT)
A firm's earnings before interest and after taxes, EBIT × $(1 - T)$. (Chapter 4)

net present value (NPV)
A capital budgeting technique that measures an investment's value by calculating the present value of its cash inflows and outflows. (Chapter 10)

net present value approach
An approach to capital rationing that is based on the use of present values to determine the group of projects that will maximize owners' wealth. (Chapter 12)

net present value profile
Graph that depicts a project's NPVs calculated at discount rates. (Chapter 10)

net proceeds
Funds actually received by the firm from the sale of a security. (Chapter 9)

net profit margin
Measures the percentage of each sales dollar remaining after all costs and expenses, *including* interest, taxes, and preferred stock dividends, have been deducted. (Chapter 3)

net working capital
The difference between the firm's current assets and its current liabilities. (Chapter 11)

no-par preferred stock
Preferred stock with no stated face value but with a stated annual dollar dividend. (Chapter 7)

nominal (stated) annual rate
Contractual annual rate of interest charged by a lender or promised by a borrower. (Chapter 5)

nominal interest rate
In the international context, the stated interest rate charged on financing when only the MNC parent's currency is involved. (Chapter 19)

nominal rate of interest
The actual rate of interest charged by the supplier of funds and paid by the demander. (Chapter 6)

non-notification basis
The basis on which a borrower, having pledged an account receivable, continues to collect the account payments without notifying the account customer. (Chapter 16)

noncash charge
An expense that is deducted on the income statement but does not involve the actual outlay of cash during the period; includes depreciation, amortization, and depletion. (Chapter 4)

noncumulative (preferred stock)
Preferred stock for which passed (unpaid) dividends do not accumulate. (Chapter 7)

nondiversifiable risk
The relevant portion of an asset's risk attributable to market factors that affect all firms; cannot be eliminated through diversification. Also called *systematic risk*. (Chapter 8)

nonrecourse basis
The basis on which accounts receivable are sold to a factor with the understanding that the factor accepts all credit risks on the purchased accounts. (Chapter 16)

nonvoting common stock
Common stock that carries no voting rights; issued when the firm wishes to raise capital through the sale of common stock but does not want to give up its voting control. (Chapter 7)

normal probability distribution
A symmetrical probability distribution whose shape resembles a "bell-shaped" curve. (Chapter 8)

normal yield curve
An upward-sloping yield curve indicates that long-term interest rates are generally higher than short-term interest rates. (Chapter 6)

North American Free Trade Agreement (NAFTA)
The treaty establishing free trade and open markets among Canada, Mexico, and the United States. (Chapter 19)

notes to the financial statements
Explanatory notes keyed to relevant accounts in the statements; they provide detailed information on the accounting policies, procedures, calculations, and transactions underlying entries in the financial statements. (Chapter 3)

notification basis
The basis on which an account customer whose account has been pledged (or factored) is notified to remit payment directly to the lender (or factor). (Chapter 16)

offshore centers
Certain cities or states (including London, Singapore, Bahrain, Nassau, Hong Kong, and Luxembourg) that have achieved prominence as major centers for Euromarket business. (Chapter 19)

open-market share repurchase
A share repurchase program in which firms simply buy back some of their outstanding shares on the open market. (Chapter 14)

operating breakeven point
The level of sales necessary to cover all *operating costs;* the point at which EBIT = $0. (Chapter 13)

operating cash flow (OCF)
The cash flow a firm generates from its normal operations; calculated as net operating profits after taxes (NOPAT) plus depreciation. (Chapter 4)

operating cash flows
The net incremental after-tax cash flows occurring each period during the project's life. (Chapter 11)

operating cycle (OC)
The time from the beginning of the production process to collection of cash from the sale of the finished product. (Chapter 15)

operating expenditure
An outlay of funds by the firm resulting in benefits received *within* 1 year. (Chapter 10)

operating lease
A cancelable contractual arrangement whereby the lessee agrees to make periodic payments to the lessor, often for 5 or fewer years, to obtain an asset's services; generally, the total payments over the term of the lease are less than the lessor's initial cost of the leased asset. (Chapter 17)

operating leverage
The use of *fixed operating costs* to magnify the effects of changes in sales on the firm's earnings before interest and taxes. (Chapter 13)

operating profit margin
Measures the percentage of each sales dollar remaining after all costs and expenses *other than* interest, taxes, and preferred stock dividends are deducted; the "pure profits" earned on each sales dollar. (Chapter 3)

operating unit
A part of a business, such as a plant, division, product line, or subsidiary, that contributes to the actual operations of the firm. (Chapter 18)

operating-change restrictions
Contractual restrictions that a bank may impose on a firm's financial condition or operations as part of a line-of-credit agreement. (Chapter 16)

opportunity costs
Cash flows that could have been realized from the best alternative use of an owned asset. (Chapter 11)

optimal capital structure
The capital structure at which the weighted average cost of capital is minimized, thereby maximizing the firm's value. (Chapter 13)

option
An instrument that provides its holder with an opportunity to purchase or sell a specified asset at a stated price on or before a set expiration date. (Chapter 17)

order costs
The fixed clerical costs of placing and receiving an inventory order. (Chapter 15)

ordinary annuity
An annuity for which the cash flow occurs at the end of each period. (Chapter 5)

ordinary income
Income earned by a business through the sale of goods or services. (Chapter 1)

originating investment bank
The investment bank initially hired by the issuing firm, it brings other investment banks in as partners to form an underwriting syndicate. (Chapter 2)

outstanding shares
Issued shares of common stock held by investors, including both private and public investors. (Chapter 7)

over-the-counter (OTC) market
Market where smaller, unlisted securities are traded. (Chapter 2)

overhanging issue
A convertible security that cannot be forced into conversion by using the call feature. (Chapter 17)

paid-in capital in excess of par
The amount of proceeds in excess of the par value received from the original sale of common stock. (Chapter 3)

par value, face value, principal
The amount of money the borrower must repay at maturity, and the value on which periodic interest payments are based. (Chapter 6)

par-value common stock
An arbitrary value that is established for legal purposes in the firm's corporate charter and that can be used to find the total number of shares outstanding by dividing it into the book value of common stock. (Chapter 7)

par-value preferred stock
Preferred stock with a stated face value that is used with the specified dividend percentage to determine the annual dollar dividend. (Chapter 7)

partnership
A business owned by two or more people and operated for profit. (Chapter 1)

payback period
The time it takes an investment to generate cash inflows sufficient to recoup the initial outlay required to make the investment. (Chapter 10)

payment date
Set by the firm's directors, the actual date on which the firm mails the dividend payment to the holders of record. (Chapter 14)

payout policy
Decisions that a firm makes regarding whether to distribute cash to shareholders, how much cash to distribute, and the means by which cash should be distributed. (Chapter 14)

pecking order theory
A hierarchy of financing that begins with retained earnings, which is followed by debt financing and finally external equity financing. (Chapter 13)

percent-of-sales method
A simple method for developing the pro forma income statement; it forecasts sales and then expresses the various income statement items as percentages of projected sales. (Chapter 4)

percentage advance
The percentage of the book value of the collateral that constitutes the principal of a secured loan. (Chapter 16)

perfectly negatively correlated
Describes two *negatively correlated* series that have a *correlation coefficient* of –1. (Chapter 8)

perfectly positively correlated
Describes two *positively correlated* series that have a *correlation coefficient* of +1. (Chapter 8)

Permanent funding requirement
A constant investment in operating assets resulting from constant sales over time. (Chapter 15)

perpetuity
An annuity with an infinite life, providing continual annual cash flow. (Chapter 5)

pledge of accounts receivable
The use of a firm's accounts receivable as security, or collateral, to obtain a short-term loan. (Chapter 16)

poison pill
A takeover defense in which a firm issues securities that give their holders certain rights that become effective when a takeover is attempted; these rights make the target firm less desirable to a hostile acquirer. (Chapter 18)

political risk
Risk that arises from the possibility that a host government will take actions harmful to foreign investors or that political turmoil will endanger investments. (Chapter 8)

political risk
The potential discontinuity or seizure of an MNC's operations in a host country via the host's implementation of specific rules and regulations. (Chapter 19)

portfolio
A collection or group of assets. (Chapter 8)

positively correlated
Describes two series that move in the same direction. (Chapter 8)

preemptive right
Allows common stockholders to maintain their proportionate ownership in the corporation when new shares are issued, thus protecting them from dilution of ownership. (Chapter 7)

preferred stock
A special form of ownership having a fixed periodic dividend that must be paid prior to payment of any dividends to common stockholders. (Chapter 2)

premium
The amount by which a bond sells above its par value. (Chapter 6)

present value
The value in today's dollars of some future cash flow. (Chapter 5)

president or chief executive officer (CEO)
Corporate official responsible for managing the firm's day-to-day operations and carrying out the policies established by the board of directors. (Chapter 1)

price/earnings (P/E) ratio
Measures the amount that investors are willing to pay for each dollar of a firm's earnings; the higher the P/E ratio, the greater the investor confidence. (Chapter 3)

price/earnings multiple approach
A popular technique used to estimate the firm's share value; calculated by multiplying the firm's expected earnings per share (EPS) by the average price/earnings (P/E) ratio for the industry. (Chapter 7)

primary market
Financial market in which securities are initially issued; the only market in which the issuer is directly involved in the transaction. (Chapter 2)

prime rate of interest (prime rate)
An interest rate charged by leading U.S. banks on business loans to creditworthy borrowers. (Chapter 16)

principal
The amount of money on which interest is paid. (Chapter 5)

principal–agent problem
A problem that arises because the owners of a firm and its managers are not the same people and the agent does not act in the interest of the principal. (Chapter 1)

private equity
External equity financing that is raised via a private placement, typically by private early-stage firms with attractive growth prospects. (Chapter 2)

private placement
The sale of a new security directly to an investor or group of investors. (Chapter 2)

privately owned (stock)
The common stock of a firm is owned by private investors; this stock is not publicly traded. (Chapter 7)

pro forma statements
Projected, or forecast, income statements and balance sheets. (Chapter 4)

probability
The *chance* that a given outcome will occur. (Chapter 8)

probability distribution
A model that relates probabilities to the associated outcomes. (Chapter 8)

proceeds from the sale of old asset
The before-tax cash inflow net of any removal costs that results from the sale of the old asset and is normally subject to some type of tax treatment. (Chapter 11)

Processing float
The time between receipt of a payment and its deposit into the firm's account. (Chapter 15)

prospectus
A portion of a security registration statement that describes the key aspects of the issue, the issuer, and its management and financial position. (Chapter 2)

proxy battle
The attempt by a nonmanagement group to gain control of the management of a firm by soliciting a sufficient number of proxy votes. (Chapter 7)

proxy statement
A statement transferring the votes of a stockholder to another party. (Chapter 7)

Public Company Accounting Oversight Board (PCAOB)
A not-for-profit corporation established by the Sarbanes-Oxley Act of 2002 to protect the interests of investors and further the public interest in the preparation of informative, fair, and independent audit reports. (Chapter 3)

public offering
The sale of either bonds or stocks to the general public. (Chapter 2)

publicly owned (stock)
The common stock of a firm is owned by public investors; this stock is publicly traded. (Chapter 7)

purchase options
Provisions frequently included in both operating and financial leases that allow the lessee to purchase the leased asset at maturity, typically for a prespecified price. (Chapter 17)

pure economic profit
A profit above and beyond the normal competitive rate of return in a line of business. (Chapter 10)

put option
An option to sell a specified number of shares of a stock (typically 100) on or before a specified future date at a stated price. (Chapter 17)

putable bonds
See Table 6.5. (Chapter 6)

pyramiding
An arrangement among holding companies wherein one holding company controls other holding companies, thereby causing an even greater magnification of earnings and losses. (Chapter 18)

quarterly compounding
Compounding of interest over four periods within the year. (Chapter 5)

quick (acid-test) ratio
A measure of liquidity calculated by dividing the firm's current assets less inventory by its current liabilities. (Chapter 3)

range
A measure of an asset's risk, which is found by subtracting the return associated with the pessimistic (worst) outcome from the return associated with the optimistic (best) outcome. (Chapter 8)

ranking approach
The ranking of capital expenditure projects on the basis of some predetermined measure, such as how much value the project creates for shareholders. (Chapter 10)

ratio analysis
Involves methods of calculating and interpreting financial ratios to analyze and monitor the firm's performance. (Chapter 3)

ratio of exchange
The ratio of the amount paid per share of the target company to the market price per share of the acquiring firm. (Chapter 18)

ratio of exchange in market price
Indicates the market price per share of the acquiring firm paid for each dollar of market price per share of the target firm. (Chapter 18)

real options
Opportunities that are embedded in capital projects and that enable managers to alter their cash flows and risk in a way that affects project acceptability (NPV). Also called *strategic options*. (Chapter 12)

real rate of interest
The rate of return on an investment measured not in dollars but in the increase in purchasing power that the investment provides. The real rate of interest measures the rate of increase in purchasing power. (Chapter 6)

recapitalization
The reorganization procedure under which a failed firm's debts are generally exchanged for equity or the maturities of existing debts are extended. (Chapter 18)

recaptured depreciation
The portion of an asset's sale price that is above its book value and below its initial purchase price. (Chapter 11)

red herring
A preliminary prospectus made available to prospective investors during the waiting period between the registration statement's filing with the SEC and its approval. (Chapter 2)

regular dividend policy
A dividend policy based on the payment of a fixed-dollar dividend in each period. (Chapter 14)

renewal options
Provisions especially common in operating leases that grant the lessee the right to re-lease assets at the expiration of the lease. (Chapter 17)

reorder point
The point at which to reorder inventory, expressed as days of lead time × daily usage. (Chapter 15)

required return
Usually applied to equity instruments such as common stock; the cost of funds obtained by selling an ownership interest. (Chapter 6)

required total financing
Amount of funds needed by the firm if the ending cash for the period is less than the desired minimum cash balance; typically represented by notes payable. (Chapter 4)

residual theory of dividends
A school of thought suggesting that the dividend paid by a firm should be viewed as a *residual*, that is, the amount left over after all acceptable investment opportunities have been undertaken. (Chapter 14)

restricted stock
Shares of stock paid out as part of a compensation package that do not fully transfer from the company to the employee until certain conditions are met. (Chapter 1)

restrictive covenants
Provisions in a bond indenture that place operating and financial constraints on the borrower. (Chapter 6)

retained earnings
The cumulative total of all earnings, net of dividends, that have been retained and reinvested in the firm since its inception. (Chapter 3)

return on equity (ROE)
Measures the return earned on the common stockholders' investment in the firm. (Chapter 3)

return on total assets (ROA)
Measures the overall effectiveness of management in generating profits with its available assets; also called the *return on investment (ROI)*. (Chapter 3)

reverse stock split
A method used to raise the market price of a firm's stock by exchanging a certain number of outstanding shares for one new share. (Chapter 14)

revolving credit agreement
A line of credit *guaranteed* to a borrower by a commercial bank regardless of the scarcity of money. (Chapter 16)

rights
Financial instruments that allow stockholders to purchase additional shares at a price below the market price, in direct proportion to their fractional ownership. (Chapter 7)

risk
The chance that actual outcomes may differ from those expected. (Chapter 1)

risk
A measure of the uncertainty surrounding the return that an investment will earn. (Chapter 8)

risk (in capital budgeting)
The uncertainty surrounding the cash flows that a project will generate or, more formally, the degree of variability of cash flows. (Chapter 12)

risk averse
Requiring compensation to bear risk. (Chapter 1)

risk averse
The attitude toward risk in which investors require an increased expected return as compensation for an increase in risk. (Chapter 8)

risk neutral
The attitude toward risk in which investors choose the investment with the higher expected return regardless of its risk. (Chapter 8)

risk seeking
The attitude toward risk in which investors prefer investments with greater risk, perhaps even if they have lower expected returns. (Chapter 8)

risk-adjusted discount rate (RADR)
The rate of return that must be earned on a given project to compensate the firm's owners adequately, that is, to maintain or improve the firm's share price. (Chapter 12)

risk-free rate of return (R_F)
The required return on a *risk-free asset,* typically a 3-month *U.S. Treasury bill.* (Chapter 8)

safety stock
Extra inventory that is held to prevent stockouts of important items. (Chapter 15)

sale-leaseback arrangement
A lease under which the lessee sells an asset to a prospective lessor and then leases back the same asset, making fixed periodic payments for its use. (Chapter 17)

sales forecast
The prediction of the firm's sales over a given period, based on external and/or internal data; used as the key input to the short-term financial planning process. (Chapter 4)

Sarbanes-Oxley Act of 2002 (SOX)
An act aimed at eliminating corporate disclosure and conflict of interest problems. Contains provisions concerning corporate financial disclosures and the relationships among corporations, analysts, auditors, attorneys, directors, officers, and shareholders. (Chapter 1)

scenario analysis
An approach for assessing risk that uses several possible alternative outcomes (scenarios) to obtain a sense of the variability among returns. (Chapter 8)

seasonal funding requirement
An investment in operating assets that varies over time as a result of cyclical sales. (Chapter 15)

secondary market
Financial market in which preowned securities (those that are not new issues) are traded. (Chapter 2)

secured bond
A bond backed by some form of collateral. (Chapter 6)

secured creditors
Creditors who have specific assets pledged as collateral and, in liquidation of the failed firm, receive proceeds from the sale of those assets. (Chapter 18)

secured short-term financing
Short-term financing (loan) that has specific assets pledged as collateral. (Chapter 16)

Securities Act of 1933
An act that regulates the sale of securities to the public via the primary market. (Chapter 2)

Securities and Exchange Commission (SEC)
The primary government agency responsible for enforcing federal securities laws. (Chapter 2)

Securities and Exchange Commission (SEC)
Federal regulatory body that governs the sale and listing of securities. (Chapter 3)

Securities Exchange Act of 1934
An act that regulates the trading of securities such as stocks and bonds in the secondary market. (Chapter 2)

securities exchanges
Organizations that provide the marketplace in which firms can raise funds through the sale of new securities and purchasers can resell securities. (Chapter 2)

securitization
The process of pooling mortgages or other types of loans and then selling claims or securities against that pool in the secondary market. (Chapter 2)

security agreement
The agreement between the borrower and the lender that specifies the collateral held against a secured loan. (Chapter 16)

security market line (SML)
The depiction of the *capital asset pricing model (CAPM)* as a graph that reflects the required return in the marketplace for each level of nondiversifiable risk (beta). (Chapter 8)

selling group
A large number of brokerage firms that join the originating investment bank(s); each accepts responsibility for selling a certain portion of a new security issue on a commission basis. (Chapter 2)

semiannual compounding
Compounding of interest over two periods within the year. (Chapter 5)

shadow banking system
A group of institutions that engage in lending activities, much like traditional banks, but that do not accept deposits and therefore are not subject to the same regulations as traditional banks. (Chapter 2)

shark repellents
Antitakeover amendments to a corporate charter that constrain the firm's ability to transfer managerial control of the firm as a result of a merger. (Chapter 18)

short-term (operating) financial plans
Plans that specify short-term financial actions and the anticipated impact of those actions. (Chapter 4)

short-term, self-liquidating loan
An unsecured short-term loan in which the use to which the borrowed money is put provides the mechanism through which the loan is repaid. (Chapter 16)

signal
A financing action by management that is believed to reflect its view of the firm's stock value; generally, debt financing is viewed as a *positive signal* that management believes the stock is "undervalued," and a stock issue is viewed as a *negative signal* that management believes the stock is "overvalued." (Chapter 13)

simple interest
Interest that is earned only on an investment's original principal and not on interest that accumulates over time. (Chapter 5)

simulation
A statistics-based behavioral approach that applies predetermined probability distributions and random numbers to estimate risky outcomes. (Chapter 12)

single-payment note
A short-term, one-time loan made to a borrower who needs funds for a specific purpose for a short period. (Chapter 16)

sinking-fund requirement
A restrictive provision often included in a bond indenture, providing for the systematic retirement of bonds prior to their maturity. (Chapter 6)

small (ordinary) stock dividend
A stock dividend representing less than 20% to 25% of the common stock outstanding when the dividend is declared. (Chapter 14)

sole proprietorship
A business owned by one person and operated for his or her own profit. (Chapter 1)

spin-off
A form of divestiture in which an operating unit becomes an independent company through the issuance of shares in it, on a pro rata basis, to the parent company's shareholders. (Chapter 18)

spontaneous liabilities
Financing that arises from the normal course of business; the two major short-term sources of such liabilities are accounts payable and accruals. (Chapter 16)

spot exchange rate
The rate of exchange between two currencies on any given day. (Chapter 19)

stakeholders
Groups such as employees, customers, suppliers, creditors, and others who have a direct economic link to the firm but are not owners. (Chapter 1)

standard debt provisions
Provisions in a bond indenture specifying certain record-keeping and general business practices that the bond issuer must follow; normally, they do not place a burden on a financially sound business. (Chapter 6)

standard deviation (σ)
The most common statistical indicator of an asset's risk; it measures the dispersion around the average. (Chapter 8)

statement of cash flows
Provides a summary of the firm's operating, investment, and financing cash flows and reconciles them with changes in its cash and marketable securities during the period. (Chapter 3)

statement of retained earnings
Reconciles the net income earned during a given year, and any cash dividends paid, with the change

in retained earnings between the start and the end of that year. An abbreviated form of the *statement of stockholders' equity.* (Chapter 3)

statement of stockholders' equity
Shows all equity account transactions that occurred during a given year. (Chapter 3)

stock
A security that represents an ownership interest in a corporation. (Chapter 1)

stock dividend
The payment, to existing owners, of a dividend in the form of stock. (Chapter 14)

stock options
Securities that allow managers to buy shares of stock at a fixed price. (Chapter 1)

stock purchase warrants
Instruments that give their holders the right to purchase a certain number of shares of the issuer's common stock at a specified price over a certain period of time. (Chapter 6)

stock purchase warrants
Instruments that give their holders the right to purchase a certain number of shares of the issuer's common stock at a specified price over a certain period of time. (Chapter 6)

stock split
A method commonly used to lower the market price of a firm's stock by increasing the number of shares belonging to each shareholder. (Chapter 14)

stock swap transaction
An acquisition method in which the acquiring firm exchanges its shares for shares of the target company according to a predetermined ratio. (Chapter 18)

stockholders
The owners of a corporation, whose ownership, or *equity,* takes the form of common stock or, less frequently, preferred stock. (Chapter 1)

stockholders' report
Annual report that publicly owned corporations must provide to stockholders; it summarizes and documents the firm's financial activities during the past year. (Chapter 3)

straight bond
A bond that is nonconvertible, having no conversion feature. (Chapter 17)

straight bond value
The price at which a convertible bond would sell in the market without the conversion feature. (Chapter 17)

straight preferred stock
Preferred stock that is nonconvertible, having no conversion feature. (Chapter 17)

strategic merger
A merger transaction undertaken to achieve economies of scale. (Chapter 18)

stretching accounts payable
Paying bills as late as possible without damaging the firm's credit rating. (Chapter 16)

strike price
The price at which the holder of a call option can buy (or the holder of a put option can sell) a specified amount of stock at any time prior to the option's expiration date. (Chapter 17)

subordination
In a bond indenture, the stipulation that subsequent creditors agree to wait until all claims of the senior debt are satisfied. (Chapter 6)

subprime mortgages
Mortgage loans made to borrowers with lower incomes and poorer credit histories as compared to "prime" borrowers. (Chapter 2)

subsidiaries
The companies controlled by a holding company. (Chapter 18)

sunk costs
Cash outlays that have already been made (past outlays) and cannot be recovered, whether or not the firm follows through and makes an investment. (Chapter 11)

supervoting shares
Stock that carries with it multiple votes per share rather than the single vote per share typically given on regular shares of common stock. (Chapter 7)

takeover defenses
Strategies for fighting hostile takeovers. (Chapter 18)

target capital structure
The mix of debt and equity financing that a firm desires over the long term. The target capital structure should reflect the optimal mix of debt and equity for a particular firm. (Chapter 9)

target company
The firm in a merger transaction that the acquiring company is pursuing. (Chapter 18)

target dividend-payout ratio
A dividend policy under which the firm attempts to pay out a certain percentage of earnings as a stated dollar dividend and adjusts that dividend toward a target payout as proven earnings increases occur. (Chapter 14)

Tax Cuts and Jobs Act of 2017
Cut personal tax rates, instituted a 21% flat corporate tax, and imposed some limits on interest deductibility, the use of operating losses to reduce taxes in other years, and dividends received by corporations.

tax loss carryforward
In a merger, the tax loss of one of the firms that can be applied against a limited amount of future income of the merged firm over an indefinite period. (Chapter 18)

tax on the sale of the old asset
Tax that depends on the relationship between the old asset's sale price and book value and on existing government tax rules. (Chapter 11)

temporal method
A method that requires specific assets and liabilities to be translated at so-called historical exchange rates and foreign-exchange translation gains or losses to be reflected in the current year's income. (Chapter 19)

tender offer share repurchase
A repurchase program in which a firm offers to repurchase a fixed number of shares, usually at a premium relative to the market value, and shareholders decide whether or not they want to sell back their shares at that price. (Chapter 14)

term structure of interest rates
The relationship between the maturity and rate of return for bonds with similar levels of risk. (Chapter 6)

terminal cash flows
The net after-tax cash flow occurring in the final year of the project. (Chapter 11)

time-series analysis
Evaluation of the firm's financial performance over time using financial ratio analysis. (Chapter 3)

timeline
A horizontal line on which time zero appears at the left and future periods appear from left to right; used to depict investment cash flows. (Chapter 5)

times interest earned ratio
Measures the firm's ability to make interest payments; also called the *interest coverage ratio.* (Chapter 3)

tombstone
The list of underwriting syndicate banks, presented in such a way to indicate a syndicate member's level of involvement, located at the bottom of the IPO prospectus cover page. (Chapter 2)

total asset turnover
Indicates the efficiency with which the firm uses its assets to generate sales. (Chapter 3)

total cash disbursements
All outlays of cash by the firm during a given financial period. (Chapter 4)

total cash receipts
All of a firm's inflows of cash during a given financial period. (Chapter 4)

total cost of inventory
The sum of order costs and carrying costs of inventory. (Chapter 15)

total leverage
The use of *fixed costs, both operating and financial,* to magnify the effects of changes in sales on the firm's earnings per share. (Chapter 13)

total proceeds
The total amount of proceeds for all shares sold in the IPO. Calculated as the IPO offer price times the number of IPO shares issued. (Chapter 2)

total rate of return
The total gain or loss experienced on an investment expressed as a percentage of the investment's value; calculated by dividing the asset's cash distributions during the period, plus change in value, by its beginning-of-period value. (Chapter 8)

total risk
The combination of a security's *nondiversifiable risk* and *diversifiable risk.* (Chapter 8)

transfer prices
Prices that subsidiaries charge each other for the goods and services traded between them. (Chapter 12)

treasurer
A key financial manager, who manages the firm's cash, oversees its pension plans, and manages key risks. (Chapter 1)

treasury stock
Issued shares of stock held by the firm; often they have been repurchased by the firm. (Chapter 7)

trust receipt inventory loan
A secured short-term loan against inventory under which the lender advances 80% to 100% of the cost of the borrower's expensive inventory items in exchange for the borrower's promise to repay the loan immediately after the sale of each item of collateral. (Chapter 16)

trustee
A paid individual, corporation, or commercial bank trust department that acts as the third party to a bond indenture and can take specified actions on behalf of the bondholders if the terms of the indenture are violated. (Chapter 6)

two-bin method
Unsophisticated inventory-monitoring technique that is typically applied to C group items and involves reordering inventory when one of two bins is empty. (Chapter 15)

two-tier offer
A tender offer in which the terms offered are more attractive to those who tender shares early. (Chapter 18)

U.S. Treasury bills (T-bills)
Short-term IOUs issued by the U.S. Treasury; considered the *risk-free asset.* (Chapter 8)

uncorrelated
Describes two series that lack any interaction and therefore have a *correlation coefficient* of zero. (Chapter 8)

underwriting
The role of the investment bank in bearing the risk of reselling, at a profit, the securities purchased from an issuing corporation at an agreed-on price. (Chapter 2)

underwriting syndicate
A group of other banks formed by the originating investment bank to share the financial risk associated with underwriting new securities. (Chapter 2)

unlimited funds
The financial situation in which a firm is able to accept all independent projects that provide an acceptable return. (Chapter 10)

unlimited liability
The condition of a sole proprietorship (or general partnership), giving creditors the right to make claims against the owner's personal assets to recover debts owed by the business. (Chapter 1)

Unsecured bond
A bond backed only by the borrower's ability to repay the debt. (Chapter 6)

unsecured short-term financing
Short-term financing obtained without pledging specific assets as collateral. (Chapter 16)

unsecured, or general, creditors
Creditors who have a general claim against all the firm's assets other than those specifically pledged as collateral. (Chapter 18)

valuation
The process that links risk and return to determine the worth of an asset. (Chapter 6)

variable-growth dividend model
A dividend valuation approach that allows for a change in the dividend growth rate. (Chapter 7)

venture capital
Equity financing provided by a firm that specializes in financing young, rapidly growing firms. Venture capital firms raise pools of money from outside investors which they then use to purchase equity stakes in small private companies. (Chapter 2)

venture capitalists (VCs)
Formal business entities that take in private equity capital from many individual investors, often institutional investors such as endowments and pension funds or individuals of high net worth, and make private equity investment decisions on their behalf. (Chapter 2)

vertical merger
A merger in which a firm acquires a supplier or a customer. (Chapter 18)

voluntary reorganization
A petition filed by a failed firm on its own behalf for reorganizing its structure and paying its creditors. (Chapter 18)

voluntary settlement
An arrangement between an insolvent or bankrupt firm and its creditors, enabling it to bypass many of the costs involved in legal bankruptcy proceedings. (Chapter 18)

warehouse receipt loan
A secured short-term loan against inventory under which the lender receives control of the pledged inventory collateral, which is stored by a designated warehousing company on the lender's behalf. (Chapter 16)

warrant premium
The difference between the market value and the theoretical value of a warrant. (Chapter 17)

weighted average cost of capital (WACC)
A weighted average of a firm's cost of debt and equity financing, where the weights reflect the percentage of each type of financing used by the firm. (Chapter 9)

white knight
A takeover defense in which the target firm finds an acquirer more to its liking than the initial hostile acquirer and prompts the two to compete to take over the firm. (Chapter 18)

widely owned (stock)
The common stock of a firm is owned by many unrelated individual and institutional investors. (Chapter 7)

wire transfer
An electronic communication that, via bookkeeping entries, removes funds from the payer's bank and deposits them in the payee's bank. (Chapter 15)

working capital
The portion of the firm's assets used in day-to-day transactions. The primary elements of working capital circulate from one form or another in the ordinary course of business. (Chapter 15)

working capital decisions
Decisions that refer to the management of a firm's short-term resources. (Chapter 1)

working capital (or short-term financial) management
Management of current assets and current liabilities. (Chapter 15)

World Trade Organization (WTO)
International body that polices world trading practices and mediates disputes among member countries. (Chapter 19)

yield curve
A graphic depiction of the term structure of interest rates. (Chapter 6)

yield to maturity (YTM)
Compound annual rate of return earned on a debt security purchased on a given day and held to maturity. An estimate of the market's required return on a particular bond. (Chapter 6)

zero-balance account (ZBA)
A disbursement account that always has an end-of-day balance of zero because the firm deposits money to cover checks drawn on the account only as they are presented for payment each day. (Chapter 15)

zero-growth dividend model
An approach to dividend valuation that assumes a constant, nongrowing dividend stream. (Chapter 7)

Index

Note: Boldface page numbers indicate pages where terms are defined.

D

E

G

H

I

FREQUENTLY USED SYMBOLS AND ABBREVIATIONS

AAI	Average Age of Inventory
ACH	Automated Clearinghouse
ACP	Average Collection Period
ANPV	Annualized Net Present Value
A/P	Accounts Payable
APP	Average Payment Period
APR	Annual Percentage Rate
APY	Annual Percentage Yield
A/R	Accounts Receivable
β_j	Beta Coefficient or Index of Nondiversifiable Risk for Asset j
β_p	Portfolio Beta
B_0	Value of a Bond
C	Carrying Cost per Unit per Period
CAPM	Capital Asset Pricing Model
CCC	Cash Conversion Cycle
CD	Stated Cash Discount in Percentage Terms
CF_0	Initial Investment
CF_t	Cash Flow in Period t
CV	Coefficient of Variation
D_p	Preferred Stock Dividend
D_t	• Per-Share Dividend Expected at the End of Year t • Depreciation Expense in Year t
DFL	Degree of Financial Leverage
DIP	Debtor in Possession
DOL	Degree of Operating Leverage
DPS	Dividends per Share
DTC	Depository Transfer Check
DTL	Degree of Total Leverage
e	Exponential Function = 2.7183
E	Exercise Price of the Warrant
EAR	Effective Annual Rate
EBIT	Earnings Before Interest and Taxes
EBITDA	Earnings Before Interest, Taxes, Depreciation, and Amortization
EOM	End of the Month
EOQ	Economic Order Quantity
EPS	Earnings per Share
ERP	Enterprise Resource Planning
EU	European Union
EVA	Economic Value Added
FC	Fixed Operating Cost
FCF	Free Cash Flow
FDI	Foreign Direct Investment
FLM	Financial Leverage Multiplier
FV	Future Value
GAAP	Generally accepted accounting principles
GATT	General Agreement on Tariffs and Trade
g	Growth Rate
I	Interest Payment
i	Expected Inflation Rate
IPO	Initial Public Offering
IRR	Internal Rate of Return
JIT	Just-In-Time System
LBO	Leveraged Buyout
m	Number of times per year interest is compounded
M	Bond's Par Value
M/B	Market/Book Ratio
MACRS	Modified Accelerated Cost Recovery System
MNC	Multinational Company
MP	Market Price per Share
MPR	Market Price Ratio of Exchange
MRP	Materials Requirement Planning
n	• Number of Outcomes Considered • Number of Periods—Typically, Years • Years to Maturity
N	• Number of Days Payment Can Be Delayed by Giving up the Cash Discount • Number of Shares of Common Stock Obtainable With One Warrant
N_d	Net Proceeds from the Sale of Debt (Bond)

FREQUENTLY USED SYMBOLS AND ABBREVIATIONS (CONTINUED)

N_n	Net Proceeds from the Sale of New Common Stock
N_p	Net Proceeds from the Sale of Preferred Stock
NAFTA	North American Free Trade Agreement
NCAI	Net Current Asset Investment
NFAI	Net Fixed Asset Investment
NOPAT	Net operating profits after taxes
NPV	Net Present Value
O	Order Cost Per Order
OC	Operating Cycle
OCF	Operating Cash Flow
P	Price (value) of asset
P_0	Value of Common Stock
PD	Preferred Stock Dividend
P/E	Price/Earnings Ratio
PI	Profitability Index
PMT	Amount of Payment
Pr	Probability
PV	Present Value
Q	• Order Quantity in Units • Sales Quantity in Units
r	• Actual, Expected ($\bar{r}$), or Required Rate of Return • Annual Rate of Interest • Cost of Capital
r^*	Real Rate of Interest
r_{wacc}	Weighted Average Cost of Capital
r_d	• Required Return on Bond • Before-Tax Cost of Debt
r_j	Required Return on Asset *j*
r_m	• Market Return • Return on the Market Portfolio of Assets
r_p	• Cost of Preferred Stock • Portfolio Return
r_r	Cost of Retained Earnings
r_s	• Required Return on Common Stock • Cost of Common Stock Equity
R_F	Risk-Free Rate of Interest
RADR	Risk-Adjusted Discount Rate
RE	Ratio of Exchange
ROA	Return on Total Assets
ROE	Return on Common Equity
S	• Usage in Units per Period • Sales in Dollars
SML	Security Market Line
t	Time
T	Firm's Marginal Tax Rate
TVW	Theoretical Value of a Warrant
V	• Value of an Asset or Firm • Venture Capital
V_C	Value of Entire Company
V_D	Value of All Debt
V_P	Value of Preferred Stock
V_S	Value of Common Stock
VC	Variable Operating Cost per Unit
w_j	• Proportion of the Portfolio's Total Dollar Value Represented by Asset *j* • Proportion of a Specific Source of Financing *j* in the Firm's Capital Structure
WACC	Weighted Average Cost of Capital
WTO	World Trade Organization
YTM	Yield to Maturity
ZBA	Zero Balance Account
σ	Standard Deviation
Σ	Summation Sign